Turkey

a travel survival kit

Tom Brosnahan

Turkey – a travel survival kit

4th edition

Published by
Lonely Planet Publications
Head Office: PO Box 617, Hawthorn, Vic 3122, Australia
Branches: PO Box 2001A, Berkeley, CA 94702, USA
12 Barley Mow Passage, Chiswick, London W4 4PH, UK

Printed by
Colorcraft Ltd, Hong Kong
Printed in China

Photographs by
Tom Brosnahan (TB)
Tony Wheeler (TW)

Front cover: Ancient Greek Ruins, Ephesus; (George Obremsk, The Image Bank)

First Published
July 1985

This Edition
November 1993

Although the authors and publisher have tried to make the information as accurate as possible, they accept no responsibility for any loss, injury or inconvenience sustained by any person using this book.

National Library of Australia Cataloguing in Publication Data

Tom Brosnahan
Turkey – a travel survival kit.

4th ed.
Includes index.
ISBN 0 86442 178 8.

1. Turkey – Guidebooks.
I. Title. (Series: Lonely Planet travel survival kit).

915.610439

text © Tom Brosnahan 1993
maps © Lonely Planet 1993
photos © photographers as indicated 1993
climate charts compiled from information supplied by Patrick J Tyson, © Patrick J Tyson, 1993

Tom Brosnahan

Tom Brosnahan was born and raised in Pennsylvania, went to college in Boston, then set out on the road. His first two years in Turkey, during which he learned to speak fluent Turkish, were spent as a US Peace Corps Volunteer. He studied Middle Eastern history and the Ottoman Turkish language for eight years, but abandoned the writing of his PhD dissertation in favour of travelling and writing guidebooks.

So far his 25 books for various publishers have sold over two million copies in twelve languages. *Turkey – a travel survival kit* is the result of over a decade of experience and travel in the country.

Tom Brosnahan is also the author of Lonely Planet's *La Ruta Maya – a travel survival kit* and the *Turkish Phrasebook*, as well as co-author of *Mexico – a travel survival kit*, *Central America on a Shoestring* and other Lonely Planet guides.

Dedication

For Josephine and John – who else?

From the Publisher

This edition of *Turkey – a travel survival kit* was edited by Frith Pike in Melbourne, Australia. Cartography, illustrations and design were coordinated by Matt King. Thanks to Dan Levin for creating the Turkish fonts and climate charts, and for computer assistance. Glenn Beanland and Louise Keppie assisted with the maps; Trudi Canavan, Graham Imeson, and Valerie Telleni assisted with the illustrations and Jane Hart advised on the design. Margaret Jung designed the cover with assistance from Matt King. Thanks also to Sharon Wertheim for her help with the index.

This Edition

From Tom Brosnahan In the 1980s, Turkey underwent a tourism boom as millions of travellers from many countries discovered its natural and historical attractions. The boom has calmed down now, but Turkey is still changing rapidly. If you find new things of interest to travellers, please let me know so I can include them in the next edition.

I'm very grateful for letters, I read each one, and I reply if I can. Send your letter to Lonely Planet Publications, PO Box 617, Hawthorn, Victoria 3122, Australia. If you have access to electronic mail, that's even better. Contact me on CompuServe at 76400,3110, on America Online at TBros, or on the Internet at 76400.3110@compuserve.com.

If you have a computer and modem, you can obtain the latest news and tips on travel to Turkey by calling my electronic information service in the USA on (508) 287 0660. (This number is for computer access only; it will not work for voice communication).

A note on money: during the past decade, the Turkish lira has been subject to high inflation (80 to 100%). Daily small devaluations of the Turkish lira keep your costs down, and the Turkish government trumpets inflation reduction as a priority. In any case, given the volatility of the economy, it is impossible to predict whether the prices given in this book will remain the same, change slightly, or change significantly.

Audio cassettes are available to help you

learn some basic Turkish. Please see the Turkish Language Guide at the back of this book for details.

Warning & Request

Things change – prices go up, schedules change, good places go bad and bad places go bankrupt – nothing stays the same. So if you find things better or worse, recently opened or long since closed, please write and tell us and help make the next edition better!

Your letters will be used to help update future editions and, where possible, important changes will also be included as a Stop Press section in reprints.

We greatly appreciate all information that is sent to us by travellers. Back at Lonely Planet we employ a hard-working readers' letters team to sort through the many letters we receive. The best ones will be rewarded with a free copy of the next edition or another Lonely Planet guide if you prefer. We give away lots of books, but, unfortunately, not every letter/postcard receives one.

(A list of thanks to readers is on pages 747-748.)

Contents

Map Legend

BOUNDARIES

▬ ▪ ▬ ▪ ▬ ▪ ▬	.... International Boundary
▬ ▪ ▬ ▪ ▬ ▪ ▬	.... Internal Boundary
+▬+▬+▬+▬+▬+	.... National Park or Reserve
▬ ▬ ▬ ▬ ▬ ▬	.... The Equator
....	.... The Tropics

SYMBOLS

◉ NATIONAL	.... National Capital
● PROVINCIAL	.... Provincial or State Capital
● Major	.... Major Town
● Minor	.... Minor Town
■	.... Places to Stay
▼	.... Places to Eat
✉	.... Post Office
✈	.... Airport
i	.... Tourist Information
⊖	.... Bus Station or Terminal
66	.... Highway Route Number
☪ ✝ 🏛 ✝	...... Mosque, Church, Cathedral
∴	.... Temple or Ruin
✚	.... Hospital
✳	.... Lookout
Ⓧ	.... Camping Area
⊓	.... Picnic Area
⌂	.... Hut or Chalet
▲	.... Mountain or Hill
╀▬▬╀	.... Railway Station
═	.... Road Bridge
+++++	.... Railway Bridge
⇒ ⇐	.... Road Tunnel
→) (←	.... Railway Tunnel
⌇⌇⌇⌇	.... Escarpment or Cliff
⌣	.... Pass
⊓⊔⊓⊔	.... Ancient or Historic Wall

ROUTES

▬▬▬▬	..... Major Road or Highway
▬ ▬ ▬ ▬	.... Unsealed Major Road
▬▬▬▬	.... Sealed Road
▬ ▬ ▬ ▬	..... Unsealed Road or Track
═══	.... City Street
+++++++++	.... Railway
●▬◉▬●	.... Subway
....	.... Walking Track
▬ ▬ ▬ ▬	.... Ferry Route
+╫+╫+╫+	.... Cable Car or Chair Lift

HYDROGRAPHIC FEATURES

～～	.... River or Creek
～⌇～	.... Intermittent Stream
⬭ ⌇	.... Lake, Intermittent Lake
～	.... Coast Line
⬮▬ ╫	.... Spring
	.... Waterfall
⌇⌇ ⌇⌇	.... Swamp
▒▒▒▒	.... Salt Lake or Reef
◎	.... Glacier

OTHER FEATURES

▤▤▤	Park, Garden or National Park
⊠	.... Built Up Area
⊞⧄	... Market or Pedestrian Mall
⊞⊠	.... Plaza or Town Square
+++++	.... Cemetery

Note: not all symbols displayed above appear in this book

Introduction

The history of Anatolia, the Turkish homeland, is simply incredible. The world's oldest 'city' was discovered here, at Çatal Höyük in 7500 BC. The Hittite Empire, little known in the west, rivalled that of ancient Egypt, and left behind captivating works of art. The heartland of classical Hellenic culture is actually in Turkey, including cities such as Troy, Pergamum, Ephesus, Miletus and Halicarnassus. Most modern Turkish cities have a Roman past, and all have a Byzantine one. The Seljuk Turkish Empire could boast of people like Omar Khayyam and Celaleddin Rumi, the poet, mystic and founder of the order of Whirling Dervishes.

The mention of Turkey conjures up vague, stereotypical visions of Oriental splendour and decadence, of mystery and intrigue, of sultans and harems, of luxury and wickedness in the minds of most Western visitors. These outdated stereotypes quickly evaporate once the visitor arrives in the country. The Turkish Republic is democratic, rapidly modernising, secular and Western-oriented with a vigorous economy.

The Turks are mostly friendly to foreign visitors, the cuisine is often excellent, the cities are dotted with majestic old buildings, and the countryside is often beautiful like a national park. The old stereotype of Oriental decadence originated in the Ottoman Empire, when the entire Middle East and much of North Africa was ruled by the Turkish sultan. The great powers of Western Europe coveted the sultan's lands, and put pressure on him by portraying him in the Western press as little better than a monster. This negative image built easily on the notion of the 'terrible Turk' left from the days, in the 1600s, when Ottoman armies threatened Vienna and central Europe.

The Turks are proud of their imperial past (not the last centuries) but the times of Mehmet the Conqueror and Süleyman the Magnificent, when the Turkish Empire was rich, powerful and envied by the West. Turks are also fascinated by the depth of history in their homeland, by the progression of kingdoms and empires which fostered a dozen great cultures: Hittite, Hellenic, Hellenistic, Roman, Byzantine, Seljuk, Ottoman and more.

Turks harbour no romantic visions of once again ruling the sultan's vast domains. But with the independence of the Turkic republics of Central Asia, Turkey has gained important influence in that region. It is seen as the model for these new countries: a democratic, secular nation-state with a free market economy.

Turkey is a big country, and the variety of things to see and do is enormous – ranging from water sports to mountain trekking, archaeology to night-clubbing, river rafting to raki drinking, Turkey can easily keep you happy for weeks or even months.

Facts about the Country

HISTORY

Turkey's history is astoundingly long – extending for almost 10,000 years. Before giving a summary, here is a table so you can keep the various periods in the right order:

7500 BC Earliest known inhabitants; earliest human community at Çatal Höyük
5000 BC Stone and Copper Age; settlement at Hacılar

2600-1900 BC Old Bronze Age; Proto-Hittite Empire in central and south-eastern Anatolia
1900-1300 BC Hittite Empire, wars with Egypt; the Patriarch Abraham departs from Harran, near Şanlıurfa, for Canaan
1250 BC Trojan War
1200-600 BC Phrygian and Mysian invasions, followed by the great period of Hellenic civilisation; Yassı Höyük settlement flourishes; King Midas and King Croesus reign; coinage is invented; kingdoms of Ionia, Lycia, Lydia, Caria, Pamphylia; Empire of Urartu

10

550 BC Cyrus of Persia invades Anatolia

334 BC Conquest of simply everything and everybody by Alexander the Great from Macedon

279 BC Celts (or Gauls) invade and set up Galatia near Ankara

250 BC Rise of the Kingdom of Pergamum (Bergama)

129 BC Rome establishes the Province of Asia ('Asia Minor'), with its capital at Ephesus (near İzmir)

47-57 AD St Paul's trips in Anatolia .

330 AD Constantine dedicates the 'New Rome' of Constantinople, and the centre of the Roman Empire moves from Rome to the Bosphorus

527-65 Reign of Justinian, greatest Byzantine emperor; construction of Sancta Sophia, greatest church in the world

570-622 Muhammed's birth; revelation of the Koran; flight *(hijra)* to Medina

1037-1109 Empire of the Great Seljuk Turks, based in Iran

1071-1243 Seljuk Sultanate of Rum, based in Konya; life and work of Celaleddin Rumi ('Mevlana'), founder of the Whirling Dervishes

1000s to 1200s Age of the crusades

1288 Birth of the Ottoman Empire, near Bursa

1453 Conquest of Constantinople by Mehmet II

1520-66 Reign of Sultan Süleyman the Magnificent, the great age of the Ottoman Empire; most of North Africa, most of Eastern Europe and all of the Middle East controlled from İstanbul; Ottoman navies patrol the Mediterranean and Red seas and the Indian Ocean

1876-1909 Reign of Sultan Abdülhamid, last of the powerful sultans; the 'Eastern Question' arises: which

European nations will be able to grab Ottoman territory when the empire topples?
1923 Proclamation of the Turkish Republic
1938 Death of Atatürk

Earliest Times

The Mediterranean region was inhabited as early as 7500 BC, during Palaeolithic, or Old Stone Age, times. By 7000 BC a Neolithic (New Stone Age) city had grown up at what's now called Çatal Höyük, 60 km south-east of Konya. These early Anatolians developed fine wall paintings, statuettes, domestic architecture and pottery. Artefacts from the site, including the wall paintings, are displayed in Ankara's Museum of Anatolian Civilisations.

The Chalcolithic (Stone and Copper Age) period saw the building of a city at Hacılar, near Burdur, in about 5000 BC. The pottery here was of finer quality, and copper implements rather than stone or clay ones were used.

Hittites – The Bronze Age

The Old Bronze Age (2600-1900 BC) was when Anatolians first developed cities of substantial size. An indigenous people now named the Proto-Hittites, or Hatti, built cities at Nesa or Kanesh (today's Kültepe), and Alacahöyük. The first known ruler of Kanesh was King Zipani (circa 2300 BC), according to Akkadian texts. You can visit the archaeological site near Kültepe, 21 km north-east of Kayseri. As for Alacahöyük, 36 km from Boğazkale (bo-AHZ-kahl-eh), it was perhaps the most important pre-Hittite city and may have been the first Hittite capital.

The Hittites, a people who spoke an Indo-European language, overran this area and established themselves as a ruling class over the local people during the Middle Bronze Age (1900-1600 BC). The Hittites took over existing cities and built a magnificent capital at Hattuşaş (Boğazkale), 212 km east of Ankara near Sungurlu. The early Hittite Kingdom (1600-1500 BC) was replaced by the greater Hittite Empire (1450-1200 BC).

The Hittites captured Syria from the Egyptians (1380-1316), clashed with the great Rameses II (1298), and meanwhile developed a wonderful culture.

Their graceful pottery, ironwork ornaments and implements, gold jewellery and figurines now fill a large section of the Museum of Anatolian Civilisations in Ankara. The striking site of Boğazkale, set in dramatic countryside, is worth a visit, as is the religious centre of Yazılıkaya nearby. The Hittite religion was based upon worship of a sun goddess and a storm god.

The Hittite Empire was weakened in its final period by the cities of Assuwa ('Asia'), subject principalities along the Aegean coast, which included the city of Troy. The Trojans were attacked by Achaean Greeks in 1250 – the Trojan War – which gave the Hittites a break. But the *coup de grâce* came with a massive invasion of 'sea peoples' from various Greek islands and city-states Driven from their homelands by the invading Dorians, the sea peoples flocked into Anatolia by way of the Aegean coast. The Hittite state survived for a few centuries longer in the south-eastern Taurus (Toros) Mountains, but the great empire was dead.

Phrygians, Urartians, Lydians & Others

With the Hittite decline, smaller states filled the power vacuum. Around 1200 BC the Phrygians and Mysians, of Indo-European stock, invaded Anatolia from Thrace and settled at Gordium (Yassı Höyük), 106 km south-west of Ankara. This Hittite city became the Phrygian capital (circa 800 BC). A huge Hittite cemetery and a royal Phrygian tomb still exist at the site. King Midas (circa 715 BC), he of the golden touch, is Phrygia's most famous son.

At the same time (after 1200 BC), the Aegean coast was populated with a mixture of native peoples and Greek invaders. The region around İzmir became Ionia, with numerous cities. To the south was Caria, between modern Milas and Fethiye, a mountainous region whose people were great traders. The Carians sided with the Trojans during the Trojan War. When the Dorians arrived they brought some Greek culture to Caria, which the great Carian king Mausolus developed even further. His tomb, the Mausoleum, was among the Seven Wonders of the Ancient World. Of his capital city, Halicarnassus (modern Bodrum), little remains.

Further east from Caria was Lycia, a kingdom stretching from Fethiye to Antalya; and Pamphylia, the land east of Antalya.

As the centuries passed, a great city grew up at Sardis, 60 km east of İzmir. Called Lydia, it dominated most of Ionia and clashed with Phrygia. Lydia is famous not only for Sardis, but for a great invention: coinage. It's also famous for King Croesus, the world's first great coin collector. Lydia's primacy lasted only from 680 to 547 BC, when Persian invaders overran it.

Meanwhile, out east on the shores of salty Lake Van (Van Gölü), yet another kingdom and culture arose. Not much is known about the Urartians who founded the Kingdom of Van (860-612 BC), except that they left interesting ruins and vast, bewildering cuneiform inscriptions in the massive Rock of Van just outside the modern town.

The Cimmerians invaded Anatolia from the west, conquered Phrygia and challenged Lydia, then settled down to take their place amongst the great jumble of Anatolian peoples. In 547 BC the Persians invaded and jumbled the situation even more. Though the Ionian cities survived the invasion and lived on under Persian rule, the great period of Hellenic culture was winding down. Ionia, with its important cities of Phocaea (Foça, north of İzmir), Teos, Ephesus, Priene and Miletus, and Aeolia centred on Smyrna (İzmir), had contributed a great deal to ancient culture, from the graceful scrolled capitals of Ionic columns to the ideas of Thales of Miletus, the first recorded philosopher in the West.

While the great city of Athens was relatively unimportant, the Ionian cities were laying the foundations of Hellenic civilisation. It is ironic that the Persian invasion which curtailed Ionia's culture caused that of Athens to flourish. On reaching Athens, the Persians were overextended. By meeting the Persian challenge, Athens grew powerful and influential, taking the lead in the further progress of Hellenic culture.

Cyrus & Alexander

Cyrus, emperor of Persia (550-530 BC), swept into Anatolia from the east, conquering everybody and everything. Though he subjected the cities of the Aegean coast to his rule, this was not easy. The independent-minded citizens gave him and his successors trouble for the next two centuries.

The Persian conquerors were defeated by Alexander the Great, who stormed out of Macedon, crossed the Hellespont (Dardanelles) in 334 BC, and within a few years had conquered the entire Middle East from Greece to India. Alexander, so it is said, was frustrated in untying the Gordian knot at Gordium, so he cut it with his sword. It seems he did the right thing, as the domination of Asia – which he was supposed to gain by untying the knot – came to be his in record time. His sword-blow proved that he was an impetuous young man.

Alexander's effects on Anatolia were profound. He was the first of many rulers who would attempt to meld Western and Eastern

Alexander the Great

cultures (the Byzantines and the Ottomans followed suit). Upon his death in 323 BC, in Babylon, Alexander's empire was divided among his generals in a flurry of civil wars. Lysimachus claimed western and central Anatolia after winning the Battle of Ipsus in 301 BC, and he set his mark on the Ionian cities. Many Hellenistic buildings went up on his orders. Ancient Smyrna was abandoned and a brand-new city was built several km away, where the modern city stands.

But the civil wars continued, and Lysimachus was slain by Seleucus (king of Seleucid lands from 305 to 280 BC), another of Alexander's generals, at the Battle of Corupedium in 281 BC. Though Seleucus was in turn slain by Ptolemy Ceraunus, the kingdom of the Seleucids, based in Antioch (Antakya), was to rule a great part of the Middle East for the next century.

Meanwhile, the next invaders, the Celts (or Gauls) this time, were storming through Macedonia on their way to Anatolia (in 279 BC) where they established the Kingdom of Galatia. The Galatians made Ancyra (Ankara) their capital, and subjected the Aegean cities to their rule. The foundations of parts of the citadel in Ankara date from Galatian times.

While the Galatians ruled western Anatolia, Mithridates I had become king of Pontus, a state based in Trebizond (Trabzon) on the eastern Black Sea coast. At its height, the Pontic Kingdom extended all the way to Cappadocia in central Anatolia.

Still other small kingdoms flourished at this time, between 300 and 200 BC. A leader named Prusias founded the Kingdom of Bithynia, and gave his name to the chief city: Prusa (Bursa). Nicaea (İznik, near Bursa) was also of great importance. And in southeastern Anatolia an Armenian kingdom grew up, centred on the town of Van. The Armenians, a Phrygian tribe, settled around Lake Van after the decline of Urartian power.

A fellow named Ardvates who ruled from 317 to 284 BC and was a Persian satrap (provincial governor) under the Seleucids, broke away from the Seleucid Kingdom to found the short-lived Kingdom of Armenia. The Seleucids later regained control, but lost it again as Armenia was split into two kingdoms, Greater and Lesser Armenia. Reunited in 94 BC under Tigranes I, the Kingdom of Armenia became very powerful for a short period (83-69 BC). Armenia finally fell to the Roman legions not long afterwards.

But the most impressive and powerful of Anatolia's many kingdoms at this time was Pergamum. Gaining tremendous power around 250 BC, the Pergamene king picked the right side to be on, siding with Rome early in the game. With Roman help, Pergamum threw off Seleucid rule and went on to challenge both King Prusias of Bithynia (186 BC) and King Pharnaces I of Pontus (183 BC).

The kings of Pergamum were great warriors, governors and also mad patrons of the arts, assembling an enormous library which rivalled that Alexandria's. The Asclepion, or medical centre, at Pergamum was flourishing at this time, and continued to flourish for centuries under Roman rule. Greatest of the Pergamene kings was Eumenes II (197-159 BC), who ruled an enormous empire stretching from the Dardanelles to the Taurus Mountains near Syria. He was responsible for building much of what's left on Pergamum's acropolis, including the grand library.

Roman Times

The Romans took Anatolia almost by default. The various Anatolian kings couldn't refrain from picking away at Roman holdings and causing other sorts of irritation, so finally the legions marched in and took over. Defeating King Antiochus III of Seleucia at Magnesia (Manisa, near İzmir) in 190 BC, the Romans were content for the time being to leave 'Asia' (Anatolia) in the hands of the kings of Pergamum. But the last king, dying without an heir, bequeathed his kingdom to Rome (133 BC). In 129 BC, the Romans established the province of Asia, with its capital at Ephesus.

An interesting postscript to this period is the story of Commagene. This small and rather unimportant little kingdom in east-central Anatolia, near Adıyaman, left few marks on history. But the one notable reminder of Commagene is very notable indeed: on top of Nemrut Dağı (NEHM-root dah-uh, Mt Nimrod), Antiochus I (62-32 BC) built a mammoth, cone-shaped funerary mound framed by twin temples filled with huge stone statues portraying himself and the gods and goddesses who were his 'peers'. A visit to Nemrut Dağı, from the nearby town of Kahta, is one of the high points of a visit to Turkey.

Roman rule brought relative peace and prosperity to Anatolia for almost three centuries, and provided the perfect conditions for the spread of a brand-new, world-class religion.

Early Christianity

Christianity began in Roman Palestine (Judaea), but its foremost proponent, St Paul, came from Tarsus in Cilicia, in what is now southern Turkey. Paul took advantage of the excellent Roman road system to spread the teachings of Jesus. When the Romans drove the Jews out of Judaea in 70 AD, Christian members of this Diaspora may have made their way to the numerous small Christian congregations in the Roman province of Asia (Anatolia).

On his first journey in about 47-49 AD, Paul went to Antioch, Seleucia (Silifke), and along the southern coast through Pamphylia (Side, Antalya) and up into the mountains. First stop was Antioch-in-Pisidia, today called Yalvaç, near Akşehir. Next he went to Iconium (Konya), the chief city in Galatia; Paul wrote an important 'Letter to the Galatians' which is now the ninth book of the New Testament.

From Iconium, Paul tramped to Lystra, 40 km south, and to Derbe nearby. Then it was back to Attaleia (Antalya) to catch a boat for Antioch. His second journey took him to some of these same cities, and later north-west to the district of Mysia where Troy (Truva) is located; then into Macedonia.

Paul's third trip (53-57) took in many of these same places, including Ancyra, Smyrna and Adramyttium (Edremit). On the way back he stopped in Ephesus, capital of Roman Asia and one of the greatest cities of the time. Here he ran into trouble because his teachings were ruining the market for silver effigies of the local favourite goddess, Cybele/Diana. The silversmiths led a riot, and Paul's companions were hustled into the great theatre for a sort of kangaroo court. Luckily, the authorities kept order: there was free speech in Ephesus; Paul and his companions had broken no laws; they were permitted to go freely. Later on this third journey Paul stopped in Miletus.

Paul got his last glimpses of Anatolia as he was being taken to Rome as a prisoner, for trial on charges of inciting a riot in Jerusalem (59-60). He changed ships at Myra (Demre); further west, he was supposed to land at Cnidos, at the tip of the peninsula west of Marmaris, but stormy seas prevented this.

Other saints played a role in the life of Roman Asia as well. Tradition has it that St John retired to Ephesus to write the fourth gospel near the end of his life, and that he brought Jesus' mother Mary with him. John was buried on top of a hill in what is now the town of Selçuk, near Ephesus. The great, now ruined basilica of St John marks the site. As for Mary, she is said to have retired to a mountaintop cottage near Ephesus. The small chapel at Meryemana ('Mother Mary') is the site of a mass to celebrate her Assumption on 15 August.

The Seven Churches of the Revelation were the Seven Churches of Asia: Ephesus (Efes), Smyrna (İzmir), Pergamum (Bergama), Sardis (Sart, east of İzmir), Philadelphia (Alaşehir), Laodicea (Goncalı, between Denizli and Pamukkale) and Thyatira (Akhisar). 'Church' of course meant 'congregation', so don't go to these sites looking for the ruins of seven buildings.

The New Rome

Christianity was a struggling faith during the centuries of Roman rule. By 250 AD, the faith had grown strong enough and Roman rule so unsteady that the Roman emperor Decius decreed a general persecution of Christians. Not only this, but the empire was falling to pieces. Goths attacked the Aegean cities with fleets, and later invaded Anatolia. The Persian Empire again threatened from the east. Diocletian (284-305) restored the empire somewhat, but continued the persecutions.

When Diocletian abdicated, Constantine battled for succession, which he won in 324. He united the empire, declared equal rights for all religions, and called the first ecumenical council to meet in Nicaea in 325.

Meanwhile, Constantine was building a great city on the site of Hellenic Byzantium. In 330 he dedicated it as New Rome, his capital city; it came to be called Constantinople. The emperor died seven years later in Nicomedia (İzmit), east of his capital. On his deathbed he adopted Christianity.

Justinian

While the barbarians of Europe were sweeping down on weakened Rome, the eastern capital grew in wealth and strength. Emperor Justinian (527-65) brought the Eastern Roman, or Byzantine, Empire to its greatest strength. He reconquered Italy, the Balkans,

Anatolia, Egypt and North Africa, and further embellished Constantinople with great buildings. His personal triumph was the Church of the Holy Wisdom, or Sancta Sophia, which remained the most splendid church in Christendom for almost 1000 years, after which it became the most splendid mosque.

Justinian's successors were generally good, but not good enough, and the empire's conquests couldn't be maintained. Besides, something quite momentous was happening in Arabia.

Birth of Islam

Five years after the death of Justinian, Muhammed was born in Mecca. In 612 or so, while meditating, he heard the voice of God command him to 'recite'. Muhammed was to become the Messenger of God, communicating His holy word to people. The written record of these recitations, collected after Muhammed's death into a book by his family and followers, is the Koran.

The people of Mecca didn't take to Muhammed's preaching all at once. In fact, they forced him to leave Mecca, which he did, according to tradition, in the year 622. This 'flight' (hijra or hegira) is the starting-point for the Muslim lunar calendar.

Setting up house in Medina, Muhammed organised a religious commonwealth which over 10 years became so powerful that it could challenge and conquer Mecca (624-30). Before Muhammed died two years later, the Muslims (adherents of Islam, 'submission to God's will') had begun the conquest of other Arab tribes.

The story of militant Islam is one of history's most astounding tales. Fifty years after the Prophet's ignominious flight from Mecca, the armies of Islam were threatening the walls of Constantinople (669-78), having conquered everything and everybody from there to Mecca, plus Persia and Egypt. The Arabic Muslim empires that followed these conquests were among the world's greatest political, social and cultural achievements.

Muhammed was succeeded by caliphs or deputies, whose job was to oversee the welfare of the Muslim commonwealth. His close companions got the job first, then his son-in-law Ali. After that, two great dynasties emerged: the Umayyads (661-750) based their empire in Damascus; the Abbasids (750-1100), in Baghdad. Both continually challenged the power and status of Byzantium.

The Coming of the Turks

The history of the Turks as excellent soldiers goes back at least to the reign of the Abbasid caliph Al-Mutasim (833-42). This ruler formed an army of Turkish captives and mercenaries that became the empire's strength, and also its undoing. Later caliphs found that their protectors had become their masters, and the Turkish 'praetorian guard' raised or toppled caliphs as it chose.

The Seljuk Empire

The first great Turkish state to rule Anatolia was the Great Seljuk Turkish Empire (1037-1109), based in Persia (Iran). Coming from Central Asia, the Turks captured Baghdad (1055). In 1071, Seljuk armies decisively defeated the Byzantines at Manzikert (Malazgırt), taking the Byzantine emperor as a prisoner. The Seljuks then took over most of Anatolia and established a provincial capital at Nicaea. Their domains now included today's Turkey, Iran and Iraq. Their empire developed a distinctive culture, with especially beautiful architecture and design; the Great Seljuks also produced Omar Khayyam (died 1123). Politically, however, the Great Seljuk Turkish Empire declined quickly, in the style of Alexander the Great's empire, with various pieces being taken by generals.

A remnant of the Seljuk empire lived on in Anatolia, based in Iconium. Called the Seljuk Sultanate of Rum ('Rome', meaning Roman Asia), it continued to flourish, producing great art and great thinkers until overrun by the Mongol hordes in 1243. Celaleddin Rumi or 'Mevlana', founder of the Mevlevi (Whirling) Dervish order, is perhaps the Sultanate of Rum's outstanding thinker.

The Crusades

These 'holy wars', created to provide work for the lesser nobles and riffraff of Europe, proved disastrous for the Byzantine emperors. Although a combined Byzantine and crusader army captured Nicaea from the Seljuks in 1097, the crusaders were mostly an unhelpful, unruly bunch. The Fourth Crusade (1202-04) saw European ragtag armies invade and plunder Christian Constantinople. This was the first and most horrible defeat for the great city, and it was carried out by 'friendly' armies.

Having barely recovered from the ravages of the crusades, the Byzantines were greeted with a new and greater threat: the Ottomans.

Founding of the Ottoman Empire

In the late 1200s, Byzantine weakness left a power vacuum which was filled by bands of Turks fleeing westwards from the Mongols. Warrior bands, each led by a warlord, took over parts of the Aegean and Marmara coasts. The Turks who moved into Bithynia, around Bursa, were followers of a man named Ertuğrul. His son, Osman, founded (circa 1288) a principality which was to grow into the Osmanlı (Ottoman) Empire.

The Ottomans took Bursa in 1326. It served them well as their first capital city. But they were vigorous and ambitious, and by 1402 they moved the capital to Adrianople (Edirne) because it was easier to rule their Balkan conquests from there. Constantinople was still in Byzantine hands.

The Turkish advance spread rapidly to both east and west, despite some setbacks. By 1452, under Mehmet the Conqueror, they were strong enough to think of taking Constantinople, capital of eastern Christendom, which they did in 1453. Mehmet's reign (1451-81) began the great era of Ottoman power.

Süleyman the Magnificent

The height of Ottoman glory was under Sultan Süleyman the Magnificent (1520-66). Called 'the Lawgiver' by the Turks, he beautified İstanbul, rebuilt Jerusalem and expanded Ottoman power to the gates of

Vienna in 1529. The Ottoman fleet under Barbaros Hayrettin Paşa seemed invincible, but by 1585 the empire had begun its long and celebrated decline. Most of the sultans after Süleyman were incapable of great rule. Luckily for the empire, there were very competent and talented men to serve as grand viziers, ruling the empire in the sultans' stead.

The Later Empire

By 1699, Europeans no longer feared an invasion by the 'terrible Turk'. The empire was still vast and powerful, but it had lost its momentum, and was rapidly dropping behind the West in terms of social, military, scientific and material progress. In the 19th century, several sultans undertook important reforms. Selim III, for instance, revised taxation, commerce and the military. But the Janissaries (members of the sultan's personal guard) and other conservative elements resisted the new measures strongly, and sometimes violently.

For centuries, the non-Turkish ethnic and religious minorities in the sultan's domains had lived side by side with their Turkish neighbours, governed by their own religious and traditional laws. (The head of each community – chief rabbi, Orthodox patriarch, etc was responsible to the sultan for the community's well-being and behaviour.) But in the 1800s, strong currents of ethnic nationalism flowed eastward from Europe. Decline and misrule made nationalism very appealing. The subject peoples of the Ottoman Empire revolted, often with the direct encouragement and assistance of the European powers. After bitter fighting in 1832, the Kingdom of Greece was formed; the Serbs, Bulgarians, Rumanians, Albanians, Armenians and Arabs would all seek their independence soon after.

As the empire broke up, the European powers (Britain, France, Italy, Germany, Russia) hovered in readiness to colonise or annex the pieces. They used religion as a reason for pressure or control, saying that it was their duty to protect the Catholic, Protestant or Orthodox subjects from misrule and

Süleyman the Magnificent

anarchy. The holy places in Palestine were a favourite target, and each power tried to obtain a foothold here for colonisation later.

The Russian emperors put pressure on the Turks to grant them powers over all Ottoman Orthodox subjects, whom the Russian emperor would thus 'protect'. The result of this pressure was the Crimean War (1853-56), with Britain and France fighting on the side of the Ottomans against the Russians.

In the midst of imperial dissolution, Western-style reforms were proposed in an attempt to revivify the moribund empire and make it compatible with modern Europe. Mithat Paşa, a successful general and powerful grand vizier, brought the young crown prince Abdülhamid II (1876-1909) to the throne along with a constitution in 1876. But the new sultan did away both with Mithat Paşa and the constitution, and established his own absolute rule.

Abdülhamid modernised without democratising, building thousands of km of railways and telegraph lines, and encouraging modern industry, keeping watch on everything through an extensive spy network all the while. But the empire continued to disintegrate, with nationalist insurrections in Crete, Armenia, Bulgaria and Macedonia.

The younger generation of the Turkish elite watched bitterly as the country fell apart, then organised into secret societies bent on toppling the sultan. The Young Turk movement for Western-style reforms gained enough power by 1908 to force the restoration of the constitution. In 1909, the Young Turk-led Ottoman parliament deposed Abdülhamid and put his weak-willed, indecisive brother Mehmet V ('Vahdettin') on the throne.

In its last years, though a sultan still sat on the throne, the Ottoman Empire was ruled by three members of the Young Turks' Committee of Union & Progress named Talat, Enver and Jemal. Their rule was vigorous, but harsh and misguided, and it only worsened an already hopeless situation. When WW I broke out, they made the fatal error of siding with Germany and the Central Powers. With their defeat, the Ottoman Empire collapsed. Istanbul and several other parts of Anatolia were occupied, and the sultan became a pawn in the hands of the victors.

The victorious Allies had been planning, since the beginning of the war, how they would carve up the Ottoman Empire. They even promised certain lands to several different peoples or factions in order to get their support for the war effort (as when Palestine was promised both to Jews and Arabs). With the end of the war, these promises came due. With more promises than territory, the Allies decided on the dismemberment of Anatolia itself in order to get more land with which to satisfy the ambitions of the victorious countries. The choicest bits of Anatolia were to be given to Christian peoples, with the Muslim Turks relegated to a small land-locked region of semi-barren steppe.

The Turkish Republic

The situation looked very bleak for the Turks as their armies were being disbanded and their country taken under the control of the Allies. But a catastrophe turned things around.

Ever since gaining independence in 1831,

the Greeks had entertained the *Megali Idea* ('Great Plan') of a new Greek empire encompassing all the lands which had once had Greek influence – in effect, the refounding of the Byzantine Empire. During WW I, the Allies had offered Greece the Ottoman city of Smyrna. King Constantine declined for various reasons, even though his prime minister, Eleutherios Venizelos, wanted to accept. After the war, however, Alexander became king, Venizelos became prime minister again, and Britain encouraged the Greeks to go ahead and take Smyrna. On 15 May 1919, they did.

The Turks, depressed and hopeless over the occupation of their country and the powerlessness of the sultan, couldn't take this: a former subject people capturing an Ottoman city, and pushing inland with great speed and ferocity. Even before the Greek invasion, an Ottoman general named Mustafa Kemal had decided that a new government must take over the destiny of the Turks from the powerless sultan. He began organising resistance on 19 May 1919. The Greek invasion was just the shock needed to galvanise the people and lead them to his way of thinking.

The Turkish War of Independence lasted from 1920 to 1922. In September 1921 the Greeks very nearly reached Ankara, the nationalist headquarters, but in desperate fighting the Turks held them off. A year later, the Turks began their counteroffensive and drove the Greek armies back to İzmir by 9 September 1922.

Victory in the bitterly fought war made Mustafa Kemal even more of a national hero. He was now fully in command of the fate of the Turks. The sultanate was abolished and after it, the Ottoman Empire. A Turkish republic was born, based in Anatolia and eastern Thrace. The treaties of WW I, which had left the Turks with almost no country, were renegotiated.

Ethnic Greeks in Turkey and ethnic Turks in Greece were required to leave their ancestral homes and move to their respective ethnic nation-states; Greeks from İzmir moved into the houses of Turks in Salonika, whose owners had moved to İzmir, and so forth. Venizelos even came to terms with Kemal, signing a treaty in 1930.

Atatürk's Reforms

Mustafa Kemal undertook the job of completely remaking a society. After the republic was declared in 1923, a constitution was adopted (1924); polygamy was abolished and the fez, mark of Ottoman backwardness, was prohibited (1925); new, Western-style law codes were instituted, and civil (not religious) marriage was required (1926); Islam was removed as the state religion, and the Arabic alphabet was replaced by a modified Latin one (1928). In 1930, Constantinople officially became İstanbul, and other city names were officially Turkified (Angora to Ankara, Smyrna to İzmir, Adrianople to Edirne etc). Women obtained the right to vote and serve in parliament in 1934.

In 1935, Mustafa Kemal sponsored one of the most curious laws of modern times. Up to this time, Muslims had only one given name. Family names were purely optional. So he decided that all Turks should choose a family name, and they did. He himself was proclaimed Atatürk, or 'Father Turk', by the Turkish parliament, and officially became Kemal Atatürk.

Atatürk lived and directed the country's destiny until 10 November 1938. He saw WW II coming, and was anxious that Turkey stay out of it. His friend and successor as president of the republic, İsmet İnönü, succeeded in preserving a precarious neutrality. Ankara became a hotbed of Allied-Axis spying, but the Turks stayed out of the conflict.

Recent Years

In the beginning years, Atatürk's Republican Peoples' Party was the only political party allowed. But between 1946 and 1950 true democracy was instituted, and the opposition Democratic Party won the election in 1950.

By 1960 the Democratic Party had acquired so much power that the democratic system was threatened. The army, charged by Atatürk to protect democracy and the constitution, stepped in and brought various Democratic Party leaders to trial on charges of violating the constitution. The popular Peron-like party leader, Adnan Menderes, was executed, though all other death sentences were commuted. Elections were held in 1961.

In 1970 there was a gentlemanly *coup d'état* again because the successor to the Democratic Party had overreached its bounds. High-ranking military officers entered the national broadcasting headquarters and read a short message, and the government fell.

Under the careful watch of those same officers, democracy returned and things went well for years, until political infighting and civil unrest brought the country to a virtual halt in 1980. On the left side of the political spectrum, Soviet-bloc countries pumped in arms and money for destabilisation and, it is claimed, supported Armenian terrorist elements who murdered Turkish diplomats and their families abroad. On the right side of the spectrum, fanatic Muslim religious groups and a neo-Nazi party caused havoc. In the centre, the two major political parties were deadlocked so badly in parliament that for months they couldn't even elect a parliamentary president.

The economy was in bad shape, inflation was 130% per year, the lawmakers were not making laws, crime in the streets by the fringe elements of left and right was epidemic. The military stepped in again on 12 September 1980, much to the relief of the general population, and restored civil, fiscal and legal order, but at the price of strict control and some human rights abuses.

The constitution was rewritten so as to avoid parliamentary impasses. In a controlled plebiscite, it was approved by the voters. The head of the military government, General Kenan Evren, resigned his military commission (as Atatürk had done) and became the country's new president. The old political leaders, seen by the new government to have been responsible for the breakdown of society, were tried (if they had committed crimes) or excluded from political life for 10 years, though many returned to politics before this time was up.

In 1983, elections under the new constitution were held, and the centre-right Anavatan Partisi (Motherland Party), the one less favoured by the military caretakers, won handily. The new prime minister was Turgut Özal, a former World Bank economist, who instituted economic liberalisations and precipitated a business boom which lasted through the 1980s. Özal's untimely death in April 1993 removed a powerful, innovative force from Turkish politics. (For details of current politics, see Political Parties under Government in the Facts for the Visitor chapter.)

ATATÜRK

It won't take you long to discover the national hero, Kemal Atatürk. Though he died on 10 November 1938, his picture is everywhere in Turkey, a bust or statue (preferably equestrian) is in every park, quotations from his speeches and writings are on every public building. He is almost synonymous with the Turkish Republic.

Kemal Atatürk

The best popular account of his life and times is Lord Kinross's *Atatürk: The Rebirth of a Nation* (Weidenfeld & Nicolson, London, 1964). Kinross portrayed Atatürk as a man of great intelligence and even greater energy and daring, possessed by the idea of giving his fellow Turks a new lease of life. Like all too few leaders, he had the capability of realising his obsession almost single-handedly. His achievement in turning a backward empire into a forward-looking nation-state was taken as a model by Nasser, the shahs of Iran and other Islamic leaders. None had the same degree of success, however.

Early Years

In 1881, a boy named Mustafa was born into the family of a minor Turkish bureaucrat living in Salonika – now the Greek city of Thessaloniki, but at that time a city in Ottoman Macedonia. Mustafa was smart, and a hard worker at school. His mathematics teacher was so impressed that he gave him the nickname Kemal (excellence). The name Mustafa Kemal stuck with him as he went through a military academy and the war college, and even as he pursued his duties as an officer.

Military Career

He served with distinction, and acquired a reputation as something of a hothead, perhaps because his commanders were not as bold as he was. By the time of the battle at Gallipoli in WW I, he was a promising lieutenant colonel of infantry.

The defence of Gallipoli, which saved Constantinople from British conquest (until the end of the war, at least), was a personal triumph for Mustafa Kemal. His strategic and tactical genius came into full play. His commanders had little to do but approve his suggestions; he led with utter disregard for his own safety. A vastly superior British force (including Anzacs from Australia and New Zealand) was driven away, and Mustafa Kemal became an Ottoman folk hero.

Though he was promoted to the rank of *paşa* ('pasha', general), the powers-that-be wanted to keep him under control. They saw him as a 'dangerous element', and they were right. When the war was lost and the empire was on the verge of being disarmed and dismembered, Mustafa Kemal Pasha began his revolution.

The Revolution

He held meetings and congresses to rally the people, began to establish democratic institutions and held off several invading armies (French, Italian, and Greek). He did all of this at the same time with severely limited resources. Several times the whole effort almost collapsed, and many of his friends and advisors were ready to ride for their lives out of Ankara. But Kemal never flinched, and was always ready to dare the worst.

He was skilful – and fortunate – enough to carry through. Many great revolutionary leaders falter or fade when the revolution is won. Atatürk lived 15 years into the republican era, and he had no doubts about what the new country's course should be. He introduced reforms and directed the country's progress with surprising foresight.

GEOGRAPHY & CLIMATE

Most first-time visitors come to Turkey expecting to find deserts, palm trees, and camel caravans. In fact, the country is geographically diverse, with snow-capped mountains, rolling steppeland, broad rivers, verdant coasts and rich agricultural valleys.

It's interesting to note that Ankara, the country's capital, is at a latitude similar to that of Naples, Lisbon, Peking, and Philadelphia. The southernmost shore of Turkey is similar in latitude to Tokyo, Seoul, Gibraltar, Norfolk (USA), and San Francisco.

Distances

Turkey is big: the distance by road from Edirne on the Bulgarian border to Kars on the Armenian one is over 1700 km. From the Black Sea shore to the Mediterranean coast is almost 1000 km. Now, 1000 km on flat ground might take only one very long day to drive, but Turkey has many mountain ranges which can lengthen travel times considerably.

Geographic Statistics

Turkey is between 35° and 42° north latitude, and 25° and 44° east longitude. It covers 779,452 sq km, and has borders with Armenia, Bulgaria, Georgia, Greece, Iran, Iraq and Syria. The coastline totals almost 8400 km – the Aegean coastline alone is 2800 km long. As for mountains, the highest is Ağrı Dağı (Mt Ararat) at 5165 metres. Uludağ (Mt Olympus) near Bursa is 2543 metres high. During imperial times, snow and ice could be taken from Uludağ, sailed across the Sea of Marmara, and presented to the sultan in İstanbul to cool his drinks.

Climatic Regions

Going from west to east, here's the lay of the land. See also the Climate graphs. For temperature conversion, see the table at the back of the book.

Marmara The Marmara region includes eastern Thrace from Edirne to İstanbul, rolling steppeland and low hills good for grazing, some farming and industry. The peninsula of Gelibolu (Gallipoli) forms the north shore of the Çanakkale Boğazı (the Dardanelles or Hellespont). On the southern shore of the Sea of Marmara are low hills and higher mountains (including Uludağ). The land is very rich, excellent for producing fruit such as grapes, peaches and apricots. Average rainfall is 668 mm; temperature extremes are 43.7°C maximum and -29.4°C minimum. This is Turkey's second most humid region, with an annual average of 73% humidity.

Aegean Fertile plains and river valleys, low hills and not-so-low mountains make up the Aegean region. The ancient river Meander, now called the Menderes, is a good example of the Aegean's rivers. When you see it from the heights of ruined Priene, you'll know where the word 'meander' comes from. When travelling, the Aegean region presents constantly changing views of olive, fig and

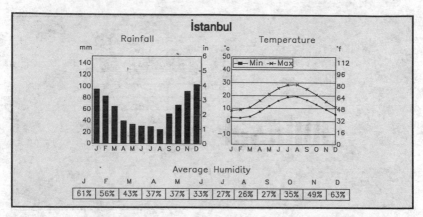

İstanbul

Rainfall

| J | F | M | A | M | J | J | A | S | O | N | D |

Temperature

Min —×— Max

Average Humidity

J	F	M	A	M	J	J	A	S	O	N	D
61%	56%	43%	37%	37%	33%	27%	26%	27%	35%	49%	63%

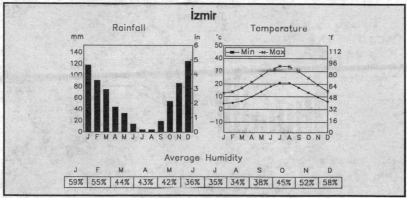

İzmir

Rainfall

Temperature

Min —×— Max

Average Humidity

J	F	M	A	M	J	J	A	S	O	N	D
59%	55%	44%	43%	42%	36%	35%	34%	38%	45%	52%	58%

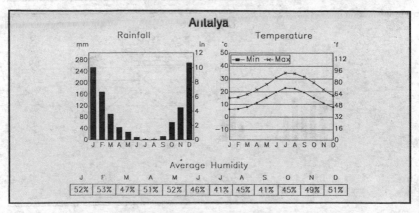

Antalya

Rainfall

Temperature

Min —×— Max

Average Humidity

J	F	M	A	M	J	J	A	S	O	N	D
52%	53%	47%	51%	52%	46%	41%	45%	41%	45%	49%	51%

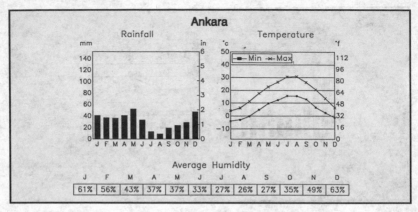

Ankara

Rainfall

Temperature

Average Humidity

J	F	M	A	M	J	J	A	S	O	N	D
61%	56%	43%	37%	37%	33%	27%	26%	27%	35%	49%	63%

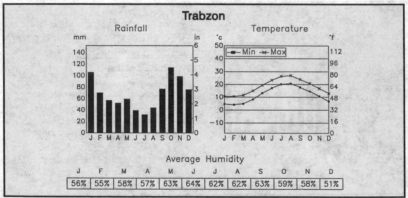

Trabzon

Rainfall

Temperature

Average Humidity

J	F	M	A	M	J	J	A	S	O	N	D
56%	55%	58%	57%	63%	64%	62%	62%	63%	59%	58%	51%

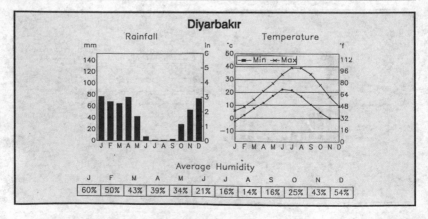

Diyarbakır

Rainfall

Temperature

Average Humidity

J	F	M	A	M	J	J	A	S	O	N	D
60%	50%	43%	39%	34%	21%	16%	14%	16%	25%	43%	54%

fruit orchards on hillsides; and broad tobacco and sunflower fields in the valleys. The maximum temperature is 44.6°C, minimum is -28°C. Average humidity is 69%; average annual rainfall is 647 mm.

Mediterranean The Mediterranean coast is mountainous without much beach between Fethiye and Antalya, but then opens up into a fertile plain between Antalya and Alanya before turning into mountains again. All along the south coast, mountains loom to the north. The great Taurus range stretches all the way from Alanya east to Adana. Temperatures at Antalya are a few degrees warmer than at İzmir. The eastern Mediterranean coast is always very humid. The maximum temperature is 45°C, minimum is -25.4°C. Annual precipitation is 777 mm; average humidity is 69%.

Central Anatolia The Turkish heartland of Central Anatolia is a vast high plateau broken by mountain ranges, including some volcanoes with snow-capped peaks. The land is mostly rolling steppe, good for growing wheat and grazing sheep. Ankara's elevation is 900 metres above sea level. In summer, Ankara is hot and dry; in winter, it's chilly and often damp. Late spring and early autumn are perfect. The maximum temperature is 41.8°C, the minimum is -34.4°C. Annual rainfall is a low 382mm; average humidity 62%.

Black Sea The Black Sea coast, 1700 km long, has a climate you might not expect to find in this part of the world. Rainfall is two to three times the national average, and temperatures are moderate. You will see hazelnut groves (on which the economy depends heavily), cherry orchards and tobacco fields. This is where cherries originated, getting their name in Roman times: the root word of 'cherry' is the Latin *cerasus* (Turkish: *kiraz)*. The cattle on the outskirts of every town provide milk, cream and butter famous throughout Turkey. At the eastern end of the Black Sea coast, the mountains come right down to the sea, and the slopes are covered with tea plantations. Rainfall and humidity are highest here. All in all, the Black Sea coast is like central Europe, but pleasantly warmer. The maximum temperature is 43°C, the minimum is -34°C. Annual rainfall is 781 mm and average humidity is 72%.

South-East Anatolia The region of southeast Anatolia is fairly dry (with 576 mm rainfall per year) and very hot in summer, with maximum temperatures reaching 47.6°C. Minimums are around -24°C. Average humidity, at 52%, is the lowest in Turkey. The land is rolling steppe with outcrops of rock. The major rivers are the Tigris (Dicle) and the Euphrates (Fırat), both of which have their sources in Turkey. The hot, dry climate produces bumper crops if there's water. The mammoth GAP hydro-electric project now provides irrigation water in abundance.

Eastern Anatolia A mountainous and somewhat forbidding zone, this is wildly beautiful like no other region in Turkey. The average temperature is a cool 9.5°C, but varies between a hot 42°C and a daunting -43.2°C. The rainfall here is average for Turkey, about 560 mm per year. It's cold out here except from June to September. The people are not as rich as in other regions, but they do well enough grazing sheep, raising wheat and producing a few other crops.

FLORA & FAUNA

Once cloaked in dense forest, after millennia of woodcutting Anatolia is now largely denuded. The government encourages conservation and reforestation, but the great forests will never return. The Mediterranean coast west of Antalya, the Black Sea area and north-eastern Anatolia still have forests of considerable size. Elsewhere, the great swaths of wild flowers which cover the rolling steppes in spring make fine splashes of colour.

Because of Turkey's temperate climate, domesticated plants such as apples, apricots, bananas, cherries, citrus fruit, cotton, date palms, grapes, sugar beet, sunflowers and tobacco thrive. The long roots of deliciously sweet *kavun* melons go deep into the dry soil of the Anatolian Plateau to find water. Turkey grows much of the world's supply of hazelnuts (filberts), and a large volume of pistachios and walnuts as well. Of the cash crops, cotton is king, and grains such as wheat and barley are important.

Turkey has similar animal life to that in the Balkans and much of Europe: bears, deer, jackals, lynx, wild boar, wolves, and rare leopards. Besides the usual domestic animals such as cattle, horses, donkeys, goats and several varieties of sheep (including the fat-tail), there are camels and water buffalo. (Though most yoghurt is made from cow's milk, that from sheep's milk is richer, and that from water buffalo's milk is richer still.)

Turkish shepherds are proud of their big, powerful and fierce Kangal sheep dogs which guard the flocks from hungry wolves. The breed is now controlled, and export is only allowed under licence. The same goes for the beautiful Van cats, with pure white fur and different-coloured eyes – one blue, one green.

Bird life is exceptionally rich, with many eagles, vultures and storks, as well as rare species such as the bald ibis, now nearly extinct. In several parts of the country reserves have been set aside as *kuş cenneti* ('bird paradises').

Turkey's coastal waters have rich varieties of fish, shellfish and other sea creatures, though overfishing and pollution are now serious problems.

GOVERNMENT
Parliament
Turkey is a parliamentary democracy. The Turkish Grand National Assembly (TGNA), elected by all citizens over 19 years of age, is the direct descendant of the congress assembled by Atatürk during the War of Independence to act as the legitimate voice of the Turkish people in place of the sultan.

President & Prime Minister
The president (usually elected by the TGNA from among its members) serves for one seven-year term and is supposed to be 'above politics,' and symbolise the nation. He (or, theoretically, she) is the head of state, with important executive powers and responsibilities and powers. But the true head of government, who decides its policies and directions, is the prime minister.

The prime minister is appointed by the president to form a government, and thus is almost always the head of the majority party, or of a likely coalition.

The judiciary, though theoretically independent, has in many instances been influenced by current government policies.

Political Parties
Though the Turks are firm believers in democracy, the tradition of popular rule and responsibility is relatively short. Real multi-party democracy came into being only after WW II (compared to England's tradition of almost 800 years). Turkish democracy has had its ups and downs.

Atatürk's Republican People's Party (RPP) enjoyed one-party rule until after WW II, when multi-party democracy became a reality. In the first elections the RPP lost out to the right-wing Democratic Party (DP), which attempted to control the government as closely as the RPP had before the war by grabbing extra-constitutional power. The Turkish armed forces, entrusted by Atatürk's legacy as guarantors of the Turkish constitution, intervened.

After the military intervention of 1960, the Democratic Party was banned, but its party faithful simply formed a successor, the similarly centre-right Justice Party (JP), and did as well in the elections as the centre-left RPP.

Under the watchful eye of the military, the RPP and JP governed as a coalition until 1965, when the JP won a parliamentary majority on its own, and its leader, Süleyman Demirel, began his first term as prime minister. He stepped down at the insistence of the military in 1971 as left-right violence and parliamentary deadlock threatened public order.

In 1973 a revivified RPP under Bülent Ecevit won election and formed a government, but was soon forced into coalition with a small far-right religious party.

During the 1970s the RPP and JP locked horns in parliament, both having around 40% of the votes. The smaller parties farther out on the political spectrum thus gained inordinate influence – their few votes making the difference between winning or losing a parliamentary vote. The Islamic fundamentalist National Salvation Party, the fascistic Nationalist Action Party, and the leftist Turkish Workers Party all traded their support for control of various government ministries through which to push their agendas. The result was widespread civil violence and government paralysis.

The bloodless military coup of September 1980 saw the dissolution of all former political parties and the exclusion from politics of their leaders (especially Ecevit and Demirel). In the elections of 1983, the armed forces supported a new centrist party formed of their supporters, but the new centre-right Motherland Party won.

Turgut Özal, founding leader of the Motherland Party, was a financial technocrat and former World Bank economist who had helped the military to revivify the economy after the 1980 intervention. His policies produced a boom in economic development, but also high inflation and charges of corruption. Throughout the decade his policies were challenged by several 'new' parties: the Social Democrat Populist Party, an heir to the RPP; the Democratic Left Party, led secretly by Ecevit, another heir to the RPP; the True Path Party, successor to Demirel's Justice Party; and the Prosperity Party, successor to the religious National Salvation Party.

Late in 1989, Turgut Özal was elected to the presidency. He remained active in Motherland Party politics, however, running the country through figurehead prime minister Yıldırım Akbulut. This was against at least the spirit if not the letter of the constitution, and raised eyebrows in political and military circles. In the hotly contested elections of February 1992 the Motherland Party gained only about a third of the vote, losing the plurality to the durable Süleyman Demirel, back from political exclusion, and his True Path Party. The centre-right True Path formed an unlikely coalition with the centre-left Social Democrat Populist Party under Professor Erdal İnönü (son of general, prime minister and president, the late İsmet İnönü) to form a government.

Demirel brought a new vigour to the government after almost a decade of Motherland leadership. With Özal's untimely death due to heart disease in April 1993, Demirel was elected to be the ninth president of the Turkish Republic. In June 1993, President Demirel asked Professor Tansu Çiller, the economics minister, to form a government, thereby making her Turkey's first female prime minister.

ECONOMY
Turkey has a strong agricultural base to its economy, being among the handful of countries which are net exporters of food. Wheat, cotton, sugar beet, sunflowers, hazelnuts, tobacco, fruit and vegetables are abundant. Sheep are the main livestock, and Turkey is the biggest wool producer in Europe. However, manufactured goods now dominate exports and much of the economy. Turkey builds motor vehicles, appliances, consumer goods and large engineering projects, and exports them throughout the region. There is still a large Turkish workforce in the industries of Europe, particularly those of Germany, which sends home remittances.

The independence of the Central Asian Turkic republics has given an important boost to the Turkish economy. These developing countries need modern goods and services of all types, from telecommunications to tyre factories, and Turkey stands ready and able to provide them.

POPULATION & PEOPLE
Turkey has a population approaching 60 million, the great majority being Sunni Muslim Turks.

Turks

The Turkic peoples originated in Central Asia, where they were a presence to be reckoned with as early as the 300s AD. The Chinese called them *Tu-küe*, which is perhaps the root of our word 'Turk'. They were related to the *Hiung-nu*, or Huns. The normally nomadic Turks ruled several vast empires in Central Asia before being pushed westward by the Mongols. Various tribes of the Oğuz Turkic group settled in Azerbaijan, northern Iran and Anatolia.

At first they were shamanist, but at one time or another these early Turks followed each of the great religions of the region, including Buddhism, Nestorian Christianity, Manichaeism and Judaism. During their western migrations they became more familiar with Islam, and it stuck.

Having begun their history as nomadic shepherds, the Turks used their skills as horsemen to become excellent soldiers. With the expansion of the Arab Empire into Turkish lands, the Turks used their renowned military prowess first to gain influence, and later to gain control. To this day most Turks are proud of their military traditions, and military prowess, courage and discipline are widely admired.

Kurds

There is a significant Kurdish minority estimated at 10 million. Some ethnologists believe that the Kurds, who speak an Indo-European language, are closely related to the Persians, and that they migrated here from northern Europe centuries before Christ. Turkey's sparsely populated eastern and south-eastern regions are home to perhaps six million Kurds and minorities of Turks, Armenians and others. Four million Kurds live elsewhere throughout the country, more or less integrated into greater Turkish society. (Yılmaz Güney's film *Yol* (The Road), winner of the best film award at Cannes in 1982, explores the dilemmas of a Kurd from a traditional family integrated into modern, urban Turkish society. Unfortunately, the subtitles do not do the script

justice, and anti-Turkish trailers were added by the foreign distributor.)

Though virtually all of Turkey's Kurds are Muslims and physically similar to the Turks, they jealously guard their language, cultural and family traditions.

Since the collapse of the Ottoman Empire, the Kurds have periodically aspired to their own ethnic nation-state with periodic revolts. Some dream of a Greater Kurdistan encompassing the millions of Kurds in neighbouring regions of Iran, Iraq and Syria. Fearing that Kurdish separatism could tear the country apart, the government in Ankara pursued a policy of assimilation. Officially, there were no 'Kurds', only 'mountain Turks,' and all were equal citizens of the republic. The Kurdish language and other overt signs of Kurdish life were outlawed.

In recent years the Kurdish question has come to the fore again. During the 1980s, Kurdistan Workers Party (PKK) guerrillas, based in neighbouring Syria, Iraq and Iran and supported clandestinely by the PLO, made hundreds of raids into south-eastern Turkey killing thousands of civilians and Turkish troops. The resulting military crackdown embittered many Turkish Kurds, but also brought the matter of Turks and Kurds to the national agenda. Some say Kurdish separatists fear that the vast South-east Anatolia Project (GAP) will bring prosperity to a historically poor region, thereby ruining their chances of ever founding an independent Kurdistan.

In 1988, Iraqi armed forces made a deadly chemical-weapon attack on the Iraqi Kurdish village of Halabja, sending thousands of refugees fleeing across the border to safety in Turkey. After the Gulf War of 1991, fearing similar attacks, three million Iraqi Kurds fled towards Turkey, threatening to overwhelm its eastern provinces.

The plight of the Kurds drew the attention of Europe and the USA, and resultant publicity led to a softening of Ankara's restrictions: Kurdish conversation and songs are now legal, and other measures such as Kurdish-language radio and TV broadcasts are being debated. But just as many Kurds are now beginning to imagine the delights of independence, their Turkish compatriots are imagining the disaster of the Turkish homeland dismembered. With the violent chaos of the former Soviet Caucasian republics and Yugoslavia in mind, one can only hope that the Kurds and Turks find some peaceful *modus vivendi*.

Other Islamic Peoples

Turkey's coasts are home to small ethnic or linguistic groups such as the Laz and Hemşin peoples along the Black Sea coast, and the Yörüks and Tahtacıs along the eastern Mediterranean coast.

Jews

The small Jewish community of about eight thousand people is centred on İstanbul, with smaller communities in İzmir, Ankara and other cities. The Turkish Jewish community is the remnant of a great influx which took place in the 1500s when the Jews of Spain (Sephardim) were forced by the Spanish Inquisition to flee their homes. They were welcomed into the Ottoman Empire, and brought with them knowledge of many recent European scientific and economic discoveries and advancements. In 1992 they celebrated 500 years of peaceful life among the Turks.

Christian Peoples

As for Christian Turkish citizens, ethnic Greeks number fewer than 100,000, they live mostly in İstanbul. Assyrian Orthodox Christians, sometimes called Jacobites, trace their roots to the church founded by Jacob Baradeus, the 6th-century bishop of Edessa (today called Şanlıurfa). Their small community has its centre south of Diyarbakır, in and around Mardin and the Tur Abdin.

Armenians

The Armenians are thought by some to be descended from the Urartians (518-330 BC), but others think they arrived from the Caucasus area after the Urartian state collapsed. Armenians have lived in eastern Anatolia for millennia, almost always as sub-jects of some greater state such as the Alexandrine empire, or of the Romans, Byzantines, Persians, Seljuks or Ottomans. They lived with their Kurdish and Turkish neighbours in relative peace and harmony under the Ottoman *millet* system of distinct religious communities. But when this system gave way to modern ethnic nationalism, they suffered one of the greatest tragedies in their history.

As ethnic groups on the fringes of the empire rose in rebellion and won their independence, the Armenians followed. Unlike other peoples, however, the Armenians lived in the Muslim heartland, where they were sometimes a plurality but never a majority. (The tragic ethnic wars of the early 1990s in the former Soviet Union and Yugoslavia arose from similarly confused ethnic situations.)

By the 1890s there were constant rebellions and Armenian terrorist attacks on Ottoman government buildings and personnel, which were inevitably answered with ferocious repression by the police and army. The revolutionaries hoped that if they triggered atrocities, the Christian powers of Europe would be persuaded to come to their aid, opening the way to independence. None of the powers, however, would allow any other to gain an advantage in the dismantling of the Ottoman Empire. Also, the tsar, like the sultan, did not want the creation of an independent Armenian state carved from his territory. The Armenians became the hopeless victims of their own small numbers, European power politics, and the Ottomans' alarm at the dissolution of their once-mighty country.

As the terrorist incidents continued, the Armenians' erstwhile Turkish and Kurdish neighbours turned against them violently. On 26 August 1896, Armenian revolutionaries seized the Ottoman Bank building in İstanbul, threatening to blow it up. Though they were unsuccessful, the incident provoked widespread massacres in the capital and elsewhere in which thousands of innocent Armenians died. The European powers raised their voices in protest, but again put no effective pressure on the sultan to stop the atrocities.

The restoration of the Ottoman constitution in 1908 provided a brief respite as all Ottoman peoples saw hope of living in harmony. But ethnic rivalries surfaced again quickly as Ottoman Bulgaria declared independence and Austria seized the former Ottoman provinces of Bosnia-Herzegovina. More Armenian demonstrations provoked massacres at Adana in April 1909. Albania and Arabia rose in revolt. War broke out with Italy, Bulgaria, Serbia and Greece. The Ottoman grand vizier was assassinated. The Ottoman Turks felt beleaguered on all sides.

As WW I approached, a triumvirate of Young Turks named Enver, Talat and Jemal seized power. When war broke out, the Christian Orthodox Armenians of eastern Turkey were seen (with some justification) as a 'fifth column' sympathetic to the advancing Russian army. On 20 April 1915 the Armenians of Van rose in revolt, massacred the local Muslims, took the *kale* (fortress) and held it until the Russian army arrived. Four days after the beginning of the Van revolt, on 24 April 1915 (now commemorated as Armenian Martyrs' Day) the Ottoman government began the deportation of the Armenian population from the war zone to Syria. Hundreds of thousands of Armenians (mostly men) were massacred in the process, the rest (mostly women and children) were marched to Syria in great privation.

With the Russian victories, a short-lived Armenian Republic was proclaimed in north-eastern Anatolia, and the victorious Armenians repaid defeated local Muslims with massacres in kind. But an offensive by the armies of Mustafa Kemal's Turkish nationalist Ankara government reclaimed Kars and Ardahan.

On 3 December 1920, the Ankara government concluded a peace treaty with the Armenian government in Erivan, now a Soviet republic. By the end of the war, the Armenian population of Anatolia had been reduced to insignificant numbers, mostly in the major cities.

The Armenians who survived the cataclysm, and their descendants in the diaspora, blame both the Ottoman government and the Turkish people as a whole for the tragedy, labelling it genocide. The Turks, while admitting that massacres occurred, deny that there was an official policy of genocide, claim that many Armenians were indeed traitorous, and that many if not most Armenian casualties were the result of civil war, disease and privation rather than massacre. Republican Turks dissociate themselves from the actions of the Ottoman government, pointing out that they themselves (or, more correctly, their parents and grandparents) fought to overthrow it.

Historians and pseudo-historians on both sides trade accusations and recriminations, dispute the actual number of casualties, the authenticity of incriminating historical documents, and the motives and actions of the other side. In the 1970s, Armenian terrorist assassinations of Turkish diplomats and their families raised the level of recrimination and bitterness. Armenians say they want the Turks to recognise and acknowledge the tragedy, and to provide compensation, perhaps even territory. Turks say they sympathise with the Armenians' great loss, but that those who were responsible are long dead, and those living today had nothing to do with it and cannot be held responsible, and thus compensation is inappropriate. It is an impasse likely to endure for generations.

EDUCATION

The Turkish Republic provides five years of compulsory primary education for all children aged from seven to 12 years. Secondary, *lise* (high school, lycée), and vocational or technical education is available at no cost to those who decide to continue. Specialised schools are available for the blind, the deaf, the mentally retarded, orphans and the very poor. There are also numerous licensed private schools and *kolej* ('colleges', like high schools) which charge tuition fees.

Turkey has 29 government-funded universities to which students are admitted through a central placement system. The language of instruction in Ankara's Middle East Technical University and Bilkent University, and İstanbul's Boğaziçi (Bosphorus) University is English.

ARTS

Ottoman Art

Art under the Ottomans was very different from art in the Turkish Republic. Until 1923 and the founding of the republic, all mainstream artistic expression had to conform to the laws of Islam, which forbade representation of any being 'with an immortal soul' (ie, animal or human). Sculpture and painting as we know them did not exist – with the notable exception of Turkish miniature painting, which was for the upper classes. Instead of painting and sculpture, Islamic artists worked at arabesque decoration, faïence, filigree, geometric stained glass, gilding, pottery and metalworking, glass-blowing, marquetry, repoussé work, calligraphy and illumination, textile design (including costumes and carpets), horticulture and landscape gardening. Turks may have invented the art of marbling paper, which is still practised today. Ottoman architecture is outstanding.

Most of these arts reached their height during the great age of Ottoman power from the early 1500s to the late 1700s. Turkish museums are full of examples of them: delicate coloured tiles from İznik, graceful glass vases and pitchers from İstanbul, carved wooden mosque doors, glittering illuminated Korans, intricate jewellery, and sumptuous costumes.

By the late 19th century educated Ottomans were taking up landscape and still-life painting in European styles.

Literature before the republic was also bound up with Islam. Treatises on history, geography and science were cast in religious

Pages from an 18th-century Turkish prayer book

terms. Ottoman poets, borrowing from the great Arabic and Persian traditions, wrote sensual love poems of attraction, longing, fulfilment and ecstasy about the search for union with God.

Republican Art
Under the republic, Atatürk encouraged European-style artistic expression. The government opened official painting and sculpture academies, encouraging this 'modern' secular art over the religious art of the past.

In this century, Turkish artists and writers have been in touch with European and US trends in the arts. Some have followed slavishly, others have borrowed judiciously, mixing in a good portion of local tradition and inspiration. By the 1970s and '80s, Turkish painting had become vigorous enough to support numerous different local schools of artists whose work is shown by museums, galleries, collectors and patrons.

By the late 19th century some Ottoman writers were adapting to European forms. With the foundation of the republic, the ponderous cadences of Ottoman courtly prose and poetry gave way to use of the vernacular. Atatürk decreed that the Turkish language be 'purified' of Arabic and Persian borrowings. This, and the introduction of the new Latin-based Turkish alphabet, brought literacy within the reach of many more citizens. Several Turkish writers, including Nazım Hikmet, Yashar Kemal and Orhan Pamuk, have been translated into other languages and have met with critical and popular acclaim abroad.

Folk Arts & Crafts
Turkish carpet-making transcends the boundaries of folk art and fine art. Embroidery and lace-making are still practised in rural Turkey, as they have been for centuries. Primitive landscape painters once used horse-drawn wagons and carts as their venue; now it's the wood-panelled sides of trucks. Turkish artisans also craft decorated wooden spoons, lathe-turned wooden items, lamps and stoves in tinplate, onyx and ala-

baster carvings, pottery and glass. Almost no one leaves the country without having bought a blue-and-white *nazar boncuğu* (evil-eye charm), usually of glass but now also of plastic.

Music
There are many kinds of Turkish music, almost all of them unfamiliar to foreign ears. Ottoman classical, religious (particularly *Mevlevi*) and some folk and popular music uses a system of *makams*, or modalities, exotic-sounding series of tones similar in function to Western scales. In addition to our whole-and half-tone intervals, much Turkish music uses quarter-tones, unfamiliar to foreign ears and perceived as 'flat' until your ear becomes accustomed to them.

Though Ottoman classical music sounds ponderous and lugubrious to the uninitiated, much Turkish folk music as played in the villages is sprightly and immediately appealing. *Türkü* music, of which you'll hear lots on the radio, falls somewhere in between: traditional folk music as performed by modern singers who live in the city.

The thousand-year-old tradition of Turkish troubadours *(aşık)*, still very much alive as late as the 1960s and '70s, is now dying out in its pure form – killed off by radio, TV, video and audio cassettes. But the songs of the great troubadours – Yunus Emre (1238?-1320?), Pir Sultan Abdal (1500s) and Aşık Veysel (who died in 1974) – are still popular and often performed and recorded.

Unfortunately, the sorts of Turkish music which are most easily comprehensible to foreign ears are the fairly vapid *taverna* styles, and the local popular songs based on European and US models. Though this music can be fun, it is also fairly mindless and forgettable.

Finally, there's Western music. Most of the groups and singers popular in Europe and the USA are popular in Turkey as well – everyone from Prince to Pavarotti. In Turkey Western classical symphony, chamber music, opera and ballet have a small but fiercely loyal following. Government-funded orchestras, dance groups and opera companies, supported by visiting artists, keep them satisfied.

Cinema

Cinema appeared in Turkey just a year after the Lumière brothers presented their first cinematic show in 1895. At first it was only foreigners and non-Muslims who watched movies, but by 1914 there were cinemas run by and for Muslims as well.

The War of Independence inspired actor Muhsin Ertuğrul, Turkey's cinema pioneer, to establish a film company in 1922 and make patriotic films. Comedies and documentaries followed. Within a decade Turkish films were winning awards in international competitions, even though a mere 23 films had been made.

After WW II the industry expanded rapidly with new companies and young directors. Lütfi Akad's *Kanun Namına* (In the Name of the Law, 1952), Turkey's first colour film, brought realism to the screen in the place of melodrama, and won first prize at the first Turkish film festival held a year later.

By the 1960s, Turkish cinema was delving deeply into social and political issues. Metin Erksan's *Susuz Yaz* (Dry Summer, 1964) won a gold medal at the Berlin Film Festival, and another award in Venice. Yılmaz Güney, the fiery actor-director, directed his first film *At, Avrat, Silah* (Horse, Woman, Gun) in 1966, and starred in Lütfi Akad's *Hudutların Kanunu* (The Law of the Borders) after he had written the script.

The 1970s brought the challenge of television, dwindling audiences, political pressures, and unionisation of the industry. The quality of films continued to improve, and social issues such as Turkish workers in Europe were treated with honesty, naturalism and dry humour. By the early 1980s, several Turkish directors were well recognised in Europe and the USA. Among current directors, Tunç Başaran, Zülfü, Halit Refiğ and Ömer Kavur bear watching.

CULTURE

At first glance, much of Turkish society is highly Europeanised. In the cities, men and women march off to jobs in offices and shops, farmers mount their tractors for a day in the fields, and bureaucrats belly up to typewriters and computer keyboards. But Turkish traditions are different from those of Europe, and glimpses of traditional attitudes and behaviour often come through.

Liberal Western attitudes born of Atatürk's reforms are strongest in the urban centres of the west and along the coasts, among the middle and upper classes. You will feel quite comfortable amongst these Turks, who look to Western culture as the ideal, and accept the validity of other religious beliefs.

The working and farming classes, particularly in the east, are more conservative, traditional and religious. There is a small but growing segment of 'born again' Muslims, fervent and strict in their religion but otherwise modern. Though always polite, these Turks may give you the feeling that East is East and West is West, and that the last echo of crusaders versus Saracens has not yet died away.

Hospitality is an honoured tradition in Turkey, from the shopkeeper who plies you with tea, coffee or soft drinks to the village family which invites you to share their home and meals for the customary three days. Commercialism has begun to corrupt traditional hospitality in tourist areas, producing the shady carpet merchant who lays on the friendliness with a trowel only to sell you shoddy goods at inflated prices. Don't let the carpet touts make you lose sight of true Turkish hospitality, which is a wonderful thing.

Customs & Practices

Under the Ottoman Empire (from the 1300s to 1923), Turkish etiquette was highly organised and very formal. Every encounter between people turned into a mini-ceremony full of the flowery 'romance of the East'. Though the Turks have adapted to the informality of 20th-century life, you'll still notice vestiges of this courtly state of mind. Were you to learn Turkish, you'd find dozens of polite phrases – actually rigid formulas – to be repeated on cue in many daily situations. Some are listed in the language section at the back of this book. Use one of these at the proper moment, and the Turks will love it.

Turks are very understanding of foreigners' different customs, but if you want to behave in accordance with local feelings, use all the polite words you can muster, at all times. This can get laborious, and even Turks complain about how one can't even get out the door without five minutes of politenesses. But even the complainers still say them.

Also note these things: don't point your finger directly towards any person. Don't show the sole of your foot or shoe towards anyone (ie, so they can see it). Don't blow your nose openly in public, especially in a restaurant; instead, turn or leave the room and blow quietly. Don't pick your teeth openly, but cover your mouth with your hand. Don't do a lot of kissing or hugging with a person of the opposite sex in public. All of these actions are considered rude and offensive.

Mosque Etiquette Always remove your shoes before stepping on a mosque's carpets, or on the clean area just in front of the mosque door. This is not a religious law, just a practical one. Worshippers kneel and touch their foreheads to the carpets, and they like to keep them clean. If there are no carpets, as in a saint's tomb, you can walk right in with your shoes on.

Wear modest clothes when visiting mosques, as you would when visiting a church. Don't wear tatty blue jeans, shorts (men or women) or weird gear. Women should have head, arms and shoulders covered, and wear modest dresses or skirts, preferably reaching to the knees. At some of the most visited mosques, attendants will lend you long robes if your clothing doesn't meet a minimum standard. The loan of the robe is free, though the attendant will probably indicate where you can give a donation to the mosque. If you donate, chances are that the money actually will go to the mosque.

Visiting Turkish mosques is generally very easy, though there are no hard and fast rules. Most times no-one will give you any trouble, but now and then there may be a stickler for propriety guarding the door, and he will keep you out if your dress or demeanour is not acceptable.

Avoid entering mosques at prayer time, (ie, at the call to prayer – dawn, noon, mid-afternoon, dusk and evening, or 20 minutes thereafter). Avoid visiting mosques at all on Fridays, especially morning and noon. Friday is the Muslim holy day.

When you're inside a mosque, even if it is not prayer time, there will usually be several people praying. Don't disturb them in any way; don't take flash photos; don't walk directly in front of them.

Everybody will love you if you drop some money into the donations box.

Body Language Turks say 'yes' (evet, eh-VEHT) by nodding the head forward and down.

To say 'no' (hayır, HAH-yuhr), nod your head up and back, lifting your eyebrows at the same time. Or just raise your eyebrows: that's 'no'.

Another way of saying 'no' is yok (YOHK): literally, 'It doesn't exist (here)', or 'We don't have any (of it)' – the same head upward, raised eyebrows applies.

Remember, when a Turkish person seems to be giving you an arch look, they're only saying 'no'. They may also make the sound 'tsk', which also means 'no'. There are lots of ways to say 'no' in Turkish.

By contrast, wagging your head from side to side doesn't mean 'no' in Turkish; it means 'I don't understand'. So if a Turkish person asks you, 'Are you looking for the bus to Ankara?' and you shake your head, they'll assume you don't understand English, and will probably ask you the same question again, this time in German.

There are other signs that can cause confusion, especially when you're out shopping. For instance, if you want to indicate length ('I want a fish this big'), don't hold your hands apart at the desired length, but hold out your arm and place a flat hand on it, measuring from your fingertips to the hand. Thus, if you want a pretty big fish, you must 'chop' your arm with your other hand at about the elbow.

Height is indicated by holding a flat hand the desired distance above the floor or some other flat surface such as a counter or table top.

If someone – a shopkeeper or restaurant waiter, for instance – wants to show you the stockroom or the kitchen, they'll signal 'Come on, follow me' by waving a hand downward and towards themselves in a scooping motion. Waggling an upright finger would never occur to them, except perhaps as a vaguely obscene gesture.

Atatürk

At the beginning of the 20th century, the Western image of the Ottoman Turks was of a decadent, sombre, ignorant and incompetent people. This Western image, which replaced that of the 'Terrible Turk' once there was no longer a threat that Turkey would conquer Europe, was based on a little truth and a lot of politics, but also on religious grounds – Turks were not Christians. Atatürk's success in holding off the Allied powers from dismembering Turkey, and his republican reforms, gave Turks a new, positive image of themselves as pro-European and modern in outlook.

Atatürk was the right man at the right time, and many Turks believe that without this particular man there is no way Turkey could be what it is today. Rather, it might have ceased to exist; at the least, it would be like one of its Islamic neighbours, with less material and social progress, and no real grounding in democratic traditions. The Turks look around them at their Islamic neighbours and think themselves lucky to have had a leader of such ability and foresight.

This all means something to the visitor. There is a law against defaming the national hero, who is still held in the highest regard by most Turks (excluding the religious right), and similar laws against showing disrespect to other patriotic symbols such as the Turkish flag. You won't see cartoons or caricatures of Atatürk, and no one mentions him in jest. A slight directed toward Atatürk or the flag is virtually the same as insulting the Turks and their country.

RELIGION

The Turkish population is 99% Muslim, mostly of the Sunni creed; there are groups of Shiites in the east and south-east. A small community of Sephardic Jews, descendants of those who were driven out of Spain by the Inquisition and welcomed into the Ottoman Empire, exists in İstanbul. There are groups of Greek Orthodox, Armenian Orthodox, Byzantine Catholic, Armenian Roman Catholic, Armenian Protestant, Assyrian and a few even smaller sects. But all of these non-Muslim groups make up less than 1% of the population, so to talk about Turkish religion is to talk about Islam.

The story of Islam's founding is covered in the History section.

Principles of Islam

The basic beliefs of Islam are these: God (Allah) created the world and everything in it pretty much according to the biblical account. In fact, the Bible is a sacred book to Muslims. Adam, Noah, Abraham, Moses and Jesus were prophets. Their teachings and revelations are accepted by Muslims, except for Jesus' divinity and his status as saviour. Jews and Christians are called 'People of the Book', meaning those with a revealed religion that preceded Islam. The Koran prohibits enslavement of any People of the Book. Jewish prophets and wise men, Christian saints and martyrs, are all accepted as holy in Islam.

However, Islam is the 'perfection' of this earlier tradition. Though Moses and Jesus were great prophets, Muhammed was the greatest and last, *the* Prophet. To him, God communicated his final revelation, and entrusted him to communicate it to the world. Muhammed is not a saviour, nor is he divine. He is God's messenger, deliverer of the final, definitive message.

Muslims do not worship Muhammed, only God. In fact, *muslim* in Arabic means, 'one who has submitted [to God's will]'; *islam* is 'submission [to God's will]'. It's all summed up in the *ezan*, the phrase called out from the minaret five times a day and said at the beginning of Muslim prayers: 'God is great! There is no god but God, and Muhammed is his Prophet.'

The Koran
God's revelations to Muhammed are contained in the *Kur'an-i Kerim*, the Holy Koran. Muhammed recited the *suras* (verses or chapters) of the Koran in an inspired state. They were written down by followers, and are still regarded as the most beautiful, melodic and poetic work in Arabic literature, sacred or profane. The Koran, being sacred, cannot be translated. It exists truly only in Arabic.

The Islamic Commonwealth
Ideally, Islam is a commonwealth, a theocracy, in which the religious law of the Koran is the only law – there is no secular law. Courts are religious courts. In Turkey and several other Muslim countries, this belief has been replaced by secular law codes. By contrast, Ayatollah Khomeini attempted to do away with secular law and return to the exclusive use of Islamic law in the Islamic Republic of Iran. In Saudi Arabia, religious law of the strict Wahhabi sect rules as well.

Religious Duties & Practices
To be a Muslim, one need only submit in one's heart to God's will and perform a few basic and simple religious duties:

One must say, understand and believe, 'There is no god but God, and Muhammed is His Prophet'.

One must pray five times daily: at dawn, at noon, at mid-afternoon, at dusk and after dark.

One must give alms to the poor.

One must keep the fast of Ramazan, if capable of doing so.

One must make a pilgrimage to Mecca once during one's life, if possible.

Muslim prayers are set rituals. Before praying, Muslims must wash hands and arms, feet and ankles, head and neck in running water; if no water is available, in clean sand; if there's no sand, the motions will suffice. Then they must cover their head, face Mecca and perform a precise series of gestures and genuflexions. If they deviate from the pattern, they must begin again.

In daily life, a Muslim must not touch or eat pork, or drink 'wine' (interpreted as any alcoholic beverage), and must refrain from fraud, usury, slander and gambling. No sort of image of any 'being with an immortal soul' (ie, human or animal) can be revered or worshipped in any way.

Islam has been split into many factions and sects since the time of Muhammed. Islamic theology has become very elaborate and complex. These tenets, however, are still the basic ones shared by all Muslims.

LANGUAGE
Turkish is the dominant language in the Turkic language group which also includes such less-than-famous tongues as Kirghiz, Kazakh and Azerbaijani. Once thought to be related to Finnish and Hungarian, the Turkic languages are now seen as comprising their own unique language group. You can find people who speak Turkish, in one form or another, from Belgrade all the way to Xinjiang in China.

In 1928, Atatürk did away with the Arabic alphabet and adopted a Latin-based alphabet much better suited to easy learning and correct pronunciation. He also instituted a language reform to purge Turkish of abstruse Arabic and Persian borrowings, in order to rationalise and simplify it. The result is a logical, systematic and expressive language which has only one irregular noun *(su,* water), one irregular verb *(etmek,* to be) and no genders. It is so logical, in fact, that Turkish grammar formed the basis for the development of Esperanto.

Word order and verb formation are very different from those belonging to the Indo-European languages, which makes Turkish somewhat difficult to learn at first despite its elegant simplicity. Verbs, for example, consist of a root plus any number of modifying suffixes. Verbs can be so complex that they constitute whole sentences in themselves, though this is rare. The standard example for blowing your mind is *Afyonkarahisarlılaştıramadıklarımızdanmısınız?* ('Aren't you one of those people whom we tried – unsuccessfully – to make to resemble the citizens of Afyonkarahisar?'). It's not the sort of word you see every day.

Turks don't expect any foreigner to know Turkish, but if you can manage a few words you'll delight them. For their part, they'll try whatever foreign words they know, usually English or German, but some French, Danish, Dutch or Swedish as well. In this guide I've written the necessary Turkish words into the text wherever possible, so that you won't be at a loss for words. For a full collection of words, see the Turkish Language Guide section and glossary at the back of this book.

Facts for the Visitor

VISAS & EMBASSIES

When visiting Turkey, citizens of Australia, Canada, Eire, Japan, New Zealand, the USA and virtually all the countries of Western Europe need only a valid passport for stays up to three months. Make sure your passport has at least three months' validity remaining, or you may not be admitted. UK and Hong Kong passport holders need a visa, obtainable at the border with no trouble for £5. Make sure your passport is good for at least another three months, and carry a cash £5 note (British, not Scottish) to pay for the visa.

Australia *(Avustralya)*
Ankara Embassy: Nene Hatun Caddesi 83, Gaziosmanpaşa, Ankara (☎ (4) 436 1240/5; fax 445 0284)
İstanbul Consulate: Tepecik Yolu 58, 80630 Etiler, İstanbul (☎ (1) 257 7050; fax 257 7054) open from 8.30 am to 12.30 pm weekdays

Austria *(Avusturya)*
Ankara Embassy: Atatürk Bulvarı 189, Kavaklıdere (☎ (4) 434 2172/4; fax 418 9454)
İstanbul Consulate: Köybaşı Caddesi 46, 80870 Yeniköy (☎ (1) 262 9315, 262 4984; fax 262 2622)
İzmir Honorary Consulate: Şehit Fethibey Caddesi 41/704 (☎ (51) 83 61 23; fax 84 81 27)

Belgium *(Belçika)*
Ankara Embassy: Nenehatun Caddesi 100, Gaziosmanpaşa (☎ (4) 436 1653; fax 436 7143)
İstanbul Consulate: Sıraselviler Caddesi 73, Taksim (☎ (1) 243 3300, 243 2068; fax 243 5074)
İzmir Honorary Consulate: Atatürk Caddesi 228/12 (☎ (51) 21 86 47; fax 22 41 61)

Bulgaria *(Bulgaristan)*
Ankara Embassy: Atatürk Bulvarı 124, Kavaklıdere (☎ (4) 426 7456; fax 427 3178)
İstanbul Consulate: Zincirlikuyu Caddesi 44, Ulus, Levent (☎ (1) 2269 0478, 269 2216)

Canada *(Kanada)*
Ankara Embassy: Nenehatun Caddesi 75, Gaziosmanpaşa (☎ (4) 436 1275/9; fax 446 4437)
İstanbul Honorary Consulate: Büyükdere Caddesi 107/3, Gayrettepe (☎ (1) 272 5174)
Commonwealth of Independent States (see Russia)

Denmark *(Danimarka)*
Ankara Embassy: Kırlangıç Sokak 42, Gaziosmanpaşa (☎ (4) 427 5258; fax 468 4559)
İstanbul Consulate: Bilezik Sokak 2, 80040 Fındıklı (☎ (1) 252 0600; fax 249 4434)
İzmir Honorary Consulate: Akdeniz Caddesi, Reyent İşhanı (☎ (51) 89 54 01; fax 25 53 88)

Egypt *(Mısır)*
Ankara Embassy: Atatürk Bulvarı 126, Kavaklıdere (☎ (4) 426 6478; fax 427 0099)
İstanbul Consulate: Bebek Sarayı, Cevdetpaşa Caddesi 173, Bebek (☎ (1) 263 6038, 265 2440; fax 257 4428)

Finland *(Finlandiya)*
Ankara Embassy: Galipdede Sokak 1/20, Farabi (☎ (4) 426 5921; fax 468 2507)
İstanbul Honorary Consulate: Mete Caddesi 24/1, 80090 Taksim (☎ (1) 245 5880, 251 2814; fax 249 2475)
İzmir Honorary Consulate: 1881 Sokak No 30/32, Balçova (☎ (51) 59 88 45; fax 85 41 77)

France *(Fransa)*
Ankara Embassy: Paris Caddesi 70, Kavaklıdere (☎ (4) 468 1154; fax 467 9434)
İstanbul Consulate: İstiklal Caddesi 8, Taksim (☎ (1) 243 1852/3; fax 249 9168)

Germany *(Almanya)*
Ankara Embassy: Atatürk Bulvarı 114, Kavaklıdere (☎ (4) 426 5451/65; fax 426 6959)
İstanbul Consulate: İnönü (Gümüşsuyu) Caddesi, Selim Hatun Camii Sokak 46, Ayazpaşa, Taksim (☎ (1) 251 5404; fax 249 9920)
İzmir Consulate: Atatürk Caddesi 260 (☎ (51) 21 69 95; fax 63 40 23)

Greece *(Yunanistan)*
Ankara Embassy: Ziya-ur-Rahman Sokak (Karagöz Sokak) 9-11, Gaziosmanpaşa (☎ (4) 436 8861; fax 446 3191)
İstanbul Consulate: Turnacıbaşı Sokak 32, Ağahamam, Kuloğlu, Beyoğlu (☎ (1) 245 0596/98; fax 252 1365)

India *(Hindistan)*
Ankara Embassy: Cinnah Caddesi 77/A, Çankaya (☎ (4) 438 2195; fax 440 3429)
İstanbul Honorary Consulate: Cumhuriyet Caddesi 257/3, Harbiye (☎ (1) 248 4864/5; fax 230 3697)
İzmir Honorary Consulate: Anadolu Caddesi 37-39, Koyuncuoğlu Han, Salhane (☎ (51) 86 10 64; fax 35 05 49)

Iran *(İran)*
Ankara Embassy: Tahran Caddesi 10, Kavaklıdere (☎ (4) 429 4320)

İstanbul Consulate: Ankara Caddesi 1/2, Cağaloğlu (☎ (1) 513 8230)

Iraq *(Irak)*
Ankara Embassy: Turan Emeksiz Sokak 11, Gaziosmanpaşa (☎ (4) 426 6118, 426 3907)
İstanbul Consulate: Halide Edip Adıvar Mahallesi, İpekböceği Sokak 1
(☎ (1) 230 2930/3; fax 234 5726)

Israel *(İsrail)*
Ankara Embassy: Farabi Sokak 43, Çankaya (☎ (4) 426 3904; fax 426 1533)
İstanbul Consulate: Valikonağı Caddesi 73/4, Nişantaşı (☎ (1) 246 4125/7)

Italy *(İtalya)*
Ankara Embassy: Atatürk Bulvarı 118, Kavaklıdere (☎ (4) 426 5460; fax 426 5800)
İstanbul Consulate: Palazzo di Venezia, Tomtom Kaptan Sokak 15, 80073 Galatasaray
(☎ (1) 243 1024, 251 3294; fax 252 5879)
İzmir Consulate: 1377 Sokak 2/1, Mutlu Apt, Alsancak (☎ (51) 63 66 96; fax 21 29 14)

Japan *(Japon)*
Ankara Embassy: Reşit Galip Caddesi 81, Gaziosmanpaşa (☎ (4) 446 0500/3; fax 437 1812)
İstanbul Consulate: İnönü Caddesi 24, Ayazpaşa, Taksim (☎ (1) 251 7605/8; fax 252 5864)

Jordan *(Ürdün Kralliyeti)*
Ankara Embassy: Dedekorkut Sokak 18, Çankaya (☎ (4) 446 0500)
İstanbul Honorary Consulate: Valikonağı Caddesi 63, Nişantaşı (☎ (1) 230 1221/2; fax 241 4331)

Lebanon *(Lübnan)*
Ankara Embassy: Cinnah Caddesi 11/3, Çankaya (☎ (4) 426 3729)
İstanbul Consulate: Saray Apt 134/1, Teşvikiye (☎ (1) 236 1365/6; fax 227 3373)

Netherlands *(Holanda)*
Ankara Embassy: Köroğlu Sokak 16, Gaziosmanpaşa (☎ (4) 446 0470; fax 446 3358)
İstanbul Consulate: İstiklal Caddesi 393, Tünel, Beyoğlu (☎ (1) 251 5030; fax 251 9289)
İzmir Honorary Consulate: Cumhuriyet Meydanı, Meydan Apt 11/2 (☎ (51) 63 49 80; fax 22 06 90)

New Zealand *(Yeni Zelanda)*
Ankara Embassy: Kızkulesi Sokak 42/1, Gaziosmanpaşa (☎ (4) 446 0768, 446 0732; fax 445 0557)

Norway *(Norveç)*
Ankara Embassy: Kelebek Sokak 20, Gaziosmanpaşa (☎ (4) 437 9950; 437 6430)
İstanbul Honorary Consulate: Rıhtım Caddesi 89, Frank Han, Kat 3, Karaköy (☎ (1) 249 9753; fax 251 3173)
İzmir Honorary Consulate: 1378 Sokak No 4/1, Kordon İşhanı 2/201 (☎ (51) 63 32 90; fax 22 06 90)

Russia *(Rusya)*
Ankara Embassy: Karyağdı Sokak 5, Çankaya (☎ (4) 439 2122/3; 438 3952)
İstanbul Consulate: İstiklal Caddesi 443, Tünel, Beyoğlu (☎ (1) 244 2610, 244 1693; fax 249 0107)

Spain *(İspanya)*
Ankara Embassy: Abdullah Cevdet Sokak 9, Çankaya (☎ (4) 438 0392/3/4; fax 439 5170)
İstanbul Consulate: Valikonağı Caddesi 33, Başaran Apt, Harbiye (☎ (1) 240 3444, 247 7452; fax 262 6530)
İzmir Honorary Consulate: Cumhuriyet Bulvarı 109, Alsancak (☎ (51) 89 79 96; fax 84 38 73)

Sweden *(İsveç)*
Ankara Embassy: Katip Çelebi Sokak 7, Kavaklıdere (☎ (4) 428 6735; fax 468 5020)
İstanbul Consulate: İstiklal Caddesi 497, Tünel, Beyoğlu (☎ (1) 243 5770/1/2; fax 252 4114)
İzmir Honorary Consulate: 1378 Sokak No 4/1, Kordon İşhanı 2/201, Alsancak (☎ (51) 22 01 38; fax 22 06 90)

Switzerland *(İsviçre)*
Ankara Embassy: Atatürk Bulvarı 247, Çankaya (☎ (4) 467 5555; fax 467 1199)
İstanbul Consulate: Hüsrev Gerede Caddesi 75/3, 80200 Teşvikiye, Şişli (☎ (1) 259 1115/7; fax 259 1118)

Syria *(Suriye)*
Ankara Embassy: Abdullah Cevdet Sokak 7, Çankaya (☎ (4) 438 8704, 439 4588)
İstanbul Consulate: Silahhane Caddesi 59/5, Ralli Apt, Teşvikiye, Şişli (☎ (1) 248 2735, 248 3284)

UK *(İngiltere, Birleşik Krallığı)*
Ankara Embassy: Şehit Ersan Caddesi 46/A, Çankaya (☎ (4) 427 4310; fax 468 3214)
İstanbul Consulate: Meşrutiyet Caddesi 34, Tepebaşı, Beyoğlu (☎ (1) 244 7540/5; fax 245 4989)
İzmir Vice Consulate: Mahmut Esat Bozkurt Caddesi, 1442 Sokak No 49 (☎ (51) 63 51 51; fax 21 29 14)

USA *(Amerika Birleşik Devletleri, Amerika)*
Ankara Embassy: Atatürk Bulvarı 110, Kavaklıdere (☎ (4) 426 5470; fax 467 0019)
Adana Consulate: Atatürk Caddesi (☎ (71) 54 21 45, 54 37 74; fax 57 65 91)
İstanbul Consulate: Meşrutiyet Caddesi 106, Tepebaşı, Beyoğlu (☎ (1) 251 3602; fax 251 3218)

Yugoslavia (former) *(Yugoslavya)*
Ankara Embassy: Paris Caddesi 47, Kavaklıdere (☎ (4) 426 2432; fax 427 8345)
İstanbul Consulate: Valikonağı Caddesi 96/A, Nişantaşı (☎ (1) 248 1133, 248 1004; fax 278 0570)

Eastern European Visas
If you travel to Turkey by rail or road (bus, car, motorcycle, bicycle), you may need visas for transit of Eastern European countries. At this writing, it is uncertain what policies the newly independent countries in the Balkans (the former Yugoslav republics, Bulgaria) may pursue. Contact the diplomatic missions of the countries through which you plan to pass.

DOCUMENTS
An International Student Identity Card (ISIC) gets you discounts at museums, historic buildings and archaeological sites, and on some transportation. See Special Discounts under Money in this chapter.

If you plan to stay in Turkey more than three months, you might want to apply for a residence permit *(ikamet tezkeresi)*. Contact a tourist office or tourism police office. You will need to show means of support: savings, a steady income from outside the country, or legal work within the country (see Work in this chapter). Most people staying for a shorter period, or working without a valid permit (as short-term private tutors of English, for example), cross the border into Greece for a day or two every three months rather than bother with the residence permit.

You need proof of vaccination against infectious diseases only if you are coming from an endemic or epidemic area.

An International Driving Permit is usually not necessary. See Customs, below, for details.

CUSTOMS
Upon entering the country, customs inspection is often very cursory for foreign tourists. There may be spot-checks, but you probably won't have to open your bags.

Arrival
A verbal declaration is usually all you need; the major airports use the red and green channel system. You can bring in up to one kg of coffee, five litres of liquor and two cartons (400) of cigarettes. Things of excep-

tional value (jewellery, unusually expensive electronic or photographic gear etc) are supposed to be declared, and may be entered in your passport to guarantee that you will take the goods out of the country when you leave.

Vehicles Automobiles, minibuses, trailers, towed watercraft, motorcycles and bicycles can be brought in for up to three months without a carnet or triptyque. Drivers must have a valid driving licence; an International Driving Permit is useful, but not normally required. Your own national driving licence should pass all right. Third-party insurance such as a Green Card valid for the entire country (not just for Thrace or European Turkey) or a Turkish policy purchased at the border is obligatory.

Departure
It is illegal to buy, sell, possess or export antiquities! Read on.

You may export valuables (except antiquities) that have been registered in your passport on entry, or that have been purchased with legally converted money. For souvenirs, the maximum export limit is US$1000 of all items combined; if two or more similar items are exported, a licence may be required. Also, you may need to show proof of exchange transactions for at least these amounts. Save your currency exchange slips, and have them ready for the customs officer in the departure area.

Your bags may well be searched when you leave the country (both for customs and security reasons), and questions may be asked about whether or not you are taking any antiquities with you. Only true antiquities are off limits, not the many artful fakes. If you buy a real Roman coin from a shepherd boy at an archaeological site, can you take it home with you? Legally not. What happens if you get caught trying to smuggle out a significant piece of ancient statuary? Big trouble.

Turkey is one of those countries with treasure-troves of antiquities, some of which are smuggled out of the country and fed into the international contraband art market. The Turkish government takes vigorous measures to defend its patrimony against theft. Antiquity smuggling, like drug smuggling, is a dirty business. Keep away from it.

Arrival Home

My own view, after decades of travel, is that customs officials in your home country encounter hundreds of travellers returning from abroad every week. They see what travellers have bought; they know pretty well what was paid. You are not the expert on souvenirs and prices, *they are!* Make a full and honest declaration to avoid expensive unpleasantness.

British readers have written to warn that you should get official-looking receipts from Turkish shopkeepers for any expensive item you purchase to take home to the UK. British customs officers may expect you to under-declare, asking 'What did you *really* pay?' If you budge from your original price (as on the receipt), they'll read you the riot act, and you'll have to cough up some duty. If you try to smuggle dutiable goods through the 'green' channel and are caught, they may offer you a choice: pay a fine equal to the price you paid for the goods abroad, or face criminal prosecution.

MONEY
Currency

The unit of currency is the Turkish *lira*, or TL, which was called the Turkish pound (LT) in the Ottoman Empire. The lira is supposedly divided into 100 *kuruş* (koo-ROOSH), but inflation of roughly 70 to 100% per year has rendered the kuruş obsolete. It may be that the Turkish government will drop several zeros from the currency in future, bringing the kuruş back to life.

Coins are 500 and 1000 liras, with 2500 and 5000-lira coins becoming more common; higher denominations may follow. Banknotes come as 1000, 5000, 10,000, 20,000, 50,000 and 100,000 liras; the introduction of 250,000 and 500,000-lira notes cannot be far off.

Exchange Rates

The exchange rates when this guide went to press were:

US$1	=	10,500TL
UK£1	=	16,300TL
A$1	=	7200TL
NZ$1	=	5700TL
C$1	=	8300TL
DM1	=	6600TL

Changing Money Wait until you arrive in Turkey to change your home currency (cash or travellers' cheques) into Turkish liras. Exchange bureaus in other countries (eg the UK, USA) usually offer terrible rates of exchange. When in doubt, check the foreign exchange listings in the business section of any important daily newspaper, or call a commercial bank. A proper tourist exchange rate will be only a few percentage points less than – and may well be better than – this published rate.

You will always need your passport when you change travellers' cheques in Turkey, and you may need it when you change cash as well.

Many tourist shops, travel agencies, expensive restaurants and most hotels accept foreign currency, though they often give bad rates of exchange. Most post office (PTT) branches will give you liras for foreign cash, but not always for travellers' cheques. Eurocheques are readily accepted by banks and also by many shops. With the value of the Turkish lira constantly dropping, it's wise to change money every few days rather than all at once at the beginning of your visit.

Travellers' Cheques Turkish banks, shops and hotels often see it as a burden to change travellers' cheques, and may try to get you to go elsewhere. You must often press the issue. The more expensive hotels, restaurants and shops will more readily accept the cheques, as will car rental agencies and travel agencies, but not at good rates of exchange. Generally it's better to change cheques to Turkish liras at a bank, although some banks may charge a fee (see Commissions in the Banks section).

Exchange Receipts Save your currency exchange receipts *(bordro)*. You may need them to change back Turkish liras at the end of your stay, and to show to the customs officer if you've purchased expensive souvenirs such as carpets or jewellery. Turkish liras are worth less outside the country, so you won't want to take any with you.

Credit & Cash Cards

Big hotels and the more expensive shops will accept your credit card. Car rental agencies certainly will. Make sure in advance because not all establishments accept all cards. If you have American Express, Visa, Diners Club, MasterCard, Access and Eurocard, you're probably equipped for any establishment that takes cards. If you only have one or two cards, ask. Turkish Airlines, for instance, may accept only Visa, MasterCard, Access and Eurocard. The Turkish State Railways doesn't accept credit cards at present, but it may soon do so. A souvenir shop may accept all major cards.

Shopkeepers may require you to pay the credit card fee from 3 to 7%, or the charges (up to US$10) for making credit card arrangements *(provizyon)* with a bank: they may not see it as a normal cost of business. Any price, whether marked or haggled for, is assumed to be for cash.

Turkey now has many of those marvellous automated teller machines (ATMs, cash machines) which pay out money from your account when you insert your credit or cash card and secret password. Some furnish operating directions in various foreign languages.

These machines can be the easiest, fastest and cheapest way to get liras, but you must be certain they will work and not just swallow your card. Show your card to the bank's officers. If they seem anything less than completely certain that it will work, be careful.

Banks

Banks are open from 8.30 am till noon, and from 1.30 to 5 pm, Monday to Friday. Outside those times it can be difficult to change money, so plan ahead, and anticipate holidays such as Şeker Bayramı and Kurban Bayramı (see Business Hours & Holidays and When to Go in this chapter). There are currency exchange desks open long hours at the major entry points to Turkey by road, air and sea. The rate at the entry point will be pretty close to the one in town, so it's a good idea to change some money when you enter – US$25 or US$50 at least.

Most banks will change money for you. Look for a sign on or near the front door reading 'Kambiyo – Exchange – Change – Wechsel', which says it all. In the large cities, big banks have branches everywhere, even within 100 metres of one another, and exchange facilities may be limited to the more convenient branches. If a particular bank can't change your money, don't worry. You won't have to walk very far to reach the next one.

In major tourist centres, non-bank currency exchange offices are becoming prominent; they prefer to change cash, but will usually change travellers' cheques if you pressure them.

Procedures Changing money, either banknotes or travellers' cheques, can take anywhere from two to 20 minutes. It depends upon the bank and how cumbersome its procedures are. Sometimes a clerk must type up a form with your name and passport number, you must sign it once or twice, it must be countersigned by one or two bank officers, and then a cashier in a glass booth *(vezne)* will give you your money. Always take your passport when changing money, and be prepared to wait a while.

Commissions Some banks charge a fee for changing travellers' cheques (though not for changing cash notes). The Türkiye İş Bankası, for instance, charges up to 3%, plus the cost of official stamps. To find out before you begin, ask *Komisyon alınır mı?* (kohmeess-YOHN ah-luh-NUHR muh, 'Is a commission taken?'). Sometimes the teller will scribble some figures on the back of the form, then pay out your liras several thousand short, saying this is a commission, but will give no receipt.

Transferring Money The speed with which you need to transfer money determines the cost of the transfer. If you have months, send a letter home, ask for a cheque, deposit the cheque in a Turkish bank for clearance, then wait. Of course, banks can telex or wire money in a matter of a day or two (usually), but this may cost as much as US$30 per transfer. Sometimes the transfer fee is a percentage of the amount transferred. Still, if you're in a hurry, you may have to do it. Have your passport with you when you go to receive your money.

The PTT in Turkey handles postal money orders, and this is fine for small amounts. For large amounts, you'd do better with a bank.

Before transferring money, consider these alternatives: some shopkeepers and other businesses will accept a personal cheque in exchange for a purchase. If you have a Turkish friend to countersign a cheque, you may well be able to get cash from a bank. With some credit cards, you may be able to get a cash advance on the card from a bank or cash machine (see above), or use the card as security to cash a cheque at the card's company office. Even if the amount is limited (from US$100 to US$150 per day), it doesn't take many days to build up a substantial sum. A bank may require you to pay a telex or fax charge of a few dollars for a credit card cash advance.

The Black Market There is no currency black market to speak of as the Turkish lira is almost fully convertible.

Costs

All costs in this book are given only in US dollars as prices in Turkish liras are ever changing.

In recent years, inflation has been 75 to 100% per annum, though the government swears it is trying hard to bring it down. The exchange rates for hard currency reflect a slow, 'creeping' devaluation which offsets this inflation and keeps the actual cost for a foreign tourist reasonable.

Turkey is Europe's low-price leader, and you can travel on as little as US$15 to US$20 (average) per day using buses, staying in pensions, and eating one restaurant meal daily. For US$20 to US$45 per person per day you can travel more comfortably by bus and train, staying in one-and two-star hotels with private baths, and eating most meals in average restaurants. For US$45 to US$75 per day you can move up to three-and four-star hotels, take the occasional airline flight, and dine in restaurants all the time. If you have over US$100 per person to spend, you can travel luxury class. Costs are highest in İstanbul, lowest in small eastern towns off the tourist track.

Here are some average costs:

Single/double room in small pension – US$8 to US$18
Single/double room with bath in one-star hotel – US$15 to US$30
Three-course meal in simple restaurant – US$6
Loaf of bread – 25c
Bottle of beer (from a shop) – 95c
Litre of petrol/gasoline – 70 to 90c
100 km by express train (1st class) – US$2.20 to US$2.70
100 km by bus – US$2 to US$2.50
Local telephone call – 10c
Turkish Daily News – 50c

Special Discounts

Holders of International Student Identity Cards are admitted to museums at sharply reduced fees. In fact, it's a good idea to show your student card before you show your money in almost every payment situation.

Students with ISICs get discounts of 10% on the Turkish State Railways and on Turkish Maritime Lines ships. Turkish Airlines, which used to give very good student discounts, does not do so any more. However, the airline does offer a 10% 'family discount' to any husband-and-wife couple, with or without children.

Turkey is part of the Wasteels and Inter-

Rail Youth discount schemes for rail, so if you have one of these cards, it will save you money on Turkish train fares.

Tipping

Restaurants In the cheapest places tipping is not necessary, though some people do leave a few coins in the change plate. In more expensive restaurants, tipping is more usual.

Some places will automatically add a service charge (servis ücreti) of 10 or 15% to your bill, but this does not absolve you from the tip, oddly enough. The service charge goes either into the pocket of the patron (owner), or to the maître d'hôtel. Leave 5% on the table for the waiter, or hand it directly to him.

If service is included, the bill may say servis dahil (service included). Still, a small tip is expected. In any situation, 5 to 10% is fine. Only in the fancy foreign-operated hotels will waiters expect those enormous 15 to 20% US-style tips. In the very plain, basic restaurants you needn't tip at all, though the price of a soft drink or a cup of coffee is always appreciated.

Hotels In the cheapest hotels there are few services and tips are not expected. In most hotels, a porter will carry your luggage and show you to your room. For doing this he'll expect about 2 or 3% of the room price. So if your room costs US$30, give about 60c to US$1. For any other chore done by a porter, a slightly smaller tip is in order.

Taxis Don't tip taxi drivers unless they've done some special service. Turks don't tip taxi drivers, though they often round off the metered fare. Thus, if the meter reads 28,600TL, it's common to give the driver 30,000TL. Taxi drivers may look for a tip from you (especially on trips to the airport), but that's only because you're a foreigner and foreigners tip taxi drivers. A driver of a dolmuş – a cab or minibus that departs only when all seats are filled – never expects a tip or a fare to be rounded upwards.

Hairdressers In barbershops and hairdressers, pay the fee for the services rendered (which goes to the shop), then about 15% to the person who cut your hair, and smaller tips to the others who provided service, down to the one who brushes stray locks from your clothing as you prepare to leave (5% for that).

Turkish Baths In a Turkish bath or hamam there will be fees for the several services, and in baths frequented mostly by Turks these will be sufficient. However, in baths with a clientele that includes tourists, everyone will expect and await tips. You needn't go overboard in this. Share out about 20 or 30% of your total bath bill to the assembled staff (and they will indeed be assembled for tips as you depart). In a few of the more tourist-frequented baths in İstanbul, the attendants are insistent. Don't let them browbeat you. Look firm and say, Yeter! (yeh-TEHR, 'It's sufficient!').

Sleeping Cars If you take a sleeping compartment on a train, the porter will come around near the end of the trip, request an official service charge of 10% of the sleeping car charge, give you a receipt for it, and hope for a small additional tip. If you give him 5% extra, he'll be pleased.

Other Situations There are other situations in which a tip is indicated, but these must be handled delicately. For instance, at a remote archaeological site, a local person may unlock the gate and show you around the ruins. He will probably have official admission tickets, which he must sell you. If that's all he does, that's all you pay. But if he goes out of his way to help you, you may want to offer a tip. He may be reluctant to accept it, and may refuse once or even twice. Try at least three times. He may well need the money, but the rules of politeness require several refusals. If he refuses three times, though, you can assume that he truly wants to help you only for friendship's sake. Don't press further, for this will insult his good intentions.

In many of these situations, a token gift will be just as happily received as a cash tip. If you have some small item, particularly something distinctive from your home country, you can offer it in lieu of money.

WHEN TO GO

Spring and autumn are best, roughly from April to June and from September to October. The climate is perfect on the Aegean and Mediterranean coasts then, and in Istanbul. It's cooler in Central Anatolia, but not unpleasantly so. Normally, there is little rain between May and October except along the Black Sea coast. If you visit before mid-June, you will avoid the mosquitoes which can be a plague in some areas.

The best months for water sports are, of course, the warmest: July and August. But the water is just right in May, June, September and October too.

In the hottest months on the coasts you may have to take a siesta during the heat of the day between noon and 3 pm. Get up early in the morning, clamber around the local ruins, then after lunch and a siesta come out again for *piyasa vakti*, 'promenade time', when everyone strolls by the sea, sits in a café, and watches the sunset.

If you plan a trip to eastern Turkey, go there in late June, July or August. As a general rule, you should not venture into the east before mid-May or after mid-October unless you're prepared, as there will still be lots of snow around, perhaps even enough to close roads and mountain passes. Unfortunately, the trip to eastern Turkey in high summer usually includes passing through the south-east, which is beastly hot at that time.

For explanations of Turkey's religious holidays and festivals, see Cultural Events in this chapter.

THE CALENDAR
January

It's rainy and cold throughout the country in January, with high air pollution in the cities – not usually a pleasant time to visit. Eastern Turkey is in the icy grip of winter; Ankara and the rest of the Anatolian Plateau may be covered in snow.

Religious Holidays
   Ramazan, the holy month which changes lots of schedules, is from 21 January to 19 February in 1996.

1 January
   New Year's Day is a public holiday. Decorations in shops, exchanges of gifts and greeting cards, make it a kind of surrogate Christmas, good for business.

15-16 January
   Camel-wrestling festival in the village of Selçuk, next to Ephesus, south of İzmir

February

In February it rains almost everywhere and is chilly and cheerless. The only fun to be had is indoors or at the ski slopes on Uludağ near Bursa, in the Beydağları mountains near Antalya, on Erciyes near Kayseri, or at Palandöken near Erzurum.

Religious Holidays
   Ramazan is from 23 February to 24 March 1993, 12 February to 13 March 1994, 1 February to 2 March 1995, and 21 January to 19 February 1996. Şeker Bayramı, the three-day festival, starts on the day after Ramazan.

March

Still rainy in most of the country, though there may be some good periods on the south Aegean and Mediterranean coasts. It's still bitterly cold in the east.

Religious Holidays
   See February for Ramazan dates.

April

April can be delightful throughout the country, except in the east, where it's still cold. There may be some rain, but there may also be virtually none, and in any case the wild flowers will be out on the Anatolian Plateau. The waters of the Aegean and Mediterranean are approaching a comfortable temperature for swimming. The south-east (Gaziantep, Urfa, Mardin, Diyarbakır), so torrid and parched in high summer, is very pleasant now, but there may still be snow on top of Nemrut Dağı. April is when the bus tours begin in earnest.

Religious Holidays
Kurban Bayramı, the most important religious holiday of the year, begins on 29 April in 1996.

20-30 April
Manisa Power Gum Festival, when a traditional remedy called *mesir macunu* or *kuvvet macunu* ('power gum'), said to restore health, youth and potency, is concocted and distributed in Manisa, near İzmir.

23 April
The big national holiday is National Sovereignty Day, when the first Grand National Assembly, or republican parliament, met in Ankara in 1920; it's also Children's Day. An international children's festival, with kids from all over the world, is held in Ankara.

Late April to early May
Tulip festival in Emirgan, the Bosphorus suburb of İstanbul

May
May usually brings perfectly beautiful weather throughout the country, with little chance of rain, though it's still chilly out east. May is a good month to visit the hot, dry south-east.

This month begins the tourist season in earnest, and also includes important civil holidays. Sound and light shows begin at the Blue Mosque in İstanbul and last until October.

In Konya, the javelin-throwing game of *cirit* (jirid), played on horseback, takes place every Saturday and Sunday until October.

Religious Holidays
Kurban Bayramı, which disrupts all Turkish schedules for a week, begins on 21 May 1994, and 10 May 1995.

1st Week
Selçuk Ephesus Festival of Culture & Art at Selçuk, south of İzmir – folk dances, concerts, exhibits, some in the Great Theatre at Ephesus

19 May
Youth & Sports Day, held to commemorate Atatürk's birthday (1881)

29 May
In İstanbul, celebrations remember the conquest of the city from the Byzantines in 1453.

Last Week
Festival of Pergamum at Bergama, north of İzmir – drama in the ancient theatre, folk dancing and handicraft exhibits

June
The weather is perfect throughout the country, but getting hot in June. There is little rain except along the Black Sea coast. Sound and light shows take place at the Blue Mosque in İstanbul all month.

Religious Holidays
Kurban Bayramı begins on 1 June 1993.

1st Week
The International Mediterranean Festival takes place in İzmir usually at this time.

4-5 June
Traditional rose-growing competition at Konya, when roses grown in the region are judged

7-13 June
Music & Art Festival at Marmaris – musical performances, folk dances, exhibitions

2nd Week
Traditional Kırkpınar Oiled Wrestling Competition at Edirne; Festival of Troy at Çanakkale, on the Dardanelles near Troy

3rd Week
The Kafkasör Festival, in a *yayla* (alpine pasture) near Artvin in north-eastern Turkey, is a true country festival featuring local dances, crafts, foods, and fights between bulls in rut.

Late June to Mid-July
The world-class International İstanbul Festival of the Arts, with top performers in music and dance, and special exhibitions

July
The weather is hot, the sky is always blue, the sea water is warm, and everything is crowded with holiday-makers, both Turkish and foreign. In İstanbul, sound and light shows at the Blue Mosque continue, as does the İstanbul Festival.

1 July
The first day of the month is Denizcilik Günü (Navy Day), when mariners, ships and various maritime pursuits are celebrated.

5-10 July
Nasreddin Hoca celebrations (in Akşehir, his traditional birthplace) are held in honour of the semi-legendary humorous master of Turkish folklore legends and tales.

7-12 July
    At Bursa, the Folklore & Music Festival is one
    of Turkey's best folk-dancing events of the year;
    the Bursa Fair (trade & tourism) starts about the
    same time.
29-31 July
    Music, Folklore & Water Sports Festival in Foça,
    north of İzmir

August

It's hot and sunny all month, and crowded
too. This is the best time to be in eastern
Turkey, when the weather is fine and crowds
are smaller than along the western beaches.
In İstanbul, sound and light shows continue
at the Blue Mosque. Similar shows begin at
the Anıt Kabir, Atatürk's mausoleum, in
Ankara.

15 August
    A special mass at the House of the Virgin Mary
    (Meryemana) near Ephesus celebrates the
    Assumption of the Virgin Mary. The Catholic
    archbishop of İzmir says mass.
15-18 August
    Çanakkale Troy Festival at Çanakkale near Troy
    with folk dances, music, tours of Mt Ida and Troy
Mid-August
    Haci Bektaş Veli commemoration at the town of
    that name in Cappadocia
20 August to 9 September
    The biggest festival is the İzmir International
    Fair; for a month the city's hotels are packed and
    transportation is crowded. The fair has amuse-
    ments, cultural and commercial-industrial dis
    plays.
30 August
    Zafer Bayramı (zah-FEHR, Victory), commem
    orating the decisive victory at Dumlupınar of the
    republican armies over the invading Greek army
    during Turkey's War of Independence in 1922.
    Towns and cities celebrate their own Kurtuluş
    Günü (Day of Liberation) on the appropriate date
    commemorating when Atatürk's armies drove
    out the foreign troops during July and August
    1922.

September

The weather is still hot and fine, moderating
a bit towards the end of the month. Swimming is still wonderful, crowds are still fairly
heavy, and the bus tours begin to make a
comeback. Sound and light shows continue
at the Blue Mosque in İstanbul and at the Anıt

Kabir in Ankara. The İzmir Fair goes on until
9 September.

1-9 September
    Bodrum Culture & Art Week, Turkish classical
    music concerts in Bodrum Castle, art exhibits
    and water sports shows
2-4 September
    Kırşehir Ahi Evran Crafts & Folklore Festival at
    Kırşehir, when Turkish handicrafts are displayed
    and modelled in shows
9 September
    In İzmir it's Kurtuluş Günü, or Liberation Day
    with lots of parades, speeches and flags.
11-12 September
    Çorum Hittite Festival, crafts shows, musical
    performances, tours of Hittite archaeological
    sites at Çorum near Ankara
15-18 September
    Cappadocia Festival, a grape harvest and folklore
    festival highlighting the 'fairy chimneys' and
    underground cities of Cappadocia
22-30 September
    Konya hosts a culinary contest.
Mid or Late September
    At Diyarbakır, there's the Watermelon Festival.
    One year when I attended, everybody was disap-
    pointed because the prize-winning watermelon
    weighed in at a mere 32 kg. A bad year, they said
    – no rain.

October

The weather is perfect again, and crowds are
diminishing, though bus tours start again in
earnest. The rains begin sometime in mid or
late October. There may also be freak snow-
storms on the Anatolian Plateau. Sound and
light shows are supposed to continue in
İstanbul at the Blue Mosque, but check in
advance.

1-9 October
    The 'Golden Orange' Film & Art Festival is held
    in Antalya, with a competition for best Turkish
    film of the year. There are other exhibits.
21-29 October
    During Turkish Troubadours' Week at Konya
    bards who continue the traditional poetic forms
    hold contests in repartee, free-form composition
    and riddles.
29 October
    Cumhuriyet Bayramı (Republic Day), commem-
    orates the proclamation of the republic by
    Atatürk in 1923. It's the biggest civil holiday,
    with lots of parades and speeches.

November

The weather is very pleasant, with cool to warm days and chilly nights, but one must play cat and mouse with the rain, which may or may not become a bore. If your luck holds, you can have a marvellous late-year beach holiday.

10 November
   The most important day of the month, it is the day Atatürk died in 1938. At precisely 9.05 am, the moment of his death, the entire country comes to a screeching halt for a moment of silence. Literally everything stops in its tracks (you should too), just for a moment. Car horns and sirens blare. In schools, in the newspapers (the names of which are normally printed in red, but are all in black on this day), on radio and television, the national hero's life and accomplishments are reviewed.

December

The weather is chilly throughout the country, though milder along the Mediterranean coast. You must expect some, perhaps heavy, rain. There are few visitors; some museums close some exhibits for renovation. In rare years, the warmth and pleasantness of a good November will stretch into early December.

All Month
   Camel wrestling at various locations in the province of Aydın, south of İzmir
6-8 December
   St Nicholas Festival, when commemorative ceremonies are held in the 4th-century church of St Nicholas, the original Santa Claus, in Demre near Antalya.
14-17 December (approximately)
   The Mevlana Festival, honouring Celaleddin Rumi, the great poet and mystic who founded the Mevlevi order of Whirling Dervishes, is held in Konya. Hotel space is tight, so try to pin down a room in advance, or be prepared to take a room below your normal standard.

SUGGESTED ITINERARIES

Any itinerary is an expression of interest, energy, time and money. You can see a lot of the country if you spend from six to eight weeks, but if your time is limited, here are some suggestions. These are *minimal* times – moving fast.

Less than a Week (three to five days)
   İstanbul, with an overnight trip to İznik and Bursa, or Troy and the Dardanelles
Basic One-Week Itinerary (seven to nine days)
   İstanbul (two nights), Bursa (one night), Dardanelles and Troy (one night), Bergama, İzmir and Kuşadası (two nights) with excursions to Ephesus, Priene, Miletus, Didyma; return to İstanbul (one night). Spend any extra time in İstanbul.
Two Weeks
   Add an excursion from Kuşadası via Aphrodisias to Pamukkale and Hierapolis (one to two nights); also take a loop excursion to Ankara, Konya and Cappadocia. Visit the Hittite cities. If you have time left over, spend a day or two on the Turquoise Coast (Kaş, Antalya, Side, Alanya).
Three Weeks
   Add a yacht cruise or coastal highway excursion from Kuşadası south to Bodrum (Halicarnassus), Marmaris, Fethiye, Kaş, Finike, Kemer and Antalya; or second-best, an excursion along the Black Sea coast. Another option is a tour to the south-east – Şanlıurfa, Mardin and Diyarbakır – best done at a time other than blazing-hot July and August.
Eastern Tour
   A 14 to 21-day tour for mid-May to early October only: a circuit beginning in Ankara or Cappadocia going to Adıyaman and Nemrut Dağı (Mt Nimrod), Diyarbakır, Van, Doğubeyazıt and Mt Ararat, Erzurum, Kars, Artvin, Hopa, Rize, Trabzon, Samsun, Amasya, and returning to Ankara via Boğazkale (Hattuşaş)

WHAT TO BRING

In high summer, that is from mid-June to mid-September, you'll need light cotton summer clothes, and a light sweater or jacket for the evenings or to wear up on the Central Anatolian Plateau. You won't need rain gear at all, except perhaps on the Black Sea coast. You would do better to duck between the showers rather than haul rain gear during your entire trip just for a possible day or two of rain on the Black Sea coast.

In spring and autumn, summer clothing will still be OK, but the evenings will be cooler. If you plan to travel extensively in Central Anatolia (to Ankara, Konya, Cappadocia or Nemrut Dağı), pack a heavier sweater and perhaps a light raincoat.

Winter wear – for December to March – is woollens and rain gear. Though it doesn't get really cold along the Mediterranean coast, it does get damp, rainy and chilly in most of the country, including along the south coast. İstanbul and İzmir get dustings of snow; Ankara gets more. Nemrut Dağı and the eastern region are frigid and covered in snow.

Formal or Informal?

How does one dress in a Muslim country? In this one, you dress pretty much as you would for Europe. In high summer, no-one will really expect men to have a coat and tie, even when visiting a government official. For the rest of the year, Turks tend to dress formally in formal situations such as at the office or in a good restaurant or nightclub, but informally at other times. Neat and tidy dress is still admired here. Tatty or careless clothes, a sign of nonchalance or independence in other societies, are looked upon as tatty or careless in Turkey. T-shirts and shorts are the mark of the summer tourist.

Anyone can visit a Turkish mosque so long as they look presentable. Clothes must be neat – no shorts or sleeveless shirts on either men or women; women require skirts of a modest length (knees) and a headscarf. Before you enter a mosque where people are praying, remove your shoes to protect the carpets from soil. Muslims pray on the carpets, so they must be kept clean.

TOURIST OFFICES

The Ministry of Tourism has a Communications Centre (☎ (4) 212 8596, -7, -8, -9; fax 212 8595) which you can call any day from 9am to 7.30 pm to help with vexing problems. The Ankara address is İletişim Merkezi, Turizm Bakanlığı, İsmet İnönü Bulvarı 5, Bahçelievler.

Local Tourist Offices

Every Turkish town of any size has a Tourism Information Office run by the Ministry of Tourism. The ministry's symbol is the fan-like Hittite sun figure. There may also be an office operated by a local tourism association called 'turizm derneği'.

In addition, a town may also have a munic-

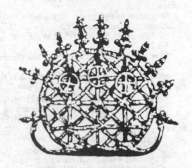

Hittite Sun Figure – symbol of the Turkish Ministry of Tourism

ipal or provincial government tourism office. If you need help and you can't find an office, ask for the Belediye Sarayı (Municipality). They'll rummage around for someone who speaks some English, and will do their best to solve your problem. Locations of tourist offices are given for each Turkish city and town in the text.

Representatives Abroad

Here are the addresses of Turkish tourism offices and diplomatic missions abroad:

Austria
    Turkische Botschaft Informationsabteilung, Singerstrasse 2/VIII, 1010 Vienna (☎ (43-222) 512 2128/9; fax 513 8326)
Belgium
    Conseiller de l'Information, Ambassade de Turquie, Rue Montoyer 4, 1040 Brussells (☎ (32-2) 513 8230/9; fax 511 7951)
Denmark
    Turkish Embassy Information Counsellor Bureau, Vesterbrogade 11A, 1620 Copenhagen V (☎ (45-31) 223 100, 228 374; fax 229 068)
Finland
    Turkish Information Office, Mikonkatu 6 C 18, 00100 Helsinki (☎ (3580) 666 044, 666 055; fax 229 068)
France
    Turquie, Service d'Information, Champs Elysées 102, 75008 Paris (☎ (33-1) 45 62 78 68, 45 62 79 84, 45 62 26 10; fax 45 63 81 05)

Germany
   Informationsabteilung des Türkischen General-
   konsulats, Baselerstrasse 37,
   6 Frankfurt-M1 (☎ (49-69) 233 081/2;
   fax 232 751)
   Informationsabteilung des Türkischen General-
   konsulats, Karlsplatz 3/1,
   8000 Munich 2 (☎ (49-89) 594 902, 594 317)
Italy
   Ambasciata di Turchia, Ufficio Informazione,
   Piazza della Republica 56, 00185 Rome
   (☎ (39-6) 487 1190, 487 1393; fax 488 2425)
Japan
   Turkish Tourism & Information Office,
   33-6, 2-Chome Jingumae, Shibuya-Ku,
   Tokyo 150 (☎ (81-3) 470 6380,
   470 5131/54/55/56; fax 470 6037)
The Netherlands
   Turkish Embassy, Information Counsellor's
   Office, Herengracht 451, 1017 BS Amsterdam
   (☎ (31-20) 626 6810, 624 4006; fax 622 2283)
Saudi Arabia
   Turkish Embassy, PO Box 94318, Riyad
   (☎ (966-1) 488 7953; fax 488 7024)
Spain
   Oficina de Información y Turismo de Turquía,
   Plaza de España, Torre de Madrid, Planta 13,
   Oficina 3, 28008 Madrid
   (☎ (34-1) 248 7014, 248 7114; fax 247 6287)
Sweden
   Turkiska Statens Informationsbyra,
   Kungsgatan 3, S-111 43 Stockholm
   (☎ (46-8) 679 8320/1; fax 611 3828)
Switzerland
   Türkisches Generalkonsulat, Talstrasse 74, 8001
   Zürich (☎ (44-1) 221 0810/2; fax 212 1749)
UK
   Turkish Tourism & Information,
   170-173 Piccadilly, 1st floor, London W1V 9DD
   (☎ (44-71) 734 8681/2, 355 4207; fax 491 0773)
USA
   Office of the Information Attaché, Turkish Con-
   sulate-General, 821 United Nations Plaza,
   New York, New York 10017
   (☎ (1-212) 687 2194/5/6; fax 599 7568)
   Turkish Information Office, 1714 Massachusetts
   Ave NW, Suite 306, Washington, DC 20036
   (☎ (202) 429 9409, 429 9844, 833 8411;
   fax 429 5649)

BUSINESS HOURS

For a list of public holidays, see The Calendar under When to Go, in this chapter. The
following are opening hours in Turkey:

Archaeological sites
   8 or 9 am to 5 or 6 pm every day, with no break
   for lunch

Banks
   8.30 am to noon and 1.30 to 5 pm Monday to
   Friday
Covered markets
   İstanbul's Grand Bazaar and covered markets in
   other cities are open from Monday to Saturday
   from 8am to 6.30 pm
Grocery stores & markets
   From Monday to Saturday from 6 or 7 am to 7 or
   8 pm. On Sunday most markets close, though one
   or two grocers open in each neighbourhood.
Mosques
   Most are open all the time. If a mosque is locked,
   there is usually a *bekçi* (guardian) with a key
   somewhere nearby. Avoid visiting mosques at
   prayer time (at or within 20 minutes after the call
   to prayer). Avoid visiting on Friday, the Muslim
   holy day, particularly in the morning.
Museums
   8.30 or 9.30 am to noon or 12.30 pm, then (in
   some cases) they close for lunch, reopening at 1
   or 1.30 pm and remaining open until 5 or 5.30
   pm, perhaps later in the summer. Most museums
   are closed on Monday, but Topkapı Palace in
   İstanbul is closed on Tuesday.
Offices
   Government and business offices may open at 8
   or 9 am, close for lunch, and reopen around 1.30
   pm, remaining open until 4 or 5 pm During the
   hot summer months in some cities the workday
   begins at 7 or 8 am and is finished at 2 pm. Also,
   during the holy month of Ramazan the workday
   is shortened.
Post offices
   Main post offices in large cities tend to be open
   every day from 8 am to 8 pm for most services
   (stamp sales, telephone *jeton* and card sales, telegrams fax etc), and the telephone centres may be
   open until midnight; but windows may be open
   only from 8.30 am to noon and 1.30 to 5 or 6 pm
   for other services such as poste restante and
   parcel service. Smaller post offices have more
   limited hours: 8.30 am to 12.30 pm and 1.30 to
   5.30 pm, and may be closed part of Saturday, and
   all day Sunday.
Restaurants
   Most restaurants serve food continuously from
   11 am to 11 pm or later. Many open early (6 or 7
   am) for breakfast. The exceptions are a few restaurants in bazaars, business and financial districts which serve primarily office workers and
   serve only lunch.
Shops
   Monday to Saturday: 9 am to noon and 1.30 or
   2.30 to 6 or 7 pm; many don't close for lunch
Tourist offices
   Usually Monday to Friday from 8.30 am to noon
   or 12.30 pm, and 1.30 to 5.30 pm, longer in
   summer in well-touristed areas

CULTURAL EVENTS
Religious Holidays

The official Turkish calendar is the Western, Gregorian one as in Europe, but religious festivals, two of which are public holidays, are celebrated according to the Muslim lunar Hijri (HIJ-ree) calendar. As the lunar calendar is about 11 days shorter than the Gregorian, the Muslim festivals arrive that many days earlier each year.

Actual dates for Muslim religious festivals are not completely systematic. Rather, they are proclaimed by Muslim authorities after the appropriate astronomical observations and calculations have been made, and then the civil authorities decide how many days should be civil holidays. To help you know what's going on, the approximate dates of all major festivals for the near future are listed under The Calendar in the When to Go section of this chapter.

Muslim days, like Jewish ones, begin at sundown. Thus a Friday holiday will begin on Thursday at sunset and last until Friday at sunset.

For major religious and civic holidays there is also a half-day vacation for 'preparation', called *arife*, preceding the start of a festival; shops and offices close about noon, and the festival begins at sunset. Friday is the Muslim Sabbath, but it is not a holiday. Mosques and baths will be crowded, especially on Friday morning. The day of rest, a secular one, is Sunday.

Only two religious holidays are public holidays: Şeker Bayramı and Kurban Bayramı.

Ramazan The Holy Month, called Ramadan in other Muslim countries, is similar in some ways to Lent. For the 30 days of Ramazan, a good Muslim lets *nothing* pass the lips during daylight hours: no eating, drinking, smoking, or even licking a postage stamp. A cannon shot, and these days a radio announcer, signal the end of the fast at sunset. The fast is broken traditionally with flat pide bread if possible. Lavish dinners are given and may last far into the night. Before dawn, drummers circulate through town to awaken the faithful so they can eat before sunrise.

During Ramazan, restaurants may be closed from dawn till nightfall, and in conservative towns it's bad form for anyone – non-Muslims included – to smoke, munch snacks or sip drinks in plain view. Business hours may change and be shorter. As non-Muslims, it's understood that you get to eat and drink when you like, and in the big cities you'll find lots of non-fasting Muslims right beside you, but it's best to be discreet and to maintain a polite low visibility.

The 27th day of Ramazan is the 'Night of Power', when the Koran was revealed and Muhammed was appointed to be the Messenger of God.

The fasting of Ramazan is a worthy, sacred act and a blessing to Muslims. Pregnant or nursing women, the infirm and aged, and travellers are excused, according to the Koran, if they feel they cannot keep the fast.

Şeker Bayramı Also called Ramazan Bayramı or İd es-Seğir, this is a three-day festival at the end of Ramazan. *Şeker* (shek-EHR) is sugar or candy; during this festival children traditionally go door to door asking for sweet treats. Muslims exchange greeting cards and pay social calls.

Everybody enjoys drinking lots of tea in broad daylight, after fasting for Ramazan. The festival is a three-day national holiday when banks and offices are closed. Hotels, buses, trains and aeroplanes are heavily booked.

Kurban Bayramı The most important religious and secular holiday of the year, Kurban Bayramı (koor-BAHN, sacrifice) is equivalent in importance to Christmas in Christian countries.

The festival commemorates Abraham's near-sacrifice of Isaac on Mt Moriah (Genesis 22; Koran, Sura 37). In the story, God orders Abraham to take Isaac, the son of his old age, up to Mt Moriah and sacrifice him.

Abraham takes Isaac up the mountain and lays him on the altar, but at the last moment

God stops Abraham, congratulates him on his faithfulness, and orders him to sacrifice instead a ram tangled in a nearby bush. Abraham does so.

Following the tradition today, 2.5 million rams are sacrificed on Kurban Bayramı in Turkey each year. For days beforehand you'll see herds of sheep parading through streets or gathered in markets. Every head of household who can afford a sheep buys one and takes it home. Right after the early morning prayers on the actual day of Bayram, the head of the household slits the sheep's throat. It's then flayed and butchered, and family and friends immediately cook up a feast. A sizeable portion of the meat is distributed to the needy, and the skin is often donated to a charity; the charity sells it to a leather products company.

Lots of people take to the road, going home to parents or friends. Everybody exchanges greeting cards. At some point you'll probably be invited to share in the festivities.

Kurban Bayramı is a four-day national holiday which you must plan for. Banks may be closed for a full week, though one or two branches will stay open in the big cities to serve foreigners. Transportation will be packed, and hotel rooms, particularly in resort areas, will be scarce and expensive.

Minor Festivals During minor religious festivals mosques are illuminated with strings of lights, and special foods are prepared.

Regaip Kandili This is the traditional date for the conception of the Prophet Muhammed. You'll see packets of small, sweetish *simit* bread rings, wrapped in coloured paper, for sale on the streets.

Miraç Kandili This is the celebration of Muhammed's miraculous nocturnal journey from Mecca to Jerusalem and to heaven astride a winged horse named Burak.

Berat Kandili This festival has various meanings in different Islamic countries.

Mevlid-i Nebi The 12th of Rebi ul-evvel is the anniversary of the Prophet's birth (in 570 AD). There are special prayers and foods, and mosque illuminations.

POST & TELECOMMUNICATIONS

Postal and telecommunication services in Turkey are handled by the PTT (peh-teh-TEH), which stands for *posta, telefon, telgraf*. Look for the yellow signs with black 'PTT' letters. For hours of operation, see Business Hours in this chapter.

Letter boxes and postal vehicles are yellow as well. Every town has a PTT, usually close to the main square. Go there to buy stamps and telephone tokens, to send letters and telegrams, or to make telephone calls if no other phone is available. It's best to post letters in the post office slots rather than in a letter box. The *Yurtdışı* slot is for mail to foreign countries, *Yurtiçi* is for mail to other Turkish cities, and *Şehiriçi* is for mail within the city.

Many of the larger railway and bus stations in Turkey have their own branch PTTs.

Anyone asking for stamps or phone cards for Australia will invariably be asked *Avusturya Avustralya?* (Austria or Australia?) The two words are similar in Turkish, and every clerk's response is Pavlovian. Get used to it.

Post

Postal Rates The constant creeping devaluation of the Turkish lira results in frequent rises in postal rates. Ask at the post office to find out current rates.

Express Mail The PTT now operates an express mail, courier-type service called *acele posta servisi* (AH-jeh-leh POHSS-tah sehr-vee-see) or APS, which competes with international express carriers such as Federal Express and DHL. If you must have something reach its destination in the fastest, most secure possible manner, ask for this. Don't confuse this courier service with the traditional *ekspres* (special delivery) service, which is slower.

Parcels To mail packages out of the country, or to receive dutiable merchandise, you must have your package opened for customs inspection, and you may have to endure a bit of frustrating red tape. (In İstanbul you may have to go to the special Paket Postahane (Parcel Post Office) near Karaköy.) Have paper, box, string, tape and marker pens with you when you go.

If you want to make certain that a parcel will get to its destination intact, send it by APS (see above) or at least *kayıtlı* (by registered mail).

Addresses Turkish postal addresses are usually written with the name of the main street first, then the minor street and then the number of the building. For example:

Bay Mustafa Adıyok
Geçilmez Sokak, Bulunmaz Çıkmazı
Lüks Apartmanı No 23/14
80200 Tophane
İSTANBUL

In this example, *Bay* means 'Mr'; for 'Mrs' or 'Miss', use *Bayan*, pronounced like the English phrase 'buy an ...'. The next line has the name of a largish street, 'Geçilmez Sokak', followed by the name of a smaller street, alley, or dead end, 'Bulunmaz Çıkmazı', which runs off it. The third line has the name of an apartment building, 'Lüks Apartmanı'. As for the numbers, the first one, '23', is the street number of the building; the second, '14', is the apartment or office number within the building. The district, 'Tophane', comes next, then the city. *Kat* in an address means floor, as in Kat 3, '3rd floor' (4th floor up if you count street level as the 1st floor).

The address can be written more simply when the desired building is on a large, well-known street. For example:

Bay Mustafa Adıyok
Büyük Caddesi No 44/10
80090 Taksim
İSTANBUL

In some cases, the district of the city is put at the beginning of the second line, eg 'Taksim, Büyük Caddesi No 44/10'. In any case, you've got to be familiar with the district names to find a certain address.

Turkey has a system of five-digit postal codes *(posta kodu)*. Use the postal code if you have it.

Poste Restante If you are having mail sent, have it addressed this way:

(Name)
Poste Restante
Merkez Postahane
(District)
(City, Province)
TURKEY

Merkez Postane means 'Central' or 'Main Post Office', which is where you should go to pick up your mail, passport in hand. The poste restante desk often keeps more limited hours than others, and may close for lunch.

Telephones
You will find the telephone useful in Turkey. The system is almost completely automated, with yellow push-button phones. You pay for a call with a jeton (zheh-TOHN, token), or perhaps several, or a *telekart* debit card. Calls are measured in usage units, each of which costs about 10c; a local call of several minutes' duration costs one usage unit.

Tokens Jetons come in three sizes. The small one-usage-unit *(küçük jeton,* kew-CHEWK zheh-TOHN) costs about 10c and is for local calls. The middle-sized five-usage-unit *(normal jeton,* nohr-MAHL), costing around 40c, is useful mostly for long-distance calls within Turkey. The large 10-usage-unit *(büyük jeton,* bew-YEWK), about 85c, is necessary for international calls. Buy your jetons at the post office, or from a disabled person (often in a wheelchair) outside a PTT or near a rank of public telephones. Most PTTs have signs saying, 'Satılmış jeton geri alınmaz', which means 'Jetons, once sold, cannot be returned'. If they insist on this, try exchanging the jetons for stamps, or sell the jetons to another traveller.

Telekarts A telekart is a telephone debit card sold at post offices. You pay for the card in advance of calling, and then as you call, your telephone usage is electronically deducted from the value of the card. Telekarts come in values of 30, 60, 100, 120, or 180 telephone-usage units. Special telekart phones take only these cards, inserted in a slot in the centre of the front panel. These phones are not yet found everywhere in Turkey; you'll see them mostly in the heavily frequented tourist areas. Try to find them, because they are by far the easiest phones to use.

There are two types of telekarts, and they are not interchangeable (each works in a separate type of phone). The more useful cards – because they work in more phones – are the yellow-and-black laminated paper ones bearing coloured pictures of touristic scenes on the back. The older red-and-silver plastic-and-metal cards are being phased out; avoid them unless you've already located a phone which accepts them.

After you've found a phone and bought a card, insert it in the slot and a liquid crystal display in the upper left-hand corner will show you the number of usage units for which the card is valid. A normal local call usually costs one usage unit; a long-distance call, four or five usage units; an international call takes lots of units. Buy only the highest-unit telekarts for international calls.

Long-Distance Calls Rates for local and intercity domestic calls are moderate, but international calls can be quite expensive: almost £1 per minute to the UK, US$3 per minute to the USA, and even higher to Australia. It can take as long as 60 seconds for the connection to be made. Calling after 10 pm and on Sunday is cheaper. Beware of hotel surcharges, which can be as high as 100%. Perhaps the best strategy is to make a quick call, give the other person the telephone number and a time at which you can be reached, and have them call you back.

AT&T customers can use the company's USADirect service from Turkey. Call 9-9-8001 2277. Though expensive (US$2.45 for the first minute, US$1.38 for each additional minute, and US$2.50 surcharge to charge the call to your AT&T credit card), it is less expensive than calling via the Turkish PTT system. In my experience you must use only jeton phones (not telekart phones) when using USADirect; you must insert jetons as for a local call. This service only works from İstanbul (calls from other cities are cut off after a few seconds.)

MCI offers a similar service called MCI World Reach. To access the service in Turkey, call 9-9-8001 1177. US Sprint's similar service, called the Sprint Express, is not available from Turkey at this writing.

Useful words, sometimes marked on the phones are *Şehirlerarası* (Intercity); or *Uluslararası* or *Milletlerarası* (International). You'll need to know the city and country codes for the place you're calling. These are on display in most PTTs and in some phone booths.

Look for the little square red light below the push buttons. If it's lit, tough luck – the phone is broken. Let's assume the phone works instead. Lift the receiver and deposit a jeton. The yellow phones have slots for all three sizes of jetons. Sometimes the jeton may fall straight through and out the return hole, so reinsert it very gently and let it fall as slowly as possible. If all else fails, try another phone or another size of jeton. The fault is with the phone, not with the jeton.

For a long-distance call, look for the little round light in the last box, to the right of the pictorial instructions above the push buttons. When this light goes out, push '9'. Then, when you hear the intercity long-distance tone, push the buttons for the city code and the local number. For international calls, push '9' twice, then the country code, followed by the city code and local number. For instance, for London, after pushing '9' twice, push '44', then the area code ('71'), then the number. For Melbourne, dial thus: 9-9-61-3 plus the local number. For the USA and Canada, dial 9-9-1 plus area code plus local number.

As you talk, watch that little round red light on top, and listen for chimes on the line. Both are indications that it's time to deposit another jeton or telekart.

Telephone Etiquette Turks answer the phone by saying *Alo?* (from 'hello'), a word which is defined in Turkish dictionaries as 'Word said when answering the telephone' because it is never used otherwise. Turks may also say *Buyurun!* (roughly, 'at your service'). When speaking to a Turk in whatever language, he or she is liable to say *hah!* now and then. This means 'yes', 'I agree', 'alright' or 'just so'.

Country Codes Here are some frequently used country codes:

Australia	61
Austria	43
Belgium	32
Canada	1
Denmark	45
Eire	353
Finland	358
France	33
Germany	49
Greece	30
India	91
Israel	972
Italy	39
Japan	81
Netherlands	31
New Zealand	64
Norway	47
South Africa	27
Spain	34
Sweden	46
Switzerland	41
Turkey	90
UK	44
USA	1

Fax, Telex & Telegraph
Turks are addicted to fax machines. Most businesses including hotels, car rental companies and airlines have them. If you must make reservations in advance, this is the fastest and often the cheapest way. Usually you can send a fax in English, German or French and the recipients will have someone translate it and reply in the same language.

Most cities have post offices with fax (*faks*) facilities, but PTT red tape turns a simple matter into a half-hour procedure. You must write your message on an official form which the PTT retains (so keep a copy if you need one). The cost is about the same as for a short phone call (it takes about a minute to send a page). You can often send a fax simply and quickly from your hotel, but the rate may be higher than from the PTT.

Most city PTTs also have telex machines, which operate by a similar procedure. If all else fails, a simple telegram to North America may cost from US$15 to $20, less to Europe, more to Australasia.

TIME
Turkish time is East European Time, two hours ahead of Coordinated Universal Time (alias GMT), except in the warm months, when clocks are turned ahead one hour. Daylight saving ('summer') time usually begins at 1 am on the last Sunday in March, and ends at 2 am on the last Sunday in September. When it's noon in İstanbul, Ankara or Erzurum, the time elsewhere is:

city	winter	summer
Paris, Rome	11 am	11 am
London	10 am	10 am
New York	5 am	5 am
Los Angeles	2 am	2 am
Perth, Hong Kong	6 pm	5 pm
Sydney	8 pm	7 pm
Auckland	10 pm	9 pm

ELECTRICITY
Electricity in Turkey is supplied at 220 volts, 50 cycles, as in Europe. Plugs are of the European variety with two round prongs, but there are two sizes in use. Most common is the small-diameter prong, so if you have these you'll be fine. The large-diameter, grounded plug used in Germany and Austria is also in use, and you'll find some outlets of this type. Plugs for these won't fit the small-diameter outlets.

Adapters are not easily available. You've got to rig something up yourself unless you've brought an adapter from Europe and it happens to be the right one. (Adapters for the flat-prong North American-style plugs are sold in many electrical shops. If you have these plugs, and 220-volt appliances, you're unusual and in luck.)

For those who have the good sense to plan ahead, here are the 'vital statistics of the Turkish plug': prongs four mm in diameter, 19 mm long; distance from the centre of one prong to the centre of the other, 19 mm; distance between the prongs 15 mm. The European grounded plug, by contrast, has prongs 4.5 mm in diameter, 19 mm apart from centre to centre, but only 14 mm long.

LAUNDRY

There are no coin-operated automatic laundries in Turkey yet, but getting laundry (çamaşır, chahm-mah-SHUR) done is a simple matter. At any hotel or boarding house, ask at the reception desk, or just short-circuit it and ask a housekeeper. They'll quickly find someone to do laundry. Agree on a price in advance. The classier the hotel, the more exorbitant their laundry rates. Even so, the rates are no higher than at home.

Figure at least on a day to get laundry done. It may be washed in a machine or by hand, but it will be dried on a line, not in a drying machine. In summer, drying takes no time at all. If you wash a T-shirt at 10.30 am in İzmir and hang it in the sun, it'll be dry by 11 am.

By the way, the word çamasır also means 'underwear' in Turkish. This can be confusing at times.

Dry-cleaning shops (kuru temizleme, koo-ROO tehm-eez-lem-MEH) are found here and there in the big cities, usually in the better residential sections or near the luxury hotels.

Service is similar to that in Europe and the USA: fast service takes an hour or two if you're willing to pay 50% more; otherwise, overnight or two-day service is normal practice. Prices are moderate to expensive, and you'll save money by taking the garments there yourself rather than having the hotel staff do it.

WEIGHTS & MEASURES

Turkey uses the metric system. For those accustomed to the British-US systems of measurement, conversion information can be found at the back of this book.

BOOKS & MAPS
Books

Everyone from St Paul to Mark Twain and Agatha Christie has written about Turkey.

Biography Atatürk, The Rebirth of a Nation (Weidenfeld & Nicolson, London, 1964) by Lord Kinross (J P D Balfour) is essential reading for anyone who wants to understand the formation of the Turkish Republic and the reverence in which modern Turks hold the father of modern Turkey. It's well written and more exciting than many novels. The US edition is Atatürk: A Biography of Mustafa Kemal (Morrow, New York, 1965).

For a fascinating look into the last years of the Ottoman Empire and the early years of the Turkish Republic, read İrfan Orga's Portrait of a Turkish Family (Eland Books, London; Hippocrene Books (new edition), New York, 1988). First published in 1950 and recently republished with an afterword by the author's son, it's an absorbing portrait of a family trying to survive the collapse of an old society and the birth of a new one.

Anthropology For a good overview of life during the great days of the empire, look for Everyday Life in Ottoman Turkey (BT Batsford, London; GP Putnam's Sons, New York, 1971) by Raphaela Lewis. The book has many photographs, but is not easily found in bookshops these days; go to a library.

Archaeology Ancient Civilisations & Ruins of Turkey (Haşet Kitabevi, İstanbul, 1973 and later editions) by Ekrem Akurgal is a very detailed and fairly scholarly guide to most of Turkey's ruins 'from Prehistoric Times until the End of the Roman Empire'. The book has 112 pages of photographs and is a good, readable English translation of the original. This is the best handbook for those with a deep interest in detailed classical archaeology.

George Bean (1903-77) was the grand old man of Western travel writers on Turkish antiquities. His four books with maps, diagrams and photos, cover the country's greatest wealth of Greek and Roman sites in depth, but in a very readable style. These four works were written as guidebooks to the ruins. They contain plenty of detail, but not so much that the fascination of exploring an ancient city or temple is taken away.

If you'd like to go deeply into a few sites, but not make the investments of time, energy and money necessary to cover the entire coast from Pergamum to Silifke, just buy Bean's *Aegean Turkey* (Ernest Benn, London; W W Norton, New York, 1979). It covers İzmir and its vicinity, Pergamum, Aeolis, sites west of İzmir to Sardis, Ephesus, Priene, Miletus, Didyma, Magnesia on the Menderes River (formerly Meander), and Heraclela.

Other books by George Bean (and from the same publishers) include:

Lycian Turkey (1978), which covers the Turkish coast roughly from Fethiye to Antalya, and its hinterland.

Turkey Beyond the Meander (1980), which covers the region south of the Menderes River, excluding Miletus, Didyma and Heracleia (covered in *Aegean Turkey*) but including sites near Bodrum, Pamukkale, Aphrodisias and Marmaris, and to the western outskirts of Fethiye.

Turkey's Southern Shore (1979), which overlaps with *Lycian Turkey* a bit, and covers eastern Lycia, Pisidia and Pamphylia, or roughly the coast from Finike east to Silifke.

Besides these archaeological guides, you'll find shorter, locally produced guides on sale at each site. Most of these include colour photographs but of varying quality. The text, however, is often badly translated, or else doesn't go into much depth. Look closely before you buy.

History *The Ottoman Centuries* (Morrow Quill, New York, 1977) by Lord Kinross covers the greatness of the empire without weighing too heavily on your consciousness.

At US$20, the paperback reads easily and has many illustrations and maps.

Professor Stanford Shaw's excellent and authoritative *History of the Ottoman Empire & Modern Turkey* (Cambridge University Press, New York, 1977 & 1984) comes in two volumes. Volume One is *Empire of the Gazis: The Rise & Decline of the Ottoman Empire 1280-1808*; Volume Two is *Reform, Revolution & Republic: The Rise of Modern Turkey 1808-1975* both by Stanford Shaw & Ezel Kural Shaw.

The Emergence of Modern Turkey (Oxford University Press, London & New York, 1968) by Bernard Lewis is a scholarly work covering Turkey's history roughly from 1850 to 1950, with a few chapters on the earlier history of the Turks. It tells you nearly everything you want to know about modern Turkey's origins.

Turkey (Frederick A Praiger, New York, 1966) by Geoffrey Lewis is a good general introduction to the country, the people and the culture through their history, but it's not easily found these days.

Gallipoli (Ballantine, New York, 1982) by Alan Moorhead is the fascinating story of the battles for the Dardanelles, which figured so significantly in the careers of Atatürk and Winston Churchill, and in the histories of Australia and New Zealand.

The Harvest of Hellenism (Simon & Schuster, New York, 1971; Allen & Unwin, London, 1972) by F E Peters details Turkey's Hellenic heritage. *Byzantine Style & Civilisation* (Penguin, New York & London, 1975) by Sir Steven Runciman is the standard work on the later Roman Empire.

The thorny subject of the Armenian tragedy is rarely dealt with in a purely scholarly fashion. Turkish and Armenian writers and scholars regularly issue 'proofs' that the other side is ignoring facts, or falsifying records, or refusing to admit the 'truth' as they see it. When a dispassionate account of the Turkish-Armenian conflict is presented, the author may find themself to be *persona non grata* with one side or the other. (When the Shaws' *History of the Ottoman Empire & Modern Turkey* was published, Armenian zealots fire-bombed their house and forced them into hiding for a time.)

It is certainly true that the more one learns on this subject, the more confusing it all becomes as rumour, fiction, press release, memory, questionable statistic, hyperbole and propaganda are all put forth as absolute truth. One work which has been favourably received by the unbiased scholarly community as a dispassionate summary of Turkish-Armenian disputes is Professor Michael M Gunter's *Pursuing the Just Cause of Their People: A Study of Contemporary Armenian Terrorism* (Greenwood Press, London & New York, 1986). Though most of the book deals with the modern problem of terrorism, the first chapter is an admirably brief and straightforward summary of both the Turkish and Armenian positions on this historical quandary.

Fiction Everybody knows about Agatha Christie's *Murder on the Orient Express*, and so they should. It has some scenes in Turkey itself, though most of the train's journey was through Europe and the Balkans. In any case, it helps to make vivid the 19th-century importance of the Turkish Empire.

Among Turkish authors, the one with the world-class reputation is Yaşar Kemal, whom some compare to Kazantzakis. Kemal's novels often take Turkish farming or working-class life as their subject matter, and are full of colourful characters and drama. There are translations in English (done by Kemal's wife) of *Memed, My Hawk; The Wind from the Plains* and several others.

Many modern 'harem' novels trade on the romance (real or wildly imagined) of the sultan's private household. Most are facile. The exception is *The Bride of Suleiman* (St Martin's Press, New York, 1981) by Aileen Crawley. The author, who lives in Northern Ireland, has written a historically faithful and very absorbing fictionalised account of the relationship between Hürrem Sultan ('Roxelana') and her husband Süleyman the Magnificent, greatest of the Ottoman

sultans. She brings alive the life of the Ottoman Empire during its golden age.

You might also want to look at *An Anthology of Modern Turkish Short Stories* (Bibliotheca Islamica, Minneapolis & Chicago, 1978) edited by Fahir İz.

Dictionaries & Phrasebooks Several companies publish Turkish-English pocket dictionaries, including Langenscheidt and McGraw-Hill. The most useful thing to have is not a dictionary, but a good phrasebook. Lonely Planet's *Turkish Phrase Book* is truly a 'language survival kit', as it contains words and phrases useful to real-life situations. Besides including all the common words and phrases needed during travel, it covers the 'unmentionable' situations in which you need to know the word for tampon or condom. An audio cassette to aid you in learning pronunciation is available from the author (see the Turkish Language Section at the back of this book for details.)

For a more detailed dictionary, look to *The Concise Oxford Turkish Dictionary*. Similar in scope and easier to find in Turkey is the *Portable Redhouse/Redhouse Elsözlüğü*; this 500-page work on thin paper was actually intended for Turkish students learning English, but it does the job well when you graduate from the pocket dictionary.

For grammar books, there's *Teach Yourself Turkish* in the popular English series, an excellent brief guide to learning the language. Also excellent is Yusuf Mardin's *Colloquial Turkish*. Longer, more expensive, and even more interesting is *Turkish Grammar* (Oxford University Press, London, 1967) by Geoffrey L Lewis. You've got to be pretty interested in Turkish (and in grammar) to get this far into it, but if a grammar book can be said to read like a novel, this one does.

Travel Guides This book was written to tell you just about everything you'd need to know on a first or even subsequent trip to Turkey. Other excellent guides exist, however, each with its own special interest.

An essential tool for hikers going to

Turkey is Lonely Planet's *Trekking in Turkey* by Marc Dubin & Enver Lucas. It does not duplicate any of the information given in this book, but rather supplements it with detailed information on the best places to hike, the finest mountains to climb, and the perfect places to camp. If you want trail maps, details on hiring guides for the trek up Mt Ararat, facts on traditional village life, and lists of essential trekking gear, this is the book in which to find them.

For the literary-minded, *Istanbul – a traveller's companion* (Atheneum/Macmillan, New York, 1987) by Laurence Kelly is a delight. The editor has combed through the writings of two millennia and collected the choicest bits, by the most interesting writers, relating to Byzantium, Constantinople and İstanbul. History, biography, diary and travellers' observations are all included.

Otherwise, the most interesting travel guides on Turkey are those published by the Redhouse Press of İstanbul. Founded under the Ottoman Empire as part of a US missionary effort, the Redhouse Press now does an admirable job of publishing dictionaries, guidebooks and general works designed to bridge the gap between the Turkish and English-speaking realms. Some of the Redhouse guides have been translated into German, French and Italian. Though only a few Redhouse books turn up in bookshops outside Turkey, you'll find them readily within the country itself, in decent editions at moderate prices. A good example of a Redhouse work is *Biblical Sites in Turkey* (1982) by Everett C Blake & Anna G Edmonds. It has colour photos, maps and costs about US$8. Other guides cover İstanbul and day trips from it.

Travellers' Accounts Mary Lee Settle's *Turkish Reflections* (Simon & Schuster, New York, 1991) is a travelogue rich with history and personal impression, fluently written by an acclaimed US novelist. To write this book, she cruised through Turkey in a chauffeur-driven Mercedes Benz; but her observations are deepened by her earlier years of residence in Turkey.

The published diaries and accounts of earlier travellers in Turkey provide fascinating glimpses of Ottoman life. One of the more familiar of these is Mark Twain's *Innocents Abroad* (New American Library, Signet Classics, New York 1982, and other editions). Twain accompanied a group of wealthy tourists on a chartered boat which sailed the Black Sea and eastern Mediterranean over a century ago. Many of the things he saw in İstanbul haven't changed much.

A more modern account of a foreigner's life in Turkey is *Scotch & Holy Water* (St Giles Press, Lafayette, California, 1981) by John D Tumpane. The author lived in Turkey for eight years as an employee of a US company, and has written a humorous and sympathetic account of his Turkish friends and adventures.

Bookshops

The major cities, and most of the resort towns, have bookshops which sell some foreign-language books, newspapers and magazines. See each city section for details.

Maps

Turkish-produced maps often lack detail or contain inaccuracies, so you'd be well advised to bring a good map from home. If you do buy a Turkish one, get the Turkish Touring & Automobile Association's *East Turkey* and/or *West Turkey* at 1:850,000 for about US$4 each. They divide the country at Kayseri; and do not show the railways. Don't trust these maps for back roads, though, particularly in the east.

Of the British maps, the Bartholomew *Euromap Turkey* (two sheets) covers the country at 1;800,000 for about US$10 per sheet; the *AA/ESR Tourist Map Turkey* is a good one as well. It covers the whole of the country at a scale of 1:2,000,000; the southwest coast at 1:750,000; and includes street plans of İstanbul, İzmir and several tourist resorts. The French *Turquie* (Série Internationale No 331) by Recta Foldex covers the entire country at 1:1,600,000. Germany produces several good series, including the Reise und Verkehrsverlag ones of eastern and western Turkey at 1:800,000. Kümmerly + Frey has a fairly good one which covers the entire country, as does Hallwag.

For İstanbul, the city publishes a very detailed map book called the *Şehir Rehberi* from time to time (latest at this writing is the 1989 edition), but it's difficult to find. More easily available is the *İstanbul A-Z Rehber-Atlas* sold in many foreign-language and tourist-oriented bookshops for about US$10.

MEDIA
Newspapers & Magazines
Local daily newspapers are produced by up-to-date computerised methods, in full colour. A few decades ago, İstanbul could boast more than a dozen Turkish-language dailies, two in Greek, one in Armenian, one in French and two in Ladino Spanish (spoken by Jews who came from Spain to the Ottoman Empire in the Middle Ages). As everywhere, the number of dailies is dwindling.

Of prime interest to visitors is the *Turkish Daily News*, an English-language daily newspaper published in Ankara and sold for 50c in most Turkish cities where tourists go. It is the cheapest source of English-language news in print. The big international papers such as the *International Herald Tribune, Le Monde, Corriere della Sera, Die Welt* etc are on sale in tourist spots as well, but are much more expensive (US$2 for the *Herald Tribune)*. Check the date on any international paper before you buy it. If it's more than a day or two old, look elsewhere.

Large-circulation magazines including *Newsweek, Time, Der Spiegel* and the like, are also sold in tourist spots.

If you can't find the foreign publication you want, go to a big hotel's newsstand or check at a foreign-language bookshop.

Radio & TV
TRT, for Türkiye Radyo ve Televizyon, is a quasi-independent establishment modelled on the BBC. Western classical and popular music, along with Turkish classic, folk, religious and pop music, are played regularly on both AM (medium-wave) and FM channels.

Short news broadcasts in English, French and German are given each morning and evening.

Turkey has recently been opened to private, commercial broadcasting. As of this writing there are only private TV stations, not radio stations, but soon there may be private radio broadcasting as well.

The BBC World Service is often receivable on AM as well as on short-wave. The Voice of America broadcasts in English on AM, relayed from Rhodes, each morning. The rest of the medium-wave band is a wonderful babel of Albanian, Arabic, Bulgarian, Greek, Hebrew, Italian, Persian, Romanian and Russian.

TRT broadcasts in colour from breakfast time till midnight on four TV channels. Independent Turkish-language stations relayed from Europe by satellite include Star 1, SHOW TV and TeleOn. The familiar Los Angeles-made series and many of the films are dubbed in Turkish. Occasionally you'll catch a film in the original language. In addition to the Turkish channels, many of the larger and more expensive hotels have satellite hook-ups to receive European channels, with programmes mostly in German, but often including the European service of the US Cable News Network (CNN) and/or the BBC.

FILM & PHOTOGRAPHY
Film is expensive in Turkey (24 Kodacolor prints about US$10, plus developing). Kodachrome slide (diapositive) film is difficult to find, and cannot be developed in Turkey, though the simpler E-6 process films such as Ektachrome, Fujichrome and Velvia are readily available and speedily (though not always perfectly) processed in city photo shops.

Do not photograph anything military, whether or not you see signs reading *Foto çekmek yasak(tır)* or *Fotoğraf çekilmez*. In areas off the tourist track, it's polite to ask *Foto çekebilir miyim?* ('May I take a photo?') before taking close-ups of people.

For camera repair, one reader recommends Mr Nazmi Kılıçer (☎ (1) 511 42 59,

527 7935), Babiali Caddesi, Başmusahip Sokak 19/1, Gün Han, 34410 Cağaloğlu, İstanbul. Though he is a Hasselblad specialist, he repairs all sorts of cameras.

HEALTH

Medical services are fairly well distributed in Turkey, though they are often fairly basic. Some doctors in the larger cities speak English, French or German, and have studied in Europe or the USA. Your embassy or consulate can recommend a good doctor or dentist (see Visas & Embassies in this chapter).

For minor problems, it's customary to ask at a pharmacy (eczane, edj-zahn-NEH) for advice. Sign language usually suffices to communicate symptoms, and the pharmacist/chemist will prescribe on the spot. Even 'prescription' drugs are sometimes sold without a prescription.

Though Turkey manufactures most modern prescription medicines, it's not good to risk running out of your medicine. If you take a drug regularly, bring a supply. If your medicine is available in Turkey, it may be less expensive here than at home. The medicine's name may not be exactly the same, though the substance may be.

Predeparture Preparations

Health Insurance A travel insurance policy to cover theft, loss and medical problems is a wise idea. There are many policies and your travel agent may have recommendations. The international student travel policies handled by STA or other student travel organisations are usually good value. Some policies offer lower and higher medical expenses options, but the higher one is chiefly for countries like the US with extremely high medical costs. Check the small print:

• Some travel insurance policies specifically exclude 'dangerous activities' which can include scuba diving, motorcycling, even trekking. If these activities are on your agenda you don't want that sort of policy.

• You may prefer to take out a policy which pays doctors or hospitals direct rather than you having to pay now and claim later. If you have to claim later make sure you keep all documentation.

Some policies ask you to call back (reverse charges) to a centre in your home country where an immediate assessment of your problem is made.

• Check if the policy covers ambulances or an emergency flight home. If you have to stretch out you will need two seats and somebody has to pay for them!

Medical Kit It is wise to carry a small, straightforward medical kit. In many countries if a medicine is available at all it will generally be available over the counter and the price will be cheaper than at home.

A possible medical kit list includes:

• Aspirin, acetaminophen, panadol or ibuprofen – for pain or fever
• Antihistamine (such as Benadryl) – useful as a decongestant for colds or allergies (especially useful in preventing ear infection from air travel with these conditions), or to ease the itch from insect bites or stings or to help prevent motion sickness
• Antibiotics – useful if you're travelling well off the beaten track, but they must be prescribed and you should carry the prescription with you.

Note that wide-spectrum antibiotics may cause sun sensitivity (redness, swelling, blistering of skin exposed to sun) in some people; consult your doctor.
• Kaolin preparation (Kaopectate), Imodium or Lomotil – for severe diarrhoea
• Rehydration mixture – for treatment of severe diarrhoea, this is particularly important if travelling with children
• Antiseptic (tincture of iodine, Mercurochrome or similar) for cuts and grazes
• Calamine lotion to ease irritation from bites or stings
• Bandages and Band-aids (sticking plaster) – for minor injuries
• Scissors, tweezers and a digital thermometer (mercury thermometers are prohibited by airlines)
• Insect repellent (which is very important along the Turkish coasts from July to September), sunblock cream, suntan lotion, chapstick and water purification tablets

Vaccinations You need no special inoculations before entering Turkey, unless you're coming from an endemic or epidemic area. If you want to get preventive shots (tetanus, typhoid etc), get cholera too. The chances are small that you'll run into cholera, but having been vaccinated may come in handy when crossing borders. Health officers far removed from the scene may not keep track of which countries have cholera.

Also, if you plan to live very cheaply and travel extensively in the eastern regions, you might consider getting an immunoglobulin injection as some protection against hepatitis.

Officially, malaria is present in south-east Anatolia from Mersin on the Mediterranean coast eastward to the Iraqi border, but the highest danger is in the muggy agricultural area called *Cukurova* north of Adana. If you just pass through, or spend most of your time in cities, the danger is low; but if you plan to spend lots of time in rural areas and camp out, consider taking chloroquine tablets weekly (consult a doctor first). At present there are no known chloroquine-resistant strains of mosquitoes in this area. I have visited south-east Anotolia repeatedly without taking medicine and have never had a problem, but you must make your own decision.

Food & Water

Travellers in Turkey experience a fair amount of Travellers' Diarrhoea ('the Sultan's Revenge'). Most people suffer some consequences from drastic change of diet and water, for each area and each cuisine has its own 'normal' bacteria and its own composition. Some people find it difficult to digest olive oil, or even to stomach pure water that has a high limestone content. Any experienced traveller knows that getting sick from food is mostly by chance, but there are still a few things you can do to improve your chances.

Dining Precautions Choose dishes that look freshly prepared and sufficiently hot. You can go into almost any Turkish kitchen (except in the very posh places) for a look at what's cooking. In fact, in most places that's what the staff will suggest, the language barrier being what it is. Except for grilled meats, Turkish dishes tend to be cooked slowly for a long time, just the thing to kill any errant bacteria. If the dishes don't sell on the day they're cooked, they might be saved, and the oil may congeal and become harder to digest.

As for grilled meats, these may be offered to you medium rare. They'll probably be all right, but if they really look pink, send them back for more cooking (no problem in this). The words you'll need are *biraz daha pişmiş* (beer-ahz da-HAH peesh-meesh) for 'cooked a bit more', and *iyi pişmiş* (ee-EE peesh-meesh) or *pişkin,* (peesh-KEEN) for 'well done'.

Beware of milk products and dishes containing milk that have not been properly refrigerated. Electricity is expensive in Turkey, and many places will scrimp on refrigeration temperature. If you want a rice pudding *(sütlaç)* or some such dish with milk in it, choose a shop that has lots of them in the window, meaning that a batch has been made recently and thus guaranteeing freshness. In general, choose things from bins, trays, cases, pots etc that are fairly full rather than almost empty. If you make a point of eating some yoghurt every day, you'll keep your digestive system in excellent condition.

Drinking Precautions Drink bottled spring water whenever possible. It's sold every-

where in clear plastic bottles in sizes of one-third of a litre, 1.5 litres and three litres. Check the date on the bottle, and don't buy water that's been around for a while as it may taste of the plastic.

Tap water in Turkey is chlorinated and not particularly poisonous (as in some countries), but neither is it certain to be safe, and it rarely tastes good.

A roadside *çeşme* (CHESH-meh, fountain or spring), may bear the word *içilmez* (eech-eel-MEHZ, 'not to be drunk'), or *içilir* (eech-eel-LEER, 'drinkable'), or *içme suyu* (EECH-meh soo-yoo, 'drinking water'), or *içilebilir* (EECH-eel-eh-bee-LEER, 'can be drunk'), but I'd avoid these if possible unless you think you really know what's upstream from them.

Alternatives to spring water include *maden suyu*, naturally fizzy mineral water, and *maden sodası* (or just *soda)*, artificially carbonated mineral water. The latter just has bigger bubbles, and more of them, than the former. Both come from mineral springs, and both are truly full of minerals. The taste is not neutral. Some people like it, some don't. It's supposed cleanse your kidneys and be good for you.

Packaged fruit juice *(meyva suyu)*, soft drinks, beer and wine are reliably pure, except in rare cases.

Toilets

Virtually every hotel above the lowest class, most apartments, many restaurants, railway stations and airports have the familiar raised-bowl commode toilet. The Turkish version is equipped with facilities for washing the user's bottom (always with the left hand): a spigot and can on the floor nearby, or, much more conveniently, a little copper tube snaking up the back and right to the spot where it's needed. As washing is the accustomed method of hygiene, toilet paper – used by Turks mostly for drying – is considered a dispensable luxury and may not be provided. In the government-rated hotels there should be paper. In public conveniences, if there's no attendant, there will be no paper. It's a good idea to carry enough paper or tissues with you at all times.

You may also meet with the traditional flat 'elephant's feet' toilet, a porcelain or concrete rectangle with two oblong foot-places and a sunken hole. Though daunting, it has much to recommend it: doctors say that the squatting position aids in the swift accomplishment of your daily duty; and since only your shod feet contact the vessel, it is more sanitary that bowl toilets.

So much for science. The first time you use it, you'll feel awkward (and older readers have found it difficult to arise from the squat). Don't despair. Think of the generations of magnificent Ottoman sultans and gracious harem ladies who did it this way. Take a tip from them: don't let all of the stuff fall out of your pockets when you squat.

Sometimes the plumbing is not built to take wads of paper, and the management will place a wastepaper basket or can next to the toilet for used paper. Signs in Turkish will plead with you not to throw the paper down the toilet. What you do depends upon your feelings on the matter. If the toilet doesn't flush, use a bucket or plastic container of water to do the job.

Serviceably clean public toilets can be found near the big tourist attractions. In other places, it depends. Look first. Every mosque has a toilet, often smelly and very basic, but it may be better than nothing, depending upon the urgency of Nature's call.

Diseases

Food Poisoning Symptoms are headaches, nausea and/or stomachache, diarrhoea, fever and chills. If you get food poisoning, go to bed and stay warm. Drink lots of fluids, preferably hot tea without sugar or milk. Camomile tea, *papatya çay*, is a specific against a queasy stomach. Some teahouses serve it, herbal markets sell the dried camomile, and in many parts of Turkey you can even pick the fragrant little daisy-like camomile flowers along the roadside and make the tea yourself.

Until the bout of food poisoning has run its course (for 24 to 30 hours), drink nothing but plain tea (no milk or sugar), and eat nothing but dry toast or rusks and maybe a little yoghurt. The day after, you'll feel weak, but the symptoms will have passed except perhaps for the diarrhoea. If you take it easy and eat only bland, easily digested foods for a few days, you'll be fine.

Do not compound the problem by ignoring it, or by continuing to travel or see the sights, or by eating whatever is easiest. Medicines can help a serious bout of the illness, but nothing can rebuild your intestinal flora, necessary to good digestion, except time and tender loving care. Most medicines for food poisoning are strong antibiotics. They kill the poisonous bacteria (which your body would have killed on its own, in time), but they also kill all the normal, healthful digestive bacteria. Thus antibiotics can actually *prolong* the diarrhoea by making it difficult for your digestive system to do its work.

Travellers' Diarrhoea The standard treatments for travellers' diarrhoea, as recommended by the US Public Health Service, include antibiotics, bismuth subsalicylate (Pepto-Bismol), and difenoxine (Lomotil). Each of these medicines has side effects; you should consult a physician before taking any of them, and you should not take any medicine as a preventative, but only if you actually become ill.

Bismuth subsalicylate coats your stomach lining and helps get rid of the harmful bacteria, but it must not be taken by people allergic to salicylates, or by those with kidney problems. The standard dosage is 30 ml of the liquid, or a similar quantity in tablet form, every half-hour for four hours.

Difenoxine usually comes as diphenoxylate (Lomotil) or loperamide (Imodium), synthetic opiate anti-motility agents. They drug your gut into passivity and also dull your senses. Don't take these pills for longer than two days, and don't take them if you have a high fever or blood in the stool.

Antibiotics can help in a bad case of travellers' diarrhoea. How do you know it's 'bad'? The US Public Health Service says that if you have three or more loose bowel movements in an eight-hour period, especially if you also suffer from nausea, vomiting, abdominal cramps, and/or fever, you probably should have a doctor prescribe an antibiotic for you. The normal prescription is for doxycycline, 100 mg twice daily; or Bactrim F (Roche), tablets of TMP and SMX (trimethoprim 160 mg and sulfamethoxazole 800 mg) twice daily. These drugs are powerful and should not be taken carelessly. Be sure not to take them if hepatitis is suspected.

Hepatitis Hepatitis (*sarılık*, SAH-ruh-LUHK) is a serious viral infection which must be treated carefully. Hepatitis A is the most common form of this disease and is spread by contaminated food and water. The chief symptoms are fatigue, loss of energy, a yellow cast to the eyes and skin, and odd-coloured brownish urine. If you rest when your body tells you to, you will have no trouble curing yourself. If you push on, the disease can cause serious liver damage or even death. Antibiotics can make it worse, even fatal, as they put great stress on the already overburdened liver which must detoxify them. At this writing, tests are being conducted on medicines designed to combat hepatitis; ask your doctor.

If you think you have hepatitis, go to a doctor and get an examination and a blood test. If the diagnosis is positive, go to bed and stay there. Eat only easily digestible non-fatty foods such as toast, yoghurt, cooked fruits and vegetables. Don't drink any alcohol for six months after diagnosis. You will have to figure on at least a week or two of bed rest, then an easy life for several months. The doctor may prescribe vitamins, especially B-complex. If any other medicine is prescribed, go to another doctor. This is no joke.

Sexually Transmitted Diseases (STDs) Sexual contact with an infected sexual partner is the most common method of contracting these diseases. Although abstinence is the only 100% preventative, use of a condom is also effective. Gonorrhoea and

A Stone head, Nemrut Dağı (TB)
B Mosaic ceiling, Kariye Museum (TB)
C Funerary stone, Aizanoi (TB)
D Marble torsos, Side Museum (TB)
E Statue of Cybele, Ephesus Museum (TB)
F Roman mosaic, Antakya Museum (TB)

Top: İstanbul as seen from the Süleymaniye minaret (TB)
Bottom: Fishing skiffs on the Bosphorus at sunset (TB)

syphilis are the most common sexually transmitted diseases, signalled by sores, blisters or rashes around the genitals, discharges or pain when urinating. Symptoms may be less marked or not observed at all in women. The symptoms of syphilis eventually disappear completely but the disease continues and can cause severe problems in later years. Antibiotics are used to treat gonorrhoea and syphilis.

There are numerous other sexually transmitted diseases, most of which have effective treatments. However, there are no cures for herpes or HIV/AIDS. Using condoms decreases – but does not eliminate – your chances of contracting these diseases.

HIV/AIDS can also be spread through infected blood transfusions or by dirty needles – vaccinations, acupuncture and tattooing can potentially be as dangerous as intravenous drug use if the equipment is not clean. If you do need an injection, be absolutely certain that the syringe used is sterile. It may be a good idea to buy a new syringe from a pharmacy and ask the doctor to use it.

Doctors, Dentists & Hospitals

You can find good doctors and dentists in Turkey's big cities, as well as hospitals (*hastane*, hahs-tah-NEH) and clinics (*klinik*, klee-NEEK). Government-supported hospitals are called *devlet hastanesi*, and you can find them by following the standard international road sign with a large 'H' on it. See the chapter or section about each city for details.

Clinics run by the Red Crescent (*Kızılay*, the Turkish equivalent of the Red Cross) are marked by a red crescent. *İlk yardım* on one of these signs means 'first aid', which may or may not be competent; a *sağlık ocağı* is a simple dispensary. All hospital and clinic costs are controlled by the government, and are quite low, even at private hospitals.

In every city and town of any size you will see signs marking the medical offices of doctors and giving their specialities. *Operatör* means surgeon. A doctor (*tıbbi doktor*, medical doctor) might treat *göz hastalıkları*, eye diseases. Some useful terms to know include *dahili*, internal medicine;

kadın hastalıkları, gynaecological ailments; *çocuk hastalıkları*, paediatric (children's) ailments.

By the way, half of all the physicians in Turkey are women. Female patients might prefer to see a woman doctor: if a woman visits a male doctor, it's customary to have a companion present during any physical examination or treatment. There is not always a nurse available to serve in this role.

Care in Turkish hospitals is sometimes not of the highest standard in terms of comfort or convenience. But medical care, as always, depends upon the particular staff members (doctors and nurses) involved. These can be quite good or not so good. The lower staff echelons may be low paid and trained on the job. As a foreigner, you will probably be given the best possible treatment and the greatest consideration.

WOMEN TRAVELLERS

I have received numerous letters from women relating their experiences at the hands (literally) of Turkish men. Some say they had no problems whatsoever, others say they thought themselves in real danger at times. I think it's fair to predict that many unescorted women will have some annoying and unpleasant moments during their travels, but that they will also be treated in a civil, even courtly, manner by many Turkish men. There's a real clash of cultures: a traditionally patriarchal Eastern society meets the modern, liberated Western woman. Less than a century ago, a proper Turkish woman was veiled from head to toe; today, most female tourists in Turkey go topless at the beach and may *even* have sex before marriage (as every Turkish man knows). The cultural adjustment may take some time.

Turkish social customs dictate that a young woman (such as a high school student) not go to a major shopping street without friends or mother; college-aged women usually stroll with friends; women in their prime look purposeful, ignore catcalls and don't walk on lonely streets after dark. If you're approached by an Eastern Romeo, ignore, ignore, ignore. It's best not to say or do anything. The key, perhaps, is respectability and hauteur: if you look and act respectably according to Turkish standards, you'll have the best chance to fend off unwanted advances. A wedding ring may help. It definitely helps to dress more formally. If you must say something at a guy who's hassling you, say *Ayıp!* (ah-YUHP), which means 'shameful'. Use it all you want to on young kids. But men may take exception if you call them shameful when they're certain you'll find their masculine charms irresistible.

When you buy a bus ticket, the ticket agent will automatically seat you next to another woman or will leave the seat next to you empty. Should you want to confirm that this is so, you can request it by saying *Yanımda erkek oturtmayın* (YAH-nuhm-DAH ehr-KEK oh-TOORT-mah-yuhn, 'Please don't seat a man next to me'). On some buses there are single seats set aside for women.

When searching for a hotel, look for one catering to families. To find a suitable hotel, look to see if there are matronly types waiting in the lobby, or just ask, *Bu otel aile için mi?* (BOO oh-tehl ah-yee-LEH ee-cheen mee, 'Is this hotel for families/ladies?') If it's not, the clerk should direct you to a more suitable place nearby.

The word 'family' *(aile)* in Turkish can mean either wife, or husband and wife, or husband, wife and children. When you go out, look for the section of the tea garden or restaurant reserved for families or women alone; sometimes this is a separate upstairs room. The magic word for a respectable spot is always *aile*, as in *aile salonu* (family dining room) or *aile çay bahçesi* (family tea garden) or *aileye mahsustur* (reserved for families). '

DANGERS & ANNOYANCES

Turkey is a safe country relative to most of the world, however, if you plan on travelling in the east read the warnings about Kurdish activity at the start of the Getting Around and Eastern Anatolia chapters.

General crime, however, is not a big problem in Turkey – yet. You may feel safer here than at home.

Police

The green-clad officers with white caps, both men and women, are part of a national force designated by the words *Polis* (poh-LEES) or *Emniyet* (ehm-nee-YEHT, security). They control traffic, patrol highways and attend to other police duties in cities and towns. Under normal circumstances you will have little to do with them. If you do encounter them, they will judge you partly by your clothes and personal appearance. If you look tidy and 'proper', they'll be on your side. If you're dressed carelessly, they may subject you to bureaucratic tedium.

The blue-clad officers are called *belediye zabıtası* (municipal inspectors), or market police. These officers are the modern expression of an age-old Islamic custom of special commercial police who make sure a loaf of bread weighs what it should, that 24-carat gold is indeed 24 carats, that scales and balances don't cheat the customer. You'll see these officials patrolling the markets and bazaars, and if you have a commercial problem they'll be glad to help. They may not speak much of a foreign language.

Soldiers in the standard Turkish army uniforms may be of three types. Without special insignia, they're regular army. With a red armband bearing the word 'jandarma', they're gendarmes who keep the peace, catch criminals on the run, stop smuggling etc. If the soldiers have white helmets emblazoned with the letters 'As İz', plus pistols in white holsters connected to lanyards around their necks, they're Askeri İnzibat, or military police who keep off-duty soldiers in line.

Most of these soldiers are draftees inducted into the enormous Turkish army, put through basic training, and sent out to guard-jobs that are usually pretty unexciting. They look ferocious – life in the Turkish army is no joke – but basically they are hometown boys waiting to get out. Every single one of them can tell you the precise number of days he has left to serve. Any request from a foreign tourist for help or directions is received as though it were a marvellous privilege.

Theft & Robbery

Theft is not much of a problem, and robbery (mugging) even less, but don't let Turkey's relative safety lull you. Take normal precautions.

Precautions include keeping track of your wallet or other valuables on crowded buses and trains and in markets; not leaving valuables in your hotel room, or at least not in view; and not walking into unknown parts of town when nobody else is around. There are isolated reports of bags being quietly slashed in İstanbul's Covered Market, and of distract, bump and grab thefts in similar crowded places.

Actually, the biggest danger of theft is probably in dormitory rooms and other open accommodation where other foreigners can see what sort of camera you have (and can guess its value pretty accurately), or where you stash your money.

There are isolated incidents of gassing and drugging. Gassing happens mostly on trains in the Balkans (ie, not in Turkey) when thieves spray anaesthetic gas into your train compartment as you sleep, then enter and relieve you of all your stuff. Drugging happens like this: your seatmate on a Turkish bus offers – nay insists – that he buy you a drink. The drink comes to you in his hand from somewhere off the bus. He's put sleeping drugs in it. After you conk out, he gets off the bus with your stuff at the next town.

In İstanbul there's a nightclub shakedown racket aimed at single men which amounts to robbery. Here's how it works: you're strolling along İstiklal Caddesi or Cumhuriyet Caddesi in the evening. You stop to look in a shop window. A well-dressed man or a couple of men approach and chat about this and that. They offer to buy you a drink in a nightclub nearby. You're given a seat next to some 'girls', and even if you protest at this point, it's too late. They say the girls' drinks are on your bill. If you resist paying an amount which conveniently equals the entire contents of your wallet, you are escorted to the back office and convinced forcibly to pay up. Moral: single men should not accept invitations from unknown Turks in large cities without sizing the situation up very carefully.

Disputes

In general, Turks view foreigners as cultured, educated and wealthy – even if many foreign visitors don't deserve such a view. This means that you will sometimes be given special consideration, jumped to the heads of queues, given the best seat on the bus etc. In a dispute, if you keep your cool and act dignified, you will generally be given the benefit of the doubt. If it is thought you have powerful friends, you will definitely be given that benefit.

It's difficult to imagine a dispute involving a foreigner coming to the point of blows, as Turks are slow to anger. Don't let it happen. A Turk rarely finds it necessary to fight, but if he does, he wants to win, *whatever* the cost. Knowing that horrible things could happen, bystanders will pull two quarrelling men apart, even if they've never seen them before.

In the case of women travellers in disputes with Turks, you should know that Turkish men feel acutely any insults to their manhood, and will retaliate. Insults to them can include being shouted at or browbeaten by a woman who is not (in their eyes) unquestionably of a higher social status. In general, keep it all formal.

Lese-Majesty

There are laws against insulting, defaming or making light of Atatürk, the Turkish flag, the Turkish people, the Turkish Republic etc. Any difficulty will probably arise from misunderstanding. At the first sign that you've inadvertently been guilty of lese-majesty, be sure to make your apologies. An apology will be readily accepted.

Natural Hazards

Earthquakes Turkey sometimes has very bad ones. The big quakes only seem to hit every eight or 10 years, though, and the same thing happens in many parts of the world, so it's up to Allah.

Undertows & Riptides At some of the swimming areas, particularly in the Black Sea near İstanbul, this is a real danger. Undertows can kill you by powerfully pulling you beneath the surface, and a riptide does the same by sweeping you out to sea so that you exhaust yourself trying to regain the shore. There may be no signs warning of the danger. Lifeguards may not be present, or may be untrained or not equipped with a boat. Don't trust to luck. You can't necessarily see these hazards or predict where they will be.

In either situation, remain calm, as panic can be fatal. Don't exhaust yourself by trying to swim straight back to the beach from a rip, because you'll never make it. Rather, swim to the left or right to escape the rip area, and make for land in that direction. These dangers are usually a problem only on long stretches of open-sea beach with surf. In coves and bays, where waves are broken or diverted by headlands, you probably won't be in danger.

Insects, Snakes & Other Animals Turkey has mosquitoes, scorpions and snakes. You will not see many of them, but be aware, as you tramp around the ruins on the Aegean and Mediterranean coasts in particular, that such beasts do live here and may be nearby, at least in summer. There are also wild boar and wolves around, though you won't encounter these unless you hike deep into the bush.

The Imperial Auto
As a pedestrian, give way to cars and trucks in all situations, even if you have to jump out of the way. The sovereignty of the pedestrian is unrecognised in Turkey. If a car hits you, the driver (if not the law courts) will blame you. This does not apply on a recognised crossing controlled by a traffic officer or a traffic signal. If you've got a 'Walk' light, you've got the right of way. Watch out, all the same. Know that every Turkish driver

considers you, a pedestrian, as merely an annoyance composed of so much vile protoplasm. A dispute with a driver will get you nowhere and may escalate into an even bigger problem.

Cigarette Smoke
If you're offended by cigarette smoke, you will have some unpleasant moments in Turkey. Though the local cancer prevention society fields a brave effort to stop smoking, this is the land of aromatic Turkish tobacco, and smoking is a national passion. The movement for no-smoking areas in public places is gaining ground, but it will be a long battle. In general, position yourself near a fresh-air source if possible. And help in my campaigns to have separate smoking and no-smoking areas: if you do not smoke, ask for the no-smoking (*sigarasız*) section whenever you board a bus. (Turkish Airlines domestic flights are all no-smoking – in principle.)

Noise
Noise is a source of great annoyance in cities and larger towns. Choose hotel rooms keeping noise in mind.

Among the most persistent and omnipresent noises is that of the call to prayer, amplified to ear-splitting levels. In the good old days before microphones and amplifiers, it must have been beautiful to hear the clear, natural voices of the muezzins calling from a hundred minarets, even before dawn, when the first call is given. Now you hear a cacophony of blaring noise five or more times a day. If there's a minaret right outside your hotel window, you'll know it.

Also, Turks are addicted to nightlife and think nothing of staying up until 1 or 2 am in the middle of the week, so watch out for highly amplified bands and singers. Nightclub noise is particularly insulting when you have spent good money to upgrade your accommodation only to find that the better the hotel, the louder its nightclub. In some resorts (such as Bodrum), atomic-powered discos rock the entire town until dawn, making sleep virtually impossible. When in doubt, ask *Sakin mi?* (sah-KEEN mee, 'Is it quiet here?').

Air Pollution

In winter, air pollution is a problem in the big cities. In Ankara it is a very serious problem, rivalling that of Tokyo and Mexico City. The traditional heating fuel is lignite (soft brown coal), which produces enormous clouds of heavy, choking particles. The situation is now improving because of a new natural gas pipeline from Russia which brings clean heating fuel to buildings in Ankara and İstanbul. But air quality in winter may still be substandard for a while. If you find your nose running, your eyes watering and itching, and your head aching, that's the pollution. The heating season lasts from 15 October to 1 April. In summer there is some pollution from cars, but it's no worse than in other big cities.

WORK

You can extend your time in Turkey by getting a job. Most people who do this teach English at one of the many private colleges or schools in İstanbul or Ankara. Others work at one of the publication offices such as the Turkish Daily News. If you're crafty and careful, you can even work without a permit.

It's best to obtain a work visa (*çalışma vizesi*) from the Turkish Embassy or consulate (in person or by mail; it takes from three weeks) in your home country before you leave. Submit the completed visa form, your passport, two photos of yourself, your proof of employment (a contract or letter from your employer) and the required fee. Your passport will be returned with the visa stamped inside.

If you're not at home and you want a work visa, apply for it outside Turkey. The Turkish consulate in Komotini in Greece, an 11-hour overnight bus ride from İstanbul, is used to such requests. It usually grants the visa within a few hours. If you plan to make a special trip, check to make sure the consulate will be open and issuing work visas when you arrive. Your own consulate or a Greek

consulate may be able to tell you (see Visas & Embassies in this chapter).

Once you arrive in Turkey on a work visa, you must obtain a 'pink book', a combined work permit and residence permit, from the Yabancılar Polisi (Foreigners' Police); in İstanbul they're in Cağaloğlu behind the İstanbul Valiliği on Ankara Caddesi. Your employer may do this for you. If not, apply with your passport, two more photos, and the US$40 processing fee. They should have your pink book ready in two or three days. The pink book, which takes over from the visa in your passport, is renewable every year, as long as you show proof of continued employment.

If you can't provide proof of employment (that is, if you're working illegally), you may still be able to get a three-month residence permit if you can show bank deposits in Turkey totalling more than about US$200. You may or may not be able to renew a three-month permit, at the whim of the officer.

When all else fails, leave the country for a day or two to Greece, Bulgaria, or to Cyprus, and get a new 90-day tourist visa as you return to Turkey. This may only be possible a few times, however, as the immigration officer will be come suspicious of too many recent Turkish stamps in your passport.

ACTIVITIES

Turkish Baths

The history of steam baths goes back millennia. Many of the natural spas in Turkey were enjoyed by the ancient Greeks and Romans. Seljuk and Ottoman Turks built beautiful, elaborate baths to serve their communities, partly because Islam demands good personal hygiene, and partly because bathing is such a pleasure.

Public baths were required in ancient times because private residences did not have bathing facilities. Everybody, rich and poor alike, went to the baths. For a workman, it was simply to get clean. For a high-born lady, it was a ritual of attendants, accessories and polite courtesies. Some baths are very fancy, others simpler, but there are still public baths to be found in virtually every neighbourhood of every town in Turkey.

The custom of going to the baths continues because the public facilities are so much grander than what is available at home, and because for the Turks it is still a social occasion. To steam clean, have a massage, relax and read, sip tea and chat with friends, is looked upon as a wonderful, affordable luxury.

The Turkish bath procedure is this: you will be shown to a cubicle where you can undress, store your clothes and wrap the cloth that's provided around you. An attendant will lead you through the cool room and the warm room to the hot room, where you sit and sweat for a while, relaxing and loosening up. You can have a massage here. Haggle with a masseur or masseuse on a price before beginning.

When you are half-asleep and soft as putty from the steamy heat, you have a choice. The cheapest bath is the one you do yourself, having brought your own soap, shampoo and towel. But the true experience is to have an attendant wash you, providing all the necessaries. You'll be led to the warm room, doused with warm water, then lathered with a sudsy swab. Next, the attendant will scrub your skin with a coarse cloth mitten loosening dirt you never suspected you had. Next comes a shampoo, another dousing with warm water, then one with cool water.

When the scrubbing is over, head for the cool room, there to be swathed in Turkish towels, then led back to your cubicle for a rest or a nap. You can order tea, coffee, a soft drink or a bottle of beer. For a nap, tell the attendant when to wake you.

Traditional Turkish baths have separate sections for men and women, or have only one set of facilities and admit men or women at different times. Bath etiquette requires that men remain clothed with the bath-wrap at all times. During the bathing, they wash their private parts themselves, without removing the modesty wrap. In the women's section modesty is less in evidence. Sexual activity has no place in the traditional bath ritual.

In touristy areas, some baths now accept that foreign men and women like to bathe together. The prices are raised substantially for the privilege, and some questionable practices have emerged. No Turkish woman would let a masseur touch her (it must be a masseuse), but masseurs are usually the only massagers available in these foreign-oriented baths. I've received complaints from women readers who suffered indignities at the hands of masseurs. Women who accept a masseur should have the massage within view of – preferably very near – their male companions or other friends, and should protest at the first sign of impropriety.

Sport

Turks are sports enthusiasts. Football (soccer), basketball and wrestling are the favoured sports. Every city of any size has a large football stadium which fills up on match days.

The famous oiled wrestling matches, where brawny strongmen in leather breeches rub themselves down with olive oil and grapple with equally slippery opponents, take place each June in Edirne. Another purely Turkish sight is the camel-wrestling matches held in the province of Aydın, south of İzmir, in the winter months. Konya is the setting for cirit, the javelin-throwing game played on horseback.

Water sports are big in Turkey because of the beautiful coasts and beaches. Yachting, rowing, water-skiing, snorkelling, diving (with or without scuba gear) and swimming are well represented. Because of the many antiquities in the depths off the Turkish coasts, scuba diving is regulated. Diving shops in Marmaris, Bodrum and other coastal towns can provide details. Turkish divers are very safety-conscious, so bring your diving credentials to prove that you are certified to dive to the depth you want to explore.

Mountain climbing (dağcılık, DAAH-juh-LUHK) is practised by a small but enthusiastic number of Turks, and Turkey has plenty of good, high mountains for it. For complete information, with addresses of out-fitters, guides, and Turkish climbing clubs, buy a copy of *Trekking in Turkey* (see Travel Guides in the Books & Maps section in this chapter).

Turkey is a good country for hunting animals, from small game to wild boar (there's a boar-hunting festival at Ephesus each spring). Check with a Turkish consulate about regulations and permits for importing a sporting gun.

Skiing is decent on Uludağ, near Bursa, at a few resorts in the Beydağları mountain range near Antalya, on Mt Erciyes near Kayseri, and at Palandöken near Erzurum. Except at Bursa, facilities are basic, even primitive, but equipment can be rented at the slopes. The reward for true skiers is on the slopes: at Palandöken, the snow is good for nine months of the year.

Bicycling through Turkey is possible, and mostly delightful. For details, see the Getting Around chapter.

HIGHLIGHTS

In İstanbul, don't miss Topkapı Palace, Aya Sofya, and the Kariye Museum. The battle-fields of Gallipoli, on the Dardanelles, are particularly moving. Many visitors find Troy disappointing, but not so Ephesus, which is the best-preserved classical city on the Mediterranean.

Seljuk Turkish architecture, earlier than Ottoman, is particularly fine. Alanya, Konya, Sivas and Erzurum have many good Seljuk buildings.

Beaches are best at Pamucak (near Ephesus), Bodrum, Patara, Antalya, Side and Alanya.

The improbable 'lunar' landscapes of Cappadocia, riddled with troglodyte dwellings and churches cut from the rock, are perhaps the single most visually impressive feature in all Turkey.

More adventurous travellers prefer eastern Turkey and the Black Sea coast to the western regions. The east is wilder, rougher, and less accustomed to foreigners. The scenery is spectacular.

ACCOMMODATION
Hotels

The cheapest hotels in Turkey are rated by each local municipality. These are the basic places that provide bed, heat, light and water. They are used mostly by working-class Turkish men travelling on business. Virtually all hotels above this basic standard are rated by the Ministry of Tourism according to a star system. One-star hotels are just a step above the cheap places rated by the municipalities. At the top, rating five stars, are the international-class places, such as the Hiltons, Sheratons, Kempinskis and Ramadas.

In this guide, hotels are listed according to price, except in places with only a few hotels which must be used by all visitors regardless of preference.

Bottom End Lodgings in this group are priced from US$4 per bed in a small town up to US$20 or US$25 for a double room in a large city. For Turks, these are the *otels* (hotels) used by farmers in town for the market, workers in town looking for a job, or the *pansiyons* (pensions) used by working-class families on holiday at the seaside. Not surprisingly, the most difficult place to find a truly cheap, good low-budget room is İstanbul. In most other cities, good, cheap beds can be found fairly easily. In out-of-the-way villages the price for a bed is surprisingly low.

Rooms priced below about US$10 do not usually have a private shower or toilet in the room, but may have a *lavabo* (washbasin). Above that price, in small towns you may get private plumbing. Cold-water showers are usually free, as they should be. Hot-water showers may cost between US$1 and US$2 in lodgings where a fire must be built in the hot-water heater. If there is solar water-heating, hot showers are often free, but the water may only be warm, as the solar tanks are generally uninsulated in the off season. On cloudy days, or if everyone else has preceded you to the showers, expect tepid water. With solar water-heating, plan to shower in the evening when the water is hottest, rather than in the morning.

At the lowest prices, the rooms will be quite bare and spartan, but functional. Hotels may quote prices per bed rather than per room. For privacy, you may have to pay for all of the beds in the room. If you find used sheets on the bed, request clean ones; the owner has got to change them sometime, and it may as well be for you. Say *Temiz çarşaf lazım* (teh-MEEZ chahr-SHAHF lyaa-zuhm, 'Clean sheets are necessary'). Bedbugs are not unheard of; let me know of any bug banquets you host so I can warn other readers.

Middle Turkey has lots of modern and comfortable hotels rated at one to three stars by the Ministry of Tourism. Facilities in this range include lifts; staff capable of speaking a smattering of German, French and English; rooms with a private shower or bath and toilet; perhaps balconies from which you can enjoy the view, and maybe guarded car parks. Prices in this range are from US$25 to US$90.

A one-star hotel will have these facilities and little else, and will price its double rooms with a bath at around US$25. A two-star hotel will probably have a restaurant and bar, a TV lounge, obsequious staff, and some pretensions to décor and architecture. Double rooms with a private bath would be priced from US$25 to US$60.

A three-star hotel may provide colour TVs and mini-bar refrigerators in all guest rooms, and may have haughty but multilingual staff, a swimming pool, nightclub, pastry shop, or other special facilities as well. Double rooms with a bath would be priced from US$50 to US$90. Fairly prosperous Turks look upon a hotel room in this range as quite luxurious accommodation.

Top End Hotels at the top-end are priced from US$90 to US$250 and up for a double room.

Hotels of an international standard, such as the Hiltons, Sheratons, Kempinskis, Ramadas, Pullman Etaps, Swissôtels etc, are rated at five stars and are mostly to be found in the three largest cities (İstanbul, Ankara, İzmir) and in the most famous tourist destinations (Antalya, Cappadocia). Just below the international chains in luxury are the Turkish chain hotels such as Turban, Emek, Dedeman, Merit and others, rated at four or five stars. These hotels sometimes provide almost the same degree of luxury as some of the top places, but at prices around 20 to 40% lower.

Besides these very expensive places, Turkey has a number of smaller, very comfortable hotels where you'll enjoy more personal and attentive service at much lower prices. These four-star luxury hotels may not have swimming pools, health clubs, ballrooms and convention centres, but they have most of the comforts an individual traveller would normally require. Prices for a double room range from $100 to $175.

Boutique Hotels In some tourist towns old Ottoman mansions, caravanserais, or other historic buildings have been refurbished or even completely rebuilt, and equipped with modern conveniences. Charm, atmosphere and history are the attractions here, and they are provided in abundance, at prices from US$75 to US$175 for a double room, breakfast included. Because of their unique character, these hotels may not be rated according to the star system. Most would rate three or four stars if they were.

Choosing a Hotel

The following are some points to watch.

Inspect the Rooms For bottom-end and middle lodgings, don't judge a hotel by its façade, tell the reception clerk you'd like to see a room. A staff member will invariably be appointed to show you one or several rooms.

In the middle range of Turkish hotels there is a tendency to put money into the lobby rather than into the rooms, and so looking at the lobby does not give you an accurate idea of the quality of the guest quarters.

Know the Price Prices should be posted prominently at the reception desk. Sometimes, particularly in low-budget hotels, the posted prices will be above what the proprietor actually expects to get for a room. Unless the hotel is obviously quite full and very busy, haggle for a lower price; you may also want to haggle to exclude the usually expensive but disappointing hotel breakfast.

Whether you haggle or not, make sure you understand the price. Is it per bed *(beher yatak,* beh-HEHR yah-TAHK) or per room *(oda fiyatı,* OH-dah fee-yah-tuh)? Is breakfast *(kahvaltı)* included *(dahil)* or excluded *(hariç)?* Is there an extra fee for a hot shower *(duş ücreti,* DOOSH urj-reh-tee)? Is the tax included *(vergi dahil,* vehr-GEE dah-HEEL)? It usually is (and should be) except at the most expensive hotels.

Beware of Noise Turkish cities and towns are noisy places, and you will soon learn to choose a hotel and a room with quiet in mind. In this guide I have done some of the work for you by recommending mostly the quieter places, but you will have to be aware when you select your room. The front rooms in a hotel, those facing the busy street, are usually looked upon as the most desirable by the hotel management, and are sometimes priced higher than rooms at the rear. Take advantage of this: take a room at the back. Ask for *sakin bir oda* (sah-KEEN beer oh-dah, 'a quiet room') and pay less.

Water Pressure In some cities, and particularly in summer, there may be temporary water problems. Water may be cut off for several hours at a time, though many hotels have roof tanks which do away with this problem. The other problem with water pressure is when the pressure remains high, but the fixtures are not in good repair, and the toilet tinkles all night.

Hot Water Except in the fanciest hotels, do not trust hot water to come out of the left-hand tap and cold water out of the right-hand one. Every time you settle into a hotel room, or use a shower, experiment with the taps. It means nothing that the left-hand one is marked in red, it may yield cold water, while the right-hand one, marked in blue, gives hot water. In the same bathroom, the sink may be marked correctly and the shower incorrectly. It's a daily struggle. Open both taps and let them run full force for a minute or so, close them, then open one and next the other to see what you get. If both are cold, let them run a few minutes more and check again. Still cold? OK, now it's time to complain to the management.

As for hot water, it's often difficult to find in summer in the cheaper hotels, unless they have solar water-heaters. Many small hotels have only a single furnace for both hot water and central heating, and they really don't want to run that furnace in summer. Since the summers are warm, even hot, this doesn't present much of a problem. Early spring and late autumn are another matter, though. Every desk clerk will say, 'Yes, we have hot water', but when you try to take a shower the new fact will be, 'Ah, the furnace just this minute broke down!'

Believe it or not, the most dependable hot water is in the cheapest pensions, because in these places the owner builds a little fire in the bottom of the hot-water tank 30 minutes before your shower appointment, and you bathe in as much steaming water as you want. The extra charge for this luxury is US$1 to US$2.

An alternative, fairly dependable hot-water method is the *şofben* (SHOHF-behn), or flash heater. This type runs on gas, and flashes into action as soon as you turn on the hot-water tap. It's activated by water flowing through the hot-water pipe. Obviously this sort of heater is not dependent on a central furnace, but it does have other problems. Gas pressure must be sufficient to heat the water, which it sometimes is not; and the flow of water must be strong enough to activate the şofben, which it sometimes is not. Often it's a balancing act, keeping the flow of water fast enough to activate the heater, yet slow enough to make sure the water is hot.

Lifts If you push the wrong button on the lift/elevator, you'll never get to ride. 'Ç' stands for *çağır* (call) which is what you want to do to the lift – call it to where you are. 'G' is for *gönder* (send), and if you push this one, you'll send the lift to the end of its run (usually to the ground floor). A little illuminated 'M' means the lift is *meşgül* (engaged); wait until the light goes out before pushing 'Ç'. If there's a little illuminated 'K', it means the car is *katta* (positioned at your floor). 'Z' or *zemin* in lift parlance means ground floor; this is the button to push to get there. If you push '1', you'll end up on the 1st floor above ground level. If the ground floor button is not 'Z' it's probably 'L' for *lobi*.

If you stay in hotels with lifts, at least once you will have the idiotic feeling that comes when you press the 'Ç' button only to have the lift respond 'K', meaning, 'The car's already here, stupid. Just pull the door open and get in.'

Electricity Electricity may go off for short periods in some locations. This is not much of a problem, however. What is a problem is the lack of reading lights in all but the more expensive hotels. Your bedside lamp will never have more than a 25-watt bulb in it. Apparently Turks don't read in bed. However, you will almost always find a *gece lambası* in your room, a low-wattage bulb, perhaps even one in a lurid colour, perhaps high on the wall. The function of this 'night light' (as the term translates) is to give an eerie glow to the room so that you do not sleep in total darkness.

Unmarried Couples Unmarried couples sharing rooms usually run into no problems, even though the desk clerk sees the obvious when he takes down the pertinent information from your passports onto the registration form. The cheaper the hotel, the more traditional and conservative its management tends to be. Very simple hotels which are clean and 'proper' want to maintain their reputations. If you look clean and proper, and act that way, there should be no trouble. Lots of allowances are made for odd foreign ways.

Hostels

As the lowest-priced hotels and pensions are already rock-bottom, there is no extensive system of hostels in Turkey. The term *yurt* (hostel or lodge) or *öğrenci yurdu* (student hostel) usually defines an extremely basic and often dingy dormitory lodging intended for low-budget Turkish students from the provinces who are attending university classes. These are not normally affiliated with the International Youth Hostel Federation, and often they are not conveniently located near the major sights, though they may open their doors to foreign students in the summertime.

Camping

Using your own equipment and bedding, it is sometimes possible to sleep on the roof of a pension or hotel, or camp in the garden, for a minimal fee of US$2 to US$4 per person, which includes use of bathing and other hotel facilities. In seaside areas and near major attractions such as Cappadocia you'll see signs marking small, scruffy *kampink* areas which often have few facilities, but may be cheap, especially if you haggle. The fancier camping grounds near seaside resorts have all facilities – showers, shops, swimming pools, gardens, games – but charge almost as much as cheap hotels.

Camping outside recognised camping grounds by the roadside is often more hassle than it's worth as the police may come and check you out, the landowner may wonder what's up, and curious villagers may decide that they'd rather sit and watch you than the *Dynasty* reruns on the telly.

Another way to save lodging money is to take night buses or trains on long hauls.

FOOD

It is worth travelling to Turkey just to eat. Turkish cuisine is the very heart of eastern Mediterranean cooking, which demands fresh ingredients and careful preparation. The ingredients are often simple but of high quality. Turkish farmers, herders and fishers bring forth a wealth of superb produce from this agriculturally rich land and its surrounding seas. Being one of only seven countries on earth which produces a surplus of food, the Turks have enough good produce to feed everyone here, with some left over for export.

Good as it is, Turkish cooking can get to be a bit monotonous after a while, as the variety of dishes found in restaurants is not as great as that found in home kitchens. And when you'd like a change from charcoal-grilled lamb, you'll rarely find an Indonesian or Mexican or Indian or Japanese restaurant just around the corner. Despite the extent of the Ottoman Empire the Turks did not trade extensively with other nations during the 18th and 19th centuries, and never received an influx of foreign populations and cuisines. This is changing, though. Some Chinese restaurants have opened, Japanese ones are sure to follow, and you can now – for better or worse – get authentic Yankee hamburgers in the largest cities.

Saving Money

Several tips can save you lots of money on food. Firstly, order as you eat. Turks order appetisers, eat them, then decide what to have next, and order it. There is no need to order your entire meal at the beginning, except perhaps in the international hotels.

Secondly, don't 'overeat with your eyes'. Often you will be directed to a steam table or cooker to select your meal, and there's a tendency to order too many courses. Order them one at a time, and remember that it takes at least 20 minutes for food to 'make you feel full' after you've eaten it.

Thirdly, eat bread. Turkish sourdough bread is delicious, fresh, plentiful and cheap. Many Turkish dishes are served with savoury sauces; dip and sop your bread and enjoy. For instance, a meal of *kuru fasulye* (beans in a rich tomato sauce with meat stock) with bread and water is delicious, nutritious and ridiculously cheap at about US$1.

Fourthly, don't accept any plate of food

which you have not specifically ordered. For example, in İstanbul's Çiçek Pasajı, near Galatasaray Square, itinerant vendors may put a dish of fresh almonds on your table. They're not a gift. They'll show up on your bill at a premium rate. The same goes for unwanted appetisers, butter, cheese etc. If you haven't ordered it, ask *Hediye mi?* (heh-dee-YEH mee, 'Is it a gift?') or *Bedava mı?* (beh-dah-VAH muh, 'Is it free?'). If the answer is no, say *İstemiyorum* (eess-TEH-mee-oh-room, 'I don't want it').

Finally, always ask prices in advance and check your restaurant bill for errors. As tourism has come to Turkey, so has the common sin of ripping off the tourist. The more touristy a place is, the more carefully you must check your bill.

Restaurants

Restaurants *(restoran, lokanta)* are everywhere, and most open early in the morning and serve until late at night. Most are very inexpensive, and although price is always some determinant of quality, often the difference between a US$6 meal and a US$15 meal is not great, at least as far as flavour is concerned. Service and ambience are fancier at the higher price. In any restaurant in Turkey, whether fancy or simple, there is a convenient washbasin *(lavabo)* so that you can wash your hands before eating. Just say the word and the waiter will point it out. Also, if you're a woman or are travelling with a woman, ask for the *aile salonu* ('family dining room', often upstairs) which will be free of the sometimes oppressive all-male atmosphere to be found in many cheap Turkish eateries.

Many Turkish waiters have the annoying habit of snatching your plate away before you're finished with it. This may be due to a rule of Eastern etiquette which holds that it is impolite to leave a finished plate sitting in front of a guest. If a waiter engages in plate-snatching, say *Kalsın* (kahl-SUHN, 'Let it stay').

Full Service First there is the familiar sort of restaurant with white tablecloths and waiter service. It may be open for three meals a day, and will probably be among the more expensive dining places. Most full-service restaurants have some 'ready food' and also prepare grilled meats, particularly in the evening. They also usually serve liquor, wine and beer, and are sometimes called *içkili* (EECH-kee-LEE, 'serving drinks') because of this.

Hazır Yemek Next there is the *hazır yemek* (hah-ZUHR yeh-mehk, 'ready food') restaurant, sometimes arranged as a *self-servis* cafeteria. Although all restaurants offer some dishes prepared in advance, these places specialise in an assortment of dishes, prepared in advance of meal time, kept warm in a steam table, and served on demand. They are basically working-class cafeterias, but with waiter service. You pass by a steam table, which is often in the front window of the restaurant to entice passers-by, you make your choices, and a waiter brings them to you. Usually there are no alcoholic beverages served in these places, but occasionally, if you order a beer, the waiter will run to a shop nearby and get one for you.

There will always be çorba (CHOR-bah, soup), often *mercimek çorbası* (mehr-jee-MEHK, lentil soup). *Ezo gelin çorbası* (EH-zoh GEH-leen) is a variation of lentil soup, with rice and lemon juice. *Domates çorbası* (doh-MAH-tess) is creamy tomato soup. *Şehriye* (SHEH-ree-yeh) is vermicelli soup, made with a chicken stock.

Pilav (pee-LAHV) of some sort will always be available. Plain pilav is rice cooked in stock. There may also (or instead) be *bulgur pilav*, cracked bulghur wheat cooked in a tomato stock.

Many of the dishes will be vegetables and meat. Most popular are *salçalı köfte* (sahl-chah-LUH kurf-teh), meatballs of lamb stewed in a sauce with vegetables; *patlıcan kebap* (paht-luh-JAHN keh-bahp), eggplant and chunks of lamb; or *orman kebap* (ohr-MAHN keh-bahp), lamb chunks, vegetables and potatoes in broth. *Kuzu haşlama* (koo-ZOO hahsh-lah-mah) is lamb hocks in a stew.

Sometimes grilled meats are available in hazır yemek restaurants. *Döner kebap* (durn-NEHR keh-bahp), lamb roasted on a vertical spit and sliced off in thin strips as it cooks, is the closest thing you'll find to a national dish. *Şiş kebap* (SHEESH keh-bahp) is meat only, small pieces of lamb grilled on real charcoal.

Beer is sometimes served in these restaurants; more often, it's not. Décor may be nonexistent and the letters on the front window may only say 'Lokanta', but the welcome will be warm, the food delicious and very cheap.

With your meal you will receive as much fresh bread as you can eat, for a nominal charge. It's easy to 'overeat with your eyes' in these places, especially when the bread is so good. Soup, pilav, a main course and bread make for a big meal.

Hazır yemek restaurants prepare most of their daily dishes for the midday meal and then just keep them heated (one hopes) until supper time. The best reason to eat a big meal at midday is that the food is freshest and best then. If you want grilled fish or meat, have it in the evening.

Kebapçı, & Köfteci Two other sorts of restaurant are the *kebapçı* (keh-BAHP-chuh) and *köfteci* (KURF-teh-jee). A kebapçı is a person who cooks *kebap* (roast meat). A köfteci roasts *köfte*, which are meatballs of minced (ground) lamb made with savoury spices. Though they may have one or two ready-food dishes, kebapçı and köfteci restaurants specialise in grilled meat, plus soups, salad, yoghurt and perhaps dessert. Döner kebap and şiş kebap are the two most common kinds of kebap. *Kuşbaşı* (KOOSH-bah-shuh, 'bird's head') is a smaller and finer lamb şiş kebap. *Çöp kebap* (CHURP keh-bahp) is tiny morsels of lamb on split bamboo skewers.

If you want any sort of kebap or köfte well done, say *iyi pişmiş* or *pişkin*.

Kebapçıs can be great fun, especially the ones that are *ocakbaşı* (oh-JAHK bah-shuh, fireside). Patrons sit around the sides of a long rectangular firepit and the kebapçı sits enthroned in the middle, grilling hundreds of small skewers of şiş kebap and şiş köfte, which is köfte wrapped around a flat skewer; *Adana köfte* (ah-DAHN-nah) is the same thing, but spicy hot. The chef hands them to you as they're done, and you eat them with flat bread, a salad and perhaps *ayran* (ah-yee-RAHN), a drink of yoghurt mixed with spring water. Alcoholic beverages are not usually served.

Pideci For those on an adventurer's low budget, the Turkish *pideci* (pizza place) is a godsend. At a pideci, the dough for flat bread is patted out and shaped something like a boat, then dabbed with butter and other toppings, immediately baked in a wood-fired oven, and served at once. It's fresh, delicious, inexpensive, sanitary and nutritious. As toppings, if you want cheese say *peynirli* (pehy-neer-LEE); if you want eggs, say *yumurtalı* (yoo-moor-tah-LUH); *kıymalı* or *etli* means with minced lamb. In some parts of Turkey a pide (pizza) with meat is called *etli ekmek*, but it's still the same freshly baked flat bread.

I've recommended numerous pidecis in the various places covered by this book. To find your own, ask *Buralarda bir pideci var mı?* ('Is there a pideci around here?'). Alcoholic beverages are usually not served in pidecis.

Pastane *Pasta* in Turkey is pastry, not noodles, which are usually designated by some Turkicised Italian name such as *makarna* or *lazanya*. Turkish *pastanes* (pastry shops) generally have supplies of *kuru pasta* (dry pastry) such as cookies/biscuits of various sorts, and *yaş pasta* (moist pastry) meaning cakes, crumpets, and syrup-soaked baked goods. Soft drinks are served, and tea and coffee are usually available. Some pastanes serve baklava, the many-layered nut-and-honey sweet; others leave this to separate shops called *baklavacıs*.

Most pastanes serve breakfast, either from their normal stock or as a *komple kahvaltı*. In Kars, out by the Armenian frontier, you can

have great gobs of the excellent local honey to mix with butter and spread on fresh bread.

Büfe & Kuru Yemiş Besides restaurants, Turkey has millions of little snack stands and quick-lunch places known as *büfe* (bew-FEH, buffet). These serve sandwiches, often grilled, puddings, portions of *börek* (bur-REHK, flaky pastry), and perhaps *lahmacun* (LAHH-mah-joon), an Arabic soft pizza made with chopped onion, lamb and tomato sauce.

A *kuru yemiş* (koo-ROO yeh-MEESH) place serves dried fruits and nuts. These places are wonderful! Along İstiklal Caddesi in İstanbul you'll find little kuru yemiş shops selling pistachios (shelled or unshelled), walnuts, hazelnuts, peanuts (salted or unsalted), dried figs and apricots, chocolate, sunflower seeds and a dozen other good things. Prices are displayed – usually per kg. Order 100 grams (*yüz gram*, YEWZ grahm), which is a good portion, and pay exactly one-tenth of the kg price displayed.

Another good place for kuru yemiş is the Mısır Çarşısı, the Egyptian Market or Spice Bazaar, in İstanbul's Eminönü district. Kuru yemiş shops here will also have *pestil* (pehs-TEEL), fruit which has been dried and pressed into flat, flexible sheets (sometimes called 'fruit leather' in English). Odd at first, but delicious, it's also relatively cheap and comes made from *kayısı* (apricots), *dut* (mulberries) and other fruits.

Hotel Restaurants These, in general, do not offer good value in Turkey. You may want to have breakfast in a hotel restaurant for convenience (or because breakfast has been included in the room price), but most other meals should be taken in independent, local places. There are exceptions, of course, as in those remote towns where the one nice hotel in town also has the one nice restaurant.

Meals
Breakfast In a hotel or pastry shop, breakfast (*komple kahvaltı*, kohm-PLEH-kah-vahl-TUH) consists of fresh, delicious *ekmek*

(ek-MEHK, Turkish bread) with jam or honey, butter, salty black olives, white sheep's milk cheese, sometimes also a slice of mild yellow *kaşar peynir* cheese, and *çay* (CHAH-yee, tea). A wedge of processed cheese, like the French La Vache Qui Rit, may be added or substituted for one of the other cheeses. In my experience, Turkish bread and tea are usually fresh and good, but the other ingredients are often of poor quality or stale. You won't know until you sit down to breakfast.

You can always order an egg (*yumurta*, yoo-moor-TAH). Soft-boiled is *üç dakikalık* (EWCH dahk-kah-luhk), hard-boiled is *sert* (SEHRT), and fried eggs are *sahanda yumurta* (sah-hahn-DAH yoo-moor-tah). Bacon is difficult to find as any pork product is forbidden to Muslims. You may find it in the big hotels in the biggest cities. Sometimes your bread will come toasted (*kızarmış*, kuh-zahr-MUSH). This is the standard breakfast for tourists. If you order an egg or another glass of tea, you may be charged a bit extra.

Breakfast is not always included in the hotel room rate, though some hotels do include it. When breakfast is included, the desk clerk will mention it when quoting the price of the room. *Kahvaltı dahil* (kah-vahl-TUH dah-HEEL) means 'breakfast is included'.

After a week or so of standard Turkish breakfasts (and a few bad ones), I generally do what many working-class Turks do. I go to a lokanta for breakfast and have a bowl of hot soup which, with lots of fresh bread, makes quite a delicious breakfast for a very low price. If that's not for you, try a lokanta or *pastane* (pastry shop) serving *su böreği* (SOO bur-reh-yee), a many-layered noodle-like pastry with white cheese and parsley among the layers, served warm.

Hot, sweetened milk (*sıcak süt*, suh-JAHK sewt) is also a traditional breakfast drink, replaced in winter by *sahlep* (sah-LEHP), which is hot, sweetened milk flavoured with tasty orchid-root (Orchis mascula) powder and a sprinkle of cinnamon.

Lunch The midday meal (*öğle yemeği*) can be big or small. In summer, many Turks prefer to eat a big meal at midday and a light supper in the evening. You might want to do this, too.

Dinner The evening meal can be a repeat of lunch, a light supper, or a sumptuous repast. In fine weather the setting might be outdoors.

Turkish Specialties

Meze A big meal starts with *meze* (MEH-zeh), all sorts of appetisers and hors d'oeuvres. You'll find börek pastry rolls, cylinders, or 'pillows' filled with white cheese and parsley, then deep-fried. There will be slabs of white cheese, *zeytin* (olives), *turşu* (toor-SHOO, pickled vegetables), *patates tava* (pah-TAH-tess tah-vah, french fries/chips) or light potato fritters called *patates köfte*. The famous stuffed vine leaves (*dolma*) come either hot (with minced lamb) or cold ('with olive oil', *zeytinyağlı*).

Salads The real stars of the meze tray, however, are the salads and purées (dips). These are mystifying at first because they all look about the same: some goo on a plate decorated with bits of carrot, peas, parsley, olives or lemon slices. Here's where you'll need words to understand:

Amerikan salatası
    a Russian salad with mayonnaise, peas, carrots etc
Beyin salatası
    sheep's brain salad, usually the whole brain served on lettuce. Food for thought.
Cacık
    that's 'jah-JUHK', yoghurt thinned with grated cucumber, then beaten and flavoured with a little garlic and a dash of olive oil
Çoban salatası
    a 'shepherd's salad', this is a mixed, chopped salad of tomatoes, cucumbers, parsley, olives and peppers (sometimes fiery). If you don't want the peppers, order the salad *bibersiz* (bee-behr-SEEZ, without pepper). But as the salad was probably chopped up all together at once, this order means some kitchen lackey will attempt to pick out the pepper, but will always miss some. Be on guard.

Karışık salata
    same as a çoban salatası
Patlıcan salatası
    this is puréed eggplant, perhaps mixed with yoghurt. The best of it has a faintly smoky, almost burnt flavour from the charcoal grilling of the eggplant.
Pilaki
    broad white beans and sliced onions in a light vinegar pickle, served cold
Rus salatası
    a Russian salad, see Amerikan salatası
Söğüş
    (pronounced 'sew-EWSH'), this indicates raw salad vegetables such as tomatoes or cucumbers peeled and sliced, but without any sauce or dressing
Taramasalata
    red caviar, yoghurt, garlic and olive oil mixed into a smooth paste, salty, fishy and delicious
Yeşil salata
    a green salad of lettuce, oil and lemon juice or vinegar

Main Courses After the meze comes the main course. The fish is marvellous all along the coast, especially in the Aegean region. Ankara has some excellent fresh fish restaurants, too.

The most popular fish are the *palamut* (tunny or bonito), a darkish, full-flavoured baby tuna. *Lüfer* (bluefish), *levrek* (sea bass), *kalkan* (turbot), *pisi* (megrim or brill) and *sardalya* (fresh sardines) are other familiar fish.

Many fish will be grilled *(ızgara)* or fried *(tava)*, especially turbot and tunny. Lüfer and levrek are particularly good poached with vegetables *(buğlama)*. Fresh sardines are best if deep-fried in a light batter.

If you prefer meat, you can order the familiar şiş kebap or köfte, but you should discover *kuzu pirzolası* (koo-ZOO peerzohl-ah-suh), tiny lamb chops, charcoal-grilled. *Karışık ızgara* (kahr-uh-SHUK uhzgahr-ah) is a mixed grill of lamb for hearty meat-eaters. For beef, order *bonfile* (bohnfee-LEH), a small fillet steak with a pat of butter on top.

Besides grilled meats there are numerous fancy kebaps, often named for the places where they originated. Best of the kebaps is *Bursa kebap* (BOOR-sah), also called

İskender kebap, since it was invented in the city of Bursa by a chef named İskender (Turkish for Alexander). The kebap is standard döner spread on a bed of fresh, chopped, flat pide bread, with a side order of yoghurt. After the plate has been brought to your table, a waiter comes with savoury tomato sauce and pours a good helping on top. Then another waiter comes with browned butter, which goes on top of the sauce. This stuff is addictive.

Of the other fancy kebaps, *Urfa kebap* comes with lots of onions and black pepper; *Adana kebap* is spicy hot, with red pepper the way the Arabs like it (Adana is down near the Syrian border).

Cheese Cheeses are not a strong point in the Turkish kitchen. Although there are some interesting peasant cheeses such as *tulum peynir* (a salty, dry, crumbly goat's milk cheese cured in a goatskin bag) or another dried cheese which looks just like twine, these interesting cheeses rarely make it to the cities, and almost never to restaurant tables. What you'll find is the ubiquitous *beyaz peynir* (bey-AHZ pey-neer), white sheep's milk cheese. To be good, this must be full-cream *(tam yağlı)* cheese, not dry and crumbly and not too salty or sour. You may also find *kaşar peynir* (kah-SHAHR peyneer), a firm, mild yellow cheese which comes *taze* (tah-ZEH, fresh) or *eski* (essKEE, aged). The eski is a bit sharper, but not very sharp for all that.

Desserts Turkish desserts tend to be very sweet, soaked in sugar syrup. Many are baked, such as crumpets, biscuits or shredded wheat, all in syrup.

Baklava comes in several varieties: *cevizli* is with chopped walnut stuffing; *fıstıklı* is with pistachio nuts; *kaymaklı* is with clotted cream. Sometimes you can order *kuru baklava*, 'dry' baklava which has less syrup. True baklava is made with honey, not syrup, and though the home-made stuff may contain honey, the store-bought stuff rarely does.

As an alternative to sweet desserts,

Turkish fruits are superb, especially in midsummer when the melon season starts, and early in winter when the first citrus crop comes in. *Kavun* is a deliciously sweet, fruity melon. *Karpuz* is watermelon.

The standard unsweetened dessert, available in most restaurants, is *krem karamel* (crème caramel or flan).

Vegetarian Food

Vegetarianism is not prevalent in Turkey. If you merely want to minimise consumption of meat, you will have no problem, as Turkish cuisine has many dishes in which meat is used merely as a flavouring rather than as a principal element. However, if you wish to avoid meat utterly, you will have to choose carefully. A good dish to try if you eat eggs is *menemen* (MEH-neh-MEHN), tomatoes topped with eggs and baked; it is fairly spicy. Salads, cheeses, pilavs and yoghurt can fill out the menu. Note that many of the bean dishes such as *nohut* (chickpeas) and *kuru fasulye* are prepared with lamb as a flavouring.

Here are some phrases so that you can explain to the waiter or the chef what you want: *Hiç et yiyemem* (HEECH eht yee-YEH-mehm, 'I can't eat any meat'); *Et suyu bile yiyemem* (EHt soo-YOO bee-leh yee-YEH-mehm, 'I can't even eat meat juices'); *Etsiz yemek var mı?* (eht-seez yeh-mehk VAHR muh, 'Do you have any dishes without meat?').

Chicken is an ingredient in two dessert puddings (*tavuk göğsü* and *kazandibi*) and you wouldn't know it from looking at them or even eating them. *Yiyemem* means 'I can't eat'. Depending upon your requirements, use it with *et* (meat), *tavuk* or *piliç* (chicken), *yumurta* (egg or roe) or *balık* (fish) to make yourself understood.

DRINKS
Tea & Coffee

The national drink is not really Turkish coffee as you might expect, but *çay* (tea). The Turks drank a lot of coffee as long as they owned Arabia, because the world's first (and best) coffee is said to have come from Yemen. With the collapse of the Ottoman Empire coffee became an imported commodity. You can get Turkish coffee anywhere in Turkey, but you'll find yourself drinking a lot more çay.

The tea plantations are along the eastern Black Sea coast, centred on the town of Rize. Turkish tea is hearty and full-flavoured, served in little tulip-shaped glasses which you hold by the rim to avoid burning your fingers. Sugar is added, but never milk. If you want your tea weaker, ask for it *açık* (ah-CHUK, 'clear'); for stronger, darker tea, order *koyu* or *demli*, 'dark'. You can get it easily either way because Turkish tea is made by pouring some very strong tea into a glass, then cutting it with hot water to the desired strength.

The tiny glasses may seem impractical at first, but in fact they assure you of drinking only fresh, hot tea. Few Turks sit down and drink only one glass. If you need lots quick at breakfast, order a *duble*, which will come in a drinking glass. For a real tea-drinking and talking session, they'll go to an outdoor tea garden and order a *semaver* (samovar) of tea so they can refill the glasses themselves, without having to call the *çaycı* (CHAH-yee-juh, tea-waiter).

Traditional herbal teas are infusions such as *adaçay* ('island tea'), made from coastal sage, and *ıhlamur*, linden-flower tea, perfumed and soothing. *Papatya çayı* is camomile tea.

A few years ago a brand-new beverage, *elma çay* (apple tea) was introduced, and it caught on quickly. Tourists love it as much as Turks do, and you may even see street vendors selling packets of it for tourists to take home with them. It's delicious, caffeine-free, slightly tart, with a mild apple flavour. There are other, similar fruit-flavoured teas as well. Surprisingly, the list of ingredients yields no mention of fruit, only sugar, citric acid, citrate, food essence and vitamin C.

As for Turkish coffee (*Türk kahvesi*, TEWRK kah-veh-see), it is better as an after-dinner drink than a breakfast drink. It's always brewed up individually, the sugar being added during the brewing. You order it one of four ways: *sade* (sah-DEH, plain, without sugar), *az* (AHZ, with a little sugar), *orta* (ohr-TAH, with moderate sugar), *çok şekerli* (CHOHK sheh-kehr-LEE, with lots of sugar).

Order *bir kahve, orta* (BEER kah-VEH, ohr-TAH) for the first time, and adjust from there. The pulverised coffee grounds lurk at the bottom of the cup – stop drinking before you get to them.

Instant coffee, called *neskafe* or *hazır kahve* (hah-ZUHR kahh-veh), is also served nearly everywhere now, but can be surprisingly expensive. *Amerikan kahvesi* (ah-mehr -ee-KAHN kahh-veh-see) is freshly brewed from grounds and is a less concentrated brew than Turkish coffee. *Fransız kahvesi* (frahn-SUHZ kahh-veh-see, 'French coffee') can be either strong Amerikan kahvesi served black or it can be coffee with milk, which may also be called *sütlü kahve* (sewt-LEW kahh-veh).

Water

Turks are connoisseurs of good water, and stories circulate of old people able to tell which spring it came from just by tasting it. *Menba suyu*, spring water, is served everywhere, even on intercity buses. The standard price for a 1.5-litre bottle of any brand, sold in a grocery, probably chilled, is around 75c. If you order it in a restaurant there will be a mark-up of 100 to 300%.

Tap water is supposedly safe to drink because it is treated, but it's not as tasty or as trustworthy as spring water. (For more information on water, see Food & Water in the Health section.)

Non-Alcoholic Drinks

Soft drinks include the usual range of Coca-Cola, Pepsi, clear lemon-flavoured soft drinks like Seven-Up, orange soda, and others. Shops and restaurants sign exclusive distribution contracts with one company or the other, so you will find either Coke or Pepsi but never Coke and Pepsi. Turks just order *kola* and take what comes.

If you want unflavoured fizzy water, ask for soda. Fizzy mineral water is maden suyu

(naturally carbonated) and maden sodası (artificially carbonated).

Fruit juice is a favourite refresher, and can be excellent. With the advent of modern marketing you will also find watery, sugared drinks with almost no food value. These are usually the ones in the paper containers. The good fruit juices tend to come in glass bottles and may be so thick that you'll want to dilute them with spring water. Try *vişne* (sour or morello cherry juice), a dark, tart, flavourful drink which may soon become your favourite. Others good ones are *şeftali* (peach), *kayısı* (apricot) and *çilek* (strawberry).

Other traditional drinks include ayran (yoghurt and water mixed), which is tangy, refreshing, healthful, and always available in kebapçıs and köftecis. *Şıra* (shur-RAH), unfermented white grape juice, is delicious but is served in only a few places, and only during the summer. *Boza* is a thick, slightly tangy, very mild-flavoured drink made from fermented millet and served only in winter. *Sahlep* or *salep* is a hot drink made with milk, flavoured with orchid root and served with a dusting of cinnamon on top. It's sweet and fortifying; it, too, is served mostly in winter.

Alcohol

Strictly observant Muslims don't touch alcoholic beverages at all, but in Turkey the strictures of religion are moderated by the 20th-century lifestyle.

Beer *Bira* is served almost everywhere. Tuborg makes light or pale *(beyaz,* bey-AHZ) and dark *(siyah,* see-YAH) beer in Turkey under licence. A local company with a European brewmaster is Efes Pilsen, which also makes light and dark beer claimed by many to be Turkey's best. The light is a good, slightly bitter pilsener. Venüs is a new brand on the market, not easily found. Tekel, the Turkish State Monopolies company, makes Tekel Birası (teh-KEHL bee-rah-suh), a small-bubbled (sort of flat), mildly flavoured brew that may be an acquired taste, and is difficult to find. Like Coke and Pepsi, shops and restaurants sign exclusive contracts for one brand, so just order *bira* as you will rarely get a choice.

As of this writing, beer is available in returnable bottles, and also in disposable cans at a premium price. You'll save money, get better flavour, and not contribute to the litter problem if you buy bottled beer.

Wine Turkish wines are surprisingly good and delightfully cheap. Tekel makes all kinds in all price ranges. Güzel Marmara is the cheap white table wine. Buzbağ (BOOZ-baah) is a hearty Burgundy-style wine with lots of tannin. Restaurants seem to carry mostly the wines of the two big private firms, Doluca (DOHL-oo-jah) and Kavaklıdere (kah-vakh-LUH-deh-reh). You'll find the premium Villa Doluca wines, white *(beyaz)* and red *(kırmızı,* KUHR-muh-ZUH) in most places. Kavaklıdere wines include the premium white named Çankaya and the medium-range wines named Kavak (white), Dikmen (red) and Lal (rose). In recent years, Turkish vineyards have begun producing some good varietal wines as well.

Strong Liquor The favourite ardent spirit in Turkey is *rakı* (rah-KUH), an aniseed-flavoured grape brandy similar to the Greek ouzo, French pastis and Arab arak. Turkish rakı is made by Tekel, the state liquor monopoly (which is no longer a strict monopoly). The standard is Yeni Rakı. Kulüp Rakısı is somewhat stronger, with a bit more anise. Altınbaş is the strongest, with the highest anise content.

It's customary (but not essential) to mix rakı with cool water, half-and-half, perhaps add ice, and to drink it with a meal.

Tekel also makes decent *cin* (JEEN, gin), *votka* and *kanyak* (kahn-YAHK, brandy). When ordering kanyak, always specify the *beş yıldız* or *kaliteli* ('five-star' or 'quality') stuff, officially named Truva Kanyak. The regular kanyak is thick and heavy, the five-star much lighter.

There is a Tekel *viski* (VEES-kee, whisky) named Ankara. You might try it once.

For after-dinner drinks, better restaurants will stock the local sweet fruit-brandies, which are OK but nothing special.

Imported spirits are available from shops in the larger cities. Though they are much more expensive than local drinks, they may not cost much more than what you'd pay at home. Hotels and restaurants usually mark up the prices of imported spirits hugely.

ENTERTAINMENT

For some background information on the lively arts in Turkey, see Arts in the Facts for the Visitor chapter.

İstanbul, Ankara and İzmir have opera, symphony, ballet and theatre. Many smaller towns have folk dance troupes. Every Turkish town has at least one cinema and one nightclub with live entertainment.

The seaside resorts throb each warm evening to the sounds of seemingly innumerable clubs and discos.

THINGS TO BUY

Most shops and shopping areas close on Sunday. For details, see Business Hours in this chapter.

Haggling

For the best buy in terms of price and quality, know the market. Spend some time shopping for similar items in various shops, asking prices. Shopkeepers will give you pointers on what makes a good *kilim* (flat-woven mat), carpet, meerschaum pipe or alabaster carving. In effect, you're getting a free course in product lore. This is not at all unpleasant, as you will often be invited to have coffee, tea or a soft drink as you talk over the goods and prices.

You can, and should, ask prices if they're not marked, but you should not make a counter-offer unless you are seriously interested in buying. No matter how often the shopkeeper asks you, 'OK, how much will you pay for it?', no matter how many glasses of tea you've drunk at his expense, don't make a counter-offer if you do not hope to buy. If the shopkeeper meets your price, you should buy. It's considered very bad form to haggle over a price, agree, and then not buy.

Some shopkeepers, even in the 'haggle capital of the world' (İstanbul's Covered Market), will offer a decent price and say, 'That's my best offer'. Many times they mean it, and they're trying to do you a favour by saving time. How will you know when they are, and when it's just another haggling technique? Only by knowing the market, by having shopped around. Remember, even if they say, 'This is my best offer', you are under no obligation to buy unless you have made a counter-offer, or have said, 'I'll buy it'.

It's perfectly acceptable to say a pleasant goodbye and walk out of the shop, even after all that free tea, if you cannot agree on a price. In fact, walking out is one of the best ways to test the authenticity of the shopkeeper's price. If they know you can surely find the item somewhere else for less, they'll stop you and say, 'OK, you win, it's yours for what you offered'. And if he doesn't stop you, there's nothing to prevent you from returning in a half-hour and buying the item for what he quoted.

If any shopkeeper puts extraordinary pressure on you to buy, walk out of the shop, and consider reporting the shop to the Market Police (see Belediye Zabıtası in the Dangers & Annoyances section).

Commissions

Read and believe: *if a Turk accompanies you into a shop, they will expect a commission from the shopkeeper on any purchase you make.* Your guide may be a wonderful person, the owner of your pension, a cheery and engaging soul, but after you buy and depart, the guide will take his cut. This is money that comes out of your pocket. It's better to go alone and strike a bargain on your own, because then you have a better chance of getting a lower price from the shopkeeper, who will have no commission to pay.

In the most touristed places, some personable young Turks (and even foreigners) make their living chatting you up, helping you find your way around, and eventually leading you to a shop (usually a carpet shop) and 'helping' you to buy a carpet at a greatly inflated price.

Value Added Tax

Turkey has a Value Added Tax (VAT), called Katma Değer Vergisi or KDV, added to and hidden in the price of most items and services, from souvenirs to hotel rooms to restaurant meals. Most establishments display a sign saying 'Fiatlarımızda KDV Dahildir' (VAT is included in our prices). Thus, it is rare that the VAT is added to your bill separately, and you should be suspicious if it is.

There is a scheme whereby tourists can reclaim the amount paid in VAT on larger purchases such as leather garments, carpets etc. Not all shops participate in the scheme, so you must ask if it is possible to get a *KDV İade Özel Fatura* (keh-deh-VEH ee-ah-DEH err-ZEHL fah-too-rah, 'Special VAT Refund Receipt'). Ask for this during the haggling rather than after you've bought. The receipt can be converted to cash at a bank in the international departures lounge at the airport (if there is a bank open!), or at your other point of exit from Turkey; or, if you submit the form to a customs officer as you leave the country, the shop will (one hopes) mail a refund cheque to your home after the government has completed its procedures (don't hold your breath).

Shipping Parcels Home

If practicable, carrying your parcels with you is the best idea, as you may escape extra duty payments when you return to your home country; parcels arriving separately may be dutiable. If you decide to ship something home from Turkey, don't close up your parcel before it has been inspected by a customs or postal official, who will check to see if you are shipping antiquities out of the country; take packing and wrapping materials with you to the post office. Wrap it very securely and insure it. Sending it by registered mail is not a bad idea, either. Unless you buy from a very posh shop (eg in one of the luxury hotels,) it's best to ship your own parcels. At least one reader has had the sad experience of buying a beautiful kilim and agreeing to have the shopkeeper ship it, only to discover that the kilim shipped was not the one bought, but a much cheaper item.

Alabaster

A translucent, fine-grained variety of either gypsum or calcite, alabaster is pretty because of its grain and colour, and because light passes through it. You'll see ashtrays, vases, chess sets, bowls, egg cups, even the eggs themselves carved from the stone.

Antiques

Turkey has a lot of fascinating stuff left over from the empire: vigorous peasant jewellery, water-pipe mouthpieces carved from amber, old Korans and illuminated manuscripts, Greek and Roman figurines and coins, tacky furniture in the Ottoman Baroque style. However, *it is illegal to buy, sell, possess or export any antiquity*, and you can go to prison for breaking the law. All antiquities must be turned over to a museum immediately upon discovery. You may be offered Greek and Roman coins and figurines for sale. Refuse at once. Items only a century or two old are not usually classed as antiquities, though, and only true antiquities are off limits, not the many artful fakes.

Carpets & Kilims

Turkey has lots of marvellous carpets and kilims, sometimes at good prices. Unless you're willing to research prices, patterns, dyes, knots per sq cm and so forth, you'll buy what you like for a price that seems reasonable. But please learn at least the basics of carpet buying before you put your money down.

The very basic examination of a carpet so that you can look like you know what you're doing, involves the following procedures. Turn a corner over and look at the closeness of the weave. Ask, 'How many knots per sq cm?'. The tighter the weave, the smaller the knots, the higher the quality and durability. Compare the colours on the back with the colours on the front. Spread the nap with your fingers and look to the bottom of the carpet's pile. Are the colours more vivid there than on the surface? If so, the surface has faded in the sun considerably, which is often a sign of modern chemical dyes. (There is nothing wrong with these dyes, but natural dyes are favoured and bring a higher price; don't pay for natural if you're getting chemical.)

Take a white handkerchief, wet it a bit, and rub it on the top surface of the carpet. Is there colour on the handkerchief? There shouldn't be; if there is, the carpet's dyes are runny, or have been retouched with watercolours.

Check the ends of the warp (lengthwise) cords: are they of wool *(yün)* or cotton *(pamuk)*? The pile should definitely be of wool; in fact, a good-quality, long-lasting carpet is 100% wool *(yüz de yüz yün)*. If the pile is of cotton or 'flosh' (mercerised cotton), sometimes misleadingly called 'floss silk', you should not pay for wool. (A real silk carpet, by the way, even a small one, will cost thousands of dollars.) Look at the carpet from one end, then from the other; the colours will be different because the pile always leans one way or the other. Take the carpet out into the sunlight and look at it there.

That's about all you can do without becoming a rug expert. If you don't trust the dealer's sworn oath that the rug is all wool, and you're serious about buying, ask him to clip a bit of the tassel and burn it for you – that is if you can differentiate between the odours of burning silk, wool, cotton or nylon.

Carpet prices are determined by demand, age, material, quality, condition, enthusiasm of the buyer and debt load of the seller. New carpets can be skilfully 'antiquated'; damaged or worn carpets can be rewoven (good work, but expensive), patched or even painted. Worn carpets look fairly good until the magic paint washes out. Give the carpet a good going-over, decide if you think it's a good price, and go from there.

Note that there is nothing wrong with dealers offering you a patched, repainted carpet so long as they point out these defects to you and price the carpet accordingly. The dishonesty is in offering you cheap goods at an inflated price.

The method of payment can be a bargaining point, or a point of contention. Some dealers will take personal cheques, but all prefer cash. If you pay with a credit card (and not all shops will have facilities for this), the dealer may require you to pay the fee which the credit card company will charge them, and even the cost of the phone call or telex to check on your credit. If the dealer doesn't require you to pay these charges, it means that you've paid a hefty enough price so that the dealer isn't bothered about another 4 to 8%. If all this seems too much trouble, be advised: it isn't. A good wool Turkish carpet will easily outlast the human body of its owner, and become an heirloom.

Ceramics

The best Turkish ceramics were made in İznik in the 17th and 18th centuries. İznik tiles from the great days are now museum-pieces, found in museums throughout the world.

Today most of the tile-making is done in

Ceramic Mosque Lamp

Kütahya, a pleasant town with few other redeeming qualities for the tourist. For the very best ceramics, you must go there. Souvenir shops will also have attractive, handmade tiles, plates, cups and bowls. They're not really high-fired so they're vulnerable to breaks and cracks, but they are still attractive.

The real, old İznik tiles from the 16th and 17th centuries qualify as antiquities and cannot be exported. If you go to İznik, you will find a reviving tile industry on a small scale. Some of the items are quite pretty and reasonably priced.

Avanos, in Cappadocia, is a centre for simple but attractive red clay pottery, made from deposits taken from the neighbouring Kızılırmak (Red River).

Copper

Gleaming copper vessels will greet you in every souvenir shop you peep into. Some are old, sometimes several centuries old. Most are handsome, and some are still eminently useful. The new copperware tends to be of lighter gauge; that's one of the ways you tell new from old. But even the new stuff will have been made by hand.

'See that old copper water pipe over there?', my friend Alaettin asked me once. We were sitting in his impossibly cluttered, closet-sized shop on İstanbul's Çadırcılar Caddesi, just outside the Covered Market. 'It dates from the time of Sultan Ahmet III (1703-30), and was used by the *Padişah* (sultan) himself. I just finished making it yesterday.'

Alaettin was a master coppersmith, and had made pieces for many luminaries, including the late Nelson Rockefeller. His pieces might well have graced the sultan's private apartments – except that the sultanate was abolished in 1922. He charged a hefty price for his fine craftwork but not for the story, which was the gift-wrapping, so to speak.

Copper vessels should not be used for cooking in or eating from unless they are tinned inside: that is, washed with molten tin which covers the toxic copper. If you intend to use a copper vessel, make sure the interior layer of tin is intact, or negotiate to have it tinned (kalaylamak). If there is a kalaycı shop nearby, ask about the price of the tinning in advance, as tin is expensive.

Inlaid Wood

Cigarette boxes, chess and tavla (backgammon) boards and other items will be inlaid with different coloured woods, silver or mother-of-pearl. It's not the finest work, but it's pretty good. Make sure there is indeed inlay. These days, alarmingly accurate decals exist. Also, check the silver: is it silver, or aluminium or pewter? Is the mother-of-pearl actually 'daughter-of-polystyrene'?

Jewellery

Turkey is a wonderful place to buy jewellery, especially the antique stuff. None of the items sold here may meet your definition of 'chic', but window-shopping is great fun. Jewellers' Row in any market is a dazzling strip of glittering shop windows filled with gold. Light bulbs, artfully rigged, show it off. In the Covered Market, a blackboard sign hung above Kuyumcular Caddesi (Street of the Jewellers) bears the daily price for unworked gold of so-many carats. Serious gold-buyers should check out this price, watch carefully as the jeweller weighs the piece in question, and then calculate what part of the price is for gold and what part for labour.

Silver is another matter. There is sterling silver jewellery (look for the hallmark), but nickel silver and pewter-like alloys are much more common. Serious dealers don't try to pass off alloy as silver.

Leather & Suede

On any given Kurban Bayramı (Sacrifice Holiday), over 2.5 million sheep get the axe in Turkey. Add to that the normal day-to-day needs of a cuisine based on mutton and lamb and you have a huge amount of raw material to be made into leather items. Shoes, bags, cushions, jackets, skirts, vests, hats, gloves and trousers are all made from soft leather. This is a big industry in Turkey, particularly

in and around the Grand Bazaar. So much leather clothing is turned out that a good deal of it will be badly cut or carelessly made, but there are lots of fine pieces as well.

The only way to assure yourself of a good piece is to examine it carefully, taking time. Try it on just as carefully; see if the sleeves are full enough, if the buttonholes are positioned well, if the collar rubs. If something is wrong, keep trying others until you find what you want. Made-to-order garments can be excellent or disappointing, as the same tailor who made the ready-made stuff will make the ordered stuff; and will be making it fast because the shopkeeper has already impressed you by saying 'No problem. I can have it for you tomorrow'. It's better to find something off the rack that fits than to order it, unless you can order without putting down a deposit or committing yourself to buy (this is often possible).

Leather items and clothing are standard tourist stuff, found in all major tourist destinations.

Meerschaum

If you smoke a pipe, you know about meerschaum. For those who don't, meerschaum ('sea foam' in German; lületaşı in Turkish) is a hydrous magnesium silicate, a soft, white, clay-like material which is very porous but heat-resistant. When carved into a pipe, it smokes cool and sweet.

Over time, it absorbs residues from the tobacco and turns a nut-brown colour. Devoted meerschaum pipe smokers even have special gloves for holding the pipe as they smoke, so that oil from their fingers won't sully the fine, even patina of the pipe.

The world's largest and finest beds of meerschaum are found in Turkey, near the city of Eskişehir. Miners climb down shafts in the earth to bring up buckets of mud, some of which contain chunks of the mineral. Artful carving of this soft stone has always been done, and blocks of meerschaum were exported to be carved abroad as well. These days, however, the export of block meerschaum is prohibited because the government realised that exporting uncarved blocks was the same as exporting the jobs to carve them. So any carved pipe will have been carved in Turkey.

You'll marvel at the artistry of the Eskişehir carvers. Pipes portraying turbaned paşas, wizened old men, fair maidens and mythological beasts, as well as many pipes in geometrical designs, will be on view in any souvenir shop. Pipes are not the only things carved from meerschaum these days. Bracelets, necklaces, pendants, earrings and cigarette holders all appear in souvenir shops. When buying, look for purity and uniformity in the stone. Carving is often used to cover up flaws in a piece of meerschaum;

do look over it carefully. For pipes, check that the bowl walls are uniform in thickness all around, and that the hole at the bottom of the bowl is centred. Purists buy uncarved, just plain pipe-shaped meerschaums that are simply but perfectly made.

Prices for pipes vary, but should be fairly low. Abroad, meerschaum is an expensive commodity, and pipes are luxury items. Here in Turkey meerschaum is cheap, the services of the carver are low-priced, and nobody smokes pipes. If you can't get the pipe you want for US$10 to US$20, or at least only half of what you'd pay at home, then you're not working at it hard enough.

STOP PRESS TELEPHONES
As this book was being printed, the Turkish PTT introduced a new system of telephone numbers and area codes. Every telephone number now has seven digits and is preceded by a three-digit area code. There are 77 codes in all. Here are the most important ones:

Ankara	312
Antalya	242
Bursa	224
İstanbul (European Side)	212
İstanbul (Asian Side)	216
İzmir	232

The access numbers to long-distance (trunk) services have also been changed. To access domestic long-distance service, press '0' (zero). to access international service, press '00' (zero-zero). ■

Getting There & Away

You can get to Turkey by air, rail, road or sea. Note that if you travel by land you may have to deal with the problem of transit visas for the Eastern European countries. (See the Embassies and Eastern European Visas sections in the Facts for the Visitor chapter.)

AIR

İstanbul's Atatürk Airport is the country's busiest. Other international airports are at Ankara, İzmir, Adana (down near the Syrian border), Antalya and Dalaman (on the southwestern Mediterranean coast).

Most foreign visitors arrive in İstanbul because the most flights go there and it is also the first place tourists want to see. İzmir has its Menderes airport south of the city on the road to Ephesus. Antalya and Dalaman receive mostly charter flights filled with vacationers headed for the south coast.

Turkish Airlines (Türk Hava Yolları, symbol TK) has flights to and from New York, Singapore, most major cities in Europe, the Middle East and North Africa. Other Turkish airlines flying from Europe (mostly Germany) to Turkey include İstanbul Airlines (symbol: IL) and Greenair, a small Turkish-Russian company.

All the fares mentioned here are subject to change, but they will give you an idea of what to expect. For more details of air travel to/from Turkey see the Getting There & Away sections under the individual Turkish destinations.

To/From Greece

Olympic Airlines and Turkish Airlines share the Athens-İstanbul route, offering at least four flights per day in summer. Fares for the 70-minute flight are US$222 one way, US$314 for a round-trip excursion (fixed-date return) ticket.

To/From Elsewhere in Europe

Both Turkish Airlines and İstanbul Airlines fly to Turkey from many points in Europe.

Most Turkish Airlines flights go to the airline's hub in İstanbul, while İstanbul Airlines (ironically) flies nonstop from Europe to cities such as Adana, Antalya, Dalaman and İzmir. İstanbul Airlines fares tend to be lower than those of the major carriers, but flights are fewer. Here are the cities served directly by Turkish carriers. (TK stands for Turkish Airlines, IL for İstanbul Airlines.)

city	airline(s)
Amsterdam	TK, IL
Athens	TK
Barcelona	IL
Basel	TK
Belgrade	TK
Bergamo	IL
Berlin (TXL)	TK, IL
Bilbao	IL
Bologna	IL
Bremen	IL
Brussels	TK, IL
Cologne	TK, IL
Copenhagen	TK
Düsseldorf	TK, IL
Geneva	TK
Graz	IL
Hamburg	TK, IL
Hannover	TK, IL
Linz	IL
London	TK, IL
Lyon	TK, IL
Madrid	TK, IL
Malpenza	IL
Manchester	IL
Marseille	IL
Milan	TK
Moscow	TK
Münster	IL
Nantes	IL
Nice	IL
Nuremberg	TK
Paris (ORY)	TK, IL
Pisa	IL
Rome	TK, IL
Salzburg	IL
Sofia	TK
Stockholm	TK
Stuttgart	TK, IL
Toulouse	IL
Verona	IL
Vienna	TK, IL

The normal one-way fare from London to İstanbul is UK£300 (US$570) and up, but there are fixed-date return (excursion) fares for as low as UK£295 (US$560) in spring and autumn. Peak-season (summer) excursion fares are higher, but there are still bargains to be had. British Airways and Turkish Airlines fly the route nonstop, and most other European airlines do it with one stop. Look at the schedules and fares of Tarom of Rumania, and Pakistan International Airlines (PIA).

Don't neglect the European and Turkish charter lines such as Condor (German) and Greenair (Turkish) which fly to Turkey from more than a dozen European centres, often for round-trip fares as low as US$350 or US$400.

To/From the Eastern Mediterranean

Eastern Mediterranean flights by Turkish Airlines include the following nonstop flights: two from Beirut (1¾ hours nonstop), three from Teheran (4½ hours nonstop), three from Tripoli (three hours nonstop) and one from Tunis (two hours nonstop).

Details of some other services to İstanbul from various Middle Eastern cities follows:

Amman Turkish Airlines and Royal Jordanian share the traffic, with about three flights per week. The nonstop 2½-hour flight costs US$260 one way. It's from US$290 to US$360 for a round-trip excursion ticket.

Cairo EgyptAir and Turkish Airlines have flights about four days per week, charging from US$333 to US$373 one way. It costs from US$368 to US$450 for a round-trip excursion ticket on the nonstop, two-hour flight.

Damascus Syrian Arab Airlines and Turkish Airlines make the 2½-hour flight four days per week and charge from US$241 to US$277 one way, from US$316 to US$326 for a round-trip excursion.

Nicosia (Turkish Side) Turkish Airlines and Cyprus-Turkish Airlines operate nonstop flights connecting Ercan Airport (ECN) in Nicosia (Lefkoşa in Turkish) with Adana (four flights weekly), Ankara (five flights weekly), Antalya (one flight weekly), İstanbul (daily, twice daily in summer) and İzmir (four flights weekly). Fares are subsidised and very reasonable.

In Nicosia, contact Turkish Airlines at Osman Paşa Caddesi 32 (☎ (20) 71 382, 71 061, 77 124, 77 344); the Cyprus-Turkish Airlines (Kıbrıs-Türk Hava Yolları) office is on Bedrettin Demirel Caddesi (☎ (20) 71 901).

İstanbul Airlines (☎ (20) 77 140/1) on Osman Paşa Caddesi, Mirata Apartımanı 4 and at Ercan Airport (☎ (23) 14 714/5) flies between Nicosia, Antalya (two flights weekly) and İstanbul (eight flights weekly), at fares lower than Turkish Airlines'.

Tel Aviv El Al has nonstop flights twice weekly, charging US$336 one way, US$506 for a round-trip excursion. Turkish Airlines has three nonstop flights weekly to İstanbul, and one direct flight a week to Dalaman. İstanbul Airlines may initiate services in the future.

To/From Azerbaijan

İstanbul Airlines has flights from Ankara to Baku in Azerbaijan on Wednesday. There are also flights between Trabzon and Baku on Turkish Airlines and Istanbul Airlines.

To/From India

Numerous airlines,including Air India, British Airways, Delta, KLM, Lufthansa, Olympic and Turkish Airlines will take you on various routes between New Delhi and İstanbul. One-way fares are a high US$700, with round-trip excursions (fixed-date return) costing only US$795. For cheap fares, try contacting Aeroflot to see what it offers via Moscow.

To/From North America

New York City has the most direct flights to Turkey, the most airlines, and the most elaborate spread of fares, so you should be able to find a fare to suit your budget. Coach-class fare is US$625 to US$965 and up, one way; excursion fares range from US$850 to US$1250 and up depending upon season, stopovers etc. From Chicago you pay from US$779 to US$854 one way, US$950 to US$1330 for a round-trip excursion. Fares from San Francisco or Los Angeles are normally from US$984 to US$1000 one way, from US$1194 to US$1444 for a round-trip excursion. You can pay an astounding US$6870 to go 1st class with all the trimmings. Of the major US airlines, only Delta flies directly to İstanbul.

Turkish Airlines operates daily flights in summer on the New York-İstanbul route, those on Tuesday and Friday going nonstop, the others laying over in Brussels. There are

---

Air Travel Glossary

Apex Apex ('advance purchase excursion') is a discounted ticket which must be paid for in advance. There are penalties if you wish to change it.

Baggage Allowance This will be written on your ticket: usually one 20-kg item to go in the hold, plus one or two items of hand luggage.

Bucket Shop (Consolidator) An unbonded travel agency specialising in discounted airline tickets

Bumped Just because you have a confirmed seat doesn't mean you're going to get on the plane – see Overbooking.

Cancellation Penalties If you have to cancel or change an Apex ticket there are often heavy penalties involved – insurance can sometimes be taken out against these penalties. Some airlines impose penalties on regular tickets as well, particularly against 'no show' passengers (see No Shows).

Check In Airlines ask you to check in a certain time ahead of the flight departure (usually 1½ hours on international flights). If you fail to check in on time and the flight is overbooked, the airline can cancel your booking and give your seat to somebody else.

Confirmation Having a ticket written out with the flight and date you want doesn't mean you have a seat until the agent has checked with the airline that your status is 'OK' or confirmed. Meanwhile, you could just be 'on request'. It's also wise to reconfirm onward or return bookings directly with the airline 72 hours before departure (see Reconfirmation).

Discounted Tickets There are two types of discounted fares: officially discounted and unofficially discounted. The lowest prices often impose drawbacks like flying with unpopular airlines, inconvenient schedules, or unfavoured routes and connections. A discounted ticket can save you things other than money – you may be able to pay Apex prices without the associated Apex advance booking and other requirements. Discounted tickets only exist where there is fierce competition.

Full Fares Airlines traditionally offer 1st-class (coded F), business-class (coded J) and economy-class (coded Y) tickets. These days there are so many discounted fares available from the regular economy class that few passengers pay full economy fare.

Lost Tickets If you lose your airline ticket, an airline will usually treat it like a travellers' cheque and, after enquiries, issue you with another one. Legally, however, an airline is entitled to treat a ticket like cash and if you lose it then it's gone forever. Take good care of your ticket and carry a photocopy or at least a record of the ticket number.

No Shows No shows are passengers who fail to show up for their flight, sometimes due to unexpected delays or disasters, sometimes due to simply forgetting, sometimes because they made more than one booking and didn't bother to cancel the one they didn't want. Full fare passengers who fail to turn up are sometimes entitled to travel on a later flight. The rest of us are penalised (see Cancellation Penalties).

On Request An unconfirmed booking for a flight (see Confirmation); wait-listed

no nonstop flights on the west-bound route from İstanbul to New York at the time of writing. Most of the European national airlines fly from New York to their home countries, then on to İstanbul. Lufthansa has especially good connections from Frankfurt.

Pakistan International Airlines has a one-stop service from Toronto, and also from New York to İstanbul, with an even lower excursion fare, but some passengers find the service less than luxurious.

From New York and Chicago, particularly during the summer months, group fares to İstanbul are sold by various tour operators. You do not have to be part of a group, nor do you have to take a tour or pay for nights in a hotel. You pay only for the flight (which is on a regular, scheduled airline, not a charter),

---

Open Jaw This is a return ticket where you fly out to one place but return from another. If available, this can save you backtracking to your arrival point.

Overbooking Airlines hate to fly empty seats, and since every flight has some passengers who fail to show up (see No Shows), airlines often book more passengers than they have seats. Usually the excess passengers balance those who fail to show up but occasionally somebody gets bumped. If this happens, guess who it is most likely to be? The passengers who check in late. If you are bumped, you'll usually get some compensation the amount and nature of which often depends heavily on your haggling skills.

Reconfirmation At least 72 hours prior to departure time of an onward or return flight you must contact the airline and 'reconfirm' that you intend to be on the flight. If you don't do this the airline can delete your name from the passenger list and you could lose your seat. You don't have to reconfirm the first flight on your itinerary or if your stopover is less than 72 hours. It doesn't hurt to reconfirm more than once.

Restrictions Discounted tickets often have various restrictions on them – advance purchase is the most usual one (see Apex). Others are restrictions on the minimum and maximum period you must be away, such as a minimum of 14 days or a maximum of one year. See Cancellation Penalties.

Standby This is a discounted ticket where you only fly if there is a seat free at the last moment. Standby fares are usually only available on domestic routes.

Tickets Out An entry requirement for many countries is that you have an onward or return ticket – in other words, a ticket out of the country. If you're not sure what you intend to do next, the easiest solution is to buy the cheapest onward ticket to a neighbouring country or a ticket from a reliable airline which can later be refunded if you do not use it.

Transferred Tickets Airline tickets cannot be transferred from one person to another. Travellers sometimes try to sell the return half of their ticket, but officials can ask you to prove that you are the person named on the ticket. This is unlikely to happen on domestic flights, but on international flights, tickets may be compared with passports. Also, if you're flying on a transferred ticket and something goes wrong with the flight (hijack, crash), there will be no record of your presence on board.

Travel Agencies Travel agencies vary widely and you should ensure you use one that suits your needs. Some simply handle tours while full-service agencies handle everything from tours and tickets to car rental and hotel bookings. A good one will do all these things and can save you a lot of money, but if all you want is a ticket at the lowest possible price, then you really need an agency specialising in discounted tickets. A discounted ticket agency, however, may not be useful for other things, like hotel bookings.

Travel Periods Some officially discounted fares, Apex fares in particular, vary with the time of year. There is often a low (off-peak) season and a high (peak) season. Sometimes there's an intermediate or shoulder season as well. At peak times, when everyone wants to fly, not only will the officially discounted fares be higher but so will unofficially discounted fares, or there may simply be no discounted tickets available. Usually the fare depends on your outward flight – if you depart in the high season and return in the low season, you pay the high-season fare. ■

but you get your ticket at a special low group rate. There may be some restrictions, such as perhaps having to stay more than seven nights and less than 180 nights. From New York, fares are about US$400 to US$600 one way, US$700 to US$850 round trip. Turkish Airlines usually has the lowest fares.

It's best to pay for these cheapie flights with a credit card so that if something goes wrong, you don't lose your money. For more information contact a travel agent or get a copy of the monthly *JAXFAX Travel Marketing Magazine*, 397 Post Rd, PO Box 4013, Darien, CT 06820-1413, USA (☎ (203) 655-8746); a subscription costs $12 per year.

It is also worth investigating the East European airlines such as Tarom, as well as alternative fares such as the 'open-jaw' ones that let you fly to one city (eg Vienna) and return from another (eg İstanbul). You have to make separate arrangements for transport between the two cities, but the overall savings can be considerable.

To/From Australia

There are now some direct flights from Australia to İstanbul offered by Malaysian Airlines (via Kuala Lumpur and Dubai) and Singapore Airlines (via Singapore and Bangkok) with round-trip fares for about A$1800. Also there are connecting flights via Athens, London and Singapore on Thai International, British Airways, Olympic, Alitalia, Turkish and Qantas.

Round-trip fares via Athens, the closest and most convenient connection to İstanbul, range from A$2506 in the off season, to A$2806 in the peak season. If you can get a cheap fare to London, you might do well to look for a cheap round-trip fare (from London to Turkey) once you arrive in London.

One of the cheapest way to get to Turkey directly from Australia is to fly to Athens (not on a charter flight! see next paragraph) and take a boat to one of the islands (Lesbos, Chios, Samos, Kos or Rhodes) and then a ferry to the Turkish mainland. This route proves the dictum that the smaller the price the greater the inconvenience.

Charter Flights

Several countries (such as Greece) which benefit greatly from charter-flight traffic have enacted a regulation which prohibits charter passengers from leaving the charter destination country for the duration of their stay. Thus, if you fly to Athens on a charter and then legally enter Turkey (ie have your passport stamped), the officials at the airport in Athens may not allow you to board your return charter flight. You may have to pay for another whole ticket to get home. (If you just take a day excursion to Turkey, and the Turkish immigration officials do not stamp your passport, you will have no problem boarding your return charter flight.) The regulation allows the charter destination country to reap all of the benefits of the low charter fare. This regulation does not apply to regular or excursion-fare flights, only to charters. It is not always enforced in Greece, but you must know about it nonetheless.

I have had no news that the Turkish officials enforce the charter regulation, which means that if you take a charter to Turkey, you probably *can* visit Greece, return to Turkey and have no trouble boarding your return charter flight. But ask in advance to avoid disappointment and expense.

OVERLAND
To/From Greece

From Greece, the major road goes to Kastanéai (Greece) and Pazarkule (Turkey), seven km south-west of Edirne on the Meriç River (mehr-EECH, Maritsa), two km past the Turkish village of Karaağaç to a border post originally meant to serve the railway line. The frontier, as determined by the Treaty of Lausanne (1923), left the Turkish line passing through Greece on its way to Edirne! A bypass line was built in the 1970s, though. The problem here is that the Greeks have declared the border area a military zone and do not permit anyone to walk in it without a military escort, so you will probably have to take a Greek taxi (US$6, two minutes) to the actual border, which is midway in the one-km-wide no-man's-land which separates the two border posts. On the

Turkish side, you can walk to and from Pazarkule. These small border posts are open during daylight hours.

From Pazarkule, or from the nearby railway station, you will probably have to take a Turkish taxi (US$5, 15 minutes) into town as there is not much traffic and hitching is not too easy, though you may be lucky.

If you are crossing from Turkey into Greece, do so as soon after 8 am as possible in order to catch one of the few trains or buses from Kastanéai heading south to Alexandroùpolis.

To/From Bulgaria

If you're travelling overland from Bulgaria see the Edirne section for border-crossing and travel details. A transit visa, good for 30 hours, costs US$12 if you buy it at the Bulgarian Consulate in Edirne; if you buy it at the border it will cost US$16. Visas for longer stays are more expensive. The rules for Bulgarian visas are liable to change due to the present instability in the region, so it's a good idea to check with the consulate in any case.

To/From Georgia

Note that the Turkish-Georgian border crossing at Sarp is presently open only to nationals of Turkey and the former Soviet republics. Citizens of other countries must cross by boat to Batumi (see Sea, following).

To/From Iran

Once you accept the cultural peculiarities of the Islamic Revolution, travel in Iran can be enjoyable. The people are mostly very friendly and helpful. To visit or travel through Iran you must have a visa, theoretically obtainable from an Iranian embassy or consulate, but this may depend on the fluctuating currents of international relations.

It may take anywhere from a week to a month or more to obtain a visa. You may have to first obtain a visa for the country you will enter when you leave Iran; you may be asked to show a bus or airline ticket out of Iran. Be prepared for some Middle Eastern bureaucratic hassles. See the Visas &

Embassies section in the Facts for the Visitor chapter, and contact your embassy in Ankara for details on current availability and requirements for visas.

The border crossing may take as little as one hour. You may be asked to pay an unofficial fee (ie, a bribe) by the Iranian officials. The Bank Melli branch at the border changes cash dollars or pounds or travellers cheques into Iranian rials (tomans). It may not change Turkish liras, but you may be able to exchange liras at banks farther into Iran.

From Doğubeyazıt (see also that section), you can catch a minibus to the Iranian frontier. From the border you can take a taxi to Maku, then an Iran Peyma bus from Maku to Tabriz.

To/From Syria

Syrian visas are not normally issued at the border, but this depends partly upon your nationality and partly upon current regulations. If you plan to travel to Syria and other Middle Eastern countries, plan ahead and obtain the necessary visas in your home country, in İstanbul or in Ankara. At the border you are no longer required to change the equivalent of US$100 into Syrian currency at the official exchange rate, which is currently only 25% of the black-market rate.

Bus

Turkish bus companies operate frequent passenger services to and from Turkey.

To/From Greece For a bus to İstanbul, go to the railway station (OSE Hellenic Railways Organisation, Plateia Peloponisu), from which the buses depart. Among other companies running to Turkey you will find Varan Turizm (☎ (1) 513 5768) which operates buses to and from İstanbul via Thessaloniki twice weekly, departing from Athens at 8 am, departing from Thessaloniki at 4 pm, and arriving in İstanbul at 6.30 am the next day; and departing from Athens at 7 pm, departing from Thessaloniki the next morning at 3 am, and arriving in İstanbul later that day at 5.30 pm.

Return trips depart from İstanbul for

Athens at 10 am and 7.30 pm, arriving 22½ hours later. In summer, when traffic is heavy, there may be extra buses. Reserve your seat in advance if you can. A one-way ticket costs US$50 from Athens, US$35 from Thessaloniki.

Other companies operating buses between İstanbul and Athens can be contacted through these offices:

Athens
    Rika Tours, Marni 44, Platia Vathis
    (☎ (1) 523-2458, 523-3686, 523-5905;
    telex 21-9473)
Thessaloniki
    Simeonidis Tours, 26 October St No 14
    (☎ (31) 54 09 71, 52 14 45)

To/From Elsewhere in Europe Several of the best Turkish companies (Ulusoy, Varan) operate big Mercedes buses which are at least as comfortable (usually more so) as the now-neglected trains, comparable in price, often faster and safer; but once you add in the cost of meals and the time involved, the price of a flight doesn't look too bad. To İstanbul (see also the İstanbul Getting There & Away section) from Basel costs US$125 one way, US$220 for a round trip; from Salzburg, US$95 one way, US$160 round trip. The major discomfort on the trip may be cigarette smoke.

Ulusoy and Varan have sales desks or representatives in the international bus terminals of several European cities. Some addresses follow:

İstanbul
    Ulusoy Turizm, Topkapı Otogar No 13, Topkapı
    Ulusoy Turizm, İnönü Caddesi 59, Taksim
    (☎ (1) 144 1271, 244 2823)
Brussels
    Ulusoy Turizm, Place de la Reine 19
    (☎ (1) 217 6382)
Karlsruhe
    Ulusoy Turizm, Sophienstrasse 126
    (☎ (721) 85 62 31)
London
    Harris Coaches, Manor Rd, West Thurrock, Grays, Essex (☎ (708) 86 49 11) or any National Travel Bureau

Paris
    Ulusoy Turizm, Gare Routière Internationale, 8 Place de Stalingrad, 75019 Paris
    (☎ (1) 12 05 12 10)

Varan Turizm operates from Metz, Nancy, Strasbourg, Colmar and Mulhouse in France, with buses departing from these cities for İstanbul on Wednesday; from St Gallen, Winterthur and Zürich in Switzerland, with departures for İstanbul on Wednesday; from Bregenz, Dornbirn, St Pölten, Linz, Salzburg, Wiener Neustadt, Vienna, Graz and Innsbruck in Austria, with departures on Wednesday, Friday or Saturday. The trip between Europe and Turkey takes anything from 32 hours (Graz to İstanbul) to 48 hours (Metz to İstanbul). Here are some addresses:

İstanbul
    Varan Turizm, İnönü Caddesi 29/B, Taksim (☎ (1) 243 1903, 244 8457)
Innsbruck
    Varan Turizm, Hofgasse 2 (☎ (5222) 35 378)
Salzburg
    Varan Turizm, Bahnhof Vorplatz Kaiser schützenstrasse 12 (☎ (662) 75 068)
Strasbourg
    Varan Turizm, 37 Faubourg de Pierre 67000 (☎ (88) 22 03 87)
Vienna
    Varan Turizm, Südbahnhof Südtirolerplatz 7 (☎ (222) 65 65 93)
Zürich
    Varan Turizm, Josefstrasse 45, 8005 Zürich (☎ (1) 44 04 77)

To/From Syria For details of bus services to/from Syria and other Middle Eastern countries see also the Adana, Antakya and Ankara Getting There & Away sections.

Direct daily buses connect Antakya, at the eastern end of Turkey's Mediterranean coast, with the Syrian cities of Aleppo (Haleb, 105 km, four hours, US$12) and Damascus (465 km, eight hours, US$20), and Amman (Jordan, 675 km, 10 hours, US$28).

Travel times to these cities do not include border-crossing formalities, which may add several hours to the trip. Get your visas in advance to hasten formalities.

For travel in Syria, you may need to obtain a visa from a Syrian consulate before you reach the border. Dolmuşes run frequently from the southern end of Antakya's bus station to the Turco-Syrian border stations at Reyhanlı (for Aleppo) and Yayladağ (for Lattakia and Beirut) throughout the day.

Train

Fares Rail tickets generally cost more than bus tickets. If you're young, you can take advantage of the Wasteels BIGE Youth Train, with special low fares. In İstanbul, buy your tickets at window *(gişe)* No 5 in Sirkeci railway station.

The Inter-Rail Youth pass is now valid for all of Turkey's railways, but it may not be valid in Bulgaria (check for current regulations). Thus if you travel on the Inter-Rail pass, you may have to go around Bulgaria by taking the Belgrade to Edirne route via Thessaloniki, which can take a long 55 hours from Munich. The alternative is to pay full fare through Bulgaria for the 39-hour *İstanbul Express* trip.

***Orient Express* Route** The *Orient Express* lives on in special excursion trains with various names, but the fares for these deluxe tours cost between US$2500 and US$5500 one way. These packages include transportation from European points to İstanbul aboard restored railway coaches, with lectures and optional side-trips. By the way, the train which now bears the name *Orient Express* goes nowhere near İstanbul on its run between London and Venice.

On the regular trains such as the *İstanbul Express* (see following), there is no romance left on this famed *Orient Express* route. You may be able to resurrect a bit of romance if you have the money to travel 1st class, preferably in a sleeping car as far as Belgrade, then in a couchette to İstanbul. Another tip is to get off the train in Edirne, the first stop in Turkey. It's an interesting city, well worth a stop. From Edirne to İstanbul the train takes at least six hours, but the bus takes less than four.

For several years I received reports of thieves who sprayed sleeping gas under compartment doors at night, and when the occupants were knocked out, stripped them of their valuables; it happened to close friends of mine. One reader even left the windows open to dilute the gas, and tried to stay awake, but they still got his stuff.

To/From Greece The 1400-km journey on the *Atina Ekspresi* (Athens Express) takes 24 hours, departing from İstanbul late in the evening, arriving in Thessaloniki late in the afternoon the next day, and Athens very late in the evening. From Athens, the train leaves at breakfast time, arrives in Thessaloniki after lunch, and gets to İstanbul at breakfast time the next morning. There's a change of trains at Thessaloniki.

To/From Munich, Vienna, Moscow & Bucharest The daily *İstanbul Express* from Munich departs each evening at dinner time, reaches Belgrade at breakfast time, Sofia at dinner time, and İstanbul at breakfast time on the third day, taking about 35 hours (if it's on time).

The train hauls sleeping and couchette *(kuşet)* coaches, a restaurant car and (three days weekly) auto-train carriages so you can take your car with you. Auto-train *(oto-kuşet)* service runs Tuesdays, Fridays and Saturdays from Munich; Wednesdays, Thursdays and Sundays from İstanbul. The fare for a car and driver from Munich to İstanbul (one way) is from US$560 to US$790; round-trip fares are discounted about 12%.

A second train, the *Skopje-İstanbul Express*, departs from Munich later each evening, reaching Sofia in about 25½ hours. At Sofia it is met by the *Sofia Express* from Moscow and Bucharest before continuing to İstanbul overnight, arriving around lunch time, 38 hours after having left Munich, 37 hours after having left Moscow.

A nightly train from Vienna connects with the *İstanbul Express* at Zagreb, departing from Vienna after dinner, arriving in Zagreb several hours after midnight. You reach İstanbul in the morning after two nights on the train. (For more details, see the İstanbul Getting There & Away section.)

To/From Armenia

The railway line from Ankara to Erzurum goes on to Kars and, in good times, goes as far as the Armenian frontier, with a connecting train to Moscow.

At the time of writing, two trains run daily from Kars to the Armenian border at Doğu Kapı. The slow *Akyaka Postası* departs from Kars each Friday afternoon for Ahuryan, just across the border in Armenia, returning to Kars in the early evening each Tuesday. You should obtain an Armenian visa from a consulate before proceeding to the border.

To/From Iran

The Van line used to go on to Iran, with a connection to Tabriz and Tehran. This connection has been severed for years, but because of recent developments in Iran it may be revived. South of Elazığ, this line branches for Diyarbakır and Kurtalan.

Car

Car ferries (see the Sea section) from Italy and Cyprus can shorten driving time considerably. No special car documents are required for visits of up to three months. The car will be entered in the driver's passport as imported goods, and must be driven out of the country by the same visitor within the time period allowed. *Do not drive someone else's car into Turkey.*

Normally, you cannot rent a car in Europe and include Turkey (or many other Eastern European countries) in your driving plans. If you want to leave your car in Turkey and return for it later, the car must be put under customs seal.

For stays longer than three months, contact the Turkish Touring & Automobile Association (Türk Turing ve Otomobil Kurumu) (☎ (1) 240 7127, 231 4631; fax 248 9661), Halaskargazi Caddesi 364, Şişli, İstanbul.

The E5 highway makes its way through the Balkans to Edirne (see also that section) and İstanbul, then onward to Ankara, Adana and the Syrian frontier. Though the road is good in most of the countries it passes through, you will encounter heavy traffic and lots of heavy vehicles along the route, as this is a very important freight route between Europe and the Middle East.

Insurance Your Green Card third-party insurance must be endorsed for *all* of Turkey, both European and Asian, not just the European portion (Thrace). If it is not, you will be required to buy a Turkish insurance policy at the border.

SEA

Several shipping lines operate car and passenger ferries from Italy, Greece and Turkish Cyprus to Turkey in summer, and small ferries shuttle between the Greek islands and the Turkish mainland. A hydrofoil service operates in high summer between Rhodes and Fethiye.

To/From Italy

Turkish Maritime Lines Turkish Maritime Lines (Denizyolları, or TML) operates modern, comfortable car and passenger ferries from Venice to İzmir and Antalya, departing from Venice every Saturday evening from mid-April to late October, arriving in İzmir on Tuesday morning. The return trip from İzmir departs on Wednesday afternoon, arriving in Venice on Saturday morning.

The one-way fare in cabins ranges from US$200 to US$470 per passenger, breakfast and port taxes included. In 'Pullman' class you get not a cabin, but a reclining seat in a large room for US$150 to US$165, breakfast and port tax included. Students can claim a 10% reduction on the fare only (not on meals). For lunch and dinner, add another US$35 to the fare. The fare for a normal car, port tax included, is around US$190; for a motorcycle it's around US$90.

For more information, contact TML at the following addresses:

İstanbul
    Türkiye Denizcilik İşletmeleri, Rıhtım Caddesi,

Top: Blue Mosque (Sultan Ahmet Camii), İstanbul (TW)
Left: Main portal, Blue Mosque, İstanbul (TB)
Right: Aya Sofya, İstanbul (TW)

Top Left: Haji selling Coca-Cola, İstanbul (TB)
Top Right: Fish seller near the Galata Bridge, İstanbul (TW)
Bottom Left: İstanbul craftsman at work on a coffee pot (TB)
Bottom Right: Selling lottery tickets, İstanbul (TB)

Karaköy
    (☎ (1) 244 0207, 249 7178; fax 251 5767)
İzmir
    Türkiye Denizcilik İşletmeleri Acenteliği,
    Yeniliman, Alsancak
    (☎ (51) 21 00 94, 21 00 77; fax 21 14 81)
London
    Sunquest Holidays Ltd, 9 Grand Parade, Green
    Lanes, London N4 1JX
    (☎ (081) 800 5455, 800 8030; fax 809 6629)
Venice
    Bassani SpA, Via 22 Marzo 2414, 30124 Venezia
    (☎ (41) 522 9544, 520 8633; fax 520 4009)

Another Turkish ferry not under TML operation is the MF *Avrasya*, which departs from Venice each Saturday evening, arriving in Kuşadası on Wednesday morning; departing from Kuşadası each Wednesday in the mid-afternoon for Venice, arriving Saturday morning during the warm months.

One-way fares are about US$300 for Pullman seats, US$325 to US$700 per person for cabins, US$420 for a car. For reservations and information, contact Tura Turizm, Cumhuriyet Caddesi 129, Elmadağ, İstanbul (☎ (1) 241 7022/3, 241 2530; fax 248 8252); in Kuşadası contact Tura Turizm, Kıbrıs Caddesi, Buyural Sokak No 9/3, Kuşadası Yolcu Limanı (☎ & fax (636) 11900).

Minoan Lines From Ancona, Minoan Lines operates weekly ferries departing each Saturday evening from mid-April to early October; stopping at Corfu, Sami, Cefalonia, Piraeus, Paros and Samos, terminating at Kuşadası, south of İzmir, on Wednesday. The 2½-day trip is actually a mini-cruise, and you are allowed one stopover at no additional cost. The return trip departs from Kuşadası on Wednesday evening, arriving back in Ancona on Saturday morning.

To/From the Greek Islands

With the boom in Turkish tourism, the traffic from the Greek islands to the Turkish mainland is intense in the warm months. From time to time, the Greek government issues regulations designed to make it difficult for travellers to go from Greece to Turkey. You may have to contend with these.

Previous efforts have included making it difficult to obtain information on boats to Turkey (the law stated that only one sign no greater than a piece of typing paper could be displayed, and only in the window of the agency selling tickets).

Greek regulations may require that passengers on trips originating in Greece must travel on Greek-flag vessels, which means that you may not be allowed to hop aboard a convenient Turkish vessel for your trip from the Greek islands to the Turkish mainland. (If you've come over from Turkey for the day, you may return on the Turkish boat.)

The most recent regulation raised port taxes for travellers to Turkey to unconscionable heights – several times the actual boat fare. The Turkish government and tourism sector – and travellers – protested at once, and you should not have to worry about excessive port taxes when you go.

There are five regular ferry services: Lesbos to Ayvalık, Chios to Çeşme, Samos to Kuşadası, Kos to Bodrum, and Rhodes to Marmaris.

The procedure is this: once you've found the ticket office, buy your ticket a day in advance. You may be asked to turn in your passport the night before the trip. The next day, before you board the boat, you'll get it back.

Here are the routes, fares and ticket agencies from Greece. For details on travelling from Turkey, see the section on each departure port (eg Ayvalık, Çeşme, Kuşadası etc).

Lesbos to Ayvalık Aeolic Cruises Travel Agency (☎ 23 960), at the port in Mytileni, is one of the ticket agencies. Both Greek and Turkish boats make this run daily in summer (from late May or early June to September). In spring, autumn and winter, boats operate about once or twice a week, weather permitting. The one-way fare is US$18; a return or round-trip ticket costs US$30.

Chios to Çeşme Boats run daily except Monday from mid-July to mid-September. In spring and autumn, service is thrice weekly on Tuesday, Thursday, and Sunday (from mid-May to mid-July and mid-September to the end of October). Winter service is once a week, on Thursday, weather permitting and if there are sufficient passengers to make the trip worthwhile. Sometimes the companies put on extra boats when demand warrants it. The voyage lasts about 45 minutes. The local boats (Greek boats from Chios, Turkish boats from Çeşme) depart at 9.30 or 10 am, making the return trip at 4 pm.

The one-way fare is US$30, same-day return fare is US$38; an open-date return ticket valid for one year costs US$38. Children from four to 12 years old are entitled to a 50% reduction on the fare. Motorcycles, cars, small caravans or minibuses can be transported on some boats. Fares for vehicles vary from US$50 to US$75, depending on their size. For details, contact Chios Tours at the port in Chios, or Ertürk Travel Agency (☎ (5492) 6768, 6876), Cumhuriyet Meydanı 11/A, on Çeşme's main square next to the fortress, facing the docks.

Samos to Kuşadası Boats sail between the Greek island of Samos and Turkish Kuşadası, near Ephesus. Services go from Samos town (daily at 8.30 am and 5 pm, a 30-minute trip) and Pythagorion (thrice weekly in summer at 8.30 am, a 45-minute trip). In spring and autumn there are four trips weekly from the town of Samos.

There is no scheduled service in winter, though this may change; check with a travel agency in Samos or Kuşadası for the latest information. The voyage costs US$32 one way, US$38 for the round trip.

Kos to Bodrum Greek ferries leave the outer harbour of Kos for Bodrum on Monday, Wednesday and Friday mornings in summer, and on other days if there are sufficient passengers. Tickets cost US$20 one way. The Greek authorities usually require you to take a Greek-flag vessel rather than the Turkish excursion boat which has come over for the day, but sometimes you can talk them into letting you take the afternoon Turkish boat. If so, buy your ticket on the boat.

Rhodes to Marmaris This is the busiest ferry service of all, with numerous boats flying Greek or Turkish flags competing for business. The Rhodes ticket office is the ANKA Travel Centre (☎ (241) 25 095), 13 Odos Galias, near the New Market. It is open from 8.30 am to 2 pm and 5.30 to 9.30 pm in summer, closed on Sunday. In Turkey, buy your tickets at any travel agency.

There are several daily boats (except on Sunday) in each direction during the summer, and if lots of passengers are waiting, they may even put on Sunday boats. The fare is US$25 one way, US$32 same-day return, US$40 open-date return. The ferry service operates all year, though service does dwindle to only one or two trips weekly in winter. Some of the ferries are large enough to carry cars; reserve space in advance.

To/From Cyprus

You should be aware that relations between the Greek Cypriot-administered Republic of Cyprus and the Turkish Republic of Northern Cyprus (TRNC) are not good, and that the border between the two regions will probably be closed. Also, if you enter the TRNC and have your passport stamped you will later be denied entry to Greece. The Greeks will reject only a stamp from the Turkish Republic of Northern Cyprus, *not* a stamp from Turkey proper. Have the Turkish Cypriot official stamp a piece of paper instead of your passport.

Famagusta to Mersin The large, comfortable MF *Yeşilada* car ferry operated by Turkish Maritime Lines departs from Famagusta (Mağusa, Magosa or Gazimagosa, northern Cyprus) on Tuesday, Thursday and Sunday at 10 pm, all year round. Departures from Mersin (Turkey) are at 10 pm on Monday, Wednesday and Friday. The overnight trip takes 10 hours, arriving at 8 am. Fares between Famagusta and Mersin range from US$75 per person in luxury cabins to US$35 for a reclining Pullman seat; port taxes are included, but meals cost extra. To transport a car one way costs about US$58.

Kyrenia to Taşucu Kyrenia (Girne in Turkish) and Taşucu, near Silifke, are connected by daily hydrofoil and car-ferry service.

The 250-passenger MV *Barbaros* is a *deniz otobüsü* ('sea bus', hydrofoil) operated by the Kıbrıs Express company (☎ (7593) 1434, 1334), Atatürk Bulvarı 82, Taşucu. It departs from Kyrenia daily at 2.30 pm on the two-hour run to Taşucu. Departures from Taşucu for Kyrenia are daily at 11.30 am. The MV *Barbaros* has comfortable aeroplane-style seats, air-con, a bar and a snack counter. Tickets cost US$28 one way, US$44 return. Children under than five years old travel free; for those aged from five to 12 years, the one-way fare is US$18. You must pay a US$8 port tax as well.

The Kyrenia office for the Kıbrıs Express hydrofoil (☎ (81) 53 544, 52 900) is at İskenderun Caddesi 4, Kyrenia; in Nicosia (Lefkoşa in Turkish) there's another office across from the İş Bankası. There's also an office in Turkey (☎ (741) 16 731, 11 550), at İnönü Bulvarı, Güvenç İş Merkezi 10, Mersin.

The *Ertürk* car ferry runs from Kyrenia at noon on Monday, Tuesday, Wednesday, Thursday and Friday, arriving in Taşucu at 4 pm. Trips from Taşucu to Kyrenia depart at midnight on Sunday, Monday, Tuesday, Wednesday and Thursday, arriving in Kyrenia the next morning at 7.30 am. One-way tickets cost US$28; a return is US$39. Contact Fatih Feribot (☎ (81) 54 880, 54 977, 52 840) in Kyrenia; in Nicosia call the Şen-Tur agency (☎ (20) 78 824). The ticket agent in Taşucu is Fatih Feribot (☎ (7593) 1249, 1386) on the main square just off the dock.

A similar car-ferry service is provided by the MV *Girne Sultanı*, operated by the Fergün Denizcilik company (☎ (81) 53 866, 52 344, 53 377) in Kyrenia and in Taşucu (☎ (7593) 1717, 1204). The MV *Girne Sultanı* departs from Kyrenia for Taşucu at 1 pm on Monday, Wednesday and Friday, arriving at 5 pm. Departures from Taşucu are at midnight on Tuesday and Thursday, arriving the next morning at 7.30 am; and at noon on Saturday, arriving in Kyrenia at 4 pm. Cabin berths are priced at US$22 to US$25 for a one-way ticket, plus US$8 port tax. Discounts are offered on return tickets and for students.

Turkish Maritime Lines runs a passenger ferry from early March to late September, departing from Taşucu daily at midnight, arriving in Kyrenia at 8 am the next morning; departing from Kyrenia at 1 pm daily, arriving in Taşucu at 5.30 pm. The fare is a flat US$20 per person, port tax included. Contact the TML (☎ 65 786, 65 995; fax 67 840) in Famagusta: Kıbrıs Türk Denizcilik Ltd, 3 Bülent Ecevit Bulvarı, PO Box 57.

To/From Georgia

Travel between Trabzon and Batumi (Georgia) by hydrofoil is possible but frustrating. First you must get a visa from the former USSR consulate in Trabzon 200 metres south-east from the south-east corner of Atatürk Alanı (look for the police guard booth). For more details see the Trabzon section.

After obtaining your visa, you must get boat tickets down by the harbour. The boat may or may not leave on time, and may or may not have a place for you. Many swindlers work the rackets concerning these boats and tickets to ride on them. One hopes the situation will soon improve.

LEAVING TURKEY
Departure Tax
As of this writing, Turkey does not levy a tax on departing travellers. Don't have any antiquities in your luggage. If you're caught smuggling them out, you'll probably go to jail.

Getting Around

Turkey has an elaborate public transport system, as private cars are still relatively expensive and Turks love to travel all the time. Even the sleepiest village seems to have minibuses darting in and out throughout the day, and buses running between İstanbul and Ankara depart every few minutes.

As this guidebook goes to press, however, I cannot recommend travel to south-eastern Turkey (Diyarbakır, Mardin, Bitlis, or points south or east of them) due to the continuing Kurdish insurgency. If you do plan to travel to this area, be sure to contact your embassy or consulate in advance, ask about current conditions, tell them your plans, and ask their advice. Travel only during daylight, only on major highways (or preferably by air), and restrict your stops to major towns and cities. (See also the Eastern Anatolia chapter.)

AIR
Local Air Services
THY & THT Türk Hava Yolları (THY, Turkish Airlines; symbol: TK) operates large jet aircraft from İstanbul, usually travelling via Ankara, to major Turkish cities. Its subsidiary, Türk Hava Taşımacılığı (THT, Turkish Air Transport; symbol: ZH) operates smaller, slower turboprop aircraft on less-travelled routes to smaller cities, and on a few of the same routes as THY. Make reservations and buy tickets for both airlines at Turkish Airlines offices. Be sure to ask about the 10% discount for couples or parent(s) with child(ren) travelling together, and discounts for youth (aged from 12 to 24 years), seniors (60 years and over), and those on their honeymoon or wedding anniversary.

The table is for *nonstop* flights only (with the exception of the Ankara-Kars route); other flights may be available by connection. Thus if you can't catch one of the two weekly THT nonstop flights from Ankara to Antalya,

you may be able to fly on THY any day via İstanbul; and there are daily one-stop flights from İstanbul to Erzurum via Ankara. Airport codes (most of these are unfamiliar to travel agents) follow the city names, and there are some sample fares.

İstanbul Airlines İstanbul Hava Yolları (symbol: IL) operates between its namesake city and Adana, Ankara, Antalya, Dalaman, İzmir, Trabzon and Van, as well as on international routes to Germany, Holland, Turkish Cyprus and Baku in Azerbaijan. The domestic flights are essentially feeder operations for the international routes, so most flights operate only once or twice per week. There are also flights connecting Antalya with Dalaman and İzmir.

Prices are usually lower than those of THY and THT. You can make reservations through the reservations centre in İstanbul at Firuzköy Yolu No 26, Avcılar (☎ (1) 509 2121; fax 593 6035) and buy tickets at the airport. (See each city section for details on each local office.) Discounts include 10% for families, youth fares (for those aged from 12 to 24 years), and seniors over 60 years of age.

Greenair Like İstanbul Airlines, Greenair flies low-cost routes between Turkey and Europe, as well as a few domestic routes, most notably İstanbul-Antalya (US$70). It offers discounts of 50% for children, for seniors over 60 years, for ladies with green eyes, and to passengers on their late-night flights. Contact Greenair in İstanbul (☎ (1) 241 0293), Cumhuriyet Caddesi 279, Adlı İşhanı, Harbiye.

Sönmez Holding Airlines Called Sönmez Holding Hava Yolları in Turkish, this is a small airline set up by a large holding company for the convenience of its employees and visitors, but they are perfectly happy to fly you between Bursa and İstanbul. The

route	frequency	carrier	fare (US$)
Adana-İzmir (ADB)	2/week	THT	112
Ankara-Adana (ADA)	1/day	THY	89
Ankara-Antalya (AYT)	2/week	THT	89
Ankara-Bursa (BTZ)	2/week	THT	89
Ankara-Batman (BAL)	2/week	THY	89
Ankara-Dalaman (DLM)	1/week	THT	101
Ankara-Diyarbakır (DIY)	1-2/day	THT	102
Ankara-Elazığ (EZS)	2/week	THT	123
Ankara-Erzincan (ERC)	2/week	THT	78
Ankara-Erzurum (ERZ)	1/day	THY	89
Ankara-Gaziantep (GZT)	1/day	THY	84
Ankara-İstanbul (IST)	11-18/day	THY & THT	106
Ankara-İzmir (ADB)	1-2/day	THY & THT	112
Ankara-Kars (KSY) (via Elazığ)	2/week	THT	101
Ankara-Malatya (MLX)	8/week	THY & THT	78
Ankara-Şanlıurfa (SFQ)	2/week	THT	123
Ankara-Trabzon (TZX)	1/day	THY	89
Ankara-Van (VAN)	1/day	THY	101
İstanbul-Adana (ADA)	3-4/day	THY	123
İstanbul-Ankara (ESB)	11-15/day	THY & THT	106
İstanbul-Antalya (AYT)	2-6/day	THY	112
İstanbul-Batman (BAL)	2/week	THY	117
İstanbul-Bursa (BTZ)	2/week	THT	34
İstanbul-Dalaman (DLM)	2-4/day	THY	112
İstanbul-Denizli (DNZ)	3/week	THY	89
İstanbul-Gaziantep (GZT)	2/week	THY	112
İstanbul-İzmir (ADB)	5-11/day	THY	106
İstanbul-Kayseri (ASR)	4/week	THT	89
İstanbul-Samsun (SSX)	3/week	THT	89
İstanbul-Trabzon (TZX)	1-2/day	THY	123

airline has one small C-212 aircraft which wings from Bursa to İstanbul and back each morning, and again each evening. There's an extra flight on Saturday, but no flights at all on Sunday. See the İstanbul and Bursa sections for details on ticketing.

Other Airlines Deregulation of Turkey's air transport system has resulted in the birth of many small commuter, charter and air-taxi firms. These companies come and go, and rarely operate scheduled flights, but you might find them of use in special circumstances.

EmAir (☎ (4) 229 0440, 229 0757), Necatibey Caddesi 88/6, Ankara, provides air-taxi services in twin-engine Cessna 421C 'Golden Eagles'. It flies frequently between İstanbul and Bodrum. Contact them in İstanbul at the Atatürk Airport domestic terminal desk No 16 (☎ (1) 574 4318, 573 7220, ext 2728). In Bodrum, the office is at Neyzen Tevfik Caddesi 138/A (☎ (6141) 2100).

SancakAir (☎ (1) 580-1517, 580 1074; fax 579 0727), Londra Asfaltı, Şefaköy, İstanbul, offers corporate jets and helicopters for hire.

Check-in Procedures
It's a good idea to get to the airport *at least* 45 minutes before flight departure time. Things can get a bit chaotic. Signs and announcements are not always provided, or understandable, so you need to keep asking to make sure you end up at the proper destination. Also, you need to make sure that your checked baggage is tagged and sent off to the

plane. Sometimes when you hand it over to the agents, they just assume you want them to keep it for you until you return.

As of this writing, there is open seating on most domestic flights; you are not assigned a specific seat number, but may sit wherever you choose. No smoking is allowed on domestic flights, but this is not always observed.

Security

As you approach the airport perimeter, your bus or taxi will be stopped and spot-checked by police looking for terrorists. On a bus, your passport and ticket will be inspected.

As you enter the terminal, you will have to put your luggage through an x-ray machine. Before you leave the terminal you will be frisked for weapons and your hand baggage will be searched. Don't try to carry even a pocketknife aboard, as it will probably be found, and you certainly won't be allowed to carry it aboard. Rather, pack it in your checked luggage.

As you approach the aircraft, all passengers' luggage will be lined up, and you will be asked to point out your bag. It will then be put on board. This is to prevent someone from checking in a bag with a bomb inside it, then not boarding the plane. So if you forget to point out your bag to the baggage handler, it may not be loaded on board and may be regarded with distrust.

BUS

The bus and the *dolmuş* (minibus) are the most widespread and popular means of transport in Turkey. Buses go literally everywhere, all the time. Virtually every first-time traveller in Turkey comments on the convenience of the bus and minibus system. The bus service runs the gamut from plain and very inexpensive to very comfortable and moderately priced. It is so cheap and convenient that many erstwhile long-distance hitchhikers opt for the bus. The eight-hour, 450-km trip between İstanbul and Ankara, for example, costs only US$12 to US$20, depending on the bus company. Though bus fares are open to competition among compa-

nies, and even to haggling for a reduction, the cost of bus travel in Turkey works out to around US$2 to US$2.50 per 100 km – a surprising bargain.

The two best companies, offering smooth service at a premium prices on national routes, are Ulusoy and Varan. Next best are Kamil Koç and Pamukkale. Many other more regional companies offer varying levels of service, some quite good, others less so.

The Otogar

Most Turkish cities and towns have a central bus terminal called variously *otogar, otobüs garajı, otobüs terminalı, santral garaj* or *şehir garajı* (city garage). In each city, I'll use the term the locals use. Besides intercity buses, the otogar often handles minibuses to outlying districts or villages. Otogars are often equipped with their own PTT branches, telephones with an international service, restaurants, snack stands, pastry shops, tourism information booths and left-luggage offices (*emanet*).

İstanbul has several mammoth garages; Ankara and İzmir each have a mammoth one. Bus companies aiming at the high-class trade may have their own small, private terminals in other parts of town, to save their privileged patrons the hassle of dealing with large crowds at the main terminal. These are mentioned in the text where appropriate.

A few small towns have only a collection of bus line offices rather than a proper terminal.

Buying Tickets

Though you can often just walk into an otogar and buy a ticket for the next bus out, it's wise to plan ahead. At the least, locate the companies' offices and note the times for your destination a day in advance. This is especially important along the south coast, where long-distance bus traffic is less frequent than in some other parts of the country.

Some bus companies will grant you a reduction on the fare if you show your ISIC student card. This may not be official policy, but just an excuse for a reduction – in any case you win.

The word for 'tomorrow', very handy to know when buying bus tickets a day in advance, is *yarın* (YAHR-uhn). Bus departure times will be given using the 24-hour clock system, eg 18.30 instead of 6.30 pm.

When you enter an otogar you'll see lots of people and baggage, buses and minibuses, plus rows of little ticket offices. Touts will invariably approach asking where you're bound. Competition on some routes is stiff. In most cases, more than one company will run to your desired destination; the cities and towns served by the company will be written prominently at that company's ticket office. Let the touts lead you to the office they work for, but then check other ticket offices, asking when the company's next bus leaves.

Seat Selection It's very important that you plan your seat strategy rather than leave it up to the ticket seller. All seats are reserved, and your ticket will bear a specific seat number. The ticket agent often has a chart of the seats in front of him, with those already sold crossed off. Look at the chart, and indicate your seating preference.

Preferable seats are in the middle of the bus (that is, not right over the wheels, which can be bumpy), and also on the side which will not get the full sun. However, unless you absolutely adore inhaling cigarette smoke, you may prefer to seize one of the front seats (Nos 1 to 4) near the driver's open window, perhaps the only fresh-air source on the bus. The problem with the front seats, however, is that they are most vulnerable in case of a traffic accident. Some buses now have *sigarasız* (no smoking) sections, and some companies (usually the premium ones such as Ulusoy and Varan) operate no-smoking buses on some routes. Ask.

Bus seat configurations are not uniform, but here are some hints. On the Mercedes 0302 bus, avoid if possible the front rows over the wheels and the last three rows (usually Nos 33 to 43); seats Nos 9 to 28 are the best, but on the shady side. On the single-deck Neoplan bus, wheel seats are Nos 5 to 8 and Nos 33 to 36; Nos 31 to 32 are right by the rear door, and Nos 45 to 48 are right on top of the motor. Avoid these. On the double-decker Neoplan bus, lower deck seats are Nos 53 to 72; you should avoid wheel seats Nos 57 to 60, and rear seats Nos 69 to 72; all of the upper deck seats are good, though Nos 31 to 36 and Nos 39 to 40 are next to the door.

Turks, it seems, are constitutionally opposed to air draughts of any strength, even on a sweltering hot day. Even if the ventilation or air-con system of the bus is excellent, it may not be turned on. 'Better to swelter than take any chance of sitting in a draught' is the Turkish rule. Thus you must choose your seat with care, keeping the glare of the hot midday sun in mind. On a four-hour summer afternoon trip from Ankara to Konya, for instance, you'll be too warm if you're on the right-hand (western) side of the bus, while the seats on the left (eastern) side will remain comfortable.

You can also join in my fresh-air campaign. Summon the *yardımcı* (assistant, also called the *muavin*) and say *çok sıcak!* ('choke' suh-jahk, 'It's very hot'). Indicate the ventilation system and say *Havalandırma açın!* (hah-vah-lahn-duhr-MAH ah-chun, 'Open the ventilation system'). If you can't manage that, just point to it here, in the book, and let the yardımcı read it. Sometimes this works.

Once you've bought a ticket, getting a refund can be difficult, though it's possible. Exchanges for other tickets within the same company are easier.

About Bus Travel

A bus trip in Turkey is usually a fairly pleasant experience if it's not too long. Buses are big, modern and comfortable. As Turks are great cigarette smokers, you may encounter a significant amount of smoke on the trip. Passengers in the seats near you will offer you cigarettes as an ice-breaker, hoping to strike up a conversation. There's no stigma in refusing. Say *Hayır, teşekkür ederim, içmem* ('No, thank you, I don't smoke') or, if this is a mouthful, just *İçmem* (eech-MEHM) with a smile. Turks, like most people, think it laudable that someone doesn't smoke (or has given up smoking). Besides, the offer was intended as a politeness, a welcome and a conversation opener. It serves this purpose whether you smoke or not.

On the subject of cigarette smoke, please join my crusade (holy war?) against smoke-filled buses. Whenever you buy an intercity bus ticket in Turkey, ask for a *sigara içilmez otobüsü* (see-GAH-rah ee-cheel-MEHZ oh-toh-bur-sur, a 'no smoking' bus). Most of your enquiries will elicit a sad smile and a *maalesef* ('unfortunately...'), indicating that there aren't any no-smoking buses on that route yet. But Turks are quick to recognise demand for a service, and future travellers may not have to suffer so much.

Once en route, your fellow passengers will be curious about where you come from, what language you speak, and how you're enjoying the country. Openers may be in German. It's polite to exchange at least a few sentences.

Shortly after you head out, the yardımcı/muavin will come through the bus with a bottle of lemon cologne with which to refresh his *sayın yolcular* (honoured passengers). He'll dribble some cologne into your cupped hands, which you then rub together, and then rub on your face and hair, ending with a sniff to clear your nasal passages. You may not be used to the custom, but if you ride buses in Turkey much you will get used to it quickly, and probably love it.

If you want a bottle of cool spring water at any time during the trip, just signal to the yardımcı and ask *Su, lütfen* ('Water, please'). There's no charge.

Stops will be made every 1½ hours or so for the toilet, snacks or meals and the inevitable çay. At some stops boys rush onto the bus selling sweets, nuts, sandwiches and the like, or a waiter from the teahouse (buses always stop at a teahouse) may come through to take orders. Most people, however, welcome the chance to stretch their legs.

Keep your bus ticket until you reach your absolutely final destination. In some cases, companies have *servis arabası* (sehr-VEES ah-rah-bah-suh, service cars) – a minibus service that will shuttle you from the bus station into the city at no extra charge, provided you can show a ticket for the company's line.

You can save money by taking night buses on long hauls (eight or 10 hours or more). Cigarette smoke will be less, the bus will be cooler, and you will save money on a hotel room. You miss the scenery, though.

Dolmuş or Minibus

A dolmuş (DOHL-moosh, 'filled') is a Turkish minibus *(minibüs* or *münübüs)*, Fiat taxi, or huge old US car serving as a jitney cab. A dolmuş departs as soon as every seat (or nearly every seat) is taken. You can catch one from point to point in a city, or from village to village, and in some cases from town to town. Though dolmuşes on some routes operate like buses by selling tickets in advance (perhaps even for reserved seats), the true dolmuş does not. Rather, it is parked at the point of departure (a town square, city otogar or beach) and waits for the seats to fill up. The dolmuş route may be painted on the side of the minibus, or on a sign posted next to the dolmuş, or in its window; or a hawker may call out the destination.

When the driver is satisfied with the load, the dolmuş heads off. Fares are collected en route or at the final stop. Often the fare is posted on the destination sign, whether it's on a signpost or in the vehicle's window. If it's not, watch what other passengers to your destination are paying and pay the same, or ask. Though passengers to intermediate stops sometimes pay a partial fare, on other routes the driver (or the law) may require that you pay the full fare. In either case, prices are low, though slightly more than for a bus on the same route.

Here are some rules of dolmuş etiquette. If your stop comes before the final destination, you may do some shuffling to ensure that you are sitting right by the door and not way up the back. Also, a woman is expected to choose a side seat, not a middle seat between two men, for her own comfort and 'protection'. If a man and a woman passenger get into the front of a car, for instance, the man should get in first and sit by the driver (contrary to everything his mother taught him about letting the lady go first), so that the woman is between 'her' man and the door. This is not a gesture against women, but rather the opposite, to show respect for their honour.

Collection of fares will begin after the car starts off, and the driver will juggle and change money as he drives. This thrilling practice costs no extra. If you're still not sure about your fare, hand over a bill large enough to cover the fare but small enough not to anger the driver, who will never have enough change and will not want a large bill. Should there be any doubt about fares or problem in payment (rare), you can always settle up at the last stop.

To signal the driver that you want to get out, say İnecek var. Other useful words are durun (DOOR-oon, 'stop') and burada (BOO-rah-dah, 'here').

TRAIN

Turkish State Railways (TC Devlet Demiryolları, TCDD or DDY) runs services to many parts of the country, on lines laid out by German companies which were supposedly paid by the km. But some newer, more direct lines have been laid during the republican era, shortening travel times for the best express trains.

It's not a good idea to plan a train trip all the way across Turkey in one stretch. Turkey is a big country, and the cross-country trains are a lot slower than the buses. The Vangölü Ekspresi from İstanbul to Lake Van (Tatvan), a 1900-km trip, takes almost two full days, for example – and that's an express! The bus would take less than 24 hours. Train travel between Ankara, İzmir and İstanbul is another matter, however. The top trains on these lines are a pleasure to ride on, whether by night or day.

Whenever you take an intercity train in Turkey, you'd do well to take only mavi tren (blue train), ekspres or mototren trains. These are fairly fast, comfortable, and often not too much more expensive than the more

Logo of the TCDD – the Turkish State Railways

cramped and smoky (but often faster) bus. Yolcu (passenger) and posta (mail) trains, however, are laughably slow and dilapidated, and should be avoided by all but sociologists wanting a long and intimate look at Turkish country life.

Note that Turkish train schedules indicate stations, not cities; the station name is usually, but not always, the city name. Thus you may not see İstanbul on a schedule, but you will see Haydarpaşa and Sirkeci, the Asian and European stations in İstanbul. For İzmir, the stations are Basmane and Alsancak. I'll mention the station names in this guide where appropriate.

Top Trains

Full information on trains is given in Getting There & Away for each city section, but here are the top trains running to the three major cities. Note that construction will soon begin on a high-speed railway between İstanbul and Ankara. Plans are to link Haydarpaşa and Sirkeci stations with a tunnel beneath the Bosphorus.

Fatih Ekspresi The pride of the Turkish State Railways, this train named for Mehmet the Conqueror (Fatih) is an air-conditioned super-1st-class day train between İstanbul (Haydarpaşa) and Ankara with Pullman seats, video, and meals served at your seat, airline-style. It leaves each city at 10.30 am, arriving in the other city before 6 pm, which is faster than most buses.

route	full fare	sleeping car fare	student fare	return fare
Ankara-Adana	$10	$22-$28	$8	$16
Ankara-Erzurum	$12.50	$27-$35	$9	$20
Ankara-İstanbul	$10.50-$13	$25-$35	$7-$10	$15-$20
Ankara-İzmir	$11-$12	$27-$35	$9-$10	$17-$20
İstanbul-Edirne	$5	–	$4	$8.50
*İstanbul-İzmir	$10	–	$8	$20

(All fares are in US dollars.) *This is the full fare for the entire journey by (top) train and boat.

İstanbul-Ankara Mavi Tren This is a daily 1st-class express between Ankara and İstanbul (Haydarpaşa). The journey takes about eight hours. The train departs from each city at 1.30 pm, arriving before 10 pm, and departing at 11 pm, arriving the next morning just after 8 am. It's a bit faster than the bus, more expensive and more comfortable.

Anadolu Ekspresi This nightly sleeping-car, couchette and coach train between Ankara and İstanbul (Haydarpaşa) takes about 9½ hours. It departs from each city at 9.30 pm, and arrives the next morning at 7 am.

Ankara Ekspresi This nightly 1st-class all-sleeping-car train between Ankara and İstanbul (Haydarpaşa), takes about 9½ hours, and departs from each city at 10.20 pm, arriving the next morning at 7.43 am.

Marmara Ekspresi This twice-daily service covers the combined ferry-train route between İstanbul and İzmir: coach train between İzmir (Basmane) and Bandırma (5½ hours), boat with seats and cabins between Bandırma and İstanbul (four hours). It leaves each city at 9 am and 9 pm, arriving about 11 hours later. The boat-train transfer at Bandırma takes from one to two hours which, on the night run, takes place in the middle of the night. The fare includes both the train and boat portions of the trip.

İzmir Mavi Tren This nightly coach and sleeping car train between İzmir (Basmane) and Ankara departs after dinner and arrives in the late morning the next day, 14 to 15 hours later.

Buying Tickets
Most seats on the best trains, and all sleeping compartments, must be reserved. As the best trains are very popular, particularly the sleeping-car trains, you should make your reservation and buy your ticket as far in advance as possible. A few days will usually suffice, except at holiday times (see The Calendar in the When to Go section of the Facts for the Visitor chapter). Weekend trains, between Friday evening and Monday morning, seem to be busiest.

If you can't buy in advance, check at the station anyway. There may be cancellations, even at the last minute.

Though Turkish State Railways now has a computerised reservations system, it is usually impossible to book sleeping-car space except in the city from which the train departs. You can buy tickets at the railway station, at many PTTs (post offices) in the major cities, and at certain travel agencies (these are mentioned in the text).

Turkish words useful in the railway station are given in the Turkish Language Guide at the back of this book.

Classes of Travel Most of the best trains, and the short-haul *mototrens* and rail-buses now have only one class of travel. Coaches on the top trains (*Fatih Ekspresi, Mavi Tren*) usually have Pullman reclining seats; the normal expresses usually have European-style compartments with six seats. The very slow trains and those in the east often have

1st and 2nd-class coaches with compartments.

Sleeping accommodation is of three classes. A *kuşetli* (couchette) wagon has six-person compartments with seats which rearrange into six shelf-like beds at night; you sleep with strangers. *Örtülü kuşetli* means the couchettes have bedding (sheets, pillows, blanket), and there may be only four beds per compartment, so two couples travelling together can get an almost private compartment. A *yataklı* wagon has European-style sleeping compartments capable of sleeping up to three people. Price depends upon the number of occupants: per person cost is lowest when three share, highest if you want a compartment all to yourself.

Discounts & Passes Inter-Rail passes are valid on the Turkish State Railways' entire network; Eurail passes are not valid on any of it.

Full fare is called *tam*. Round-trip (return) fares, called *Gidiş-Dönüş*, are discounted by 20%. Student *(öğrenci* or *talebe)* fares discounted by 20 to 30% are offered on most routes (show your ISIC). If you are under 26 years of age or over 55, you can buy a Tren-Tur card which allows you one month's unlimited rail travel. Ask at Sirkeci Station in İstanbul, or at the station in Ankara. Families *(aile)* travelling together are entitled to a 20 to 30% discount; disabled persons get 30% off, press card holders 30% off.

Cancellation Penalties If you decide not to travel and you seek a refund for your rail ticket up to 24 hours before the train's departure, you must pay a cancellation fee of 10% of the ticket price. Within 24 hours of departure the fee rises to 25%. After the train has departed the fee is 50%.

Fares

Normal train fares are cheaper than or the same as bus fares for the same journey; the top trains are usually a bit more expensive than the bus. Train fares are set by the railway bureaucracy, however, and are not revised as frequently as bus fares. Thus with the creeping devaluation of the lira, you may find trains cheaper than buses if you ride several months after the last price-fixing.

The table shows fares (in US dollars) on the top trains. The low sleeping-car fare is for a berth in a shared three-bed compartment; highest is for a private compartment.

BOAT

Turkish Maritime Administration (Türkiye Denizcilik İşletmeleri), also called Turkish Maritime Lines (TML) operates car and passenger ferry services from İstanbul eastward along the Black Sea coast and southward along the Aegean coast, as well as passenger services in the Sea of Marmara and shuttle services across the Dardanelles and the Bay of İzmit.

Ferry

Car and passenger ferries save you days of driving. Even if you have no car, they offer the opportunity to take mini-cruises along the Turkish coasts. Room on these ships is usually in hot demand, so reserve as far in advance as possible through one of TML's agents (see below), or directly with the İstanbul Karaköy office by fax.

İstanbul to İzmir The overnight car ferries running between İstanbul and İzmir (19 hours) demand advance reservations for both car space and cabins. Schedules are like this: Friday departure from İstanbul at 3 pm, arriving in İzmir on Saturday at 9 am; departing from İzmir on Sunday at 2 pm, arriving in İstanbul on Monday at 9 am, year round. In high summer, extra trips are added on Monday and Wednesday from İstanbul departing at 2 pm, Tuesday and Thursday from İzmir departing at 2 pm; arrivals are at 9 am the next morning.

Fares range from US$20 for a Pullman reclining seat to US$80 per person in the most luxurious cabin. You can turn the trip into a mini-cruise by staying aboard and using the ship as your hotel in İzmir for a night, then returning to İstanbul. The extra charge for this night in port is 80% of the regular fare. Meals cost extra, about US$3 for breakfast, and US$8 for lunch or dinner. The fare for a car is US$35; it's US$12 for a motorcycle.

İstanbul to Trabzon Car ferries operate each week from late May to September, departing from İstanbul on Monday at 3.30 pm, stopping briefly in Zonguldak and Sinop, arriving in Samsun on Tuesday at 7.30 pm and departing at 10.30 pm, arriving in Trabzon on Wednesday at 11.30 am. The boat continues to Rize, returning to Trabzon and departing on the return voyage to İstanbul at 7.30 pm. The returning ferry stops briefly at Giresun and Ordu, arrives in Samsun on Thursday at 12.30 pm, departs at 1.30 pm, stops briefly in Sinop, and arrives in İstanbul on Friday at 3 pm.

Per-person fares between İstanbul and Trabzon are US$26 for a Pullman seat, US$34 to US$75 for cabin berths. Cars cost US$40; motorcycles, US$10.

İstanbul to Bursa If you're headed from İstanbul to Bursa, you'll doubtless want to take the speedy and enjoyable hydrofoil trip across the Sea of Marmara and the Bay of İzmit to Yalova, where you catch the bus for İznik or Bursa. Details of this route are given in the South of the Sea of Marmara chapter.

There is also a car ferry service every half hour between Gebze (Eskihisar docks), on the coast east of Üsküdar, and Topçular, east of Yalova on the Sea of Marmara's southern shore. A similar car ferry shuttles between Hereke and Karamürsel, farther east. The drive (or bus ride) east around the Bay of İzmit is long, boring, congested and the scenery's ugly. Take one of these ferries instead.

Sea of Marmara Services
Turkish State Railways and TML team up to provide an inexpensive and enjoyable ride between İstanbul and İzmir on the *Marmara Ekspresi* boat-train. See the previous Top Trains section of this chapter.

You can take just the boat portion if you like. Departures from İstanbul are at 9 am

and 9 pm, reaching the port of Bandırma about four hours later.

TML operates other services which link İstanbul with the Marmara ports and islands of İmralı, Armutlu, Mudanya, Asmalı, Avşa and Marmara. Other services run from the island of Gökçeada (Imbros), west of Gallipoli, to the Dardanelles port of Çanakkale, and to the Gallipoli peninsula at Kabatepe.

DRIVING
Having your own car in Turkey, whether owned or rented, gives you unparalleled freedom to enjoy the marvellous countryside and coastline. If you can manage it, car travel in Turkey is rewarding despite the draw-backs.

In theory, Turks drive on the right and yield to traffic approaching them from the right. In practice, Turks drive in the middle and yield to no person. You must accustom yourself to drivers overtaking you on blind curves. If a car approaches from the opposite direction, all three drivers stand on their brakes and trust to Allah.

The international driving signs are erected, but rarely observed. Speed limits, for the record, are 50 km/h in towns, 90 km/h on highways, unless otherwise posted.

As there are only a few divided highways and many two-lane roads are serpentine, you must reconcile yourself to spending some hours sniffing the stinky diesel exhaust of pokey, seriously overladen trucks. At night you will encounter cars without lights or with lights missing; vehicles stopped in the middle of the road; and oncoming drivers who play inscrutable light games, flashing and flashing whether you have your 'brights' on or not.

Driving Permits
You don't really need an International Driving Permit (IDP) when you drive in Turkey, despite what some travel books say. Your home driving licence, unless it's something unusual (say, from Upper Volta), will be accepted by traffic police and by car rental firms. If you'd feel more secure against

bureaucratic hassle by carrying an IDP, you can get one through your automobile club in your home country.

Road Safety

The quality of Turkish highways is passable. The Türkiye Cumhuriyeti Karayolları (Turkish Republic Highways Department or TCK) undertakes ambitious improvements constantly, but despite its efforts most roads still have only two lanes, perhaps with overtaking lanes on long uphill grades. Expressways/motorways are to be found mostly near the four largest cities; a new toll motorway now connects İstanbul and Ankara. In eastern Turkey, with its severe winter weather, roads are easily destroyed by frost, and potholes are a tyre-breaking nuisance any time of year.

The major commerce routes (E5, E24) are often busy but not impossible; the lesser highways can be pleasantly traffic-free. City streets are usually thronged.

Turkish drivers are not particularly discourteous out on the highway, but give the impression of being inexperienced and incautious: they drive at high speed; they simply must overtake you whatever the cost; and, most regrettably, they believe absolutely in *kısmet* (fate). If a Turkish driver, careening along a slippery highway in a car with smooth tyres and the accelerator pedal flat to the floor and their mind engaged in heated conversation, swerves to avoid an errant sheep and crashes into a tree, that's kısmet, and it can't be helped. Moderating speed, getting better tyres or paying attention to the road are not really possible options, as kısmet will get you if it's going to, no matter what you do. So why bother?

In the cities *düzensizlik* – disorder resulting from illogic and discourtesy – is universal. In addition to the customary and very appropriate *Allah Korusun* ('May God Protect Me') emblazoned somewhere on every Turkish car, bus and truck, imagine the additional motto *Önce Ben* ('Me First').

To survive Turkish driving, drive very defensively, avoid driving at night, and *never* let emotions affect what you do.

Fuel

Fuel stations are everywhere, operated by some familiar international companies (BP, Shell, Mobil) and unfamiliar Turkish ones (Türk Petrol, Petrol Ofisi). Many never close, others stay open long hours, so refuelling is usually no problem. All the same, it's a good idea to have a full tank when you start out in the morning across the vast spaces of central and Eastern Anatolia.

Benzin (gasoline/petrol) comes as *normal, süper* and *kurşunsuz* (the last being unleaded, which is not found easily outside the major cities and the heavily touristed western region). Normal costs about 70c per litre (US$2.65 per US gallon); süper, about 80c per litre (US$3.02 per US gallon); kurşunsuz, about 85c per litre (US$3.21 per US gallon). *Dizel* (diesel) costs about 55c per litre (US$2.08 per US gallon).

Spares & Repairs

Turkey's equivalent of the Automobile Association (UK) and American Automobile Association (USA) is the Türkiye Turing ve Otomobile Kurumu (TTOK), the Turkish Touring & Automobile Association (☎ (1) 240 7127, 231 4631; fax 248 9661), Halaskargazi Caddesi 364, Şişli, İstanbul. It is useful mostly for driving aids (maps, lists of repair shops, legal necessities) rather than for repairs.

Spare parts for most cars may be available, if not readily so, outside the big cities. European models (especially Renaults, Fiats and Mercedes-Benz) are preferred, though ingenious Turkish mechanics contrive to keep all manner of huge US models – some half a century old – in daily service.

If you have a model with which Turkish mechanics are familiar (such as a Mercedes, simple Renault or Fiat) repairs can be swift and very cheap. Don't be afraid of little roadside repair shops, which can often provide excellent, virtually immediate service, though they (or you) may have to go somewhere else to get the parts. It's always good to get an estimate of the repair cost in advance. Ask *Tamirat kaç para?* ('How much will repairs cost?'). For tyre repairs find a *lâstikçi* (tyre-repairer). Repair shops are closed on Sunday, but even so, if you go to the repair shop district of town (every town has one) and look around, you may still find someone willing and able to help you out.

Traffic Police

Police in black-and-white cars (usually Renaults) and green uniforms with white peaked caps set up checkpoints on major highways in order to make sure that vehicle documents are in order, that you are wearing your seatbelt, and that vehicle safety features are in working condition. They busy themselves mostly with trucks and buses, and will usually wave you on, but you should slow down and prepare to stop until you get the wave.

If you are stopped, officers may ask for your car registration, insurance certificate and driving licence. They may ask you to turn on your headlights (high and low beam), hoot your horn, switch on your turning signals and windscreen wipers etc, to see that all are working properly. They'll certainly ask your nationality, and try to chat, because one of the reasons you've been stopped was to break the monotony of checking trucks by throwing in a curious foreigner.

Car Rental

Renting a car is expensive, but gives you wonderful freedom. If you share the cost among several people, renting can be reasonable.

Minimum age is generally 19 years for the cheaper cars, 24 for some larger cars, and 27 for the best. You must have a major credit card to pay with, or you will be required to make a large cash deposit.

Cars may be rented in Adana, Alanya, Ankara, Antalya, Bodrum, Bursa, Çeşme, Dalaman, Gaziantep, İstanbul, İzmir, Kuşadası, Marmaris, Mersin, Samsun, Side and Trabzon from the larger international rental firms (Avis, Budget, Dollar, Europcar, Hertz, Inter-Rent, Kemwel, National) or from smaller local ones. Avis has the most extensive and experienced network of agen-

cies and staff, and the highest prices. Some firms will be happy to deliver your car to another place, or arrange for pick-up, at no extra charge; others will charge you.

You should not be afraid to try (with caution) one of the small local agencies. Though there is no far-flung network for repairs and people in theses places have little fluency in English; they are friendly, helpful and charge from 10 to 20% less than the large firms, particularly if you're willing to haggle a bit.

The most popular rental cars are the Fiat 124 (Serçe), a small four-passenger car with limited space and power; Fiat 131 (Şahin), more powerful and comfortable; Fiat 131SW (Kartal), more powerful and comfortable; and Fiat Mirafiori (Doğan), big enough for five. Of the Renaults, the 12TX is similar to the Fiat 131, but more economical with fuel; the Renault 9 is larger and more powerful, the 12 STW, better still. All of these cars have standard gear shift. Only the most expensive cars (big Fords, Mercedes etc) have automatic transmission and air-conditioning.

Costs Rental cars are very expensive in Turkey, partly due to huge excise taxes paid when the cars are purchased. Total costs of a rental arranged on the spot in Turkey during the busy summer months, for a week with unlimited km, including full insurance and tax, might be from US$400 to US$700. If you reserve a car in advance from your home country, however, prices may be significantly lower. Ask your travel agent to shop around, or to set up a fly-drive arrangement. Renting from the USA, friends of mine recently found that Kemwel had the lowest prices, but this may change.

If you rent from abroad, the Collision Damage Waiver (CDW) is usually included in the all-inclusive price quoted to you. Those with credit cards (to which collision damage in rental cars can be charged) who might not normally pay for this, thus end up paying for it. Even so, you will end up saving perhaps as much as 20 or 25%. The CDW is not a bad thing to have, because a renter is liable not merely for damage, but for rental revenue lost while the car is being repaired or, in the case of a stolen car (uncommon in Turkey), until the car is recovered. Note that in most cases you do not need the personal injury insurance, as your health insurance from home should cover any medical costs.

As for fuel, you'll pay about 65c per litre for fuel (US$2.30 per US gallon, UK£1.60 per imperial gallon). The fuel cost to operate a small car is about 9c per km.

When you look at a rental company's current price list, keep in mind that the daily or weekly rental charge is only a small portion of what you will actually end up paying, unless it includes unlimited km. The charge for km normally ends up being higher, per day, than the daily rental charge. By the way, VAT (KDV) should be included in the rental, insurance and km prices quoted to you. It should not be added to your bill.

Safety & Accidents Child safety seats are usually available from the larger companies if you order them at least 48 hours in advance. Rental costs about US$5 per day.

If your car incurs any damage at all, or if you cause any, do not move the car before finding a police officer and asking for a *kaza raporu* (accident report). The officer may ask you to submit to an alcohol test. Contact your car rental company within 48 hours. Your insurance coverage may be void if it can be shown that you were operating under the influence of alcohol or other drugs, were speeding, or if you did not submit the required accident report within 48 hours.

Any traffic fines you incur will be charged to you. Normally, the company charges your credit card.

Car rental insurance does not normally pay for breakage of windscreens or headlights, or puncture or theft of a spare tyre or other equipment. If you encounter these misfortunes, it's usually best and cheapest to arrange for repair or replacement yourself, en route.

MOTORCYCLE
Motorcycles and mopeds are becoming more popular in Turkey because they are cheaper

to buy and to run than cars. These days, Austrian and German mopeds are the popular items. Motorcycles tend to be large old Czechoslovak Jawa models that make a distinctive hollow putt-putt sound.

You can bring your motorcycle to Turkey and have a fine time seeing the country. Spare parts will probably be hard to come by, so bring what you may need, or rely on the boundless ingenuity of Turkish mechanics to find, adapt or make you a part. Or else be prepared to call home, have the part flown in, and endure considerable hassles from customs.

BICYCLE
Though Turks use bicycles primarily as utilitarian vehicles to go short distances, long-distance bicycling for sport is being introduced by European tourists, mostly Germans with mountain bikes. You can cycle pleasurably through Turkey if you plan ahead, pick your routes carefully and avoid certain perils.

The pleasures are in the spectacular scenery, the friendly people, the easy access to archaeological sites and the ready availability of natural camping sites both official and unofficial. The best routes are those along the coasts, particularly the western Mediterranean coast between Marmaris and Antalya. You may be wheeling merrily along, overtaken by a truck loaded with fruit, and handed some on the run by the laughing children who have just picked it.

The perils are more specific. Road conditions are not ideal. The road surface, particularly on the newer roads, is of rough limestone and marble chips. Turkish car and bus drivers tend to believe more in kısmet (fate) than in good driving to protect them; truck drivers are usually more reasonable, if only because their heavily overladen vehicles can't go very fast. *Every* driver will hoot at you (this is safe but annoying). Maps available in Turkey are sometimes incorrect on such things as grades and altitudes, so search out a suitable map before leaving home.

As a cyclist, you may find your relations

with Turks somewhat extreme. Along the road, some children not used to cyclists may toss stones. This is often more of an annoyance than a danger, and as cyclists become more familiar sights it should subside. In hotels and pensions, and on those occasional bus and train rides, you may find people so accommodating and helpful in storing your valuable cycle 'safely' that lights, carriers and reflectors may get damaged unintentionally, so supervise and say *yavaş yavaş* (yah-VAHSH yah-VAHSH, 'slowly') frequently.

Whenever you stop for a rest or to camp, the rural staring squads of the curious will appear, instantly, as if by magic. You may find, like the royal family, that constant scrutiny, even if friendly, can be wearisome.

You can usually transport you bike by air, bus, train and ferry, sometimes at no extra charge.

Here are some tips on equipment and repairs. You cannot depend upon finding spare parts, so bring whatever you think you may need. Moped and motorcycle repair shops are often helpful, and if they can't do the repairs they will seek out someone who can. High-pressure pumps are not yet available in Turkey; fuel-station pumps may or may not go to 90 psi (high pressure). Inner tubes of 69 cm by three cm are available, but not everywhere; most of the tubes sold are larger, and they won't fit 69 cm by 2½ cm rims because of the large valve seat. Be prepared for frequent chain maintenance because of the effects of dust and mud.

HITCHING

When you hitchhike (*otostop*), Turkish custom requires that you offer to pay for your ride, though these days some drivers pick up foreign hitchers for the curiosity value. The amount is more or less equivalent to the bus fare on the same route. (Say *Borcum kaç?*, bohr-JOOM kahtch, 'How much do I owe you?' as you prepare to get out). Long-distance hitchhiking, though possible in Turkey, is not all that common. The bus and minibus network is so elaborate and cheap

that most people opt for that, figuring that if bus fare must be paid, bus comforts might as well be enjoyed. Private cars are not as plentiful as in Europe, and owners here are not as inclined to pick up hitchers.

Short-distance hitching is somewhat different. As the country is large and vehicles not so plentiful outside the towns, short-distance country hops are the norm. If you need to get from the highway (where the bus dropped you) into an archaeological site (Ephesus, Troy or wherever), you hitch a ride with whatever comes along. Again, private cars are the least amenable, but delivery vans, heavy machinery, oil tankers, farm tractors etc are all fair game. You should still offer to pay for the ride; in most cases your offer will be declined (though appreciated) because you are a 'guest' in Turkey.

The signal used in hitchhiking is not an upturned thumb. In Turkey, you face the traffic, hold your arm out towards the road, and wave your hand and arm up and down as though bouncing a basketball.

Women Hitchhikers

When it comes to women hitchhiking, Turkey is like the rest of the world, perhaps a bit more so: it is done, but you really should not do it, especially alone. A Turkish woman would rather die than hitchhike; she'd feel like she was offering herself to every man in every car that picked her up. With buses so cheap, why set yourself up for hassle?

Hitching as a couple is usually OK, but avoid vehicles with more than one or two men in them. Two women hitching together is preferable to one alone. If you're determined to hitch, take the normal precautions: don't accept a ride in a car or truck which is already occupied by men only (especially if it's only one man, the driver). Look for vehicles carrying women and/or children as well as men. Be appreciative and polite, but cool, dignified and formal, to the driver who picks you up. Avoid hitching across long, empty spaces, and never hitch at night. As for regional variances, you'll have the easiest time where foreigners and their strange customs are most familiar, naturally. The Aegean coast is the least dangerous. The further east you go, the more misunderstood you'll be.

LOCAL TRANSPORT
To/From the Airport
Transport to and from each airport in Turkey is covered within the section on each city.

Bus
Turkish cities have lots of buses, but they are usually crowded to capacity. Buses run by the city government often have *(city-name) belediyesi* (municipality) marked on them. Most municipal buses now work on a ticket system, and you must buy a ticket *(otobüs bileti,* or simply *bilet,* bee-LEHT) at a special ticket kiosk. These kiosks are at major bus termini or transfer points; some shops may sell them as well, and scalpers may hang around bus stops selling them for a marked-up price.

Dolmuş
Besides the previously mentioned intercity dolmuş system, a similar system exists within every town of any size. You'll find yourself using it frequently as it is usually faster, more comfortable and only slightly more expensive than the bus (and still very cheap). Intra-city dolmuş stops are near major squares, termini or intersections, and you'll have to ask: (name of destination) *dolmuş var mı?* (DOHL-mõosh VAHR muh). If you are in Laleli or Aksaray in İstanbul, for instance, and you want to get to Taksim Square, you ask, *Taksim dolmuş var mı?* Someone will point you to the dolmuş stop on Atatürk Bulvarı.

Often there is not a direct dolmuş route from where you are to where you're going. Maps of the system don't exist. If the person you ask seems to hem and haw, they're probably trying to tell you that you must take one dolmuş to a certain point, and then another.

Once you know a few convenient routes, you'll feel confident about picking up a dolmuş at the kerb. In the larger cities, stopping-places are regulated and sometimes

marked by signs with a black 'D' on a blue-and-white background reading *Dolmuş İndirme Bindirme Yeri* (Dolmuş Boarding and Alighting Place). You'll see minibuses, old US cars and new little Turkish-made cars stopping.

A true city dolmuş has a solid-colour band, usually yellow or black, painted horizontally around the car just below the windows. Sometimes taxis with a black and yellow chequered band operate like the dolmuş. You've got to be careful. If you climb into an empty car, the driver might assume (honestly, or for his own benefit) that you want a taxi, and he will charge you the taxi fare. Always ask, *Dolmuş mu?* (dohl-MOOSH moo? 'Is this a dolmuş?') when you climb into an empty car.

You'll get the hang of the dolmuş way of life after only a few days in Turkey, and will find it very useful.

Taxi
Most taxis in most cities have digital meters, and they use them. If yours doesn't, mention it right away by saying, *Saatiniz* (saa-AHT-EE-NEEZ, 'Your meter'). The starting rate is about 70c, more late at night. The average taxi ride costs from US$2 to US$3 during the day time, more at night.

With the flood of tourists arriving in Turkey, some taxi drivers – especially İstanbul's many crooks-on-wheels – have begun to demand flat payment from foreigners. In some cases the driver will actually offer you a decent fare, and will then pocket all the money instead of giving the owner of the cab his share. But most of the time the driver will offer an exorbitant fare, give you trouble, and refuse to run the meter. City regulations against this sort of behaviour are strict, and the fines are huge, so drivers don't want to be caught at it. All the same, do you want to get into a guy's cab just after having chewed him out for illegal gouging? If you call the police, they'll probably smooth it over, and the driver will agree to take you to your destination, and you'll feel obliged to accept the offer, and then the driver will take you where you're going by way of the Paris suburbs, running up an astronomical fare. Perhaps the best course of action if you are asked to pay a flat fare is to find another cab.

Ferry

In İstanbul and İzmir, public transport is delightfully augmented by ferries. White with orange trim (the TML's colours), these sturdy craft steam up, down and across the Bosphorus and the Bay of İzmir, providing city dwellers with cheap, convenient transport, views of open water and (in summer) fresh cool breezes. They are not nostalgic transport toys but a real, even vital, part of each city's transport system. You should take the ferry in each city at least once, enjoying the cityscapes that are revealed from the decks, sipping a glass of fresh tea or a soft drink. The ferries can be crowded during rush hour but there's still lots of air and scenery; and while buses sit trapped in traffic the ferries glide through the water effortlessly, at speed.

In İstanbul, special daily ferry sailings on a touristic route.

TOURS

As Turkey's tourist boom continues, the number of companies offering guided tours of cities or regions expands apace. Along with legitimate operators, the sleazy ones are moving in, so you should be careful when choosing a tour company. The actual tour you get depends greatly on the competence, character and personality of your particular guide; but it's difficult to pick a tour by guide rather than company, so you must go by the tour company's reputation. The best course of action is to ask about at your hotel for recommendations. Other foreign visitors may be able to give you tips about which companies to use and which to avoid.

Watch out for the following rip-offs: a tour bus that spends the first hour or two of your 'tour' circulating through the city to various hotels, picking up tour participants; a tour that includes an extended stop at some particular shop (from which the tour company or guide gets a kickback); a tour that includes a lunch which turns out to be mediocre.

Most of the time, it is a lot cheaper and quicker to see things on your own by bus, dolmuş, or even taxi. Tours can cost from US$20 to US$40 per person; you may be able to hire a taxi and driver for the entire day for less than that, after a bit of haggling.

İstanbul

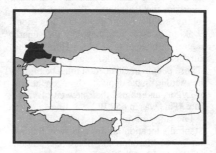

For many centuries this city was the capital of the civilised world. Even though Ankara became the capital of the newly proclaimed Turkish Republic in 1922, İstanbul continues to be the Turkish metropolis. It is the largest city (with almost 10 million residents), the business and cultural centre, the largest port and the first destination for tourists, Turkish or foreign.

In recent years İstanbul has yielded some of its pre-eminence to up-and-coming towns such as Ankara, İzmir and Antalya. However, it is still, without doubt, the heartbeat of the Turkish spirit. For Ankara (the up-tempo, 20th-century capital city) Turks feel pride, but it is İstanbul, the well-worn but still glorious metropolis, which they love. Its place in the country's history, folklore, commerce and culture is unchallenged.

No matter how you arrive in İstanbul, you'll be impressed. The train skirts the southern coast of the Thracian peninsula, following the city walls until it comes around Seraglio Point and terminates right below Topkapı Palace. The bus comes in along an expressway built on the path of the Roman road. From the bus station, you'll approach the city walls and pass through the Topkapı (Cannon Gate, not to be confused with the palace of the same name). Flying in on a clear day may reveal the great mosques and palaces, the wide Bosphorus (Boğaziçi) and the narrower Golden Horn (Haliç), in a wonderful panorama.

But nothing beats 'sailing to Byzantium' – gliding across the Sea of Marmara, watching the slender minarets and bulbous mosque domes rise on the horizon. Even Mark Twain, who certainly had control of his emotions, waxed rhapsodic in his *Innocents Abroad* on the beauties of arriving by sea. Today, though fumes from fossil fuels may obscure the view a bit, it's still impressive. (If you take the boat-train from İzmir via Bandırma, or the ferry from Bursa and Yalova, you'll approach the city by sea.)

İstanbul has grown ferociously in the past decade, and now sprawls westward as far as the airport, 23 km from the centre, northward halfway to the Black Sea, and eastward deep into Anatolia. It is crowded. The Bosphorus, the strait which connects the Black Sea and the Sea of Marmara, is more than 1.5 km wide, and the narrower Golden Horn, a freshwater estuary, also helps to preserve a sense of openness and space. More than that, the Bosphorus provides an uncrowded maritime highway for transport to various sections of the city. For several thousand years before the construction of the Bosphorus Bridge in 1973, the only way to go between the European and Asian parts of the city was by boat. The second Bosphorus bridge, named Fatih Köprüsü, north of the first one at Bebek/Beylerbeyi, was finished in 1988. A third bridge, farther north, is being built, and a metro is being developed.

As an introduction to Turkey and the Turks, İstanbul is something of a rich diet – too rich for some people. You might enjoy the city more if you come here after having first seen some smaller, more comprehensible and easily manageable Turkish town, such as Edirne (see the end of this chapter) or a port on the Aegean Sea.

HISTORY

İstanbul today is interesting as the Turkish

metropolis, but nobody visits just for that reason when the city is 3000 years old. The greatest part of the city's fascination comes from its place in history and from the buildings that remain from ancient times. Without knowing something of its history, a tour of İstanbul's ancient monuments will leave you impressed but bewildered.

Here's a quick summary of its past, so that you'll be able to distinguish a hippodrome from a harem.

1000-657 BC
Ancient fishing villages on this site
657 BC - 330 AD
Byzantium, a Greek city-state, later subject to Rome
330-1453 AD
Constantinople, the 'New Rome', capital of the Later or Eastern Roman ('Byzantine') Empire – reached its height in the 1100s
1453-1922
İstanbul, capital of the Ottoman Turkish Empire, which reached the height of its glory in the 1500s
1922-84
Ankara becomes the capital of the Turkish Republic. İstanbul continues to be the country's largest city and port, and its commercial and cultural centre.
1984 to the Present
İstanbul begins to enjoy a renaissance as 'capital of the East'. A new municipal government undertakes vast schemes to modernise and beautify the city, and to attract international business operations. New parks, museums and cultural centres are opened, old ones are restored and refurbished.

Early Times

The earliest settlement, Semistra, was probably around 1000 BC, a few hundred years after the Trojan War and in the same period that kings David and Solomon ruled in Jerusalem.

This was followed by a fishing village named Lygos, which occupied Seraglio Point where Topkapı Palace stands today. Later, around 700 BC, colonists from Megara (near Corinth) in Greece settled at Chalcedon (now Kadıköy) on the Asian shore of the Bosphorus.

Byzantium

The first settlement to have historic significance was founded by another Megarian colonist, a fellow named Byzas. Before leaving Greece, he asked the oracle at Delphi where he should establish his new colony. The enigmatic answer was 'Opposite the blind'. When Byzas and his fellow colonists sailed up the Bosphorus, they noticed the colony on the Asian shore at Chalcedon. Looking to their left, they saw the superb natural harbour of the Golden Horn, on the European shore. Thinking, as legend has it, 'Those people in Chalcedon must be blind', they settled on the opposite shore, on the site of Lygos, and named their new city Byzantium. This was in 657 BC.

The legend might as well be true. İstanbul's location on the waterway linking the Sea of Marmara and Black Sea, and on the 'land bridge' linking Europe and Asia, is still of tremendous importance today, 2600 years after the oracle spoke. The Megarian colonists at Chalcedon must certainly have been blind to have missed such a site.

Byzantium submitted willingly to Rome and fought Rome's battles for centuries, but finally got caught supporting the wrong side in a civil war. The winner, Septimius Severus, razed the city walls and took away its privileges in 196 AD. When he relented and rebuilt the city, he named it Augusta Antonina.

Constantinople

Another struggle for control of the Roman Empire determined the city's fate for the next 1000 years. Constantine pursued his rival Licinius to Augusta Antonina, then across the Bosphorus to Chrysopolis (Üsküdar). Defeating his rival in 324 AD, Constantine solidified his control and declared this city to be 'New Rome'. He laid out a vast new city to serve as capital of his empire, and inaugurated it with much pomp in 330 AD. The place which had been first settled as a fishing village over 1000 years earlier was now the capital of the world, and would remain so for almost another 1000 years.

The Later Roman, or Byzantine, Empire lasted from the re-founding of the city in 330 AD to the Ottoman Turkish conquest in 1453, an impressive 1123 years. Much remains of ancient Constantinople, and you'll be able to visit churches, palaces, cisterns and the Hippodrome during your stay. In fact, there's more of Constantinople left than anyone knows about. Any sort of excavation reveals streets, mosaics, tunnels, water and sewer systems, houses and public buildings. Construction of a modern building may be held up for months while archaeologists investigate. Rediscovering Byzantium, to a modern real-estate developer, is an unmitigated disaster.

The Conquest Westerners usually refer to 'The Fall of Constantinople', whereas to Muslims it was 'The Conquest of İstanbul'. Though the Byzantine Empire had been moribund for several centuries, the Ottomans were quite content to accept tribute from the weak Byzantine emperor as they progressively captured all the lands which surrounded his well-fortified city. By the time of the Conquest, the emperor had control over little more than the city itself and a few territories in Greece.

When Mehmet II, 'the Conqueror' *(Fatih)*, came to power in 1451 as a young man, he needed an impressive military victory to solidify his dominance of the powerful noble class. As the Ottomans controlled all of Anatolia and most of the Balkans by this time, it was obvious that the great city should be theirs. Mehmet decided it should be sooner rather than later.

The story of the Conquest is thrilling, full of bold strokes and daring exploits, heroism, treachery and intrigue. Mehmet started by readying the two great fortresses on the Bosphorus. Rumeli Hisar, the larger one, on the European side, was built in an incredibly short three months. Anadolu Hisar, the smaller one on the Asian side, had been built half a century earlier by Yıldırım Beyazıt, so Mehmet had it repaired and brought to readiness. Together they controlled the strait's narrowest point.

The Byzantines had closed the mouth of the Golden Horn with a heavy chain to prevent Ottoman boats from sailing in and attacking the city walls on the north side. In another bold stroke, Mehmet marshalled his boats at a cove (now covered by Dolmabahçe Palace) and had them transported overland on rollers and slides, by night, up the valley (where the Hilton now stands) and down the other side into the Golden Horn at Kasım Paşa. He caught the Byzantine defenders completely by surprise and soon had the Golden Horn under control.

The last great obstacle was the mighty bastion of the land walls on the western side. No matter how Mehmet's cannons battered them by day, the Byzantines would rebuild them by night, and the impetuous young sultan would find himself back where he started come daybreak. Then he received a proposal. A Hungarian cannon founder named Urban had come to offer his services to the Byzantine emperor, for the defence of Christendom, to repel the infidel. Finding that the emperor had no money, he went to Mehmet and offered to make the most enormous cannon ever. Mehmet, who had lots of money, accepted the offer, and the cannon was cast and tested in Edirne.

Sultan Mehmet II

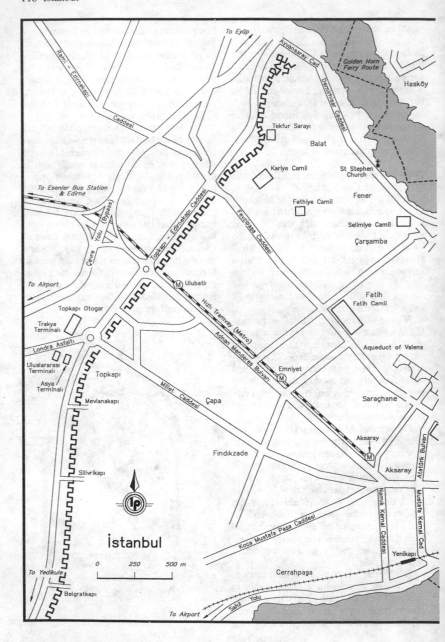

İstanbul

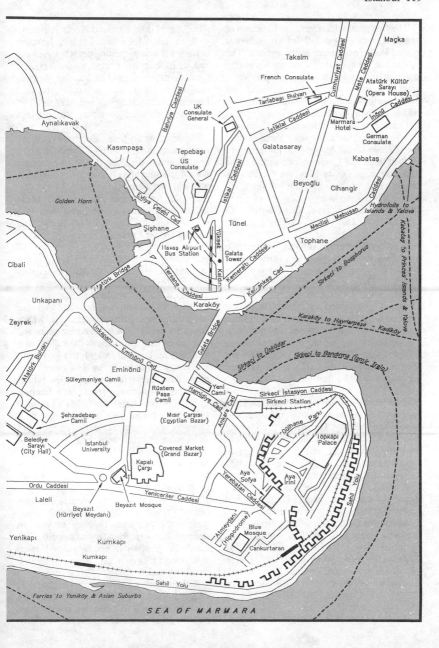

The first shot, which terrified hundreds of peasants, sent a huge ball 1.5 km, where it buried itself two metres in the ground. The jubilant sultan had his new toy transported to the front lines and set to firing. A special crew worked hours to ready it for each shot, for every firing wrecked the mount, and the gun had to be cooled with buckets of water.

Despite the inevitability of the Conquest, the emperor refused surrender terms offered by Mehmet on 23 May 1453, preferring to wait in hope that Christendom would come and save him. On 28 May the final attack began, and by the evening of the 29th Mehmet's troops were in control of every quarter. The emperor, Constantine XI Dragases, died in battle – fighting on the walls.

Mehmet's triumphant entry into 'the world's greatest city' on the evening of 29 May is commemorated every year in İstanbul. Those parts of the city which did not resist his troops were spared, and their churches guaranteed to them. Those that resisted were sacked for the customary three days, and the churches turned into mosques. As for Sancta Sophia, the greatest church in Christendom (St Peter's in Rome was not begun until 1506), it was converted immediately into a mosque.

The Ottoman Centuries Mehmet the Conqueror began at once to rebuild and repopulate the city. He saw himself as the successor to the glories and powers of Constantine, Justinian and the other great emperors who had reigned here. He built a mosque (Fatih Camii) on one of the city's seven hills, repaired the walls and made İstanbul the administrative, commercial and cultural centre of his growing empire.

Süleyman the Magnificent (1520-66) was perhaps İstanbul's greatest builder. His mosque, the Süleymaniye (1550), is İstanbul's largest. Other sultans added more grand mosques, and in the 19th century numerous palaces were built along the Bosphorus: Çirağan, Dolmabahçe, Yıldız, Beylerbeyi, Küçük Su.

As the Ottoman Empire grew to include all of the Middle East and North Africa as well as half of Eastern Europe, İstanbul became a fabulous melting pot. On its streets and in its bazaars, people spoke Turkish, Greek, Armenian, Ladino, Russian, Arabic, Bulgarian, Rumanian, Albanian, Italian, French, German, English and Maltese. The parade of national costumes was no less varied.

However, from being the most civilised city on earth in the time of Süleyman, the city and the empire declined. By the 19th century it had lost some of its former glory, though it was still the 'Paris of the East'. Its importance was reaffirmed by the first great international luxury express train ever run, which connected İstanbul with Paris – the famous *Orient Express*.

Republican İstanbul Atatürk's campaign for national salvation and independence was directed from Ankara. The founder of the Turkish Republic decided to get away from the imperial memories of İstanbul, and also to set up the new government in a city which could not easily be threatened by gunboats. Robbed of its importance as the capital of a vast empire, İstanbul lost a lot of its wealth and glitter. From being the East's most cosmopolitan place, it relaxed into a new role as an important national, rather than international, city. But during the 1980s it began to return to its former role. More liveable than Cairo or Beirut, more attractive than Tel Aviv, more in touch with the Islamic world than Athens, it is fast becoming the 'capital' of the eastern Mediterranean again.

ORIENTATION

It's a daunting prospect to arrive in a strange city of almost 10 million people whose language is a complete mystery to you. In general, Turks are friendly and helpful, even amidst the frustrations of a language barrier. It shouldn't take you long to get set up in a suitable hotel.

The first thing you'll see in İstanbul will be the impressive skyline of the Old City (Eski İstanbul). It will take you at least three days to get around and see the major sights.

You can easily spend a week at it, for İstanbul offers a great deal to see.

The sightseeing plan here is organised to show you the most important and accessible sights first, so you can see as much as possible in even a short time. If you have a week, you should be able to see just about everything described.

A glance at the map will show you that İstanbul is divided down the middle, from north to south, by the wide strait of the Bosphorus. The areas of prime attraction for hotels, restaurants and sightseeing are in the European (Avrupa) portion of the city, on the western shore of the Bosphorus.

European İstanbul is divided by the Golden Horn into the Old City to the south and Beyoğlu (BEY-oh-loo) to the north.

Eski İstanbul

The Old City is ancient Byzantium/Constantinople/İstanbul. It's here, from Seraglio Point (Sarayburnu) jutting into the Bosphorus to the mammoth land walls some seven km eastward, that you'll find the great palaces and mosques, hippodromes and monumental columns, ancient churches and the Covered Market. The Old City also harbours the best areas for inexpensive and moderate hotel choices: Laleli near Aksaray, and Sultanahmet.

When referring to the Old City, Turks usually mention the name of a particular district such as Sultanahmet, Aksaray or Beyazıt. They do not say Stamboul, as Europeans sometimes do. Nor do they use the term Old City – in Turkish this is Eskişehir which is also the name of a completely different municipality hundreds of km away in Anatolia. Get used to asking for a district, not for Stamboul.

Beyoğlu

North of the Golden Horn is Beyoğlu, the Turkish name for the two old cities of Pera and Galata, or roughly all the land from the Golden Horn to Taksim Square. Here is where you'll find the Hilton, the Sheraton, the Pera Palas and other luxury hotels; airline offices and banks; the European consulates

and hospitals; Taksim Square, the very hub of European İstanbul; and the 19th-century palace of Dolmabahçe.

Under the Byzantines, this was a separate city built and inhabited by Genoese traders. Called Galata then, it extended from the shore up to the Galata Tower, which still stands and which now serves as a convenient landmark. Galata is now usually called Karaköy (KAHR-ah-keuy).

Under the sultans, the non-Muslim European population of Galata spread up the hill and along the ridge, founding the sister city of Pera. In modern times this part of the city has been the fastest growing and has stretched far beyond the limits of old Galata and Pera. The name Beyoğlu still refers to just those two old cities.

Galata Bridge

One landmark you will get to know at once is the new Galata Köprüsü (Galata Bridge), opened in 1992 to replace the old Ottoman pontoon bridge. Connecting Karaköy with Eminönü (eh-MEEN-eu-neu), it is İstanbul's jugular vein, always packed with traffic and lively with activity. Views of the Old City, Beyoğlu, the Golden Horn and the Bosphorus are fantastic from the bridge.

Karaköy and Eminönü, by the way, are the areas from which Bosphorus ferries depart. The ferries from Karaköy go exclusively to Haydarpaşa Station and Kadıköy (a lighted signboard tells you which one is the destination); ferries from the Eminönü side go to Üsküdar and the Bosphorus. See Getting Around at the end of this chapter for more information.

Asia

The Asian part of the city, on the eastern shore of the Bosphorus, is of less interest to tourists, being mostly dormitory suburbs such as Üsküdar (EU-skeu-dahr, Scutari) and Kadıköy (KAH-duh-keuy). One landmark you'll want to know about is Haydarpaşa Station (Haydarpaşa İstasyonu), right between Üsküdar and Kadıköy. This is the terminus for Anatolian trains, which means any Turkish train except the one from Europe via Edirne. If you're headed for Ankara, Cappadocia or any point east of İstanbul, you'll board at Haydarpaşa.

INFORMATION
Tourist Offices
Ministry of Tourism offices are at Atatürk Airport (☎ 573 7399) in the international arrivals area, and at the western end of the Hippodrome in Sultanahmet Square (☎ 522 4903), near the Blue Mosque, Aya Sofya and Topkapı Palace (open from 9 am to 5 pm daily).

In Beyoğlu, there is an office at the Karaköy Yolcu Salonu (Karaköy International Maritime Passenger Terminal) (☎ 249 5776); another in the Hilton Hotel arcade (☎ 233 0592), just off Cumhuriyet Caddesi (open from 9 am to 5 pm, closed on Sunday), two long blocks north of Taksim Square on the right-hand side of the street. Yet another office is more or less across the street from the British Consulate-General at Meşrutiyet Caddesi 57, Tepebaşı (☎ 245 6875; fax 252 4346).

Automobile Club
The Turkish Touring & Automobile Association (☎ 231 4631), Halaskargazi Caddesi, Şişli, about two km north of Taksim, sells road maps and many books on Turkish history and culture, especially concerning İstanbul.

Money
For general information on banks, see the Money section in the Facts for the Visitor chapter. Remember that you can change money (preferably cash) at PTT branches; see Post for locations. Currency exchange booths at Atatürk Airport's international arrivals area are open whenever flights arrive.

İstanbul has a growing number of non-bank currency exchange offices, usually identifiable by the word *döviz* (foreign currency) in their names. They offer quick service, longer opening hours, no commission; they often have competitive rates, so you may want to use them in preference to banks.

Bamka Döviz (☎ 253 5500), Cumhuriyet Caddesi 23 near Aydede Caddesi, two blocks north of Taksim across the boulevard from Pizza Hut, is open every day from 8 am to 10 pm. A similar place is Turkom Döviz (☎ 232 0011), Cumhuriyet Caddesi 55, Elmadağ, a few short blocks farther north, across Cumhuriyet Caddesi from the Divan Oteli. Çetin Döviz (☎ 252 6428), İstiklal Caddesi 39, Beyoğlu, across from the French Consulate a block off Taksim, does not offer as good a rate as Bamka. The cheapest rate in town is at the döviz office on the west side of Şişli Meydanı, two km north of Taksim, but there's usually a long queue.

Post & Telecommunications
İstanbul's Main Post Office (*Merkez Postane*) is several blocks west of Sirkeci railway station on Yeni Postane Sokak. It's open daily from 8 am to 8 pm, though many services such as poste restante have more restricted hours and close at lunch time. The phone centre, however, is open until midnight. There are other convenient PTT branches near Taksim Square, on İstiklal Caddesi in Galatasaray, in Aksaray and in the Covered Market near the Havuzlu Lokantası.

Consulates
For details of the many consulates in İstanbul, see the Facts for the Visitor chapter.

Bookshops
In general, the place to find foreign-language books is in and around Tünel Square, at the southern end of İstiklal Caddesi.

Haşet Kitabevi (Hachette, ☎ 243 1343), İstiklal Caddesi 469, Tünel, Beyoğlu, has perhaps the best selection of French and English books and periodicals. Haşet has branches in several of the larger hotels, including the Hilton (in the arcade at the entrance and also inside the hotel) and the Divan. The big luxury hotels all have little bookshops or newsstands.

ABC Kitabevi, near Haşet at İstiklal

Caddesi 461, has mostly language-learning aids, but some other books as well. The nearby Metro Kitabevi (☎ 249 5827), İstiklal Caddesi 513, facing Tünel Square, sells guide books and maps.

For antiquarian booksellers, try the Narmanlı Han, İstiklal Caddesi 390, more or less across the street from Haşet. Also, walk down Galipdede Caddesi from Tünel towards the Galata Tower to the Librairie de Péra (Beyoğlu Kitapçılık, ☎ 245 4998) at No 141/5.

Redhouse Kitabevi (☎ 522 8100) at Rıza Paşa Yokuşu, Uzunçarşı, in the Old City down the hill from the Covered Market, publishes books in English and Turkish, including excellent guides and dictionaries. It has an English-language bookstore as well. You will find Redhouse books for sale in many English-language bookshops in Turkey.

Aypa (☎ 516 0100), Mimar Mehmet Ağa Caddesi 19, Sultanahmet, is just down the hill from Aya Sofya and the Blue Mosque on the way to the hotels and pensions of Cankurtaran. It has a good selection of guides, maps and magazines in English, French and German.

Sahaflar Çarşısı, the used-book bazaar, is great fun for browsing in. It's just west of the Covered Market across Çadırcılar Caddesi, sandwiched between that street and the Beyazıt Camii.

Laundry

If you don't do your own laundry, ask for prices at your hotel. The alternative is Hobby Laundry (☎ 513 6150), Caferiye Sokak 6/1, Sultanahmet, adjoining the Yücelt Interyouth Hostel and across the street from Aya Sofya. Posted hours are from 9 am to 8 pm every day, actual hours may be different. The charge is less than US$1 per kg to wash (minimum two kg), about 50c per kg to dry, but 'dry' means dampish. Attendants take your clothes and run the machines.

İstanbul has numerous dry-cleaning shops (kuru temizleme), usually open every day except Sunday from 8 am to 7 pm. Bring items in early for same-day service. In Laleli, try Universal Kuru Temizleme (☎ 511 6380), Ağa Yokuşu 16. Just two blocks westward uphill from the southern end of the Hippodrome in Sultanahmet is Doğu Expres (☎ 526 0725), Peykhane Sokak 61 (also called Üçler Sokak). In Tepebaşı, try Reforma Kuru Temizleme (☎ 243 6862), Meşrutiyet Caddesi 131, near the Büyük Londra Oteli. West of Taksim down the hill towards Dolmabahçe is Cevat Kuru Temizleme (☎ 249 0578), İnönü Caddesi 30.

Travel Agents

The most convenient travel agents are on the north side of Divan Yolu in Sultanahmet, and along Cumhuriyet Caddesi near Taksim between the Divan and Hilton hotels. For airline, bus and railway information, see the İstanbul Getting There & Away section at the end of this chapter.

Admission Hours & Days

Most museums are closed on Monday, but some – including the most important one of all, Topkapı Palace – are closed on Tuesday instead. Dolmabahçe Palace is closed on both Monday and Thursday at present, but I expect that this may change. The Covered Market (Kapalı Çarşı) is closed on Sunday.

Mosques are open every day. Avoid visiting mosques right after the call to prayer (wait 30 minutes) and on Friday morning (the Muslim sabbath), when congregations assemble for prayers and sermons.

Holders of an International Student Identity Card are admitted free or at reduced rates to sites controlled by the Ministry of Tourism and Ministry of Culture.

Emergency

In case of hassles, stolen or lost documents and the like, you might get some help from the Tourism Police (☎ 527 4503), Yerebatan Caddesi 2, Sultanahmet, across the street from Yerebatan Saray (the 'Sunken Palace' cistern). They have some multilingual staff and some experience with foreigners. The ordinary police (☎ 055 in an emergency) don't seem to be the right ones to call first.

For details of health concerns in Turkey,

see Health in the Facts for the Visitor chapter. You should contact your country's consulate in İstanbul or embassy in Ankara (see Visas & Embassies in the Facts for the Visitor chapter) for advice about suitable doctors, dentists, hospitals, and other medical care. İstanbul has several private hospitals which provide good quality care at low government-controlled prices. These include:

Amerikan Bristol Hastanesi, Güzelbahçe Sokak, Nişantaşı (☎ 231 4050), about two km north-east of Taksim, with US administration

Florence Nightingale Hospital, Abidei Hürriyet Caddesi 290, Çağlayan, Şişli (☎ 231 2021)

Intermed Check-up Centre, Teşvikiye Caddesi, Bayar Apt 143, Nişantaşı (☎ 234 5146)

International Hospital, İstanbul Caddesi 82, Yeşilyurt (☎ 574 7802; fax 573 4939)

La Paix Hastanesi, Büyükdere Caddesi 22-24, Şişli, (☎ 246 1020), with French administration

Alman Hastanesi, Sıraselviler Caddesi 119, Taksim (☎ 251 7100), a few hundred metres south of Taksim on the left-hand side, with German administration

OLD İSTANBUL

In the Old City, Topkapı Palace is right next to Aya Sofya, which is right next to the Blue Mosque, which is right on the Hippodrome, which is right next to the Cistern Basilica, which is only a few steps from the museum complex, which is right next to Topkapı Palace. You can spend at least two days just completing this loop. Start with the palace, which is among the world's great museums.

You can get there from Aksaray and Laleli by the free Aksaray-Sirkeci tram (tramvay) or on foot along Ordu Caddesi, which changes its name to Yeniçeriler Caddesi, and finally to Divan Yolu. From Taksim take a dolmuş or bus to Aksaray or Sirkeci and board the free tram, or walk. A taxi from Taksim to Sultanahmet costs about US\$3.

Topkapı Palace

Topkapı Sarayı (TOHP-kahp-uh, ☎ 512 0480) was the residence of the sultans for almost three centuries. Mehmet the Conqueror built the first palace shortly after the Conquest in 1453, and lived here until his death in 1481. Sultan after sultan played out the drama of the Ottoman sovereign here until the 19th century. Mahmut II (1808-39) was the last emperor to occupy the palace. After him, the sultans preferred to live in new European-style palaces – Dolmabahçe, Çirağan, Yıldız – which they built on the Bosphorus. Under the republic, the palace is Turkey's finest museum.

Topkapı Palace is open from 9.30 am to 5 pm, till 7 pm during July and August; closed on Tuesday. Admission to the palace costs US\$3, half-price for students; you will buy a separate ticket for the Harem (open from 10 am to 4 pm, US\$1.50) at the Harem entrance as you begin the tour.

I suggest that you head straight for the Harem when you enter the palace, note the tour times posted on the board by the entry, buy your ticket, and return in time to catch the next tour. In summer this may not work; the crowds are so thick and the tour groups so numerous that individual travellers sometimes are out of luck as the groups book all of the Harem tours in advance. I expect that in seasons to come the palace (and the Harem) will have to remain open on Tuesday in order to accommodate the crowds. Also, it may be possible to schedule a Harem tour with a private guide. The cost is about US\$10 for a group of six or so. Ask at the Harem ticket kiosk.

Foreigners called Topkapı the Seraglio, an Italian word. Mozart's famous opera Abduction from the Seraglio is performed in the palace every summer in late June-early July during the International İstanbul Festival.

It will take you the better part of a day to explore Topkapı Palace. You should be at the door when it opens if you plan to visit in the busy summer months. Though it's tempting to nip into Aya Sofya for a look as you go by on your way to Topkapı, I strongly recommend that you resist the urge. Aya Sofya has been there for 1500 years, and it will be there when you come out of Topkapı.

Court of the Janissaries Topkapı grew and changed with the centuries, but its basic four-

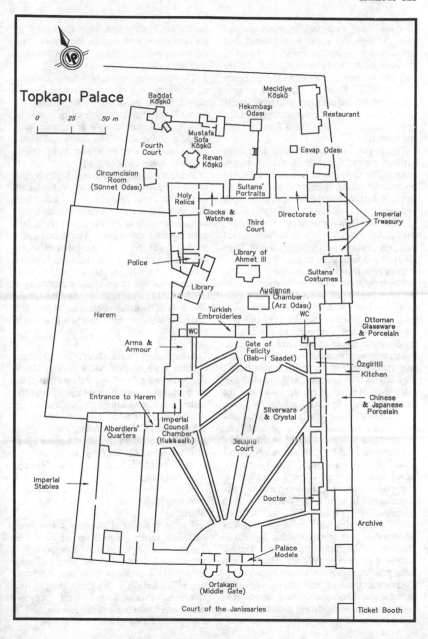

Topkapı Palace

0   25   50 m

Bağdat Köşkü

Mecidiye Köşkü

Hekimbaşı Odası

Restaurant

Fourth Court

Mustafa Sofa Köşkü

Esvap Odası

Revan Köşkü

Circumcision Room (Sünnet Odası)

Holy Relics

Sultans' Portraits

Clocks & Watches

Third Court

Directorate

Imperial Treasury

Police

Library of Ahmet III

Sultans' Costumes

Library

Audience Chamber (Arz Odası)

Harem

Turkish Embroideries

WC

WC

Ottoman Glassware & Porcelain

Arms & Armour

Gate of Felicity (Bab-i Saadet)

Özgiritli Kitchen

Entrance to Harem

Imperial Council Chamber (Kubbaaltı)

Silverware & Crystal

Chinese & Japanese Porcelain

Alberdiers' Quarters

Second Court

Imperial Stables

Doctor

Archive

Palace Models

Ortakapı (Middle Gate)

Court of the Janissaries

Ticket Booth

courtyard plan remained the same. As you pass through the great gate behind Aya Sofya, you enter the first court, the Court of the Janissaries. On your left is the former **Aya İrini Kilisesi** or Church of Divine Peace (☎ 520-6952), Sarayiçi 35, now a concert hall where recitals are given during the International İstanbul Festival, and soon perhaps to be a museum dedicated to Atatürk's life and career.

There was a Christian church here from earliest times, and before that, a pagan temple. The early church was replaced by the present one during the reign of the Byzantine emperor Justinian in the 540s, so the church you see is as old as Aya Sofya. When Mehmet the Conqueror began building his palace, the church was within the grounds and thus couldn't be used for worship. Ironically, it was used as an arsenal for centuries, then as an artillery museum.

The large Court of the Janissaries, stretching from the church to the Ortakapı (Middle Gate), is now a shady park and tour-bus parking area, but in the old days this was where the sultan's elite corps of guards gathered to eat the hearty pilav provided by him. When they were dissatisfied with the sultan's rule (which meant his treatment of them), they would overturn the great cauldrons of pilav as a symbol of revolt. After that the sultan usually didn't last too long.

'Janissary' comes from *yeni çeri*, 'new levies'. These soldiers were personal servants of the sultan, 'owned' by him, paid regularly and fed by him, and subject to his will. They were full-time soldiers in an age when most soldiers – and all soldiers in Europe – were farmers in spring and autumn, homebodies in winter, and warriors only in summer.

The Janissaries were mostly recruited as 10-year-old boys from Christian families in the Balkans. The boys were taught Turkish and were instructed in Islam. The brightest went into the palace service, and many eventually rose to the highest offices, including grand vizier. This ensured that the top government posts were always held by 'slaves' of the sultan. Those not quite so bright made

up the Janissary corps. More than once, in the later years of the empire, they proved that the sultan was their 'slave', and not the other way around.

The reforming sultan, Mahmut II, decided to do away with this dangerous and corrupted palace guard in 1826. Risking his throne, his life and his dynasty, he readied a new, loyal European-style army, then provoked a revolt of the Janissaries and wiped them out, ending their 350 years in this courtyard headquarters.

Janissaries, merchants and tradespeople could circulate as they wished in the Court of the Janissaries, but the second court was different. The same is in a way true today, because you must buy your tickets before entering the Second Court. The ticket booths are on your right as you approach the entrance. Just past them is a little fountain where the imperial executioner used to wash the tools of his trade after decapitating a noble or rebel who had displeased the sultan. The head of the unfortunate was put on a pike and exhibited above the gate you're about to enter.

Ortakapı & Second Court The Ortakapı (Middle Gate, also called the Gate of Greeting) led to the palace's second court, used for the business of running the empire. Only the sultan was allowed through the Ortakapı on horseback. Everyone else, including the grand vizier, had to dismount. The gate you see was constructed by Süleyman the Magnificent in 1524, utilising architects and workers he had brought back from his conquest of Hungary.

To the right after you enter is a map and model of the palace to help you get your bearings.

Within the second court is a beautiful, park-like setting. You'll see at once that Topkapı is not a palace on the European plan (one large building with outlying gardens), rather it is a series of pavilions, kitchens, barracks, audience chambers, kiosks and sleeping quarters built around a central enclosure, much like a fortified camp. It is a delightful castle and palace all in one.

As you walk into the second court, the great **palace kitchens** will be on your right. They now contain a small portion of Topkapı's incredibly large and varied collection of Chinese celadon porcelain. The greater part of the collection, which is quite vast, is in storage. Another room holds a fine collection of European and especially interesting Ottoman porcelain and glassware. The last of the kitchens, the Helvahane in which all the palace sweets were made, is now set up as a kitchen, and you can easily imagine what went on in these rooms as the staff prepared food for the 5000 inhabitants of the palace.

On the left side of the second court is the ornate **Kubbealtı** or Imperial Council Chamber where the grand vizier met with the Imperial Divan (council) on matters of state. The sultan did not participate in these discussions, but kept track sometimes by sitting behind a screen and listening. (Kubbealtı means 'beneath the cupola'.) The squarish tower which is one of Topkapı's most noticeable features is just above the Imperial Council Chamber.

Next to the Kübbealtı, to the right, is the armoury *(silahlar)* exhibit, with all sorts of fearsome Ottoman and European weaponry.

Harem The entrance to the Harem is just behind the Kubbealtı. You will have to buy a ticket and take the guided tour. Tour times and languages are listed on a board at the Harem ticket office. A little snacks and drinks stand here serves refreshments to those waiting for the tour. It's a good idea to see the Harem as soon as possible, because it is open only from 10 am to 4 pm. Reserve your place for the Harem tour before visiting the other parts of the palace. Make sure the guide will be speaking a language that you understand.

Fraught with legend and wild romance, the Harem is everything that you've imagined, even though the legends and stories are not really quite true.

The usual stereotype has an army of gorgeous women petting and caressing, amusing and entertaining, and doing their best to exhaust a very pampered man. Well, there's no denying that the sultan had it good, but every detail of Harem life was governed by tradition, obligation and ceremony. The sultan could not, unfortunately, just leap into a roomful of beauties and go to it.

Every traditional Muslim household had two distinct parts: the *selamlık* ('greeting room') where the master greeted friends, business associates and tradespeople; and the *harem* ('private apartments'), reserved for himself and his family. The Harem, then, was something akin to the private apartments in Buckingham Palace or the White House. The selamlık was what outsiders saw when they visited.

The women of the Harem had to be foreigners, as Islam forbade enslaving Muslims, Christians or Jews (Christians and Jews could be enslaved in the Balkans due to a loophole in Islamic law, or if taken as war prisoners, or if bought as slaves in a legitimate slave market). Besides war prisoners, girls were bought as slaves (often sold by their parents at a good price), or received as gifts from nobles and potentates. A favourite source of girls was Circassia, north of the Caucasus Mountains in Russia, as Circassian women were noted for their beauty, and parents were often glad to sell their 10-year-old girls.

Upon entering the Harem, the girls would be schooled in Islam and Turkish culture and language, plus such arts as make-up and dress, music, reading and writing, embroidery and dancing. They then entered a meritocracy, first as ladies-in-waiting to the sultan's concubines and children, then to the sultan's mother and finally, if they were good enough, to the sultan himself.

Ruler of the Harem was the *valide sultan* or queen mother, the mother of the reigning sultan. She often owned large landed estates in her own name and controlled them through Black eunuch servants. She was allowed to give orders directly to the grand vizier. Her influence on the sultan, on the selection of his wives and concubines, and on matters of state, was very great.

The sultan was allowed by Islamic law to

have four legitimate wives, who received the title of *kadın* (wife). If a wife bore him a child, she was called *haseki sultan* if it was a son; *haseki kadın* if it was a daughter. The Ottoman dynasty did not observe primogeniture, succession by the first-born son. The throne was basically up for grabs to any imperial son. Each lady of the Harem would do almost anything to get her son proclaimed heir to the throne, thus assuring her own role as the new valide sultan.

As for concubines, Islam permits as many as a man can support in proper style. The Ottoman sultan could support a lot. Some of the early sultans had as many as 300 concubines, though not all in the Harem at the same time. The domestic thrills of the sultans were usually less spectacular. Mehmet the Conqueror, builder of Topkapı, was the last sultan to have the four official wives. After him, sultans did not officially marry, but instead kept four chosen concubines without the legal encumbrances, thereby saving themselves the embarrassments and inconveniences suffered by another famous Renaissance monarch, King Henry VIII of England.

The Harem was much like a small village with all the necessary services. About 400 or 500 people lived in this distinct section of the palace at any one time. Not many of the ladies stayed in the Harem forever: sometimes the sultan granted them their freedom, and they were snapped up as wives by powerful men who wanted the company of these supremely graceful and intelligent women, not to mention their connections with the palace.

The *kızlarağası* (kuhz-LAHR-ah-ah-suh, chief Black eunuch), was the sultan's personal representative in the running of the Harem and other important affairs of state. In fact, he was the third most powerful official in the empire, after the grand vizier and the supreme Islamic judge.

The imperial princes were brought up in the Harem, taught and cared for by the women. The tradition of the *kafes* (cage) was one of many things which led to the decline of the great empire. In the early centuries imperial princes were schooled in combat and statecraft by direct experience: they practised soldiering, fought in battles and were given provinces to administer.

In the later centuries they spent their lives more or less imprisoned in the Harem, where the sultan could keep an eye on them and prevent any move to dethrone him. This meant that the princes were prey to the intrigues of the women and eunuchs; and when one of them did succeed to the throne he was corrupted by the pleasures of the Harem, and completely ignorant of war and statecraft. Luckily for the empire in this latter period, there were very able generals and grand viziers to carry on.

Tour When you walk into the Harem, think of it as the family quarters; as a place of art, culture and refinement; and as a political entity subject to intense manoeuvring and intrigue. Much of it was constructed during the reign of Süleyman the Magnificent (1520-66), but a lot was added over the years.

The door through which you enter was for tradespeople, who brought their wares here to the Black eunuch guards. The tilework in the second room is some of Turkey's finest: the green and yellow colours are unusual in İznik faïence (tin-glazed earthenware). A corridor leads past the rooms of the Black eunuchs who guarded the sultan's ladies. In the early days White eunuchs were used, but Black eunuchs sent as presents by the Ottoman governor of Egypt later took control. As many as 200 lived here, guarding the doors and waiting on the women.

The sultan, when he walked these corridors, wore slippers with silver soles. They were noisy, and that was the point: no woman was allowed to show herself to the 'imperial regard' without specific orders. When they heard the clatter of silver on stone, they all ran to hide. This rule no doubt solidified the valide sultan's control: *she* would choose the girls to be presented to the sultan. There was to be no flirting in the hallways.

You enter a small courtyard, around which were the private apartments of the four kadıns. A larger courtyard beyond was the domain of the valide sultan. Besides being the centre of power in the Harem, this was where each new sultan came after accession to the throne, to receive the allegiance and congratulations of the people of the Harem.

The sultan's private Turkish bath is next. His mother and his four wives each had their own private bath. Other private baths went to the lady responsible for discipline in the Harem and to her assistant, the treasurer. After that, all the women shared common baths.

Next you enter a few of the sultan's private chambers. There is a 17th-century room with a beautifully decorated fireplace, and a reception room with a fountain. Here the sultan received the ladies of the Harem, or his married female relatives – sisters, cousins and aunts. The fountain obscured the sounds of their conversation so that no one, in this hotbed of intrigue, could eavesdrop.

The sultan's private chamber was first built by Sinan, Süleyman the Magnificent's great architect, but the present décor dates from the 18th century.

Sultan Ahmet I (1603-17), builder of the Blue Mosque, added a nice little library. In 1705 his successor Ahmet III added the pretty dining room with all the appetising bowls of fruit painted on the walls.

The **Veliaht Dairesi** is the apartment of the crown prince, where in later centuries he was kept secluded from the world. Note the ingenious little fountains in the windows and the leather-covered domed ceiling. Next to the crown prince's suite are the sumptuous rooms of his mother, the haseki sultan.

These are the last rooms you see on the tour. You exit into the third, innermost courtyard.

Third Court If you enter the Third Court through the Harem, and thus by the back door, you should head for the main gate into the court. Get the full effect of entering this holy of holies by going out through the gate, and back in again.

This gate, the **Bab-i Saadet** or Gate of

Felicity, also sometimes called the Akağalar Kapısı or Gate of the White Eunuchs, was the entrance into the sultan's private domain. A new sultan, after girding on the sword which symbolised imperial power, would sit enthroned before this gate and receive the congratulations and allegiance of the empire's high and mighty. Before the annual military campaigns in summertime, the sultan would appear before this gate bearing the standard of the Prophet Muhammed to inspire his generals to go out and win one for Islam. Today the Bab-i Saadet is the backdrop for the annual performance of Mozart's *Abduction from the Seraglio* during the International İstanbul Festival in late June and early July.

The Third Court was staffed and guarded by White eunuchs, who allowed only very few, very important people to enter. Just inside the Bab-i Saadet is the **Arz Odası** or Audience Chamber. The sultan preserved the imperial mystique by appearing in public very seldom.

To conduct official business, important officials and foreign ambassadors came to this little room. An ambassador, frisked for weapons and held on each arm by a White eunuch, would approach the sultan. At the proper moment, he knelt and kowtowed; if he didn't, the White eunuchs would urge him ever so forcefully to do so.

The sultan, seated on the divans whose cushions are embroidered with over 15,000 seed pearls, inspected the ambassador's gifts and offerings as they were passed by the small doorway on the left. Even if the sultan and the ambassador could converse in the same language (sultans in the later years knew French, and ambassadors often learned Turkish), all conversation went through an interpreter. One couldn't have just anybody putting words into the imperial ear.

During the great days of the empire, foreign ambassadors were received on days when the Janissaries were to get their pay. Huge sacks of silver coins were brought to the Kubbealtı. High court officers would dispense the coins to long lines of the tough, impeccably costumed and faultlessly disciplined troops as the ambassadors looked on in admiration.

As you stroll into the Third Court, imagine it alive with the movements of imperial pages and White eunuchs scurrying here and there in their palace costumes. Every now and then the chief White eunuch or the chief Black eunuch would appear, and all would bow deferentially. If the sultan walked across the courtyard, all activity stopped until the event was over.

Right behind the Arz Odası is the pretty little **Library of Ahmet III** (1718). Walk to the right as you leave the Arz Odası, and enter the rooms which were once the **Turkish baths** of the Third Court staff. They now contain a fascinating collection of imperial robes, kaftans and uniforms worked in thread of silver and gold. You'll be surprised at the Oriental, almost Chinese, design of these garments.

The Turks came originally from the borders of China, and their cultural history was tied closely with that of the Persian Empire and Central Asia. In fact, tribes in China's westernmost province of Xinjiang still speak a dialect of Turkish. The masterful artists of Süleyman the Magnificent's palace workshops created wonderful designs of a high aesthetic for the royal raiment.

Next to the baths are the chambers of the **Imperial Treasury**. This you won't believe. After a while the display cases filled with rubies, emeralds, jade, pearls and more diamonds than you ever imagined will cause you to think, 'These are not all real, they must be glass'. They're real.

One of my favourite items in the Imperial Treasury is the solid gold throne given by Nadir Shah of Persia to Mahmud I (1730-54). Other thrones are almost as breathtaking. Look also for the tiny figurine of a sultan sitting under a baldachin (canopy). His body is one enormous pearl.

The Kaşıkçının Elması or Spoonmaker's Diamond is an 86-carat mammoth surrounded by several dozen smaller stones. But the prize for biggest precious stone goes to the uncut emerald which weighs 3.26 kg. When you are surrounded by this heavy-duty

show of wealth, remember that the craftwork, design and artistry of many items is extraordinary in itself.

Next door to the Treasury is the **Hayat Balkonu** or the Balcony of Life. From here the breeze is cool and there's a marvellous view of the Bosphorus and the Sea of Marmara.

Fourth Court Four imperial pleasure domes occupy the north-easternmost part of the palace, sometimes called the gardens, or Fourth Court. The **Mecidiye Köşkü** built by Abdülmecit (1839-61) was designed according to 19th-century European models and now serves as the entrance to the palace's Konyalı restaurant. Tour groups fill it around lunch time, so plan your visit after noon, or at least half an hour before.

In the other direction (north-east) is the **Mustafa Paşa Köşkü** or Kiosk of Mustafa Pasha, sometimes called the Sofa Köşkü. Also here is the room of the *hekimbaşı* or chief physician to the sultan, who was always one of the sultan's Jewish subjects.

During the reign of Sultan Ahmet III (1703-30), known as the Tulip Period because of the rage for these flowers which spread through the upper classes, the gardens around the Sofa Köşkü were filled with tulips. Little lamps would be set out among the hundreds of varieties at night. A new variety of the flower earned its creator fame, money and social recognition. Tulips had been grown in Turkey from very early times, having come originally from Persia. Some bulbs were brought to Holland during the Renaissance. The Dutch, fascinated by the possibilities in the flower, developed and created many varieties, some of which made their way back to Turkey and began the tulip craze there.

Up the stairs at the end of the tulip garden are two of the most enchanting kiosks. Sultan Murat IV (1623-40) built the **Revan Köşkü** or Erivan Kiosk in 1635 after reclaiming the city of Yerevan (now in Armenia) from Persia. He also constructed the **Bağdat Köşkü** or Baghdad Kiosk in 1638 to commemorate his victory over that city. Notice the İznik tiles, the inlay and woodwork, and the views all around.

Just off the open terrace with the wishing well is the **Sünnet Odası** or Circumcision Room, used for the ritual which admits Muslim boys to manhood. (Circumcision is usually performed when the boy is nine or 10 years old.) Be sure to see the beautiful tile panels.

Back in the Third Court Re-enter the Third Court for a look at yet another set of wonders, the holy relics in the **Hırka-i Saadet** or Suite of the Felicitous Cloak. These rooms, sumptuously decorated with İznik faïence, in a way constituted a holy of holies. Only the chosen could enter the Third Court, but entry into the Hırka-i Saadet rooms was for the chosen of the chosen on special ceremonial occasions.

For in these rooms reside the cloak of the Prophet Muhammed himself, his battle standard, two of his swords, a hair from his beard, a tooth, his footprint and a letter in his own handwriting.

The 'felicitous cloak' itself resides in a golden casket in a special alcove along with the battle standard. This suite of rooms was opened only once a year so that the imperial family could pay homage to the memory of the Prophet on the 15th day of the holy month of Ramazan. Even though anyone, prince or commoner, faithful or infidel, can enter the rooms now, you should respect the sacred atmosphere by observing decorous behaviour.

Other exhibits in the Third Court include **Ağalar Camii** or Mosque of the Eunuchs, another little **library**, Turkish miniature paintings, imperial monograms, seals and arms, calligraphy, and portraits of the sultans. These exhibits are sometimes moved around or closed to make room for special exhibits. In the room with the seals, notice the graceful, elaborate *tuğra* (TOO-rah, monogram) of the sultans. The tuğra was at the top of any imperial proclamation. It actually contains elaborate calligraphic rendering of the names of the sultan and his father. The formula reads like this:

'Abdülhamid Khan, son of Abdülmecit Khan, Ever Victorious'.

Imperial Stables Enter the Imperial Stables (Has Ahırları) from the Second Court, just to the north-east of the main entrance (Ortakapı). Go down the cobbled slope.

The stables are now a museum for the carriages, saddles and other horse-related gear used by the sultans. The usual collection of gold-encrusted coaches, diamond-studded bridles, etc fill the rooms. One gets the impression that the imperial lifestyle was at least soft, even though it had its complications.

As you leave the palace proper through the Ortakapı, you can walk to your right and down the slope along Osman Hamdi Bey Yokuşu to the archaeological museums, or straight to Aya Sofya. I'll assume, for the moment, that you're heading for Aya Sofya, only a few steps away. Thus you can ignore the taxi drivers who will confront you with ever more original ways of increasing the cost of a simple ride from point A to B.

Soğukçeşme Sokak Just after you leave the tall gate of the Court of the Janissaries, take a look at the ornate little structure on your left. It's the **Fountain of Ahmet III**, the one who liked tulips so much. Built in 1728, it replaced a Byzantine fountain at the same spring. There's no water these days, though.

The fancy gate across the road from the fountain was where the Sultan entered Aya Sofya for his prayers. It led to a special elevated imperial pavilion inside, which you will see when you explore the inside.

The gate is at the beginning of Soğukçeşme Sokak (Street of the Cold Fountain), to the right, a street entirely restored by the Turkish Touring & Automobile Association. The houses clinging to the palace walls are the Ayasofya Pansiyonları or Sancta Sophia Pensions. At the far (western) end of the street is the entrance to the Restaurant Sarnıç or Cistern Restaurant, in a restored Byzantine cistern, and across the street from it the Konuk Evi, a new hotel and garden restaurant built in the old İstanbul manner. (For details, see the following Places to Stay and Places to Eat sections.)

Aya Sofya (Sancta Sophia)

The Church of the Divine Wisdom (Sancta Sophia in Latin, Hagia Sofia in Greek, Aya Sofya in Turkish) was not named for a saint; *sofia* means wisdom. Aya Sofya (☎ 522 1750) is open daily except Monday, from 9.30 am to 4.30 pm (to 7 pm in July and August); the galleries are open from 9.30 to 11.30 am and from 1 to 4 pm; there's a multivision show at 3 pm daily except Saturday. Admission costs US$3, half-price for students.

Emperor Justinian (527-65) had the church built as yet another effort to restore the greatness of the Roman Empire. It was completed in 548 and reigned as the greatest church in Christendom until the conquest of Constantinople in 1453. St Peter's in Rome is larger than Aya Sofya, but it was built more than 1000 years later.

A lot can happen to a building in 14 centuries, especially in an earthquake zone, and a lot has certainly happened to Aya Sofya. But it is still a wonder and a joy to behold. Ignore the clutter of buttresses and supports, kiosks, tombs and outbuildings which hug its massive walls, and the renovations which are under way.

It is not enough to 'see' Aya Sofya, you must experience it as the architects intended. Although you can no longer approach the church exactly as a Byzantine would have, walking along a street which led up a hill and straight to the great main door, you can experience the church proper as you enter.

Pay your admission fee and walk to the terrace before the main entrance. Here are the sunken ruins of a Theodosian church (404-15), and the low original steps. Now enter the church slowly, one step at a time, and watch what happens: at first there is only darkness broken by the brilliant colours of stained-glass windows. As your eyes adjust to the dark, two massive doorways appear within, and far beyond them in the dim light, a semi-dome blazing with gold mosaics portraying the Madonna and Child – she as Queen of Heaven. Take a few steps and stop just inside the threshold of the first door: the far mosaic is clear and beautiful, and the apse beneath it makes a harmonious whole.

Look up from where you are standing now, and you see a gorgeous mosaic of Christ as Pantocrator (Ruler of All) above the third and largest door, visible except for the august expression on the face.

Take a few more steps and the face of the Pantocrator becomes visible. Look deep into the church again, and you'll see that the semi-dome of the Madonna and Child is topped by another semi-dome, and above that is the famous, gigantic main dome of the church; at the same time, you are facing the Pantocrator in all His majesty.

Walk through the second door and towards the immense Imperial Door, and surprise! The 'gigantic main dome' turns out to be only another semi-dome: halfway to the Imperial Door, a row of windows peeks out above the larger semi-dome and betrays the secret. As you approach the Imperial Threshold the real, magnificent main dome soars above you and seems to be held up by nothing. It's no wonder that Justinian, when he slowly entered his great creation for the first time almost 1500 years ago, came this far and exclaimed, 'Glory to God that I have been judged worthy of such a work. Oh Solomon! I have outdone you!'

During its years as a church (almost 1000), only imperial processions were permitted to enter through the central, Imperial Door. You can still notice the depressions in the stone by each door just inside the threshold where imperial guards stood. It was through the Imperial Door that Mehmet the Conqueror came in 1453 to take possession for Islam of the greatest religious edifice in the world. Before he entered, so historians tell us, he sprinkled earth on his head in a gesture of humility. Aya Sofya remained a mosque for almost 500 years. In 1935 Atatürk proclaimed it a museum; the wisdom in this decision is apparent when you consider that both devout Muslims and Christians would like to have it as a place of worship for their religions.

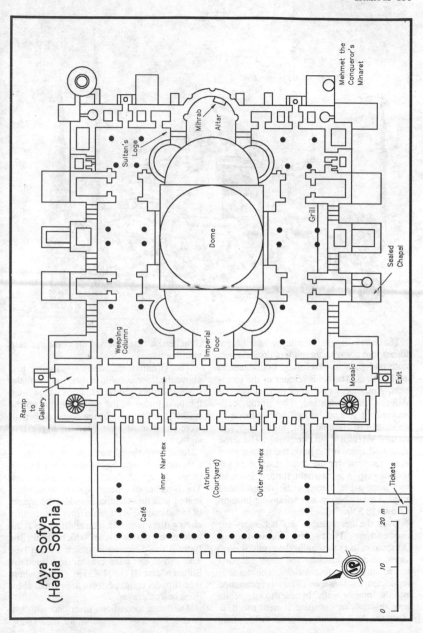

Aya Sofya (Hagia Sophia)

Mehmet the Conqueror's Minaret

Sultan's Loge

Mihrab

Altar

Dome

Grill

Sealed Chapel

Weeping Column

Imperial Door

Ramp to Gallery

Mosaic

Exit

Inner Narthex

Atrium (Courtyard)

Outer Narthex

Café

Tickets

0   10   20 m

Aya Sofya

There are bigger buildings, and bigger domes, but not without modern construction materials such as reinforced concrete and steel girders. The achievement of the architects, Anthemius of Tralles and Isidorus of Miletus, is unequalled. The dome, constructed of special hollow bricks made in Rhodes from a unique light, porous clay, was a daring attempt at the impossible. The sense of air and space in the nave and the apparent lack of support for the dome made the Byzantines gasp in amazement. Indeed, it almost was impossible, because the dome lasted only 11 years before an earthquake brought it down in 559.

Over the centuries it was necessary for succeeding Byzantine emperors and Ottoman sultans to rebuild the dome several times, to add buttresses and other supports and to steady the foundations. The dome is supported by massive pillars incorporated into the interior walls. In order to appreciate how this works, compare it with the Blue Mosque. And for an acoustic thrill, stand right beneath the centre of the dome and clap your hands.

The Ottoman chandeliers, hanging low above the floor, combined their light with the rows and rows of little oil lamps which lined the balustrades of the gallery and even the walkway at the base of the dome. When all were lit, it must have been an impressive sight.

Justinian ordered the most precious materials for his church. Note the matched marble panels in the walls, and the breccia columns. The Byzantine emperor was crowned while seated in a throne placed within the square of inlaid marble in the main floor. The nearby choir gallery is an Ottoman addition, as is the *mihrab* or prayer niche, which shows the faithful the direction in which Mecca lies. The large alabaster urns were added by Sultan Murat III (1574-95) as a place where worshippers could perform their ritual ablutions before prayer.

The large medallions inscribed with gilt Arabic letters were added in the mid-1800s.

Calligraphy is a highly prized art in Islam, and these medallions were done by Mustafa İzzet Efendi, a master calligrapher of the time. You'll see these words over and over in Turkish mosques. They are the names of God (Allah), Muhammed and the early caliphs Ali and Abu Bakr.

The curious elevated kiosk, screened from public view, is the **Hünkar Mahfili** or Sultan's Loge. Ahmet III (1703-30) had it built so he could come, pray, and go unseen, preserving the imperial mystique.

If you wander around enough you'll come to the 'weeping column'. A copper facing with a hole in it has been put on a column (to the left after you enter through the Imperial Door). Stick your finger in the hole and make a wish. Legend has it that if the tip of your finger emerges damp, you're supposed to get your wish. If your wish is that a feeling of silliness sweep over you as soon as you poke your finger in the hole, your wish is certain to be fulfilled whether your finger's damp or dry.

Mosaics Justinian filled his church with gorgeous mosaics. The Byzantine church and state later went through a fierce civil war (726-87) over the question of whether images were to be allowed or not. The debated biblical passage was Exodus 20:4:

Thou shalt not make unto thee any graven image, or any likeness of anything that is in heaven above, or that is in the earth beneath, or that is in the water under the earth: Thou shalt not bow down thyself to them, nor serve them.

Though the Bible seems clear, the people liked images a lot, and the iconoclasts ('image-breakers') were defeated. It's interesting to speculate whether iconoclastic Islam, militant and triumphant at this time, had any influence on Byzantine theology.

When the Turks took Constantinople there was no controversy. The Koran repeatedly rails against idolatry, as in Sura 16:

We sent a Messenger into every nation saying, Serve God and give up idols.

Consequently Islamic art is supposed to have no saints' portraits, no pictures of animals, fish or fowl, nor anything else with an immortal soul, and the mosaics had to go. Luckily they were covered with plaster rather than destroyed. Restoration work is still going on.

From the floor of Aya Sofya you can see several saints' portraits high up in the semicircles of the side walls. The best are in the galleries, reserved for female worshippers in Byzantine times. Climb to the galleries by a switchback ramp which starts at the northern end of the narthex.

Some of the work, though partially lost, is superb. The best mosaics are in the southern gallery. Most famous of all is the beautiful Deesis, dating from the early 1300s. Christ is at the centre, with the Virgin Mary on one side, John the Baptist on the other.

Be sure to go all the way to the far ends of the galleries. At the apse end of the south (right-hand) gallery are portraits of emperors, with a difference. The Empress Zoe (1028-50), for instance, had three husbands. When her portrait was put here in mosaic her husband was Romanus III Argyrus, but he died in 1034. So when she married Michael IV in that year, she had Romanus's portrait taken out and Michael's put in, but Michael didn't last that long either. In 1042 his portrait was removed to make way for that of Constantine IX Monomachus. Constantine outlived Zoe, so it is his portrait that you see today. The inscription reads, 'Constantine, by the Divine Christ, Faithful King of the Romans'.

As you leave Aya Sofya, pass all the way through the corridor-like narthex and through the door at the end of it. Then turn and look up. Above the door is one of the church's finest mosaics, a Madonna and Child dating from the late 900s; on the left, Constantine the Great offers her the city of Constantinople; on the right, Justinian offers her Sancta Sophia.

A few more steps and you're out of the museum. The fountain to the right was for Muslim ablutions. Immediately to your left is the church's baptistry, converted after the

Conquest to a tomb for sultans Mustafa and Ibrahim. Other tombs are clustered behind it: those of Murat III, Selim II, Mehmet III and various princes. By the way, the minarets were added by Mehmet the Conqueror (1451-81), Beyazıt II (1481-1512) and Selim II (1566-74).

Baths of Lady Hürrem Every mosque had a Turkish steam bath nearby. Aya Sofya's is across the road to the left (east) of the park with the fountain. It's the Haseki Hürrem Hamamı or Turkish baths of Lady Hürrem, built in 1556 by the great Sinan, and now fixed up as a government-run carpet gallery and shop ('Turkish Handwoven Carpets Sale Centre') (☎ 511 8192), open daily except Tuesday from 9.30 am to 5 pm; admission is free.

Designed as a 'double hamam' with identical baths for men and women, it had a centre wall dividing the two; it's now been breached by a small doorway. Both sides have the three traditional rooms: first the square frigidarium for disrobing (on the men's side, this has a pretty marble fountain and stained glass windows); then the long tepidarium for washing, finally the octagonal caldarium for sweating and massage. In the caldarium, note the four *eyvan* niches and the four semi-private washing rooms. The *göbektaşı* (hot platform) in the men's bath is inlaid with coloured marble.

The carpet shop, by the way, is an excellent place to learn about traditional Turkish carpets and how to get the real thing when you buy. Carpets of guaranteed quality are sold here for a fixed price.

The Blue Mosque
There used to be palaces where the Blue Mosque now stands. The Byzantine emperors built several of them, stretching from near Aya Sofya all the way to the site of the mosque. You can see a mosaic from one of these palaces, still in place, in the Mosaic Museum (described later).

Sultan Ahmet I (1603-17) set out to build a mosque that would rival and even surpass the achievement of Justinian. He came pretty

close to his goal. The Sultan Ahmet Camii or Mosque of Sultan Ahmet, the Blue Mosque, is a triumph of harmony, proportion and elegance, and its architect, Mehmet Ağa, achieves the sort of visual experience on the exterior which Aya Sofya has on the interior.

As at Aya Sofya, you must approach the Blue Mosque properly in order to appreciate its architectural mastery. Don't walk straight from Aya Sofya to the Blue Mosque through the crowd of touts. Rather, go out to the middle of the Hippodrome and approach the mosque from the front.

Walk towards the mosque and through the gate in the peripheral wall. Note the small dome atop the gate: this is the motif Mehmet Ağa uses to lift your eyes to heaven. As you walk through the gate, your eyes follow a flight of stairs up to another gate topped by another dome; through this gate is yet another dome, that of the *şadırvan*, or ablutions fountain, in the centre of the mosque

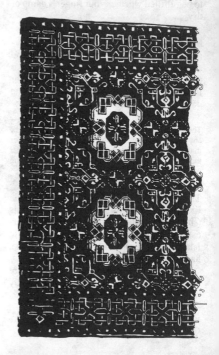

courtyard. As you ascend the stairs, semi-domes come into view, one after another: first the one over the mosque's main door, then the one above it, and another, and another. Finally the main dome crowns the whole, and your eyes ascend to heaven pointed by the six minarets.

The layout of the Blue Mosque is classic Ottoman design. The forecourt contains an ablutions fountain in its centre. The portico around three sides could be used for prayer, meditation or study during warm weather.

The Blue Mosque is such a popular tourist sight that worshippers were in danger of being lost in the tourist crowds. So you'll be asked to turn left and enter through the north side door, not through the main door.

At the side door an attendant will take your shoes; if your clothing is unpresentable, you'll be lent a robe to wear while you see the mosque. There's no charge for this, but you may be asked for a donation for the mosque, to which the money will actually go.

Though the stained-glass windows are replacements, they still create the marvellous coloured effects of the originals. The semi-domes and the dome are painted in graceful arabesques. The 'blue' of the mosque's name comes from the İznik tiles which line the walls, particularly in the gallery (which is not open to the public). You'll be able to get up close to equally beautiful tiles in the Rüstem Paşa Camii.

You can see immediately why the Blue Mosque, constructed between 1606 and 1616, over 1000 years after Aya Sofya, is not as great an architectural triumph as Aya Sofya. Although the four massive pillars which hold up the dome don't detract from the mosque's breathtaking beauty, they show what an impressive achievement Aya Sofya is, by demonstrating what's usually needed to hold up a massive dome.

Other things to notice are: the imperial loge, covered with marble latticework, to the left; the piece of the sacred Black Stone from the Kaaba in Mecca, embedded in the mihrab; the grandfather clock, making sure the faithful know the exact times of the five-times-daily prayers; the high, elaborate chair (*mahfil*) from which the *imam* or teacher gives the sermon on Friday; and the *mimber*, or pulpit. The mimber is the structure with a curtained doorway at floor level, a flight of steps and a small kiosk topped by a spire. This one is particularly notable because of its fine carving (it's all marble), and because it was from here that the destruction of the Janissary corps was proclaimed in 1826 (see the Topkapı Palace section).

Mosques built by the great and powerful usually included numerous public-service institutions. Clustered around the Sultan Ahmet Camii were a *medrese* or theological school; an *imaret* or soup kitchen serving the poor; a hamam so that the faithful could wash on Friday, the holy day; and shops, the rent from which supported the upkeep of the mosque. The tomb (*türbe*) of the mosque's great patron, Sultan Ahmet I, is on the north side facing the fountain park (open for visits daily except Monday and Tuesday from 9.30 am to 4.30 pm). Buried with Ahmet are his brothers, Sultan Osman II and Sultan Murat IV.

Textile Museum Parts of the Blue Mosque cellars have been turned into a textile museum officially called the **Kilim ve Düz Dokuma Yaygılar Müzesi** or Museum of Kilims & Flat-Woven Rugs. The cellars, entered from the north side (towards Aya Sofya) are where you buy your ticket. (Opening hours are from 9 am to 4 pm, closed Sunday and Monday; admission costs less than US$1.)

Inside the building are impressive stone-vaulted chambers. Huge kilims are stretched on boards, with descriptive tags written in Turkish and English.

The napped carpets are housed upstairs in the Halı Müzesi or Carpet Museum, at the end of the stone ramp which you can see from the side door where you entered the mosque. The ramp was so that the sultans could ride their nobly caparisoned steeds right up into the shelter of the mosque, dismount, and walk to their loge in safety and imperial privacy.

Turkish oriental carpets are among the finest works of art. The collection here provides a look at some of the best examples.

Mosaic Museum Before the Blue Mosque was built, its site was occupied by the palaces of the Byzantine emperors. The Roman art of mosaic moved, with most other Roman traditions, to Byzantium, and so the palace floors were covered in this beautiful artwork. Though the palaces have long since disappeared, some of the mosaics have survived.

When archaeologists from the University of Ankara and the University of St Andrew's (in Scotland) dug at the back (east) of the Blue Mosque in the mid-1950s, they uncovered a mosaic pavement dating from early Byzantine times, circa 500 AD. The pavement, filled with wonderful hunting and mythological scenes and emperors' portraits, was a triumphal way which led from the palace down to the harbour of Boucoleon. The dust and rubble of 1500 years have sunk the pavement considerably below ground level.

Other 5th-century mosaics were saved providentially when Sultan Ahmet had shops built on top of them. The row of shops, called the **Arasta**, was intended to provide rent revenues for the upkeep of the mosque. Now they house numerous souvenir vendors, a little teahouse, and the entrance to the Mosaic Museum. The museum is open daily except Tuesday from 9 am to 5 pm, for US$1.

After you've paid your admission fee, descend to the walkways around the sunken mosaics. The intricate work is impressive, with lots of hunters and beasts and maidens and swains. Note the ribbon border with heart-shaped leaves which surrounds the mosaic. In the western-most room is the most colourful and dramatic picture, that of two men in leggings carrying spears and holding off a raging tiger. If you can convince the custodian to wipe the mosaics with a wet cloth, the colours will become much more vivid.

The Hippodrome

The Hippodrome was the centre of Byzantium's life for 1000 years and of Ottoman life for another 400 years. The Hippodrome (At Meydanı, 'Horse Grounds') was the scene of countless political and military dramas during the long life of this city.

History In Byzantine times, the rival chariot teams of 'Greens' and 'Blues' were politically connected. Support for a team was the same as membership in a political party, and a team victory had important effects on policy. A Byzantine emperor might lose his throne as the result of a post-match riot.

Ottoman sultans kept an eye on activities in the Hippodrome. If things were going badly in the empire, a surly crowd gathering here could signal the start of a disturbance, then a riot, then a revolution. In 1826, the slaughter of the debased and unruly Janissary corps was carried out by the reformer-sultan, Mahmut II. Almost a century later, in 1909, there were riots here which caused the downfall of Abdülhamid II and the repromulgation of the Ottoman constitution.

Though the Hippodrome might be the scene of their downfall, Byzantine emperors and Ottoman sultans outdid one another in beautifying it. Many of the priceless statues carved by ancient masters have disappeared. The soldiers of the Fourth Crusade sacked Constantinople (a Christian ally city!) in 1204, tearing all the bronze plates from the magnificent stone obelisk at the Hippodrome's southern end, in the mistaken belief that they were gold. The crusaders also stole the famous 'quadriga', or team of four horses cast in bronze, which now sits atop the main door to St Mark's Church in Venice.

Monuments Near the northern end of the Hippodrome, the little gazebo in beautiful stonework, is actually **Kaiser Wilhelm's fountain**. The German emperor paid a state visit to Abdülhamid II in 1901, and presented this fountain to the sultan and his people as a token of friendship. According to the Ottoman inscription, the fountain was built in the Hijri (Muslim lunar calendar) year of 1316 (1898-99 to us). The monograms in the stonework are those of Abdülhamid II and Wilhelm II.

The impressive granite obelisk with hieroglyphs is called the **Obelisk of Theodosius**, carved in Egypt around 1500 BC. According to the hieroglyphs, it was erected in Heliopolis (now a suburb of Cairo) to commemorate the victories of Thutmose III (1504-1450 BC). The Byzantine emperor, Theodosius, had it brought from Egypt to Constantinople in 390 AD. He then had it erected on a marble pedestal engraved with scenes of himself in the midst of various imperial pastimes. Theodosius' marble billboards have weathered badly over the centuries. The magnificent obelisk, spaced above the pedestal by four bronze blocks, is as crisply cut and as shiny bright as when it was carved from the living rock in Upper Egypt 3500 years ago.

Many obelisks were transported over the centuries to Paris (Place de la Concorde), London (Cleopatra's Needle), New York, Rome and Florence. A few still remain in Egypt as well.

South of the obelisk is a strange **spiral column** coming up out of a hole in the ground. It was once much taller and was topped by three serpents' heads. Originally cast to commemorate a victory of the Hellenic confederation over the Persians, it stood in front of the temple of Apollo at Delphi from 478 BC, until Constantine the Great had it brought to his new capital city around 330 AD. Though badly bashed up in the Byzantine struggle over the place of images in the church (called the Iconoclastic Controversy), the serpents' heads survived until the early 1700s. Now all that remains of them is one upper jaw in the Archaeological Museum.

The level of the Hippodrome rose over the centuries, as civilisation piled up its dust and refuse here. The obelisk and serpentine column were cleaned out and tidied up by the English troops who occupied the city after the Ottoman defeat in WW I.

No-one is quite sure who built the large **rough-stone obelisk** at the southern end of the Hippodrome. All we know is that it was repaired by Constantine VII Porphyrogenetus (913-59), and that the bronze plates were ripped off by the boys during the Fourth Crusade.

Turkish & Islamic Arts Museum

The Palace of İbrahim Paşa (1524) is on the western side of the Hippodrome. Now housing the Türk ve İslam Eserleri Müzesi or Turkish & Islamic Arts Museum (☎ 522 1888), it gives you a glimpse into the opulent life of the Ottoman upper class in the time of Süleyman the Magnificent. İbrahim Paşa was Süleyman's close friend, son-in-law and grand vizier. He was enormously wealthy and so powerful that the sultan was finally convinced by İbrahim's enemies to have him murdered. Roxelana, Süleyman's wife, had convinced the sultan that İbrahim was a rival and a threat.

The museum is open from 9.30 am to 4 pm daily; closed on Monday. Admission costs US$2. Labels are in Turkish and English. A video show on the 1st floor of the museum gives you a quick summary of Turkish history, and explains the sultan's tuğra (monogram) and *ferman* (imperial edict). The coffee shop in the museum is a welcome refuge from the press of crowds and touts in the Hippodrome.

Highlights among the exhibits, which date from the 8th and 9th centuries up to the 19th century, are the decorated wooden Koran cases from the high Ottoman period; the calligraphy exhibits, including fermans with tuğras, Turkish miniatures, and illuminated manuscripts. You'll also want to have a look at the *rahles* or Koran stands, and the many carpets from all periods.

The lower floor of the museum houses ethnographic exhibits. At the entry is a black tent *(kara çadır)* like those used by nomads in eastern Turkey. Inside the tent is an explanation of nomadic customs, in English. Inside the museum building are village looms on which carpets and kilims are woven, and an exhibit of the plants and materials used to make natural textile dyes for the carpets. Perhaps most fascinating are the domestic interiors, including those of a yurt

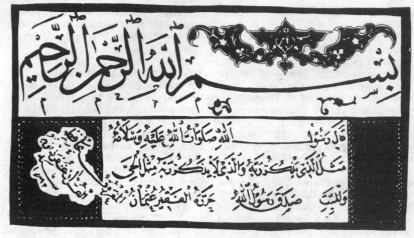

Murakka (17th Century), Turkish & Islamic Arts Museum, İstanbul

or Central Asian felt hut, a village house from Yuntdağ, and a late-19th-century house from Bursa. One display shows women shopping for cloth; another, a scene of daily life in an İstanbul home of the early 20th century.

The buildings behind and beside İbrahim Paşa's palace are İstanbul's law courts and legal administration buildings.

'Little' Sancta Sophia

Take a detour into İstanbul's lively little back streets for a look at the Byzantine feat of engineering called the Sphendoneh: the southern end of the Hippodrome is artificially supported by a system of brick arches. While you're down there, you can visit the Little Sancta Sophia Mosque or Küçük Aya Sofya Camii (formerly the Byzantine Church of St Sergius & St Bacchus), and also the Sokollu Mehmet Paşa Camii.

Facing south, with the Blue Mosque on your left, go to the end of the Hippodrome and turn left, then right, onto Aksakal Sokak. Soon you'll be able to recognise the filled-in arches of the Byzantine Sphendoneh on your right. Follow the curve around to the right

and onto Kaleci Sokak. The next intersecting street is Mehmet Paşa Sokak; turn left and the Küçük Aya Sofya Camii is right there. If the mosque is not open, just hang around or signal to a boy on the street, and someone will come with the key.

Justinian and Theodora built this little church sometime between 527 and 536. Inside, the layout and décor are typical of an early Byzantine church, though the building was repaired and expanded several times during its life as a mosque, after the conquest of Constantinople in 1453. Repairs and enlargements to convert the church to a mosque were added by the chief White eunuch Hüseyin Ağa around 1500. His tomb is to the left as you enter.

Go north on Mehmet Paşa Sokak, back up the hill to the neighbouring **Sokollu Mehmet Paşa Camii**. This one was built during the height of Ottoman architectural development in 1571 by the empire's greatest architect, Sinan. Though named for the grand vizier of the time, it was really sponsored by his wife Esmahan, daughter of Sultan Selim II. Besides its architectural harmony, typical of Sinan's great works, the mosque is unique because the medrese is not a separate building but actually part of the mosque structure, built around the forecourt.

If the mosque is not open, wait for the German-speaking guard to appear. When you enter, notice the harmonious architecture, the coloured marble, and the beautiful İznik tiles, some of the best ever made. Also, check out the four fragments from the sacred Black Stone in the Kaaba at Mecca: one above the mosque entrance (framed in gold), two in the mimber, and one in the mihrab. The marble pillars by the mimber revolve if the foundations have been disturbed by earthquake – an ingenious signalling device.

Walk back up the hill on Suterazisi Sokak to return to the Hippodrome.

Yerebatan Saray

Cross the main road, Divan Yolu, from the Hippodrome. On the north side of the street is a little park with a curious stone tower rising from it. The tower is part of an ancient aqueduct, a segment of this timeless city's elaborate water system. Beneath the park, entered by a little doorway on its north side (on Yerebatan Caddesi) is the Yerebatan Saray ('Sunken Palace') (☎ 522 1259), formerly called the Cistern Basilica.

Admission, from 9 am to 5 pm (7 pm in summer) costs US$2. You can stay down in the cool darkness as long as you want. If you have a hand torch (flashlight), take it along, as the lights tend to go out for short periods every now and again.

Yerebatan Saray is actually a grand Byzantine cistern, 70 metres wide and 140 metres long. It has been completely restored, and now has atmospheric low lighting, classical music playing from hidden speakers, and a maze of walkways spreading throughout the 'palace'. The Byzantines never had it so good.

The cistern was built by Justinian the Great (527-65), who was incapable of thinking in small terms. The roof is held up by 336 columns. At the back of the cistern is a column with an upside-down capital as its plinth, an anomaly that's rated as one of the big attractions here. But the mood of the place is what you'll remember; water still drips and tinkles in the dank shadows as it has for centuries.

Gülhane Park & Sublime Porte

Walk down the hill from Yerebatan Saray, along the main street called Alemdar Caddesi. Aya Sofya will be on your right. Just past a big tree in the middle of the road, the street turns left, but just in front of you is the arched gateway to Gülhane Parkı or Gülhane Park.

Before entering the park, look to the left. That bulbous little kiosk built into the park walls at the next street corner is the **Alay Köşkü** or Parade Kiosk, from which the sultan would watch the periodic parades of troops and trade guilds which commemorated great holidays and military victories.

Across the street from the Alay Köşkü (not quite visible right from the Gülhane gate) is a gate to the Sublime Porte. The gate leads into the precincts of what was once the grand vizierate, or prime ministry, of the Ottoman Empire. Westerners called the Ottoman prime ministry the 'sublime porte' because of a phrase in Ottoman official documents: 'The Ambassador of (wherever) having come to my Sublime Porte...'

In Islamic societies, and in other societies with strong clan roots, it was customary for the chief or ruler to adjudicate disputes and grant favours. To petition the leader, you went to his tent, or house, or palace, stood at the door (hence 'porte'), and waited for a chance to lay it on him. When a Western ambassador arrived at the sultan's 'sublime porte', he was looked on as just another petitioner asking favours. In later centuries, ambassadors reported not to the palace but to the grand vizierate, which was thus thought to be the Sublime Porte. Today the buildings beyond the gate hold the Ottoman archives and various offices of the İstanbul provincial government.

Back up the street and inside the gates of Gülhane Park you'll find a shady refuge. Gülhane was once the palace park of Topkapı; admission costs less than US$1. There's a small zoo here. At the far (north) end of the park, up the hill, is a flight of steps used as seats, and a small tea garden. Few tourists (except Lonely Planet readers) know about this quiet refuge, where you can sip a bracing glass of tea or a cool drink, gaze at the Bosphorus, and shake off the stresses of travel.

Archaeological Museums

İstanbul's major collection of 'serious' museums is right behind Gülhane Park and Topkapı. As you pass beneath the arched gateway from Alemdar Caddesi into Gülhane, bear right and walk up the slope along a cobbled road, Osman Hamdi Bey Yokuşu, which then turns to the right. After the turn you'll see a gate on the left. Within the gate are the İstanbul Archaeological Museum, Tiled Kiosk and Museum of the Ancient Orient.

You can also reach the museum complex from Topkapı. As you come out the Ortakapı gate from the palace, walk into the Court of the Janissaries, then turn right and walk

down the hill before you get to Aya İrini, the Church of Divine Peace.

The museum complex (☎ 520 7740) is open daily from 9.30 am to 4.30 pm, closed Monday. Admission to the complex, and thus to all three museums, costs US$2.

These museums were the palace collections, formed during the 19th century and added to greatly during the republic. While not immediately as dazzling as Topkapı, they contain an incredible wealth of artefacts from the 50 centuries of Anatolia's history.

The **Archaeological Museum** (Arkeoloji Müzesi) houses a vast collection of classical statues and sarcophagi. The Ottoman Turkish inscription over the door of this imposing structure reads 'Eser-i Atika Müzesi' or Museum of Ancient Works. Extensive renovations during the 1980s have rendered it very attractive, with good lighting and signs in Turkish and English. A Roman statue in archaic style of the daemonic god Bes, greets you as you enter. The

Relief of Alexander (Sarcophagus, Archaeological Museum)

classical sculpture rooms are to the right, with lots of pieces from Aphrodisias. To the left are other exhibits, including sarcophagi. The ancient, monolithic basalt sarcophagus of King Tabnit of Egypt is on display, as is its former occupant in a glass case. The famous Lycian sarcophagus should not be missed; even better ones are beyond the staircase at the museum's northern end. Upstairs are exhibits of figurines, pottery and jewellery which trace the history of Troy and Anatolia through the ages. Through the windows there's a fine view of the neighbouring Çinili Köşk.

The **Tiled Kiosk** of Sultan Mehmet the Conqueror (Çinili Köşk), faces the Archaeological Museum. Though once completely covered in fine tilework, you'll see tiles only on the façade these days. Mehmet II had this built in 1472 not long after the Conquest, which makes it the oldest surviving non-religious Turkish building in İstanbul. It now houses an excellent collection of Turkish faience, including many good examples of fine İznik tiles from the period in the 1600s and 1700s when that city produced the finest coloured tiles in the world.

Last of the museums in the complex is the **Museum of the Ancient Orient** (Eski Şark Eserler Müzesi). Go here for a glimpse at the gates of ancient Babylon in the time of Nebuchadnezzar II (604-562 BC), for clay tablets bearing Hammurabi's famous law code (in cuneiform, of course), ancient Egyptian scarabs, and artefacts from the Assyrian and Hittite empires.

Divan Yolu

Divan Yolu, the main thoroughfare of the Old City, stretches between the gate named Topkapı and the palace named Topkapı. Starting from the Hippodrome and Yerebatan Saray, it heads due west, up one of İstanbul's seven hills, past the Covered Market, through Beyazıt Square and past İstanbul University to Aksaray Square. Turning north a bit, it continues to the Topkapı (Cannon Gate) in the ancient city walls. In its progress through the city, its

name changes from Divan Yolu to become Yeniçeriler Caddesi, Ordu Caddesi and Millet Caddesi. At the eastern end, near the Hippodrome, it's Divan Yolu, the Road to the Imperial Council. Today you can ride along it in a free tram running between Sirkeci and Aksaray.

The street dates from the early times of Constantinople. Roman engineers laid it out to connect with the great Roman roads heading west. The great milestone from which all distances were measured was near the tall shaft of stones which rises above Yerebatan Saray. The street held its importance in Ottoman times, as Mehmet the Conqueror's first palace was in Beyazıt Square, and his new one, Topkapı, was under construction.

If you start from Aya Sofya and the Hippodrome and go up the slope on Divan Yolu, you will see the little **Firuz Ağa Camii** on the left. Firuz Ağa was chief treasurer to Beyazıt II (1481-1512). The mosque was built in 1491, in the simple style of the early Ottomans: a dome on a square base, with a simple porch out the front. The Ottomans brought this style with them from the east or borrowed it from the Seljuk Turks. It changed greatly after they conquered İstanbul, inspected Aya Sofya and put the great architect Sinan to work.

Just behind Firuz Ağa Camii are the ruins of the **Palace of Antiochus** (5th century), not much to look at these days.

The first major intersection on the right is that with Babıali Caddesi. Turn right here and after walking a block you'll be in **Cağaloğlu Square**, once the centre of İstanbul's newspaper publishing. Most of the publishers have moved to large, modern buildings outside the city walls. The **Cağaloğlu Hamamı**, is just off the square, on the right (see the Entertainment section for details).

If instead you turn left (south) from Divan Yolu, you'll be on Klodfarer Caddesi (not a German word, but the name of the Turcophile French novelist Claude Farrère). It leads to a large open area beneath which lies the Byzantine cistern now called **Binbirdirek**,

'A Thousand-and-One Columns'. You'll see the little doorway to the stairs. If the door is locked, call to a child, who will find the guard. Not as large as Yerebatan Saray, Binbirdirek is still very impressive, but woefully neglected these days. Watch out for con men hanging around the entrance.

Back on Divan Yolu, the impressive enclosure right at the corner of Babiali Caddesi is filled with **tombs** of the Ottoman high and mighty. The first one to be built here was the mausoleum of Sultan Mahmut II (1808-39), the reforming emperor who got rid of the Janissaries and revamped the Ottoman army. After Mahmut, other notables chose to be buried here, including sultans Abdülaziz (1861-76) and Abdülhamid II (1876-1909).

Right across Divan Yolu from the tombs is a small stone **library** built by the Köprülü family in 1659. The Köprülüs rose to prominence in the mid-1600s and furnished the empire with an outstanding succession of grand viziers, generals and grand admirals for centuries. They basically ran the empire during a time when the scions of the Ottoman dynasty did not live up to the standards of Mehmet the Conqueror and Süleyman the Magnificent.

Stroll a bit further along Divan Yolu. On the left, the curious tomb with wrought-iron grillework on top is that of Köprülü Mehmet Paşa (1575-1661). Across the street, that strange building with a row of streetfront shops is actually an ancient Turkish bath, the **Çemberlitaş Hamamı** (1580).

The derelict, time-worn column rising from a little plaza is one of İstanbul's most ancient and revered monuments. Called **Çemberlitaş** ('The Banded Stone') or the Burnt Column, it was erected by Constantine the Great (324-37) to celebrate the dedication of Constantinople as capital of the Roman Empire in 330. This area was the grand Forum of Constantine, and the column was topped by a statue of the great emperor himself. In an earthquake zone erecting columns can be a risky business. This one has survived, though it needed iron bands for support within a century after it was built.

The statue crashed to the ground almost 1000 years ago.

The little **mosque** nearby is that of Atik Ali Paşa, a eunuch and grand vizier of Beyazıt II.

The Covered Market

İstanbul's Kapalı Çarşı ('Covered Market' or Grand Bazaar) is 4000 shops and several km of streets, mosques, banks, police stations, restaurants and workshops open daily except Sunday from 8.30 am to 6.30 pm. Today it is very touristy, with touts badgering bus tour groups everywhere. For real shopping in a more relaxed atmosphere, the Egyptian Market in Eminönü is better. But you must take a spin through the Covered Market in any case, or you haven't seen İstanbul.

Starting from a small *bedesten* or warehouse built in the time of Mehmet the Conqueror, the bazaar grew to cover a vast area as neighbouring shopkeepers decided to put up roofs and porches so that commerce could be conducted comfortably in all weather. Great people built *hans*, or caravanserais, at the edges of the bazaar so that caravans could bring wealth from all parts of the empire, unload and trade right in the bazaar's precincts. Finally, a system of locked gates and doors was provided so that the entire mini-city could be closed up tight at the end of the business day.

Though tourist shops now crowd the bazaar, it is also still a place where an İstanbullu (citizen of İstanbul) may come to buy a few metres of printed cloth, a gold bangle for a daughter's birthday gift, an antique carpet or a fluffy sheepskin. Whether you want to buy or not, you should see the bazaar (remember that it's closed on Sunday). Also, I've had a report from a reader that his flight bag was slashed while strolling in the bazaar, and again while walking down the busy market streets to the Egyptian Market. Guard your belongings.

Turn right off Divan Yolu at the Çemberlitaş and walk down Vezir Hanı Caddesi. The big mosque before you is **Nuruosmaniye Camii** or Light of Osman Mosque, built between 1748 and 1755 by

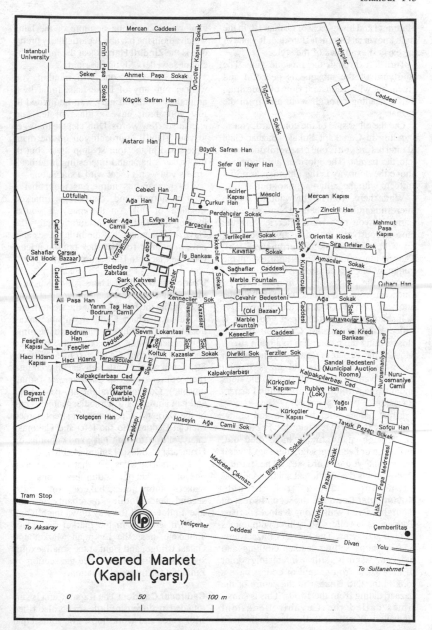

Covered Market
(Kapalı Çarşı)

0   50   100 m

Mahmut I and his successor Osman III, in the style known as Ottoman Baroque. It's one of the earliest examples of the style.

Turn left through the mosque gate. The courtyard of the mosque is peaceful and green, but with a constant flow of pedestrian traffic heading through it, to and from the bazaar.

Out the other side of the courtyard, you're standing in Çarşıkapı Sokak (Bazaar Gate St) and before you is one of several doorways into the bazaar. The glorious gold emblem above the doorway is the Ottoman armorial emblem with the sultan's monogram.

While here, you might want to see an interesting little street behind Nuruosmaniye Camii. If you turn right after leaving the mosque courtyard, then right again, you'll be on **Kılıççılar Sokak** (Swordmakers' St). They no longer make swords here, except the miniature ones to be used as letter openers. Most of the metalwork is brass souvenirs. Once you've taken a look, head back to the doorway with the Ottoman arms above it.

Inside the bazaar, the street you're on is called **Kalpakçılarbaşı Caddesi**. It's the closest thing the bazaar has to a main street. Most of the bazaar is down to your right in the maze of tiny streets and alleys, though you will want to take a left turn up the steps and into the **Kürkçüler Çarşışı**, the Furriers Bazaar.

Street names refer to trades and crafts: Jewellers St, Pearl Merchants St, Fez Makers St. Though many trades have died out, moved on or been replaced, there are several areas that you should see. The **Sandal Bedesteni** is the municipal auction hall and pawn shop – take a stroll through. **Kuyumcular Caddesi**, the second street on the right as you walk along Kalpakçılarbaşı Caddesi, is Jewellers St, aglitter with tonnes of gold and gems. The Furriers Bazaar now houses shops selling leather clothing and other goods, but it's still an interesting corner of the bazaar. You should of course have a look in the **Old Bazaar** at the centre of the bazaar, dating from the 1400s. This is sometimes called the Cevahir Bedesteni (Jewellery Warehouse). I'd also recommend

explorations into one or more of the hans which adjoin the bazaar. A particularly pretty one is the **Zincirli Han**: it's at the far (north) end of Jewellers St, on the right.

By the way, no one will mind if you wander into any of these hans for a look around. In fact, you may well be invited to rest your feet, have a glass of tea and exchange a few words. Don't let the touts get to you. They'll approach you on the main streets and in the tourist-shop areas, but in the bazaar's hans and interesting little back streets you won't meet with a single one.

The bazaar has numerous inexpensive little restaurants and 'cookshops' (marked 'lokanta' or 'lok' on the map). If you're looking for a full-scale restaurant there's the Havuzlu Lokantası, but the little places also have very tasty food at rock-bottom prices. (See the Places to Eat section for details.)

Uzunçarşı Caddesi There is another very interesting route you can follow by starting from within the bazaar. Near the western end of Kalpakçılarbaşı Caddesi, Sipahi Sokak heads north, changes names to become Feraceciler Sokak (Cloakmakers St), then becomes Yağcılar Caddesi (Oil Merchants St). You'll see the Şark Kahvesi on your left, then some steps up to a *mescit* (small mosque). Continue straight on, past shops and han entrances to Örücüler Kapısı (Gate of the Darners). Cross a main street named Mercan Caddesi (to the left) and Çakmakçılar Yokuşu (to the right), and continue on Uzunçarşı Caddesi (Longmarket St).

'Longmarket St' is just what its name says: one long market of woodturners' shops, clog makers' cubbyholes, bakeries for simits, second-hand clothing merchants and the like. Follow it all the way down the hill and you will end up in the market district of Tahtakale, near the Egyptian Market and Galata Bridge, and right at the small, exquisite Rüstem Paşa Camii. See the section on Eminönü for more information.

Çadırcılar Caddesi The Kapalı Çarşı is surrounded by dozens of little streets also filled with stores and workshops. For your actual purchases, you might do well to escape the bazaar and look for shops with lower rents and thus lower prices. Chief among these, and fascinating in its own right, is Çadırcılar Caddesi (Tentmakers St). Exit from the bazaar by walking to the west end of Kalpakçılarbaşı Caddesi. Once outside, turn right and you'll be on Çadırcılar Caddesi.

Old Book Bazaar Just after leaving the bazaar, if you turn right onto Çadırcılar Caddesi, then left through a doorway, you'll enter the Sahaflar Çarşısı or Old Book Bazaar. Go up the steps and along to the shady little courtyard. Actually, the wares in the shops are both new and old. Of the new, most are in Turkish. Of the old, many are in other languages. It's unlikely that you'll uncover any treasures here, but you can certainly find a curiosity or two.

The book bazaar dates from the Byzantine Empire. Many of the booksellers are members of a dervish order called the Halveti after its founder, Hazreti Mehmet Nureddin-i Cerrahi-i Halveti. Their *sema* or religious ceremony includes chanting from the Koran, praying, and rhythmic dancing and breathing to the accompaniment of classical Turkish liturgical music. As with all dervish orders, the sema is an attempt at close knowledge of and communion with God. The Mevlevi dervishes attempt it by their whirling dance, the Halveti through their circular dance and hyperventilation. Don't, however, expect to wander into a den of mystics. What you'll see are normal Turkish booksellers who just happen to be members of this dervish order.

Out the north gate of the Sahaflar Çarşısı is a daily flea market; on Sunday the flea market expands and spills out into Beyazıt Square.

Beyazıt & İstanbul University
The Sahaflar Çarşısı is right next to **Beyazıt Camii** or Mosque of Sultan Beyazıt II (1481-1512). Beyazıt used an exceptional amount of fine stone in his mosque, which he built in 1501-06 on a plan similar to that for Aya Sofya, but smaller. It's well worth a look.

The main street here, which started out as Divan Yolu, is now called Yeniçeriler Caddesi. It runs past Beyazıt Square, officially called Hürriyet Meydanı (Freedom Square), though everyone knows it simply as Beyazıt. The plaza is backed by the impressive portal of İstanbul University.

Under the Byzantines, this was the largest of the city's many forums, the **Forum of Theodosius**, built by that emperor in 393. Mehmet the Conqueror built his first palace here, a wooden structure which burnt down centuries ago. After Mehmet built Topkapı he used his wooden palace as a home for aging harem women.

The grand gates, main building and tall tower of the university were originally built as the Ottoman War Ministry, which explains why they are so grandiose and somewhat martial. You used to be allowed up into the tower, which is no doubt still used as a fire lookout post.

The small building at the west side of the square is now **Beyazıt Hat Sanatları Müzesi** or Beyazıt Calligraphy Museum, open from 9.30 am to 4 pm every day, for 50c admission. Though you may not be fascinated by Ottoman calligraphy, the building, once a theological college, is certainly worth a look.

Laleli & Aksaray
As you continue west along the main street, now named Ordu Caddesi (Army or 'Horde' Ave), notice the huge broken marble columns decorated with peacock-tail designs on the left-hand side of the roadway. These were part of the decoration in the Forum of Theodosius. There was a monumental arch hereabouts.

A bit further along, on the right, are more university buildings, and beyond them the hotel district of Laleli. Stay on Ordu Caddesi and just past the Ramada Hotel you'll come to the **Laleli Camii**, an Ottoman Baroque mosque built between 1759 and 1763 by Sultan Mustafa III. The ornate Baroque architecture houses a sumptuous interior. Underneath the mosque are shops and a plaza with a fountain. These were partly to produce rent for the upkeep of the mosque, partly to show off the architect's skill and cunning.

Continue down the hill on Ordu Caddesi and you will enter the confused clamour of Aksaray Square, where there's nothing particularly interesting to see or do. The **Valide Camii** on the square's north-west side is, well, highly ornamented to say the least. It does not date from any great period of Ottoman architecture, having been built in 1871 by Valide Sultan Pertevniyal, mother of Sultan Abdülaziz.

It used to be attractive, in a way, because it looked like a white wedding cake among the dull, normal structures of Aksaray, but now – with all the exhaust fumes – it's not even white anymore, and traffic flyovers block a good, full view.

Süleymaniye Camii

The Süleymaniye Camii or Mosque of Sultan Süleyman the Magnificent, is İstanbul's largest mosque. To get to the Süleymaniye from Beyazıt Square, walk around the university. The mosque is directly north of (behind) the university enclosure. Facing the university portal in Beyazıt, go to the left along Takvimhane Caddesi. The mosque is open every day, but the impressive tombs (see following) are usually inaccessible on Monday and Tuesday, when the caretaker takes his 'weekend'.

The Süleymaniye Camii crowns one of İstanbul's hills, dominating the Golden Horn and providing a magnificent landmark for all of the city. This, the grandest of all Turkish mosques, was built between 1550 and 1557 by the greatest, richest, and most powerful of Ottoman sultans, Süleyman I (1520-66), 'The Magnificent'. The Turks call this sultan Kanuni, 'The Lawgiver', and remember him more for his codification of the empire's laws than for his magnificent style.

Süleyman the Magnificent was a great builder who restored the mighty walls of Jerusalem (an Ottoman city from 1516) and built countless other monuments throughout his empire. He was the patron of Mimar Sinan (MEE-mahr see-NAHN), Turkey's greatest architect. Though the smaller Selimiye Camii in Edirne is generally counted as Sinan's masterpiece, the Süleymaniye is without doubt his grandest work.

Ottoman imperial mosques were instrumental in repopulating the capital after its conquest. In 1453, much of the city had been abandoned, the Byzantine population had shrunk, and huge areas were vacant or derelict.

When a sultan built an imperial mosque, it quickly became the centre of a new quarter – residences and workshops were soon built nearby.

Each imperial mosque had a *külliye*, or collection of charitable institutions, clustered around it. These might include a hospital, insane asylum, orphanage, soup kitchen, hospice for travellers, religious school, library, baths and a cemetery in which the mosque's imperial patron, his family and other notables could be buried.

The külliye of the Süleymaniye is particularly elaborate, and includes all of these institutions. Those are the impressive buildings you see surrounding the mosque, one of which now houses an excellent restaurant.

Most visitors enter the mosque precincts by a side door. Though this is the most convenient entrance, coming from Beyazıt, the effect of entering from the north-west side and seeing the four towering minarets and the enormous, billowing domes is better.

Inside, the mosque is breathtaking in its size and pleasing in its simplicity. There is little in the way of decoration, except for some very fine İznik tiles in the mihrab, gorgeous stained-glass windows done by one İbrahim the Drunkard, and four massive columns, one from Baalbek, one from Alexandria and two from Byzantine palaces in İstanbul. The painted arabesques on the dome are 19th-century additions, recently renewed.

Near the south-east wall of the mosque is the cemetery. Ask for the *bekçi* (BEHK-chee, caretaker) so you can see the *türbeler* (tombs) of Süleyman and his wife Haseki Hürrem Sultan (known in the West as Roxelana), and of his architect, the great Mimar

Süleymaniye Camii

Sinan. The tombs are high points of rich, high Ottoman decoration. The İznik tiles in Hürrem's tomb are particularly fine.

Şehzadebaşı Caddesi

Aqueduct of Valens Walk along Süleymaniye Caddesi, which goes south-west from the mosque, and turn right onto Şehzadebaşı Caddesi. You can see remnants of the high Bozdoğan Kemeri or Aqueduct of Valens on the left side of the street. It's not really certain that the aqueduct was constructed by the Emperor Valens (364-78), though we do know it was repaired in 1019, and in later times by several sultans. After the reign of Süleyman the Magnificent, parts of it collapsed, but restoration work was begun in the late 1980s.

Şehzade Camii On the south side of the aqueduct is the Şehzade Camii, the Mosque of the Prince. Süleyman had it built between

1544 and 1548 as a memorial to his son Mehmet, who died in 1543. It was the first important mosque to be designed by Mimar Sinan, who spent the first part of his long career as a military architect. Among the many important people buried in tile-encrusted tombs here are Prince Mehmet, his brothers and sisters, and Süleyman's grand viziers, Rüstem Paşa and İbrahim Paşa.

Gazanfer Ağa Medresesi If you have a few minutes to spare, walk west on Şehzadebaşı Caddesi. The dusty modern building on the left is Belediye Sarayı, İstanbul's Municipality or town hall. Turn right (north) and pass under the aqueduct, then take your life in your hands and cross Atatürk Bulvarı. Just on the other side of the street is the former medrese of Gazanfer Ağa (1599), now the **İstanbul Karikatür ve Mizah Müzesi** or Cartoon & Humour Museum. Turkish cartoon artistry is lively and politically important. Though the exhibits may not hold much interest for you, the pleasant sunny courtyard, with its fountain, grapevines, café and toilets, is an excellent place for a rest-stop. Hours are from 10 am to 6 pm daily except Sunday; admission is free.

EMİNÖNÜ

No doubt you've already seen Eminönü. The view of the Galata Bridge, crowded with ferries and dominated by the Yeni Cami (YEHN-nee jahm-mee, New Mosque), also called the Pigeon Mosque because of the ever present flocks of these birds, is a favourite for advertisements and magazine articles about İstanbul. The Yeni Cami sits comfortably and serenely in the midst of bustling Eminönü as the traffic, both vehicular and pedestrian, swirls around it. Visitors to İstanbul find themselves passing through Eminönü time after time.

In a way, Eminönü is the inner city's transportation hub. Not only do the Bosphorus ferries dock here, not only does all Galata Bridge traffic pass through, but Sirkeci Station is just around the corner.

Galata Bridge

Until June 1992, the Galata Bridge floated on pontoons. Ramshackle fish restaurants, teahouses and hookah joints filled the dark recesses beneath the roadway. The stream of traffic, both pedestrian and vehicular, was intense at all times.

The pontoon bridge blocked the natural flow of water and kept the Golden Horn from flushing itself of pollution, so it was replaced by a new bridge which allows the water to flow. Within weeks of the new bridge's opening, it was damaged by a terrorist bomb which blew up a ferry.

At this writing the new bridge has yet to acquire the shops and restaurants expected to occupy its nether portions, but this should happen soon.

In Byzantine times the Golden Horn provided a perfect natural harbour for the city's commerce. Suppliers of fresh vegetables and fruits, grain and staple goods set up shop in the harbour. Until only a few years ago, their successors in İstanbul's wholesale vegetable, fruit and fish markets performed the same services, in the same area to the west of the Galata Bridge in Eminönü. With the drive to clean up and beautify the Golden Horn, the wholesale markets have been moved to the outskirts of the city.

Still picturesque and interesting is the retail market district which surrounds the Egyptian Market. But before wandering into this maze of market streets, take a look inside the Yeni Cami.

Yeni Cami

The imperial mosque Yeni Cami was begun in 1597, commissioned by Valide Sultan Safiye, mother of Sultan Mehmet III (1595-1603). The site was earlier occupied by a community of Karaite Jews, radical dissenters from orthodox Judaism. When the valide sultan decided to build her grand mosque here, the community was moved to Hasköy, a district further up the Golden Horn which still bears traces of the Karaite presence.

The valide sultan lost her august position when her son the sultan died, and the mosque had to be completed in 1663 six sultans later by Valide Sultan Turhan Hatice, mother of Sultan Mehmet IV (1648-87).

In plan, the Yeni Cami is much like the Blue Mosque and the Süleymaniye Camii, with a large forecourt and a square sanctuary surmounted by a series of half-domes crowned by a grand dome. The interior is richly decorated with gold, coloured tiles and carved marble. The mosque and its tiles are 'late', past the period when Ottoman architecture was at its peak. The tilemakers of İznik were turning out slightly inferior products by the late 1600s. Compare these tiles to the ones in the Rüstem Paşa Camii, which are from the high period of İznik tilework. Only in İstanbul would a 400-year-old mosque be called 'New'.

Egyptian (Spice) Market

The Mısır Çarşısı (MUH-suhr chahr-shuh-shuh, Egyptian Market) is also called the Spice Bazaar because of its many spice shops. A century or two ago, it was twice as fascinating as it is now. Its merchants sold such things as cinnamon, gunpowder, rabbit fat, pine gum, peach-pit powder, sesame seeds, sarsaparilla root, aloe, saffron, liquorice root, donkey's milk and parsley seeds, all to be used as folk remedies.

Gunpowder, for instance, was prescribed as a remedy for haemorrhoids: you'd boil a little gunpowder with the juice of a whole lemon, strain off the liquid, dry the powder and swallow it the next morning with a little water, on an empty stomach. It was also supposed to be a good cure for pimples when mixed with a little crushed garlic. Whatever its values as a pharmaceutical, it was finally banned from the market because the shops in which it was sold kept blowing up.

The market was constructed in the 1660s as part of the Yeni Cami complex, the rents from the shops going to support upkeep of the mosque and its charitable activities. These included a school, baths, hospital and public fountains.

Enter the market (open Monday to Saturday from 8.30 am to 6.30 pm, closed Sunday) through the big armoured doors which open onto Eminönü Square. Just inside the doors, to the left, is the little stairway which leads up to the Pandeli restaurant (see the Places to Eat section).

Strolling through the market, the number of shops selling tourist trinkets is increasing annually, though there are still some shops which sell *baharat* (bah-hah-RAHT, spices) and even a few which specialise in the old-time remedies. Some of the hottest items are bee pollen and royal jelly, used to restore virility. You'll see also shops selling nuts, candied fruits, chocolate and other snacks. Try some *incir* (een-JEER, figs) or *lokum* (low-KOOM, Turkish delight). Fruit pressed into sheets and dried (looks like leather) is called pestil. It's often made from apricots or mulberries, and is delicious and relatively cheap. Buy 50 grams or 100 grams to start with.

When you come to the crossroads within the market, you have a choice. I'd suggest you turn left, see the rest of the market, then return to the crossroads and take the street to

the right. Going left, you'll come to the Ulus Lokantası, on the right-hand side next to a postcard booth, a good cheap place for a meal if you need one.

Turning left will reveal shops selling toys, clothing and various household goods. You may see a shop which specialises in the white outfits little boys wear on the day of their circumcision *(sünnet)*. The white suit is supplemented with a pillbox hat and a red sash which bears the word *Maşallah* (MAH-shah-lah, 'What wonders God has willed!'). When you see a little kid in such an outfit, you'll know that today he's going to get his. He will probably be riding around in the midst of musicians and merrymakers, for a boy's circumcision is his coming of age (at around eight to 10 years) and an excellent excuse for a tremendous party.

Turn left again at the first opportunity, and you'll leave the bazaar and enter its busy courtyard, backed by the Yeni Cami. This is the city's major market for flowers, plants, seeds and songbirds. There's a WC to your left, down the stairs, subject to a small fee. To the right, across the courtyard, is the **tomb of Valide Sultan Turhan Hatice**, founder of the Yeni Cami. Buried with her are no less than six other sultans, including her son Mehmet IV, plus dozens of imperial princes and princesses.

Now, back at that crossroads within the bazaar, take the right turning and exit through another set of armoured doors. Just outside the doors is another crossroads of bustling market streets. You can always smell coffee here, because right across the intersection is the shop of Kurukahveci Mehmet Efendi. Clerks wrap customer's parcels with lightning speed (they take great pride in this), and there always seems to be a queue of people waiting to make a purchase. To the right, down towards the Golden Horn, is a small fish market with a few butchers' shops thrown in for good measure. Up to the left, the shops and street pedlars sell mostly household and kitchen items.

Head out the bazaar doors and straight across the intersection. This is **Hasırcılar Caddesi**, Mat Makers St. Shops along it sell fresh fruits, spices, nuts, condiments, knives and other cutlery, coffee, tea, cocoa, hardware and similar retail necessities. The colours, smells, sights and sounds make this one of the liveliest and most interesting streets in the city.

Rüstem Paşa Camii

Keep walking a few short blocks along Hasırcılar Caddesi, and on the right-hand side, you'll come to the Rüstem Paşa Mosque. Keep your eyes peeled – it's easy to miss as it is not at street level. All you'll see is a tidy stone doorway and a flight of steps leading up; there is also a small marble fountain and plaque. This mosque is used heavily by the merchants and artisans of the bazaar. At this writing the mosque is closed for renovation; check to see if repairs have been completed.

At the top of the steps is a terrace and the mosque's colonnaded porch. You'll notice at once the panels of dazzling İznik faïence set into the mosque's façade. The interior is covered in similarly gorgeous tiles, so take off your shoes (women should also cover their head and shoulders), and venture inside. This particularly beautiful mosque was built by Sinan, the greatest Ottoman architect, for Rüstem Paşa, son-in-law and grand vizier of Süleyman the Magnificent. Ottoman power, glory, architecture and tilework were all at their zenith when the mosque was built in 1561. You won't forget this one.

After your visit to the mosque, you might want to spend some more time wandering the streets of this fascinating market quarter, called Tahtakale. If you need a goal, head up the hill (south) on Uzunçarşı Caddesi, which begins right near the Rüstem Paşa Camii and ends at the Covered Market (see that section for more details).

Outer City

From early times the heart of this ancient city has been near the tip of Seraglio Point. As the city grew over the centuries, its boundaries moved westward. That process continues.

There are several points of interest farther out, and if you have at least four days to tour İstanbul you should be able to see all the centre's essential sights and still have time for these outlying ones. They include the Fatih Camii, the Church of the Holy Saviour in Chora (Kariye Müzesi) famous for its Byzantine mosaics, the Palace of Constantine Porphyrogenetus (Tekfur Saray), several other mosques, the mammoth city walls, and the village of Eyüp up the Golden Horn. On your way back downtown you can stop at the Ecumenical Orthodox Patriarchate and also at a curious Bulgarian church made of cast iron.

A detour to Yedikule is described at the end of this section.

Fatih Camii The Mosque of the Conqueror or Fatih Camii is just west of the Aqueduct of Valens, on Fevzi Paşa Caddesi. You can get a dolmuş from Aksaray or Taksim to the town hall (ask for the Belediye Sarayı, behl-eh-DEE-yeh sar-rah-yuh) near the Aqueduct and walk five blocks; or you can catch any bus that has 'Fatih' or 'Edirnekapı' listed on its itinerary board.

When Mehmet the Conqueror entered Constantinople in 1453, he found a once-great city depopulated and shrunken in size within the walls. Large tracts of urban land had reverted to grass and shrubs, and many buildings were in ruins. He sought to repopulate the city with groups from the various nations of his empire, sometimes commanding that they move to İstanbul.

A prime method of repopulating a district was to commission the construction of an imperial mosque there. The mosque would become the nucleus of a city quarter, first providing work for construction crews and the merchants and pedlars who served them, then providing a focus of religious and social life. The mosque's külliye would also encourage people to move to the quarter.

The Fatih Camii was the first great imperial mosque to be built in İstanbul following the Conquest. For its location, Fatih Sultan Mehmet (Mehmet the Conqueror) chose the hilltop site of the ruined Church of the Apostles. The mosque complex, finished in 1470, was enormous, and included in its külliye 15 charitable establishments – religious schools, a hospice for travellers, a caravanserai etc. The mosque you see, however, is not the one he built. The original mosque stood for 300 years before toppling in an earthquake in 1766. It was rebuilt, but to a completely different plan. The exterior of the mosque still bears some of the original decoration; the interior is not all that impressive.

While you're here, be sure to visit the tomb of Mehmet the Conqueror behind the mosque. His wife Gülbahar, whose tomb is next to the sultan's, is rumoured to have been a French princess.

Mihrimah Camii When you're finished at the Fatih mosque, go back to Fevzi Paşa Caddesi and catch a bus or dolmuş headed north-west towards Edirnekapı. Get off the bus just before the massive city walls. You'll see the Mihrimah Camii, a mosque built by Süleyman the Magnificent's favourite daughter, Mihrimah, in the 1560s. The architect was Sinan, and the mosque marks a departure from his usual style. The inevitable earthquakes worked their destruction, and the building has been restored several times, most recently around 1900. Mihrimah married Rüstem Paşa, Süleyman's brilliant and powerful grand vizier (his little tile-covered mosque is down by the Egyptian Market). You can visit her tomb on the south-east side of the mosque.

Take a look at the **city walls** (you can hardly help it!). You'll get a closer look, and even a climb up top, in a little while.

Cross the road from the Mihrimah Camii and, still inside the walls, head north towards the Golden Horn. You'll see signs, and children pointing the way, to the Chora church.

Chora Church Mosaics If we translate the original name *(Chora)* for this building, it comes out 'Church of the Holy Saviour Outside the Walls' or 'in the Country', because the original church on this site was indeed outside the walls built by Constantine the Great. But just as London's church of St Martin-in-the-Fields is hardly surrounded by bucolic scenery these days, the Church of the Holy Saviour was soon engulfed by Byzantine urban sprawl. It was enclosed within the walls built by the Emperor Theodosius II in 413, less than 100 years after Constantine. So the Holy Saviour in the Country was 'in the country' for about 80 years, and has been 'in the city' for 1550 years. It was not only the environs of the church which changed: for four centuries it served as a mosque (Kariye Camii), and is now a museum, the Kariye Müzesi.

The **Kariye Müzesi** (☎ 523-3009) is open daily from 9.30 am to 4.30 pm, closed Tuesday; admission costs US$3. You reach it by taking any Edirnekapı bus along Fevzi Paşa Caddesi.

The building you see is not the original church-outside-the-walls. Rather, this one was built in the late 11th century, with lots of repairs and restructuring in the following centuries. Virtually all of the interior decoration – the famous mosaics and the less renowned but equally striking mural paintings – dates from about 1320. Between 1948 and 1959 the decoration was carefully restored under the auspices of the Byzantine Society of America.

The mosaics are breathtaking. There is a definite order to the arrangement of the pictures. The first ones are those of the dedication, to Christ and to the Virgin Mary. Then come the offertory ones: Theodore Metochites, builder of the church, offering it to Christ. The two small domes of the inner narthex have portraits of all Christ's ancestors back to Adam. A series outlines the Virgin Mary's life, and another, Christ's early years. Yet another series concentrates on Christ's ministry. There are lots of representations of saints and martyrs everywhere.

In the nave are three mosaics: of Christ, of the Virgin as Teacher, and of the Dormition (Assumption) of the Blessed Virgin – turn around to see this one, it's over the main door you just entered.

By the way, the baby in the painting is actually Mary's soul, being held by Jesus, while her body lies 'asleep' on its bier.

South of the nave is the parecclesion, a side chapel built to hold the tombs of the church's founder and his relatives, close friends and associates. The frescoes appropriately deal with the theme of death and resurrection. The striking painting in the apse shows Christ breaking down the gates of Hell and raising Adam and Eve, with saints and kings in attendance.

Kariye Pudding Shop Just across from the Kariye Müzesi is the Kariye Muhallebicisi or Pudding Shop, an old İstanbul structure restored by the Turkish Touring & Automobile Association. *Muhallebi* (Arabic) means pudding, and there were lots of such 'pudding shops' in Ottoman İstanbul. Today the word generally refers to a bland rosewater jelly served alone as a sweet. You can have some or another sweet or beverage on the patio on the ground floor, or on the neighbouring shady terrace with its dovecote. The upper floor of the building has been arranged as a traditional Ottoman salon. One room of the structure serves as a souvenir shop.

Constantine's Palace From Kariye, head west to the city walls, then north again, and you'll soon come to the Palace of Constantine Porphyrogenetus, the Tekfur Saray (tehk-FOOR sar-rah-yuh). It's nominally open on Wednesday, Thursday and Sunday from 9 am to 5 pm, but you can usually just wander in on any day. The caretaker may appear and sell you a ticket for 25c.

Though the building is only a shell these days, it is remarkably preserved for a Byzantine palace built in the 1300s. Sacred buildings often survive the ravages of time because they continue to be used even though they may be converted for use in another religion. Secular buildings, however, are often torn down and used as quarries for building materials once their owners die. The Byzantine palaces which once crowded Sultanahmet Square are all gone; so is the great Palace of Blachernae, which adjoined the Tekfur Saray. Only this one remains.

The caretaker may have put a ladder against the wall for you, and you can climb up onto the walls for a view of the palace, the city walls, the Golden Horn, and much of the city.

The City Walls Since being built in the 400s, the city walls have been breached by hostile forces only twice. The first time was in the 1200s, when Byzantium's 'allies', the armies of the Fourth Crusade, broke through and pillaged the town, deposing the emperor and setting up a king of their own. The second time was in 1453 under Mehmet the Conqueror. Even though Mehmet was ultimately successful, he was continually frustrated during the siege as the walls withstood admirably even the heaviest bombardments by the largest cannon in existence at the time.

The walls were kept defensible and in good repair until about a century ago, when the development of mighty naval guns made such expense pointless: if İstanbul was going to fall, it would fall to ships firing from the Bosphorus, not to soldiers advancing on the land walls.

During the late 1980s, the city undertook to rebuild the major gates for the delight of tourists. Debates raged in the Turkish newspapers over the style of the reconstruction. Some said the restorations were too theatrical, while others said that if the walls never actually did look like that, perhaps they *should* have. Anyway, the work allows you to imagine what it must have looked like in the Middle Ages. The gates which have been completed include the Topkapı, Mevlanakapı, and Belgrat Kapısı.

For a look at the most spectacular of the defences in the walls see Yedikule following.

By now you've seen the high points in this part of the city. If you've still got time and stamina, take your bearings for these places while you're up on the walls: outside the walls, on the Golden Horn, is the suburb of Eyüp, with a famous mosque and coffee house. Inside the walls, near the Golden Horn but back towards the centre, is the Rum Patrikhanesi, the seat of the Ecumenical Patriarch of the Orthodox Church. You can't see it, but you'll notice the prominent cupola of a Greek school near it.

Heading North or East Heading north, you can make your way on foot to the Golden Horn at Balat or Ayvansaray and then take a bus, dolmuş or ferry to Eyüp. Otherwise, return to the Kariye Müzesi and make your way through the maze of streets to the Fethiye Camii, where there are more magnificent Byzantine mosaics. From the Fethiye Camii it's only a few minutes' walk to the seat of the Ecumenical Orthodox Patriarchate.

Fethiye Camii Fethiye Camii or the Mosque of the Conquest was built in the 1100s as the Church of the Theotokos Pammakaristos or Church of the Joyous Mother of God. To reach it, ask someone to point you towards Draman Caddesi; follow this street until it changes names to become Fethiye Caddesi, then look left (north) to see the mosque, set in the midst of an open space.

The original monastery church was added to several times over the centuries, then converted to a mosque in 1591 to commemorate Sultan Murat III's victories in Georgia and Azerbaijan. Before its conversion it served as the headquarters of the Ecumenical Orthodox Patriarch (1456-1568); Mehmet the Conqueror visited to discuss theological questions here with Patriarch Gennadios not long after the conquest of the city. They talked things over in the side chapel known as the parecclesion, which has been restored to its former Byzantine splendour; the rest of the building remains a mosque. Visit the parecclesion to see the wonderful mosaics showing Jesus, the Apostles, the Virgin Mary, St John the Baptist, angels and saints. Entry to the parecclesion costs US$1; it is open daily from 9.30 am to 4.30 pm, closed on Tuesday.

From the Fethiye Camii, ask directions for the walk of three short blocks to the Ecumenical Orthodox Patriarchate. If your goal is Eyüp, catch a bus or ferry from Fener, near the patriarchate.

Eyüp The suburb of Eyüp, once a village outside the walls, is named for the standard-bearer of the Prophet Muhammed. Eyüp Ensari (Ayoub in Arabic, Job in English) fell in battle here while carrying the banner of Islam during the Arab assault and siege of the city in 674-78. Eyüp had been a friend of the Prophet and a revered member of Islam's early leadership. His tomb and the **Eyüp Sultan Camii** are very sacred places for most Musiims, almost ranking with Mecca, Medina and Jerusalem.

The most pleasant way to reach Eyüp is on a Golden Horn ferry, boarded at Galata Bridge (Eminönü side) or at one of the little landing stages along the route westward. Otherwise, take bus No 55 (Taksim to Eyüp Üçşehitler) or bus No 99 (Eminönü to Alibeyköyü), and get off at the 'Eyüp' stop. There are also dolmuşes: Edirnekapı to Eyüp, Topkapı to Eyüp, Aksaray to Eyüp, or Aksaray to Alibeyköyü. The mosque is open long hours every day, for free; avoid visiting on Friday and on Muslim holy days, when the mosque and tomb will be very busy with worshippers, and infidels may be looked upon as interlopers. For a snack or a lunch, there are little pastry shops and snack stands on Kalenderhane Caddesi across from the mosque.

Ironically, Eyüp's tomb was first venerated by the Byzantines after the Arab armies withdrew, long before the coming of the Turks.

When Mehmet the Conqueror besieged the city in 1453, the tomb was no doubt known to him, and he undertook to build a grander and more fitting structure to commemorate it. A legend persists though, that the tomb had been lost and was miraculously rediscovered by Mehmet's Şeyh-ül-İslam (Supreme Islamic Judge). Perhaps both are true. If the tomb was known to Mehmet Fatih and his leadership, but not generally known by the common soldiers, it could be used for inspiration – have it miraculously 're-discovered', and the army would take it as a good omen for the holy war in which they were engaged.

Whatever the truth, the tomb has been a

very holy place ever since the Conquest. Mehmet had a mosque built here within five years of his victory, and succeeding sultans came to it to be girded with the Sword of Osman, in a coronation-style ceremony. Mehmet's mosque was levelled by an earthquake in 1766, and a new mosque was built on the site by Sultan Selim III in 1800.

From the open space next to the complex, enter the great doorway to a large courtyard, then to a smaller court shaded by a huge, ancient plane tree. Note the wealth of brilliant İznik tilework on the walls here. To the left, behind the tilework and the gilded grillework, is Eyüp's tomb; to the right is the mosque. Be careful to observe the Islamic proprieties when visiting: decent clothing (no shorts), and modest dresses for women, who should also have their head, shoulders and arms covered. Take your shoes off before entering the small tomb enclosure, rich with silver, gold, crystal chandeliers, and coloured tiles. Try not to stand in front of those at prayer; act respectfully; don't use a camera.

During your visit you may see boys dressed up in white satin suits with spangled caps and red sashes emblazoned with the word 'Maşallah'. These lads are on the way to their circumcision and have made a stop beforehand at this holy place. After the actual operation, they'll be treated to huge celebration parties.

Across the court from the tomb is the **Eyüp Sultan Camii** or Mosque of the Great Eyüp, where for centuries the Ottoman princes came for the Turkish equivalent of coronation: to gird on the Sword of Osman, signifying their power and title as *padişah* ('king of kings') or sultan. The Baroque style of the mosque, gilding, marble, windows, calligraphy and other decoration lavished on it, is elegant and even simple – if Baroque can ever be described as simple.

As the Eyüp Sultan Camii is such a sacred place, many important people including lots of grand viziers wanted to be buried in its precincts. Between the mosque-tomb complex and the Golden Horn you will see a virtual 'village' of octagonal tombs. Even

those who were not to be buried here left their marks. The Valide Sultan Mihrişah, Queen Mother of Selim III, built important charitable institutions such as schools, baths and soup kitchens. Sokollu Mehmet Paşa, among the greatest of Ottoman grand viziers, donated a hospital which still functions as a medical clinic to this day.

Museum of Contemporary Art About 500 metres south of the Eyüp Sultan Camii on the Golden Horn shore stands the Feshane (FESS-hah-neh, fez factory). Built in the mid-1800s to manufacture the distinctive headgear of the Ottomans, the Feshane was converted to other textile production when Atatürk's reforms did away with the fez in 1925. The factory, after being abandoned in the 1980s, was given a new life by philanthropist Dr Nejat Eczacıbaşı, head of Turkey's largest pharmaceutical company, who provided the funds and the inspiration to restore and modernise the landmark building.

It is now the Museum of Contemporary Art (Çağrılı Sanat Müzesi), with a permanent collection of works by Turkish artists and space for changing exhibits. The museum plays a prominent role in the staging of the İstanbul Biennale; the fourth Biennale is scheduled for autumn 1994. Opening hours are from 9.30 am to 5 pm (closed on Monday); admission costs US$1.

Pierre Loti Café Up the hill to the north of the mosque is a café where 'Pierre Loti' (Louis Marie Julien Viaud, 1850-1923) used to sit and admire the city. Loti pursued a distinguished career in the French navy, and at the same time became his country's most celebrated novelist. Though a hard-headed mariner, he was also an inspired and incurable romantic who fell in love with the graceful and mysterious way of life he discovered in Ottoman İstanbul.

Loti set up house in Eyüp for several years and had a love affair, fraught with peril, with a married Turkish woman whom he called Aziyadé (the title of his most romantic and successful novel). He was transferred back to France and forced to leave his mistress and his beloved İstanbul, but he decorated his French home in Ottoman style and begged Aziyadé to flee and join him. Instead, her infidelity was discovered and then she 'disappeared'.

Pierre Loti's romantic novels about the daily life of İstanbul under the last sultans introduced millions of European readers to Turkish customs and habits, and helped to counteract the politically inspired Turkophobia then spreading through Europe.

Loti loved the city, the decadent grandeur of the empire, and the fascinating late-medieval customs of a society in decline. When he sat in this café, under a shady grapevine, sipping some çay, he saw a Golden Horn busy with caiques, schooners and a few steam vessels. The water in the Golden Horn was still clean enough for boys to swim in, and the vicinity of the café was all pastureland.

The café which today bears his name may not have any actual connection to Loti, but it occupies a spot and enjoys a view which he must have enjoyed. It's in a warren of little streets on a promontory surrounded by the Eyüp Sultan Mezarlığı (Cemetery of the Great Eyüp), just north of the Eyüp mosque. The surest way to find it is to ask the way to the café via Karyağdı Sokak. Walk out of the mosque enclosure, turn right, and walk around the mosque complex keeping it on your right until you see the street going uphill into the cemetery. There's a little sign, 'Pierre Loti'. Hike up the steep hill on Karyağdı Sokak for 15 minutes to reach the café. If you take a taxi, it will follow a completely different route because of one-way streets. At my last visit, tea was 35c, soft drinks were about twice as much. They serve a few snacks and sandwiches as well.

Back to the Centre
The ferry service on the Golden Horn will take you from the dock at Eyüp, not far from the mosque, down to the Galata Bridge at Eminönü. Ferries are not frequent, however, and you may instead find yourself going by bus or taxi. You can get a bus or dolmuş from Eyüp along the shore of the Golden Horn or up along the walls and into the city that way.

From the ferry, you'll view the old city walls, shipyards, warehouses, residential and industrial quarters, a government dry-dock, naval buildings and the cast-iron Bulgarian church.

Until a few years ago the Golden Horn was quite a sewer, but now a cleanup of the waters has begun, and green parks line much of its banks. Taking the shore road allows you to stop at the Ecumenical Orthodox Patriarchate, the Sultan Selim Camii and the Bulgarian church, all very interesting sights.

Balat
The quarter on the Golden Horn called Balat used to house a large portion of the city's Jewish population. Spanish Jews driven from their country by the judges of the Spanish Inquisition found refuge in the Ottoman Empire in the late 1400s and early 1500s. The quincentenary (500th anniversary) of their migration to Ottoman lands was celebrated in 1992. As the sultan recognised, they were a boon to his empire: they brought news of the latest Western advances in medicine, clockmaking, ballistics and other means of warfare. The refugees from the Inquisition set up the first printing presses in Turkey. Like all other religious 'nations' within the empire, the Jewish people were governed by a supreme religious leader, the Chief Rabbi, who oversaw their adherence to biblical law and who was responsible to the sultan for their good conduct.

Balat used to have many synagogues. Only two working synagogues remain, the recently restored Ahrida and the nearby Yanbol. Admission is by guided tour only. Contact a tour company for information.

Most of the city's Jewish residents have long since moved to more attractive quarters or emigrated to Europe or Israel. There is one İstanbul newspaper published in Ladino Spanish, the language brought by the immigrants in Renaissance times and still spoken in this city today.

Church of St Stephen

The Church of St Stephen of the Bulgars, between Balat and Fener on the Golden Horn, is made completely of cast iron. Most of the interior decoration is of cast iron as well. The building is unusual, and its history even more so.

The church is not normally open for visits. The best time to try visiting is, of course, Sunday morning when services for the tiny, aging congregation are held.

During the 19th century the spirit of ethnic nationalism swept through the Ottoman Empire. Each of the many ethnic groups in the empire wanted to rule its own affairs. Groups identified themselves on the bases of language, religion and racial heritage. This sometimes led to problems, as with the Bulgarians.

The Bulgars, originally a Turkic-speaking people, came from the Volga in about 680 AD and overwhelmed the Slavic peoples living in what is today Bulgaria. They adopted the Slavic language and customs, and founded an empire which threatened the power of Byzantium. In the 800s they were converted to Christianity.

The head of the Orthodox church in the Ottoman Empire was an ethnic Greek; in order to retain as much power as possible, the patriarch was opposed to any ethnic divisions within the Orthodox church. He put pressure on the sultan not to allow the Bulgarians, Macedonians and Rumanians to establish their own groups.

The pressures of nationalism became too great, and the sultan was finally forced to recognise some sort of autonomy for the Bulgars. What he did was establish not a Bulgarian patriarchate, but an 'exarchate'. The Bulgarian exarch would be 'less important' than, but independent of, the Greek Orthodox patriarch. In this way the Bulgarians would get their desired ethnic recognition, and would get out from under the dominance of the Greeks.

St Stephen's is the Bulgarian exarch's church. The Gothic church was cast in Vienna, shipped down the Danube on 100 barges, and assembled in İstanbul in 1871. A duplicate church, erected in Vienna, was destroyed by aerial bombing during WW II. The Viennese cast-iron church factory produced no other products, so far as we know.

A number of years ago St Stephen's was repaired and repainted. The first coat, of course, was metal primer. The whole procedure seemed to fit in well, what with a shipyard on the opposite shore of the Golden Horn.

Fener

The next quarter along the Golden Horn from Balat is Fener (fehn-EHR; Greek: *Phanari*, lantern or lighthouse), where the Ecumenical Orthodox patriarch has his seat. To find the patriarchate (*patrikhane*), you'll have to head inland from the Fener ferry dock on the Golden Horn, and ask. People will point the way.

Ecumenical Orthodox Patriarchate The Ecumenical patriarch is a ceremonial head of the Orthodox churches, though most of the churches – in Greece, Cyprus, Russia and other countries – have their own patriarchs or archbishops who are independent of İstanbul. Nevertheless, the 'sentimental' importance of the patriarchate, here in the city which saw the great era of Byzantine and Orthodox influence, is considerable.

These days the patriarch is a Turkish citizen. He is nominated by the church and appointed by the Turkish government to be an official in the Directorate of Religious Affairs. In this capacity he is the religious leader of the country's Orthodox citizens.

The **Church of St George**, within the patriarchate compound, is a modest place, built in 1720. The ornate patriarchal throne may date from the last years of Byzantium. The patriarchate itself has been in this spot since about 1600. In 1941 a disastrous fire destroyed many of the buildings, but spared the church.

Selimiye Camii

Only a few blocks south-east of the patriarchate (ask someone to point the way) is the mosque of Yavuz Selim (Selim I, 1512-20) on a hilltop overlooking the Golden Horn. Sultan Selim 'the Grim' laid the foundations of Ottoman greatness for his son and successor, Süleyman the Magnificent. Though he ruled for a very short time, Selim virtually doubled the empire's territory, solidified its institutions and filled its treasury. He came to power by deposing his father, Beyazıt II (1481-1512), who died 'mysteriously' soon thereafter. To avoid any threat to his power, and thus the sort of disastrous civil war which had torn the empire apart in the days before Mehmet the Conqueror, Selim had all his brothers put to death, and in the eight years of his reign he had eight grand viziers beheaded. So 'Grim' is indeed the word.

But all of this violence was in the interests of empire-building, at which he was a master. He doubled the empire's extent during his short reign, conquering part of Persia, and all of Syria and Egypt. He took from Egypt's decadent, defeated rulers the title Caliph of Islam, which was borne by his successors until 1924. In his spare time he liked to write poetry in Persian, the literary language of the time. When he died, the empire was well on the way to becoming the most powerful and brilliant in the world.

The mosque was built mostly during the reign of Selim's son Süleyman. It is especially pretty, with lots of fine, very early İznik tiles (the yellow colour is a clue to their 'earliness') and a shallow dome similar to that of Aya Sofya. Selim's tomb behind the mosque is also very fine. Among the others buried nearby are Sultan Abdülmecit (1839-61) and several children of Süleyman the Magnificent.

To the Galata Bridge

You can walk back down the hill to the Fener ferry dock and catch a ferry down to the Galata Bridge. Ferries aren't all that frequent, so check the schedule first. Otherwise, catch a bus or dolmuş (along the waterfront street Abdülezel Paşa Caddesi) headed for Eminönü.

Yedikule

Yedikule or the Fortress of the Seven Towers is a long way from most other sights of interest in İstanbul, and involves a special trip. Situated where the great city walls meet the Sea of Marmara, it's accessible by cheap train from Sirkeci. Take any *banliyö* train and hop off at Yedikule, then walk around to the entrance in the north-east. You can take bus No 80 ('Yedikule') from Eminönü, Sultanahmet and Divan Yolu, but the ride may take the better part of an hour if there's any sort of traffic. The castle is open every day from 9.30 am to 5 pm; admission costs US$1.

If you arrived in İstanbul by train from Europe, or if you rode in from the airport along the seashore, you've already had a glance of Yedikule towering over the southern approaches to the city.

Theodosius I built a triumphal arch here in the late 300s. When the next Theodosius (408-50) built his great land walls, he incorporated the arch. Four of the fortress' seven towers were built as part of the Emperor Theodosius' walls; the other three, inside the walls, were added by Mehmet the Conqueror. Under the Byzantines, the triumphal arch became known as the **Golden Gate**, and was used for triumphal state processions into and out of the city. For a time, its gates were indeed plated with gold. The doorway was sealed in the late Byzantine period.

In Ottoman times the fortress was used for defence, as a repository for the imperial treasury, as a prison and as a place of execution. Diplomatic practice in Renaissance times included chucking into loathsome prisons the ambassadors of countries with which yours didn't get along. For foreign ambassadors to the Sublime Porte, Yedikule was that prison. Latin and German inscriptions still visible in the Ambassadors' Tower bring the place's history to light. It was also here that Sultan Osman II, a 17-year-old youth, was executed in 1622 during a revolt of the Janissary corps. The kaftan he was wearing when he was murdered is now on display in Topkapı Palace's costumes collection.

The best view of the city walls and of the fortress is from the **Tower of Sultan Ahmet III**, near the gate in the city wall.

Beyond the fortress are the city's leather-tanning industries. Even in medieval times, the tanners were required to work outside the city walls because their work generated such terrible odours. Plans now call for them to be moved to the Asian suburbs (downwind) soon.

Right down at the shoreline, where the land walls meet the Sea of Marmara, is the **Marble Tower**, once part of a small Byzantine imperial seaside villa.

BEYOĞLU

Beyoğlu (BEY-oh-loo) is fascinating because it holds the architectural evidence of the Ottoman Empire's frantic attempts to modernise and reform itself, and the evidence of the European powers' attempts to undermine and subvert it. The Ottomans were struggling for their very existence as a state; the Europeans were struggling for domination of the entire Middle East, and especially its oil (already important at that time), holy places and sea lanes through the Suez Canal to India.

New ideas walked into Ottoman daily life down the streets of Pera (which with Galata comprises Beyoğlu). The Europeans, who lived in Pera, brought new fashions, machines, arts and manners, and rules for the diplomatic game. The Old City across the Golden Horn was content to sit tight and continue living in the Middle Ages with its Oriental bazaars, great mosques and palaces, narrow streets and traditional values. But Pera was to have telephones, underground trains, tramways, electric light and modern municipal government. Even the sultans got into the act. From the reign of Abdülmecit (1839-61) onwards, no sultan lived in Mehmet the Conqueror's palace at Topkapı. Rather, they built opulent European-style palaces in Pera and along the shores of the Bosphorus to the north.

The easiest way to tour Beyoğlu is to start from its busy nerve-centre: Taksim Square. You can get a dolmuş directly to Taksim from Aksaray or Sirkeci; buses to Taksim are even more plentiful.

History

Often called the New City, Beyoğlu is 'new' just in a relative sense. There was a settlement on the northern shore of the Golden Horn, near Karaköy Square, before the birth of Jesus. By the time of Theodosius II (408-50), it was large enough to become an official suburb of Constantinople. Theodosius built a fortress here, no doubt to complete the defence system of his great land walls, and called it Galata (gah-LAH-tah), as the suburb was then the home of many Galatians.

During the height of the Byzantine Empire, Galata became a favourite place for foreign trading companies to set up business. To this day, it still harbours the offices of many non-Muslim businesses and foreign representatives.

The word 'new' actually applies more to Pera, the quarter above Galata, running along the crest of the hill from the Galata Tower to Taksim Square. This was built up only in later Ottoman times.

In the 19th century, the European powers were waiting eagerly for the 'Sick Man of Europe' (the decadent Ottoman Empire) to collapse so that they could grab territory and spheres of influence. All the great colonial powers – the British, Russian, Austro-Hungarian and German empires, France and the kingdom of Italy – maintained lavish embassies and tried to cajole and pressure the Sublime Porte into concessions of territory, trade and influence.

The embassy buildings, as lavish as ever, still stand in Pera. Ironically, most of the great empires which built them collapsed along with that of the Ottomans. Only the British and French survived to grab any of the spoils. Their occupation of Middle Eastern countries under League of Nations 'mandates' has given us the Middle East we have today.

Taksim Square

The name could mean 'my taxi' in Turkish, but it doesn't; after a look at the square, you may wonder why not. Rather, it is named after the *taksim* (tahk-SEEM), or distribution point, in the city's water-conduit system. The main water line from the Belgrade Forest, north of the city, was laid to this point in 1732 by Sultan Mahmut I (1730-54), and the branch lines lead from the taksim to all parts of the city.

The first thing you'll notice in the elongated 'square' is the **Atatürk Kültür Sarayı** or Atatürk Cultural Palace (sometimes called the Opera House), the large building at the eastern end. In the summertime, during the International İstanbul Festival, tickets for the various concerts are on sale in the ticket kiosks here, and numerous performances are staged in its various halls.

To the south of the grassy mall stretching from the cultural palace to the traffic roundabout is the luxury Marmara Hotel. To the north is the **Taksim Gezi Yeri**, Taksim Park or Promenade, with the İstanbul Sheraton Hotel at its northern end.

In the midst of the roundabout swirling with traffic is the **Cumhuriyet ve İstiklal Abidesi**, Monument to the Republic & Independence, one of the earliest monuments erected during the time of the republic. It was done by an Italian sculptor in 1928. Atatürk, his assistant and successor İsmet İnönü and other revolutionary leaders appear prominently on the monument.

North of Taksim
From the roundabout, Cumhuriyet Caddesi (Republic Avenue) leads north past several streetside cafés and restaurants, banks, travel agencies, airline offices, nightclubs and the Divan and İstanbul Hilton hotels to the districts called Harbiye and Şişli.

Military Museum A km north of Taksim in Harbiye is the Askeri Müzesi or Military Museum (☎ 248 7115), open Wednesday to Sunday, from 9 am to noon and 1 to 5 pm; admission costs US$1.50. Concerts by the Mehter, the medieval Ottoman Military Band, are at 3 and 4 pm. To reach the museum, walk north out of Taksim Square along the eastern side of Cumhuriyet Caddesi (by Taksim Park) and up past the Hilton. When you come to Harbiye, the point where Valikonağı Caddesi bears right off

Cumhuriyet Caddesi, you'll see the gate to the Military Museum on your right.

The museum, within a military complex, has two parts. Entering from Cumhuriyet Caddesi, you'll come first to the new section. On the ground floor are displays of weapons, a 'heroes' gallery' *(şehit galerisi)* with artefacts from fallen Turkish soldiers of many wars, displays of Turkish military uniforms through the ages, and many glass cases holding battle standards, both Turkish and captured. The captured ones include Byzantine, Greek, British, Italian, Austro-Hungarian, and imperial Russian. Perhaps the most interesting of the exhibits are the *sayebanlar* or imperial pavilions. These luxurious cloth shelters, heavily worked with thread of silver and gold, jewels, precious silks and elegant tracery, were the battle headquarters for sultans during the summer campaign season.

The upper floor of the new section has fascinating displays of Ottoman tents, and more imperial pavilions, as well as a room devoted to Atatürk who was, of course, a famous Ottoman general before he became founder and commander-in-chief of the Turkish republican army, and first president of the Turkish Republic.

To reach the old section of the Military Museum, walk out of the new section, turn right, and walk down the hill past displays of old cannon, then turn right again, and climb the steps into the museum. Signs along the way read 'To the Other Departments'. The cannons, by the way, include Gatling guns bearing the sultan's monogram, cast in Vienna.

The old section is where you really feel the spirit of the Ottoman Empire. It has exhibits of armour (including cavalry), uniforms, field furniture made out of weapons (chairs with rifles for legs, etc), and a *Türk-Alman Dostluk Köşesi* (Turco-German Friendship Corner) with mementoes of Turkish and German military collaboration before and during WW I. Some of the exhibits here are truly amazing. My favourites are the great chain that the Byzantines spread across the mouth of the Golden Horn to keep Mehmet the Conqueror's ships out during the battle for Constantinople in 1453; and a tapestry woven by Ottoman sailors (who must have had lots of time on their hands) showing the flags of all of the world's important maritime nations.

Perhaps the best reason to visit the Military Museum is for a little concert by the Mehter. The Mehter, according to historians, was the first true military band in the world. Its purpose was not to make pretty music for dancing, but to precede the conquering Ottoman paşas into vanquished towns, impressing upon the defeated populace that everything was going to be different now. They would march in with a steady, measured pace, turning all together to face the left side of the line of march, then the right side. With tall Janissary headdresses, fierce moustaches, brilliant instruments and even kettledrums, they did their job admirably.

South of Taksim

To the south, two streets meet just before the roundabout. Sıraselviler Caddesi goes south and İstiklal Caddesi goes south-west. The famous **taksim** is to the south-west of the roundabout, just to the right of İstiklal Caddesi. It is a little octagonal building of stone. You'll also notice fountains and a pool, a little public celebration of the city's water system.

Nestled in the small triangle formed by the two mentioned streets, rising above the shops and restaurants which hide its foundations, is the **Aya Triada Kilisesi** or Greek Orthodox Church of the Holy Trinity. If it's open, as it is often during the day, you can visit: take either street out of Taksim Square, and look for the first possibility to turn towards the church.

Now head down İstiklal Caddesi for a look at the vestiges of 19th-century Ottoman life. The restored turn-of-the-century tram runs from Taksim via Galatasaray to Tünel for about 35c. It's fun, but it runs too seldom to be very useful, and is always crowded.

İstiklal Caddesi

Stretching between Taksim Square and Tünel Square, İstiklal Caddesi (ees-teek-LAHL, Independence Ave) was once known as the Grande Rue de Péra. It was the street with all the smart shops, several large embassies and churches, many impressive residential buildings and a scattering of tea shops and restaurants. Renovation efforts in 1990-91 have restored much of the street's appeal. It's now a pedestrian way. In Turkey this means that there are fewer cars, not no cars.

As you stroll along İstiklal, try to imagine it during its heyday a century ago, peopled by frock-coated merchants and Ottoman officials, European officers in colourful uniforms, women with parasols, and even some lightly veiled Turkish women.

Just out of Taksim Square, the first building you'll come to on your right is the former French plague hospital (1719), for years used as the French Consulate General in İstanbul. There's a French library here as well.

İstiklal Caddesi is packed with little restaurants and snack shops, bank branches, clothing stores, itinerant pedlars, shoppers and strollers. If you have the time, take a few detours down the narrow side streets. Any one will reveal glimpses of Beyoğlu life. The street names alone are intriguing: Büyükparmakkapı Sokak, 'Gate of the Thumb St'; Sakızağacı Sokak, 'Pine-Gum Tree St'; Kuloğlu Sokak, 'Slave's Son St'.

This used to be the cinema centre of İstanbul. With the advent of television, the cinemas found it necessary to appeal to baser appetites, which is what many of them do now. Baser appetites are also satisfied by going up some of the stairways which lead from the back streets. Though I wouldn't recommend doing a lot of wandering along narrow, dark streets here late at night, the area is perfectly safe during the day and early evening.

A few streets before coming to Galatasaray Square, look on the left for Suterazisi Sokak. Turn into this street, and at its end you'll find the **Tarihi Galatasaray Hamamı** or Historic Galatasaray Turkish Bath. The bath is one of the city's best, with lots of marble decoration, comfy little cubicles for resting and sipping tea after the bath, pretty fountains and even a shoeshine service. However, the staff are very hungry for tips, and this can result in an unpleasant bathing experience. If you go, you'll enjoy it more if you don't go alone; best of all, go with a Turkish friend. The women's section of the bath, by the way, is not nearly so elegant or pleasant as the men's.

Galatasaray Square Halfway along the length of İstiklal Caddesi is Galatasaray (gah-LAH-tah-sah-rah-yee), named for the imperial lycée you can see behind the huge gates on your left. This building once housed the country's most prestigious school, established in its present form by Sultan Abdülaziz in 1868, who wanted a place where Ottoman youth could hear lectures in both Turkish and French. Across İstiklal Caddesi from the school is the Galatasaray post office.

Çiçek Pasajı Before coming into the square (really just an intersection) of Galatasaray, you'll notice on your right a small street with some flower-sellers' stalls. This is İstanbul's renowned Çiçek Pasajı (chee-CHEHK pah-sah-zhuh) or 'Flower Passage'. Besides the flowers, there is a charming market called the Balık Pazar, literally the 'fish market', although meats, fruits, vegetables, condiments and kitchen items are sold as well. You can do a lot of interesting exploring here.

Turn right from İstiklal into Sahne Sokak, the flower-lined street, and then right again into a courtyard. On the lintel of the doorway into the courtyard you can see the legend 'Cité de Pera', for this was a 'modern' building which symbolised Pera's growth as the 'modern' European-style city. For years the courtyard held a dozen cheap little restaurant-taverns. In good weather beer barrels were rolled out onto the pavement, marble slabs were balanced on top, little stools were put around, and enthusiastic revellers filled the stools as soon as they hit the ground.

In the late 1980s, the venerable Çiçek Pasajı was 'beautified'. The makeshift tables and little stools have been replaced by comfortable, solid wooden tables and benches, the broken pavement has been replaced with smooth tiles, and the courtyard has been covered with a glass canopy to keep out foul weather. The clientele is better behaved now, and its smattering of adventurous tourists has become a significant proportion. It's a favourite destination for local guys who have picked up foreign women and want to show them some tame İstanbul nightlife. But for all that, the Çiçek Pasajı is still OK for an evening of beer drinking, food and conversation.

Pick a good place, pull up a stool and order a mug of beer, beyaz (pale) or siyah (dark). For something stronger, ask for *Bir kadeh rakı* (BEER kah-deh rah-KUH), 'A shot of rakı'. As for food, printed menus, even if you can find them, mean little here. If you already know a few Turkish dishes you like, order them, but ask prices first. Otherwise, the waiter will lead you to the kitchen so you can see what's cooking. As you eat and drink, at least three nearby revellers will want to know where you are from; when you tell them, the response is always *Çok iyi*, 'Very good!'

Many regulars have now abandoned the Çiçek Pasajı to the tourists and their attendant carpet and leather-apparel touts, opting instead to dine at little *meyhanes* (tavernas) deeper in the market. (See Places to Eat for some suggestions.)

Balık Pazar Walk out of the courtyard to the flower stalls on Sahne Sokak, turn right, then look for a little passage off to the left. This is the Avrupa Pasajı, the 'European Passage', a small gallery with marble paving and little shops selling this and that. In Pera's heyday it was undoubtedly very elegant, and present restoration aims to make it so again.

Further up the market street, another little street (Duduodaları Sokak) leads off to the left, down to the British Consulate General (more of that in a moment). Continuing along Sahne Sokak, though, near this junction on your right is the entrance to the **Üç Horan Ermeni Kilisesi**, the Armenian

Church of Three Altars. You can visit if the doors are open.

Past the Armenian church, Sahne Sokak changes names to become Balık Sokak. Leading off to the right from Balık Sokak are narrow streets harbouring numerous meyhanes where the old-time life of the Çiçek Pasajı continues, untrammelled by the glossy overlays of tourist İstanbul. Feel free to wander in and have a meal and a drink. You will probably not encounter much English, either on menus or on waiters' lips.

Unless you want to continue down the slope among the fishmongers on Balık Sokak, turn back and then right into Duduodalari Sokak, and stroll down this little street past fancy food shops, butchers', bakers', and greengrocers' shops to the British Consulate General. Along the way you may notice small stands where *midye* (skewered mussels) are frying in hot oil, and others where *kokoreç* (lamb intestines packed with more lamb intestines) is being grilled over charcoal. I recommend the mussels, but get a skewer that's been freshly cooked.

At the end of the market street you emerge into the light. Right in front of you is Meşrutiyet Caddesi, which makes its way down to the Pera Palas Oteli and the American Consulate General. On the corner here are the huge gates to the **British Consulate General**, an Italian palazzo designed by Sir Charles Barry and built in 1845. Sir Charles is the one who did the Houses of Parliament in London.

Walk past the British Consulate General along Meşrutiyet Caddesi. Watch for an iron gate and a small passage on the left, leading into a little courtyard with a derelict lamp-post in the centre. Enter the courtyard, turn right up the stairs, and you'll discover the Greek Orthodox **Church of Panaya Isodyon**. It's quiet and very tidy, hidden away in the midst of other buildings. The doors are open to visitors most of the day.

When you've seen the church, go down the stairs *behind* it (not the stairs you came up). Several little streets here are lined with tiny shops, many bearing their Greek

proprietors' names. Turn right, and just past the church property on the right-hand side you will see the entrance to the **Yeni Rejans Lokantası** or New Regency Restaurant. Founded, as legend would have it, by three White Russian dancing girls who fled the Russian Revolution, the restaurant is still operated by their Russian-speaking descendants.

This area of Beyoğlu was a favourite with Russian émigrés after the revolution. The Yeni Rejans, by the look of it, was a cabaret complete with orchestra loft and grand piano. Lunch and dinner are still served except on Sunday. The food is good, though you pay quite a bit for the seedy nostalgia.

When you go out the restaurant door, down the steps, turn right, then left along the narrow alley called Olivo Çıkmazı, which brings you back to İstiklal Caddesi.

Back on İstiklal Caddesi Across İstiklal, Caddesi notice the large Italian Gothic church behind a fence. The Franciscan **Church of San Antonio di Padua** was founded here in 1725; the brick building dates from 1913.

Cross over to the church, turn right, and head down İstiklal Caddesi once more. After the church you will pass Eskiçiçekçi Sokak on the left, then Nuriziya Sokak. The third street, a little cul-de-sac, ends at the gates of the **Palais de France**, once the French embassy to the Ottoman sultan. The grounds of the palace are extensive. The buildings include the chapel of St Louis of the French, founded here in 1581, though the present chapel building dates from the 1830s. You can get a better look at the palace and grounds another way: read on.

A few steps along İstiklal Caddesi brings you to the pretty **Netherlands Consulate General** (1855), built by the former architect to the Russian tsar. The first embassy building here dated from 1612. Past the consulate, turn left down the hill on Postacılar Sokak. You'll see the **Dutch Chapel** on the left side of the street. If it's open, take a look inside. The chapel is now the home of the Union Church of İstanbul, a multinational Protestant congregation that holds services in English.

The narrow street turns right, bringing you face to face with the former Spanish Embassy. The little chapel, founded in 1670, is still in use though the embassy is not.

The street then bends left and changes names to become Tomtom Kaptan Sokak. At the foot of the slope, on the right, is the **Palazzo di Venezia**, once the embassy for Venice, now the Italian Consulate. Venice was one of the great Mediterranean maritime powers during Renaissance times, and when Venetian and Ottoman fleets were not madly trading with one another, they were locked in ferocious combat.

To the left across the open space is a side gate to the Palais de France. Peek through the gates for another, better view of the old French embassy grounds. Then you've got to slog back up that hill to İstiklal Caddesi.

Continuing along İstiklal Caddesi, the **Church of St Mary Draperis** (built in 1678 and extensively reconstructed in 1789) is behind an iron fence and down a flight of steps. It's rarely open to visitors. Past the church, still on the left-hand side, is the grand Russian Consulate General, once the embassy of imperial Russia.

Now take a detour: turn right (north-west) off İstiklal Caddesi along Asmalımescit Sokak, a narrow, typical Beyoğlu street which holds some fusty antique shops, food shops, suspect hotels and little eateries. After 50 metres the street intersects Meşrutiyet Caddesi. To the left of the intersection is the American Library & Cultural Center, and just beyond it the pretty marble mansion which was first the US embassy, now the American Consulate General. Built as a pleasure palace for a rich man's mistress, it is now heavily fortified. A new consulate, more easily defensible, is to be built on a site up the Bosphorus. To the right of the consulate is the grand old Pera Palas Oteli.

Pera Palas Oteli The Pera Palas was built in the 1890s by Georges Nagelmackers, the Belgian entrepreneur who founded the Compagnie International des Wagons-Lits et Grands Express Européens in 1868. Nagelmackers, who had succeeded in linking Paris and Constantinople by luxury train, found that once he got his esteemed passengers to the Ottoman imperial capital there was no suitable place for them to stay. So he built the hotel here in the section today called Tepebaşı. It opened in the 1890s, advertised as having 'a thoroughly healthy situation, being high up and isolated on all four sides', and 'overlooking the Golden Horn and the whole panorama of Stamboul'.

The Pera Palaş Oteli is a grand place, with huge public rooms, a pleasant bar, a good but very pricey pastry shop, and a birdcage lift. Atatürk often stayed here; his luxurious suite on the 2nd floor (room No 101) is now a museum, preserved as it was when he used it (ask at the reception desk). The hotel was a favourite of Agatha Christie. The author usually stayed in room No 411, which at the time enjoyed a view of a little park and wooden theatre building. The view is now of the city's new meeting and exhibition centre. Once you've taken a turn through the hotel, and perhaps had a drink in the bar or tea in the salon (not for the budget-minded), head back to İstiklal Caddesi.

Near Tünel Square Back on İstiklal Caddesi, you will notice, on your left, the **Royal Swedish Consulate**, once the Swedish embassy, and after it the Four Seasons Restaurant. The road curves to the right; the open space here is Tünel Square.

Tünel

You now have a chance to take a peek at İstanbul's underground railway. Built by French engineers in 1875, the Tünel allowed the European merchants to get from their offices in Galata to their homes in Pera without hiking up the steep hillside. Until the 1970s, the carriages were of dark wood with numerous coats of bright lacquer. A modernisation programme replaced them with modern rubber-tyred Paris metro-type trains.

The fare is 40c. Trains run as frequently as necessary during rush hours, about every five or 10 minutes at other times. Though you may want to use the Tünel later to ascend the hill, right now you should stay on foot. There's a lot to see as you descend slowly towards Karaköy: a Whirling Dervish monastery, the Galata Tower and glimpses of Beyoğlu daily life.

Whirling Dervish Monastery Though the main road (İstiklal Caddesi) bears right as you come into Tünel Square, you should continue walking straight on. The street narrows and takes the name of Galipdede Caddesi, and on your left you'll notice the doorway into the Museum of Divan Literature (Divan Edebiyatı Müzesi), open from 9.30 am to 5 pm, closed on Monday. Admission costs 75c.

The dervishes still occasionally whirl here, usually on the last Sunday. of each month. Ask for current times and dates.

The dervish orders were banned in the early days of the republic because of their ultraconservative religious politics, and this hall, once the Galata Whirling Dervish Monastery (Galata Mevlevi Tekkesi) now holds exhibits of *hattat* (Arabic calligraphy) and *Divan* (Ottoman) poetry.

The Whirling Dervishes, or Mevlevi, took their name from the great Sufi mystic and poet, Celaleddin Rumi (1207-73). Rumi was called Mevlana ('Our Leader') by his disciples. Sufis (Muslim mystics) seek mystical communion with God through various means. For Mevlana, it was through a sema, involving chants, prayers, music and a whirling dance. The whirling induced a trance-like state which made it easier for the mystic to 'get close to God'. The dervish order, founded in Konya during the 1200s, flourished throughout the Ottoman Empire and survives in Konya even today. The Galata Mevlevihane (Whirling Dervish Hall) was open to foreign, non-Muslim visitors, who could witness the sema. The dervishes stressed the unity of humankind before God regardless of creed.

The modest frame *tekke* (a place where dervishes hold religious meetings and ceremonies) was restored between 1967 and 1972, but the first building here was erected by a high officer in the court of Sultan Beyazıt II in 1491. Its first *şeyh* (sheik, or leader) was Şeyh Muhammed Şemai Sultan Divani, a grandson of the great Mevlana. The building burned in 1766, but was repaired that same year by Sultan Mustafa III.

In the midst of the city, this former monastery is an oasis of flowers and shady nooks. As you approach the building, notice the little graveyard on the left. The stones are very beautiful with their graceful Arabic lettering. The shapes on top of them are of hats of the deceased; each hat denotes a different religious rank. Note also the tomb of the sheik by the entrance passage, and the *şadırvan* (ablutions fountain).

Inside the tekke, the central area was where the dervishes whirled. Several times a year Mevlevi groups from Konya (now supposedly organised as 'social clubs') come to perform the sema here. In the galleries above, visitors sit and watch. Separate areas were set aside for the orchestra and for female visitors (behind the lattices). Don't neglect the exhibits of calligraphy, writing instruments and other paraphernalia associated with this highly developed Ottoman art.

Leaving the Whirling Dervish monastery, turn left down Galipdede Caddesi, lined with shops selling books, Turkish and European musical instruments, plumbing supplies and cabinetmakers' necessities such as wood veneers. The hillside here is covered with winding streets, little passageways, alleys of stairs and European-style houses built mostly in the 19th century. There are some older 'Frankish' houses, a glimpse of what life was like for the European émigrés who came to live here and make their fortunes centuries ago. A few minutes' walk along Galipdede Caddesi will bring you to Beyoğlu's oldest landmark, the Galata Tower.

Galata Tower

The ancient Galata Kulesi or Galata Tower was the highpoint in the Genoese fortifications of Galata, and has been rebuilt many times. Today it holds an observatory and a restaurant/nightclub. The circular tower's lofty **panorama balcony** is open to visitors from 9 am to 9 pm every day, for US$1. In the evening the restaurant, bar and nightclub swing into action, but I'd recommend a daytime visit. A set-price meal, often forgettable, with drinks and the show, costs from US$35 to US$40 per person; single drinks without dinner cost from US$3 to US$6.

Daily life in the vicinity of the tower is a fascinating sight. There are woodworking shops, turners' lathes, workshops making veneer and other materials for interior decoration, and a few dusty antique stores. During the 19th century Galata had a large Sephardic Jewish population, but most of this community has now moved to more desirable residential areas. **Neve Shalom Synagogue**, a block north-east of the Galata Tower towards Şişhane Square on Büyük Hendek Caddesi, was the site of a horrible massacre by Arab gunmen during the summer of 1986. Now restored, it is used by İstanbul's Jewish community for weddings, funerals and other ceremonies.

From the Galata Tower, continue downhill on the street called Yüksek Kaldırım to reach Karaköy.

Karaköy

In order to avoid 'contamination' of their way of life, both the later Byzantine emperors and the Ottoman sultans relegated European traders to Galata. Under the late Byzantines, Genoese traders got such a hold on the town that it was virtually a little Genoa. Though Galata, now usually called Karaköy, still harbours many shipping and commercial offices, and some large banks, it is also busy with small traders.

As you approach the Galata Bridge from Karaköy, the busy ferry docks and also the docks for Mediterranean cruise ships are to your left. To your right is a warren of little streets filled with hardware stores and plumbing-supply houses. Scattered throughout this neighbourhood are Greek and Armenian churches and schools and a large Ashkenazi synagogue, reminders of the time when virtually all of the empire's business-people were non-Muslims.

At the far end of the square from the Galata Bridge, right at the lower end of Yüksek Kaldırım, Voyvoda Caddesi (also called Bankalar Caddesi) leads up a slope to the right towards Şişhane Square. This street was the banking centre during the days of the empire, and many merchant banks still have headquarters or branches here. The biggest building was that of the Ottoman Bank, now a branch of the Turkish Republic's Central Bank. On 26 August 1896, Armenian revolutionaries seized the Ottoman Bank building and threatened to blow it up if their demands were not met. They were not, and the terrorists surrendered, but anti-Armenian riots following the incident caused many Armenian casualties.

Karaköy has busy bus stops, dolmuş queues and the lower station of the Tünel. To find the Tünel station descend into the hubbub of the square from Yüksek Kaldırım, and turn into the next major street on the right, Sabahattin Evron Caddesi. The Tünel is a few steps along this street, on the right, in a concrete bunker.

Aynalıkavak

İstanbul has many marvellous imperial palaces. Perhaps more charming are its lodges, or *kasrs*, built on a more human scale, not to impress visitors but to please the monarchs themselves. Among the least frequently visited is Aynalıkavak Kasrı, an early 19th-century hunting lodge in the district called Hasköy, on the northern shore of the Golden Horn about six km from Karaköy.

The only practical way to reach it is by taxi (US$3 from Beyoğlu). Tell the driver to take you to the Hasköy Polis Karakolu (police station) or the Şükrü Urcan Spor Tesisleri (athletic facilities), which are well known. A minute's walk south-east of the Hasköy police station along the Kasımpaşa-Hasköy Yolu brings you to Aynalıkavak Kasrı (☎ 250 4094) open from 9.30 am to 4 pm (closed Monday and Thursday); admission costs less than US$1, with reductions for students.

Several centuries ago an imperial naval arsenal was established at Kasımpaşa, southeast of Hasköy, and near it a shipyard *(tersane)*. The collection of imperial hunting lodges and pleasure kiosks at Hasköy became known as the Tersane Palace, after the shipyard. A wooden palace was built on this site by Sultan Ahmet III (1703-30), and restored by Selim III (1789-1807). What you see today is mostly the work of Sultan Mahmut II (1808-39).

With its Lale Devri (Tulip Period, early 18th century) decoration and Ottoman furnishings, the pavilion is a splendid dusty old place, giving a good impression of what life was like for the Ottoman ruling class at the turn of the 19th century, when Hasköy was a thriving Jewish neighbourhood.

When sultans came here to relax, European culture was intruding on traditional Ottoman Oriental life. The lodge has some rooms – much the most comfortable – furnished in Eastern style, others in less commodious European style. Selim III composed poetry and music in one of its eastern rooms; futon-like beds were tucked away into cabinets during the day. The Bekleme Salonu (Waiting Room) has the only extant Tulip Period ceiling. In the European-style rooms, don't miss the room filled with sumptuous mother-of-pearl furniture. There's a small museum of Turkish musical instruments as well.

The pavilion's gardens and grounds provide a welcome respite from the city's concrete landscape.

THE BOSPHORUS

The strait which connects the Black Sea and Sea of Marmara, 32 km long, from 500 metres to three km wide and 50 to 120 metres (average 60 metres) deep, has determined the history not only of İstanbul, but even of the empires governed from this city. In earlier centuries it was one of the city's strongest defences. Until the age of armoured gunboats, the city was never seriously threatened from the sea.

In Turkish, the strait is the Boğaziçi, from *boğaz*, throat or strait, and *iç*, inside or interior: 'within the strait'.

The Bosphorus provides a convenient boundary for geographers. As it was a military bottleneck, armies marching from the east tended to stop on the eastern side, and those from the west on the western. So the western side was always more like Europe, the eastern more like Asia. Though the modern Turks think of themselves as Europeans, it is still common to say that Europe ends and Asia begins at the Bosphorus.

Except for the few occasions when the Bosphorus froze solid, crossing it always meant going by boat – until 1973. Late in that year, the Bosphorus Bridge, the fourth longest in the world, was opened to travellers. For the first time in history there was a firm physical link across the straits from Europe to Asia. (Interestingly, there had been a plan for a bridge during the late years of the Ottoman Empire, but nothing came of it.)

Traffic was so heavy over the new bridge that it paid for itself in less than a decade. Now there is a second bridge, the Fatih Köprüsü, (named after Mehmet the Conqueror, Mehmet Fatih) just north of Rumeli Hisar. A third bridge, even farther north, is already in the works.

History

Greek legend recounts that Zeus, unfaithful to his wife Hera in an affair with Io, tried to make up for it by turning his erstwhile lover into a cow. Hera, for good measure, provided a horsefly to sting Io on the rump and drive her across the strait. In ancient Greek, *bous* is cow, and *poros* is crossing place, giving us Bosphorus: the place where the cow crossed.

From earliest times it has been a maritime road to adventure. It is thought that Ulysses' travels brought him through the Bosphorus. Byzas, founder of Byzantium, explored these waters before the time of Jesus. Mehmet the Conqueror built two mighty fortresses at the strait's narrowest point so he could close it off to allies of the Byzantines. Each spring, enormous Ottoman armies would take several days to cross the Bosphorus on their way to campaigns in Asia. At the end of WW I, the defeated Ottoman capital cowered under the guns of Allied frigates anchored in the strait. And when the republic was proclaimed, the last sultan of the Ottoman Empire snuck quietly down to the Bosphorus shore, boarded a launch, and sailed away to exile in a British man-of-war.

Touring the Bosphorus

You could spend several days exploring the sights of the Bosphorus. It holds five Ottoman palaces, four castles, the mammoth suburb of Üsküdar, and dozens of interesting little towns. But if you're pressed for time, you can see the main points in a day.

The essential feature of any Bosphorus tour is a cruise along the strait. You just can't appreciate its grandeur and beauty completely if you're in a bus or car. On the other hand, it's time-consuming to take a ferry to a certain dock, disembark, visit a palace or castle, and return to the dock to wait for the next boat, so a trip combining travel by both land and sea is best. I recommend that you begin your explorations with a ferry cruise, get a glimpse of everything, and decide which sites you'd like to visit.

A Bosphorus Cruise Though tour agencies and luxury hotels have private boats for cruises on the Bosphorus, it's considerably cheaper to go on one of the orange-and-white ferries of the Denizyolları (Turkish Maritime Lines). Special Bosphorus cruise trips are operated twice daily on summer weekdays and Saturdays, and five times a day on summer Sundays and holidays. If you can't afford the time for the whole trip, you can get off at one of the four stops en route.

Reading the Ferry Schedule The special cruise ferries are called *Boğaziçi Özel Gezi Seferleri*. Look for this heading on the schedules, which are posted in the waiting area of each ferry dock. By tradition, European ports of call are printed on the schedules in black, Asian ports in red.

Times will be close to the following, but check to be sure. Eminönü departures are on summer weekdays at 10.30 am, 12.30 and 2.10 pm; in winter daily at 10.30 am and 1.30 pm. Anadolu Kavağı departures are on summer weekdays at 1.30, 3 and 5.10 pm; in

winter daily departures are at 3 and 5.10 pm. On Sunday and holidays in summer, departure times from Eminönü are 10 and 11 am, noon, 1.30 and 3 pm. From Anadolu Kavağı, Sunday departures are at 12.30, 1.30, 2.30, 4 and 5.30 pm.

The fare for the 1¾-hour cruise from Eminönü to Anadolu Kavağı, or vice versa, is US$4. Buy your ticket only from a ticket-seller in a booth; ignore the touts and con men. Prices are printed on all tickets. Save your ticket to show the ticket-collector when you leave the ferry at your destination. The special cruise ferries call at only five docks: Beşiktaş on the European shore, Kanlıca on the Asian shore, Yeniköy and Sarıyer on the European shore, and Anadolu Kavağı on the Asian shore (the turn-around point).

If you visit in the cooler months and the special ferries aren't running, look at the schedule for the heading 'Boğaz'a Gidiş' ('To the Bosphorus'), and also 'Boğaz'dan Geliş' ('From the Bosphorus'), for long-distance boats that make good substitutes. Heaviest traffic will naturally be southward down the Bosphorus in the morning rush hour, and northward up the Bosphorus in the evening.

The special cruise ferries are popular, and they fill up early and quickly. It's a good idea to get to the dock well ahead of departure (say, 30 minutes or even more), locate the boat, board and seize a seat. Keep the sun in mind when you choose your place; you may want some shade as you head north.

Cross-Bosphorus Ferries At several points along the Bosphorus, passenger ferries run between the European and Asian shores, allowing you to cross easily from one side to the other. If you can't catch one of these ferries, you can often hire a boatman to motor you across the Bosphorus for a few dollars.

Southernmost are the routes from Eminönü, Kabataş and Beşiktaş in Europe to Üsküdar in Asia. See Sights on the Asian Shore for details.

Another ring route is from Kanlıca to Anadolu Hisar on the Asian shore, thence across the Bosphorus to Bebek on the European shore. Departures from Kanlıca are at 8.30, 9.30, 10.30 and 11.30 am, and 12.30, 2.30, 4, 5.15 and 6.15 pm. The voyage to Bebek takes 25 minutes and costs 50c.

Other ring ferries run from İstinye on the European side to Beykoz and Paşabahçe on the Asian side. Yet another ring ferry operates from Sarıyer and Rumeli Kavağı in Europe to Anadolu Kavağı in Asia.

Sights on the European Shore

If you've cruised up the Bosphorus on a ferry, catch any bus or dolmuş headed south. To be safe, mention the name of your destination, Rumeli Hisar for example, when you board, and this way you won't miss your stop.

Coming from Aksaray, Sultanahmet, or Eminönü to visit the sights along the Bosphorus, your best bet is to take a bus or dolmuş to reach Dolmabahçe, one km down the hill from Taksim Square. From Taksim, the downhill walk is short (about 10 minutes) and pleasant with views of the Bosphorus and the palace. Starting in Taksim Square, walk towards the Atatürk Cultural Palace (Opera House). As you stand facing it, the tree-lined, divided street on your right is İnönü Caddesi, formerly called Gümüşsuyu Caddesi. It leads directly to Dolmabahçe. On the right-hand side of İnönü Caddesi, just out of Taksim, you'll see ranks of dolmuşes. Routes are mostly long ones up the European Bosphorus shore, but you may find a dolmuş going to Beşiktaş. Take this one to Dolmabahçe if you need to ride.

Coming from other parts of the city, catch a bus that goes via Eminönü and Karaköy to Beşiktaş. Any bus heading out of Karaköy along the Bosphorus shore road will take you to Dolmabahçe. Get off at the Kabataş stop. Just north of the stop you will see the Dolmabahçe Camii, and beyond it the palace.

Dolmabahçe Palace For centuries the padişah, the Ottoman sultan, had been the envy of all other monarchs in the world. Cultured, urbane, sensitive, courageous; controller of vast territories, great wealth and

Dolmabahçe Palace

invincible armies and navies, he was the Grand Turk. The principalities, city-states and small kingdoms of Europe, Africa and the Near East cowered before him, and all stood in fear of a Turkish conquest. Indeed, the Turks conquered all of North Africa, parts of southern Italy, and eastern Europe to the gates of Vienna. The opulent palace of Dolmabahçe might be seen as an apt expression of this Ottoman glory – but it's not.

Dolmabahçe was built between 1843 and 1856, when the homeland of the once-mighty padişah had become 'the Sick Man of Europe'. His many peoples, aroused by a wave of European nationalism, were in revolt; his wealth was mostly mortgaged to, or under the control of, European interests; his armies, while still considerable, were obsolescent and disorganised. The European, Western, Christian way of life had triumphed over the Asian, Eastern, Muslim one. Attempting to turn the tide, 19th-century sultans 'went European' modernising the army and civil service, granting autonomy to subject peoples, and adopting – sometimes wholesale – European ways of doing things.

The palace is open from 9 am to noon and from 1.30 to 4.30 pm, closed Monday and Thursday; I predict that the press of crowds will soon force it to open on Monday and/or Thursday as well, at least in summer. Admission costs US$5. There is a camera fee, but

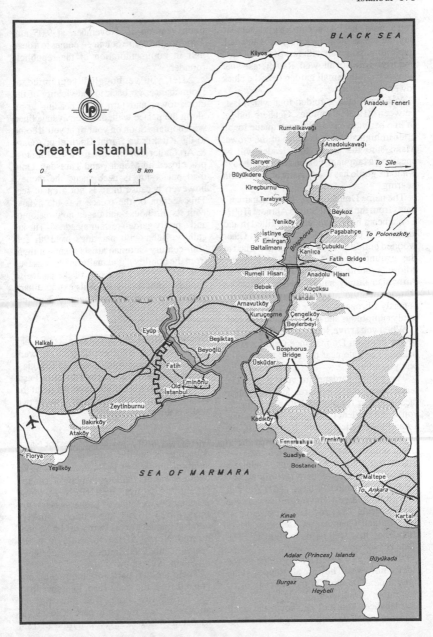

Greater İstanbul

0   4   8 km

you should check your camera in rather than pay the fee as the palace interior is too dark to photograph (even with fast film) and flash and tripod are not allowed. Rather, take your photos from the small garden near the clock tower.

You must take a guided tour which lasts between 60 and 90 minutes. Get here and get in line early: even so, you may queue for an hour in high summer because of the crowd. Make sure the palace tour leader will be speaking a language you understand, though what the guide has to say is not always worth hearing.

The name Dolmabahçe, 'filled-in garden', dates from the reign of Sultan Ahmet I (1607-17), when a little cove here was filled in and an imperial pleasure kiosk built on it. Other wooden buildings followed, but all burned to the ground in 1814. Sultan Abdülmecit, whose favourite architects were scions of an Armenian family named Balyan, wanted a 'European-style' marble palace. What he got is partly European, partly Oriental, and certainly sumptuous and heavily overdecorated.

When you arrive, look for the ornate **clock tower** between Dolmabahçe Camii and the palace. The gate near the clock tower is the one you enter.

The palace gardens are very pretty. The fence along the Bosphorus and the palace façade go on for almost half a km. Inside, you'll see opulent public and private rooms, a harem with steel doors, lots of stuff like Sèvres vases and Bohemian chandeliers, and also a staircase with a crystal balustrade.

One room was used by Sultan Abdülaziz (1861-76), an enormously fat fellow who needed an enormously large bed. (You will see just how large.) The magnificent throne room, used in 1877 for the first meeting of the Ottoman Chamber of Deputies, has a chandelier that weighs over 4000 kg. The place is awesome.

Don't set your watch by any of the palace clocks, however. They are all stopped at the same time: 9.05 am. On the morning of 10 November 1938, Kemal Atatürk died in Dolmabahçe. You will be shown the small bedroom which he used during his last days.

Each year on 10 November, at 9.05 am, Turkey – the entire country – comes to a dead halt in commemoration of the republic's founder.

After you've boggled your mind at Dolmabahçe, go back to the vicinity of the clock tower and turn right, heading north along the palace wall, down an avenue lined with poplars. Soon on your right you'll come to the **Kuşluk ve Sanat Galerisi** or Aviary & Art Gallery, open daily from 9.30 am to 4 pm, closed on Monday and Thursday. Only mad palace-lovers need spend the money, however, because there is not a lot to see. This section of the palace was the aviary, with its birdhouse and cages now restored, and a pretty garden restaurant added. The art gallery, lined with paintings by 19th and 20th-century Ottoman artists (many of them from the nobility), is actually an old passageway leading from one part of the palace to another. That accounts for its extraordinary shape, a single corridor over 100 metres long.

Beşiktaş When you've finished at the aviary and gallery, turn right (north) again and walk for five minutes to the suburb of Beşiktaş, sometimes called Barbaros Hayrettin Paşa. It's not a long walk if you're willing, but the heavy traffic in this corridor between two walls is noisy and smelly.

Naval Museum The Deniz Müzesi or Naval Museum, is on the Bosphorus shore just south of the flyover in Beşiktaş. Among its exhibits are an outdoor display of cannon (including Selim the Grim's 21-tonne monster) and a statue of Barbaros Hayrettin Paşa (1483-1546), the famous Turkish admiral known also as Barbarossa who conquered North Africa for Süleyman the Magnificent. The admiral's tomb, designed by Sinan, is close by.

There are two parts to the museum, one entered from the main road, the other from the Bosphorus shore. You must pay an admission fee for each part. The Naval Museum (☎ 261-0225) is open from 9.30 am to 5 pm, closed on Monday and Tuesday. Admission costs US$1 in each part.

Though the Ottoman Empire is most remembered for its conquests on land, its maritime power was equally impressive. During the reign of Süleyman the Magnificent (1520-66), the eastern Mediterranean was virtually an Ottoman lake. The sultan's navies cut a swath in the Indian Ocean as well. Sea power was instrumental in the conquests of the Aegean coasts and islands, Egypt and North Africa. Discipline, well-organised supply and good ship design contributed to Ottoman victories.

However, the navy, like the army and the government, lagged behind the West in modernisation during the later centuries. The great battle which broke the spell of Ottoman naval invincibility was fought in 1571 at Lepanto, in the Gulf of Patras off the Greek coast. (Cervantes fought on the Christian side, and was badly wounded.) Though the Turkish fleet was destroyed, the sultan quickly produced another, partly with the help of rich Greek shipowners who were his subjects.

In the Bosphorus section of the museum, be sure to see the sleek, swift imperial barges in which the sultan would speed up and down the Bosphorus from palace to palace (in those days the roads were not very smooth or fast). Over 30 metres in length but only two metres wide, with 13 banks of oars, the barges were obviously the rocket boats of their day. The ones with latticework screens were for the imperial ladies. There's also a war galley with 24 pairs of oars.

You may also be curious to see a replica of the *Map of Piri Reis*, an early Ottoman map (1513) which purports to show the coasts and continents of the New World. It's assumed that Piri Reis ('Captain Piri') got hold of the work of Columbus for his map. The original map is in Topkapı Palace; this one is on the wall above the door as you enter the Bosphorus section. Colourful copies are on sale here in the museum.

Ihlamur Kasrı Inland to the north of Dolmabahçe Palace and the Naval Museum,

sheltered in a narrow valley surrounded by a maze of twisting little streets, is the Ihlamur Kasrı (UHH-lah-moor kahss-ruh) or Kiosk of the Linden Tree (☎ 261-2991). The pretty park actually has two small, ornate imperial pavilions.

The park and two kiosks are open from 9.30 am to 4 pm every day except Monday and Thursday. Admission to the park and kiosks costs 75c, or 25c if you just want to stroll through the park. The fee for using a camera is US$6. The easiest way to find this place in its maze of streets is to take a taxi which, from Dolmabahçe or Beşiktaş, should cost only US$1 or so. Bus No 26 (from Dikilitaş to Eminönü) departs from Eminönü, stops at Karaköy, Dolmabahçe and Beşiktaş, before heading inland to the Ihlamur stop and continuing to Dikilitaş (DEE-kee-LEE-tahsh), which is not far past Ihlamur. Other buses are No 26A, 26B or 26C.

Once a quiet, sheltered valley neighbouring the imperial palaces of Yıldız and Dolmabahçe, the Ihlamur Valley now hums with the noise of traffic and is surrounded by modern apartment blocks. It's not difficult to imagine, however, what it must have been like when these two miniature palaces stood here alone, in the midst of a forest, waiting for the sultan to drop by for a few hours away from his duties. Near the entry gate the park is open and formal, with grassy lawns, ornamental trees, and a quiet pool. To the right behind the Maiyet Köşkü the gardens are more rustic, shady and cool, with naturalistic spring-like fountains.

As you enter, look across the pool to find the **Merasim Köşkü** or Sultan's Kiosk, built on the orders of Sultan Abdülmecit between 1849 and 1855 by Nikogos Balyan, of the family of imperial architects. As you enter, a guide will approach to offer you a free guided tour. Up the marble stairway and through the ornate door is the Hall of Mirrors, with crystal from Bohemia and vases from France. The Baroque décor includes patterns of shells, flowers, vines, fruits and lots of gold leaf.

The music room which is to the right of

the entrance has precious Hereke fabrics on the chairs and a beautiful enamelled coal-grate fireplace painted with flowers. You'll see similarly beautiful fireplaces in the other rooms as well. The 'marble' walls of the music room are fake.

Next comes the Imperial Water Closet, with an interesting flat Turkish toilet, demonstrating that even the sultan had to hunker down.

The room to the left of the entrance was a reception salon with a sofa-throne and 'marble' decoration of plaster with gold flecks. The tour ends downstairs, where displays of photographs show details of the restoration work carried out in the 1980s.

The **Maiyet Köşkü** or Retinue Kiosk, was for the sultan's suite of attendants, guests or harem. It's now a teahouse serving tea, coffee and snacks (for around US$2). Downstairs are WCs and a shop selling books and other publications.

Çirağan Palace From the Naval Museum and the flyover in Beşiktaş, you can walk north for 10 minutes, or catch a bus or dolmuş heading north along the shore, to reach the entrance to Yıldız Park (bus stop Galatasaray Lisesi). Before you reach the entrance, you'll be passing Çirağan Palace on your right. The palace, now restored as the posh Çirağan Palace Hotel Kempinski, is hidden from the road by a high wall, though you can get a glimpse of it through the huge gates. If you're dressed like an affluent tourist you can even go in and take a turn around the sumptuous hotel and its grounds.

Unsatisfied with the architectural exertions of his predecessor at Dolmabahçe, Sultan Abdülaziz (1861-76) had to build his own palace. He built Çirağan on the Bosphorus shore only a km north of Dolmabahçe, replacing an earlier wooden palace. The architect was the self-same Balyan as for Dolmabahçe. The sultan didn't get to live here much, however. Instead, it served as a detention place for his successor, the mentally unbalanced Sultan Murat V, who was deposed before he had even reigned

a year. Later the palace housed the Ottoman Chamber of Deputies and Senate in 1909, but in 1910 it was destroyed by fire under suspicious circumstances.

Yıldız Palace & Park Sultan Abdülhamid II (1876-1909), who succeeded Murat V, also had to build his own palace. He added considerably to the structures built by earlier sultans in Yıldız Park, on the hillside above Çirağan. The kiosks and summer palaces, as well as the park itself, have been restored by the Turkish Touring & Automobile Association, and several now have become delightful restaurants and teahouses.

The park is open from 9 am to 6 pm every day; admission costs 25c for pedestrians, 85c for cars (including taxis). The park began life as the imperial reserve for Çirağan Palace, but when Abdülhamid built the Şale Köşkü, the park served that palace. Under Abdülhamid, the park was planted with exotic and valuable trees, shrubs and flowers, and was provided with manicured paths and a superior electric lighting and drainage system. The sultan could reach Çirağan Palace by a private bridge over the roadway from the park. If you come to the park by taxi, you might as well have it take you up the steep slope to the Şale Köşkü. You can visit the other kiosks on the walk down. A taxi from Taksim Square to the top of the hill might cost around US$5 or $6.

As you toil up the hill along the road, near the top of the slope to the left you'll see the **Çadır Köşkü**. This pretty, ornate little kiosk was built between 1865 and 1870 as a place for the sultan to enjoy the view, rest from a walk, and have a cup of tea or coffee. It serves the same purpose today for visitors. Only drinks are served (no food), but you can enjoy them on the marble terrace overlooking the Bosphorus, and afterwards walk around the artificial lake complete with island.

To the right (north) as you are hiking up the road from the gate, you will notice two greenhouses and another kiosk. These are the **Kış Bahçesi** (Winter Garden), the **Yeşil**

Sera (Green Nursery), and the **Malta Köşkü** (Malta Kiosk) (☎ 260-2752). The Malta Kiosk, restored in 1979, is now a café serving refreshments, alcoholic drinks and light meals. The view from here is the best in the park, much better than that at the Çadır Köşkü. If you sit down to a plate of grilled lamb and then finish up with something sweet, your bill will add up to US$4 to $6.

Also to the right are the **Yıldız Porselen Fabrikası** or Yıldız Porcelain Factories, constructed to manufacture dinner services for the palace. They still operate and are open to visits.

At the very top of the hill, enclosed by a separate, lofty wall, is the **Şale Köşkü** or Chalet Kiosk, a 'guesthouse' put up in 1882 and expanded in 1898 by Abdülhamid for use by Kaiser Wilhelm II of Germany during a state visit. You must pay a separate admission fee of US$3 to see the Chalet Kiosk (☎ 258-3080) which is open from 9.30 am to 4 pm daily and closed on Monday.

I expect the Kaiser had enough space to move in, as the 'chalet' has 64 rooms. After his imperial guest departed, the sultan became quite attached to his 'rustic' creation, and decided to live here himself, forsaking the more lavish but less well-protected palaces on the Bosphorus shore. Abdülhamid was paranoid, and for good reason. Fate determined that his fears would come true. He was deposed, left this wooden palace in April 1909 and boarded a special train which took him to house arrest in Ottoman Salonika (today Thessaloniki, in Greece). He was later allowed by the Young Turks' government to return to İstanbul and live out his years in Beylerbeyi Palace, on the Asian shore of the Bosphorus.

As though this were not enough dolorous history for the place, the last sultan of the Ottoman Empire, Mehmet V (Vahideddin), lived here until, at 6 am on 11 November 1922, he and his first chamberlain, bandmaster, doctor, two secretaries, valet, barber and two eunuchs accompanied by trunks full of jewels, gold and antiques, boarded two British Red Cross ambulances for the secret journey to the naval dockyard at Tophane.

There they boarded the British battleship HMS *Malaya* for a trip into exile, ending the Ottoman Empire forever. On the way to the quay one of the tyres on the sultan's ambulance went flat; while it was being changed, the Shadow of God on Earth quaked, fearing that he might be discovered.

In the republican era, the Chalet Kiosk has served as a guesthouse for visiting heads of state, including Charles de Gaulle, Pope Paul VI, and the Empress Soraya. The gravel walkways along which you approach the palace are said to have been ordered by Abdülhamid as a security measure. It's impossible for anyone to walk on them without making a lot of noise. As you enter the palace, a guide will approach you to give you the tour, which is required. The guide will tell you that all of the carpets in the palace are from the imperial factory at Hereke, east of İstanbul.

The first section you visit was the original chalet, built in 1882. The first room on the tour was used by Abdülhamid's mother for her religious devotions, the second was her guest reception room, with a very fine mosaic tabletop. Then comes a women's resting room, and afterwards a tearoom with furniture marked with a gold star on a blue background, which reminds one that this was the 'star' (*yıldız*) palace.

In 1898 the chalet was expanded, and the older section became the harem (with steel doors), while the new section was the selamlık. In the selamlık are a bathroom with tiles from the Yıldız Porcelain Factories, and several reception rooms, one of which has furniture made by Abdülhamid himself, an accomplished woodworker. The grand hall of the selamlık is vast, its floor covered by a 7½-tonne Hereke carpet woven just for this room. So huge is the rug that it had to be brought in through the far (north) wall before the building was finished and the wall was closed.

Other buildings at Yıldız include the **Merasim Köşkü** or Ceremonial Kiosk and barracks. Part of the Ceremonial Kiosk was restored in 1988 and opened as the **İstanbul Şehir Müzesi** or İstanbul City Museum, open daily except Thursday from 9 am to 4.30 pm; admission costs US$1. It's reached from Barbaros Bulvarı, the road along the south side of the park, not from within the park itself.

After seeing Yıldız, you can take a bus or dolmuş north to Bebek and Rumeli Hisar, or return to Beşiktaş to catch a shuttle ferry over to Üsküdar, on the Asian side, in order to continue your sightseeing. The ferries operate every 15 or 20 minutes in each direction, from 6 am to midnight. There are also boats between Üsküdar and Eminönü. Ferries going to Eminönü may bear the sign 'Köprü' or 'Bridge', meaning the Galata Bridge.

Ortaköy Literally 'middle village', this Bosphorus suburb of İstanbul has had an interesting ethnic history. Even today, church, synagogue and mosque coexist peacefully in its narrow streets. For a closer look at the ornate mosque called the **Ortaköy Camii**, get out of the bus or dolmuş at Osmanzade Sokak, near the doorway to the Etz Ahayim Synagogue, and walk eastward. The narrow streets are filled with art and craft galleries and trendy cafés (such as the one named A La Turka). At the water's edge are more cafés with lots of open-air tables in fair weather. It's a pleasant place to wander around and to sip a drink.

The mosque, officially named the Büyük Mecidiye Camii, is currently under restoration. There was an earlier mosque here, but the present eclectic-Baroque building is the work of Nikogos Balyan, architect of Dolmabahçe Palace, who designed it for Sultan Abdülmecit in 1854. Within the mosque hang several masterful examples of Arabic calligraphy executed by the sultan, who was an accomplished calligrapher.

Bebek & Rumeli Hisar Bebek is a prosperous suburb of İstanbul with a surprising foreign and academic presence because of Boğaziçi Üniversitesi (Bosphorus University). A ring ferry service here joins Bebek with Kanlıca and Anadolu Hisar on the Asian

shore. (For dining suggestions in Bebek, see Places to Eat.)

Just north of Bebek on the European shore is **Rumeli Hisar**, the Fortress of Europe. The fortress is open from 9.30 am to 5 pm daily; closed on Monday. Admission costs US$2.50, half-price on Sundays and holidays.

Here at the narrowest part of the Bosphorus, Mehmet the Conqueror had this fortress built in a mere four months during 1452, in preparation for his planned siege of Byzantine Constantinople. To speed its completion in line with his impatience to conquer Constantinople, Mehmet the Conqueror ordered each of his three viziers to take responsibility for one of the three main towers. If the tower's construction was not completed on schedule, the vizier would pay with his life, or so legend has it. Not surprisingly, the work was completed on time, with Mehmet's three generals competing fiercely with one another to finish.

Once completed, Rumeli Hisar, in concert with Anadolu Hisar on the Asian shore just opposite, controlled all traffic on the Bosphorus, and cut the city off from resupply by sea from the north. The mighty fortress's useful military life lasted less than one year. After the conquest of Constantinople, it was used as a glorified Bosphorus toll booth for a while, then as a barracks, later as a prison, and finally as an open-air theatre, but never again as a fortress.

Above the town you'll notice the New England 19th-century-style architecture of the **Boğaziçi Üniversitesi** (Bosphorus University) on a hilltop above the town of Bebek.

Founded as Robert College in the mid-19th century by the American Board of Foreign Missions, the college had an important influence on the modernisation of political, social, economic and scientific thought in Turkey. Though donated by the board to the Turkish Republic in the early 1970s, instruction is still in English and Turkish.

Robert College, having joined forces with the American College for Girls in nearby

Arnavutköy, survives as a special school to prepare bright students for university.

Emirgan & Yeniköy Each spring a tulip festival takes place in Emirgan, a well-to-do suburb north of the Fatih Bridge. North of Emirgan, at İstinye, is a cove with a dry dock. A ring ferry service runs from İstinye to Beykoz and Paşabahçe on the Asian shore and will soon be replaced by a third Bosphorus bridge.

On a point jutting out from the European shore is Yeniköy, first settled in classical times. This place later became a favourite summer resort, indicated by the lavish 19th-century Ottoman *yalı* or seaside villa, of the one-time grand vizier, Sait Halim Paşa. Not too many of these luxurious timber villas survive. Fire destroyed many. Economics and desire for modern conveniences caused many others to be torn down before preservation laws were promulgated. Today it is against the law to remove a yalı from the Bosphorus – it must either be repaired or rebuilt.

Tarabya Originally called Therapeia for its healthful climate, the little cove of Tarabya has been a favourite summer watering place for İstanbul's well-to-do for centuries. Little restaurants, specialising in fish, ring the cove (for details, see Places to Eat). North of the village are some of the old summer embassies of foreign powers. When the heat and fear of disease increased in the warm months, foreign ambassadors and their staffs would retire to palatial residences, complete with lush gardens, on this shore. The region for such embassy residences extended north to the next village, Büyükdere.

Sarıyer The villagers of Sarıyer have occupied themselves for most of their history by fishing in the currents of the Bosphorus. Fishing is still a pastime and a livelihood here, and Sarıyer is justly noted for its several good fish restaurants. Turn right as you leave the ferry dock, stay as close to the shore as possible, and you will soon come to the village's active fish market and several

fish restaurants – both cheap and expensive (see the Places to Eat section for details). Dolmuşes for the beach at **Kilyos** leave from a point just to the north of the ferry dock.

Dolmuş minibuses link Sarıyer and Taksim Square (US$1). The stop in Taksim is on Mete Caddesi north of the Gezi Oteli, east of the İstanbul Sheraton Hotel.

Of particular interest in Sarıyer is the **Sadberk Hanım Museum** (☎ 242-3813), Piyasa Caddesi 27-29, Büyükdere, a private museum of Anatolian antiquities and Ottoman heirlooms from one of Turkey's richest families. If you come to Sarıyer by ferry, look to the left as you leave the dock, and you will see a yellow wooden house on the shore road about 300 metres to the south – that's the museum. It's open in summer from 10.30 am to 6 pm, in winter from 10 am to 5 pm; it's closed on Wednesday all year. Admission costs US$1. Plaques are in English and Turkish.

Sadberk Hanım, who gathered the collections now housed in the museum, was the wife of Mr Vehbi Koç, one of the country's foremost businessmen, who made much of his fortune as Turkish agent for many international firms such as Coca-Cola, Avis and IBM. After her death in the 1970s, the family established the museum in this graceful old Bosphorus yalı, once the summer residence of Manuk Azaryan Efendi, an Armenian who was once speaker of the upper house of the Ottoman parliament.

The original museum building houses artefacts and exhibits from Turkey's Islamic past. The non-Islamic collections are displayed in a separate building at the rear.

In my opinion, the most fascinating of the museum's collections are those in the original yalı, dating from Ottoman times: worry beads of solid gold; golden, bejewelled tobacco boxes and watches (one bears the sultan's monogram in diamonds); beautiful Kütahya pottery; even a table that once belonged to Napoleon (he's pictured on it, surrounded by his generals). A number of rooms in the great old house have been arranged and decorated in Ottoman style – the style of the ruling class, obviously.

There's a sumptuous maternity room with embroidered cloth and lots of lace, a salon with all the paraphernalia of the Ottoman coffee ceremony, and a third set up as a circumcision room. A display case holds a fine collection of Ottoman spoons (the prime dining utensil) made from tortoiseshell, ebony, ivory, and similarly precious materials.

The collections in the new building include very choice artefacts dating from as early as the 500s BC, and continuing through Roman and Byzantine times. There is also a well-chosen collection of Chinese celadon ware from the 1300s to 1500s, later Chinese blue-and-white porcelain, and some 18th-century Chinese porcelain made specifically for the Ottoman market.

Rumeli Kavağı North of Rumeli Kavağı, the village farthest north on the European shore, is a military zone. The sleepy little town gets most of its excitement from the arrival and departure of ferries. There is a little public beach named Altınkum near the village.

Kilyos From Sarıyer you can get a bus (No 151, for 50c) or dolmuş ('Sarıyer-Kilyos', 65c) to Kilyos, on the Black Sea coast. The 20-minute ride takes you up into the hills past posh villas built by Arab oil potentates and traders, and little impromptu open-air roadside restaurants featuring *kuzu çevirme* (spit-roasted lamb). I can recommend the lamb highly. These places are usually open every day in high summer, but at weekends only in the off season. Prices range from low to moderate.

There are some little pensions, hotels and guesthouses in Kilyos, open during the summer for beach fanciers (see Places to Stay for details). The best beach is the fenced one in front of the Turban Kilyos Moteli, open daily in warm weather from 8 am to 6 pm; it's very crowded on summer weekends, but not bad during the week. You can use it without staying at the motel if you pay US$3.50 per person; a private changing cabin for two costs US$7.50. Parking costs US$2, so if you drive, park elsewhere in the village and walk over to the beach.

If you go to Kilyos for swimming, keep in mind that the waters of the Black Sea are fairly chilly. More importantly, there is a deadly undertow on many beaches. Swim only in protected areas or where there is an attentive lifeguard, and don't swim alone.

Sights on the Asian Shore

The Asian shore of the Bosphorus has a number of possibilities for interesting excursions, with the advantage that you will meet far fewer tourists than in European İstanbul.

Crossing the Bosphorus To reach the Asian shore, hop on the Üsküdar ferry from Eminönü (Dock No 2), which runs every 20 minutes between 6 am and midnight, even more frequently during rush hours, for 50c. A similar, frequent ferry service operates between Beşiktaş and Üsküdar. From Kabataş, just south of Dolmabahçe Palace, ferries run to Üsküdar every 30 minutes on the hour and half-hour from 7 am to 8 pm. There are also city buses and dolmuşes departing from Taksim Square for Üsküdar. The ferries are faster and much more enjoyable, though.

If you take the ferry to Üsküdar, you'll notice **Leander's Tower**, called the Kız Kulesi (Maiden's Tower) in Turkish. The tower was a toll booth and defence point in ancient times; the Bosphorus could be closed off by means of a chain stretching from here to Seraglio Point. The tower has really nothing to do with Leander, who was no maiden, and who swam not the Bosphorus but the Hellespont (Dardanelles), 340 km from here. The tower is subject to the usual legends: oracle says maiden will die by snakebite; concerned father puts maiden in snake-proof tower; fruit vendor comes by in boat, sells basket of fruit (complete with snake) to maiden; maiden gets hers etc. The legend seems to crop up wherever there are offshore towers, and maidens. Anyway, it's a pretty tower, and an İstanbul landmark.

Another landmark is the tall spear of a

television tower on Büyük Çamlıca hilltop, a lookout you can visit from Üsküdar.

A landmark especially for travellers is the German-style **Haydarpaşa Station**, south of Üsküdar, the city's terminus for Asian trains. During the late 19th century, when Kaiser Wilhelm was trying to charm the sultan into economic and military cooperation, he gave him the station as a little gift.

You will also notice the large **Selimiye Barracks** (Selimiye Kışlası), a square building with towers at the corners. It dates from the early 19th century, when Selim III and Mahmut II reorganised the Ottoman armed forces along European lines. Not far away is the **Selimiye Camii** (1805). During the Crimean War (1853-56), when Britain and France fought on the Ottoman side against the Russian Empire, the Selimiye Barracks served as a military hospital as well. It was here that the English nurse Florence Nightingale, horrified at the conditions suffered by the wounded, established with 38 companion nurses the first model military hospital with modern standards of discipline, order, sanitation and care. In effect, her work at the Selimiye Barracks laid down the norms of modern nursing, and turned nursing into a skilled, respected profession. A small museum (☎ 343 7310) in the barracks, open from 9 am to 5 pm on Saturday (other days by appointment), is dedicated to her work.

That other highly ornamented building, very storybook Ottoman, was formerly a rest home for aging palace ladies. It's now a school.

Üsküdar Üsküdar (ER-sker-dahr) is the Turkish form of the name Scutari. Legend has it that the first ancient colonists established themselves at Chalcedon, the modern Kadıköy, south of Üsküdar. Byzas, bearing the oracle's message to found a colony 'Opposite the blind', thought the Chalcedonites blind to the advantages of Seraglio Point as a town site, and founded his town on the European shore. Still, people have lived on this, the Asian shore, longer than they've lived on the other.

Today Üsküdar is a busy dormitory suburb for İstanbul, and you will enjoy several hours' browse through its streets, markets and mosques. Highlights of the area include the exquisite Tiled Mosque (Çinili Cami), the hilltop lookouts of Büyük Çamlıca and Küçük Çamlıca, and Beylerbeyi Palace.

As you leave the ferry dock in Üsküdar, the **main square**, Hakimiyet-i Milliye Meydanı, is right before you. North-east of the square behind the dolmuş ranks and near the ferry landing is the **Mihrimah Sultan Camii** (1547), sometimes called the İskele Camii (Dock Mosque), designed by Sinan for a daughter of Süleyman the Magnificent. To the south of the square is the **Yeni Valide Camii** or New Queen Mother's Mosque (1710), built by Sultan Ahmet III for his mother. It resembles the Rüstem Paşa Camii near the Egyptian Market in Eminönü. Built late in the period of classical Ottoman architecture, it is not as fine as earlier works.

West of the square, overlooking the harbour, is the **Şemsi Paşa Camii** (1580), also designed by Sinan.

If you need a place to eat in Üsküdar, try the *Kanaat Restaurant*, near the ferry dock on Selmanipak Caddesi.

After you have explored downtown Üsküdar a bit, head up to the Çamlıca hilltops.

Büyük Çamlıca The hilltop park, highest point in İstanbul at 261 metres, has long been enjoyed by İstanbul's nobility, poets and common folk. Once favoured by Sultan Mahmut II (1808-39), by the late 1970s it was a dusty (or muddy), unkempt car park threatened by illegal and unplanned construction. In 1980 the municipal government and the Turkish Touring & Automobile Association collaborated on a plan to restore and beautify the hilltop and to build a coffeehouse restaurant such as Mahmut might have enjoyed. The plan was a great success, yielding a park to be enjoyed by locals as well as visitors.

To reach the hilltop from Üsküdar's main square, you can take a taxi (US$2.50 to US$3) all the way to the summit, or a dolmuş most of the way. For the latter, walk to the dolmuş ranks in front of the Mihrimah Sultan Mosque near the ferry dock, take a dolmuş headed for Ümraniye, and ask for Büyük Çamlıca. The dolmuş will pass the entrance to Küçük Çamlıca and drop you off shortly thereafter in a district called Kısıklı. The walk uphill following the signs to the summit takes from 20 to 30 minutes, depending on your speed and stamina.

At the car park you'll find the **Museum of Illuminating & Heating Appliances** (Aydınlatma ve Isıtma Araçları Müzesi), which might well escape your interest, even though it has its own café and gift shop.

Once at the top you can rest and marvel at the view (and the crowds, if it's a weekend). From Büyük Çamlıca the Bosphorus is laid out like a map, with its twists and turns, and the minaretted skyline of Old İstanbul looks just like the picture postcards.

The *kahvehane* (coffee house) (☎ 335 3301) serves full meals (daily, from 9 am to 10 pm) for about US$10 to US$15, or snacks such as peynirli tost (grilled cheese sandwich) for US$2.50 to US$3, soft drink included. There's full bar service, and drinks are even a bit cheaper in the shady garden out the front; you save little by ordering in the less attractive cafés lower down the hill.

Neighbouring **Küçük Çamlıca hilltop**, with its tea garden, is not quite as fancy as its loftier sibling, and is thus likelier to be quiet on weekends.

Tiled Mosque The Tiled Mosque or Çinili Cami (CHEE-nee-lee jah-mee) is Üsküdar's jewel, a small and unassuming building harbouring a wealth of brilliant İznik faïence on its interior walls.

It's a neighbourhood mosque in the quarter called Tabaklar, up the hillside a way from Üsküdar's main square. It can be tricky to find on your own (a 30-minute walk); a taxi costs less than US$2. If you're descending from Büyük Çamlıca, a taxi is the way to go.

To get there on foot from Üsküdar's main square, walk out of the square along the main street south, Hakimiyet-i Milliye Caddesi. Turn left (south-east) onto Toptaşı Caddesi

and follow it for several blocks to Valide İmareti Sokak, on the left. Take this street up to Çinili Cami Sokak and the mosque.

It's unprepossessing from the outside: just a shady little neighbourhood mosque with the usual collection of bearded old men sitting around. Inside, it is brilliant with İznik faïence, the bequest of Mahpeyker Kösem (1640), wife of Sultan Ahmet I (1603-17) and mother of sultans Murat IV (1623-40) and İbrahim (1640-48). As it is used heavily by local people for prayer, be properly dressed and on your best behaviour when you visit.

Beylerbeyi Palace Both shores of the Bosphorus have their Ottoman palaces. The grandest on the Asian side is Beylerbeyi, a few km north of Üsküdar. Catch a bus or dolmuş north along the shore road from Üsküdar's main square, and get out at the Çayırbaşı stop, just north of Beylerbeyi and the Asian pylons of the Bosphorus Bridge.

Beylerbeyi Palace (☎ 333-6940) is open from 9.30 am to 5 pm, closed on Monday and Thursday; admission for the obligatory guided tour costs US$3; camera permits (no flash or tripod) cost US$6, and are a waste of money.

The entrance to the palace is down a long, vaulted stone passage which used to be a vehicular tunnel on the coast road; traffic was rerouted when the Bosphorus Bridge was built. The tunnel is now a gallery for small exhibits. At its southern end is a beautiful small garden (with a bamboo grove) and the entrance to the palace.

Today the palace, for all its grandeur, is a bit musty, but still impressive, particularly on a sunny afternoon when golden light floods the rooms. The tour goes too fast. Soon you are overwhelmed by Bohemian crystal chandeliers, Sèvres and Ming vases and sumptuous carpets.

Every emperor needs some little place to get away to, and 30-room Beylerbeyi Palace was the place for Abdülaziz (1861-76). Mahmut II had built a wooden palace here, but like so many other wooden palaces it burned down. Abdülaziz wanted stone and marble, so he ordered Serkis Balyan to get to work on Beylerbeyi Palace. The architect came up with an Ottoman gem, complete with fountain in the entrance hall, and two little tent-like kiosks in the sea wall. The sultan provided much of the decorating expertise himself.

Abdülaziz spent a lot of time here. But so did other monarchs and royal guests, for this was, in effect, the sultan's guest quarters. Empress Eugénie of France stayed here on a long visit in 1869. Other royal guests included Nasruddin, shah of Persia; Nicholas, grand duke of Russia; and Nicholas, king of Montenegro. The palace's last imperial 'guest' was none other than the former sultan, Abdülhamid II, who was brought here to spend the remainder of his life (from 1913 to 1918), having spent the four years since his deposition in 1909 in Ottoman Salonika. He had the dubious pleasure of gazing across the Bosphorus at Yıldız, and watching the great empire which he had ruled for over 30 years crumble before his eyes.

Küçüksu Lodge If Beylerbeyi Palace was a sultan's favourite retreat, Küçüksu was preferred for picnics and 'rustic' parties. Sultan Abdülmecit was responsible for building the Küçüksu Kasrı, an ornate lodge, actually a tiny palace, in 1856. Earlier sultans had wooden kiosks here, but architect Nikogos Balyan, son of the designer of Dolmabahçe, produced a Rococo gem in marble. The Büyük Göksu Deresi (Great Heavenly Stream) and Küçük Göksu Deresi (Small Heavenly Stream) were two brooks which descended from the Asian hills into the Bosphorus. Between them was a flat, fertile delta, grassy and shady, just perfect for picnics, which the Ottoman upper classes enjoyed here frequently. Foreign residents, referring to the place as 'The Sweet Waters of Asia', would often join them.

Take a bus or dolmuş along the shore road north from Beylerbeyi to reach Küçüksu Kasrı (☎ 332-0237), open from 9.30 am to 5 pm, closed on Monday and Thursday; admission costs US$2.

Anadolu Hisar North of Küçüksu, in the shadow of the Fatih Köprüsü (second Bosphorus bridge) is the castle and village of Anadolu Hisar. This small castle had been built by Sultan Beyazıt I in 1391. It was repaired and strengthened as the Asian strong-point in Mehmet the Conqueror's stranglehold on Byzantine Constantinople. Anadolu Hisar is a fraction the size of its great European counterpart, Rumeli Hisar. You're free to wander about the ruined walls.

Khedive's Villa The Fatih Bridge soars across the Bosphorus just north of Rumeli Hisar and Anadolu Hisar. North of the bridge are more small Asian Bosphorus towns, including Kanlıca, famous for its yoghurt. The mosque in the shady town square dates from 1560. High on a promontory above the town, overlooking the Bosphorus, is a delightful Art-Nouveau villa built by the khedive of Egypt to be his summer cottage during visits to İstanbul. Here's a bit of its history:

Having ruled Egypt for centuries, the Ottomans lost control to an adventurer named Muhammed Ali, who took over the government of Egypt and defied the sultan in İstanbul to dislodge him. The sultan, unable to do so, gave him quasi-independence and had to be satisfied with reigning over Egypt rather than ruling. The ruling was left to Muhammed Ali and his line, and the ruler of Egypt was styled *hıdiv*, 'khedive' (not 'king', as that would be unbearably independent). The khedives of Egypt kept up the pretence of Ottoman suzerainty by paying tribute to İstanbul.

The Egyptian royal family, which looked upon themselves as Turkish and spoke Turkish rather than Arabic as the court language, often spent their summers in a traditional yalı on the Bosphorus shore. In 1906, Khedive Abbas Hilmi built himself a palatial villa on the most dramatic promontory on the Bosphorus, a place commanding a magnificent view. The Egyptian royal family occupied it into the 1930s, after which it became the property of the municipality.

Restored by the Turkish Touring & Automobile Association after decades of neglect, the Khedive's Villa (Hıdiv Kasrı, ☎ 331-2651) is now a hotel, restaurant and tea garden. (For details on accommodation, see Places to Stay.) Come for a stroll in the park, to gaze at the marvellous view, and to see the elegant villa (no charge to look round). Stay for tea (US$2 to US$4) or a meal (US$10 to US$15) in the wood-panelled semi-circular dining room, in the solarium or on the curved porch.

The villa is a few minutes by taxi (US$1.50) uphill from Kanlıca or Çubuklu. To walk, go north from Kanlıca's main square and mosque and turn right at the first street (Kafadar Sokak) which winds up to the villa car park in 15 or 20 minutes.

A much nicer walk is the one up from Çubuklu through the villa's grounds. Take a bus or dolmuş north to the stop marked 'Çubuklu Dalgıç Okulu' (a naval installation). Just north of the stop is a fire station (look for signs saying 'Dikkat İtfaiye' and 'İstanbul Büyükşehir Belediye Başkanlığı İtfaiye Müdürlüğü Çubuklu Müfrezesi'). Walk in the gate and to the right of the fire station, then up the winding forest road to the villa, a 20 to 30-minute walk.

Paşabahçe & Beykoz North of Çubuklu, the town of Paşabahçe has a large glassware factory whose products you have no doubt already used, perhaps unwittingly. In Beykoz, legend says that one of Jason's Argonauts, Pollux by name, had a boxing match with the local king, Amicus. Pollux was the son of Leda (she of the swan); Amicus was a son of Poseidon. Pollux won. At Hünkar İskelesi, farther north, is a former imperial palace not now open to the public.

From Beykoz, a road heads eastward towards the Polish village of Polonezköy and the Black Sea beach resort of Şile. Much of the land along the Bosphorus shore north of Beykoz is in a military zone, and you may be denied entry. You can, however, reach the village of Anadolu Kavağı by ferry, either on the Bosphorus touristic cruise from Eminönü or from Sarıyer and Rumeli Kavağı on the European shore.

Anadolu Kavağı Perched above the village are the ruins of Anadolu Kavağı a medieval castle with seven massive towers in its walls. First built by the Byzantines, it was restored and reinforced by the Genoese in 1350, and later by the Ottomans. As the straits are

narrow here, it was a good choice for a defensive site to control traffic. Two more fortresses, put up by Sultan Murat IV, are north of here. But Anadolu Kavağı is the final stop on the special cruise-ferry route, and the land to the north is in a military zone. If you have a picnic lunch, climb up to the fortress, which provides a comfortable picnic location with spectacular views. Check the ferry schedules before you decide to spend time here, however. You don't want to end up waiting hours for a ferry to get you out.

Polonezköy What's a Polish village doing in İstanbul? Polonezköy is a quaint and dying anachronism, a relic of 19th-century politics and the Crimean War.

Founded in 1842 as Adampol, it was named for Prince Adam Jerzy Czartoryski (1770-1861), once the imperial Russian foreign minister and later head of a short-lived Polish revolutionary government (1830-31). When his revolution failed, he bought land in the Ottoman Empire for some of his former soldiers. In 1853 Russia provoked war with the Ottoman Empire; England, France and Sardinia joined the Ottomans in battling the Russians in the Crimea. The men of Adampol organised a regiment of Ottoman Cossacks and fought with such bravery that Sultan Abdülmecit exempted them and their heirs from taxation.

A generation ago, Polish was still the lingua franca in the village. But with modern media, the language and customs of old Poland are dying out. Once Poles in a time warp, the people of Polonezköy are now Turkish citizens of Polish ancestry. Even so, the Pope (who is Polish) visited the village in 1979.

For more than a century, city people would come here for the delicious and authentic Polish farm food: wild mushrooms, wild boar, omelettes with eggs from free-range chickens, excellent fruit. Farmhouses provided simple lodgings as well as meals, and this attracted another, non-culinary clientele: lovers who, unable to show a marriage licence, could not shack up in İstanbul's hotels.

Alas, Polonezköy has lost much of its charm. Simple meals and lodgings are still available, but at relatively high prices; lovers still make up a hefty segment of the trade. Transport is a problem also; it's only easily reachable if you have your own vehicle. If you do, stop and take a turn through the village, have a look at the tiny church, and ponder the vicissitudes of history.

Şile Seaside getaways from İstanbul tend to be disappointing. Ataköy and Florya, on the Sea of Marmara, are crowded and citified. Kilyos is small and crowded. But Şile, 70 km north-east of Üsküdar on the Black Sea coast, has wonderful long sand beaches and a fairly laid-back atmosphere – at least on weekdays.

Buses (US$2.50) depart from the western side of Üsküdar's main square on the hour from 9 am to 4 pm on the two-hour journey.

Known as Kalpe in classical times, Şile was a port of call for ships sailing east from the Bosphorus. As an important port, it was visited by Xenophon and his Ten Thousand on their way back to Greece from their disastrous campaign against Artaxerxes II of Persia in the 4th century BC. Unable to find ships to sail them to Greece, Xenophon and his men marched to Chrysopolis (Üsküdar) along the route now followed by the modern road.

Şile's other claim to fame is Şile bezi, an open-weave cotton cloth with hand embroidery, usually made up into shirts and blouses which are wonderfully cool in the summer heat.

Numerous hotels provide accommodation, with highest prices on weekends. The *Kumbaba Hotel* (☎ (1992) 1038), two km south of town, is among the oldest yet still the most congenial, with rooms for US$50 to US$70 a double. They have a camping ground as well. The similarly priced *Değirmen Hotel* (☎ (1992) 1048; fax 1248), Plaj Yolu 24, has two stars, 76 rooms, restaurants and bars, and overlooks the beach. *Rüya Motel* (☎ (1992) 1070), also on the

beach, is considerably cheaper: two people in a little cabin pay US$20. There's a restaurant as well.

As İstanbul expands, so do the getaway spots on its outskirts. If Şile is too busy for you, hop on the bus to the village of Ağva, less than an hour eastward on the coast. Accommodation is limited, there are good possibilities for camping – and peace and quiet.

THE PRINCES' ISLANDS

The Turks call the Princes' Islands, which lie about 20 km south-east of the city in the Sea of Marmara, the Kızıl Adalar, 'Red Islands'. Most İstanbullus get along with 'Adalar' ('The Islands'), however, as there are no other islands nearby.

It's convenient to have islands near a big city, as they serve all sorts of useful purposes. In Byzantine times, so the story goes, refractory princes, deposed monarchs and others who were a threat to the powers that be, were interned here. A Greek Orthodox monastery and seminary on Heybeliada turned out Orthodox priests until the 1970s.

In the 19th century the empire's business community of Greeks, Jews and Armenians favoured the islands as summer resorts. The population was heavily Greek up to the end of the empire. Many of the pretty Victorian holiday villas and hotels built by these wealthy Ottoman subjects survive, and make the larger islands, Büyükada and Heybeli ada, charming places.

Touring the Islands

Hydrofoils and ferries depart from İstanbul's Kabataş docks for the trip to the islands. The summer schedules heavily favour commuters, with frequent morning boats from the islands and frequent evening boats from the city. But you'll have no trouble getting a convenient boat if you check the schedules in advance. Board the vessel and seize a seat at least half an hour before departure time unless you want to stand.

The fastest way to reach the islands is by hydrofoil (22 minutes, US$5, or US$3.50 for students), operating between Kabataş and

Büyükada. There are 11 departures from Kabataş on weekdays, six on weekend days.

Cheaper and more leisurely (50 minutes) are the conventional ferries to the islands, which depart from Kabataş on weekdays at 9.30 am, 2, 6.30 and 7.30 pm in summer for US$3.50 (US$2.50 for students). The first two boats go to Heybeliada first, then Büyükada before continuing to Yalova; the 6.30 boat goes only to Heybeli (island) and Yalova, and the 7.30 boat stops at Kınalı, Burgaz and Heybeli before continuing to Yalova.

Perhaps the best plan is to take the cruise out on the conventional ferry at 9.30 am, then return by hydrofoil.

The ferry steams out of the Golden Horn, with good views all around. To the right is a magnificent panorama of Topkapı Palace, Aya Sofya and the Blue Mosque; to the left, Üsküdar, Haydarpaşa and Kadıköy. Along the southern coast of Asia are more suburbs of İstanbul, some of them industrial. Before coming to the bigger islands, you'll pass the small ones named Kınalı and Burgaz. Heybeliada is next. Finally, you disembark at Büyükada.

Büyükada

The first thing you will notice about this delightful place is that cars are not allowed. Except for the necessary police, fire and sanitation vehicles, transportation is by bicycle, horse-drawn carriage and foot. It's wonderful!

Something you may not notice, but that you should be aware of, is that there is no naturally occurring fresh water on the islands; it must be brought in tanks from the mainland.

Walk from the ferry to the clock tower and the main street. The business district, with some fairly expensive restaurants, is to the left. For a stroll up the hill and through the lovely old houses, bear right. If you need a goal for your wanderings, head for the Greek Monastery of St George, in the 'saddle' between Büyükada's two main hills.

Horse-drawn carriage tours of the island are available. You can take either the 'long tour' *(büyük tur)* for about US$12, or the 'short tour' *(küçük tur)* which gives you a look mostly at the town, not the shores or hills, for US$8. You may have to haggle.

Hotels on the island move inexorably upmarket, but the many restaurants range from cheap to moderate in price.

Between the islands of Büyükada and Heybeliada there are fairly frequent ferries making the 15-minute trip.

Heybeliada

Called Heybeli for short, the small island Heybeliada holds the Turkish Naval Academy. Within the academy grounds is the grave of Sir Edward Barton (died 1598), ambassador of Queen Elizabeth I to the Sublime Porte. Much less touristed than Büyükada, it's a delightful place for walking in the pine groves and swimming from the tiny (but still crowded) beaches. There's not much in the way of accommodation if you don't have your own villa (or an invitation to a friend's), but there are several restaurants with good food and decent prices.

Burgaz & Kınalı

Two smaller islands are also accessible by ferry, but offer less reward for the trouble. Burgaz has a church, a synagogue, and the home of the late writer Sait Faik, which is now a museum; but it's mostly for the well-to-do İstanbullus who have summer villas here.

Kınalı, flat and fairly featureless, is even more a site for these summer villas, and is favoured by Armenian families. If you stop here to have a meal (there are no hotels), you'll probably be the only foreigner in sight.

PLACES TO STAY

İstanbul is well provided with hotels in all categories, particularly in the middle price range. Hotel clusters in various areas of the city make it easy to find the room you want at an affordable price. If the first hotel you look at is full, there will be another one around the corner, or even right next door.

Unfortunately for low-budget travellers,

the trend in hotels is to modernise and upgrade cheap hotels to higher price brackets. But there will always be cheap beds to be found in İstanbul.

The prices given here were carefully researched, but they may rise or fall according to İstanbul's volatile hotel situation.

As everywhere in Turkey, you should inspect the hotel room before you register. It may be better or worse than the lobby or façade. Also, one room may be better than another. If you don't like what you see, you can look at something else; just ask, *Başka var mı* (BAHSH-kah VAHR-muh, 'Are there others?').

Generally speaking, the lowest priced hotels and pensions are near Sultanahmet or Sirkeci Station. The best selection of moderate rooms is in the quarter named Laleli. Most luxury places are around Taksim Square and up the Bosphorus. Camping areas are in the beach sections named Ataköy and Florya. Kilyos, on the Black Sea coast, has moderate pensions and small hotels.

Places to Stay – bottom end

Among the hotels in this section are those which will provide you with a place to roll out your sleeping bag on the roof for as little as US\$6 or US\$8, and those offering double rooms with private hot-water shower for as much as US\$40. Mostly though, these places have simple but adequate double rooms with a sink or private shower for US\$20 to US\$30.

Sultanahmet The Blue Mosque is officially the Sultan Ahmet Camii. It gave the square and the quarter its name, contracted to Sultanahmet. The Blue Mosque faces the ancient Hippodrome, now a public park.

Around the Hippodrome are grouped the premier sights of İstanbul: Topkapı Palace, Aya Sofya, the Blue Mosque and the Yerebatan Saray, so when you stay here the sights are mere steps from your hotel door. Unless otherwise noted, the postal code for all hotels in this area is 34400 Sultanahmet.

The best place to look for a cheap room is in the *mahalle* (district) called Cankurtaran,

east of the Blue Mosque. There are other places scattered around the Hippodrome area as well.

Cankurtaran The quiet neighbourhood down towards the Bosphorus, east of Aya Sofya and the Blue Mosque, is called Cankurtaran ('Life-saver') because of the naval life-saving station which was once on the shore nearby. You can walk here easily from Sultanahmet, or take the banliyö train from Sirkeci to the Cankurtaran station.

Sleepy and untouristed until just a few years ago, this area promises to be the new Laleli, with hotels popping up like mushrooms overnight. It's still fairly quiet and cheap, though, and supremely convenient. To reach Cankurtaran, find the expensive Yeşil Ev hotel just south-east of the park with the fountain, and walk down Tevkifhane Sokak which is just to the left of the Yeşil Ev.

A walking tour of the lodgings in this district follows. *Tay Hotel* (☎ (1) 517 6909), Tevkifhane Sokak 6, is pleasant and modern enough. Its 22 small rooms (10 with bath) are priced from US\$25 to US\$35 a double and very little English is spoken.

Hotel Park (☎ (1) 517 6596), Utangaç Sokak 26, a few steps farther along, is one of the best deals in the district with 11 rooms (five with shower) priced from US\$12 to US\$18 a single, US\$35 a double, breakfast included. Rooms in this tidy place have been modernised, and there's a nice roof garden with a view of the Sea of Marmara.

Hotel Side Pansiyon (☎ (1) 517 6590), Utangaç Sokak 22, right next door to the Hotel Park, has 25 rooms, five with showers, many of them refreshingly large. The décor is plain but pleasant; a beautiful little garden is great for tea, drinks and light meals. Rates are from US\$14 to US\$20 a single, US\$18 to US\$26 a double; higher priced rooms have private facilities.

Continue down Tevkifhane Sokak to Kutlugün Sokak and turn left.

Guesthouse Berk (☎ (1) 516 9671, fax 517 7715), Kutlugün Sokak 27, is comfortable, congenial, family-run, dependable, and a good choice for single women. The half-

■ PLACES TO STAY

4 Hotel Ema
5 Elit Hotel
6 Hotel Anadolu
7 Konuk Evi & Conservatory Restaurant
9 Ayasofya Pansiyonları
11 Yücelt Interyouth Hostel & Hobby
   Laundry
12 And Otel
17 Hotel Nomade
33 Hotel Halı
42 Hotel Ferhat
43 Optimist Guesthouse
46 Hipodrom Pansiyon
47 Ottoman Hotel
48 Piyerloti Pansiyon
50 Hotel Turkuaz
52 Küçük Ayasofya Hotel
53 Hotel Sokullu Paşa
55 Hotel Ayasofya
63 Yeşil Ev Hotel
65 Tay Hotel
66 Topkapı Hostel & Yusuf Guesthouse
68 Hotel Park
69 Hotel Side Pansiyon
70 Pension Violette
71 Guesthouse Berk
72 Barut's Guesthouse
73 Alp Pension
74 Hanedan Hostel
75 Orient Youth Hostel
76 Pembe Ev Pansiyonu
77 Cem Guesthouse
80 Hotel Arasta
82 Hotel Obelisk
83 Hotel Sümengen
84 Hotel Avicenna

▼ PLACES TO EAT

8 Taverna-Restaurant Sarnıç
14 Akdeniz Lokanta & Karadeniz Pide ve
   Kebap Salonu
16 Tarihi Halk Köftecisi
18 Meşhur Halk Köftecisi
19 Cafeterya Medusa
20 Meşhur Halk Köftecisi Selim Usta
21 Can Restaurant
22 Pudding Shop
23 Sultan Pub
27 Dedem Börekçisi
28 Kardeşler Köftecisi
29 Sultanahmet Sütiş
35 Sultan Sofrası
37 Saray Köftecisi
40 Lezzet Lokantası

41 Karadeniz Aile Pide Salonu
62 Derviş Aile Çay Bahçesi
78 Mehtap Aile Tea Garden

OTHER

1 Cağaloğlu Hamamı
2 Gülhane Park
3 Aya İrini (Hagia Eirene Church)
10 Caferağa Medresesi Handicrafts Centre
13 Imperial Tombs
15 Tarihi Park Hamamı
24 Yerebatan Saray
25 Imperial Gate, Topkapı Palace

Sultanahmet Area

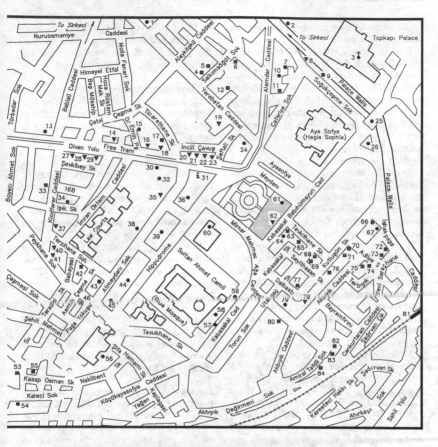

dozen rooms all have private bath and prices of US$35/45 a single/double.

Topkapı Hostel (☎ (1) 517 6558), Kutlugün Sokak 1, 34400 Cankurtaran, at the intersection of Kutlugün Sokak and İshakpaşa Caddesi, is congenial. A room for one or two people costs US$20/10 with/ without a private shower, but you can also get a bed in a dormitory for only US$8, or sleep on the roof with your own bedding for US$6, and hot showers are free.

Yusuf Guesthouse (☎ (1) 516 5878, fax 517 7287), İshakpaşa Caddesi, Kutlugün Sokak 3, 34400 Sultanahmet, is next door to the Topkapı Hostel and charges US$23 a double (private shower and family-style breakfast included) for clean but cramped rooms – some without windows – and difficult plumbing. The friendly manager, Mr Erol Canpolat, speaks English and German.

Had you turned right instead of left into Kutlugün Sokak, you would have come to two more pensions, the unfortunately named *Pink House (Pembe Ev) Pansiyonu* at No 47, and the *Cem Guesthouse* on the corner of Dalbastı Sokak. Check these out if the others are full.

Walk downhill on Adliye Sokak (the little street by the Pension Violette on Kutlugün Sokak) to find more pensions. Continue across Akbıyık Caddesi – there's a fine street market here on Wednesday – to the *Alp Pension* (☎ (1) 517 9570), Adliye Sokak 4, a clean, simple family-run place with double rooms priced at US$35, private shower and breakfast included. This part of the street is especially quiet. Across the street is the *Hanedan Hostel* which is similar.

Walk the few steps back up to Akbıyık Caddesi and turn left. *Orient Youth Hostel* (☎ (1) 516 0171), Akbıyık Caddesi 13, is a friendly place popular with backpackers. The atmosphere is one drawing card, the other is the price: US$12 a double for a room with sink. I've had several complaints, however, of female travellers being harassed.

Continue walking south-west on Akbıyık Caddesi to Mimar Mehmet Ağa Caddesi and turn right. On the left-hand side you'll see the *Hotel Arasta* (☎ (1) 516 1817), a modern but plain, unexciting place where serviceable rooms with private shower go for US$34 a double, breakfast included.

Off Yerebatan Caddesi Another few cheap hotels are a short walk north-west from Aya Sofya along Yerebatan Caddesi to Salkımsöğüt Sokak, on the right. This area is not as desirable as Cankurtaran, but will do at a pinch.

Elit Hotel (☎ (1) 511 5179, 519 0466; fax 511 4437), Salkımsöğüt Sokak 14, has 12 clean, simple, fairly quiet rooms with private facilities, above a carpet shop. The price is US$30 a double. The adjoining *Hotel Ema* is a bit more expensive, but well worth the money.

Down Salkımsöğüt Sokak a few more steps the street narrows. At this point, on the right, is the *Hotel Anadolu* (☎ (1) 512 1035), Salkımsöğüt Sokak 3, 34000 Cağaloğlu, perhaps the oldest hotel in the quarter, but also the quietest. By the front door are a few little tables overlooking a car park, a good place to sip a tea or write a letter. The rooms are tiny and just have sinks, but beds are priced at only US$8 per person, and hot showers are free.

Beside Aya Sofya Right beside Aya Sofya, running along its western side, is Caferiye Sokak, and the *Yücelt Interyouth Hostel* (☎ (1) 513-6150/1), Caferiye Sokak 6/1, literally across the street from the front door of Aya Sofya. Though called a hostel, it's actually a hotel for young backpackers. It has a restaurant, bulletin board, TV room, terrace, and a Turkish bath. Prices are not low as in hostels: doubles with bath cost US$28, rooms with three or four beds go for US$10 per person, and dormitory beds (eight to a room) cost US$7 each.

On & Off the Hippodrome Hotel *Nomade* (☎ (1) 511 1236, fax 513 2404), Divanyolu, Ticarethane Sokak 7-9, is just a few steps off busy Divan Yolu, friendly and French-oriented. *On parle français* here, and prices are quoted in francs working out at US$34 to

US$38 a double; the higher price includes private shower. You mount a narrow flight of steps to reach the lobby.

Optimist Guesthouse (☎ (1) 516 2398, fax 516 1928), Atmeydanı 68, 34400 Sultanahmet, is a tiny private home-turned-pension, in a superb location near the southern end of the Hippodrome on the western side, across the Hippodrome from the Blue Mosque. The six rooms (two with private shower) are priced at US$30 to US$38 a double, breakfast included.

Hipodrom Pansiyon (☎ (1) 516 0902), Üçler Sokak 9, is simple but clean and convenient, just a few steps up Üçler Sokak from the south-western corner of the Hippodrome. Waterless rooms go for US$23 a double, US$28 a triple.

Piyerloti Pansiyon (☎ (1) 517 8070), Piyerloti Caddesi, Kadırga Hamamı Sokak 4, Çemberlitaş, is a favourite with those travelling far, long and cheaply. Beds in six-bed dormitories go for US$5, in double rooms (no water) US$7. The historic Kadırga Hamamı (Turkish bath, built in 1724) is right across the street, and there's a bakery nearby for breakfast goods. The staff are helpful, and the clientele international. To find this pension, take the free tram up Divan Yolu to the Çemberlitaş stop, then walk south to Piyerloti Caddesi, and south-west to Kadırga Hamamı Sokak.

Student Hostels In the summer (July and August), several university dormitories open their doors to foreign students. These dorms tend to be extremely basic and cheap. They're not for all tastes, but if you want to look into one, ask for the latest information from the Tourism Information Office in Sultanahmet, right at the northern end of the Hippodrome.

Sirkeci Railway Station Most of the hotels near Sirkeci tend to be noisy, run-down or 'off-colour', but there is a street full of good hotels only five minutes' walk from the station. Walk out of the station's main (west) door, turn left, then left again onto Muradiye Hüdavendigar Caddesi. A block up on the right you'll see Orhaniye Caddesi going up a gentle slope. Follow it up to the top, two very short blocks. At the top is the recently renovated (and fairly expensive) İpek Palas Hotel and İbni Kemal Caddesi. Turn left onto İbni Kemal Caddesi, where there are eight hotels, all fairly quiet, most reasonably priced. The postal code is 34000 Sirkeci.

Hotel Fahri (☎ (1) 522 4785, 520 5686), İbni Kemal Caddesi 14-16, is not fancy but will do for a night at US$15/22 a single/double for rooms with shower. It's quiet because the street in front of it is used as an unofficial car park. A much better bet is the *Hotel Fahri II* (☎ (1) 527 9636), Nöbethane Caddesi 32, a few streets to the north, even nearer to Sirkeci Station (leave the station by the west door, turn left up the steps, then left along Muradiye Caddesi to Nöbethane Caddesi). All rooms cost US$18/22 a single/double and have private showers; there's TV and free tea in the lounge.

Back on İbni Kemal Caddesi you'll see the *Hotel Meram* (☎ (1) 527 6295), İbni Kemal Caddesi 19, which is simpler, but even cheaper, with singles/doubles for only US$12/18, with sink. The *Hotel İnci Palas* is even more basic, and still cheaper.

Should you have a mind to spend some money on comfort, the *Hotel Karacabay* (☎ (1) 526 0902, fax 527 8952), İbni Kemal Caddesi 38, is the 'high-priced' lodging on the block. I haggled them down to US$26 for a double room with private shower, buffet breakfast included. A similar single would have cost US$16. The advantage here is a roof terrace with views of Aya Sofya, and some rooms with TVs. Avoid the expensive bar. The Karacabay operates two other hotels on this street as well.

İpek Palas Oteli (☎ (1) 520 9724/5), Orhaniye Caddesi 9, on the corner with İbni Kemal Caddesi, has been gutted and renovated, and is now out of the cheap price range.

Aksaray-Laleli The district of Laleli (LAA-leh-LEE) is just east of Aksaray, just west of İstanbul University and north of Ordu Caddesi, about 1.5 km west of Aya Sofya.

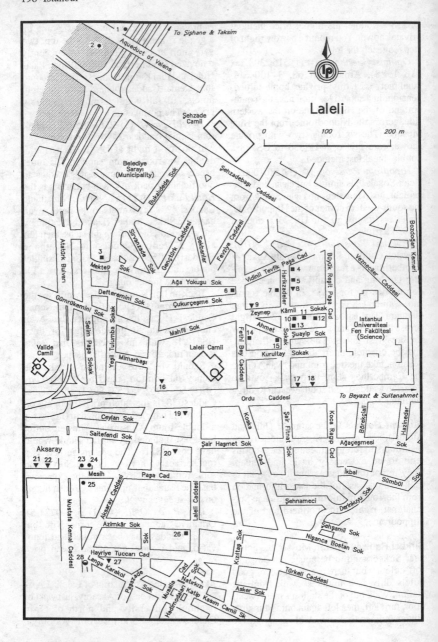

Laleli

To Şişhane & Taksim

Aqueduct of Valens

0   100   200 m

Şehzade Camii

Belediye Sarayı (Municipality)

Şehzadebaşı Caddesi

Bozdoğan Kemeri

Bubalidede Sok

Sekbanlar

Feyziye Caddesi

Şirvanzade Sok

Genctürk Caddesi

Veznecıler Caddesi

Büyük Reşit Paşa Cad

Vidinli Tevfik Paşa Cad

Harikzadeler

3

Mektep Sok

Ağa Yokuşu Sok

Defteremini Sok

6

Çukurçeşme Sok

4

5

8

7

9

Zeynep Kâmil

11 Sokak

10

13

12

İstanbul Üniversitesi Fen Fakültesi (Science)

Atatürk Bulvarı

Gümrükemini Sok

Yeşil Tulumba Sokak

Selim Paşa Sokak

Mahfil Sok

Ahmet

Şuayip Sok

Fethi Bey Caddesi

14

15

Kurultay Sokak

Laleli Camii

Mimarbaşı

16

17   18

Valide Camii

Ordu   Caddesi

To Beyazıt & Sultanahmet

Ceylan Sok

19

Koska

Şair Fıtrat Sok

Koca Ragıp Cad

Ağaçeşmesi

Börekçiali

Hazinedar Sok

Saitefendi Sok

Şair Haşmet Sok

Cad

20

İkbal

Sümbül Sok

Aksaray

21   22

23   24

Mesih

25

Paşa Cad

Şehnameci

Derinkuyu Sok

Azimkâr Sok

Sok

Laleli Caddesi

26

Kızıltaş Sok

Şehsamil Sok

Nişanca Bostan Sok

Aksaray Caddesi

Mustafa Kemal Caddesi

Hayriye Tuccarı Cad

28   Langa Karakol   27

Paşazade Sok

Musalla

Natırkızı Cad

Hacımodası Katip Kasım Camii Sk

Asker Sok

Türkeli Caddesi

The landmark here is the Ramada Hotel İstanbul, fitted into a large old apartment building beautifully restored. Laleli was once a pleasant residential and hotel district with relatively quiet, shady, narrow streets, but in recent years the pedlars have become increasingly numerous and insistent, as have the pickpockets. Though it is not really dangerous, you must be a bit more cautious here at night when streets are empty.

The northern part of this district is named Şehzadebaşı (sheh-ZAH-deh-bosh-uh). It's really all one area, but some hotels will have Laleli in their addresses, others Şehzadebaşı. Refer to the map of this area to find your way.

The postal code is 34470 Laleli unless otherwise noted.

Laleli must have over 100 hotels in all price ranges, and as they upgrade facilities and raise prices, it gets more difficult to find a clean, quiet double room that's within our low-budget price range. Off-season, or if you intend to stay for more than just a few days, you can haggle for a reduction. Most places will grant it willingly.

Start your explorations by walking up Harikzadeler Sokak from Ordu Caddesi into the heart of Laleli.

Hotel Öz Fethiye (☎ (1) 511 2663), Harikzadeler Sokak 11, formerly the Hotel Ayda, is simple and old-fashioned, but the management is accommodating and not averse to granting cuts in price if business is slow. Rooms with private shower cost US$10 per bed.

Ömür Hotel (☎ (1) 526 3030), at the intersection of Zeynep Kamil Sokak and Harikzadeler Sokak, has a tradition of low prices, but renovations have begun, and it will undoubtedly raise prices.

Turn right onto Zeynep Kamil Sokak to find the *Hotel Kul-1* (☎ (1) 526 0127, 528 2892), Büyük Reşit Paşa Caddesi, Zeynep Kamil Sokak 27, recently a very basic, old-fashioned place, but now modernised. Posted prices are US$20/34 a single/double, but they should quote you only about US$16/28 for a nice room with private shower.

Hotel Kaya (☎ (1) 528 2663), Zeynep Kamil Sokak 35, has not yet been modernised and still charges only US$16 for a decent double room with shower – but it may not last long. The management is very helpful, friendly and accommodating.

Hotel Burak (☎ (1) 522-7904, 511-8679), Ağa Yokuşu Sokak 1-3, 34470 Laleli, is older than many of the other hotels in this area, with prices that reflect this difference. Furnishings are well used, and the décor is perhaps a bit drabber than at other places, but the tiny private bathrooms are bright and shiny. There's a lift and the staff are friendly. The best rooms in the hotel are the corner rooms, whose numbers end in '3' (Nos 203,

303, 403 etc); try to get one of these high up. You'll pay US$24/30 a single/double for any room, breakfast included.

Taksim Believe it or not, there are a few inexpensive hostelries near up-market Taksim Square, amidst the banks, airline offices, nightclubs and towering luxury hotels.

Otel Avrupa (☎ (1) 250 9420), Topçu Caddesi 32, Talimhane, 80090 Taksim, on the corner of Şehit Muhtar Caddesi, is in the warren of little streets north of Taksim Square. It's a converted apartment house with an entrance at street level, a cheerful breakfast room one flight up, and guest rooms of varying sizes on the upper floors. Hallways are dingy, but the guest rooms are fine. Prices are the best in the Taksim area: US$22/28 a single/double without private shower, or US$32 a double with private shower. To find the Avrupa, locate the Air France office, and walk north on either Şehit Muhtar or Lamartin caddesis which are nearby. When you come to Topçu Caddesi, look for the hotel's sign.

İstanbul Plaza Hotel (☎ (1) 245 3273/4), Sıraselviler, Aslan Yatağı Sokak 19/21, 80090 Taksim, has older, somewhat drab, unrenovated 1950s-style rooms and facilities, but some rooms have good Bosphorus views (though a new building is encroaching upon them). Rooms are priced at US$28/44 a single/double for a room with bath, somewhat less for a room without private bath. Rooms Nos 21, 31, 41 etc (all large corner rooms with little sun-porches and big baths) offer the best value for money. Water may be available only at certain times during the summer. The ageing staff speak French, Greek and Turkish. Walk south along Sıraselviler Caddesi and turn left at a sign reading 'Plaza Hotel' just before the Alman Hastanesi (German Hospital). The hotel is hidden away on quiet Aslan Yatağı Sokak (Lion's Bed St).

Tepebaşı *Otel Alibaba* (☎ (1) 244 0781), Meşrutiyet Caddesi 119, 80050 Tepebaşı, next door to the Büyük Londra Oteli (Grand London Hotel), was under construction at my last visit. When it reopens, room prices may be out of our bottom-end range. Before construction a double room cost a mere US$18, with shower.

Kilyos On the Black Sea coast, an hour's drive (35 km) north of the Galata Bridge, lies Kilyos, a seaside resort village protected from development by the Ministry of Tourism. The village itself is not particularly charming, but the sand beach is a nice one, and the waters of the Black Sea are wonderfully cooling on a hot summer's day. Several hotels, motels, and pensions provide lodging; most are priced in our middle range, but there are a few in the bottom end.

On summer weekends all Kilyos lodgings are likely to be filled from advance reservations. You will have a better chance of finding a room if you plan your visit for the middle of the week, reserve ahead, or visit outside the high season (which lasts from mid-July to the end of August).

To get to Kilyos from Taksim Square, you can take bus No 40 ('Sarıyer-Taksim') and then bus No 151 ('Sarıyer-Kilyos') for a total cost of 85c; or a dolmuş minibus from Taksim to Sarıyer (US$1) and another dolmuş from Sarıyer to Kilyos, for only a little more. Catch the Sarıyer dolmuş at the northern end of Mete Caddesi, just past the Hotel Gezi.

Yuva Motel (☎ (1) 882 1043), Kilyos, İstanbul, near the beach, has a few rooms with views of the sea. All rooms have little porches, but the rooms on the sea side of the motel are preferable. The price for a small double room with private shower, breakfast included, is US$28.

Yalı Pansiyon (☎ (1) 882 1018), Kilyos, İstanbul, is a tidy little place at the eastern end of the beach. The rooms are simple, neat and clean, but have no running water; washing facilities are down the hall. Rooms on the lower level, with no sea view, cost US$24 a double; upstairs, with sea views, the price is US$32 a double. The upstairs rooms have one double and one single bed each, perfect for a couple with one child. The

Top: İstanbul ferries (TW)
Middle: Süleymaniye Mosque from across the Golden Horn,İstanbul (TB)
Bottom: Fishing on the Marmara shore, İstanbul (TB)

Top: Interior, Baghdad Kiosk, Topkapl Palace, İstanbul (TB)
Bottom: Salon, the Harem, Topkapı Palace, İstanbul (TB)

pension's kitchen facilities are available for your use.

Camping İstanbul's camping areas are ranged along the shore in Florya, Yeşilköy and Ataköy near the airport, about 20 km from Aya Sofya. They have good sea-view locations and average prices of US$8 for two persons in a tent. All are served by the frequent commuter trains (banliyö trenleri) which run between Sirkeci Station and the suburb of Halkalı. Thus, once you've set up camp you can hop on the train and ride to within 400 metres of Aya Sofya and Topkapı Palace for less than a dollar.

Yeşilyurt Kamping (yeh-SHEEL-yoort) (☎ (1) 572 4961) is on the shore road, Sahil Yolu, near the village of Yeşilköy.

In Ataköy is the camping place closest to the city, the *Ataköy Mokamp* (AH-tah-kury) (☎ (1) 572 4961), part of a hotel, restaurant and beach complex with all sorts of facilities. The cost is US$10 for two in a tent. From Ataköy, hitch or take a bus east along the shore road about four km to Kazlıçeşme, where there's a railway station; otherwise, rely on bus No 81 to trundle you between Eminönü and Ataköy, or bus No 71 or 72 to and from Taksim Square.

Londra Kamping is on the south side of the Londra Asfaltı highway between the airport and Topkapı gate. Right on the highway is a truck fuel and service station, but behind it, farther off the road, are grassy plots with small trees. You won't escape the noise and pollution completely here, but it will do at a pinch. To reach it you must be going eastward from the airport towards Topkapı gate and turn into the *servis yolu* (service road), watch carefully for the sign. About 300 metres after the turn, the camping ground is on the right-hand side.

There are also several camping places south of the highway in the suburb of Küçükçekmece, on the Sea of Marmara shore.

Places to Stay – middle

Middle-range hotels vary in size from 40 or 50 to 150 rooms, and charge from US$40 to US$100 for a double with bath; but most rooms fall in the range of US$45 to US$65. Except for a few hotels in Sultanahmet and Taksim, virtually all of these middle-range places are rated at two or three stars by the Ministry of Tourism, which means they can be depended upon to have lifts, restaurants, bars, and staff who speak foreign languages. Many places provide TVs, and some have minibars, in their guest rooms. They're usually newer buildings constructed during the past decade or so.

Sultanahmet Middle-range hotels in this area fall into two categories: restored Ottoman mansions several blocks off the Hippodrome, and modern buildings much nearer. Let's look at the Ottoman places first, then the modern ones.

Ottoman Mansions There are several excellent choices not far from the south-western end of the Hippodrome in the Küçük Ayasofya mahalle, near the mosque of that name. Sinan's famous mosque Sokollu Mehmet Paşa Camii is around here as well. The postal code is 34410 Sultanahmet.

To reach this area, walk to the south-western end of the Hippodrome, turn right then take the third left into Suterazisi Sokak and walk downhill.

At the bottom of Suterazisi Sokak is the *Küçük Ayasofya Hotel* (☎ (1) 516 1988, fax 516 8356), Şehit Mehmetpaşa Sokak 25, a restored 19th-century house. The helpful English-speaking manager, Mr Vural Orun, obviously enjoys hosting foreign visitors, and often offers substantial discounts from the posted rates of US$45/65 a single/double, with breakfast included. All rooms have private shower, phones and central heating.

Hotel Sokullu Paşa (☎ (1) 518 1790/1/2, fax 518 1793), Şehit Mehmetpaşa Sokak 5/7, is a larger, grander restored Ottoman house with its own small terrace and Turkish bath (hamam). Rooms are small and close together but otherwise suitable, with some nice old-time touches; all have private facilities. Rates are US$65/85 a single/double, breakfast included.

Go east (downhill) along Şehit Mehmetpaşa Sokak to find the *Hotel Ayasofya* (☎ (1) 516 9446, fax 513 7622), Demirci Reşit Sokak 28. Another nicely renovated house, this one charges about the same as the Küçük Ayasofya for its rooms with shower, and likewise the staff is ready to haggle with you for lower rates. It's very quiet here.

Go west along Şehit Mehmetpaşa Sokak to Kadırga Limanı Caddesi and the *Ottoman Hotel* (☎ (1) 516 0211, 517 1486; fax 512 7628), Kadırga Limanı Caddesi 85, 34490 Kumkapı, on the corner of Sarayiçi Sokak near the Kumkapı Polis Karakolu (police station). Operated by the same people who run the Yücelt Hostel, the hotel is Ottoman only in name. It's actually a modern 40-room place with lots of services at moderate prices, including a café, bar, shop and car park. Rooms cost US$35/45 a single/double and US$55 a triple, breakfast and tax included.

Not far from the Ottoman Hotel, the *Hotel Turkuaz* (☎ (1) 518 1897, fax 517 3380), Cinci Meydanı 36, Kadırga, is a restored Ottoman mansion with lots of old-time charm, only 14 rooms (all with private shower), a very un-Ottoman roof bar, and prices at the top of our middle range.

The mahalle called Cankurtaran, described under Places to Stay – bottom end, has a few good lodging places that reach almost into our middle range. There are also a number of restored mansion hotels which are right at the top of our middle range. To find them, walk down Mimar Mehmetağa Caddesi behind the Blue Mosque to Amiral Tafdil Sokak.

Hotel Sümengen (☎ (1) 517 6869; fax 516 8282), Amiral Tafdil Sokak 21 is an Ottoman town house with its own marble-covered Turkish bath, an airy and light restaurant with excellent views of the Sea of Marmara, an ornate lobby with parquet floors and Turkish carpets everywhere, and Turkish-style sofas to relax upon. On the top floor is an open-air terrace with the same fine views of the Sea of Marmara. The 30 guest rooms are small with tiny showers and twin or double beds. A few of the rooms have views of the sea but many rooms open only onto corridors, giving their inhabitants little privacy. Rates are US$75/95/115 a single/double/triple, breakfast included. Turkish baths cost US$10 extra.

Just to the left of the Sümengen stands the *Otel Obelisk* (☎ (1) 517 7173, fax 517 6861), Amiral Tafdil Sokak 17/19, another restored mansion with Ottoman period furnishings, a roof terrace with Marmara view, and prices of US$75/95 a single/double, breakfast included.

To the right of the Sümengen are two more restored hotels one of which, the *Hotel Avicenna* (☎ (1) 517 0550, fax 516 6555), Amiral Tafdil Sokak 31-33, has lots of shiny marble but slightly lower prices than the others in this group. Though Ottoman on the outside, it is more modern on the inside, with satellite TV, a roof-terrace café-bar, and small though pleasant rooms for US$65/85 a single/double.

The Yeşil Ev and Ayasofya Pansiyonları are described under Places to Stay – top end.

Pensions *Barut's Guesthouse* (☎ (1) 517 6841; fax 516 2944), İshakpaşa Caddesi 8, is a 23-room pension run by artists Hikmet and Füsun Barut (Hikmet Bey specialises in the old Turkish craft of paper marbling). The lobby, furnished with Turkish carpets, is a good place for tea and conversation, as is the small breakfast terrace (with water view) on the top floor. Guest rooms are a bit disappointing, with creaky plumbing, but the family atmosphere is exceptional. Rates are $36/44 for a single/double and US$55/66, a triple/quad.

Modern Hotels The trend in this area is for restored hotels, but there are several good, modern places in convenient locations offering excellent value.

Hotel Ferhat (☎ (1) 516 9642, fax 516 9650), Binbirdirek Mahallesi, Terzihane Sokak 9, looks much fancier than its three-star rating would warrant. There's lots of shiny marble, as well as helpful staff, a restaurant and bar, and 64 up-to-date air-con rooms with bath. Rates are US$65/85/105 a single/double/triple. Walk southward on the Hippodrome and turn right onto Terzihane Sokak just past the big Adliye Sarayı (Law Courts) building which stands on the north-west side of the Hippodrome.

Hotel Halı (☎ (1) 516 2170, fax 516 2172), Klodfarer Caddesi 20, Çemberlitaş, uphill to the north-west of the Hippodrome, is a good choice at an even lower price. Clean and bright, it charges US$42/58 a single/double for its rooms with bath, breakfast included.

And Otel (☎ (1) 512 0208/9), Yerebatan Caddesi, Cami Çıkmazı 46, more or less across the street from Yerebatan Saray, opened late in 1992 and offers double rooms with bath for US$60, breakfast included. The location is excellent, and the view from the top floor restaurant of the Golden Horn and Bosphorus superb. The staff may haggle if business is slow.

Aksaray-Laleli In recent years the area around Aksaray Square has become a 'hotel ghetto'. Every narrow street is lined with hotels rating two, three or four stars (with very few one-or five-stars), tour buses jockey to get into narrow parking places, and construction on yet another hotel begins. A babble of languages fills the air, many of them spoken by Eastern European shoppers who regard İstanbul as one huge department store for modern consumer goods scarce in their home countries.

Two major roads form a cross at Aksaray Square. Of this cross, the north-west quadrant has few hotels; all the other quadrants are packed with them. Busiest is the north-east quadrant, called Laleli after the mosque of that name. The postal code is 34470 Laleli unless otherwise noted.

My current favourite accommodation here is hidden away on a tiny back street. *Hotel Birbey* (☎ (1) 512 4675, fax 512 4674), Kemalpaşa Mahallesi, Mektep Sokak 1-3 is new, bright and shiny, with 32 comfy if small rooms going for US$45/65 a single/double; haggling is possible. There's a bar and breakfast room, and virtually no

traffic noise. Mektep Sokak is the western continuation of Ağa Yokuşu; the Birbey is up at the northern end of the street from the much more easily visible Hotel Hanzade.

Metro Oteli (☎ (1) 511 3019), Ahmet Şuayip Sokak 17, just off the right-hand side of Harikzadeler Sokak on the corner with Ahmet Şuayip, is a three-star hotel, thoroughly modern in architecture and décor. Each comfortable room has its own small tiled private bath and a fan; some have TVs. Prices are US$40/52 a single/double, US$12 for an extra bed, breakfast included.

Mati Pansiyon (☎ (1) 526 4299), Harikzadeler Sokak 29, is quite small but pleasing with its honey-coloured natural wood, tiled private baths, and small breakfast room. Though it calls itself a pension, this is actually a small, simple hotel which is a good choice for families: rooms have either a double bed and a single bed, or three single beds. Rooms are priced at US$40/50 a single/double, breakfast included.

Uran Hotel (☎ (1) 513 8200; fax 513 8205), Harikzadeler Sokak 36-42, has a modern décor seemingly inspired by the Art-Deco movement. Guest rooms have 'tub and shower' baths, TVs, minibars and direct-dial phones. The hotel has a lift, nice lobby, restaurant and bar. It's good value for money at US$46/60 a single/double, breakfast included.

Klas Hotel (☎ (1) 511 7874, fax 512 3354), Harikzadeler Sokak 48, is at the northern end of Harikzadeler Sokak where it meets Vidinli Tevfik Paşa Caddesi. The advantages here are a new building, good location, 60 tidy rooms with little balconies, two lifts, restaurant and bar and even a sauna, all for good prices of US$45/60/70 a single/double/triple.

Hotel Keçik (☎ (1) 511 2310, fax 528 1400), Fethi Bey Caddesi 18, is very near the fancy Ramada Hotel, which may be why it looks and feels a bit more elegant than the rest. The modern lobby has antique touches; the 75 guest rooms are attractively modern, with solid-colour drapes, halo-light vanity mirrors, and bathrooms with mini-tub and shower; some rooms have TVs. Services include hairdressers, restaurant, bar, lounge, small outdoor terrace, TV room and even a fitness room equipped with sauna and Turkish bath. Prices are US$56/78 a single/double, breakfast included.

The south-east quadrant of Aksaray, across Ordu Caddesi from Laleli, has a similar plethora of hotels, and if you haven't found what you want in Laleli, look here. The postal code is 34480 Laleli.

My favourite in this district is the three-star *Hotel Erden* (☎ (1) 518 4852, fax 518 4857), Azimkar Sokak 62-68, with 68 nicely decorated air-con rooms of decent size, all with private facilities. It's on a back street and fairly quiet, there's a restaurant, bar and terrace. Rates are US$50/70/90 a single/double/triple, tax and breakfast included.

The south-west quadrant of Aksaray holds even more lodging possibilities. These are less 'discovered' than those in the north-east and south-east, and can be more amenable to reductions in price.

Taksim Airline offices, foreign banks and luxury hotels are mostly near Taksim Square. Because of the district's up-market reputation, a double hotel room that costs US$75 in Laleli costs US$100 near Taksim. The postal code is 80090 Taksim unless otherwise noted.

Hotel Lamartine (☎ (1) 254 6270, fax 256 2776), Lamartin Caddesi 25, is a modern four-star hotel on a quiet street just 1½ blocks north of Taksim. The 58 rooms are carpeted and comfy, with minibars and TV sets. The basement restaurant is uninspiring but serviceable at a pinch. Normal rates are US$80/100 a single/double, breakfast included, but can be lower if they're not busy.

Another, similar four-star place just around the corner is the *Riva Otel* (☎ (1) 256 4420, fax 256 2033), Aydede Caddesi 8, with prices that are about the same. The Riva has its own currency exchange office as well.

Hotel Nippon (☎ (1) 254 9900, fax 250 4553), Topçu Caddesi 10, another four-star place around the corner from the Lamartine, is bigger (94 rooms), a bit fancier, and

slightly more expensive. It's a popular lodging for small tour groups.

The four-star *Dilson Hotel* (DEEL-sohn) (☎ (1) 252 9600, fax 249 7077), Sıraselviler Caddesi 49, a block south of Taksim, has 115 very comfortable rooms priced at US$90/110 a single/double, but don't get one facing the street because of the noise. The restaurant is fairly good, the pastry shop even better, and experienced staff provide service.

Hotel Star (☎ (1) 245 0050), Sağlık Sokak 11, is very close to Taksim. The 24 rooms are quite small and well used, as are the hallways, lift and lobby, but rates are a moderate US$50/70 a single/double, breakfast included. Rooms with numbers ending in '4' are the corner ones, larger and lighter. To find the hotel, walk down İnönü Caddesi on the right-hand side and look on the right for the hotel's sign.

Family House (☎ (1) 249 7351, fax 249 9667), Kutlu Sokak 53, Gümüşsuyu, has five three-room apartments for rent in a well-kept building. The manager, Mr Atıl Erman, is available to answer any question or solve any problem. Apartments have two single beds and one double bed, telephone, colour TV with video hook-up, kitchen with refrigerator, two-burner gas cooker and utensils. In summer it's US$115 per day for up to four people; in winter, US$95. To find Family House, follow the directions to the Hotel Star, then go downhill one more flight of steps, following the signs.

Tepebaşı Between Galatasaray Square and Tünel Square, west of İstiklal Caddesi, is the district called Tepebaşı (TEH-peh-bah-shuh), which was the first luxury hotel district in the city. The main road through Tepebaşı is Meşrutiyet Caddesi, where one finds the British and US consulates-general, the Pera Palas Oteli and the Pullman Etap İstanbul Hotel. To get there from Taksim, take the restored tram along İstiklal Caddesi to Galatasaray, or go by taxi, or by dolmuş; you may have to use a dolmuş that goes past Tepebaşı (say, to Aksaray) and pay the full fare. You can catch a bus along Tarlabaşı Bulvarı (TAHR-la-bash-uh), just out of

Taksim near the Air France office. Coming from Karaköy, take the Tünel to the top station and walk the several blocks to the hotels.

Just behind the towering Etap İstanbul Hotel is the three-star *Yenişehir Palas* (☎ (1) 252 7160, fax 249 7507), Meşrutiyet Caddesi, Oteller Sokak 1/3, 80050 Tepebaşı, renovated in recent times. It is a hotel of eight floors, with little in the way of views but in a good location, with 138 comfortable and attractive rooms with baths; many have TVs and minibars. Its moderate prices have made it popular with Greek tourists and small groups. Rooms are priced from US$35 to US$45 a single, US$50 to US$60 a double.

Büyük Londra Oteli (☎ (1) 249 1025, fax 249 0438), Meşrutiyet Caddesi 117, 80050 Tepebaşı, dates from the same era as the Pera Palas Oteli, but has much smaller rooms and bathrooms, and is a bit the worse for wear. But it does preserve some of the Victorian-era glory (in the public rooms at least) at a price considerably below that of its larger and more famous neighbour. A room with shower costs US$50 with one double bed, US$60 with two beds.

Kilyos For a description of Kilyos and how to get there, refer to the Kilyos section in Places to Stay – bottom end.

The prime hostelry in Kilyos is the *Turban Kilyos Moteli* (☎ (1) 242 0288; fax 882 1259), right on the beach. The several two-storey motel buildings hold 144 rooms of three types. There are twin-bedded rooms with bath, rooms with twin beds and a double bed, and two-room four-bedded suites. All of the rooms, designed in a simple, modern Mediterranean style with white stucco walls, dark wood and plaid blankets, have bathrooms and porches with some sea views.

Prices depend upon the number of beds, the position of the building (whether it's nearer or farther from the beach), and the season of the year; you are required to take breakfast and dinner with your room. Services at the motel include a tennis court, sea-view restaurant and bar, tea terrace and beer garden, and of course the fine beach just steps away. In high summer (from mid-July to August), prices range from US$45 to US$50 a single, US$68 to US$78 a double, breakfast and dinner included. In rooms with four beds, three people pay US$110, four pay US$130, breakfast and dinner included. Prices in 'mid-season' (from mid-May to early July and all of September) are 20% lower; off-season (early to mid-May) prices are 33% lower. The motel is closed from October to April.

The next-best lodging at Kilyos is the *Kilyos Kale Hotel* (☎ (1) 882 1054, fax 882 1295), Kale Caddesi 78, Kilyos, İstanbul, up the hill from the centre of the village. This modern, comfortable but simple hotel has 27 rooms with bath, many of which have beach and sea views; there's a fine view from the restaurant as well. Rooms cost US$30/40 a single/double; add US$4.50 more per person for breakfast, US$10 per person for breakfast and dinner, or US$13 per person for all three meals.

Gurup Hotel (☎ (1) 882 1194, fax 882 1266), Kale Caddesi 21/1, Kilyos, İstanbul, has a nice hillside location with fine views of the sea and the beach, a sunny patio and a vine-covered restaurant. It's a small place with 33 tidy little rooms, each with twin beds, a private shower and vine-covered porch with sea view (in late summer you can pick the grapes right on your own porch). The aptly named Gurup ('abundant') is a favourite with British holiday groups. You must take breakfast and dinner with your room; the price for room and half board is US$44 a double.

Kilyos Erzurumlu Motel (☎ (1) 882 1003), Kilyos, İstanbul, is next door to the Kilyos Kale Hotel. It's somewhat older but very tidy and quiet. Rooms have splendid views and cost US$40 a double with breakfast.

Places to Stay – top end
The centre of the posh hotel district is certainly Taksim Square, but there are numerous luxury hotels in other parts of the city as well. Prices range from US$125 to

US$300 and higher for a double, but most rooms cost from US$140 to US$180. At the big international hotels, try not to pay the 'normal' published rates ('rack rates'), which are quite high. Often these hotels offer special packages; ask when you make reservations. The big international chains usually allow children (of any age) to share a double room with their parents at no extra charge or, if two rooms are needed, they charge only the single rate.

Sultanahmet has several restored Ottoman mansions. In Tepebaşı is the famous Pera Palas Oteli, built for the passengers on the original *Orient Express*. Çirağan Palace is now a luxurious Kempinski hotel. And up the Bosphorus at Çubuklu is the Hıdiv Kasrı, the former mansion of the khedives of Egypt, now converted into a fabulous villa hotel. Here you can sleep in the bed of King Faruk if you like.

Sultanahmet The Turkish Touring & Automobile Association has restored historic buildings throughout the city, including several Ottoman mansions very near Aya Sofya and the Blue Mosque.

Konuk Evi (☎ (1) 513 3660, fax 513 3669), Soğukçeşme Sokak, 34400 Sultanahmet, is on the corner of Soğukçeşme and Caferiye sokaks, facing Aya Sofya. Built in 1992, it duplicates an historic mansion which stood on this site during the reign of Sultan Abdülhamit, but has all the modern hotel conveniences. Besides the 20 guest rooms with bath, there is a garden, conservatory restaurant and, right next door, the Caferağa Medresesi Handicrafts Centre. Prices are US$100/135 a single/double, breakfast included.

Yeşil Ev (☎ (1) 517 6785, fax 517 6780), Kabasakal Caddesi 5, 34400 Sultanahmet is a rebuilt Ottoman house with 22 rooms furnished with period pieces and antiques in fine taste. To its right is the İstanbul Handicrafts Centre, a restored Ottoman medrese in which the rooms that were once student cells are now shops. Behind the hotel is a lovely shaded garden-terrace restaurant. Though

the hotel is charming, recent reports from readers indicate that service may be slipping, and the food can be uninspiring. It costs US$105/135/165 a single/double/triple or US$200 for the Pasha's Room, with its own private Turkish bath. Breakfast, service and tax are included in the rates.

Not far from the Yeşil Ev, behind Aya Sofya against the walls of Topkapı Palace, is a row of Ottoman houses which have also been rebuilt and refitted by the Turkish Touring & Automobile Association as lodgings for travellers. These are the *Ayasofya Pansiyonları* (☎ (1) 513 3660, fax 513 3669), Soğukçeşme Sokak, 34400 Sultanahmet. The location is unbeatable, which is why all the rooms are often filled. The 58 rooms with private baths are in 19th-century Ottoman style with brass or antique wooden beds, glass lamps, Turkish carpets and period wall hangings. Prices are from US$75 to US$85 a single, US$100 to US$110 a double, US$120 to US$130 a triple, breakfast included. The cheaper rooms are at the back, with little light. The complex's dining rooms provide good food and moderate prices, and the Sarnıç Restaurant, set up in a Roman cistern, is right next door (see Places to Eat for details). The reception desk, by the way, is at the north-western end of the street, on the way to Gülhane Park.

Laleli *Ramada Hotel İstanbul* (☎ (1) 513 9300, fax 512 6390), Ordu Caddesi 226, 34470 Laleli, is installed in a renovated apartment complex. The narrow courtyards and walks of the original building have been enclosed and covered with glass canopies. Services include shops, a courtyard pastryshop café and bar, an enclosed heated swimming pool and fitness centre, a Turkish restaurant and a formal Chinese restaurant.

The 275 guest rooms tend to be small by luxury standards, with small bathrooms, but they are certainly comfortable. Some overlook the enclosed courtyards, others the busy street or side streets. Prices are US$145/175 a single/double for 'standard' rooms which are the smaller ones; larger, deluxe rooms cost US$285 single or double, tax and service included, but breakfast costs extra.

Taksim *Divan Oteli* (dee-VAHN) (☎ (1) 231 4100; fax 248 8527), Cumhuriyet Caddesi 2, Elmadağ, 80200 Taksim, was founded by Vehbi Koç, Turkey's millionaire industrialist whose family also founded the Sadberk Hanım Museum in the Bosphorus town of Sarıyer. Though it is one of the city's older luxury hotels, and with 180 rooms one of the smaller ones, it has built an enduring reputation as a small European-style hotel with excellent cuisine and personal service by well-trained English-speaking staff. The location, almost facing the Sheraton and two blocks from Taksim Square or the Hilton, is very convenient. Prices here are US$140 a single, US$195 a double.

The 437-room *Sheraton İstanbul Hotel and Towers* (☎ (1) 231 2121; fax 231 2180), Taksim Park, 80174 Taksim, is a 23-storey asymmetrical tower with wonderful Bosphorus and Golden Horn views. All conceivable luxury hotel services are here, including an enclosed heated swimming pool, health club, rooftop restaurant and bar and an indoor car park. Rooms are large, airy and furnished with every luxury including marbled bathrooms. Prices depend partly upon the view from the room: singles cost from US$135 to US$185, doubles are US$175 to US$225, tax and service included.

A bit farther from Taksim along Cumhuriyet Caddesi on the right is the *İstanbul Hilton* (☎ (1) 231 4650; fax 240 4165), Cumhuriyet Caddesi, 80200 Harbiye, set in its own spacious park with tennis courts, swimming pool, helicopter pad and even its own convention centre. It gives one the feeling of staying at a private luxury club. The public rooms and guest rooms are done in creamy marble, gleaming brass and rich textiles. Guest rooms are in several locations, with varied décor and special services, and so the price range is broad: from US$190 to US$215 a single, US$225 to US$260 a double, tax and service included. Pricier rooms have more services (hair dryers, TVs

with remote control etc), are larger, and have Bosphorus views. Weekend prices can be as low as US$170 a double per night, tax, service and continental breakfast included.

The Marmara (☎ (1) 251 4696; fax 244 0509), 80090 Taksim, towers over the busy square and offers splendid views of the Old City, Beyoğlu and the Bosphorus from its upper floors. Several restaurants, an enclosed swimming pool, sun deck, nightclub, gambling casino and rooftop restaurant are among the services. The 424 guest rooms have colour TVs and minibars. The plumbing is a bit noisy. Prices range from US$175 to US$200 a single, US$200 to US$250 a double, with tax, service and buffet breakfast included.

Tepebaşı In the heart of Beyoğlu, midway between Galata and Taksim, is Tepebaşı.

Hotel Pullman Etap İstanbul (☎ (1) 251 4646; fax 249 8033), Meşrutiyet Caddesi, 80050 Tepebaşı is a modern 22-storey tower rising across the street from the Pera Palas Oteli. The 200 simple rooms have satellite TVs and minibars; some have splendid views of the Golden Horn, the Old City and the Bosphorus. The view from the rooftop's tiny swimming pool is the best of all. The Etap İstanbul has a pastry-shop café, disco, restaurant, coffee shop, bar and lounge. Rates are US$100/135 a single/double.

Pera Palas Oteli (PEH-ra pa-LAHS) (☎ (1) 251 4560, fax 251 4089), Meşrutiyet Caddesi 98-100, 80050 Tepebaşı, fills up regularly with individual tourists and groups looking to relive the great age of Constantinople. It is a worthy place.

It used to be fairly cheap, too, but the management has discovered what foreigners will pay for nostalgia – a lot – and have upped the prices. The Pera Palas Oteli has 145 rooms. Many of those in the original building have high ceilings, period furnishings and bathrooms to match; those in the annex are less romantic. Some rooms have views of the Golden Horn. Nostalgia and atmosphere are what you're paying for here, as there are few luxury services other than the excellent but very expensive pastry shop.

The restaurant could be a lot better. But the atmosphere in the public salons and the wonderful bar is certainly bewitching. Rooms with bath and breakfast are priced from US$70 to US$120 a single, US$100 to US$180 a double; lower prices are for the annexe. Rooms on the lower floors of the original building can be very noisy, and west-facing rooms can get quite hot from the setting sun in summer.

While we're on the subject of the Pera Palas Oteli, I should let you know that Agatha Christie's favourite room was No 411, while the great Atatürk preferred No 101, a vast suite which, kept just as he used it, is now a museum (ask at the reception desk for admission).

Bosphorus The shores of the Bosphorus have several new luxury hotels, all of which (except the Hıdiv Kasrı) rate five stars, and have toll-free reservations numbers in Europe and North America.

Conrad Istanbul (☎ (1) 274 1000, fax 274 1088), Yıldız Caddesi, 80700 Beşiktaş, opened in June 1992, quickly earned a reputation for having some of the most accommodating, best-trained staff in the city. Off Barbaros Bulvarı just west of Yıldız Palace, the Conrad's 614 rooms and suites have fine Bosphorus views and all the luxuries. Hotel services run the gamut from indoor and outdoor swimming pools to in-room faxes (on request) to a casino. Rates range from US$165 to US$275 a single, US$220 to US$290 a double, tax included.

Swissôtel Istanbul The Bosphorus (☎ (1) 259 0101, fax 259 0105), Bayıldım Caddesi 2, Maçka, 80680 Beşiktaş, capitalises upon its magnificent Bosphorus views: the lobby, restaurant and guest rooms all benefit. Lavish use of marble gives it a luxury feel, and all services give it luxury for real. Rates range from US$175 to US$290 a single, US$195 to US$320 a double, tax included. One drawback: you must take taxis almost everywhere.

Çirağan Palace Hotel Kempinski İstanbul (☎ (1) 258 3377, fax 259 6687), Çirağan Caddesi 84, 80700 Beşiktaş, is a modern hotel built next to the historic Cirağan Palace, on the shore at the foot of the Yıldız Palace park. Destroyed by fire in 1911, the rebuilt marble palace holds VIP suites, a ballroom, casino, restaurants and boutiques. Sharing the palace garden is a modern 312-room luxury hotel annexe where guests stay. All luxury services are available, and prices are İstanbul's highest: from US$200 to US$320 a single, and from US$235 to US$360 a double, tax included. You can book rooms through Lufthansa.

Istanbul Mövenpick Hotel (☎ (1) 285 0900, fax 285 0951/2), Büyükdere Caddesi 49, Üçyol Mevkii, 80670 Maslak, opened in late 1992, a dramatic 30-storey high-rise jutting up from on top of the Bosphorus hills. Of moderate size (305 rooms), it aims at both business and holiday travellers, and provides all luxury services with Swiss efficiency. Rooms are priced at US$150 to US$235 a single, US$170 to US$260 a double, tax included.

Hıdiv Kasrı (☎ (1) 331 2651; fax 322 3436), restored by the Turkish Touring & Automobile Association, stands on a promontory above the village of Çubuklu, far up the eastern shore of the Bosphorus. (For a full description of the villa, see Sights on the Asian Shore under Khedive's Villa.)

Set in its own large park, it is a treasure of pure, delicious Art-Nouveau style, with a circular entry hall complete with fountain. There is room for only 50 guests. Rooms are priced from US$40 to US$110 a double, depending upon size and location; all share baths. The khedive's suite, with private bath, goes for US$150. Çubuklu is about a 30 to 45-minute drive (costing around US$16 in a taxi) north of the city centre.

PLACES TO EAT

In İstanbul you will eat some very tasty food, no matter if you eat in a simple workers' cafeteria or in a luxury restaurant. Good food has been a Turkish passion for centuries. In fact, the fearsome Janissary corps, the sultan's shock troops, were organised along the lines of a kitchen staff. They had a habit of signalling revolt by overturning the cauldrons which held their dinner of pilav. The message from these elite troops to their sovereign might be phrased, 'If you call this food, we have confidence in neither your taste buds nor your leadership'.

Little local places, mostly hazır yemek (ready-food) restaurants, kebapçıs and pidecis, will charge from US$2 or US$3 for a simple main-course lunch to perhaps US$5 or US$6 for a several-course budget tuck-in. They do not normally serve alcoholic beverages. These are the places listed in the Places to Eat – bottom end section.

In slightly nicer places with white tablecloths and waiters, if you order a good portion of meat, with wine or beer and a sweet (dessert), expect to pay from US$8 to US$20 per person. These are the restaurants listed in the 'middle' section, most of which serve alcohol.

In the Places to Eat – top end section are those restaurants in which a meal will normally cost US$25 or more per person, all included. A meal costing more than US$40 per person is a rarity in Turkey except in a few trendy eateries and the big international-class hotels. The following places to eat are organised according to district, and type of eatery within each district.

Places to Eat – bottom end

Sultanahmet Several little restaurants are open along Divan Yolu, the main street which goes from Sultanahmet Square up the hill towards the university and the Covered Market.

Köftecis My favourite eateries in this area are the many little köfteci shops. Order your köfte (grilled meatballs) or şiş kebap by the *porsyon*: if you're not all that hungry, order *bir porsyon* (BEER porss-yohn, one portion), if you'd like a bit more, ask for *bir buçuk porsyon* (BEER boo-CHOOK, one and a half); if you're hungry, order a *duble porsyon* (DOOB-leh, double). An order of köfte, a plate of salad, bread and a glass of ayran (a yoghurt drink) should cost around US$3.

Meşhur Halk Köftecisi Selim Usta ('Chef Selim, Famous Popular Köfte-maker'), Divan Yolu 12/A, is a classic Turkish workers' eatery which has somehow survived in the midst of this touristy area. It's crowded, noisy and always busy because the food's good and cheap.

Another, similar place named *Meşhur Halk Köftecisi* is up Divan Yolu a short distance, facing the Hippodrome.

Yet another is the *Tarihi Halk Köftecisi* ('Historic Popular Köfte-maker') nearby at No 28.

Down the street towards Aya Sofya is the *Sultanahmet Köftecisi*, also good.

For bright, modern surroundings, seek out the *Kardeşler Köftecisi*, Divan Yolu 13, up the hill a block near the expensive Çamlık Restaurant. It's new, cheap, clean and good, with soup, köfte, sweet and drink going for less than US$4.

Restaurants Across Divan Yolu from the Hippodrome is the famous *Pudding Shop*, where the drop-out generation of the 1960s kept alive and happy on various nutritious, tasty, inexpensive puddings such as sütlaç or its even tastier baked version, fırın sütlaç, served cold. Today the Pudding Shop is a self-service cafeteria with a variety of foods. Prices are higher and food quality not the same as in the hippy heyday, but if you want to meet other travellers, you can have a meal here for US$4 to US$6, or a sandwich and soft drink for less.

A few doors down Divan Yolu, overlooking the small park atop Yerebatan Saray, is the *Sultan Pub*. The upper floor holds a middle-range restaurant, but the ground-floor café serves sandwiches and drinks for US$5 or so. It's a favourite place to meet and talk.

Up the street from the Pudding Shop is the *Can Restaurant*, a cafeteria-style place. Prices are about the same as at the Pudding Shop, the food quite tasty. It's generally preferred to the nearby *Vitamin Restaurant* (VEE-tah-meen) (☎ 526 5086). Divan Yolu 16, at which you must check your bill carefully.

Up Divan Yolu about a block, on the south side, is the *Dedem Börekçisi,* Divan Yolu 21, a streetside booth selling savoury börek filled with cheese made from white sheep's milk, eaten either hot or cold. You order by weight, so you can have as much as you like; a normal serving is 200 grams, 250 grams if you're quite hungry. With a soft drink, lunch would cost less than US$2.

Sultanahmet Süt-iş (☎ 516 0539), nearby on Divan Yolu, is bright, modern and open long hours (from 6.30 am to midnight every day). Sandwiches go for a little over US$1, kebaps and roast chicken for US$3 or so. Sweets are served as well. The neighbouring Çamlık Restaurant, once recommended in this book, is now overpriced.

Other very cheap meals can be had by exploring the side streets north of Divan Yolu. *Akdeniz Lokanta* and *Karadeniz Pide ve Kebap Salonu* are up the street by the Sağlık Müzesi (Health Museum). Because they don't draw in passers-by, their prices are lower.

For a light meal and a drink in the evening, the popular place is the *Cafeterya Medusa,* on Yerebatan Caddesi near the corner with Şeftali Sokak just a block from the Yerebatan Saray. The open-air terrace is often filled with travellers. Have a pizza or another snack, plus a drink, for about US$4.

So much for the tourist-frequented restaurants along Divan Yolu. For some very cheap and good places patronised largely by local people, walk towards the far (south-west) end of the Hippodrome. Before coming to the end of the Hippodrome, turn right onto Terzihane Sokak, and walk up the slope to find some small restaurants patronised mostly by lawyers pleading cases in the law courts (Adliye Sarayı) facing the Hippodrome.

Lezzet Lokantası (Flavour Restaurant), Terzihane Sokak 13, near the Hotel Ferhat, is simple with very tasty food, waiter service and quite low prices. My lunch of kuru fasulye, pilav, bread, and melon for dessert, along with a soft drink, cost US$3.50. Around the corner on Klodfarer Caddesi is yet another köfte joint, *Saray Köftecisi.*

Even less expensive? Turn left (south) on Klodfarer Caddesi and at the intersection with Peykhane/Üçler Sokak is the *Karadeniz Aile Pide Salonu,* where hot, made-to-order Turkish pizza is served up for US$1.50 or less. The price depends upon the toppings you request, which may include cheese, minced lamb or eggs.

Cafés For refreshments and snacks, the most obvious place to go to is the *Sultan Sofrası,* a café-restaurant facing the Hippodrome on its north-west side, with good people-watching possibilities. Though it is a restaurant with indoor and outdoor seating areas, most customers are here for drinks: coffee, tea, beer or fizzy refreshers. Most of the food served is snacks and sandwiches: hamburgers, fried cheese toast and plates of chips. A drink and a sandwich should cost less than US$2. Directly across the Hippodrome from the Sultan Sofrası, hugging the wall of the Blue Mosque, is another small teahouse operated by the same management.

If you prefer shade to sun, seek out the *Derviş Aile Çay Bahçesi* (Dervish Family Tea Garden), Kabasakal Caddesi 2/1 near the Yeşil Ev Hotel. In the cool, dark shadows cast by big old trees, this pleasant café offers tea, coffee, and small sandwiches for less than US$1. Try peynirli tost, a cheese sandwich mashed in a vice-like sandwich cooker. Prices are listed on the menu placed at each table.

To make your own picnics, don't forget the street market on Wednesday on Akbıyık Caddesi in Cankurtaran, down the hill behind the Blue Mosque.

Sirkeci & Eminönü There is a serviceable – if a bit pricey – restaurant right in Sirkeci railway station, and lots of good small restaurants nearby in the neighbourhood called Hocapaşa (HO-ja pah-shah).

Hocapaşa Eateries Leave the railway station by the main (west) door, turn left and walk up the slope on Ankara Caddesi, turning into the third little street on the left. This will bring you to İbni Kemal Caddesi and the Hoca Paşa Camii (mosque). Within a few steps of the mosque are one dozen small restaurants.

Bozkurt Döner Kebap Salonu serves that succulent lamb roasted on a vertical spit; the *Yıldız Et Lokantası* (Star Meat Restaurant) serves a variety of grilled meats; the *Hoca-paşa İskender ve Et Lokantası* specialises in savoury grilled lamb Bursa-style (with browned butter and tomato sauce); the *Hocapaşa Pidecisi* specialises in freshly made Turkish pizza. There are others: *Kardeşler Anadolu Lokantası* has lots of ready food, the *Karadeniz Pide ve Kebap Salonu* serves pide and kebaps. At the restaurants, you can get a full meal for US$3 or US$4. The köftecis and pidecis will have meals for even less.

If you want something to finish off your meal at the lowest possible price, buy fresh fruit from a vendor and wash it at the tap by the mosque.

Boza Facing the plaza in Eminönü, to the right of the Denizcilik Bankası and to the left of the Yeni Cami, is a tiny stand which bears the name *Vefa Bozacısı*. Boza (a thick millet drink) is all they serve here from October to June; from June to October they switch to refreshing white grape juice called *şıra*. A fortifying glass of boza, favourite drink of the Ottoman Janissary corps, costs 50c, şıra the same; prices are posted prominently. By the way, Vefa is also noted for its flavourful vinegar *(sirke)*. Don't mistake this for şıra or boza.

Fish Sandwiches About the cheapest way to enjoy fresh fish from the waters round İstanbul is to buy a fish sandwich from a boatman. Go to the Eminönü end of the old Galata Bridge, and on the right-hand (Bosphorus) side, tied to the quay railing just east of the bridge, you'll see a boat bobbing in the water. In the boat, two men tend a tinplate cooker and fry fish fillets in oil. The quick-cooked fish is slid into the cleft made in a quarter of a loaf of fresh Turkish bread, the whole is wrapped in newspaper, and handed up to a hungry, waiting customer, who forks over about US$1 for the meal. Once you get over the shock of seeing a fire in a boat, order one. I've never been disappointed, nor made sick, by one of these.

Turkish Delight For another traditional Ottoman treat, walk through the archway to the left of the Yeni Cami in Eminönü, and turn left onto Hamidiye Caddesi. One short block along, on the right-hand (south) side of the street near the corner with Şeyhülislam Hayri Efendi Caddesi, is the original shop of Ali Muhiddin Hacı Bekir, inventor of Turkish delight.

History notes that Ali Muhiddin came to İstanbul from the Black Sea mountain town of Kastamonu and established himself as a confectioner in the Ottoman capital in the late 1700s. Dissatisfaction with hard candies and traditional sweets led the impetuous Ali Muhiddin to invent a new confection that would be easy to chew and swallow. He called his soft, gummy creation rahat lokum, the 'comfortable morsel'. 'Lokum', as it soon came to be called, was an immediate hit with the denizens of the imperial palace, and anything that goes well with the palace goes well with the populace.

Ali Muhiddin elaborated on his original confection, as did his offspring (the shop is still owned by his family), and now you can buy lokum made with various fillings: cevizli (JEH-veez-LEE, with walnuts), şam fıstıklı (SHAHM fuhss-tuhk-LUH, with pistachios), portakkallı (POIIR-tah-kahl-LUH, orange-flavoured), or bademli (BAH-dehm-LEE, with almonds). You can also get a çeşitli (CHEH-sheet-LEE, assortment). Price is according to weight; a kg costs US$3, more or less, depending upon which flavour you choose. If you'd like to taste before you buy, ask for a free sample by indicating your choice and saying *Denelim!* (DEH-neh-LEEM, 'Let's try it').

During the winter, a cool-weather speciality is added to the list of treats for sale. Helvah, a crumbly sweet block of sesame mash, is flavoured with chocolate or pistachio nuts or sold plain. Ali Muhiddin Hacı Bekir has another, more modern shop on

İstiklal Caddesi between Taksim Square and Galatasaray.

Karaköy & Galata Bridge

On shore at Karaköy, facing the ferry docks, are numerous snack shops, including several *börekçis*. A börekçi (bur-REK-CHEE) makes various sorts of flaky pastries filled with cheese and chopped parsley. Each type of börek has its own name. Su böreği (SOO bur-reh-yee, water pastry) is a thick, noodle-like affair with sprinklings of cheese made from white sheep's milk and chopped parsley. Ask for 200 grams (ee-KEE yurz gram), and the clerk will cut out a square, chop it into manageable bites, and hand it to you on a plastic plate with a fork. It will cost perhaps US$1. Other sorts of börek are the more familiar flaky pastries with filling, like sosisli (sohsees-LEE, sausage) or cheese.

Karaköy is also noted for its baklava, which comes with various stuffings. Prices are marked per kg and per portion (usually 150 grams, though you can order more or less). Stuffings include pistachios, walnuts and even clotted cream. İstanbul's most famous *baklavacı* (baklava maker), is *Güllüoğlu*, in a shop on the street level of the big parking garage across from the Yolcu Salonu (International Maritime Passenger Terminal), 100 metres east of the Galata Bridge.

Çemberlitaş & Covered Market

Facing the Çemberlitaş and its tram stop on the south side of Yeniçeriler Caddesi is a building called the Fırat Kültür Merkezi or FKM, holding several cinemas. Walk into the building and look for the *Büyük Muhallebici* on the ground floor. A *muhallebici* traditionally serves puddings, especially the bland rose-water pudding called muhallebi. This, however, is a full-service pastry shop serving light meals including soup, böreks, pilavs and pastries. You can eat for US$2 to US$4 easily. It's closed on Sunday.

Within the Kapalı Çarşı (Covered Market) you will come across several little restaurants. With one exception, these are tiny, basic places where bazaar workers eat or from which prepared meals are taken to their workshops on trays.

Some of these little places rarely see a foreign tourist, but some are accustomed to serving foreigners. All will welcome you and make extra efforts to please. The ones that are used to foreigners, where the menus may be in English and where the waiter will know at least a few words of a foreign language, are grouped on Koltuk Kazazlar and Kahvehane sokaks. The most prominent one is the *Sevim Lokantası*, founded (a sign proudly states) in 1945. Take a seat in the little dining room, or sit at a table set out in one of the little streets and order two or three plates of food. The bill shouldn't exceed US$5.

Another place is the *Balkan Restaurant* at Perdahçılar Sokak 60, on the corner of Takkeciler Caddesi. Don't let its tiny entrance fool you, as the dining room is larger and there is another dining room upstairs. Choose one of the ready-food items or order döner kebap. I had a çerkez kebabı (Circassian kebap) of peas, aubergine, lamb, potatoes, tomatoes and peppers in a rich sauce, plus bulgur pilav with beans, ayran and bread for US$4.50.

You will no doubt pass the Şark Kahvesi (SHARK kahh-veh-see, Oriental Café), at the end of Fesçiler Caddesi. It's always filled with locals and tourists, and finding a seat can be difficult. The arched ceilings betray its former existence as part of a bazaar street; some enterprising *kahveci* (coffee-house owner) walled up several sides and turned it into a café. On the grimy walls hang paintings of Ottoman scenes and framed portraits of sultans and champion Turkish freestyle wrestlers. A cup of Turkish coffee, a soft drink or a glass of tea costs around 50c; Nescafé is overpriced at US$1.

Laleli & Aksaray

Perhaps the best and most popular ready-food restaurant in Laleli is the *Murat Lokanta ve Kebap Salonu* (☎ 528 1928), Ordu Caddesi 212/A, half a flight down from street level near the Ramada Hotel. Bright, clean and attractive, the Murat is open for all three meals and is busy with tourists and locals all day. Meal bills usually come to US$4 to US$6, depending upon what and how much you eat. Everything is available.

For kebaps, a favourite in this district has the daunting name of *Hacıbozanoğulları Kebap Salonu* (☎ 528 4492), Ordu Caddesi 214, up the hill from the big Ramada Hotel between Harikzadeler Sokak and Büyük Reşit Paşa Caddesi. The restaurant is one flight up from the street; menus at street level by the doorway show pictures of various kebaps and announce prices. A portion of kebap is 100 grams and costs only about US$2; you may want to order a double portion. With your kebap you may get yufka, the paper-thin unleavened peasant flat bread; or pide, the thicker, leavened flat bread. For a drink, try ayran. Hacıbozanoğulları (that's ha-JUH-bo-ZAHN-oh-ool-lah-ruh) also has a separate baklavacı (sweet shop) across the street and down the hill one block, on the corner of Ordu and Laleli caddesis.

Hacı Dayı Kebap Salonu (☎ 528 2043), Harikzadeler Sokak, is deep in the midst of the Laleli hotel district, next door to the Oran Hotel. Fairly dressy as kebap restaurants go, it is quite narrow, and low priced, with a meal of soup, kebap, bread and beverage costing US$5.

Gaziantep Emek Saray Kebapçısı (☎ 522 4556), Gençtürk Caddesi 6, just a few steps north from Ordu Caddesi, will serve you a portion of Urfa kebap plus a glass of ayran for US$4. When you order your kebaps here, specify whether you want them *acısız* (ah-juh-SUHZ, without hot pepper) or *acılı* (ah-juh-LUH, with hot pepper). The restaurant's speciality is çiğ köfte (CHEE kerf-teh), uncooked minced lamb with spices.

Two blocks south of Aksaray Square, on the corner of Mustafa Kemal and Mesihpaşa caddesis, are several eateries specialising in spit-roasted chicken (çevirme piliç) and charcoal-grilled chicken (kömürde piliç). To find them walk from Laleli along Ordu Caddesi to Aksaray Caddesi. Walk down Aksaray Caddesi to Mesih Paşa Caddesi (the

second street), turn right, and walk to Mustafa Kemal Caddesi.

Best is *Arjantin Piliç* (☎ 512 1475), Mustafa Kemal Caddesi 76, with marble floors and a quieter, more sedate dining room upstairs for women, couples and families. You can order a quarter chicken (US$2), half chicken (US$4) or whole chicken (US$7), other dishes such as salads, pilav etc (US$1), and a glass of draught lager (US$1.50). Directly across the street is the similar *Şölen Piliç* (☎ 528 6166), Mustafa Kemal Caddesi 78. A *piliç*, by the way, is a pullet (young chicken); a *tavuk* is a stewing chicken, tough as a football.

One short block up Mesihpaşa Caddesi from these two places is *Mudurnu Barbekü* (☎ 518 5268), İhtisapağası Sokak 16, a popular chicken-chain eatery offering barbecued birds.

Across Mustafa Kemal Caddesi from the chicken restaurants are the kebap places. Taking your life in your hands, cross the street, and walk west along İnkilap Caddesi, the continuation of Mesih Paşa Caddesi.

İskender Kebapçısı (☎ 586 6073), İnkilap Caddesi 4, serves Bursa-style döner kebap, with the meat spread on a bed of fresh flat pide bread, and the whole topped with savoury tomato sauce and browned butter. The restaurant is just a little local eatery, but the kebap is delicious and, with a bowl of soup and a drink, makes a fine meal for US$4 or US$5.

A few doors to the west is *Konyalı Kebabcı Osman* (☎ 586 6083), İnkilap Caddesi 10, specialising in Konya's fırın kebap (rich chunks of oven-roasted mutton), and etli ekmek, the type of Turkish pizza made in Konya, topped with ground lamb. At the *Güneş Kebap & Baklava Salonu* right next door, the speciality is tandır kebap, a savoury lamb and vegetable stew traditionally cooked in an earthenware crock. The crock should be buried in a fire pit, but here in the city they settle for an oven. Etli ekmek is served here as well and is the cheapest choice for a good, simple meal.

For cheap seafood, or at least for seafood as cheap as it's going to come in this city, head for the *Dergâh Restaurant* (☎ 588 0895), İnkilap Caddesi 39. Portions are huge, the fish is good, and service is courteous – at least until it is discovered by more tourists. A meal with wine might cost US$9.

Taksim The McDonald's hamburger restaurant, Pizza Hut and streetside cafés on the east side of Cumhuriyet Caddesi are slated for destruction when they start building the Taksim metro station.

Altın Şiş (☎ 244 9640), Osmanlı Sokak 22/1, is very near Taksim, yet patronised mostly by local folk. Facing The Marmara Hotel in Taksim, walk down the steep street which runs along the hotel's left side one long block to the restaurant. Soup, various kebaps, a few ready-food dishes, and sweets are available, and a full meal costs around US$3 or US$4. No alcohol is served.

There's a wonderful tea garden near Taksim, open every day in summer from mid-morning to evening. *Cennet Bahçesi* (jeh-NEHT bahh-cheh-see, Heavenly Garden) overlooks the Bosphorus, Old İstanbul and the Asian shore, and is a favourite rendezvous for young lovers and those who need a respite from the city's bustle.

Snacks and light meals are served as well as tea, coffee, beer and soft drinks. From Taksim, walk down İnönü Caddesi and turn right on the little street named Ayazpaşa Camii Sokak just before the palatial German Consulate (Alman Konsolosluğu). One short block down, just after it turns right you turn left, keeping the little mosque on your right side. Two blocks along at Saray Arkası Sokak turn right and follow it around to the left and into the Cennet Bahçesi.

Otherwise, it's best to look for a meal on İstiklal Caddesi.

Antep Restaurant, İstiklal Caddesi 3, is just off the traffic roundabout. This bright, plain place has the standard cafeteria line, steam tables and low prices. They're not as low as they might be, however: this is Taksim. Be careful not to order too much: three selections (two will usually suffice), plus that good Turkish bread, is plenty for anyone. You can always go back. Fill up at lunch or dinner for US$4 to US$6.

Continuing along İstiklal Caddesi takes you past several little side streets. Perhaps the best and most plentiful food for the lowest price in the Taksim area is to be found at the *Ada Lokantası* (☎ 245 1633), at No 25 on a narrow side street called Büyükparmakkapı Sokak (Thumb Gate St) going left (south) from İstiklal Caddesi opposite the posh Beymen clothing store; it's the third little street on the left as you come from Taksim. A bright, fairly large restaurant, it is open seven days a week from early morning to late evening, with lots of ready-food choices on which you can fill up easily for US$2 to US$4.

Büyükparmakkapı Sokak, by the way, is a colourful introduction to the local street life of Beyoğlu, with a shoe-repair shop, barber shop, bridge salon, record shop, sporting goods shop and cheap nightclubs. The population of the street seems to be 99% male, but all are good natured and the area is safe enough. The scene looks like something out of an Oriental movie.

On the north side of İstiklal Caddesi, opposite Büyükparmakkapı Sokak, is Mis Sokak and the *Sohbet Ocakbaşı*, at No 9/1. 'Ocakbaşı' means 'right at the grill' which is where you sit in this type of restaurant. The speciality here is Kozan kebap, a spicy shish from south-eastern Turkey where the Arabic influence is strong. A full meal can cost under US$6.

Other food bargains can be had just off of İstiklal Caddesi. Walk from Taksim until you see the Ağa Camii (on the right), the only little mosque on the street. Walk around behind it to Mahyacı Sokak to find the *Meşhur Sultanahmet Köftecisi* (☎ 244 1355) and the *Kristal Köftecisi* (☎ 245 8462), serving cheap grilled meatballs, lahmacun (Arabic pizza) and pide.

For sweets, try the *Saray Muhallebi ve Tatlı Salonu* (☎ 244 5724), İstiklal Caddesi 102, on the right-hand side of İstiklal Caddesi as you approach Galatasaray. A tall glass façade shields a high-ceilinged, airy salon with a mezzanine floor. The baklava, puddings and other sweets are in refrigerator cases at the front. Look them over, point out your choice to a waiter, order a beverage (tea, coffee, a soft drink or just water), take a table, and enjoy. My usual here is burma kadayıf (BOOR-mah kah-dah-yuf), a shredded wheat roll stuffed with pistachios and doused in honey and syrup, plus a büyük çay, (ber-YERK chah-yee) – a large glass of tea, costing US$2.

Approaching Galatasaray, *Hasır Fast Food*, between Balo and Solakzade streets, is clean, bright, attractive and fairly cheap, with börek (flaky pastry), pide, lahmacun and içli köfte (filled fritters) for around US$1 and Italian-style pizzas for around US$2.50.

Tepebaşı & Tünel Just north of Galatasaray there's the Balık Pazar (fish market), actually a full food market spread out in two little streets, Sahne and Duduodaları, next to the touristy Çiçek Pasajı. Most of the meyhanes (tavernas) are in our middle-price range, but a few simple eateries can fill your needs.

The cheapest and tastiest snack is midye tavası, mussels deep-fried on a skewer for about 30c, a bit more sandviçli (in bread). There are many interesting şarküteri (charcuterie, delicatessen) shops as well, offering cheeses, dried meats such as pastırma, pickled fish etc, but prices are not really low-end. If you want to put together an up-market picnic, try the shop named *Şütte* (☎ 244 9292) at Duduodaları Sokak 21, which has been here for decades.

From Galatasaray, Meşrutiyet Caddesi leads north, then west, then south, roughly parallel to İstiklal Caddesi. Several middle-range restaurants are of interest on these two streets, but there's not a lot of good, cheap eating to be had.

For a light lunch or snack, go to the *Karadeniz Pide Salonu* behind and to the left of the Etap İstanbul Hotel, where you can get a fresh pide with butter and cheese for US$1. No alcohol is served.

Down the hill near the Galata Tower is the *Mengen Restaurant* (☎ 249 9430), Büyük-hendek Caddesi 26 at Şair Ziyapaşa Caddesi, a small local place between the tower and

Şişhane Square, next to the Yapı Kredi Bankası. A simple storefront sort of place, it serves meals for about US$3 to US$5 from 8 am to late at night every day except Sunday.

Bosphorus In Üsküdar, try the *Kanaat Restaurant* near the Mihrimah Sultan (İskele) Camii (mosque) on the north side of the main square. Founded in 1933, it still serves good food at low prices. A full meal of meze, şiş kebap, pilav and drinks need cost only US$5 per person.

Fish is expensive, but in the Bosphorus fishing village of Sarıyer, several restaurants serve it up at affordable prices.

Sahil Aile Lokantası, next to the sea just north of the town's fish market, is extremely simple. You'll recognise it by the several rickety little tables set out under a shady grapevine, or by its combination 'sign and menu' slate. Prices are marked (if something's not priced be sure to ask), and depending upon the fish in season, you should be able to have a tasty fish dinner in summer for less than US$7. The cheapest thing to have is simply a grilled or fried fish fillet of whatever's in season, with salad – the Turkish equivalent of fish and chips.

Places to Eat – middle
Be sure to read Places to Eat – bottom end for tips on where to find good simple snacks and meals, even though your budget can afford a bit more.

Sultanahmet The indefatigable Turkish Touring & Automobile Association has established no fewer than four restaurants within a few steps of Aya Sofya. The *Yeşil Ev* hotel's garden restaurant has a very pretty setting, but mediocre food.

Meals are tastier at the Ottoman-Victorian dining rooms of the *Ayasofya Pansiyonları* on Soğukçeşme Sokak. The menu is Turkish, with grilled aubergine (eggplant), lamb chops, mutton stews and veal cutlets. Full meals cost around US$14 to US$18.

At the intersection of Caferiye and Soğukçeşme sokaks is the *Taverna-Restau-*

rant Sarnıç (☎ 512 4291), set up in a vast old Roman cistern. The baronial fireplace hardly belongs in a sunken stone cistern, but the rosy glow is welcome on rainy evenings. Continental dishes fill the menu, from onion soup to goulasch, with a few Turkish favourites thrown in. Meals cost from US$20 to US$30 per person with drinks, tax and tip. It's open Wednesday to Sunday from 11.30 am to 11 pm.

Just across the street from the Sarnıç, next to the Konuk Evi hotel, is its *Conservatory Restaurant* (☎ 513 3660), in a glass greenhouse with a nice open-air terrace. Dishes served here tend to be those which do not require a large or elaborate kitchen: soups, pastas, grills and böreks. The setting is lovely, the hours long – from 8 am to 11 pm every day. Light meals cost US$10, full meals with drinks, from US$16 to US$20.

Sultan Pub (☎ 526 6347), Divan Yolu 2, between the Pudding Shop and the small park atop Yerebatan Saray, has a café on the ground floor and a nicer restaurant one flight up, both fairly noisy. A sandwich and soft drink in the café, patronised mostly by tourists, cost from US$3 to US$5. A full meal upstairs costs between US$8 and US$12. Alcoholic and other drinks are served in both places.

Topkapı Palace Everyone who visits Topkapı Palace has a problem: since it can take almost a whole day to see the palace properly (including the Harem), where does one eat lunch? There is a restaurant in the palace, the *Konyalı Restaurant* (☎ 526 2727), all the way down at the northern end; find the Mecidiye Köşkü, the Kiosk of Sultan Abdülmecit, and the restaurant is below. You'll find tables inside and outside under an awning (with very fine views of Üsküdar, the Bosphorus and the Sea of Marmara).

Because the restaurant has a captive market of tourists (not locals, who might complain), food and service are mediocre, and prices high for what you get. Even so, the restaurant is always crowded at lunch time. The trick is to arrive by 11.30 am to beat the lunch rush, or to come later in the

afternoon. For a meal of soup, şiş kebap, salad and drink with tax and tip included, figure on paying about US$12 or US$15.

If it's just a good seat, a sandwich and a cool drink you're looking for, go to the café terrace just below the restaurant, where there are even better views, and a snack won't set back your budget so much.

The only other food in the palace is at the little snacks-and-drinks stand by the entrance to the Harem.

Laleli & Aksaray Besides the numerous restaurants described in Places to Eat – bottom end, this district has several fancier places, both of them south of Ordu Caddesi.

Çağrı Restaurant (☎ 516 5623), Mustafa Kemal Caddesi 54, has tables spread with white cloths and set with flowers, attentive service, and an interesting menu of Turkish and European classics (I had a good şiş kebap garni). The clientele is local and foreign, the conversation a babble of languages. One whole wall is the wine cellar. Meals are served from noon to 11 pm every day. To find it, walk south towards the Sea of Marmara along Mustafa Kemal Caddesi on the left-hand side. Look for the restaurant behind the bus stop at the intersection of Aksaray Caddesi.

Kervan Restaurant (☎ 518 1484), Saitefendi Sokak 38/A, between Laleli and Aksaray caddesis, is bright and busy with an international clientele. Have the tavuk şiş (chicken chunks grilled on skewers), or a meat kebap. With soup, beer and bread, the bill should be about US$10. It's open every day.

Özlale Restaurant (☎ 511 4775), Zeynep Kamil Sokak 64 on the corner of Fethibey Caddesi, is fairly touristy – being in this tourist bedroom neighbourhood – but still good, with tablecloths, an English menu, and air-con. Have something as simple as an omelette for US$3, or go for a full meal of soup, meat course and sweet for about US$8 to US$12. A 10% service charge is added to your bill. It's open for lunch and dinner every day.

Sirkeci & Eminönü Go out the station door, turn left, then left again onto Muradiye Caddesi. The first street to the right is Orhaniye Caddesi. Across the street from the Küçük Karadeniz Oteli is the *Şehir Lokantası* (sheh-HEER), with white table-cloths, waiter service, decent surroundings, lots of ready-food choices as well as grilled-to-order kebaps. It costs from US$8 to US$10 for a full meal.

In Sirkeci Station there is a restaurant offering good meals at similar prices.

Ümit Restaurant ve Kebap Salonu, Ebusuud Caddesi, Mehmet Murat Sokak 4, serves consistently good Turkish food at very decent prices. It's a local place, not a tourist one. A full meal with wine should cost under US$10 per person. Ebusuud Caddesi is the next street to the south of İbni Kemal Caddesi; Mehmet Murat Sokak is the second street west of Alemdar Caddesi.

Karaköy & Galata Bridge The Yolcu Salonu (YOHL-joo sah-loh-noo, International Maritime Passenger Terminal), on Kemankeş Caddesi 100 metres north-east of the Galata Bridge, contains two of İstanbul's best restaurants. As headquarters for Turkish Maritime Lines, the Yolcu Salonu must have a showplace seafood restaurant. In fact, it has two. Enter on the building's right (south-west) end and go to either the *Liman Lokantası* or the *Liman Kafeteryası* (☎ 244 1033). Both are open from noon to 4 pm (lunch only) every day except Sunday.

The Kafeteryası is a less elegant, less expensive version of the restaurant. You pay a set price (about US$10) and help yourself to the various courses at the steam tables.

Upstairs in the Liman Lokantası, a spacious, simple, somewhat old-fashioned dining room overlooks the mouth of the Golden Horn and the Old City. (If there's a cruise ship moored at the Yolcu Salonu dock, the ship will block the view.) Service is polite and refined, fish is the speciality, and a full, elegant, delicious lunch from soup to baklava and coffee, with wine, will cost between US$14 and US$18 per person.

Covered Market Though most Covered Market eateries are low budget (see Places to Eat – low end), at the *Havuzlu Lokantası* (☎ 527 3346), Gani Çelebi Sokak 3, prices are in the moderate range. The food is about the same as at the bottom-end places in this area, but you get a lofty dining room made of several bazaar streets (walled off for the purpose long ago) and a few tables set out in front of the entrance by a little stone pool *(havuzlu* means 'with pool'), which I suspect was a deep well centuries ago. Waiter service here is more polite and unhurried. If you want to escape from the activity of the bazaar into a haven of quiet and calm, spend a little more (from US$8 to US$10) and go to the Havuzlu. It's next to the PTT. Follow the yellow-and-black signs and ask for the PTT or the restaurant.

Taksim & İstiklal Caddesi Taksim Square and the surrounding area have numerous restaurants and sweets shops. I'll start by describing some full-service restaurants, and then give you a few hints on where to have a light meal or refreshments.

Hacı Baba Restaurant (ha-JUH bah-bah) (☎ 244 1886), at İstiklal Caddesi 49, deserves special mention. The nondescript doorway opens onto a flight of stairs leading to the restaurant, which is much nicer than the appearance of the entrance suggests. For a better first impression, continue down İstiklal Caddesi, turn left at the next corner, and enter the Hacı Baba from the side street (Meşelik Sokak).

It's here, on Meşelik Sokak, that you'll see the restaurant's strong point: a pleasant little outdoor porch set with tables overlooking the courtyard of the Greek Orthodox Church of the Holy Trinity next door – a bit of open space, peace and quiet in the midst of the city. Hacı Baba is a full-menu, full-service restaurant with fish and grilled meats, ready-food dishes and specialties. The food is good, the service usually competent; some English is spoken. Prices have risen dramatically in recent years, however, and now you must expect to pay from US$12 to US$20 per person for a full lunch or dinner with wine or beer.

Two other good full-service restaurants are a short walk from the square, down the hill on İnönü Caddesi by the Atatürk Cultural Palace. Walk down the hill on the right-hand side of the tree-lined street and around the curve until you see the huge rectangular bulk of the German Consulate General on the opposite side of the road. These restaurants are more or less opposite the consulate.

The *C Fischer Restaurant* (☎ 245 2576, 245 3375), İnönü Caddesi 51/A, is the latest expression of a famous old İstanbul dining place which was previously near the British Consulate General in Galatasaray. Now the pleasant dining room, a half-flight down from street level, caters to the German diplomats with Turkish and continental dishes including lamb şiş kebap and delicious tiny lamb chops, beef tournedos and wiener-schnitzel. The traditional starter course at Fischer's is savoury borsch, and for a sweet, apple strudel or palaçinka (crêpes filled with fruit jam). Lunch or dinner at the Fischer costs US$8 to US$12 per person, with wine or beer, tax and tip included.

In the same block is the *Russian Restaurant* (☎ 243 4892), İnönü Caddesi 77/1, operated by the same management as the Fischer. Walk down the hill to the end of the block and turn left onto Miralay Şefik Bey Sokak, from which you enter the restaurant's small low-ceilinged dining room with white-clothed tables. The feeling here is of a local bistro.

Many years ago, when I first came to İstanbul and lived in this quarter, one could buy a big bowl of borsch here for 1 TL. Well, the lira has fallen, but the borsch has improved considerably.

The Russian menu features chicken Kiev (boned chicken stuffed with spiced butter, rewrapped around a bone, dusted with batter and deep fried), beef stroganoff or beefsteak with mushrooms. Your bill might be from US$8 to US$12 per person, all inclusive. Opening hours are from noon to 3 pm and 6 to 11 pm daily, and from 2 to 10 pm on Sunday.

Asian Food The Turks were not colonisers, so İstanbul has few 'ethnic' restaurants. An exception is *Tegik* (☎ 254 7172), Receppaşa Caddesi 20, Elmadağ, in the warren of little streets north of the square. Korean, Japanese and Chinese dishes are on the menu, and are served daily from noon to 3 and 6 to 11 (no lunch on Sunday) in a very pleasant triangular dining room. Expect to pay from US$15 to US$22 per person for a full meal with wine or beer.

Also in this neighbourhood is the *Çin Lokantası* (China Restaurant) (☎ 250 6263), Lamartin Caddesi 17/1, near the Lamartine and Riva hotels, more or less behind the Air France office off Cumhuriyet Caddesi. Standard Chinese restaurant decorations bring some gaiety to this little place, and white tablecloths add a touch of elegance. The standard fare is offered, nothing too adventurous: wonton soup and egg rolls, then beef, shrimp, chicken and fish prepared with various vegetables. A full meal costs about US$15 per person. Avoid the overpriced coffee. The Çin Lokantası is open from noon to 3 pm and 7 to 11 pm, closed Sunday.

İstiklal Caddesi & Galatasaray Now head west along İstiklal Caddesi. *Hacı Salih* (☎ 243 4528), İstiklal Caddesi 201, in the Anadolu Han, is open for lunch only. It's been serving lunch for over 25 years, with good standard Turkish fare with no pretensions, at very reasonable prices, about US$5 to US$10 for a full meal.

At Galatasaray, 700 metres along, the big Galatasaray Lycée rises on the south side of the street. On the north side (at İstiklal Caddesi 172) is an entrance to the Çicek Pasajı, the 'Flower Passage', a collection of taverna-restaurants open long hours every day in the courtyard of a historic building.

This used to be a marvellous place where locals gathered for drinking, singing and lots of good, cheap food. It has now been tarted up for tourists, and while the food can still be good, the hassle factor has increased dramatically: overcharging, giving you items you didn't order etc. If you want to eat here anyway, try the *Huzur Restaurant* (☎ 244

7129), at the far end on the left as you come in from İstiklal Caddesi.

The locals who used to eat here have moved on to the meyhanes (tavernas) deeper in the market. Walk along Sahne Sokak into the market to the first street on the right, Nevizade Sokak, to find the *Çağlar Restaurant* (☎ 249 7665) at No 6, and also *Kadri'nin Yeri* (☎ 243 6130). There are at least eight restaurants here with streetside tables in fine weather charging about US$1 to US$1.75 for plates of meze, about twice that for kebaps. Alcohol is served – enthusiastically.

Tepebaşi & Tünel Popular with the diplomatic set at lunch time is the *Dört Mevsim* (Four Seasons) (☎ 245 8941), İstiklal 509, almost in Tünel Square. Under English management, it is well located to draw diners from the US, British, Dutch, Russian and Swedish consulates. The food is continental with several delicious concessions to Turkish cuisine, preparation and service are first-rate. Lunch is served from noon to 3 pm, dinner from 6 pm to midnight; closed Sunday. If you order the fixed menu at lunch, you might pay US$10, drink and tip included. Ordering from the regular menu at dinner can drive your bill up to US$20 or US$25 per person.

Çati Restaurant (☎ 251 0000), İstiklal Caddesi, Peremeci Sokak 20/7, is on the 7th (top) floor of a building on a small side street which runs between İstiklal and Meşrutiyet caddesis; it's south of Balyoz Sokak and north of Asmalımescit Sokak. Though the view is vestigial at best, the greenhouse-style dining room is pleasant, the food quite good and not expensive. Try the Çatı Böreği for an appetiser; it's halfway between a Turkish börek and a turnover, made with cheese.

Main courses are mostly Turkish, with a few European specialities. Expect to spend from US$10 to US$15 per person. If you don't like syrupy organ music, come early for dinner. It's open for lunch and dinner every day.

Yakup 2 Restaurant (yah-KOOP ee-KEE) (☎ 249 2925), Asmalımescit Caddesi 35/37,

just up the street from the Pera Palas, is popular with local artists, musicians and actors. It hasn't been fancied up for tourists, so the décor is minimal but the food is quite good and moderately priced. Strike up a conversation with those at a neighbouring table; they may well speak a foreign language. Full meals with wine, beer or rakı cost about US$8 to US$15. It's open every day for dinner, and for lunch daily except Sunday.

At Meşrutiyet Caddesi 129 between the Büyük Londra Hotel and the Etap İstanbul Hotel is the *Restaurant Tuncel* (toon-JEHL) (☎ 245 5566), a small place with an attractive, modern décor and black-coated waiters. Have a meal of soup, grilled meat, a side dish of vegetables and something to drink, and you'll pay around US$9 to US$12 per person.

Vagabondo's (☎ 249 0481), İstiklal Caddesi 315-318, about 100 metres northeast of Tünel Square, serves big portions of good Italian food, garlic bread and all, at moderate prices, though you must be careful when you order the expensive drinks. Order an appetiser or soup, spaghetti and a sweet, finish off your meal with cappuccino, and you'll pay about US$10 per person.

Galata Tower When you're poking around in the neighbourhood of the Galata Tower, try *Güney Kardeşler Restaurant*, Şahkapısı Sokak, between Galipdede Caddesi and the tower. It's clean, pleasant, and moderate in price.

Bosphorus The Bosphorus is lined with villages, each with its several little seafood restaurants catering to a more or less distinguished clientele. Some of these places charge prices at the top end of the scale, a very few charge bottom-end prices (see those sections for details).

One place in the middle range is *Hanedan Restaurant* (☎ 260 4854), near the ferry terminal in Beşiktaş, just north of Dolmabahçe. Seafood is the speciality, but meats and traditional dishes are cheaper. It's clean and pleasant, and you'll pay only about US$8 to US$10 for a meal.

Aksaray & Kumkapı The Ramada Hotel in Aksaray has an excellent Chinese restaurant called *Dynasty Asian* (☎ 513 9300), with dim sum at lunch (from noon to 2.30 pm); dinner is from 7 to 11 pm. You can spend US$40 to US$50 per person here, all in.

Kumkapı In Byzantine times, the fishers' harbour called Kontoscalion was due south of Laleli. The gate into the city from that port came to be called Kumkapı by the Turks. The harbour has been filled in and the gate is long gone, but the district is still filled with fishers who moor their boats in a more modern version of the old harbour. Each evening the narrow streets of the neighbourhood resound to the footsteps of people hungry for fish. In fine weather restaurant tables crowd the narrow streets, and happy diners clatter plates and cutlery between bolts of pungent rakı.

In recent years the scene has become a bit too hectic for some visitors, with touts pushing menus at you as you approach. Ignore them, find a seat, order carefully (and don't accept anything you haven't ordered), and you'll enjoy yourself. Expect to part with US$18 to US$30 per person for the meal, appetisers, salads, wine, sweet, tax and tip all included.

Here are a few tips on seasons. From March to the end of June is a good time to order *kalkan* (turbot), *uskumru* (mackerel), and *hamsi* (fresh anchovies), but from July to mid-August is spawning season for many species, and fishing them is prohibited. In high summer, these are the easiest to find in the markets and on the restaurant tables: *çinakop* (a small bluefish), *lüfer* (medium-size bluefish), *palamut* (bonito), *tekir* (red mullet: *Mullus surmuletus*), *barbunya* (red mullet: *Mullus barbatus*), and *istavrit* (scad, horse mackerel).

Kumkapı has dozens of seafood restaurants, many operated by Turkish citizens of Greek or Armenian ancestry. Among the favourite things to order is swordfish şiş kebap, chunks of fresh fish skewered and grilled over charcoal, but there are fish soups and stews, fish poached with vegetables, pan-fried fish and pickled fish.

Typical of Kumkapı's seafood eateries is *Minas* (MEE-nahss) (☎ 522 9646) at Samsa Sokak 7, Kumkapı, facing the square. Minas is not one of the cheaper places; you can dine for less elsewhere. If you're not in the mood for seafood but would like to explore Kumkapı in any case, come for a kebap, and you'll spend a mere US$4 or so.

Also facing the square is *Köşem Cemal Restaurant* (☎ 520 1229), Samsa Sokak 1, Kumkapı, with similar prices, cuisine and advantages. Here there are white tablecloths, good careful service and a mixed clientele of Turks and tourists. Upstairs is another pleasant dining room.

Ördekli Bakkal Sokak, the street which runs from the railway station to Kumkapı Meydanı (as the little square is named), has another half-dozen good seafood restaurants, including *Üçler Balık Restaurant* (☎ 517 2339), Ördekli Bakkal Sokak 3, just off the square. Another which can be recommended is the *Deniz Restaurant* (☎ 528 0858), Ördekli Bakkal Sokak 12/A. Yet other side streets hold more restaurants. Two that have been recommended to me are the *Yengeç Balık Lokantası* (☎ 516 3227), Telli Odalar Sokak 6, and the *Kumkapı Restaurant* (☎ 522 6590), Üstad Sokak 7.

To/From Kumkapı You can get to Kumkapı by one of three methods. From Laleli, Beyazıt or the Covered Market, walk. Just opposite the Beyazıt Camii in Beyazıt Square, on the south side of Yeniçeriler Caddesi, is the beginning of Tiyatro Caddesi. Follow this street south for 10 short blocks (for the last block, it veers to the left), and you'll find yourself in Kumkapı's main square.

You can also take a taxi, but it may be a bit expensive as the driver might choose to cruise all the way around the old city in order to enter this congested district from the sea side; figure on US$3 or so from Sultanahmet, US$5 or US$6 from Taksim.

Kumkapı

0   50   100 m

1 Köşem Cemal Restaurant
2 Kumkapı Meydanı
3 Yengeç Balık Lokantası
4 Deniz Restaurant
5 Minas
6 Kumkapı Restaurant
7 Üçler Balık Restaurant

SEA OF MARMARA

The cheapest way to go is by train from Sirkeci Station. Enter the station, bear to the right and buy a ticket at one of the kiosks marked 'Banliyö' for 40c, and board any of the electric commuter trains on the right-hand platforms. Most will be for Halkalı, but in fact any train will do, as they all pass Kumkapı. The trains are run-down, but the ride is short.

You will round Seraglio Point, offering marvellous views of the Sea of Marmara and Topkapı Palace, and stop briefly at Cankurtaran Station before pulling into Kumkapı Station. Leave the train and the station, and walk down the most prominent street, which is Ördekli Bakkal Sokak, (Grocer with a Duck St).

By the way, the next station on the railway line after Kumkapı is Aksaray (Yenikapı). You can use the train to come and go from that district as well, for the same fare.

Sirkeci & Eminönü Here, at the Mısır Çarşışı, Egyptian Market, a famous old restaurant has been serving for decades.

Pandeli (☎ 527 3909), over the main entrance (facing the Galata Bridge) of the Mısır Çarşışı, is a series of small chambers covered in beautiful faïence. Only lunch is served (from Monday to Saturday), and seafood is the speciality, but grilled meats are served as well. In recent years the food has not improved though prices have risen steeply. They even charge you to hang up your coat. Though beautiful, it is not the place it once was, so you may spend upwards of US$16 to US$20 for a complete meal.

Karaköy The place for a good fish lunch here (and lunch only) is the *Liman Lokantası*. For details see Places to Eat – middle.

Taksim The fanciest places to eat in Taksim Square are the various restaurants of the big hotels. Usually rated the best is the *Divan Oteli* (☎ 231 4100), which serves continental and Turkish cuisine in posh surroundings at decent prices, about US$35 to US$40 per person for a fine meal, all in. *Divan Pub*, adjoining, is still fairly fancy but signifi-

cantly cheaper. The speciality here is excellent Turkish döner kebap.

The *Roof Rotisserie* at the İstanbul Hilton is also very good, with fine views and excellent food at similar prices. The Hilton's main dining room, the *Dragon Restaurant*, serves Asian fare. There are many good restaurants in the bottom-end and middle-range categories as well (see those sections).

Sea of Marmara İstanbul's longtime favourite for grilled meats is *Beyti* (☎ 573 9373, 573 9212), Orman Sokak 33, in Florya, just west of Atatürk Airport. A dramatic, opulent place with a domed stained-glass canopy and a dozen different dining rooms, Beyti moved here from the village of Büyükçekmece, which used to be the butchery for İstanbul. Vegetarians should stay away, but meat-eaters will love the Beyti kebap, a feast of successive plates of various meats prepared in various ways – you finish one and another appears, hot and savoury, and then another, until you can't eat one more thing. Beyti is open for lunch and dinner (closed on Monday); expect to pay about US$20 to US$30 per person for a full dinner, wine, tax and tip included.

To get to Beyti, take a taxi (US$10 to US$14 each way), or to save some money take any banliyö train from Sirkeci Station to the Yeşilköy stop, then a taxi (cabs are rare at Florya Station).

Bosphorus – European Shore The shores of the Bosphorus bear many excellent restaurants. Here are my favourites at the top of the price spectrum. These 'high' Turkish prices would be considered low in any other major European city.

Bebek In the interesting Bosphorus village of Bebek are several excellent restaurants, including the *Yeni Bebek Restaurant* (yeh-NEE beh-BEHK) (☎ 263 3447), Cevdet Paşa Caddesi 123, next to the Hotel Bebek on the shore road. Heavy velvet drapes, white high-backed chairs and tables spread with snowy cloths make for a formal atmosphere, and the quiet, careful service reinforces the formality. The array of dishes offered is vast, with appetisers, then fish (but the meat dishes are equally tasty and much cheaper). With wine or beer, your meal might cost US$16 to US$25 per person. To reach the restaurant, take bus No 23 'Bebek-Taksim' or a dolmuş from Taksim Square.

'S' Restoran (☎ 263 8326), Vezirköşkü Sokak 2, Bebek, is on the upper floor of a fuel station on the coast road. Don't let this put you off, the imaginative Turkish and French-style dishes are excellent, as is the view of the Bosphorus. Make reservations for lunch (from noon to 4 pm) or dinner (7 pm to midnight); closed on Sunday. Dinner for two can cost as high as US$80 – higher if you're reckless.

İstinye Continue northward from Bebek, under the Fatih Bridge, to the village of İstinye and the famous restaurant called Süreyya (☎ 263 8385), İstinye Caddesi 26. The cuisine is superb and varied, with Russian, Turkish and continental dishes to choose from. Chicken Kiev is a favourite here, but there's also good borsch and various French-inspired dishes. Hours are from noon to 3 pm and from 8 pm to midnight, reservations are essential, and dinner for two can hit US$100 unless you're careful.

Tarabya Farther north along the European shore of the Bosphorus is the village of Tarabya, which takes its name from the Greek word Therapia, or treatment for an illness. Under the Byzantines and Ottomans, this little village surrounding a cove was a favourite resort away from the ills of the big city. Today the cove is surrounded with seafood restaurants, and in summer a carnival atmosphere prevails.

On the south side of the cove is the Garaj Restaurant (☎ 262 0032, 262 0474), Yeniköy Caddesi 30, where the fish is fresh and in vast array, but the waiters have a tendency to load your table (and your bill) with items you did not order. A delicious seafood lunch or dinner here costs from

US$18 to US$30 per person, wine, tax and tip included.

On the north side of the cove, the inland side of the road is lined solidly with little seafood restaurants. All have streetside tables, but the traffic makes these unpleasant at times, unfortunately.

Palet 1 (☎ 262 0118), Kefeliköy Caddesi 110, is small and overdecorated, but it dares to be different by offering seafood soufflé, shrimp in a Mexican barbecue sauce, octopus in a cheese sauce, and even paella. In trying these exotic items, I would not expect authenticity, though they will be tasty enough. A fish dinner is about US$15 or US$20 per person, meat about half that, all included. The Palet's sister establishments, Palet 2 and Palet 3, provide additional seating when Palet 1 is heavily booked.

Most famous and exclusive of Tarabya's seafood restaurants is Façyo (☎ 262 0024), Kireçburnu Caddesi 13, some distance north of the cove on the shore road. The waiters are experienced, the seafood superb, the views good, the prices high – up to US$90 or so for two if you order whatever you like. Dining for just over half that much is possible, though. Reserve in advance, and arrive between noon and midnight any day.

Sarıyer Even farther up the Bosphorus, in Sarıyer, is a cheap seafood restaurant described in Places to Eat – bottom end.

Urcan Balık Lokantası (☎ 242 0367), Orta Çeşme Caddesi 2/1, displays live fish in aquaria, fresh fish laid out on beds of crushed ice, baskets of live crabs and lobsters, buckets of shellfish and shrimp. Try to get a table next to the windows overlooking the Bosphorus, choose a fish, determine the price, then order wine, soup or mezes and salads. Expect to pay from US$25 to US$40 per person, all in, for dinners based on fish in season. Lobster and fish out of season can be breathtakingly expensive.

Mücahit Körfez Balık Lokantası, right next door, is similar. I have not yet had a chance to try the Aquarius (☎ 271 3434), Cami Arkası, in the old fish market, but the setting is certainly appropriate. It's open daily from noon to midnight, and charges from US$28 to US$30 for a full meal.

Bosphorus – Asian Shore
There are fewer good restaurants on the eastern shore of the Bosphorus, and they are more expensive or inconvenient to reach.

Halfway to the Black Sea, north of the Fatih Bridge, is the village of Kanlıca and the *Körfez Restaurant* (☎ 332 0108), Körfez Caddesi 78. Call for reservations, then meet the restaurant's boat on the European shore for the ride across. The speciality here is sea bass baked in salt, and it also does a famous zucchini (marrow) salad. Lunch is served from noon to 3 pm, dinner from 8 pm to midnight, for US$28 to US$38 per person, all in.

On a promontory above the village of Çubuklu, is the *Hıdiv Kasrı* (☎ 331 2651), described in Places to Stay. The dining room of the villa is a wonderful place to enjoy a lunch or dinner, with the blue of the Bosphorus glistening below you. In the evening, a string trio plays songs from between the two world wars as you dine. The cuisine here is pure Turkish. Soup, or a selection of appetisers, followed by a lamb dish, then a sweet, will cost from US$15 to US$20 per person, drinks included. Allow enough time (and daylight) to stroll around the grounds and inspect the marvellous villa as well.

The only practical way to the Hıdiv Kasrı is by taxi. You may have to take a taxi. If you do, you may want to ask the driver to wait while you dine, an old İstanbul practice which avoids the hassle of finding scarce taxis later. Drivers may oblige for no extra charge (which deserves a tip), or may charge you a negotiable amount. From the city, a taxi should cost about US$10 or US$12 each way. Lunch and dinner are served every day.

ENTERTAINMENT
The name 'İstanbul' often conjures up thoughts of mysterious intrigues in dusky streets, dens in which sultry belly dancers do what they do, and who knows what else? As with most aged stereotypes, the reality is somewhat different.

International İstanbul Festival
This, the most prominent entertainment event in İstanbul, begins in late June and continues to mid-July. World-class performers – soloists and virtuosos, orchestras, dance companies, rock and jazz groups – give recitals and performances in numerous concert halls, historic buildings and palaces. The highlight is Mozart's *Abduction from the Seraglio* performed in Topkapı Palace, with the Sultan's private Gate of Felicity as a backdrop. Check at the box offices in the Atatürk Cultural Palace (☎ 251 5600, fax 245 3916) for schedules, ticket prices and availability, or contact the festival office (☎ 260 4533, 260 9072; fax 261 8823), İstanbul Kültür ve Sanat Vakfı, Yıldız Kültür ve Sanat Merkezi, 80700 Beşiktaş, İstanbul.

Another good bet during the festival, and on other warm summer evenings as well, is a performance of drama or folk dance given in Rumeli Hisar, up the Bosphorus.

Another open-air theatre, the Açık Hava Tiyatrosu, is just north of the İstanbul Hilton Hotel, off Cumhuriyet Caddesi.

Folklore
Turks are enthusiastic folklore fans, and many are still close enough in tradition to their regional dances to jump in and dance along at a performance. It's usually pretty easy to find a dance performance. University groups, good amateur companies and professionals all schedule performances throughout the year. The Turkish Folklore Association usually has something going on. For current offerings, ask at a Tourist Information Office or at one of the larger hotels.

High Culture
There are symphony, opera and ballet seasons, and occasional tour performances by the likes of Jean-Pierre Rampal or Paul Badura-Skoda. Many but not all of these performances are given in the Atatürk Cultural Centre (☎ 251 5600) in Taksim Square.

The box offices have schedules, as do many of the luxury hotels.

Theatre

The Turks are enthusiastic theatre-goers, and as a people they seem to have a special genius for dramatic art. The problem, of course, is language. If you're a true theatre-buff you might well enjoy a performance of a familiar classic, provided you know the play well enough to follow the action without benefit of dialogue.

Cinema

İstiklal Caddesi between Taksim and Galatasaray is the centre of İstanbul's cinema (*sinema*) district, with many foreign films being shown. The advent of television has put many cinemas out of business, and some of the survivors screen the racier movies, plus the much-beloved Turkish melodramas. Many first-run foreign feature films do make it to İstanbul, however, and you will be able to enjoy them at bargain prices. For current listings, buy the *Turkish Daily News* on Friday to get their special *Weekend* supplement.

You may need some words on your cinema outing. Look on the cinema posters for the words *Renkli* and *Türkçe* or *Orijinal* (ohr-zhee-NAHL). If you see *Renkli Orijinal*, that means the film is in colour and in the original language with Turkish subtitles. If you see *Renkli Türkçe* the film is in colour, but has been dubbed in Turkish, in which case you may understand nothing.

There are three general seating areas, and you pay according to which you choose: *koltuk* (kohl-TOOK), on the floor in the midsection to the rear; *birinci* (beer-EEN-jee), on the floor near the screen; and *balkon* (bahl-KOHN), in the balcony where the young lovers congregate. If you're going to the cinema to watch the film, ask for koltuk.

When possible, buy your tickets a few hours in advance. Tickets cost from US\$1.75 to US\$2.50. Also, the usher will expect a small tip for showing you to your seat.

Beyoğlu Along İstiklal Caddesi, look for these:

Atlas (☎ 243 7576), İstiklal Caddesi 209, Kuyumcular Pasajı
Beyoğlu (☎ 251 3240), İstiklal Caddesi 140, Halep Pasajı
Dünya (☎ 249 9361), İstiklal Caddesi 24-26, Fitaş Pasajı
Emek (☎ 244 8439), İstiklal Caddesi, Yeşilçam Sokak 5
Fitaş & Fitaş Cep (☎ 249 0166), İstiklal Caddesi 24-26, Fitaş Pasajı
Sinepop (☎ 251 1176), İstiklal Caddesi, Yeşilçam Sokak 22

Harbiye & Şişli Cumhuriyet Caddesi goes north from Taksim past the Hilton to Harbiye, where it changes names to become Halaskargazi Caddesi. From Harbiye northward through Osmanbey to Şişli Square about two km) are several more cinemas:

Gazi (☎ 247 9665), Halaskargazi Caddesi 214, Osmanbey
Harbiye As (☎ 247 6315), Cumhuriyet Caddesi, Cebeltopu Sokak 7, Harbiye
Kent (☎ 241 6203), Halaskargazi Caddesi 281, Şişli
Nova Baran (☎ 240 3558), Nova Baran Plaza, Şişli
Site (☎ 247 6947), Halaskargazi Caddesi 291, Şişli

Çemberlitaş In Old İstanbul, on Yeniçeriler Caddesi between Sultanahmet and Beyazıt, is another good cinema area. Look for the Fırat Kültür Merkezi (FKM) cinema complex opposite the Çemberlitaş tramway stop. Also here are the Şafak cinemas (☎ 516 2660), in the Darüşşafaka Pasajı, with three screens.

Nightclubs

Belly dancers do still perform in Turkey, of course. Clubs are mostly in Beyoğlu and along the Bosphorus shores. Several nightclubs along Cumhuriyet Caddesi between Taksim and the Hilton feature belly dancers, folk-dance troupes, singers and bands, and are generally safe to attend, though very expensive (as high as US\$50 or US\$60 per person for dinner and the show).

Nightclubs in the big hotels are expensive also, but safe. Nightclub ripoffs are a big problem in this city, particularly for single

foreign males. Avoid any club which is recommended by any source except a reliable one, such as a longtime Turkish friend.

İstiklal Caddesi and the side streets running from it have many clubs, but one of İstanbul's oldest and richest con games works like this:

You're a single male out for a stroll in the afternoon or evening. A well-spoken, well-dressed Turk strikes up a conversation, and says he knows 'a good place where we can have a drink and chat' or 'a great nightspot' etc. You enter, sit down, and immediately several women move to your table and order drinks. When they come, you're asked to pay – anywhere from US$100 to however much money you have with you. It's a mugging, and if you don't pay up they take you into the back office and take it from you. It's a situation to avoid.

An exotic variation is a single foreign male having a drink and a meal at the Çiçek Pasajı. Several Turkish friends strike up a conversation, then suggest you all take a taxi to another place. In the taxi, they forcefully relieve you of your wallet.

Casinos & Gazinos

Many of the large luxury hotels (Hilton, Conrad, Sheraton, The Marmara etc) have casinos where you can play the slots, blackjack, roulette, and other games. It's fun, but remember: casinos are not successful because gamblers win, but because they lose.

A Turkish *gazino*, on the other hand, has nothing to do with gambling. Rather, gazinos are open-air nightclubs popular in the summertime. (Some have been built up and operate in winter to the point that they are actually nightclubs with a gazino heritage.) The best of these are along the European shore of the Bosphorus. You won't find much belly dancing here. The shows are mostly Turkish popular singers. Dinner and drinks are served. If the name of the place has the word 'aile' in it, as in Bebek Aile Gazinosu, it means the proprietor wants to appeal to a respectable, mixed crowd and avoid all-male or heavy-drinking audiences.

Night Cruises

About the cheapest yet most enjoyable nighttime activity in İstanbul is to take a Bosphorus ferry somewhere. It doesn't really matter where, as long as you don't end up on the southern coast of the Sea of Marmara or out in the Princes' Islands. Catch one over to Üsküdar or any town up the Bosphorus, and enjoy the view, the twinkling lights, the fishing boats bobbing in the waves, the powerful searchlights of the ferries sweeping the sea lanes. Have a glass of tea (a waiter will bring it round regularly). Get off anywhere, and take a bus or dolmuş home if you can't catch a ferry back directly.

Perhaps the easiest ferry to catch for this purpose is the one from Eminönü to Üsküdar. Just go to Eminönü's Üsküdar dock, buy two jetons (for the voyages out and back), and walk aboard. From Üsküdar, just come back; or wait for one of the frequent ferries to Beşiktaş or Kabataş, from whence you can catch a bus or dolmuş back to your part of town.

A similar ride is the one to Haydarpaşa or Kadıköy, from Karaköy. These two Asian suburbs are the only destinations for ferries from these docks, so you can't end up way off somewhere. Return boats bring you back to Karaköy. Each way, the voyage takes 20 minutes.

Turkish Baths

For a description of taking a Turkish bath, see the Facts for the Visitor chapter. Actually, you're not confined to bathing only in the evenings, but it does feel wonderful after a tiring day.

The price for the entire experience can be US$3 or US$4 in a local bath if you bring your own soap, shampoo and towel, and bathe yourself; from US$8 to US$10 for an assisted bath; from US$16 to US$25 at a 'historic' bath, including a perfunctory massage. Tips will be expected all around.

After you're all done, you'll be utterly refreshed, squeaky clean, and almost unable to walk due to the wonderful relaxation of muscles, mind and spirit.

Tourist Baths İstanbul has several beautiful historic baths. Unfortunately, they have been ruined by tourism and now offer gruff, careless service at high prices, especially in the women's sections.

Cağaloğlu Hamamı (jaa-AHL-oh-loo) (☎ 522 2424), on Yerebatan Caddesi at Babıali Caddesi, just 200 metres from Aya Sofya near Cağaloğlu Square, was built over three centuries ago. It boasts (without evidence) that King Edward VIII, Kaiser Wilhelm II, Franz Liszt and Florence Nightingale have all enjoyed its pleasures, in the future they'll probably claim that they all bathed at the same time. Hours are from 7 am to 10 pm (men) or 8 am to 9 pm (women). Several female readers of this book have written to complain of the service.

The other bath is the Tarihi Galatasaray Hamamı (☎ 244 1412) at the end of Suterazi Sokak, a little street going south-east from İstiklal Caddesi, just north of Galatasaray. Look for the sign on İstiklal Caddesi that points the way. The men's section is filled with gleaming marble and bath attendants hungry for tips; the women's section has less marble, but the same sort of service.

Local Baths If it's a bath you're interested in, ask at your hotel for directions to a *mahalli hamam* (local baths) where locals go. Neighbourhood baths will treat you much better for much less money than the touristy baths, though as more foreigners patronise these local baths they might suffer the same fate. Here are some suggestions near Sultanahmet:

Tarihi Park Hamamı
> a small and unpretentious place at Doktor Emin Paşa Sokak 10; turn off Divan Yolu opposite the Hippodrome by the Hotel Petrol

Kadırga Hamamı
> on Kadırga Hamamı Sokak, just off Piyerloti Caddesi a few blocks west of the south-western end of the Hippodrome near the Piyerloti Pansion and Ottoman Hotel (see Places to Stay for directions)

Tarihi Hocapaşa Hamamı,
> at İbni Kemal Caddesi 23 near the Hocapaşa mosque near Sirkeci railway station, the area is described in Places to Eat

Tarihi Çemberlitaş Hamamı is on Yeniçeriler Caddesi at Çemberlitaş.

In Beyoğlu, look for the *Tarihi Ağa Hamamı*, very near the Galatasaray Hamamı on Turnacıbaşı Sokak (the street just north-east of the big Galatasaray Lycée).

If you find another good, untouristy hamam, please write and let me know. And if your experience at any of the aforementioned baths is bad, let me know so I can warn other readers.

THINGS TO BUY

İstanbul has it all, and prices for craft items are not necessarily higher than at the source. Leather apparel offers good value, but you must shop around, get to know the market a bit, and inspect your prospective purchase carefully for flaws and bad craftwork.

Carpets

There must be as many carpet shops as there are taxis. The carpet shop touts become exceedingly tedious very early in your visit, but a Turkish carpet – a good one at a fair price – is still a wonderful souvenir.

The government-run carpet shop in the

Haseki Hürrem Hamamı between Aya Sofya and the Blue Mosque, described previously, is an excellent choice: with honest, well-informed and helpful service, with guaranteed quality and fair prices that are fixed. Also check out the Halı Evi, next to the Konuk Evi (in front of Aya Sofya), both places run by the Turkish Touring & Automobile Association.

If you haggle for a carpet, at least shop around and get to know price levels a bit. Beware of this scam:

You make friends with a charming Turk, or perhaps a Turkish-American or Turkish-European couple, they recommend a friend's shop, you go and have a look. There's no pressure to buy. Indeed, your new friends wine and dine you (always in a jolly group with others), paying for everything. Before you leave İstanbul you decide to buy a carpet. You go to the shop, choose one you like, and ask the price. So far so good; if you can buy that carpet at a good price, everything's fine. But if the owner strongly urges you to buy a 'better' carpet, more expensive because it's 'old' or 'Persian' or 'rare', or 'makes a good investment', beware. You may return home with it to find you've paid many times more than the carpet is worth.

You choose the carpet, inspect it carefully, compare prices for similar work at other shops, then buy and take it with you or ship it yourself (don't have the shopkeeper ship it).

Leather Apparel

Turkey has lots of leather clothing for sale. Shops in the Kürkçüler Çarşısı section of the Kapalı Çarşı (Covered Market) have a good selection, as do many shops outside the market in the streets surrounding Beyazıt Square.

Handicrafts

Several historic medreses (theological colleges) have been restored and turned into handicrafts bazaars. İstanbul Arts & Crafts Market is just to the right of the Yeşil Ev hotel on Kabasakal Caddesi, between Aya Sofya and the Blue Mosque.

More lively and interesting, with a café for hot and cold drinks, is the Caferağa

Medresesi Handicrafts Centre to the right of the Yücelt Interyouth Hostel, and to the left of the Konuk Evi hotel on Caferiye Sokak, facing Aya Sofya. Shops set up in the old student cells offer carpets, jewellery, leather goods, embroidery, calligraphy and Turkish miniature paintings.

A few steps away on Soğukçeşme Sokak is the Turkish Touring & Automobile Association's Halı Evi ('carpet house'), with a good selection of carpets at fair prices.

For posher shops, head north-east from Eminönü along the Golden Horn to the Golden Horn Handicrafts Centre (☎ 512 4270), Ragıp Gümüşpala Caddesi. An ancient four-storey Genoese-Ottoman prison called the Zindan Han has been converted into a beautiful but pricey store selling jewellery, leather and fine art. There's a restaurant with a view of the Golden Horn as well.

Shopping Malls

Grandest of them all is, of course, the Kapalı Çarşı, described above. İstanbul's fanciest mall so far is the Galleria (gah-LEHR-ree-yah), on the Marmara shore road at Ataköy, west of the city walls. Built as a typical US-style shopping mall, it features posh shops selling international goods – so why come all the way to İstanbul to find a mall? A bonus is the small indoor ice-skating rink in winter.

GETTING THERE & AWAY

All roads lead to İstanbul. As the country's foremost transportation hub, the question is not how to get there (see the Getting There & Away chapter at the front of this book), but how to negotiate this sprawling urban mass when you arrive. Here is the information you may need on arrival.

Air

Atatürk Airport, formerly known as Yeşilköy Airport, has a decent, modern terminal for international flights, and an upgraded domestic terminal. A new, larger airport is already under construction at a site nearby.

The Ministry of Tourism maintains an

information office in the international arrivals terminal and will be happy to help with questions or problems. There is also a hotel-reservation desk in the arrivals terminal, but some readers of this guide have written to say that they always recommend the same expensive, inconvenient hotel to everyone, regardless of their preference. This may change, so check anyway.

Also in the arrivals terminal are various currency exchange offices operated by Turkish banks. If you change money here, count your money carefully and make sure it agrees with the total on the exchange slip. These guys will often short-change you by several thousand liras, relying upon your confusion as a new arrival to get away with it. Also, don't accept an excuse that they 'have no small change'. It's their business to have the proper change.

Before you pass through customs, avail yourself of the opportunity to buy duty-free goods at decent prices, with no transcontinental carrying problems. They're on sale at the Tekel shop; sales are for foreign currency only.

For examples of airfares from İstanbul to other Turkish cities, see the Getting Around chapter. For details on transport to and from İstanbul's Atatürk Airport, see the Getting Around section following.

Airline Offices Most of the offices are on Cumhuriyet Caddesi between Taksim Square and Harbiye, in the Elmadağ area, but Turkish Airlines has offices around the city. Travel agencies can also sell tickets and make reservations. Some addresses follow:

Aeroflot
(☎ 243 4725) in Taksim
Air France
(☎ 256 4356) in Taksim; (☎ 573 9453) at the airport
Alitalia
(☎ 231 3391) in Elmadağ;(☎ 573 8103) at the airport
American Airlines
(☎ 230 2211) in Harbiye
British Airways
(☎ 234 1300) in Elmadağ; (☎ 573 8107) at the airport

Delta Airlines
(☎ 231 2339) in the Hilton arcade; (☎ 573 7709) at the airport
El Al
(☎ 246 5303) in Elmadağ; (☎ 573 889) at the airport
Greenair
(☎ 241 0293), Cumhuriyet Caddesi 279, Adlı İşhanı, Harbiye
Iberia
(☎ 255 1968) in Elmadağ; (☎ 574 377) at the airport
İstanbul Airlines
(☎ 231 7526/7; fax 246 4967), Cumhuriyet Caddesi 111, Elmadağ; or at Atatürk Airport, international (☎ 573 4093; fax 574 4455); domestic (☎ 574 2443)
KLM
(☎ 230 0311) in Nişantaşı, north-east of Harbiye; (☎ 573 8635) at the airport
Lufthansa
(☎ 251 7180) in Elmadağ; (☎ 573 3750) at the airport
Olympic Airways
(☎ 246 5081 573) in Elmadağ; (☎ 573 8730) at the airport
Qantas Airways
(☎ 240 5032) in Elmadağ
Sabena
(☎ 254 7254) in Taksim; (☎ 573 4623) at the airport
SAS
(☎ 246 6075) in Elmadağ; (☎ 574 4498) at the airport
Singapore Airlines
(☎ 232 3706) in Harbiye; (☎ 574 2656) at the airport
Sönmez Holding Airlines
(☎ 249 8510), c/o Moris Seyahat Acentalığı, Tünel Pasajı 11, Beyoğlu
Swissair
(☎ 231 2811) in Taksim; (☎ 573 2573) at the airport
Turkish Airlines
reservations (☎ 574 8200; fax 240 2984); (☎ 574 7300) at the airport
offices (☎ 586 7514), Mustafa Kemal Paşa Caddesi 27, Aksaray
(☎ 522 8888), Hamidiye Caddesi, Doğubank İşhanı 26, Sirkeci
(☎ 246 4017), Cumhuriyet Caddesi 199-201, Harbiye; across from the Hilton
(☎ 245 2454), in Taksim, in the row of shops on the east side of Cumhuriyet Caddesi (soon to be razed)
(☎ 247 7021) Hilton arcade

Road

The E5/100 expressway from Europe takes you past Atatürk Airport and a bypass heading north and east to cross the Bosphorus bridges. If you're headed for Aksaray, don't take the bypass, but rather go straight on, through the city walls and you will end up in Aksaray Square. For Taksim, stay on the bypass and follow the signs.

If you're a bit more daring, leave the expressway at the airport, following signs for Yeşilköy or Ataköy. You can make your way to the shore of the Sea of Marmara and drive into the city along the water's edge. You'll pass the city walls near Yedikule, the Fortress of the Seven Towers and the Marble Tower, which has one foot in the water. The city's southern wall will be on your left as you drive. Across the Bosphorus, the view of Üsküdar, Haydarpaşa and Kadıköy is impressive. You can turn left onto Mustafa Kemal Caddesi for Aksaray and Laleli; or continue around Seraglio Point to Sirkeci, Eminönü and the Galata Bridge.

Bus

İstanbul has two major bus stations, the European one at Topkapı, and the Asian one at Harem. A new otogar is being built at Esenler to replace the chaotic Topkapı one. Most long-distance buses stop at both the European and Asian bus terminals, though some buses from Europe do not cross to Asia.

Topkapı Otogar Coming from Europe or Edirne, until the new Esenler otogar is open, your bus will drop you at Topkapı Otogar (☎ 577 5617), which straddles the Londra Asfaltı, the road to the airport, right outside the city walls next to the Topkapı or Cannon Gate. (Similarly named Topkapı Palace, by the way, lies five km to the east, on the Bosphorus.) Topkapı Otogar is a bewildering chaos of little bus offices, snack stands, taxi shills, mud, dust, noise and air pollution. For transport information, see the following Getting Around section.

Trakya Terminalı (Thrace Terminal), on the north side of the Londra Asfaltı highway, is mostly for European Turkey, the Marmara region and the coast to around Antalya. Anadolu Terminalı (Anatolia Terminal), on the south side, is for most travel through the middle of Turkey and for Greece and all European destinations. The Uluslalarası Terminalı (International Terminal), west of the Anatolia Terminal, has all the super-cheap unlicensed lines to Europe, the Middle East and Asia. Ignore the touts and shop around; you'll be surprised at the range of schedules and fares.

Esenler Otogar A new, modern bus terminal to replace the chaos at Topkapı is being built at Ferhat Paşa Çiftliği in Esenler, on the new motorway (expressway) from Edirne to İstanbul. It's almost completed, and may be open by the time you arrive. It is a good, modern facility, quite a distance west of the city.

Harem Otogar There is also a bus station (☎ 333 3763) on the eastern shore of the Bosphorus at Harem, between Üsküdar and Haydarpaşa. Many buses entering and leaving the city make a stop at Harem to serve residents of the Asian suburbs.

Bus Ticket Offices Bus-company ticket offices are found clustered at the north-east end of the Hippodrome in Sultanahmet (try the Tur-Ista office), in Laleli on Ordu Caddesi, and near Sirkeci Station on Muradiye Caddesi.

In Taksim, try the offices of the Pamukkale company (☎ 245 2946) at Mete Caddesi 16, to the left (north) of the Atatürk Cultural Palace. Pamukkale has a reputation as one of Turkey's best bus companies. It operates services to many points in Turkey, as well as to Europe.

Three more offices near Taksim are to the right (south) of the cultural centre, down the hill a block along İnönü Caddesi, on the left-hand side of the road. Varan (☎ 249 1903, 244 8457), at İnönü Caddesi 29/B, is also one of Turkey's best companies; its routes include those to Ankara, Athens, Çanakkale, Dornbirn, Edirne, Innsbruck, İzmir, Salzburg, Strasburg and Zürich, and to the more popular holiday destinations in Turkey.

Kamil Koç, another good line, is represented by Arama Turizm (☎ 245 2795), İnönü Caddesi 31, where you can also buy tickets for the TCDD (Turkish State Railways).

Ulusoy (☎ 249 4373, 248 8449), also among the best, has an office down the hill another block along İnönü Caddesi, facing the German Consulate General. Also here are As Turizm and Hakiki Koç lines (☎ 245 4244).

Fares & Travel Times Here are some examples of bus fares and travel times from İstanbul. Fares vary among companies, and sometimes can be reduced by haggling or by showing a student card. Departures to major destinations are very frequent; you can usually just go to the bus terminal and buy a ticket.

Ankara – 450 km, six hours, US$9 to US$20
Antakya – 1115 km, 20 hours, US$19 to US$26
Antalya – 725 km, 12 hours, US$14 to US$22
Artvin – 1352 km, 24 hours, US$30 to US$35
Ayvalık – 570 km, 9 hours, US$12 to US$15
Bodrum – 830 km, 14 hours, US$17 to US$24
Bursa – 230 km, four hours, US$6
Çanakkale – 340 km, six hours, US$8 to US$11
Denizli (for Pamukkale) – 665 km, 10 hours, US$13 to US$20
Edirne – 235 km, four hours, US$5.75
Erzurum – 1276 km, 22 hours, US$17 to US$23
Fethiye – 980 km, 15 hours, US$20 to US$26
Gaziantep – 1150 km, 20 hours, US$22 to US$30
İzmir – 605 km, nine hours, US$12 to US$20
Konya – 660 km, 11 hours, US$14 to US$18
Kuşadası – 700 km, 11 hours, US$14 to US$22
Marmaris – 900 km, 15 hours, US$20 to US$25
Nevşehir (Cappadocia) – 725 km, 10 to 12 hours, US$15 to US$20
Side – 790 km, 14 hours, US$15 to US$24
Trabzon – 1110 km, 19 hours, US$20 to US$32

Train

Sirkeci Station All trains from Europe terminate at Sirkeci (SEER-keh-jee) Station, right next to Eminönü in the shadow of Topkapı Palace. The station has its own small Tourism Information Office, post office and currency exchange booth, as well as a restaurant and café.

The main (west) station door of Sirkeci now is a modern structure. But take a look on the north side of the station, facing the Bosphorus: this more ornate façade was the original front of the station, more in keeping with the romantic ideas of what the terminus for the *Orient Express* should look like.

Right outside the station's west door is the free tram up the hill to Sultanahmet, Beyazıt, Laleli and Aksaray.

If you're headed for Taksim, go out the station door and turn right. Walk towards the sea and you'll see the Eminönü bus ranks to your left. Catch a bus to Taksim from here.

Departures The *İstanbul Express*, the train for Athens and for cities in Europe, departs from Sirkeci Station, on the European side of the Bosphorus, at 10.15 pm each evening in summer, at 11 pm in winter, arriving at the Turkish frontier the following morning about 9½ hours later (check these times, as they may change). The *Orient Express* no longer runs between İstanbul and Paris, but this evening train carries with it a whiff of the old romance, with carriages destined for points in Austria, Bulgaria, Croatia, Germany, Greece, Hungary, Romania, Russia, Serbia and Slovenia. It has 1st and 2nd-class seats to Belgrade and Munich, couchettes to Munich and Vienna; sleeping carriages once a week to Bucharest and Moscow; extra couchettes to Munich on Tuesday and Wednesday, and extra couchettes to Sofia on Sunday and Monday. Remember that you may need transit visas for some of the countries you'll be passing through.

Haydarpaşa Station To continue a train journey eastward into Turkey (meaning Anatolia), you must get to Haydarpaşa Station on the Asian side. The best way is by ferry (50c, 20 minutes) from Karaköy. Cross the Galata Bridge from Eminönü to Karaköy (by bus, dolmuş or taxi if your luggage is heavy), go to the prominent ferry dock, buy a token, go through the turnstile and look for the illuminated sign saying Haydarpaşa. Some ferries stop both at Haydarpaşa and Kadıköy; but you should be careful not to get a ferry that goes *only* to Kadıköy. If in doubt, just say *Haydarpaşa'ya mı?* ('To Haydarpaşa?') to anyone while pointing at the boat.

By the way, don't let anyone suggest that you take a taxi to Haydarpaşa. Ferries are scheduled to depart from Kadıköy and arrive at Haydarpaşa in time for the departure of all major trains. The ferry is cheap, convenient, pleasant and speedy. A taxi would be expensive and slow.

Ferries depart from Kadıköy for Haydarpaşa every 15 to 30 minutes. The special ferries, timed to connect with the departures of the major expresses, leave Karaköy about a half-hour before express train departures.

Departures The major trains departing from Haydarpaşa for Ankara, and fares for the journey, are detailed in the Getting Around chapter. For trains to Edirne, see the Edirne section. Here are details of other trains and services:

Anadolu Ekspresi
This train, described in the Getting Around chapter, connects at Ankara with the *Güney Ekspresi*, which departs from Ankara on Monday, Wednesday, Friday and Saturday via Kayseri, Sivas and Malatya to Diyarbakır and Kurtalan; and the *Van Gölü Ekspresi*, which departs from Ankara on Tuesday, Thursday and Sunday via Kayseri, Sivas, Malatya, Elazığ and Muş to Tatvan on Lake Van. If you plan to take these trains, remember that you must leave İstanbul the day before (eg, take the *Anadolu Ekspresi* from Haydarpaşa on Sunday evening to connect with the *Güney Ekspresi* at Ankara on Monday morning).

Doğu Ekspresi
Though this train departs from Haydarpaşa on time each morning at 8.30 am, it is usually late thereafter on its long trip via Ankara, Sivas, Erzincan and Erzurum to Kars on the Armenian border. It is a long and not particularly pleasant trip, but it is certainly cheap, costing only US$20/15 in 1st/2nd class for the 2½-day trip across the country. There are coaches only, no sleeping accommodation.

İç Anadolu Mavi Tren
This train departs at 11.15 pm via Eskişehir and Afyon to Konya (US$12; couchette US$15), and

arrives at 12.35 pm the next day before continuing to Karaman, arriving at 2.25 pm.

Meram Ekspresi
This train departs daily at 6.40 pm via Eskişehir and Afyon, arriving in Konya at 8.10 am. The fare to Konya is US$10/7.50 in 1st/2nd class; for sleeping compartments, total fares are US$32/50/75 for singles/doubles/triples.

Pamukkale Ekspresi
This train departs daily at 5.30 pm, arriving in Denizli at 7.27 am. Fares are US$10/7.50 in 1st/2nd class; for sleeping compartments, total fares are US$32/50/75 for singles/doubles/triples.

Toros Ekspresi
This train departs from Söğütlüçeşme Station on Tuesday, Thursday and Sunday at 9 am, and heads for the south-east, arriving in Adana at 6.55 am the next morning, and Gaziantep at 2.56 pm. Fares to Adana are US$13/9 in 1st/2nd class; for sleeping compartments, total fares are US$26/46/66 a single/double/triple. Fares to Gaziantep are around 22% higher.

Train Ticket Agencies You needn't go to the station to buy a ticket. Several travel agencies can make reservations and sell you tickets. In Sultanahmet, try Genç Turizm Seyahat Acentesi (☎ 526 5409 or 512 0457), Yerebatan Caddesi 15/3.

North of Taksim Square, between the Divan and Hilton hotels, go to Çelebi Turizm ve Seyahat (☎ 230 0900; fax 230 6147), Cumhuriyet Caddesi 141/1, Elmadağ; or Sultan Turizm Seyahat (☎ 240 3771; fax 230 0419), Cumhuriyet Caddesi 87/1, Elmadağ; or Setur Servis Turistik (☎ 230 0336; fax 230 3219), Cumhuriyet Caddesi 107, Harbiye.

Boat
Passenger ships dock at Karaköy, near the Yolcu Salonu (YOHL-joo sahl-oh-noo) or International Maritime Passenger Terminal on Rıhtım Caddesi. The Ministry of Tourism has an information office (☎ 249 5776) in the Yolcu Salonu, near the front (street) doors.

The international dock is next to the Karaköy ferry dock and only 100 metres east of the Galata Bridge. Bus and dolmuş routes to Taksim pass right in front of the Yolcu Salonu. For destinations in the Old City such as Sultanahmet, Laleli and Aksaray, go to the western side of Karaköy Square itself, right

Top: Carpet shop, Grand Bazaar, İstanbul (TB)
Left: Lone Pine Cemetery & Memorial, Gallipoli (TB)
Right: A latter-day Trojan Horse in Troy (TB)

Top: Rural life near the Byzantine walls, İznik (TB)
Bottom: Bakery, Bursa (TB)

at the end of the Galata Bridge. You'll have to find the pedestrian underpass to get to the dolmuş and bus stops.

Some domestic-line ships dock at Kabataş (KAH-bah-tahsh), about two km north of Karaköy on the Bosphorus shore, just south of Dolmabahçe Palace and Mosque. As you leave the dock at Kabataş, buses and dolmuşes heading left will be going to Karaköy and the Old City; those travelling right will be going to Taksim or north along the Bosphorus shore.

Boats arriving from Bandırma on the İzmir to İstanbul train-boat route dock at Sarayburnu (Seraglio Point), one km east of the Galata Bridge, north and east of Sirkeci Station.

GETTING AROUND

Transport within İstanbul moves slowly. The medieval street patterns do not receive automobiles well, let alone buses. Several conflagrations in the 19th century cleared large areas of the city and allowed new avenues to be opened. Were it not for these providential disasters, traffic would be even slower.

To/From the Airport

Free shuttle buses leave the airport's international terminal for the domestic terminal every 20 minutes or so throughout the day. Just walk out of the international arrivals terminal and look for the Havaş shuttle bus.

Airport to City The fastest way to get into town from the airport is by taxi (from 20 to 30 minutes), but this may cost US$10 to US$18, depending upon what part of the city you're headed for and whether it's night or day. A far cheaper alternative is the airport bus (operated by Havaş, from 35 to 60 minutes) for US$2.75, which departs from the domestic terminal and goes into the city, stopping at Bakırköy (Cevizlik), and on Mustafa Kemal Paşa Bulvarı in Aksaray (near Laleli), before ending its run in Beyoğlu at Şişhane Square, near the Galata Tower. Buses leave every half-hour from 5.30 to 10 am, every hour from 10 am to 2

pm, every half-hour from 2 to 8 pm, and every hour from 9 to 11 pm; there are no buses between 11 pm and 5.30 am.

You can cut the cost down to 50c if you take the No 96 red-and-beige İETT city bus to Yenikapı, a few blocks south of Aksaray, but the nine buses per day leave only about every 1½ hours. Catch the bus at the bus stop by the big taxi-parking area more or less between the two terminals (ask for the *belediye otobüsü*).

For only slightly more, find two or three other thrifty travellers and share a taxi (US$3 total; make sure the driver runs the meter) from the airport to the Yeşilköy banliyö tren istasyonu, the suburban railway station in the neighbouring town of Yeşilköy. From here, battered trains (50c) run every half hour or less to Sirkeci Station. Get off at Yenikapı for Aksaray and Laleli, at Cankurtaran for Sultanahmet hotels, or at Sirkeci for Beyoğlu.

City to Airport You must be at the airport for check-in *at least* 30 minutes before departure time for domestic flights, and it's not a bad idea to be there earlier, say 45 to 60 minutes before. For international flights, be at the airport at least an hour before take-off or, better still, 1½ or two hours before. Remember, there are three security checks, customs, check-in and immigration procedures to pass through before you board, and if the aircraft is wide-bodied, the officials will have to process about 400 passengers before boarding is completed.

If you're staying in Old İstanbul and you have plenty of time (45 minutes to an hour) for the return trip to the airport, catch the No 96 bus (50c) on the east side of Mustafa Kemal Paşa Bulvarı south of Aksaray, across the street from McDonald's. Departures are at 7, 8.40, 10.15 and 11.45 am, and 1.35, 2.45, 4.05, 5.55 and 7.40 pm. Otherwise, get on a suburban train ('Halkalı', 50c) at Sirkeci, Cankurtaran or Yenikapı, and get out at Yeşilköy, then take a taxi (US$3) to the airport.

If you're staying in Beyoğlu, the cheapest and most convenient way to the airport is the

Havaş bus (US$2.75) from the Şişhane terminal near Galata Tower.

Some cheap hotels in Aksaray and Sultanahmet can arrange to have a minibus take you to the airport for about US$3 or US$4. Ask at the reception desk.

To/From the Bus Terminal

If you arrive at the new otogar at Esenler, take the metro (Hızlı Tramvay) to Aksaray, then a taxi or the free tram to Sultanahmet and Sirkeci; or a dolmuş, bus or taxi to Taksim Square.

If the new otogar is not yet open, and you arrive at the old Topkapı Otogar, transport is a more complicated matter. The better bus lines such as Varan and Ulusoy will provide a *servis arabası*, or minibus, to take you from the bus station into the city. Both minibuses terminate at Taksim Square, but if you ask to be dropped in Aksaray or Laleli, the driver will doubtless oblige. From Aksaray you can hop on the free tram to Sultanahmet and Sirkeci.

If your bus company doesn't have a servis arabası, you'll have to make your own way into the city. Taxi drivers will be waiting to buttonhole you as you alight. Otherwise, make your way out of the bus station and across to the Topkapı gate itself. Just inside the gate (on the other side of the walls from the bus station) is a city bus stop, from which you can catch a bus or a dolmuş to Aksaray. If Aksaray or Laleli is not your final destination, you must change in Aksaray for the free tram to Sultanahmet and Sirkeci/Eminönü, or take a bus or dolmuş from Aksaray to Taksim.

To return to the Topkapı Otogar, take bus No 82, 84, 89, 89-S, 92, 93, 93-A, 95 or 97. There are also direct dolmuşes between Topkapı and Taksim (60c), stopping in Aksaray. To find one in Taksim, from the Air France office walk downhill (south-west) on Tarlabaşı Bulvarı two blocks to Abdülhak Hamit Caddesi and the dolmuş stand.

If you buy your bus ticket at a company office or travel agency in the city, be sure to ask about minibus service to the otogar.

To get to the Harem bus terminal, take a ferry from Karaköy to Haydarpaşa or Kadıköy, then catch a dolmuş northward along the shore to Harem; they run very frequently. You can also take a ferry from Eminönü, Kabataş or Beşiktaş to Üsküdar, then a dolmuş or bus south 2.5 km to Harem.

Metro

A metro system is under construction, but will take many years to complete. One problem is the city's history: every time a Roman or Byzantine structure is discovered, construction must be halted and the archaeologists brought in for weeks, perhaps months of study.

A metro line already in operation is the Hızlı Tramvay from Aksaray north-westward out along Adnan Menderes Bulvarı (formerly Vatan Caddesi) through the Bayrampaşa and Sağmalcılar districts to the new otogar (bus terminal) in Esenler. Another is the free tram from Aksaray along Ordu Caddesi/ Yeniçeriler Caddesi/Divan Yolu through Beyazıt to Sultanahmet and Sirkeci. The suburban train lines (see following) will also become part of the metro system.

Bus

İstanbul's red-and-beige İETT city buses run almost everywhere. Fares are 40c per ride, around half-price for students, but you may need a Turkish student ID card to get the discount. Fares are paid on a ticket system (see the Getting Around chapter). Hawkers near the major bus stops usually sell tickets for a markup of 20% for your convenience. On the kerb side of each bus is a list of stops along the route.

Most buses require one ticket for passage (look for *Tek* or *Bir Bilet Geçerlidir* in the windscreen), others on longer routes require two tickets (*Çift* or *İki Bilet Geçerlidir*).

Some buses fill to capacity right at the departure point, leaving no room for passengers en route. It's frustrating to wait five or 10 minutes for a bus, only to have it pass right by due to wall-to-wall flesh inside. If you're jammed in the middle of the bus when your stop comes, you may not be able to get off.

What you do in this situation is let the driver and other passengers know you must get out by saying, *İnecek var!* (een-eh-JEK vahr, 'Someone will alight!').

Dolmuş

For a definition of 'dolmuş', see the Getting Around chapter. The İstanbul city government has banned dolmuşes from some streets and routes, but several important routes survive. Unlike city buses, dolmuşes are rarely overcrowded. Major dolmuş termini of use to tourists are Taksim and Aksaray.

At these major dolmuş termini, look for the rows of cars and lines of people being matched up. If there's no sign indicating your destination, look in the cars' front windows, or ask just by saying the name of your destination. A hawker or driver will point you to the appropriate vehicle.

Tünel

İstanbul's little underground train, the Tünel, runs between Karaköy and the southern end of İstiklal Caddesi called Tünel Meydanı (Tünel Square). The fare is 35c. There are only two stations on the line, the upper and lower, so there's no getting lost. Buy a token, enter through the turnstile and board the train. They run every five or 10 minutes from early morning until about 10 pm.

Taxi

Taxis are plentiful, and it is usually not difficult to find one, though finding an honest driver can be a lot more difficult. All taxis have digital meters, and it is an offence (punishable by a large fine) to take a passenger and refuse to run the meter. Some drivers, however, particularly those who loiter in areas frequently visited by tourists, may demand that you pay a flat rate (see the warning under Taxi in the Getting Around chapter), or may try to charge you ten times what the meter reads.

The base (drop) rate is about US$1 during the daytime (*gündüz*); the night-time (*gece*) rate is higher, and you should be careful that the driver is not running the night-time rate on his meter during the day. A trip between Aksaray and Sultanahmet costs about US$1.25; between Taksim and Karaköy about US$2.25; between Taksim and Sultanahmet about US$4.

Ferry

Without doubt the nicest way to travel any considerable distance in İstanbul is by ferry. You will (and should) use the boats whenever possible. The alternatives are bus and dolmuş along the coastal roads or across the Bosphorus Bridge. These can be faster, but they will also be less comfortable and sometimes more expensive. Most ferry rides cost around 50c.

The mouth of the Golden Horn by the Galata Bridge is a seething maelstrom of the white ferries at rush hour. The Eminönü docks are being reorganised at this writing, so some of the dock information which follows may have changed by the time you arrive. Each dock serves a certain route, though a few routes may overlap.

Schedules At each dock is a framed copy of the *tarife* (tah-ree-FEH, timetable) outlining the service. It's only in Turkish, so I'll give you the necessary translations. Each route (*hat* or *hattı*) is designated by the names of the principal stops. Please note that the tarife has two completely different parts, one for weekdays (*normal günleri*) and Saturday (*Cumartesi*), and another for Sunday (*Pazar*) and holidays (*bayram günleri*). Make sure you're looking at the proper part.

Special Touristic Excursions The ferry most tourists use is the Eminönü-Kavaklar Boğaziçi Özel Gezi Seferleri (Eminönü Special Touristic Excursion, US$5) up the Bosphorus. These ferries depart from Eminönü daily at 10.35 am, 12.35 and 2.10 pm each weekday, arriving at Sarıyer, on the European shore about three quarters of the way up the Bosphorus, at 11.50 am, 1.50 and 3.30 pm respectively. The schedule is fuller on Sunday and holidays, with boats departing from Eminönü at 10 and 11 am, noon, 1.30 and 3 pm. Hold onto your ticket; you need to show it to re-board the boat for the return trip.

Departures from Sarıyer for the trip back down the Bosphorus are at 2.20, 3.10 and 5.50 pm on weekdays.

These special voyages go all the way to Rumeli Kavağı and Anadolu Kavağı (1¾ hours), but you may want to go only as far as Sarıyer, then take a dolmuş or bus back down, stopping at various sights along the way. These boats fill up early, so buy your ticket and walk aboard at least 30 or 45 minutes prior to departure in order to get a seat.

Karaköy to Haydarpaşa/Kadıköy To get to the Asia railway station at Haydarpaşa, or for a little cruise around Seraglio Point (good for photos of Topkapı Palace, Aya Sofya and the Blue Mosque) and across the Bosphorus, catch a boat from dock No 7 or 8 in Karaköy; they depart every 15 minutes (every 20 minutes on weekends). (If you're going to the station, be sure it's a Hyadarpaşa boat.) The trip over to Haydarpaşa or Kadıköy and back will take about an hour, and cost about US$1 for the round trip.

İstanbul to Üsküdar Ferries depart from Eminönü (dock No 2), every 15 minutes between 6 am and midnight for Üsküdar, even more frequently during rush hours, for 50c. From Kabataş, just south of Dolmabahçe Palace, ferries run to Üsküdar every 30 minutes on the hour and half-hour from 7 am to 8 pm. A similarly frequent ferry service operates between Beşiktaş and Üsküdar.

Cross-Bosphorus Ferry Other ferry routes link the eastern and western shores of the Bosphorus, running from breakfast time to dinner time for about 50 c. Here are the routes: Bebek-Kanlıca-Anadolu Hisar-Kandilli (about every hour); Yeniköy-Beykoz (about every half-hour, with a few boats calling at İstinye and Paşabahçe); Sarıyer-Rumeli Kavağı-Anadolu Kavağı (about every hour). If you don't catch one of these boats, you can always hire a boatman

as a private water taxi to take you across from one shore to the other.

Hydrofoil
Called *deniz otobüsü* (sea-buses), hydrofoils run from Old İstanbul to the Asian suburbs on the north Marmara shore, and from Kabataş (just south of Dolmabahçe Palace) to the Princes' Islands and Yalova (the port for Bursa), on the south shore of the Marmara. For details, see Getting There & Away in the Yalova section of the South of the Sea of Marmara chapter.

Hydrofoil trips cost several times more than ferries, but are much faster. There are presently hydrofoil docks at Kabataş (the main one), Karaköy and Yenikapı (south of Aksaray, east of Kumkapı on the Sea of Marmara shore). Yenikapı is slated to become the main hydrofoil port.

Car
It makes no sense to drive in İstanbul. If you have a car, park it and use public transport except for excursions up the Bosphorus. If you plan to rent a car, do so when you're ready to leave İstanbul.

The best rates are those you arrange from home before travelling to Turkey. See the introductory Getting Around chapter for details.

The well-known international car-rental firms have desks at Atatürk Airport and downtown, mostly near Taksim Square.

Avis has offices at Atatürk Airport in both the international (☎ 573 6445) and domestic (☎ 573 1452) terminals. The city office is just off of Cumhuriyet Caddesi, across that street from the Divan Hotel, at Yedikuyular Caddesi 4/A, Elmadağ (☎ 241 2917). Other offices are in the Hilton and Divan hotels.

Budget is at the airport's domestic terminal (☎ 574 1635), and near Taksim Square at İnönü Caddesi, Kunt Apartıman 33/1, Gümüşsuyu (☎ 245 1276; fax 249 5894).

Europcar (National, Tilden, Inter-rent, Nippon) is represented by Esin Turizm in the international terminal (☎ 573 7024), the domestic terminal (☎ 574 1908), and in their head office near Taksim at Cumhuriyet

Caddesi 47/2 (☎ 254 7788; fax 250 7649 or 250 8888).

Hertz is in the international terminal (☎ 573 5987), and in the İstanbul Sheraton Hotel (☎ 231 2121), as well as at Cumhuriyet Caddesi 295, north of Taksim in Harbiye (☎ 234 4300).

In addition to the international names, there are small local companies which may offer better deals, at perhaps 15% lower than the big companies' standard rates, but you'll have to haggle. Nothing beats deals arranged from home before you arrive in Turkey.

On Foot

With an overburdened public transport system, walking can often be faster and more rewarding. The street scenes are never dull, and the views from one hill to the next are often extraordinary. While walking, watch out for broken pavement, bits of pipe sticking a few cm out of the pavement, and all manner of other obstacles.

Don't expect any car driver to stop for you in any situation. In Turkey, the automobile seems to have the right of way virtually everywhere, and drivers get very annoyed at pedestrians who assert ridiculous and specious rights. It is obvious, isn't it? The automobile, being such a marvellous and expensive machine, should go wherever its driver is capable of taking it, without hindrance from mere pedestrians. This, at least, seems to be the common belief.

Edirne & Thrace

The land to the north of the Aegean Sea was called Thrace by the Romans. Today this ancient Roman province is divided between Turkey, Bulgaria and Greece, with Turkey holding the easternmost part. Turkish Thrace (Trakya) is not particularly exciting except for its major city, Edirne.

EDİRNE

A glance at the map seems to tell you all about Edirne (eh-DEER-neh, altitude 40 metres, population 90,000): it's the first town you come to if you're travelling overland from Europe to Turkey, it's a way-station on the road to İstanbul. It wouldn't be surprising if this had been Edirne's role throughout history, even in the old days when the town was called Adrianople. But there's more to Edirne than this. Because of its role in history, several of the finest examples from the greatest periods of Turkish mosque architecture were built here, and if you have the chance you should take time to visit.

If you're coming from İstanbul, you can make the 250-km trip to Edirne (four hours) and back to İstanbul in a long day. Get an early morning bus, plan to have lunch and see the sights, and catch a return bus in the late afternoon.

History

This town was indeed built as a defence post for the larger city on the Bosphorus. The Roman emperor Hadrian founded Edirne in the 2nd century as Hadrianopolis, a name which was later shortened by Europeans to Adrianople, then again by the Turks to Edirne.

It played a very important role in the early centuries of the Ottoman Empire which grew from a small Turkish emirate in northwestern Anatolia. By the mid-1300s, the emirate of the Ottomans with its capital at Bursa had become very powerful, but not enough to threaten the mighty walls of Constantinople. Bent on more conquest, the Ottoman armies crossed the Dardanelles into Thrace, skirting the great capital. Capturing Adrianople in 1363, they made it their new capital and base of operations for military campaigns in Europe.

For almost 100 years, this was the city from which the Ottoman sultan would set out on his campaigns to Europe and Asia. When, at last, the time was ripe for the final conquest of the Byzantine Empire, Mehmet the Conqueror set out from Edirne on the road to Constantinople. Even after this great city was captured, Edirne played an important role in Ottoman life and society, for it was still a forward post en route to other conquests in Europe.

When the Ottoman Empire disintegrated after WW I, the Allies had decided to grant all of Thrace to the Greek kingdom. Constantinople was to become an international city. In the summer of 1920, Greek armies occupied Edirne. But Atatürk's republican armies were ultimately victorious and the Treaty of Lausanne left Edirne and eastern Thrace to the Turks. Edirne returned to its role as 'the town on the way to İstanbul'.

Edirne is largely disregarded by tourists, which has helped preserve its Turkish character and appeal. While the towns along the Aegean and Mediterranean coasts are clogged with foreigners and with vast new European-style building projects, Edirne attracts the discerning few who come to enjoy the harmony and history of its mosques, covered bazaars, bridges and caravanserais, and the easy pace of life.

These days it has also taken on a little importance as an international shopping town. As many Turkish prices are lower than those in neighbouring Greece, Greeks from border towns cross over to Edirne to do their shopping. You'll see numerous shops in Edirne's market streets with window notices written in Greek.

Orientation

The centre of town is Hürriyet Meydanı or Freedom Square, at the intersection of the two main streets, Saraçlar/Hükümet Caddesi and Talat Paşa Caddesi. Just west of the square is the Üçşerefeli Cami. Going east east along Talat Paşa Caddesi and north-east along Mimar Sinan Caddesi will bring you to Edirne's masterpiece, the Selimiye Camii. On the way to the Selimiye, you'll pass the Eski Cami and south of Hürriyet Square is the Ali Paşa Çarşısı, Edirne's covered bazaar.

The main dolmuş station downtown is right next to the Eski Cami and the Hotel Rüstempaşa Kervansaray. There is a major city bus stop across the street from the Eski Cami which is only a few minutes' walk from most important points in town.

Information

The main Tourism Information Office (☎ (181) 15260, 21490) is west of the centre at Talat Paşa Caddesi 76/A, open from 8.30 am to 9 pm in summer, till 5 pm in winter. A smaller office (☎ (181) 11518) is just off the main square, a half-block south-west of Hürriyet Meydanı on Talat Paşa Caddesi; there's yet another office in the Turing building at the Kapıkule border post (☎ (181) 81019) as you enter from Bulgaria. The office at Hürriyet Meydanı can help you with finding places to stay (many of these are within finger-pointing distance) and transport questions. The staff speak some English and have maps and brochures in English.

The postal code for all of Edirne is 22100.

Consulates & Visas The Bulgarian Consulate (☎ (181) 11069) is on Talat Paşa Asfaltı on the way to the otogar, open Monday to Friday from 9 am to 12.30 pm. A transit visa good for 30 hours costs US$12; if you buy it at the border it will cost US$16. Visas for longer stays are more expensive. The rules for Bulgarian visas are liable to change due to the present instability in the region, so it's a good idea to check with the consulate in any case.

The Greek Consulate (☎ (181) 11074), is in the Kaleiçi district on Cumhuriyet Caddesi, open Monday to Friday from 9 am to 12.30 pm.

Üçşerefeli Cami

The principal reason to stop in Edirne is to see mosques, so start out from Hürriyet Meydanı and go the few steps north-east to the Üçşerefeli Cami.

The name means 'mosque with three galleries (balconies)'. Actually it's one of the mosque's four minarets which has the three balconies. The minarets, built at different times, are all wonderfully varied.

Enter at the far end of the courtyard rather than through a side gate. That way you can enjoy the full effect of the architect's genius. The courtyard at the Üçşerefeli (EWCH-sheh-reh-feh-LEE) with its şadırvan (ablutions fountain) was a prototype for the

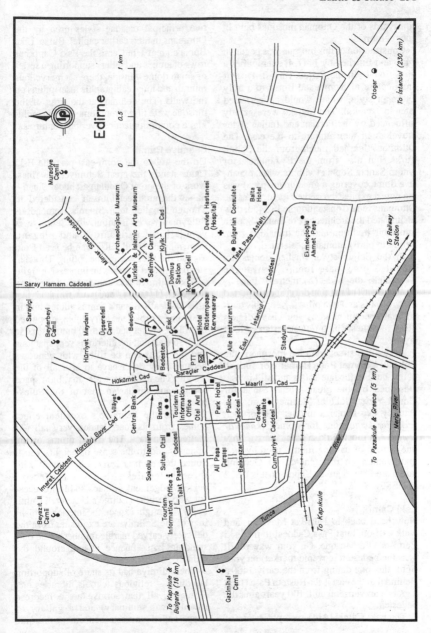

courtyards of the Ottoman mosques built in later centuries.

Construction of this mosque was begun in 1440 and finished by 1447. It exemplifies a transition from the Seljuk Turkish type of architecture of Konya and Bursa to a truly Ottoman style, which would be perfected later in İstanbul. The Seljuks were greatly influenced by the Persian and Indian styles prevalent in their empire to the east. The Ottomans learned much from the Seljuk Turks, but also from the Byzantines, for whom Sancta Sophia (with its wide, expansive dome covering a great open space) was the purest expression of their ideal. After the Ottomans took Constantinople in 1453, they assimilated the architecture of Sancta Sophia into their tradition and the transition from Seljuk to pure Ottoman accelerated.

In the Seljuk style, smaller domes are mounted on square rooms. But at the Üçşerefeli, the wide (24 metres) dome is mounted on a hexagonal drum and supported by two walls and two pillars. Keep this transitional style in mind as you visit Edirne's other mosques which reflect earlier or later styles.

Across the street from the mosque is the **Sokollu Mehmet Paşa Hamamı** or Turkish baths, built in the late 1500s and still in use. Designed by the great Mimar Sinan for Grand Vizier Sokollu Mehmet Paşa, it is actually two hamams in one: one for men (*erkekler kısmı*), one for women (*kadınlar kısmı*). (At most Turkish baths there is only one system of bathing rooms, used by men and women on different days.) Opening hours are from 6 am to 10 pm; cost is US$2 to US$5.

Eski Cami

Now head back to Hürriyet Meydanı, and walk east on Talat Paşa Caddesi to the Eski Cami or Old Mosque. On your way you'll pass the bedesten (covered market) on your right, this one dating from the early 1400s. Behind it to the east is the Rüstem Paşa Hanı, a grand caravanserai built 100 years after the bedesten.

The Eski Cami (1414) exemplifies one of two principal mosque styles used by the Ottomans in their earlier capital, Bursa. Like Bursa's great Ulu Cami, the Eski Cami has rows of arches and pillars supporting a series of small domes. Inside, there's a marvellous mihrab and huge calligraphic inscriptions on the walls. The columns at the front of the mosque were lifted from some Roman building, a common practice over the centuries.

Selimiye Camii

Up the hill to the north-east past the Eski Cami stands the great Selimiye, the finest work of the great Ottoman architect Sinan – or so the architect himself considered it. Though smaller than Sinan's tremendous Süleymaniye in İstanbul, the Selimiye is wonderfully harmonious and elegant. Crowning its small hill, it can be seen from a good distance across the rolling Thracian steppeland and it makes an impressive sight.

The Selimiye was constructed for Sultan Selim II (1566-74) and was finished just after his death. Sinan's genius guided him in designing a broad and lofty dome, supported by pillars, arches and external buttresses. He did it so well that the interior is very spacious and the walls can be filled with windows because they don't have to bear all of the weight. The result is a wide, airy, light space for prayer, similar to that of the Süleymaniye.

Part of the Selimiye's excellent effect comes from its four slender, very tall (71 metres) minarets. The fluted drums of the minarets add to the sense of height. You'll notice that each is *üçşerefeli*, or built with three balconies – Sinan's respectful acknowledgement, perhaps, to his predecessor who designed Edirne's Üçşerefeli Cami.

As you might expect, the interior furnishings of the Selimiye are exquisite, from the delicately carved marble mimber to the outstanding İznik faïence in and around the mihrab.

The Selimiye had its share of supporting buildings – religious schools, libraries etc. However, all that survive are a medrese (theological seminary) and a gallery of shops, called the arasta, beneath the mosque.

The shops have been restored and are still in use; rents are dedicated to the upkeep of the mosque, as they have been for over 400 years. The medrese now houses the Turkish & Islamic Arts Museum (Türk-Islam Eserleri Müzesi), open daily except Monday from 8 am to 5.30 pm, for less than US$1.

The town's main museum, the Archaeological Museum (Arkeoloji ve Etnoloji Müzesi) is across the street, a few steps east of the Türk-İslam Eserleri Müzesi, open from 8.30 am to noon and 1 to 5.30 pm, for US$1.

Muradiye Camii

A short walk (10 to 15 minutes) north-east of the Selimiye and the museum along Mimar Sinan Caddesi brings you to the Muradiye Camii, a mosque built on the orders of Sultan Murat II and finished in 1436. Its T-shaped plan with twin eyvans is reminiscent of the Yeşil Cami in Bursa, and its fine İznik tiles remind one that Bursa (near İznik) was the first Ottoman capital and Edirne, the second. Turkish mosque architecture would change dramatically after the Turks conquered Constantinople (1453) and studied Sancta Sophia.

The Muradiye Camii was once part of a complex of buildings housing the local Mevlevis (Whirling Dervishes). It is not always open to visits. If you are at the Selimiye around prayer time, walk out to the Muradiye and arrive about 20 minutes after the call to prayer has been sounded from the minarets, and you'll probably find the door open.

Beyazıt II Camii

Edirne's last great imperial mosque is that of Sultan Beyazıt II (1481-1512), on the far side (north-west of the town) of the Tunca River (TOON-jah). From Hürriyet Meydanı, the pleasant walk to the mosque will take you about 15 or 20 minutes. Walk along Hükümet Caddesi past the Üçşerefeli Cami (on your right), and turn left immediately after its Turkish bath. Walk one block and bear right at the ornate little fountain. This street is Horozlu Bayır Caddesi; it changes names later to İmaret Caddesi, but it will take you right to the bridge (1488) across the Tunca to Sultan Beyazıt's mosque.

The Beyazıt complex (the İkinci Beyazıt Külliyesi, 1484-88) was fully restored in the late 1970s, so it now looks as good as new. The architect, a fellow named Hayrettin, didn't have the genius of Mimar Sinan, but did a very creditable job nonetheless.

The mosque's style is between that of the Üçşerefeli and the Selimiye, moving back a bit rather than advancing: its large prayer hall has one large dome, more like in Bursa's mosques, but it has a courtyard and sadırvan like the Üçşerefeli Cami's. Though it's certainly of a high standard, it can't compare with the Selimiye, built less than a century later.

The mosque's külliye is extensive and includes a *tabhane* (hostel for travellers), medrese, bakery, imaret (soup kitchen), *tımarhane* (insane asylum) and *darüşşifa* (hospital). Some of the buildings are now in use, appropriately, by the faculties of art and medicine of the Thracian University (Trakya Üniversitesi).

Eski Saray & Sarayiçi

Saray means 'palace' in Turkish. Upriver (east) from the Sultan Beyazıt II mosque complex are the ruins of the Eski Saray (Old Palace). Begun by Sultan Beyazıt II in 1450, this palace once rivalled İstanbul's Topkapı in luxury and size. Today, little is left of it: only a few bits of the kitchen buildings. But it's a pleasant walk along the river (less than a half-hour) to reach Eski Saray from the Beyazıt mosque, and if the day is nice you might want to go there. From the Eski Saray, Saraçhane Köprüsü (bridge) will take you back across the Tunca; Saraçhane Caddesi then leads directly back to Hürriyet Meydanı.

East of Eski Saray, across a branch of the Tunca (there's a bridge called Fatih Sultan Köprüsü), is Sarayiçi ('Within the Palace'). This scrub-covered island, once the sultans' hunting preserve, was for years the site of the famous annual Kırkpınar oiled wrestling matches or Tarihi Kırkpınar Yağlı Güreş

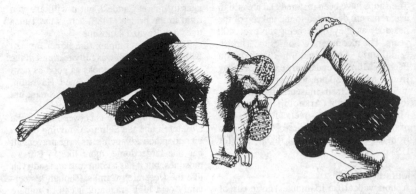

Festivali (yah-LUH gew-RESH, 'oiled wrestling'). In late May and early June, huge wrestlers slathered with olive oil and clad only in leather knickers take part in freestyle matches now held in a nearby stadium. An early sultan is said to have invented the sport to keep his troops in shape. Whatever the origin, a *pehlivan* (wrestler) at the Kırkpınar matches is something to behold. Folk-dancing exhibitions are organised as part of the festivities.

If you've made it all the way to Sarayiçi, look for the Kanuni Köprüsü to get you back to the south bank of the Tunca. Bear right coming off the bridge, and the road will lead you to Hükümet Caddesi, and eventually to Hürriyet Meydanı.

The Old Town (Kaleiçi)
While you're here, don't forget to take a stroll through the old town of Edirne to discover some scenes of Turkish daily life. The Old Town, called Kaleiçi ('Within the Fortress') by the locals, was the original medieval town with streets laid out on a grid plan. Some fragments of Byzantine city walls are still visible at the edges of the grid, down by the Tunca River. The Old Town, bounded by Saraçlar Caddesi and Talat Paşa Caddesi, is basically the area behind and to the west of the Ali Paşa Çarşısı.

Places to Stay
It's relatively easy to find inexpensive pen-sions and rooming houses in Edirne, as this is the first stop within Turkey en route from Europe. Travellers who know the route will often push on through northern Greece or Bulgaria in order to get into Turkey so they can enjoy the lower prices and incomparably better food. Edirne is where they spend their first night.

However, this route is heavily travelled by Turkish workers on their way to and from Europe, and by international truck-drivers heading to or from Iran and the Arabic countries. So your companions in the inexpensive hostelries may be mostly men on the road. Also, many places will be filled by crowds at holiday time.

Places to Stay – bottom end
The first area to look for low-cost lodging is behind the Tourism Information Office near Hürriyet Meydanı along Maarif Caddesi. Several grand old town houses here have been converted into fairly dingy but cheap budget hotels.

First along the street is the *Otel Anıl* (☎ (181) 21482), Hürriyet Meydanı, Maarif Caddesi 8, among the better places with simple but acceptable waterless rooms costing US$12 a double. Bathrooms are down the hall; showers here have electric shower heads for heating the water.

Next door to the Anıl, but not nearly so clean or suitable, is the *Konak Hotel* (☎ (181) 11348), Hürriyet Meydanı, Maarif

Caddesi 6. Rooms here are also waterless; some have five or six beds, renting for US$4 per person.

Only slightly more expensive and much more pleasant is the *Otel Açıkgöz* (☎ (181) 11944), Tüfekçiler Çarşısı, Sümerbank Arkası 74, a block off Saraçlar Caddesi behind the Sümerbank building. Modest but cheerful, the price for a clean room with private shower is US$8 to US$10 a single, US$14 to US$18 a double.

Camping Open from April to mid-October, the *Fifi Mocamp* (☎ (181) 11554), E-5 Karayolu, Demirkapı Mevkii, is eight km east of town on the İstanbul road. It has a full range of hook-ups and services for tents and caravans, and even a few motel rooms available for rent the year round. Others are the *Turing* on the Kapıkule/Svilengrad road; and *Kervansaray Ayşekadın Mocamp* (☎ (181) 11290), on İstanbul Caddesi near the bus station. You might also be able to camp at Söğütlük Orman Parkı, a park on the south edge of the city between the Tunca and Meriç rivers.

Places to Stay – middle
Were you to ask any Edirneli the name of the best hotel in town, they would no doubt answer with the name of the two-star, 80-room *Balta Hotel* (☎ (181) 15210, fax 13529), Talat Paşa Asfaltı 97, halfway from the bus terminal (otogar) to Hürriyet Meydanı. This is where the important business executives and government officials stay. It does offer the town's newest and most comfortable rooms, a bar, restaurant and similar two-star services, but it has the disadvantage of being several km from Hürriyet Meydanı, facing a noisy street. Rooms are priced at US$30/38 a single/double with breakfast included.

A more convenient choice is the 83-room *Sultan Oteli* (☎ (181) 11372; fax 15763), Talat Paşa Caddesi 170. It's several decades old but nicely renovated. The advantages here are two-star comforts just off Hürriyet Meydanı across the street from the Tourism Information Office. The Sultan has a restau-

rant and bar and a clientele that's a mix of Turkish and foreign, tourist and business travellers. Rooms are priced at US$30/36 a single/double.

Less posh, but still quite comfortable, very quiet and less expensive is the *Park Hotel* (☎ (181) 14610), Maarif Caddesi 7, down the end of this street of bottom-end lodgings which starts behind the Tourism Information Office. Though this hotel does not face a park, it's still quiet, clean, comfortable and convenient. Rooms cost US$22/28 a single/double for a room with bath, breakfast included; rooms with only a washbasin go for US$16/24 a single/double.

Kervan Oteli (☎ (181) 11382) on Talat Paşa Caddesi, Kadirhane Sokak 134, was the city's prime place to stay several decades ago. Even though it is now a bit faded and old-fashioned, it still provides serviceable if noisy rooms with bath for US$34 a double in summer, less in the off season.

The most intriguing place to stay is undoubtedly the *Hotel Rüstempaşa Kervansaray* (☎ (181) 12195), Eski Cami Yanı, to the right of the Eski Cami beyond the dolmuş lot. The hotel's name means 'Caravanserai of Rüstem Paşa'. The eponymous Rüstem Paşa was a grand vizier of Süleyman the Magnificent who ordered the caravanserai to be built in the mid-1500s. The camel caravans on the road between Europe, İstanbul and points further east rested here for the night, their valuable freight safe within the building's massive stone walls and great armoured doors.

Several decades ago the caravanserai was renovated and turned into a hotel for a tourist boom that has yet to arrive; tourists come to Edirne in twos and threes, not by the busload. Though the rooms are comfortable enough and certainly atmospheric, it is the hotel's nightclub which brings in the profit. The club can be noisy, which can make the rooms less than suitable; so if you stay here, get a quiet room. The price is US$38/54 a single/double, breakfast included.

Places to Eat
The hotels have the best dining rooms in

town, and it may be possible to spend from US$12 to US$15 per person for a meal in one. In the rest of Edirne, it's very difficult to spend that much on dinner.

My longtime favourite is the *Aile Restaurant*, Saraçlar Caddesi, Belediye İş Hanı, which has been good for decades. To find it, walk south from Hürriyet Meydanı along Saraçlar Caddesi, looking for the building named Belediye İş Hanı on the left-hand side; it's just past the PTT. The entrance is on the side street by the post office. Climb the stairs to the upper level where you'll find a pleasant, if simple, dining room with windows overlooking Saraçlar Caddesi. Kebaps, stews and other traditional Turkish dishes are served, and a meal need cost no more than US$5 or US$7 per person.

On the opposite side of the PTT from the Aile is the *Café M Restaurant* (☎ 23448), Saraçlar Caddesi, Vakıf İş Hanı, on the upper floor of a building named the Vakıf İş Hanı. Actually, there are two establishments here: the Café Muharipler (Veterans' Café), and the Café M Restaurant. The first is a typical no-nonsense Turkish teahouse, always filled with men and smoke. The second is the genteel gathering-place of Edirne's young, well-dressed and upwardly mobile types. The décor is white: little café tables, bent-wood chairs and wall benches. The menu features snacks and confections, coffee, tea and soft drinks. You can have an omelette, a sausage plate, chips or some other light fare for about US$4, with a drink included.

For simple, tasty fare at simple, low prices, stop at a kebap or köfte place on Saraçlar Caddesi or anywhere else in town for that matter. Side by side on Saraçlar Caddesi, a few steps from Hürriyet Meydanı just past the park, are the *Rumeli Köftecisi* and the *Serhad Köftecisi*, two plain little places selling those good grilled Turkish meatballs with yoghurt, salad, bread and drink for US$2 or so. Down the street a bit farther, just past the PTT but on the opposite (right-hand) side of the street, is the *Şark Kebap ve Lahmacun*, a tiny, very basic place with a few tables downstairs and a few more upstairs in the aile salonu. I had a filling meal

of soup, pide with cheese (Turkish pizza), salad, a soft drink and a glass of tea for US$3.75. The pide was freshly made and delicious.

Getting There & Away

For information on consulates, see Information at the beginning of this section.

Bulgarian Border Crossing On the E5/100 highway from Svilengrad, Bulgaria, you come to the busy border post of Kapıkule, open 24 hours. After the formalities, you enter the town by crossing the river Tunca at the Gazi Mihal Bridge and passing some fragments of Byzantine city walls. The red-and-cream city bus No 1 runs along the route from Kapıkule to the Eski Cami; there are dolmuşes on this route as well, but both are infrequent in early morning and late at night. By the way, you may not be allowed to walk to the border on the Bulgarian side; you may be required to hitch a ride or rent a taxi.

Greek Border Crossing From Greece, the major road goes to Kastanéai (Greece) and Pazarkule (Turkey), seven km south-west of Edirne on the Meriç River (mehr-EECH, Maritsa), two km past the Turkish village of Karaağaç to a border post originally meant to serve the railway line. The frontier, as determined by the Treaty of Lausanne (1923), left the Turkish line passing through Greece on its way to Edirne! A bypass line was built in the 1970s, though. The problem here is that the Greeks have declared the border area a military zone and do not permit anyone to walk in it without a military escort, so you will probably have to take a Greek taxi (US$6, two minutes) to the actual border, which is mid-way in the one-km-wide no-man's-land which separates the two border posts. On the Turkish side, you can walk to and from Pazarkule. These small border posts are open during daylight hours.

From Pazarkule, or from the nearby railway station, you will probably have to take a Turkish taxi (US$5, 15 minutes) into town as there is not much traffic and hitching is not too easy, though you may be lucky.

If you are crossing from Turkey into Greece, do so as soon after 8 am as possible in order to catch one of the few trains or buses from Kastanéai heading south to Alexandroùpolis.

Road The E5/100 highway between Europe and İstanbul follows very closely the Via Egnatia, the ancient road which connected Rome and Constantinople. It follows the river valleys past Niš and Sofia, on between the mountain ranges of the Stara and Rhodopi to Plovdiv, and along the Maritsa riverbank into Edirne which stands alone on the gently undulating plain, snuggled into a bend of the Tunca River. After Edirne, the road heads out into the rolling, steppe-like terrain of eastern Thrace towards İstanbul.

Bus Intercity buses operate very frequently throughout the day (about every 20 minutes or so) and take four hours to make the 235-km journey to İstanbul, tickets cost US$5.75. In Edirne, buses operate out of the city's Otobüs Garajı on the outskirts of town. Take a city bus or dolmuş from the Eski Cami to get to the Otobüs Garajı.

Along the way, the bus will stop in Lüleburgaz and Çorlu before joining the new motorway into İstanbul.

The terminus in İstanbul is the Topkapı Otogar, the big bus station just outside the city walls at Topkapı gate, on the E5/100 highway (also called the Londra Asfaltı). When the new bus station at Esenler is completed, this will no doubt be the terminus.

Train You may be coming to Turkey by train, in which case you will probably be ready for a break. Rail service through the Balkans is slow and tedious. The international train can take another eight to 10 hours to reach İstanbul. Get off. Don't miss Edirne.

If you are leaving Turkey for Europe, note that the daily westbound *İstanbul Express* passes through Edirne each morning around breakfast time (usually between 8 and 9 am). Get up-to-date schedule information from the tourism office.

Edirne has two railway stations: the city station (Edirne Garı), and the one at Kapıkule on the Bulgarian border. There is also the station at Uzunköprü 60 km to the south. (Uzunköprü is the last station in Turkey on the route via Alexandroùpolis to Athens.)

Train service between Edirne and İstanbul is slow and inconvenient. The train departs from İstanbul's Sirkeci Station at 3.40 pm, arriving in Edirne about six hours later. The railway station is out of town, reachable by dolmuş, bus or taxi. Tickets on the run from Edirne to İstanbul cost US$4 one way, with a 10% discount for students. You'd be better off taking the bus.

It's interesting to note that the original *Midnight Express* ran between İstanbul and Edirne through Greece. When the Ottoman Empire collapsed, the new Turkish-Greek border was drawn so that the old rail line was partly in Greece. Greek border police would board when the train entered Greek territory and get off when it re-entered Turkish territory. There used to be a slow, late-night train on this run. Foreigners convicted of drug-related offences in Turkey would be released by the Turkish government while their convictions were being appealed. They'd be given all of their possessions except their passports, and told in a whisper about the *Midnight Express*.

They'd climb aboard and jump off the train in Greece, where Greek border police would pick them up and jail them. They'd call their consulate, arrange for a new passport, be let out of jail and sent on their way. This system allowed the Turkish government to meet foreign governments' demands that it be strict with drug smugglers, but it avoided the expense and bother of actually incarcerating the convicted smugglers. In the late 1970s, the Turkish State Railways built a bypass line and the Greek corridor route was abandoned. The truth of the *Midnight Express* is quite different from that portrayed in the blatantly anti-Turkish movie of the same name.

East of Edirne
The ride to İstanbul is largely uneventful,

even though this part of the country has had a tumultuous history. Enemy armies from the west intent on seizing Constantinople/ İstanbul passed easily over this rolling countryside. In 1877 the Russians held all of Turkish Thrace, and got to within a few km of the city walls. During WW I, Allied armies marched this way; in WW II Thrace was heavily militarised by the Turks to fend off the Germans and to protect Turkey's fragile neutrality. A Turkish friend tells the story of his time on the line in Thrace:

It was late in a bitter winter. The wolves found little to eat in the countryside, and began coming dangerously close to our outpost. Ammunition was very scarce, but we asked permission to use a few rounds to defend ourselves against the wolves. Our commander said, 'You are Turkish soldiers. Use your bayonets'.

Havsa & Lüleburgaz The first town along the İstanbul road is Havsa (population 8000), a town of some importance during Ottoman times. The **Sokollu Kasım Paşa Külliyesi** is a mosque complex designed by Sinan and built in 1576-77 on orders of the son of Sokollu Mehmet Paşa, a grand vizier under Sultan Süleyman the Magnificent.

About an hour's ride east of Edirne (75 km) is the market town of Lüleburgaz (population 45,000), the ancient Arcadiopolis. Unremarkable in itself, Lüleburgaz holds the fine **Sokollu Mehmet Paşa Camii**, a mosque built on the orders (1549) of Sokollu Mehmet Paşa, the *beylerbey* of Rumeli (governor of European Turkey) and later grand vizier to sultan Süleyman the Magnificent. The mosque was part of a larger complex which was finally completed in 1569. Incorporated into the mosque's design is a medrese (theological college).

Çorlu Though wonderfully ancient, having been founded by the Phrygians around 1000 BC, Çorlu (population 60,000) has little to show for its long history. A farmers' market town at best, it was a way-station on the İstanbul-Edirne road and thus received its share of mosque-building, as well as a caravanserai and hamam. The **Sultan Süleyman**

Camii (1521) is its most noteworthy old building. A few small hotels and restaurants provide for travellers.

Tekirdağ Once known for its luxuriant vineyards and excellent wines, Tekirdağ (population 65,000), once called Rodosto, today is a bustling modern place with little to hold your interest. Traces of Early Bronze Age life have been found in the vicinity.

The Ottomans – particularly Süleyman the Magnificent's grand vizier Rüstem Paşa – left Tekirdağ a legacy of great buildings, including the mosque, bedesten and medrese named after Rüstem.

Also here is the **Rakoczi Museum** (☎ (186) 12082) on Barbaros Caddesi just in from the waterfront near the centre of the town, with memorabilia of the great Hungarian nobleman Prince Francis II Rakoczy (1676-1735). Prince Rakoczy led rebellious Hungarians in their struggle against Hapsburg repression in the early 1700s. Forced to flee in 1711, he went into exile in Poland, then France, and finally in Turkey, where he died. Rakoczy's remains were returned to Hungary in 1906, and his Tekirdağ home (1720-35) became a museum in 1932.

East & West of Tekirdağ Most maps show the road east of Tekirdağ, leading to Silivri and İstanbul, as a major highway. In fact, it is very narrow for the volume of traffic that must pass through, so you should expect some slow going.

West of Tekirdağ the coast road is passable as far as Kumbağ, but then degenerates to a track, very rough and not recommended except for the adventurous. The better road heads due west to İnecik and Keşan. About 48 km west of Tekirdağ a rough road heads south over the mountains to Ballı, Gölcük and Şarköy (32 km). The latter is a seaside resort for İstanbullus and a handful of enterprising Europeans, with a decent beach and several typically noisy Turkish nightclubs.

South of Edirne
If you've come from İstanbul, it might make sense to head due south after looking around

Edirne and go directly to the Dardanelles and Troy. There are few direct buses between Edirne and Çanakkale; most probably you will have to change buses at Keşan. By doing this you miss the ferry cruise across the Sea of Marmara as well as the delightful cities of İznik (ancient Nicaea) and Bursa, the first Ottoman capital. So if you've got the time, head back to İstanbul and catch a ferry to Yalova, first stop on your explorations of the south Marmara shore.

Uzunköprü Named 'Long Bridge' for the long Ottoman aqueduct with 173 arches on the north side of the town, Uzunköprü has the nearest railway station to the border on the line connecting İstanbul and Athens. You can catch the daily train to Athens here, but transport is much easier and convenient via either Edirne to the north or İpsala to the south.

İpsala & Keşan İpsala is the main border-crossing point between Turkey and Greece, on the E25/110 highway; the Greek station is named Kipi. Both stations are open 24 hours a day.

The actual Turkish border station is five km west of the town of İpsala, reachable by taxi (US$4). There is a Turkish Touring & Automobile Association office at the border station (☎ (1846) 1574) and also a Tourism Information Office (☎ (1846) 1577). If you're coming from Greece, ignore İpsala and get a ride or a taxi (US$12) all the way to Keşan, from which bus connections to Edirne, İstanbul, Gelibolu and Çanakkale are far easier and more numerous.

Gelibolu & Çanakkale For details of these towns and the Gallipoli peninsula battle-fields see the South of the Sea of Marmara chapter.

South of the Sea of Marmara

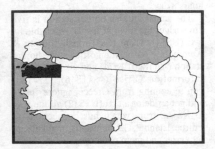

The southern shore of the Sea of Marmara is a land of small villages surrounded by olive groves, orchards, sunflower fields, rolling hills and rich valleys. During the time of the Ottoman Empire the choice olives for the sultan's table came from here, and snow from the slopes of Bursa's Uludağ (the Bithynian Mt Olympus) cooled his drinks. The region's few cities are of moderate size and significant interest.

You can enjoy this region and its sights in only two days: catch an early hydrofoil from İstanbul to Yalova, make a quick tour of İznik (the ancient city of Nicaea) and spend the night in Bursa. After seeing the sights of Bursa, the next morning catch a bus westward to Çanakkale. You'll reach that town on the Dardanelles in time for a late supper. But spending from three to five days is more realistic if you want also to enjoy the mineral baths of Termal and Cekirge, to visit Troy and the Gallipoli battlefields.

Plan to spend some of your extra time in Bursa, where the mosques and museums are particularly fine (this was the Ottomans' first capital city, before Edirne and İstanbul). You can also ride a cable car to the top of Uludağ, which is snow-capped for most of the year, and offers skiing in winter.

If you must, you can rocket down to Bursa from İstanbul just for the day. But this means a lot of travel time for only a few hours' sightseeing, when the city really deserves an overnight stay.

On your way to Bursa, you will probably pass through the port of Yalova on the Sea of Marmara.

YALOVA

The small town of Yalova (pronounced YAH-loh-vah; population 60,000) is a farming and transportation centre. The highway between the industrial cities of Bursa and İzmit (not to be confused with İznik) passes near here, as does the hydrofoil-ferry/bus link between Bursa and İstanbul. It's a pleasant enough town, with a few modest hotels and restaurants, most within two blocks of the ferry dock. Everything else you'd need is here as well, including banks, chemists etc. The market area is a short stroll straight from the wharf.

Other than these few amusements, there's nothing to detain you in Yalova. You can plan to head for the spa at Termal, the ancient city of İznik or booming Bursa without delay.

Getting There & Away

Bus On arrival in Yalova, disembark from the hydrofoil, and as you walk from the wharf you will see a traffic circle centred on an enormous statue of Atatürk. Just off the dock, look to the left. You'll see rows of buses and minibuses. Approach them, and a man will approach you to find out where you're going. Say 'İznik' (EEZ-neek) or 'Bursa' (BOOR-sah) as the case may be, and he'll lead you to a waiting minibus. Be certain that your bus is going to İznik, not İzmit, which is a different city entirely. Climb in and find a seat; buses to these cities leave about every 30 minutes. The fare is US$2 to İznik, US$2.50 to Bursa, and it will be collected en route.

Yalova city bus No 4 (Taşköprü-Termal) will take you to Termal for 40c; a dolmuş charges 55c. Both leave from a parking area only a block from the ferry dock. Coming off the ferry, walk to the traffic circle with the statue and turn right, walk a block and the parking area is on the left.

Boat To reach Yalova, Termal, İznik and Bursa from İstanbul, most people board a hydrofoil (deniz otobüsü, for US$6 or US$3.50 for students) at Kabataş, just south of Dolmabahçe Palace, and whizz across the Sea of Marmara to Yalova in about an hour, then continue by bus to Termal, İznik or Bursa. Hydrofoils depart from Kabataş on weekdays at 8.30 and 11 am, and 1.35, 4 and 6.15 pm; and on weekends at 9.15 and 11.35 am, 1.30, 2.45 and 5.30 pm.

Return voyages from Yalova to Kabataş depart on weekdays at 7.30 and 9.45 am, and 12.30, 2.45, 5.05 and 7.20 pm; on weekends departures are at 10.30 am, 1.30, 4.15 and 6.30 pm.

Also less expensive but more time-consuming are the normal ferries (US$3.50) which depart from Kabataş for Yalova at 9.30 am, 2, 6.30 and 7.30 pm on weekdays only, stopping at the Princes Islands and taking about 2½ hours to reach Yalova.

An alternative route, involving slightly less expense but more time and bother, is to take a ferry (50c) from Karaköy to Haydarpaşa, then a suburban train (35c) from Haydarpaşa south-eastward to Kartal, and from Kartal a hydrofoil (US$3.50, or US$1.75 for students) to Yalova. Hydrofoils depart from Kartal for Yalova nine times on weekdays between 7 am and 7.45 pm; on weekends there are 13 departures between 8.30 am and 7.45 pm.

There are also slower, cheaper conventional ferries between Kartal and Yalova, departing from Kartal at 8.15 am and noon, 6 and 9 pm; and departing from Yalova at 6.30 and 10 am, and 3 and 7.30 pm.

Car Ferry If you're driving, do yourself a favour and take the car ferry from Eskihisar (near Darıca, south-west of Gebze) south across the Bay of İzmit to Topçular, on the south shore east of Yalova. You'll save yourself 100 km of driving along chaotic roads through an industrial wasteland. Ferries run every 30 minutes round the clock on the 25-minute voyage; the fare for car and driver is US$10.

TERMAL

Twelve km west of Yalova, off the road to Çınarcık, is Termal (tehr-MAHL), a spa. The baths here take advantage of hot, mineral-rich waters that gush from the earth and were first exploited in Roman times. The Ottomans used the baths from the 1500s and Abdülhamit II repaired and refurbished them in 1900 to celebrate the 25th anniversary of his accession to the throne.

He had the work done in the wonderfully gaudy Ottoman Baroque style. Atatürk added a simple but comfortable spa hotel, where time seems to stand still: at luncheon you may still hear a violin-and-piano duo play a lilting rendition of 'Santa Lucia', it's as though the great Turkish leader were resting and taking the waters here, as he did in the 1930s. You can come just to stroll through the shady gardens and have a look at the facilities, or you can come to bathe or stay the night.

Things to See

The gardens and greenery at Termal are worth the trip. But then there are the baths. At the Valide Banyo you get a locker for your clothes, then take a shower and enter a pool. An admission charge of around US$1 gets you 1½ hours of bathing. Soap and shampoo cost extra, so bring your own. The Sultan Banyo is even grander and much pricier at US$3/4 a single/double; you can rent a swimsuit here. The Kurşunlu Banyo features an open-air pool for US$2, an enclosed pool and sauna for US$2.50, and small private cubicles for US$2/2.50 a single/double.

Atatürk had a small house here, which is now a museum you can visit.

Places to Stay – bottom end

The villages several km from the centre of Termal have numerous modest little pensions charging from US$5 to US$8 per person for rooms with and without running water. The only problem with these places is that they are a long walk from the baths. You may find yourself hitchhiking in, or waiting for the infrequent buses and dolmuşes.

Places to Stay – top end

Though fairly simple, befitting a health resort, the two hotels here are extremely pleasant, but both are in the upper price range. The *Turban Yalova Termal Hotel* (☎ (1938) 4905) and the *Çınar Oteli* (same telephone) charge from US$40 to US$55 a single, US$45 to US$60 a double, the price depends on whether the room is at the front or the back of the hotel; breakfast is included in these high-season summer prices. Off-season rates are from 25 to 30% lower, but do not include breakfast.

Places to Eat

Termal has several restaurants and cafés, but all are fairly pricey. A cup of Nescafé, for example, costs around US$1.

İZNİK

The road from Yalova to İznik (population of 18,000) runs along fertile green hills punctuated by tall, spiky cypress trees, passing peach orchards, cornfields and vineyards. The journey of 60 km takes about one hour.

As you approach İznik you may notice fruit-packing plants among the orchards. You will certainly have admired the vast İznik Gölü (İznik Lake). Watch for the great Byzantine city walls: the road passes through the old İstanbul Kapısı (İstanbul Gate) and then becomes Atatürk Caddesi, and leads to the ruined Sancta Sophia (Aya Sofya) Church (now a museum) in the very centre of town. The otogar is a few blocks southeast of the church.

History

This ancient city may well have been founded around 1000 BC. We know for sure that it was revitalised by one of Alexander the Great's generals in 316 BC. Another of the generals, Lysimachus, soon got hold of it and named it for his wife Nikaea. It became the capital city of the province of Bithynia.

Nicaea lost some of its prominence with the founding of Nicomedia (today's İzmit) in 264 BC, and by 74 BC the entire area had been incorporated into the Roman Empire.

Nicaea flourished under Rome; the emperors built a new system of walls, plus temples, theatres and baths. But invasions by the Goths and the Persians brought ruin by 300 AD.

Ecumenical Councils With the rise of Constantinople, Nicaea took on a new importance. In 325, the First Ecumenical Council was held here to condemn the heresy of Arianism. During the great Justinian's reign, Nicaea was grandly refurbished and embellished with new buildings and defences, which served the city well a few centuries later when the Arabs invaded. Like Constantinople, Nicaea never fell to its Arab besiegers.

In 787 yet another Ecumenical Council, the seventh, was held in Nicaea's Sancta Sophia Church. The deliberations solved the problem of iconoclasm: henceforth it would be church policy not to destroy icons. Theologians who saw icons as 'images', prohibited by the Bible, were dismayed. But Byzantine artists were delighted, and went to work on their art with even more vigour.

Nicaea and Constantinople did, however, fall to the crusaders. During the period from 1204 to 1261 when a Latin king sat on the throne of Byzantium, the true Byzantine emperor Theodore Lascaris reigned over the 'Empire of Nicaea'. When the crusaders cleared out, the emperor moved his court back to the traditional capital.

The Turks The Seljuk Turks had a flourishing empire in Central Anatolia before 1250, and various tribes of nomadic warriors had circulated near the walls of Nicaea during those times. In fact, Turkish soldiers had served as mercenaries in the interminable battles which raged among rival claimants to the Byzantine throne. At one point, a Byzantine battle over Nicaea ended with a Turkish emir as its ruler.

It was Orhan, son of Osman and first true sultan (1326-61) of the Ottoman Empire, who conquered İznik on 2 March 1331. The city soon had the honour of harbouring the first Ottoman college. Proussa (Bursa) had fallen to the Ottomans on 6 April 1326, and became their first capital city. In 1337 they took Nicomedia and effectively blocked the Byzantines from entering Anatolia.

Sultan Selim I (1512-20), a mighty conqueror nicknamed 'The Grim', rolled his armies over Azerbaijan in 1514 and took the Persian city of Tabriz. Packing up all of the region's artisans, he sent them westward to İznik. They brought with them a high level of expertise in the making of coloured tiles. Soon İznik's kilns were turning out faïence which is unequalled even today. The great period of İznik faïence continued almost to 1700. At one point, artisans were sent to Tunisia, then an Ottoman possession, to begin a high-quality faïence industry there.

The art of coloured tile-making is being revived in İznik today; you can buy some good examples at moderate prices in the shops. Be aware that true İznik tiles from the great period are considered antiquities, and cannot legally be exported from Turkey.

Orientation

In İznik the famous Aya Sofya (Hagia Sophia) church is at the very centre, a good vantage point from which to consider the town's classical Roman layout: two dead-straight boulevards, north-south (Atatürk Caddesi) and east-west (Kılıçaslan Caddesi), leading to the four principal gates in the city walls. To the north is the İstanbul Kapısı, to the south is the Yenişehir Kapısı, to the east is Lefke Kapısı and to the west, the Göl Kapısı. More details about the walls and gates follow.

Information

İznik's Tourism Information Office (☎ (252) 71933) is on the main east-west street, Kılıçaslan Caddesi 71, east of Aya Sofya – follow the signs. Hours are from 8.30 am to noon and from 1 to 5.30 pm every day in the warm months, with shorter hours (and no hours on weekends) off-season.

Aya Sofya

Start your sightseeing in the centre of town, at the Aya Sofya Church or Church of the Divine Wisdom.

Aya Sofya is open from 9 am to noon and from 2 to 5 pm daily, closed on Monday. If there's no-one about when you visit, continue with your tour. The key is probably at the museum. After visiting there, ask to be let into the church.

This former church is hardly striking in its grandeur, but it has a fascinating past. What you see is the ruin of three different buildings. Inside you can inspect a mosaic floor and a mural of Jesus with Mary and John the Baptist which dates from the time of Justinian (during the 500s). That original church was destroyed by earthquake in 1065 but later rebuilt. Mosaics were set into the walls at that time. With the Ottoman conquest (1331), the church became a mosque. A fire in the 1500s ruined everything, but reconstruction was carried out under the expert eye of Mimar Sinan, who added İznik tiles to the decoration.

Behind Aya Sofya is the **II. Murat Hamamı**, also called the Hacı Hamza Hamamı, a Turkish bath constructed during the reign of Sultan Murat II, in the first half of the 15th century. It's still in operation.

The Main Street

Now walk east towards Lefke Kapısı (Lefke Gate), along İznik's main street, Kılıçaslan Caddesi. On the left is the Belediye Sarayı or Municipality, with a sign out the front that reads (in Turkish) 'Our motto is, Clean City, Green City'. It really is a very pleasant, quiet, peaceful and agreeable place with its big poplars shading the commercial district from the summer sun.

A bit farther along on the left is the **Hacı Özbek Camii**, one of the town's oldest mosques, dating from 1332.

A short detour along the street opposite the Hacı Özbek Camii, to the south, will bring you to the **Süleyman Paşa Medresesi**. Founded by Sultan Orhan shortly after he captured Nicaea, it has the distinction of being the very first college (actually a theo-

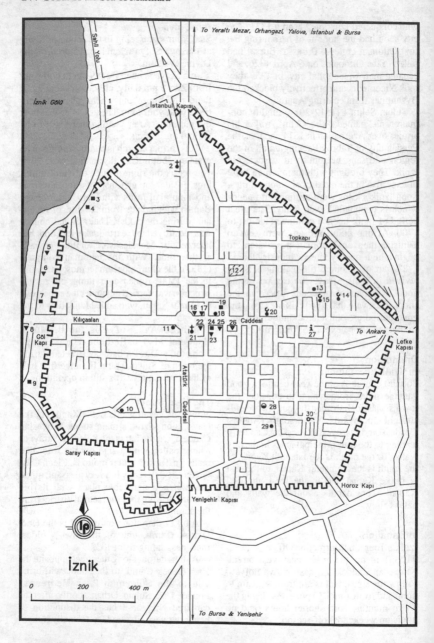

İznik Gölü

Sahil Yolu

To Yeraltı Mezar, Orhangazi, Yalova, İstanbul & Bursa

İstanbul Kapısı

1

2

3

4

5

6

7

Kılıçaslan

Göl Kapı

8

9

10

11

12

13

15

14

16 17

19

18

20

22 24 25 26 Caddesi

21 23

27

To Ankara

Lefke Kapısı

Topkapı

Atatürk

Caddesi

28

30

29

Saray Kapısı

Yenişehir Kapısı

Horoz Kapı

İznik

0   200   400 m

To Bursa & Yenişehir

■ PLACES TO STAY

1   Berlin Motel
3   Cem Pansiyon
4   Pensiyon-Café Murat
7   Motel Burçum
9   Çamlık Motel
19 Hotel Şener
24 Hotel Babacan

▼ PLACES TO EAT

4   Café Murat-Pensiyon
5   Savarona Restaurant
6   Kırıkçatal Restaurant
8   Dallas Restaurant
16 Lambada Café
17 Konya Etil Pide Salonu
22 Inegöl Köftecisi
23 Saray Pastanesi
25 Ergün Restaurant
26 Köşk Restaurant

OTHER

3   Aya Trifon Kilisesi
10 Roman Theatre
11 Bank
12 Pazar Alanı (Marketplace)
13 Museum
14 Yeşil Cami
15 Şeyh Kutbettin Camii
18 Belediye Sarayı Municipality
20 Hacı Özbek Camii
21 Aya Sofya
27 Tourism Information Office
28 Otogar
29 Yakup Çelebi Zaviyesi
30 Ayazma (Sacred Spring)

logical seminary) founded by a member of
the Ottoman dynasty.

Back on the main street, you will come to
the Tourism Information Office on the right-
hand side. Soon, to the left, you can see the
tile-covered minaret of the Yeşil Cami.

Yeşil Cami

Built in the year that Columbus discovered
America (1492), the Yeşil Cami or Green
Mosque has Seljuk Turkish proportions
influenced more by Persia (the Seljuk homeland) than by İstanbul. The green-glazed

bricks of the minaret foreshadowed the tile
industry that arose a few decades after the
mosque was built. Sultan Selim, impatient to
have a tile industry of his own, simply moved
a large number of artisans from Tabriz.

Archaeological Museum

Across the road from the Yeşil Cami is the
Nilüfer Hatun İmareti or Soup Kitchen of
Lady Nilüfer (1388), now set up as the
town's museum. Opening hours are from
8.30 am to noon and 1 to 5.30 pm, closed
Monday (usually). Admission costs 75c.

Begun in 1388, it was built by Sultan
Murat I for his mother, Nilüfer Hatun, who
was born a Byzantine princess but was
married off to Orhan, second sultan of the
Ottoman state, to cement a diplomatic alliance. I'll wager that Lady Nilüfer would be
pleased to see her pious gift in its present
state.

Though intended as a place where the poor
could come for free food, it now dispenses
culture to the masses. The front court is filled
with marble statuary, bits of cornice and
column, and similar archaeological flotsam
and jetsam. In the lofty, cool halls are exhibits of İznik faïence, Ottoman weaponry,
embroidery and calligraphy, and several
items from the city's Roman past. Many of
the little signs are in French and English, but
you'll need to know the word *yüzyıl* –
'century', as in 'XVI Yüzyıl', '16th century'.

While at the museum, enquire about a visit
to the Byzantine tomb **Yeraltı Mezar** or
Katakom on the outskirts of town. You must
have a museum official accompany you with
the key; there is a small charge for admission,
and the official should receive a small tip.
Also, you will have to haggle with a taxi
driver for a return-trip price. But once these
arrangements have been made, you're in for
a treat. The little tomb, discovered by accident in the 1960s, has delightful Byzantine
murals covering walls and ceiling. There is
another tomb nearby, but it's not really worth
the bother or expense to see.

Across the road to the south of the
museum is the **Şeyh Kutbettin Camii**
(1492), now undergoing restoration. One

used to be allowed to climb its minaret for the view. Perhaps after restorations are completed it will be opened again.

City Walls

Go back to Kılıçaslan Caddesi and continue east to the **Lefke Kapısı**. This charming old monument is actually three gates in a row, all dating from Byzantine times. The middle one has an inscription which tells us it was built by Proconsul Plancius Varus in 123 AD. It's possible to clamber up to the top of the gate and the walls here, a good vantage point for inspecting the ancient walls.

Outside the gate is an **aqueduct**, and the **tomb of Çandarlı Halil Hayrettin Paşa** (late 1300s), with the graves of many lesser mortals nearby.

Lefke, by the way, is now called Osmaneli. In Byzantine times it was a city of considerable size, though now it's just a small town.

Re-enter the city through the Lefke Kapısı, and turn left. Follow the walls south and west to the **Yenişehir Kapısı**. On the way you will pass near the ruined **Church of the Koimesis**, which dates from about 800. Only some bits of the foundation remain, but it is famous as the burial place of the Byzantine emperor Theodore I Lascaris. When the crusaders took Constantinople in 1204, Lascaris fled to Nicaea and established his court here. He never made it back to his beloved capital. When the court did move back to Constantinople in 1261, it was under the guidance of Michael VIII Palaeologus. By the way, it was Lascaris who built the outer ring of walls, supported by over 100 towers and protected by a wide moat. No doubt he didn't trust the crusaders, having lost one city to them.

Near the church is an ayazma *(aghiasma)* or **sacred fountain**, also called a *yeraltı çeşme* (underground spring).

After admiring the Yenişehir Kapısı, start towards the centre along Atatürk Caddesi. Halfway to Aya Sofya, a road on the left leads to the ruins of a Roman theatre. Nearby is the **Saray Kapısı** or Palace Gate in the city walls. Sultan Orhan had a palace near here in the 1300s.

The Lake

Make your way to the lakeshore where there's a bathing beach (the water tends to be chilly except in high summer), teahouses and little restaurants. This is the place to rest your feet, and have an ice cream, soft drink or glass of tea, and ponder the history of battles which raged around this city. It is obviously much better off as a sleepy fruit-growing centre and weekend getaway spot for citizens of İstanbul, İzmit and Bursa.

Places to Stay – bottom end

Hotels in İznik may fill up with Turks from nearby cities on summer weekends, and you may need to reserve a room in advance.

İznik has a few modest hostelries good for a one-night stay. In the centre, just across the street from the Belediye, is the plain, fairly drab *Hotel Babacan* (☎ (252) 71211, 71623) at Kılıçaslan Caddesi 86. Thirty of the rooms come with sinks and are priced at US$8/10 a single/double. With private shower, the prices are US$12 and US$15, respectively.

A bit newer, and thus nicer, are the *Cem Pansiyon* (☎ (252) 71687) and the *Pension Café Murat* (☎ (252) 72651), on the Sahil Yolu (shore road) in the north-west part of town facing the lake. Both charge US$8/11 a single/double for rooms without water or with sink.

Camping Both of the following places have very basic camping areas.

Places to Stay – middle

Motel Burcum (☎ (252) 71011) has nice verdant grounds, and tidy rooms, some with views of the lake, for US$15 a double, breakfast included. Get a room on the 2nd or 3rd floor if you want that view. You can camp in the garden for a few dollars per night.

The tidy *Çamlık Motel* (CHAHM-luhk) (☎ (252) 71631), at the southern end of the lake-front road, has nice rooms and a pretty restaurant, with prices identical to those at the Burcum. There is camping here as well, and it's perhaps a bit quieter.

Berlin Motel-Restaurant (☎ (252) 73355, -6; fax 74333), Sahil Yolu 36, north-west of the centre on the Sahil Yolu, offers simple but adequate rooms, a well-stocked bar, a popular restaurant, and loud nightly entertainment (watch out for this if you're a light sleeper). Rates are a fairly high US$18/22 a single/double, with bath.

Hotel Şener (☎ (252) 71338, -9; fax 72280), Belediye Arkası, H Oktay Sokak 7, prides itself on being the fanciest hotel in the centre, with a lift, lounge, restaurant, and presentable rooms going for US$18/22 a single/double with bath, which is expensive for İznik, but better than some of the alternatives.

Places to Eat

Near the Belediye look for the *Köşk* (☎ 71843) and *Ergün* restaurants, facing one another across the main street. The nearby *Çiçek* serves no alcohol. At any of these places, a meal can be had for US$4 or less.

Another choice near the Belediye is the *İnegöl*, specialising in İnegöl köftesi, rich grilled meatballs of minced lamb in the style used in the nearby town of İnegöl. They have typical ready-food dishes as well.

Facing the İnegöl is the *Konya Etli Pide Salonu*, serving good, cheap, freshly made Turkish-style pizzas for US$1 to US$2, depending upon toppings. Arab-style lahmacun costs less than 50c per portion.

About the most modern, up-market eatery in the centre is the *Lambada Café*, across Kılıçaslan Caddesi from Aya Sofya. Despite its more contemporary décor, prices are still low to moderate.

There are also several pastahanes hereabouts, including the *Saray Pastanesi*, good for breakfast, tea or a snack.

The lakeside restaurants are the most pleasant and popular for a meal if the weather is fine, and Turkish patrons will enjoy themselves here for hours each evening. Alcoholic beverages are served: expect to spend about US$8 to US$12 for a full meal, less for a light supper.

Dallas Restaurant, named for the US television series, is just south of where Kılıçaslan Caddesi meets the lake, with a pleasant waterfront situation. *Kırıkçatal* (Broken Fork) is north of the Motel Burcum, and has a longstanding reputation. Yet a bit farther north, the *Savarona*, named for Atatürk's sumptuous yacht, is perhaps the busiest. There's live entertainment, Turkish-style, at the *Berlin Motel-Restaurant* yet farther north.

Things to Buy

Coloured tiles, of course, are the natural souvenir from İznik. Several small shops along the main street sell these. (Note that classic tiles from the 1700s are antiquities and may not legally be exported from Turkey without a permit.) There is also embroidery, a local cottage industry.

Getting There & Away

Bursa has a much better selection of hotels and restaurants than İznik. Unless you are unusually interested in İznik, take one of the hourly buses from İznik's otogar to Bursa. Don't wait until too late in the day, however, as the last bus heads out at 6 or 7 pm on the 1½-hour trip. A ticket costs from US$1.50 to US$2, depending upon the company.

BURSA

Bursa, with a population of one million, has a special place in the hearts of the Turks. It was the first capital city of the enormous Ottoman Empire and, in a real sense, the birthplace of modern Turkish culture. The city, at an altitude of 155 metres, has its pretty parts despite its industrial base.

History

Called Prusa by the Byzantines, Bursa is a very old and important city. It was founded – according to legend, by Prusias, king of Bithynia – before 200 BC; there may have been an even older settlement on the site. It soon came under the sway of Eumenes II of Pergamum, and thereafter under direct Roman control.

Bursa grew to importance in the early centuries of Christianity, when the thermal baths at Çekirge were first developed on a large scale and when a silk trade was founded here. The importation of silkworms and the establishment of looms began an industry which survives to this day. It was Justinian (527-65) who really put Bursa on the map. Besides favouring the silk trade, he built a palace for himself and bathhouses in Çekirge.

With the decline of Byzantium, Bursa's location near İstanbul drew the interest of would-be conquerors, including the Arab armies (circa 700 AD) and the Seljuk Turks. The Seljuks, having conquered much of Anatolia by 1075, took Bursa with ease that same year, and planted the seeds of the great Ottoman Empire to come.

With the arrival of the First Crusade in

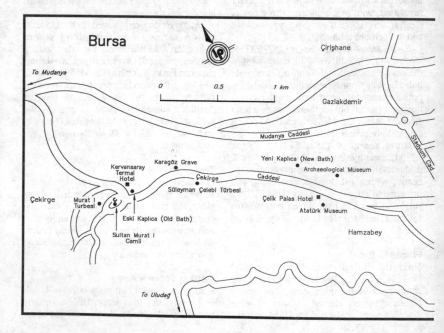

1097, Bursa reverted to Christian hands, though it was to be conquered and reconquered by both sides for the next 100 years. When the rapacious armies of the Fourth Crusade sacked Constantinople in 1204, the Byzantine emperor fled to İznik and set up his capital there. He succeeded in controlling the hinterland of İznik, including Bursa, until he moved back to Constantinople in 1261.

Ever since the Turkish migration into Anatolia during the 11th and 12th centuries, small principalities had risen here and there around Turkish military leaders. A *gazi* (warrior chieftain or 'Hero of the Faith') would rally a group of followers, gain control of a territory, govern it and seek to expand its borders. One such prince was Ertuğrul Gazi (died 1281), who formed a small state near Bursa. Under the rule of his son Osman Gazi (1281-1326) the small state grew to a nascent empire and took Osman's name *(Osmanlı*, 'Ottoman'). Bursa was besieged by Osman's forces in 1317 and was

finally starved into submission on 6 April 1326 when it immediately became the Ottoman capital.

After Osman had expanded and enriched his principality, he was succeeded by Orhan Gazi (1326-61) who, from his base at Bursa, expanded the empire to include everything from what is now Ankara in Central Anatolia to Thrace in Europe. The Byzantine capital at Constantinople was thus surrounded, and the Byzantine Empire had only about a century to survive. Orhan took the title of *sultan* (lord), struck the first Ottoman coinage and near the end of his reign was able to dictate to the Byzantine emperors. One of them, John VI Cantacuzene, was Orhan's close ally and later even his father-in-law (Orhan married the Princess Theodora).

Even though the Ottoman capital moved to Adrianople (Edirne) in 1402, Bursa remained an important, even revered, Ottoman city throughout the long history of

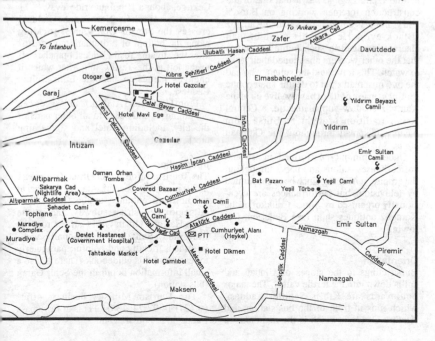

the empire. Both Osman and Orhan were buried there; their tombs are still proud, important monuments in Turkish history.

With the founding of the Turkish Republic, Bursa's industrial development began in earnest. What really brought the boom was the automobile assembly plants, set up in the 1960s and 1970s. Large factories here assemble Renaults, Fiats and other motor vehicles. Also, Bursa has always been noted for its fruit; it was logical that a large fruit juice and soft drink industry should be centred here. Tourism is also important.

Karagöz Bursa is traditionally regarded as the 'birthplace' of the Turkish Karagöz shadow-puppet theatre. The puppets, cut from camel hide, treated with oil to promote translucency, and painted with colours, are manipulated behind a white cloth onto which their coloured shadows are cast by a light behind them. Legend has it that one of the construction foremen working on Bursa's Ulu Cami was a hunch-back called Karagöz (Black-eye). He and his straight-man Hacivat indulged in such humorous antics that the other workers abandoned their tasks to watch. This infuriated the sultan, who had the two miscreants put to death. Their comic routines (many of them bawdy) live on in the Karagöz shadow-puppet theatre, a Central Asian tradition brought to Bursa from whence it spread throughout the Ottoman lands.

Once commonly performed in tea and coffee houses, salons and parks throughout the empire, it has long since been supplanted by television, but performances are occasionally organised by Şinasi Çelikkol of the Karagöz antiques shop (see Bedesten, following).

Orientation
Bursa clings to the slopes of Uludağ and spills down into the fertile valley. The major boulevards are Kıbrıs Şehitler Caddesi, which runs in front of the bus station, and Atatürk Caddesi, which is the main axis in the commercial district. Both run across the slope, not up and down it.

Bursa's main square is Cumhuriyet Alanı (Republic Square), where you will see an equestrian statue of Atatürk. Most people refer to the square as Heykel (hey-KEHL, statue), and this is what you will see on the illuminated signs atop dolmuşes which wait near the bus station to take you up to the city centre.

Bursa's main street, Atatürk Caddesi, runs west from Heykel to the Ulu Cami (oo-LOO jah-mee, Great Mosque), a distance of about 700 metres. This is the business section, the centre of Bursa. Heavy traffic makes it almost impossible to cross the street, so use the pedestrian subways (altgeçidi, underpass), each of which bears a name (see following).

The westward continuation of Atatürk Caddesi becomes Cemal Nadir Caddesi, then Altıparmak Caddesi, then Çekirge Caddesi. It leads to the spa suburb of Çekirge, about a 10-minute ride away.

East of Heykel, Namazgah Caddesi crosses the stream Gök Deresi trickling along the bottom of a dramatic gorge. Just after the stream, Yeşil Caddesi branches off to the left to the Yeşil Cami, after which it changes names to become Emir Sultan Caddesi.

From Heykel and Atatürk Caddesi you can get dolmuşes and buses to all other parts of the city, including hotel and sightseeing areas.

Information
The Tourism Information Office (☎ (24) 21 2359) is actually beneath Atatürk Caddesi at the northern entrance to the Orhan Gazi Altgeçidi pedestrian subway, facing the Koza Han and Orhan Gazi Camii across the little park. Staff are exceptionally well-informed, friendly and helpful, particularly to readers of this guidebook. There is also a small information booth in the Şehir Garajı (bus station).

The Tourism Ministry business office (☎ (24) 14 22 74, 13 04 11) is at Fevzipaşa Caddesi 75, Fomara Han.

Bookstores TAŞ Kitapçılık & Yayıncılık (☎ 22 94 53), Adliye Karşısı, Kültür Sokak 8/A, just a few steps uphill from Heykel, has Penguins and a number of other English titles as well as some English-language newspapers and periodicals. The local branch of Haşet Kitabevi (☎ 22 55 58) is at Altıparmak Caddesi 48-50, on the way between Bursa and Çekirge.

Emir Sultan Camii

You can see most of Bursa's sights in one full day, though a leisurely tour will take a little more time. Start with the city's most famous architectural monuments, east of the city centre. You can go by dolmuş (look for the Emir Sultan dolmuş stand on the north side of the square), or by bus 18 (Emir Sultan-Heykel-Santral Garajı). You'll pass by the Yeşil Cami and Yeşil Türbe before coming to the Emir Sultan Camii, but this way you can walk downhill, not up.

This mosque is a favourite of Bursa's pious Muslims. Rebuilt by Selim III in 1805 and restored in the early 1990s, it echoes the romantic decadence of Ottoman Rococo style. The setting, next to a large hillside cemetery surrounded by huge trees and overlooking the city and valley, is as pleasant as the mosque itself.

Yıldırım Beyazıt Camii

Gazing across the valley from the Emir Sultan Camii, you'll see the two domes of the Yıldırım Beyazıt Camii, the Mosque of Beyazıt the Thunderbolt. It was built earlier (in 1391) than Bursa's famous Yeşil Cami, and forms part of the same architectural evolution. You can walk through the city to this mosque if you like, but go and see the Yeşil Cami first. Dolmuşes (Heykel-Beyazıt Yıldırım or Heykel-Fakülte) depart from Heykel and pass near the mosque.

Next to the Yıldırım Beyazıt Camii is its medrese, once a theological seminary, now a public health centre. Here also are the tombs of the mosque's founder, Sultan Beyazıt I, and his son İsa. This peaceful spot gives one no sense of the turbulent times which brought Beyazıt to his death.

Yıldırım Beyazıt (Sultan Beyazıt I, 1389-1402) led his Ottoman armies into Yugoslavia and Hungary, and captured even more of Anatolia for the Ottomans. But he was brought down by Tamerlane, who defeated him and took him prisoner at the Battle of Ankara in 1402. Beyazıt died a year later in captivity, and Tamerlane marched all the way to İzmir and Bursa. With this blow, the Ottoman Empire all but collapsed.

Yeşil Cami

After the disastrous victories of Tamerlane, Beyazıt's sons argued over the succession to the weakened Ottoman throne. The civil war amongst them lasted for 10 years until 1413, when one son, Mehmet Çelebi, was able to gain supreme power. Six years after becoming sultan, Mehmet I (1413-21) ordered his architect Hacı İvaz to begin construction on Bursa's greatest monument, the Yeşil Cami or Green Mosque. It was finished in 1424.

The mosque is a supremely beautiful building in a fine setting and represents a turning-point in Turkish architectural style. Before this, Turkish mosques echoed the style of the Great Seljuks which was basically Persian, but in the Yeşil Cami a purely Turkish style emerges. Notice the harmonious façade and the beautiful carved marble work around the central doorway. As you enter, you will pass beneath the sultan's private apartments into a domed central hall. The rooms to the left and right, if not being used for prayer, were used by high court officials for transacting government business. The room straight ahead, with the 15-metre-high mihrab, is the main prayer room. Greenish-blue tiles on the interior walls gave the mosque its name.

Much of Bursa, including the Yeşil Cami, was destroyed in an earthquake in 1855 but the mosque was restored, authentically, by 1864.

Just inside the mosque's main entrance, a narrow stairway leads up to the **hünkar mahfili** or sultan's loge, above the main door. The loge is sumptuously tiled and decorated. This is where the sultan actually lived (or at least it was one of his residences), with his

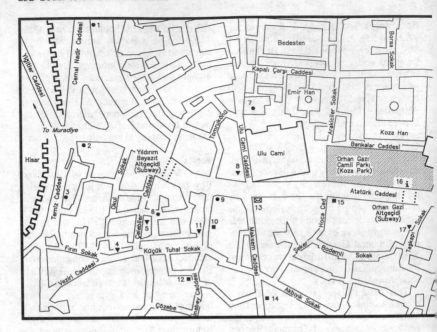

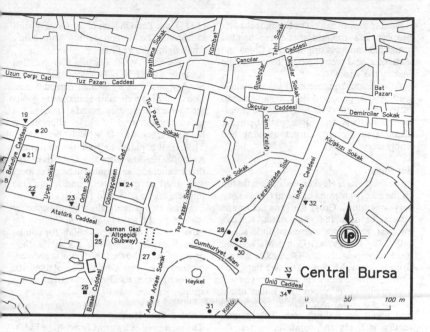

Central Bursa

harem and household staff in less plush quarters on either side. The caretaker used to choose single travellers or couples, give them a conspiratorial wink, and lead them up for a peek, after which he would receive a tip. Somebody higher up must have caught on, as he no longer seems to be doing it.

Yeşil Türbe
Sharing the small park surrounding the Yeşil Cami is the Yeşil Türbe or Green Tomb. It's not green, of course. The blue exterior tiles were put on during restoration work in the 1800s; the lavish use of tiles inside is original work, however. No need to remove your shoes to enter here. The tomb is open from 8.30 am to noon and 1 to 5.30 pm; admission is free.

The most prominent tomb is that of the Yeşil Cami's founder, Mehmet I (Çelebi). Others include those of his children. The huge tiled mihrab here is very impressive. Take a walk around the outside of the tomb

to look at the tiled calligraphy above several windows.

After seeing the mosque and the tomb, you might want to take a rest and have something to drink at one of the cafés on the east side of the mosque. They have wonderful views of the valley.

Turkish & Islamic Arts Museum
Down the road a few steps from the Yeşil Cami is its medrese, now called the Türk ve İslam Eserleri Müzesi. The building is in the Seljuk style of religious schools, and is open from 8.30 am to noon and 1 to 5 pm, closed on Monday; admission costs 75c, half-price for students. Start to the right to see a recreation of an Ottoman *sünnet odası* (circumcision room), then, in the eyvan or niche-like hall, there's an exhibit of ceramics from the Selçuk period (12th and 13th centuries), İznik ware from the 14th to 18th centuries, and more modern Kütahya ware (from the 18th to 20th centuries).

Next comes an exhibit of Karagöz shadow puppets. It's thought that these painted camel-hide puppets originated in China and Mongolia, and were brought to the Middle East by the Turks.

After Karagöz, museum displays include costumes, carpets, jewellery, metalwork and arms; *dergah* (dervish-hall) musical instruments, turbans and other paraphernalia; illuminated Korans, carpet weaving and embroidery.

Bat Pazarı

From the plaza at Heykel, walk down the hill on the east (right) side of İnönü Caddesi one very long block. Cross Kirişkızı Sokak and turn right onto the next street, Kayhan Caddesi, to enter a warren of little streets called the Bat Pazarı (Goose Market), or, more appropriately, the Demirciler Çarşısı (Ironmongers' Market). The one thing you won't find here today are geese, but you will find ironmongers' shops and pedlars of old clothes, carpets, rope, utensils, potions and just about everything else. This market section is lively and colourful, perfect for photographing. When you snap a shot of the blacksmith at his forge, chances are he will ask you to send him a copy. It's only fair; you should try to do so.

Bedesten

After a half-hour's stroll through the Bat Pazarı, head back to İnönü Caddesi and ask someone to point the way to the Bedesten or Covered Bazaar. Cross İnönü Caddesi and head into the side streets, following their directions. The actual covered market is surrounded by a network of small shopping streets.

The Bedesten was originally built in the late 1300s by Yıldırım Beyazıt, but the earthquake of 1855 brought it down. The reconstructed Bedesten retains the look and feel of the original, though it is obviously much tidier. This is not a tourist trap; most of the shoppers are local people. As you wander around, look for the **Eski Aynalı Çarşı**, which, though now a market, was originally built as the Orhangazi Hamamı

(1335), the Turkish bath of the Orhan Camii külliyesi. The domed ceiling with many small lights shows this.

In the Eski Aynalı Çarşı is a shop called Karagöz (☎ 21 87 27), open daily except Sunday, and run by a man named Şinasi Çelikkol. Şinasi specialises in quality goods (copper and brass, carpets and kilims, knitted gloves and embroidery, old jewellery etc) at fair prices, as did his father Rafet before him. This is the place to find the delightful Karagöz shadow-puppets. Cut from flat, dried camel leather, painted in bright colours and oiled to make them translucent, the puppets are an authentic Turkish craft item.

Şinasi Bey periodically organises performances of the shadow plays in English for groups, charging several dollars for admission. If you're interested, ask at the shop about the next shows. If one is not scheduled, he may give you a brief idea of how the shadow-puppet theatre works right in his shop.

Koza & Emir Hans

The raising of silkworms is a cottage industry in Bursa. Each April, villagers buy the worms from their cooperatives, take them home and raise them on mulberry leaves. After a month the worms spin their cocoons and are soon ready for the trip to the **Koza Han** or Silk Cocoon Caravanserai, just outside the Bedesten's eastern entrance, built in 1490 and lively with cocoon dealers in June and also in September when there is a second harvest. (Another way to enter the Koza Han is from the park just north of Atatürk Caddesi.)

When you visit, you may well see huge sacks of the precious little white cocoons being haggled over by some of the 14,000 villagers who engage in the trade. In the centre of the Koza Han's courtyard is a small mosque constructed by Yıldırım Beyazıt in 1493, restored by the guild of silk traders in 1948, and again in 1985 by the Aga Khan. The product of all this industry, silk cloth *(ipek)*, is for sale in the Bedesten.

Another place you ought to visit in the Bedesten is the **Emir Han**, adjoining the north-east corner of the Ulu Cami, a caravanserai used by many of Bursa's silk brokers today as it has been for centuries. There's a lovely fountain in the centre of the courtyard, and a tea garden for refreshments. Camels from the silk caravans used to be corralled in the courtyard, while goods were stored in the ground-floor rooms and drovers and merchants slept and did business in the rooms above.

Ulu Cami

Next to the Bedesten and Emir Han is Bursa's Ulu Cami or Great Mosque. This one is completely Seljuk in style, a big rectangular building with immense portals and a forest of supporting columns inside, similar to the much older Ulu Cami in the eastern city of Erzurum. The roof is a mass of 20 small domes. A şadırvan (ablutions fountain) plays peacefully at the centre of the interior. It was Yıldırım Beyazıt who put up the money for the building in 1396; it was finished in 1399. Notice the fine work of the mimber and the preacher's chair, also the calligraphy on the walls.

Hisar

From the Ulu Cami, walk west and up Yiğitler Caddesi, a ramp-like street which leads up to the section known as Hisar (Fortress). This section, the oldest in Bursa, was once enclosed by stone ramparts and walls, bits of which survive.

Coming by dolmuş from Heykel, get in a car labelled 'Muradiye', parked on a side street on the north side of the plaza, to the left of the T C Ziraat Bankası; by bus, hop in bus 1-A, 'Muradiye-Heykel' or any bus with 'Dev. Hst.' (Devlet Hastanesi) or 'Muradiye' on its signboard. Get off at the 'Tophane' stop. (The Devlet Hastanesi, by the way, is a large government hospital just west of the tombs of sultans Osman and Orhan.)

Near a sign which reads 'İstiklal Savaşı Şehitler', in a little park near the edge of the cliff overlooking Cemal Nadir Caddesi and the valley, are the **tombs of sultans Osman and Orhan**, founders of the Ottoman Empire. The originals were destroyed in the

earthquake of 1855 and rebuilt in Ottoman Baroque style by Sultan Abdülaziz in 1868. The tomb of Orhan Gazi was built on the foundations of a small Byzantine church, and you can see some remnants of the church's floor. The park here is attractive, as is the view of the city.

Hop in a bus or dolmuş marked 'Muradiye' to continue along Hasta Yurdu Caddesi to Muradiye, about 2.5 km to the west. You'll dip down into the valley of the Cılımboz Deresi stream before arriving in the verdant residential quarter of Muradiye.

Muradiye Complex

With a shady park in front and a quiet cemetery behind, the Sultan Murat II (Muradiye) Camii, also called the Hüdavendigar Camii, is pretty and peaceful. The mosque proper dates from 1426 and follows the style of the Yeşil Cami.

Beside the mosque are 12 tombs dating from the 1400s and 1500s, including that of Sultan Murat II (1404-51) himself. The Ottoman dynasty, like other Islamic and Asiatic dynasties, did not practice primogeniture, or succession of the first-born. Any son of a sultan could claim the throne upon his father's death, so the designated heir (or the strongest son) would have his brothers put to death rather than see civil war rend the empire. Many of the occupants of tombs here, including all the şehzades ('imperial sons', died at the hands of their close relatives.

Tomb-visiting may not be high on your list of priorities but you should see the beautiful decoration in some of the tombs. The superb decoration on the woodwork porch of the **Murat II Türbesi** contrasts with the rest of the tomb's austerity. The sultan's tomb has an opening to the sky so that his grave could be washed by the rain, and his unadorned sarcophagus has no lid, following common Muslim custom rather than imperial tradition. The tomb's architect did add a bit of Byzantine grandeur by borrowing some old Corinthian columns, but he used capitals as both capitals and plinths.

The beautiful coloured İznik tilework in

the gaudy **Cem Türbesi** celebrates Cem Sultan (1459-95), the youngest son of Sultan Mehmet the Conqueror. Cem reigned for 18 days, but was chased from the throne by Beyazıt II and fled to Europe, where he became a hostage of the pope and a pawn in Ottoman-European diplomacy.

The İznik tiles in the **Şehzade Mustafa Türbesi** are as fine as those in the Rüstem Paşa Camii in İstanbul. Mustafa (1515-53), son of Süleyman the Magnificent, was governor of Amasya when Süleyman's wife Roxelana intrigued against him, causing the sultan to order his execution – which he soon regretted bitterly.

The **Şehzade Ahmet Türbesi** is elegant in its simplicity of light and dark blue tiles framed by a vine-patterned blue-and-white border. The stained glass window is restrained as well. Ahmet's mother Bülbül Hatun is buried beside him.

Also here is the **Tarihi II. Murat Hamamı**, or Historic Turkish Bath of Sultan Murat II, still in use (see Mineral Baths, following).

Across the park from the mosque and tombs is an old Ottoman house (the sign says '17 Y. Y. Osmanlı Evi Müzesi', or '17th-century Ottoman House Museum'. Visit for a fascinating glimpse into the daily life of the Ottoman nobility in the 1600s. Carpets and furnishings are all authentic. Hours are from 8.30 am to noon, and 1 to 5 pm, closed on Monday; admission costs less than US$1.

Kültür Parkı

Bursa's Kültür Parkı (kewl-TEWR pahr-kuh) or Cultural Park, is laid out to the north of the Muradiye complex, down the hill some distance. You can reach it from Heykel by any bus or dolmuş going to Çekirge (see the following Getting Around section). Besides offering a pleasant stroll, the Kültür Parkı is good for lunch in one of its shady outdoor restaurants (see Places to Eat).

The park also houses the **Bursa Archaeological Museum**. Bursa's history goes back to the time of Hannibal (200 BC), and Roman artefacts are preserved here. The collection is nice, but not at all exceptional. If you've seen another good Turkish collection, this is more of the same. Find the bus stop named 'Arkeoloji Müzesi', and enter the park by the gate nearby. The museum is open from 8.30 am to noon and 1 to 5.30 pm, closed on Monday; admission costs US$2.

Mineral Baths

The warm, mineral-rich waters which spring from the slopes of Uludağ have been famous for their curative powers since ancient times. Today the ailing and the infirm come here for several weeks at a time, take a daily soak or two in the tub, spend the rest of the time chatting, reading or dining. Most people stay in hotels which have their own mineral bath facilities. There are independent baths *(kaplıca)* as well, some of historical importance.

For details on bathing procedure, see the Turkish Baths section of the Facts for the Visitor chapter. Baths will be crowded on Friday, the Muslim sabbath, as local people clean up for the holy day.

The **Yeni Kaplıca** (☎ 36 69 55, -6), Mudanya Caddesi 10, on the north-west side of the Kültür Parkı, is a bath renovated in 1522 by Sultan Süleyman the Magnificent's grand vizier Rüstem Paşa on the site of a much older one built by Justinian. Besides the Yeni ('New') baths, you'll find the Kaynarca ('Boiling') limited to women, and the Karamustafa, which has facilities for family bathing. All baths in the complex are open from 6 am to 11 pm (last admission at 10 pm).

Perhaps the most attractive place is the **Eski Kaplıcaları** or Old Baths, right next door to the new Kervansaray Termal Hotel on the eastern outskirts of Çekirge. Beautifully restored, the baths now cater to an up-market clientele of business travellers, tourists and local notables who stay at or socialise in the new hotel.

The bathing rooms are covered in creamy marble; in the hot room on the men's side there's a plunging pool (I haven't seen the women's side); use of the nice swimming pool downstairs is subject to a hefty additional charge. The cool room has lounge chairs for relaxing, and a bar with waiter service. Prices are higher here than at unrestored local baths, but the building is beautiful, though service is fairly unattentive. Hours are daily from 7 am to 11 pm for men, from 7.30 am to 11 pm for women. There's an entry fee of US$4, and a similar fee to have an attendant wash you; the cost of soap is additional, so figure on spending US$15 for the works, including massage and tips. You can bring your own soap and wash yourself for little more than the basic entry fee.

For a simpler, less expensive bath in the centre of Bursa, try the Çakır Ağa Hamamı, at the corner of Atatürk Caddesi and Temiz Caddesi, just west of the Tahtakale/İnebey district. Posted prices are US$2 for a wash, another dollar or so for soap and scrub, US$3 for a massage, or the works for US$7 or so.

Next to the Muradiye mosque is the Tarihi II. Murat Hamamı (that's 'İkinci Murat'), open to men on Friday and Sunday, to women all other days, from 10 am to 6 pm.

Excursions to Villages

Cumalı Kızık It is said that Osman Gazi, founder of the Ottoman Empire, founded seven villages for his seven sons and their brides about 700 years ago on lands just east of Bursa. Five of the villages, built before the Ottoman conquest of Bursa, survive to this day and retain many features of Ottoman domestic architecture.

The village of Cumalı Kızık, set on the slopes of Uludağ amidst fruit and nut orchards, is registered as a national monument and protected from development. Transportation is difficult without your own vehicle. Go 12 km eastward from Bursa along the main road to İnegöl and Ankara, then 3.5 km south to Cumalı Kızık. Facilities are limited, so you might want to bring a picnic.

The other four old villages, all south of the Bursa-Ankara highway, are Hamamlı Kızık, not far from Cumalı Kızık; Dere Kızık farther east; and Fidye Kızık and Değirmenli Kızık, closer to Bursa.

Güneybudaklar With your own vehicle, go west from Bursa, and on the outskirts turn south on the road marked for Keles. The road winds around Uludağ and climbs its southern slopes, passing through the wine-making village of Misi before reaching a road, 45 km from Bursa, marked for Güneybudaklar. The village, three km north of the main road, was founded some 500 years ago by Turcoman nomads on the site of a Roman-Byzantine settlement. The land around is planted with strawberries and other fruits, beans, potatoes, wheat and barley. Flocks graze on the rich mountain grasses while the women of the village weave colourful cloths at their looms. There are few tourists and no services, but you can stop, enjoy the views and the air, and have a satisfying glass of tea before retracing your way to Bursa.

Places to Stay

Though there are a few hotels in the centre of town, many of Bursa's best lodgings in terms of both quality and price are in the western suburb of Çekirge. I'll mention those in Bursa's centre first, then those in Çekirge. Hotels atop Uludağ are mentioned in that section following the Bursa section.

Places to Stay – bottom end

Bursa You can find a very cheap room in Bursa near the Şehir Garajı (bus station), in the centre, or in Çekirge, but you must choose carefully. Hotels near the bus station tend to be horribly noisy and not well kept.

I strongly recommend that you look for lodgings away from the bus station. If you must stay here, at least find a quiet place. Walk out the front door of the bus station and cross Kıbrıs Şehitler Caddesi, the big avenue. There are several hotels here, but they are noisy and expensive. Turn left, then right, and walk along this small street (Şirin Sokak) to the *Mavi Ege Oteli* (☎ (24) 14 84 20), Fırın Sokak 17. The 'Blue Aegean' is very plain and simple but quieter than most places, and charges from US$6 to US$8 a single, US$8 to US$10 a double, US$10 to US$12 a triple. Some rooms have sinks. Check the sheets and have the management change them if they've been used. Soon they may price themselves too high.

Just around the corner is the similar *Hotel Şirin*, charging the same prices; you'll see its sign.

A few steps up the street from the Mavi Ege and Şirin is Celal Bayar Caddesi (formerly Gazcılar Caddesi) and two even better lodgings. *Hotel Belkis* (☎ (24) 14 83 22), Celal Bayar Caddesi 168, charges the same as the Mavi Ege, but has nicer rooms; there's no running water in the rooms, though. *Öz Uludağ Hotel*, a few doors to the left (west) of the Belkis is similar.

For better accommodation at a higher price, find the *Gazcılar Oteli* (GAHZ-juh-LAHR) (☎ (24) 14 94 77), Celal Bayar Caddesi 156/A. Neat and clean, the Gazcılar has central heating and a *lüks* (deluxe) rating from the municipal government, which has lower standards than most. Rooms with sinks only are fairly good value at US$12 a double; those with shower are overpriced at US$18, but you can haggle.

Even better is *Otel Geçit* (☎ (24) 14 10 32), Celal Bayar Caddesi 175, with better rooms and prices presently lower than at the Gazcılar Oteli at US$14 for a double with private shower. But price will soon catch up with quality as this place has a lift, central heating, and all sorts of other modern conveniences.

The Tahtakale/İnebey district just south of the Ulu Cami is an interesting area with many narrow streets and historic houses. Some of the houses are being restored, and will no doubt soon be turned into expensive shops and moderately priced 'boutique' hotels. There's a good produce market here as well. The traditional lodging choice here is the *Otel Çamlıbel* (CHAHM-luh-behl) (☎ (24) 21 25 65, 22 55 65), İnebey Caddesi 71, an old and well-worn place with these advantages: a quiet location, rooms with constant hot water and good cross-ventilation, a lift and a few parking places in front of the hotel. Rates are US$12/15/18 a single/double/triple, a few dollars more with private shower. You can have breakfast served in the hotel. To find the Çamlıbel,

walk one block west from the PTT on Atatürk Caddesi (it's across from the Ulu Cami), pass the Türkiye Emlak Kredi Bankası and turn left. This is İnebey Caddesi. Walk two blocks up the hill on İnebey Caddesi, and the hotel is on the right-hand side.

Also on this street is the simpler, drabber but cheaper *Yeni Ankara Oteli* (☎ (24) 21 73 77), İnebey Caddesi 48, across from the Şehir Lokantası. Rooms are waterless, but the general baths are clean enough, and prices are a low at US$6/8/10 a single/double/triple. The location is fine.

Çekirge Most Çekirge hotels have their own facilities for 'taking the waters', since that's the reason people come here. You may find that the bathtub or shower in your hotel room runs only mineral water, or there may be separate private or public bathing-rooms in the basement of the hotel. One day's dip in the mineral waters is no great thrill. The therapeutic benefits are supposedly acquired over a term of weeks. All the same, you may find that a soak in a private tub is included in the price of the room, even in the very cheapest hotels, so take advantage of it.

The main street here is named I. Murat Caddesi (that's 'Birinci Murat Caddesi').

For all of the Çekirge hotels, get a bus or dolmuş from Heykel or along Atatürk Caddesi, and get out at the bus stop mentioned.

Konak Palas Oteli (☎ (24) 36 51 13, 35 52 74), Birinci Murat Camii Arkası 11, Çekirge, more or less behind the Ada Palas Hotel near the entrance to Çekirge, is very simple but adequate, quite friendly and well located. Posted rates are US$10/16 a single/double for bed and breakfast in a room with washbasin, but I easily obtained rates 40% lower with a bit of haggling. The mineral bath in the basement is rich with marble, and costs no more.

Nearby, the acceptable, if unexciting, *Hotel Eren* (☎ (24) 36 80 99, 36 71 05), Birinci Murat Camii Aralığı 2, is up the hill a few steps from the Konak Palas, behind the Ada Palas. It has usable, quiet rooms with showers, and a nice terrace in front, but charges US$16/20 a single/double for a room with private shower.

The *Yeşil Yayla Oteli* (☎ (24) 36 80 26), Çekirge Caddesi, behind the Yıldız Hotel at the upper end of the village just off the main road, has similar simple rooms at identical prices. Daily use of the hotel's mineral bath facilities is included, as always.

Camping There are no camping facilities in the city. The best you can do is out on the Yalova road. *Nur Camping* (☎ (24) 14 74 53), at Km 8 on the Yalova road, caters especially for caravans. *Kervansaray Kumluk Mocamp* (☎ (24) 14 89 68) is more accustomed to tents.

Places to Stay – middle

Bursa In central Bursa noise is a big problem, but the best hotels are off the main streets in any case.

My favourite is the *Hotel Çeşmeli* (☎ (24) 24 15 11, -2), Gümüşçeken Caddesi 6, Heykel, just a few steps north of the main square. Clean, quiet, friendly, simple but pleasant and conveniently located, it charges US$17/20 a single/double for a room with shower and breakfast. Check it out.

Equally good value is offered by the nearby *Hotel Bilgiç* (☎ (24) 20 31 90; fax 22 76 33), Başak Caddesi 30, one block southwest of Heykel. The décor is an amusing melange of Art Deco and Art Nouveau which you may never get used to, but the hotel has cheerful staff, good and fairly quiet rooms, and decent prices of US$17/20 a single/double with shower.

Hotel Dikmen (☎ (24) 24 18 40; fax 24 18 44), Maksem Caddesi 78, is farther west, then south. This 50-room two-star hotel's lobby is pleasant, with a small enclosed garden terrace, complete with fountain, at the back; a lift takes you up to your room. Rooms with little luxuries such as bathtubs, TVs and minibar refrigerators rent for US$27/34 a single/double, slightly cheaper without the frills. Remember to ask for *sakin bir oda* (a quiet room). The hotel is about 50 metres uphill on the street, sometimes called

Fevzi Çakmak Caddesi, which begins beside the main PTT, across from the Ulu Cami.

Finally, *Kent Hotel* (☎ (24) 21 87 00; fax 21 74 12), Atatürk Caddesi 119, is the most comfortable place right in the centre, rating three stars for its 64 rooms. All rooms are air-conditioned and have private showers, minibars and satellite TVs, and cost US$38/52/64 a single/double/triple, tax and service included. The hotel's terrace restaurant (serving alcohol), one flight up, overlooks busy Atatürk Caddesi. Do not take a room facing the noisy street.

Çekirge The 60-room *Termal Hotel Gönlü Ferah* (☎ (24) 36 27 00; fax 36 77 96), I. Murat Caddesi 24, Çekirge, 16090 Bursa, in the very centre of the village, is one of the old reliables, and is among the more deluxe three-star hotels in Çekirge. Some of the 62 rooms have wonderful views over the valley, all have very comfortable furnishings and TVs. The ambience here is 'European spa', the service attentive and experienced. Rates are US$56 a double on the street side, US$62 a double on the panoramic side, with breakfast included.

Next door, the *Hotel Dilmen* (☎ (24) 36 61 14; fax 35 25 68), I. Murat Caddesi, Çekirge, 16090 Bursa, rates four stars, boasts a lobby replete with stained glass, a pleasant garden terrace with restaurant and bar service, an exercise room with sauna and mineral-water baths, and 100 modern, posh rooms complete with satellite TV hook-ups. Prices are US$75 a double for a room facing the village, US$85 a double for a room with a valley view. Take a room with the valley view, for sure.

Places to Stay – top end

Bursa's most famous spa hotel is the five-star, 173-room *Hotel Çelik Palas* (☎ (24) 33 38 00; fax 36 19 10), Çekirge Caddesi 79, 16070 Bursa. Given its name in 1935 by Atatürk himself, the hotel had been a favourite resort for the Turkish leader and his peers; King Idris of Libya was taking the waters here when he was ousted by Colonel Muammar Gaddafi. Set in pretty grounds, the hotel consists of a historic older building dating from between the wars, and a newer section. The décor is an odd combination of the modern and the traditional elements.

All 173 rooms have TVs, minibars, direct-dial phones, air-con and bathrooms with separate mineral-water taps. The Çelik Palas's mineral-water bath facilities are the most sumptuous in town, with lots of marble and tile, stained glass and a huge circular pool. Restaurants, bars, nightclub and disco, shopping and exercise room are all available. Though not on a par with the great spa hotels of Europe, it is quite comfortable. Rates range from US$70 to US$98 a single, from US$90 to US$125 a double. Breakfast costs US$7, other meals from around US$10 to US$16. The Çelik Palas is part of the Emek chain.

Çekirge's other five-star hotel is the 211-room *Hotel Kervansaray Termal* (☎ (24) 35 30 00; fax 35 30 24), Çekirge Meydanı, Çekirge, 16080 Bursa, opened in late 1988. The architecture and decoration here are updated subdued Art Deco, and your first impression will be one of comfort and old richness. Marble, brass and mirrors shine, tawny travertine with brick and wood trim links the building with its past; a nice little swimming pool is open for use in summer.

The Eski Kaplıcaları mineral baths are right next door to the hotel, which is on the eastern outskirts of Çekirge set well back from a major crossroad. Rates at the hotel are US$75/105 a single/double. It's part of the Kervansaray hotel chain, which also has a hotel in Bursa, and another atop Uludağ.

Places to Eat

Bursa's culinary specialities include fresh fruit (especially peaches in season), candied chestnuts *(kestane şekeri)* and two types of roast meat. Bursa kebap or İskender kebap is the most famous, made from döner kebap laid on a bed of fresh pide bread and topped with savoury tomato sauce and browned butter. When I'm in Bursa, I have this every single day. The other speciality is İnegöl köftesi, a type of very rich grilled meatball which is actually the speciality of the nearby

town called İnegöl. You will see several restaurants which specialise in these dishes exclusively, called Bursa kebapçısı or İnegöl köftecisi.

Most of Bursa's eateries are quite inexpensive and would suit a bottom-end budget, while the food is good enough for the top end.

The following places to eat are arranged according to the type of food, location or style of place.

Bursa Kebapçıs Locals and foreigners debate the relative merits of the town's many Bursa kebapçıs. On my last visit I dined in all of them again. Price differences were small due to fixed municipal prices, but quality differences were notable. You'll pay about US$5 or US$6 for a one-porsyon plate of kebap with yoghurt, plus a soft drink (no alcohol is served at any kebapçı). Add US$2 if you order *bir buçuk porsyon* (1½ portions). All these places are open seven days a week from 11 am until 9 or 10 pm.

I judged the best kebap and service for the price to be at *Kebapçı İskender* (☎ 21 46 15), Ünlü Cadde 7, a half-block south-east of Heykel. The elaborate Ottomanesque façade and semi-formal waiters belie moderate prices (US$6.50 for 1½ portions of Bursa kebap with yoghurt, plus a soft drink). You get a smile and a splash of refreshing lemon cologne as you leave.

Directly across Ünlü Cadde is *Adanur Hacıbey* (☎ 21 64 40), a simpler, but neat and tidy place where the Bursa kebap comes with a dab of smoky aubergine purée on the side. Price is the same as at Kebapçı İskender. Remember, after your kebap is served, don't begin eating until the waiter brings the tomato sauce and browned butter.

The original *Hacıbey Kebapçısı* (☎ 22 66 04), Taşkapı Sokak 4/11, is just south-west of Heykel on a side street south off Atatürk Caddesi. Two floors of narrow rooms have marble floors, beautiful tiled walls and dark polished woodwork. Waiters in waistcoats serve politely and efficiently, and the kebap is very good.

Bursa kebap was invented in a small restaurant now called *Kebabcı İskenderoğlu Nurettin* (Iskender's Son) at Atatürk Caddesi 60, between Heykel and the Ulu Cami. The surroundings are basic and simple, the kebap good but unremarkable.

The main advantage of *Sultan İskender Kebap*, on the east side of the Koza Park, is its view over the park, though the kebap is quite edible.

Çiçek Izgara (☎ 21 65 26), Belediye Caddesi 15, is a modern grill a block north of Atatürk Caddesi. Though it does not specialise in Bursa kebap, it serves excellent grills in an atmosphere that's especially comfortable for single women. Prices range from US$2 for köfte to US$5 for the big mixed grill; a bonfile (small beef filet steak) costs US$3.50. To find it, look for the old Belediye building, a curious half-timbered Ottoman relic, and walk downhill through the flower market to the restaurant, which is one flight up.

İnegöl Köfteci For İnegöl köftesi, try the *İnegöl Köftecisi* on a little side street by Atatürk Caddesi 48. On your second visit you might try the köfte made with onions or cheese as a variation on the basic stuff. A full lunch need cost only US$4.

Another good köfteci is the *Özömür*, on the western side of the Ulu Cami, in the historic arasta, the complex of shops attached to the mosque. Here you can dine in an old stone building, and order from an English-language menu. *Köfte*, salad and soft drink go for for about US$3.50, şiş kebap for a bit more.

Hazır Yemek Ready-food restaurants have steam tables and pre-cooked soups, stews, pilavs and stuffed vegetables. Many close by 7 pm.

The Tahtakale/İnebey district is a particularly good place to look for a good, cheap meal. *Şehir Lokantası* (☎ 22 62 03), İnebey Caddesi 85, a half-block up from Atatürk Caddesi, is near the Çamlıbel and Yeni Ankara hotels in the Tahtakale/İnebey district. Simple, clean and attractive, it serves filling hazır-yemek (ready-food) meals for around US$3.

Just up the street from the Şehir, turn right (west) and walk to the market area known as the *Tahtakale Çarşısı*. Just west of it is Çelebiler Caddesi and the *Lokanta Alış*, at No 18, and the adjoining *Tahtakale Lokantası*. But my favourite is a bit farther south. Walk uphill on Çelebiler Caddesi two blocks to a T-intersection, turn right and walk half a block to the *Yeşil İnci Lokantası*, a very tidy and pleasant restaurant with a separate 10-table aile salonu (ladies' dining room). The 'Green Pearl' stays open later than many other local eateries serving ready food accompanied by its own freshly baked pide bread. You need spend no more than US$4 to fill up, and you can spend less.

Near Heykel, try the *Saray Lokantası*, on the east (right) side of İnönü Caddesi as you go downhill. It's white, with bare walls, fluorescent light, and a mostly male clientele, but there's lots of good food and it's cheap. I had soup and etli nohut (chickpeas in a meat sauce) for less than US$2.

Kültür Parkı Strolling around the Cultural Park is pleasant, and having a meal here is more so. The *Selçuk Restaurant* (☎ 20 96 95) is good, quiet, shady and not overly expensive. I paid US$7 for a full lunch here, beverage and tip included. There are lots of other pleasant little restaurants in the park as well.

Çekirge The more expensive hotels in Çekirge have their own dining rooms. Besides these, there's the *Sezen Restaurant* (☎ 36 91 56), on Çekirge Caddesi to the right of the Ada Palas Hotel. Plain white walls, white tablecloths, white plates – in short, very simple surroundings. But the food is fine and the prices fairly low, at US$5 or US$6 for a full meal.

Markets The Tahtakale Çarşısı is the nicest and most convenient market area in central Bursa. Walk west from the Ulu Cami along Atatürk Caddesi to the subway (pedestrian underpass) named Yıldırım Beyazıt

Altgeçidi. From the south end of the subway, go left or right a few steps, then south along a narrow street to the market area.

Cafés *Café Koza*, above the Koza Park on Atatürk Caddesi near the Ulu Cami is Bursa's central people-watching place, but it's not cheap. A simple tea costs 60c, coffee twice as much.

Tora Café-Bar is at Setbaşı, the place 2½ short blocks east of Heykel where Namazgah Caddesi crosses the Gök Deresi gorge. Enter the Setbaşı Pasajı on the north side of the road and take the stairs on the right side down to the bar, which has a small terrace overlooking the gorge. Alcohol is served.

Entertainment

Bursa's equivalent of İstanbul's Kumkapı district is Sakarya Caddesi, a small street lined with small restaurants and wineshops, some of them serving fish. The street is on the north side of the Hisar district, just south of Altıparmak Caddesi. To find it, take a bus or dolmuş from Heykel bound for Çekirge and get out at the Çatal Fırın bus stop across from the Sabahettin Paşa Camii. Cross to the south side of Altıparmak Caddesi and walk west into Sakarya Caddesi.

This was once the main street of Bursa's Jewish quarter, which throve from 1492 until recent times. There are still several operating synagogues on the street, most notably the 500-year-old Geruş Havrası (visits by special arrangement only).

Among Sakarya Caddesi's most famous restaurants is *Arap Şükrü*, which now has several outlets here. For wine only, try the *Misi Wine Shop*, famous for the vintages brought from a village in the Bursa hinterland.

Things to Buy

I've already mentioned those Bursa exclusives, silk cloth (especially scarves), hand-knitted woollen mittens, gloves and socks, Karagöz shadow-puppets and candied chestnuts. Other good items are thick Bursa Turkish towels (some say they were invented

here, for those taking the waters). If you have lots of room in your luggage, buy a *bornoz*, a huge thick, heavy terry-cloth bathrobe.

Getting There & Away

The best way to reach Bursa is by ferry and bus. There is limited air service. The railway line bypasses Bursa to the east, going between Adapazarı, Bozüyük and Eskisehir.

Air Two small airlines link Bursa with İstanbul and Ankara. Both have ticket offices in the Çakırhamam district just off Cemal Nadir Caddesi, a few minutes' stroll west of the Ulu Cami.

Türk Hava Taşımacılığı (THT; ☎ (24) 21 11 67, 21 28 38), Temiz Caddesi 16/B, Çakırhamam, operates nonstop flights to and from İstanbul and Ankara on Tuesday and Thursday; the Ankara flight continues to Şanlıurfa. Walk west on Atatürk Caddesi and when it veers to the right to become Cemal Nadir Caddesi, go left (south) on Temiz Caddesi.

Sönmez Holding Hava Yolları at Bursa's airport (☎ (24) 46 54 45); in İstanbul (☎ (1) 573 9323, 573 7240 ext 712) runs flights from Bursa to İstanbul at 8.30 am and 3 pm from Monday to Friday, and 9 am Saturday, for US$35 each way. Return flights from İstanbul to Bursa run at 9.30 am and 4 pm on weekdays, 10.30 am on Saturday; no flights on Sunday. In Bursa, tickets can be bought at Ottomantur (☎ (24) 21 00 99, 22 20 97; fax 21 89 48), Cemal Nadir Caddesi, Kızılay Pasajı, Çakırhamam. A bus departs from the Ottomantur office 45 minutes prior to flight time. Buy your tickets in İstanbul at the Moris Seyahat Agentalığı (☎ (1) 249 8510, -1; fax 251 7140), Tünel Pasajı 11, Beyoğlu, opposite the upper station of the little Tünel subway at the southern end of İstiklal Caddesi.

Bus For information on reaching Bursa from İstanbul or Yalova, see the previous Yalova section. For local transport, see the Getting Around section, which follows this one.

You will probably arrive in Bursa by bus or minibus from the ferry dock at Yalova, or from İznik. These services come into Bursa's otogar, officially called the Şehir Garajı.

When the time comes to leave Bursa, go to the otogar. The fastest way to İstanbul is to take a minibus to Yalova, then a hydrofoil to İstanbul's Kabataş docks. To do this, be sure to get a bus that departs at least 90 minutes before the scheduled hydrofoil or ferry departure. (See the Yalova section for details.)

If you plan to take a bus all the way to İstanbul, be careful when you buy your ticket. Buses designated *karayolu ile* (by road) take four hours and drag you all around the Bay of İzmit; those designated *feribot ile* take you to Topçular, east of Yalova, and drive aboard the car ferry to Eskihisar, a much quicker and more pleasant way to go. You must also determine whether your chosen bus terminates its journey at İstanbul's Harem bus station on the Asian shore, or at Topkapı bus station on the European shore (some buses stop at both).

For other destinations, buy your ticket in advance to ensure a good seat and departure time. Here are some routes from Bursa:

Afyon – 290 km, 4½ hours, US$9; eight buses daily
Ankara – 400 km, 5½ hours, US$11; hourly buses
Bandırma – 115 km, two hours, US$3.75; 12 buses daily
Çanakkale (for Troy and Gallipoli) – 310 km, five hours, US$9; a dozen buses daily
Erdek – 135 km, 2¼ hours, US$4; three buses daily
Eskişehir – 155 km, 2½ hours, US$5.50; hourly buses
İstanbul – 230 km, four to five hours *karayolu ile* (by road) or 2½ hours *feribot ile* (by car ferry: 135 km by road plus 25 minutes by sea), US$7.50 to US$9; hourly buses
İzmir – 375 km, six hours, US$5; hourly buses
İznik – 82 km, 1½ hours, US$1.50 to US$2; hourly buses until 6 or 7 pm
Kütahya – 200 km, three hours, US$7; several buses daily
Yalova – 60 km, 70 minutes, US$2.75; minibuses every 30 minutes (see the Yalova section)

Getting Around

Bus Station Transport In front of Bursa's Şehir Garajı is a big street named Kıbrıs Şehitler Caddesi; a few metres west of the bus station it intersects with Fevzi Çakmak Caddesi. Here you will find dolmuşes, taxis

and city buses. For the city buses, you will need to buy a 35c ticket *before* you board the bus. Look for the ticket kiosk. Bus No 18 goes from the Garaj via Heykel to Emir Sultan.

You will most likely be looking for transport to the centre of town and its hotels, or to the hotels at Çekirge. To reach Heykel, walk out the front door of the otogar, cross the street, and look for the rank of cars filling up with people; most of these dolmuşes bear rooftop signs for Heykel (40c). To get to the Ulu Cami and Tahtakale/İnebey from the otogar, go out the door, turn right, cross Fevzi Çakmak Caddesi and catch a bus or dolmuş heading south up the slope. Most will pass the Ulu Cami (ask for OO-loo JAH-mee).

City Buses Bursa's city buses (35c) are useful and go to many sites you'll want to reach, but do not necessarily show signs indicating the places you may be going. Here are translations followed by descriptions of the bus routes:

Catch a bus marked...	to get to...
Devlet Hastanesi (Dev. Hst)	Hisar, Orhan Gazi & Osman Gazi tombs
Emir Sultan	Yeşil Cami, Emir Sultan
Muradiye	Hisar, Muradiye
Ş. Garaj	Şehir Garajı (bus station)
Sigorta	Kültür Parkı, Eski Kaplıca baths
SSK Hast(anesi)	Kültür Parkı, Çekirge
Yeşil	Heykel, Setbaşı, Yeşil Cami

Bus No 1
    travels the entire 'tourist route' through the city from Emir Sultan via Heykel and the Kültür Parkı to Çekirge and back
Bus No 1-A
    travels between Muradiye and Heykel
Bus No 3 (3-A, 3-B, 3-C etc)
    go to and from the Teleferik, the cable car up Uludağ
Bus No 18
    travels between Heykel and Emir Sultan

Dolmuş In Bursa, sedans operate as dolmuşes along with the minibuses. The destination is indicated by the illuminated sign on the roof. The minimum fare is 40c.

From Heykel, dolmuşes depart for most parts of the city. See the map of central Bursa for routes and departure points. Other useful routes are mentioned previously in the text.

Taxis As everywhere in Turkey, taxis are readily available and not wildly expensive. In Bursa, a ride halfway across the city from the bus station to Heykel, Muradiye or Tahtakale costs less than US$2.

ULUDAĞ

In the ancient world, a number of mountains bore the name 'Olympus'. Uludağ (Great Mountain) was on the outskirts of the ancient city of Bithynia (now Bursa), so this was the Bithynian Olympus.

The gods no longer live on top of Uludağ, but there is a cable car *(teleferik)*, a selection of hotels, a national park, cool forests and often snow. Even if you don't plan to hike to the summit (three hours each way from the hotel zone) or to go skiing (in winter only), you might want to take the cable car up for the view and a draught of the cool, fresh air. You can also reach the top by dolmuş.

Skiing

Though a fairly sleepy place in summer, the hotel and ski area on Uludağ comes to life during the ski season from late December to March. Hotels have equipment to rent: boots and skis cost about US$8 per day. Each hotel also has its own ski lift, so when you buy a day pass, you are buying it for that lift alone. If you want to try other slopes, buy only a few rides on any particular lift.

Places to Stay

More than a dozen inns and hotels are scattered about the mountaintop. All are meant for skiers, so they close for much of the year. A few places stay open all the time, though they have little business in summer unless they can schedule a commercial meeting.

Among the better places to stay is the 80-room, three-star *Beceren Hotel* (BEH-jeh-REHN) (☎ (2418) 1111; fax 1119). For US$40 a double you get a room with bath and satellite TV. For US$60 two people can

have a room and all three meals in summer. Prices almost double in winter, but all three meals are included.

Hotel Aylin Yalçın, farthest up the road on the right, offers good value during the ski season. Rooms and meals are simple but acceptable, and the price is US$75 a double, meals included.

Of the other hotels, the two-star, 100-room *Büyük Otel* (☎ (2418) 1216; fax 1220) is a traditional favourite. It's an older place with small rooms, with showers or baths, renting for US$40/55 a single/double in winter, with breakfast and dinner included; prices are lower in summer, of course.

The four-star status address on the mountain is the *Grand Hotel Yazıcı* (YAH-zuh-juh) (☎ (2418) 1050; fax 1048), where a lot of the status is in the lobby, the minds of the staff and the prices: US$75/100 a single/double, for one of the 162 rooms with shower, minibar, satellite TV and hair dryer.

Getting There & Away

Cable Car For a summer visit to Uludağ, getting there is most of the fun. Take a Bursa city bus (3, 3-A, 3-B, 3-C etc), a dolmuş from Heykel, or a taxi to the lower terminus of the teleferik (cable car), called Teleferuç (☎ 21 36 35) – a 15-minute ride from Heykel at the city's eastern edge. In summer when crowds abound, the cable cars depart when full or at least every 30 to 45 minutes, weather and winds permitting. The trip to the top takes about 30 minutes and the trip costs US$4 each way.

The cable car stops at an intermediate point named Kadıyayla, from whence you continue upward to the terminus at Sarıalan (sah-RUH-ah-lahn) at an altitude of 1635 metres. From Sarıalan, there is a smaller ski lift *(telekabin)* which runs to Çobankaya, but it's not worth the time or money.

At Sarıalan there are a few snack and refreshment stands, a national-park camping area (always full, it seems), some walking trails *(patika)* and the occasional dolmuş to the hotel zone (called the *Oteller Mevkii)*, six km farther up the mountain slope. That's all there is to do, except enjoy the scenery.

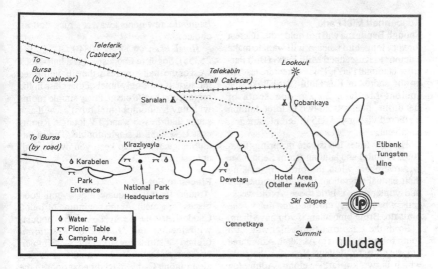

Dolmuş Dolmuşes depart from Bursa's otogar to the hotel zone on Uludağ several times daily in summer, more frequently in winter, for about US$6 each way, which is more than the cable car. On the winding, 22-km trip you pass the İnkaya Çınarı, a gigantic ancient plane tree about three km beyond Çekirge. The tree, set in a little park, is said to have been alive when the Ottomans conquered Bursa in 1326.

At the 11 km marker you must stop and pay an entry fee for the national park of 50 c per person, US$1.50 for a car and driver. The hotel zone is 11 km farther up from the national park entrance. Almost half of the entire 22 km is on rough granite-block pavement.

The return ride can be difficult in summer as there are few dolmuşes or taxis in evidence. In winter there are usually plenty, and they are eager to get at least some fare before they head back down, so you may be able to get back to Bursa for less – haggle.

BANDIRMA

The port town of Bandırma with 80,000 residents has an ancient history, but nothing to show for it. What you see is a 20th-century creation which might well be nicknamed *Betonbol* (Concreteville). It has little to offer the tourist except the junction between the İzmir to Bandırma rail line and the Bandırma to İstanbul ferry line. You'd do well to pass straight through, but if you must stop, there are hotels and restaurants enough.

Orientation

Bandırma's bus station is several km southeast of the centre, out by the main highway; get a servis arabası (shuttle bus) to reach the centre. (There is a separate, small bus station west of the centre for buses to Erdek and Gönen.)

If you arrive by train or boat, walk east for one km to reach the main square.

From the main square, the main road going east is İnönü Caddesi, which has most of the services you may want, including cheap hotels and restaurants, and bus ticket offices. The Kamil Koç ticket office is right across from the Hotel Marmara. Behind it down the side street are several others, including As Turizm, Uludağ, Doğan Körfez, and Yılmaz.

Kuşcenneti Milli Parkı

Though Bandırma will not hold your interest for very long, bird fanciers will want to make a detour to Kuşcenneti Milli Parkı (Bird Paradise National Park). This 64-hectare reserve on the shores of Kuş Gölü (Bird Lake, the ancient Manias), 20 km due south of Bandırma, boasts from two to three million feathered visitors, of 255 different varieties, each year.

The best times to visit are in spring (from April to June) and autumn (from September to November) when the birds are making their annual migration. In high summer and mid-winter there is little to see. Avoid weekends, when it's very crowded and noisy – the birds do. Bring binoculars if you have them.

From the Bandırma-Bursa highway, turn south following signs to Aksakal. After three km, turn west following signs for the park, which is two km farther along. Admission costs 75c (half-price for students).

The Visitors Centre has exhibits – reminiscent of 19th-century natural history museums – of stuffed birds in simulated habitats. From the centre, walk along the *patika* (path) to the observation tower for the view over the lake.

No camping or picnicking is permitted. For lodgings, try the simple *Gölbaşı Pension-Restaurant*, one km to the south in the village of Sığırcıatik.

Places to Stay

There are several cheap hotels on and east of the main square on İnönü Caddesi. Facing the square is the *Sahil Hotel* (☎ (198) 14485, -6), İnönü Caddesi 10, a simple and convenient place favoured by Turkish businessmen. It is proper, has a lift, and offers rooms for US$7/9 a single/double with sink, US$12/14 a single/double with private shower.

Farther east, the *Marmara Otel* (☎ (198) 22080), İnönü Caddesi 44, is simpler and cheaper.

Özdil Hotel (☎ (198) 12200), east of the square near the water, facing the Haydar Çavuş Camii, is quieter as it is off the main street. Rates are about the same. *Otel İstanbul* a few doors away is a rock-bottom choice.

Hotel Eken (☎ (198) 10840, -1, -2; fax 25355), Soğuksu Caddesi 11, is a half-block west of the main square up the hill: you'll see the sign. It's the only hotel of this class in the region, and has 78 clean, fairly simple rooms with tiny bathrooms (mini-tubs),as well as a sauna, hairdresser's and TV lounge. Rooms cost US$30/38 a single/double. The nightclub is guaranteed to keep you awake until at least midnight.

Places to Eat

Around the main square are several good places for a meal. At the beginning of İnönü Caddesi, try the *Saray Lokantası* (popular with locals) and *Moby Dick Restaurant* (aimed at attracting foreigners). Simpler, cheaper places are to be found farther east along İnönü Caddesi. Right next door to the Özdil Hotel is the *Mercan Tandır Kebap & Izgara Salonu*, specialising in tandır kebap, a stew of meat and vegetables baked in an earthenware crock.

Getting There & Away

For information on the *Marmara Ekspresi*, the train/boat connection between İstanbul and İzmir, see the Getting Around chapter at the front of this book under Train.

Bandırma is midway on the run between Bursa (115 km, two hours, US$3.75; 12 buses daily) and Çanakkale (195 km, three hours, US$5.75;12 buses daily). There are also buses southward to Balıkesir and points beyond. For route, schedule and fare information, ask at the otogar, or at the bus-company ticket offices on İnönü Caddesi.

For information on the cities south of Bursa and Bandırma, see the Aegean Turkey chapter under Aegean Hinterland.

The Dardanelles

A tremendous amount of world commerce depends on sea travel. Since commerce means wealth and wealth means power, the people who control the sea have enormous commercial – not to mention military – power. The best place for a small group of people to control a lot of sea is at a strait.

The name 'Dardanelles' comes from Dardanus, ruler of a very early city-state at Çanakkale, who controlled the straits. The story of the Dardanelles (Çanakkale Boğazı in Turkish) is one of people battling each another for control of this narrow passage which unites the Mediterranean and Aegean seas with the Marmara and Black seas. In ancient times it was the Achaeans attacking the Trojans; in modern times the Anzacs facing Mustafa Kemal (Atatürk) at Gallipoli.

The story of the Dardanelles is not all war and commerce; romance, too, has been central to its mythical associations: legend says that the goddess Helle fell from a golden-winged ram into the water here, giving the straits the name of Hellespont. The lovesick Leander, separated from his beloved Hero, swam to her through the fierce currents each night, until one night he didn't make it. 'Swimming the Hellespont' is a challenge for amateur and professional swimmers to this day.

The height of romance is the story of two ancient peoples battling over the love and honour of Helen, the most beautiful woman in the world. Historians now tell us that Helen was just a pawn in the fierce commercial and military rivalries between Achaea and Troy. Still, no one says she wasn't beautiful, or that the Trojan horse didn't actually fool the Trojans and lead to their defeat by the Achaeans.

In Ottoman times, Çanakkale saw the birth of Piri Reis, the famous Ottoman cartographer who compiled a surprisingly accurate map of the New World from various sources.

The area of the straits holds these attractions: the town of Çanakkale, a fast-growing agricultural centre on the south-east shore; the fortifications, ancient and modern, which guarded the straits; the battlefields of Gallipoli on the north-west side of the straits; and the excavated ruins of ancient Troy (Truva) 32 km to the south. You can make your base at the town of Gelibolu on the Gallipoli peninsula, but Çanakkale has more facilities.

As you approach from Bandırma, you pass the car-ferry docks at Lapseki, 33 km north-east of Çanakkale. For ferry schedules and information, see Gelibolu in the Gallipoli Peninsula section.

ÇANAKKALE
Orientation

The heart of Çanakkale (population 55,000) is its docks, and the town has grown from the docks inland. An Ottoman clock tower, the town's symbol, stands just west of the docks, and makes a convenient landmark for hotel searches. Hotels, restaurants, banks and bus ticket offices are within an easy walk of the docks if your luggage is not too heavy. The otogar is one km from the docks, the dolmuş stop for Troy is also one km; the Archaeology Museum just over two km.

From the otogar, turn left, walk to the first turning to the right and follow signs straight to the 'Feribot'. Just before you come to the docks you'll see the vaguely Teutonic clock tower, Saat Kulesi, on your left. To reach the market area (çarşı), walk behind the clock tower and turn into one of the streets on the left-hand side.

The Tarihi Yalı Hamamı (Turkish bath) is a few short blocks south of the clock tower (see the Central Çanakkale map).

Information

The town's Tourism Information Office (☎ (196) 71187) is in a little booth near the quay, between the clock tower and the ferry docks. Çanakkale's postal code is 17100.

Cannon Monument

In the broad main street in the town's centre is a monument constructed of old WW I cannons. The words on the plaque translate

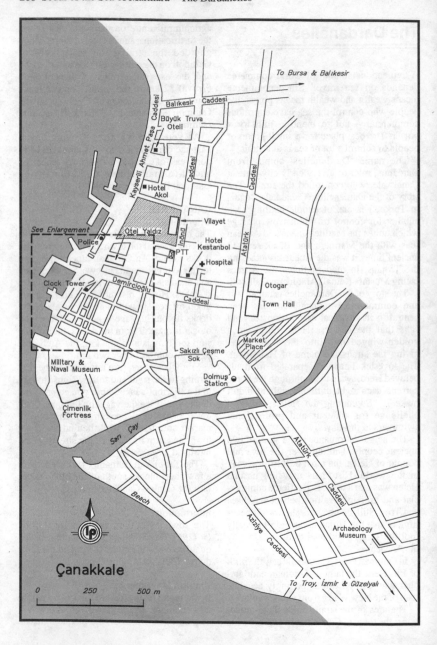

To Bursa & Balıkesir

Balıkesir Caddesi

Kayserili Ahmet Paşa Caddesi

Büyük Truva Oteli

Caddesi

Atatürk Caddesi

Hotel Akol

See Enlargement

Vilayet

Otel Yaldız

İnönü

Hotel Kestanbol

Police

PTT

Hospital

Clock Tower

Demircioğlu

Otogar

Town Hall

Caddesi

Market Place

Sakızlı Çeşme Sok

Military & Naval Museum

Dolmuş Station

Çimenlik Fortress

Sarı Çay

Atatürk Caddesi

Beach

Aziziye Caddesi

Archaeology Museum

Çanakkale

0   250   500 m

To Troy, İzmir & Güzelyalı

as 'Turkish soldiers used these cannons on 18 March 1915 to ensure the impassability of the Çanakkale strait'.

Military & Naval Museum

There is an interesting Military & Naval Museum (Askeri ve Deniz Müzesi) in the Military Zone at the southern end of the quay, open from 9 am to noon and from 1.30 to 5 pm; admission is free. It's supposedly closed on Monday and Thursday, but I visited on a Thursday with no problem. The nice lawns and gardens are open for strolling until 10 pm. Start from the ferry docks and walk along the quay to the zone and its fortress. If you walk inland, the zone is two blocks beyond the Hotel Konak.

You'll see a mock-up of the old minelayer *Nusrat*, which had a heroic role in the Gallipoli campaign. The day before the Allied fleet was to steam through the straits, Allied minesweepers proclaimed the water cleared. At night the *Nusrat* went out, picked up loose mines and relaid them, helping to keep the Allies from penetrating the straits the next day.

There's also a small museum with memorabilia of Atatürk and the battles of Gallipoli.

The impressive fortress, built by Mehmet the Conqueror in the mid-1400s, is still considered active in the defence of the straits. So it is forbidden to climb to the top of the walls or keep, but you're free to examine the wonderful old cannons left from various wars; many were made in French, English and German foundries. The keep is now a gallery with changing exhibits.

Archaeology Museum

Çanakkale's Archaeology Museum (Arkeoloji Müzesi) is on the southern outskirts of town, just over two km south-east of the clock tower, on the road to Troy. Opening hours are from 10 am to 5 pm, closed on Monday. Admission costs US$1. City buses (to İntepe or Güzelyalı) and dolmuşes (same destinations) run past the museum from the centre of town.

The museum's exhibits are arranged chronologically, starting with prehistoric fossils and continuing with Bronze Age and later artefacts. Perhaps the most interesting exhibits are those from Troy, labelled (in Turkish and English) by 'city', that is: Troy I, Troy II etc; and the exhibits from Dardanos, the ancient town near Çanakkale. Don't miss the glass case of bone pins and small implements near the exit.

Gallipoli Tours

Several companies run tours of the Gallipoli battlefields (see the Gallipoli Peninsula section, following). Tours include car or minibus, driver and guide and cost from US$10 to US$20 per person, depending upon the company and the number of people signed up to go.

The longtime favourite is Troy-Anzac Tours (☎ (196) 75047, 75049), Saat Kulesi Yanı 2, Çanakkale, near the clock tower. A newer company which readers of this guide have found good is Ana-Tur (☎ (196) 75482; fax 72906), Cumhuriyet Meydani, Özay İşhanı, Kat 3, No 3, which also markets its tours through the Otel Meydan (Anzac House) on Çanakkale's main square.

Whichever tour you take, before you tour drop in at Anzac House for the daily viewing of a video about the Gallipoli campaign, and a screening of the movie *Gallipoli*, which really helps you to understand the campaign and the terrain.

Festivals

The great battles of Gallipoli are commemorated each year during March (usually from 12 to 19 March), with the biggest celebrations being on 18 March, 'Victory Day', the anniversary of the great naval battle which began the Gallipoli campaign. Australian, British, French and New Zealand representatives usually take part. Hotels, particularly the better ones, are often full during the ceremonies.

For a week in mid-August, the Çanakkale Festival also fills the hotels in town. If you plan to be there then, arrive early in the day and start your search for a hotel room at once.

Places to Stay

Çanakkale has a good, if small, selection of hotels in all price ranges. There are also comfortable hotels in a seaside setting at Güzelyalı on the road to Troy, and a few small places in the village of Tevfikiye right next to the ruins of Troy.

Places to Stay – bottom end

The hotels in the centre of town are clustered near the clock tower. Perhaps the most friendly place is the *Otel Meydan* (☎ (196) 70156, 71392), Cumhuriyet Meydanı 61, better known as Anzac House (not to be confused with the Anzac Hotel), facing the main square (on the right-hand side as you walk from the docks, past the clock tower). Noisy, ramshackle and somewhat disorderly, it is nonetheless the lodging of choice for many backpackers because of its congenial atmosphere. Hanifi, the proprietor, provides Vegemite breakfasts for his guests from Oz, and can sign you up for Ana-Tur's Gallipoli tours. Waterless rooms cost US$6 a double. Even if you don't stay here, come for the showings of the documentary and film *Gallipoli* each evening.

Hotel Erdem and *Hotel Hülya*, on either side of Anzac House, take the overflow, but there are quieter and better places around the corner behind the clock tower in the neighbourhood called Kemal Paşa Mahallesi. There are numerous cheap places to stay here, including the quaint old brick *Hotel Kervansaray*, Fetvahane Sokak 13, just behind the clock tower, the 200-year-old former home of a Turkish paşa. It has a delightful garden with a fountain, cooking facilities you can use, and rooms for US$5/7 a single/double without running water, or US$14 a triple with shower.

Hotel Efes (☎ (196) 73256), farther west along Fetvahane Sokak at Aralık Sokak 5, is a similar place: good and cheap, kept clean and airy by an energetic woman. Waterless doubles cost US$7, or US$10 with shower. *Hotel Akgün* (☎ (196) 73049), across the street from the Efes, is similar.

Hotel Konak (koh-NAHK) (☎ (196) 71150), Fetvahane Sokak, boasts central heating, constant hot water and prices of US$8 a double with sink, or US$12.50 a double with private shower.

For a clean, friendly family pension, the place to go is the *Avrupa Pansiyon* (☎ (196) 74084), Matbaa Sokak 8, past the Hotel Kervansaray a bit further on from the clock tower. It's quiet here, as the pension is on a block-long side street. It is run by Mehmet Özcan's family; it's clean and safe, and you can use the kitchen. Rooms cost US$6/9/12 a single/double/triple, or US$8/12/14 with private shower. Breakfast costs extra. If the Avrupa is full, try the *Hotel Fatih*, directly opposite, which shares the advantage of the quiet location.

Yellow Rose Pension Yetimoğlu (☎ (196) 73343), Yeni Sokak 5, 50 metres south-east of the clock tower, is an altogether tidier and nicer place to stay. Operated by Osman Yetimoğlu, it is an accommodating house with a quiet garden, washing machine and kitchen for guests' use, English-language TV, and flyscreens on the windows. Prices are US$8/12 a single/double with bath.

Koç Pansiyon (☎ (196) 70121), Kızılay Sokak, on the south-east side of the Hotel Yaldız, is tiny, neat, quiet, and priced at US$14 a double with shower.

Güzelyalı This seaside resort suburb has numerous little pensions patronised mostly by Turkish families on holiday. *Yalı Pansiyon* in the centre is nice, and right on the water; *Pınar Pansiyon* on 10. Sokak is near the İris Otel. The price for either is US$12 a double with shared bath.

Camping There are several small camping places 16 km from Çanakkale along the Troy road at Güzelyalı, including *Truva Mocamp* and *Pinna Camping*. There are also a few across the straits in the Gallipoli National Historic Park (see that section).

Places to Stay – middle

Çanakkale You can't miss the three-star, 70-room *Otel Anafartalar* (☎ (196) 74454, -5, -6; fax 74457), İskele Meydanı, on the north side of the ferry docks. The front rooms in this seven-floor structure have good views of the water and cost US$28/36 a single/double with bath. The hotel has a pleasant restaurant on its roof, and a supremely convenient location.

Anzac Hotel (☎ (196) 77777, 72017; fax 72018), Saat Kulesi Meydanı 8, very near the clock tower, is a newish, modern building with 27 rooms, all with showers (some with tubs) going for US$14/20 a single/double – great value, comfortable rooms, prime location.

Büyük Truva Oteli (☎ (196) 71024, 71886; fax 70903), Kayserili Ahmet Paşa Caddesi, Yalıboyu, is a special two-star place as it is owned and operated by a hotel training school. Most of the staff are students for whom serving you well means good grades in class, so the service is careful, if perhaps a bit earnest. The 66 rooms are comfortable without being fancy; some in the older front section have sea views, while the ones at the back are newer. Rates are from US$23 to US$27 a single, US$30 to US$36 a double, breakfast included. Higher-priced rooms have bathrooms, with tub and shower, while lower-priced rooms have shower alone. The hotel is a short 200-metre walk north-east of the main square, along the waterfront.

The one-star, 35-room *Hotel Bakır* (bah-KUHR) (☎ (196) 72908, 74088, -9; fax 74090), Rıhtım Caddesi 12 (also called Yalı Caddesi), is very near the clock tower. A clean if old and well-used room with bath and view of the straits, breakfast included, costs US$12/20/28 a single/double/triple. Note that the Kilitbahir ferry leaves from in front of the hotel, making noise periodically all night. Rooms on the landward side are quieter and a bit cheaper.

Just a block from the ferry docks is the one-star, 33-room *Otel Yaldız* (☎ (196) 71793, 71069), Kızılay Sokak 20, on a quiet side street. It is a comfortable enough place renting rooms with private shower for US$18 with a double bed, US$21 with twin beds. A restaurant, bar, a lift and several English-speaking staff make your stay pleasant here. To find the hotel, get to the front door of the Hotel Anafartalar, walk out that door and head straight down the side street and you'll see it.

Otel Kestanbol (☎ (196) 70857, 79173), Hasan Mevsuf Sokak 5, inland a few blocks and across the street from the Emniyet Sarayı (police station), is a modern place with 26 rooms, all with bath, costing US$24 a double with breakfast. It's quiet and proper, with a rooftop bar that's pleasant on summer evenings.

The fanciest of the town's lodgings is the new *Hotel Akol* (☎ (196) 79456; fax 72897), Kordonboyu, a four-star place with 129 rooms. It's often filled by tour groups. The very comfy rooms with bath go for US$35/50 a single/double. Services include a swimming pool, several restaurants and bars, a disco, and satellite TV (with CNN) in guest rooms.

Güzelyalı This seaside suburb, 16 km south-west of Çanakkale, has a number of hotels, pensions and camping grounds. Only someone with a car would be interested in staying here, however. To get here, leave Çanakkale by the road to Truva, drive about 14 km and take the turning for Güzelyalı.

Tusan Hotel (☎ (1973) 8210; fax 8226), Güzelyalı Mevkii, in a pine forest, has views of the straits and the ambience of a small, quiet retreat. Its 64 rooms are priced at US$38 a double with shower and breakfast, which is a bit expensive. The hotel closes between November and March. Follow the motel's signs for about 2.5 km after you turn off the Truva road.

İris Otel (☎ (1973) 8100; fax 8028) is the big new three-star place favoured by tour groups, with its 74 comfortable rooms and big swimming pool. Rates are US$30/40 a single/double, breakfast included. It's open all winter.

Places to Eat – bottom end

Çanakkale has inexpensive places to eat throughout town. Right by the clock tower is the clean, bright, friendly and convenient *Meydan Restaurant* (☎ (196) 72703), where I had lentil soup, yoghurt, bread and water for less than US$2.

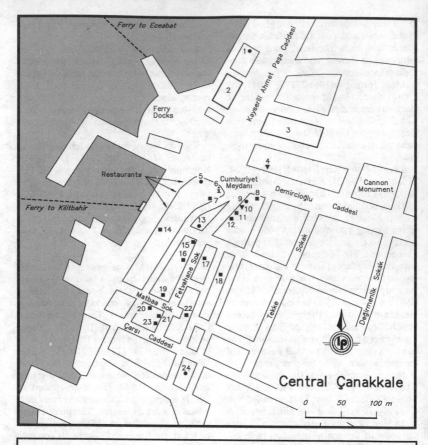

Central Çanakkale

0   50   100 m

PLACES TO STAY

2   Otel Anafartalar
3   Otel Yaldız
7   Aras Oteli
8   Otel Meydan (Anzac House)
11 Hotel Anzac
12 Hotel Erdem
14 Hotel Bakır
15 Küçük Truva Oteli
16 Hotel Konak
17 Hotel Kervansaray
18 Yellow Rose Pension Yetimoğlu
19 Hotel Fatih
20 Avrupa Pansiyon
21 Hotel Can

22 Hotel Efes
23 Hotel Akgün

PLACES TO EAT

4   Trakya Restaurant
10 Meydan Restaurant

OTHER

1   Police
5   Çanakkale Bus Office
6   Tourism Information Office
9   Yılmaz & Kâmil Koç Bus Offices
13 Clock Tower
24 Tarihi Yalı Hamamı

For even cheaper food, head inland along the main street or past the clock tower until you see a köfteci or pideci shop. At a pideci, fresh flat pide bread is topped with such things as whole eggs, cheese or minced lamb, dabbed with butter, then baked. It's filling, delicious and very cheap. The price depends on the toppings. Ask for pide yumurtalı, peynirli or kıymalı.

Gaziantep Aile Kebap ve Pide Salonu, good for kebaps, is a few steps behind the clock tower. A meal of soup, pide or köfte, bread and a soft drink should cost about US$3.75.

Anzac House Café in the Otel Meydan is the favourite gathering-place of the young and adventurous, featuring Vegemite breakfasts, Nescafé, and cheap meals all day long.

Across the square from Anzac House, *Trakya Restaurant* (☎ (196) 77257) is bright and cheerful, always with a big selection of ready food in the steam tables. It's supposedly open 24 hours a day.

Places to Eat – middle range

The most enjoyable places to dine are those right along the quay to the left of the ferry docks as you face the water. *Rıhtım* is one place of long-standing, as is *Bizim Entellektüel* (Our Intellectuals' Restaurant), and *Yalova Liman Restaurant*; the last has a 3rd-floor patio with a fine view of the straits and of Kilitbahir fortress on the opposite shore. A meal of an appetiser, fried or grilled fish, salad and a bottle of beer might cost from US$8 to US$12. Be sure to ask prices, as bill-fiddling is a tradition at these places.

For similar food in fancier surroundings, try the dining rooms in the Büyük Truva and Akol hotels.

Getting There & Away

Bus Çanakkale's otogar is one km east of the ferry docks and clock tower. Walk straight inland from the docks and when you must turn, turn left; the otogar is 100 metres or so along, on the right. For transport to Troy (30 km), see that section, following.

You can buy bus tickets at the otogar, or at the bus company offices on the main street in the centre of Çanakkale near the ferry docks.

For information on buses to, from and around Gallipoli, see the Gallipoli Peninsula section. Details of some daily bus services from Çanakkale follow:

Ankara – 700 km, 12 hours, US$15; several buses
Behramkale (Assos) – 100 km, two hours (or more, depending upon dolmuşes), US$5; many buses; change to dolmuş at Ayvacık
Ayvalık – 200 km, 3½ hours, US$7; many buses
Bandırma – 195 km, three hours, US$5.75;12 buses
Bursa – 310 km, five hours, US$9; a dozen buses
Edirne – 230 km, 3½ hours, US$7; five direct buses, or change at Keşan
Gelibolu – 49 km plus ferry ride, less than two hours, US$3: take a bus or minibus north-east to the Lapseki-Gelibolu ferry or take the ferry to Eceabat or Kilitbahir and then the minibus to Gelibolu
Lapseki – 33 km, 45 minutes, US$1; take a Gönen, Bandırma or Bursa-bound bus, but make sure you'll be allowed to get off at Lapseki
İstanbul – 340 km, six hours, US$8 to US$11; 12 buses
İzmir – 340 km, six hours, US$10; many buses

Boat Two ferries serve Çanakkale, connecting it with Kilitbahir and Eceabat; both carry cars as well as passengers. For information on the Gelibolu-Lapseki car ferry, see Gelibolu in the Gallipoli Peninsula section.

The Çanakkale-Eceabat car ferries are large vessels which take about 25 minutes to cross in good weather. From 6 am to 11 pm boats run in each direction every hour on the hour. There are also boats at midnight and 2 and 4 am from Eceabat and at 1, 3 and 5 am from Çanakkale. Fares are 40c per person, US$10 per car.

The Çanakkale-Kilitbahir ferry is a much more modest affair, a small boat which takes mostly passengers but manages to take a handful of cars aboard as well. It departs from in front of the Hotel Bakır, to the south-west of the main docks, by the Rıhtım and Bizim Entellektüel restaurants. There is only one boat, and if it is not in port there is nothing to mark its departure point, so just wait by the hotel. It runs an irregular schedule, but crosses in only 15 minutes for fares lower than the big boat to Eceabat.

GALLIPOLI PENINSULA

The slender peninsula which forms the north-western side of the straits, across the water from Çanakkale, is called Gelibolu in Turkish. For a millennium it has been the key to İstanbul: the navy that could force the straits had a good chance of capturing the capital of the Eastern world. Many fleets have tried to force the straits. Most, including the mighty Allied fleet mustered in WW I, have failed.

Since Byzantine times the straits have been well defended. The Ottomans maintained four pairs of fortresses: Seddülbahir and Kumkale at the southern end of the straits; Çamburun and Karaburun, and Bigali and Nara within the straits; Bozcaada on the island at the southern mouth; Çimenlik in the town of Çanakkale, and Kilitbahir, the 'Lock on the Sea', on the Gallipoli side across from Çanakkale.

On the hillside by Kilitbahir, clearly visible from Çanakkale on the far shore, are gigantic letters spelling out the first few words of a poem by Necmettin Halil Onan commemorating the momentous 1915 struggle for Gallipoli:

Dur yolcu! Bilmeden gelip bastığın
bu toprak bir devrin battığı yerdir.
Eğil de kulak ver, bu sessiz yığın
bir vatan kalbinin attığı yerdir.

Traveller, halt! The soil you tread
once witnessed the end of an era.
Listen! In this quiet mound
there once beat the heart of a nation.

History

With the intention of capturing the Ottoman capital and the road to Eastern Europe during WW I, Winston Churchill, British First Lord of the Admiralty, organised a naval assault on the straits. A strong Franco-British fleet tried first to force them in March 1915 but failed. Then, in April, British, Australian, New Zealand and Indian troops were landed on Gallipoli, and French troops near Çanakkale. Both Turkish and Allied troops fought desperately and fearlessly, and devastated one another. After nine months of ferocious combat but little progress, the Allied forces were withdrawn.

The Turkish success at Gallipoli was partly due to bad luck and bad leadership on the Allied side, and partly due to the timely provision of reinforcements coming to the aid of the Turkish side under the command of General Liman von Sanders. But a crucial element in the defeat was that the Allied troops happened to land in a sector where they faced Lieutenant-Colonel Mustafa Kemal (Atatürk).

Though a relatively minor officer, he had General von Sanders' confidence. He guessed the Allied battle plan correctly when his commanders did not, and stalled the invasion by bitter fighting which wiped out his division. Though suffering from malaria, he commanded in full view of his troops and of the enemy, and miraculously escaped death several times. At one point a piece of shrapnel tore through the breast pocket of his uniform, but was stopped by his pocket watch (now in the Çanakkale Military & Naval Museum). His brilliant performance made him a folk hero and paved the way for his promotion to pasha (general).

The Gallipoli campaign lasted for nine months, until January 1916, and resulted in huge numbers of casualties on both sides. The British Empire suffered over 200,000 casualties, with the loss of some 36,000 lives.

French casualties of 47,000 were over half of the entire French contingent. Of the half-million Turkish troops who participated in the battle, one out of every two became a casualty, with more than 55,000 dead. There are now 31 war cemeteries on the peninsula, as well as several important monuments.

Orientation

Gallipoli is a fairly large area to tour, especially without your own transport. It's over 35 km as the crow flies from the northernmost battlefield to the southern tip of the peninsula. The towns of Eceabat and Gelibolu are 45 km apart.

Ferries run from Çanakkale across the Dardanelles to Kilitbahir and Eceabat (see

Getting There & Away in the Çanakkale section for details).

The principal battles took place on the western shore of the peninsula near Anzac Cove and Arıburnu, and in the hills just to the east. Anzac Cove is about 12 km from Eceabat, 19 km from Kilitbahir. If your time is limited or if you're touring by public transport, head for these places first.

Transport & Tours

With your own transport you can tour the battlefields easily in a day or less. Touring by public transport is possible, but dolmuşes serve only certain sites or nearby villages, and you must expect to do some waiting and walking. In summer, hitchhiking greatly facilitates getting around on your own, but in other seasons traffic may not be sufficient. The most important group of monuments and cemeteries, from Lone Pine uphill to Chunuk Bair, can be toured on foot, an excellent idea in fine weather.

Joining an organised tour is a good idea as you save time and trouble, and get the benefit of a guide who can relate the history and explain the battles. Some readers have complained that tours go too fast, and allow too little time at the beach, so you'd be well advised to talk with other travellers who have just taken a tour and find out what they recommend. Most tours include a picnic and some time at a Gallipoli beach for swimming. Tours are organised by several agencies in Çanakkale, and in the town of Gelibolu on the Gallipoli Peninsula. (See the sections on those towns for details.)

Gelibolu

Coming from Edirne or Keşan, or from İstanbul along the northern shore of the Sea of Marmara, the little town of Gelibolu (population 17,000) is a good place to look for transport or a bed.

Orientation As at Çanakkale, the centre of Gelibolu is right by the docks for the car ferry to and from Lapseki, and everything you may need is within 50 metres of here. The ruined stone tower which looms above the little ancient harbour is a remnant of the Byzantine town of Kallipolis, which gave the present town and the peninsula their names. The otogar is in the shadow of the tower.

Gallipoli Tours As you will see within minutes of arriving in Gelibolu, most of the town's touristic infrastructure is controlled by the Yılmaz family, who also run Yılmaz Tours and Yılmaz Taxi. Reserve a place on a tour of the Gallipoli battlefields through any of the Yılmaz hotels described below.

Places to Stay To find the hotels, walk off the ferry, go 50 metres straight ahead, then turn right and walk between the little harbour and the Byzantine stone tower.

About the cheapest beds in town are at the very basic *Ersöz Otell*, which charges US$6.50/7.50 a single/double in waterless rooms. *Hotel Yılmaz* (☎ (1891) 1256), a bit farther along, is newish and two-star comfortable but overpriced at US$20 for a double with private shower, breakfast included. The older *Pension Yılmaz* across the street (says 'Hotel Yılmaz' over the door) is a better deal at US$10 for a double with sink, breakfast included, but the pension is quite cheerless. The Yılmaz family also controls the *Motel Anzac* on the outskirts of the town.

Camping Obidi is 1.5 km from the bus station off the road south-west to Eceabat and Kilitbahir (follow the signs). It's on the shore in a military-industrial zone, and is fairly unappealing but will do for one night.

Places to Eat Amidst the hotels are several dozen restaurants, kebapçıs and büfes serving everything from stand-up snacks to white-tablecloth sit-down dinners with wine. Just east of the Hotel Yılmaz is the *Çakırlar Can Restaurant* with white tablecloths but moderate prices. To the left of that is the *İpek Urfa Kebap Salonu* for kebaps. Overlooking the ancient harbour, the *İmren, Sahil* and *Liman* restaurants have nice views, tables on the pavement, and fish menus (sardalya or fresh sardines are the local speciality).

Expect to spend from US$8 to US$12 here. The *Gelibolu Restaurant* is much fancier, with prices for full dinners ranging from US$12 to US$18.

Waiting for the ferry? Note that several of the cafés in the square have signs which read 'Ön iki sıra aileye mahsustur' (The front two rows of tables are reserved for ladies and families).

Getting There & Away Gelibolu's otogar is just inland from the ancient harbour. Dolmuşes or buses run hourly via Eceabat to Kilitbahir; there are ferries from both these towns to Çanakkale. To get to the Gallipoli battlefields, go to Eceabat, then look for a dolmuş (or hitch a ride) to Kabatepe. Details of services follow:

Balıkesir – change at Çanakkale

Bursa – change at Çanakkale

Çanakkale – 49 km plus ferry ride, less than two hours, US$3: take the Gelibolu-Lapseki ferry and catch a bus or minibus going to Çanakkale; or take the minibus to Eceabat or Kilitbahir and then the ferry to Çanakkale

Eceabat – 45 km, 50 minutes, US$1.75; hourly buses or minibuses

Edirne – three hours, US$7; three direct buses daily; or take one of the frequent buses to Keşan and change

İstanbul – 288 km, 4½ hours, US$6 to US$7.75; hourly buses from 7 am to 7 pm, plus some later buses

İzmir – 384 km, 6½ hours, US$7 to US$9.75; frequent buses

Keşan – 100 km, two hours, US$4.50; frequent buses

Kilitbahir – 52 km, one hour, US$2; hourly minibuses

The Gelibolu-Lapseki car ferry departs from Gelibolu at 6.30, 7.30, 8.15, 9 and 11 am, and 1, 3, 5, 6, 7, 8, 9, 10 and 11 pm and midnight. Departures from Lapseki are at 6.30, 7.30, 8.15 and 10 am, noon, 2, 4, 5, 6, 7, 8, 9, 10 and 11 pm and midnight. The fare is 50c per person, US$2 for a bicycle or moped, US$10 for a car. If you miss this boat, you can go south-west to Eceabat (45 km, one hour) and catch the similar car ferry, or to Kilitbahir seven km farther on and catch the small private ferry, which can take a few cars as well, and charges less than the other ferries. See the Çanakkale section for details.

Eceabat

The small town of Eceabat (population 4500) exists for the car ferries to Çanakkale and for the Gallipoli National Park headquarters and visitors centre, two km south of the town. For details on the car ferries to Çanakkale, see that section.

Grouped at Eceabat's ferry dock are the *Hotel Ece* and *Hotel Boss*, noisy and nothing special but useful in emergencies; the *Atlantik Restaurant* for cheap meals and the *Saros Restaurant-Bar* in the Hotel Ece for slightly more up-market (and expensive) food and drink; and the Yılmaz bus company ticket office.

Buses or minibuses run hourly north-east to Gelibolu (45 km, one hour). In summer there are several dolmuşes daily to the ferry dock at Kabatepe (10 km, 15 minutes) on the western shore of the peninsula, and these can drop you at the national park's Kabatepe information centre and museum, or at the base of the road up to Lone Pine and Chunuk Bair. Dolmuşes also run down the coast to Kilitbahir, from whence there are dolmuşes south to Abide at the southern tip of the peninsula.

Kilitbahir

The small hamlet of Kilitbahir at the foot of the Kilitbahir castle hosts the small private ferry from Canakkale, which arrives at a dock just north-east of the castle walls. There are a few small teahouses and restaurants, but Kilitbahir is essentially a pass-through place. Dolmuşes and taxis await the ferry to shuttle you north-east to Eceabat (seven km), or south-west via Alçıtepe (19.5 km) to Çanakkale Abidesi ('Abide', 28 km).

Gallipoli National Park

Gallipoli National Park (Gelibolu Tarihi Milli Park) covers much of the peninsula and all of the significant battle sites. Park headquarters is two km south-west of Eceabat (five km north-east of Kilitbahir) at the Ziyaretçi Merkezi (Visitors Centre); there's a picnic ground here as well.

In the national park there are several different signage systems: the normal Turkish highway signs, those erected by the national park administration, and those posted by the Commonwealth War Graves Commission. This leads to confusion because the foreign troops had a completely different nomenclature for battlefield sites than the Turks did, and the Turkish battlefield markings do not necessarily agree with the ones erected by the highway department. In the text below and on the Gallipoli map I've attempted to lessen the confusion by adding alternate site names in brackets (parentheses).

There are camping grounds at Kabatepe, Kum Limanı and Seddülbahir, and simple accommodation at Kum Limanı, Seddülbahir and Abide.

Three km north of Eceabat a road marked for Kabatepe and Kemalyeri heads west.

Kabatepe Information Centre & Museum

The Kabatepe Tanıtma Merkezi, nine km from Eceabat and a km or so east of the village of Kabatepe, holds a small museum (30c) with period uniforms, soldiers' letters, rusty weapons and other battlefield finds such as the skull of a luckless Turkish soldier with a ball lodged right in the forehead.

Kabatepe Village

This small harbour was the object of the Allied landing on 25 April 1915, but in the pitch dark of early morning the landing craft were swept northwards to the steep cliffs of Arıburnu – a bit of bad luck which was crucial to the course of the campaign. Today there is little here but the dock for the ferries to the Turkish Aegean island of Gökçeada, but just south of the village there will soon be a national park camping ground and picnic area.

Anzac Cove

About three km north along the coast from Kabatepe, passing the road on the right for Lone Pine and Chunuk Bair, and the Shell Green (Yeşil Tarla) and Shrapnel Valley (Korku Dere) sites, is Anzac Cove. The ill-fated Allied landing was made here on 25 April 1915, beneath and just south of the Arıburnu cliffs. The Allied forces were ordered to advance inland, but met with

fierce resistance from the Ottoman forces under Mustafa Kemal (Atatürk), who had foreseen the landing here and was prepared. After this first failed effort, the Anzacs concentrated on consolidating and expanding the beachhead, which they did until June while awaiting reinforcements.

In August a major offensive was staged in an attempt to advance beyond the beachhead and up to the ridges of Chunuk Bair and Sarı Bair, and resulted in the bloodiest battles of the campaign, but little progress was made.

Anzac Cove is marked by a Turkish monument which repeats Atatürk's famous words uttered in 1934 for the Anzac troops:

Those heroes that shed their blood and lost their lives...you are now lying in the soil of a friendly country. Therefore rest in peace. There is no difference between the Johnnies and the Mehmets to us where they lie side by side here in this country of ours.... You, the mothers, who sent their sons from far away countries, wipe away your tears; your sons are now lying in our bosom and are in peace. After having lost their lives on this land they have become our sons as well.

As a memorial reserve, the beach here is off-limits to swimmers and picnickers.

Lone Pine to Chunuk Bair

Retrace your steps and follow the signs up the hill for Lone Pine (Kanlı Sırt), perhaps the most poignant and affecting of all the Anzac cemeteries. The small tombstones carry touching epitaphs: 'Only son', 'He died for his country' and 'If I could hold your hand once more just to say well done'.

As you progress up the hill, you quickly come to understand the ferocity of the battles here. At some points the trenches were only a few metres apart. The order to attack meant certain death to all who followed it, and virtually all – on both the Ottoman and Allied sides – followed the order.

At Johnston's Jolly (Meçhul Asker) and Quinn's Post (Bomba Sırt, Yüzbaşı Mehmet Şehitliği), the trenches were separated only by the width of the modern road. On the eastern side at **Jonston's Jolly** is the Turkish monument to the unknown soldiers who died

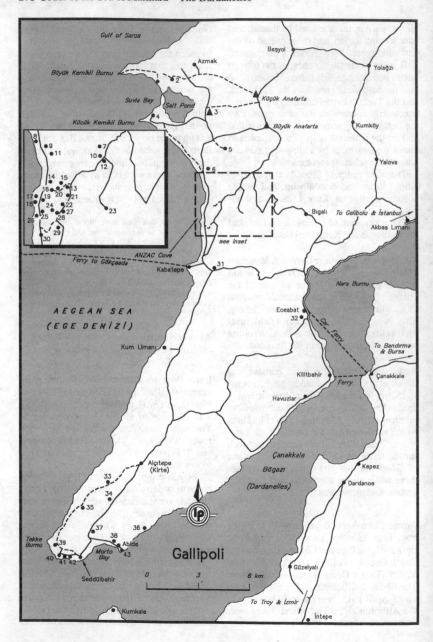

Gulf of Saros

Büyük Kemikli Burnu

Azmak

Besyol

Yolağzı

Suvla Bay

Salt Pond

Küçük Anafarta

Küçük Kemikli Burnu

Büyük Anafarta

Kumköy

Yalova

Bıgalı

To Gelibolu & İstanbul

Akbaş Limanı

see inset

ANZAC Cove

Ferry to Gökçeada

Kabatepe

Nara Burnu

AEGEAN SEA
(EGE DENİZİ)

Eceabat

Cer Ferry

Kum Limanı

To Bandırma
& Bursa

Kilitbahir

Çanakkale

Ferry

Havuzlar

Alçıtepe
(Kirte)

Çanakkale
Boğazı
(Dardanelles)

Kepez

Dardanos

Tekke
Burnu

Abide

Gallipoli

Morto
Bay

Güzelyalı

Seddülbahir

0   3   6 km

Kumkale

To Troy & İzmir

İntepe

1 Büyük Kemikli Picnic Area & Beach
2 Hill 10
3 Green Hill
4 Lala Baba
5 Hill 60 New Zealand Memorial
6 7th Field Ambulance Cemetery
7 The Farm Cemetery
8 Embarkation Pier Cemetery
9 NZ No 2 Outpost Cemetery
10 Chunuk Bair New Zealand Memorial
11 No 2 Outpost Cemetery
12 Conkbayırı Mehmetçik Memorials
13 Baby 700 Cemetery
14 Canterbury Cemetery
15 The Neck Cemetery
16 Walker's Ridge New Zealand
   Memorial
17 Arı Burnu Cemetery
18 ANZAC Memorial
19 Plugge's Plateau
20 The Nek (Cesaret Tepe)
21 Quinn's Post (Bombasırt) Cemetery
22 Courtney Steele's Post (Boyun)
   Cemetery
23 Kemalyeri (Scrubby Knoll,Turkish HQ)
24 4th Battalion Parade Ground
   Cemetery
25 Shrapnel Valley (Korkudere)
   Cemetery
26 Beach (Hell Spit) Cemetery
27 Meçhul Asker (Unknown Soldier)
   Memorial
28 Johnston's Jolly Cemetery
29 Lone Pine (Kanlı Sırt) Cemetery
30 Shell Green (Yeşil Tarla) Memorial
31 Kabatepe Information Centre &
   Museum
32 Gelibolu Tarihi Milli Park Ziyaretçi
   Merkezi
   (Park Visitors' Centre) & Picnic Area
33 Twelve Tree Copse Cemetery & NZ
   Memorial
34 Redoubt Cemetery
35 Pink Farm Cemetery
36 Kerevizdere Picnic Area
37 Skew Bridge Cemetery
38 French Memorial & Museum
39 Lancashire Landing Cemetery
40 Cape Helles British Memorial
41 İlk Şehitler & Yahya Çavuş Memorials
42 'V' Beach Cemetery
43 Çanakkale Şehitleri Abidesi Memorial

(Conkbayırı), the first objective of the Allied landing in April 1915. As the Anzac troops made their way up the scrub-covered slopes, Group Commander Mustafa Kemal (Atatürk) gave this famous order to the troops of his 57th Infantry Regiment: 'I order you not just to attack, but to die. In the time it takes us to die, other troops and commanders will arrive to take our places.' The 57th was wiped out, but held the line and inflicted equally heavy casualties on the Anzacs below.

Chunuk Bair was also at the heart of the struggle from 6 to 9 August 1915, when 28,000 men died on this ridge. The peaceful pine grove of today makes it difficult to imagine the blasted wasteland of almost a century ago, when bullets and bombs mowed down men and trees as the fighting went on day and night with huge numbers of casualties. The Anzac attack on 6 August was deadly but the attack on the following day was of a ferocity which, according to Atatürk, 'could scarcely be described'.

To the east, a side road leads up to the **Turkish memorial**, five gigantic tablets with inscriptions (in Turkish) describing the progress of the battle. On the western side of the road is the **New Zealand memorial** and some **reconstructed Turkish trenches** *(Türk Siperleri)*. A sign indicates the spots at which Mustafa Kemal (Atatürk) stood, known to every Turkish schoolchild: the spot where shrapnel would have hit his heart, but was stopped by his pocket watch (Atatürk' ün saatinin parçaladığı yeri); where he watched the progress of the battle (Savaş gözetleme yeri); and where he gave the order to attack (Atatürk'ün taarruz emrini verdiği yer).

From this hilltop the **Dardanelles** strait is clearly visible, but the Anzac troops never got to see it. It also becomes clear how crucial Atatürk's role in the battle was, and why he became an Ottoman folk hero almost overnight.

Beyond Chunuk Bair the road leads to **Kemalyeri** (Scrubby Knoll), Atatürk's command post, and to **Büyük Anafarta** and **Küçük Anafarta** hilltops, other important strategic points in the battle.

here. At **Quinn's Post** is the memorial to Sergeant Mehmet, who fought with rocks and his fists after he ran out of ammunition.

At the top of the hill is **Chunuk Bair**

Kabatepe to Seddülbahir A road goes south from near the Kabatepe Information Centre past the side road (one km) to **Kum Limanı**, where there is a good swimming beach, camping ground, and the *Kum Motel* (☎ (1964) 1455), charging US$12 per person in a waterless A-frame cabin, or US$22 per person in motel rooms with shower. This is the place to stop for a swim; if you're on a guided tour, you will probably swim here.

From Kabatepe it's about 12 km to the village of **Alçıtepe**, formerly known as Kirte. In the village, signs point out the road south-west to **Twelve Tree Copse** and **Pink Farm** cemeteries, and north to the **Turkish Sargı Yeri cemetery** and **Nuri Yamut monument**.

Heading south, the road passes the **Redoubt Cemetery**. About 5.5 km south of Alçıtepe, just south of the **Skew Bridge Cemetery**, the road divides, the right fork for the village of Seddülbahir and several Allied memorials. **Seddülbahir**, 1.5 km from the intersection, is a sleepy farming village with a few small pensions, including the *Helles Panorama* (☎ (1964) 1429 x 34), *Evim* (☎ (1964) 1429 x 20), *Kale* and *Fulda*, a PTT, ruined Ottoman/Byzantine fortress, army post, and a small harbour.

Follow the signs for Yahya Çavuş Şehitliği to reach the **Helles Memorial**, one km beyond the Seddülbahir village square.

The initial Allied attack was two-pronged, with the southern landing being here at the tip of the peninsula on 'V' Beach. Yahya Çavuş (Sergeant Yahya) was the Turkish officer who led the first resistance to the Allied landing on 25 April 1915, causing heavy casualties. The cemetery named for him (**Yahya Çavuş Şehitliği**) is between the Helles Memorial and 'V' Beach.

Lancashire Landing cemetery is off to the north along a road marked by a sign; another sign points south to **'V' Beach**, 550 metres downhill. Right next to the beach is the *Mocamp Seddülbahir*, with tent and caravan sites and a few pension-like rooms.

From the Helles Memorial there are fine views of the straits, with ships cruising placidly up and down. A half million men died or were wounded in the dispute over which ships should (or should not) go through.

Retrace your steps to the road division and go east following signs for Abide and/or Çanakkale Şehitleri Abidesi (Çanakkale Martyrs' Memorial) at Morto Bay. Along the way you pass the **French cemetery** and the simple little *Abide Motel*, less than two km west of the Turkish War Memorial. At the foot of the monument hill is a fine pine-shaded picnic area.

The **Çanakkale Şehitleri Abidesi** commemorates all of the Turkish soldiers who fought and died at Gallipoli. It's a gigantic four-legged stone table almost 42 metres high surrounded by landscaped grounds which stands above a war museum (admission 50c). Exhibits include interesting bits of metal turned up by farmers' ploughs, including English forks and spoons, soldiers' seals and medals, scimitars, French bayonets and machine guns. The poem inscribed on the side of the memorial translates:

Soldiers who have fallen on this land defending this land!
Would that your ancestors might descend from the skies to kiss your pure brows.
Who could dig the grave that was not too small for you?
All of history itself is too small a place for you.

The most touching exhibit is a letter (in Ottoman Turkish) from a young officer who had left law school in Constantinople to volunteer in the Gallipoli campaign. He writes to his mother in poetic terms about the beauty of the landscape and of his love for life. Two days later he died in battle.

TEVFİKİYE & TROY

The approach to Troy (Truva) is across low, rolling grainfields, with villages here and there. This is the Troad of ancient times, all but lost to legend until German-born Californian entrepreneur and amateur archaeologist Heinrich Schliemann (1822-90) rediscovered it in 1871. The poetry of Homer was at that time assumed to be based on legend, not history, but Schliemann got permission from the Ottoman government to excavate here at his own expense. He uncovered four superimposed ancient towns and went on to make notable excavations at other Homeric sites.

History

The first people lived here during the Early Bronze Age. The cities called Troy I to Troy V (3000-1800 BC) had a similar culture, but Troy VI (1800-1275 BC) took on a new character, with a new population of Indo-European stock related to the Mycenaeans. The town doubled in size and carried on a prosperous trade with Mycenae. It also held the key, as defender of the straits, to the prosperous trade with Greek colonies on the Black Sea. Troy VI is the city of Priam which engaged in the Trojan War. A bad earthquake brought down the walls in 1275 and hastened the Achaean victory.

This heroic Troy was followed by Troy VII (1275-1100 BC). The Achaeans may have burned the city in 1240; an invading Balkan people moved in around 1190 BC

and Troy sank into a torpor for four centuries. It was revived as a Greek city (Troy VIII, 700-300 BC) and then as a Roman one (Troy IX, 300 BC-300 AD). At one point Constantine the Great thought of building his new eastern Roman capital here, but he chose Byzantium instead. As a Byzantine town, Troy didn't amount to much.

Now for Homer's history of Troy. In the *Iliad*, this is the town of Ilium. The battle took place in the 13th century BC, with Agamemnon, Achilles, Odysseus (Ulysses), Patroclus and Nestor on the Achaean (Greek) side, and Priam with his sons Hector and Paris on the Trojan side. Homer alludes to no commercial rivalries as cause for the war. Rather, he says that Paris kidnapped the beautiful Helen from her husband Menelaus, King of Sparta, and the king asked the Achaeans to help him get her back.

The war went on for a decade, during which Hector killed Patroclus and Achilles killed Hector. When the time came for Paris

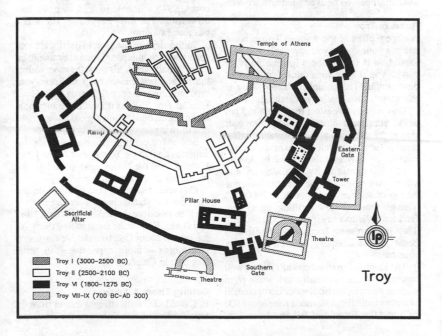

Troy I (3000–2500 BC)
Troy II (2500–2100 BC)
Troy VI (1800–1275 BC)
Troy VIII–IX (700 BC–AD 300)

Temple of Athena

Ramp

Eastern Gate

Tower

Pillar House

Sacrificial Altar

Theatre

Southern Gate

Theatre

Troy

to kill Achilles, he was up to the task. Paris knew that Achilles' mother had dipped her son in the River Styx, holding him by his heel, and had thus protected Achilles from wounds anywhere that the water had touched. So Paris shot Achilles in the heel.

Even this carnage didn't end the war, so Odysseus came up with the idea of the wooden horse filled with soldiers. That's the way Homer reported it.

One theory has it that the earthquake of 1275 BC gave the Achaeans the break they needed, bringing down Troy's formidable walls and allowing them to battle their way into the city. In gratitude to Poseidon, the Earth-Shaker, they built a monumental wooden statue of his horse. Thus there may well have been a real Trojan horse, even though Homer's account is less than fully historical.

The last people to live here were Turkish soldiers and their families, subjects of the emir of Karası, in the 1300s. After them, the town disappeared until Schliemann arrived.

Ruins of Troy

A huge replica of the wooden Trojan horse catches your eye as you approach, and so it should, as it was put here for that purpose, and so you'd have something distinctive to photograph. The complaint about Troy is that there's little that's eye-catching.

Troy is open to visitors from 8 am to 5 pm daily; admission costs US$2.50. On your way to the site, stop at the Excavation Information Centre, which has exhibits on the work under way, and also a small bookshop.

The excavations by Schliemann and others have revealed nine ancient cities, one on top of another, going back to 3000 BC. Though there are few thrilling sights here (and some visitors say it's not worth the trip), Troy is interesting because of the Troad's beauty, great antiquity and semilegendary character.

The identifiable structures at Troy are well marked. Notice especially the walls from various periods, the **bouleuterion** or council chamber built about Homer's time (circa 800 BC) and the **Temple of Athena** from Troy

VIII, rebuilt by the Romans. Also, don't miss the beautiful views of the Troad, particularly over towards the straits. On a clear day you can see the Çanakkale Martyrs' Memorial on the far shore, and ships passing through the Dardanelles. You can almost imagine the Achaean fleet beached on the Troad's shores, ready to begin a battle that would be remembered over 3000 years later.

Tevfikiye

Just half a km before the archaeological site is the village of Tevfikiye, with a Tourism Information Office, drink stands, restaurants, souvenir shops, replicas of the Trojan treasure, etc. Several little pensions can put you up.

On the western side of the village, about 600 metres from the archaeological site, are the *Hotel Hisarlık* (☎ (1973) 1026 or 1992), Tevfikiye Köyü, 17120 Çanakkale, a new and reasonably comfortable but overpriced lodging. Rooms with bath on the upper floor cost US$25 a double in high summer, less off-season. The *İlion Restaurant* below is a bus tour favourite.

To the right of the Hotel Hisarlık are two 'Houses of Schliemann', one claiming to be the original (which it's not); the other claims that *neither* house is the original. Spend your time looking at the one right next to the Hotel Hisarlık (for free), as it's the more authentic, having been built following old photographs and drawings.

Several camping grounds provide for tenters, such as the *Bozkır* east of the Hotel Hisarlık, and the *Helen*, next to the bus tour restaurant of the same name.

On the eastern side of the village, over one km from the archaeological site, are most of the little pensions, including the *Akçın*, *Varol* and *Deniz*. Follow the signs to find them. All are priced about US$10 a double for waterless rooms – more expensive than better lodgings in Çanakkale.

Getting There & Away

In Çanakkale, walk straight inland from the ferry docks and turn right onto the Troy road;

the dolmuş station for minibuses to Tevfikiye and Troy is several hundred metres along by a small bridge.

Dolmuşes head for Troy every 30 to 60 minutes in high summer. Troy is 30 km, less than an hour's drive away; the fare is US$1 each way. If you are here in winter, early spring or late fall, the dolmuşes may not be running all the way to Troy, but only as far as the village of Tevfikiye, and you may have to walk the last half km to the archaeological area. Otherwise, it's a tour by taxi.

If you plan to visit Troy and then head south, you should try to buy a ticket on a southbound bus a day in advance, let the ticket seller know you want to be picked up at Troy, do your sightseeing at Troy, then be out on the main highway in plenty of time to catch the bus. Without a ticket, you can hitch out to the highway from Troy and hope a bus will come by, and that it will have vacant seats. This often works, though it entails some waiting and some uncertainty regarding the availability of seats.

If you're coming from the south, ask to be let out on the highway at the access road to Troy, which is 4.5 km north of the big Geyikli/Çimento Fabrikası crossroads. From the highway it's almost five km west to Troy. Hitch, or wait for a dolmuş.

Aegean Turkey

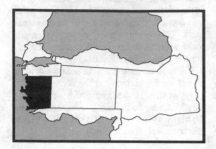

Turkey's Aegean region is one of the country's richest in many ways. Agriculture has been very important here for millennia. The many small to medium-sized cities support light manufacturing and commerce. The number, variety and state of preservation of the region's ancient ruins is incomparable. The coast offers excellent opportunities for swimming, boating and other water sports.

The Aegean coast is a beautiful procession of golden wheat fields, fig and olive orchards, fishing villages and holiday resort towns. Assos (Behramkale) is an out-of-the-way village built on an ancient city. Ayvalık is a pleasant fishing and resort town with good beaches, good seafood restaurants and beautiful panoramas of pine forest and Aegean islands. At Bergama, the ancient Pergamum, you should see the impressive ruins of the Acropolis and the Asclepion, an early medical centre. Many visitors make their base in İzmir and go north to Bergama or east to Sardis for the day.

South of İzmir the main attractions are the many Ionian cities, including Ephesus, the best-preserved classical city in the world, and also Priene, Miletus, Didyma, Labranda, and several others. The resort town of Kuşadası can serve as a base for visits to many of these sites.

At the southern end of the Aegean coast is the beautiful little resort and yachting port of Bodrum, with its crusader castle, just across the water from the Greek island of Kos.

Inland from the coast (several hours eastward by bus), the cities of the Aegean hinterland are much less visited by tourists, and – despite their lack of coastline – this makes them all the more appealing for travellers wanting to see the 'real' Turkey. Eskişehir, Balıkesir, Kütahya, Afyon, Denizli and Pamukkale, Isparta and Eğirdir all have their good points. Whether you stop for the night or just for some tea, these cities yield interesting experiences and lasting memories.

This chapter is divided into three parts: the North Aegean, from Assos (Behramkale) south to İzmir; the South Aegean, from Selçuk/Ephesus south to Bodrum; and the Aegean Hinterland, covering the cities east of İzmir but west of Ankara and Konya.

Here's what you'll find on the coastal highway (E24), heading south from Çanakkale and Troy (which are covered in the preceding chapter).

North Aegean

Heading south from Çanakkale and Troy on the main highway (as the buses do), there is little to stop for until you reach the town of Ayvacık, from which dolmuşes run west to Assos (Behramkale). If you have your own transport, consider taking a much more interesting side road through the western part of the Biga Peninsula which takes you to little-visited minor ruins and soon-to-be-discovered beaches which are good for camping, while they last.

COASTAL ROUTE
South of the Troy road 4.5 km is a paved if narrow road heading west and marked for 'Çimento Fabrikası'' (cement factory) and

Geyikli. After passing the obvious cement factory the road proceeds south-west to the small towns of Geyikli and Oduniskelesi. Geyikli, 24 km along, has a few simple restaurants and basic hotels. Oduniskelesi, five km west of Geyikli, is the terminus for the ferry to the Turkish island Bozcaada.

Oduniskelesi & Bozcaada

Bozcaada, formerly known as Tenedos, has always been known to Anatolian oenophiles for its wines (Dimitrakopulo, Doruk, Talay) and to soldiers for its defences. A huge medi-eval fortress towers over the north-eastern tip of the island, and vineyards blanket its sunny slopes. The island has the advantage of being small (about five or six km across) and easy to explore, and the disadvantage of being too small to host much accommodation. Rooms and beds are usually filled by İstanbullus with reservations in summer, so advance bookings are essential unless you just plan to come for the day.

Ferries depart from the mainland village of Oduniskelesi year-round at 10 am and 5 pm; departures from Bozcaada are at 7.30 am and 3 pm. Fares are 50c per passenger, US$9 per car. There may be additional boat services in high summer.

The village of Oduniskelesi has a few simple pensions and camping grounds about one km south of the ferry dock.

On Bozcaada, poke around the enormous fortress, then hike across the island to the beaches for a dip.

Alexandria Troas

Five km south of Oduniskelesi the road passes right through the widely scattered ruins of Alexandria Troas near the Turkish village of Dalyan. (Some signs read 'Alexandria (Truva)', but this is not Troy.)

Antigonus, one of Alexander the Great's generals, took control of this land after the collapse of the Alexandrine empire, and founded the city of Antigoneia in 310 BC in his own honour. He was later defeated in battle by Lysimachus, another of Alexander's generals, who took the city and renamed it in honour of his late commander. An earthquake later destroyed much of the city.

Nowadays dolmuşes run infrequently between Ezine, on the main highway, and Dalyan.

Archaeologists have identified bits of the city's theatre, palace, temple, agora, baths, necropolis, harbour and city walls amidst the farmers' fields. But for most visitors Alexandria Troas is a mood, a place which, like so many places in Turkey, conjures up that feeling of great antiquity disappearing beneath the slowly grinding wheels of time. Don't make a special trip here, but if you pass by, stop and climb a ruined wall for the view.

Neandria When Antigonus founded the city of Antigoneia, he forced the inhabitants of nearby Neandria, settled around 700 BC, to move to his new city and populate it. The ruins of Neandria, 1.5 km north-east of the village of Kayacık and 500 metres inland from the sea, offer nothing to the casual visitor today, but archaeologists have discovered here the oldest Aeolian temple with a clearly distinguishable plan.

Gülpınar

Three km south of Alexandria Troas are the hot springs of Kestanbol Kaplıcaları (13 km south of Geyikli), with a small bathhouse. Continue south 32 km to Gülpınar, a small farming town with no services but for a fuel station. This was once the ancient city of Khrysa, famous for its Ionic temple to Apollo and mice. The **Apollo Smintheion**, 400 metres down a steep hill from the centre of the town, has some bits of marble column on top of a short flight of steps. The cult statue of the god, now disappeared, had mice carved in marble at its feet, in accordance with an old legend. Reliefs on the temple's walls illustrated scenes from the Iliad.

Babakale & Akliman

In Gülpınar a road going west is marked for Babakale (Lekton), nine km away. Three km along it is the road to Akliman, a coastal settlement with a nice long beach backed by olive groves, and several good, cheap camping places and motels. About six km farther on is Babakale (Lekton), with a small village clustered at the base of a ruined fortress overlooking a long sweep of sea. A new yacht and fishing harbour is being completed, and the first touristic hotels – the Karayel and Ser-Tur – have been opened, with undoubtedly many more to follow. Some İstanbullus have already fixed up stone village houses (and one windmill) as villas.

From Gülpınar the road east to Assos (25 km) passes through a half-dozen small villages. From some, unpaved roads head down to the shore where there is sure to be some beach shack with a primitive toilet and perhaps fresh water for the ever-increasing number of camper-van owners who have discovered this road.

ASSOS (BEHRAMKALE)

Called Assos in ancient times, the ruins and the Turkish village of Behramkale share a gorgeous setting west of Ayvacık, overlooking the Aegean and the nearby island of Lesbos (Midilli, MEE-dee-lee in Turkish).

It's 73 km from Çanakkale along the main

highway (E 90) to Ayvacık (not to be confused with nearby Ayvalık), a ride of less than two hours. From Ayvacık, dolmuşes run the 19 km to Behramkale, and it's often possible to hitch as well.

The main part of the village and the acropolis ruins are perched on top of a hill, but down the far (sea) side of the hill at the iskele (wharf) a tiny cluster of little stone buildings clings to the cliff in an incredibly romantic, not to mention unlikely, setting. It's a picture-postcard sight, but crowded with tourists in summer. The swimming is difficult here, but there's a good beach at Kadırga, four km to the east.

History
Assos was founded in the 8th century BC by colonists from Lesbos. Aristotle stayed here for three years, and St Paul visited briefly. In its long history, Assos has flourished as a port, agricultural town and centre for Platonic learning. Today the main part of the village on top of the hill is just a Turkish farming village. The iskele is crammed if a few dozen foreigners show up.

Things to See
There's a fine **Ottoman hump-back bridge**, built in the 1300s, to the left of the road as you approach the village. When you get to a fork in the road, go left up to the village proper, or right to see the massive city walls, necropolis and iskele.

Taking the village road, you wind up to a small square with a few shops and a small restaurant or two. Continue upwards on the road, and you'll come to a small square with a teahouse and a bust of Atatürk. At the very top of the hill you will get a spectacular view, and perhaps meet some village girls crocheting lace and importuning you to buy some.

You'll also get a look at the **Murad Hüdavendigar Camii** (1359-89). This early mosque is very simple – a dome on squinches set on top of a square box of a room. The mihrab is nothing special. The Ottomans had not yet conquered Constantinople and begun to elaborate on the theme of Sancta Sophia at the time this mosque was built. Curious, though, is the lintel above the entrance, which bears Greek crosses and inscriptions. It probably was left over from a Byzantine church.

The principal sight on top of the hill is the **Temple of Athena**, partly (and badly) reconstructed. Its short, tapered columns with plain capitals are hardly elegant, and the concrete reconstruction hurts more than helps. But the site and the view are, as with so many ancient cities, spectacular and worth the US$1 admission fee.

By taking the right fork of the entry road, you'll reach the impressive **city walls** and the **necropolis** or cemetery. Just 2.5 km past the fork, on a block-paved road which winds down the cliff side, is the iskele, the most picturesque spot in Assos. There are lodging and eating possibilities here, and crowds of bodies in summer. Try to plan your Assos visit for spring or autumn.

Places to Stay
The building boom has hit Assos with hotels, motels and pensions opening up all over the place. Room prices are 35% lower in the off season (April, May and October). Virtually all places are atmospheric old stone buildings. For reservations, write to the hotel, Behramkale/Ayvacık, 17860 Çanakkale.

Places to Stay – bottom end
The upper town, near the Temple of Athena, has some pensions, including the simple *Gök Köşe Pansiyon* and *Athena Pansiyon*, both US$12 a double. The cheapest way to stay in Assos is to camp in the olive groves just east (inland) where there are five small camping grounds in a row, charging about US$2 per person.

In the iskele area, the *Aristo Motel* (☎ (1969) 7042), just north-east of the prominent Hotel Kervansaray, has a little vine-covered stone building with shower-equipped rooms renting for US$18 a double, breakfast included, in the high summer season. They also have camp sites among the fig trees along the shore for US$6. Right above the Aristo is *Dost Camping*, at the same price.

Assos Şen Pansiyon (☎ (1969) 7076), inland from the Hotel Kervansaray up the hill, is a stone building wherein the front rooms (which have sun and views) are reached by perilous-looking wooden walkways; rooms at the back are dark but cooler. The roof restaurant has a good view and interesting architectural information on the Assos ruins. A double room with shower and breakfast costs US$19 in season.

Otel Behram (☎ (1969) 7044) is another old stone building with a restaurant, bar and comfortable shower-equipped guest rooms renting for US$22 in summer, breakfast included.

Places to Stay – middle
Hotel Assos Kervansaray (☎ (1969) 7093, 7198, -9; fax 7200) is the best in town, with three-star comforts, a stone fireplace and rattan/bamboo furniture in the lobby. Rates are US$35 a double in season, breakfast included.

Hotel Yıldız Saray (☎ (1969) 7169, 7025), to the left as you come into iskele, is famous for its roof-terrace fish restaurant ('since 1966'). Rooms are good, some with partial sea views, for US$25 a double. The Yıldız has a sister hotel on Kadırga beach (☎ (1969) 7204).

Otel Nazlıhan (☎ & fax (1969) 7064), beyond the jandarma post, has been nicely restored. The rooms and baths are quite small but attractive. Rates are US$28 a double with sea view, slightly less without.

Hotel Assos (☎ (1969) 7017, 7034), right on the harbour, has the iskele's most popular restaurant, and charges from US$26 a double for its comfy rooms in summer.

Places to Eat
There are no especially cheap places to eat in Assos, particularly around the iskele. Meals at the hotel restaurants generally cost from US$6 to US$15.

Getting There & Away
Dolmuşes depart from Ayvacık hourly in high summer for Assos. In the off season, they are less frequent, perhaps only a few times per day. If you visit off-season (which I recommend), leave from Ayvalık or Çanakkale early in the day, get to Ayvacık as soon as possible, then hang out on the road to Assos to catch a dolmuş or hitch a ride.

Küçükkuyu to Ören
After you've seen Assos and are back on the highway, heading south, you will come round the Bay of Edremit. At the eastern end of the bay are the holiday resorts of **Küçükkuyu, Altınoluk, Akçay** and **Ören**, with moderately priced hotels and motels. At Akçay is a fine five-km-long beach with sulphur springs issuing from parts of it; the beach at Ören is nine km long. Ayvalık, your most likely destination, is 130 km (over two hours) from Assos, 110 km (two hours) from Ayvacık.

AYVALIK
Across a narrow strait from the Greek island of Lesbos, Ayvalık (EYE-vah-luhk, population 50,000) is a beach resort, fishing town, olive oil and soap-making centre, and terminus for boats to and from Lesbos. The coast here is cloaked in pine forests and olive orchards; the offshore waters, sprinkled with 23 islands.

Orientation & Information
The town of Ayvalık is small and manageable, but with some inconveniences: the otogar (bus station) is 1.5 km north of the centre; the Tourism Information Office (☎ (663) 12121) is a km south of the main square around the curve of the bay, opposite the yacht harbour.

Three km farther to the south are the areas called Çamlık and Orta Çamlık, with a scattering of pensions popular with Turks on holiday. Eight km south of the centre is Sarımsaklı (SAHR-uhm-SAHK-luh, Garlic Beach), sometimes called Plajlar (The Beaches), a nice if not spectacular beach lined with hotels, motels and a few pensions. The island Alibey Adası, sometimes called Cunda, is 8.3 km north-west of Ayvalık centre by road.

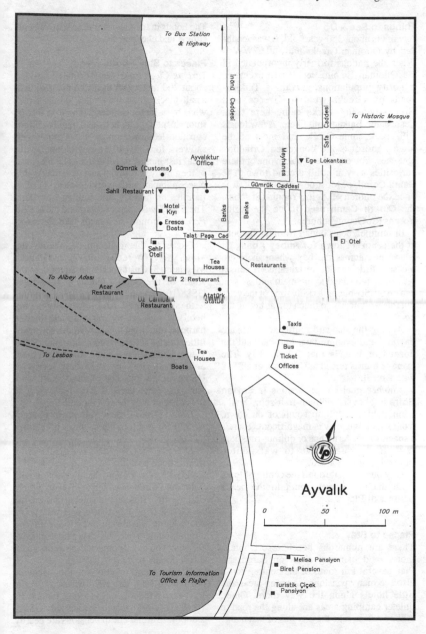

To Bus Station & Highway

İnönü Caddesi

To Historic Mosque

Caddesi

Safa Caddesi

Meyhanes

▼ Ege Lokantası

Ayvalıktur Office

Gümrük (Customs)

Gümrük Caddesi

Sahil Restaurant ▼

Banks

Banks

■ Motel Kıyı

● Eresos Boats

Talat Paşa Cad

■ El Otel

■ Şehir Oteli

Tea Houses

Restaurants

To Alibey Adası

▼ ▼ ▼ Elif 2 Restaurant

Acar Restaurant

Üç Camlıdik Restaurant

Atatürk Statue

● Taxis

To Lesbos

Bus Ticket Offices

Tea Houses

Boats

Ayvalık

0   50   100 m

To Tourism Information Office & Plajlar

■ Melisa Pansiyon

● Biret Pension

■ Turistik Çiçek Pansiyon

Things to See & Do

Ayvalık is about 350 years old. It was inhabited by Ottoman Greeks until after WW I. When the nations formerly incorporated in the Ottoman Empire decided to exchange minority populations, Ayvalık's Turkish-speaking Greeks went to Greece, and Greek-speaking Turks came here from Lesbos, the Balkans and Crete. A few locals still speak some Greek, and most of the town's mosques are converted Orthodox churches. You can take a look in one of these curiosities as you stroll around town. The **Saatli Camii**, or Mosque with a Clock, was once the church of Agios Yannis (St John); the **Çınarlı Camii** used to be the Agios Yorgos (St George) church.

In summer, boats depart from the harbour at the centre of town for **Alibey Adası**, an island just across the bay where there are pleasant little seaside restaurants. A causeway links the island to the mainland, so you can go by city bus or taxi any time of the year, but this isn't nearly so much fun as taking the boat.

Among the standard tourist activities are daytime and evening boat tours around the dozens of islands that fill the bay. The average tour is priced at US$3.50, or US$12 with a meal.

Another goal for excursions is **Şeytan Sofrası** (shey-TAHN soh-frah-suh, Devil's Dinnertable), a hilltop south of the town, from which the view is magnificent. There's a snack stand. As no bus or dolmuş runs here regularly, you'll have to walk, hitch (unlikely) or take a taxi.

City buses run through the centre of town from the bus station south to the beach Sarımsaklı Plaj.

Places to Stay

There are numerous beach resort hotels, motels and camping areas on Sarımsaklı Plaj, several km south of the centre. You'll also see many pensions, camping areas and little hotels along the way there. Other, quieter camping areas are along the road to Alibey Adası; take the city bus of that name. The hotels in the town centre are convenient, simple and cheap.

Places to Stay – bottom end

Turistik Çiçek Pansiyon (☎ (663) 11201) is about 200 metres south of the main square, a half-block off the main road, hidden somewhat by a larger building. There is lots of fluorescent lighting here, and bare but bright corridors leading to simple, clean rooms with showers, for US$10/12 a single/double with breakfast included. Mr Ismail Öztürk, head of the family, is a jovial sort who makes this place popular with working-class Turkish families on holiday, and foreign travellers. The *Biret Pansiyon* next door and the *Melisa Pansiyon* around the corner take the overflow.

Closer to the main square, there's the *Motel Kıyı* (☎ (663) 16677) at Gümrük Meydanı 18 (Customs House Square), to the south of the Sahil Lokantası. It charges US$8/16/24 a single/double/triple for rooms with shower. The motel (actually a tiny hotel) is just off the main square by the harbour, out along the quay in the warren of little streets. The front rooms have nice water views. Right on this same square is the old *Şehir Oteli*, with very cheap, basic rooms for US$5 per person. The plumbing (with hot water) is down the hall. This place may be noisy because of the restaurant below.

Hotel Kaptan, near the Kıyı, charges US$30 for nice double rooms with shower and ocean view.

El Otel (☎ (663) 12217) is a block off the main street near the main square, at Safa Caddesi 3, overlooking the intersection with Talat Paşa Caddesi which leads to a church-like mosque. It is very clean and correct, run by God-fearing types who will rent you a room with washbasin for US$7/10/14 a single/double/triple, which is a bit expensive for what you get. Rooms with showers go for a few dollars more.

If you want to stay on the beach at Sarımsaklı Plaj, turn right when you get to the beach and look for the *Motel Samanyolu* (☎ (663) 41093), which charges only US$18 a double. Similar cheap pensions are nearby.

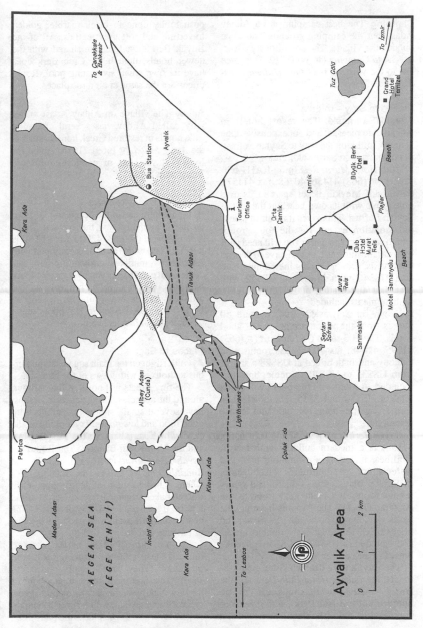

Ayvalık Area

0   1   2 km

Camping The best camping is on Alibey Adası, but the camping grounds tend to be outside the village. The ubiquitously advertised *Ada Camping* (☎ (663) 71211) is three km to the west, as is *Ortunç Hidden Paradise*.

Places to Stay – middle

Ayvalık/Sarımsaklı The resort hotels in Ayvalık are pleasant and not expensive. One is near Çamlık on the way to Şeytan Sofrası, the others are on Sarımsaklı Plaj.

Club Hotel Murat Reis (moo-RAHT reh-yeess) (☎ (663) 41456, 40788; fax 41457), Sarımsaklı Mevkii, is set apart in its own pine grove with its own beach at the foot of Şeytan Sofrası. This gives it an air of splendid isolation except for the tour groups which come and go daily. You will need your own car for transport, or will have to depend upon taxis. Double rooms including a bath cost US$40 with breakfast, US$52 with breakfast and dinner, or US$60 (for two) with all meals included.

Down on Sarımsaklı Plaj, a mere 50 metres from the water, are numerous good hotels. The 100-room *Otel Ankara* (☎ (663) 41195, 41048; fax 40022) has rooms with balcony and bath priced at US$28 a single, from US$35 to US$40 a double, breakfast included. A room with full board will cost a total of US$50 or US$55. The hotel has a card-and-game room, bar, café and terrace restaurant.

Büyük Berk Oteli (☎ (663) 41045, -6; fax 41194) is a modern building with lots of facilities, including a swimming pool and water-sports paraphernalia, discotheque, children's playground, billiard and table-tennis room. It's right next door to the Ankara. The 112 guest rooms have private baths, balconies (some with sea views) and prices of US$32 to US$40 a double, breakfast included or US$42 to US$56 a double, breakfast and dinner included.

The Büyük Berk has two sister establishments, the fancier *Hotel Club Berk* and the *Hotel Zeytinci* (with the same phone numbers as the Büyük Berk), with even more comfortable and up-to-date guest rooms, a

posh lobby done in black marble, golden travertine and soft grey textiles. All of the Büyük Berk's facilities are shared with the newer hotels, though the Club Berk does have its own small swimming pool. Room prices are the same at all three places.

Alibey The village on Alibey Adası, officially called Alibey, has several charming little hotels in restored Greek houses, such as the *Artur Motel* (☎ (663) 71014) suited for longer stays. Lots of condominiums are being built here.

Places to Stay – top end

At the western end of the beach, not far from the north-south highway, the five-star *Grand Hotel Temizel* (☎ (663) 42000; fax 41274) is the class act, with 164 rooms equipped with satellite TV, minibars, air-conditioning, balconies and even hair dryers. Water sports, six bars and a disco, a health club and casino – all the services are yours for US$60 to US$70 a single, US$65 to US$80 a double or triple, breakfast included.

Places to Eat

Ayvalık Right on the main square are numerous teahouses, with views of the harbour.

The tiny streets just north of the harbour, around the agencies selling tickets to Lesbos, have several small, simple restaurants with good food and low prices. Try looking on the street which starts between the Tariş Bankası and the Yapı Kredi Bankası. You'll find the *Ayvalık Restaurant* (☎ 16759), and also the *Anadolu Pide ve Kebap Salonu* (☎ 16759), where I had a lunch of lentil soup, türlü (mixed baked vegetables), pilav, a soft drink, lots of fresh bread and tea for US$3. The nearby *Sultan Pastanesi* is good for biscuits or pastries and tea.

Ege Lokantası, inland at the market, remains cheap while the waterfront places go up-market. They have lots of good cheap steam-table fare ready to eat at any hour of the day. Nearby in the narrow market streets are various meyhanes, the Turkish equivalent of tavernas. These places are patronised by local men, and have good food and lots of drink at untouristy prices.

The cheapest full-service restaurant in the area is the *Sahil Restaurant* (☎ 11418), on Gümrük Meydanı near the Motel Kıyı. With both indoor and outdoor dining areas, the Sahil serves in all weather. Seafood is the speciality, but you'll pay a lot less if you order meat. A full dinner based on meat, beverage and tip included, costs about US$5; for seafood, figure on spending at least twice as much.

Out on the quay by the main square are several good waterfront fish restaurants, including the *Elif 2*, *Öz Canlıbalık* and *Acar*. Spacious, airy dining rooms, well-dressed clientele, and nicely lit terrace dining areas make dining here pleasant. One even advertises *elleniki kouzina* (Greek cuisine) to attract Greek tourists from Lesbos. The price for a full dinner rounds out to about US$20 per person.

Alibey One of the reasons people visit Ayvalık is to take the boat out to Alibey Adası and have lunch or dinner. You can expect to spend from US$12 to US$20 per person for a full seafood dinner with wine.

The west end of the village's seaside promenade is given over to tea gardens, cafés and pastry shops.

The eastern extent of the promenade is all restaurants, mostly named after the owner: *Günay'ın Yeri* (Günay's Place), *Arif'in Yeri* (Arif's Place etc). Cheapest among them, and still good currently, is Günay'ın Yeri at the east end of the promenade. At the west end, *Poseidon Restaurant*, one block north (inland), faces a parking lot, has no sea view and is thus a bit cheaper than the others.

Getting There & Away

Bus Ayvalık is served by the frequent bus service running up and down the Aegean coast between Çanakkale and İzmir, but you may have to hitchhike in from the highway. See the following Getting Around section.

When it comes time to leave Ayvalık, you should know that you can buy bus tickets at offices in the main square. Check departure times and availability early in the day. Buses stop running in late afternoon. Here are some details of services, from Ayvalık to:

Assos (Behramkale, via Ayvacık) – 130 km, over two hours, US$5; many buses to Ayvacık
Bergama – 50 km, 45 minutes, US$2; many buses to highway junction, few into town
Bursa – 300 km, 4½ hours, US$8; a dozen buses daily, continuing to İstanbul or Ankara
Çanakkale – 200 km, 3½ hours, US$7; many buses
İzmir – 240 km, 3½ hours, US$5.50; many buses

Boat – to/from Lesbos Greek and Turkish boats share the trade and make the two-hour voyage daily in summer (roughly from late May/early June to the end of September). Thus you can leave from Ayvalık on any day at 9 am with the Turkish boat, or 5 pm with the Greek boat. From Lesbos the weekday times are 8.30 am for the Greek boat and 1.30 pm for the Turkish boat (I've heard that Greek law states you must leave Greece on a Greek-flag vessel, unless you arrived on a Turkish-flag vessel with a round-trip ticket; thus, you may not be able to take the Turkish boat). On weekends the departure times are different: Saturday at 5.30 am, Sunday at 6 pm from Ayvalık; Saturday at 9 am, Sunday at 8 or 9 pm from Lesbos for the Turkish boat. Off-season (from October to April) boats operate about three times a week, but may halt completely in bad winter weather.

The cost of a one-way ticket is US$18, a round-trip ticket costs US$35; children up to six years of age sail free, those aged from six to 12 years pay half-price. Cars are carried for US$50 to US$70, motorcycles for US$20. Usually you must buy your ticket and hand over your passport for paperwork a day in advance of the voyage, whether you are departing from Turkey or from Greece.

For information and tickets, contact one of the several shipping agencies in the warren of little streets north and west of the main square, near the Motel Kıyı and the Sahil Restaurant. Eresos Tur has an agent, Ali Barış Erener (☎ 11756), Talat Paşa Caddesi 67, who can fill you in on schedules and fares, as can Ayvalık Tur (☎ (663) 12740).

In summer there are often afternoon boats departing from Lesbos at 4 pm for Piraeus, which means that you may be able to leave Ayvalık by the morning boat, spend a pleasant day in Lesbos, depart for Piraeus in the late afternoon, and arrive in Athens about 24 hours after leaving Ayvalık.

Getting Around

Buses along the highway will drop you at the northern turn-off for Ayvalık, exactly five km from the centre, unless the bus company specifically designates Ayvalık Otogar as a stop. From the highway you must hitchhike into town; drivers of most vehicles will understand your situation and stop to give you a lift. If you are dropped in town, it will be at the Şehirlerarası Otobüs Garajı (Intercity Bus Garage), which is 1.5 km (15 or 20 minutes' walk) north of the main square. City buses marked 'Ayvalık Belediyesi' run all the way through the town from north to south and will carry you from the bus station to the main square, south to the Tourism Information Office, and farther south to Çamlık, Orta Çamlık and Sarımsaklı, for a minimal fare.

BERGAMA (PERGAMUM)

Modern Bergama (BEHR-gah-mah, population 50,000), in the province of İzmir, is an agricultural market town in the midst of a well-watered plain. There has been a town here since Trojan times, but Pergamum's heyday was during the period after Alexander the Great and before Roman domination of all Asia Minor. At that time, Pergamum was one of the richest and most powerful small kingdoms in the Middle East.

History

Pergamum owes its prosperity to Lysimachus and to his downfall. Lysimachus, one of Alexander the Great's generals, controlled much of the Aegean region when Alexander's far-flung empire fell apart after his death in 323 BC. In the battles over the spoils Lysimachus captured a great treasure, which he secured in Pergamum before going

---

■ PLACES TO STAY

6   Acroteria Pension
10 Şehir Oteli
12 Pergamon Pension
21 Park Otel
23 Pension Aktan
25 Böblingen Pension
26 Hotel Berksoy

▼ PLACES TO EAT

3   Meydan Restaurant
4   Sarmaşık Lokantası
7   Gözde Yemek ve Kebap Salonu
9   Doyum 2

    OTHER

1   Kızıl Avlu (Red Basilica)
2   Fruit & Vegetable Market
5   Kulaksız Camii
8   Çarşı Hamamı (Turkish Bath)
11 Yeni Cami
13 Police Station
14 Belediye (City Hall)
15 Kurşunlu Cami
16 Government Building
17 School
18 High School
19 Arkeoloji Müzesi (Archaeology
    Museum)
20 Hospital
22 Bus Station
24 Tourism Information Office

---

off to fight Seleucus for control of all Asia Minor. But Lysimachus lost and was slain in 281 BC, so Philetarus, the commander he had posted at Pergamum to protect the treasure, set himself up as governor.

Philetarus was a eunuch, but he was succeeded by his nephew Eumenes I (263-241 BC), and Eumenes was followed by his adopted son Attalus I (241-197 BC). Attalus took the title of king, expanded his power and made an alliance with Rome. He was succeeded by his son Eumenes II, and that's when the fun began.

Eumenes II (197-159 BC) was the man who really built Pergamum. Rich and powerful, he added the library and the Altar of

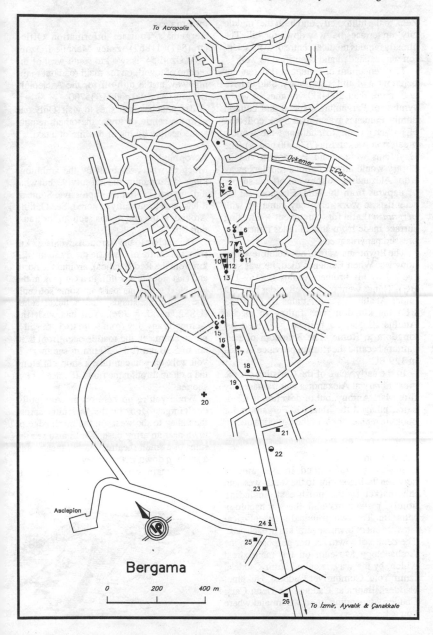

To Acropolis

Öçkemer

E Çay

5

6

7

8

9

10

11

12

13

14

15

16

17

18

19

20

21

22

23

24

25

26

Asclepion

Bergama

0   200   400 m

To İzmir, Ayvalık & Çanakkale

Zeus to the hilltop city, and built the 'middle city' on terraces halfway down the hill. The already famous medical centre of the Asclepion was expanded and beautified as well.

The Pergamum of Eumenes II is remembered most of all for its library. Said to have held more than 200,000 volumes, it was a symbol of Pergamum's social and cultural climb. Eumenes was a mad book collector. His library came to challenge the world's greatest in Alexandria (700,000 books). The Egyptians were afraid Pergamum and its library would attract famous scholars away from Alexandria, so they cut off the supply of papyrus from the Nile. Eumenes set his scientists to work, and they came up with *pergamen* (Latin for 'parchment'), a writing surface made from animal hides rather than pressed papyrus reeds.

The Egyptians were to have their revenge, however. When Eumenes died, he was succeeded by his brother Attalus II (159-138 BC). Things went pretty well under him, but under Attalus II's son Attalus III (138-133 BC) the kingdom was falling to pieces. Attalus III had no heir so he willed his kingdom to Rome. The Kingdom of Pergamum became the Roman province of Asia in 129 BC.

In the early years of the Christian era the great library at Alexandria was damaged by fire. Marc Antony, out of devotion to Cleopatra, pillaged the library at Pergamum for books to replace those of the Egyptian queen.

Orientation

Everything you'll need in Bergama is between the bus station to the south-west and the market to the north-east, including hotels, restaurants and the Archaeology Museum. The two principal archaeological sites are out of town, several km in each case. The centre of town, for our purposes, is the Archaeology Museum on the main street which, by the way, is called İzmir Caddesi, İzmir Yolu, Cumhuriyet Caddesi, Hükümet Caddesi, Bankalar Caddesi, or Uzun Çarşı Caddesi, depending upon whom and where you ask.

Information

Bergama's Tourism Information Office (☎ (541) 11862), Zafer Mahallesi, İzmir Yolu Üzeri 54, is two km south-west of the 'centre of town', on the main road out to the highway, at the turn-off for the Asclepion. Bergama's postal code is 35700.

Bergama has four sites to visit. Only one is in the centre of town; the others require some healthy hiking or the hire of a taxi.

Acropolis

Much of what was built by the ambitious kings of Pergamum did not survive, but what did survive is certainly impressive. Some of it has been beautifully restored. See Getting Around, at the end of this section, for transport tips.

The road up to the Acropolis winds six km from the centre of town (ie the museum; 4.3 km from the Red Basilica), around the north and east sides of the hill, to a car park at the top. Next to the car park are some souvenir and soft-drink stands, and a ticket seller (US$2, parking 70c). You can visit the Acropolis any day from 9 am to 5 pm (till 7 pm in summer); the road is open from 8.30 am to 5.30 pm (till 7.30 pm in summer). If you walk up you can take a short cut along the path up through the ruins. It's steeper but shorter.

While you're up here on the Acropolis, don't forget to look for the Asclepion, across the valley to the west, on the north edge of town near an army base. You'll also see the ruins of a small theatre, a larger theatre and a stadium down in the valley.

The main structures on the Acropolis

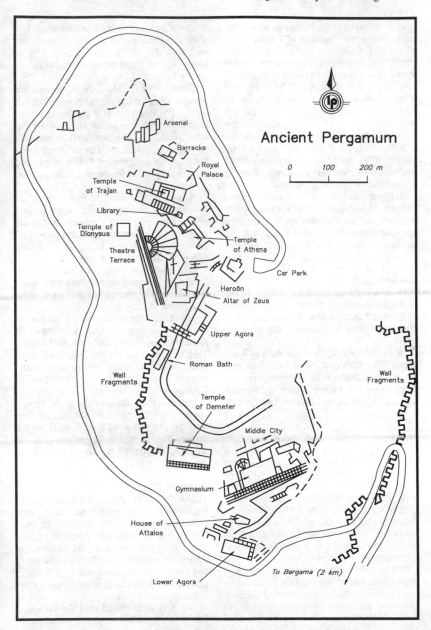

Ancient Pergamum

0   100   200 m

- Arsenal
- Barracks
- Royal Palace
- Temple of Trajan
- Library
- Temple of Dionysus
- Temple of Athena
- Theatre Terrace
- Car Park
- Heroön
- Altar of Zeus
- Upper Agora
- Roman Bath
- Wall Fragments
- Wall Fragments
- Temple of Demeter
- Middle City
- Gymnasium
- House of Attalos
- Lower Agora
- To Bergama (2 km)

include (of course) the **library** as well as the marble-columned **Temple of Trajan**, being rebuilt by the German Archaeological Institute. The great **theatre** is impressive (10,000 seats) and unusual. Pergamum borrowed from Hellenistic architecture, but in the case of the theatre made major modifications. To take advantage of the spectacular view and to conserve precious building space on top of the hill, it was decided to build the theatre into the hillside. Hellenistic theatres are usually more rounded, but because of this one's location, rounding was impossible, so it was increased in height instead.

Below the stage of the theatre is the ruined **Temple of Dionysus**. The **Altar of Zeus**, south of the theatre, shaded by evergreen trees, is in an idyllic setting. Most of the building is now in Berlin, taken there (with the sultan's permission) by the 19th-century German excavators of Pergamum. Only the base remains.

Otherwise, several piles of rubble on top of the Acropolis are marked as the **palaces of Attalus I and Eumenes II**, and there is an **agora** as well as fragments of the defensive walls.

Walk down the hill from the Altar of Zeus, through the **Middle City**, and you will pass the **Altar & Temple of Demeter, gymnasium** or school, **Lower Agora** and **Roman bath**. The path down is not well marked.

Asclepion

The Asclepion of Pergamum was not the first nor the only ancient medical centre. In fact, this one was founded by Archias, a citizen of Pergamum who had been treated and cured at the Asclepion of Epidaurus in Greece. But Pergamum's centre came to the fore under Galen (131-210 AD), who was born here, studied in Alexandria and Greece as well as in Asia Minor, and set up shop as physician to Pergamum's gladiators.

Recognised as perhaps the greatest early physician, Galen added considerably to knowledge of the circulatory and nervous systems, and also systematised medical theory. Under his influence, the medical school at Pergamum became renowned. His work was the basis for all Western medicine well into the 1500s. Around 162 AD, he moved to Rome and became personal physician to Emperor Marcus Aurelius.

There are two roads to the Asclepion, the handier being the one from the centre of town (see map). The other is at the western edge of town on the way to the highway. By the latter road, the ruins are 3.5 km from the Archaeology Museum, about 1.5 km from the Tourism Information Office. Asclepion opening hours and fees are the same as at the Acropolis.

As you walk around the ruins, you'll see bas-reliefs or carvings of a snake, the symbol of Aesculapius, god of medicine. Just as the snake shed its skin and gained a 'new life', so the patients at the Asclepion were supposed to 'shed' their illnesses.

Diagnosis was often by dream analysis. Treatment included massage and mud baths, drinking sacred waters, and the use of herbs and ointments.

A **Sacred Way** leads from the car park to the centre. Signs mark a **Temple to Aesculapius, library** and **Roman Theatre**. Take a drink of cool water from the **Sacred Well**, then pass along the vaulted underground corridor to the **Temple of Telesphorus**.

It is said that patients slept in the temple hoping that Telesphorus, another god of medicine, would send a cure, or at least a diagnosis, in a dream. Telesphorus, by the way, had two daughters named Hygeia and Panacea.

Sights in Town

The **Arkeoloji Müzesi** (Archaeology Museum) is in the town centre next to the hillside tea gardens, not far from the Park Otel. It has a substantial collection of artefacts for so small a town, and an excellent ethnology section as well. It's open every day from 9 am to noon and 1 to 7 pm in summer (to 5.30 pm in winter), every day; admission costs US$2.

The **Kızıl Avlu** (KUH-zuhl ahv-loo), Red Basilica or Red Courtyard, 150 metres north-

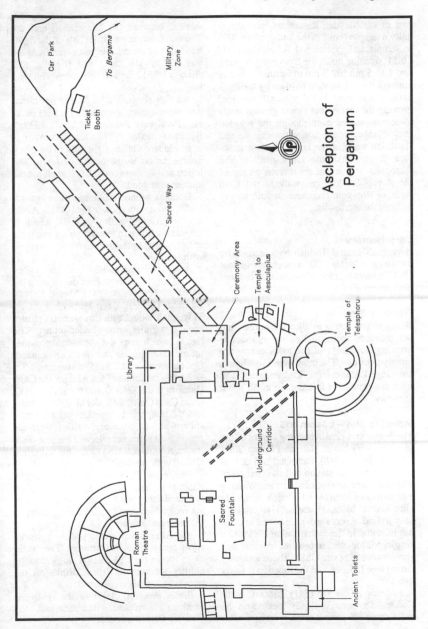

Asclepion of Pergamum

Car Park

To Bergama

Military Zone

Ticket Booth

Sacred Way

Ceremony Area

Temple to Aesculapius

Temple of Telesphorus

Library

Underground Corridor

Roman Theatre

Sacred Fountain

Ancient Toilets

east of the Meydan Restaurant, was originally a temple (built in the 2nd century AD) to Serapis, an Egyptian god. Admission costs US$1; opening hours are from 9 am to noon and 1 to 5 pm (till 7 pm in summer). It was converted to a Christian basilica by the Byzantines and now holds a small mosque, proving the theory that sacred ground tends to remain sacred even though the religion may change. You'll notice the curious red flat-brick walls of the large, roofless structure if you take the main road to the Acropolis or you can see it from on top of the Acropolis. You can walk to the Kızıl Avlu, or stop your taxi there on your way to or from the Acropolis.

Çarşı Hamamı

Bergama's central Turkish bath is used by tourists and locals alike, and charges about US$2, a mere fraction of the inflated İstanbul bath prices.

Places to Stay

Bergama has hotels in all price ranges, but not many of them, though the number is growing. Lodgings in the town centre are mostly pensions. The more expensive hotels are ranged along İzmir Caddesi, the road from the centre out to the main north-south highway.

Places to Stay – bottom end

The hotels and pensions at the centre of the town are very basic, plain and cheap. *Park Otel* (☎ (541) 11246), Park Otel Sokak 6, is closest to the bus station and the first place where most people look for a room. Walking east into town from the bus station, turn right after several blocks; there's a sign, and it's easy to find. Rooms are quite bare and plain but tidy, and in fierce demand at US$9/12 a single/double without water rooms; hot showers cost an extra US$1. There's a shady sitting area in front, and the location is fairly quiet.

Pension Aktan (☎ (541) 14000), İzmir Caddesi 18, is conveniently located on the main street 120 metres south-west of the bus

station, between the bus station and the Tourism Information Office; it's on the right-hand side of the road as you come from the bus station. It's clean and friendly, and charges US$12 for a double room with twin beds.

Another pension, a bit farther north-east past the museum, also caters for backpackers. *Pergamon Pension* (☎ (541) 12395), Bankalar Caddesi 3, Polis Karakolu Yanı, is in an old stone house right next to the city's police station in the centre of town. The toilets and showers could be cleaner, but the ambience is good.

Doubles without running water go for US$8, those with shower for US$12. Avoid the 'large room' with five beds, which is subject to kitchen smells. Meals are available at tables in the pleasant courtyard complete with fountain.

Across the street and down a narrow alley by the Çarşı Hamamı (follow the signs) is the *Acroteria Pension* (☎ (541) 12469, 21047), Bankalar Caddesi, Çarşı Hamamı Yanı 11. Tidy small rooms with tiny showers cluster around a quiet, vine-shaded court. The family which runs the Acroteria provides informative tips, tea and meals on demand. Double rooms cost US$15 in summer.

Also in the centre of town facing the Çarşı Hamamı is the *Şehir Oteli* (☎ (541) 11031), Uzun Çarşı Caddesi 45, an old-style farmers' hotel. Though it is spartan, has no atmosphere and is certainly noisier than the pensions, it is respectable, and the low-price leader. Rooms cost US$7 a double with sink, US$10 with shower.

Böblingen Pension (☎ (541) 12153), Zafer Mahallesi, Asclepion Caddesi 2, is a quiet and cheap place on the western Asclepion road which goes uphill from the Tourism Information Office.

The Altın family, owners of the pension, spent many years in Germany. They offer clean rooms for US$10/14 a single/double, clothes-washing facilities, drinks on the terrace and meals on demand.

Berlin Pension, closer to the centre, is another pleasant place with a patio and good view for US$12 a double.

Camping *Hotel Berksoy* (see following) has a mocamp for tents, caravans and camper vans, but prices rival those at the pensions, and it's two km out of town. Farther out towards the highway, about five km from the centre, are the cheaper *Küçükkaya* and *Gülgün* camping grounds, two km east of the highway junction.

Places to Stay – middle
Bergama's nicest place to stay is the *Hotel Berksoy* (☎ (541) 12595; fax 15346), PK 19, two km west of the centre on the road out to the main highway. The three-star Berksoy, set in verdant grounds, offers four-star comforts including a restaurant, bar, tennis court and swimming pool for US$55 a double in season, breakfast included, in one of its 57 rooms. There is a mocamp as well.

Also out on the road west of the centre is the equally comfortable three-star *Asude Hotel* (☎ (541) 11669, 13067; fax 13143), İzmir Asfaltı 93, with similar rates. Its 52 rooms have satellite TV, minibars and so forth; other services include a Turkish bath, sauna, and indoor swimming pool.

Efsune Hotel (☎ (541) 12936, 21614; fax 12510), İzmir Caddesi 86, rates two stars for its 22 bath-equipped rooms. With two bars, a restaurant and swimming pool, it offers good value within a longish walk of the otogar. Room prices are from US$25 to US$35 a double.

The 42-room *Tusan Bergama Moteli* (☎ (541) 11173), Çatı Mevkii, near the junction of the highway and the road into town, is Bergama's oldest touristic hotel, but is still nice. It has a restaurant and a quiet location with pretty gardens, in the middle of nowhere. Rooms with a bath cost US$24/35 a single/double; breakfast costs another US$4.

Serapion Hotel (☎ (541) 12663), İzmir Caddesi 75, is on the road as you come into town about one km from the centre. The Serapion has 20 double rooms with shower priced at US$15/24 a single/double.

Places to Eat
The three types of restaurant in Bergama are those used by tour groups, those used by individual travellers, and those used by locals. Places in the first two categories are used to tourists and are at that stage when you should ask prices, protest if they seem unreasonable, and check your bill for 'errors'.

There are several small eateries near the Pergamon and Acroteria pensions, near the Çarşı Hamamı on the main street. *Gözde Yemek ve Kebap Salonu* has tidy streetside tables and an assortment of ready foods and grills. The nearby *Adil Lokanta ve Kebap Salonu* is similar, but without the streetside tables. *Doyum 2* is on the main street just east of the Şehir Oteli. Any of these places can provide a good three-course meal for US$4 to US$6. *Doyum Tabldot Restaurant*, advertising a full three-course meal for under US$2, is down the little street directly across the main street from the mosque Yeni Cami (look for the gate with the marble Ottoman inscription above it).

About 400 metres north-east of these restaurants and 150 metres before the Red Basilica is a small plaza (meydan) surrounded by restaurants right next to Bergama's open-air fruit and vegetable market. *Meydan Restaurant* is among the most prominent of these, serving shish kebap for US$2, and half a roasted chicken for US$2.75. *Çiçek Birahanesi* and *Yüksel Birahanesi*, despite their names as beerhalls, are in fact full-service restaurants, similar to the Meydan, with vine-shaded streetside tables.

Across the plaza from the Meydan is the *Sarmaşık Lokantası*, a less touristed place with only indoor dining (no streetside tables) but lower prices. For more cheap places, walk south-west along the main street to find simpler places such as *Şen Kardeşler* and *Çiçek Sever Kebap Salonu*, where full meals can be had for US$3 or so.

At the Acropolis and Asclepion there are soft drinks for sale, but no food.

Getting There & Away
Whether you approach Bergama from the north or south, check to see if your bus actually stops *in* Bergama. Any bus will be glad to drop you along the highway at the

turn-off to Bergama, but you will have to hitchhike seven km into town in this case. Hitching is pretty easy, except in the evening. It's better to be on a bus which goes right to Bergama's Santral Garaj (otogar).

Ask the driver, *Bergama Santral Garajına gidiyor musunuz?* (BEHR-gah-mah sahn-tral gah-rah-zhuh-nah gee-dee-YOHR-moo-soo-nooz, 'Do you go to Bergama's central garage?') Be advised that many drivers will nod *Evet!* (Yes!), and then blithely drop you out at the highway.

The otogar is on the main street, which is also the road between the town and the highway.

Following are the major routes; note that bus traffic dies down dramatically in late afternoon and evening.

Ayvalık – 50 km, 45 minutes, US$2; many buses from highway junction, few from Bergama's Santral Garaj

Dikili – 30 km, 35 minutes, US$1; frequent minibuses

İstanbul – Though there are a few direct night buses between Bergama and İstanbul, it is far cheaper and, surprisingly, quicker to travel via İzmir.

İzmir – 100 km, 1¾ hours, US$3; Pamukkale runs buses almost every half-hour; Bergama municipal buses ('Bergama Belediyesi') run eight times daily

Buses to other destinations are not all that frequent. In winter, you may find yourself changing buses in İzmir or Balıkesir to get to Ankara, Bursa or İstanbul.

Getting Around

On Foot Bergama can be a tiring town if you aren't used to walking. Here are some distances from the bus station:

To Museum – 200 metres
To Pergamon Pension – 600 metres
To Acropolis – 6.2 km
To Asclepion – two km

If you're in good shape and don't mind walking, but you have limited time, find others to share a taxi to the top of the Acropolis, then walk down the hill to the Kızıl Avlu. Walking down through the various levels of the ruined city is the best way to see the site in any case. From the Kızıl Avlu, walk through the market district into town, have lunch and take a taxi, or hitch, or walk to the Asclepion, depending upon your budget, your level of fatigue and your schedule.

Taxi Tours The standard taxi-tour rates (per car) are from:

Town to Acropolis
    (one way) – US$4
Town to Acropolis
    (one hour's waiting) then return to town – US$14
Town to Acropolis
    (one hour's waiting), to Kızıl Avlu (short stop), to museum (15 minutes' waiting), to Asclepion (30 minutes' waiting), return to town – US$18

Taxis for hire cluster near the Belediye, just north-east of the museum; and near the market by the Meydan Restaurant.

DİKİLİ

Travelling 41 km south from Ayvalık along the coast road, there is a turn-off on the right for Dikili (population 20,000), four km west of the coastal highway, and 30 km west of Bergama. A new wharf capable of serving ocean liners is bringing cruise ships to Dikili; the passengers then take a bus to Bergama to see the ruins. Dikili is a pleasant place to stop for a few days by the sea if you've got the time.

Orientation

The town's main beach (of coarse, dark sand) starts about 600 metres north of the main square and goes west for about one km. The post office (PTT) is a few steps north of the main square, towards the beach. The otogar is 400 metres north of the main square and 200 metres south of the beach.

Places to Stay

Following is a list of the lodgings closest to the bus station. *Dörtler Camping* is on the beach 400 metres north of the bus station. *Özdemir Pansiyon* (☎ (5419) 1295), 100 metres north of the main square along the main street, is good if you expect to spend only a night or two and want to do it cheaply; likewise the *Güneş Pansiyon* (☎ (5419) 1847), a bit farther north from the Özdemir, then east (inland) 100 metres (follow the signs). Either charges about US$6 per person.

Tanrıverdi Perla Hotel (☎ (5419) 1849) is on the western shore of the bay, 800 metres from the main square, and offers two-star comforts for US$35 to US$40 a double.

For beach fun, there are many small pensions and hotels north of the centre along the beach.

Getting There & Away

Though there are direct buses between İzmir and Dikili via Çandarlı, most long-distance bus traffic goes via Bergama. Take one of the frequent minibuses to Bergama (35 minutes, US$1) for connections with more distant points.

ÇANDARLI

Heading south from Dikili, after 18.5 km you come to Çandarlı, marked by a small but stately Genoese castle. The castle and the village at its feet are on a peninsula which juts southward into the Aegean. It's a nice hideaway, without too much tourism yet.

The main square and the commercial section of the village are to the east of the castle, the nicer hotels and pensions are to the west. The post office is on the market square, a few dozen metres south of the main square.

Places to Stay & Eat

Near the main square on the eastern side of the castle, *Kaya Pension* (☎ (5415) 1058) is central but noisy, with beds for US$6 per person. Get a room high up, with less noise and better views. Locals prefer the little restaurants around the main square which, though not as pleasant as the 'touristic' places to the west, are cheaper. The simple *Lokanta* to the left of the Kaya Pension has cheap fare. The *Temiz Ocak Pide Salonu* ('Tidy Hearth') just a bit farther along, serves pides for around US$1 at a few streetside tables. *Azim Lokantası*, to the right of the

post office, facing the market square, does good cheap grilled meats.

Walk along the western shore and you'll quickly see most of the village's lodging and dining possibilities: *Martı Motel* (☎ (5415) 1441), 400 metres west of the main square, overlooks the sea and has a nice, verdant terrace restaurant. Rooms cost US$22 a double. *Philippi Pansiyon* is 200 metres south of the Martı, a modern house converted to a pension, with a little terrace café. Rates are US$8/16 a single/double, which is what most places in town charge.

Halil'in Yeri Restaurant, 100 metres north of the Martı Motel is good. There's also the *Kale Kafeteryası* and the *Atamer Restaurant*, the latter next to the Papatya Pansiyon.

Senger Pansiyon is similar to the Papatya, but 300 metres north of it. Next to the Senger is the *Kalender Restaurant*, a white-table-cloth place which seems to be Çandarlı's best. Finally, the *Oral Pansiyon* is 100 metres north of the Senger, and the *Hotel Emirgan* and *Hotel Kibele* are two modern places 100 metres north of the Oral.

Getting There & Away

Sebat Otobüsleri runs buses between Çandarlı and İzmir and Dikili several times daily. It also operates several daily minibuses to and from Bergama.

FOÇA & YENİ FOÇA

Old Ottoman-Greek stone houses line a sinuous shore crowded with fishing boats. On a hill behind the town a Genoese fortress (1275) continues its slow centuries of crumbling. Turkish sailors in nautical whites crowd the cheaper cafés, while the more expensive ones are a babble of European languages. This is Foça (FOH-chah), a pleasant little resort town which resembles Kuşadası in the 1970s, before Kuşadası exploded into hyper-tourism.

Eski Foça, the ancient Phocaea, was founded before 600 BC and flourished during the 500s BC. During their golden age, the Phocaeans were famous mariners, sending swift vessels powered by 50 oars into the Aegean, Mediterranean and Black seas. They were also great colonists, having founded Samsun on the Black Sea as well as towns in southern Italy, Corsica, France and Spain.

Nothing remains of the ancient city. In recent centuries this was an Ottoman Greek fishing and trading town, but it's now a middle-class Turkish resort with yachts bobbing in the harbour and condos being built on the quay. Near Yeni Foça, to the north of Foça, there's a Club Méditerranée holiday village *(tatil köyü)*, which feeds groups of European holiday-makers into the local economy.

Yeni Foça, 25 km north of Foça, has a few old stone houses, lots more new houses, hotels, condos and holiday villages, all ranged around a picture-perfect bay which must have been created by nature expressly for water sports. It's nice, but without the charm of Foça proper.

Orientation & Information

The bus station is only a few metres off the main square. Walk north through the square with its Tourism Information Office (☎ (5431) 11222), post office and shady park. Pass the post office (PTT) keeping it on your right to find the town's restaurants (350 metres from the bus station) and pensions (600 to 700 metres from the bus station). Foça's postal code is 35680.

Places to Stay

Most of Foça's lodgings are little pensions charging between US$7 and US$12 for a double room, and small hotels charging up to US$30 for double rooms with bath. Here is what you'll encounter as you walk north from the bus station.

Hotel Kaan and *Zümrüt Pension*, a few steps from the bus station, are cheap at US$7 a double, but not very comfortable or quiet. Keep walking, and go along the waterfront street (Sahil Caddesi).

Hotel Karaçam (☎ (5431) 1416; fax 2042), Sahil Caddesi 70, is an Ottoman house (1881) fixed up, fairly comfortable, with friendly management and the advantages of a roof-terrace bar, streetside café,

fancy furniture in the lobby, and lots of cats. A few of the 22 rooms have water views. Rates are US$20/30 a single/double in season, breakfast included. The adjoining *Villa Dedem* is similar.

Ensar Aile Pansiyonu (☎ (5431) 1401, 1777), İsmetpaşa Mahallesi, 161 Sokak No 15, is a new, modern building one block inland from the water. It charges US$12 a double for nice rooms with private showers. The adjoining *Siren Pansiyon* (☎ (5431) 2660) is similar. *Hotel Melaike*, at the end of the street, is new, modern, quiet, and charges US$19 a double with shower. There are no water views here.

Sempatik Hotel Güneş (☎ (5431) 2195), 206 Sokak No 11, is nice, new, comfy, and as the name indicates, 'sympathetic'. Rates for the rooms, done in stucco and honey-coloured pine, are US$22 a double.

Even farther along, *Hotel Celep* has plain rooms with bath for US$20 a double, and its own very popular restaurant with water views. Near the Celep are several other pensions, including the *İyigün Pension* across the street, which charges US$6 per person and also has its own restaurant. Behind the Celep, the *İyon Pension* (☎ (5431) 1415), is one of the cheaper ones at US$6 per person.

Camping The coast north of Foça is sculpted into small coves with sandy beaches, mostly backed by holiday condominium developments, but a few have primitive café-restaurant-camping places. The nicest of these is the *Pınar*, six km north of Foça, with electrical and water hook-ups in an olive grove on the beach, and no condos.

Places to Eat

For cheap fare, try the *Sahil Pide Salonu* on the south-west side of the bus station, popular with sailors at Foça's naval base because it's the cheapest place in town. *Zümrüt*, in the pension of the same name facing the main square, is also cheap, with meat stews for US$1.50 or so.

Be sure to ask prices first at any of the restaurants along the water, particularly if you are ordering fish. All waterfront restaurants – Foça, Celep, Çetin, Gaziantep, all in a row – charge from US$12 to US$20 for a full fish dinner, half that for meat. The Celep was best at my last visit. All are good, particularly for sunset dining.

Getting There & Away

Foça is 83 km south of Bergama, 73 km south of Çandarlı, and 70 km north-west of İzmir. Virtually all bus traffic is to and from İzmir (1¼ hours, US$2), with a stop midway in Menemen (37 km, 35 minutes, US$1.25). If you're bound for somewhere other than İzmir (Manisa in particular), it's best to change buses in Menemen rather than to wait out on the highway.

MENEMEN

Menemen (MEHN-eh-mehn), 33 km north of İzmir, is famous for a reactionary riot which took place in 1930. Atatürk's cultural reforms such as abolishing religious law, separating religion from the state and recognising the equality of women were not received well by religious conservatives. A band of fanatical dervishes staged a riot in Menemen's town square. When a young army officer named Mustafa Fehmi Kubilay attempted to quell the disturbance, he was shot and beheaded by the dervishes. The government took immediate action to quash the fanatics' revolt, and proclaimed Kubilay a republican hero. The statue here honours the young officer.

MANİSA

A road goes east 30 km to the town of Manisa (mah-NEES-ah, population 160,000), the ancient town of Magnesia ad Sipylus. It's a modern little city with an ancient past. An early king was Tantalus, from whose name we get the word 'tantalise'. The early, great Ottoman sultans favoured it as a residence, and for a while the province of Manisa was the training ground for promising Ottoman princes.

During the War of Independence, retreating Greek soldiers wreaked terrible destruction on the town. After they passed through, Manisa's 18,000 historic buildings had been reduced to only 500.

Orientation

Doğu Caddesi is the main street in the commercial district. The historic mosques are only a few hundred metres to the south along İbrahim Gökçen Caddesi. The railway station is less than one km north-east of the centre; the otogar, 600 metres north-west.

Information

Manisa's Tourism Information Office (☎ (551) 12541) is in the Özel İdare İşhanı building, Yarhasanlar Mahallesi, Doğu Caddesi 14/3.

Things to See

As you might expect, there are several old mosques, among them the **Muradiye Camii** (1586) with nice tilework. The adjoining building, constructed originally as a soup kitchen, is now the **Manisa Müzesi** (open from 9 am to noon and 1 to 5 pm, closed on Monday), with the standard collections, including some fine mosaics from the ruins of Sardis. Near the museum is the ancient tomb of **Saruhan Bey**. The **Sultan Camii** (1572) has some gaudy painting, but an agreeable hamam next door. Perched on the steep hillside above the town centre is the **Ulu Cami** (1366), ravished by the ages, and not as impressive as the view from the teahouse next to it. Other historic mosques in town are the **Hatuniye** (1490) and the **İlyas Bey** (1363).

Festivals

On four days around the spring equinox (in late March) each year, Manisa rejoices in the Mesir Şenlikleri, a festival celebrating *Mesir macunu* (power gum). Legend says that over 450 years ago, a local pharmacist named Merkez Müslihiddin Efendi concocted a potion to cure a mysterious ailment of Hafza Sultan, mother of Sultan Süleyman the Magnificent. The queen mother, delighted with her swift recovery, ordered that the amazing elixir be distributed to the people of Manisa at her expense. In fact, the Ottomans had a long-standing custom of eating spiced sweets at *Nevruz*, the Persian new year (spring equinox).

Hafza Sultan's bank account is long closed, so the municipal authorities pick up the tab for the 10 tonnes of Mesir, mixed from sugar and 40 spices and ingredients. Townsfolk in period costumes re-enact the mixing of the potion, then throw it from the dome of the Sultan Camii. Mesir is credited by locals with improving the circulation, calming the nerves, stimulating hormones, increasing appetite, immunising one against poisonous stings and bites, and doubling tourist revenues.

Places to Stay

The 34-room, two-star *Hotel Arma* (☎ (551) 11980), Doğu Caddesi 14, is the town's best. It has a willing and helpful staff, a restaurant and bar, clean and presentable rooms, a lift and prices of US$20/28 a single/double. Other than the Arma, there are few decent places to stay – everyone, whatever their business, stays in İzmir and drives to Manisa for the day.

Into İzmir

If you approach İzmir from Menemen, you will pass a road at Çiğli to İzmir's old airport. İzmir's new Adnan Menderes Airport – the one you'll use – is at Cumaovası, south of the city halfway to Ephesus. Past Çiğli, the highway passes the suburb of Karşıyaka (KAHR-shuh-YAH-kah), then curves around the end of the bay to the otogar.

Coming from Manisa, the road passes through the suburb of Bornova, once the residence of wealthy Levantine traders. Some of their mansions still stand, most now converted for public use as municipal offices, schools, and the like. There's a university here. İzmir city buses run from Bornova to the centre of İzmir.

İZMİR

İzmir (EEZ-meer, population two million), is Turkey's third-largest city and its major port on the Aegean. It has a different feeling

about it: something Mediterranean, something more than just being a large and prosperous Turkish city. The setting is certainly dramatic, for İzmir rings a great bay and is backed to the east and south by mountains. Most of the city is quite modern and well laid-out, with broad boulevards radiating from a series of hubs. The streets are lined with waffle-front, stucco-and-glass apartment and office blocks, and dotted with shady streetside cafés, though here and there the red-tile roof and bull's-eye window of a 19th-century warehouse hide in the shadow of an office tower. When you see an old mosque in İzmir it comes as a surprise, as though it doesn't really fit in.

You may enjoy a short stay in İzmir, with its palm-lined waterfront promenade. The city can be explored and enjoyed in a fairly short time because there's not a whole lot to see: most of the remains from its long and eventful history have been swept away by war, fire and earthquake. Compared with most Turkish towns, İzmir does not have a large number of antiquities. You can also use İzmir as a base for excursions to a few nearby points: Sardis, for instance. But in most cases you will be ready to move on in a day, as you may find İzmir to be a big, busy, noisy and impersonal city.

History

İzmir owes its special atmosphere, indeed its entire appearance, to an eventful and turbulent history. What you see today is new because it has risen from the ashes of Ottoman İzmir since 1923, when a Greek invasion and a disastrous fire razed most of the city. Before that year, İzmir was Smyrna, the most Western and cosmopolitan of Turkish cities, where more citizens were Christian and Jewish than Muslim, and there were thousands of foreign diplomats, traders, merchants and sailors. Its connections with Greece and Europe were close and continuous. To the Turks it was 'Infidel Smyrna'.

İzmir's commercial connections with Europe began in 1535, but the city is far, far older than that. The first settlement that we know of, at Bayraklı near the eastern end of the bay, was by Aeolians in the 10th century BC, but there were probably people here as far back as 3000 BC. The city's name comes from the goddess Myrina, the prevalent deity before the coming of the Aeolians who also worshipped Nemesis. Famous early citizens of Smyrna included the poet Homer, the founder of Western literature, who lived before 700 BC.

The city began its history of war and destruction early, for the Aeolians were overcome by the Ionians, who in turn were conquered by the Lydians from Sardis. Around 600 BC, the Lydians destroyed the city and it lay in ruins until the coming of Alexander the Great.

Alexander the Great (356-323 BC) refounded Smyrna on Mt Pagus, now called Kadifekale (kah-dee-FEH-kah-leh, Velvet Fortress), in the centre of the modern city. He erected the fortification that you can still see crowning the hill, and made many other improvements.

Smyrna's luck changed during the struggles over the spoils of Alexander's empire. The city sided with Pergamum, the Aegean

power-to-be. Later it welcomed Roman rule and benefited greatly from it. When an earthquake destroyed the city in 178 AD, Emperor Marcus Aurelius sent money and men to aid in the reconstruction. Under Byzantium, the later Roman Empire, it became one of the busiest ports along the coast.

As Byzantium's power declined, various armies including the Arabs, Seljuk Turks, Genoese and crusaders marched in, and often out again. When Tamerlane arrived in 1402 he destroyed the city, true to form, but after he left, the Ottomans took over in 1415 and things began to look better.

In 1535, Süleyman the Magnificent signed the Ottomans' first-ever commercial treaty (with François I of France), which permitted foreign merchants to reside in the sultan's dominions. After that humble start, İzmir became Turkey's most sophisticated commercial city. Its streets and buildings took on a quasi-European appearance, and a dozen languages were spoken in its cafés. Any merchant worth his salt was expected to be fluent in Turkish, Greek, Italian, German, English and Arabic, and perhaps a few other languages as well.

The Ottoman Empire was defeated along with Germany in WW I, and the victorious Allies sought to carve the sultan's vast dominions into spheres of influence. Some Greeks had always dreamed of re-creating the long-lost Byzantine Empire. In 1920, with Allied encouragement, the Greeks took a gamble, invaded İzmir, seized Bursa and headed towards Ankara. In fierce fighting on the outskirts of Ankara, where Atatürk's provisional government had its headquarters, the foreign forces were stopped, then turned around and pushed back. The Greek defeat turned to a rout and the once-powerful army, half its ranks taken prisoner, scorched the earth and fled to ships waiting in İzmir. The day Atatürk took İzmir, 9 September 1922, was the moment of victory in the Turkish War of Independence. (It's now the big local holiday.)

A disastrous fire broke out during the final mopping-up operations and destroyed most of the city. Though a tragedy, it allowed a modern city of wide streets to rise from the ashes.

Orientation

İzmir has wide boulevards and an apparent sense of orderliness, but it is in fact somewhat difficult to negotiate. This is because the numerous roundabouts (traffic circles), with their streets radiating like spokes from a hub, don't give you the sense of direction a street grid does. Here are some tips on getting your bearings.

First of all, the city's two main avenues run parallel to the waterfront, downtown. The waterfront street is officially Atatürk Caddesi, which is what you will see in written addresses, but everyone in town calls it the Birinci Kordon (beer-EEN-jee kohr-DOHN, First Cordon). Just inland from it is Cumhuriyet Bulvarı (joom-hoor-ee-YEHT bool-vahr-uh, Republic Blvd), which is called by everyone the İkinci Kordon (ee-KEEN-jee, Second Cordon).

The city's two main squares are along these two parallel avenues. The very centre of town is Konak Meydanı (Government House Square), or simply Konak. Here you will find the municipality buildings, the Ottoman clock tower (İzmir's symbol) and a little old tiled mosque set in a spacious park, and a dock for ferries to Karşıyaka, the suburb across the bay.

Konak also has an entrance to the bazaar. Anafartalar Caddesi, the bazaar's main street, winds through İzmir's most picturesque quarters all the way to the Basmane Garı (railway station).

The other main square, Cumhuriyet Meydanı, holds the equestrian statue of Atatürk. It is about a km north of Konak along the two kordons. The PTT, Tourism Information Office, Turkish Airlines office, car-rental offices and Büyük Efes Oteli are here.

The section called Çankaya (CHAN-kah-yah) is two long blocks inland, south-east of Cumhuriyet Meydanı.

Another İzmir landmark is the Kültür Parkı (kewl-TEWR pahr-kuh), the city's Culture Park, site of the annual İzmir Inter-national Fair (see Festivals). When it's not fair time the grounds provide a pleasant, shady place to walk, sit and rest in, as well as some amusements.

Finally, the hill directly behind the main part of town is crowned by Kadifekale, the 'Velvet Fortress'.

Information

The Tourism Information Office (☎ (51) 19 92 78, 14 21 47), Gaziosmanpaşa Bulvarı 1/C, is next to the Büyük Efes Oteli, in the row of offices which includes the Turkish Airlines office. Opening hours are from 8.30 am to 7 pm daily June to October, till 5.30 pm and closed on Sunday in the off season. Other offices are at the Yeni Liman (☎ (51) 63 16 00) and at Adnan Menderes Airport (☎ (51) 51 26 26 x 1081, 51 19 50). The bus station has a small office as well. The administrative office (☎ (51) 21 68 41, 22 02 07, -8; fax 21 68 41) is at Atatürk Caddesi 418, Alsancak.

The Tourism Police can be reached on (51) 21 86 52.

Consulates See Visas & Embassies in the Facts for the Visitor chapter.

Bookshops Net is at Cumhuriyet Bulvarı 142-A, behind the NATO building; Haşet is at Şehit Nevres Bey Bulvarı 3-B, and near it is Kuydaş (☎ 63 29 97), Şehit Nevres Bey Bulvarı 9-A. Try also the bookshop in the İzmir Hilton on Gaziosmanpaşa Bulvarı.

If you want to read English-language periodicals, there's the Türk-Amerikan Derneği (Turkish-American Association, ☎ 21 52 06), Şehit Nevres Bey Bulvarı 23-A, on the corner of 1379 Sokak, just north-east of the Büyük Efes Oteli. Opening hours are Monday to Friday from 1.30 to 6.30 pm.

Hospitals Call your consulate for a recommendation of a doctor or hospital.

Banks Many banks have offices in Konak. You can exchange currency at the PTT on Cumhuriyet Meydanı as well. Bamka Döviz, is a currency exchange office on the corner

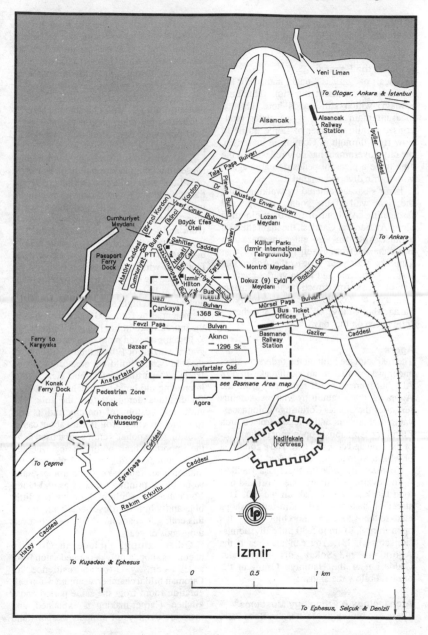

İzmir

of 1369 and 1364 sokaks, 1½ blocks west of the little hotels on 1369 Sokak.

Konak & the Bazaar

The heart of İzmir is Konak, named for the Ottoman government mansion (Hükümet Konağı) which still stands here. Once a pleasant main square, it was later modernised to allow a river of fierce traffic to flow right through it. Coming to its senses, the city government has now redesigned the area to be a pleasant pedestrian area again, with traffic diverted around it.

İzmir's bazaar, entered by walking along the right wall of the konak, is large and fascinating. An hour or two of exploration along Anafartalar Caddesi, the main street, is a must. You can also enter the bazaar at Basmane, or from Eşrefpaşa Caddesi near Çankaya after your visit to the Agora. Get lost in the bazaar, and when you're ready to get out, ask for directions to Basmane, Çankaya, or Konak. Note that virtually all bazaar shops close on Sunday, and there's little to see on that day.

Agora

The marketplace built on the orders of Alexander was ruined in an earthquake in 178 AD, but there is much remaining from the Agora as it was rebuilt by Marcus Aurelius just after the quake. Corinthian colonnades, vaulted chambers and a reconstructed arch fill this conspicuously open spot in the midst of the crowded city, and give you a good idea of what a Roman 'bazaar' looked like.

To reach it, walk up Eşrefpaşa Caddesi from Fevzipaşa Bulvarı, one short and one long block, to 816 Sokak on the left. This street of bakeries and radio-repair shops leads to the Agora, one short block away. It's open from 8.30 am to 5.30 pm daily; admission costs US$1. You can also reach the Agora via 943 Sokak, off Anafartalar Caddesi near the Hatuniye Camii in the bazaar. Follow the signs.

Archaeology & Ethnology Museums

These two museums are in Bahri Baba Park, just a short walk up the hill from Konak, along the road up to Kadifekale called the Varyant. The entrance is positioned on the one-way road which brings traffic down the hillside so, to reach the museums, walk up that way. If you walk up the road for uphill traffic, you'll walk all the way around the museums but you won't be able to enter.

The two museums are open from 9 am to 5.30 pm every day; admission costs US$1 per museum.

The Arkeoloji Müzesi or Archaeology Museum is in a modern building. You enter on a floor with quite fine exhibits of Egyptian, Greek and Roman statuary, then move to an upper level dedicated to terracotta objects, tools and vessels, glassware, metalwork and jewellery of silver and gold. The lower level has tomb statuary and sarcophagi, and also the head of a gigantic statue of Domitian which once stood at Ephesus. Be sure to see the beautiful frieze from the mausoleum at Belevi (250 BC), south of İzmir, and also the high relief of Poseidon and Demeter dating from 200 AD. All plaques in the museum are in English and Turkish.

Perhaps of even more interest is the Etnoğrafya Müzesi or Ethnography Museum, in the old stone building next door. Once İzmir's Department of Public Health, this interesting old building now houses colourful displays demonstrating the folk arts, crafts and customs of the city and its surrounding province. You'll learn about camel wrestling, the potter's craft as practised here, the important craft of tin-plating whereby toxic copper vessels were made safe for kitchen use, felt-making, embroidery, and wood-block printing for scarves and cloth. You can even see how those curious little blue-and-white 'evil eye' beads are made; this craft goes back hundreds, perhaps even thousands of years.

Other exhibits include an Ottoman chemist's shop, a fully decorated salon from a 19th-century Ottoman residence, an Ottoman bridal chamber, a circumcision celebration room from the same period and a kitchen. Carpet-making is explained, and there are displays of armour, weapons and local costumes. The museum is well worth a visit.

Kadifekale

The time to ride up the mountain is an hour before sunset. Catch a dolmuş in Konak (it may say only 'K Kale' on the sign) and allow 15 or 20 minutes for the ride. The view on all sides is spectacular. Look inside the walls, and even climb up on them if you like. Just on sunset, the muezzins will give the call to prayer from İzmir's minarets. A wave of sound rolls across the city as the lights twinkle.

Near the gate in the walls are a few little terrace teahouses where you can have a seat and a tea, soft drink or beer.

Other Sights

As you make your way around town, you will certainly see the equestrian statue of Atatürk in Cumhuriyet Meydanı. It symbol ises Atatürk's leadership as he began the counteroffensive from Ankara during the War of Independence. His battle order to the troops on the first day of the offensive (26 August 1922) read 'Soldiers, your goal is the Aegean'.

A few blocks north of Cumhuriyet Meydanı is the South-Eastern Headquarters of NATO, in a building with a long row of flags in front. Here and there along the Birinci Kordon you can see the few old stone houses which survived the Great Fire of 1922.

The Kültür Parkı or Culture Park is pleas-ant, and you can dodge in here any time of day for a quiet walk or picnic away from the city bustle. In late August and early Septem-ber, the fairgrounds hold centre stage in this city, during the İzmir International Fair.

Had it with the crowded, noisy city? Head down to the ferry dock on the waterfront in Konak, and board a ferry for the ride over to Karşıyaka, on the far side of the bay. The view is beautiful, the air fresh and cool. The voyage over and back takes an hour, perhaps 75 minutes, and the whole trip costs less than US$1.

Festivals

From mid-June to mid-July, performances of music and dance are organised under the rubric of the International İzmir Festival. Venues are often Çeşme and Ephesus as well as İzmir. Check with the İzmir Kültür Vakfı (İzmir Culture Foundation), Mahmut Esat Bozkurt Caddesi 4-6, Alsancak, or the Tourism Information Office for current per-formances and locations.

The annual İzmir International Fair is an amusement and industry show which takes place from 20 August to 9 September. Empty hotel space can be difficult to find during the fair unless you've reserved in advance.

Places to Stay

İzmir has lots and lots of good, very cheap places to stay, and several nice expensive places. The middle-range establishments, unfortunately, often suffer from street noise so you must choose your room carefully. The magic word for low prices is Basmane; there are several middle-range places near that railway station as well. The top-end places tend to be on the waterfront near Cumhuriyet Meydanı.

Places to Stay – bottom end

The quarter named Akıncı (also called Yenigün) is bounded by Fevzipaşa Bulvarı, Basmane Meydanı, Anafartalar Caddesi and Eşrefpaşa Caddesi. Right next to Basmane, İzmir's main railway station, it's a low-budget traveller's dream come true. Several entire streets are lined with clean, cheap, safe places to stay. The Basmane Hamamı, adjoining the Basmane mosque facing the station, is a convenient Turkish bath.

1296 Sokak Walk out the front door of Basmane Station, turn left, fight your way across the flood of traffic and walk up shady Anafartalar Caddesi. Take the first small street on your right, which is 1296 Sokak, lined with small hotels, some in new build-ings, others in once-grand old İzmir houses with coloured glass, fancy woodwork and mosaic floors, now somewhat dilapidated.

A few steps along 1296 Sokak, on the

left-hand side, is the *Yıldız Palas Oteli* (☎ (51) 25 15 18), 1296 Sokak No 50. Bright and airy, it is quite simple, and so are its prices: US$7 for a double bed without running water, US$10 for twin beds with a sink and telephone.

Slightly farther along 1296 Sokak, look left down a side street and you'll see the *Otel Gümüş Palas* (gerr-MERSH pah-lahss) (☎ 13 41 53), 1299 Sokak No 12, a more modern place (but hardly ultramodern) where a double room without running water costs only US$3 per bed.

Güzel Konya Oteli (☎ (51) 13 69 39), 1296 Sokak No 37, is the low-price leader, with run-down rooms going for US$2.50 per person without running water. *Otel Reşat* (☎ (51) 19 93 88), 1296 Sokak No 43, is better, at the same prices. There are lots more.

In the Bazaar Walk along Anafartalar Caddesi through the bazaar and turn left at No 828, opposite 1297 Sokak, to find the *Otel Gülistan* (☎ (51) 25 49 75), an old mansion, beat-up but serviceable, and blissfully quiet. A marble-paved garden courtyard with shade trees offers fine possibilities for tea-drinking. It's cheap, at US$6 for two, without water.

Continue along Anafartalar Caddesi and soon you'll pass the entrance (on the left) to the Mum Yakmaz Camii, and just beyond it, on the right, 1298 Sokak and the *Kervansaray Oteli* (☎ (51) 14 06 99), at No 5. It's a dark but fairly well-kept old mansion, quiet, and deep in the bazaar.

After the Mum Yakmaz you come to the Hatuniye Camii (mosque, also called the Kuşlu Cami). Just past it, on the right, is the *Otel Saray* (☎ (51) 13 69 46), Anafartalar Caddesi 635, Tilkilik. It's a backpackers' favourite charging US$10 for a clean double room with sink, opening onto a small enclosed central courtyard. Get a room on the upper floor if you can.

Across from the Hatuniye Camii is the *Otel Aksu* (☎ (51) 13 54 95), a second choice to the Hotel Saray.

Otel Hikmet (☎ (51) 14 26 72, 41 36 01),

945 Sokak No 26, Tilkilik/Dönertaş, up the side street opposite the Hatuniye Camii, is a step up in quality, with newer, clean double rooms with sinks and showers costing US$14; toilets are down the hall, not in the rooms.

1368 & 1369 Sokaks Should you want a slightly better class of hotel, head for a different area equally close to Basmane Station, packed with hotels and with good restaurants as well. Go out the station door and straight down the right-hand side of Fevzipaşa Bulvarı to the three-star Hotel Hisar. Turn right and you will be on 1368 Sokak, which is lined with little hotels charging about US$12 to US$20 for a double room with a private shower.

Güzel İzmir (☎ (51) 13 50 69, 14 66 93), 1368 Sokak 8, is a bit fancier in its lobby, but the rooms are about the same as others on the street and go for US$6 to US$9 per person with washbasin or with shower. The *Otel Çiçek Palas* (☎ (51) 13 48 03), 1368 Sokak No 10, charges US$11 a double with sink, US$13 with private shower.

Walk along 1368 Sokak and at the end, on 1369 Sokak, are several more: *Gönen Palas Oteli* (☎ (51) 13 55 68), 1369 Sokak No 66, is good for US$7/10 a single/double with sink; *Ömür Palas Oteli* (☎ (51) 13 14 03), 1369 Sokak No 56, charges the same, as do the *Otel Akgün* (☎ (51) 13 55 63) and the clean and friendly *Otel Oba* (☎ (51) 13 54 74), 1369 Sokak 59, just to name two. Most of these hotels give you a choice between rooms with a shower and rooms without one, and most are quiet, even in this noisy city.

Places to Stay – middle

Basmane Of the moderately priced hotels in the Basmane area, the quietest and best is the marble-fronted *Hotel Baylan* (☎ (51) 13 14 26, 13 01 52; fax 13 38 44), 1299 Sokak No 8. Accommodating staff, clean, modern rooms with shower and TV, private car park and good prices of US$24/34 a single/double make this two-star, 33-room place the first choice. Walk up 1296 Sokak and turn left onto 1299 Sokak by the Otel Gümüş Palas.

Tanık Otel (☎ (51) 41 20 07, -8, -9; fax 13 11 19), 1364 Sokak No 13, Çankaya, is also rated two-star. It's new and modern, but a bit farther from Basmane. Walk down Gazi Bulvarı two blocks to find this two-star, 36-room hotel charging US$25/37 a single/double, breakfast included. Rooms have bathroom, TV and sound insulation, but avoid rooms on busy, noisy Gazi Bulvarı all the same.

Otel Saysen (☎ (51) 25 45 45; fax 13 63 44), Dokuz (90) Eylül Meydanı 787, 35230 Basmane, has 31 bath-equipped rooms, and is just across the street from Basmane Station. Convenient and friendly, it is moderately priced for what you get: US$35/42 a single/double with bathroom, breakfast included. The Saysen has a restaurant and bar.

Right next door is the 60-room *Otel Billûr* (☎ (51) 14 84 68, 13 62 50; fax 13 97 35), Basmane Meydanı 783, 35230 Basmane. Though cheaper, it is noisier and older, charging US$24/34 a single/double, or from US$40 to US$50 for a suite/apartment, with breakfast included.

Down Fevzipaşa Bulvarı a block from the station is the 63-room *Hotel Hisar* (☎ (51) 14 54 00; fax 25 88 30), Fevzipaşa Bulvarı 153 (or 1368 Sokak No 2), an older but still comfy three-star place featuring rooms with bath, TV, minibar and air-con for US$40/46 a single/double, breakfast included.

Just around the corner on 1368 Sokak, which is much quieter, is the two-star, 36-room *Hotel Zeybek* (☎ (51) 19 66 94, 19 74 71; fax 13 50 20), 1368 Sokak No 5, 35230 Basmane. Light wood, gleaming brass and coloured marble fill the small lobby. The tiny guest rooms have TVs, fans and bathrooms (some with small tubs), and cost US$36/42 a single/double. By the time you read this, a new three-star Hotel Zeybek should be open across the street.

Cumhuriyet Meydanı *Otel Marla* (☎ (51) 41 40 00; fax 41 11 50), Kazım Dirik Caddesi 7, 35210 Pasaport, advertises 'five-star comforts at three-star-prices'. Its 68 rooms almost meet this claim, with marble vanities in the baths, trendy décor, satellite TVs, minibars and air-conditioning. The location is quiet, yet only a block from Cumhuriyet Meydanı. rates are US$65/85/100 for a single/double/suite.

Behind the Büyük Efes Oteli, in a fairly quiet residential section, is the three-star, 73-room *Otel Karaca* (☎ (51) 19 19 40, 14 44 45; fax 13 14 98), Necati Bey Bulvarı, 1379 Sokak No 55, 35210 Alsancak, between the Hilton and the Büyük Efes. The quiet yet convenient location, comfortable, modern rooms with TVs and minibars, and English-speaking staff make this a favourite of NATO military and diplomatic families. Rooms cost US$48/68 a single/double, breakfast included.

Otel İzmir Palas (☎ (51) 21 55 83; fax 22 68 70), on Vasıf Çınar Bulvarı 2 near Atatürk Bulvarı, 35210 Alsancak, is a short walk north of Cumhuriyet Meydanı. Well located in the centre, it is a comfy if older three-star, 148-room place, with sea views from many rooms. Prices are good: US$64/81/95 a single/double/triple officially, but I was quoted a price 30% lower when I asked.

Places to Stay – top end
As you enter İzmir, you can't help noticing the *İzmir Hilton* (☎ (51) 41 60 60; fax 41 22 77), Gaziosmanpaşa Bulvarı 7, 35210 İzmir, which soars above the centre – the tallest building by far. Its 381 rooms and suites have all the luxuries. There are two tennis courts, two squash courts and an indoor pool. Within the same complex is a shopping centre and car park. Rooms cost from US$110 to US$155 a single, from US$120 to US$180 a double, with tax included. This is İzmir's best.

The five-star, 400-room *Büyük Efes Oteli* (Grand Ephesus Hotel) (☎ 14 43 00; fax 25 86 95), Gaziosmanpaşa Bulvarı 1, 35210 İzmir, on Cumhuriyet Meydanı right next to the Hilton, was İzmir's status address for decades. It is still comfortable and has these advantages: pretty gardens with a swimming pool, a good dining room and patio restaurant, a nightclub and rooms with bath, TV, minibar, air-con and perhaps a view of the

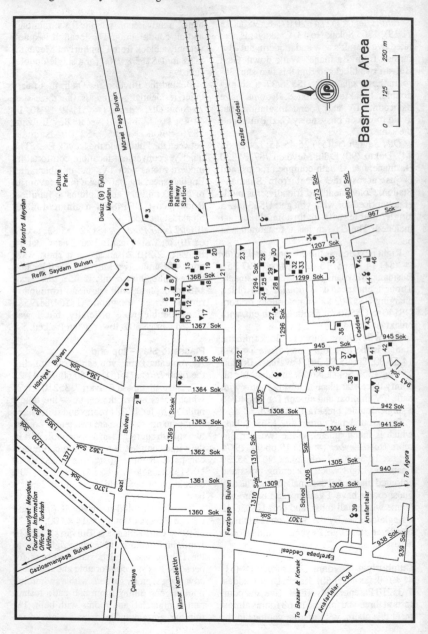

Basmane Area

bay. From April to October is the summer season, with rooms renting for US$95 to US$145 a single, for US$105 to US$155 a double.

The four-star, 127-room *Pullman Etap İzmir Hotel* (☎ (51) 19 40 90; fax 19 40 89) is just around the corner from the Büyük Efes, across from the PTT, at Cumhuriyet Bulvarı 138, 35210 İzmir. The Etap has a good pastry-shop café in its lobby; there's also a nice, garden-style ground-floor restaurant serving a buffet luncheon and dinner daily. Part of the worldwide French chain, its air-con, minibar and TV-equipped rooms cost US$95/126/140 a single/double/triple in high summer.

There's another Etap, the *Pullman Etap Konak* (☎ (51) 19 15 00; fax 19 17 09), Mithatpaşa Caddesi 128, 35260 Konak, just south-west of Konak on the way to the archaeology and ethnography museums. It's also rated at four stars, but is smaller (76 rooms) and a bit cheaper. Many rooms have fine sea views.

Places to Eat – bottom end

The lowest priced meals are to be found in the same areas as the lowest priced hotels. Some of the most delightful places are along Anafartalar Caddesi in the bazaar. Start from the Basmane end, and hazır yemek restaurants, kebapçıs and köftecis will appear all along the way as you wander. A few will have one or two small tables outside; none serve alcoholic beverages.

Basmane Right across from Basmane Station at the beginning of Anafartalar Caddesi are four noisy restaurants – good for a quick meal before boarding a train: *Aydin-Denizli-Nazilli, Ödemiş Azim, Tokat,* and *Ankara* restaurants.

On 1296 Sokak, look for the cheap *Ödemiş Kebap Salonu, Güneydoğu Kebap Salonu* and the *Şanlıurfa Kebap Salonu*, each serving kebap meals for US$4 or less.

Anafartalar Caddesi Heading into the bazaar from Basmane, check out the *Ömür Lokantası* (☎ 19 26 25), near the Mum

Yakmaz Camii at Anafartalar Caddesi 794/A. It's bright, clean and cheap, with a good selection of hazır-yemek dishes for around US$1 each. It's open every day from breakfast through to late supper.

Just before the little square with the Hatuniye mosque, look for the *Ege Lezzet Lokantası* on Anafartalar Caddesi. The front window is filled with steam tables holding hearty pilav, stews and vegetable dishes. Lunch for US$3 or US$4 is a simple matter. The *Konya Lezzet Lokantası*, 50 metres past the mosque, is a bit fancier, but priced about the same.

1368 & 1369 Sokaks The *Zeybek Mangal Restaurant* (☎ 13 52 31), 1368 Sokak No 6/A, specialises in döner kebaps and has pleasant streetside tables. A portion of döner or one of their many other kebaps, with a salad and something to drink, costs about US$5.

The *Güzel İzmir Restaurant* (☎ 14 05 01), 1368 Sokak No 8/B, across the street from the Zeybek Mangal, has more hazır-yemek dishes, streetside tables and similar prices.

At the junction of 1368 and 1369 sokaks, the *Marmara Börekçisi* serves large portions of flaky börek and freshly baked pide for about US$2, soft drink included.

On 1369 Sokak, look for the similarly cheap *İnci Kebap, Pide ve Lahmacun Salonu* – the restaurant's name is its menu.

For decently priced seafood, walk south on 1369 Sokak to 1367 Sokak and turn left to find *Lidaki Balıkevi* (☎ 14 71 61), 1367 Sokak No 14, just around the corner from the Ömür Palas hotel. It serves mainly fish and meze, and a full meal with wine need cost only US$10 to US$15. It's open every day for lunch and dinner.

Near Konak Enter the bazaar along Anafartalar Caddesi from Konak to find even more cheap places. The second street on the right is 846 Sokak, which holds the *Ekmekçibaşı Lokantası*, a tidy and popular local place which is, like the bazaar, closed on Sunday.

A bit farther on at No 61, to the right of the Osmanlı Bankası in the courtyard of the dilapidated 19th-century Yeni Şükran Oteli, is the *Şükran Lokantası*. It's a bazaar merchants' hang-out which serves booze and decent food in the atmospheric courtyard. Expect to pay from US$5 to US$7 for a full dinner; it's closed on Sunday.

When you get to a T-intersection, Anafartalar Caddesi goes right, but if you turn left onto 853 Sokak you'll find the *Bolulu Hasan Usta Lokantası*, behind the Polis Karakolu (police station). The town of Bolu is famous for its chefs, and Hasan Usta (Chef Hasan) keeps up the tradition with lots of ready food and grills, served every day of the week. Full meals cost US$4 or US$5.

Farther into the bazaar along Anafartalar Caddesi, near the mosque Başdurak Camii are more good restaurants. Turn left onto 875 Sokak (between Nos 199 and 201 Anafartalar Caddesi), and the first cross-street is 872 Sokak. Right at this corner is the *Afiyet Pide Salonu* (☎ 19 85 77), 872 Sokak No 124. The pide (Turkish pizza) here is fresh, hot, delicious and cheap, costing less than US$2 for the fanciest type. It's closed on Sunday.

Turn left onto 872 Sokak and walk one block past the songbird sellers' shops to a little plaza in the midst of the fish market with a şadırvan (ablutions fountain) which serves the adjacent Başdurak Camii. Around this little plaza are several other restaurants, including the *Halikarnas Balık Lokantası*, an appropriately located fresh fish restaurant. Expect to spend about US$8 for a fish dinner, less if you order carefully.

Arı Kebap Salonu, also on the plaza, is good for a quick kebap, but it's closed on Sunday.

Places to Eat – middle

Birinci Kordon For medium-priced meals, the city's most interesting section is the waterfront. Most of the following restaurants serve alcoholic beverages.

South of Cumhuriyet Meydanı are several trendy cafés – *Carnevale, L'Aventure* and *Deux Mégots* for Turkish yuppies, where conversation and big glasses of draught beer

(US$2) are the whole point. But just south of the cafés are three moderately priced fish restaurants overlooking the water.

Mangal Restaurant (☎ 25 28 60, 14 75 90), Atatürk Caddesi 110, with white table-cloths and experienced service, has a good seafood dinner for US$12 to US$16 per person, all included. If you order lamb as your main course, the cost will only be half that much. The few streetside tables fill up early in the evening, so come early or late if you want one of them. The *Kazan* and *Ahtapot* restaurants, right next door beneath the Kilim Oteli, are similar in all regards.

For equally good food at substantially lower prices, but without the waterfront ambience, go one block inland along Kazım-paşa (Kazım Dirik) Caddesi, which begins right by the aforementioned Ahtapot Restaurant and Kilim Oteli. Cross the İkinci Kordon and you'll see several cheaper restaurants: *Cevat'in Yeri, Topçu'nun Yeri, Köz Kebap Salonu*, etc. In the evening the streetside tables are pleasant.

North of Cumhuriyet Meydanı along the Birinci Kordon, many of the restaurants have streetside tables, views of the harbour activity, lots of good meze dishes and fresh fish prepared various ways.

Sisim and *Gördüm* cafés serve draught beer (US$2) at streetside tables, but just a bit farther north is *Pizzeria Z*, Atatürk Caddesi 186, serving hamburgers and pizza at streetside tables for US$1.25 to US$8.

The seafood restaurant of choice for İzmir's business community (look for all the cellular phones) is *Deniz Restaurant* (☎ 22 06 01, 22 47 52), Atatürk Caddesi 188-B on the corner of Vasıf Çınar Bulvarı, on the ground floor of the Otel İzmir Palas. Prices are not much higher than at the aforementioned Mangal, but the ambience is classier, with outdoor tables in fine weather.

Just one-half block south of the NATO headquarters building is *Orfoz Balık Restaurant* (☎ 21 41 89), Atatürk Caddesi 192-C, between 1380 and 1382 sokaks. Simple and pleasant, with water views, it offers the Turkish equivalent of sushi (raw fish) as well as fish buğlama (poached with vegetables –

try it). Fish meals cost from US$12 to US$16.

Inland from Cumhuriyet Meydanı *Chinese Restaurant* (☎ 13 00 79), 1379 Sokak No 57/A, adjoining the Otel Karaca, is a branch of the Turkish chain. It's more or less behind the Büyük Efes Oteli. The narrow dining room has rows of tables with red cloths, bits of Chinese decoration and a menu listing the more popular Chinese dishes. Expect to pay from US$12 to US$18 per person for a full dinner. The restaurant is open every day for lunch and dinner.

Alsancak North of Cumhuriyet Meydanı, inland from the water, is the wealthy residential district of Alsancak, which has many good restaurants. For Italian fare in attractive surroundings, try *Pizza Venedik* (☎ 22 27 35, 22 18 26), 1382 Sokak No 10-B, a half-block inland from the NATO headquarters. Its attractive dining rooms and outdoor tables are open from 11 am to 11 pm every day, and customers typically include several native speakers of Italian. The 16 types of pizza are supplemented by various Italian specialties. Expect to spend from US$8 to US$17 per person; alcohol is served.

Entertainment

There are discos and nightclubs in the top hotels, but in fine weather most of İzmir goes outdoors. The Birinci Kordon north of Cumhuriyet Meydanı is closed to motor vehicles on summer evenings, allowing the İzmirlis to stroll along the waterfront, which they do in droves. When not walking, the locals are sitting in cafés or open-air restaurants, deep in conversation, music and drink. See the previous Places to Eat section for suggestions.

İzmir Devlet Opera ve Balesi (İzmir State Opera and Ballet, ☎ 14 64 45) and the İzmir Devlet Senfoni Orkestrası (İzmir State Symphony Orchestra, ☎ 25 41 15) perform during the winter season from September to May. For current performance schedules, check the *Turkish Daily News* or *Key*, a free pamphlet available at the Tourism Information Office and in top-class hotels. You can also try the Atatürk Kültür Merkezi (Atatürk Cultural Centre, ☎ 14 85 26), in Konak.

Getting There & Away

Air For information on flights and fares, see the Getting Around chapter at the front of this book. For airport transport, see the following Getting Around section. The information number at Adnan Menderes Airport is (51) 51 26 26.

Turkish Airlines (☎ (51) 14 12 20; for reservations 25 82 80; fax 13 62 81), both THY and THT, is in the arcade of shops in the Büyük Efes Oteli at Gaziosmanpaşa Bulvarı 1-F, open from 8.30 am to 7.30 pm (until 5.30 pm on Sunday). At Adnan Menderes Airport the number is (51) 51 25 25.

İstanbul Airlines (☎ (51) 19 05 41, -2; fax 19 05 42), Gaziosmanpaşa Caddesi 2-E, is across the street from the Büyük Efes Oteli and Turkish Airlines. It can also be contacted at Menderes airport (☎ (51) 51 30 65; fax 51 07 77).

Details of the offices of foreign airlines, all close to Cumhuriyet Meydanı follow:

Air France
    (☎ (51) 25 90 04), Gaziosmanpaşa Bulvarı, 1353 Sokak No 1, two blocks south of the Tourism Information Office
Austrian Airlines
    (☎ (51) 25 80 20), Şair Eşref Bulvarı, 1371 Sokak No 5, Çankaya
British Airways
    (☎ (51) 14 17 88), Şehit Fethi Bey Bulvarı 120, on the third street inland from the waterfront south of Cumhuriyet Meydanı
KLM
    (☎ (51) 21 47 57), Cumhuriyet Meydanı 11/2, on the south side of the square
Lufthansa
    (☎ (51) 22 36 22), Atatürk Caddesi 244, north of Cumhuriyet Meydanı
Swissair
    (☎ (51) 21 47 57), Cumhuriyet Meydanı 11/2, on the south side of the square

Bus Buses arrive at İzmir's Yeni Garajlar (☎ (51) 16 31 06), a mammoth and seemingly chaotic establishment almost three km north-east of the city's centre. Buses roar

around outside while throngs of passengers move through the interior past rows of shops selling snacks, trinkets and refreshing lemon cologne. There's a small Tourism Information Office and complaints office near the terminal's main gate, ask to be directed to it. If you're at the otogar to buy a ticket to another city, ask for directions to the *bilet gişeleri* (bee-LEHT gee-sheh-leh-ree, ticket windows).

For transport to and from the otogar, see the following Getting Around section.

To buy bus tickets in the city centre without having to drag yourself all the way out to the otogar, go to Dokuz (9) Eylül Meydanı. Here, at the beginning of Gazi Bulvarı, are numerous bus ticket offices, including those for Aydın, Dadaş, Hakiki Koç, İzmir Seyahat, Kamil Koç, Karadeveci, Kent, Kontaş, Vantur and other companies. You should be able to buy a ticket to any point in the country from here.

Here are details on travel from İzmir to:

Ankara – 600 km, 8½ hours, US$14.50; buses at least every hour
Antalya – 550 km, nine hours, US$14.50; buses at least every two hours
Bergama – 100 km, 1¾ hours, US$3; Pammukale company buses every half-hour from 6 am to 7.30 pm; also several Bergama municipality ('Bergama Belediyesi') buses
Bodrum – 250 km, four hours, US$8; buses every hour in summer
Bursa – 375 km, six hours, US$10; hourly buses
Çanakkale – 340 km, six hours, US$10; buses at least every two hours
Çeşme (for Chios) – 85 km, 1½ hours, US$2; frequent buses (at least hourly) depart from a separate bus station in Güzelyalı, 6.5 km south-west of Konak; take a Güzelyalı or Balçova minibus from Konak to Güzelyalı
Denizli – 250 km, four hours, US$8; buses every hour
İstanbul – 610 km, nine hours, US$12 to US$20; buses at least every hour
Konya – 575 km, eight hours, US$14; buses at least every two hours
Kuşadası – 95 km, 1½ hours, US$2.25; buses at least every 30 minutes from 6.30 am to 7 pm in summer
Marmaris – 320 km, six hours, US$10; buses at least every two hours
Sardis – 90 km, 1¼ hours, US$2; buses for Salihli (get off at Sartmustafa) at least every 30 minutes

Selçuk (for Ephesus) – 80 km, 1¼ hours, US$2; buses every 15 minutes from 6.30 am to 7 pm in summer

Trabzon – 1375 km, 22 hours, US$33; several buses daily

Van – 1600 km, 28 hours, US$40; several buses daily

Train Most intercity trains come into Basmane Garı (Basmane Station, ☎ (51) 14 86 38; for reservations 14 53 50), whence there are buses and dolmuşes to other sections, and numerous hotels close by. İzmir's other terminus, Alsancak Garı (☎ (51) 21 01 14), at the northern end of the city near the international passenger ship docks, is mostly for commuter and suburban lines, including some trains for Adnan Menderes Airport.

Here's how to reach these destinations; all train services are daily unless otherwise noted:

Afyon
Some Ankara-bound trains from Basmane stop at Afyon. Consult the station schedule.

Ankara
The fastest and most comfortable train is the *Ankara Mavi Tren*, departing from Basmane at 8.30 pm, arriving in Ankara at 10.35 am. The one-way fare is US$13; sleeping compartments cost US$32 for one person, US$55 for two people, US$75 for three. Table d'hôte dinner on board costs from US$6 to US$10. The next best train is the *İzmir Ekspresi*, departing from Basmane at 6 pm, arriving in Ankara at 9.17 am. The one-way fare is US$12/8 in 1st/2nd class. The *Ege Ekspresi* departs from Basmane at 6.40 am, arriving in Ankara at 6.23 pm, for US$8 one way (one-class service).

Balıkesir
Marmara Ekspresi trains to and from Bandırma stop in Balıkesir, as do some Ankara-bound trains.

Bandırma
The *Marmara Ekspresi* is a combined boat-train service between İzmir and İstanbul, with the change between boat and train being made at Bandırma. For details, see the introductory Getting Around chapter.

Denizli (Pamukkale)
Three express trains depart from Basmane for Denizli (near Pamukkale), stopping at Adnan Menderes Airport; Selçuk (for Ephesus and Kuşadası); Aydın; and Nazilli (for Aphrodisias). The train departs at 8.15 am (arrives at 1.42 pm), 3.15 pm (arrives at 10 pm), and 6.05 pm (arrives

at 11.28 pm). The one-way fare is US$2, US$1.50 for students.

Eskişehir
All Ankara-bound trains stop at Eskişehir, a major railway switching station.

Kütahya
All Ankara-bound trains stop at Kütahya.

İstanbul
The *Marmara Ekspresi* is a combined boat-train service between İzmir and İstanbul, with the change between boat and train being made at Bandırma. For details, see the introductory Getting Around chapter.

Manisa
All trains bound for Bandırma/İstanbul and Ankara stop at Manisa.

Selçuk (Ephesus)
The three Denizli-bound trains and the one Söke-bound train (departs at 6.46 pm), all from Basmane, stop at Selçuk. The one-way fare is US$1, 75c for students.

Besides all these trains, there are also daily trains to Alaşehir, Ödemiş, Söke and Uşak.

Boat For maritime passenger services to İzmir, see the introductory Getting Around chapter. If you are lucky enough to arrive in İzmir by sea, the city will present itself to you wonderfully as you glide by, and your ship will come into Alsancak Limanı (Alsancak Harbour, ☎ (51) 21 00 77), also called Yeni Liman (New Harbour), at the northern tip of Alsancak. The harbour is about equidistant (two km) from the otogar and the centre of the city, Konak. For transport, turn left as you leave the dock area and walk the block to Alsancak railway station, from which No 2 buses (40c), dolmuşes (50c) and taxis (US$2) will take you to the centre.

Getting Around

To/From the Airport You can travel between the centre of İzmir and Adnan Menderes Airport (25 km south of the city near Cumaovası on the road to Ephesus and Kuşadası) by airport bus, city bus, intercity bus, commuter train or express train.

Havaş airport buses leave for the half-hour trip from the Turkish Airlines office periodically throughout the day. Plan to catch a bus that leaves at least 90 minutes before domestic flight departures, or two hours before international departures; the bus fare is US$2.

City buses trundle – fairly slowly – between Menderes airport and Montrö Meydanı, next to İzmir's Kültür Parkı, every half-hour throughout the day for even less, but the trip takes twice as long.

A taxi between İzmir and Menderes airport can cost between US$14 and US$30, depending upon your haggling abilities.

There are frequent suburban trains (75c) which connect the station at Menderes airport with Alsancak Station, so you'll probably wait between 30 and 60 minutes to catch one. There are also a few intercity express trains to and from Basmane Station (for schedules, see the previous Train section and also the Selçuk/Ephesus section, following).

To/From the Otogar If you've come on a premium bus line such as Varan or Ulusoy, there may be a servis arabası to take you into town at no extra charge. Otherwise, take a city bus (*şehir otobüsü*) No 50, 51 or 52, 'Yeni Garaj-Konak', which stops at Alsancak railway station and Çankaya as well. Find the tourism and complaints office, go out the gate nearby, turn right, walk to the bus shelter, and buy a ticket at the kiosk.

Dolmuşes depart from in front of this bus rank. Most convenient is the dolmuş marked 'Çankaya-Mersinli', which will take you to the bus ticket offices on Gazi Bulvarı at Dokuz (9) Eylül Meydanı (doh-KOOZ ey-LEWL), just a few steps from Basmane Station, then on to Çankaya. For the moderate and more expensive hotels, take something to Konak, but get out at Cumhuriyet Meydanı.

If you're arriving in İzmir by bus from the south, ask to be let out at Tepecik (TEH-peh-jeek), which is 700 metres east of Basmane Station, and closer to the centre than the otogar. Minibuses and dolmuşes run from Tepecik via Basmane to the centre at Konak.

To get to Çeşme, catch any bus or dolmuş bound from Konak for Güzelyalı, Altay Meydanı or Balçova, and get out at Güzel-yalı/Altay Meydanı to board a bus bound for Çeşme.

Bus & Dolmuş Within the city, blue-and-silver city buses lumber along the major thoroughfares, but dolmuşes are much faster. Dolmuşes in İzmir tend to be Fiat taxis, which provide fast, convenient service. One of these running between Alsancak Station and Konak via Cumhuriyet Meydanı charges 50c.

İzmir Metro Ground was broken in 1992 for İzmir's underground train system. The first line of the Metro, 9.2 km in length, will connect Basmane with Konak, then run west along the shore via Üçyol to Altay Meydanı in Güzelyalı, the beginning of the Çeşme Otoyol (highway) where buses leave for Çeşme.

Car Rental The large international franchises and many small local companies rent cars in İzmir. There's a cluster of offices on Şehit Fethi Bey Caddesi, the street between the Büyük Efes Oteli and the İkinci Kordon, near the Otel Anba; and also on the İkinci Kordon north of Cumhuriyet Meydanı.

Some addresses of the offices follow. Avis, Budget, Europcar/Interrent, Hertz and some of the smaller companies have offices at Menderes airport as well:

Avis
   (☎ (51) 21 12 26), Şehit Nevres Bey Bulvarı 19-A
Budget: Camel Oto Kiralama
   (☎ (51) 25 80 12, -3; fax 25 26 74), Gaziosmanpaşa Bulvarı 1-E, in the Büyük Efes Oteli
Europcar/Interrent: Esin Turizm
   (☎ (51) 25 46 98; fax 13 00 31), Şehit Fethi Bey Caddesi 122-F
Hertz
   (☎ (51) 21 70 02), Cumhuriyet Bulvarı 123/1
Yes Rent a Car
   (☎ (51) 22 71 07; fax 22 24 99), 1377 Sokak No 8-B; this agency is partly owned by the Tourism Bank
Zafer Rent a Car
   (☎ (51) 14 60 96, 14 71 81; fax 13 09 04), Akdeniz; Caddesi 8, Anba İşhanı; this is a small local agency with good service

Top: İzmir (TB)
Bottom: Travertine pools at Pamukkale (TB)

Top: Harbour, Bodrum (TB)
Bottom: Angelic figure in high relief, Ephesus (TB)

SARDIS (SART)

The phrase 'rich as Croesus' made its way into language early, in the 6th century BC to be precise. Croesus was the king of Lydia, and Sardis was its capital city. It was here that one of humankind's most popular and valuable inventions appeared: coinage. No doubt the Greeks thought Croesus (560-546 BC) rich because he could store so much wealth in such a small place. Rather than having vast estates and far-ranging herds of livestock, Croesus kept his wealth in his pockets, and they were deep pockets at that.

History

For all his wealth, Croesus was defeated and captured by Cyrus and his Persians, after which he leapt onto a funeral pyre. Even Croesus couldn't take it with him.

The Lydian kingdom had dominated much of the Aegean area before the Persians came. Besides being the kingdom's wealthy capital, Sardis was a great trading centre as well, obviously because coinage facilitated trade.

After the Persians, Alexander the Great took the city in 334 BC and embellished it even more. The inevitable earthquake brought its fine buildings down in 17 AD, but it was rebuilt by Tiberius and developed into a thriving provincial Roman town. It became part of the Ottoman Empire at the end of the 14th century.

Orientation

There are actually two small villages at Sardis, nestled in a valley rich in vineyards (for sultanas, not wine grapes), olive groves, melon fields and tobacco fields. Sartmustafa (SART-MOOS-tah-fah) is the village on the highway, with a few teahouses and grocery shops. Sartmahmut (SART-mah-MOOT) is north of the highway, clustered around the railway station. The station is precisely one km north of the highway.

During the day the farmers come into town, park their tractors in front of the teahouses, sit down for a few glasses and discuss the crops. In early August the harvest is in progress, and little stalls by the roadside, attended by children, sell huge bunches of luscious, crisp, sweet sultanas to passers-by.

The teahouses in town are where you wait to catch a bus back to İzmir.

Things to See

The ruins of Sardis are scattered throughout the valley which lies beneath the striking ragged mountain range to the south. Two concentrations of ruins are of interest.

Just east of the village (away from İzmir), on the north side of the highway, lies the most extensive part of the ruins, open virtually all the time during daylight hours, every day, for US$2.

Buy your ticket at the little booth, then enter the ruins along the Marble Way past rows of Byzantine-era shops. Many of them once belonged to Jewish merchants and artisans, as they backed onto the wall of the great synagogue. Note the elaborate drainage system, with pipes buried in the stone walls. Some of the shops have been identified from inscriptions. There's a restaurant, Jacob's Paint Shop, an office, a hardware shop, the shop of Sabbatios and the shop of Jacob, an elder of the synagogue. At the end of the Marble Way is an inscription on the marble paving-stones done in either 17 or 43 AD, honouring Prince Germanicus.

Turn left from the Marble Way and enter the **synagogue**, impressive because of its size and beautiful decoration. It has lots of fine mosaic paving, and coloured stone on its walls. A modern plaque lists donors to the Sardis American Excavation Fund, who supported the excavations carried out between 1965 and 1973.

The striking restored façade to the right of the synagogue is that of the **gymnasium**. Note especially the finely chiselled inscriptions in Greek, and the serpentine fluting on the columns. Behind the façade is a swimming pool and rest area.

Just over one km south of the village (take the road beside the teahouse) is the **Temple of Artemis**, a once-magnificent building which was actually never completed. Today only a few columns stand untoppled, but the temple's plan is clearly visible and quite impressive. Next to the temple is an **altar** used since ancient times, refurbished by Alexander the Great and later by the Romans. Clinging to the south-eastern corner of the temple is a small brick **Byzantine church**. From archaic times until the Hellenistic, Roman and Byzantine periods, this was a sacred spot, no matter what the religion was.

Getting There & Away

Sardis is 90 km east of İzmir along the Ankara road. In high summer, start out early so you're not tramping around the ruins in the heat of the day, which can be oppressive.

Bus Buses depart frequently – at least every 30 minutes – for the 90-km, 1¼-hour trip from İzmir's otogar. You needn't buy a ticket in advance, just go out to the bus station and buy a ticket for the next bus to Salihli (US$2). Tell them you want to get out at Sart.

Dolmuş minibuses run between Sartmustafa and Manisa for US$1.25 per ride.

Train There are several daily trains from İzmir (Basmane) which stop here; they are slower than the buses. Take the bus out to Sardis, but then ask in town about trains returning to İzmir, as you may find one at a convenient time.

Tours Alternatively, local travel agencies in İzmir operate full-day tours to Sardis and Manisa for about US$30, lunch included.

ÇEŞME

The name of this town and resort area (population 100,000), 85 km due west of İzmir, means 'fountain' or 'spring' (*çeşme*, CHESH-meh). From the town, it's only about 10 km across the water to the Greek island of Chios. The ferries to the Greek islands are the main reason people go to Çeşme, though the fast-growing resort area encircling the town is popular with weekend-trippers from İzmir.

Çeşme is a pleasant seaside town, but the land to the east of it is rolling steppe, a foretaste of Anatolia, though this barrenness

subsides as one approaches İzmir, giving way to wheat fields, lush orchards, olive groves and tobacco fields. About 23 km east of Çeşme is the pretty Uzunkuyu Piknik Yeri, a roadside picnic area in a pine forest. One passes the official city limits of İzmir a full 30 km west of Konak Meydanı (50 km east of Çeşme).

Orientation

Çeşme is right on the coast. Ilıca, a seaside resort town six km to the east of Çeşme, has lots of hotels in all price ranges, from family pensions to big luxury hotels. Dolmuşes run between Ilıca and Çeşme frequently (50c), but unless you want to spend all your time at the beach you're better off staying in Çeşme proper.

Çeşme's otogar is less than one km south of the main square and the fortress. In Çeşme everything you need is very near the main square on the waterfront, with its inevitable statue of Atatürk. The Tourism Information Office, Customs House (Gümrük), ferry ticket offices, bus ticket offices, restaurants and hotels are all here, or within two blocks.

Information

The Tourism Information Office (☎ (549) 26653) is down by the dock at İskele Meydanı No 6.

Things to See

The old fortress in the centre of town was built by the Genoese but repaired by Beyazıt, son of Sultan Mehmet the Conqueror, to defend the coast from attack by the Knights of St John of Jerusalem based on Rhodes, and from pirates. It now holds the museum and is called the **Çeşme Kalesi ve Müzesi** (Çeşme Fortress & Museum) open every day from 8.30 to 11.45 am and from 1 to 5.15 pm, for US$1. The entrance is up the hill on the right-hand side as you face the fort from the main square.

Facing the main square, with its back to the fortress, is a **statue of Cezayirli Gazi Hasan Paşa** (1714-90), together with a lion which symbolises his temperament. As a boy he was captured in a battle on the Iranian border, sold into slavery by the Ottoman army and bought by a Turkish tradesman who raised him with his own sons. Having joined the Janissary corps at the age of 25, he began a brilliant military, naval and political career which included fierce battles with the Russian fleet off Çeşme. He retired an extremely wealthy man, having served as the sultan's grand vizier and having built public monuments, fountains and mosques on Lesbos, Limnos, Chios, Kos and Rhodes (all were Ottoman islands at the time).

In the evening the people of Çeşme still observe the custom of dressing up and coming down to the main square for a stroll, a glass of tea, a bit of conversation and some people-watching. That's nightlife in Çeşme, and it's pleasant enough. The men, some with their wives, will linger in the seaside restaurants and teahouses.

The area around Çeşme is developing rapidly. Some say Çeşme is spoiled already, and the place to spend your time in is **Alaçatı** instead (dolmuşes run the two km to Alaçatı from Ilıca). There's a nice beach about three or four km out of the village.

Places to Stay

Çeşme has several inexpensive pensions and hotels, several moderately priced hotels, a restored caravanserai and a luxury resort. All charge more than normal, and many lodgings are often booked solid in the summer season. The accommodation situation in Çeşme is thus not particularly good in any respect.

Places to Stay – bottom end

The best, cheap lodgings are at the several little pensions in private homes.

Walk up the hill along the walls of the fortress and follow the signs to reach the *Anıt Pansiyon,* (☎ (549) 27697) in a nicely restored old Çeşme house across from the fortress museum entrance. If it's full, follow the signs from the Anıt to the *Çelik Pansiyon* (☎ (549) 26153), and the *Kısaoğlu Pansiyon* (☎ (549) 27467) which charge US$7.50/12 a single/double for a room without private shower. The *Kervan Pansiyon* (☎ (549)

26061), just south of the main square and the docks past the Çeşme Kervansaray hotel, charges the same, but will allow you to roll out your sleeping bag on the roof for US$3. Just past the Kervan pension is the town's hamam, and beyond it are even more cheap pensions.

There are several small, fairly noisy and severely plain hotels along the main shopping street, which heads inland towards İzmir. These are last-ditch lodgings, unless some renovation is done to them.

Places to Stay – middle

Right on the shore, facing the main square, is the two-star *Ertan Oteli* (☎ (549) 26795, -6), Cumhuriyet Meydanı 12, with a lift, an open-air terrace bar, an air-conditioned restaurant, and 60 guest rooms with bath, some of them facing the sea, priced at US$40/50 a single/double. This is a bit expensive for what you get, but demand is high in Çeşme, rooms are scarce and the Ertan is often filled with tour groups.

Next door to the Ertan, the newer 35-room *Rıdvan Oteli* (☎ (549) 26336, -7) also rates two stars and has similar facilities, but here most rooms have balconies. Prices are identical at US$40/50 a single/double.

Çeşme Kervansaray (☎ (549) 26490; in İzmir call (51) 14 17 20), just south of the main square, dates from 1528 during the reign of Süleyman the Magnificent. Restored by the same company that operates the Golden Dolphin resort (see following), it is now a beautiful hotel decorated with a mixture of modern and traditional Turkish styles. Rates for room with a bath, breakfast included, in the summer season (from mid-June to mid-September) are US$42/58/76 a single/double/suite; off-season, rates are about 20% lower. Note that the hotel is closed from October to the end of March. A table d'hôte meal in the hotel is priced from US$10 to US$12.

At Ilıca/Boyalık, four km from Çeşme proper, is the *Turban Ilıca Motel* (☎ (549) 32183; fax 32128), Çeşme, Ilıca, İzmir. It's a newer two-storey motel at the seaside with

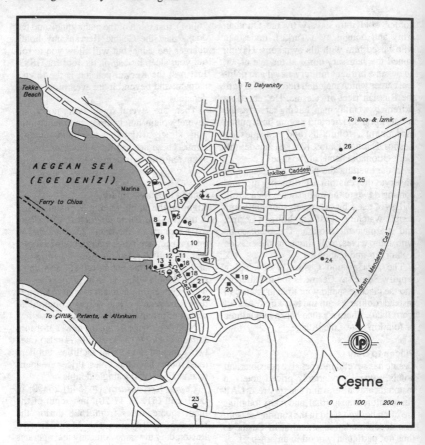

Çeşme

0   100   200 m

65 rooms going for US$45/65 a single/ double in the high summer season (from early July to the end of August), tax and service, breakfast and dinner included. Off-season prices are substantially lower; the hotel is closed from November to April. The motel is moderately well kept up, with a swimming pool, beach, sun deck, restaurant, bar and games room. Many other medium-priced hotels are nearby, with new ones being built.

Places to Stay – top end

About four km outside of Çeşme proper is the luxury *Golden Dolphin Holiday Village* (Altın Yunus Tatilköyü) (☎ (549) 31250; fax 32252), Boyalık Mevkii, Ilıca, İzmir, a complete resort with facilities for all water sports, a yacht harbour and luxury accommodation. Facilities at this lavish spread include 540 guest rooms in three buildings; five restaurants; cafés and bars; a disco; seven tennis courts (two of them floodlit); two swimming pools and another one for children; a health and fitness centre; and facilities for water sports, hunting, horseriding and bicycling. Rates change with the seasons but are about US$125 to US$140 a double per night with near the İmren, is much cheaper, with vegetable plates for US$1, and salçalı köfte for US$1.25.

Hasan Abi Lokantası, on the right (east) side, is similar. Tiny, ugly, crowded and always busy, 'Big Brother Hasan' (that's the name) serves kebaps and hazır-yemek dishes throughout the day. I had salçalı kebap (a stew in a rich sauce), pilav, a glass of ayran, bread, and water for US$3.

Also on the main street, the *Nil Patisserie* serves breakfast for less than US$1; it's across the street from the Tekbank in the second block in from the main square.

Down on the waterfront at the main square is the *Sahil Restaurant*, perhaps the most popular eatery, with lots of outdoor tables, some facing the square; others, the sea. The bill of fare includes a lot of seafood, and full meals cost from US$5 to US$7, more if you order fish. It serves an early breakfast but it's a bit expensive at US$3 for the same bread, honey, tea, cheese and olives that you get inland for US$2.

For a local taste treat, try the sakızlı dondurma (sah-kuhz-LUH dohn-door-mah), ice cream flavoured with pine resin, the same stuff they put in Greek retsina wine. It tastes like you think it will, there's no mystery or discovery involved. If you like retsina, you may like this weird incarnation of the flavour.

tax, service charge, breakfast and dinner included.

Places to Eat

Except for meals in the more expensive hotels, Çeşme's restaurants are all fairly cheap, but some are cheaper than others. *İmren Lokantası* on the main street inland from the main square has white tablecloths, a garden seating area, and grilled meats for around US$3. *Castle Restoran & Bar* (☎ 28339), in a tower of the fortress, is under the same management.

Lezzet Aş Evi ('Flavour Cook-House'),

Getting There & Away

The Çeşme-İzmir highway should be finished by the time you arrive, alleviating the weekend traffic jams which used to clog the narrow coastal road.

When the highway is completed, car ferries bound for İzmir from Venice and other ports may terminate at Çeşme rather than in İzmir's harbour, thereby cutting several hours off the voyage.

Bus It's simple. Çeşme Turizm buses and minibuses make the 85-km, 1¼-hour run into the big city every 15 minutes or so from 6 am to 6 pm, for US$2. Çeşme buses operate out of a separate terminal in Güzelyalı, a

neighbourhood west of Konak, not from
İzmir's big otogar. From Güzelyalı, you take
city buses and dolmuşes into the centre of
town.

Ferry – to/from Chios The reason you've
come to Çeşme is probably to catch the ferry
between this town and the Greek island of
Chios. Boats run on Thursday at 10 am
during winter, weather and customers permitting; on Sunday and Thursday in early
May; on Tuesday, Thursday, Friday and
Sunday from mid-May till mid-July. In high
summer there are daily boats (except on
Monday) from mid-July to mid-September.
From mid-September to the end of October
the boats run on Tuesday, Thursday, and
Sunday. At other times, extra boats may run
if there is enough traffic. Most of these boats
depart in the morning at 9.30 or 10 am, but
a few depart at 4 pm.

A one-way fare between Çeşme and Chios
is US$30, to go there and back in a day costs
US$38. Children aged from four to 12 years
get a 50% reduction. Motorcycles, cars, even
caravans, minibuses and buses can be carried
on some of the ferries. The fare for a car is
between US$45 and US$80.

You can make your boat trip into a day trip
to Chios by leaving from Çeşme in the
morning, spend the better part of the day on
Chios and return to Çeşme in the evening.

For details, reservations and tickets,
contact the Ertürk Travel Agency (EHR-
tewrk) (☎ (549) 26768, 26876) in Çeşme's
main square at Cumhuriyet Meydanı 11/A,
near the fortress and across from the docks.
The head office is at İnkilap Caddesi 42/1
(☎ (549) 26147, 26223). It's a good idea to
buy your ticket at least a day in advance, if
possible. By the way, the Ertürk people
usually have information about onward connections from Chios to Piraeus (daily except
on Saturday at 8 pm), to Athens by air, and
to Samos, Lesbos and Thessaloniki by boat,
as well as multiple connections to other
Greek islands.

SOUTH TO EPHESUS

The route from Çeşme via Seferihisar and
Gümüldür to Pamucak beach, Ephesus,
Selçuk and Kuşadası (about 150 km) follows
shallow river valleys, passes through
farming towns, then skirts the coast at points.
The region has a dozen ancient cities (Colo-
phon, Claros, Notion, Teos) in an advanced
state of ruin; a few of them are of no great
interest except to archaeologists.

At the time of writing there were no direct
buses between Çeşme and Selçuk, but services will no doubt begin soon. For now, take
a bus to Urla and the Seferihisar turn-off, and
wait there for a bus or dolmuş to Seferihisar.
Coming from Selçuk, catch a minibus to
Seferihisar (72 km). From Seferihisar, city
buses run west to Sığacık (4.5 km) and
Akkum (7.2 km) every few hours.

Sığacık & Akkum

Before the road to Sığacık and Akkum was
improved, yachters had discovered the
beauty of the fishing village of Sığacık with
its mood-enhancing little medieval fortress
set on a perfect natural harbour. Following
the yachters came the water-sports types.
Though beaches are small and few, the mood
is sunny, laid back and restful. Scattered
amidst the farmers' fields near Akkum are
the ruins of ancient Teos.

The centre of the village is Atatürk
Meydanı, the park bordered by the PTT,
teahouses and restaurants. The *Burç Restaurant* is right over the yacht harbour, as is the
fancier *Liman Restaurant*, just off the square
by the fortress. For a good view of the town,
go around the harbour to the *Deniz Restaurant*, on the road to Akkum. For lodging,
there's the *Burg Pansiyon* (☎ (5448) 1716),
Atatürk Meydanı 14, a modern building in
traditional dark-wood-and-white-stucco
style charging US$15 for a double with
shower. Some rooms have harbour views.
Liman Pansiyon (☎ (5448) 2019), Akkum
Caddesi 19, is a clean family-run place with
a pide salonu downstairs charging the same
prices. The nearby *Deniz Moteli* (☎ (5448)
2533) is a bit fancier.

Two km around the bay and over the hills
is the turn-off westward to Akkum, another
700 metres along. The protected cove here is

always busy with sailboarders in summer, and a small but smooth sand beach backed by an olive grove accommodates non-sailing companions. It's idyllic, but the new five-star, 500-bed hotel may ruin it as the beach is far too small for such a crowd.

Hotel Neptun, at the head of the cove inland from the beach, caters to the sailboarders, with rooms, meals and rental equipment available. Several small camping grounds adjoining have simple lean-to shelters – no need to bring a tent. The very basic *Canlı Balık Restaurant* can provide simple meals, and as the big hotel gears up, there will be more and fancier places.

From Akkum, go up to the road and turn right to reach the Teos Orman İçi Dinlenme Yeri, 1100 metres east of the turn-off, a pine-shaded picnic grove run by the forestry department. Another 600 metres along, the road splits: the left fork goes to the ruins of Teos (800 metres); the right, to the Teos-Emeksiz Plajı, a *Çadırlı Kamp-Günnübirlik Plaj* (beach, day-use and tent-camping ground), one km over the hill.

The **ruins of ancient Teos**, 3.2 km from Akkum, are scattered in fields and olive groves by the roadside. The few fluted column bases and chunks of marble rubble only hint that this was once a major Ionian city, home of the poet Anacreon and noted for its devotion to Dionysus and the pleasures of the cup and the table.

Ephesus Region

It's often said that Turkey has more ancient cities and classical ruins than Greece. Well, it's true, and the Aegean coast holds a great number of sites, including Ephesus, the grandest and best preserved of them all.

Even if you are not fascinated by archaeology, there's great pleasure in riding through a countryside rich in fields of tobacco, passing orchards of fig trees, tramping among verdant fields bright with sunflowers, resting in little village tea-houses, and strolling along marble streets which once witnessed the passing of the people who practically invented architecture, philosophy, mathematics and science. And when it gets hot, there's always the beach.

History

This was Ionia. About 1000 BC, colonists from Greece arrived on these shores, fleeing an invasion by the Dorians. The Ionian culture flourished, and its cities exported these cultural refinements back to Greece.

The history of Ionia is much the same as that of İzmir, with the original Ionian league of cities being conquered by the Lydians of Sardis, then the Persians, then Alexander. They prospered until their harbours silted up, or until the predominance of İzmir siphoned off their local trade.

Ephesus (Efes) was a great trading and religious city, centre for the cult of Cybele,

Statue of Diana the Huntress

the Anatolian fertility goddess. Under the influence of the Ionians, Cybele became Artemis, the virgin goddess of the hunt and the moon, and a fabulous temple was built in her honour. When the Romans took over and made this the province of Asia, Artemis became Diana and Ephesus became the Roman provincial capital. Its Temple of Diana was counted among the Seven Wonders of the World.

As a large and busy Roman town with ships and caravans coming from all over, it had an important Christian congregation very early. St Paul visited Ephesus and later wrote the most profound of his epistles to the Ephesians.

Ephesus was renowned for its wealth and beauty even before it was pillaged by Gothic invaders in 262 AD, and it was still an important enough place in 431 AD for a church council to be held there. Much of the city remains for you to see. As for the other Ionian ports, sometimes a sleepy Turkish village rose among the ruins, sometimes not. Today several of those once-sleepy villages are bustling seaside resort towns.

Orientation

The region around Ephesus is rich in attractions. The city itself is an archaeological zone, but only three km away is Selçuk, a Turkish town of 20,000 people, where you catch buses and dolmuşes, have meals and find pensions to sleep in for the night. On a hilltop 10 km south of Selçuk is Meryemana, the House of the Virgin Mary. About seven km from Selçuk, past Ephesus, is the Aegean coast and Pamucak beach, a long, wide swath of dark sand backed by some beach-shack eateries and hotels.

Farther south along the coast, 20 km from Selçuk, is Kuşadası, a resort town of 40,000 people and a port for Aegean cruise ships doing the Greek islands route. Kuşadası is also where you can catch a ferry to Samos. Inland 15 km from Kuşadası and about 35 km due south of Selçuk is the farming town of Söke with a population of 50,000. Söke is a bit of the 'real' (untouristed) Turkey, a transportation point on the way to three

nearby archaeological sites of great importance: Priene, Miletus and Didyma.

It is easy to spend at least three days seeing the sights in this region. Plan a day for Selçuk and Ephesus, another for Priene, Miletus and Didyma, and a third for Pamucak, Kuşadası and the beach.

Accommodation

You can make your base in Selçuk, the small town three km from the Ephesus ruins, or you can stay in the seaside resort of Kuşadası, 20 km away. Selçuk is closer to Ephesus proper and has a large number of inexpensive pensions, and is thus the choice for younger, more adventurous travellers. Kuşadası is closer to Priene, Miletus and Didyma, and has a greater number and variety of lodgings, especially in the higher price ranges, but is bigger, noisier and more hectic. Details appear in the Places to Stay sections of each town.

Getting There & Away

İzmir is the transportation hub for the region. It has the major air service, and the only rail service from İstanbul and Ankara except for one İstanbul-Denizli train.

Air An airstrip for small planes is under construction just north of the Ephesus ruins in Selçuk. Flights on THT (Turkish Airlines' short-hop line) or smaller companies may be available to Bodrum, İstanbul and İzmir by the time you arrive.

Bus Buses, of course, go everywhere. Direct services run from İzmir otogar to:

Selçuk – 80 km, 1¼ hours, US$2; buses every 15 minutes from 6.30 am to 7 pm in summer
Kuşadası – 100 km, 1⅔ hours, US$2.25; buses at least every 30 minutes from 6.30 am to 7 pm in summer
Söke – 125 km, two hours, US$2.75

Selçuk is a stopping-place for many buses travelling between İzmir and Denizli, Pamukkale, Marmaris, Bodrum, Fethiye, Antalya and other south-western points.

Kuşadası has lots of direct bus services to İzmir, some direct bus services to Denizli and Pamukkale, and minibus dolmuş services to many other parts of the region.

Train The schedule below is for long-distance ekspres and mototren trains on the İzmir to Denizli run, and return. Check these times locally before you travel, as they are subject to change.

Fares are low, about 60c between İzmir and Menderes airport, US$1 between İzmir and Selçuk, US$2 between İzmir and Denizli, and US$1.75 between Selçuk and Denizli.

Car Rental It's simple but expensive to rent a car in İzmir or Kuşadası. The big international companies as well as many small local ones offer cars at varying rates. You will probably have to return the car to the same city. If you give it up in Antalya or Ankara, you may have to pay a hefty charge to get the car back to its home base. See the Getting Around chapter for more information.

SELÇUK

Once a modest farming town with a sideline in tourism, Selçuk has been transformed by Turkey's tourism boom of the 1980s.

Tourism is now the driving force behind the economy, and the town grows apace.

Unless you require luxury lodging, Selçuk is an excellent place to use as a base for visiting Ephesus, the beach at Pamucak, and the other interesting spots in the region.

Orientation

The layout of Selçuk is easy to comprehend, and easy to walk around. Landmarks in town include the castle-topped Ayasoluk Hill, north-west of the centre; Cengiz Topel Caddesi, the pedestrian way which is the heart of the commercial and tourist district, running from an elaborate round fountain at the intersection with the main road to the Selçuk railway station; and, a few hundred metres south of the fountain on the main road, the bus station. On the west side of the main road is a park, and west of it the famous Ephesus Museum. On the south side of the park is the Tourism Information Office.

The İzmir-Aydın bypass highway will probably be finished by the time you arrive, reducing the amount of noisy traffic on Selçuk's main street.

Information

Selçuk has a Tourism Information Office (☎ (5451) 1328) in a group of modern shops near the museum and across the highway

Train Schedule

Depart İzmir (Basmane)	Depart Menderes Airport	Depart Selçuk (Ephesus)	Arrive Denizli
8.15 am	8.39 am	9.53 am	1.24 pm
3.15 pm	3.59 pm	5.12 pm	9.14 pm
6.05 pm	6.20 pm	7.42 pm	11.30 pm
6.45 pm	7.15 pm	8.58 pm	–

Depart Denizli	Depart Selçuk (Ephesus)	Depart Menderes Airport	Arrive İzmir (Basmane)
5.40 am	8.45 am	10.10 am	12.14 am
7.30 am	12.29 pm	1.50 pm	12.57 pm
8.40 am	1.45 pm	3.05 pm	2 pm
3 pm	7.53 pm	9.22 pm	9.07 pm

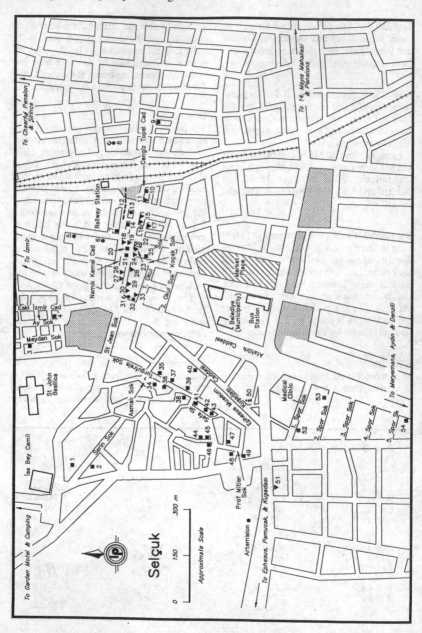

Selçuk

■ PLACES TO STAY

1 Hotel Akay
2 Amazon Pension
3 Pension Sİ
4 Tuncay Pension
7 Hotel Aksoy
9 Nur Pansiyon
10 Otel Gazi
14 Victoria Hotel
20 Hotel Subaşı
21 Ürkmez Otel
25 Hotel Hasanağa
34 Homeros Pension
35 Sevil Pansiyon
36 Akgüneş Pension
37 Abasız Pansiyon
38 Star Pension
39 Ak Otel (rear)
40 Ak Otel
41 Pension Kırhan
42 Gedik Pansiyon
43 Barım Pansiyon
44 İlayda Pension
45 Australian Pension
46 Deniz Pansiyon
47 Semiramis Manolya Pension
48 Sultan Pension
49 Pension Gözde
52 Hotel Mekan
53 Pension Akbulut
54 Hotel Katibim

▼ PLACES TO EAT

11 Efes Çorba Salonu
15 Efes Birahanesi
16 Bayraklı Restaurant
17 Selçuk Köftecisi
18 Ephesus Restaurant
19 Turhan Restaurant
23 Bizim Restaurant
24 Firuze Restaurant
26 Barbaros Cafe Bar
27 Seçkin Restaurant
28 Dilek Patisserie
29 Seçil Restaurant
30 Özdamar Restaurant
33 Doyum Pide Salonu

OTHER

5 Selçuk Hamamı (Turkish Bath)
6 Police Station
8 Mosque
12 Byzantine Aquoduct
13 Teahouse
22 PTT (Post Office)
31 Akıncılar Mosque
32 Toilets
50 Tourism Information Office
51 Villa Restaurant

from the bus station. It's open every day from 8.30 am to 6.30 or 7 pm (outside the busy summer months, Sunday hours are from 9 am to 2 pm). The staff will be glad to help you with accommodation here, particularly if you want a bed in a small, inexpensive pension.

The PTT on Cengiz Topel Caddesi is open 24 hours every day, and will change cash, travellers cheques or Eurocheques anytime. Selçuk's postal code is 35920.

At my last visit, the exchange office on Cengiz Topel Caddesi near the fountain and the main highway gave the best exchange rate.

If you park a car near the Tourism Information Office, Ephesus Museum, St John Basilica, or a few other touristy places in Selçuk you may be approached by a man

wanting to collect a parking fee of up to US$1.50. Ask for a *bilet* (ticket) or *makbuz* (receipt) and if he doesn't have a book of them, and doesn't give you one, ignore him. If he does show you his receipts, move your car and park a few blocks away for free.

Ayasoluk Hill
Before going to Ephesus, take an hour or two to visit the ancient buildings in Selçuk. The best place to start is the St John Basilica on top of the hill; look for signs pointing the way to St Jean.

It is said that St John came to Ephesus at the end of his life and wrote his Gospel here. A tomb built in the 300s was thought to be his, so Justinian erected this magnificent church above it in the 500s. Earthquakes and scavengers for building materials had left the church a heap of rubble until a century ago when restoration began. Virtually all of what you see is restored. The church site is open every day from 8 am to 5.30 pm (later in summer) for US$2. Parking at the entrance costs almost as much, so park a block or two away.

This hill, including the higher peak with the fortress, is called Ayasoluk. The view is attractive. Look west: at the foot of the hill is the **İsa Bey Camii**, built in 1307 by the Emir of Aydın in a transitional style which was post-Seljuk and pre-Ottoman. Keep a picture of it in your mind if you plan to venture deep into Anatolia for a look at more Seljuk buildings.

Beyond the mosque you can see how the Aegean Sea once invaded this plain, allowing Ephesus to prosper from maritime commerce. When the harbour silted up, Ephesus began to lose its famous wealth.

Early in the town's existence it had earned money from pilgrims coming to pay homage to Cybele or Artemis. The many-breasted Anatolian fertility goddess had a fabulous temple, the **Artemision**, to the south-west of the St John Basilica. A sign on the road to Ephesus marks the spot today, and you can see a re-erected column and the outline of the foundation. When you visit the huge temple at Didyma you can get an idea of what the great temple looked like, as the one at Didyma is thought to be similar. But the cult of the fertility goddess has now moved from Ephesus to men's magazines.

By the way, the **citadel** on top of the hill to the north of the St John Basilica was originally constructed by the Byzantines in the 500s, rebuilt by the Seljuks and restored in modern times. A small Seljuk mosque and a ruined church are inside.

Ephesus Museum

Don't miss the beautiful museum in the centre of Selçuk just a few steps from the Tourism Information Office, open from 8.30 am to 6.30 pm for US$2. The collection is a significant one, and its statuary, mosaics and artefacts are attractively displayed. In the late 1980s exhibit space was expanded by incorporating the historic hamam next door.

Among the prime attractions in this rich collection are several marble statues of Cybele/Artemis, with rows of egg-like breasts representing fertility, elaborate head-dresses and several effigies of Priapus, the phallic god. There are also good mosaics and frescoes.

Other Sites

Selçuk has some **tombs** and a little **mosque** dating from the Seljuk period just south of the bus station. Also, on the streets between the highway and the railway station you can see the remains of a **Byzantine aqueduct**, now a favourite nesting-place for a large population of storks. Eggs are laid in late April or May, and the storks are in residence into September.

Festivals

The Ephesus Festival, held during the 2nd week of May, brings world-class performers to the Great Theatre at Ephesus, and other venues. From mid-June to mid-July, performances of music and dance are organised under the rubric of the International İzmir Festival, with some performances being held at Ephesus.

Places to Stay – bottom end

Selçuk has almost 100 small pensions, and the Tourism Information Office will help you find one with rooms available. Touts at the bus station will lead you to one or another of the pensions, but unless they actually own the pension they will collect a commission from the owner, thereby raising your price.

Pensions fall into several groups according to location and price. Cheapest are those east of the centre in the section called Zafer Mahallesi, across the railway tracks and up the hill, a 10 or 15-minute walk from the centre; and north-east of Ayasoluk Hill, reached by going north along the main road towards İzmir, then left. The most convenient and congenial, but also a bit more expensive, are those in the sections called Atatürk Mahallesi and İsabey Mahallesi, on the hill behind (north and west of) the museum. Finally, there are a few smaller pensions on the south side of the Ephesus road.

Rooms in these modest, friendly, cheap places cost from $US3.50 to US$5 a single, US$7 to US$10 a double without bath; or from US$4 to US$6 a single, US$10 to US$12 a double with private shower. In some cases it's possible to sleep on the roof or camp in the garden for US$2 to US$3 per person.

Following are some of the pensions which Lonely Planet readers have found to be particularly good value.

Behind the Museum There are at least 60 pensions on and around the hill behind the museum. Facing the museum, walk up the street to the right of it. You will soon encounter the *Pension Kırhan* (☎ (5451) 2257), Turgutreis Sokak 7, with four rooms in a convenient location.

Turn right to find the *Star Pension* (☎ (5451) 3858), Ova Sokak 22, just off Turgutreis Sokak, where the five rooms all have baths and are thus a bit more expensive. Farther along Turgutreis Sokak, *Abasız Pansiyon* (☎ (5451) 1367), Turgutreis Sokak 13, is very friendly, with nine rooms, some with views. *Akgüneş Pension* (☎ (5451) 3869), Turgutreis Sokak 14, across the street, has eight rooms, some with bath. A bit farther on, *Sevil Pansiyon* (☎ (5451) 2340), Turgutreis Sokak 17, has nine rooms, some with three beds, and a nice roof terrace.

Walk past the Sevil and turn left to find the popular *Homeros Pension* (☎ (5451) 3995), Asmalı Sokak 17, with lots of 'character' and a nice terrace and rooftop bar with panoramic view. The Homeros is high enough to get a cooling breeze on those burning hot days.

Back down Turgutreis Sokak past the Kırhan are two more pensions: the *Gedik Pansiyon* (☎ 5451) 2452), Turgutreis Sokak 5, with 11 rooms, some with showers, and some singles; and beyond it, the *Barım Pansiyon* (☎ (5451) 1927), Turgutreis Sokak 34, has lots of fancy brickwork and iron-work, and six clean rooms.

Just to the right of the Pension Kırhan, Sefa Sokak winds uphill to the *Australian Pension* (☎ (5451) 1050), Profesör Mitler Sokak 17, run by the Toparlak family which spent 12 years Down Under. The 12 clean, modern rooms around a courtyard have no private baths, but common facilities are fine. You can use the kitchen and washing machine. The Toparlaks also operate the Australian Carpet Shop and New Zealand Carpet Shop, where readers have reported fair dealing and no pressure tactics.

İlayda Pension (☎ (5451) 3276), Profesör Mitler Sokak 15, behind the Australian Pension, has eight clean, good bathless rooms if the Australian is full. Another nearby choice is the five-room *Deniz Pansiyon* (☎ (5451) 1741), Sefa Sokak 9, just beyond the Australian.

Just beyond the Deniz, turn left and descend the hill to find yet more pensions, most of them cheaper. *Semiramis Manolya Pansiyon* (☎ (5451) 1690), Profesör Mitler Sokak 6, has 12 beds jammed into four rooms, and a relatively quiet location. *Sultan Pension* (☎ (5451) 2862), Profesör Mitler Sokak 3, is also small, un-fancy and cheap, with three rooms. A bit farther along, the *Pension Gözde* (☎ (5451) 2814), Profesör Mitler Sokak 2, also has three bathless rooms.

Try also the *Amazon Pension* (☎ (5451) 3215), Serin Sokak 8, near the İsabey Camii and Hotel Akay. It has seven bathless rooms and a pretty garden where breakfast is served.

Other pensions that readers have liked in this area include the four-room *Anatolia Pension 1* (☎ (5451) 1254), St Jean (Senjan) Caddesi 2, and the larger, quieter *Anatolia Pension 2* (☎ (5451), 1001 Sokak No 23.

East of Ayasoluk Hill East of Ayasoluk Hill and the castle, west of the main road, are several other pensions and hotels. Because they are slightly out of the way, they offer slightly better prices and service than those more readily evident in the centre. *Hülya Pansiyon* (☎ (5451) 2120), Özgür Sokak 15, is small but friendly and quite cheap, with three bathless rooms. *Pension Si* (☎ (5451) 2088), Meydan Sokak 45, officially the 'Pension Selçuk International', is also a good choice, with 11 rooms. *Tuncay Pension* (☎ (5451) 1260), Ay Sokak 3, is the best choice here, with cool, quiet, clean rooms, and a washing machine for guests' use.

South of the Ephesus Road South of the Ephesus road and west of the main street is a quiet neighbourhood of unremarkable modern apartment blocks. Some of the apartments have been converted to small pensions. *Yılmaz Pension* (☎ (5451) 2163), 3. Spor Sokak No 2, is typical, with three bathless rooms. *Pension Akbulut* (☎ (5451) 1139), 2. Spor Sokak No 4, has five quiet rooms with shared facilities.

The small four-room *Pamukkale Pension* (☎ (5451) 2388), Zafer Mahallesi, Kaner Sokak 3, is another good choice in this area.

East of the Centre Come out of the bus station, turn left (south) and walk to the big street, then turn left (east) and walk until you cross the railway tracks. By this time you will see signs which will lead you to several pensions. Readers of this guide have particularly enjoyed the *Nur Pansiyon* (☎ (5451) 1595), Zafer Mahallesi, Dere Sokak 16, with seven bathless rooms; the aptly named *Cheerful Pension* (☎ (5451) 2732), Zafer Mahallesi, Çimenlik Sokak 3, with eight bathless rooms; and the *Ayla Pension*, about 15 minute's walk from the centre.

In 14. Mayıs Mahallesi, farther up the hill and to the right, is the *Yayla Pension* (☎ (5451) 2903), İnce Sokak 19. The 10 rooms have showers and toilets, and some have balconies. English is spoken by the friendly family proprietors. The nearby *Zümrüt Pension* (☎ (5451) 1887), İnce Sokak 13, is simpler but cheaper, and just as welcoming.

Camping On the west side of Ayasoluk Hill 200 metres beyond the İsabey Camii, *Garden Motel & Camping* (☎ (5451) 1163) offers simple camp sites amidst orange trees and fields, as well as basic 'motel' rooms and (surprise!) a carpet shop. At US$5 for a two-person tent, it's only a bit cheaper than the cheapest pensions, but the setting is nice. There's also camping at Pamucak (see following).

Places to Stay – middle
Selçuk has a good number of those suitable if simple two-star hotels with elevators, restaurants, and guest rooms featuring private baths. Breakfast is usually included in the price.

Most convenient and relatively quiet are those on Cengiz Topel Caddesi between the fountain and the railway station. The two-star *Victoria Hotel* (☎ (5451) 3203), Cengiz Topel Caddesi 4, is decorated in light natural wood and creamy marble, with a decent dining room on the ground floor and a lift to take you up to your room. The 14 small rooms cost US$35 a double with shower, breakfast included, in the high summer season. By the way, some rooms here have views of the storks' nests in the old aqueduct, but the storks are in residence only during the warm months (from mid-April to September).

Not far from the railway station, behind the Victoria Hotel, is the simple 20-room *Ürkmez Otel* (☎ (5451) 1312), Namık Kemal Caddesi 18, with willing staff, some rooms with balconies, some with shower, costing US$25 a double.

Otel Gazi (☎ (5451) 1464), at Cengiz Topel Caddesi 1, facing the bust of Atatürk on the little plaza right by the railway station, is in the centre of the action. A terrace café out the front is good for people-watching, and the rooftop bar is perfect for breakfast. Rooms with bath and balcony cost US$18 a double, breakfast included.

Hotel Subaşı (☎ (5451) 1359), Cengiz Topel Caddesi 12 across from the PTT, is comfortable. Owner Ziya Subaşı and his French wife live in Paris most of the year, but run the hotel from April to October. All 16 rooms have baths, and rent for US$18 a double; breakfast costs extra.

A half-block south of Cengiz Topel Caddesi, *Hotel Hasanağa* (☎ (5451) 1317),

Koçak Sokak 5, is a second choice if the previously mentioned ones are full. It has 23 quiet rooms, all with private baths, going for US$18 a double. *Hotel Aksoy* (☎ (5451) 1040), Namık Kemal Caddesi 2, is among the oldest hotels in town, and shows it in some places, but charges US$18 a double. Some rooms have private showers.

Another good choice is just west of the park, to the right of the museum. The two-star *Ak Otel* (☎ (5451) 2161; fax 3142), Kuşadası Caddesi 14, owned by a Turkish family which spent many years in Belgium, boasts two stars and has 60 rooms in two buildings, all with showers. Rooms at the back are quieter. Rates are US$15/25 a single/double, breakfast included. The rear building is usually filled by groups such as Elderhostel tours.

The 16-room *Hotel Akay* (☎ (5451) 3009, 3172), İsa Bey Camii Karşısı, Serin Sokak 3, is near the İsa Bey Camii and thus well away from the noise of the town. A TV thrums in the lounge, and a waiter takes orders at the rooftop (3rd floor) terrace restaurant. The simple guest rooms are built around an interior court and reached by walkways, motel-style. All is white stucco except for the honey-coloured pine doors, windows, and other trim. All rooms have tiled baths with telephone booth-style showers, and go for US$16/25 a single/double.

Hotel Mekan (☎ (5451) 1299; fax 1331), 1. Spor Sokak 19, just south of the museum across the Ephesus road, also rates two stars for its 24 rooms and charges US$15/25 a single/double, breakfast included.

For somewhat greater comfort at a higher price, try the three-star, 40-room *Otel Pınar* (☎ (5451) 2561, -3), on Şahabettin Dede Caddesi, a short distance east of the bus station along Pazaryeri Caddesi. The one-star, 28-room *Hotel Katibim* (☎ (5451) 2417, 2498), six short blocks south of the Tourism Information Office along the main road, is another choice with comfortable rooms, but the ones at the front may be noisy.

Best in town is the new four-star *Hitit Hotel* (☎ (5451) 1007; fax 2372), Atatürk Caddesi 2 (the main road), with 96 air-conditioned rooms, satellite TV, minibars, a nice swimming pool and various restaurants and bars. Rates in summer are US$50/70 a single/double.

Places to Eat

The first place to look for a meal is along Cengiz Topel Caddesi, between the highway and the railway station. There are numerous restaurants, including several with pleasant outdoor tables by the street. Prices are set by the town government for each class of restaurant. On average, soups cost US$1, meze (hors d'oeuvres, salads etc) from US$1 to US$1.50, meat dishes from US$1.75 to US$3. Alcoholic beverages are available at most restaurants, the exceptions being the simple pide and köfte joints.

The pide and köfte joints just off of Cengiz Topel Caddesi are the cheapest eateries, as well. Try the *Doyum Pide Salonu*, a block south of the fountain, where Turkish-style pizza goes for US$1 to US$2; kebaps from US$1.75 to US$2.25; salads and soups, less than US$1. *Selçuk Köftecisi*, a few blocks east and a block south of Cengiz Topel Caddesi, is also cheap. Another good, cheap place is the *Kodalak Restaurant* at the bus terminal; there's also a good pastane (pastry shop), the *Efes Pastanesi*.

On Cengiz Topel Caddesi, start from the round fountain by the main road, and you'll come first to the *Özdamar Restaurant*, facing the fountain, and next to it the popular *Seçil*. The Seçil is the eatery of choice these days, but these things change quickly. The similarly named *Seçkin Restaurant* (☎ 1698), Cengiz Topel Caddesi 22, across the street, has gone up-market, is more expensive, and seems to have suffered a loss of clientele. The *Barbaros Cafe-Bar* adjoining the Seçkin is a fairly up-market drinking hang-out. For pastries and puddings, try the *Dilek Patisserie*, a bit farther along.

In the next block, the *Firuze* and the *Bizim* restaurants are a bit cheaper. Cheaper still are the family-run *Ephesus Restaurant*, on Namık Kemal Caddesi near the Hotel Aksoy; the *Selçuk Restaurant* nearby; and the *Bayraklı Restaurant* at the eastern end of

Cengiz Topel Caddesi. Next to the popular Bayraklı is the *Efes Birahanesi*, more of a restaurant than a beerhall, despite its name.

The restaurant in the *Hotel Victoria* serves a good variety of tasty food (from spaghetti to şiş kebap) at value-for-money prices, and has maintained a good reputation over the years.

The *Efes Çorba Salonu* ('soup salon') on the square at the eastern end of Cengiz Topel Caddesi actually serves full meals, but the food can be disappointing.

By the railway station there are some shaded tea gardens where you can sit, sip tea and watch the storks on top of the aqueduct (in summer only). For a sweet treat, drop in for a taste at *Tadım Şekerleme* (☎ 3999), next to the Sümerbank a short block south of Cengiz Topel Caddesi. A 125-gram package of Turkish Delight costs less than US$1, and you can choose from 40 different types, from the fruity to the creamy. Hikmet Bey, the confectioner, makes candied chestnuts as well.

For a different ambience, try the *Villa Restaurant* (☎ 1299), at the beginning of the road to Ephesus. Vines and lattices shade the tables here, and in summer they erect a wooden rig which holds a large barrel-like churn for ayran, as the best of this drink is churned (yayık ayran), not simply mixed. Prices for meals are a bit higher (from US$8 to US$12), and there's sometimes a service charge added to your bill. Try çöp şiş (pronounced 'churp sheesh'), delicate small morsels of lamb grilled on little wooden skewers. The Villa Restaurant is open only in summer.

Entertainment

Sipping and talking are the main evening entertainments in Selçuk. Besides the restaurants along Cengiz Topel Caddesi, there's the *Ekselans Bar*, 1. Okul Sokak No 18/1, with outdoor tables and rock music.

The local Turkish bath is the Selçuk Hamamı, north of the Hotel Aksoy and the police station. Ladies' hours are from noon to 5 pm; men bathe in the mornings and evenings.

Getting Around

Bus Selçuk's bus station is a few blocks south of the fountain, on the east side of the main road across it from the Tourism Information Office and the Ephesus-Kuşadası road. Service is mostly local. For long-distance intercity bus service, transfer to İzmir or Kuşadası.

Details of some of the main bus services follow:

Ephesus – three km, five minutes, 50c; frequent minibuses in summer, but it's also pleasant to walk (see the following)

İzmir – 80 km, 1¼ hours, US$2; buses every 15 minutes from 6.30 am to 7 pm in summer

Kuşadası – 20 km, 30 minutes, 80c; minibuses run frequently in summer, with the last minibus departing from Selçuk at 8.30 pm, from Kuşadası at 9 pm. After hours, look for a more expensive taxi lurking near the museum.

Pamucak – seven km, 10 minutes, 70c; last minibus departs well before sunset; a taxi costs US$8

Tours For details of minibus tours to Priene, Miletus, Didyma and Altınkum, see that section, following.

If the tours are not running, or if you'd rather go on your own, catch a bus or minibus to Söke. From there, minibuses run to points throughout the region, including to Priene, Didyma and Altınkum. Going on your own is cheaper, but can take much more time.

Taxi Taxi drivers charge about US$2.50 to take you the three km to the Ephesus ruins, about US$8 to Meryemana and back. For US$15, they'll take you to the main ruins, wait, take you to Meryemana, and return you to Selçuk. All of these rates are per carload, not per person.

EPHESUS

Ephesus is the best-preserved classical city on the Mediterranean, and perhaps the best place in the world to get the feeling for what life was like in Roman times. Needless to say, it is a major tourist destination.

In high summer it gets very hot here. It's best to start your tramping early in the morning, then retire to a shady restaurant for lunch at the peak of the heat. If your interest in ancient ruins is slight, a half-day may suffice, but real ruins buffs will want to continue their explorations in the afternoon as well.

Ephesus is three km from the Tourism Information Office in Selçuk to the admission gate at Ephesus, a pleasant 30 to 45-minute walk in the morning or evening, but a hot trek at midday. Vehicles take the new, sunny highway; walkers follow Doktor Sabri Yayla Bulvarı, the old tree-shaded road just north of the highway, named for the late mayor of Selçuk who planted the trees.

Things to See

As you walk into the site from the highway, you will see a road to the left marked to the **Grotto of the Seven Sleepers**, on the north-east side of Mt Pion (Panayir Dağı) about a 10-minute walk away. A legend says that seven persecuted Christian youths fled from Ephesus in the 3rd century and took refuge in this cave. Agents of the Emperor Decius, a terror to Christians, found the cave and sealed it. Two centuries later an earthquake broke down the wall, awakening the sleepers, and they ambled back to town for a meal. Finding that all of their old friends were long dead, they concluded that they had undergone a sort of resurrection – Ephesus was by this time a Christian city. When they died they were buried in the cave, and a cult following developed. The grotto is actually a fairly elaborate Byzantine era necropolis with scores of tombs cut into the rock. You must pay an extra admission charge to enter, which many people feel is hardly worth it.

Back on the entry road you pass the **Gymnasium of Vedius** (2nd century AD) on your left, which had exercise fields, baths, latrines, covered exercise rooms, a swimming pool and a ceremonial hall. Just south of it is the **Stadium**, dating from about the same period. Most of its finely cut stones were taken by the Byzantines to build the citadel and walls of Ayasoluk. This 'quarrying' of precut building stone from older, often earthquake-ruined structures

continued through the entire history of Ephesus.

The road comes over a low rise and descends to the parking lot, where there are teahouses, restaurants, souvenir shops, a post office and banks. To the right (west) of the road are the ruins of the **Church of the Virgin Mary**, also called the Double Church.

Admission to the archaeological site costs US\$3, half-price for students; parking costs US\$1.25. The site is open from 8.30 am to 5.30 pm (till 6.30 pm in summer) every day.

As you walk down a lane bordered by evergreen trees, a few colossal remains of the **Harbour Gymnasium** are off to the right (west). Then you come to the marble-paved **Arcadian Way**. This was the grandest street in Ephesus. Constructed with water and sewer lines beneath the paving, installed with streetlighting along the colonnades, lined with shops and finished with triumphal columns, it was and still is a grand sight. The builder was the Byzantine emperor Arcadius (395-408). At the far (western) end was the harbour of Ephesus, long since silted up. Near the western (harbour) end of the street is the **Nymphaeum**, a fountain and pool.

At the east end of the Arcadian Way is the **Great Theatre**, still used for performances. Its design is Hellenistic; construction was begun in 41 AD and finished in 117. It could – and can – hold almost 25,000 spectators. When you visit, no doubt someone will be standing on the orchestra floor of the theatre, speaking to someone seated high up in the auditorium to demonstrate the fine acoustics.

Behind the Great Theatre is **Mt Pion**, which bears a few traces of the ruined city walls.

From the theatre, continue along the marble-paved **Sacred Way**, also called the Marble Way. Note the remains of the city's elaborate water and sewer systems. The large open space to the right, once surrounded by a colonnade and shops, was the **Agora** (3 BC) or marketplace, heart of Ephesus' business life.

At the end of the Sacred Way, Curetes Way heads east up a slope. This corner was 'central Ephesus'. The beautiful **Library of**

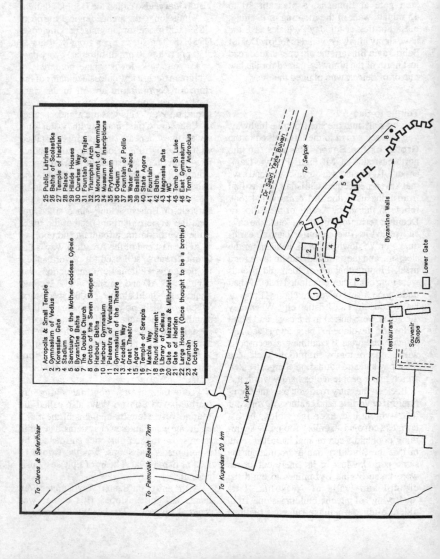

1 Acropolis & Small Temple
2 Gymnasium of Vedius
3 Koressian Gate
4 Stadium
5 Sanctuary of the Mother Goddess Cybele
6 Byzantine Baths
7 The Double Church
8 Grotto of the Seven Sleepers
9 Harbour Baths
10 Harbour Gymnasium
11 Palaestra of Verulanus
12 Gymnasium of the Theatre
13 Arcadian Way
14 Great Theatre
15 Agora
16 Temple of Serapis
17 Marble Way
18 Round Monument
19 Library of Celsus
20 Gate of Mazeus & Mithridates
21 Gate of Hadrian
22 Large House (Once thought to be a brothel)
23 Fountain
24 Octagon
25 Public Latrines
26 Baths of Scolastika
27 Temple of Hadrian
28 Palace
29 Hillside Houses
30 Curetes Way
31 Fountain of Trajan
32 Triumphal Arch
33 Monument of Memmius
34 Museum of Inscriptions
35 Prytaneum
36 Odeum
37 Fountain of Pollio
38 Water Palace
39 Basilica
40 State Agora
41 Fountain
42 Baths
43 Magnesia Gate
44 WC
45 Tomb of St Luke
46 East Gymnasium
47 Tomb of Androclus

To Claros & Seferihisar

To Pamucak Beach 7km

To Kuşadası 20 km

Airport

Dr Sabri Yayla Bulvarı

To Selçuk

Byzantine Walls

Lower Gate

Restaurant

Souvenir Shops

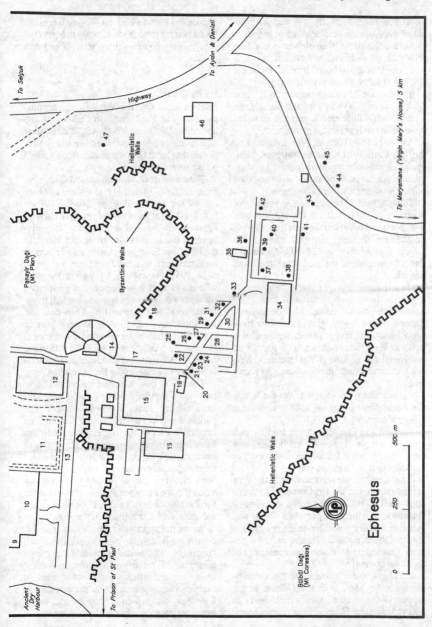

Celsus is here, carefully restored with the aid of the Austrian Archaeological Institute.

Across the street is an elaborate building with rich mosaics and several fountains. It was once thought to be the brothel, but some say it was just a grand private residence.

In the maze of ruined walls you'll come upon a **spring** served by a hand pump from which, with a little effort, you can coax the most deliciously refreshing cool water.

As you head up Curetes Way, a passage on the left leads to the **public latrines**, their design demonstrating their function unmistakably. These posh premises were for men only. The women's were elsewhere.

You can't miss the impressive **Temple of Hadrian**, on the left. It's in Corinthian style, with beautiful reliefs in the porch and a head of Medusa to keep out evil spirits. The temple was finished in 138 AD. Across the street is an elaborate house from the same period.

On the right side of Curetes Way across from the Temple of Hadrian, a path leads uphill to the Yamaç Evleri (hillside houses), Several of the larger, grander houses have been excavated and restored, and are now open to visitors from 8 am to 5 pm for an additional fee of US$1. The mosaics, frescoes, columns and marble facing are very fine.

Further along Curetes Way, on the left, is the **Fountain of Trajan**, who was Roman emperor from 98-117 AD.

To the right is a side street leading to a colossal temple dedicated to the Emperor Domitian (81-96 AD), which now serves as the **Museum of Inscriptions**.

Up the hill on the left (north) are the very ruined remains of the **Prytaneum**, a municipal hall; and the **Temple of Hestia Boulaea**, in which the perpetual flame was guarded. Finally you come to the pretty little marble **Odeum**, a small theatre used for lectures, musical performances and meetings of the town council.

There is another entrance to the archaeological zone here, near the Odeum at the Upper Gate, on the road which leads to Meryemana, the House of the Virgin Mary,

also called Panaya Kapulu. You will need to take a taxi for the 5.5 km journey to Meryemana, unless you are willing to walk or hitch there.

MERYEMANA

Legend has it that the Virgin Mary, accompanied by St Paul, came to Ephesus at the end of her life, circa 37-45 AD. Renaissance church historians mentioned the trip, and it is said that local Christians venerated a small house near Ephesus as Mary's.

Then a German woman named Catherine Emmerich (1774-1824) had visions of Mary and of her surroundings at Ephesus. When Lazarist clergy from İzmir followed Emmerich's detailed descriptions, they discovered the foundations of an old house in the hills near Ephesus; a tomb, also described by Emmerich, was not found.

In 1967 Pope Paul VI visited the site, where a chapel now stands, and confirmed the authenticity of the legend. A small traditional service, celebrated by Orthodox and Muslim clergy on 15 August each year in honour of Mary's Assumption into heaven, is now the major event here. To Muslims, Mary is Meryemana, Mother Mary, who bore İsa Peygamber, the Prophet Jesus.

The site is now a Selçuk municipal park; there is no regular dolmuş service, so you'll have to hitch, rent a taxi or take a tour. The park is seven km from Ephesus' Lower Gate (or 5.5 km from the Upper Gate, nine km from Selçuk), up steep grades. The views of Ephesus, Selçuk, Ayasoluk Hill, and the surrounding countryside are wonderful along the way. At the top of the hill you must pay a small park entrance fee of 25c, and a fee for the site of 50c, then ride or walk down the other side a short way to the site.

Along the approach to the house are signboards explaining its significance in various languages. The house is usually busy with pilgrims, the devout and the curious. A small restaurant and snack stand provide meals at fairly moderate prices. If you're travelling on a budget, bring picnic supplies and enjoy lunch on your own in the shady park.

PAMUCAK

About seven km west of Selçuk (three km west of the highway junction with the Kuşadası and Seferihisar roads) lies Pamucak (PAH-moo-jahk) beach, a long wide crescent of dark sand. Often used by free campers and Turkish families, Pamucak's dramatic sand is often heavily littered, though the water is still refreshing. Gigantic hotels are rising to north and south, and soon this uncrowded beach may be cleared of litter only to be paved in bodies.

Places to Stay

The first and oldest hotel on the beach is the very shady *Dereli Motel* (☎ (5451) 3636), to the left as you come to the beach. It has little double or twin-bedded motel-style rooms with bath, facing the beach (US$25) or the land (US$20); slightly more comfortable rooms in bungalows, inland a bit cost US$30 a double. The whole place could do with a bit more maintenance, but it does offer a restaurant, food shop, camping area (US$5 for a tent, more for a caravan or camper van), horse rides, and that lovely deep shade.

Beyond the Dereli to the south (follow the road that goes behind the Dereli) is the *Selçuk Belediyesi Halk Plajları*, the municipal beach and camping ground. The rate is US$3 for up to four people in a tent. There are showers and a snack shop, and you can avail yourself of many of the services at the adjoining Dereli.

Moonlight Camping, which you passed on your way from Selçuk to Pamucak, is cheaper, scruffier, and not on the beach.

Inland from the beach about 250 metres is the four-star, 150-room *Otel Tamsa* (☎ 1190; fax 2771), Çorak Mevkii, Pamucak, a big, white box designed for the pleasure of tour groups. Though the exterior has all the charm of a barracks, the interior is comfortable, even plush. Guest rooms have TV, bath and refrigerator. The many services include tennis court, water sports equipment, restaurant and bar. Rates are US$30/50 a single/double during the high-summer season.

Getting There & Away

There are regular minibuses from Selçuk and Kuşadası in summer; hitching is easy in the hot months as well. Be sure to find out when the last minibus departs from the beach; it may leave before sunset.

ŞİRİNCE

Eight km east of Selçuk up in the hills, in the midst of grapevines, peach and apple orchards, lies Şirince (population 800). The old-fashioned stone-and-stucco houses have red-tile roofs, and the villagers, who were moved here from Salonica and its vicinity during the exchange of populations (1924) after WW I, are ardent fruit farmers. They make an interesting apple wine. People here will regale you proudly with the story that this village used to be named Çirkince ('ugliness'), but that it was changed to Şirince ('pleasantness') shortly after they arrived.

There's not much to do in Şirince except look at a few old Byzantine churches and monasteries, walk in the hills, and hang out, but that's exactly why people come here, away from the touristy bustle of Selçuk.

The minibus drops you at the centre of town. For services, Şirince has the *Köy Restaurant*, *Sultanhan Cafe*, and *Restaurant Dido Sotiruyu*, and several small pensions. These include Mr Metin Ozan's simple *Village of Maria's Pension*, which you pass on the road in; and the more charming, German-run *Erdem Pansion* (☎ (5451) 1430; in İzmir (51) 11 49 28). Beds at Maria's are US$3 each. At the Erdem you pay DM20 (US$14) for a bed, DM7 (US$5) for breakfast.

Getting There & Away

Three or four minibuses run daily between Selçuk and Şirince for 40c. If you go on a day trip, start out early in the morning as the last minibus back might leave by mid-afternoon.

BELEVİ

North and east of Selçuk nine km on the İzmir highway is the village of Belevi, and about two km east of the village, just to the side of the new İzmir-Aydın highway, stands the Belevi Mausoleum (Belevi Mezar Anıtı), a large and very ancient funerary monument resting on a base about 30 metres square cut from the limestone bedrock. The roof was decorated with lion-griffins (now in the Ephesus Museum at Selçuk and in İzmir's Archaeological Museum), and the interior held a large sarcophagus with a carved effigy of its occupant; the sarcophagus is now in the museum at Selçuk. Archaeologists are not certain who built this great tomb. It may have been the Seleucid ruler Antiochus II Theos (261-246 BC), or it may have been the work of the Persian invaders a century or more earlier.

Just west of the mausoleum is a tumulus, or burial mound, thought to date from the 300s BC, but little remains.

KUŞADASI

On the Aegean coast, 20 km from Selçuk, is Kuşadası (koo-SHAH-dah-suh, Bird Island). A seaside resort town with a population of 50,000, it is, like Selçuk, a base for excursions to the ancient cities of Ephesus, Priene, Miletus and Didyma, and even inland to Aphrodisias and Pamukkale.

Many Aegean cruise ships on tours of the Greek islands stop at Kuşadası so that their passengers can take a tour to Ephesus and haggle for trinkets in Kuşadası's shops. Day-trippers come over on the daily ferries from Samos. The package-tour business has also affected this once-sleepy fishing village, so that today it is littered with characterless high-rise apartment and hotel blocks and noisy with traffic. The town centre is all shops, and in front of the shops, beside the shops, in the streets, on the waterfront and climbing the walls are *işportacılar*, itinerant pedlars and touts ready to sell you anything and everything. The pleasant, easy atmosphere which made it popular in the 1970s is long gone, even though Kuşadası still has some businesses serving the farmers, bee-keepers and fishers who still make up an ever-dwindling portion of the town's population.

Kuşadası gets its name from a small island, now connected to the mainland by a causeway, called Güvercinada (Pigeon Island). You can recognise it by the small stone fort which is the tiny island's most prominent feature.

History

The natural port here may have been in use several centuries BC, and was probably known to the Byzantines, but modern Kuşadası's history begins in medieval times when Venetian and Genoese traders came here, calling it Scala Nuova. Two centuries after the Ottoman conquest in 1413, Öküz Mehmet Paşa, vizier and sometime grand vizier to sultans Ahmet I and Osman II, ordered the building of the Kaleiçi mosque and hamam, the city walls, and the caravanserai, in order to improve Kuşadası's prospects as a trading port with Europe and Africa.

Useful for exporting agricultural goods, Kuşadası was also an important defensive port along the Ottoman Aegean coast. In 1834 the little fortress on Güvercinada was restored and improved. It maintained its modest trade, farming and fishing economy and its quiet character until the tourism boom of the 1980s turned it into a brash resort.

Orientation

Kuşadası's central landmark is the Öküz Mehmet Paşa Kervansarayı, an Ottoman caravanserai which is now a hotel called the Hotel Kervansaray. It's 100 metres inland from the cruise-ship docks, at the intersection of the waterfront boulevard and the town's main street.

The waterfront road is named Atatürk Bulvarı. The main street (now a pedestrian way) heading from the caravanserai inland is officially named Barbaros Hayrettin Caddesi. The post office is on Barbaros Hayrettin Caddesi near the caravanserai. Just beyond the post office on the same (north) side of Barbaros Hayrettin Caddesi, a narrow passage leads to the Öküz Mehmet Paşa mosque and the Kaleiçi Hamamı (Turkish bath). At the little stone tower that was once part of the town's defensive walls, Barbaros Hayrettin Caddesi crosses Sağlık Caddesi and changes names to become Kahramanlar Caddesi, lined with shops and restaurants. Turn left onto Sağlık Caddesi to explore Kuşadası's market and the old Kaleiçi neighbourhood of narrow streets, little restaurants and pensions. Turn right to find more restaurants and pensions up on the hill which overlooks the harbour.

The little mosque about 100 metres along Kahramanlar Caddesi, called the Hacı Hatice Hanım Camii (Hanım Camii for short), is a convenient landmark.

The bus and dolmuş station is more than one km east of the caravanserai on the bypass road.

Information

The Tourism Information Office (☎ (636) 11103), on İskele Meydanı, is down by the wharf where the cruise ships dock, about 100 metres west of the Hotel Kervansaray. Hours are officially from 7.30 am to 8 pm every day in July and August, 8 am to 6 pm in May, June, September and October, and Monday to Friday from 8.30 am to 5.30 pm, but these hours are not strictly observed.

Kuşadası has a government-run hospital (☎ (636) 11026) and many private doctors and dentists.

Kuşadası's postal code is 09400.

Bookshops Try Kuydaş (☎ 11828), Kıbrıs Caddesi 10/A, which has some foreign books, newspapers and periodicals. Art Kitabevi (☎ 15435), Kahramanlar Caddesi 70, near the Hanım Camii, has a similar collection.

Beaches

After a stroll through the caravanserai and out to Güvercinada (Güvercin Adası), you'll want to find the beaches. You can swim from the rocky shores of Güvercin Adası and its causeway, but Yılancı Burnu, the peninsula less than one km to the south, is more enticing. Or catch the shuttle to the northern beach near the yacht marina, or catch a Şehiriçi ('In-town') dolmuş and take it all the way

north past the Kuştur holiday village to the beach opposite the Kervansaray Mocamp. Even farther along is the Tusan Hotel, which is on a nice beach. The hotel rents water sports equipment.

Kuşadası's most famous beach is Kadınlar Denizi ('Ladies' Sea'), 2.5 km south of town. To get there, wait along the road between the Tourism Information Office and Güvercin Adası for a minibus. Kadınlar Denizi is a small beach crowded by big hotels. It is woefully inadequate for the crowds in high summer, when the hotel pool is often more inviting. The coast south of Kadınlar Denizi has several more small beaches, each backed by its ranks of new hotels.

There's also Pamucak, 15 km to the north near Selçuk. Dolmuşes run from Kuşadası's otogar to Pamucak several times daily in high summer; at other times you must go to Selçuk and change to a Pamucak dolmuş, or get out at the Pamucak road and walk over two km. (See the previous section on Pamucak, following Selçuk.)

Nearby Sites

Kuşadası is a convenient base for visits to Ephesus, Priene, Miletus, Didyma, Altınkum beach, and Dilek Milli Park (a national park). See the following for more information.

Turkish Baths

Kuşadası's hamams are of the New Age type, allowing men and women to bathe at the same time. The cost ranges from US$4 to US$8; be sure to ask costs in advance.

The Belediye Hamamı (☎ 11219) is up the hill behind the Hotel Akdeniz; take the street which goes along the left side of the hotel. Kaleiçi Hamamı (☎ 11292) is just west of the Öküz Mehmet Paşa mosque.

Places to Stay

Prices for rooms in Kuşadası are highest in July and August, about 20% lower in June and September, and up to 50% lower in other months. Rates quoted below are the high-summer rates. Many hotels and pensions close from November to March.

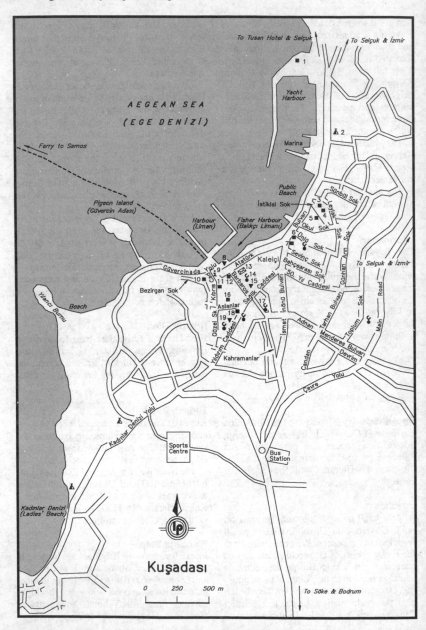

AEGEAN SEA
(EGE DENİZİ)

Ferry to Samos

Pigeon Island
(Güvercin Adası)

Harbour
(Liman)

Fisher Harbour
(Balıkçı Limanı)

Güvercinada Yolu

Yılancı Burnu

Beach

Bezirgan Sok

Yıldırım Caddesi

Güzel Sk

I Kıbrıs Cd

Atatürk

Kaleiçi

Barbaros

Sağlık Caddesi

İnönü Bulvarı

İsmet

Aslanlar

Kahramanlar

Kadınlar Denizi Yolu

Kadınlar Denizi
(Ladies' Beach)

Sports
Centre

Bus
Station

To Tusan Hotel & Selçuk

To Selçuk & İzmir

Yacht
Harbour

Marina

Public
Beach

İstiklal Sok

Sümbül Sok

Leylak

Bülvarı

Okul Sok

Ünlü Sok

Üniv

Sevinç Sok

Bahçearası Sok

50. Yıl Caddesi

Günhan Arın Sok

To Selçuk & İzmir

Tarhan Bulvarı

Lopium Sok

Main Road

Adnan Menderes Bulvarı

Candan

Devrim

Çevre Yolu

Kuşadası

0   250   500 m

To Söke & Bodrum

The big five-star hotels are on the outskirts of town. In the centre are small, moderately priced hotels and cheap pensions. The rule of thumb is the same for any seaside resort: the farther you go inland (away from the sea), the cheaper the room.

Places to Stay – bottom end

Cheap rooms can be pleasant or stark. Most have sinks, a few have private baths. The price for a double ranges from US$10 to US$16.

Pension touts await you at the otogar and ferry dock, and taxi drivers will want to take you to a pension or hotel which pays them a fat commission. The cheapest pensions are farther inland, and can be difficult to find on your own, so you may have to trust in the touts; many are in fact helpful. But say goodbye at the first sign of improper dealing to avoid rip-offs. Among Kuşadası pension owners are a small number of sleazy charac-

ters, so it's good to size a pension up carefully before staying there. The tourism officials at the otogar are helpful, but may try to book you in a hotel charging more than you want to spend.

There are several convenient clusters of pensions and small hotels near the centre; here's how to find them. Walk up Barbaros Hayrettin Caddesi, turn right towards the Akdeniz Hotel, and take Aslanlar Caddesi, the road on the right side of the hotel. This takes you into the neighbourhood called Camiatik Mahallesi which will take you up past half a dozen pensions and inexpensive hotels.

Aslanlar Caddesi *Hotel İzmirli* (☎ (636) 14861), on Aslanlar Caddesi near the Hotel Akdeniz, is right in the thick of things, but if you choose your room carefully it can be quiet and pleasant. Rooms cost US$10/14/18 a single/double/triple, breakfast included.

Follow signs to the family-run *Pansiyon Golden Bed* (☎ (636) 18708), Aslanlar Caddesi, Uğurlu 1. Çıkmazı No 4, on a quiet little cul-de-sac not far from the centre. Some rooms have balconies and sea views. The roof terrace is delightful, the family welcome is cordial. Rooms with shower cost US$13 a double.

Farther uphill on Aslanlar Caddesi past the Hotel Flash, look for the *Hotel Ada* (☎ (636) 12491) and nearby the very simple but cheap *Pansiyon Su* (☎ (636) 11453), Aslanlar Caddesi 13, with basic waterless rooms for US$5 per person.

Kıbrıs Caddesi At the top of the slope, Kıbrıs Caddesi goes downhill on your right. There's a good place here as well.

Özhan Pansiyon (☎ (636) 12932), Kıbrıs Caddesi 5, is very central and normally quiet, with a nice roof terrace with bar and – occasionally – pension-sponsored belly-dance parties. Rooms with shower go for US$8/14 a single/double; breakfast costs extra, but is very pleasant on the terrace.

Bezirgan Sokak Back up at the top of the hill, turn right and follow Bezirgan Sokak, looking for signs to the *Pansiyon Dinç* (☎ (636) 14249), Mercan Sokak, small, simple, and cheap at US$12 a double, breakfast included, in a waterless room. Past the Hotel Stella are several more, including the *King Pansiyon* (☎ (636) 13128), Enişte Pansiyon (☎ (636) 12171) and Pansiyon Hasgül (☎ (636) 13641), all in a quiet area, some with sea views.

Güzel Sokak At the top of Aslanlar and Kıbrıs caddesis, instead of turning right onto Bezirgan Sokak, if you turn left you'll be on Güzel Sokak. Two blocks along is the 15-room *Hülya Pension* (☎ (636) 12075), İleri Sokak 39 near Güzel Sokak, which charges US$5 per person in a room, slightly less if you roll out your own sleeping bag on a bed on the roof. Some rooms have sinks or private showers. Laundry is done for an additional fee; cheap, good meals are available, or you may use the kitchen yourself.

Farther inland, *Pansiyon Sympathy* (☎ (636) 44388), Güvercin Sokak, is run by a smiling dynamo of a woman who provides good, cheap meals in a rooftop dining room as well as clean, cheap lodgings. Rates are from US$8/15 a single/double in summer; meals cost extra.

Şefik Pension (☎ (636) 14222), Camiatik Mahallesi, Doğan Sokak 11, is similar, at comparable rates, with good food and friendly family proprietors.

Camping North of the centre about one km, inland from the yacht marina, are three decent camping areas. Best is *Önder Camping* (☎ (636) 12413), open all year, with lots of facilities: tennis, swimming pool, laundry, and a good restaurant (open from March to October only). If the Önder is full, the adjoining *Yat Motel & Camping* and *Selam Motel & Camping* take the overflow.

Kervansaray Mocamp, several km north of these on the shore just before the Tusan Hotel, is a larger camping ground open from mid-April or late May until mid to late October. Nicely laid out with lots of services, it charges US$3 per person, US$2 for a car and US$4 for a tent. Little cabins cost

US$28/40/52 a single/double/ triple, breakfast and dinner included.

Places to Stay – middle
Mid-range hotels are scattered throughout the town, with some inland from the yacht marina, some on the pension streets of Aslanlar and Kıbrıs caddesis and Bezirgan Sokak, and many more farther inland along Kahramanlar Caddesi.

In Kaleiçi, just off Barbaros Hayrettin Caddesi opposite the caravanserai is Cephane Sokak (JEHP-hah-neh) and the *Bahar Pansiyon* (☎ (636) 11191), Cephane Sokak 12, a charming inn with a façade full of balconies and flower boxes, and a rooftop restaurant. The 13 rooms offer a step up in comfort, and also in price, at US$18/28 a single/double, breakfast included. Note that the Bahar is closed from November to February.

Also right in the centre is the 22-room *Hotel Aynalı* (☎ (636) 14582), PTT Sokak 6 (walk north one block on the little street by the post office), a modern building with old Turkish wood trim. Many rooms have balconies, all have baths, and breakfast is included in the price of US$28 a double.

Up at the end of Barbaros Hayrettin Caddesi, to the right, is the *Otel Akdeniz* (☎ (636) 11120) with a pleasant vine-shaded patio in front, a spacious lobby and 42 rooms of varying sizes, shapes, and number of beds, with or without a bath. Finnish tour groups sometimes fill the hotel. If you find a room vacant, look at it and listen to the noise level, as some rooms face streets that have heavy volumes of traffic. A double without a bath costs US$26, with a bath from US$32 to US$38; breakfast is included in room prices.

Walk up Aslanlar Caddesi, which mounts the slope to the right of the Otel Akdeniz, to find the *Hotel Flash* (☎ (636) 13806; fax 14225), Aslanlar 70-A, across from the Hotel Ada. Popular with groups, it has a nice swimming pool and bar, and charges from US$20 to US$25 a double, breakfast included.

Turn right onto Bezirgan Sokak to find the two-star, 22-room *Hotel Stella* (☎ (636) 11632, 13787), Bezirgan Sokak 44. It's a tidy, airy place with fabulous views of the town and the harbour; friendly and personable management; and bright, modern rooms priced at US$40 a double with shower, breakfast included.

About one km north of the centre is another group of moderately priced lodgings on İstiklal Sokak.

Hotel Köken (☎ (636) 15723), İstiklal Sokak 5, is operated by a retired medical doctor and features rooms with private baths for US$24, breakfast included.

Next door to the Köken is the Yunus Pension, and beyond that the 20-room *Çidem Pansiyon* (chee-DEHM) (☎ (636) 11895), İstiklal Sokak 9, a clean and cheerful place with single rooms for US$22 to US$26, doubles for US$28 to US$34; cheaper rooms have sinks, more expensive rooms have private showers.

The nearby *Hotel Akman* (☎ (636) 11501), İstiklal Caddesi 13, is a neat little two-star, 46-room place open from mid-March to the end of October, used by tour groups. Some rooms have bathtubs, and all rooms are priced at US$28/36 a single/double, breakfast included.

Facing the sea, only a few hundred metres north of the caravanserai on Atatürk Bulvarı, are two modern hotels offering a convenient location and comfortable rooms for moderate prices. *Atınç Otel* (☎ (636) 17608; fax 14967) has 75 rooms with bath (and many with sea-view balconies), a rooftop swimming pool, satellite TV, sauna and fitness room, all for US$35/50 a single/double. *Otel Derici* (☎ (636) 18222; fax 18226), next door at Atatürk Bulvarı 40, has 87 rooms (all with bath) and a similar list of services at similar rates.

Places to Stay – top end

In the centre, there is little in the way of luxury lodging. For a fairly convenient location and a dramatic setting you can't beat the *Hotel Kısmet* (☎ (636) 12005; fax 14914), Akyar Mevkii, just north of the yacht marina perched on a little peninsula. Though relatively small (100 rooms) and older, it is well maintained, and has the feel of a private club.

Rates are US$70/95/105 a single/double/triple, breakfast included.

The refurbished Ottoman Öküz Mehmet Paşa Kervansaray at the centre of town is called the *Hotel Kervansaray* (or Club Caravansérail; ☎ (636) 14115; fax 12423). Once managed by the Club Méditerrannée, it is now under local management, and maintenance standards have fallen noticeably. The rooms are quite small, as they were when it was a working caravanserai, but are decorated with local crafts. The charming, verdant courtyard has been spoilt by the addition of a canopied bar at the centre, and a loud floor show keeps everybody awake until at least midnight. Overnight rates are from US$50 to US$60 a single, US$70 to US$85 a double, breakfast included.

The coast to the north and south of Kuşadası is crowded with huge, gleaming white four and five-star hotels, mostly dedicated to the group-tour and package-holiday trade. Rooms for single travellers cost from US$95 to US$125 a double in summer. To the north rises the assertive bulk of the *Adakule Hotel* (☎ (636) 19270; fax 15085), with 275 rooms and a distinctive tower.

South of the centre on Kadınlar Denizi are comfortable hotels priced from US$50 to US$100 a double. These include the five-star, 250-room *İmbat Oteli* (☎ (636) 12000; fax 14960), and the much cheaper three-star *Martı Oteli* (☎ (636) 13650; fax 14700), an older 112-room place that offers a superb location at good value-for-money prices.

Five km south of the centre beyond Kadınlar Denizi at Yavansu Mevkii, the five-star *Onur Hotel* (☎ (636) 18505; fax 13727) is perched on a cliff right above the sea, offering 330 comfortable rooms and lots of facilities.

Places to Eat – bottom end

The cheapest food – other than that you prepare yourself – is in the low-budget pensions mentioned above. Ask about pension meals when you book a room.

For other cheap meals, the farther you get away from the sea, the lower the price. About the best you can do in the centre is the little

Kuşadası Hazır Yemek Restaurant, next to the Kaleiçi Hamamı on the north side of the Kaleiçi mosque. Ready-food dishes are served up for an average of US$1 to US$1.40 apiece.

Walk inland on Kahramanlar Caddesi to the Hacı Hatice Hanım Camii, look to the left and you'll find several little restaurants serving delicious köfte, flat pide bread, salad and soft drinks, all for less than US$4. Walk even farther inland along Kahramanlar Caddesi for even cheaper snacks.

Places to Eat – middle

The big surprise in resorty Kuşadası is the *Restaurant Ada*, on Güvercin Adası, which has good food at low prices right on the water. It's almost too good to last.

On Cephane Sokak, the street of the Bahar Pension, look for two restaurants with several outdoor tables. The *Öz Urfa Kebapçısı* (☎ 16070) is strong on roast meats (from US$1.25 to US$2). The adjoining *Çamtepe Restaurant* (☎ 18348) specialises in kalamar (squid) and octopus salads and fries, and does a good tomato kebap (each for US$1.40).

For more good seafood, try *Hacı Dede* (☎ 13546), on Barbaros Hayrettin Caddesi across from the PTT above the pizza restaurant. Prices are lower than those at the more expensive waterfront places.

Go up Barbaros Hayrettin Caddesi past the stone tower, continue on Kahramanlar Caddesi, and find the *Konya Restoran*, good for a moderately priced feed. Across from the Konya, the *Loretta Cafe & Restaurant* (☎ 14470) is run by Şerif and Jill Peksen (he's Turkish, she's Welsh). The food is delicious, the welcome and the clientele international.

Farther along and to the left, the *Deniz Restaurant* (☎ 11397) offers decent food at good prices. On my last visit they even made patates köfe, delicious potato fritters, to go with the inexpensive fish.

Places to Eat – top end

The town's prime dining location is on the waterfront by the fishers' harbour, so a full fish dinner with wine at the *Toros Canlı Balık* (☎ 11144), *Kâzım Usta'nın Yeri* (☎ 11226) or *Diba* (☎ 11063) may cost from US$15 to US$25 per person. Perhaps the best prices, with equally good food, are at the nearby *Çam Restaurant* (☎ 11051).

Şanlı Restaurant (☎ 19528), Aslanlar Caddesi 54, about 200 metres uphill from the stone tower, is another favourite. Start with drinks and the buffet of mezes and salads, go on to a main meat course, finish with fresh fruit. Each person pays from US$10 to US$15, drinks included. The century-old house has several dining rooms and a shady terrace for dining. Lunch and dinner are offered daily in summer.

In Kaleiçi, everybody enjoys the *Yaba Restaurant & Bar* (☎ 12441), a few steps east (inland) from the Kaleiçi Hamamı. Rough stone, baked tiles, dark wood and soft music make the mood in this secluded courtyard eatery. Start with mezes, go on to fish shish kebap, finish with a sweet, and the bill might be from US$18 to US$24 per person, with wine or beer. The Yaba is open every day for lunch and dinner; closed in winter.

Sultan Han Restoran (☎ 13849), Bahar Sokak 8, also in Kaleiçi, is a large old han (caravanserai) with lots of nice old wood detail and local crafts. Food is offered in great variety, including lots of fish and Turkish meat choices, a smattering of continental dishes, good mezes and traditional Turkish sweets. Some evenings there's a belly-dancer. Lunch and dinner are served daily from 11 am to 11 pm, for US$14 to US$20 per person, all in.

Entertainment

Much of Kuşadası's nightlife is aimed at specific national groups. Narrow streets near the Hotel Akdeniz are choked with Olde English-style 'pubs' and Deutsches 'bierstuben' where patrons suffer excesses of jollity. The quieter, classier bars are in Kaleiçi's narrow streets. Wander around to find *Olive*, the *Jazz Club*, *She*, and newer places. Most have dusky courtyards, cushy upholstered seats/benches, drinks, conversation and hip music.

The nightclub-style show in the Hotel Kervansaray costs US$35 per person with drinks. The show includes Turkish and international songs and some folkloric entertainment.

Out on Güvercinada, the little fort is usually let to disco organisers (the disco name changes frequently). Even if the latest incarnation is not to your liking, the walk out to the island and back is pleasant.

Things to Buy
While you're in Kuşadası, however, you might want to shop for onyx, meerschaum, leather clothing and accessories, copper, brass, carpets and jewellery. Don't shop while the cruise ships are in port, however, as prices are higher and dealers ruder.

Getting There & Around
Bus & Dolmuş *Şehiriçi* (intra-city) minibuses run from the otogar to the centre, and up and down the coast within the town.

Kuşadası's otogar is out on the main highway to Aydın and Selçuk. Direct buses leave for several far-flung points in the country; or you can transfer at İzmir. And speaking of transfers, note that ticket-sellers sometimes sell you tickets on 'direct buses' which do not exist; your 'bus to Priene' may turn out to be a bus to Söke, from which you must await a minibus to Priene. Ask and be certain of what you're getting.

Dodlum – 131 km, 2½ hours, US$7; frequent buses in summer
Didyma – see Söke
İzmir – 95 km, 1½ hours, US$2.25; Elbirlik buses at least every 30 minutes from 6.30 am to 7 pm in summer
Menderes Airport – 80 km, 1¼ hours, US$2; take an Elbirlik İzmir bus and ask to be let off at the airport
Miletus – see Söke
Pamukkale – 220 km, three hours, US$6; some direct buses, or change at Denizli
Priene – see Söke
Selçuk – 20 km, 30 minutes, 80c; minibuses run frequently in summer, with the last minibus departing from Selçuk at 8.30 pm, and from Kuşadası at 9 pm

Söke – 20 km, 30 minutes, 80c; frequent minibuses, especially on Wednesday (Söke's market day). From Söke otogar, transfer to minibuses for Priene (Güllübahçe), Miletus (Balat), Didyma (Didim) or Altınkum beach.

Tours In summer, minibus drivers organise tours to various sites in the region for one flat fee. The tours may cost a bit more than normal dolmuş and bus fare, but save you the time you'd spend waiting on the road to hitch or find an onward minibus.

In spring and autumn, tours to Priene, Miletus and Didyma may run on Wednesday, Saturday and/or Sunday, or only when a group can be gathered.

Minibus drivers at the Kuşadası bus station also run tours to Ephesus and Meryemana for about US$10 per person.

Dolmuşes for Kadınlar Plajı, south of town, and for Pamucak, to the north, depart from the bus station as well.

Boat – to/from Samos Any travel agency in Kuşadası will sell you a ticket for a boat to Samos. You can go over for the day and return in the evening, or go there to stay. Boats depart from each port, Samos and Kuşadası, at 8.30 am and 5 pm daily in high summer, about four times weekly in spring and autumn. Service is usually suspended in winter except for special excursions. The trip costs a high US$32 one way, US$38 same-day round-trip, or US$45 for a round-trip ticket good for a year. You may have to surrender your passport for immigration processing the evening before you travel. Some agencies discount these expensive tickets, so ask, and flash your student card if you have one.

DİLEK NATIONAL PARK
Thirty km south of Kuşadası the Dilek peninsula juts westward into the Aegean, almost touching the island of Samos. West of the village of Güzelçamlı the land has been set aside as Dilek Milli Parkı (Dilek National Park), a nature reserve with some day-use areas; no camping is allowed. The mountain

slopes here are clad in pines, the air is clean and the sun, bright.

The park is open daily from 8 am to 6 pm for 50c per person, US$2.50 per car.

Approaching Dilek from Kuşadası or Söke, the road passes through the village of Davutlar and, seven km farther west, Güzelçamlı. This village has numerous simple, cheap pensions used mostly by Turkish families on holiday, and a few other basic services (see following).

It's two km from Güzelçamlı to the national park entrance, then another km to **İçmeler Köyü**, a protected cove with a small but beautiful beach, lounge chairs and umbrellas, a restaurant and picnic area.

Three km beyond İçmeler Köyü an unpaved road goes off to the right, downhill one km to **Aydınlık beach**, a pebble-and-sand strand about 800 metres long with surf, backed by pines, and served by a small café. (If you continue another 1.2 km on the main road you'll come to the far entrance to the same beach.)

Less than one km farther along is a jandarma post. Another km brings you to **Kavaklı Burun**, another sand-and-pebble surf beach 500 metres to the right of the road. As at Aydınlık, there is another entrance to the beach at the far end, another km along. West of that is a military zone, entry forbidden. It's 8.5 km back to the park entrance.

Places to Stay & Eat

Of the several dozen pensions in town, among the friendliest is the *Valley Pension* (☎ (6366) 1870), just outside the village near the national park entrance. Osman, the retired owner, has five rooms with private shower and toilet; rooms have two or three beds. The roof is available for sleeping if you have your own gear. The cost is US$8 per person, full breakfast included.

Park Pansiyon (☎ (6366) 1359), near the village square, is similarly accommodating, at similar prices.

The *Orkide Restaurant* is currently the fanciest and most popular place in Güzelçamlı, serving good food at decent prices.

There are several bars and discos down by the shore.

Getting There & Away

You can walk the three km from Güzelçamlı to İçmeler Köyü in about 30 minutes. Otherwise, without your own transport you must rely on dolmuşes from Kuşadası and Söke (45 minutes, US$1). They run from 8 am to dusk in summer, especially on weekends, and usually run all the way to the far end of Kavaklı Burun. It's a good idea to leave the park not too long after mid-afternoon, as the later dolmuşes fill up quickly.

PRIENE, MILETUS & DIDYMA

South of Kuşadası lie the ruins of three very ancient and important settlements well worth a day trip. Priene occupies a dramatic position overlooking the plain of the River Menderes (formerly Meander). Miletus preserves a great theatre, and Didyma's Temple of Apollo is among the world's most impressive religious structures. Beyond Didyma is Altınkum Beach, good for an after-ruins swim.

Priene

Priene was important around 300 BC because it was where the League of Ionian Cities held its congresses and festivals. Otherwise, the city was smaller and less important than nearby Miletus, which means that its Hellenistic buildings were not buried by Roman buildings. What you see in Priene is mostly what one saw in the city over 2000 years ago.

The setting is dramatic, with steep Mt Mykale rising behind the town, and the broad flood plain of the River Menderes spread out at its feet.

As you approach the archaeological zone, you'll come to a shady rest spot in a romantic setting: water cascades from an old aqueduct next to the *Şelale Restaurant* (☎ (6357) 1009), where you can get a cool drink or hot tea, make a telephone call or have a meal. There are three smaller, cheaper restaurants as well as the simple *Priene Pension & Camping* (☎ (6357) 1249).

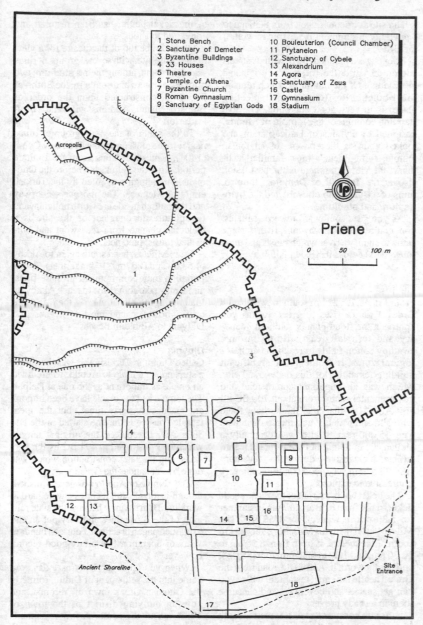

1 Stone Bench
2 Sanctuary of Demeter
3 Byzantine Buildings
4 33 Houses
5 Theatre
6 Temple of Athena
7 Byzantine Church
8 Roman Gymnasium
9 Sanctuary of Egyptian Gods
10 Bouleuterion (Council Chamber)
11 Prytaneion
12 Sanctuary of Cybele
13 Alexandrium
14 Agora
15 Sanctuary of Zeus
16 Castle
17 Gymnasium
18 Stadium

Acropolis

Priene

0   50   100 m

Ancient Shoreline

Site
Entrance

The site at Priene is open from 8.30 am to 7 pm daily in summer (to 5.30 pm in winter) for US$2.

Priene was a planned town, with its streets laid out in a grid (the grid system originated in Miletus). Of the buildings which remain, the **bouleuterion** (city council meeting place) is in very good condition. The five standing columns of the **Temple of Athena**, designed by Pythius of Halicarnassus and looked upon as the epitome of an Ionian temple, form Priene's most familiar landmark; the view from here is the best. Look also at the **Temple of Demeter**; **theatre**; ruins of a **Byzantine church**; and the **gymnasium** and **stadium**.

As you gaze southward towards Miletus, you realise at once why this river's name came to signify a river which twists and turns (meanders) across its flood plain.

Miletus

From Priene, it's 22 km south to Miletus. Its **Great Theatre** rises to greet you as you approach the flood plain's southern boundary and turn left (east), riding through swampy cotton fields to reach the archaeological zone. It is the most significant building remaining of this once-grand city, which was an important commercial and governmental centre from about 700 BC till 700 AD. After that time the harbour filled with silt, and Miletus' commerce dwindled. The 15,000-seat theatre was originally a Hellenistic building, but the Romans reconstructed it extensively during the 1st century AD. It's still in very good condition and very impressive to explore.

The ticket booth in front of the theatre sells tickets daily from 8.30 am to 7 pm in summer (to 5.30 pm in winter), for US$1.25. The Milet Müzesi (Miletus Museum), about a km south of the theatre, is open from 8.30 am to 12.30 pm, and 1.30 to 5.30 pm, for US$1.25, and hardly worth it. Across the road from the Great Theatre is a small restaurant where you can get snacks and beverages and consume them in a shady grove.

A **Seljuk caravanserai**, 100 metres south of the ticket booth, has been restored and converted to shops.

Climb to the top of the theatre for a view of the entire site, with several groups of ruins scattered about, among them a **stadium**; two **agoras**, northern and southern; the **Baths of Faustina**, constructed upon the order of Emperor Marcus Aurelius' wife; and a **bouleuterion**.

To the south of the main group of ruins, nearer to the museum, is the **İlyas Bey Camii** (1404), a mosque dating from the Emirate period. After the Seljuks but before the Ottomans, this region was ruled by the Turkish emirs of Menteşe. The mosque's doorway and the mihrab inside are worth noticing, and the picturesque neglect of the site is a welcome change from the swept and burnished tourist precincts.

From Miletus, head south again to Akköy (4.5 km) and Didyma (14 km farther). Transportation may be infrequent in these parts, and it may take some time to reach Akköy by hitchhiking. South of Akköy there is more traffic, however, and most of it goes past Didyma to Altınkum Beach.

Didyma

Called Didim in Turkish, this was the site of a stupendous temple to Apollo, where lived an oracle as important as the one at Delphi. The temple and the oracle have been important since very early times, but the great temple you see is the one started in the late 300s AD. It replaced the original temple which was destroyed in 494 BC by the Persians, and the later construction which was done by Alexander the Great.

The Temple of Apollo was never finished, though its oracle and its priests were hard at work until Christianity became the state religion of the Byzantines and they put an end to all such pagan practices. Fourteen hundred years of operation is a pretty good record, however.

When you approach Didyma today, you come into the settlement of Didim, formerly the Ottoman Greek town of Yeronda, and now an outlying district of the town of Yenihisar, to the south. A few restaurants

Top: Great Theatre, Ephesus (TB)
Left: Distinctive Ottoman gravestone (TB)
Right: Crusader inscriptions, Castle of St Peter, Bodrum (TB)

The Temple of Zeus, Aizanoi (TB)

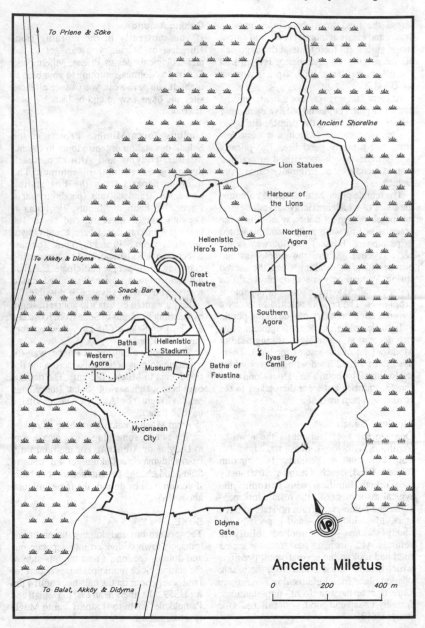

To Priene & Söke

Ancient Shoreline

Lion Statues

Harbour of
the Lions

Northern
Agora

Hellenistic
Hero's Tomb

To Akköy & Didyma

Great
Theatre

Snack Bar ▼

Southern
Agora

Baths

Hellenistic
Stadium

Western
Agora

İlyas Bey
Camii

Museum

Baths of
Faustina

Mycenaean
City

Didyma
Gate

Ancient Miletus

0   200   400 m

To Balat, Akköy & Didyma

across the road from the temple provide drinks and meals at tourist prices, and carpet shops gush forth their touts at the approach of each new tour bus. Admission is from 8.30 am to 7 pm in summer (in 5.30 pm in winter), for US$1.25.

Ancient Didyma was not a town, but the home of a god. People did not live there, only priests. I assume that the priests, sitting on the temple treasure (which was considerable) had a pretty good life. The priestly family there, which specialised in oracular temple management, originally came from Delphi.

The temple porch held 120 huge columns, the bases of which are richly carved. Behind the porch is a great doorway at which the oracular poems were written and presented to petitioners. Beyond the doorway is the *cella* or court, where the oracle sat and prophesied after drinking from the sacred spring. We can only speculate on what that water contained to make someone capable of prophesies. The cella is reached today by a covered ramp on the right side of the porch.

In the temple grounds are fragments of its rich decoration, including a striking head of Medusa (she of the snakes for hair). There used to be a road lined with statuary which led to a small harbour. The statues stood there for 23 centuries but were then taken to the British Museum in 1858.

Altınkum Beach

One km south of Didyma is the town of Yenihisar, with shops, pensions, banks etc. Four km south of Yenihisar is Altınkum (Golden Sand) Beach, a resort visited mostly by Turkish families, who patronise the typical assortment of little restaurants, pensions and hotels rated from no stars to three stars. Most lodgings – and especially the cheapest ones – are booked solidly in summer. At a pinch, go west from the access road and look at the several small pensions which stand a block inland from the beach. A good place for a light meal is *The Family Cafe*, right on the waterfront – unpretentious, friendly, cheap and good, with full meals for under US$3.

Getting Around

If you start early in the morning from Kuşadası or Selçuk, you can get to the archaeological sites of Priene, Miletus and Didyma by dolmuş, returning to your base at night. If you have a car, you can see all three sites and have a swim and be back by mid-afternoon.

Minibus Tours Minibus drivers at the Selçuk bus station organise tours to Priene, Miletus, Didyma and Altınkum Beach during good weather in summer. The minibus departs from the bus station between 8.30 and 9.30 am, spends an hour at Priene, 1½ hours at Miletus, 2½ hours at Didyma and its museum, and about 1½ hours at Altınkum Beach before returning to Selçuk between 5.30 and 6.30 pm. The cost is between US$10 and US$18, depending upon how many people participate. Lunch is not included in this price. It's a good idea to reserve your seat in advance, if possible.

If you want to do this trip yourself, begin by catching a dolmuş to Söke from Kuşadası (20 km) or Selçuk (40 km), then another onward to Priene.

When you've finished at Priene, wait for a passing dolmuş or hitchhike across the flat flood plain to Miletus (22 km). The dolmuş may bear a sign saying 'Balat' (the village next to Miletus) or 'Akköy', a larger village beyond Balat.

From Miletus, catch something to Akköy or, if you can, something going all the way to Didyma or Altınkum. For the return trip from Didyma or Altınkum get a dolmuş to Söke, and change for another to your base. If you do it all by dolmuş the fares will total about US$6.

SÖKE

The modern bus and dolmuş station in this transport town is divided into separate bus and dolmuş sections. From the bus side of the station, Söke municipal buses depart for İzmir every hour on the half-hour until 4 pm for US$2.50. Others head east to Denizli and Pamukkale, south to Bodrum and to Muğla (for Marmaris).

The dolmuş side of the station serves vehicles going to the following towns:

Altınkum Beach – 61 km, US$2
Aydın – 55 km, US$1.75 (the provincial capital on the way to Aphrodisias, Denizli and Pamukkale)
Balat – 35 km, US$1.25 (the village near Miletus)
Davutlar – 13 km, US$1 (on the way to Dilek National Park)
Didyma – 56 km, US$1.50
Güllübahçe – 14 km, 80c (the village next to Priene)
Güzelçamlı – 22 km, US$1 (near Dilek National Park)
Kuşadası – 20 km, 80c
Milas – 82 km, US$2 (on the way to Bodrum)

Aphrodisias & Pamukkale Region

Hot calcium-laden mineral waters burst from the earth to run through a ruined Hellenistic city before cascading over a cliff at Pamukkale (pah-MOO-kah-leh, Cotton Fortress), the spa 220 km due east of Kuşadası. As the water cools, the calcium precipitates and clings to the cliffs, forming snowy white travertines, waterfalls of white stone, which give the spa its name. Nearby are the ruins of Laodicea, one of the Seven Churches of Asia.

On the way from Selçuk or Kuşadası to Pamukkale you can make several detours to significant archaeological sites, including the hilltop city of Nyssa about 100 km east of Kuşadası, and, about 150 km east of Kuşadası, Aphrodisias, one of Turkey's most complete and elaborate archaeological sites.

As you begin your trip you may pass through the ruins of Magnesia ad Meander, which lie on the road between Söke and Ortaklar. This ancient city is not really worth a stop, but the fragments of wall easily visible from the road are certainly impressive. From Ortaklar to the provincial capital of Aydın it's 33 km.

AYDIN

Framed by the mountains of Aydın Dağı to the north and Menteşe Dağı to the south, Aydın (altitude 64 metres, population 120,000) is at the centre of the agriculturally rich Menderes river valley. Olives, figs, cotton, grain and fruit grow in abundance. The valley has always been an important natural travel route, which today includes an east-west highway and the railway to Denizli, Burdur and Isparta.

Aydın was formerly Tralles, which flourished during Roman times. Its most famous son was perhaps the architect Anthemius of Tralles who, at the order of the Emperor Justinian and with the help of Isidore of Miletus, designed and built between 532 and 537 the great church of Sancta Sophia in Constantinople. During the War of Independence Aydın was occupied by the invading Greek forces for several years, and burned to the ground on their departure. Being at the centre of an earthquake zone has not helped Aydın's ancient buildings much either. What you see today is mostly modern.

Orientation

The otogar is on the main highway a few hundred metres west of a large traffic roundabout which marks the beginning of Adnan Menderes Bulvarı. The centre of town is one km north of the highway along Adnan Menderes Bulvarı. At the centre, marked by the main square and a park, are various hotels, the post office and railway station.

Information

The Tourism Information Office (☎ (631) 14145, 26226) is on the traffic roundabout on the main highway just east of the otogar. It's helpful and has an excellent map. Aydın's postal code is 09000.

Things to See

Though Aydın retains a good number of **Ottoman mosques**, they are in somewhat distant neighbourhoods and not really worth seeking out unless you're doing a close study of Ottoman religious architecture. Have a look at the **Süleyman Bey Camii** (1683), between the railway station and the park right on the main square, designed by one of Sinan's apprentices.

The **Archaeology Museum** is 750 metres

north-west of the main square (follow the signs), open from 9 am to noon and 1.30 to 5 pm for US$1. There are finds from Aphrodisias, Didyma, Miletus, Priene and Tralles, including good statues of Athena and Nike, and a fine bust of Marcus Aurelius.

Places to Stay & Eat
Just north of the main square are several hotels which will do nicely for a night. Perhaps the best value for money is the *Hotel Kabaçam* (☎ (631) 12794), Hükümet Bulvarı, 11 Sokak No 2, where comfortable rooms with private shower go for US$14/18 a single/double. Across the street is the *Hotel Vardar*, somewhat cheaper but certainly less comfortable.

The *Hotel Baltacı* (☎ (631) 11321), Gazi Bulvarı, 3. Sokak (a bit farther up the hill from the Kabaçam, then bear right), charges about the same as the Kabaçam, but is not as nice.

The 28-room *Orhan Hotel* (☎ (631) 21713; fax 11781), Gazi Bulvarı 63, and the 30-room *Otel Özlü* (☎ (631) 13371), Adnan Menderes Bulvarı 71, both offer two-star comforts for slightly more than the Kabaçam, but the Özlü can be fairly noisy.

The best place in town is actually out of town on the road to Muğla. It's the four-star *Turtay Hotel* (☎ (631) 33003; fax 30351), with 70 air-con, satellite TV-equipped rooms priced at US$38/48 a single/double. The hotel offers private helicopter and aeroplane service as well.

The centre of the city has the usual good collection of small kebap and ready-food restaurants at your service.

Getting There & Away
Bus Service is very good if you're going to Denizli, Pamukkale, Kuşadası, Selçuk or İzmir. For other destinations, you may have to change at one of those places.

Train Four daily trains connect Aydın with Denizli, Selçuk, Menderes airport and İzmir. See those sections for details.

NYSSA
East of Aydın, you are deep in the fertile farming country of the Büyük Menderes river valley. Cotton fields sweep away from the road in every direction. During the cotton harvest in late October, the highways are jammed (dangerously so) with tractors hauling wagons overladen with the white puffy stuff. Other crops prevalent in the valley, all the way to Denizli, are pomegranates, pears, citrus fruits, apples, melons, olives and tobacco.

Heading 31 km east from Aydın brings you to the town of Sultanhisar and, three km to the north uphill, ancient Nyssa, set on a hilltop amid olive groves. You'll have to walk or hitch to the site, as there is no public transport. When you reach the ruins you'll find public toilets, a soft-drink stand, and a guard who will charge you US$1 admission during daylight hours. The guard will show you around the site if you wish; a tip is expected.

The major ruins here are of the **theatre**, and a 115-metre-long **tunnel** beneath the road and the parking area which was once the main square of the ancient city. A five-minute walk up the hill along the road and through a field brings you to the **bouleuterion**, which has some nice fragments of sculpture.

What you will remember about Nyssa, however, is the peacefulness and bucolic beauty of its site, very different from tourist metropolises such as Ephesus. The walk back down to Sultanhisar and the highway is very nice in late afternoon.

Though Sultanhisar has a few simple eateries, there are no real hotels. The İzmir-Denizli trains stop in town, and the highway carries many east-west buses.

NAZİLLİ
Nazilli (NAH-zee-lee, altitude 87 metres, population 100,000), 14 km east of Nyssa and Sultanhisar, is a market town and the transfer point for a trip to Aphrodisias. The otogar is just north of the main highway, one block west of the main traffic roundabout. The railway station is south of the highway.

Places to Stay & Eat

Unfortunately, Nazilli has no cluster of cheap little hotels around its otogar, as one might expect, though there are a few small places near the railway station. The new two-star, 40-room *Hotel Metya* (☎ 637) 28888; fax 28891), in Karaçay Mahallesi at 92. Sokak No 10, is a few steps west of the otogar across from the Shell fuel station. It's the best hotel in town at this writing, charging US$18/28 singles/doubles for a bath-equipped room and breakfast.

Go north 200 metres from the main traffic roundabout on the highway east of the otogar to reach the comfortable three-star, 54-room *Ticaret Odası Oteli* (Chamber of Commerce Hotel) (☎ (637) 19678, -9), Hürriyet Caddesi. Quite decent rooms with a bath and balcony rent for US$16/26 a single/double, breakfast included. There's a restaurant and bar of course, and also a decent pastry shop adjoining the hotel.

There are several little eateries in the bus station area.

Getting There & Away

Bus Nazilli is the local transportation hub, with buses to and from İzmir and Selçuk about every 45 minutes or less in the morning and afternoon, but infrequent in the evening.

One stops at Nazilli on the way to or from Aphrodisias, probably to change buses or to stay in Nazilli's hotels, which are better than anything in Karacasu, 42 km south of Nazilli near Aphrodisias.

Details of some other daily services from Nazilli follow:

Ankara – 545 km, eight hours, US$12; several buses
Antalya – 360 km, six hours, US$8; several buses
Bodrum – 225 km, four hours, US$6; several buses
Denizli – 65 km, one hour, US$1.50; very frequent buses and dolmuşes
İstanbul – 600 km, 12 hours, US$18; several buses
İzmir – 170 km, 2½ to three hours, US$4; very frequent buses
Konya – 505 km, eight hours, US$6; several buses
Kuşadası – 150 km, 2½ hours, US$4; several buses
Pamukkale – 85 km, 1½ hours, US$2; several buses
Selçuk – 130 km, 1½ hours, US$3.75; buses at least every hour

Train The four trains running daily between Denizli and İzmir stop at Nazilli. See the Denizli, Selçuk and İzmir sections for details.

Car For those driving, Aphrodisias is 55 km from Nazilli, 101 km from Denizli and 38 km off the east-west highway.

APHRODISIAS

The city's name quickly brings to mind 'aphrodisiac'. Both words come from the Greek name for the goddess of love, Aphrodite, called Venus by the Romans. Aphrodite was many things to many people. As Aphrodite Urania she was the goddess of pure, spiritual love; as Aphrodite Pandemos she was the goddess of sensual love, married to Hephaestus but lover also of Ares, Hermes, Dionysus and Adonis. Her children included Harmonia, Eros, Hermaphroditus, Aeneas and Priapus, the phallic god. All in all, she was the complete goddess of fertility, fornication and fun.

You come to Aphrodisias from Nazilli by way of the town of Karacasu (KAH-rah-jah-soo) surrounded by tobacco fields, fig trees and orchards. Besides farming, Karacasu is famous for its potters, who work with the local reddish-brown clay, firing it in 30 wood-fired kilns. To see the potters at work, ask to be directed to the *bardakçı ocakları*.

History

Excavations have shown the acropolis of Aphrodısıas to be not a natural hill but a prehistoric mound built up by successive settlements beginning in the Early Bronze Age (2800-2200 BC). From the 8th century BC, the temple at Aphrodisias was famous and a favourite goal of pilgrims for over 1000 years, and the city prospered. But under the Byzantines the city changed substantially: the steamy Temple of Aphrodite was transformed into a chaste Christian church, and ancient buildings were pulled down to provide building stones for defensive walls (circa 350 AD).

The town, diminished from its former glory, was attacked by Tamerlane on his

Anatolian rampage in 1402 and never recovered. The Turkish village of Geyre sprang up on the site sometime later. In 1956 an earthquake devastated the village, which was rebuilt to the west at its present location, allowing excavations to be more easily carried out at the site. The pleasant plaza by the big plane tree in front of the museum was the main square of pre-1956 Geyre.

Preliminary explorations of Aphrodisias were carried out by French and Italian archaeologists early in this century. After the earthquake of 1956, US and Turkish archaeologists began to resurrect the city. They found a surprisingly well-preserved stadium, odeum and theatre. The National Geographic Society (USA) supported some of the excavation and restoration. From 1961 to 1990 the work at the site was directed by Professor Kenan T Erim of New York University. His book, *Aphrodisias: City of Venus Aphrodite* (1986) tells the story of his work. After his death, Professor Erim was buried at the site he had done so much to reveal and explain.

Museum

The site and museum at Aphrodisias, 13 km past Karacasu, are open from 8 am to 6.30 or 7 pm in summer, 8 am to 5 pm in winter. Admission costs US$2 to the ruins, and the same again to the museum. No photography is permitted in the museum, and you are also prohibited from photographing excavations in progress here. Signs in the car park advise that no camping is allowed; they're afraid of antiquity thieves.

During Roman times Aphrodisias was home to a famous school for sculptors who were attracted by the beds of high-grade white and blue-grey marble two km away at the foot of Babadağ mountain. The statuary in the museum reflects the excellence of their work. Note especially the 'cult statue of Aphrodite, second century' and the 'cuirassed statue of an emperor or high official, second century, signed by Appolonius Aster'. The 'portrait statue of Flavius Palmatus, governor of the province of Asia', looks like a man with big problems. Did they make his head that small on purpose, or as an insult?

The Ruins

The site is not yet well marked, so it can be confusing to get around, even with our handy map. Follow the path to the right as you come from the museum. Most of what you see is from no earlier than the 2nd century AD.

The first site you pass, on your left, is an unmarked collection of serpentine **columns** in a murky pool. Farther along on the left is the **Tetrapylon**, or monumental gateway, which greeted pilgrims as they approached the temple of Aphrodite. The tomb of Professor Erim is just south-west of it.

The footpath next leads you towards the **stadium**, off to the right. It is wonderfully preserved, and most of its 30,000 seats would be usable right now.

Back to the main path, continue to the **Temple of Aphrodite**. Aphrodisias' claim to fame was completely rebuilt when it was converted into a basilica church (circa 500 AD): its cella was removed, its columns shifted to form a nave, and an apse added at the eastern end. It's now difficult to picture the place in which orgies to Aphrodite were held. Near the temple-church is the **Bishop's Palace**, dating from Byzantine times.

Just south of the Bishop's Palace is a side path eastward to the beautiful marble **odeum**, preserved for millennia by being covered in mud.

South of the Bishop's Palace and the odeum was Aphrodisias' main **agora**, once enclosed by Ionic porticoes but now little more than a grassy field. Next the path leads you to the **Baths of Hadrian**, five large **galleries** and a **colonnaded palaestra** or playing field; and the grand **Portico of Tiberius**.

The dazzling white marble **theatre** is beautiful, and virtually complete. South of it was a large baths complex.

Antiocheia

On the road between the main highway and Karacasu you may notice signs pointing the

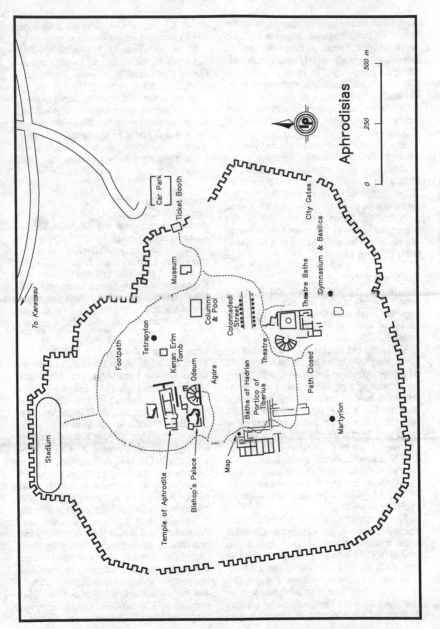

Aphrodisias

To Karaesu

Car Park
Ticket Booth
Museum
Tetrapylon
Footpath
Stadium
Kenan Erim Tomb
Odeum
Agora
Bishop's Palace
Temple of Aphrodite
Columne & Pool
Colonnaded Street
Baths of Hadrian
Portico of Tiberius
Map
Theatre
Path Closed
Martyrion
Theatre Baths
Gymnasium & Basilica
City Gates

0   250   500 m

way to Antiocheia; you turn north at the centre of the village of Başaran, 18.3 km north-west of Karacasu. From Başaran it's one km to the impressively sited ruins of this ancient hilltop city. The ruins are extensive but in very bad condition, and totally unexcavated and unrestored. If you'd like to see what the archaeologists see on the day they begin their fieldwork, come and have a look at Antiocheia.

If you have your own vehicle, you can return to the Nazilli-Denizli highway, six km to the north, by continuing past Antiocheia across the intensely fertile flood plain of the Büyük Menderes river and through the farming village of Azizabat, which has some very fine fieldstone walls and houses. You regain the highway at a point 5.6 km east of the Karacasu turn-off, 21 km east of Nazilli. Turn right for Denizli.

Places to Stay

Nazilli has the nearest two and three-star hotels, Karacasu has a few emergency lodgings, but there are a few suitable places near Geyre as well, all of which offer camping possibilities.

Half a km before coming to the ruins from Karacasu you'll spot *Chez Mestan* (☎ (6379) 5120/46), Afrodisias, Karacasu, Aydın, a big house with an airy, shady front porch on the left-hand side of the road. Mestan Bey is Turkish; his wife, French. You can stay the night here in a simple but clean room decorated with Turkish crafts and equipped with a private hand-held 'telephone' shower for US$12 a double, breakfast included, less if they're not busy or if you're good at haggling. Meals on the front porch cost around US$3. They have an area set aside for camping as well.

The proprietors of Chez Mestan have opened a simple, modern hotel a half-km back towards Karacasu: the *Aphrodisias Moteli* (☎ (6379) 5120/132), where a double with bath, breakfast included costs US$24.

Nearer the ruins is the *Bayar Pension*, 200 metres up from the crossroads closest to the ruins. It's a simple village house which may or may not be receiving visitors when you

arrive. Up behind Chez Mestan is the *Belle Vue Pension*, charging the same rates.

Nine km from Geyre back towards Karacasu in the village of Dandalaz is the *Elmas Pension & Restaurant* – new, nice, quiet, and cheap.

In the town of Karacasu, there is an *otel* on the upper floor of the bus station building where you can sleep for US$3 per person, but it is really only for emergencies. I expect that the enterprising souls in Karacasu will begin opening comfy pensions and small hotels soon.

Places to Eat

Besides at *Chez Mestan*, you can get simple meals in Karacasu at the *Köseoğlu Restaurant* and at the *Öztekin* on the main street. A cut above the rest is the *Bonjour Restaurant* at the main traffic circle in Karacasu. Fancier restaurants, patronised mostly by coach tour groups, are to be found along the road between Karacasu and Nazilli. If you stop at one of these, you'll get better service if you arrive half an hour before or after a group.

Getting There & Away

There are a few direct buses a day between Karacasu and İzmir (210 km, 3½ hours, US$9) and Selçuk (130 km, two hours, US$7.50). If you don't get one of these, take a bus from İzmir, Selçuk, Ortaklar, Aydın or Denizli to Nazilli, and from there a dolmuş to Geyre, the village 13 km beyond Karacasu and right next to the ruins. If you can't find a dolmuş to Geyre or Aphrodisias, take one to Karacasu. Then take a dolmuş, hitch a ride or hire a taxi (US$8 round-trip) in Karacasu for the final 13 km to Geyre and the ruins. You should be able to hitch easily in summer.

Several bus companies, including Pamukkale and Kamil Koç, operate special minibuses in summer, departing from Pamukkale town at 10 am on the 1½-hour trip to Aphrodisias, returning at 3 pm, thus leaving you ample time to explore the ruins and have a picnic lunch. The cost is US$10 per person. The minibus is a special service for those based in Pamukkale who want to visit Aphrodisias, and it does not stop to take on or discharge passengers in Denizli.

For transport from other points, see the Nazilli section.

DENİZLİ

Denizli (deh-NEEZ-lee, altitude 354 metres, population 350,000) is a prosperous and bustling agricultural city with some light industry as well. It is also noisy, dusty and smoky, but it has a number of hotels and restaurants in all price ranges, which are of interest because accommodation in Pamukkale is usually more expensive and often full.

Denizli's main Tourism Information Office (☎ (621) 47621, 43971) is at Atatürk Caddesi 8, 2nd floor, office 4. A smaller office (☎ (621) 13393) is in the railway station, but it is often inexplicably closed. The railway station is on the main highway, only one block west of the bus station, a short distance west of the three-point traffic roundabout called Üçgen by which one goes to Pamukkale 19 km to the north. Delikli Çınar Meydanı, the city's main square, is two km from the railway station and the bus station. Denizli's postal code is 20100.

Places to Stay

If all accommodation at Pamukkale is full, you must stay in Denizli. There are numerous cheaper lodgings near the otogar and railway station, and more expensive hotels between the railway station and Delikli Çınar Meydanı.

Places to Stay – bottom end

Behind the otogar is the district named Topraklık Mahallesi, with many small numbered streets. The aptly named *Garaj Oteli* (☎ (621) 15603), 630 Sokak No 7, just south of the otogar, has those cheap Turkish hotel rooms with which you are by now all too familiar, charging US$7 a double without running water, US$8.50 a double with private shower.

The tidy 16-room *Yetkin Pansiyon* (☎ (621) 51266), Halk Caddesi, 452 Sokak 13, is on a quietish side street between İstas-

yon Caddesi and the otogar, a five-minute walk away. The old building has been spruced up with paint and carpeting, and the guest rooms have neat tiled showers. Rates are US$11 a double in a room with a shower; breakfast is included. The pension has no lift.

Among the favourite spots with budget travellers is the *Denizli Pansiyon* (☎ (621) 18738), Deliktaş Mahallesi, 1993 Sokak 14. It's slightly more than a km (a 15-minute walk) from the bus station, away from the centre of town in the section called Deliktaş; signs point the way. All rooms have private showers and toilets, and go for US$15 a double in summer, cheaper off season; breakfast costs another US$2 per person. The pension has a courtyard with a fountain and lots of fruit trees, and it's quiet; there's space for camping, too. The owner, Süleyman Can (pronounced 'john'), also sells carpets; he'll sometimes shuttle you to and from the bus station in his car. His wife cooks delicious Turkish meals for around US$3 each.

Other places to stay are nearby. Turn right onto Cumhuriyet Caddesi from İstasyon Caddesi at the Halley Oteli, and one block along on the left is the 22-room *Otel Gong* (☎ (621) 111178, 38803), Cumhuriyet Caddesi 13, an older hotel that's had a facelift. It now has a lift and suitable rooms renting for US$10/14/18 a single/double/triple, breakfast included. Some rooms without private shower cost less. Right across the street, the *Otel Gökdağ* (☎ (621) 50402) is also suitable and somewhat cheaper. Both of these hotels suffer from street noise, though.

Places to Stay – middle

The two-star, 84-room *Otel Laodikya* (☎ (621) 51506, 51513; fax 15512), right behind the otogar, is new and comfortable, offering great value with air-conditioned, TV-equipped rooms priced at US$30/42 a single/double, though I was quoted a figure considerably lower when I haggled a bit. The hotel has a restaurant and bar.

Otel Ben-Hur Yıldırım (☎ & fax (621) 333590), 632 Sokak No 3, has 44 rooms,

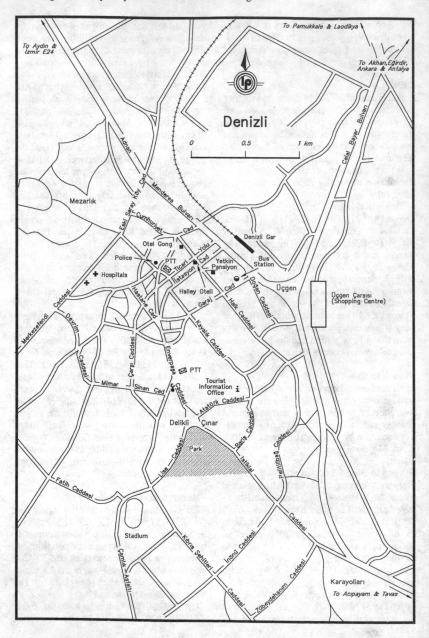

To Pamukkale & Laodikya

To Akhan, Eğirdir, Ankara & Antalya

To Aydın & İzmir E24

Celal Bayar Bulvarı

Denizli

0   0.5   1 km

Adnan

Köy

Menderes Bulvarı

Mezarlık

Eski Saray

Cumhuriyet

Cad

Denizli Gar

Otel Gong

Yolu

Police

PTT

Ticari

Cad

Yetkin Pansiyon

Bus Station

İstasyon

Üçgen

Hospitals

Hastane Cad

Halley Oteli

Garaj

Halk Caddesi

Doğan Caddesi

Üçgen Çarşısı (Shopping Centre)

Merkezefendi

Devrim

Caddesi

Kayalık Caddesi

Caddesi

Çarşı Caddesi

Enverpaşa

PTT

Mimar

Sinan Cad

Caddesi

Tourist Information Office

Delikli

Çınar

Atatürk Caddesi

Park

Lise Caddesi

Barış Caddesi

İstiklal

Pelitlibağ Caddesi

Fatih Caddesi

Stadium

Çamlık Asfaltı

Kıbrıs Şehitleri

İnönü Caddesi

Caddesi

Zübeydehanım Caddesi

Caddesi

Karayolları

To Acıpayam & Tavas

rates two stars, and will rent you a bath-equipped room for US$28, breakfast included. Have your room without breakfast if you like.

Also here is the *Otel Seza* (☎ (621) 46844, 51770; fax 24630), Halk Caddesi 6, is older, but its 28 bath-equipped rooms cost substantially less: US20/30 a single/double. Have a look at the roof bar in the evening.

Up the hill from the railway station along İstasyon Caddesi are several more hotels, including the two-star, 60-room *Halley Oteli* (named for the comet) (☎ (621) 19544, 21843); and the two-star, 30-room *Keskinkaya Oteli* (☎ (621) 11325), İstasyon Caddesi 83, at slightly lower prices, with the same noise problem.

Just a step or two off Delikli Çınar Meydanı, two km from the bus and train stations, are the two-star, 75-room *Kuyumcu Oteli* (☎ (621) 13749,-50); and the similar but smaller *Arar Hotel* (☎ (621) 37195; fax 15093), Delikli Çınar Meydanı 9, charging US$22/34 a single/double.

Places to Stay – top end

Grand Hotel Keskin (☎ (621) 33565; fax 33564), İstasyon Caddesi 11, is the best in town, boasting four stars, and 111 air-con rooms, all with bath and satellite TV. Rates are US$50/65 a single/double.

Places to Eat

Denizli's bus station has several inexpensive restaurants, including the *Doyuran Kafeteryası* ('filling up'), serving kıymalı pide (flat bread topped with ground lamb) for US$1.25. I recommend this because they bake the bread and make up the pide fresh to your order. The *Self-Servis Hamburg Restaurant* is open long hours, and is good for ready-food meals such as soups, stews and salads. Two plates, with bread and drink cost around US$3.

Right behind the bus station at the northwest corner of the Hotel Yıldırım is the *Özlem Lokantası*, another cheap possibility.

If you're staying near Delikli Çınar Meydanı, there are numerous restaurants a few steps away from the square. The *Sevimli*

Kardeşler Döner Kebap Salonu (☎ 14700) will serve you a portion of döner kebap, a soft drink and a slice of watermelon (in season) for about US$3.50.

Getting There & Away

Bus There are frequent buses between İzmir and Denizli Belediyesi Oto Santral Garajı, the Denizli Municipal Central Bus Station; these buses take a route via Selçuk, Ortaklar, Aydın and Nazilli. City buses and dolmuş minibuses depart frequently from the otogar for Pamukkale, though service drops off in late afternoon and ceases in the evening.

For your onward journey, you can catch a bus in Denizli for virtually any major city in Turkey, including these daily routes:

Ankara – 480 km, seven hours, US$12; frequent buses
Antalya – 300 km, five hours, US$8; several buses
Bodrum – 290 km, five hours, US$8; several buses
Bursa – 532 km, nine hours, US$17; several buses
Eğirdir – 208 km, 3½ hours, US$7; frequent buses
Fethiye – 280 km, five hours, US$8; several buses
Göreme/Ürgüp – 674 km, 11 hours, US$18; a few buses
İstanbul – 665 km, 13 hours, US$13 to US$20; frequent buses
İzmir – 250 km, four hours, US$8; frequent buses
Konya – 440 km, seven hours, US$11; several buses
Kuşadası – 215 km, 3½ hours, US$6; frequent buses
Marmaris – 185 km, three hours, US$5.75; several buses
Selçuk – 195 km, three hours, US$5.75; hourly buses

Train Four trains a day ply between Denizli and İzmir; for the schedule, refer to the beginning of the Ephesus section. Tickets go on sale at Denizli station an hour before departure.

The *Pamukkale Ekspresi* is a nightly train between Denizli and İstanbul via Afyon hauling sleeping, couchette and Pullman cars, departing from İstanbul (Haydarpaşa) at 5.30 pm, arriving in Denizli the next morning at 7.27 am. Departure from Denizli is at 6 pm, arriving in İstanbul (Haydarpaşa) at 8.35 am the next morning. A 1st/2nd-class seat ticket costs US$12/9; sleeping compartments range from US$35 for one person to US$80 for three people.

There is also a daily mototren between Denizli and Afyon, departing from Denizli at 7.30 am on the five-hour journey; and departing from Afyon at 5.55 pm for the return to Denizli, arriving at 11.08 pm.

When you arrive at the railway station, walk out the front door, go out to the highway, cross over, turn left and walk one block to the otogar, where you can catch a dolmuş or bus to Pamukkale. İstasyon Caddesi, an important thoroughfare for hotels, begins just on the other (south) side of the main highway from the railway station.

PAMUKKALE

From afar, the gleaming white travertines of Pamukkale (pah-MOO-kah-leh), 19 km north of Denizli, form a white scar on the side of the ridge. As you come closer, they take on a more distinct shape, giving credence to the name, which means 'cotton castle.' The travertines, filled with warm, calcium-rich mineral water, form shallow pools supported by stalactites of white and black.

Beneath the travertines in the valley is the town of Pamukkale, filled with little pensions, restaurants, and the inevitable carpet shops. On the plateau above are several motels lining the ridge, a municipal bathing establishment with various swimming pools and bath houses, and the ruined city of Hierapolis. An overnight stay here is recommended for several reasons. The site is beautiful, the waters deliciously warm and inviting, the accommodation good and the ruins – especially the restored theatre – worth visiting.

Orientation

The ridge on top of the travertines within the national park is littered with the ruins of Roman Hierapolis. This area is known as Örenyeri or Ören Mevkii (the Ruins District). At the base of the travertines, outside the park, is Pamukkale Kasabası (Pamukkale town), once a farming village, now a fully fledged town with dozens of lodging and dining places.

Information

Pamukkale has a Tourism Information Office (☎ (6218) 1077) at Örenyeri, and also a PTT, souvenir shops, a museum and a first aid station. Pamukkale's postal code is 20210.

Hierapolis

After you've sampled the warm mineral waters (see the Swimming section following), tour the extensive ruins of Hierapolis. To inspect the ancient city carefully can take almost a full day, though most visitors settle for an hour or two. It was a cure centre (founded around 190 BC by Eumenes II, king of Pergamum) which prospered under the Romans and even more under the Byzantines. It had a large Jewish community and therefore an early Christian church. Earthquakes did their worst a few times, and after the one in 1334 the people decided it was actually an unhealthy spot to live in, and moved on.

Perhaps the centre of Hierapolis was the sacred pool, now the swimming pool in the courtyard of the Pamukkale Motel. If the motel is torn down as planned, perhaps the pool will again be visible as it was to the ancients. The city's **Roman baths**, parts of which are now the **Pamukkale Museum**, are in front of the Pamukkale Motel. The museum is open from 8.30 am to noon, and 1 to 5.30 pm. Your national park ticket gets you into the museum as well.

Near the museum is a ruined **Byzantine**

Pamukkale – Travertines

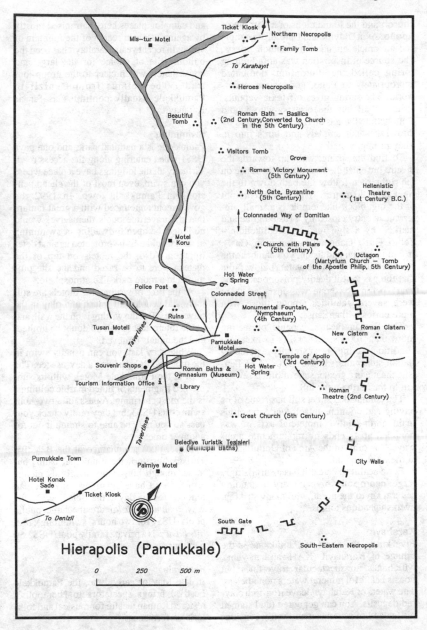

Ticket Kiosk

Northern Necropolis

Mis–tur Motel

Family Tomb

To Karahayıt

Heroes Necropolis

Beautiful
Tomb

Roman Bath – Basilica
(2nd Century, Converted to Church
in the 5th Century)

Visitors Tomb

Grove

Roman Victory Monument
(5th Century)

Hellenistic
Theatre
(1st Century B.C.)

North Gate, Byzantine
(5th Century)

Colonnaded Way of Domitian

Motel
Koru

Church with Pillars
(5th Century)

Octagon
(Martyrium Church – Tomb
of the Apostle Philip, 5th Century)

Hot Water
Spring

Police Post

Colonnaded Street

Ruins

Monumental Fountain,
'Nymphaeum'
(4th Century)

Tusan Motel

Roman Cistern

New Cistern

Travertines

Pamukkale
Motel

Souvenir Shops

Roman Baths &
Gymnasium (Museum)

Hot Water
Spring

Temple of Apollo
(3rd Century)

Tourism Information Office

Library

Roman
Theatre (2nd Century)

Great Church (5th Century)

Travertines

Beledìye Turistik Tesisleri
(Municipal Baths)

Pumukkale Town

City Walls

Hotel Konak
Sade

Palmiye Motel

Ticket Kiosk

To Denizli

South Gate

South-Eastern Necropolis

Hierapolis (Pamukkale)

0   250   500 m

church and the foundations of a **Temple of Apollo**. As at Didyma and Delphi, the temple had an oracle attended by eunuch priests. The source of inspiration was an adjoining spring called the Plutonium, dedicated appropriately to Pluto, god of the underworld. The spring gives off toxic vapours, lethal to all but the priests, who would demonstrate the gas's powers to visitors by throwing small animals and birds into it. They promptly died.

To find the spring, walk up towards the theatre but enter the first gate in the fence on the right, then follow the path down to the right about 30 metres. To the left and in front of the big, block-like temple is a small subterranean entry closed by a rusted grate and marked by a sign reading 'Tehlikelidir – Zehirli Gaz' ('Dangerous – Poisonous Gas'). If you approach and listen, you can hear the gas bubbling up from the waters below. Note that the gas is still deadly poisonous. In the years before the grate was installed there were several fatalities among those with more curiosity than sense.

The Roman theatre, capable of seating more than 7000 spectators, is in excellent condition, having been carefully restored by Italian stonecutters in the 1970s. A Hellenistic theatre in a greater state of ruin is several km to the north up the hill.

The colonnaded street still has some of its paving and columns intact. Once the city's main north-south commercial axis, it was bounded at its ends by monumental archways. The ruins of the Arch of Domitian are at the northern end.

For a health spa area, it has a surprisingly large **necropolis** or cemetery, extending several km to the north, with many striking, even stupendous tombs.

Karahayıt

Five km to the north of Pamukkale is the village of Karahayıt (KAH-rah-hah-yuht), which has no spectacular travertines but boasts healthful mineral waters nonetheless. The waters of Karahayıt leave iron-rich clay-red deposits. You can get cured (and stained red) at any of several small family pensions

and camping places here, patronised mostly by ageing locals in search of the fountain of youth. In recent years Karahayıt has been the building-site of choice for the large and lavish hotels which cater to the group-tour trade. The dolmuş from Denizli to Pamukkale usually continues as far as Karahayıt.

Swimming

Pamukkale is a national park, and one pays US$1 when entering along the access road. Virtually all the lodgings have a place where you can swim, even most of the cheap pensions in Pamukkale town. In 1992 the government announced with a great fanfare that the travertine pools themselves would no longer be open for wading or swimming in, and would thus be protected against deterioration. Also, the motels on top of the plateau were to be razed and the site promoted to a more park-like atmosphere.

At the time of writing, the motels are still there and people still splash and play in the travertines. But the writing is on the wall, and in the future access will no doubt be limited, and the motels removed.

While they last, you can usually swim in the motel pools by paying a day-use fee. The pool at the Pamukkale Motel, with its submerged fragments of fluted marble columns, is the most charming. A pass for a two-hour swim costs US$3, but they rarely check your pass so you may be able to stretch it out for a longer time.

Lower rates are charged at the Belediye Turistik Tesisleri, the municipal baths, but these, though bigger, are hardly as picturesque. Don't have a bathing suit? You can rent one for the day at the Belediye. By the way, *umumi havuzlar* are the large public pools (US$1 for two hours' swimming); *özel aile havuzu* is a private family pool (US$2.50 per hour).

Festivals

In late May or early June, the Pamukkale Festival brings spectators to Hierapolis's restored Roman theatre for musical and folk-loric performances.

Places to Stay

The Turkish government, in league with UNESCO and the World Bank, plans to raze the hotels on top of the ridge at Pamukkale. When they do, all the available lodgings will be in Pamukkale town and at Karahayıt.

On weekends you may find the pensions and motels at Pamukkale full, and may have to seek lodgings in Denizli. To avoid the crush, come during the week, or very early in the day on Friday or Saturday, and preferably in spring or autumn, not high summer.

Prices vary a great deal according to the season, being highest in midsummer. In general, the inexpensive places to stay are in Pamukkale town, moderate places are at Örenyeri, and the new luxury hotels are at Karahayıt.

Pamukkale Town The town at the base of the ridge is filled with little family pensions, some more elaborate and expensive than others. Many have little swimming pools, often oddly shaped and filled with the calcium mineral water – cool by the time it gets here – and shady places to sit, read, sip tea or have a meal. If rooms are available, you will have no problem finding one, as pension owners will crowd around your bus as it arrives and importune you with offers. Those with rooms available after the mêlée will intercept you as you walk along the road into the village.

A walking tour of some of the better places to stay follows. Right at the entrance to Pamukkale town, just off the highway, is the *Hotel Konak Sade* (☎ (6218) 1002), the first lodging place in the village, opened more than 25 years ago. It's an old village house decorated with Turkish carpets, kilims and copperware. The shady rear garden holds a small swimming pool surrounded by tables and chairs for drinks, snacks or meals; the view of the travertines from here is the best around. The rooms are simple, in character with the old village house, but many have private showers. You pay US$30 a double with breakfast, or US$40 a double with breakfast and dinner. Readers report that the food is good.

Motels are squeezing out some cheap pensions as the demand for accommodation grows. The 58-room *Yörük Motel* (☎ (6218) 1073; fax 1102), just a short walk down the hill in the village centre, is nice. Guest rooms are on two levels, surrounding a courtyard with swimming pool. Balconies allow you to sit outside and enjoy the sun while watching the swimmers. The restaurant is often busy with group tours. Double rooms with shower, breakfast included, cost US$25/35 a single/double in summer.

Walk past the Yörük and turn left to find the *Fatih Motel* (☎ (6218) 1054), a great bargain. Smaller and slightly less fancy, it has an even quieter situation, though the pool is smaller and murkier. The price is the best part: US$18 a double, breakfast included.

Continue along the road past the Fatih, and turn left on İnönü Caddesi for the *Kervansaray Pension* (☎ (6218) 1209), which offers rooms with shower for US$18, a swimming pool, and a friendly family atmosphere. It's been a favourite for years.

If the Kervansaray is full, go back to the road and the next place along is the *Aspawa Pension* (☎ (6218) 1094), which is modern, friendly, and priced similarly.

Four hundred metres farther along is the *Koray Motel* (☎ (6218) 1300), an excellent choice. Away from the noise and bustle, it is well kept, friendly, and filled with plants. A double room with shower costs US$18. For US$9 more you get breakfast and dinner as well. Recommended.

Hulley Hotel (☎ (6218) 1204), next to the mosque in the town centre, has a few plain, clean rooms for US$12 a double without running water, or US$18 a double for the newer 'motel-style' rooms with nice tiled showers.

Other pensions are similar, such as the *Ziya Pension* (☎ (6218) 1195), Pamukkale town, Denizli, which offers rooms without bath for US$5/10/15 a single/double/triple. If the rooms are full, you'll be able to sleep on the roof for less.

Near the highway is the *Pension Mustafa* (☎ (6218) 1240) in which anyone over 140 cm tall must be careful not to bump their

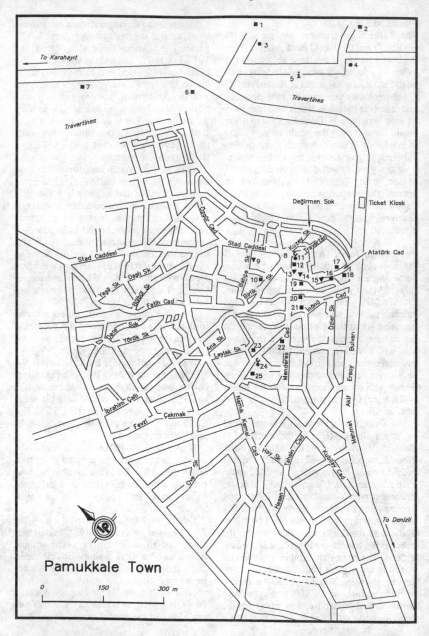

Pamukkale Town

■ PLACES TO STAY

1 Pamukkale Motel
2 Çankur Turizm Camping
6 Tusan Moteli
7 Motel Koru
10 Ziya Pansiyon
12 Halley Hotel
16 Hotel Turku
17 Hotel Konak Sade
18 Pension Mustafa
19 Yörük Motel
20 Fatih Motel
21 Kervansaray Pansiyon
22 Aspawa Pansiyon
23 Rose (Gül) Pansiyon
25 Koray Motel

▼ PLACES TO EAT

9 Ünal Restaurant
13 Han Restaurant
14 Gürsoy 2 Restaurant
15 Pizzeria

OTHER

3 Museum
4 First Aid Post
5 Tourism Information Office
8 Main Square & Belediye
11 Mosque
24 Mosque

head on the interior staircase. The rooms are sort of jerry-built; some have showers, others do not. The owner is open to haggling. There is a small swimming pool and restaurant. A room alone, without running water, costs US$14 a double.

Hotel Turku (☎ (6218) 1181) is fancier, with tidy rooms with private showers, a pool, and tasty meals in the dining room, but charges slightly higher prices (about US$25 a double). *Pension Rose* (☎ (6218) 1205), also called the Gül Pansiyon (the translation) has a small camping area as well as cheap rooms.

Camping There are several camping grounds along the road between Denizli and

Pamukkale, and others in Karahayıt. There is also the *Çankur Turizm Camping* at Örenyeri, behind the Belediye Turistik Tesisleri swimming pools. Shady sites for tents and camper vans cost US$6 a double. Little A-frame shelters nearby cost a bit more.

Örenyeri The motels amidst the ruins at Pamukkale may not last long. If you plan to stay here, make reservations in advance to be sure the establishment is still in existence.

Pamukkale Motel (☎ (6218) 1024; fax 1026) is the one with the garden swimming pool littered with broken marble columns that you see in photographs so often. This was the sacred pool of ancient Hierapolis. With its column-studded pool, the Pamukkale Motel is in demand, though it is hardly luxurious. Rooms with a bath rent for US$55/75 a single/double.

The three-star, 47-room *Tusan Moteli* (☎ (6218) 1010; fax 1059), was the first comfortable motel here, and still commands premium prices of US$65/80 for a single/double. The Tusan is off by itself a bit, surrounded by gardens and away from the crowds, yet still very close to the ruins of Hierapolis.

The *Mis-tur Motel* (MEESS-toor) (☎ (6218) 1130; fax 1013) is another middle-range place to stay. It is at the northern end of 'motel row', slightly away from things. Its odd beehive rooms produce unnerving echoes (you will scare yourself silly if you snore), but it's well kept and attractive, with live entertainment around the pool most evenings. Rates are US$40/58 a single/double, breakfast included. The motel is in a slightly inconvenient location, a bit of a walk from the centre of things.

At the *Palmiye Motel* (☎ (6218) 1014; fax 1018), you can choose from several styles of accommodation. The older rooms (Nos 101 to 129) are arranged so that you have your own individual section of swimming pool right near your room, with a magnificent view of the valley. Newer rooms (Nos 130 and up) do not share this fabulous valley view, but rather surround a big swimming pool. All are simple Turkish-style motel rooms, comfortable but fairly basic. In the busy summer season the motel, with one of the best situations on the ridge, can get away with charging US$50 a double for a room around the main pool, or US$75 for a room with an individual pool. Breakfast and dinner are included in these prices.

To one side of the main swimming pool, an 'antique bar' has caryatid (draped female-statue) barstools so tacky they're good. The bar is a fine pergola-observatory for gazing at the valley or watching the sunset.

The conveniently located 130-room *Motel Koru* (☎ (6218) 1020; fax 1023), is the largest lodging place here, with a big, beautiful swimming pool and pleasant gardens. It's a mecca for bus tours, and always seems to be thronged with groups settling in for a good feed. The air-conditioned rooms with shower go for US$40/60 a single/double. Service to individual travellers may suffer as a result of the groups.

Karahayıt There are lots of new, large, comfortable hotels at Karahayıt, five km beyond Pamukkale Örenyeri. Most are patronised by tour groups, but will provide for individual travellers as well.

Merit Hierapolis (☎ (6228) 4116, 4147; fax 2416), opened in 1988, is among the older hotels, with more established gardens and good guest rooms in two-storey sugar-cube-white blocks. Doubles cost US$80, breakfast included.

Other good, new places in Karahayıt include the four-star, 225-room *Polat Hotel* (☎ (6228) 4111; fax 4092); the three-star, 158-room *Pam Hotel* (☎ (6228) 4140; fax 4097); the 208-room *Hierapolis Thermal Hotel* (☎ (6228) 4105; fax (621) 24816); and the smaller 69-room *Kur-Tur Motel* (☎ (6228) 4117; fax (621) 30818).

Places to Eat – bottom end

The inexpensive places (and they're not all that cheap for what you get) are at the bottom of the ridge in Pamukkale town. Most of the pensions serve meals, and I recommend that you take a room with breakfast and dinner included. Chances are very good that your pension will serve you better food, with larger portions at lower prices, than any of the eateries in the village.

The famous *Pizzeria* on the main street between the highway and the Yörük Motel was built to resemble a Pizza Hut in Australia, in which its builder worked for several years. Don't expect a shiny plastic fast-food place; this one's far more 'Turkish villagey', with prices to match, and excellent fresh pizza. The upper deck gives you a view with your meal. *Pizzaland* next door is also good, though the food is a bit more bland.

On top of the ridge there is a pide restaurant and a café selling soft drinks, with tables overlooking the travertines, but at prices somewhat higher than those in the valley. You'd be well advised to pack a picnic before you climb the ridge from Pamukkale town.

Places to Eat – middle

All of the motels at Örenyeri have dining rooms, mostly geared to group tours. In Pamukkale town, try the *Gürsoy 2 Restaurant*, facing the Yörük Motel on the main street. With its small, shady front terrace, it's great for people-watching. A three-course meal with drink costs about US$5. Similarly priced is the popular *Han Restaurant*, facing the main square. The menu has many popular dishes, and all prices are posted. The *Ünal*, below the square, has less of a view and simpler décor, but is a bit cheaper. The *Mustafa Restaurant*, on top of the Mustafa Pension, has good views. For a drink, try the *Harem Restaurant & Bar*, on the main street, with a good view of the foot traffic.

Getting There & Away

Bus In summertime, Pamukkale has a surprising number of direct buses to and from other cities. Many of these buses are continuations of the Denizli service. Companies serving the town with direct buses include Kamil Koç, Köseoğlu, Pamukkale and Paklale. For distances and prices, see the Denizli section.

At the time of writing the town has no proper otogar. Ticket offices are near the junction of the highway and the town's main street.

Municipal buses make the half-hour trip between Denizli and Pamukkale every 45 minutes or so, more frequently on Saturday and Sunday, for 50c. Dolmuşes go more frequently, and faster, and charge 60c. If you arrive in the evening the dolmuşes and buses may have ceased to run, and you may have to take a taxi, which will cost about US$8.

Car If you're driving from Aphrodisias and Nazilli, you might want to know that there's a short cut to Pamukkale. About 600 metres after you pass the exit sign from Sarayköy ('Sarayköy' with a red diagonal stripe through it), there is a narrow road on the left going to Pamukkale via the villages of Sığma (SUH-mah), Akköy, and Karahayıt. The road is not well marked, so you should ask directions for Pamukkale in each village. If enough people ask directions, the locals might erect signs.

LAODİKYA

Laodicea was a prosperous commercial city at the junction of two major trade routes running north to south and east to west. Famed for its black wool, banking and medicines, it had a large Jewish community and a prominent Christian congregation. It is one of the Seven Churches of Asia mentioned in the New Testament Book of Revelation. Cicero lived here a few years before he was put to death at the request of Marc Antony.

To reach the ruins of Laodikya, you will need a car, a taxi, a hired minibus, or good strong legs. Head north towards Pamukkale from the Üçgen, the large traffic roundabout near Denizli's bus station. Take the left turn marked for Pamukkale, and then almost immediately another left marked (badly) for Laodikya.

From this point it is just over three km to the edge of the archaeological site, or just over four km from Laodikya's most prominent theatre. There are actually several routes to the ruins, but this one takes you through a little farming village; the road is unmarked, so ask, or when in doubt, go to the right. You should soon come to a railway level crossing; on the other side of the tracks, the ruins are visible. (Another route leaves the main road closer to Pamukkale, and brings you to the theatre first.)

At present there is no guard at the site, no fee and no appointed visiting hours, so you can come anytime during daylight hours.

Though the city was a big one, as you see by the ruins spread over a large area, there is not much of interest left for the casual tourist. The **stadium** is visible, but most of the cut stones were purloined for construction of the railway. One of the **two theatres** is in better shape, with many of its upper tiers of seats remaining, though the bottom ones have collapsed. Unless you have a car or are interested in church history, you can bypass Laodikya.

AK HAN

While you're digging about out here, consider taking a look at the Ak Han (White Caravanserai), a marble Seljuk Turkish caravan 'motel' just one km past the Pamukkale turn-off from the main road. (Heading north from the Üçgen in Denizli, don't take the Pamukkale road, but continue in the direction marked for Dinar for one more km.) The caravanserai is set just off the highway on the left as you come down the slope of a hill. Somewhat neglected these days, the caravanserai awaits preservation, but it is still in quite marvellous shape considering that it dates from the early 1250s.

South Aegean

The south-western corner of Anatolia is mountainous and somewhat isolated. In ancient times this was the Kingdom of Caria, with its own indigenous customs and people, who later took on a veneer of Hellenic civilisation. Later, Christian anchorites (hermits) sought out the mountains and lake islands of Caria to be alone, and to escape the invading Arab armies. Ottoman sultans used the mountainous region to exile political troublemakers in Bodrum, secure in the belief that they could raise no turmoil from such a remote spot.

Your goal is probably Bodrum, the sea-coast town in which sleek yachts are anchored in twin bays beneath the walls of a medieval crusaders' castle. Along the way are a number of ancient cities and temples worth stopping to see.

SÖKE TO MİLAS

The 86-km ride from Söke, near Selçuk and Kuşadası, to Milas need take only 1¼ hours if you go nonstop. But there are so many interesting detours and stops to make that it may take you several days.

About 29 km south of Söke there is a turn-off, on the right, for Akköy (seven km), Miletus and Didyma, described above. Soon afterwards, the highway skirts the southern shore of Bafa Gölü (Bafa Lake). The lake was once a gulf of the Aegean Sea, but became a lake as the sea retreated. Thirteen km beyond the Akköy turn-off are several restaurants, motels and camping areas, most prominently the *Turgut*.

Four km farther along (heading south-east) is a small island bearing traces of a ruined Byzantine monastery, and just beyond it is *Ceri'nin Yeri* (☎ (6131) 4498), a good restaurant serving sea bass, eel, carp and grey mullet which find their way into the lake to spawn. Ceri'nin's has a few pension and motel rooms, and a camp site as well. Sometimes you can arrange for a tour by boat to Latmos.

Latmos

At the south-eastern end of the lake is a settlement named Çamiçi, from which an unpaved road on the left is marked for Kapıkırı, 10 km to the north, though it's actually only eight km. You will have to hike or hitch unless you can catch one of the infrequent dolmuşes. The road is rough and dusty but easily drivable (30 km/h), unless it's very wet. At the end of the road, in and around the village of Kapıkırı (population 350), are the ruins of Herakleia ad Latmos. Behind the village is Beşparmak Dağı, the

Five-fingered Mountain (1500 metres), named for its five peaks. This was the ancient Mt Latmos.

History Latmos is famous because of Endymion, the legendary shepherd-boy. As the story goes, the incredibly handsome Endymion was asleep on Mt Latmos when Selene, the moon goddess, fell in love with him. The myth-sayers tend to disagree on what happened next, though you can easily imagine. It seems that Endymion slept forever, and Selene (also called Diana) got to come down and sleep with him every night. What Endymion did in the hot daytime sun, when Selene was hidden, is not report-ed. Selene somehow saw to the care of his flocks, and on he slept. No more to report. When the male lead sleeps through, it makes for a short play.

This area, ringed by mountains, was one of refuge for Christian hermits during the Arab invasions of the 700s AD, which accounts for the ruined churches and monas-teries. The monks reputedly thought Endymion a Christian saint because they admired his powers of self-denial, though catatonia is more the word for it.

Things to See As you enter the village in summer (at other times they don't seem to bother), you may be asked to pay an admis-sion fee of US$1. Bear right at the ticket booth, pass the *Duran Restaurant*, which has fine lake views, and you come to the *Agora Restaurant*. A yellow sign in German announces that the road only continues for another 30 metres, so you should park in the car park by the sign and explore on foot.

A path behind the car park leads westward up to the **Temple of Athena**, on a promon-tory overlooking the lake. Also from the car park, paths lead eastward to the **agora**, and then several hundred metres through stone-walled pastures and across a valley to the unrestored **theatre**. The theatre is oddly sited, with no spectacular view; it's badly ruined. Its most interesting feature is the several rows of seats and flights of steps cut into the rock. You will also see many remnants of the **city walls** dating from 300 BC.

Much of the fun of a visit to Latmos is to observe real Turkish farming village life, as you will when you walk about this relatively untouristed spot. Beehives dot the fields, and camomile flowers *(papatya)* grow wild by the roadsides in spring and summer.

When you're finished in the village, follow the road down to the lake, past the **Endymion Temple** built partly into the rock, the ruins of a **Byzantine castle** and the city's **necropolis**.

Down at the lakeside, near the ruins of a Byzantine church, are several small restaurants for fish (if they've caught any that day), including the *Zeybek, Kaya* and *Selene*. All offer camping and boat tours of the lake as well. There's a small beach of coarse white sand. Just offshore is an 'island' which is often connected to the shore as the level of the lake has fallen in recent years. Around its base are foundations of ancient buildings.

Though there were no pensions at my last visit, it can't be long before some enterprising village matron decides to provide simple lodging for travellers.

Euromos

About 15 km past the lake Bafa Gölü and one km south of the village of **Selimiye**, keep your eyes open for the extremely picturesque **Temple of Zeus**, on the left-hand side of the road in the midst of what was once the city of Euromos. The Corinthian colonnades set in green olive groves seem too good to be true, like a Hollywood idea for a classical scene. Once there was a town here, but now only the temple remains. But it's enough, and well worth a stop.

First settled in the 6th century BC, Euromos held a sanctuary to a local deity. With the coming of Greek, then Roman culture, the local god's place was taken by Zeus. Euromos reached the height of its prosperity between 200 BC and 200 AD. Emperor Hadrian (117-38 AD), who built so many monuments in Anatolia, is thought to have built this one as well. From the several

columns which remain unfluted, it appears that the work was never really finished.

The site is open from 8.30 am to 5 pm (to 7 pm in summer) for US$1. There are no services but there may be some soft drinks on sale.

If you're interested in ruins, you can explore the slopes around to find other bits of the town. Look north-east (more or less towards İzmir) and find the big stone fortification walls up on the hillside. Climb up to them through the olive groves, go over the wall, and continue at the same altitude (the path dips a bit, which is OK, but don't climb higher). After 100 metres you'll cross another stone wall and find yourself on flat ground which was the stage of the ancient **theatre**. It's badly ruined now, with olive trees growing among the few remaining rows of seats. Besides the theatre, the town's **agora** is down by the highway to the north of the temple, with only a few toppled column drums to mark it.

The city of Milas is about 12 km south of Euromos, but before you come to this city, there are other places to visit.

Iasos

A sleepy Aegean fishing village built amidst the tumbled ruins of an ancient city: the Turkish coasts used to be liberally sprinkled with such places, but tourism has brought development to most of them by now. Iasos is next, but for a few short years it may retain some of its unspoilt charm.

About four km south-east of Euromos (eight km north-west of Milas) is a road on the right (west) marked for Kıyıkışlacık (Iasos) about 18 km to the south-west over a twisting road. The Turkish name means 'Little Barracks on the Coast', but Iasos was in fact a fine city set on its dramatic perch several centuries before Christ. Earliest settlement may date from the Old Bronze Age, and may have included a civilisation much like the Minoan one on Crete.

As you approach, the road takes you right by a large Roman mausoleum, perhaps the best-preserved structure in the area. Though it's closed to visitors, you can see much of it without venturing inside. Farther along at the village, recent excavations have revealed the city's bouleuterion and agora, a gymnasium, a basilica, a Roman temple of Artemis Astias (190 AD) and numerous other buildings besides the prominent Byzantine fortress.

Iasos was built on a hill at the tip of a peninsula framed by two picture-perfect bays. Today the hill is covered with ruins, including a walled acropolis-fortress (admission costs US$1 if there's anyone around to sell you a ticket). Olive groves surround the town and reach nearly to its centre. Southwest of the hill on the bay is a small yacht harbour. Fishing smacks crowd the quay, and a handful of small pensions and restaurants cater to travellers who want to get away from it all for a few days: *Hotel Iasos* (run by Esin Şerbetçi) is a friendly, family-run place and often full because of it. *Iasos Pension* and *Mandalya Pension* also have cheap rooms. *Ergül Camping* is 6.5 km out of town over the hills. Have *çipura* (gilt head bream), if it's in season, at the *Iasos Deniz Restaurant*, the tour-group favourite right down on the water, or at the *Yıldız* or the *Dilek*, directly behind the Iasos Deniz.

Boats come over to Iasos from Güllük to the south (see following) in summer, ferrying tourists and visiting beaches accessible by water (there are no good beaches in Iasos proper). Iasos' peaceful idyll is soon to be ended as the Ankara Journalists' Cooperative is developing villas nearby.

Labranda

Labranda was a sanctuary to Zeus Stratius, controlled for a long time by Milas. There may have been an oracle here. It's known that festivals and Olympic games were held at the site. Set into a steep hillside at 600 metres elevation in an area from which the ancient city of Mylasa and the modern town of Milas took their water supplies, Labranda today is surrounded by fragrant pine forests peopled by beekeepers. Late in the season (October) you can see their tents pitched in cool groves as they go about their business of extracting the honey and rendering the wax from the honeycombs. It's a beautiful

site, worth seeing partly because so few people come here – yet.

The junction for the road to Labranda is 12 km south of Euromos, just before Milas. It's 14 km to the site: the first six km are paved and fast to travel on, the remaining eight km are on a very rough and slow but scenic road which winds tortuously up into the mountains. In rainy weather (from October to April) the road turns to a slough of mud that may require 4WD. The village of Kargıcak is eight km along the way, and though you may be able to get a dolmuş from Milas to Kargacık, that leaves six km to walk. Hitching is possible but not reliable. A taxi from Milas charges about US$15 for the trip to the site and back.

Labranda was a holy place, not a settlement. Worship of a god at this site had been going on by the 7th century BC, and perhaps long before. The site seems to have been abandoned circa 1000 AD. Today there is no settlement here either, just a caretaker who will welcome you, have you sign the guest book and show you around the site; he speaks only Turkish, with a few words of other languages, but the site is well marked.

The great **Temple of Zeus** honours the god's warlike aspect (Stratius, or Labrayndus, 'Axe-bearing'). Two men's religious gathering places, the **First Andron** and the **Second Andron**, are in surprisingly good condition, as is a large 4th-century **tomb** of fine construction, and other buildings. The ruins, excavated by a Swedish team in the early part of this century, are interesting, but it is the site of the sanctuary which is most impressive. The view over the valley is spectacular.

MİLAS

Milas (MEE-lahs, altitude 46 metres, population 35,000) is a very old town. As Mylasa, it was capital of the Kingdom of Caria, except during the period when Mausolus ruled the kingdom from Halicarnassus (now Bodrum). Today it is an agricultural town and has many homes in which carpets are woven by hand.

Orientation

Approaching Milas from the north-west, you pass Milas' new otogar one km (along 19 Mayıs Bulvarı) before coming to the Labranda road to the left; to the right (along İnönü Caddesi) the road is marked 'Şehir Merkezi' (City Centre). It's another km to the centre of town at the park (Milas Belediye Parkı).

Things to See

The road into town from the north passes the city's **museum** on the left, after which you'll see a little yellow-arrow sign on the left pointing the way to the **Baltalı Kapı**, or 'Gate with Axe'. Follow the sign, cross a little bridge, and you come to a T-intersection. Look to the right to see a ruined gate in ancient Milas' defensive walls, but turn left to reach the more impressive and well-preserved Baltalı Kapı, which has marble posts and lintel and Corinthian capitals.

Continuing into the centre of town, you'll come to a traffic roundabout next to the shady Belediye Parkı. Follow the little yellow-arrow signs from the roundabout to the **Gümüşkesen** ('That Which Cuts Silver'), 1.4 km from the roundabout on a hill west of the centre (along Gümüşkesen Caddesi).

The Gümüşkesen, set in a little park, is a Roman tomb dating from the 1st century AD, thought to have been modelled on the great Tomb of Mausolus at Halicarnassus. A guardian will let you into the enclosure and allow you to climb a ladder up to the platform; the view of the city from this perch is very good. The Corinthian columns support a pyramidal roof, just as at the Tomb of Mausolus. Beneath the platform is the tomb chamber, which you can enter. A hole in the platform floor allowed devotees to pour libations into the tomb chamber to quench the dead soul's thirst.

You might also want to see some of Milas' fine mosques, especially the **Ulu Cami** (1378) and **Orhan Bey Camii** (1330), built when Milas was the capital of the Turkish principality of Menteşe. The larger, more impressive **Firuz Bey Camii** (1394) was built shortly after Menteşe became part of the new and growing Ottoman Empire.

Places to Stay

Otel Arıcan (☎ (6131) 1215), near the Hacı İlyas Camii, has decent cheap rooms for US$7 a double without bath, or US$8 with private shower. *Hotel Akdeniz* (☎ (6131) 2217), across the street, is nicer but a bit more expensive. The entrance is around to the side. The Yeni Hamam, across Hacı İlyas Sokak from the Otel Arıcan, fills the need for a Turkish bath.

Hotel Çınar (☎ & fax (6131) 2102), Kadıağa Caddesi 52, is nice, new and clean, with a lobby one flight up. Take a room at the back as front rooms may be noisy. Rates are US$10 for two in one bed, US$14 with two beds, with private bath and breakfast.

Otel Sürücü (☎ (6131) 4001; fax 4000), on Atatürk Bulvarı more or less across from the statue of Atatürk, is Milas' best, a serviceable modern hotel where the Rotary and Lions clubs meet. Double rooms with bath cost US$20. There's a terrace café in front, and a decent dining room.

Places to Eat

Pamukkale Pide Salonu, beneath the Hotel Akdeniz, satisfies the need for Turkish pizza quickly and cheaply. The Otel Arıcan across the street has its own *Arıcan Bolu Lokantası* with soups, stews and kebaps. There are numerous other small restaurants in the area where a three-course meal can be had for US$2 to US$3.

Fifty metres south-west of the traffic roundabout by the Belediye Parkı is the *Karya Restaurant* (☎ 2908), a fairly simple place with a front terrace set with tables. *Otel Sürücü*, 200 metres farther along, has a good restaurant and also a fast-food burger place.

Peçin Kale & Ören

Three km south of Milas is an intersection: right to Bodrum, left to Ören, Muğla and Marmaris. Turn left and there's a road on the right marked for Ören, 50 km along where the road ends at the Gulf of Gökova.

A few km along the Ören road, watch for

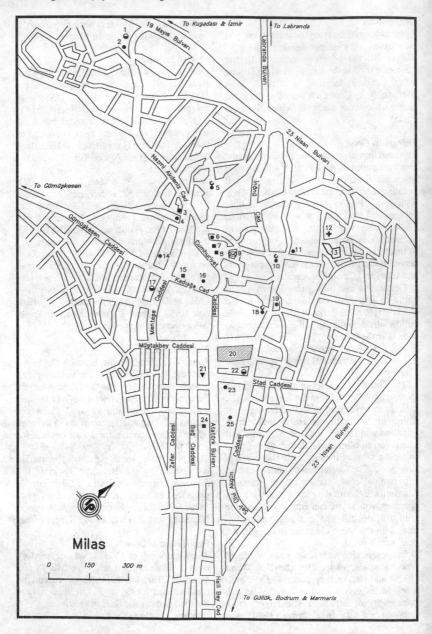

Milas

0   150   300 m

■ PLACES TO STAY

7 Otel Arıcan & Arıcan Bolu Lokantası
8 Hotel Akdeniz & Pamukkale Pide
   Salonu
15 Hotel Çınar
24 Otel Sürücü

▼ PLACES TO EAT

21 Karya Restaurant

OTHER

1 Otogar
2 Taşkıran Market
3 Bank
4 Bank
5 Firuz Bey Camii
6 Belediye
9 PTT
10 Orhan Bey Camii
11 Weekly Market
12 Hospital
13 Baltalı Kapı
14 Fruit & Vegetable Market
16 Hamam
17 Ören Dolmuş Station
18 Ulu Cami
19 Archaeological Museum
20 Milas Belediye Parkı
22 Güllük Dolmuş Station
23 Government Building
25 Police Headquarters

an unpaved road which leads after 800
metres to **Peçin Kale**, a Byzantine fortress
later pressed into service by the Turkish
emirs of Menteşe. The fortress is open from
8 am to dusk (US$1), but there is not a lot to
see inside. Less than 500 metres on are remnants of the Menteşe settlement (dating from
the 1300s), including the Kızıl Han caravanserai, Orhanbey Camii, and the Ahmet Gazi
tomb and medrese.

Because the Ören road is a dead end, Ören
has been slow to lose that tranquil atmosphere which was once common to villages
along the Turkish coasts. The village actually
consists of two parts. Inland from the beach
is the centre, with its post office, shops, and
old Ottoman houses set amidst the **ruins of**

the ancient city of **Keramos** (or Ceramus),
which flourished from the 6th century BC
until at least the 3rd century AD. The **beach**
is the centre of visitor interest, however.

The sand-and-pebble beach is one km
long and draws Turkish holiday-makers
from the big cities. They come for stays of a
week, two weeks or more in the village's few
cheap lodgings. If you bother to travel the 50
km to the village, you too will want to stay
more than a night.

Places to Stay & Eat If you plan to stay in
high summer, come early in the morning to
find a room, or call ahead and reserve one.
Among cheap lodgings, try the *Karya Oteli*
(☎ (6134) 1115), the *Otel Göksu* (☎ (6134)
1112) or the *Hotel Marçalı* (☎ (6134) 1063),
with double rooms for US$12. *Yıltur Motel*
(☎ (6134) 1108), at the eastern end of the
beach, is a bit cheaper but simpler. For more
comfort there's the *Hotel Salihağa*
(☎ (6134) 1138) and the *Keramos Motel*
(☎ (6134) 1065), which also has a camping
ground. Ören also has a few restaurants to
serve its transient population.

Güllük
Turn right at the intersection three km south
of Milas, and after another 15 km you come
to the turn-off for Güllük, a beach resort with
several little pensions. In a short while this
will be the home to the south Aegean's large
new airport.

Eight km west of the highway through
olive groves lies Güllük, a little fishing
village with a harbour occupied predominantly by fishing boats, not yachts or
excursion ships. Fishers still repair their nets
on the quays, and town life still centres on
the teahouse, not the noisy disco. There are
actually three little bays here, with the
central bay at the centre of town. To the left,
the Türk Petrol company has a company
resort which monopolises the southern bay;
to the right, the northern bay is lined mostly
with posh summer villas. The north bay is
the best for swimming, but in fact there is no
beach here.

One comes to Güllük for a few days' easy

relaxation after the trials of life on the road. It's still quieter and more laid back than Bodrum or Marmaris, though less interesting as well. Most of the activity has to do with fishing, with the Türk Petrol resort, and with the nearby Etibank bauxite mines. A few simple pensions and restaurants provide the necessities. Mr Fadıl Deniz Yıldıran's *Kaptan Pansiyon*, at the right-hand (northeast) end of the waterfront, is cheapest and best, with a marvellous view of the bay and sunset. Double rooms cost from US$8 to US$10.

Dolmuşes run to Güllük from Milas, and also from the village of Koru, on the highway a few km north of the Güllük turn-off.

For an excursion, haggle with a boat owner to take you north across the bay to Iasos for the day, a voyage of less than an hour each way.

BODRUM

The road to Bodrum winds through pine forests and along beautiful unspoilt coastline, finally cresting a hill to reveal the panorama of Bodrum with its striking crusader castle.

It is strange that a town should owe its fame to a man long dead and a building long since disappeared, but that's the way it is with Bodrum (population 50,000). It's the South Aegean's prettiest resort town with a yacht harbour and a port for ferries to the Greek island of Kos.

The man long dead is King Mausolus, and the building his tomb, the Mausoleum, but Bodrum has many other attractions. Most striking is the fairytale crusaders' castle in the middle of town, guarding twin bays now crowded with yachts. Palm-lined streets ring the bays, and white sugar-cube houses are scattered on the hillside. Yachting, boating, swimming, snorkelling and scuba diving are prime Bodrum activities. For daytime diversion, you can take boat or jeep trips to nearby secluded beaches and villages (see the Bodrum Peninsula section), or over to the Greek island of Kos. At night, Bodrum's famous discos throb, boom and blare at will, keeping much of the town awake until dawn.

Both Turkish and foreign visitors complain about the ear-splitting cacophony, but no one does anything about it.

Bodrum's economy is now dedicated to tourism, though in winter there is a bounteous citrus crop (especially tangerines), and you will still see a few sponge-fishing boats.

History

Following the Persian invasion, Caria was ruled by a satrap named Mausolus (circa 376-353 BC), who moved the capital here from Mylasa and called this town Halicarnassus. After the satrap's death, his wife undertook construction of a monumental tomb which Mausolus had planned for himself. The Mausoleum, an enormous white-marble tomb topped by a stepped pyramid, came to be considered one of the Seven Wonders of the World. It stood relatively intact for almost 19 centuries, until it was broken up by the crusaders and the pieces used as building material in 1522.

Bodrum's other claim to fame comes from Herodotus (485?-425? BC), the 'Father of History', who was born here. Herodotus was the first person to write a comprehensive 'world history', and all other histories in Western civilisation owe him a debt.

Orientation

The bus station is several hundred metres inland from the water, on Cevat Şakir the main street into the centre. Walk down from the bus station towards the castle, and you will come to a small white mosque called the Adliye Camii (AHD-lee-yeh jah-mee), Courthouse Mosque), or Yeni Cami. Turn right, and you'll be heading west on Neyzen Tevfik Caddesi towards the Yat Limanı (Yacht Marina); turn left and you will go through the bazaar, then walk along Doktor Alim Bey Caddesi, which later becomes Cumhuriyet Caddesi, past dozens of hotels and pensions in all price ranges. The array of lodgings continues all the way around the bay, then along the shore of another bay farther on.

Go straight on towards the castle and

you'll be walking along Kale Caddesi, the tourist axis of Bodrum, lined with boutiques selling clothing, carpets, souvenirs and such. At the end of Kale Caddesi beneath the castle walls, is Oniki Eylül Meydanı (12 September Square), also called İskele Meydanı (Dock Square), the main plaza. It has the Tourism Information Office, customs office, teahouses and lots of activity.

Information

The Tourism Information Office (☎ (614) 11091; fax 17694) is on Oniki Eylül Meydanı, with yachts moored alongside. Summer hours are Monday to Friday from 8 am to 8 pm, Saturday from 9 am to noon and 3.30 to 7.30 pm, closed on Sunday. The staff are helpful and well informed, with bus and ferry schedules and accommodation lists. Several bus and ferry companies have ticket offices nearby. Bodrum's postal code is 48400.

Market There is a fresh vegetable and fruit market held just inland from the Adliye Camii from Thursday noon to Friday noon each week. Another market area is just north of the otogar.

Laundry The yachters don't have hotel staff to do their laundry, so the town's most convenient laundry places are near the yacht marina. Try Fatih's Self-Service Laundry, past the Herodot Pansiyon and the marina entrance, but before the Hotel Gala. Minik Laundry is farther along, uphill and around the corner to the right. There's also a Fatih's Laundry near the Halikarnas Disco (follow the signs).

Castle of St Peter

The castle, of course, is first on anyone's list of things to see in Bodrum. When Tamerlane invaded Anatolia in 1402, throwing the nascent Ottoman Empire off balance for a time, the Knights Hospitaller or Knights of St John of Jerusalem based on Rhodes took the opportunity to capture Bodrum. They built the Castle of St Peter, and it defended Bodrum (not always successfully) until the end of WW I. It now holds Bodrum's famous **Museum of Underwater Archaeology** and an open-air theatre. Hours are from 8.30 am to noon and 3 to 7 pm every day from June to mid-September; 9 am to noon and 1 to 5 pm in winter. The exhibit of the world's oldest shipwreck is open for limited hours, Tuesday to Friday from 10 to 11 am and 2 to 4 pm only. Admission costs US$2; students pay half-price.

As you find your way up into the castle, you'll pass several coats of arms carved in marble and mounted in the walls. Many of the stones in these walls came from the ruined Mausoleum. As always, the question which the knights put to themselves was this: with all this lovely cut stone from some old fellow's tomb, why bother to cut our own?

Many of the museum's exhibits are the result of underwater archaeology conducted by Professor George Bass of Texas A&M University and his international team of marine archaeologists. Numerous ancient coastal cargo ships have been found sunk off Bodrum, and divers have recovered many artefacts. One of these was the oldest shipwreck ever discovered, raised from the bottom of the Aegean off Bodrum and now in the 'glass wreck hall', built especially for it.

Within the French Tower, the highest point in the castle, is the Sub-Mycenaean Archaic Age Hall, with the very oldest finds. The Italian Tower holds the Hellenistic Hall and the Classical Hall. Then, in descending order, you come to the Medieval Hall, the Hall of Coins and Jewellery, a collection of tombstones (outdoors), and the Snake Tower with a collection of ancient amphorae. Finally, there is the Bronze Age Hall.

Mausoleum

Though the Mausoleum is long gone, you might like to visit the site. In a handsome gallery here, archaeologists have arranged models, drawings and documents to give you an idea of why this tomb was among the

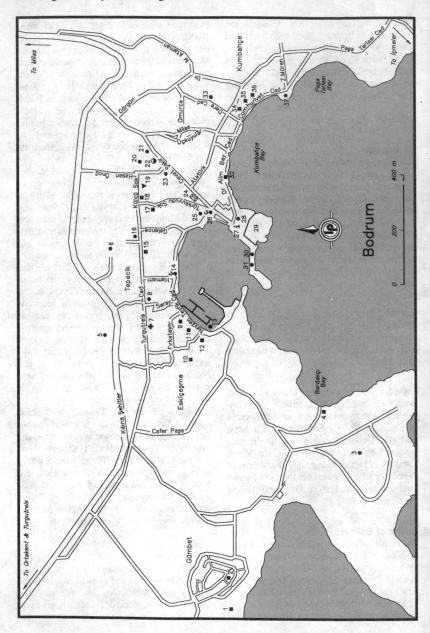

Bodrum

■ PLACES TO STAY

1 Hotel Seray
2 Ayhan Pension
4 Azka Otel
9 Otel Bodrum
10 Hotel Karia Princess
11 Herodot Pansiyon
12 Hotel Gala
15 Su Otel
17 Melis Pansiyon
18 Pension Espri
32 Otel Baraz
34 Artemis Pansiyon
35 Dinç Pansiyon
36 Karya Otel

▼ PLACES TO EAT

19 Sapa Restaurant

OTHER

3 Windmills
5 Ancient Theatre
6 Temple of Mars
7 Hospital
8 Mausoleum
13 Yacht Marina
14 Tepecik Camii
16 Medical Clinic
20 Marketplace
21 Mobil Station
22 Otogar (Bus Station)
23 Shell Station
24 Post Office (PTT)
25 Belediye
26 Adliye Camii
27 Tourism Information Office
28 Police
29 Castle of St Peter
30 Passport Police
31 Ferries to Datça & Greece
33 Hamam
37 Halikarnas Disco

Seven Wonders of the (ancient) World. It's a few blocks inland from Neyzen Tevfik Caddesi. Turn near the little white Tepecik Camii on the shore of the western bay, then left onto the road to Turgutreis Caddesi, following the signs.

The site is open every day from 8 am to 5 or 6 pm; though officially closed on Monday, you can usually get in by asking at the little grocery shop across the street. Admission costs 50c. Most labels and documents are in English as well as Turkish; a few are in French.

The site has pleasant gardens, with the excavations to the right and the exhibition galleries to the left. Exhibits include bits of sculpted marble found at the site, a model of Halicarnassus at the time of King Mausolus, a model of the Mausoleum and its precincts, and various diagrams and plans.

Written descriptions taken from ancient documents (1581) tell the alarming story: The Knights Hospitaller from Rhodes discovered the Mausoleum, largely buried and preserved by the dust of ages. They uncovered it, admired it for a while, then went back to the castle for the night. During the night, pirates broke in and stole the tomb treasures, which had been safe as long as the Mausoleum was buried. The next day the knights returned and broke the tomb to pieces for use as building stone. Some of the bits were pulverised to make lime for mortar. They used these materials to repair their castle in anticipation of an attack by Süleyman the Magnificent. They knew he would attack, and they knew they would lose and have to abandon the castle, but they saw the effort as a holding action. So the Mausoleum was sacrificed to the honour of a crusader military order.

In the large exhibition room is a copy of the famous frieze found in the castle walls; the original is now in the British Museum. Four fragments of the frieze here are original, having been discovered more recently.

In the archaeologists' hole itself there is little to see: a few pre-Mausolean stairways and tomb chambers, the Mausolean drainage system, the entry to Mausolus' tomb chamber, a few bits of precinct wall and some large, fluted, marble column drums.

Theatre

The theatre, behind the town up on the hillside by the bypass road, is cut into the rock

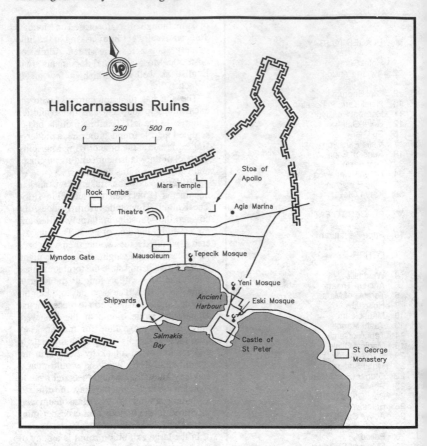

Halicarnassus Ruins

0   250   500 m

Rock Tombs

Mars Temple

Stoa of Apollo

Theatre

Agia Marina

Myndos Gate

Mausoleum

Tepecik Mosque

Yeni Mosque

Shipyards

Ancient Harbour

Eski Mosque

Salmakis Bay

Castle of St Peter

St George Monastery

of the hillside. The view is splendid, the traffic on the busy road noisy, smelly, and disturbing.

Turkish Bath

Bodrum's hamam is near the mosque beneath the castle walls just off of İskele Meydanı. Opening hours are from 8 am to 5 pm; the hamam is open to women on Wednesday and Saturday, to men on the other days. Admission and a wash cost US$2 at least until the hamam goes up-market, allows men and women to bathe together, and charges five times as much. This may

happen soon. There is another hamam on Dere Caddesi in the Kumbahçe district.

Boat Excursion

Dozens of yachts are moored along Neyzen Tevfik Caddesi on the western bay, and most have sales agents who will try and cajole you into taking a day trip. Most boat excursions depart at 10 or 11 am, return at 4.30 or 5 pm and cost US$6.

Here's a typical itinerary. First you sail to Karaada (Black Island) due south of Bodrum, where there are hot springs issuing in a strong current from a cave. Swimmers

Castle of St Peter, Bodrum

here rub the orange mud from the springs on their bodies, hoping for some aesthetic improvement. After a half-hour stop at Karaada, the boat makes for the coarse sand and pebble beach at Ortakent Yalısı, due west of Bodrum. There's a lovely little cove here with a few beach-front restaurants, small pensions and camping areas, but big hotels nearby as well.

You can have lunch at the *Ökalyptos Restaurant* for about US$5 or US$6. After Ortakent, the boat sails to the 'Aquarium', a small cove deserted except for other excursion boats. The water is beautifully clear, and the idea is that you'll see lots of fish, but much of the time the boating and swimming activity scares the fish away. After the Aquarium, it's back to Bodrum.

Festivals

The Bodrum Festival is held annually during the first week in September. Lodgings may be especially crowded then.

Places to Stay

In high summer, especially on weekends, Bodrum can fill up with holiday-makers. Try to arrive early in the day to find a room. The Tourism Information Office may be able to help you find a room if space is tight.

Places to Stay – bottom end

North of the western bay are narrow streets harbouring good little pensions. These tend to be quieter than those on the eastern bay because they are farther from the nuclear-powered Halikarnas Disco.

Türkkuyusu Sokak This street with a tongue-twister name starts just north of the Adliye Camii and goes north past several good, cheap, convenient pensions charging from US$10 to US$16 a double for rooms with private shower. *Metin Pansiyon* (☎ (614) 12125) is first, followed by the *Sevin Pansiyon* (☎ (614) 18361). Turn right at the Metin onto Eski Belediye Sokak for the *Pansiyon Kaya* (☎ (614) 15745).

Farther along Türkkuyusu Sokak are more pensions, including the *Melis Pansiyon* (☎ (614) 11487), at No 50, a tidy place with a shady garden terrace away from the street. It's fairly quiet, and charges US$14 a double in summer. Nearby on Gencel Çıkmazı, a short cul-de-sac off Türkkuyusu Soksk, is the *Pension Rainbow* ('Mike's Home', ☎ (614) 15170), which is even quieter.

Pension Espri (☎ (614) 11129), Türkkuyusu Sokak 98, on the corner of Külcü Sokak, is actually quite a comfortable hotel with a swimming pool, tennis possibilities, and 40 rooms with bath costing US$20 a double.

Very near the Espri is the *Otel Nur* (☎ (614) 15329), Türkkuyusu Sokak 139, a modern, pleasant, fairly quiet little hotel charging US$18 a double in summer, less in the off season.

Off Neyzen Tevfik Caddesi The way to find these places is to walk along Neyzen Tevfik Caddesi and look for little signs pointing the way. *Albatros Motel & Pansiyon* (☎ (614) 11329), Menekşe Sokak 8, built of cool stone, is covered in flowers and is quiet and proper, with an assortment of shower-equipped rooms going for US$10/US$16 a single/double, breakfast included. Up the street beyond it are two undistinguished modern pensions, the *Menekşe* (☎ (614) 13416) and the *Yenilmez* (☎ (614) 12520), for use if all else is full.

Ataer Pansiyon (☎ (614) 15357), Neyzen Tevfik Caddesi 102, is just east of the Tepecik Camii, set back from the waterfront street a bit so it's quieter. The cost of a double room is US$14 in season, breakfast included.

Doktor Alim Bey/Cumhuriyet Caddesi The eastern bay has some pensions worth considering. The 17-bed *Kemer Pansiyon* (☎ (614) 11473), at Uslu Çıkmazı 36, a small street off Cumhuriyet Caddesi, is typical of Bodrum's little pensions. Some rooms have private shower; rates vary from US$5 to US$10 per person, depending upon the room and the season. The pension is swathed in bougainvillea and morning glory, and is on a quiet back street.

If the Kemer is full, there are two other pensions just a few steps away – the *Aşkın Pansiyon* (☎ (614) 11499) and the *Billûr Pansiyon* – but they are badly affected by disco noise. The Billûr has some rooms with a private shower. Another pension nearby on Cumhuriyet Caddesi is the *Uslu Pansiyon* (☎ (614) 11486).

Though the address of the *Elvan Pension*, is 'off Atatürk Caddesi at 426 Sokak No 4', it's actually a block north of the waterfront. It's run by a Turkish-Australian couple who rent clean, simple rooms for US$10 to US$16. Excellent meals are served in the rooftop restaurant-bar.

There are many pensions clustered along Rasathane Sokak in the Kumbahçe district near the Halikarnas Disco – *Berlin Pansiyon* (☎ (614) 12524), *Durak Pansiyon* (☎ (614) 11564), *Uğur Pansiyon* (☎ (614) 12106).

You can find them by following their signs, but the noctural disco noise in this neighbourhood often prevents sleep.

Camping The construction boom of the 1980s wiped out most of Bodrum's camping grounds. For dependable camping you must leave Bodrum proper and make your base in one of the smaller villages on the peninsula. Bitez Yalısı and Ortakent Yalısı, for instance, are beach villages west of Bodrum with many small pensions and camp sites. There are more on the peninsula's north shore.

Places to Stay – middle
Western Bay My first choice is the charming *Su Otel* (☎ (614) 16906; fax 17391), Turgutreis Caddesi, 1201 Sokak, hidden away at the end of a narrow cul-de-sac. The bi-national management (he's Turkish, she's British) have used lots of local crafts to decorate the hotel with flair and good taste, and have let nature do the rest with an abundance of flowers. Rooms overlook a courtyard with a central swimming pool. With only 30 beds, it's often full, so reserve in advance if you can. Rates are US$40, buffet breakfast included, for a room with bath. To find this hotel, walk north on the street directly opposite the Tepecik Camii, turn right at the 'T' intersection, and walk several hundred metres following the signs.

Facing the western bay, along Neyzen Tevfik Caddesi, you'll find the *Herodot Pansiyon* (☎ (614) 11093), Neyzen Tevfik Caddesi 116, with 15 rooms near the marina priced at US$15/24 a single/double. It's quiet and tidy, and therefore usually full up. Also on Neyzen Tevfik Caddesi, at No 164/1, is *Seçkin Konaklar* (☎ (614) 11351) with multi-bed apartments sleeping up to six persons priced from US$18 to US$20 per person. This place is a good choice for families or small groups.

Next door is the *Hotel Gala* (☎ (614) 12216, 1673), Yat Limanı, nothing fancy, but not unreasonable at US$35 a double with shower, breakfast included. The lobby, bar and garden-terrace breakfast area are more attractive than the guest rooms, which are pretty simple and small.

The three-star *Otel Bodrum* (☎ (614) 12269, 12270, 12347), Yat Limanı Karşısı, Neyzen Tevfik Caddesi 212, is fancier than these other places, and advertises that 'there is no disco close by, and the windows are double insulated'. Besides the 84 comfortable guest rooms with wall-to-wall carpeting and private baths with showers, the hotel has two freshwater swimming pools, two restaurants and three bars. Décor is the standard Bodrum idiom of white stucco and natural wood with Turkish carpets, textiles and crafts for colour. A double room with breakfast and dinner costs US$65 in the high season.

Eastern Bay Along Cumhuriyet Caddesi on the eastern bay you'll see the two-star *Otel Baraz* (bah-RAHZ) (☎ (614) 11857, 11714; fax 14430), at No 62, right on the water. It has 24 clean and comfortable rooms with private bath priced at US$35/48 a single/double, breakfast included. Rooms with sea views are preferable, but all rooms suffer from disco noise. The Baraz is open all year.

Farther east along Cumhuriyet Caddesi is the *Artemis Pansiyon* (☎ (614) 12530), at No 117, a 22-room place facing the bay and charging US$28 a double, breakfast included.

The 16-room *Dinç Pansiyon* (☎ (614) 11141, 12051), Cumhuriyet Caddesi 123, near the Artemis, is similar. Newer than both is the *Karya Otel* (☎ (614) 11535; fax 12907), at No 127, charging the same. Its 12 bath-equipped rooms all have water views. There's a narrow strip of beach shaded by palm trees just across the street from these places. These pensions are comfy, but the dreaded Halikarnas Disco blares its music at hundreds of decibels all night long.

Gümbet Other lodging possibilities are to be found at Gümbet, the bay to the west of Bodrum over the hills. Dolmuşes run regularly between Bodrum and Gümbet, or you can take a short taxi ride or hitchhike.

Down the slope from the hilltop Hotel

Kıvanç is the *Ayhan Pension*, Esendemir Sokak 38. Clean and well run, its front terrace becomes a pide/pizza restaurant in the evenings. The adjoining *Berg Pension* is similar. Other, similar places here are the *Hotel Mafar* (☎ (614) 11837) and the *Hotel Gümbet* (☎ (614) 15935, 15936), providing clean, if spartan, double rooms with shower for about US$25. They're popular with young British and German holiday-makers on package trips.

Right down by the beach at Gümbet is the *Hotel Seray* (☎ (614) 11969, 14891, 16544). It's a welcoming family-run hostelry with pleasant little two-storey stucco units grouped around a small swimming pool. Jasmine, bougainvillea and other flowers surround the shaded terrace dining area and bar. Guest rooms have brown tiled floors, honey-coloured wood furniture, balconies with clotheslines for drying things, insect screens, and – surprise of surprises – decent reading lamps by the beds. The little marble-floored bathrooms have showers. Rooms go for US$35 to US$40 in season, breakfast included. It's an easy walk to the beach. The adjoining *Hotel Serhan* (☎ (614) 13044) is quite similar. Both hotels close at the end of October, re-opening in April.

Places to Stay – top end
Bodrum has lots of luxury accommodation on the outskirts. If you prefer to stay close to the centre, try the excellent *Hotel Karia Princess* (☎ (614) 18971; fax 18979), Canlıdere Sokak 15. It's small (58 rooms), with the feel of a private club. Guest rooms have air-con, satellite TV, minibars, and king-size beds imported from France. Facilities include a marble-walled Turkish bath, sauna, fitness room, tennis court, a large swimming pool, even two private hotel yachts. Rates are US$140/160 for a single/double with breakfast, dinner, tax and service included.

Just around the headland to the south of the yacht harbour is the *Azka Otel* (☎ (614) 18992; fax 18214), Bardakçı Köyü, a luxurious four-star hotel right on the beach (this is rare) with 118 air-con rooms. Guest rooms and public spaces have good views of the water across spacious grounds, and the list of guest services is long. You pay US$90/135 a single/double, breakfast and dinner included. It's popular with tour groups, so reserve ahead if you can.

Places to Eat

You will have no trouble finding places to eat, but you may encounter a good deal of mediocre food. Many of the restaurants are seasonal, with part-time staff.

Places to Eat – bottom end

For sitting and sipping, the teahouses on İskele Meydanı, near the castle, are the best places, though prices tend to be high due to the popular location. There are also numerous little teahouses along the promenade on Neyzen Tevfik Caddesi.

Walk along Kale Caddesi, the narrow shopping street which runs from the Adliye Camii to the castle. Turn left just after the Tütünbank into a narrow alley crowded with cheap tavernas. Long tables line the sides, and if the crowd is right – jolly without being raucous – it's a fine place for a drink and supper. The names are not particularly encouraging: *No Restaurant, Hades Restaurant*. But then, culinary excellence is hardly the point here.

For better cheap food, look for the little eateries in the bazaar, the grid of market streets just to the east of Adliye Camii. Most have signboards listing prices.

Hacı Baba'nin Yeri, just east of the Adliye Camii, serves döner kebap, pide and pizza that's not bad, but you can do better farther along. *Ziya'nin Yeri* is cheap and popular with locals as well as foreigners. Try their İnegöl köfte if you like rich meatballs; even richer is the kaşarlı variety, with cheese. The nearby *Üsküdarlı* and *Kardeşler* provide similar meals at similar prices at around US$3 per meal.

The *Durak Lokantası* (☎ 11880), just a few steps east of Adliye Camii, has equally cheap prices, as does the *Sakallı Köfteci*, ('Bearded Meatball-Maker') near the Garanti Bankası, serving full meals of grilled lamb meatballs, salad, bread and a drink for

US$3. The few outdoor tables here permit you to enjoy the market atmosphere as you eat.

Just east of the bazaar is Hilmi Uran Meydanı, called Kilise Meydanı (Church Square) by the locals; it once had an Orthodox church on its east side. Today Kilise Meydanı is chock-a-block with cheap cafés, snack shops, pidecis, restaurants and tavernas. The *Nazilli*, the *Şahin*, the *Anatolian* and the *Karadeniz* all serve cheap pide, kebaps, or hazır yemek and all have streetside seating areas. It's a good place for people-watching. Fresh pides and Italian-style pizzas are priced between US$1.50 and US$2.50. For very cheap eats, buy a dönerli sandviç (dur-nehr-LEE sahn-DVEECH, sandwich with roast lamb).

For breakfasts, try the *Karadeniz Börekçisi*, just east of the Karadeniz Restaurant at the eastern edge of Kilise Meydanı. Fresh, filling börek (flaky pastry with cheese) goes for US$1 a serving in the morning. Otherwise, for snacks or picnics, walk along Cumhuriyet Caddesi to the *Yunuslar Karadeniz Fırını* (Dolphins Black Sea Bakery), which has a good selection of breads, rolls and sweet treats. Try lokma, light spherical fritters dipped in syrup, sold in a paper cone.

Near the Kemer, Billûr and Aşkın pensions on Uslu Sokak, off Cumhuriyet Caddesi, is the *Hora Köftecisi*, a little streetside place serving up cheap meatball meals for US$2 or US$2.50. Follow Cumhuriyet Caddesi eastward, and just before the beach appears on the right-hand side you'll see the *06 Lokanta*, which takes its odd name from the motor vehicle licence plate prefix for Ankara. The 06 is a relic of Bodrum's simpler past: a cheap lokanta serving good hazır yemek (ready food) at low prices.

Places to Eat – middle

The best restaurants are out along the western bay on Neyzen Tevfik Caddesi. When dining in Bodrum, remember always to ask the price of fish, and choose those in season, as out-of-season fish are much more expensive than the already expensive seasonal ones. When in doubt, ask *Mevsimli mi?* (mehv-seem-LEE mee, Is it in season?).

Halfway between Adliye Camii and the Amphora Restaurant on Neyzen Tevfik Caddesi is the *Mauzolos Restaurant*, a modest place with a simple indoor dining room (used in winter), and an awning-shaded seaside open-air dining area across the street. The seaside tables are much more pleasant. Though they do serve meat here, the fish is usually delicious and reasonably priced, about US$10 to US$15 per person for a full three or four-course fish dinner with wine.

Kocadon Restaurant (☎ (13705; fax 15338), Neyzen Tevfik Caddesi 160, is Bodrum's best. Sheltered from the street by several atmospheric old stone houses, it fills a quiet courtyard. Soft music and lighting, good service, and Turkish and continental cuisine keep it busy every day. Try the revived Ottoman dishes, such as Hünkar Beğendi (with aubergines). You can pay from US$10 to US$20 per person all in, or choose the fixed-price menu at US$8, plus drinks and tip. Make reservations in high summer; it's open every day for dinner only.

Sapa Restaurant (☎ 12553, 13507), Külcüoğlu Sokak 6, is bit difficult to find, but worth the effort. Perhaps the simplest way to find it is to follow Türkkuyusu Sokak from the Adliye Camii to its end at the Pension Espri and turn right onto Külcü Sokak. The restaurant's door is 50 metres along on the right-hand side, and easy to miss. Secluded in a walled garden setting, Sapa is a delightful hideaway serving international cuisine. Expect to pay from US$10 to US$18 for a full meal you won't soon forget.

Café Sandal (☎ 15828), Neyzen Tevfik 132, is that rarest of things in Turkey, a good Thai-Chinese restaurant. Sit inside or at one of the open-air terrace tables and order vegetable mint curry, sweet-and-sour beef or fish, or prawn satay with peanut sauce. Full meals go for around US$10 to US$12.

Amphora Restaurant (☎ 12368) is at Neyzen Tevfik Caddesi 164, across from the yacht marina and near the Herodot Pansiyon on the western bay. It's a pleasant place with streetside tables under a broad awning and several inside dining rooms in an old, stone commercial building. Turkish carpets here and there add colour, and bits of seafaring equipment add visual interest to the décor. The clientele is drawn largely from the yachting crowd, who seem to want meat when they come ashore after days of cruising and eating fish, so the Amphora serves very little fish, though they do have fish soup. Grilled meats are the thing here, but start with a selection of mezes. You can expect to spend from US$7 to US$10 per person for a full dinner with wine or beer.

Ristorante Italiano (☎ 10792), Neyzen Tevfik Caddesi 196, a short distance past the Amphora, is a cheery place with streetside tables and decent Italian food for about US$10 to US$12 per person, all inclusive.

On the eastern bay along Cumhuriyet Caddesi, try the *İstanbul Restaurant*, at No 122, with tables set out along the water's edge overlooking the castle. The menu is Turkish with several concessions to international taste, and prices are moderate.

Entertainment

Bodrum has lots of entertainment; some would say too much. Staff at the famous Halikarnas Disco, on the eastern bay at the end of Cumhuriyet Caddesi, look you up and down for proper mod dress and take a cover charge of between US$8 to US$12 before admitting you to Turkey's classiest, loudest and most presumptuous disco. Inside it's like a Hollywood set, but with a laser light show most evenings.

If the Halikarnas is too rich for your blood or budget, stroll along Cumhuriyet Caddesi and drop in at one of the ever-changing clubs, lounges and bars. Another good place to look is along Neyzen Tevfik Caddesi on the western bay.

Getting There & Away

There are a few boat routes serving Bodrum, and a small commuter airline operates planes from İstanbul, but most transport is by bus. There is no rail service south of Söke.

Air The closest air service to Bodrum is at Imsık, 30 km to the north along the İzmir road. The nearest large airports to Bodrum are at İzmir, 220 km away, and Dalaman (near Fethiye), 220 km away. Muğla, the provincial capital, only 110 km from Bodrum, may get a sizeable airport soon.

Imsık Airways has small planes departing from Bodrum in the morning and afternoon to İzmir (US$50) and İstanbul (US$120). Also, an air taxi company called EmAir operates single-engine Cessna 172 and 206, and twin-engine Cessna 412C aircraft carrying from four to seven passengers between İstanbul and Imsık on weekends in summer. Prices are high, because this is basically an aircraft charter. In İstanbul contact EmAir at Atatürk Airport, Desk 16 in the Domestic Terminal (☎ (1) 574 4318, 573 7220 ext 2728); in Bodrum the office is at Neyzen Tevfik Caddesi 138/A (☎ 12100).

Bus As usual, Bodrum's bus service is frequent and far flung. Companies serving the Bodrum bus station include Aydın Turizm, Hakiki Koç, Kamil Koç, Karadeveci, Kontaş, Pamukkale and Varan. Here are some services; there are lots of others as well:

Ankara – 785 km, 13 hours, US$20; a dozen buses daily
Antalya – 640 km, 11 hours, US$20; one bus daily
Dalaman – 220 km, four hours, US$10; six buses daily
Fethiye – 265 km, 4½ hours, US$12; six buses daily
Gökova – 135 km, 2½ hours, US$8; Marmaris bus, then a dolmuş or hitch
İzmir – 250 km, four hours, US$8; buses at least every hour in summer
İstanbul – 830 km, 14 hours, US$17 to US$24; hourly buses in summer
Kaş – 400 km, six hours, US$11; Fethiye bus, then change
Konya – 750 km, 12 hours, US$22; one bus daily
Kuşadası – 151 km, 2½ hours, US$7; buses every half-hour in summer
Marmaris – 165 km, three hours, US$6.50; hourly buses in summer

Ören – 95 km, two hours, US$5; bus to Milas and change
Pamukkale – 310 km, five hours, US$11; two direct buses daily
Trabzon – 1565 km, 28 hours, US$30; one bus daily

Boat You can take boats to the Greek island of Kos, and to the Datça Peninsula west of Marmaris.

Ferries carry passengers and cars on the short voyage (less than an hour) to Kos at 9 am on Monday, Wednesday and Friday in summer, and on other days if demand warrants; return trips from Kos are at 5 pm. Make reservations and buy tickets at least a day in advance at the boat offices on İskele Meydanı, the square just beneath the castle walls, or farther along out by the harbour entrance. Fares are US$20 one way, US$24 same-day round trip, or US$40 open-date round trip. These prices include the Greek taxes of US$8 per person per trip.

Ferries between Bodrum and Datça, operate daily in summer, taking from 1½ to two hours, depending upon the boat. Passenger fares are US$8 one way, US$14 round trip; cars are carried as well for US$22. Buy your ticket at the boat ticket offices on the wharf near the Tourism Information Office beneath the castle. The ferry actually docks at Körmen on the peninsula's northern coast, then you drive 10 or 15 minutes due south to reach Datça.

BODRUM PENINSULA

If tourist-crowded Bodrum is not your cup of tea, escape to one of the little seaside villages on the Bodrum Peninsula. Volcanic action has produced a landscape of high hills, fantastical rock outcrops and wonderful scenery. It comes as a surprise to see so much traditional life in the midst of booming touristic modernisation, but in peninsula villages you may see local women wearing the traditional *şalvar* (pantaloons) and white headscarves or shawls. Donkeys laden with sticks for fuel plod stubbornly to the domed, beehive-shaped earthen ovens still used to bake bread and roast mutton. But the distinctive white-domed stone cisterns (*gümbet,* 'dome') are falling into ruin since the advent of electric and petrol-powered pumps and piping.

The slow, easy pace of life in the villages contrasts markedly with the crowded streets and noisy discos of cosmopolitan Bodrum. Although there are no really splendid beaches easily accessible on the peninsula, there are at least several serviceable ones.

Dolmuşes depart from Bodrum's bus station several times daily to all of these points.

Southern Shore

The southern shore of the peninsula has many small bays and inlets, but a number of them are being developed as tourist resorts, and the land behind the beaches is covered in construction. The beach at **Gümbet**, backed by lots of hotels and pensions, with more being built, is only a five-km, 10-minute ride from Bodrum; or you can walk to Gümbet in about 45 minutes over the hills west of the yacht marina. It has numerous restaurants to provide sustenance.

West of Gümbet, past the next peninsula, are the bays of **Bitez Yalısı** and **Ortakent Yalısı**, backed by white hotels, resort villas and holiday villages, but still offering good swimming possibilities. At Bitez Yalısı there's a windsurfing school. At Ortakent Yalısı there are numerous small pensions, including the *Erkal Bahçe Pansiyon*, the *Nautilus Pansiyon & Camping*, the *Zeferya Motel & Camping* and several restaurants including the *Ökaliptus Restaurant & Camping* and the *Yalım Restaurant*.

From Ortakent Yalısı you must travel inland to continue your circuit of the peninsula, as there is not a coastal road yet. Take a dolmuş to Ortakent, 13 km west of Bodrum, then via Gürece to Akçaalan, where you can hitch south to **Akyarlar**, 30 km from Bodrum. This is a pretty village, formerly inhabited by Ottoman Greeks, with a narrow beach, several little pensions and hotels and a small yacht and fishing port. It's something like Bodrum was a half century ago. Just east of Akyarlar is **Karaincir**, a similar cove with a beach, hotels, a few pensions and a holiday village. East of here there are dirt roads leading to more holiday villages.

Western Shore

Following the coastal road west and north from Akyarlar brings you to **Akçabük**, where there is another pretty cove and beach. North of Akçabük all the way to Turgutreis the coast is covered in Turkish holiday villages. Most of these are reserved for employees of large government organisations such as the various ministries and the PTT.

The newly developed town of **Turgutreis** (toor GOOT-reh-yeess), 20 km west of Bodrum, has a nice beach, many little hotels, pensions, and restaurants. Dolmuşes run frequently between Turgutreis and Bodrum. The town, formerly known as Karatoprak, was renamed for the Turkish admiral Turgut Reis (died 1560) who was born here. A statue of the admiral stands south of the town on the shore.

From Turgutreis, an unpaved road goes north along the shore to **Kadıkalesi**, a sleepy little village on the water with several small pension-restaurants. You can camp here as well. The village has an old fortress, cistern, disused church, a few big old trees and new condominium developments.

Farther north is **Gümüşlük**, reachable by direct dolmuş from Bodrum. The village has a few little pensions and fish restaurants, a fine beach and, on the rocky islet south of the hamlet, the ruins (some underwater) of ancient **Mindos**. All vehicles are stopped at a car park 100 metres from the beach to preserve the village's tranquillity.

As you walk down to the beach you'll see several restaurants to your right (north): *Tertib'in Yeri*, the *Yacht Club*, the *Teras* and the *Batı*, with tables set out by the water. To the left (south) are several small hotels and pensions, and also a few more restaurants. The *Gümüşlük Motel* has simple rooms with balconies. The restaurants include the *Batık Şehri* (Sunken City), which also has rooms to rent, *Nazim'in Yeri*, the *Mindos* and the *Siesta*. The *Fenerci Pansiyon & Restaurant* (☎ (614) 71420/51), out on the point, has a

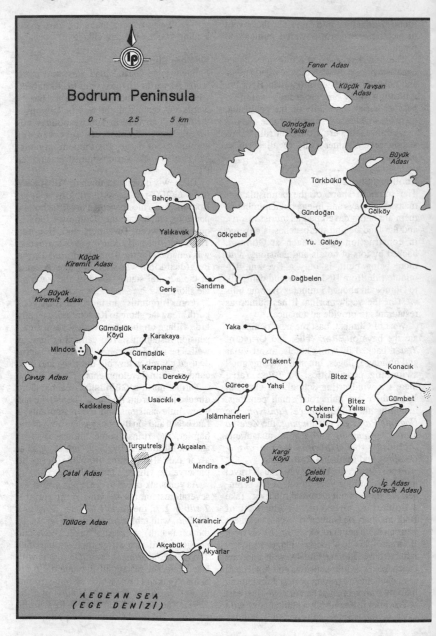

Bodrum Peninsula

0   2.5   5 km

Fener Adası
Küçük Tavşan Adası
Gündoğan Yalısı
Büyük Adası
Türkbükü
Bahçe
Yalıkavak
Gökçebel
Gündoğan
Gölköy
Yu. Gölköy
Küçük Kiremit Adası
Geriş
Sandıma
Dağbelen
Büyük Kiremit Adası
Gümüşlük Köyü
Karakaya
Yaka
Mindos
Gümüslük
Ortakent
Konacık
Çavuş Adası
Karapınar
Dereköy
Bitez
Gürece
Yahşi
Gümbet
Kadıkalesi
Usacıklı
Bitez Yalısı
Ortakent Yalısı
İslâmhaneleri
Turgutreis
Akçaalan
Kargı Köyü
Çelebi Adası
Çatal Adası
Mandıra
Bağla
İç Adası (Gürecik Adası)
Tülluce Adası
Karaincir
Akçabük
Akyarlar

A E G E A N   S E A
(E G E   D E N İ Z İ)

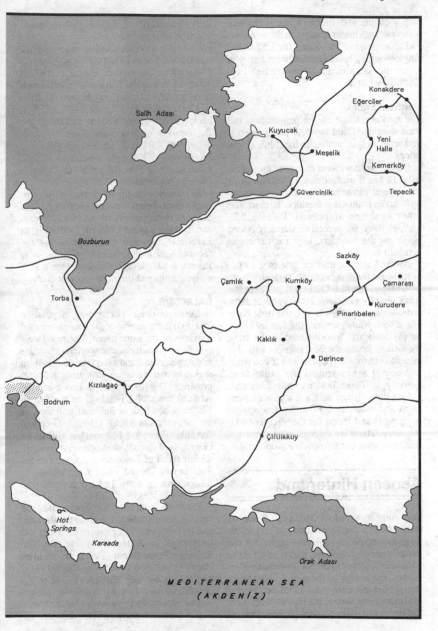

nice location and rooms without running water but with insect screens on the windows and nice views of the water, for US$8/12 a single/double, breakfast included. If you want the simple, laid-back, quiet life, Gümüşlük has it.

Northern Shore

The northern shore of the peninsula is the least developed and the best place to go if you want simple, authentic local life at low prices.

On the north-western corner of the peninsula, 18 km from Bodrum, is **Yalıkavak**. It has several old windmills, a village square with taxis, teahouses, tractors, farmers and other evidence of normal Turkish life. Though there are several moderately priced hotels on the outskirts, look for the cheap pensions in town.

Arrayed along a perfect little bay, 17 km north of Bodrum, is the small Turkish village of **Gölköy**. It's like Gümüşlük without the ruins. Family pensions accommodate most arrivals, though there is also the little *Sahil Motel* with pretty gardens, and fancier hotels on the outskirts. Wooden boat docks serve the fishing boats; the boat owners will also take you out for short excursions if you wish.

About 1.5 km around the point from Gölköy is **Türkbükü**, another beautiful, simple little village with a few modest pensions and motels, a PTT and a few simple restaurants and shops for the yachters who stop here. There are signs of more construction of course, but for now it's wonderful.

Aegean Hinterland

The Aegean coast is Turkey's foremost tourist mecca. The cities farther inland, in the Aegean hinterland, have less appeal for the casual holiday visitor, but plenty to offer the adventurous traveller. As everywhere in Turkey, the history of these hinterland cities is involved and eventful. Unlike the Aegean coast towns, however, the inland cities offer the interested visitor a look at real Turkish daily life and culture, without the overheated prices of the resorts.

For most travellers, Balıkesir is a transit point, but if you need to stay the night you'll find it interesting enough. Eskişehir, 150 km south of Bursa, is Turkey's meerschaum mining centre. The soft white stone is artistically carved into bracelets, earrings, necklaces, cigarette holders, and of course the famous meerschaum pipes. A short detour of 90 km south-east of Eskişehir brings you to Kütahya, a pleasant historic town which is now the centre of Turkey's faïence (coloured-tile) industry.

Afyon, the centre of Turkey's government-controlled opium industry, is a pleasant town famous for its clotted cream and Turkish delight (lokum). Denizli is an industrial city and transit point for the famous spa at Pamukkale. Eğirdir, near Isparta, is a relatively untouristed town with a pretty setting at the edge of a vast lake.

BALIKESİR

Balıkesir (altitude 147 metres, population 200,000) is the capital of the triangle-shaped province of the same name. The province's odd shape gives it coastlines on the Marmara and Aegean seas, and a mountainous eastern region bordering on neighbouring Kütahya province. The resort town of Erdek and the railhead town of Bandırma, on the Sea of Marmara, are both in Balıkesir province, as are the resorts at Akçay, Edremit, Ören and Ayvalık. There are historic hot springs at Gönen, used since Roman times. At Sındırgı, 63 km south of Balıkesir town, the famous Yağcıbeydir Turkish carpets are woven by descendants of early Turkish nomads who came to this area from Central Asia.

Balıkesir is at least 5000 years old, and was known as Palaeokastron to the Romans and Byzantines. Though there are a few old buildings in Balıkesir, including the **Zağanos Paşa Camii** (1461), the **Yıldırım Camii** (1388), the **Umur Bey Camii** (1412) and the **Karesi Bey Türbesi** (1336), this is not really a touristic town. No doubt you will just be passing through on the bus or train.

For answers to questions, contact the

Tourism Directorate (☎ (661) 11820, 17611, 10505), Gazi Bulvarı, Kamil Bey Apt 27.

There are numerous cheap hotels near the bus station. The best hotel rated by the Ministry of Tourism is the two-star *İmanoğlu Hotel* (☎ (661) 17144), on Örücüler Caddesi. It's a 36-room place charging US$24/30 a single/double for its rooms.

ESKİŞEHİR

Though first settled by the Phrygians 3000 years ago, Eskişehir (altitude 788 metres, population 500,000) is today a modern city despite its name which translates as 'Old City'. The scant ruins of Graeco-Roman Dorylaeum, which earlier occupied this place, lie mostly beneath modern buildings.

Dorylaeum and Eskişehir have this in common: they both stand at an important transit point in the natural routes from north, south, east and west. Perhaps because of its central location, Eskişehir is important to the railways, as both a transfer point and as Turkey's major manufacturer of railway locomotives and carriages. And perhaps because of the railways, there are thriving cement, sugar, textile and other industries. The city is also home to a large Turkish airforce base (you'll hear the crack and whoosh of fighter jets as they thunder overhead) and the quieter Anatolia University (Anadolu Üniversitesi).

Eskişehir is dusty in summer and muddy in winter. But its pleasant riverside promenade with streetside cafés in the city centre, and its bustling market make it interesting enough for a short overnight stop. Be sure to try the local *nuga helvası* (nougat), on sale at the many confectioners' shops in the otogar.

Orientation

The city centre is easily negotiated on foot. Hotels, restaurants, banks and other services are all within a few minutes' walk of the otogar, and just a bit farther from the railway station, which is north-west of the centre.

Information

The provincial authorities sponsor the local tourist office (☎ (22) 10 17 52), in the Vilayet (provincial government headquarters) at İki Eylül Caddesi 175, which has little to offer beyond a basic map.

Meerschaum

Most tourists pass through Eskişehir on the bus or the train, but those who shop are usually looking for meerschaum (German for 'sea foam', *lületaşı* in Turkish). This soft, light, porous white stone, a hydrous magnesium silicate called sepiolite by mineralogists, is mined at numerous villages east of Eskişehir, including Başören, Karahöyük (Karatepe), Kemikli, Kozlubel Köyü, Nemli, Sarısıva, Sepetçi Köyü, Söğütçük and Yarmalar. Eskişehir has the world's largest and most easily accessible deposits, though meerschaum is also found near Madrid in Spain, in France's Seine-et-Marne, in the Crimea, in Kenya, and in the US states of Pennsylvania, South Carolina and Utah.

Miners are lowered into vertical shafts which penetrate the meerschaum beds to depths from 10 to 150 metres. The miners fill buckets with heavy mud, which is hauled to the surface, dumped and sluiced, revealing rough chunks of meerschaum. It's dark, dirty, dangerous work. There are no veins where large blocks can be cut. The larger the chunk, the higher its value.

Though once pulverised and used as tooth powder, meerschaum is now used for carving. While the stone is still wet and as soft as soap, carvers in the villages and in Eskişehir work it into fanciful shapes and decorative objects, most of which are exported. Block meerschaum was also exported until 1979, when someone figured out that to export the material was to export the carving jobs as well. Now it is illegal to export block meerschaum. Prayer beads, necklaces, belts, earrings, baubles and cigarette-holders are common items, but the most popular item by far is the meerschaum pipe.

A good carver can make about four pipes a day. More elaborate pieces can take a week. Meerschaum pipes are valued because the strong, light, porous material smokes cool and sweet, drawing off the burning tobacco's heat and some of the tar. Devoted meerschaum smokers wear special gloves while smoking to protect their prized pipes from tarnish by skin oils. With time, a coddled pipe will take on an even nut-brown patina that is highly valued by devotees.

You can view carvers at work and buy their art in Eskişehir Monday to Saturday from 9 am to about 7 pm at Işık Pipo (☎ 13 87 02), Sakarya Caddesi, Konya İşhanı 12/17; and Pipo Burhan Yücel, both in the city centre near the Büyük Otel. Burhan Yücel also has a shop in the collection of shops beneath the otogar.

Meerschaum Mining Villages Those truly fascinated by meerschaum may want to visit the mining villages of **Sepetçi Köyü** and **Kozlubel**. Sepetçi, obviously more prosperous than its neighbours with its tidy white houses with windows trimmed in blue, has recently changed its name to Beyaz Altın (White Gold) in honour of its most valuable commodity. There are poultry and grain farmers here as well, but 85% of the village's wealth comes from meerschaum.

There are no services in the village, but if you ask for Mr Bülent Girgin, he will take you to his prominent carving workshop at the eastern edge of the village, and even show you a mining pit *(lületaşı ocağı)* farther east if you wish.

Transport can be difficult without your own vehicle. Ask at the otogar for the minibus to Yakakayı, which sometimes proceeds beyond its primary destination to Sepetçi. If you have wheels, drive north-east from Eskişehir on the road to Alpu as far as Çavlum (18.5 km), then turn left (north) and go via Kızılcaören, Yakakayı and Gündüzler to Sepetçi/Beyaz Altın (40 km) and, six km beyond it, to Kozlubel.

Festivals

The International White Gold Festival is held in Eskişehir and surrounding villages in the 3rd week in September. Meerschaum (the 'white gold') is celebrated with art, photo and craft exhibitions, football (soccer) matches, musical performances and folk dances.

Places to Stay

There's no problem finding a good, convenient room at the right price. You're probably best off staying right near the otogar as the hotels in the city centre are even noisier.

The main street running north-south in front of the otogar is Yunusemre Caddesi. Come out of the otogar, turn left, and the street on the otogar's south side is Asarcıklı Caddesi. *Otel Beşik* (☎ (22) 11 28 43), Asarcıklı Caddesi, Sanayi Sokak 1-F, is clean, proper and cheap at US$5/8 a single/double without running water.

Even cheaper is the *Görgün Oteli* (☎ & fax (22) 11 24 57), Yunusemre Caddesi 111-B, just north across the bridge on the left-hand side, above the hardware store of the same name. It's plain but tidy, charging US$6 for a waterless double. In addition, there are many small, cheap hotels in and around the market.

The two-star *Emek Otel* (☎ (22) 11 29 40), Yunusemre Caddesi, adjoins the otogar on its north side. Though well worn, it's serviceable and friendly. Rooms with bath go for US$12/16 a single/double; breakfast costs US$1.75 more.

Across Yunusemre Caddesi from the otogar are three more two-star hotels: the older but cheaper the *Otel Dural* (☎ (22) 13 30 60) at No 97, charging US$14 a double with sink, US$18 with private shower; the *Soyiç Hotel* (☎ (22) 10 71 90) at No 101, newer and very friendly, charging US$24 for a double with bath; and the *Porsuk Otel* (☎ (22) 11 50 05), at No 103, newest in this area and quite comfy at US$26 a double.

In the city centre at the confluence of İnönü, Cengiz Topel, Sakarya, Muttalip and Sivrihisar caddesis (in the district called Köprübaşı) are two more hotels. *Büyük Otel* (☎ (22) 11 12 46), Sivrihisar Caddesi 40, is an older three-star place charging US$28 a double with bath and breakfast. Avoid the noisy front rooms.

Otel Şale (☎ (22) 11 41 44), İsmet İnönü Caddesi 17/1, across the street from the prominent Ordu Evi (ask for that to find the hotel) above the Tütünbank, is central but quite noisy. It charges US$12/17 for a single/double room with shower.

Places to Eat

For a quick, good, cheap kebap, leave the otogar, cross Yunusemre Caddesi and walk along the polluted river to the *Uğurlu Lokanta ve Kebap Salonu* (☎ 12 09 38), where soup, pilav and etli nohut (chickpeas with lamb in a tomato sauce), bread and water cost only US$2.25. It's quieter here than at the kebap places on Yunusemre Caddesi.

Getting There & Away

As Eskişehir is an important stop on the İstanbul-Ankara line, there is frequent train service to those cities throughout the day and night. (See the Getting Around chapter for information on the major train services.) Bus service is equally convenient and includes the following services:

Ankara – 230 km, 3¼ hours, US$8; hourly
Bursa – 155 km, 2½ hours, US$5.50; hourly
İstanbul – 310 km, 4½ hours, US$10; hourly
Konya – 420 km, six hours, US$14; several direct buses, or change at Afyon
Kütahya – 91 km, 1¼ hours, US$2.50; hourly

KÜTAHYA

In the midst of hill country, Kütahya (population 150,000, altitude 949 metres) is a small city famous for the manufacture of coloured tiles. It's spread beneath the walls of an imposing hilltop fortress. Not far away is the Temple of Zeus at Aizanoi, the best-preserved Roman temple in Anatolia.

History

No one knows for sure when Kütahya was founded; its earliest known inhabitants were Phrygians. In 546 BC it was captured by the Persians, and then saw the usual succession of rulers, from Alexander the Great to the kings of Bithynia, to the emperors of Rome and Byzantium, who called the town Cotyaeum.

The first Turks to arrive were the Seljuks, in 1182. They were later pushed out by the crusaders, but they returned to found the Emirate of Germiyan (1302-1428), with Kütahya as its capital. The emirs cooperated with the Ottomans in nearby Bursa, and upon the death of the last emir, his lands were incorporated in the growing Ottoman Empire. When Tamerlane swept in at the beginning of the 15th century, he upset everyone's applecart, made Kütahya his headquarters for a while and then went back to where he came from.

As an Ottoman province, Kütahya settled down to tile-making. After Selim I took Tabriz in 1514, he brought all of its ceramic artisans to Kütahya and İznik, and set them to work. The two towns rivalled one another in the excellence of their faïence.

After the collapse of the 1848 Hungarian revolution, the great leader Lajos Kossuth fled to the Ottoman Empire, where he was given refuge and settled in Kütahya for a short time. His house is now a museum.

During the Turkish War of Independence, Greek armies pushed inland from İzmir, occupied Kütahya and threatened the fledgling republican government at Ankara. Twice the Greek advance was checked by the Turks at the village of İnönü, north-east of Kütahya, but the invading forces finally broke through and took Eskişehir and Afyon. On 26 August 1922, the Turkish forces began a bold and risky counterattack, breaking through the Greek defences along the valley of Dumlupınar, due south of Kütahya, near the highway from İzmir to Afyon. In the battle for the valley, half of the Greek expeditionary force was annihilated or imprisoned, while the other half was soon beating a hasty retreat towards İzmir. The Dumlupınar victory (30 August 1922) was the turning point in the war.

When you arrive in the main square, you can see what this town does for a living. There before you, in the middle of a traffic roundabout, is a huge coloured-pottery vase in a circular fountain. You'll see faïence (coloured tiles) used everywhere, on façades of buildings, in floors and walls, and in some

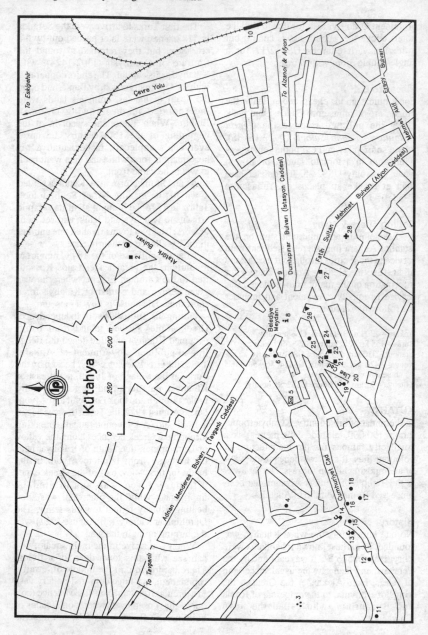

Kütahya

unexpected places. Every year scholars come here from many countries to attend the International Faïence & Ceramics Congress. The Dumlupınar Fuarı, held each year in the fairgrounds of the same name not far from the otogar, is Turkey's largest handicraft fair. Besides decorative tiles, Kütahya's factories turn out industrial ceramics such as water pipes and conduits.

Orientation
After the confusing layouts of İstanbul and Bursa, Kütahya's uncomplicated street plan is a joy. The roundabout with the vase in the fountain is the city's main square, called Belediye Meydanı, with the Vilayet (the provincial government headquarters) here as well. The bus station, called the Kütahya Çinigar ('Tile-Garage') is less than one km (north-east) from Belediye Meydanı; go out the otogar's front gateway (which is tiled, naturally), turn right and walk straight on to reach Belediye Meydanı. There are lots of good hotels, restaurants and tile shops within 100 metres of the square.

The town's main commercial street is Cumhuriyet Caddesi, which goes south-west from the Vilayet building on Belediye Meydanı. Follow it to find the post office.

Information
Kütahya's local information office (☎ (231) 31962) is in the Vilayet building on Belediye Meydanı, up one flight. In summer an information kiosk in the park just east of Belediye Meydanı is sometimes open. Kütahya's postal code is 43000.

Things to See
You can find Kütahya pottery in any souvenir shop in Turkey, but the shops in the city's bazaar have the widest selection and the lowest prices. Surprisingly, tile shops are not the city's proudest feature. Rather, Kütahyans pride themselves on the old houses, picturesque places of wood and stucco found in several old neighbourhoods near Belediye Meydanı. The city hosts a Historic Turkish Houses week each year. Many of the buildings have been beautifully restored, among them the Kossuth Evi, where Lajos Kossuth lived while in Kütahya.

Kütahya Museum
The best way to see what there is to see in town is to follow signs from Belediye Meydanı along Cumhuriyet Caddesi, the town's main commercial street, to the Kütahya Museum (Kütahya Müzesi), 750 metres from Belediye Meydanı. It's open from 8 am to noon and 1.30 to 5.30 pm, closed on Monday; admission costs 50c. The museum is in the Vacidiye Medresesi, built by Umur bin Savcı of the princely family of

Germiyan in 1314. It's worth a visit for the building alone, which has been nicely restored, with a beautiful central dome, now closed by a glass light, over a central marble pool. The museum exhibits are the usual collection, from Chalcolithic to Ottoman, including finds from the precincts of the great Temple of Zeus at Aizanoi (see the following).

Great Mosque & Bazaar

The Great Mosque (Ulu Cami), adjoining the Vacidiye Medresesi, was built in 1410, and restored several times later, including during this century. It's surrounded by Kütahya's colourful bazaar, in which you might stumble upon the **Kavaflar Pazarı**, a 16th-century market building; the **İshak Fakih Camii** (1434) and the **İmaret Mescidi** (1440), a former medrese.

Kossuth Evi

Walk around behind the Ulu Cami and follow the signs to the Kossuth Evi (Kossuth House), also called the Macar Evi (Hungarian House), 250 metres more or less straight on up the slope; look for the house on the left, marked by plaques in Turkish and Hungarian.

Lajos Kossuth (1802-94) was a prominent member of the Hungarian parliament. In 1848, chafing at Hapsburg rule from Vienna, he and others rose in revolt, declaring Hungary an independent republic in 1849. When Russian troops intervened on the side of the Austrians, he was forced to flee, was welcomed to the Ottoman domains, and lived in Kütahya in 1850-51.

His house, beautifully restored, is open from 8 am to noon and 1.30 to 5.30 pm, closed on Monday; admission costs 50c. It's a virtual ethnographic museum, with its perfectly preserved kitchen, dining room, bedroom, and Kossuth's office, showing how an upper-class Kütahyan lived in the mid-1800s.

Kütahya Fortress

Continue past the Kossuth House and watch for signs to the kale to find your way to the top of the hill and Kütahya's fortress. The western walls are still standing, the eastern ones are mostly ruined. Built originally by the Byzantines, the castle was restored and used by their successors, the Selçuks, the emirs of Germiyan, and the Ottomans. A few traces of buildings can be seen, but mostly one comes up here for the hike and the view.

Places to Stay

As tourism has yet to hit Kütahya, the range of lodgings is limited, but usually adequate.

On the south-west side of the Belediye building, to the left of the Hotel Gül Palas and the TZDK (Türkiye Zirai Donatım Kurumu) building is the *Güneş Oteli* (☎ (231) 20848). It's tidy, central, fairly quiet, and charges only US$7 for a waterless double room. *Hotel Yüksel 2* (☎ (231) 20111), Belediye Meydanı 1, is clean and central, though hardly fancy, charging US$9 for a waterless double.

The town's old standards are the old-fashioned *Gül Palas 1* (☎ (231) 11759, 11233), Belediye Meydanı, and newer *Gül Palas 2* (☎ 12325), on Lise Caddesi, just around the corner. Both hotels have lifts and simple sagging but serviceable rooms with showers going for US$12/17 a single/double. In some rooms, the shower is a 'phone' attached to the sink faucet. Gül Palas 1 has seen better days, but offers views of the square. Gül Palas 2 is newer and also quieter. Staff at both are as yet unjaded by tourists, and thus are quite eager to please.

In between the two Gül Palas hotels is the *Otel Köşk* (☎ (231) 30644), Belediye Önü, Lise Caddesi 1, offering simple double rooms with sinks for US$7.50.

Hotel Erbaylar (☎ (231) 36960; fax 11046), Afyon Caddesi 14, is a modern, three-star, 42-room place which is simple but quite comfortable. All rooms have solid-colour carpeting, bedspreads and drapes, private baths (without any Kütahya tiles), and some rooms have TVs with satellite hook-ups receiving US programmes. There's a restaurant and the Çini Bar (Faïence Bar). Posted rates are US$40/55 a single/double, but unless it's nearly full you will pay from 25 to 35% less. Breakfast costs extra.

The 52-room *Hotel Bakır Sözer* (☎ (231) 15027; fax 12874), Çinigar Caddesi, on the south side of the otogar, is a few years newer than the Erbaylar and a few dollars cheaper. All rooms have private showers, and cost US$16/28 a single/double, a bit more if you want a TV set in your room.

Places to Eat

The *Hotel Erbaylar* has the poshest dining in town. For cheaper meals, try the very decent restaurant in the otogar, or *Çınar Köfte* (☎ 11130), Lise Caddesi 7, near the Hotel Gül Palas 2 and the Otel Köşk. Köfte, soup, salad, bread and beverage are yours for US$3. Beneath the Otel Köşk is the *Cumhuriyet Lokantası*, a dependably good eatery. Also good is *Restaurant Çinili International* (☎ 13879), Afyon Caddesi 2, a white-tablecloth place only a few steps from the vase fountain on Belediye Meydanı. Try the İskender (Dursa) kebap, with soup, salad and soft drink. The bill will come to less than US$5.

On the north-east side of Belediye Meydanı across Dumlupınar Bulvarı and Fatih Caddesi are several other good kebapçıs and a pastry shop. For fresh fruit, vegetables and picnic supplies, browse through the open-air market one block south up the hill on Lise Caddesi from Çınar Köfte and the Hotel Gül Palas 2.

Getting There & Away

The bus station Kütahya Çinigar has an emanet (left luggage/checkroom). Because Kütahya is a provincial capital, its otogar supports fairly busy traffic. Here are details on bus trips from Kütahya to:

Afyon – 100 km, under two hours, US$4; many buses daily
Aizanoi – see Çavdarhisar
Ankara – 315 km, five hours, US$9; a dozen buses daily
Antalya – 375 km, eight hours, US$14; a few buses daily in summer, fewer in winter
Bursa – 190 km, three hours, US$8; a dozen buses daily

Çavdarhisar – 60 km, one hour, US$2; take a Gediz or Emet minibus and get out at Çavdarhisar
Eskişehir – 91 km, 1¼ hours, US$2.50; very frequent buses daily
İstanbul – 355 km, six hours, US$11; a dozen buses daily
İzmir – 385 km, six hours, US$11; a dozen buses daily
Konya (via Afyon) – 335 km, five hours, US$13; several direct buses, or change at Afyon

AIZANOI (ÇAVDARHİSAR)

Aizanoi (or Aezani), 60 km south-west of Kütahya, is the site of Anatolia's best-preserved Roman temple. The Temple of Zeus (or Jupiter) dates from the reign of Hadrian (117-38 AD), and was dedicated to the worship of Zeus and also the Anatolian fertility goddess Cybele (Artemis, Diana).

Hours are officially from 9 am to noon and 1 to 5 pm, but in fact there is no fence and the guard, Mr Nazim Ertaş, will find you after you arrive to sell you a ticket for US$1. He will also take you down to the sanctuary of Cybele beneath the temple and open the locked gate so you can see the goddess's special prayer place.

The temple stands on a broad terrace built to hold it, and which served as the temple precinct. Like some ancient Hollywood set, the north and west faces of the temple have their double rows of columns intact, but the south and east rows are fallen in a picturesque jumble. The three columns at the north-east corner were toppled by the disastrous Gediz earthquake of 1970, but have been re-erected. The cella (interior) walls are intact enough to give you a good picture of the whole. It is quite impressive. On the north-west edge of the temple precinct is a wire enclosure holding some of the best bits of sculpture found at the site.

From the height of the temple you can survey the surrounding gardens and fields to see bits of the other Roman and Byzantine ruins, including the easily identifiable but badly ruined amphitheatre 800 metres to the north. Elsewhere in the town and surrounding fields and orchards are ruins of the main baths (off to the north-west), a smaller baths with some surviving mosaics (near the minaret); a stadium between the temple and the amphitheatre; and an old Roman bridge.

Getting There & Away

The town of Çavdarhisar (population 4100) is on the Kütahya-Uşak road. Take a Gediz or Emet minibus from Kütahya's Çinigar (one hour, US$2), which will follow the Afyon road for 10 km, then turn right (west) on the road marked for Aezani, Uşak and Gediz for another 50 km. The Temple of Zeus is 800 metres north-west of the Kütahya-Uşak road along the road to Emet.

Çavdarhisar has a few very basic lodgings and eateries, good only for emergencies. You may be able to get permission to camp somewhere at the edge of the village, but there are no facilities except at the fuel stations and the toilets at the temple. If you have questions, ask at the Belediye, at the main crossroads in the town centre.

The best way to visit Aizanoi from Kütahya is to start early in the morning and bring a picnic to eat at the ruins. When you arrive in Çavdarhisar, ask about return minibuses to Kütahya or onward minibuses to Gediz (37 km) and Uşak (65 km more), from whence you can easily catch a bus to Afyon, Ankara, Denizli/Pamukkale, İzmir, Konya or Manisa.

AFYON

Formerly called Afyonkarahisar (The Black Fortress of Opium), this workaday agricultural and carpet-weaving town (population 100,000, altitude 1015 metres), capital of the province of the same name, hardly lives up to its sinister moniker. There is indeed a steep hill, crowned with a fortress, in the historic centre of town. This is still an important region for producing legal opium for legitimate pharmaceutical use. But Afyon's claim to fame among Turks is its kaymak or clotted cream.

The story is this: Afyon's opium farmers never used the stuff themselves, but they used every other part of the plant. The juice was made into opium, the seeds were sprinkled on bread and pastries, the tender leaves were good in salads and the left-over plants

Opium Flowers

were fed to the cattle. The cattle became very, very contented and produced rich cream in abundance.

The clotted cream became famous perched on top of a serving of *kadayıf* (crumpet in syrup), used in baklava, or even stuffed in lokum (Turkish delight). Whether it was the clotted cream which inspired locals to become confectioners is anybody's guess, but today you will see dozens of *şekerleme* (confectioners') shops in the town centre and at the otogar.

Today the opium – more than a third of the world's legal crop – is grown by the 'poppy straw' method, which is easier to police and control. The young plants are cut down before the narcotic sap begins to flow, and the 'straw' is processed in special government-operated factories. But the local cattle still seem to be contented.

Afyon is also important to the marble-cutting industry, with numerous marble factories on the outskirts.

History

As with so many Anatolian towns, Afyon's history starts some 3000 years ago. After occupation by the Hittites, Phrygians, Lydians and Persians, Afyon was settled by the Romans and then the Byzantines, who called the town Akroenos, and later Nikopolis. Following the Selçuk victory at Manzikert (Malazgirt) in 1071, Afyon passed into the control of the Selçuk Turks. The important Selçuk vizier Sahip Ata took direct control of the town, and it was called

Karahisar-i Sahip even through Ottoman times (1428-1923).

During the War of Independence, Greek expeditionary forces occupied the town during their push towards Ankara. During the Battle of the Sakarya, in late August 1921, within earshot of Ankara, the republican armies under Mustafa Kemal (Atatürk) stopped the invading force in one of the longest pitched battles in history. The Greek forces retreated and dug in for the winter near Eskişehir and Afyon.

On 26 August 1922 the Turkish forces began their counteroffensive, achieving complete surprise and advancing rapidly on the startled Greek army. Within days Kemal had set up his headquarters in Afyon's Belediye building, and had surrounded half of the Greek army at Dumlupınar, 40 km to the west. The Battle of the Commander-in-Chief, as it was to be known, destroyed the Greek expeditionary army as a fighting force, and sent its survivors storming towards İzmir, where they would flee to ships waiting in the harbour.

Orientation

The main square, called Hükümet Meydanı, is at the north-east foot of the citadel, at the intersection of Ordu Bulvarı and Bankalar (or Eski İzmir) Caddesi. You'll know it by its fountain. About 250 metres east of it is another traffic roundabout, the starting point for Ambar Yolu (which goes north-east two km to the otogar) among other streets. Almost everything important is on or just off Bankalar Caddesi between the two traffic roundabouts, including the post office, several hotels, restaurants, and the local hamam. The railway station is two km from the centre, at the northern end of Ordu Bulvarı. Minibuses connect both the gar (railway station) and the otogar (bus terminus) to the centre.

Information

The local tourism office (☎ (491) 15271), Ordu Bulvarı 22, is near the high school (Lise) a few blocks north of Hükümet Meydanı on the right-hand side. Opening hours are from 9 am to 5 pm Monday to Friday. Afyon's postal code is 03000.

Historic Mosques

The finest of the historic mosques in the centre is the **İmaret Camii**, just east of the traffic roundabout at the eastern end of Bankalar Caddesi. Built on the orders of Gedik Ahmet Paşa in 1472, it has an interesting design which shows the transition from Selçuk to Ottoman style. The spiral-fluted minaret is decorated with blue tiles in an excellent state of preservation. The entrance on the northern side is like an eyvan, or large niche, which leads to a main sanctuary topped by two domes, front and back. A shady park with fountain provides a peaceful refuge from bustling Bankalar Caddesi. The mosque's medrese, now the city's Ethnographic Museum, is on the south side; its hamam (still in use) is nearer to the busy traffic roundabout.

The **Ulu Cami** or Great Mosque, is in the warren of narrow streets on the south-east side of the fortress hill. Dating from 1273, it is one of the most important remaining examples of the Selçuk architectural style which used brick construction supported by carved wooden columns and beams. Its brick minaret is decorated with green tiles.

Not far away is the **Mevlevi Camii**, next to which is the Afyonkarahisar Mevlevihanesi, or dervish meeting-place, both dating from Selçuk times (1200s). Sultan Veled, son of Celaleddin Rumi, the founder of the Mevlevi (Whirling Dervish) order, established Afyon as the second most important Mevlevi centre in the empire. The mosque has twin domes and a pyramidal roof above its courtyard. The Mevlevihane, once used for the *sema* (whirling ceremony) is now a museum of Mevlevi life. Ask at the mosque for someone to let you in.

Citadel

Near the Ulu Cami is the beginning of a long flight of steps leading up to the citadel, 226 metres high. Despite its eventful history (or perhaps because of it), there is little to see in the enclosure itself. The first fortress here is thought to have been built by the Hittite king Mursil II circa 1350 BC, and elaborated upon by every conqueror ever since.

Archaeology Museum

Afyon's modern museum, 1.5 km east of Bankalar Caddesi along Kurtuluş Caddesi (the eastward continuation of Bankalar Caddesi) near İnönü Caddesi, is open from 9 am to 5.30 pm for 75c. The Roman collection is particularly nice.

Places to Stay

Afyon's hotels are mostly old fashioned, a bit dowdy, and certainly overpriced.

Otel Mesut (☎ (491) 20429), Dumlupınar 2. Cadde No 5, on the west side of the post office a half-block north of Bankalar Caddesi, offers perhaps the cheapest good rooms at the very centre. Clean, quiet accommodation costs US$16 a double with shower here. There are several even cheaper hotels farther along this street as well.

Otel Afyon Palas (☎ (491) 17429), Dumlupınar 15, one street west of the Mesut and just around the corner from the Otel Oruçoğlu, is clean, cheap and quietish, charging US$5/7 a single/double in waterless rooms.

Otel Oruçoğlu (☎ (491) 20120, -1, -2; fax 31313), Bankalar Caddesi, facing Hükümet Meydanı on the corner of Ordu Bulvarı, is well used but serviceable, with a decent dining room. Rooms with private shower rent for US$16/23/33 a single/double/triple.

Hotel Ece (☎ (491) 16070; fax 16265), Ordu Bulvarı 2, around the corner, is a 39-room, nominally two-star place charging US$20/25 a single/double, but open to haggling if business is slow. It's the best place in town at this writing, but that's not saying a lot.

Places to Eat

Follow the little streets south from Hükümet Meydanı towards the fortress hill and you'll easily find a number of good, cheap little restaurants where a good meal of soup, kebap or stew and pilav will cost less than

US$3. For slightly fancier dining, try the two top hotels, the Ece and the Oruçoğlu.

Don't forget to pop into one of the local şekerleme (confectioners' shops) for a taste of Afyon's famous lokum. Usually there are free samples to be had (point to something and say *Denelim!*, 'Let's try it!'). Cost for a half-kilo is between US$1.50 and US$2, depending upon the type.

You can leave your sweets purchase until the last minute, as there are numerous şekerleme at Afyon otogar. I like the shop called Ogaş (pronounced 'oh-gosh'), as much for the name as for the lokum.

Getting There & Away

Afyon is on the inland routes connecting İstanbul with Antalya and Konya, and İzmir to Ankara and the east, so bus traffic is heavy. Trains will take you to Eskişehir, İstanbul, İzmir, Konya and Kütahya (see the Getting Around chapter for details.).

Bus Details of daily bus services follow:

Ankara – 260 km, four hours, US$8; buses at least
  hourly
Antalya – 300 km, five hours, US$11; frequent buses
  passing through
Eskişehir – 191 km, three hours, US$6; hourly buses
Isparta – 165 km, three hours, US$6; several buses
İstanbul – 455 km, eight hours, US$14; hourly buses
İzmir – 340 km, 5½ hours, US$12; hourly buses
Konya – 235 km, 3¾ hours, US$8; several buses
Kütahya – 100 km, 1½ hours, US$3.50; hourly buses
Pamukkale – 240 km, four hours, US$9; several buses

ISPARTA

Famous for its kilims, carpets and *attar* (rose oil), Isparta (population 125,000, altitude 1035 metres) is at an important highway junction. Many buses plying the route to and from Antalya stop here. Of the several cities in the Aegean hinterland, however, Isparta has the least to draw your attention

Though there is little to hold you, the scenery around here is quite beautiful. Isparta lies in the midst of the Aegean hinterland's lakes region. The play of tectonic plates long ago resulted in depressions which, when they filled with water, became the lakes of Burdur, Eğirdir, Beyşehir etc.

Isparta's sandy soil is well suited to the growing of roses for oil. In the late 19th century, rose varieties were brought from Bulgaria and established here. Each year on 20 May the rose harvest begins. The attar produced is mostly exported to France.

The main reason any traveller comes to Isparta is to change buses and head 36 km east to the pretty lakeside resort town of Eğirdir.

Orientation

The main square, Kaymakkapı Meydanı, is a traffic roundabout near the Otel Bolat. The otogar is 1.5 km away; the railway station, a bit farther.

Information

The local tourism office (☎ (327) 14438), Mimar Sinan Caddesi, 1742 Sokak No 1, is open from 9 am to 5 pm Monday to Friday. Isparta's postal code is 32000.

Things to See

Should you have to spend some time here, stop in at the **Ulu Cami** (1417) and the **Archaeology Museum** on Kenan Evren Caddesi, open from 8.30 am to 6 pm for 75c.

Places to Stay & Eat

The very central one-star *Otel Bolat* (☎ (327) 18998, 13506), Demirel Bulvarı 71, offers decent rooms for US$10/16 a single/double with sink, US$14/20 with private shower. Along nearby Mimar Sinan Caddesi past the Belediye are several cheaper hotels with double rooms costing US$9 with a sink, US$13 with a shower.

Also here is the four-star, 63-room *Büyük Isparta Hotel* (☎ (327) 21017; fax 21801), offering the relative comfort of rooms equipped with private baths and satellite TVs for US$26/38 a single/double.

The centre of town near the hotels has the usual assortment of eateries, which will do nicely for a meal or two.

Getting There & Away

Living up to its reputation as a transfer point, Isparta's otogar, 1.5 km from the main traffic roundabout in the centre, has daily buses to many destinations including:

Afyon – 175 km, 2½ hours, US$5; frequent buses
Antalya – 175 km, two hours, US$5; hourly buses passing through
Denizli – 175 km, 2½ hours, US$5; several buses
Eğirdir – 36 km, 30 minutes, US$1; minibuses every half-hour
İzmir – 425 km, seven hours, US$14; several buses
Konya – 270 km, four hours, US$9; frequent buses passing through

EĞİRDİR

Eğirdir (pronounced eh-YEER-deer; population 15,000, altitude 950 metres) enjoys a beautiful situation on the road from Konya to the Aegean, near the southern tip of Eğirdir Gölü (Lake Eğirdir). It is Turkey's fourth-largest lake, covering 517 sq km, with an average depth of 12 metres and a maximum depth of 16.5 metres.

In Lydian times the highway was the Royal Road, the main route between Ephesus and Babylon, and Eğirdir was a beautiful and convenient place to stop, so the town prospered.

Today the town, clinging to the base of the steep slopes of Davras Dağı (2635 metres), serves something of the same purpose. Travellers on their way to or from Konya stop for a day or two to enjoy views of the lake, dine on its fish, and generally relax in one of the small pensions on the small island (now connected to the shore by a causeway) which stands a short distance out into the lake. The town is proud of its carpet and kilim weaving, mostly carried out by descendants of the Yörük nomads, and of its apple orchards and rose gardens, but really what it does best is relax the visitor.

History

Founded by the Hittites, it was taken by the Phrygians circa 1200 BC, and was later ruled by the Lydians, captured by the Persians, conquered by Alexander the Great, followed by the Romans. Its Roman name was Prostanna, and documents from the period hint that it was large and prosperous, but no excavations have been done at the site, which now lies within a large military reservation.

In Byzantine times, as Akrotiri ('steep mountain'), it was the seat of a bishopric. With the coming of the Turks, it became first a Selçuk city (circa 1080-1280), then the capital of a small principality covering the lakes region and ruled by the Hamidoğulları (1280-1381). Most of the historic buildings in town date from the Selçuk and Hamidoğulları periods. The Ottomans took control in 1417.

Under the Turks, Akrotiri was transformed into Eğridir, a word which carries meanings of 'crooked' and 'wrong'. In the 1980s, however, public relations caught up with Eğridir and the town officially changed its name to Eğirdir, a word which instead carries pretty references to spinning, sweet flag (a flower), and propolis (a sticky sap used by bees in hive-building).

Orientation

Eğirdir stretches along the lakeshore for several km. Its centre is on a point of land jutting into the lake, marked by the statue of Atatürk, the historic Hızır Bey Camii, Dündar Bey Medresesi, the otogar (☎ 1159), and most other important buildings.

A few hundred metres north-west of the centre, the kale (fortress) rises at the beginning of the isthmus and causeway which leads to the peninsula Yeşilada, 1.5 km north-west of the otogar. Many of the town's good cheap pensions are on Yeşilada, or around the kale's crumbling walls. The railway station is three km from the centre of town on the Isparta road.

Information

The Tourism Information Office (☎ (3281) 2098, 1388) is at 2. Sahil Yolu No 13. It's 600 km north-west of the otogar on the shore road towards Isparta. The Hotel Eğirdir is at the northern side of the town centre. The police station (☎ 1875) and post office (☎ 1004) are in between the Hotel Eğirdir

and the tourism office. Eğirdir's postal code is 32500.

Things to See

You can see Eğirdir's sights on a walking tour in an hour or two. Start at the centre.

The **Hızır Bey Camii** is a Selçuk work built as a warehouse in 1237, but restored as a mosque in 1308 by Hızır Bey, the Hamidoğulları emir. Note especially the finely carved wooden doors, and the bits of blue tile still to be seen on the minaret. Otherwise, the mask is quite simple, with a clerestory above the central hall. The tiles around the mihrab are new work.

Facing the mosque is the **Dündar Bey Medresesi**, a theological school built first by the Selçuk sultan Alaeddin Keykubat as a caravanserai in 1218, but converted to a medrese in 1285 at the order of Felekeddin Dündar Bey, the Hamidoğulları emir. It was restored most lately in 1979, and is now filled with shops. You can enter by the door near the **Atatürk statue**, but the grand main portal is the one facing the mosque. Note the Kufic inscription around the doorway, translated on a sign into Turkish and fractured English.

A few hundred metres out towards Yeşilada, the massive but crumbling walls of the **kale** rise above the beach. Its foundations may have been laid on the order of Croesus, the 5th-century king of Lydia. It was restored by successive rulers, including the Byzantines, Hamidoğulları, Selçuks and Ottomans. Near one of its walls is the **tomb of Devran Dede**, a local Muslim mystic.

Beaches & Boat Tours

The best beaches are out of the centre – Yeşilada has no real beaches to speak of. All of the following beaches have facilities such as changing cabins and food stands or restaurants. **Belediye Plajı** is less than one km from the centre on the Isparta road in the district called Yazla. **Altınkum Plajı** is several km farther north, near the railway station, three km from the centre along the Isparta road. Yet farther north (about 11 km) on the road to Barla is **Bedre Plajı**, perhaps

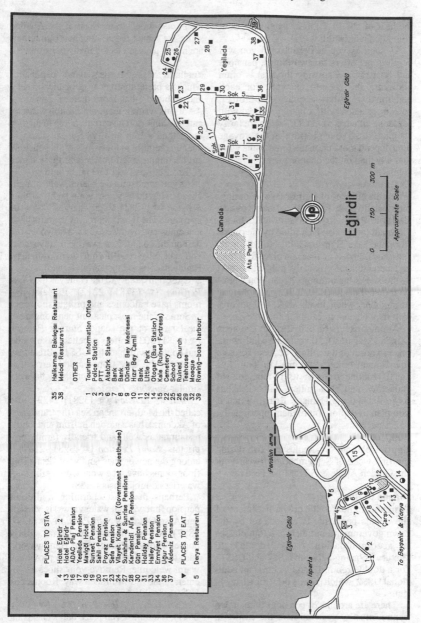

Egirdir

Approximate Scale

0   150   300 m

PLACES TO STAY
4   Hotel Eğirdir 2
13   Hotel Eğirdir
16   ADAC Plaj Pension
17   Yeşilada Pension
18   Mavigöl Hotel
19   Sunset Pension
20   Sahil Pension
21   Poyraz Pension
23   Sefa Pension
24   Vilayet Konuk Evi (Government Guesthouse)
27   Sunshine & Sunrise Pensions
28   Karadenizli Ali's Pension
30   Gün Pension
31   Holiday Pension
33   Halley Pension
34   Emniyet Pension
36   Uğur Pension
37   Akdeniz Pension

PLACES TO EAT
5   Derya Restaurant

35   Halikarnas Balıkçısı Restaurant
38   Melodi Restaurant

OTHER
1   Tourism Information Office
2   Police Station
3   PTT
6   Atatürk Statue
7   Bank
8   Bank
9   Dündar Bey Medresesi
10   Hızır Bey Camii
11   Bank
12   Little Park
14   Otogar (Bus Station)
15   Kale (Ruined Fortress)
22   Cemetery
25   School
26   Ruined Church
29   Teahouse
32   Mosque
39   Rowing-boat harbour

the best of all – 1.5 km of sand and water with adequate facilities.

As soon as you arrive in town you will begin to get offers for two things: pensions and boat tours. Choosing the first is often choosing the second as well, for each pension owner has a boat or a brother, cousin, or a son with a boat, or a deal with someone who has a boat. Offerings are fairly standard, and your pleasure in the voyage may depend more upon the force of the wind that day than on the boat or owner.

Excursions

When the citizens of Eğirdir take an outing, they usually go 25 km south to **Lake Kovada National Park** (Kovada Gölü Milli Park), the small (40 sq km) lake filled by the runoff from the lake Eğirdir Gölü. Noted for its flora and fauna, it's a pleasant place for a hike and a picnic. Unfortunately, public transport to the site is uncommon. If you don't have your own transport, try hitching on a Sunday in summer, when locals make excursions. You may be able to camp on the lakeshore.

Another excursion is to **Zindan Caverns** (Zından Mağarası), 30 km to the south-west, one km north of the village of Aksu across a fine Roman bridge. The one-km-long cave has Byzantine ruins at its mouth, lots of stalactites and stalagmites, and a curious room dubbed the Hamam. Bring a torch if you plan to explore more than superficially.

Festivals

Eğirdir celebrates its apples and fish during the first week of September each year with the Golden Apple & Silver Fish Festival.

Places to Stay

A signboard next to the otogar lists many of the town's pensions. Prices are set by the town government, but there are four classes of accommodation, from 3rd class to 'luxury', costing between US$7 and US$12 for a double room. Breakfast costs an additional US$2, which is quite high for what you get.

There are around 20 pensions in the town centre, mostly clustered near the castle. In the bazaar streets to the west of the Atatürk statue are some typical small hotels, but they are not as pleasant as the many pensions.

Yeşilada Yeşilada, the 'island' peninsula, which is preferable because of the scenery and ambience, has more than 16 pensions. As of this writing there are no noisy discos and few importunate carpet sellers to disturb the island's tranquillity. But Yeşilada is adapting rapidly to tourism, simple pensions are becoming small hotels, and these banes of Turkish travel can't be far behind.

As you come onto the island, walk straight ahead with the sea on your right. *Halley Pension* (☎ (3281) 3625) charges US$9 for its rooms. The two front rooms upstairs have balconies and showers, and are two of the best on the island. Reserve one in advance if you can, else you'll find them full. The Halley has a good restaurant as well.

Closest in quality to the Halley is the *Uğur Pension* (☎ (3281) 2212). Its lakeview rooms have balconies and private showers.

Some of the most pleasant pensions are at the far end of the island. *Sunrise Pension* (☎ (3281) 3032) offers excellent lake views and doubles with bath for US$13. Breakfast, taken on the tidy front garden terrace, is included. Adjoining the Sunrise is the very similar *Sunshine Pension*.

Akdeniz Pension (☎ (3281) 2432), also called the Mediterranean Sea (the translation of Akdeniz), has a garden in front and a little restaurant as well, and friendly family proprietors. *Sahil Pension* (☎ (3281) 2167) is among the newer ones, and very clean. Top-floor rooms have nice woodwork ceilings. A waterless double costs US$8.

Perhaps the most charming traditional pension (but without water views) is Mustafa and Ayşe Gökdal's *Sefa Pension* (☎ (3281) 1877), a very homy, traditional village house. Though retired, Ayşe Hanım works hard to keep it tidy, and Mustafa provides a warm welcome. Remove your shoes as you enter, in the old-fashioned way. Rooms cost US$9 a double without water.

Karadenizli Ali's Pension (☎ (3281) 2547), is a family-run place that's cheap and good, at US$8 for a double without running water.

Halikarnas Balıkçısı Pension (☎ (3281) 1926) is most noted for its Fish House Restaurant. If its rooms are full, try the *Emniyet* (☎ (3281) 2370) beside it, or the *Holiday* behind it.

ADAC Plaj Pension (☎ (3281) 3074), which you'll see as you approach the island on the causeway, rents modern waterless rooms for US$6/10 a single/double. The ground-floor restaurant with a water view is popular, though breakfast is overpriced.

Near the Castle As you pass the kale on your way out to Yeşilada, look up to the left to see the *Fulya Pension* (☎ (3281) 2175), among the best in town with its roof terrace, restaurant and panoramic views. Double rooms with shower and breakfast cost US$12. Down the hill from the Fulya is the five-room, friendly and family-run *Çetin* (☎ (3281) 2154). Rates are US$6/9/14 a single/double/triple for rooms, some with fine lake views. Breakfast and dinner are served. Other places nearby include the *Kale*, the *Mehtap* or Moonlight, ☎ (3281) 1517), and the *Eğirdir* (☎ (3281) 2033), 'where you live just like one of the family'.

Hotels At this writing, Eğirdir has only a few tourist-class hotels, but more will undoubtedly be built soon. For now, content yourself with the central *Hotel Eğirdir* (☎ (3281) 1798), where serviceable rooms with bath rent for US$33 a double, breakfast included.

The *Hotel Eğirdir 2*, around the corner, charges a bit less and closes in winter.

Places to Eat
On Yeşilada, many pensions have their own little restaurants. You may also want to try the *Melodi Restaurant*, next to the Akdeniz Pension at the tip of the island, where every dish except the fish fillet seems to cost 75c or US$1. There are good lake views from the dining room. In the centre, the *Derya Restaurant*, across the street from the Hotel Eğirdir, is the class act, with outdoor tables set by the water, and a pleasant indoor dining room as well. Full meals range from US$4 to US$10 here. For cheaper kebapçıs, look in the narrow bazaar streets on the opposite side of the Atatürk statue.

Getting There & Away
By bus is the easiest and fastest way of travelling to and from Eğirdir. Though there are trains to the spur which comes in from the İzmir-Aydın line via Isparta, they are not frequent or fast. If there is no bus leaving soon for your destination, hop on a minibus to Isparta and catch a bus there. Details of some services from Eğirdir follow:

Ankara – 457 km, seven hours, US$12
Antalya – 186 km, 2½ hours, US$6
Denizli – 203 km, three hours, US$6
Isparta – 36 km, 30 minutes, US$1;
    minibuses every half-hour
İstanbul – 638 km, 11 hours, US$20
İzmir – 418 km, seven hours, US$12
Konya – 306 km, four hours, US$8
Nevşehir – 443 km, eight hours, US$15

Mediterranean Turkey

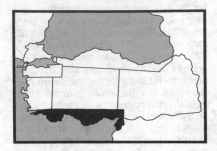

The southern coast of Turkey is delightful: a succession of scenic roads, interesting villages and picturesque ancient ruins. Only a few decades ago one had to explore parts of this coast with a sturdy vehicle, a pack animal or a boat. New highway construction has changed all that and now you can ride easily from Marmaris where the Aegean and Mediterranean seas meet, to Antakya near the Syrian border, enjoying the countryside rather than battling against it.

For all its natural beauty, the coast is still relatively undeveloped. This is no Riviera with miles of waffle-front hotels, but a succession of small settlements separated by miles of rocky coastline, with the occasional sweep of beach.

The most idyllic way to explore the coast is by private yacht – not as outrageously expensive as it sounds. While yachts chartered in the Greek islands may charge over US$100 per person per day, you can charter a beautiful wooden yacht in Turkey in spring or autumn for as little as US$40 to US$70 per person per day, meals included. The meals, made by the crew, will include fish and octopus pulled fresh from the blue waters, and herbs gathered along the shore. There's more information on yacht chartering in the Marmaris section.

You can spend as much or as little time as you like on the coast. Those without a lot of time can see the coast from Marmaris as far as Alanya pretty well in a week. The Greek island of Rhodes is close enough for a day trip from Marmaris. In this chapter I'll describe the towns and sights along the coast, from west to east.

Getting There & Away
Air The airport at Dalaman, 120 km east of Marmaris and 50 km west of Fethiye, is used mostly for charter flights from abroad, and services operated by İstanbul Airlines, though in summer there are daily flights to and from İstanbul by Turkish Airlines, and one flight weekly to Ankara by THT.

İstanbul Airlines has direct or nonstop flights once a week between Dalaman and Amsterdam, Antalya, Bologna, Brussels, Düsseldorf, Frankfurt, Graz, Hannover, İstanbul, İzmir, Cologne, Linz, Munich, Münster, Paris and Vienna.

For detailed information on land transport from Dalaman to other points on the Mediterranean coast refer to the Dalaman section.

There's a small airport being built at Ula, 15 km south of Muğla, 10 km north-east of Gökova, 40 km north of Marmaris, and 50 km north-west of Köyceğiz. The other south coast airports are at Antalya and Adana.

Bus Your coastal explorations will be by bus, car or hired yacht. With the yacht and car you travel at your own pace. With the bus you must be aware that traffic can be sparse along the coast at some times and in some areas. There may be only a few buses a day between points. As with most parts of Turkey, service dwindles and disappears in the late afternoon or early evening, so do your travelling early in the day and relax in the evening. With fewer buses it's all the more important to buy your reserved-seat tickets a day or so in advance.

Train There is no rail service south of Söke, Denizli and Isparta; trains do run from

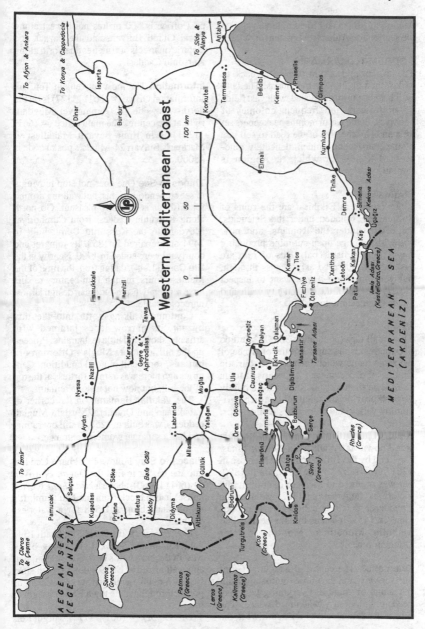

Ankara to Adana and Mersin, however. See the sections on Ankara and Adana for details.

BODRUM TO MARMARİS

The trip from Bodrum takes you back to Milas, then up into the mountains. The land is rich and heavily cultivated, with vast fields of sunflowers and frequent colonies of beehives. In the warm months beekeepers set up stands by the side of the road to sell jars of the translucent, golden, delicately pine-scented honey for which the region is famous.

Stratonikea

Near Yatağan at Eskihisar are the ruins of Stratonikea, founded under the Seleucids, important under the Romans, and now sullied by a huge open-cut mine producing *linyit* (lignite, hard coal). Bits of ruin are visible from the road as you pass through, but you must stop if you want to inspect closely the bits of the Roman city walls and gates, gymnasium, tomb etc.

Muğla

This small city (population 30,000, altitude 650 metres) is the capital of the province of the same name which includes the touristic centres of Bodrum and Marmaris. Muğla itself is hardly touristic. Rather, it's a purely Turkish provincial capital set in a rich agricultural valley, and therein lies its interest.

History First settled around 1200 BC, Muğla was known as Alinda until Selçuk times. Captured by the Turkish emirs of Menteşe in 1261, it was seized by the Ottomans in 1390, but was returned to Menteşe control by the victorious Tamerlane in 1402. Mehmet the Conqueror regained control for the Ottomans in 1451. It seems to have been called Mabolla, Mobella or Mobolia in later Ottoman times.

Orientation The centre of Muğla is Cumhuriyet Meydanı, the traffic roundabout with the statue of Atatürk. Everything you may need is within easy walking distance. The otogar is a few blocks to the south-west, the post office is 500 metres north-west along Recai Güreli Bulvarı, and the bazaar and historic quarter is 500 metres due north along Kurşunlu Caddesi.

Information The most convenient Tourism Information Office (☎ (661) 13127) is on the north-west side of Cumhuriyet Meydanı right at the centre. The main office (☎ (661) 11261) is in Emir Beyazıt Mahallesi at Marmaris Bulvarı 24. Muğla's postal code is 48000.

Things to See One does not stop in Muğla to see stupendous sights, but walking around for an hour is certainly pleasant. Go north along Kurşunlu Caddesi from Cumhuriyet Meydanı to the **Kurşunlu Cami**, built in 1494 and repaired in 1853. Its minaret and courtyard were added in 1900. Nearby is the **Ulu Cami** (1344), dating from the time of the Menteşe emirs, though 19th-century repairs have rendered its pre-Ottoman design almost unrecognisable.

Continue walking north into the tidy **bazaar**, its narrow lanes jammed with artisans' shops and little restaurants. Proceed up the hillside to see Muğla's **Ottoman-era houses**, some still in good condition. Centuries ago there was a small fortress at the top of the hill, but now not a stone remains.

The **Vakıflar Hamamı**, on the corner of Tabakhane and Orgeneral Mustafa Muğlalı caddesi, was built in 1258, is still operating, and has a separate women's entrance.

Places to Stay Follow Tabakhane Caddesi into the bazaar to find the *Doğan Pansiyon* (☎ (661) 13960), above a *kiraathane* (coffee house) half a block from the Ulu Cami. It's simple and cheap at US$8 for a waterless double.

Otel Tuncer (☎ (661) 18251), Saatli Kule Altı, Kütüphane Sokak 1, is a long block west of the bazaar. It's new, tidy, fairly quiet, and well priced at US$9 a double with sink, US$11 a double with private shower. Signs posted throughout the town lead you right to it.

Otel Zeybek (☎ (661) 11774), Turgut Reis

Caddesi 5, two blocks from the Kurşunlu Cami, is older and a bit noisier, but also a bit cheaper than the Tuncer.

The 48-room *Hotel Yalçın* (☎ (661) 11599), Garaj Caddesi 7, is half a block north-west of the otogar on a quiet street. Though three decades old, it is one of the town's better hotels, charging US$14/25 a single/double for a comfortable room with bath.

Walk east on Orgeneral Mustafa Muğlalı Caddesi several blocks to the *açık pazar yeri* (marketplace), look to your left (north) and you'll find the *Hotel Saray* (☎ (661) 11594), among the town's newer hotels. Good, clean, newish rooms with shower and views of the marketplace go for US$12/17 a single/double.

Muğla's best is the three-star *Hotel Petek* (☎ (661) 11897, 13135), Marmaris Bulvarı 27, 400 metres east of Cumhuriyet Meydanı. This is where the coach groups stay. If you do too, it'll cost US$22/28 a single/double, perhaps a bit more in summer.

Places to Eat The bazaar holds many tiny köfte grills, pide-makers and ready-food eateries. Try *Hayati'nin Yeri* on Kurşunlu Caddesi as it enters the bazaar, or the *88 Pideci*, off to the right just a bit farther into the bazaar. Just a few doors to the left of the Otel Zeybek is the *Berlin 92 Pideci*, good for a cheap, quick Turkish pizza and a glass of ayran. Near the Otel Tuncer are the *Sezer Izgara* and the *Koç Pide ve Pasta Salonu*, two cheap little hole-in-the-wall eateries.

For fancier fare, go east along Orgeneral Mustafa Muğlalı Caddesi to the marketplace. Just south of the market is a big office building called the Orgeneral Mustafa Muğlalı İşhanı, and on its north-east side are two fancier places, the *Mabolla Restaurant* and the *Bulvar Restaurant*. Both have indoor and outdoor seating, and a good meal at either should cost no more than US$5 to US$7.

Getting There & Away Muğla's touristic importance means its otogar is a busy one, with fairly frequent buses to all major destinations in the region. For points along the Mediterranean coast east of Marmaris, you may have to take a bus to Marmaris and change there to an eastbound bus. Details of some services follow:

Aydın – 100 km, 1¾ hours, US$4
Bodrum – 110 km, two hours, US$4.25
Dalaman – 86 km, 1½ hours, US$4
Denizli – 130 km, two hours, US$4.25
  (the road is now improved)
İzmir – 265 km, 4½ hours, US$9
İstanbul – 875 km, 14 hours, US$22
Köyceğiz – 57 km, one hour, US$2
Marmaris – 55 km, one hour, US$2

Gökova

Thirty km north of Marmaris the road comes over the Sakar Geçidi (Sakar Pass, at 670 metres) to reveal breathtaking views of Gökova bay before descending by switchbacks into a fertile valley.

At the base of the hill, signs point the way right (west) to the village of Akyaka, often called Gökova after the beautiful bay. This little resort village is built on a hillside which descends to the shore at a little sand beach by a river mouth. Much favoured by British holiday-makers, Gökova has many small pensions, as well as hotels rating from two to four stars.

About 700 metres beyond the village of Akyaka is an orman piknik yeri (forest picnic ground), and another 500 metres beyond that is the port hamlet of İskele. The tiny beach at the end of a small cove is served by a few basic restaurants. No doubt a few out-of-the-way pensions will be in business soon.

From the base of the hill at the Gökova turn-off, the Marmaris road crosses the floor of the broad river valley beside a magnificent double row – over two km in length – of great eucalyptus trees. (The old highway went right between the trees; the new one bypasses them on the west side.) At the far end of the trees the road ascends into the hills again before coming down into Marmaris.

MARMARİS

The once-sleepy fishing village of Marmaris (MAHR-mahr-ees, population 10,000) is situated on the marvellous natural harbour where Lord Nelson once (in 1798) organised his fleet for the attack on the French at Abukir. During the last several decades, Marmaris has become the 'in' place for Turkey's rich and famous, who are followed in their choice of holiday places by the hoi polloi.

Marmaris is not as cosmopolitan as Kuşadası, it does not have as fine a castle as Bodrum, nor does it have impressive ruins like Side. It does have Turkey's largest and most modern yacht marina, however, and is consequently Turkey's busiest yacht-charter port.

Besides the yachters, throngs of middle-class locals and the occasional newsworthy Turk, the streets and shores of Marmaris play host to an interesting variety of international tourists, ranging from Saudi princes to university students, including a surprisingly large number of Finns. There are also day-trippers from Rhodes who – ignoring the dire warnings of Greeks that Turkey is expensive, unfriendly and dangerous – come over to find just the opposite. If it's an idyllic little resort town you're looking for, take only a brief look at Marmaris then rush on to Datça.

Orientation

The town centre is the little plaza called İskele Meydanı, beneath the hill topped by a small fortress (now a museum), next to the Tourism Information Office and the dock for boats to Rhodes. Inland from İskele Meydanı is the shopping district. Most of the town centre is reserved for pedestrian traffic in summer.

South and east of İskele Meydanı is the Netsel Marina; just north of it is the otogar. South-east of these one km is Günnücek, a forest park reserve.

The waterfront road heading north-west from İskele Meydanı is officially named Atatürk Caddesi, though most locals refer to it as Kordon Caddesi. A landmark is the equestrian statue of Atatürk on Kordon Caddesi 500 metres north-west of İskele Meydanı. This is Atatürk Meydanı. Heading inland from it is the wide Ulusal Egemenlik (National Sovereignty) Bulvarı, the unoffi-

cial dividing line between 'old' Marmaris (to the east) and 'new' Marmaris (to the west).

A few hundred metres west of the Atatürk statue is Abdi İpekçi Park, with park benches and children's playground equipment shaded by palms. Yet another few hundred metres west is the Fountain Park, with its namesake fountain and bits of ancient columns and statuary.

Uzunyalı, a beach district with many hotels, is three to four km west of İskele Meydanı. İçmeler, another beach resort area, is eight km south-west of İskele Meydanı.

Information

The Tourism Information Office (☎ (612) 11035) is at İskele Meydanı 39. Opening hours are from 8 am to 8 pm every day in summer, 8 am to noon and 1 to 5 pm Monday to Friday in winter.

Marmaris' postal code is 48700.

Money Some of the exchange booths at the wharf, next to the tourism office, stay open on summer evenings and weekends when other banking facilities are closed.

Post The PTT is open until about 8 pm and will change foreign currency.

British Consulate The consulate (☎ (081) 53232), Hacı Mustafa Sokak 118 near the Hotel Begonya, is open Monday to Friday from 9 am to noon and 2.30 to 5 pm in summer.

Beaches

There are beaches along the Kordon in Marmaris, and even better, cleaner ones outside of town, although they are all small. The better beaches are near the fancy hotels, and still others can be reached by excursion boat.

Menzilhane

Take a look at the *menzilhane*, behind and to the left of the tourism office, at the foot of the path up to the little fortress. It's an Ottoman 'pony express' way-station built by Sultan Süleyman the Magnificent in 1545.

The historic stone building has been visually ruined by being used for souvenir shops.

Fortress Museum

The small castle on the hill behind the tourism office was built during the reign of Sultan Süleyman the Magnificent, when (in 1522) the sultan massed 200,000 troops here for the attack and seige of Rhodes, defended by the Knights of St John. The fortress is now a museum open from 9 am to 1 pm and 2.30 to 7 pm, closed on Monday; admission costs less than US$1. Exhibits are predictably nautical, historical and unexciting, though the building itself and the views are nice. To reach the fortress, walk up the narrow street to the left of the menzilhane opposite the Hotel İmbat, then go around the back of the menzilhane and through a village-scape very reminiscent of the Greek islands.

Atatürk Statue

The equestrian statue of Atatürk at the foot of Ulusal Egemenlik Bulvarı gives a quick lesson in Turkish civic history. Plaques on the plinth bear the sayings 'Türk Öğün Çalış Güven' (Turk! Be Proud, Work, Trust) and 'Ne Mutlu Türküm Diyene' (What joy to him who says, 'I am a Turk'). Both sayings were meant to dispel the feeling of inferiority towards Europeans suffered by Ottoman Turks. Another plaque bears the words 'Egemenlik Ulusundur' (Sovereignty belongs to the Nation), Atatürk's statement signifying that the Turkish people, and not the imperial House of Osman, were in charge of the country's destiny. The final plaque in this statuary history lesson reads 'İzindeyiz' (We Follow in Your Footsteps); the 'footsteps' being Atatürk's, of course.

İçmeler

Catch a dolmuş just inland from the Atatürk statue to get to İçmeler, a beautiful little seaside holiday spot eight km west and south around the bay from Marmaris. You may decide you like İçmeler better than Marmaris, and can then move to one of the hotels or camping grounds there.

Boat Excursions

Besides the daily boats to Rhodes there are numerous boats ranged along the waterfront offering day tours of the harbour, its beaches and islands. Departures are usually at 9 am. About half an hour before then, walk along Kordon Caddesi, check out the boats and talk to the captains about the *gezi* (excursion): where it goes, what it costs, whether lunch is included and, if so, what's on the menu. An average price for a day's pleasure outing is around US$6 to US$10, more if lunch is included.

There are longer, more serious excursions by boat, including trips to Datça and Knidos, well out along the hilly peninsula west of Marmaris. Ask at a travel agency or haggle with a boatman for a day's excursion to the secluded coves, beaches and ruins scattered along the peninsula.

Blue Voyage

Between the world wars writer Cevat Şakir Kabaağaç lived in Bodrum and wrote an account of his idyllic sailing excursions along Turkey's Carian (southern Aegean) and Lycian (western Mediterranean) coasts. The area was completely untouched by tourism at the time. Kabaağaç entitled his book *Mavi Yolculuk* (Blue Voyage), and any cruise along these coasts now shares that name.

You can charter a comfortable yacht in Turkey and, out of season, the cost can be as low as US$40 to US$70 per person daily. The larger the yacht (up to 12 berths) and the earlier (in spring) or later (in autumn) the cruise, the cheaper it is. For instance, an 11-berth yacht rented for a week in late April can cost a mere US$40 per person per day. The same yacht rented in July or August would cost several times as much. You can have the crew make the meals (for an extra charge) or you can plan to buy supplies and cook on board yourself, planning also to eat in little village restaurants much of the time. It is much cheaper to self-cater, especially if you have booked your charter through a yacht-charter broker abroad. The broker will

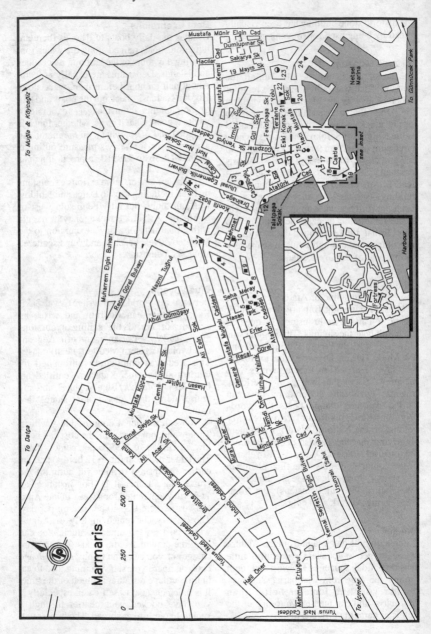

Marmaris

■ PLACES TO STAY

1   Interyouth Hostel
3   Özcan & Maltepe Pensions
4   Ayçe Otel
5   Ay-Ti Otel
6   Otel Yavuz
9   Otel 47
10 Çubuk Otel
18 Hotel Kaptan
20 Dilek Aile Pansiyon
21 Hotel Begonya

▼ PLACES TO EAT

19 Birat Restaurant
22 The Door Restaurant
24 Pineapple International Restaurant

OTHER

2   Devlet Hastanesi (Hospital)
7   Turkish Airlines' Office
8   Fountain Park
11 Abdi İpekçi Park
12 Atatürk Statue
13 İçmeler Dolmuş
14 PTT
15 Mosque
16 İskele Meydanı
17 Tourism Information Office
23 Otogar

mark up the price of meals to well above the actual cost.

Smaller boats tend to be more expensive per person but, even if you hire a larger yacht and cruise with some of the berths empty the charges are still quite reasonable. A yacht designed to sleep eight people (10 at a pinch) will be all the more comfortable for five or six people. In May or October, with crew and meals included, the charge for such a boat will still be only US$55 to US$70 daily per person, compared to US$45 if there were eight people. Considering that this includes lodging, meals, transport and a luxurious, unforgettable experience, the cost is quite moderate.

Occasionally, charter yachts sell berths individually, allowing you to enjoy a cruise even if you can't find half a dozen people to

share the cost. Prices depend upon the season, the yacht, the number of people signed up and the length of the cruise. For current information ask at any travel agency in town.

As for yachting itineraries, virtually everything described in this book from Bodrum to Antalya is open to you, as well as many secluded coves and islands.

For more information on yachting and lists of yachts and brokers, contact the Marmaris International Yacht Club (☎ (612) 23835; fax 28416 or 26550), PO Box 132, 48700 Marmaris. You can usually book through a yacht broker or travel agency near your home. If not, contact Yeşil Marmaris (☎ (612) 16486; fax 15077), Barbaros Caddesi 249 (PO Box 8), 48700 Marmaris. For bareboat charters (no captain or crew – you sail it), contact Albatros Yachting (☎ (612) 12456; fax 14470), Barbaros Caddesi 7, 48700 Marmaris.

Festivals
The Marmaris Yacht Festival is usually held in the 2nd week in May. Though this is a private convention for yacht owners and brokers, anyone interested in yachts will enjoy seeing all the boats in the harbour and marina. For information, contact the Marmaris International Yacht Club (☎ (612) 23835; fax 28416 or 26550), PO Box 132, 48700 Marmaris.

Places to Stay
Marmaris has several hundred lodging places. The cheapest are fairly central. There are many moderately priced hotels a short walk from İskele Meydanı, and even more several km along the bay. Most of the expensive hotels are well around the bay from the town, some as far as the beach suburb of İçmeler, eight km from İskele Meydanı.

Places to Stay – bottom end
The cheapest lodgings are called *ev pansiyon* (home pensions), where you rent a room in a private home. The Tourism Information Office can help you locate one of these. This simple, homy accommodation is where

thrifty Turkish families and couples stay, paying only US$8 to US$12 for a double room depending upon facilities. Some rooms have three and four beds – good for families. Ev pansiyons are dwindling in number as Marmaris grows, but a few survive.

Directly east (inland) from the tourism office several hundred metres is Hacı Mustafa Sokak and the *Dilek Aile Pansiyon* (☎ (612) 13591), at No 108, across the street from the Hotel Begonya.

Walk from İskele Meydanı along the shore road until you see the little Abdi İpekçi Park on the right-hand side; the Çubuk Otel is here as well. Walk through the park and inland one block to 3. Sokak to find these pensions: the *Altun* at No 3, the *Kınalı* (☎ (612) 11322) at No 9, the *Cihan* (☎ (612) 14372) at No 14, and the *Etem* at No 16.

For other pensions, walk from Abdi İpekçi Park westward in front of the Çubuk Otel. Turn right at the second street, walk down past the Ayçe Otel and cross a footbridge to reach the *Özcan Pension* (☎ (612) 17761), a quiet place with a nice front terrace shaded by grapevines. Adjoining it is the similar *Maltepe Pension*; both places have rooms for US$10/16 a single/double in summer.

Keep walking inland from the Maltepe, cross the road and look for the *Interyouth Hostel* (☎ (612) 16432), Kemeraltı Mahallesi, İyiliktaş Mevkii. This modern facility has double, triple, quadruple and dormitory rooms, a roof-terrace bar, laundry, restaurant, baggage storage room, and free hot showers. The top rate is US$12 for two beds in a double room; other sleeping arrangements are cheaper.

A few small hotels survive right near İskele Meydanı from when Marmaris was a small fishing village. One by one they are being modernised or converted to other uses. They also tend to be noisy, but are certainly convenient. Have a look at the *Hotel İmbat* (☎ (612) 11413), Kemeraltı Eski Çarşı Sokak 30, with very plain but clean double rooms for US$12 without facilities, US$14 with shower. Also here is the *Otel Karaaslan* (☎ (612) 11867), Kemeraltı Eski Çarşı Sokak 36, charging the same prices for

similar rooms. Some top-floor rooms have good water views.

About two km west of the centre is the Uzunyalı district, its shore lined with four and five-star hotels. But inland from these palaces are many smaller, cheaper lodging places. The area is still developing rapidly. Take a minibus to Uzunyalı, get out at the Hotel Karacan, and walk inland, and you should be able to find good lodgings for under US$20 a double with private shower.

Another money-saving strategy is to take a Siteler-Turban minibus from the centre via Uzunyalı to its final stop at the Turban Tatil Köyü (Turban Holiday Village). Just east of this luxury complex are several small hotels patronised mostly by Turkish families: *Rol Motel, Hotel Yüzbaşı, Lembol 3, Panorama Motel* and *Tümer Hotel*, where rooms are often available for under US$20 a double, with bath.

Camping Camping areas are disappearing as the building boom races on. *Berk Camping*, just east of the previously mentioned Turban Tatil Köyü, has tent sites, little cabins and all services for about US$3 per person (more for the cabins). There's also camping in Günnücek Park, a forest park one km south-east of the otogar.

Places to Stay – middle

In the very centre of Marmaris is the *Hotel Kaptan* (☎ (612) 11251) facing the wharf for boats to Rhodes. A double with shower and breakfast costs US$34. Right next door to the Tourism Information Office, facing İskele Meydanı, is the *Hotel Anatolia* (☎ (612) 12665, 12851), with small but decent rooms and tiled showers for the same price.

Hotel Begonya (☎ (612) 14095; fax 11518), Kısayalı Hacı Mustafa Sokak 71, is a different and delightful place. Here an old village house on a quiet back street has been renovated, its rooms equipped with tiled showers and decorated simply. Outside the house is a delightful private garden terrace with a fountain and lots of greenery. Prices are US$30/35/48 a single/double/triple; breakfast (taken at tables on the terrace) costs an extra US$2.50 per person. Unfortunately, the Begonya is open only from April to October, and it's often full in high summer, but check anyway. From the mosque and fountain in the market (see map) head north along the narrow street for 200 metres; the hotel is on the left.

A block inland on the western side of Abdi İpekçi Park is the *Çubuk Otel* (☎ (612) 16774; fax 16776), Atatürk Caddesi, Konti Sokak 1. Done in the standard Turkish-Mediterranean idiom of white stucco and varnished pine trim, the hotel's six floors of rooms are tidy, simple and less noisy than the more expensive hotels right on the Kordon. Prices for singles/doubles are US$15/25, breakfast and shower included.

Across the street from the Çubuk is the *Palmen Otel* (☎ (612) 11805), Kemeraltı Mahallesi, 99. Sokak No 4. It's small, tidy, and similar to the Çubuk in every way, including price.

Around the corner on Çam Sokak is the Ayçe Otel (☎ & fax (612) 13136), at No 4. Though small, it has a quality feel and a swimming pool. Rooms rent for US$18/28 a single/double.

On Atatürk Caddesi a bit farther west is the three-star *Otel 47* (kirk-yeh-DEE) (☎ (612) 11700, 12730), Atatürk Caddesi 10, a fairly lavish place for this district with a streetside restaurant, shops and comfortable rooms with balconies overlooking the bay for US$40/50 for singles/doubles including breakfast.

Otel Yavuz (☎ (612) 12937; fax 14112), farther west along the Kordon, has three-star comforts, 54 rooms and a small swimming pool on top of the building. Chances are good that your room (with bath) will have a balcony with a view of the bay. The price is US$30/40 a single/double, with bath.

Around the corner from the Yavuz and inland one block on Hacı Selim Sokak is the *Ay-Ti Otel* (☎ (612) 15431; fax 13056), at No 27, offering clean rooms in a convenient location at similar prices.

On Uzunyalı beach, two km west of the centre, are many more hotels offering greater comfort at higher prices. *Otel Zarif* (☎ (612)

14306; fax 13112), Uzunyalı 94, has air-con rooms with sea views, a beautiful oval pool, deck chairs on the beach, and prices of US$55 a double, breakfast and dinner included.

If the Zarif is full (as it often is), try the similar but cheaper *Yeşil Hurma Oteli* (☎ (612) 16778; fax 16779), 100 metres farther north. Other choices nearby are the *Green Hotel* and the *Sun Gezgin*.

Places to Stay – top end
Marmaris now has numerous five-star hotels. My favourite from the standpoint of location is the 285-room *Hotel Grand Azur* (☎ (612) 18201; fax 13530), Kenan Evren Bulvarı 11 in Uzunyalı, three km west of the centre. The circular lobby with blue-veined marble floors and fluted columns sets a classic mood. A full range of services, facilities and activities keep guests happy. The price is US$125 a double in summer, breakfast and dinner included.

Places to Eat – bottom end
The centre of Marmaris near İskele Meydanı is now completely touristy, with matching prices. Small restaurants open, operate and go out of business at an alarming rate. Still, you won't starve and you won't go broke either. Following are a few suggestions. For the very cheapest fare, walk inland and look for untouristy, local Turkish places selling pide, kebaps and ready food. Find where the farmers eat and you'll save 40% on the price of your meal.

Ayyıldız Lokantası (☎ 12158), between the menzilhane and the mosque in the bazaar, has been dependably good for almost a decade. A meal of döner kebap, bulgur pilav, salad and drink costs about US$5.

Fevzi Paşa Caddesi, the street with the post office, is closed to vehicles and in fine weather several restaurants along the street set tables outdoors. My favourite here is the *Toros Çorba ve Yemek Salonu* at the inland end of the street on the left. Vegetable stew (sebzeli kebap), pilav, yoghurt, bread, beer and tea cost US$5.25 at my last visit.

Near Abdi İpekçi Park, walk inland on the

street between the park and the Çubuk Otel, and look on the left for *Altun Mantı ve Kebap Salonu*, specialising in cheap kebaps and mantı (Turkish ravioli). Keep walking down this street to the end, and turn right. Up at the far end on the left is *Aslan Usta'nin Yeri*, a small place which raised its level of service – and its prices – after it was mentioned in this guidebook. Kebaps cost from US$2.50 to US$4, breakfast goes for US$2.

Places to Eat – middle

My favourite Marmaris restaurant is *The Door* (☎ 13939), Kısayalı Sokak 123, on the street also called Hacı Mustafa Sokak, not far from the Hotel Begonya and Dilek Aile Pansiyon. Ms Gülsevil Sümter provides Turkish home cooking in a pleasant dining room (no outdoor tables). The welcome is warm, the service efficient, the food excellent, the price around US$12 to US$15 per person, all included. The Door is open daily for dinner only.

This street has several other interesting dining places. You'll find something you like if you stroll along it in early evening. *Beyoğlu Café-bar* sometimes has set-price meals for US$3 to US$5. *Pizza Napoli* offers pizzas for US$3.75, a big Niçoise salad for even less. *Mutfak Restaurant & Steak House* has a full menu at prices lower than at the waterfront places.

In the bazaar, the *Yeni Liman Restaurant* is good and cheap, with full meals for US$8 to US$10, but the surging tide of souvenir shops, leather boutiques and jewellery stores is lapping at its table legs, and it may soon be swept away.

Just outside the bazaar near the hospital, the *Avrasya Restaurant* offers some of the best food, service and value for money in town. Alcohol is not served, but that won't matter after the first bite.

Waterfront restaurants east of the tourism office along the quay have pleasant outdoor dining areas and moderate prices. The *Birtat* (BEER-taht, 'one taste') (☎ 11076) is well established, has a good reputation, and the food was good when I last had dinner there. Plan to spend between US$8 and US$14 per

person for a full meal with wine. Farther along towards the yacht harbour, the *Yakamoz* is similar. Even farther along, the *Restaurant-Pizzeria O'Yes* (☎ 12350) is modern, pleasant, and a bit cheaper.

In the Netsel Marina complex shopping centre is the excellent *Pineapple International Restaurant* (☎ 14999, 12078), which looks expensive with its international menu, formal dining room and open-air tables. But prices are moderate: a good full dinner with wine or beer need cost only US$15 to US$20 – recommended.

At the western end of the footbridge leading to the marina, the *Marina Meat & Fish House* is popular, atmospheric on a fine summer evening, and moderately priced with meals costing from US$5 to US$8.

Entertainment

You'll have no trouble finding a congenial place for a drink and a chat in Marmaris. *Daily News Bar-Club* is among the oldest bars in town, but it now has a disco as well. *Café Kale* in the fortress doesn't advertise that it serves food, but it does, and it's good, though the selection is limited.

In the marina next to the Pineapple Restaurant is the small, quiet *Captain's Pub*, with good food and good service.

Quieter places are east along the quay from the tourism office, and on Hacı Mustafa Sokak inland from the bazaar. The larger, noisier nightclubs tend to be along the Kordon west of the Atatürk statue.

Things to Buy

Marmaris is a honey-producing region. Those who know honey will want to sample several of the local varieties, most famous of which is *çam balı* (CHAHM bah-luh, also called *wald*, from the German). It's a pine-scented honey from young forest growth and is rich, dark and full-flavoured. There's also *siyah çam balı*, black-pine honey, with a deep, rich flavour and a colour almost as dark as molasses. Others are *portakkal*, orange-blossom, very light-coloured, thin in texture, with a light, sweet flavour; *akasya balı*, locust-tree blossom; slightly darker and more flavoursome *çiçek* (flower honey); and *oğul balı*, virgin honey (the first honey from a new swarm). You can buy the honey in jars priced from US$2 to US$4, or in larger tins for US$5 to US$10.

One shop which has many varieties is Nur-Bal (☎ 13731), Fevzi Paşa Caddesi 9-C, one block inland from the post office on the same side of the street. A few steps farther inland, on the opposite side, Hobim ('My Hobby'), Fevzi Paşa Caddesi 8-D, also sells honey, as well as Turkish delight and other traditional Turkish sweets.

Speaking of shopping, Marmaris has lots of possibilities. Because the boats from Rhodes bring lots of shoppers on day trips, Marmaris merchants stock everything: onyx, leather clothing and accessories, carpets, jewellery, crafts, Turkish delight, meerschaum pipes and baubles, sandals, apple tea powder, copper and beach-wear.

Getting There & Away

Air There's a small airport being built at Ula, 15 km south of Muğla, 10 km north-east of Gökova, and 40 km north of Marmaris. When finished, it will be able to receive aircraft seating up to 50 passengers.

The region's principal airport is at Dalaman, 120 km east of Marmaris. İstanbul Airlines (☎ (612) 13222), Kemal Elgin Bulvarı 50-B, has direct or nonstop flights once a week between Dalaman and Amsterdam, Antalya, Bologna, Brussels, Düsseldorf, Frankfurt, Graz, Hannover, İstanbul, İzmir, Cologne, Linz, Munich, Münster, Paris and Vienna.

In summer there are daily flights between Dalaman and İstanbul by Turkish Airlines (☎ (612) 13751), Kordon Caddesi 30-B, and one flight weekly between Dalaman and Ankara by THT.

Airport buses operated by Havaş and Marmaris Belediyesi serve Turkish Airlines' flights using Dalaman. Buses depart from the Turkish Airlines office on the Kordon about three hours before flight departure. You're probably better off going to the otogar and catching a regular bus to Dalaman, then taking a taxi to the airport. For more information on land transport to and from Dalaman, refer to the Dalaman section.

Bus The otogar in Marmaris is just northwest of the Netsel Marina, a few hundred metres from İskele Meydanı. Convenient bus company ticket offices are concentrated on the waterfront street near the equestrian statue of Atatürk. Look for the names Pamukkale, Kamil Koç, Kontaş and Köseoğlu. The Varan office is farther west along the Kordon, near the Yavuz and Karadeniz hotels.

In summer bus traffic is furiously active, with dozens of the huge growling machines rolling in and out of town all day long, but in winter service drops off to what's required by a small farming town. Destinations include:

Adana – 1025 km, 20 hours, US$32; change buses at Antalya
Ankara – 780 km, 13 hours, US$22; a dozen buses daily in summer
Antalya – 590 km, nine hours, US$14; a few buses daily
Bodrum – 165 km, three hours, US$6.50; hourly buses in summer
Dalaman – 120 km, 2½ to three hours, US$5 to US$6; hourly buses in summer
Datça – 75 km, 1¾ hours, US$3.75; hourly buses in summer
İstanbul – 900 km, 15 hours, US$20 to US$25; a dozen buses daily in summer
İzmir – 320 km, six hours, US$10; hourly buses in summer
Fethiye – 170 km, four hours, US$6.50; hourly buses in summer
Kaş – 305 km, five hours, US$8; several buses daily
Köyceğiz – 75 km, 1½ hours, US$2.75; at least nine buses daily in summer
Muğla – 55 km, one hour, US$2; very frequent buses and dolmuşes
Pamukkale – 185 km, three hours, US$5.75; via Muğla and Tavas, several buses daily

Boats – to/from Rhodes Boats to and from Rhodes run daily in high summer on the 2½-hour voyage. Turkish boats depart from Marmaris in the morning, returning from Rhodes in the late afternoon; Greek boats depart from Rhodes in the morning, returning from Marmaris in the late afternoon.

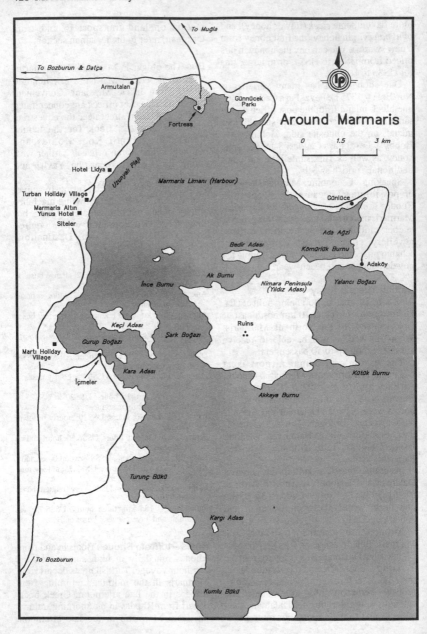

To Muğla

To Bozburun & Datça

Armutalan

Günnücek Parkı

Fortress

Around Marmaris

0   1.5   3 km

Hotel Lidya

Uzunyalı Plajı

Marmaris Limanı (Harbour)

Turban Holiday Village

Günlüce

Marmaris Altın Yunus Hotel

Siteler

Ada Ağzı

Bedir Adası

Kömürlük Burnu

İnce Burnu

Ak Burnu

Nimara Peninsula
(Yıldız Adası)

Adaköy

Yalancı Boğazı

Keçi Adası

Ruins

Gurup Boğazı

Şark Boğazı

Martı Holiday Village

Kara Adası

Kütük Burnu

İçmeler

Akkaya Burnu

Turunç Bükü

To Bozburun

Kargı Adası

Kumlu Bükü

Some of these ferries are capable of carrying cars as well as passengers. Buy your ticket on a Turkish boat (US$25 one way, US$32 same-day return, US$40 open-date return) at any travel agency in Marmaris (you'll see them along the Kordon) at least a day in advance if you can. For the Greek boat go to All Star, Barbaros Caddesi 228, near the otogar. When departing from Greece, passengers are subject to a US$8 port tax.

At other times of the year there may be fewer boats but you can depend on at least two boats per week except in times of stormy weather.

Getting Around

Dolmuşes run frequently around the bay, beginning just inland from the Atatürk statue on Ulusal Egemenlik Bulvarı and going to Uzunyalı (three km), Turban-Siteler (four km) and İçmeler (eight km).

REŞADİYE & DARAÇYA PENINSULAS

A narrow, mountainous finger of land points westward from Marmaris, stretching 100 km into the Aegean between the Greek islands of Kos and Rhodes. Known in ancient times as the Peraea, it is now called the Reşadiye Peninsula, Datça Peninsula or Hisarönü; its southern branch is known as the Daraçya or Loryma peninsula, with the ruins of the ancient city of Loryma at its southern tip.

Until recently, access to the peninsula was mostly by sea, as the road was primitive, long and slow. Now a paved, though twisting, road stretches from Marmaris westward beyond Reşadiye and Datça, and visits are possible by land as well.

Besides the joy of sailing near the peninsula's pine-clad coasts and anchoring in some of its hundreds of secluded coves, visitors come to Reşadiye to explore Bozburun, a small fishing village 56 km south-west of Marmaris; Datça, a fast-growing 'mini-Marmaris' resort town about 75 km west of Marmaris; and the hamlet and ruins of Knidos, the ancient city of the great sculptor Praxiteles, 35 km west of Datça.

Leave Marmaris by road, and you immediately climb into the mountains of the peninsula. About 20 km west of Marmaris the road divides. Go straight on for Datça and Knidos, turn left (south) for Bozburun.

The Road to Bozburun

At this writing, the seaside village of Bozburun is perfect for a quiet getaway from the tourist madness of the more developed towns along the Turkish coasts. Fishing and farming occupy most villagers, though some work in little bars and 'markets' (shops) set up to serve the yachters who drop anchor in Sömbeki bay. Though there's no good beach, there are rocks from which to swim, many interesting walks in the countryside, and excursions to be made by boat.

The road in to Bozburun is being widened and improved. When it's suitable for large buses, the village will be utterly changed. Heading south from the main road, travelling two km brings you to the village of Hisarönü. **Orhaniye**, set on a beautiful bay, is eight km farther along. You might want to stop for a meal here at the *Kadir* or *Iskele* restaurants.

Nine km south of Orhaniye is an intersection with roads to Başık and Bozburun. Follow the Bozburun road to reach the village of **Selimiye**, on its own lovely bay facing an islet topped by ruined bits of ancient wall. Selimiye has many pleasant cheap restaurants supplying the yachters, and also the *Emre Motel*, renting singles/doubles with shower for US$10/14. Old village houses are being rebuilt as villas; hotels and pensions will follow, and the condos can't be far behind.

Bozburun

Twelve km beyond Selimiye is Bozburun. As you descend the slope and enter the town, notice the Sağlık Ocağı (Health Clinic), a convenient landmark.

Behind the Sağlık Ocağı, a road runs down to the outer bay, with boatyards, yacht moorings and fishing skiffs. As you approach the beach on the outer bay, a new hotel is off to the left about 100 metres. To the right is a track which takes you to several of the better pensions and, ultimately, to the centre of the village.

Two km east of the Sağlık Ocağı is a smaller cove with several boatyards, a few yachts moored, and one small pension, but no transport.

If you stay on the main road past the Sağlık Ocağı, you'll reach a the village centre after a 2.5-km ride.

Swimming Bozburun is not known for its beaches, but you can swim from the rocks by the İlkokul (primary school) south-east of the Atatürk statue.

Places to Stay Bozburun's little pensions charge from US$2.50 to US$7 per person, depending upon the pension, the season and the demand. Haggling is advisable.

In town is the *Keskin Pension*, next to the big Akvaryum Yacht Club restaurant, and *Başçavuşun Yeri* (☎ (6216) 1365 or 1048), next to the Atatürk statue, offering rooms for US$4 per person with toilet and solar-heated shower. But pensions out along the shore from the Atatürk statue are preferable as they are quieter, and have better sea views.

First along the shore is the *Yılmaz Pension* – well kept, with nice views, priced at US$4 per person. Just beyond it is the *Nail Pension* (that's nah-YEEL), similar to the Yılmaz down to the chairs and tables on its porch from where you can enjoy views of the bay.

Out on a point of land beyond the Nail is the local primary school (İlkokul), and just beyond it is the *Erdinç Pension* (☎ (6126) 1153), slightly more expensive than the others.

There are several more pensions along this beach, and finally the *Motel Pembe Yunus* (☎ (6126) 1154), 250 metres beyond the İlkokul. Though not much fancier than a pension, the Pembe Yunus (Pink Dolphin) has a roof terrace for sunning and dining, and the inimitable Ms Fatma Doğanyılmaz as a manager. Fatma Hanım will rent you one of her clean but basic, shower-equipped rooms for US$10/18 a single/double, breakfast and dinner included.

Places to Eat The restaurants started out catering to the yachters, still their major clientele. *Başçavuşun Yeri*, next to the Atatürk statue, is among the cheapest, though *Kandil* and *Osman'ın Yeri* are nicer and more popular. Classiest is the upper-storey terrace restaurant of the *Akvaryum Yacht Club*. Meals for around US$3 are available at all of these places.

Getting There & Away At least three minibuses daily run between Marmaris and Bozburun; the fare is US$2. Departures from Bozburun for Marmaris are at 6.30 and 11 am and 12.30 pm. Return trips from Marmaris are in the afternoon, the last being at 5 pm. Service is more frequent in summer.

Datça

About 50 km past the Bozburun turn-off is Reşadiye, where a road goes off to the left (south) for Datça while the main road continues westward to Knidos.

Orientation Datça is essentially a one-street town. The road into Datça passes near the hospital, past the jandarma and through a commercial district of shops selling scented honey and spices. Past several small teahouses and restaurants, you reach the main plaza with its marketplace and bus area. The street then climbs a hill, curves to the left down the other side, scoots across an isthmus and ends on a hill at the end of a short peninsula, once an island called Esenada. This whole distance is about one km.

Information Datça's Tourism Information Office (☎ (6145) 1163) is next to the main square. Accommodation lists are posted in its windows.

Things to See There is nothing to see in Datça apart from the town itself, which is small and quiet except for the altogether too friendly carpet hawkers. To the east is a long beach, and to the south is another one on the cove.

Datça is a place for hanging around and relaxing in. For exciting sights you must take an excursion to Knidos.

Places to Stay – bottom end Datça has about 50 small pensions with a total of perhaps 400 or 500 beds costing around US$3 to US$5. A list of the pensions is on display at the Tourism Information Office. Among the quieter pensions are the *Bora* (☎ (6145) 1327), *Karaoğlu* (kah-RAH-oh-loo; ☎ (6145) 1079), *Huzur* (☎ (6145) 1052), *Sadık* (☎ (6145) 1196) and *Çağla* (☎ (6145) 1084). The *Pansiyon Yılmaz* is actually much fancier and has higher prices.

Readers of this guide have enjoyed staying at the *Oya Pansiyon* and the *Pansiyon Şahin*. The latter offers rooms with or without shower for US$12, use of the kitchen, the fridge, the iron and ironing board included. The Şahin is a favourite with British tour groups.

If you prefer a small, cheap hotel to a pension try the *Esenada Oteli* (☎ (6145) 1014), almost at the end of the main street, out on the little peninsula. Though it's right next door to the town's only fancy hotel and has pleasant gardens, the Esenada charges only US$8/12 for a double/triple room without running water. The showers have hot water, but the insect screens leave something to be desired. If there's no-one around ask for assistance in the Çimen Kardeşler clothing shop next door.

On the main square facing the bus area is the *Deniz Motel* (☎ (6145) 1038), actually a little hotel charging US$8 for a double room without water.

Camping There's camping in the district called Ilıca, on the eastern bay, at Camping Ilıca.

Places to Stay – middle Datça's premier hostelry is the *Hotel Club Dorya* (☎ (6145) 1593; fax 1303), İskele Mahallesi, Esenada, at the end of the main street, out on the little peninsula amidst nice gardens, with good views all round. Rooms with bath and perhaps a view cost US$30/$45 a single/double.

The three-star *Hotel Mare* (☎ (6145) 1211), Yanık Harman Mevkii, is a newish 50-room hotel on the main beach (not on the peninsula) near the Club Datça. Besides comfortable rooms with tiled showers and balconies with sea views, there is a pretty circular swimming pool, and the beach is only metres away. Rooms cost US$45/60 a single/double. The hotel is not open from November to March.

The *Club Datça* (☎ (6145) 1170), İskele Mahallesi, is a 95-room holiday village, with lots of water-sports facilities, charging somewhat more than the Mare.

Places to Eat Except for the dining rooms at the more expensive hotels, Datça's restaurants tend to charge US$2 for the standard komple kahvaltı Turkish breakfast, and from US$3 to US$6 for a full lunch or dinner with a meat course. The *Taraça* doesn't look like much from the street, but enter it and you'll find a nice terrace with very good views of the harbour. The *Liman*, on the upper floor, has similarly fine views. The *Köşem* has bits of sculpture in front, a few outdoor tables and slightly lower prices. The *Dutdibi*, a shady restaurant run by friendly people on the small beach right in the village, is good and cheap. The *Marina Café* by the yacht harbour is good – surprisingly posh for Datça but also a bit more expensive.

Getting There & Away Datça is served by the Pamukkale and Kamil Koç companies, which together run at least a dozen buses from Datça to Marmaris (75 km, 1¾ hours, US$4), where you can change for a bus to any other destination.

Boat There are often boat excursions to Datça from Marmaris and sometimes you can buy a one-way ticket.

There are scheduled ferry services between Bodrum and Datça during the summer months, organised by Karya Tour Yachting & Travel Agency (☎ (6141) 1759, 1914), Karantina Caddesi 13, Bodrum. Daily departures are at 8.30 am from Bodrum, 5 pm from Datça, with the following exceptions:

Friday
  a second boat leaves Bodrum at 5.30 pm
Saturday
  the boat departs from Bodrum at 6 pm and Datça
  at 8 am
Sunday
  boats depart from Datça at 7.30 am and 5 pm

The one-way fare is US$8, return it's US$14; a car costs US$22. The ferry actually departs from Körmen, about a 15-minute ride due north of Datça on the peninsula's northern coast.

Knidos

At Knidos, 35 km west of Datça at the very tip of the peninsula, are ruins of a prosperous port city dating from about 400 BC. The Dorians who founded it were smart: the winds change as one rounds the peninsula and ships in ancient times often had to wait at Knidos for good winds. This happened to the ship carrying St Paul to Rome for trial.

Being rich, Knidos commissioned the great Praxiteles to make a large cult statue of Aphrodite. It was housed in a circular temple in view of the sea. The statue, said to be the sculptor's masterpiece, has been lost, though copies or derivative versions exist in museums in Munich, New York and Rome.

Other than the ruins, Knidos consists of a tiny jandarma post with a telephone for emergencies, four little makeshift restaurants (the *Bora* and the *Knidos* were most popular on my last visit), and a repository for artefacts found on the site (no entry). At present staying in the village overnight is forbidden, and thus there are no facilities. You can swim in the bays from wooden piers, but the beaches are several km out of town. The nearest PTT is in Çeşme Köyü, the last village you pass through on the road to Knidos.

The Ruins The ruins of Knidos are scattered along the three km at the end of the peninsula. The setting is dramatic – steep hillsides terraced and planted with groves of olive, almond and fruit trees – and the peninsula here is occupied by goatherds and the occasional wild boar. All this surrounds two picture-perfect bays in which a handful of yachts rest at anchor. Few of the ancient buildings are in recognisable shape, but you can appreciate easily the importance of the town by exploring the site. The guardian will show you around for a small tip.

Getting There & Away The trip to Knidos must be made by private car, taxi (about US$30 for a day trip from Datça) or boat. There is not really any dependable minibus service. A ferry departs from Datça each morning in summer at 9 am for a day trip to Knidos, returning at 5 pm and charging US$8 per person.

EASTWARD TO KÖYCEĞİZ

Leaving Marmaris and heading north, the road climbs into mountains with beautiful panoramas and fertile valleys in between. At the end of that two-km-long double row of eucalyptus trees is a highway junction where you turn right towards Köyceğiz and Fethiye. Along the way are fields of cotton and tobacco, orchards of fruits and nuts, and cool pine forests buzzing with honey bees. At Kadırga and Günlük there are forest picnic areas.

Near Köyceğiz, a local agricultural centre, is the town of Dalyan, with an archaeological site named Caunus – worth a side-trip.

KÖYCEĞİZ

Less than 50 km east of the turn-off from the Muğla-to-Marmaris road lies Köyceğiz (population 7000), a small lakeside town only now being discovered by foreign tourists. Turks in on the secret of Köyceğiz's beauty have been coming here quietly for years.

Köyceğiz sits at the northern end of the large lake Köyceğiz Gölü, which connects with the Mediterranean Sea via the stream Dalyan Çayı. The attraction here is the lake – broad, beautiful and serene. Except for its small (but growing) tourist trade, Köyceğiz is a farming and fishing town. Among the goods produced here are citrus fruit, olives, honey and cotton. This region is also famous for its liquidambar trees, the sort which produced that precious petrified gum ages ago. The government is now sponsoring large-scale reafforestation projects in this region using liquidambar evergreens.

Orientation

The local hospital is near the highway turn-off. Proceed along the tree-lined boulevard from the highway for two km until you reach a small mosque right by the waterfront park, the Atapark. Just west of the mosque is the Belediye.

Information

The town's Tourism Information Office (☎ (6114) 1703) is opposite the mosque, on the eastern edge of the square. It has a simple map and several historical hand-outs.

Walks

Walk along the lakeshore on the promenade, officially called the Atatürk Kordonu, past the pleasant town park, a children's playground, shady tea gardens and several lakeside restaurants. If there's not a lot of activity on the lake, you can see the fish jump. Enjoy the quiet pace of the town.

Boat Excursions

When you get restless take a boat excursion on the lake; boats can be hired along the promenade. Take a boat to the **Sultaniye Kaplıcaları** or thermal springs, 30 km by road or eight nautical miles across the lake on the southern shore. The hot mineral waters are rich in calcium, sulphur, iron, nitrates, potassium and other mineral salts; temperatures sometimes reach 40°C. Admission costs 50c, and you should allow an hour if you plan to bathe in the mud, let it dry, and wash it off.

Other than the hot springs, you can take boat trips to Dalyan and its ruins, and to points along the Mediterranean coast. For details see the Dalyan/Caunus section following.

Places to Stay – bottom end

As you come into town there are many signs advertising pensions along the main boule-vard. Most prominent of the pensions is the *Pension & Café Deniz Feneri* (☎ (6114) 2560), an old-fashioned building recently fixed up with white stucco, Ottoman-style lattice screens on the windows and decorated with handicrafts and carved wood. The ground-floor café has been fixed up as a frontier saloon of sorts; Turkish and Greek flags fly happily together behind the bar. Wooden tables outside allow you to enjoy the fresh air. The high-ceilinged rooms are similarly decorated with handicrafts and, though simple, are fairly authentic period pieces, but have the useful addition of insect screens. Bath and shower are down the hall, and are primitive but serviceable. Rates are US$16 for a double, breakfast included.

Other pensions around the main square can be noisy, but head inland to the east and follow signs for these better, quieter places: *Oba* (☎ (6114) 1181 or 1306), charging from US$5 to US$7 per person; and *Atilla* (☎ (6114) 2703), run by a Turkish-German couple, charging US$18 a double for very clean rooms.

Behind the Hotel Kaunos is the *Motel Beyaz Konak* (☎ (6114) 1893), a simple, modern building with double rooms renting for US$15 with shower. Also here, and cheaper, are the *Myra* and the *Özbek*.

Inland a block from the Beyaz Konak (400 metres west of the main square) is the *Özbek Pension* (☎ (6114) 2840), modern and tidy, with rooms for US$14 in summer.

Camping One km west of the mosque along the shore is *Anatolia Camping* (☎ (6114) 1750), a forest camping ground among liquidambar trees, with a small beach nearby.

Places to Stay – middle

Walk past the mosque and the Belediye to the two-star, 20-room *Hotel Özay* (☎ (6114) 1300, 1361), Kordonboyu 11, a nice little modern place with a small pool in front surrounded by shady vine-covered arbours. Rooms have private showers, tiny balconies with partial lake views, and cost US$30 for a double in the tourist season, breakfast included.

Farther along in the same direction (west) is the *Hotel Kaunos* (☎ (6114) 1288; fax 1836), Cengiz Topel Caddesi 37, also rated at two stars. The 40 rooms have private showers and balconies overlooking the placid lake. In front of the hotel is a pretty terrace where you can relax and enjoy the view. There's a restaurant and bar as well. Rates are US$32 a double, breakfast included.

A bit farther west and inland a few blocks is the new *Evceğiz Otel* (☎ (6114) 2343; fax 2342), Ulucami Mahallesi, Ali İhsan Kalmaz Caddesi, 300 metres from the main square. The nice atmosphere, friendly welcome and clean comfortable rooms make the price, US$15 a double with shower, excellent value.

Places to Eat
As always, the market has the cheapest eats. For special occasions, the *Gölbaşı*, next to the Tourism Information Office, is good for fish. The *Şamdan*, near the Hotel-Pension Villa, is as good but doesn't have the lakeshore location. *Meşhur Ali Baba Pide Salonu*, on the east side of the main park, has good cheap Turkish pizza. The *Nokta Pide Salonu* is north (inland) a short distance; the *Penguen Pide Salonu* is opposite the Nokta, so there's no shortage of cheap eats.

Getting There & Away
Unless you don't mind walking that last two km into town, make sure your bus will drop you at the Köyceğiz otogar on the west side of the main street a few hundred metres north of the Atapark behind the Kamil Koç bus-company office.

Kamil Koç runs nine buses daily to Marmaris (75 km, 1½ hours, US$2.75), and nine to Fethiye (95 km, two hours, US$4). Pamukkale has about a dozen buses to Marmaris. Köyceğiz Minibüs Kooperatifi operates frequent minibuses to Marmaris, Muğla (57 km, one hour, US$2.25), to Ortaca (for Dalyan, 20 km, 25 minutes, US$1), and Dalaman (34 km, 40 minutes, US$1.50).

Bicycles are for rent next to the mosque.

DALYAN/CAUNUS
Fishing for bass and mullet in the placid waters of Köyceğiz Gölü (Köyceğiz Lake) and at broad weirs near the mouth of the stream Dalyan Çayı, and farming the rich alluvial soil of the flood plain is what the Dalyanlıs do when not catering to tourists.

The tourists come to this lush alluvial plain and cruise the calm river and lake in motor launches, usually having the ruins of ancient Caunus as their ultimate destination. Above the river on sheer cliffs are the weathered façades of Lycian tombs cut from the living rock. To the south, on the Mediterranean, lies İztuzu beach, a fine place for sunning and swimming, but more famous as the nesting place of *Caretta caretta*, the loggerhead sea turtle.

Orientation
It's 13 km from the highway at Ortaca to Dalyan's centre by the mosque and the towering post office building. To the north along the riverbank are the requisite tea terraces and, inland from them, pensions, hotels and restaurants. To the south are most of the town's hotels and pensions along Maraş

Lycian Rock Tombs

Caddesi, which runs one km south and ends at the riverbank.

Information

Dalyan has no official Tourism Information Office. Ask your questions at the big Belediye building at the northern end of Maraş Caddesi. There is a Sağlık Ocağı (medical clinic) near the Hotel Dalyan, south of the centre. Dalyan's postal code is 48840.

Boat Excursions

On the town's tidy quay you can choose an excursion boat for a cruise to the ruins of Caunus, the pretty cove at Ekincik, the beach at İztuzu on the Mediterranean coast or up the stream Dalyan Çayı to Köyceğiz Gölü and the Sultaniye hot springs and mud baths. Single fares are from US$3 to US$4. If you can organise a small group, it's often more economical to hire an entire passenger boat which holds from eight to 12 people. Do some haggling to get the best price, particularly if there are many boats without work, as is the case early and late in the season.

A two-hour tour just to the Caunus ruins costs from US$30 to US$40 for the entire boat; if you want to visit the Sultaniye hot springs as well, figure on three hours and US$50 for the boat. To charter a boat just for Caunus costs US$14.

Want to do it yourself? Rowing boats are for rent as well, at US$8 per day.

Boats belonging to the Dalyan Kooperatifi operate a 'river dolmuş' service between the town and İztuzu beach, charging U3$1.75 for the round trip. In high summer there may be five or more boats per day, heading out from 9 to 11 am, returning between 4 and 6 pm. (In high summer minibuses serve İztuzu by land as well.) Take some food as you might not like the few little kebap stands on the beach, which has few other facilities.

Caunus

This was an important Carian city by 400 BC, having been founded perhaps five centuries before. Right on the border with the kingdom of Lycia, its culture shared aspects of both kingdoms. The **tombs**, for instance,

are in Lycian style (you'll see many more of them at Fethiye, Kaş and other points east). If you don't hire a boat for a cruise on the river, walk south from town along Maraş Caddesi and you can get a fairly good view of the tombs.

Those curious wooden structures in the river are **fishing weirs** *(dalyan)*. No doubt the ancient Caunians benefited from such an industry as well.

Your boat pulls up to the western bank, from whence it's a five-minute walk up to the site. Admission is from 8.30 am to 5.30 pm for US$1.

When Mausolus of Halicarnassus was ruler of Caria, his Hellenising influence reached the Caunians, who eagerly adopted Hellenistic culture. Though of good size, Caunus suffered from endemic malaria; according to Herodotus, its people were famous for the yellow cast to their skin and eyes. The Caunians' prosperity was also threatened by the silting of their harbour. The Mediterranean, which once surrounded the hill on which the archaeological site stands, has now retreated five km to the south, pushed back by silt from the Dalyan Çayı.

Besides the tombs, the **theatre** is very well preserved; parts of an **acropolis** and other structures (baths, a basilica, defensive walls) are nearby.

İztuzu Beach

This stretch of sand near the mouth of the Dalyan Çayı, six km south of the town, is an excellent swimming beach, and has some camping possibilities as well. A parking fee of US$1 is charged.

Hotel development was stopped several years ago when foreign visitors alerted ecologically minded locals to the significance of the beach as a breeding ground for the loggerhead turtle *(deniz kaplumbağa* in Turkish).

The turtles come here to lay their eggs at night in the soft sand from May to September when the beach is open during the day but closed between 10 pm and 8 am. Though local tour agencies and guides will tell you that it's alright to visit the beach at night to

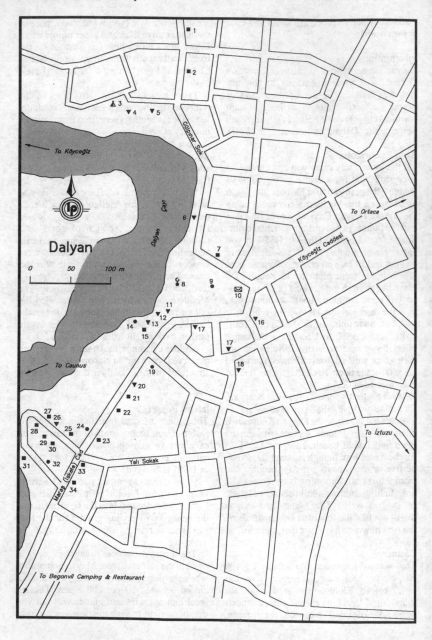

■ PLACES TO STAY

1 Nil Motel
2 Motel Patio
3 Dost Camping
7 Atay Pension
15 Kaunos Otel
21 Hakan Pansiyon
22 Albatros Pansiyon
23 Nur Pansiyon
25 Motel Özalp 1
27 Çınar Sahil Pansiyon
28 Hotel Caria
29 Otel Yalı
30 Hotel Dönmez
31 Hotel Dalyan
33 Dipdağ Motel & Pension
34 Beyaz Gül Pansiyon

▼ PLACES TO EAT

4 Sürmen Restaurant
5 Denizatı Restaurant
6 Tea Gardens
11 Köşem Restaurant
12 Kordon Restaurant
15 Kaunos Otel Restaurant
16 Derya Kebap ve Çorba Salonu
17 Café Natural
18 Very Special Turkish Meals
20 Çiçek Restaurant
26 Pembe Restaurant

OTHER

8 Mosque
9 Atatürk Statue
10 PTT
14 Dalyan Kooperatifi Boat Office
19 Belediye (Municipality)
24 İlk Okulu (School)
32 Sağlık Ocağı (Medical Clinic)

see the turtles, taking care not to disturb them, the best thing you can do is refrain from going near the beach at all at night during nesting season.

During the day the beach is open, but you must be careful to avoid the nesting sites, often identifiable by the marks which the turtles have made in the sand as they approach and lay. (If we were really interested in the turtles, we'd let them have this beach altogether, allowing no one to approach at any time.)

Places to Stay

Once known for its many cheap ev pansiyons (house pensions), Dalyan is fast going up-market. Waterless rooms are being given plumbing, and pensions are being razed to make way for hotels. At present, however, there are still good lodgings in all price ranges. Most of the town's accommodation is south of the centre along Maraş Caddesi. The road continues for just over one km before ending at the river bank, where there are several restaurants and a camping ground.

Places to Stay – bottom end

There are several pensions in the centre, but the ones along Maraş Caddesi to the south are preferable as they are quieter, and some have views of the river and the rock-cut tombs. Prices are generally US$5 per person in waterless rooms, US$6 with a private shower. Cheap hotels are usually priced from US$18 to US$22 for a double with shower.

Walking south along Maraş Caddesi, look for the family-run *Hakan Paynsion* and the similar *Albatros*, with no views, and therefore among the cheaper ones. *Nur Pansiyon* (☎ (6116) 1007), across from the İlk Okul (primary school) is similar. The *Aktaş* (☎ (6116) 1042) is on the water, however, with views of the river and tombs; all rooms have showers. The *Sahil* (☎ (6116) 1187), despite its name ('shore') actually has two locations, one on the water and one inland. The *Beyaz Gül Pansiyon*, just past the Dipdağ Motel, is among the most atmospheric.

Dipdağ Motel & Pension (☎ (6116) 1401, 1778) is on the corner of Maraş Caddesi and Yalı Sokak, a short street running to the river. All rooms have showers, and cost US$16 a double, but there are newer, nicer places at the same price on the street to the river.

Turn right (north-west towards the water) at the Dipdağ onto Yalı Sokak to find the 35-room *Hotel Dönmez* (☎ (6116) 1107; fax 1201). It's new and nice, offering the best value on this street with bath-equipped hotel rooms going for US$20. *Motel Özalp 1*, across the street, is a simpler place with a breezy roof terrace.

Otel Yalı (☎ (6116) 1134; fax 1086) follows the modern Turkish architectural canon of white stucco and pine trim, and charges US$20 a double for its tiny balcony and bath-equipped rooms. The neighbouring *Hotel Caria* is similar in price and facilities, with balconies as well.

At the end of Yalı Sokak on the shore is the nice *Çınar Sahil Pension* (☎ (6116) 1117), with a shady terrace from where you can gaze at the river.

In the centre of the town, the prominent *Atay Pension* (☎ (6116) 1156) across from the mosque has a convenient location and rooms on the second and third storeys up from the street, but it suffers from minaret noise.

There are more simple lodgings to the north of the centre past the Denizatı and Sürmen restaurants. They have no views to speak of. *Motel Patio* (☎ (6116) 1214) is new and tidy, as is the *Nil Motel* (☎ (6116 1383), charging US$18 a double with shower. A bit farther on is the *Can Pansiyon* (☎ (6116) 1252), an older and cheaper place, and the newer *Sun Motel*.

Camping Perhaps the best place for camping is the *Begonvil*, adjoining the restaurant of the same name at the southern end of Maraş Caddesi by the river. More camping areas are north of the centre. *Dost Camping* adjoins the Sürmen Restaurant; *Mehtap* is several hundred metres farther north. All of these places are quite primitive, with just running water and toilets, but more facilities will doubtless be provided soon.

Places to Stay – middle

Dalyan's old standby is the *Kaunos Otel & Restaurant* (☎ (6116) 1057), between the mosque and the river bank. It advertises *klima* (air-conditioning), which is weak at best. Its location is certainly convenient, and its price of US$35 a double, reasonable.

About one km north of the centre in the midst of farmers' fields is the three-star, 42-room *Antik Hotel* (☎ (6116) 1136, 1137; fax 1138), a modern place with rooms grouped around a nice swimming pool. It's an obvious choice for those with their own transport, charging US$35 for a double, breakfast included.

The town's best is the *Hotel Dalyan* (☎ (6116) 1239; fax 1240), at the end of Yalı Sokak around the corner to the right. Set on a point of land at a bend in the river, an emerald carpet of lawn surrounds comfortable, modern facilities priced at US$68 a double, breakfast included. It is often filled by German tour groups, so reserve ahead if you can.

Places to Eat

Café Natural has two locations, a small eatery on a shopping street at the centre, and a small terrace facing the main square where it serves döner kebap and toasted sandwiches. Prices are good, with three-course meals possible for US$2.50 to US$3.50.

'Very Special Turkish Meals' says the sign across the street from the Café Natural. This place serves the more unusual Turkish fare such as mantı (Turkish ravioli) and gözleme (thin bread griddle fried, sprinkled with meat, or cheese and folded over to make a many-layered sandwich).

Derya Kebap ve Çorba Salonu is inland behind the big post office building and a bit to the east. It's not touristy, which is why it's still good and cheap.

Çiçek Restaurant (☎ 1676), on Maraş Caddesi south of the centre, is dependably good and cheap.

Facing a terrace leading down to the river at the centre of town are three nice semi-open-air restaurants: the *Köşem Restaurant, Kordon Restaurant* and *Kaunos Hotel Restaurant*. The prices and situations are nearly identical, with breakfast priced at under US$2, meat-based meals for US$5 to US$8, fish for slightly more.

North of the centre, try the *Denizatı*, Dalyan's longest-lived restaurant, specialising in fish, or the neighbouring *Sürmen*, both of which have excellent views of the river and town from their river-bank locations. A full fish dinner costs from US$10 to US$12.

Getting There & Away

Dolmuşes run frequently between Dalyan, Ortaca, Köyceğiz, and Dalaman. You can often catch buses to more distant points at the highway in Ortaca, or take a minibus to Dalaman (23 km, 30 minutes, US$1.25) and change there.

DALAMAN

This agricultural town (population 15,000) was quite sleepy until the regional airport was built on the neighbouring river delta. Now the town stirs whenever a jet arrives, but otherwise slumbers as in the past. Most visitors pass right through, as they should. Bus connections are good. If you need to stay the night, Dalaman has a small but good selection of hotels.

Orientation

It is 5.5 km from the airport to the town, and another 5.5 km from the town to the east-west highway. The road connecting the highway with the airport is called Kenan Evren Bulvarı. The town itself has one main street named (surprise!) Atatürk Caddesi. It's about 500 metres long, running east from Kenan Evren Bulvarı, with banks, shops and simple restaurants. The bus station, served by the Pamukkale, Aydın and Köseoğlu companies, is near the junction of Evren Bulvarı and Atatürk Caddesi. The PTT is a block north of Atatürk Caddesi.

Places to Stay

As its air traffic grows Dalaman grows along with it. Look for the *Dalaman Pansiyon* (☎ (6119) 1543, 1550), 200 metres south of the traffic roundabout near the bus station, out towards the airport, where a double room with bath costs US$12.

The wonderfully named *Affable Pension* is a small village house run by an affable woman who charges from US$8 to US$10 for a waterless room, depending upon the season and your bargaining ability.

You can camp in the shade of fragrant pines in the *Belediye Koru Parkı* (Municipal Forest Park), 300 metres north of the otogar along Kenan Evren Bulvarı.

The well kept *Otel Hafızoğlu* (☎ (6119) 1078), on Meltem Sokak, one block south of the bus station across Atatürk Caddesi, charges US$8/14/17 a single/double/triple for its standard one-star rooms with bath.

The two-star *Hotel Meltem* (☎ (6119) 2901), Kenan Evren Bulvarı 65, has 27 rooms with bath, a restaurant and bar, and charges from US$18 to US$22 a double, depending upon demand.

The *Airport Apart-Hotel* (☎ (6119) 1073; fax 2450), Kenan Evren Bulvarı, is not far away, just a few hundred metres south towards the airport. It has tidy rooms with private shower and air-conditioning which cost US$28 a double, breakfast included. There are 50 rooms; suites and apartments with more facilities cost a bit more.

The best place in town is the new *Hotel Dalaman Park* (☎ (6119 3158; fax 3332), with restaurant, bar, lifts, and a swimming pool. It's just a few hundred metres from the otogar on the airport road. Facilities almost rate three stars, and cost US$45/60 a single/double, breakfast included.

Getting There & Away

Unless you can hitch a ride into town from the airport, take a taxi to the bus station (US$2). At Dalaman's small otogar you can buy tickets to many destinations.

All routes north and east pass through either Muğla or Fethiye. Details of some services follow:

Antalya – 345 km, seven hours, US$9 (coastal route)
Bodrum – 201 km, 3½ hours, US$7
Denizli – 221 km, four hours, US$8
Fethiye – 50 km, one hour, US$2
Göcek – 23 km, 30 minutes, US$1
Gökova – 80 km, 1½ hours, US$3
İstanbul – 966 km, 16 hours, US$24
İzmir – 356 km, six hours, US$11
Kalkan – 131 km, three hours, US$6.25
Kaş – 160 km, 3½ hours, US$9
Köyceğiz – 34 km, 40 minutes, US$1.50
Marmaris – 120 km, 2½ to three hours, US$5 to US$6
Muğla – 91 km, 1½ hours, US$3.25

Pamukkale – 240 km, 4½ hours, US$10 (take the cheaper bus to Denizli, then a cheap city bus or minibus)
Patara – 125 km, 2¾ hours, US$5.50
Selçuk – 285 km, 5¼ hours, US$10

DALAMAN TO FETHİYE

The highway east of Dalaman winds through mountains cloaked in fragrant evergreen forests, with many liquidambar trees, before reaching Fethiye 50 km to the south-east. The road is slow to drive on but beautiful. Along the way the local foresters, anxious about forest fires, have erected dozens of signs bearing slogans which cry out for translation:

A huge forest fire hides in each tiny match.
Love of the forest is love of the Motherland.
Love, not rangers, protects the forest.
Lush green forest or charred wasteland: the choice is yours.
Love is as important to a tree as sunlight and water.
Every sapling brings hope for the future.

Göcek

About 23 km east of Dalaman a road on the right (south) is marked for Göcek, a delightful little hamlet on a bay at the foot of the mountains. Yachts stop in the harbour and fishing boats ply their trade. Near the village is a wharf from which chromium ore and forest products are shipped out.

Dolmuşes run to Göcek from behind the PTT in Fethiye several times daily, and frequently on summer weekends.

It's one km from the highway to the village square with its mosque, Belediye and Atatürk statue. All along the way are signs advertising small pensions and shady camping grounds. The road is being improved, and Göcek is obviously preparing for its tourism boom, when pensions will be razed to make way for hotels. For the time being, though, Göcek is largely unsullied by mass tourism. Come and sit in one of the waterfront restaurants for a sunset dinner.

Küçük Kargı & Katrancı

At a place called Küçük Kargı, 33 km east of Dalaman, is a forest picnic area with a camping place and beach. Two km farther east is Katrancı, another picnic and camping spot with a small restaurant, on a beautiful little cove with a beach. If you can plan it, stop here. It's a further 18 km to Fethiye.

FETHİYE

Fethiye (FEH-tee-yeh, population 25,000) is a very, very old town with few old buildings. An earthquake in 1958 levelled the town, leaving very little standing. Most of what was left were tombs from the time when Fethiye was called Telmessos (400 BC).

Fethiye's inner bay, protected by the island Şövalye Adası, is an excellent natural harbour, well protected from storms. The much larger outer bay has 11 more islands. Beaches are good here, and even better at nearby Ölüdeniz, one of Turkey's seaside hot spots. The Fethiye region has many interesting sites to explore, including the ghost town of Karmylassos, just over the hill.

Orientation

Fethiye's ötogar is one km west of the highway, and the centre of town is another km to the west. Mid-range and top-end hotels are near the centre, but most inexpensive pensions are either east of the centre near the bus station, or west of the centre overlooking the yacht harbour. Dolmuşes run to and fro along Fethiye's main street, Atatürk Caddesi.

The all-important beach at Ölüdeniz is 15 km south of Fethiye. For full information see the Ölüdeniz section.

Information

Fethiye's Tourism Information Office (☎ (615) 11527), open from 8 am to 8 pm daily in summer (from 8 am to 5 pm in winter) is on İskele Meydanı next to the Dedeoğlu Hotel, near the yacht harbour at the downtown end of Atatürk Caddesi. The staff will help you with lodgings and inexpensive yacht charters. Right next door is the office of the Fethiye Turizm Derneği (Fethiye Tourism Association), a local group which can also provide helpful information. On Atatürk Caddesi across from the Kordon Oteli is the Fethiye Belediyesi Turizm Ofisi, the city's contribution to the tourism information game.

Should you need a doctor, a reader of this book recommends Doktor Hasan Ali Bulak (☎ (615) 16812), who speaks English.

Fethiye's postal code is 48300.

Things to See & Do
Throughout the town you will notice curious Lycian stone **sarcophagi** dating from around 450 BC. There is a sarcophagus near the PTT, and others in the middle of streets or in private gardens; the town was built around them. All have been broken into by tomb robbers millennia ago, of course.

Carved into the rock face behind the town is the so-called **Tomb of Amyntas** (350 BC), a Doric temple façade carved in the sheer rock face. It's open from 8 am to 7 pm for US$1, and is very crowded at sunset in summer, the most pleasant time to visit. Other smaller tombs are near it, off to the left. Follow the signs, or take a taxi for a look at the tomb and the fine view of the town and bay.

Fethiye's **museum** is open from 8 am to 5 pm (closed on Monday) and charges US$1 for admission. It's small and dull, with the exception of some nice small statues and votive stones (the so-called 'Stelae of Graves' and 'Stelae of Promise'). The trilingual stele (Lycian-Greek-Aramaic) from Letoön, describing the dedication of a pious foundation to the mythical King Kaunos in 358 BC, was instrumental in deciphering the Lycian language.

On the hillside behind the town, just north of the road to Karmylassos, notice the ruined tower of a **crusader fortress** constructed by the Knights of St John on earlier foundations dating back perhaps to 400 BC.

Beaches Five km north-east of the centre is **Çalış**, a wide swath of beach several km long lined with little hotels and pensions. It was once Fethiye's claim to fame, but now is somewhat ignored by the crowds racing to Ölüdeniz (described following). Dolmuşes depart from behind the PTT for Çalış frequently all day.

Other beaches are on Şövalye island, and at Katrancı and Küçük Kargı, described just before the Fethiye section. Gemile beach, opposite the island of the same name, is five km beyond Kayaköy (see following) along a rough road.

Still more secluded beaches become available if you sign up for a boat tour or hire a boat for a day's outing.

Archaeological Sites You can arrange to take a boat or minibus tour to some of the archaeological sites and beaches along the nearby coasts. Standard tours are those which go west to Günlük (Küçük Kargı), Pınarbaşı, Dalyan and Caunus, and east to Letoön, Kalkan, Kaş, Patara and Xanthos. See those sections for details on the sites.

Kayaköy (Karmylassos) Called Levissi for much of its history, this town of 2000 stone houses eight km south of Fethiye was deserted by its mostly Ottoman Greek inhabitants after WW I and the Turkish War of Independence. The League of Nations established rules for an exchange of populations between Turkey and Greece, with most Greek Muslims coming from Greece to Turkey, and most Ottoman Christians moving to Greece. The people of Levissi, most of whom were Orthodox Christians, moved to the outskirts of Athens and founded a neighbourhood called Nea Levissi.

As there were far more Ottoman Greeks than Greek Muslims, many of the towns vacated by the Ottoman Greeks were left unoccupied after the exchange of populations. Kayaköy, as it is called now, has only a handful of Turkish inhabitants – farmers and herders who trek to the fertile Kaya Çukuru (Rock Basin) each day.

With the tourism boom of the 1980s, a development company sought permission to restore Kayaköy's stone houses and turn the town into a holiday village. The local inhabitants were delighted, as their property values would rise dramatically. Turkish artists and architects, however, were

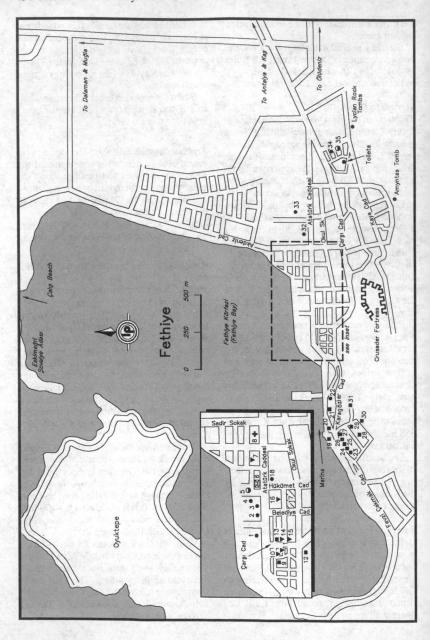

alarmed, and saw to it that the Ministry of Culture declared Kayaköy a historical monument, safe from unregulated development.

Plans now call for some careful restoration of the town, and its use as a venue for cultural presentations. A few simple pensions and restaurants provide for those who want to stay awhile.

Two churches are still prominent, the Panayia Pirgiotissa in the lower part of the town, and the Taxiarhis farther up the slope. Some carving and murals are still preserved.

Tours run to Kayaköy along the paved road from Fethiye daily, but it is much more enjoyable to leave Fethiye early in the morning and hike the two hours up to the site. After a look at Kayaköy and a cool drink, you can continue along a marked trail to Ölüdeniz, another two to 2½ hours (eight km) away.

12-Island Cruise Be sure to sign up for the 12-island tour, a boat trip around Fethiye Bay which takes most of a day (from 9 am to 6 or 7 pm) and costs between US$6 and US$8 per person. Any hotel or travel agency can sign you up, or just ask around at the harbour.

A normal tour visits **Şövalye island**, at the mouth of the inner bay, with a beach and restaurant; **Gemile**, with the unrestored ruins of an ancient city; **Katrancı**, offshore from the beach of the same name to the west of Fethiye; **Göcek**, opposite the town 27 km west of Fethiye; and the **islands** named Kızılada, Tersane, Domuz, Yassıcalar, Delikli, Şeytanlı, and Karacaören.

Scuba Diving European Divers, a scuba-diving company founded by two Welshmen, offers day trips for US$55, including two dives and lunch. The diving is well organised and visibility is excellent, though the seabed is somewhat littered and overfishing has robbed the area of much of its marine life. If you do not have your diver's certification, you can take a certification course for US$300. There are other dive companies in Fethiye as well, including the Fethiye Diving Centre (☎ (615) 16582), on Fevzi Çakmak Caddesi.

Places to Stay
Fethiye has a good selection of budget and mid-range lodgings, but little in the way of luxury.

Places to Stay – bottom end
Fethiye has several dozen small downtown hotels and almost 100 small pensions so

Around Fethiye

0   10   20 km

MEDITERRANEAN SEA
(AKDENİZ)

you're sure to find suitable cheap lodgings. Pension owners with vacant rooms await your bus at the otogar. Some of these bottom-end places are on quiet back streets a five or 10-minute walk from the centre, and would be difficult to find without the owner as guide.

East of the Centre The following are several pensions which readers of this book have found to be excellent.

Next to the stadium, *Göreme Pansiyon* (☎ (615) 16944), Dolgu Sahası, Stadyum Yanı 25, is run by the very friendly and

helpful Ali Duvarcı. Mr and Mrs Duvarcı lived in London for a while, and speak English. The rate for bed and breakfast is US$10/14 a single/double.

Amintas Pension (☎ (615) 12883, 11732), Dolgu Sahası, 2. Park Geçidi No 6, is run by the estimable Erol Süleyman Sivri, whose sons speak some English.

Olimpiyat Pansiyon (☎ (615) 13444; fax 13445), Stadyum Yanı, Yerguz Caddesi 48, run by Mr Osman Toklu, has big, clean rooms for US$14 a double, breakfast included.

On the road to Çalış beach, try the *Konak*

Pension (☎ (615) 13393), with rooms set around a beautiful orchard. The charming, helpful owners charge US$12 a double, breakfast included.

West of the Centre The main concentration of pensions at the centre is west of the tourism office, up the hill behind the Likya Hotel in the district called 1. Karagözler Mahallesi: look for the little 'pansiyon' signs. Some places provide rooms with shower, but most rooms are waterless and cost from US$3 to US$5 per person, depending upon whether your room has a shower; breakfast usually costs another US$1. Some of these pensions close in winter.

Walking up the hill along Fevzi Çakmak Caddesi, you'll come to the *Yıldırım* (☎ (615) 13913); the *Pınara* (☎ (615) 12151), at No 39; *Derelioğlu* (☎ (615) 15983); *Polat* (☎ (615) 12347); and *İrem* (☎ (615) 13985) at No 45.

Up the hill behind these places on Zafer Caddesi (follow signs for the Hotel Pırlanta) are several excellent choices, including the *Pension Ideal* (☎ (615) 11981), Zafer Caddesi 1, with a fine terrace overlooking the bay. Built more as a hotel, all rooms have showers and cost US$12/18 a single/double in season, breakfast included.

Farther uphill are even cheaper places, the clean and friendly *İnci Pension* (☎ (615) 13325), with clean, shower-equipped rooms for US$10/14 a single/double; and the similar *Cesur* (☎ (615) 13398) across the street.

The Centre If you want a simple central hotel try the modern *Hotel Kaya* (KAH-yah) (☎ (615) 11161, 12469), Cumhuriyet Caddesi 6, next to the Güneş Restaurant a block inland from the main road on a narrow market street. Graced with a wonderful jasmine vine on its façade, the Kaya charges US$11/15 for a single/double with private shower. The *Hotel Kent* facing the Kaya is similar in price and comforts.

There's a good pension at the centre as well, the *Ülgen Pansiyon* (☎ (615) 13491), up a flight of steps off Çarşı Caddesi. Con-

venient to everything in the centre, it also offers fine views, and charges only US$7/12 a single/double in friendly surroundings.

Places to Stay – middle
The four-star *Hotel Pırlanta* (☎ (615) 14959; fax 11686), 1. Karagözler Mevkii, up the hill behind the Hotel Likya, is the fanciest city-centre hotel. Many of its 72 rooms have wonderful water views; all have balconies and, of course, bathrooms. Rates are US$40/55 a single/double, and worth it.

Just opposite the yacht marina is Fethiye's old standard, the 40-room *Hotel Likya* (☎ (615) 12233, 11169; fax 13100), 1. Karagözler Mahallesi. Its older rooms open onto the sea and Fethiye's most pleasant gardens, and cost US$28/36/44 for singles/doubles/triples, breakfast included. The Likya has a swimming pool and a Chinese restaurant (see following).

The new two-star, 27-room *Hotel Statüs* (☎ (615) 11068), between the Hotel Likya and the pensions on Fevzi Çakmak Caddesi, has good views across the marina and bay, but rooms with those views may suffer from noise from the disco below. Rooms cost US$18/22 a single/double.

The older two-star *Otel Dedeoğlu* (☎ (615) 14010; fax 11707), İskele Meydanı, next to the Tourism Information Office, has 41 rooms with sea view and private bathrooms priced at US$20/26 for singles/doubles, breakfast included. It's far from elegant, with a leather shop crowding the lobby, but it will do nicely.

In town at the intersection of Çarşı and Atatürk caddesis stands the *Hotel Sema* (☎ (615) 11015; fax 31061). Though it was among the first hotels built in the city, it has been kept up-to-date and its modest comforts are yours for US$16/22 a single/double.

Places to Eat
Fethiye is fast earning a reputation as a place where restaurateurs cheat you in many small ways. At any restaurant be sure to ask prices – at least the price of the main course, and especially the price of fish – before you order. Don't let waiters put items on your

table which you have not ordered. If they do, ask *Bedava mı?* (Is it free?) It rarely is. Also, check your bill carefully. I've found more 'errors' here than in İstanbul.

Places to Eat – bottom end

For really cheap fare in Fethiye you must go off the beaten path to where the workers eat – no English menus, no fancy tablecloths. Go east along the street behind the PTT to find the *Osman Bey Restaurant* and the *Canbaba Çorba & Köfte Salonu*, serving filling meals of soup, grilled köfte and ready food for US$2 to US$4. There are more places farther along.

Among the least expensive restaurants in the bazaar are two on Çarşı Caddesi: the *Tuna Merkez*, and the *Tahirağa Lokantası* (☎ 16308), across the street at Çarşı Caddesi 12. Both always have good selections of ready food as well as numerous kebaps, both serve beer and wine, and both also have a few streetside tables and charge from US$5 to US$7 for a meal. Around the corner on Tütün Sokak is the *Tuna Merkez 2*, which is a bit quieter. Farther down this street on the left-hand side is *Nefis Pide Salonu* which serves cheap pide, and more: soup, şiş kebap, bread and a soft drink costs only about US$3.

Around the corner is *Pizza Pepino* – nice, quiet, and not overly expensive.

Places to Eat – middle

In the bazaar, *Afrodit Restaurant* (☎ 12005), also called Üsküdarlı'nın Yeri, is half a block west of Çarşı Caddesi on the first street south of Atatürk Caddesi. It gets good marks for food, service, and value for money. The menu is heavy in snacks, good cheap soups, and light-meal items such as börek.

The *Güneş*, recommended in earlier editions of this guide, is usually busy, but some readers have not been fully pleased.

The *Peking Restaurant* has good Thai-style oriental food, but you must beware of the waiters who bring you dishes you did not order.

For atmosphere, try the *Yacht Restaurant*, facing the yacht harbour right by the Hotel Likya. The outdoor tables are very pleasant,

the service polite, and the food quite good. A fish dinner might cost about US$12, drinks included. Another good choice is the *Rafet Restaurant* on the waterfront.

The *Happy Chinese Restaurant* at the Hotel Likya is good for a change, with tables set out right by the water. Expect to spend about US$15 per person for good, if not purely authentic, Chinese cuisine.

Getting There & Away

Bus Isolated by the mountains behind it, Fethiye's transport goes east and west and for many routes you must change at Antalya or Muğla. There are, however, buses eastward along the coast at least every two hours in summer.

The otogar is one km east of the centre, and one km west of the highway. A neighbouring garage handles much of the minibus dolmuş traffic to intermediate-distance destinations, but a separate lot behind the PTT in the centre is for short-distance trips to Ölüdeniz, Çalış beach, and Katrancı.

The Pamukkale bus company has a city-centre ticket office at Atatürk Caddesi 30, near the Atatürk statue and the Garanti Bankası.

The archaeological sites eastward (Xanthos, Letoön, Patara etc) can be reached by frequent dolmuşes from Fethiye – you needn't take an expensive tour. Bus fares along this stretch of coast tend to be high as the passengers are mostly tourists. The highways in this region are being greatly improved, with new routings, wider curves and more gentle grades. These improvements shorten highway distances and decrease travel times. Some approximate times and distances include:

Antalya – 295 km, seven hours, US$12 (*sahil*, coastal route); 222 km, 4½ hours, US$8 (*yayla*, inland route)
Dalaman – 50 km, one hour, US$2
Demre – 155 km, 3½ hours, US$5
Denizli – 290 km, 5½ hours, US$8
Kalkan – 81 km, two hours, US$2.75
Kaş – 110 km, 2½ hours, US$3
Letoön – 60 km, 1½ hours, US$2
Marmaris – 170 km, four hours, US$6.50

Muğla – 150 km, three hours, US$6
Ölüdeniz – 15 km, 25 minutes, US$1;
    catch this bus behind the PTT
Pamukkale – 309 km, six hours, US$10
Patara – 75 km, two hours, US$2.75
Pınara – 52 km, one hour, US$1.75; take a minibus to
    Akşam Belen Makası, then walk six km, or
    bargain with the driver to take you all the way
Tlos – 40 km, one hour, US$1.75; one morning depar-
    ture from Tlos, one afternoon from Fethiye;
    arrange a price with the driver to return to Fethiye
    the same evening
Xanthos (Kınık) – 65 km, 1½ hours, US$1.75

Boat A hydrofoil service operates in high summer between Rhodes (Greece) and Fethiye. Contact the tourism office for details.

ÖLÜDENİZ

Ölüdeniz (eur-LUR-deh-neez, Dead or 'Calm' Sea) is not dead like its biblical namesake. Rather, it is a very sheltered lagoon not at all visible from the open sea. The scene as you come down from the pine-forested hills is absolutely beautiful: in the distance is open sea, in the foreground a peaceful lagoon bordered by forest, in the middle a long sand spit of perfect beach. Yachts stand at anchor in the blue water, or glide gracefully along the hidden channel out to sea. The discordant note is the rampant and unplanned development taking place all along the road to the beach.

The development of Ölüdeniz has been somewhat haphazard, with a jumble of makeshift camping areas and rentable shacks beginning several km inland from the shore. The beach area itself has been laid out as a park with stone walkways, dressing and toilet facilities. Admission to the beach area costs US$2.

Orientation

As you approach Ölüdeniz, the road passes through the village of Ovacık. Dozens of pensions line the road, and if you want to stay near the beach and stay cheaply, this is the place. Four km beyond Ovacık the road descends towards the great and beautiful swath of beach.

When you reach the beach you are at the centre of things. Most of the beach is closed to vehicular traffic, though you can drive as far as the Hotel Meri and nearby camping grounds.

To your right (north-west) is a jandarma post, a PTT and the entrance to the Ölüdeniz Piknik Yeri (picnic ground). Beyond these are five camping grounds and the Hotel Meri overlooking the lagoon.

To your left (south-east), just inland from the beach promenade, are restaurants backed by 'camps' with small cabins, dependably full in high season. Behind these cabin camps are more of the same, then some cultivated fields, then small hotels and camping grounds.

At the far left end of the beach the road climbs up a slope and clings to the mountainside for two km before descending to Kıdrak Orman Parkı (Kıdrak Forest Park), with the most beautiful camping facilities for tenters. A hotel is being developed a short way past Kıdrak.

You can rent water-sports equipment on the main beach. Excursion boats leave the main beach to explore the coast, charging from US$6 to US$8 per person.

Places to Stay

My suggestion is to stay in Fethiye at least one night, then – if you must stay at the beach – come out to Ölüdeniz the next morning and reserve a place to stay.

To the left towards the Hotel Meri are five camping areas: *Ölüdeniz Kamp*, one km past the jandarma post; then *Ölüdeniz Asmalı*, with bungalows as well as tent spaces; *Suara*, with a restaurant; *Bambus* and *Genç Camping*, which has bungalows, too. The last two are right in front of the Hotel Meri.

The two-star *Hotel Meri* (☎ (615) 14388) has 75 rooms scattered down a steep hillside amidst pretty gardens. The views from many of the rooms are very fine. Some of the rooms are a bit musty, but this place has a lock on the market here so the price for a double with bath, breakfast and dinner included is US$55; similar singles cost US$40, triples are US$70. The motel has its own beach and seaside restaurant.

Places to Eat

The *Han Restaurant*, facing the beach, is the cheapest and most popular beachfront spot. You can save a bit of money by walking inland along the access road to the *Pirate's Inn Restaurant & Bar* which, because it is 100 metres from the beach, has lower prices. The *Kum Tur*, on the beach south-east of Deniz Camp, is cheap, with good food and atmosphere.

The imported beach culture at Ölüdeniz includes the concept of a Happy Hour, when drinks are cheaper. Try the Buzz Bar if you want a lively place, Harry's Bar if you take your happiness more quietly.

FETHİYE TO KAŞ

This portion of the Lycian coast, sometimes called the Lycian Peninsula because it extends well south into the Mediterranean, is littered with the remains of ancient cities. If you have your own transport you can visit as many of these as you like by making a few short detours. Without a car you can still make your way to many of them by dolmuş or bus, with perhaps a bit of a hike here and there.

The highways in the Lycian peninsula are rapidly being improved. This sometimes means changes in their routings. Keep this in mind as you travel to the many sites described below.

Tlos

Tlos was one of the oldest and most important cities in ancient Lycia. Its prominence is matched by its promontory, as the city has a dramatic setting high on a rocky outcrop. As you climb the winding road to Tlos, look for the fortress-topped **acropolis** on the right. On a rock wall beneath it is the impressive **Tomb of Bellerophon**, a pseudo-temple façade carved into the rock-face. You can reach the tomb by a winding path which descends along a stream bed, turns left, then climbs a crude ladder to the site.

At the ticket kiosk, pay the US$1 admission fee. One of the men there will offer to be your guide (for a tip), which is a good idea if you want to see all of the rock-cut tombs,

as he knows the paths and can save you some time.

The **fortress** crowns the acropolis; what you see is Ottoman-era work, but the Lycians had a fort in the same place. Beneath it, reached by narrow paths, are the familiar **rock-cut tombs**, including that of Bellerophon, which has a fine bas relief of the hero riding Pegasus, the winged horse.

The **theatre** is 100 metres farther up the road from the ticket kiosk, and is in excellent condition, with most of its marble seating intact, though the stage wall is gone. There's a fine view of the acropolis from here. Off to the right of the theatre (as you sit in the centre rows) is one of those ancient **Lycian sarcophagi** in a farmer's field. The **necropolis** on the path up to the fortress has many stone sarcophagi.

You can buy drinks and snacks in the small village here but there are few other services.

Back on the highway heading south towards Kaş, the road takes you up into fragrant evergreen forests and down to fertile valleys. Herds of sheep and goats (and a few cattle) skitter along the road near the villages. The road is curvy and the journey somewhat slow. Farm tractors pulling trailers can slow you down as well.

Getting There & Away Follow the road 23 km east from Fethiye to the village of Kemer, where the road to Antalya divides at a traffic roundabout into the coastal (sahil) route via Kaş, to the right ('Kaş-Antalya'), and the inland (yayla) route via Korkuteli straight on ('Korkuteli-Antalya'). Go straight on for the inland route and, about one km later, just after crossing the bridge over the stream Esençay, take the first road on the right, marked for Tlos and several villages including Güneşli and Yaka. It's eight km to Güneşli, where you turn left onto an unpaved road to Yaka (four km), which is the village next to Tlos.

One minibus a day leaves Yaka in the morning for Fethiye, returning in the afternoon. If you take the afternoon minibus up, you can haggle with the driver to take you back down to Fethiye. Agree on the fare in advance.

Pınara

Some 46 km east of Fethiye, near the village of Esen, is the turn-off (to the right) for Pınara, which lies another six km up in the mountains. Minibuses from Fethiye (one hour, US$1.75) drop you at the start of the Pınara road, at a place called Akşam Belen Makası, from which you can walk six km to the site, or bargain with the driver to take you all the way. (Note: the highway is being improved hereabouts, and may have been rerouted somewhat by the time you arrive.)

The road winds through tobacco and corn-fields and alongside irrigation channels for over three km to the village of Minare, then takes a sharp left turn to climb the slope. The last two-plus km are extremely steep and rough, and not all cars can make it. If yours has trouble, try doing it in reverse as that is often a car's lowest gear, or get out and walk.

At the top of the slope is an open parking area, and near it a cool, shady spring with refreshing water. The guardian may appear and offer to show you around the ruins, and it is wise to take him up on his offer as the path around the site (which is always open) is not easy to follow. You may want to tip the guardian if he gives you a tour.

Pınara was among the most important cities in ancient Lycia and, though the site is vast, there are only a few features which make a lasting impression. The sheer column of rock behind the site, and the rock walls to its left, are pock-marked with many **rock-cut tombs**. To reach any one of them would take several hours. Other tombs are within the ruined city itself. The one called the Royal (or King's) Tomb has particularly fine reliefs, including several showing walled cities.

Pınara's **theatre** is in good condition; its **odeum**, badly ruined. The **temples** of Apollo, Aphrodite and Athena (with heart-shaped columns) are also badly ruined, but in a fine location.

The village at **Esen**, three km south-east

of the Pınara turn-off, has a few basic pensions and restaurants.

Sidyma

About four km south and east of Esen, a road goes off to the left for Sidyma, 12 km over a rough dirt road. The ruins are not spectacular. If you've seen all the other Lycian cities and are simply aching for more, then take the time to visit Sidyma. Otherwise, head onward.

Letoön

Seventeen km east of the Pınara turn-off is the road to Letoön, on the right-hand (south-west) side near the village of Kumluova. (Dolmuşes run from Fethiye via Esen to Kumluova, get out at the Letoön turn-off.) Turn right off the highway, go 3.2 km to a T junction, turn left, go 100 metres, then turn right (this turn-off is easy to miss) and proceed one km to the site through fertile fields and orchards, and past greenhouses full of tomato plants. If you miss the second turn you'll end up (after one km) in the village on the main square with its bust of Atatürk. There are no services as this is still a farming village largely unaffected by tourism.

When you get to the ruins, a person selling soft drinks and admission tickets (US$1) will greet you.

Letoön takes its name and importance from a large and impressive shrine to Leto, who according to legend was loved by Zeus. Hera, Zeus' wife, was upset by this arrangement and commanded that Leto spend an eternity wandering from country to country. According to local legends she spent a lot of this enforced holiday time in Lycia. In any case, she became the Lycian national deity, and the federation of Lycian cities built this impressive religious sanctuary for worship of her.

The site consists of three **temples** side by side, to Apollo (on the left), Artemis (in the middle) and Leto (on the right). The Temple of Apollo has a nice mosaic showing a lyre and a bow and arrow. There's also a **nymphaeum** which is permanently flooded and inhabited by frogs, which is appropriate as worship of Leto was somehow associated with water. Nearby is a large Hellenistic **theatre** in excellent condition, with a corn-field for a stage.

Xanthos

At Kınık, 63 km from Fethiye, the road crosses a river. Up to the left on a rock outcrop is the ruined city of Xanthos, once the capital and grandest city of Lycia, with a fine **Roman theatre** and **Lycian pillar tombs** with Lycian inscriptions. Dolmuşes run here from Fethiye, and some long-distance buses will stop if you ask.

Walk up the hill to the site. Xanthos, for all its importance and grandeur, had a chequered history of wars and destruction. Several times, when besieged by clearly superior enemy forces, the city was destroyed by its own inhabitants. You'll see the **theatre** at once, and opposite it is the **agora**. Though Xanthos was a large and important city, the **acropolis** is now badly ruined. Many of the finest sculptures and inscriptions were carried off to the British Museum in 1842; many of the inscriptions and decorations you see here today are copies of the originals. Excavations by a French team in the 1950s have made Xanthos worth visiting, however. One enjoys the spicy smells of sage and mint which waft up while trudging through the ruins. Try to get here before the heat of the day.

Patara

Heading east again, after seven km you'll reach the turn-off for Patara. The ruins here are of some interest and they come with a bonus in the form of a wonderful white sand beach some 50 metres wide and 20 km long.

Patara was the birthplace of Santa Claus. Yes! The 4th-century Byzantine bishop who was later canonised as St Nicholas was a Patara native. Most of his life and work was in Myra (Demre), farther east along the coast, and his church there is still much visited.

Before St Nicholas, Patara had a famous temple and oracle of Apollo, of which little remains.

Orientation Look for the Patara turn-off just east of the village of Ovaköy; from here it's 3.5 km to the village of Patara, with its pensions, hotels and restaurants, or five km to the ruins; the beach is one km past the ruins.

The Ruins Admission to the ruins costs US$1, and includes admission to the beach. The ruins at Patara include a triple-arched **triumphal gate** at the entrance to the site and just past it a **necropolis** with a **Lycian tomb**. Next are the **baths** and a much later **basilica**.

The good sized **theatre** is striking because it is half-covered by wind-driven sand, which seems intent on making a dune out of it. Climb to the top of the theatre for a good view of the whole site.

Several other **baths**, two **temples** as well as a Corinthian temple by the lake are also here, though the swampy ground may make them difficult to approach. Across the lake is a **granary**. What is now a swamp was once the city's harbour. When it silted up, the city declined, as usual.

The Beach The beach is simply splendid, and the problems of litter and itinerant vendors have been addressed, if not completely solved. You can get to the beach by following the road in through the ruins, or by turning right at the Golden Pension and following the track which heads for the sand dunes on the other (western) side of the archaeological zone. It's about a 30-minute walk. Sometimes you can hitch a ride with vehicles passing along the main road.

Be sure to bring footwear for crossing the 50 metres of scorching sand to the water's edge, and also something for shelter if you can as there are few places to get out of the sun, and bad burns are a real problem. If you don't have your own shelter, rent a beach umbrella for US$2 at the beach.

Two little restaurants, the *Patara* and the *Harabe*, provide shade and sustenance, though you might do well to bring a picnic.

There is a public telephone at the Patara.
There's an admission fee of US$1. The beach
closes at dusk, as it is a nesting ground for
sea turtles. Camping is prohibited.

Places to Stay – bottom end Patara has
grown at an unbelievable rate and somewhat
chaotically in recent years, and now has
lodgings in all price ranges.

The best known of the cheap pensions is
the *Golden Pension & Restaurant* (☎ (3215)
1166), right in the village centre, with 15
rooms – six with private shower, nine
without – and a restaurant on the roof. The
charge for a double room with shower is
US$15 in season, slightly less in the off
season. The owner, Muzaffer Otlu, speaks
some English and French and is very
friendly.

There are many similarly priced pensions
around, including the *St Nicholas*, the *Akgül*
and the *Sisyphos*. The *Patara Pension* also
calls itself the Patara Motel and is a newer
building with double rooms with shower for
US$18 to US$20 in season, almost half-price
in the off season. Go up the hill by the
Eucalyptus Pension to the *Topaloğlu* and
Lighthouse for cheaper beds.

On the opposite side of the valley from
these, on the road to the Otel Beyhan, are
four more modern 'pensions' (actually small
hotels), the *Apollon, Sülü, Zeybek 1* and
Zeybek 2, charging US$18 a double, break-
fast included. Some rooms have fine views.

Camping In the village, there are several
little camping grounds which are relocated
frequently as construction pushes them from
one lot to the next. Camping on the beach is
prohibited because of the antiquities nearby
and because the beach is a nesting area for
sea turtles.

Places to Stay – middle Up on the hillside
to the left as you enter the village, above the
road, are several hotels and lots of holiday
villas. The *Hotel Delfin* has nice little standard Turkish hotel rooms with shower and
balcony, and a terrace restaurant. The *Hotel
Xanthos*, higher on the hill above the Delfin,

even has a swimming pool and tennis court.
Another place on this hillside is the *Ekizoğlu
Motel* (☎ (3215) 4007) where double rooms
with bath and breakfast cost US$20. Build-
ing is so furious here that by the time you
arrive there will be many other lodging
choices, both cheap and not so cheap.

The best in town is the *Otel Beyhan
Patara* (☎ (3215) 5096; fax 5097), more luxurious than its three stars might suggest.
Facilities include a tennis court, hamam,
sauna, sundecks, rooftop restaurant, volleyball and basketball courts, exercise room,
and 128 air-con rooms priced at US$40 per
person, breakfast and dinner included.

Places to Eat Most of the hotels and some
of the pensions (including the Golden and
the Patara) have restaurants. Others open and
close by the month, it seems. The *Sinbad
Restaurant*, near the Golden Pension, has
good food and reasonable prices – about
US$4 for a full meal – as do the *Maestro* and
the *Antalya*. Many of the shops in the village
sell stale packaged food. The *Patara Market*
seemed to have the edge on freshness.

Getting There & Away A small airport is
being built inland from Patara and Kalkan,
and may soon have service by small
'commuter' aircraft.

Dolmuşes run at least five times a day –
and in high summer more than a dozen times
a day – to Patara from Fethiye and Kaş. They
tend to fill up so you should make careful
arrangements about getting there and back.
Buy your tickets in advance to assure a seat.

Kalkan
About 11 km east of the Patara turn-off (81
km east of Fethiye, 26 km west of Kaş) the
highway skirts Kalkan, a fishing village formerly occupied by Ottoman Greeks and
called Kalamaki, but now completely
devoted to tourism. Discovered a decade ago
by intrepid travellers in search of the simple,
cheap, quiet life, this perfect Mediterranean
village soon saw development. First came a
yacht marina, then some modern hotels, and
now a vast holiday village complex (the

Hotel Patara Prince and Club Patara) covering an entire hillside to the south.

Still, Kalkan retains some of its charm. Since 1989 the Kalkan Foundation (Kalkan Vakfı), an association of public officers and private individuals, has been working to preserve the town's architecture, ambience and environment.

Orientation Kalkan is built on a hillside sloping down to the bay, and you will find yourself trekking up and down it all day. Coming in from the highway the road descends past the Belediye then takes a switchback turn by the Ziraat Bankası to pass the Orman Genel Müdürlüğü (Directorate of Forests) office and the PTT before entering the main commercial area, where it descends the hill and is renamed as Hasan Altan Caddesi, also known as 6 Sokak. The Kalkan Han hotel is one street above on Süleyman Yılmaz Caddesi (also known as 7 Sokak), though most other little hotels and restaurants are on terraces below the shopping area, all the way down to the harbour's edge.

Information The town maintains a small information booth near the Belediye, just before the Kalkan Han. The postal code for Kalkan is 07960.

Places to Stay – bottom end Cheapest are the pensions rated 2nd class by the town, some of which are near the Kalkan Han on 7 Sokak.

Very near the Kalkan Han, the excitable Mehmet Özalp, proprietor of the *Özalp Pansiyon* (☎ (3215) 1486), charges US$12 for his good, modern rooms with shower and balcony. Some are tiny, others larger. There's a restaurant on the ground floor, and the Smile and Köşk restaurants are nearby.

The neighbouring *Çelik Pansiyon* (☎ (3215) 1022), Yalıboyu 9, more or less across from the Kalkan Han, is a standard simple pension charging US$10 a double, breakfast included. Up the hill across the street from it (follow the signs) is the *Deniz Pansiyon* (☎ (3215) 1133), and the *Gül*

Pansiyon (☎ (3215) 1099), more primitive and slightly cheaper.

Also cheap is the *Cengiz Pansiyon* (☎ (3215) 1196), just up from the Mekan restaurant. The posted price is US$16 a double with breakfast, but the owner is ready to drop the price if he's not busy. Rooms in this old house are small, with tiny add-on showers, but it's a friendly family-run place.

Deren Pension (☎ (3215) 1848) is new, modern, and a bit out of the way, on the hillside north of the centre. But the views from its vine-covered terrace are spectacular, and it's quieter here. It's worth the walk and rooms cost US$12 a double.

Farther down the hill, the *Akın Pansiyon* (☎ (3215) 1025) has some waterless rooms on the top floor priced at US$12 a double, and rooms lower down with private showers cost US$18, breakfast included. The *Akgül* (☎ (3215) 1270) around the corner is similar.

Çetin Pansiyon (☎ (3215) 1094), in the southern part of town, is out of the central bustle, quieter, and done in traditional style. Rooms cost US$16 a double.

Readers of this guide have also liked the *Hakan Pansiyon*, a 120-year-old house nicely restored with private baths and good insect screens on the windows.

Places to Stay – middle Among the hotels, perhaps the most atmospheric is the *Kalkan Han* (kahl-KAHN) (☎ (3215) 1151), on 7 Sokak. It's built to resemble an old village house and is equipped with 16 rooms, each with private bath. Rates are US$38/55 a single/double, breakfast included. The décor is stone and wood, local crafts and Turkish carpets. The Star Bar on the rooftop terrace provides a good view of the stars at night.

Daphne Pansion (☎ (3215) 1380) is nicely decorated with kilims and carpets, and the rooms have good reading lights. You pay US$20 a double, breakfast included.

Another old village house beautifully restored is the *Balıkçı Han* (☎ (3215) 1075), with several old fireplaces, red-tile floors throughout, and panels of coloured faïence in the walls, with Turkish carpets and craft items added as accents. Some rooms have brass beds. Rooms with private shower cost US$40 a double, breakfast included.

Nicely updated is the *Patara Pansiyon* (☎ (3215) 1076), an old stone house with views from the roof terrace. Rooms cost US$24 a double with shower and breakfast.

Among the newer additions to Kalkan's range of accommodation is the *Famous Pansiyon* (☎ (3215) 1286), a five-minute walk from the centre of the village on the hillside to the north-west of the harbour. The bright guest rooms have nice touches such as wooden latticework on the wardrobes and glass-enclosed shower stalls (toilets are shared, down the hall), as well as views of the bay, and the surrounding olive groves. Rates are US$35 for a double with shower and breakfast.

Hotel Diva (☎ (3215) 1175; fax 1139) is a new small hotel built to look like an old village house, with vine-covered trellises shading the roof terrace and 17 comfy rooms with bath for US$20 to US$30 a double, breakfast included. The neighbouring 25-room *Dionysia Pension* (☎ (3215) 1681), under the same management, is more like a hotel, but still quite comfortable. Rooms cost from US$22 to US$34 a double, breakfast included.

The three-star *Hotel Pirat* (☎ (3215) 1178; fax 1183) has added an unwelcome six storeys to the village skyline, but does provide 65 comfortable, modern rooms with balconies for US$40/60 a single/double, breakfast included. It was built to cater for tour groups, which it often does. The morning-glory-covered terrace restaurant is a good place from which to gaze at the harbour just to the east.

There are several other good hotels in town, including the *Grida Apart-Hotel* (☎ (3215) 1434; fax 1585) renting fully furnished apartments; the three-star *Club Patara* (☎ (3215) 1210) on the hillside to the south; and the neighbouring, elaborate five-star *Patara Prince* (☎ (3215) 1338; fax 1337).

Places to Eat Dining has yet to approach the level of an art in Kalkan, but you can have pleasant and not overly expensive meals if you choose carefully.

In the commercial district at the top of the town, the *Smile Restaurant* is still relatively cheap, with meals for US$4 to US$6, as is the *Mekan*. The *Köşk* (☎ 1046) has become more expensive, but does offer fine views from its terrace seating area.

Farther south along Hasan Altan Caddesi (6 Sokak) from the Köşk, the little *Alternatif Restaurant* (☎ 1571), on an upper-storey terrace, is simpler and cheaper.

Down on the waterfront by the marina are numerous restaurants which are fun to patronise in the evening, but tend to be more expensive. To the left are the *Yakamoz, Deniz, Kalamaki, Korsan* and *Lipsos*; to the right, *İlayda, Han, Panorama* and *King*. Off-season, pick the one that's busiest. In season, you may have to take one of the rare vacant tables where you can find it. Expect to spend from US$15 to US$18 for a meal with wine or beer.

Kalkan to Kaş

Eighty-seven km from Fethiye is Kaputaş (or Kapıtaş), a striking mountain gorge crossed by a small highway bridge. The marble plaque on the east side of the bridge, embedded in the rock wall, commemorates four road workers who were killed during the dangerous construction of this part of the highway. Below the bridge is a perfect little sandy cove and beach, accessible by a long flight of stairs.

A short distance past Kaputaş, 20 km before Kaş, is the Blue Cave (Mavi Mağara). It is beneath the highway and marked by a sign. You may see boats approaching, bringing tourists for a glimpse of this Turkish Capri. You can climb down from the road for a look and a swim.

KAŞ

Fishing boats and a few yachts in the harbour, a town square with teahouses and restaurants in which one can hear half a dozen languages spoken, inexpensive pensions and hotels, classical ruins scattered about: this is Kaş (KAHSH, population

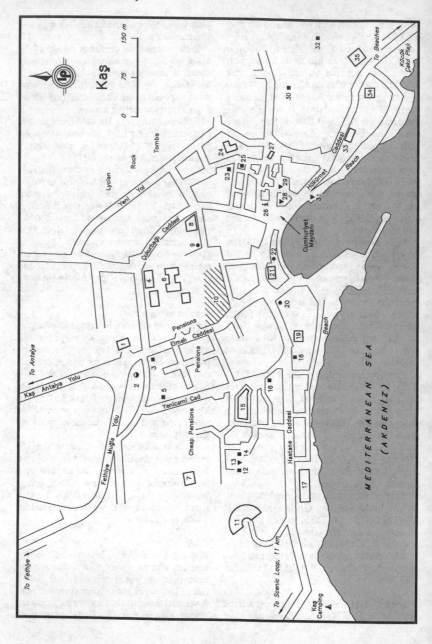

■ PLACES TO STAY

3	Hotel Mimosa
5	Pension Orion
12	Kale Pansiyon
14	Çetin Pansiyon
16	Ay Pansiyon
18	Andifilı Oteli
23	Mini Pansiyon
25	Kısmet Pansiyon
30	Hotel Ekici
32	Hotel Club Phellos

▼ PLACES TO EAT

13	Efecan Winehouse
28	Eriş Restaurant
29	Roosters Restaurant
31	Mercan Restaurant

OTHER

1	Fuel Station
2	Bus Station
4	Toilet
6	Schools
7	Tomb
8	PTT
9	Ziraat Bankası
10	Market
11	Theatre
15	Yeni Camii
17	Hospital
19	Hellenistic Temple
20	Eczane (Pharmacy)
21	Mosque
22	Toilet
24	School
26	Tourism Information Office
27	Doric Tomb
33	Police
34	Jandarma
35	New Hükümet Konağı (Government Building)

a base for boat excursions to several fascinating spots along the coast.

Life centres on the town square by the harbour, with its teahouses, restaurants, mosque, police station and shops. A well-preserved ancient theatre is about all that's left of ancient Antiphellus, which was the Lycian town here. On the sheer rock mountain wall above the town are a number of Lycian rock tombs, which are illuminated at night.

Orientation

The otogar is just off the highway, a few hundred metres uphill from the town centre. Descend the hill to the harbour and turn left to reach the main square Cumhuriyet Meydanı. Beyond the main square over the hill are more hotels and a few tiny pebble beaches. Turning right at the harbour, onto Hastane Caddesi, takes you to the hospital, theatre, and camping ground.

Information

The Tourism Information Office (☎ (3226) 1238) is on the main square. The staff speak English and have numerous hand-outs on local lodgings and sights.

The Kaş Turizm ve Tanıtma Derneği (☎ (3226) 2659), behind the Mercan Restaurant just off the main square, is the Kaş Tourism & Publicity Association, which can also help with questions. The postal code for Kaş is 07580.

Laundry The Laundry (*Çamaşırhane*) Habessos (☎ 1263) is near the Kısmet, Kanber and Antique pensions up the hill from the main square (turn left at the Lycian sarcophagus). There is another small laundry nearby.

Antiphellus Ruins

Walk up the hill on the street to the left of the Tourist Information Office to reach the **Monument Tomb**, a Lycian sarcophagus mounted on a high base. It is said that Kaş was once littered with such sarcophagi but that over the years most were broken apart to

5000), the quintessential Turkish seaside town.

Although Kaş has been discovered by foreign travellers and Turks on holiday, somehow it retains much of its charm.

Kaş is not popular because of its beaches – they are small, not sandy but pebbly and some are a good distance out of town. But Kaş is pleasant in itself, and it can be used as provide building materials. This one, on its lofty perch, survived very well.

Walk to the **theatre**, 500 metres west of the main square, for a look. It's in very good condition and was restored some time ago. Over the hill behind the theatre is the **Doric Tomb**, cut into the hillside rock in the 3rd century BC. You can also walk to the rock tombs in the cliffs above the town, but as the walk is strenuous go at a cool time of day.

Excursions

Local boatmen will take you along the coast for cruising and swimming on several standard excursions. No matter which excursion you take, check to see what the provisions are for lunch. If you take an all-day trip you'll have to eat, and I've had some reports of rip-offs on the price of lunch.

One popular excursion is to Kekova and Üçağız, about two hours away by boat, where there are several interesting ruins. It's also accessible by road (see the following). The cost is from US$5 to US$8 per person.

You can go over to Kastellorizon (Meis Adası in Turkish), the Greek island just off the coast and visible from Kaş, for the day, returning to Kaş in the evening, or perhaps enter Greece and go on to other islands. Check on the current diplomatic status of Kastellorizon as a port of entry. The cost to charter a fishing boat for the excursion is about US$50; a single (individual) fare is about US$6 for the round trip.

Other standard excursions go to the Blue Cave, Patara and Kalkan for US$7 per person, lunch included; or to Liman Ağzı, Longos and several small islands for the same price, lunch included.

For a three-day (two-night) yacht cruise along the coast, expect to pay about US$100 per day for the entire boat.

If you have a car, drive out of town on Hastane Caddesi past the theatre, and make the 11-km scenic loop around the western peninsula, which has nice views though not really any good swimming spots. At the tip of the peninsula you're surprisingly close to Kastellorizon.

Places to Stay

You can ignore the hawkers who will greet you at the bus station and want to take you to a hotel, or you can ask some questions about price and facilities, and then follow them home. Most of the town's lodgings are within a five-minute walk, the rest are within 10 minutes' walk.

Places to Stay – bottom end

Pensions are everywhere. The cheapest charge from US$5 or US$6 per bed in high season, but prices range up to US$8 or US$10 per bed in places with more comforts. Find the stairway going down at the back of the otogar; at the bottom, turn left, cross the main road and walk uphill on Yenicami Caddesi (also called Recep Bilgin Caddesi) to reach the following pensions.

Pension Orion (☎ (32256) 1938; fax 1819), Yenicami Caddesi, is just up the hill on the left. The top floor is a quiet terrace with a fine view of the town and the sea, and tidy rooms go for US$16 a double, breakfast included. Some rooms have balconies, and a few are triples.

Farther along the street or just off it are many other pensions, including the *Akkın Pansiyon*, the *Anı Motel* (☎ (3226) 1791), *Hilal Pansiyon* (☎ (3226) 1207), and the *Melisa Pansiyon* (☎ (3226) 1162). At the (southern) end of the street, by the mosque, is the *Ay Pansiyon* (☎ (3226) 1562), where the front rooms have sea views.

Turn right at the Ay Pansiyon and follow the signs to the *Çetin Pansiyon* and the *Kale Pansiyon* (☎ (3226) 1094), which are quieter. The good *Efecan Winehouse* restaurant is here as well.

On the other (eastern) side of town are many more pensions offering similar accommodation. Try the *Koştur* (☎ (3226) 1264), which readers have liked.

Over the hill to the south-east is Küçük Çakıl Plajı (Little Gravel Beach), and behind it, along with the big hotels (Ekici, Club Phellos), a row of small places offering good simple rooms, vine-shaded terraces with sea views, and congenial atmosphere. Prices depend upon season and demand, but

Top: Site & Valley of Olimpos (TB)
Left: Back streets of Antalya (TB)
Right: A çaycı (tea waiter) in his filigree vest (TB)

Top: Old Roman harbour, Antalya (TB)
Bottom: An antique and carpet shop, Side (TB)

average from US$14 to US$18 a double, with private shower. Try the *Golden*, *Cemil* (☎ (3226) 1554), *Antiphellos*, *Talay*, *Defne* (☎ (3226) 1932), and the *Çakıl* (☎ (3226) 1532).

Camping The most popular place is *Kaş Camping* (☎ (3226) 1050), one km west of the centre out along Hastane Caddesi past the theatre. Two persons in their own tent pay US$3; you can rent a little waterless 'bungalow' shelter for US$10 a double if you don't have your own camping equipment. The site is very pleasant, with a small swimming area, restaurant and bar.

Places to Stay – middle

Hotel Kayahan (☎ (3226) 2001; fax 1313), up the hill from Küçük Çakıl beach, is two-star, attractive and family-run, with front rooms having fine sea views, even though the sun makes them hot by afternoon. All have baths, and cost US$24/30 a single/double. There's a roof terrace as well.

The three-star *Hotel Ekici* (☎ (3226) 1417, 1823; fax 1823), with 75 rooms, a swimming pool, terrace restaurant, Turkish bath, lifts and central air-con, seems to suffer from dispirited staff, and is overpriced. All rooms have balconies (some with sea views) and private baths, and cost US$44/54 for singles/doubles, buffet breakfast included.

Hotel Club Phellos (☎ (3226) 1953; fax 1890), on Doğruyol Sokak, up from Küçük Çakıl beach, rates three stars, and is built to recall the historic houses of Kaş, now mostly swept away. It has a nice airy restaurant and swimming pool, and 81 air-con rooms with bath going for US$55/88/110 a single/double/triple.

Even fancier? Try the four-star *Aqua-Park Hotel* (☎ (3226) 1901; fax 1906), five km out of Kaş, with 106 fairly luxurious rooms equipped with TV and fridge.

Places to Eat

Prices for restaurant dishes are established and fixed by the municipal authorities, so all of the various restaurants in a given class should charge exactly the same for any item you order. Restaurant quality varies with the seasons and the patronage, and nothing is certain, but here are some tips.

My favourite for dinner is the *Efecan Winehouse* (☎ 2443), near the Çetin and Kale pensions west of the Yeni Cami. Set in an old Turkish house decorated with kilims, Ms Arife Aydemir, the owner, makes up the meals fresh each day, taking suggestions from customers. Meze (hors d'oeuvres) and vegetable dishes are the strong points, not grilled meats. Wine-tasting is encouraged. Meals cost from US$5 to US$8, drinks included.

In the centre, three much-patronised restaurants occupy an awning-shaded passage running between the waterfront and the marketplace. Closest to the water is the *Derya Restaurant* (☎ 1093), where many dishes are set out for you to choose from, which simplifies ordering somewhat. A lunch or dinner consisting of several plates of meze should cost no more than US$4. Up the passage are the *Orkinos* and *Eva Kent*, essentially similar – it's difficult to tell where one stops and the next begins.

Other restaurants are at the eastern edge of the square near the Belediye. The *Mercan* (☎ 1209) is noted for its waterfront location and its seafood. Choose a fish, have it weighed, get the price, then say 'evet' if you want it, or 'hayır' if you don't. A fish dinner with mezes and wine can cost from US$12 to US$16 per person.

Across the street, the *Morning Star Café* (☎ 1517), Hükümet Caddesi 15, has a small street-level dining room, but upstairs there's a covered terrace with a view of the harbour and the traffic along Hükümet Caddesi. Choose your dinner before you climb the stairs; it has a good selection of salads and mezes, fish and kebaps.

Among the prominent restaurants on the main square is the *Eriş* (☎ 1057), with shady pseudo-rustic tables in front. Prices are not bad, better food can be found elsewhere, but the candlelight dining atmosphere makes it a very popular place in the evenings.

Up on the hillside behind the Eriş is *Roosters*, run by Osman Horoz ('horoz' means rooster), a Turkish Cypriot who started two successful restaurants in Melbourne, Australia. The menu is eclectic: pizzas for US$1.25 to US$3, grilled meats for US$2 to US$5, and spaghetti and böreks. It's open from April to October.

Behind Roosters, the *King Restaurant* (☎ 1871) provides cheap pides and kebaps.

For breakfast, snacks, pastries and puddings, the *Noel Baba Pastanesi* (Father Christmas) on the main square is the favourite, and the best for people-watching when its outdoor tables are in shade.

Getting There & Away

Air A small airport is to be built inland from Patara and Kalkan, and this would serve Kaş with small-aircraft flights as well.

Bus Most of the buses in and out of Kaş are handled by the Pamukkale, Kaş Turizm and Kamil Koç companies. Some daily services include:

Antalya – 185 km, four hours, US$7.50; at least four buses
Bodrum – 400 km, six hours, US$11; three buses
Fethiye – 110 km, 2½ hours, US$3; at least eight buses, dolmuşes as well, some going directly to Ölüdeniz
Göreme (Cappadocia) via Antalya – 775 km, 15 hours, US$20; several
İzmir (via Selçuk) – 510 km, nine hours, US$18; two night buses
Kalkan – 29 km, 35 minutes, US$1; frequent service
Kekova – 34 km, 40 minutes, US$1.25; several dolmuşes in summer
Marmaris – 305 km, five hours, US$8; four buses
Pamukkale (via Muğla) – 400 km, seven hours, US$12; two buses
Patara – 36 km, one hour, US$2; several dolmuşes

KEKOVA

Fourteen km east of Kaş you will see signs for a turn-off (south, right) to Kekova. A 20-minute, 19-km drive along a paved road brings you to the village of Üçağız, the ancient **Teimiussa**, in an area of ancient ruined cities, some of them partly submerged in the Mediterranean's waters. This area is regularly visited by day-trippers on boats and yachts from Kaş, but is just now being

discovered by travellers wanting to stay overnight. Declared off-limits to development by the government, it remains a relatively unspoilt Turkish fishing and farming village.

The setting of the village is absolutely idyllic, on a bay amidst islands and peninsulas. The old village houses, many whitewashed, are of the local stone, not breeze block. The largest building in town is the modern İlkokul (primary school). Cows and chickens wander the streets, villagers heft sacks of carob beans down to the town wharf, fishers repair their nets on the quay as yachts glide through the harbour. Village girls sell hand-printed scarves (*yazma*) with handmade lace borders; you can see village women sitting outside making lace and doing embroidery. Here and there, perhaps by a football pitch or in a house's back garden, are remnants of ancient Lycian tombs. A few carpet shops have already opened, however, and the dreaded discos cannot be far behind.

Orientation

The village you enter is Üçağız ('Three Mouths'; that is, entrances to the harbour), the ancient Teimiussa. Across the water to the east is Kale, a village on the site of the ancient city of Simena, accessible by boat. South of the villages is a larger harbour called Ölüdeniz (not to be confused with the famous beach spot near Fethiye), and south of that is the channel entrance, shielded from the Mediterranean's sometime fury by a long island named Kekova.

Walking Tour

Don't neglect to walk around Üçağız itself as it has a few old Lycian tombs also. Next to the football field are two Lycian sarcophagi (one of them in the shape of a house) and a rock-cut tomb.

Kale

Though Üçağız is where you arrive, Kale is where you will go by motorboat (10 minutes) or on foot (one hour) to see the **ruins of ancient Simena** and the **medieval Byzan-**

tine **fortress** perched above the picture-perfect hamlet. Within the fortress is a little **theatre** cut into the rock. Near the fortress are **ruins** of several temples and public baths, several sarcophagi and Lycian tombs; the **city walls** are visible on the outskirts. It's a delightfully pretty spot.

Boat Excursions

Boats from Üçağız will take you on a tour of the area lasting from one to 1½ hours. Chartering an entire boat costs around US$10 to US$16, but haggle as prices are subject to what the traffic will bear. For a taxi boat to Kale (one way) you pay US$5.

Beware blandishments for the 'glass-bottomed boat', a regular skiff which the owner has equipped with a glass-bottomed bucket. The water is so clear, there's no need to pay more for such a primitive contraption.

The Tour Your boat excursion may follow this route around the bay clockwise. First you go to Kale, where there are a dozen little seaside restaurants (*Palmiye, Balıkçı'nın Restaurant* and *Mehtap* up on the hillside, *Simena* and *Yacht* down by the harbour) and a few tiny pensions. The restaurants tend to be a bit expensive as everything comes by boat, and yachting types are the most frequent customers.

From Kale, the boat goes to the **sunken Lycian tombs** just offshore, and then to **Kekova Adası** (Kekova Island, also called Tersane). Along the shore of the island are more foundations and ruins, partly submerged in the sea, and called the Batık Şehir, the Sunken City. Signs say 'No Skin-Diving Allowed', indicating that this is an archaeological zone and the authorities are afraid of antiquity theft.

The boat stops at the island dock in a little cove to let you have a swim and wander around and explore the ruins on land. The town here dates from Byzantine times. After a swim it's back to Üçağız.

Places to Stay

There are only small pensions in Üçağız, charging from US$4 to US$6 per person.

Among the best is the *Koş Pension* at the eastern end of town. The *Kekova* is in a restored village house.

The *Onur Pansiyon* has rooms with two or three beds; all rooms have solar-heated water, some have water views. There's an agreeable water-front terrace dining area and you are allowed to use the fridge.

Antique Pension has very tiny, basic rooms with bed and wardrobe only (no plumbing), but trim is natural wood and the shared bathroom is tiled, with a fired hot-water tank guaranteeing lots of hot water if you notify the owners in advance.

The *Ekin Pansiyon* is behind the Kekova Restaurant. Look also at the *Likya, Koç* and the *Huzur* (☎ (3191) 1031).

Places to Eat

On the waterfront are a half-dozen little eateries, including the *Kordon, Liman, Hassan's* and *Kekova*, all charging around US$4 or US$5 for a meal. The Liman is currently favoured. Some readers have liked the *Koç*, farther along by the football pitch as well.

A typical lunch includes a salad of beans in tomato sauce, cubes of white cheese with sliced green olives, sigara böreği (tubes of flaky pastry filled with white cheese), marrow (squash) fritters, potato and egg

salad, and fish or lamb kebap, followed by fruit. Wine and beer are served.

There are a few simple shops in the village at which you can buy basic food supplies and, of course, souvenirs and Turkish carpets.

Getting There & Away

There is minibus service between Üçağız and Kaş several times daily in summer, and at least once daily in winter. Coming from Demre, motorboats can be chartered at the western beach, called Çayağzı, for US$30; often it is possible to buy one place in the boat for a one-way journey for about US$3. You may be able to do this from Kaş as well.

KYANEAI

From the main highway at the Kekova turn-off, it's eight km east and south to the turn-off for Kyaneai, two km off the highway, where a few barely distinguishable ruins stand amidst the houses and paddocks of a farming hamlet. A track starts in the town and leads three km uphill to the main part of this ancient city, founded in Lycian times, which flourished under the Romans and was the seat of a bishop during the Byzantine era. It was abandoned in the 10th century.

The site has some interesting tombs, and traces of other buildings, but the rough terrain and undergrowth make exploration difficult. This is one for those dedicated antiquities buffs who enjoy having a little-visited site to themselves except for the inevitable village boys and curious goats.

DEMRE

Winding through rough, rocky, scrubby terrain from Kaş, the road descends from the mountains to a fertile river delta, much of it covered in greenhouses. At Demre (DEHM-reh) also called Kale, sometimes even Kale-Demre, 40 km east of Kaş, is the Church of St Nicholas. It is said that the legend of Father Christmas (Santa Claus) began here when a 4th-century Christian bishop gave anonymous gifts to village girls who had no dowry. He would drop bags of coins down the chimneys of their houses, and

the 'gift from heaven' would allow them to marry. This is perhaps why he is the patron saint of virgins; he went on to add sailors, children, pawnbrokers and Holy Russia to his conquests. His fame grew, and in 1087 a raiding party from the Italian city of Bari stole his mortal remains from the church. In medieval Europe relics were hot items. (They missed a few bones, which are now in the Antalya Museum.)

This, the Roman city of Myra (the name comes from myrrh), was important enough to have a bishop by the 4th century. Several centuries before, St Paul stopped here on his voyage to Rome.

Though Myra had a long and significant history as a religious, commercial and administrative town, Arab raids in the 7th century and the silting of the harbour led to its decline.

Today that same silting is the foundation of the town's wealth. The rich alluvial soil supports the intensive greenhouse production of flowers and vegetables.

Orientation

Demre sprawls over the alluvial plain. At the centre is the main square, near which are several cheap hotels and restaurants. The street going west from it is Müze Caddesi (also called St Nicholas Caddesi), on which is the Church of St Nicholas. Going north is Yenicami Caddesi, which leads two km to the Lycian rock tombs of Myra. The street going east is PTT Caddesi (also called Ortaokul Caddesi), which leads to the post office and the town's best hotel. The street going south from the square passes the otogar (100 metres) and continues to a cluster of three cheap hotels (800 metres) across from the İlkokul (primary school), near the junction with the road to Antalya.

Five km west of the centre is Çayağzı beach, with several places to camp for free and several which charge a small amount. This was Andriake in Roman times, an important entrepôt for grain on the sea route to Rome. The great granary built by Hadrian (finished in 139 AD) still stands, off to the south of the road.

Church of St Nicholas

The Church of St Nicholas ('Noel Baba' in Turkish) was first built in the 3rd century, and became a Byzantine basilica when it was restored in 1043. Later restorations sponsored by Tsar Nicholas I of Russia in 1862 changed the building even more. Restoration during the last decade by Turkish archaeologists was designed to protect it from deterioration.

Not vast like Aya Sofya, not brilliant with mosaics like İstanbul's Chora Church, the Church of St Nicholas at Demre is, at first, a disappointment. What redeems it is the venerable dignity lent it by its age and the stories which surround it.

A symposium on St Nicholas is held here each year in December. Admission to the church costs US$2, half-price for students.

Myra

Two few km inland from the main square of Demre are the ruins of Myra, with a striking honeycomb of rock hewn **Lycian tombs** and a very well-preserved **Roman theatre**. Climb up the ladders for a closer look at these tombs, which were thought to have been carved to resemble Lycian houses, wood beams and all. Around to the left as you climb is a tomb topped by a deathbed scene; there are other reliefs to discover as well.

Admission costs US$1; hours are from 8 am to 5.30 pm, till 6.30 pm in summer. In summer, the best time to visit is early in the morning or late in the afternoon, to avoid the crowds. Taxi drivers in town will offer to take you on a tour but that's not really necessary. The walk from the main square takes only about 20 minutes and the site is pretty much self-explanatory.

Places to Stay

Demre does not have a lot of accommodation. In the centre are several basic, well-used places, including the *Myra Pansiyon* (☎ (3224) 1026), just off the main square by the Akdeniz Restaurant at the beginning of St Nicholas Caddesi. Doubles with sink cost US$8, with shower US$11; look at the room before you take it.

A few steps closer to the church on the opposite side of St Nicholas Caddesi is the *Hotel Şahin* (☎ (3224) 1686), also an older place, where simple rooms cost US$14 a double with shower. Some rooms have one double and one single bed, good for couples with a child.

About 300 metres north of the main square on the way to the Myra rock tombs are the *Noel Pansiyon* (☎ (3224) 2304) and next door the *Ümit Pansiyon*, both fairly cheap (US$6/10 a single/double) but also noisy.

Three more hotels are less than one km south of the main square near the junction with the highway to Antalya. The *Kekova Pansiyon* is the one preferred by readers of this guide. Next to it is the *Otel Topçu* (☎ (3224) 2200). Across the street is the *Kıyak Otel* (☎ (3224) 2092). All these places charge US$14 for a double room with private shower and one large bed, US$16 for a double with two beds; prices drop in the off season.

The best (and quietest) in town is the *Hotel Simge* (☎ (3224) 3674; fax 3677), PTT Caddesi, Kaparlar Çıkmazı, a block east of the square down a side street on the right. Rooms with bath are comfortable without being luxurious, and are priced right at US$20 a double, breakfast included.

Places to Eat

The food from the little restaurants near the main square *(Akdeniz* and *Çınar)* and along Müze Caddesi between the square and the church can fill you up, but for a pleasant (if somewhat more expensive) lunch or dinner, head for the restaurants at Çayağzı beach, Demre's harbour, the ancient port settlement of Andriake. To find it, head south from the main square, past the Kekova Pansiyon and Topçu Otel, and turn right. When the highway turns sharp right, continue straight along the river bank to the port, about five km from the main square. Apart from the pleasant restaurants (with meals from US$8 to US$12) there is also a good beach.

ÇAĞILLI & GÖKLİMAN

Going east from Demre towards Antalya, 20

km brings you to Çağıllı, a small secluded cove with a nice pebble beach just off the highway. At Gökliman, another four km along, is a longer and wider beach good for a swim stop.

FİNİKE

Thirty km along the twisting mountain road brings you to Finike (FEE-nee-keh, population 7000), the ancient Phoenicus, now a sleepy fishing port and way-station on the burgeoning tourist route. Most of the tourists are Turks who have built ramshackle dwellings on the long pebble beach to the east of the town. The beach looks very inviting but parts of it have pollution problems and insects can be a problem at certain times of the year.

About 10 km inland from Finike are the ruins of ancient Limyra, not really worth the effort unless you're out to see every ancient town along the coast. Arycanda, 35 km north along the Elmalı road, is well worth seeing with its dramatic setting and many well-preserved buildings, but this requires a special excursion. Finike itself is uninteresting and you should not make a special plan to stop here.

Places to Stay

If you must stay, there are places, as Finike wants to get in on the seaside tourism boom. The *Kale Pansiyon* (☎ (3225) 1457), up above the modern Limyra Pansiyon overlooking the yacht harbour, is on the west side of town. Look for it up the steep hillside on the left as you enter from Demre. The pension, an Ottoman town house which retains much of its ornate décor, takes its name from its situation on top of the ruins of Finike's kale (fortress). Rooms cost US$6/10 a single/double. Inland from the Kale is the *Şendil Pansiyon* (follow the signs).

In the centre near the otogar are several inexpensive, suitable hotels, including the *Hotel Bahar* (☎ (3225) 2020), the *Hotel Bilal* (☎ (3225) 2199), and the older *Hotel Sedir* (☎ (3225) 1183, 1256) at Cumhuriyet Caddesi 37. All of these are in the market

district behind the Belediye building. A double room with shower costs from US$16 to US$18, breakfast included.

On the eastern outskirts of town is Sahilkent (literally 'Shore City'), which is not a city but a scattering of seaside villas, hotels and camping grounds, including the *Uralli Motel* and the *Hotel Finike*.

Baba Camping, three km east of Finike centre, is on the landward side of the very wide highway; *Karaca Camping*, two km farther east, is cheaper, simpler, and on the beach side. The *Hotel Eker* (☎ (3229) 1427), eight km east of Finike, charges US$32 for a double with shower, breakfast included.

FİNİKE TO KEMER

As you leave Finike the highway skirts a sand-and-pebble beach which runs for about 15 km. Signs at intervals read 'Plaj Sahası Halka Açıktır', which means 'The Beach Area is Open to the Public'.

Upon leaving the long beach the road passes through the town of **Kumluca** (population 13,000), a farmers' market town surrounded by citrus orchards and plastic-roofed greenhouses. A few small pensions can put you up in an emergency. After Kumluca the highway winds back up into the mountains.

About 28 km from Finike there is an especially good panorama. Three km later you enter **Beydağları Sahil Milli Parkı**, the Bey Mountains Coastal National Park. After another six km you'll get splendid views of the mountains.

Olimpos

Though a very ancient city, the early history of Olimpos is shrouded in mystery. We know that it was an important Lycian city by the 2nd century BC, and that the Olympians worshipped Hephaestos (Vulcan), the god of fire. No doubt this veneration sprang from reverence for the mysterious Chimaera, an eternal flame which still springs from the earth not far from the city. With the decline in the fortunes of the Lycian coastal cities in the 1st century BC, Olimpos suffered along with the rest. With the coming of the Romans in the 1st century AD, things improved, and Olimpos held some importance until the Turkish invasion, when it was abandoned.

Today Olimpos is fascinating, not for its ruins (which are fragmentary and widely scattered amidst the thick verdure of wild grapevines, flowering oleander, bay trees, wild figs and pines) but for its site just inland from a beautiful beach along the course of a stream which runs through a rocky gorge. The stream dries to a rivulet in high summer, and a ramble along its course, listening to the wind in the trees and the songs of innumerable birds, is a rare treat, with nary a tour bus in sight.

At present there is no admission fee, and the site is open all the time. You must park in a designated car park and walk to explore the site.

The Chimaera From Çıralı, follow the track marked for the Chimaera (Yanartaş, 'burning rock' in Turkish) three km down another valley to the car park, then climb along a marked path for another 20 to 30 minutes to the site.

The Chimaera, a spontaneous and inextinguishable flame which blazes from crevices on the rocky slopes of Mt Olimpos, is the stuff of legends. It's not difficult to see why ancient peoples attributed this extraordinary flame to the breath of a monster part lion, part goat and part dragon. Even today, it is has not been explained.

A gas seeps from the earth, and bursts into flame upon contact with the air. The exact composition of the gas is unknown, though it is thought to contain some methane. Though the flame can be extinguished now by being covered, it will reignite when uncovered. In ancient times it was much more vigorous, being easily recognised at night by mariners sailing along the coast.

In mythology, the Chimaera was the son of Typhon, the fierce and monstrous son of Gaia, the earth goddess, who was so frightening a being that Zeus set him on fire and buried him alive under Mt Aetna, thereby creating the volcano. Typhon's offspring, the Chimaera, was killed by the hero Belle-

rophon on the orders of King Iobates of Lycia. Bellerophon killed the monster by aerial bombardment – mounting Pegasus, the winged horse, and pouring molten lead into the Chimaera's mouth.

Places to Stay & Eat The ideal place to stay is Çıralı, as you'll be able to walk to Olimpos, the beach and the Chimaera easily. There are many pensions here, including the *Barış, Sahil, Bizim Cennet, Can* and *Karakuş*, charging US$4 or US$5 per person. The *Çıralı Pansiyon* is actually a hotel, with balconied rooms with bath for US$14 a double. The *Chimère Hotel*, on the way to the village, rates one star and charges about the same.

Nicest of all is *Olympos Lodge* (☎ & fax (3214) 3848), PO Box 38, Çıralı, Kemer, Antalya. It's a peaceful, beautiful lodge and villas set amidst citrus orchards and well-tended gardens very near the beach. The management is German, everything is well maintained, and the price is US$80 a double, breakfast and dinner included. The lodge is within walking distance of the Olimpos archaeological site.

In Çavuşköy proper are lots of places, including the *Atıcı Motel & Pension*, the *Çizmeci Hotel* (☎ & fax (3217) 5243), the *Gelidonya Pension, Yasemin Motel*, and the *Koreli Motel*. Rates vary from US$5 per person to US$24 a double, depending on the place and the season.

After turning off the macadamed road from Çavuşköy, it's three km to the car park at Olimpos. Along the way are several rustic restaurants which allow camping as well. *Kadir's Restaurant & Free Camping* is at the edge of a citrus orchard 800 metres before the car park; 600 metres from the car park are the *Atalay* and *Vadi* pension-restaurants. At 350 metres are *Kadir's Bungalows*, and at 200 metres *Hasan's Restaurant & Free Camping*.

Getting There & Away After a half-hour's drive east of Kumluca a road on the right (east) is marked for 'Olimpos-Çavuşköy-Adrasan'. This is the western approach to the site. With your own transport you can follow this road two km to a turn-off, then another six km to the village of Çavuşköy, where you turn left onto a rough dirt road which follows the rocky riverbed to the site, almost 12 km from the highway. When you make your way from the car park to the sea, you will be at the western end of Adrasan beach.

There is another way to approach the site, from the east. On the highway, 700 metres east of the Çavuşköy turn-off, is another road marked for 'Olimpos-Çıralı-Yanartaş/Chimaera', which leads through citrus groves to the village of Çıralı (seven km), and then another km to the eastern end of Adrasan beach. Olimpos is another five km along by road, shorter if you walk along the beach to the Olimpos Örenyeri (the archaeological site).

Tekirova

About 13 km north-east of Olimpos is the turn-off for Tekirova, a resort area with several large luxury hotels, including the *Phaselis Princess Hotel*, and a number of small pensions and camping grounds.

Phaselis

Three km north of the Tekirova turn-off, 12 km before the turn-off to Kemer, is a road marked for Phaselis, a ruined Lycian city two km off the highway on the shore. Shaded by soughing pines, the ruins of Phaselis are arranged around three small perfect bays, each with its own small beach. Among the ruins there is not a lot to see, and it is all from Roman and Byzantine times, but the setting is incomparably romantic. You will want to have a look at the aqueduct, but that's about all. Prominent signs read 'No Picnicking in the Ruins!', and point the way to a designated picnic area. Turkish visitors largely ignore the signs and picnic where they like.

The site is open from 8 am to 6 pm daily, for US$2. One km from the highway is the entrance to the site, with a small modern building where you can buy soft drinks, snacks and souvenirs, use the WC, and visit a one-room museum. The ruins and the shore are another km farther on. The nearest

accommodation is at the previously mentioned Tekirova.

Kemer

Kemer (population 10,000), 103 km from Demre, 12 km north of Phaselis and 42 km south-west of Antalya, is a burgeoning beach holiday resort with its face turned to the rough, rocky beaches of the Mediterranean and its back to the steep, pine-clad Beydağları (Bey Mountains). It was designed as a holding tank for planeloads of sun-seeking charter and group tours, and built to a government master plan. Besides its appealing situation and the standard pleasures of Turkish hotels, carpet shops and street hawkers, it has little to offer.

Passing through, you can stop for a meal and a look at the Yörük Parkı, an outdoor ethnological exhibit. Accommodation is available in all price ranges, should you want to stay.

Orientation The main street in town, Liman Caddesi (Harbour Ave), is a typically narrow Turkish noise-canyon lined with white hotels, palm trees, banks, cafés, as well as leather, jewellery and carpet shops. At the end of the main street to the north is the large yacht marina and dry-dock; to the south is a peaceful cove with a beautiful crescent of sand-and-pebble beach backed by emerald grass and fragrant pine trees. Stands here rent equipment for parasailing, water-skiing and windsurfing. Motorboat excursions run from the beach as well.

The minibus (dolmuş) station is 500 metres north of the centre on the old Antalya road, which is between the shore and the new highway. Most of the best cheap pensions and camping grounds are here as well.

Information The Tourism Information Office is in the Belediye Binası (municipal building) (☎ (3268) 1536; fax 1116). Kemer's postal code is 07980.

Yörük Parkı On a promontory north of the cove beach is Kemer's Yörük Parkı, an ethnographic exhibit meant to introduce you to

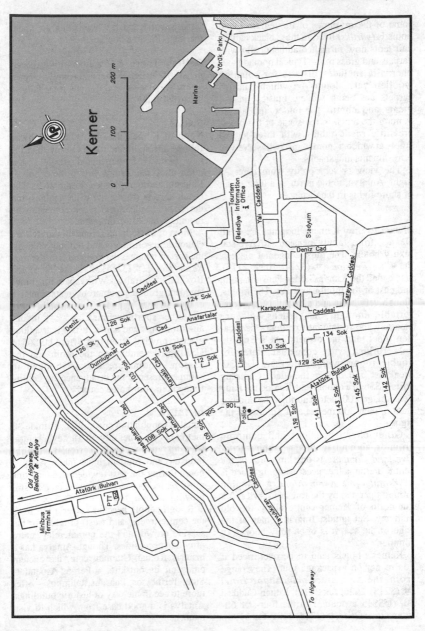

some of the mysteries of the region. Local nomads *(yörüks)* lived in these black camel-hair tents now furnished authentically with carpets and grass mats. Typical nomad paraphernalia includes distaffs for spinning woollen yarn, looms on which Turkish carpets are being woven, musical instruments and churns for butter and ayran. Among the tents, in the shade of the pines, are little rustic tables with three-legged stools at which a 'nomad girl' will serve you refreshments and snacks.

The view is very pretty from here. At night, Antalya, to the north, is a long string of shore lights in the distance.

Places to Stay Kemer's lodgings are of all classes, from family pensions to five-star luxury hotels. The most congenial place is the *King Pension* (☎ (3214) 1039, 2119), also called the King's Garden Pension, north and east of the minibus station. The rooms, though very basic and a bit musty, are comfortable enough; the gardens are very pleasant; the restaurant excellent; the location quiet; and the owners (she's English, he's Turkish) very congenial. Rates for double rooms with shower are US$30, breakfast and dinner included. Camping costs US$6 in a double tent. To find the King Pension, go 100 metres north of the minibus station, then 300 metres east, following the signs.

Other cheap pensions and camping grounds abound in this neighbourhood. *Overland Camping* is one km north of the centre. Perhaps the nicest camping place is at *Kındılçeşme Kamp Alanı*, a camping ground operated by the forestry service, 3.5 km north of Kemer centre along the old highway. Set amidst fragrant pines at the edge of the sea, it is often fully booked in summer.

Kemer's hotels tend to be overpriced if you're not on a package tour. They range from the two-star *Ambassador Hotel* (☎ (3214) 2626; fax 3111), Liman Caddesi 10, (US$45 a double) to the four-star 60-room *Otem Oteli* (☎ (3214) 3181; fax 3190),

Yat Limanı Karşısı, which faces the yacht marina (US$80 a double).

Getting There & Away Dolmuşes run nonstop between Kemer and Antalya all day. There are also several dolmuş runs daily to Tekirova and Phaselis.

Beldibi
North of Kemer, the old Antalya highway follows the shoreline more closely than the new highway, farther inland. About 12 km north of Kemer brings you to the centre of Beldibi, another planned resort area. The beach here is stones, not even pebbles, but the water is clear, the pines cool and the mountain backdrop dramatic.

Most of the lodgings along this stretch are elaborate resort hotels and holiday villages, the best of which is the *Ramada Renaissance Resort Hotel* (☎ (3214) 3255; fax 3256), PO Box 654, Antalya. With spacious pine-studded grounds, numerous restaurants, a casino, swimming pools, Turkish bath, water and other sports facilities, and 341 luxury air-con rooms and suites. It is a marvellous place to unwind. Rates range from US$65 to US$145, depending on the room and the season. Rooms are heavily booked in summer; reservé far in advance by calling Ramada in your home country.

ANTALYA
Antalya (population one million, altitude 38 metres) is the chief city on Turkey's central Mediterranean coast. Agriculture, light industry and tourism have made Antalya boom during the past few decades, and this mostly modern Mediterranean city is still growing at a fast pace.

Rough pebble beaches (several km from the centre to east and west) provide for the seaside crowd, and the commercial centre provides necessities. Though Antalya has a historic Roman-Ottoman core, the ancient cities on its outskirts – Perge, Aspendos, Side, Termessos, Phaselis, Olimpos – offer more to see in the way of historic buildings. Antalya is a good base from which to visit them.

History

This area has been inhabited since the earliest times. The oldest artefacts found in the Karain caves, 25 km from Antalya, have been dated to the Palaeolithic period. Antalya as a city, however, is not as old as many other cities which once lined this coast but it is still prospering while the older cities are dead. Founded by Attalus II of Pergamum in the 1st century BC, the city was named Attaleia after its founder. When the Pergamene kingdom was willed to Rome, Attaleia became a Roman city. Emperor Hadrian visited here in 130 AD and a triumphal arch (Hadrian Kapısı) was built in his honour.

The Byzantines took over from the Romans. In 1207 the Seljuk Turks based in Konya took the city from the Byzantines and gave Antalya a new version of its name, and also its symbol, the Yivli Minare (Grooved Minaret). After the Mongols broke Seljuk power, Antalya was held for a while by the Turkish Hamidoğulları emirs. It was later taken by the Ottomans in 1391.

During WW I the Allies made plans to divide up the Ottoman Empire, and at the end of the war they parcelled it out. Italy got Antalya in 1918, but by 1921 Atatürk's armies had put an end to all such foreign holdings in Anatolia.

Though always a busy port (trading to Crete, Cyprus and Egypt), Antalya has grown explosively since the 1960s because of the tourism boom. Its airport, the busiest on the Turkish Mediterranean, funnels travellers to the whole coast and beyond.

Orientation

At the centre of the historic city is the Roman harbour, now the yacht marina. Around it is the historic district called Kaleiçi ('Within the Fortress') of old Ottoman houses sprinkled with Roman ruins. Many of the graceful old houses have been restored and converted to restaurants, pensions and small hotels – some simple, some of them quite luxurious.

Around Kaleiçi, outside the Roman walls, is the commercial centre of the city. Antalya's central landmark and symbol is the Yivli Minare (yeev-LEE mee-nah-reh, the Grooved Minaret), a monument from the Seljuk period which rises near the main square, called Kale Kapısı (Fortress Gate), marked by an ancient stone clock tower (saat kulesi). The broad plaza with the bombastic equestrian statue is Cumhuriyet Meydanı (Republic Square).

From Kale Kapısı, Cumhuriyet Caddesi goes west past the Tourism Information Office and Turkish Airlines office, then changes names to become Kenan Evren Bulvarı, which continues several km to the Antalya Museum and Konyaaltı Plajı, a pebble beach 10 km long, and now partly sullied by industrial development.

North-west from Kale Kapısı, Kazım Özalp Caddesi, also called Şarampol Caddesi, goes to the otogar and the ring road. Antalya's nice bazaar is east of Kazım Özalp Caddesi. As Kazım Özalp Caddesi heads north-west from the bus station the name changes to Abdi İpekçi Caddesi, then Vatan Bulvarı before it meets the ring road (Gazi Bulvarı). The bus station is a 10 or 15-minute walk from Kaleiçi.

East from Kale Kapısı, Ali Çetinkaya Caddesi goes to the Doğu Garaj (Eastern Garage), a mustering-point for eastbound minibuses, then onward to Perge, Aspendos, Side and beyond. Atatürk Bulvarı goes south-east from Ali Çetinkaya Caddesi, skirting Kaleiçi through more of the commercial district to the large Karaali Parkı before heading for Lara beach (12 km from the centre), lined with hotels and pensions.

A çevreyolu (ring road or bypass) named Gazi Bulvarı carries long-distance traffic around the city centre.

Information

There are two Tourism Information offices, reputedly open from 9 am to 5.30 pm (5 pm on Saturday and Sunday in summer). The main office (☎ (31) 47 05 41; fax 47 62 98) is in Kaleiçi, Selçuk Mahallesi, Mermerli Sokak, Ahiyusuf Camii Yanı, across the street from the Hotel Aspen. I have never found anyone on duty to answer questions here.

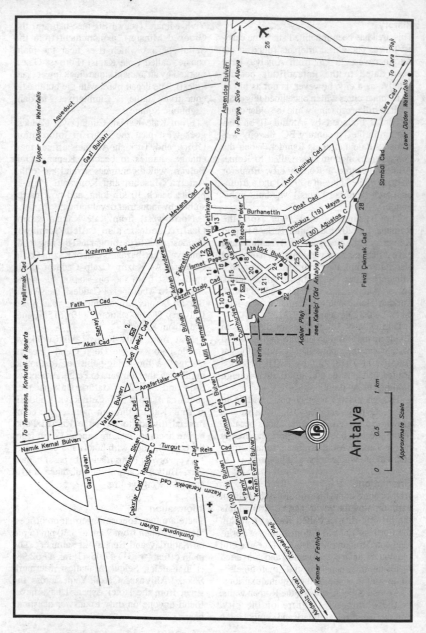

Antalya

Approximate Scale

0   0.5   1 km

■ PLACES TO STAY

5   Sheraton Voyager Hotel
27 Talya Hotel
28 Hotel Antalya Dedeman

▼ PLACES TO EAT

16 Eski Sebzeciler İçi Sokak
    (Meat Restaurants)

    OTHER

1   Police
2   PTT
3   Otogar (Bus Station)
4   Hospital
6   Antalya Museum
7   Turkish Maritime Lines Office
8   Merkez PTT (Central Post Office)
9   Tourism & Airline Offices
10 Government House
11 Hamams (Turkish Baths)
12 PTT
13 Doğu Garaj (Eastern Garage)
14 Yivli Minare (Grooved Minaret)
15 Kale Kapısı
17 PTT
18 Hadrian's Gate
19 Vegetable & Fruit Market
20 Kesik Minare (Cut Minaret)
21 Tourism & Airline Offices
22 Hıdırlık Kulesi (Tower)
23 Karaali Parkı
24 Police
25 Belediye (Municipality)
26 Antalya Airport

The other, less convenient office (☎ (31) 41 17 47) is at Cumhuriyet Caddesi 91. It's 600 metres west of Kale Kapısı on the right-hand side in the Özel İdare Çarşısı building (the same building as Turkish Airlines). This building is after the big jandarma headquarters but before the pedestrian bridge over the roadway. Look for 'Antalya Devlet Tiyatrosu' emblazoned on it.

Antalya's postal code is 07100.

Banks There are many banks along Şarampol (Kazım Özalp) Caddesi. I got a good rate of exchange at the Halkbank (go up two flights of stairs to find the foreign exchange desk). A bank exchange kiosk is open on summer evenings at Kale Kapısı.

Bookshops Try the Owl Bookshop, Barbaros Mahallesi, Akarçeşme Sokak 21, in Kaleiçi. The owner, Kemal Özkurt, stocks old and new books in English, French, German and Turkish.

Yivli Minare & the Bazaar

Start your sightseeing at the Yivli Minare, just downhill from the clock tower. The handsome and unique minaret was erected by the Seljuk sultan Alaeddin Keykubat I in the early 13th century, next to a church which the sultan had converted to a mosque. It's now the **Fine Arts Gallery** (Güzel Sanatlar Galerisi) with changing exhibits. To its north-west is a Whirling Dervish (Mevlevi) tekke (monastery) which probably dates from the 13th century, and nearby are two **tombs**, that of Zincirkıran Mehmet Paşa (1378) and the lady Nigar Hatun.

The view from the plaza, taking in Kaleiçi, the bay and the distant ragged summits of the Beydağları (Bey Mountains), is spectacular. Teahouses behind Cumhuriyet Meydanı and the Atatürk statue offer the opportunity to enjoy the view at leisure.

Antalya's bazaar is the cluster of small streets and passages on the right (east) side of Kazım Özalp Caddesi as you walk north from Kale Kapısı. The shops near Kale Kapısı inevitably specialise in the more expensive items such as jewellery and tourist souvenirs. Farther along, the streets are more authentic and interesting.

Kaleiçi (Old Antalya)

Go down the street by the clock tower. On the left is the **Tekeli Mehmet Paşa Camii**, built by the Beylerbey (Governor of Governors) Tekeli Mehmet Paşa. No inscription dates the building, which was repaired extensively in 1886 and 1926. Note the beautiful Arabic inscriptions in the coloured tiles above the doors and windows.

Wander into Kaleiçi, now a historic zone protected from modern development. Many

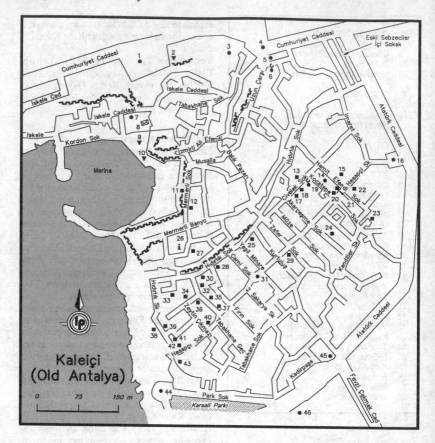

Kaleiçi
(Old Antalya)

of the gracious old Ottoman houses have been restored, then immediately converted to pensions and hotels or – worse – carpet shops.

The Roman harbour at the base of the slope was restored during the 1980s and is now used for yachts and excursion boats. It was Antalya's lifeline from the 2nd century BC up until very recently when a new port was constructed about 12 km west of the city, at the far end of Konyaaltı beach.

In the eastern reaches of Kaleiçi is the **Kesik Minare** (the Cut Minaret), a stump of a minaret which is famous because it's

famous, being mentioned in all the guidebooks. It's not much to look at, but it marks the location of the 5th-century Byzantine church of the Virgin Mary. Converted to use as a mosque by Korkut Bey, son of Sultan Beyazıt II, the church suffered a fire in 1896 which destroyed the wooden superstructure of its minaret.

At the south-western edge of Kaleiçi, on the corner with Karaali Parkı, rises the Hıdırlık Kulesi, a 14-metre-high tower in the ancient walls which dates from the 1st century AD, and may have been used as a lighthouse.

Hadrian's Gate & Karaali Park

Down Atatürk Caddesi is Hadrianüs Kapısı, (Hadrian's Gate; also called Üçkapılar, the Three Gates) erected during the reign of that Roman emperor (117-38). The monumental marble arch, which now leads to Kaleiçi, makes a shady little park in the midst of the city.

Farther along Atatürk Caddesi towards the sea is Karaali Parkı, a large, attractive, flower-filled park good for a stroll and for views of the sea. Sunset, the prettiest time, is when most Turks come here to stroll.

Antalya Museum

Antalya's large and rich museum Antalya Müzesi is in the western part of town, just over two km from the Yivli Minare, reached by bus along Cumhuriyet Caddesi. Ask the driver: *Müzeye gider mi?* (mur-zeh-YEH gee-DEHR mee?), 'Does this go to the museum?'. The collections include fascinating glimpses into the popular life of the region, with crafts and costume displays as well as a wealth of ancient artefacts. Opening hours are from 9 am to 5 pm (Monday 10 am to 1 pm); admission costs US$1.50.

The exhibits, most of them labelled in English as well as Turkish, start with fossils, proceed chronologically through the Stone and Bronze ages (in which Turkey is especially rich in artefacts) and continue through the Mycenaean, classical and Hellenistic periods. The Gods Gallery has statues of 15 classical gods from Aphrodite to Zeus, some of them very fine. Among the exceptionally good smaller objects are jewellery, vases, glass items and statuettes. The Tomb Room is also quite good.

The museum has a small collection of Christian art, including a room for icons which also contains a few of the bones of St Nicholas. There are also several sections of mosaic pavement.

The collection continues through Seljuk and Ottoman times, with costumes, armour, calligraphy, implements, faïence, musical instruments, carpets and saddlebags. The ethnographic exhibits are fascinating and include a fully furnished nomad's tent, a room with a carpet loom from a village home and several rooms from a typical Ottoman household.

A shady patio has tables where you can sit and have a cool drink or hot tea.

Hamams

If you'd rather have a Turkish bath than a shower, try the Sefa Hamamı, on Kocatepe Sokak in Kaleiçi, just around the corner from the Sabah, Hadriyanüs, Atelya and Adler pensions. It's untouristy (at this writing – subject to change!), and open to women from 11 am to 5 pm, men from 5 to 10 pm.

Boat Excursions

Excursion boats moored at the yacht harbour in Kaleiçi make tours of the nearby coast. A normal tour takes 4½ or five hours, visits the lower Düden waterfall, islands in the gulf, and beaches for a swim, includes lunch, and costs US$14 per person.

Festivals

Antalya is famous in Turkey for its Golden Orange Film Festival (Altın Portakkal Filim Festivali), held in late September or early October, and the Mediterranean Song Festival (Akdeniz Şarkı Festivali), a juried performance contest held immediately afterwards. Hotels are more heavily booked during the festivities.

Places to Stay

Antalya has hundreds of lodging places in all price ranges. Undoubtedly the most interesting area to stay in is Kaleiçi, which has simple, basic pensions, comfortable and charming mid-range 'boutique' hotels, and luxurious restored mansion hotels. There are numerous homy pensions and cheap ones near the otogar which offer beds at cheaper rates than those in Kaleiçi; and lavish luxury hotels within a km or two of the centre. In addition, there are dozens more hotels strung out along Lara Plajı, the city's eastern beach.

Kaleiçi's pensions and small hotels fall into three categories. Cheapest are the run-down old houses and new breeze-block buildings which may or may not have charm

– and private plumbing – but which charge from US$12 to US$16. Next come the houses renovated in the old style, most with lots of charm, private bathrooms, and rates of US$16 to US$34. Finally come the 'boutique' hotels, one or more adjoining houses perfectly restored and lavishly furnished, perhaps with a swimming pool, costing from US$60 to US$100 and up. Surprisingly, you don't get much more guest room for US$100 than you do for US$30.

Places to Stay – bottom end

Near the Otogar Pensions near the bus station tend to be somewhat cheaper and less atmospheric than those in Kaleiçi. As you emerge from the otogar, small signs hung on lampposts point the way to nearby pensions in private homes: *Tekin Aile, Phaselis, Erkal, Yemen, Sima.* The last two of these offer vegetarian meals. All charge from US$10 to US$12 a double with shared showers. The *Fatih Aile Pansiyon* (☎ (31) 42 27 63), Teoman Paşa Caddesi, 161 Sokak No 5, has rooms with shower for US$14 a double, but is 800 metres from the otogar.

If you walk several blocks south (towards Kale Kapısı) on Şarampol (Kazım Özalp) Caddesi from the otogar, you will come to an area of small hotels and pensions. Fifty metres south of the otogar off Şarampol Caddesi, 461 Sokak has several pensions, including the *Bilgin* (☎ (31) 48 49 60) and the *Esin* (☎ (31) 48 48 98), which are tidy and modern, and the *Ocak* (☎ (31) 41 84 23) which is a big old Ottoman house with a garden. Rates vary from US$10 to US$16, depending upon the season and the room.

One very short block south of 461 Sokak is the quaint old *Otel Süngül* (☎ (31) 41 14 08), Tahıl Pazarı, 459 Sokak No 3. A real traditional old Turkish marketplace hotel in a stone building, the Süngül charges US$14 for double rooms (some have washbasins), and US$1 for a hot shower.

There are a number of other small, cheap hotels in this area. Across the street from the Süngül is the modern white *Kaya Oteli* (☎ (31) 41 13 91), Kazım Özalp Caddesi, 459 Sokak 12, which, having been mentioned in the previous edition of this guide, raised its prices, and does not now offer good value for money. You can do better in Kaleiçi.

Kaleiçi Perhaps the best way to guide you to cheap pensions through the labyrinthine streets of Kaleiçi is to describe a route which you can follow, looking at the various pensions, seeing which have the right prices and also beds available. Almost every pension in Kaleiçi will be glad to rent you a car as well.

Start your explorations at Hadrian's Gate, on Atatürk Caddesi. Walk through the gate, bear left around the Urartu Rug Store and you're on Hesapçı Sokak. If you follow this street straight to its end you'll reach the Kesik Minare (Cut Minaret).

Near the corner of Hesapçı and Hamit Efendi sokaks are four pensions, including the *Hasbahçe Pension* (☎ (31) 48 53 67), a neat, tidy restored house renting rooms for US$20 a double with shower.

Across the street is the *Yunus Pansiyon* (☎ (31) 41 89 73; 42 61 42), Hesapçı Sokak 14, a friendly place with rough-and-ready rooms in an old, obviously unrestored house. The small interior court is half-sheltered and half-open to the sun so you can choose your level of exposure. Yalçın Paşa, the genial Falstaffian owner serves as your cook and car-rental agent as well. Rates are US$18/15 for a double with/without shower.

Turn left on Hamit Efendi Sokak just after the Hasbahçe to find the quiet *Patara Pansiyon* (☎ (31) 41 33 68), Barbaros Mahallesi, Kandiller Sokak 21, a newer building with a large garden and spartan but clean rooms with showers for a high US$24 a double, breakfast included. All the tea and hot showers you want are included in the price. Haggle like mad, though, and you'll get a better rate, especially if you're staying more than a day or two.

Turn right at the Hasbahçe to find the *Ninova Pension* (☎ (31) 48 61 14; fax in İstanbul (1) 352 0479), a beautifully and artistically restored house with a pleasant, peaceful garden renting double rooms for US$32, breakfast included.

The fancy Villa Perla Hotel is on the corner of Hesapçı and Kocatepe sokaks. Turn right onto Kocatepe Sokak, walk down past the Sefa Hamamı and turn left around the mosque to find the *Adler Pension* (☎ (31) 41 78 18), Barbaros Mahallesi, Civelek Sokak 16, which, being unrestored, is among the cheapest pensions in the neighbourhood at US$8/13 a single/double, with shared baths.

While we're here on Civelek Sokak, walk past the Adler to find the *Atelya Pension* (☎ (31) 41 64 16), Civelek Sokak 21, a beautifully restored stone house with a vine-shaded garden on a quiet street. All rooms have private baths; there's a bar. Room rates are US$18/28 a single/double, breakfast included – excellent value.

For nice but slightly cheaper rooms, walk a few steps farther to the *Pansion Mini Orient* (☎ (31) 42 44 17), Civelek Sokak 30, an old house nicely restored but still simple. The four double and six triple rooms grouped around the small but pleasant courtyard all have tiny private facilities, and there's a cosy little dining room for meals. Prices in summer are US$20/26/38 for a single/double/triple, with reductions in the off season.

Turn left onto Akarçeşme Sokak and walk two blocks to the *Bahar Aile Pansiyon* (☎ (31) 48 20 89), Akarçeşme Sokak 5, an unrestored old house with refreshingly low prices (for US$12 a double) for simple, basic clean waterless rooms (good for men or women). The showers are clean, tiled and fired by şofbens.

Garden Pansiyon & Bar (☎ (31) 47 19 30), Zafer Sokak 16 (or Hesapçı Sokak 44, on the corner of Zafer and Hesapçı sokaks), has a nice quiet garden and seven rooms with bath for US$20 a double. A few older rooms without bath go for half that price, and offer excellent cheap value.

Go north-west along Zafer Sokak to Hıdırlık Sokak and turn left to find the *Erken Pansiyon* (☎ (31) 47 60 92), Kilinçaslan Mahallesi, Hıdırlık Sokak 5, a well-preserved (not restored) old Antalya house with lots of dark wood and white plaster. Ottoman times come alive here. One room on the ground floor has its own private bath; the upstairs rooms have no running water but are large and airy with high ceilings. You pay a bit for the antiquity here – the charge per person is US$10.

Hıdırlık Sokak has two more good but more expensive choices. The *Turistik Frankfurt Pansiyon* (☎ (31) 47 62 24), Hıdırlık Sokak 17, is a restored house with white plaster walls, bright honey-coloured wood trim on door frames and lattice-covered windows, and German-style management. A little marble fountain burbles in the courtyard. It's pleasant, and excellent value at US$26/32 a single/double in high summer for a room with shower, a good breakfast included. The nearby *Pansiyon Dedekonak* (☎ (31) 47 51 70), Hıdırlık Sokak 11, is a good choice at US$14/24 a single/double, if the Frankfurt is full. Or try the *Villa Mine* (☎ (31) 47 62 29), in the opposite direction (south-west) at Hıdırlık Sokak 25, also with private showers and a garden café. The price is US$26/32 a single/double in high summer, breakfast included.

Down past the Kesik Minare (Cut Minaret), on and off Hesapçı Sokak, are many more pensions.

The *Sabah Pansiyon* (☎ (31) 47 53 45), Hesapçı Sokak 60/A, is famous for good value among backpackers. It's run by the friendly Sabah family (Ali, the manager, speaks English and German) and its more modern building (constructed in 1991) has its own garden and dining room serving three meals a day. Rates for the 16 rooms with shower are from US$16 to US$18 a double, or US$10 a double for the rooms with shared bath. Breakfast is included, and the owners promise a 10% discount to guests who show this guidebook. You can roll out your sleeping bag on the sleeping terrace for US$3 – breakfast, showers, and gallons of tea included. The Sabahs can also rent you small cars and motorbikes at quite good rates.

There is a concentration of good, cheap pensions near the corner of Hesapçı Geçidi and Zeytin Çıkmazı, a block and a half from the Sabah Pansiyon. Best is the *Hadriyanüs*

Pansiyon (☎ (31) 41 23 13), Kılınçarslan Mahallesi, Zeytin Çıkmazı 4/A-B, an old house fronting on to a refreshingly green walled garden. The owners are very friendly and charge US$14/20 for a single/double room with shower, breakfast included. Other possibilities in this area include the *Tamer*, the *White Garden*, and the somewhat drab *Anatolia*.

At the south-western end of Hesapçı Sokak are a half-dozen pensions which, being somewhat out of the way, may be willing to haggle over the price. The *Saltur Pansion* (☎ (31) 47 62 38), on the corner of Hesapçı and Hıdırlık sokaks, has a nice garden and overlooks verdant Karaali Parkı. It charges US$15 for a double with shower and breakfast. The *Bermuda* and *Senem* across the street are other good bets.

A few doors down on Hıdırlık Sokak, the *Keskin Pansiyon* (☎ (31) 41 28 65), at No 35, is two converted houses (one built to look old). All rooms have baths, some have sea views, all come with breakfast and rent for US$17 in summer. Watch out for the smell of drains here.

The *Pansiyon Falez* (☎ (31) 42 31 88), facing the Keskin at Hıdırlık Sokak 48, is an unsightly modern building with bare rooms that offer splendid views of the bay and mountains. Prices are a bit high, though, at US$11/14 a single/double for rooms without plumbing, breakfast included.

Places to Stay – middle
For pensions and small hotels priced from US$20 to US$40 a double, follow the walking tour of Kaleiçi pensions in the previous Places to Stay – bottom end section.

Places to Stay – top end
Kaleiçi Old Antalya has some excellent charming 'boutique' hotels. Among the best for the money is the *Abadotel Pansiyon* (☎ (31) 47 66 62; fax 48 92 05), Kılıçaslan Mahallesi, Hesapçı Sokak 52, on the corner of Hesapçı Geçidi. It's a newish, very nice Ottoman-style hotel with a large garden and prices of US$45/60 a single/double. Reduc-

tions are offered for longer stays, and in the off season.

The more luxurious places are ranged along Mermerli Sokak, just to the east of the yacht harbour.

Tütav Türk Evi Otelleri (☎ (31) 48 65 91; fax 41 94 19), Mermerli Sokak 2, is three beautifully restored Ottoman houses with 20 guest rooms, all done in late Ottoman Baroque décor with lots of gold leaf and Turkish carpets. There's a small octagonal swimming pool, and the terrace café-bar overlooks the yacht harbour. All rooms have private baths and air-con, and cost US$60/85 a single/double, breakfast included.

Just down the street is the *Marina Hotel* (☎ (31) 47 54 90; fax 41 17 65), Mermerli Sokak 15, managed by Kuoni of Switzerland. If the restored pensions of Kaleiçi are village houses, this is an Ottoman mansion, with opulent decoration and all the comforts (except lifts), including air-con, TV, minibars and direct-dial phones in the rooms, as well as a swimming pool and courtyard garden café. Turkish carpets, kilims, mirrors and gilt are used throughout. Depending on the size of your room and its view, prices range from US$112 to US$160 a double, breakfast included.

The four-star *Hotel Aspen* (☎ (31) 47 05 90; fax 41 33 64), Mermerli Sokak 16-18, across from the tourism office, is a perfect gem of a hotel, beautifully restored with bevelled glass, marble and gilt. The 36 rooms and four suites have air-con, satellite TV, minibars and all the comforts. Indulge yourself in the swimming pool, Turkish restaurant and bar, and sauna. Rates are US$65/88 a single/double, breakfast included.

Big Luxury Hotels Without doubt, Antalya's most prestigious and luxurious address is the five-star, 409-room *Sheraton Voyager Antalya* (☎ (31) 48 21 82; fax 41 89 95), 100 Yıl Bulvarı, at the western end of Kenan Evren Bulvarı, eastern end of Konya-altı beach, about 2.5 km west of Kale Kapısı. All the five-star services are here, in a strikingly modern and appealing building with

lavish terraced gardens. Rooms cost from US$170 to US$190 a single, US$200 to US$220 a double, including taxes, service and a full buffet breakfast.

Closer to the centre, the best local effort is the five-star *Talya Hotel* (☎ (31) 41 68 00; fax 41 54 00), Fevzi Çakmak Caddesi 30, a bright and modern 204-room palace dramatically sited overlooking the sea. For US$135 a single or from US$165 to US$200 a double, you get a modern air-conditioned room of international-standard, swimming pool, tennis court, restaurant, bar and nightclub, hairdressers and exercise room.

Near Lara beach the best address is the five-star *Hotel Antalya Dedeman* (☎ (31) 21 79 10; fax 21 38 73), Lara Yolu, a high-rise property of the Turkish chain with 482 rooms perched on a cliff overlooking the beach. Prices are quite reasonable, considering what you get: US$80 to US$100 a single, US$100 to US$140 a double, all included.

Places to Eat
Antalya is renowned among Turks for its fruit jams and preserves, which come in a surprising array of flavours. Stroll to the corner of Cumhuriyet and Atatürk caddesis and have a look in the shop windows. Here are some of the flavours:

Bergamot (bergamot)
Çilek (strawberry)
Greyfurt (grapefruit)
Gül (rose)
İncir (fig)
Karpuz (watermelon)
Kayısı (apricot)
Kiraz (cherry)
Limon (lemon)
Limon çiçeği (lemon blossom)
Patlıcan (aubergine/eggplant)
Portakal (orange)
Turunç (Seville orange)

Places to Eat – bottom end
Go to the intersection of Cumhuriyet and Atatürk caddesis and find the little street (parallel to Atatürk Caddesi) called Eski Sebzeciler İçi Sokak. The name means 'the Old Inner Street of the Greengrocers' Market'. The narrow street is now shaded by

awnings and lined with little restaurants and pastry shops, many of which have outdoor tables. It's now quite touristy, but still enjoyable if you're careful not to let yourself be cheated.

The food is kebaps, mostly the ever-popular döner kebap, but you'll also find Antalya's speciality, tandır kebap – mutton baked in an earthenware pot buried in a fire pit; it's rich, flavourful and greasy, served on a bed of fresh pide with vegetable garnish. It's sold by weight so you can have as many grams as you like. A normal portion is 150 grams *(yüz elli gram)*, a small portion 100 grams *(yüz gram)*. A full meal costs anywhere from US$4 to US$8; ask prices before you sit down.

On my last visit I had 150 grams of döner kebap, soslu, and a glass of ayran for US$4 at *Azim Döner ve İskender Salonu* (☎ 41 66 10), at No 6.

The little pedestrian-only street parallel to and just south-west of this one, 2 İnönü Caddesi, is developing into a similar eating-street.

Another place to look for good cheap restaurants – these are mostly patronised by Turks – is Kazım Özalp (Şarampol) Caddesi. Just a few steps up Şarampol Caddesi from Kale Kapısı on the left-hand side is the entrance to a bare courtyard and the *Parlak Restaurant* (☎ 41 65 53), an old Antalya standby for grills. The impressively long grill pit belches smoke generated by its load of skewered chickens and lamb kebaps. Talk and rakı flow freely, and the evening passes quickly. If the atmosphere is too basic (there is none), escape to the aile salonu on the left. A full meal of meze, grills and rakı costs from US$8 to US$12 a person.

Farther along Şarampol Caddesi on the left-hand side is the *Topçu Kebap Salonu* (☎ 41 16 16), another plain place famed for its kebaps. Good, simple, cheap and clean, it offers İskender kebap (Bursa-style döner) for US$1.75, but it's open for lunch only, every day.

Across Şarampol Caddesi from the Topçu, penetrate the bazaar to find similarly cheap places serving sulu yemekleri (soups and stews). On 461 Sokak, on the east side of Şarampol Caddesi, is the *İnci Börek Salonu*, specialising in Turkish flaky pastry, which makes an excellent cheap light meal. Nearby is the *Öz Şiş Kebap ve Piyaz Salonu*, with cheap kebaps accompanied by piyaz (cold beans vinaigrette).

Also east of Şarampol Caddesi, behind the Çarşı branch of the PTT (post office), the *Üç Yıldız Lokantası* has meaty kuru fasulye (white beans in tomato sauce with lamb) and buttery pilav for less than US$2. Walk through to the back where there are outside tables. The nicer *İkbal Lokantası*, just north of the Üç Yıldız, has grills, stews, and lots of shady outdoor tables.

Just a few blocks south of the otogar on the east side of Şarampol Caddesi, the *Tektat Börekçisi ve Pidecisi* has excellent cheap börek at lunch time. It's usually gone by 1 pm, after which you can still have a good, fresh pide for US$1.50 or less, or one of their excellent pastries. Look for the tables outside at the back, away from the street noise. The *Deniz Restaurant* just south of the Tektat has ready food dishes.

Places to Eat – middle

One goes to the *Hisar Restaurant* (☎ 41 52 81) more for the view than the food. Diners peer out from holes in the sheer cliff behind Cumhuriyet Meydanı to the harbour and the sea beyond. As you might have guessed, the restaurant is set up in some old vaulted stone chambers within the retaining wall. The stone is exposed, with Turkish kilims and copper utensils added for decoration.

The cuisine is Turkish and a three-course meal with wine or beer should cost only US$10 to US$14 per person. Come early for lunch (noon) or dinner (from 6 to 7 pm) if you want to get one of the few tables with the view. To get to the restaurant walk from the Atatürk statue to the edge of the cliff and find the flight of stairs descending to the harbour. The restaurant has erected some signs.

Down by the yacht harbour are numerous patio restaurants such as the *Ahtapot*, featuring standard Turkish cuisine with prices marked on a signboard and meals of meat or fowl for US$7 to US$10, of fish for about US$10 to US$16, appetisers, main course, sweet and beverage included. The *Yat Restoran* (☎ 42 48 55) is in a stone building close by, with a nice terrace dining area out the front graced by two marble fountains. The Yat is ambitious in its menu, listing onion soup, beef stroganoff and other such non-Turkish dishes. Prices are similar to those at the Ahtapot.

The clientele at the *Şehir Halepişi Restaurant* (☎ 41 51 27), not far from Kale Kapısı, is mostly locals, not tourists. In fine weather streetside tables are set up. First, the waiter rolls up a cart with dozens of mezes, from which you choose. With drinks, you can make a meal of mezes; or you can order a kebap, perhaps halepişi (in the style of Aleppo). Food is not expensive, but the drinks are dear, so ask prices. To find the restaurant, from Kale Kapısı cross Cumhuriyet Caddesi to its northern side. More or less parallel, and just a few more steps up a rise to the north, is Birinci Sokak (written '1 Sokak' on street signs). Turn left on Birinci Sokak and look down the second street on the right to see the restaurant.

Entertainment

Kaleiçi and the yacht harbour have numerous bars and lounges good for drinks and conversation. Many visitors find that their pension owners – particularly in the cheaper places – organise evenings of singing, dancing and storytelling.

Getting There & Away

Air The Antalya airport is 10 km east of the city centre on the Alanya highway. Turkish Airlines (☎ (31) 41 28 30; fax 48 47 61), Cumhuriyet Caddesi 91, in the same building as the tourism office, has two nonstop flights daily in summer between İstanbul and Antalya. Direct flights to many other destinations in Turkey, Europe and the Middle East stop in İstanbul en route.

THT (Türk Hava Taşımacılığı), a subsidiary of Turkish Airlines, has two nonstop flights weekly between Antalya and Ankara.

İstanbul Airlines (☎ (31) 42 48 88; at the airport 42 24 44), Anafartalar Caddesi 2, Selekler Çarşısı 82, has direct flights between Antalya and Amsterdam, Berlin, Brussels, Düsseldorf, Lefkoşa (Nicosia), Frankfurt, Graz, Hamburg, Cologne, Linz, Munich, Rome, Salzburg, Stuttgart, Verona and Vienna. They also have flights five days a week to and from İstanbul, and on Sunday to and from Dalaman. Discounts are offered to families (10%), youth (aged from 12 to 24 years, 25%) and Golden Agers (60 years and over, 25%).

Greenair, a joint Turkish-Russian line, has daily flights between Antalya and İstanbul. Discounts of 50% are offered to children from two to 12 years old, passengers taking middle-of-the-night flights, and women with green eyes. Those aged 60 years and over get 50% off round-trip tickets. The Antalya agency for Greenair and İstanbul Airlines is Doğal/Natur (☎ (31) 48 77 68; fax 41 40 97), Cumhuriyet Caddesi, Özel İdare İşhanı, in the same building as Turkish Airlines and the tourism office.

Bus Because Antalya is such a popular tourist and commercial city, bus transport is frequent and convenient from all points in Turkey.

Antalya's Oto Garajı (bus station) is on Kazım Özalp (Şarampol) Caddesi, about 700 metres north of Kale Kapısı and the Yivli Minare.

For minibuses to places east of Antalya (such as Perge, Aspendos, Manavgat, Side and Alanya) go to the Doğu Garajı, not a building but a parking lot and staging area for the minibus traffic. It's 600 metres east of Kale Kapısı along Ali Çetinkaya Caddesi. You can take a dolmuş (D Garajı) between the Oto Garajı and the Doğu Garajı. The minibus to Lara Plaj leaves from the Doğu Garajı.

Some destinations served from Antalya's Oto Garajı include:

Adana – 555 km, 12 hours, US$20; a few buses daily
Alanya – 115 km, two hours, US$4; hourly buses in summer

Ankara – 550 km, 10 hours, US$17; frequent buses daily

Denizli (Pamukkale) – 300 km, five hours, US$8; several buses daily

Eğirdir – 186 km, 2½ hours, US$6

Fethiye – 295 km, seven hours, US$12 (sahil or coastal route); 222 km, 4½ hours, US$ 8 (yayla, inland route); several buses daily on each route

Göreme/Ürgüp – 485 km, 11 hours, US$20; several buses daily in summer

İstanbul – 725 km, 12 hours, US$14 to US$22; frequent buses daily

Kaş – 185 km, four hours, US$7.50; at least four buses daily

Konya – 365 km, seven hours, US$12; several buses daily

Marmaris – 590 km, nine hours, US$14; a few buses daily

Side/Manavgat – 65 km, 1½ hours, US$3; very frequent buses and dolmuşes in summer

AROUND ANTALYA

You can use Antalya as a base for excursions to Olimpos and Phaselis, Termessos, Perge, Aspendos and Side, but you might find it easier to visit Olimpos and Phaselis on your way to or from Kaş, and Perge and Aspendos on your way to Side. With your own car you can stop at Termessos on your way north or west to Ankara, Denizli/Pamukkale, Eğirdir, İstanbul or İzmir.

Travel agencies in Antalya operate tours to all of these sites. For instance, a half-day tour to the Düden waterfalls (Düden Şelalesi) and Termessos costs US$20 per person and is perhaps a bit rushed – there's a lot to see at Termessos.

A full-day tour to Perge, Aspendos and Side costs almost US$40. Or you can organise your own transport. If you can scrape together a party of four or five people you can negotiate with a taxi or minibus driver for a private excursion. The private taxi method is especially pleasant and useful for getting to Termessos, and is a lot cheaper than taking an organised tour.

Beaches

Antalya's reputation as a tourist centre is built not on its own beaches, but of those not far away, like Side's. Antalya's Konyaaltı beach to the west is pebbly, shadeless and relatively cheerless. Lara Plajı, to the east, is much better, but access is restricted and fees are charged. For a real beach holiday, spend your time at Side, Alanya or Patara.

Düden Waterfalls

The Upper Düden Falls, less than 10 km north of the city centre, can be reached by dolmuş from the Doğu Garajı. Within view of the falls is a nice park and teahouse. This can be a relaxing spot on a hot summer afternoon, but avoid Düden on summer weekends when the park is crowded.

The Lower Düden Falls are down where the stream Düden Çayı, meets the Mediterranean at Lara Plajı. Excursion boats include a visit to Lower Düden Falls on their rounds of the Gulf of Antalya. See Boat Excursions in the Antalya section for details.

Termessos

High in a rugged mountain valley 34 km inland from Antalya lies the ruined city of Termessos. The warlike Termessians, a Pisidian people, lived in their impregnable fortress city and guarded their independence fiercely. Alexander the Great was fought off in 333 BC, and the Romans accepted Termessos as an independent ally, not as a subject city in 70 BC.

Start early in the day as you have to walk and climb a good deal to see the ruins. Though it's cooler up in the mountains than on the shore, the sun is still quite hot. Take good shoes, a supply of drinking water, and perhaps a picnic lunch. Make this visit in the morning and spend the afternoon at the beach.

The Termessos archaeological site is open daily from 8 am to 7 pm (until 5.30 pm in winter); admission costs US$1, half-price for students.

At the agora are the remains of a small **Temple of Hadrian**, now little more than a doorway. Head up the path to the **city gate**, the impressive **theatre** (the best preserved building here) with its spectacular view, **gymnasium**, a **Corinthian temple** and the **upper city walls**.

Your goal is the **necropolis**(*mezarlık*) at the very top of the valley, three km up from

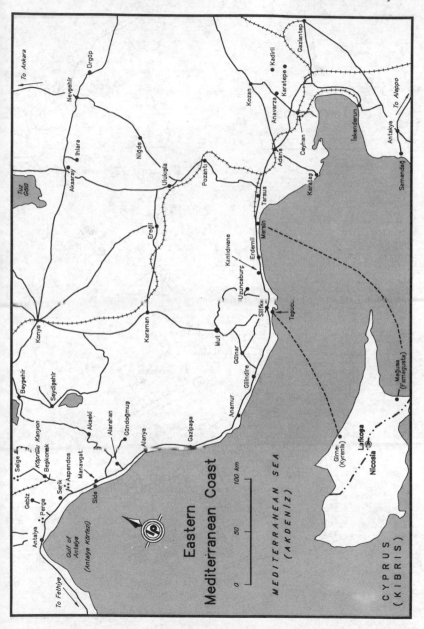

Eastern Mediterranean Coast

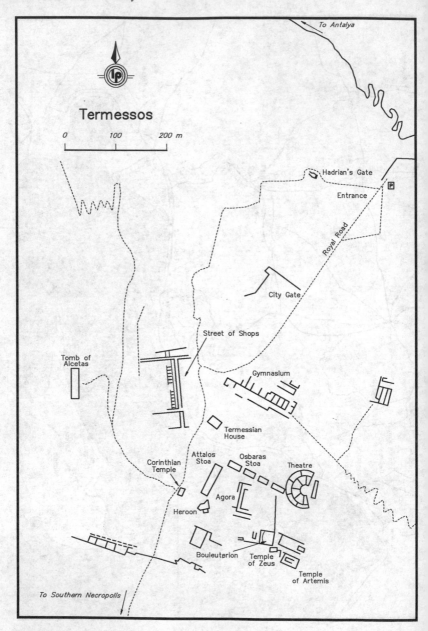

Termessos

To Antalya

Hadrian's Gate

Entrance

Royal Road

City Gate

Street of Shops

Tomb of Alcetas

Gymnasium

Termessian House

Corinthian Temple

Attalos Stoa

Osbaras Stoa

Theatre

Agora

Heroon

Bouleuterion

Temple of Zeus

Temple of Artemis

To Southern Necropolis

the agora. It's a hike but the necropolis is a fantastic sight and the mountain vistas are breathtaking. As you toil upward you'll notice a wire running alongside the path. It goes to a fire tower at the top of the valley, where a man sits, drinks tea, smokes cigarettes, reads newspapers and keeps a lookout for fires.

The necropolis is really something – a vast field of huge stone sarcophagi tumbled about by earthquakes and grave-robbers. The scene is reminiscent of medieval paintings portraying the Judgement Day, when all tombs are to be cast open. Most famous of the tombs here is that of Alcatus, a successor general of Alexander's, with fine reliefs on its façade.

Getting There & Away Taxis hang around Antalya's otogar offering trips to Termessos for US$35 to US$50, for the round trip, for up to four people. If you don't have your own transport, travelling like this probably makes the most sense.

Leave Antalya by the highway towards Burdur and Isparta, turning after about 12 km onto the road marked for Korkuteli. About 25 km from Antalya, look for a road on the right marked for Karain (nine km), the cave where important Palaeolithic artefacts were found.

Just after the Karain road, look on the left for the entrance to **Güllükdağı (Termessos) Milli Parkı**, the national park. Entry to the park costs US$3.50 for a car, 75c per person; you will pay again to enter the ruins of Termessos. About 800 metres into the park is a small **museum** with photographs and artefacts from the ruins, plus displays touching on the botany and zoology of the park. Near the museum are picnic sites. Continue another nine km up the road to the ruins. The road winds up through several gates in the city walls to the agora, the largest flat space in this steep valley. From here you must explore the ruins on foot.

Termessos to Denizli
If your itinerary takes you north from Termessos towards Denizli, you pass through Korkuteli and Tefenni, two undistinguished

farming towns on the Anatolian Plateau. But onward, near Yeşilova, is Salda Gölü, a beautiful lake with a few simple camp sites and restaurants with signs in German.

Kurşunlu Şelalesi
About seven km east of Antalya and the same distance north from the Antalya-Aksu highway is Kurşunlu Şelalesi (Leaded Waterfall), a shady park set in a pine forest with a waterfall and pool. It's a good place to get away from the noise and activity of Turkish cities, except on weekends, when the cityfolk move here. Opening hours are from 8 am to 5.30 pm; admission costs 35c.

Bring a picnic (there are lots of tables), then follow the *geziyolu* (scenic trail) down the steps to the pool and the falls, actually a number of rivulets cascading down a rock wall festooned with ferns, vines and moss.

Perge
Perge (PEHR-geh), 13 km east of Antalya just north of the town of Aksu, is one of those very ancient towns. Greek colonists came here after the Trojan War and probably displaced even earlier inhabitants. The city prospered under Alexander the Great and the Romans but dwindled under the Byzantines. Opening hours are from 8 am to 6 pm in summer; admission is US$2.

The substantial remains of a great theatre, stadium, huge Hellenistic and Roman gates and an impressive colonnaded street are worth seeing. At the acropolis, on a rise behind the other ruins, there is nothing much to see. For a fine view of the site climb to the top of the theatre.

Getting There & Away A visit to Perge can be included in the trip eastward to Aspendos and Side, doing it all in a day if you're pressed for time. Leave early in the morning.

Dolmuşes leave for Aksu from the Doğu Garajı or, better still, get an Aksu Belediyesi bus from the otogar. Ride the 13 km east from Antalya to Aksu and the turn-off for Perge, then walk (20 to 25 minutes) or hitch the remaining two km north to the ruins.

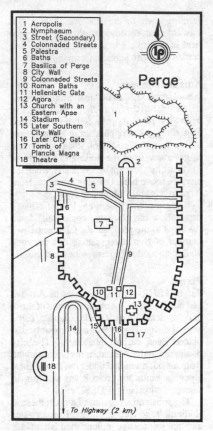

1 Acropolis
2 Nymphaeum
3 Street (Secondary)
4 Colonnaded Streets
5 Palestra
6 Baths
7 Basilica of Perge
8 City Wall
9 Colonnaded Streets
10 Roman Baths
11 Hellenistic Gate
12 Agora
13 Church with an
   Eastern Apse
14 Stadium
15 Later Southern
   City Wall
16 Later City Gate
17 Tomb of
   Plancia Magna
18 Theatre

Perge

To Highway (2 km)

Sillyon

East from Perge and Aksu seven km, a road on the left (north) is marked for Gebiz and Sillyon. Set on a mesa usually visible from the highway, Sillyon was a thriving city when Alexander the Great came through in the 4th century BC. Unable to take the city, the conqueror passed it by.

Sillyon offers little to the casual visitor. Bits of the ruined theatre, gymnasium and temple remain, but most of the ruins were destroyed by a landslide in 1969. The greatest curiosity here is an inscription in the Pamphylian dialect of ancient Greek, a unique example of this otherwise little-seen language.

Getting There & Away The ruins, near the village of Asar Köyü, are difficult to reach without your own vehicle. Despite the sign reading 'Sillyon 8 km' on the highway, it is farther: 7.2 km to a road on the right marked for Sillyon, then 2.2 km to another right turn (unmarked). Go 900 metres and bear left, then another 100 metres, and turn left at a farm. The ruins are clearly visible one km farther along.

Aspendos

The land east of Antalya was called Pamphylia in ancient times. The Taurus Mountains (Toros Dağları) form a beautiful backdrop to the fertile coast, rich with fields of cotton and vegetables. Concrete irrigation troughs radiate like spider webs through the lush agricultural land.

Aspendos (Belkis) lies 47 km east of Antalya in the Pamphylian plain. Go as far as the stream Köprüçayı, and notice the old Seljuk humpback bridge. Turn left (north) along the western bank of the stream, following the signs to Aspendos. The great theatre is less than four km from the highway. Opening hours for the site are from 8 am to 7 pm daily in summer; admission is US$2.

What you see here remains from Roman times, though the history of the settlement goes back to the Hittite Empire (800 BC). In 468 BC the Greeks and Persians fought a great battle here (the Greeks won, but not for long). Under the Romans, during the reign of Marcus Aurelius (161-80 AD), Aspendos got its theatre.

There are many fine Hellenistic and Roman theatres in Anatolia but the one at Aspendos is the finest of all. Built by the Romans, maintained by the Byzantines and Seljuks, it was restored after a visit by Atatürk. A plaque by the entrance states that when Atatürk saw the theatre he declared that it should be restored and used again for performances and sports.

Purists may question the authenticity of the restorations, but more than any other, the theatre at Aspendos allows the modern visitor to see and feel a true classical theatre: its acoustics, its lighting by day and night, and how the audiences moved in and out. Don't miss it.

Facing the theatre from the car park, a path to the right of the theatre is marked for Theatre Hill, which takes you up above the theatre for the stunning view. Follow the 'Aqueduct' fork in the trail for a good look at the remains of the city's aqueduct, and of the modern village to the left of it.

Other ruins of a stadium, agora and basilica offer little to look at. Follow the aqueduct trail along the ridge to reach them.

Getting There & Away From the Doğu Garajı take a minibus which passes by the Aspendos turn-off, then walk (45 minutes) or hitch the remaining four km to the site. Often there are taxis waiting at the highway junction to shuttle you to Aspendos.

Selge & Köprülü Kanyon

High in the mountains north of the lush Mediterranean littoral, about 44 km from the Antalya-Alanya highway, a Roman bridge spans the picturesque canyon of the Köprü Irmağı (Bridge River, anciently called the Eurymedon). Above it in the mountain fastness, less than 12 km away, are the ruins of the Roman city of Selge, scattered amidst the stone houses of the Turkish village of Altınkaya (Zerk, altitude 1050 metres) in a forest of Mediterranean cypresses. The setting, high in this mountainous country, is spectacular. The local people make their living cultivating wheat, corn, barley, apples, plums, chestnuts, walnuts, and vetch for fodder.

Roman Selge was thought to have a population of some 20,000 at its height, though how such a thriving city was sufficiently supplied with water in these arid mountains is something of a mystery. Selge was famous for storax, the balsam of the Asiatic liquidambar tree, which was highly prized for medicinal purposes and for use in perfumes. The city survived into Byzantine times.

Selge Ruins The vine-covered theatre rises dramatically behind the town. Though it is fairly well preserved, with only some rows of seats collapsed, the rest of the city is badly ruined. According to the locals, the stage wall of the theatre stood intact until 1948, when it was felled by lightning. As you approach the theatre's left side, traces of the stadium are visible off to the left. Climb up past the hamam to the agora. Not much remains, but the situation and views are satisfying. On a hill near the agora is a ruined church and, on a higher hill behind it, a temple of Zeus now completely ruined. Traces of the 2.5 km of city walls are still visible.

Mountain Hikes Villagers can guide you on hikes up from Köprülü Kanyon along the original Roman road, about two hours up, or 1½ hours down, for about US$10 each way. They can also arrange mountain treks for groups to Bozburun Dağı (2504 metres) and other points in the Kuyucak range, with a guide, katırcı (muleteer) and yemekçi (cook) for about US$50 per day.

Canoe & Raft Trips Medraft (☎ (31) 48 00 83; fax 42 71 18), Cumhuriyet Caddesi 76/6, Işık Apt, Antalya, operates daily multiperson raft and two-person inflatable 'canoe' trips in summer along the Köprülü River in Köprülü Kanyon.

The company's buses pick you up at your hotel in the morning and drive you to the river. You paddle about 15 km downstream, stopping on the way for a picnic lunch. Buses return you to your hotel late in the afternoon. The price per person is US$50 (half-price for children aged under 13 years), which includes lunch, insurance, guides and equipment.

Places to Stay At this writing there is little in the way of accommodation, though a request for a *misafir odası* (guest room) will sometimes produce a bed in a village house at a low price. There is camping farther down the valley. Altınkaya will not develop much because there is a shortage of water; the village's meagre supply is now brought from many km away. There is camping in the national park (see the following Getting There & Away section).

Getting There & Away Köprülü Kanyon and Selge are included in some tours run from Antalya, Side and Alanya for about US$20 per person. If you'd rather do it independently, the one daily minibus departs from Altınkaya in the morning for Serik (1½ hours, $4) on the Antalya-Alanya highway, returning to Altınkaya in the evening. Thus you must plan to spend the night in the mountains, or haggle for a return fare, if you take the minibus.

With your own vehicle, you can make the visit in a half-day, though it deserves more time. About six km east of the Aspendos road (48 km east of Antalya) along the main highway, a paved road on the left (north) is marked for Beşkonak, Selge and Köprülü Kanyon Milli Parkı (Bridge Canyon National Park).

The road is paved and travelling is fast for the first 32 km. About four km before the town of Beşkonak, an unpaved road on the left is marked for Selge (22 km). The shorter route is straight on through Beşkonak. From the end of the paved road in Beşkonak, it's 6.5 km to the canyon and the graceful old arched Oluk bridge. Erosion by wind and water has sculpted the surrounding rock into fantastic shapes. Cross the bridge, ignore the road on the right marked for Selge and continue 600 metres past the Selge turn-off to the second bridge, named Böğrüm. Nearby is a pine-shaded camping ground, and two km farther along the unpaved road is the *Kanyon Pansion ve Camping*, a tidy place for lodging and meals right by the river.

Retrace your steps to the unpaved road marked for Altınkaya (or Zerk), the modern Turkish names for Selge, and climb 11.7 km from the canyon bridge to the village.

When you enter the village, local boys will urge you to park next to refreshment stands which charge a parking fee. You can ignore the fee, or have one of the lads show you around for a tip.

SİDE

Cleopatra and Mark Antony chose Side (SEE-deh, population 2000) as the spot for a romantic tryst, and today lots of Turkish couples follow their example. Side has everything: a km of fine sand beach on either side of the settlement, good Hellenistic ruins, an excellent little museum and a Turkish village.

It is perhaps too good. In recent years Side has been overrun in summer by tourists mostly from Ankara but also from Germany and the UK. During the tourist season even moving down the streets can be difficult. The quaint main street is now lined with carpet and clothing shops, some with air-cons roaring and venting their hot blasts into the street. You may want to avoid Side entirely in high summer, and lower your expectations in spring and autumn.

History

Ancient Side's great wealth was built on piracy and slavery. Many of its great buildings were raised with the profits of such dastardly activities. Slavery flourished only under the Greeks and was stopped when the city came under Roman control.

No-one knows where Side got its name, though it probably means 'pomegranate' in some ancient Anatolian language. The site was colonised by Aeolians around 600 BC but by the time Alexander the Great swept through, the inhabitants had abandoned much of their Greek culture and language.

After the period of piracy and slave-trading, Side turned to legitimate commerce and still prospered. Under the Byzantines it was still large enough to rate a bishop. The Arab raids of the 7th century AD diminished the town, which was dead within two centuries, but it revived in the late 19th century under the Ottomans.

Orientation

Side is several km south of the east-west highway. The road to the village is littered with trashy signs and billboards and is dotted with little hotels and pensions, often bearing signs which read 'Boş Oda Var' (Rooms

Side

1	Tourism Information Office
2	Otogar (Bus Station)
3	Aqueduct
4	Nymphaeum
5	Houses
6	Colonnaded Street
7	Colonnaded Street
8	Baths
9	Houses
10	Basilica
11	Triumphal Arch
12	Round Building & Agora
13	Museum
14	Baptistry
15	Bishop's Palace
16	Theatre
17	City Gates
18	Main Agora
19	Baths
20	Temples
21	Nymphaeum

Available). The road passes through the archaeological zone and past the museum, beneath an arch and around the theatre. In high season you will not be allowed to drive a car into the village proper. You must pay a fee and park in the car park outside the village, before the ruins.

Side's otogar is near the Tourism Information Office, about one km from the village centre, on the road in from Manavgat.

Information

The Tourism Information Office (☎ (321) 31265) is on the outskirts of the village near

the otogar, around one km from the village centre. Side's postal code is 07330.

The Ruins

Side's impressive ruins are an easy walk from the village. Look first at the **theatre**, one of the largest in Anatolia, with 15,000 seats. Originally constructed during Hellenistic times, it was enlarged under the Romans.

Next to the theatre and across the road from the museum is the **agora**. The **museum** is built on the site of the Roman baths. It has a very fine small collection of

statuary and reliefs. Opening hours are from
8 am to 5.15 pm daily; admission costs
US$1.50.

To the east, between these buildings and
the Hellenistic city walls, lie a **Byzantine
basilica** and some foundations of Byzantine
houses. Down at the edge of the eastern
beach is another agora.

At the very southern tip of the point of land
upon which Side lies are two temples, the
Temple of Athena and **Temple of Apollo**,
which date from the 2nd century AD. Who
knows that Cleopatra and Mark Antony
didn't meet at exactly this spot? Though they
met (in 42 BC) before these great columns
(some of limestone, newly erected) were
standing, might they not have sat in earlier
marble temples to enjoy one of Side's spectacular sunsets? Long after their meeting, the
Byzantines constructed an immense basilica
over and around the temple sites. Parts of the
basilica walls remain.

Wandering among these marble remains
at dusk is one of the finest things to do here.

Manavgat

The larger town, five km to the north and east
of Side, is a farmers' market and commercial
town, with good shopping for souvenirs. Its
Manavgat Şelalesi (waterfall) is famous
and has a cool, shady teahouse by it. About
six km past the falls are the ruins of the
ancient city of Seleucia, with many buildings
still recognisable.

Horseriding

The Özcan Atlı Spor Kulübü (Equestrian
Sport Club) (☎ 1230), on the road to the
motels on the western beach, has horses you
can ride.

Places to Stay

You may have difficulty finding a room in
high summer so try to arrive early in the day.
Before May and after early October you
should have no problem finding the lodgings
you want, but the 'tourist season' lasts from
April to October these days. Prices are
highest from June to September, slightly
lower in April, May and October, and much

lower in winter at the few places which
remain open.

Places to Stay – bottom end

In the village proper, little pensions abound.
There are dozens to choose from and your
choice is dictated by availability as much as
price. I can't help you much with these
because ownership and facilities change
every season to a surprising degree. Prices
depend upon season, demand, facilities, and
even your nationality, and range from US$14
to US$18 for double rooms with running
water; some have private showers.

The *Şen Pansiyon* (Shen) is a simple place
on a quiet street not far from the water. A
good one near the eastern beach is the *Martı*
(mahr-TUH). Some readers of this book
have enjoyed the *Çiğdem* and the small
wooden bungalows at the *İkimiz*. *Heaven's
Gate Pension* has cheap triple rooms with
toilet and shower. The *Morning Star,
Pension Başak* and *Türköz* are other favourites. As you comb the town for good lodgings
look for little signs which say 'Boş Oda Var'
(Room Available).

Camping There are camping grounds on the
road into town from the main highway, and
along the roads going to motels on the
western beach.

Places to Stay – middle

Near the Köseoğlu is the *Sidemara Motel*
(☎ (321) 31083), not far from the eastern
beach. Double rooms with private shower go
for US$34 to US$38, breakfast included.

Side has a few comfortable motels on its
western beach, among which the best is the
Motel Side (☎ (321) 31022). Close to the
village, attractive and with a pretty patio
restaurant, the motel charges US$30 for a
double room, breakfast and dinner included.

Other motels along the western beach are
reached by a road going west, outside the
antique city walls. Lodgings here include the
Subaşı Motel (SOO-bah-shuh) (☎ (321)
31215, 31047), one of the first places you
come to along this road. The location is good
as it's only a 15-minute walk to the village,

and the motel's rooms (with balconies) face east and west to take full advantage of beach views, sunrises and sunsets. Two people pay US$42 for a double room with bath and breakfast. If the Subaşı is full, the nearby *Temple Motel* (☎ (321) 31119, 31414) is the place to check next. It's considerably cheaper at US$22 a double but is not right on the beach.

Places to Stay – top end

Among the several luxury hotels which have sprung up around Side in recent years, my favourite is the five-star, 154-room *Hotel Asteria* (☎ (321) 31830; fax 31830), about three km north-west of the village proper, on the western beach. Set on a rise overlooking the beach and the sea, the hotel's extensive grounds are fenced and kept private. Between the hotel and the beach are swimming pools, sunning areas, bars and cafés, and lots of equipment for water sports.

Rooms have good quality furnishings, minibar, TV, private baths with marble vanities and both tubs and showers. Each room has a *lanai*, or patio, with chairs and table, and plants. Ask for a room with an eastern sea view. The hotel's restaurant is excellent, and a casino with one-armed bandits will take your money if you like. Rates are US$100/140 for a single/double in high summer, breakfast included.

Places to Eat

When looking for a pension, ask about cooking facilities. Most places have them and this allows you to make substantial savings. At the motels you may be required to buy at least two meals a day, so the food problem is solved that way whether you like it or not. As for cheap restaurants, there aren't any. The names, prices, staff and quality of food change every season.

The cheapest food is pizza, served in many places. For a full restaurant, try *Bademaltı* (☎ 1403), at the top of the main street on the way to the theatre. The selection of dishes is vast, and prices are reasonable, at US$5 to US$8 for a full meal.

For a gratifying lunch or romantic dinner try the very pleasant *Afrodit Restaurant* (☎ 31171) at the beach end of the main street. A large place with lots of garden-terrace dining tables, the Afrodit usually has a very good selection of mezes and salads, as well as fish. To eat lightly and cheaply, order three or four meze plates with bread and a drink. If you go for fish, remember to ask prices; they speak English and German here. The average meal costs around US$12 per person.

Soundwaves Restaurant, beside the Otel Pamphylia, has a terrace surrounded by tall grasses, a woody pine interior, soft lighting, and a different menu: garlic prawns, honey-baked chicken, and onion steak, along with some Turkish standards. Full meals cost from US$10 to US$20 per person, drinks included.

Konak Beer Garden Restaurant, down at the waterfront to the left, is popular as well, and costs about as much as the aforementioned Bademaltı.

For drinks, snacks and perhaps a fondue in the evening, drop by the *Dionysos*, just west of the temples (walk down the main street to the water and turn left). A woody décor, soft classical music, and good views of the water set the mood. Drinks cost from US$1.50 to US$3 and up.

Getting There & Away

Side, 75 km east of Antalya, is so popular as a resort that it has its own direct bus service to Ankara, İzmir and İstanbul. The numerous buses which run along the coast between Antalya and Alanya will drop you in Side or in Manavgat, the town on the highway. From Manavgat dolmuşes frequently travel the few km down to the shore.

To catch the bus eastward to Alanya you may find it best to take a dolmuş from Side to the highway junction or to Manavgat.

NORTH TO KONYA

About 12 km east of Manavgat (45 km west of Alanya) a highway heads north up to the Anatolian Plateau and Konya (280 km) via Akseki, twisting its way through an endless expanse of mountains. The road is narrow (often a single lane) and twisty, but is being improved. The first 30 km is along a good, fast new road, but when you hit the construction work, your speed slows. If you get caught behind a bus or truck, there are few safe places for overtaking. However, the scenery is spectacular and it is an area rarely seen by tourists. At present it takes about four hours to drive to Konya on this route. The time may drop to three hours as work progresses.

EAST TO ALANYA

The journey from Manavgat to Alanya is 60 km and takes about an hour by bus. The coastal highway skirts good **sandy beaches** virtually the whole way to Alanya. Here and there a modern motel, posh holiday village or government rest camp has been built to exploit the holiday potential. On the landward side you see the occasional bit of aqueduct or the foundations of some old caravanserai or baths.

About 23 km west of Alanya you pass İncekum (Fine Sand) and Avsallar. At İncekum is the **İncekum Orman İçi Dinlenme Yeri** (Fine Sand Forest Rest Area) with a camping ground in a pine grove near the beach. Thirteen km before Alanya notice the **Şarapsa Hanı**, a Seljuk caravanserai. Another one, the **Alarahan**, is accessible (nine km) by a side road heading north.

ALANYA

The Seljuk Turks built a powerful empire, the Sultanate of Rum (ROOM, Rome), which thrived from 1071 to 1243. Its capital was in Konya, but its prime port was Alanya.

Like Side, Alanya (ah-LAHN-yah, population 200,000) occupies a point of land flanked by two great sweeping beaches. Once a pleasant, sleepy small agricultural and tourist town, Alanya was heavily affected by the tourism boom of the late 1980s. With its wide swath of sandy beach stretching more than six km eastward from the town, it has become Turkey's mini-Miami, with a similar clutter of high-rise towers and resort hotels, lots of carpet-shop touts and high prices. Most of its charm has

been buried in the process. If you want beach, Alanya has it. If you want more than beach, look elsewhere.

Orientation

The bus station is on the coastal highway (Atatürk Caddesi) three km west of the centre. It is served by city buses which take you into town every half-hour for 40c.

Information

The Tourism Information Office (☎ (323) 11240), Çarşı Mahallesi, Kalearkası Caddesi, is at the north-western foot of the promontory, near the Alanya Müzesi and Damlataş cave. The staff are surprisingly unhelpful and ill-informed. City buses to the top of the promontory depart from the office every hour.

Alanya's postal code is 07400.

Seljuk Sites

Head for the Seljuk sites early in the day as Alanya gets very hot in summer. Walk down to the harbour for a look at the **Kızıl Kule** (Red Tower), constructed in 1226 during the reign of the Seljuk sultan Alaeddin Keykubad I by a Syrian Arab architect. The five-storey octagonal tower, now restored to its former glory and outfitted as an ethnographic museum, was the key to Alanya's harbour defences. The tower/museum is open from 8 am to noon, and 1.30 to 5.30 pm (closed on Monday) for US$1.

Climb the 78 steps to the top of the battlements for five views of the harbour and the town. Past the tower, out towards the sea, a path leads to the old **Seljuk Tersane**, or shipyard (1228).

Fortress

Alanya's most exciting historical site is of course the Kale (fortress) on top of the promontory, reached by hourly city bus from the Tourism Information Office. Otherwise it's a very hot one-hour walk (three km), or take a taxi (US$5); with your own car you can drive right up to the fort.

The ancient city was enclosed by the rambling wall (1226) which makes its way all

Top: Yacht near Uğurlu (TB)
Bottom: Kız Kalesi, near Silifke (TB)

Top: Anıtkabir, Atatürk's mausoleum, Ankara (TB)
Bottom: Turkey's first republican parliament building in Ankara (TB)

around the peninsula. At the top is the **Ehmedek Kapısı**, the major portal into the enclosure. From the İç Kale (inner fort or keep) you get a dazzling view of the peninsula, walls, town and great expanses of beautiful coast backed by the blue Taurus Mountains, as well as of the amazing amount of litter that visitors have thrown down from the lookout. The İç Kale holds ruins of a Byzantine church, cisterns and store-rooms.

Admission to the Kale is from 8 am to 5.30 pm daily, and costs US$1.50, half-price for students.

Atatürk's House

Atatürk visited Alanya on 18 February 1935 when he was president of the republic, and spent the night in a house on Azaklar Sokak, off Fatih Sultan Mehmet Caddesi. His stay here has little historical importance, but the owner of the house, Mr Rifat Azakoğlu, left it to be preserved as a museum. By visiting the house you will learn little about Atatürk, but much about the lifestyle of a well-to-do Turkish family in provincial Alanya during the 1930s.

Opening hours are from 8.30 am to noon, and 1.30 to 5.30 pm (closed on Monday); admission costs 40c. Among the attractions of the house is a paucity of visitors; you may have it to yourself. The kitchen is fully equipped with period utensils, and the bedrooms upstairs have period furnishings.

Museum

Alanya has a tidy little museum on the west side of the peninsula, near the Tourism Information Office on the way to Damlataş cave; it's open daily from 8 am to noon and 1.30 to 5.30 pm; admission costs US$1. Exhibits span the ages from Old Bronze through Greek and Roman to Ottoman. Don't miss the Ethnology Room at the back, with a fine assortment of kilims (woven mats), *cicims* (embroidered mats), Turkish carpets, wood and copper-inlay work, gold and silver, and beautifully written and illuminated religious books.

Damlataş Cave

A hundred metres seaward from the museum and tourism office is the entrance to Damlataş (Dripping-stone), a cave noted for its moisture-laden air. The stalactites do indeed drip, encouraged by the heavy-breathing exhalations of asthma sufferers and troops of curious tourists. If you have heart problems, the heavy atmosphere may be dangerous for you. In any case, it's hardly a world-class thrill. Admission costs US$1, from 10 am to 5 pm daily.

Boat Excursions

You can hire a boat for a coastal tour around the promontory, during which you'll approach several caves, including those called Aşıklar Mağarası (the Lovers' Grotto), Korsanlar Mağarası (Pirates' Cave), Fosforlu Mağarası (Phosphorescent Cave), as well as Kleopatra Plajı (Cleopatra's Beach) on the west side of the promontory. To hire the entire boat for a short tour of one hour costs about US$20, for the long tour of 2½ hours, about twice as much. A boat can take seven or eight passengers.

By the way, Damlataş and Cleopatra's Beach are accessible on foot from the western side of the promontory, not far from the museum and the Tourism Information Office.

Places to Stay

The most comfortable and luxurious lodgings are well out on the eastern beach, but they're inconvenient if you want to stroll in town. The downtown hotels are moderately priced or quite cheap.

Places to Stay – bottom end

The cheapest pensions are out of the centre near the otogar. Descend from your bus and follow the signs. Pension owners with rooms vacant often collar new arrivals right at the otogar.

In the centre, small hotels and pensions rent rooms for as little as US$10 to US$15 a double. *Pension Best* (☎ (323) 10446), Damlataş Caddesi, Müze Yanı, is a good one

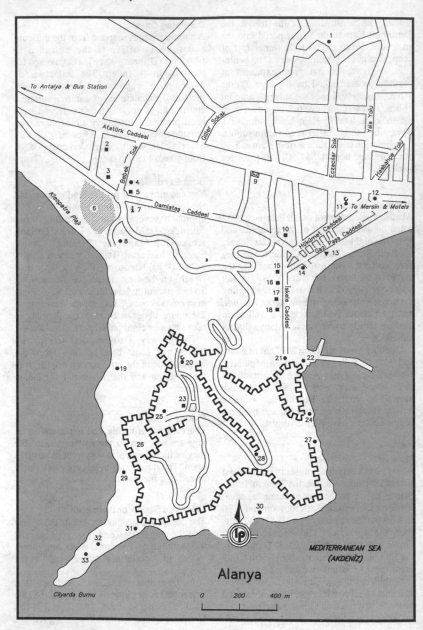

To Antalya & Bus Station

Atatürk Caddesi

Çiler Sokak

Eczacılar Sok

Yalı Yolu

Hasbahçe Yolu

2

3

Bebek   Sok

4

5

6

Kleopatra Plaji

i 7

Damlataş   Caddesi

9

8

10

11

&

To Mersin & Motels

12

Hükümet Caddesi

Gazı Paşa Caddesi

13

14

15

16

17

18

İskele Caddesi

19

&
20

21

22

23

25

24

26

27

28

29

30

31

32

33

MEDITERRANEAN SEA
(AKDENİZ)

Alanya

Ciyarda Burnu

0   200   400 m

right next to the Alanya Museum, across from the tourism office.

Nearby on Bebek Sokak are several middle-range hotels (Bebek, Sunway, Baverya) and also two cheap pensions, the *Aras* and the *Peker*, charging US$15 a double for waterless rooms. The street is a quiet one.

At the *Hotel Baba* (☎ (323) 11032), İskele Caddesi 8, rooms cost US$8/12 a single/

double without shower, or US$14/17 a double/triple with private shower. Some rooms higher up have sea views.

Özen Otel (☎ (323) 12220), Müftüler Caddesi 38, is a half-block south of the highway on the east side of the promontory, in the market at the centre of the town. Ms Cemile Sayar runs this tidy one-star lodging place charging US$20/30 a single/double, breakfast included.

Günaydın Otel (☎ (323) 11943), Kültür Caddesi 26/B, one long block inland from the hotels along İskele Caddesi, provides reliably enjoyable accommodation, but prices have risen considerably since it was first mentioned in this guide. Though staff are helpful and the rooms are clean, it is now a bit expensive at US$22 a double, breakfast included.

Places to Stay – middle

I prefer hotels in the centre of the town as they allow you to walk easily to restaurants and attractions. If you prefer them too, head for the three-star *Kaptan Otel* (☎ (323) 14900; fax 12000), İskele Caddesi 62, near the Red Tower. The modern 45-room hotel faces the harbour, town and beach; air-con singles cost from US$32 to US$40, doubles are US$44 to US$55, breakfast included.

The nearby, newer *Emek Otel* (☎ (323) 14060), İskele Caddesi 12, has clean shower-equipped rooms with balconies (some with water views) for US$28 a double. Look for it next to the Hotel Baba, right above the Emlak Bankası.

Also on İskele Caddesi down towards the Red Tower is the *Bayırlı Otel* (☎ (323) 16487; fax 14320), with 54 shower-equipped rooms, many with nice balconies overlooking the town and the bay. You pay US$28/46 for a single/double, with breakfast included.

Near the museum and the tourism office are more moderately priced hotels. *Bebek Hotel* (☎ (323) 11827), Güzelyalı Caddesi, Bebek Sokak 3, is small and decently priced at US$32 a double, breakfast included. Across the street is the similar *Hotel Baverya* (☎ (323) 14512), and nearby is yet another likely place, the *Sunway Hotel* (☎ (323) 14545) at Bebek Sokak 4.

Otel Modena (☎ (323) 23399; fax 22252), Saray Mahallesi, Kalearkası Sokak, is past the Pension Best on a quiet street. Used by Scandinavian tour groups, it offers good value if there's a room available: US$28 a double, breakfast included.

Up on top of the promontory within the Kale walls is perhaps the most atmospheric place to stay. *Bedesten Hotel* (☎ (323) 21236; fax 17934), İç Kale, has gardens, restaurants, tea terraces, places for Turkish folk dancing, swimming pools for adults and children, and simple but pleasant guest rooms arranged around a small courtyard in an old bedesten (caravanserai). All rooms have private baths, and cost US$45 a double with breakfast.

Places to Eat

Alanya is another of those towns where the waiters are liable to bring you expensive dishes you didn't order. If you don't want them, be sure they're taken away. Then make sure they don't reappear on your food bill.

The cheapest meals are to be found in the narrow streets of Alanya's bazaar, in the centre of town on the eastern side of the promontory. Lots of the little market eateries style themselves 'İnegöl Köftecisi', and serve cheap grilled meatballs and salad for US$3 or so. In fine weather, streetside tables are set up.

Many of these places are patronised mostly by tourists, but if you search you may find one which serves mostly Turks. I found the *İmren Kebap Salonu* (☎ 15167), in a little courtyard entered at Hayati Hanım Sokak 22/C. I had kuru fasulye (beans in tomato sauce), salad, pilav, bread, soft drink and tea for US$3.

On the waterfront promenade are several restaurants with attractive terraces looking out towards the sea. The *Mahperi Restaurant* (☎ 11099) is one of long standing, serving at this location for more than 30 years. Seafood is the speciality, of course, but it also does a good chicken shish kebap (US$3.50). Just east of the Mahperi are the newer *La Luna* and the older, more traditional *Yönet*.

Getting There & Away

Bus Much of Alanya's bus traffic travels via Antalya and you may find yourself switching buses there. When the Manavgat to Beyşehir road is finally widened and straightened you can expect to find direct buses between Alanya and Konya, making the 340-km trip in about six hours. Travel times and distances to other northern cities (Ankara, Nevşehir/ Ürgüp) will be shortened by about three hours also.

Compared to the rest of Turkey, traffic is sparse eastward around the 'bulge' of Anamur. Few buses originate in Alanya so you have to rely on passing buses having empty seats, which they don't always have, so make your departure arrangements as far in advance as possible. Also keep in mind that the road eastward is mountainous and curvy and takes a good deal longer to traverse than you might think from looking at the map.

Some destinations include:

Adana – 440 km, 10 hours, US$18; eight buses daily in summer
Anamur – 135 km, three hours, US$6; several buses daily in summer
Antalya – 115 km, two hours, US$4; hourly buses in summer
İstanbul – 840 km, 17 hours, US$23; several buses daily, more from Antalya
İzmir – 660 km, 12 hours, US$20; via Antalya
Kaş – 300 km, seven hours, US$14; via Antalya
Konya – 480 km, 10 hours, US$18; via Antalya
Marmaris – 700 km, 11½ hours, US$20; via Antalya
Mersin – 375 km, 8½ hours, US$16; eight buses daily in summer
Silifke – 275 km, seven hours, US$12; eight buses daily in summer
Ürgüp – 600 km, 13 hours, US$22; via Antalya

Boat – to Cyprus You can make arrangements in Alanya to catch a ferry to northern Cyprus. Boats leave from Taşucu, just west of Silifke, 265 km east of Alanya. At Alanya's otogar you can make a boat reservation and also buy a ticket for the very early morning bus from Alanya to the ferry docks.

For more information on these boats, see the Taşucu section.

ALANYA TO SİLİFKE

From Alanya you may want to head north to Konya, Cappadocia and Ankara. The eastern Mediterranean coast has a few sights worth seeing, but the cities of Mersin, Tarsus, Adana and İskenderun have very little to hold your interest. Agriculture, commerce and shipping, not the tourist trade, are what keep them going.

From Alanya to Silifke is 275 km along a twisting road cut into the cliffs which rise steeply from the sea. Every now and then the road passes through the fertile delta of a stream, planted with bananas or figs. Views of the sea and stretches of cool evergreen forest are nice but there's little else to look at until Anamur.

This region was called Cilicia by the ancients, a somewhat forbidding part of the world because of the mountains. Anyone wanting to conquer Cilicia had to have a navy, as the only practicable transport was by sea. If you just had a ship, you were in for it as this coast was a favourite lair of pirates. In the late 1960s the Turks put the finishing touches on a good paved road stretching from Alanya to Silifke. Though this has opened the country to progress considerably, transport is still slow, though the going is scenic.

Anamur

Anamur (population 32,000), at the southernmost point along the Turkish coast, is near the ruined Byzantine city of Anamurium, which you should see, south-west of the town on the beach. To the east of the town are two crusader castles, the Mamure Kalesi and the Softa Kalesi, also worth a look. Each of these points of interest has a beach close by.

Orientation The town itself is to the north of the highway (one km to the main square) but it has a beachside 'suburb' two km south of the highway. The otogar is at the junction of the highway and the main street north of the

main square. To reach the beach head east a short distance and turn right (south) at the signs; the beach is two km down the road in the district called İskele (dock).

Anamurium The ruins of Anamurium are 8.5 km west of the centre of the modern town of Anamur. Coming down from the Cilician mountains the highway finally reaches some level ground and a straight section. At this point, six km from the main square in Anamur, a road on the right (south) is marked for the ruins. Another 2.5 km brings you past fields and through the ruins to a dead end at the beach. There is no regular dolmuş service to the ruins; you will probably have to take a taxi.

Founded by the Phoenicians, Anamurium flourished through the Roman period. Its Golden Age may have been around 250 AD, after which it lost some importance, but nothing like what it was about to lose. When the Arab armies stormed out of Arabia in the 7th century they raided and pillaged this coast, including Anamurium. Despite its mighty walls and remote location, the city fell. It never recovered from the devastation and no-one was interested in settling here afterwards.

Had new settlers come, they doubtless would have torn down these old buildings and used the cut stones to build their own houses, stores, wharves and bridges, as they did everywhere until this century. Anamurium escaped this pillage and today it is an authentic Byzantine ghost town, with dozens of buildings perched eerily on this rocky hillside above an unsullied pebble beach. Churches, aqueducts, houses and defensive walls stand silent and empty, their roofs caved in but their walls largely intact. It's quite surprising that Anatolia's earthquakes did so little damage.

Anamurium's **baths** are well-preserved, even to some of the wall decoration; many of the tombs in the **necropolis** have traces of decoration as well.

Mamure Kalesi Seven km east of Anamur, just off the highway, stands Mamure Kalesi

– you can't miss it. There has been a fortress at this point since the 3rd century AD, but the present structure dates from the time of the crusades when it was used by the crusader rulers of Cyprus, and later the emirs of Karaman. The Ottomans took over in the middle of the 15th century and kept the castle in good repair until the empire ended this century. The fortifications, with crenellated walls and towers, are very impressive. You can visit every day from 8 am to 5 or 6 pm; admission costs US$1.

Softa Kalesi Heading east from Anamur, 2.8 km past the Mamure Kalesi, is a new harbour (a yacht marina?), and four km east of the harbour the town of **Bozyazı**, a town spread (like Anamur) on a fertile alluvial plain backed by rugged mountains. Eastward across the plain, clearly visible as you travel, is the Softa Kalesi, surrounded by the little hamlet of **Çubukkoyağı**. As you leave Bozyazı, a road on the left (north, inland) is marked for the Softa Kalesi, perched on top of its rocky crag and looming over the highway. This castle, built by the Armenian kings who ruled Cilicia for a short while during the crusades, is now fairly ruined inside but the walls and situation are still quite impressive. From the Softa Kalesi it's 20 km west back to Anamur, or 140 km east to Silifke.

Places to Stay There are cheap pensions and camping grounds near each of the three points of interest. On the road to ancient Anamurium you pass the *Alper Pension* and the *Anamuryum Pension & Restaurant*, open in summer only. Down on the beach (bear left at the Alper Pension and go 650 metres) is the fancy *Anamuryum Mocamp* for campers. Prices are the standard US$4 to US$6 per person, depending upon season and demand.

Just across the road from the Mamure Kalesi is the *Mamure Pension*, a tidy place which is handy but suffers from road noise. To the east of the castle in the next 1.5 km are lots more little pensions, including the

very tidy *Ak Pansiyon*, charging US$12 a night, breakfast included. Staying at one of these places allows you to visit the castle and take a swim from the same base. Exactly 1.5 km east of the castle is the *Pullu Orman İçi Dinlenme Yeri*, a forest camping ground operated by the General Directorate of Forests. The cost is US$1 for a tent, US$2 for a caravan, plus 40c per person. There is a fine sandy beach just below.

On the little cove beneath the Softa Kalesi are several little pensions, some condominiums and the *Alinko Motel*.

Down at Anamur beach, called the İskele (dock) district, are numerous little pensions and camping grounds. The configuration changes every few months as new construction gets under way. The one-star *Dragon Motel* (☎ (7571) 4140; fax 3005), İskele Caddesi, has 35 rooms with shower in little bungalows set amid evergreens on the beach, for which the charge is US$24/36 for a single/double, breakfast included. The three-star, 70-room *Hermes Hotel* (☎ (7571) 4045; fax 3995), is Anamur's best, charging US$30/44 a single/double, breakfast included. The hotel has a swimming pool, and is right on the beach.

In the town of Anamur itself the *Hotel Saray* (☎ (7571) 1191), Tahsin Soylu Caddesi, near the Otel Alahan, is simple and cheap, with cleanish rooms for US$14 a double.

The two-star *Otel Anahan* (☎ (7571) 3511; fax 1045), Tahsin Soylu Caddesi 109, is fairly simple. It has 30 fairly comfy rooms (with balcony and private shower) reached by a marble staircase (no lift), a restaurant and a café-bar. It's one km east of the main square, 1.5 km from the otogar, and almost three km from the beach.

Places to Eat Many pensions provide meals, as do the hotels and motels. A few metres south of the main square is the *Bulvar Restaurant*. It's nothing fancy, but it provides food.

Getting Around Anamur is spread out and somewhat difficult to get around if you haven't got your own wheels. To get to Anamurium, ask at the bus station; sometimes drivers going a longer distance will drop you at the crossroads, from where it's 1.5 km to the archaeological zone entrance. A taxi will no doubt run you out to the ruins, wait for an hour, and take you back into town for US$5 to US$7.

During the summer there are sometimes dolmuşes to the beach south of Anamur, and you may also be able to hitch here. East of Anamur the transport situation brightens as there are frequent dolmuşes to Bozyazı from the Anamur otogar. You can use these to visit the Mamure Kalesi, the Softa Kalesi and the beach.

East to Silifke

From Anamur it's 160 km to Silifke. The highway winds up into the mountains again, and then winds on and on, occasionally dipping down to another alluvial valley with its requisite farming hamlet and semi-tropical crops. If you'd like to climb into the mountains and see yet another medieval castle, turn left (north) a few km east of Gilindire and head up towards Gülnar (25 km) for a look at the **Meydancık Kalesi**, which has stood here in one form or another since Hittite times.

After interminable curves and switchbacks the highway finally comes down from the cliffside to the Cilician Plain, the fertile littoral at the foot of the Taurus Mountains which stretches from Silifke to Adana. Before coming to Silifke proper, you pass its port of Taşucu, from where ferries and hydrofoils depart for northern Cyprus.

Taşucu

Taşucu (TAHSH-oo-joo) lives for the ferries. This pleasant little village has always been the port for Silifke. Hotels put up voyagers, and car ferries and hydrofoils take them to and fro across the sea.

Orientation & Information The main square by the ferry dock has a PTT, a customs house, a Tourism Information Office (☎ (7593) 1234), various shipping offices and a few restaurants. It's only a few dozen metres south of the highway. The village bazaar is east of the main square.

Places to Stay About the cheapest place to stay is the *Işık Otel* (☎ (7593) 1026), on Atatürk Caddesi, an old waterfront building facing the main square with rooms for US$10 a double without running water. It's right next door to a *pavyon* (Turkish nightclub) and thus may be noisy.

The *Hotel Fatih* (☎ (7593) 1125, 1248) is better. It's on the highway behind the Gümrük only metres from the square. Rooms have private showers, little balconies and prices of US$18/26/34 a single/double/triple, though you can haggle them down out of season. There's a restaurant as well.

You may have noticed two motels on the highway as you approached Taşucu. The *Lades Motel* (☎ (7593) 1008, 1190) is the older of the two. It is also comfortable and commodious with a swimming pool, a wading pool for children, a playground, a restaurant and rooms with private bath. Many rooms also have balconies looking right out to the ferry dock directly below.

The *Taştur Motel* (☎ (7593) 1045; fax 1290), 100 metres west of the Lades, has 54 quite comfortable rooms with private showers and sea-view balconies furnished with table and chairs. Public spaces include a dramatic restaurant and terrace, a lobby, and a bar all done in sea blues with bits of nautical decoration. A small garden reaches down to the seashore beyond the large swimming pool and the smaller children's pool. Rates in summer are US$50/66 for a single/double, breakfast included.

Places to Eat The *Denizkızı Restaurant*, opposite the bust of Atatürk in the main square, is the locals' favourite at lunch and dinner time, and is fairly cheap. The fancy *Baba Restaurant* (☎ 1210) adjoining the Taştur Motel has good views of the harbour, good fish and moderate prices (about US$6 for a meat meal, US$12 or more for fish).

Getting There & Away Passenger boats to Kyrenia (Girne, northern Cyprus) depart from Taşucu, 11 km west of Silifke's otogar.

The air-con, 250-passenger MV *Barbaros*, a deniz otobüsü, is operated by Kıbrıs Express (☎ (7593) 1434, 1334), Atatürk Caddesi 82. It departs from Taşucu on the two-hour voyage to Kyrenia daily at 11.30 am, returning from Kyrenia at 2.30 pm. Tickets cost US$28 one way, US$44 for the round trip; children under four years of age travel free, those aged from five to 12 years pay US$20 one way. There is a Cypriot port tax which is added to your fare. The *Barbaros* has a snack bar but no restaurant so bring your own supplies. Tickets are on sale at the Kıbrıs Express office on Taşucu's main square.

Tickets are also sold at Mersin Seyahat (☎ (741) 18789, 13644) in Mersin's bus station. Direct Mersin-to-Taşucu buses depart daily at 8.30 am, arriving in Taşucu in time for the *Barbaros*' departure. Other Kıbrıs Express offices are in Kyrenia at İskenderun Caddesi 4 (☎ (581) 53544, 52900); in Mersin at İnönü Bulvarı, Güvenç İş Merkezi 10 (☎ (741) 16731, 11550); and in Lefkoşa (Nicosia, northern Cyprus) across from the İş Bankası.

Turkish Maritime Lines also operates a passenger service between Taşucu and Kyrenia from March to September. Departure from Taşucu is at midnight daily, with arrival in Kyrenia at 8 am. Departure from Kyrenia is at 1 pm, with arrival back in Taşucu at 5.30 pm. The fare is US$24 each way.

For the car ferry, tickets cost less but the trip is longer. The Ertürk company operates boats at midnight on Sunday, Monday, Tuesday, Wednesday and Thursday, arriving in Kyrenia the next day at 7.30 am. From Kyrenia the ferries depart at noon on Monday, Tuesday, Wednesday, Thursday and Friday, arriving in Taşucu at 4 pm. Tickets cost US$28 one way, US$39 round trip. Buy your tickets at Fatih Ferryboat

(☎ (7593) 1249, 1386) in Taşucu's main square, or at these offices: in Kyrenia (☎ (081) 54880, 54977, 52840); in Lefkoşa call the Jen-Tur agency (☎ (020) 78824).

Getting Around Dolmuşes run between Taşucu and Silifke's otogar frequently throughout the day. The Silifke terminus is not the otogar proper, but a fuel station across the road from bit.

SİLİFKE

Silifke (population 25,000) is the ancient Seleucia, founded by Seleucus I Nicator in the 3rd century BC. Seleucus was one of Alexander the Great's most able generals and founder of the Seleucid dynasty which ruled Syria after Alexander's death.

Silifke's other claim to fame is as the place where Emperor Frederick I Barbarossa (1125-90), while leading his troops on the Third Crusade, drowned in the river – an ignominious end for a soldier.

A striking castle dominates the town from a Taurus hillside and promises good sightseeing. To many people, however, Silifke is just a place to catch the boat to Cyprus or a bus to Mersin, Adana or Konya.

Orientation

The bus terminal is near the junction of highways to Alanya, Mersin and Konya. From the bus terminal into the centre of the town is exactly one km; halfway you pass the Temple of Jupiter.

The town is divided by the Göksu River, called the Calycadnus in ancient times. Most of the services are on the southern bank of the river, along with the bus station. Exceptions are the Tourism Information Office, several hotels and the dolmuş to Uzuncaburç, which are on the river's northern bank.

Information

At Silifke's Tourism Information Office (☎ (7591) 1151), Atatürk Caddesi 1/2 on the traffic roundabout just at the northern end of the bridge across the river, the staff speak some English and French and have interesting material on Silifke and its history.

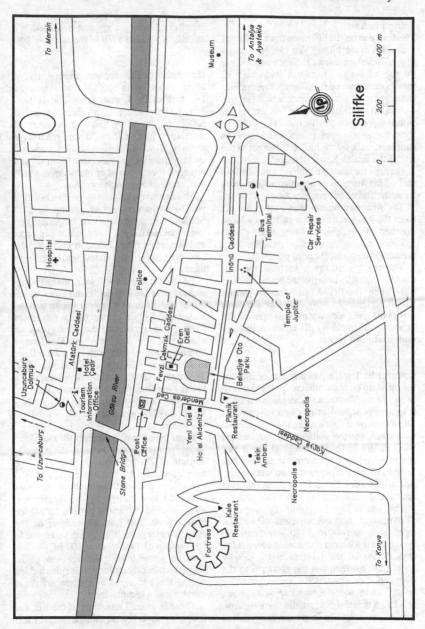

Silifke

Things to See

The **fortress** on the hill dates from medieval times. From the hilltop you can gaze down at the **Tekir Ambarı**, an ancient cistern some 46 metres long, 23 metres wide and 12 metres deep, carved from the rock. A circular stone staircase provides access to what was an important feature of the ancient city's water supply. To get to the Tekir Ambarı from the junction of İnönü and Menderes caddesis, walk up the hill on the street to the left of the Emlak Kredi Bankası.

Perhaps the most striking ruin in Silifke is that of the **Temple of Jupiter**, which dates from the 2nd or 3rd century AD.

The **Archaeological Museum** is not far from the bus terminal, and includes a large number of Hellenistic coins and several mosaics, among many other exhibits from the area's deep and eventful past.

The town's mosques include the **Ulu Camii**, originally constructed by the Seljuks but much modified, and the **Reşadiye Camii**, an Ottoman work. The **stone bridge** across the river, which you cross to reach the Tourism Information Office, was originally built in Roman times.

Cave of St Thecla Another site of interest for those up on their biblical lore is the cave of St Thecla. The saint (Ayatekla in Turkish) is known as St Paul's first Christian convert. She was also the first woman to be threatened with death for the young faith. An outcast from family and society, legend has it that she retreated to a cave outside present-day Silifke, where she pursued good works, particularly healing the sick. The church over the cave in her honour in 480 AD.

The site is four km from the otogar in Silifke, south past the museum, then to the right up a narrow road. Rubble from the Byzantine settlement is scattered over a large area. Ruins of the basilica and a nearby cistern are evident, but the entrance to the cave is not. As soon as you arrive (probably by taxi or on foot), a guardian will appear, sell you a ticket (US$1) and unlock the iron gate to the cave. In it are several vaulted chambers, some arches and columns. It's exciting if you are a fan of the saint.

Uzuncaburç The ancient temple-city of Olbia, 28 km north of Silifke, was renamed Diocaesarea in Roman times and is now called Uzuncaburç. The place began its history (as far as we know) as a centre of worship to Zeus Olbius. It was ruled by a dynasty of priest-kings, who also managed the ceremonies in the large temple and arranged for the burial of many devout visitors, some of them quite wealthy.

You can take a dolmuş to the site, but then you have the problem of getting back to Silifke – dolmuşes are not frequent. You might decide to find a few other explorers and hire a taxi (from US$6 to US$8 for the car, for the round trip, waiting time included).

Because it was a holy place, many people wanted to be buried near it, and you will see lots of curious **tombs** on your detour into the mountains. Only eight km up the road from Silifke you encounter the first group of tombs, and at 8.7 km the **Twin Monument Tombs** (Çifte Anıt Mezarları) in the village of Demircili, plainly visible from the road. Turn right at 22.7 km and proceed through a lovely pine forest to the archaeological site, just over 28 km from Silifke. Entry costs US$2. A village girl will find you out and sell you a ticket.

From the car park you enter the site along a colonnaded way, passing the famous **Temple of Zeus Olbius** on your left. The temple, among the earliest (circa 300 BC) examples of Corinthian architecture, was converted to a church by the Byzantines, who removed its central portion (cella) for this purpose. Just past the temple, on the right, is a **city gate**, after which you come to the **Temple of Tyche** (circa 100 BC).

Along a road leaving the right side of the car park is the **city tower**. Other ruins hidden among the undergrowth include a Roman **theatre** and a **temple-tomb**.

There is a small restaurant at the site, the *Burç*, but no lodgings, though I expect that simple pensions will open some time in the future.

If you are driving you may be curious about what lies farther along the road. You can indeed continue via Kırobası to Mut and thus to Konya. Winding up into the forests you may pass huge stacks of logs cut by the Tahtacılar, the mountain woodcutters who live a secluded life in the forest.

About 40 km before coming to Mut the road skirts a fantastic limestone **canyon** which extends for quite a number of km. High above in the limestone cliffs are **caves** which seem to have been inhabited at one time or another. The land in the valleys here is rich and well-watered, exploited by diligent farmers. The air is cool, clean and sweet.

Places to Stay

There are comfortable motels along the highway at Taşucu, 11 km west of Silifke. In Silifke proper the hotels are much more modest. As this is a transportation junction, hotels can fill up. Arrive early in the day or, better still, make your connection and head out of town the same day.

The *Hotel Akdeniz* (AHK-deh-neez) (☎ (7591) 1285), Menderes Caddesi 96, is at the western end of İnönü Caddesi. Simple but presentable, it charges US$7 for a double without private bath, or US$9 for a double with private shower. The *Hotel Taylan* next door is similar. Menderes Caddesi was formerly named Mut Caddesi and may still be called that by locals.

The nearby *Eren Oteli* (☎ (7591) 1289) is in a quiet location north of İnönü Caddesi. It charges US$7/11 for a single/double room with private shower.

Across the river on the north side is the *Hotel Çadır* (☎ (7591) 1244, 2449), Gazi Mahallesi, Atatürk Caddesi 8, which currently can boast of being this town's finest hotel. In the past comfort and style were not its hallmarks but renovations are underway and the future promises better. Its situation, overlooking the river, is pleasant and convenient. Rates range from US$20 to US$22 for a double room with shower.

Places to Eat

The best place in town at my last visit (not counting the seaside restaurants in Taşucu and other shoreline enclaves) was the *Piknik Restaurant* (☎ 2810), İnönü Caddesi 17, on the corner of Menderes Caddesi in the centre of town. It provides ready food or grills for about US$3 or US$4 per person.

Up near the fort on the hilltop above the town is the aptly named *Kale Restaurant* (☎ 1521), right at the upper end of the road. It's a wonderful place for lunch or dinner in summer, with meals costing from US$6 to US$8 per person.

Getting There & Away

Being at the junction of the coastal highway and the road into the mountains and up to the plateau, Silifke is an important transportation point with pretty good bus service.

Frequent dolmuşes to Taşucu for the Cyprus ferries depart frequently from a Mobil fuel station across the highway from the bus station.

Dolmuşes north to Uzuncaburç depart from near the Tourism Information Office at 11 am and noon daily (but check these schedules at the Tourism Information Office).

The highway east from Silifke to Adana is well travelled by buses. The Silifke Koop company buses depart for Adana about every 20 minutes throughout the morning and afternoon and will stop to pick you up on the road should you be visiting one of the many archaeological sites east of town.

Some other likely destinations include:

Adana – 155 km, two hours, US$3.50; three buses per hour until early evening

Alanya – 275 km, seven hours, US$12; eight buses daily in summer

Ankara – 520 km (via Konya), eight hours, US$14; frequent buses daily

Antalya – 390 km, nine hours, US$16; eight buses daily in summer

Kızkalesi – 20 km, 30 minutes, US$1.25; three buses per hour

Konya – 260 km, 4½ hours, US$8; frequent buses daily

Mersin – 85 km, two hours, US$3.50; three buses per hour

Narlıkuyu – 23 km, 30 minutes, US$1.25; three buses
    per hour
Ürgüp (via Mersin) – 400 km, 6½ hours, US$13;
    several buses daily (change at Mersin)

SİLİFKE TO ADANA

East of Silifke the Cilician Plain opens to an
ever-widening swath of arable land which
allowed civilisation to flourish. The ruins
come thick and fast until Mersin, where
modern commerce and industrialisation
takes over.

Susanoğlu is a holiday village 16 km east
of Silifke with a very nice little beach, but
also an enormous amount of construction
underway. With all the condos for well-to-do
Mersinli and Adanalı vacationers, there's
little room for the passing traveller. The four-
star, 108-room *Altınorfoz Hotel* (☎ (7596)
1211; fax 1215) has surprisingly reasonable
rates of US$45/55 a single/double.

The wildly romantic castle offshore, about
20 km east of Silifke, is the **Maiden's Castle**
(Kız Kalesi); another, much more ruined
castle, is near it on the shore. These two
edifices account for many legends, but historically the castles were built by the
Byzantines and later used by the Armenian
kings with the support of the crusaders. The
castles and good beach are served by a few
small restaurants, some pensions, camping
areas and a motel or two. The clientele is
mostly Turkish, with the occasional Yank
from İncirlik Air Base near Adana, so prices
remain low. *Kaktüs Kamping* (☎ (7584)
1216), at nearby Erdemli, is a good place to
camp.

Inland from the Kız Kalesi a road winds
two km north-west up the mountainside to
the **Caves of Heaven & Hell** (Cennet ve
Cehennem). This limestone coast is riddled
with caverns but the Cennet (jeh-NEHT) is
among the most impressive. Little soft-drink
and snack stands cluster at the top. Walk
down a long path of many steps to reach the
cavern mouth. Along the way notice the
strips of cloth and paper tied to twigs and tree
branches by those who have come to this
'mystical' place in search of cures. The bits
of cloth and paper are reminders to a saint or

spirit that a supplicant has asked for interces-
sion. At the mouth of the cave are the ruins
of a small Byzantine church. The cave is not
lit so the immense mouth is about as far as
you can go without a guide. Near Cennet is
Cehennem (jeh-HEHN-nehm), or Hell, a
deep gorge which is entered by a ladder.

The village of **Narlıkuyu**, on the seashore
at the turn-off for Cennet ve Cehennem, has
a few seaside restaurants, a little shop for
snacks and necessities, a water pump, a little
pension and the remains of a Roman bath
(4th century AD) with a nice mosaic of the
Three Graces – Aglaia, Thalia and Euphro-
syne. Admission to the museum which
protects the mosaic costs US$1. The fish
restaurants here are very nice but surprisingly expensive; a little tea garden and
kebapçı serves meals for much less.

Some 8.5 km east of Kız Kalesi, at a place
called Kumkuyu (KOOM-koo-yoo), is a
turn-off to **Kanlıdivane**, the ruins of ancient
Elaiussa-Sebaste-Kanytelis, which lie three
km off the highway. The ancient city occupies a vast site around limestone caverns. As
you ride the four km up into the hills the ruins
become more prolific. The main part of the
old city has many buildings, mostly in great
ruin. The necropolis, with its tombs built as
little temples, is interesting. If you have
camping equipment you can set up camp at
Kumkuyu.

Back on the highway you see unmarked
ruins at various points along the roadside,
testifying to the long and confused history of
the area. It served as a pathway between the
Anatolian Plateau and Syria.

Just before Mersin, at a place called
Mezikli, is a turn-off on the right (south) to
Viranşehir, the ancient Soles or Pompei-
opolis. Two km down the road is a row of
Corinthian columns in a field, while in the
distance is part of an aqueduct; all date from
the 3rd century AD.

MERSİN

Mersin (mehr-SEEN, population 500,000),
capital of the province of İçel, is a modern
city built half a century ago to give Anatolia
a large port conveniently close to Adana and

its agriculturally rich hinterland. It has several good hotels in each price range and can serve as an emergency stop on your way through.

Information

The Tourism Information Office (☎ (74) 11 63 58) is down near the docks, east of the park, at Yenimahalle, İnönü Bulvarı, Liman Giriş Sahası. Near the office is the stop for city buses going out to Viranşehir. Mersin's postal code is 33000.

Places to Stay – bottom end

Downtown, several small hotels are at the centre of the action. The *Hotel Kent* (☎ (74) 11 16 55), İstiklal Caddesi 51 near Kuvayi Milliye Caddesi, charges US$16 for a double with shower. The *Erden Palas Oteli* (☎ (74) 11 13 29), Cami Şerifi Mahallesi, 3 Sokak 19, is just off Uray Caddesi east of Kuvayi Milliye Caddesi (follow the narrow street between the little square mosque and the Türkiye Vakıflar Bankası). Quiet except for the amplified call of the muezzin, it charges a mere US$14 for a double.

Places to Stay – middle

The two-star *Ezgi Hotel* (☎ (74) 12 48 26; fax 11 20 14), Yeni Otogar Yanı, is right next to Mersin's bus station. The price for one of its 52 comfortable rooms is US$28/36 for a single/double.

Rooms cost about the same at the two-star, 52-room *Hosta Otel* (☎ (74) 11 47 60; fax 12 41 97), Fasih Kayabalı Caddesi 4, Yeni Hal Civarı, near the wholesale vegetable markets just a few blocks from the Mersin Oteli. Singles/doubles with shower cost US$24/32. The two-star, 42-room *Sargın Hotel* (☎ (74) 13 58 15; fax 13 58 16), Fasih Kayabalı Caddesi 10, charges about the same for similar comfort.

Places to Stay – top end

The four-star *Mersin Oteli* (☎ (74) 12 16 40; fax 11 26 25), Gümrük Meydanı 112 at the seaward end of Kuvayi Milliye Caddesi, is down on the waterfront in the very centre of town. Its 116 air-con rooms have comfort-able beds, refrigerator, private bath, minibar, telephone and balcony, and are quite comfortable. Underground parking is available nearby.

Rates are US$50/66/86 for a single/double/triple, but you can get a reduction if it's not too busy. There's a restaurant on the hotel roof.

The other four-star place in town is the *Hotel Atlıhan* (☎ (74) 12 41 53), İstiklal Caddesi 16, on the western side of the city, with 80 very pleasant rooms which cost slightly more than those at the Mersin Oteli. You can find the hotel easily by following its signs.

For luxury, there's the five-star *Ramada Hotel Mersin* (☎ (74) 16 10 10; fax 16 10 30), Kuvayi Milliye Caddesi 165, with 249 rooms in Mersin's tallest building – yes, that immense one which towers above all else. The *Mersin Hilton* (☎ (74) 26 50 00; fax 26 50 50), Adnan Menderes Bulvarı, right by the docks on the waterfront, is rumoured to be changing hands at this writing, and may be managed by another company by the time you arrive.

Places to Eat

Try the *Ali Baba Restaurant* (☎ 13 37 37), off Silifke Caddesi (one block inland from Atatürk Caddesi), on a little side street between the Türkiye Emlak Kredi Bankası and the Türk Ticaret Bankası; it's across from the Silifke Garajı. Fairly quiet, with bright lights, café chairs and a good selection of food, it is very reasonably priced with average meals costing from US$3 to US$5 (somewhat more for seafood). Some English and German are spoken; seafood is the speciality.

Getting There & Away

Bus From Mersin's otogar on the eastern outskirts of the city buses depart for all points, including up to the Anatolian Plateau through the Cilician Gates. Distances, travel times and prices are similar to those from Adana, 70 km to the east on a fast four-lane highway.

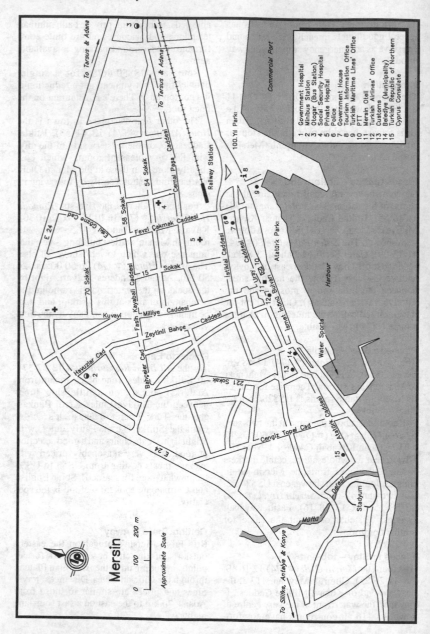

Mersin

Approximate Scale

0   100   200 m

To Silifke, Antalya & Konya

To Tarsus & Adana

To Tarsus & Adana

To Tarsus & Adana

Commercial Port

Harbour

Railway Station

100. Yıl Parkı

Atatürk Parkı

Water Sports

Stadyum

Müfta

Dersesi

E 24

E 24

Eski Gözne Cad

70 Sokak

58 Sokak

54 Sokak

Cemal Paşa Caddesi

Fevzi Çakmak Caddesi

15   Sokak

İstiklal Caddesi

Uray Caddesi

İsmet İnönü Bulvarı

Milliye Caddesi

Fasih Kayabalı Caddesi

Zeytinli Bahçe   Caddesi

Bahçeler Cad

Havuzlar Cad

221 Sokak

Cengiz Topal Cad

Atatürk Caddesi

Kuvayi

1 Government Hospital
2 Minibus Station
3 Otogar (Bus Station)
4 Social Security Hospital
5 Private Hospital
6 Police
7 Government House
8 Tourism Information Office
9 Turkish Maritime Lines' Office
10 PTT
11 Mersin Otell
12 Turkish Airlines' Office
13 Customs
14 Belediye (Municipality)
15 Turkish Republic of Northern
   Cyprus Consulate

Ferry – to/from Cyprus Turkish Maritime Lines operates the MF *Yeşilada* car-ferry service to Famagusta (Mağusa or Magosa, mah-GOH-sah) in Cyprus from Mersin all year. Ferries depart from Mersin at 10 pm on Monday, Wednesday and Friday arriving in Famagusta the next day at 8 am. Departures from Famagusta are at 10 pm on Tuesday, Thursday and Sunday, with arrival in Mersin the next day at 8 am.

Fares for the trip between Mersin and Famagusta range from US$35 for a Pullman chair to US$75 per person for a luxury cabin; mid-range cabins rent for US$40 per person. The fare for a car is US$58.

Agents for the ferry service are Kuzeymanlar Gemi Acenteliği (☎ (74) 11 25 36; fax 11 10 69), İstiklal Caddesi, 31 Sokak No 5/4 (PO Box 38), Mersin; and the Kıbrıs Türk Denizcilik Şirketi Ltd, (☎ 65995; fax 67840), 3 Bülent Ecevit Bulvarı (PO Box 37), Famagusta.

MERSİN TO ADANA

Transport between Mersin and Adana is fast and frequent, with buses leaving every few minutes. There are even some trains.

Going east for 27 km brings you to **Tarsus**, where St Paul was born almost 2000 years ago. There is very little left of old Tarsus. Bus tour groups are shown **Cleopatra's Gate**, a Roman city gate which really has nothing to do with Cleopatra, though the Egyptian queen is thought to have met Mark Antony in Tarsus; **St Paul's Well**, a hole in the ground with water in it; and remnants of **Roman baths**. Don't waste your time here.

Three km east of Tarsus the E5 highway heads north through the Cilician Gates, a wide gap in the Taurus Mountains, to Ankara, Nevşehir and Kayseri.

ADANA

Turkey's fourth largest city, Adana (AH-dah-nah, population 1.2 million), is commercial. Its wealth comes from the intensely fertile Çukurova the ancient Cilician Plain formed by the rivers Seyhan and Ceyhan, and by the traffic passing through the Cilician Gates. The city has grown rapidly and chaotically

during the last few decades. Though the local people take pride in their city, many look upon it as an overgrown village – an adolescent metropolis.

Adana has one or two sights of touristic interest, but if you are not here on business you will find yourself in and out of town in no time. This is good, as Adana suffers from high humidity in summer and the clammy air doesn't cool off much even at night.

Orientation

The Seyhan River (Seyhan Nehri) skirts the eastern edge of the city; the highway heads right through the centre from west to east. Adana's airport (Şakirpaşa Havaalanı) is several km west of the centre on the highway. The bus station is in the eastern part of town, a 15-minute walk from the centre just north of the highway, on the west bank of the river. The railway station is at the northern end of Ziyapaşa Bulvarı, several km north of the centre. The main commercial and hotel street is İnönü Caddesi; it will serve as your reference point for everything else in town.

Information

The Tourism Information Office (☎ (71) 11 13 23) is at Atatürk Caddesi 13, a block north of İnönü Caddesi, in the centre of town. Adana's postal code is 01000.

Museums

Adana has a little gem of a museum, the **Adana Ethnography Museum** (Adana Etnoğrafya Müzesi; ☎ 12 24 17), housed in a former church built by the crusaders. Nicely restored, the building now holds displays of carpets and kilims, weapons, manuscripts, inscriptions and funeral monuments. Opening hours are from 9 am to noon and 1.30 to 5.30 pm, closed on Monday; admission costs US$1. The museum is on a little side street off İnönü Caddesi, just to the east of the Adana Sürmeli Oteli.

Adana's other museum is the **Adana Regional Museum** (Adana Bölge Müzesi; ☎ 14 38 56), beside the otogar on the bank of the Seyhan just north of the east-west highway. Admission costs US$2, and

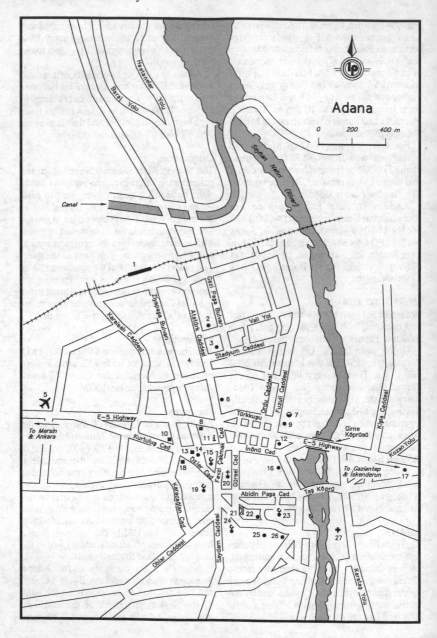

Adana

0   200   400 m

Seyhan Nehri (River)

Hastaneler Yolu

Baral Yolu

Canal

Gazi Paşa Bulvarı

Atatürk Caddesi

Vali Yol

Ziyapaşa Bulvarı

Karaisalı Caddesi

Stadyum Caddesi

Kışla Caddesi

Ordu Caddesi

Fuzuli Caddesi

2

3

4

5

6

7

9

8

10

11

12

13 14
15
18
20
19

16

17

Türkkuşu

İnönü Cad

Girne Köprüsü

E-5 Highway

E-5 Highway

Kurtuluş Cad

To Mersin & Ankara

Fevzi Çakmak Cad

Gürsel Cad

Özler Cad

Karacoğlan Cad

Abidin Paşa Cad

Taş Köprü

To Gaziantep & İskenderun

Saydam Caddesi

21
24

22

23

25 26

27

Oblar Caddesi

Karataş Yolu

opening hours are from 8.30 am to 12.30 pm and 1.30 to 5.30 pm. This museum has lots of Roman statuary as the Cilician Gates were an important transit point even in Roman times.

Other Sights
Have a look at the long Taş Köprü, or **Roman bridge**, built by Hadrian and repaired by Justinian, which spans the Seyhan River. Sullied by lots of modern traffic, it is impressive, though not romantic. The bridge is one long block south of the Adana Regional Museum.

Places to Stay
Adana has lots of hotels in all classes. There are a few cheap hotels (useful in an emergency) near the otogar but most of the mid-range and top-end hotels are in the city centre on İnönü Caddesi. There are no hotels near the airport or the railway station.

Places to Stay – bottom end
The *Otel Köşk Palas* (☎ (71) 13 72 15), on the corner of Türkkuşu and Ordu caddesis one block west of the otogar, is a big old building on a back street well away from the intense traffic noise, yet conveniently close to the otogar. The plain rooms contain nothing but beds and rent for US$5/8/11 a single/double/triple. To find this place, leave the otogar, cross the boulevard (Fuzuli Caddesi), turn left and look for a little sign pointing the way west (right) to the hotel.

The downtown hotels are more congenial and comfortable. They include the little *Mehtap Oteli* (☎ (71) 12 19 54), İnönü Caddesi, 123 Sokak No 6, on a tiny street opposite the Adana Sürmeli Oteli. The entrance to the Mehtap is populated with public scribes banging out citizens' petitions to the government. It's quiet here, yet central, and waterless rooms cost only US$4/7 a single/double.

The *Öz Otel* (☎ (71) 11 78 44), İnönü Caddesi 34, is right on the main street and so is noisy. Doubles with/without shower go for US$14/10.

Two hotels on İnönü Caddesi offer a good deal more comfort for a modest increase in price. The *Otel Duygu* (☎ (71) 11 67 41), İnönü Caddesi 14/1, has a lift, a bar and 27 rooms with private baths and fans for US$14/20 a single/double. Nearby, the two-star, 50-room *Otel İpek Palas* (☎ (71) 11 87 41; fax 11 87 45), İnönü Caddesi 103, charges just US$16/24 for singles/doubles with private bath and ceiling fan.

Across the street from the prominent Büyük Sürmeli Oteli (see Places to Stay – middle, following), the modest old *Pehlivan Palas* charges only US$12 for a huge old room with private bath, although there may be no hot water.

Places to Stay – middle
The 94-room *Otel İnci* (☎ (71) 15 83 68, 15 82 34), Kuruköprü Meydanı, Kurtuluş

Caddesi, is rated at four stars, and has two lifts, air-con and baths in the rooms, and offers a sauna and Turkish bath as well as the standard restaurant and bar. All rooms have natural wood trim and some come with TV and fridge. Prices in summer are a very reasonable: US$34/44 for a single/double.

The *Otel Çavuşoğlu* (☎ (71) 11 69 83), Ziyapaşa Bulvarı 115, Atilla Altıkat Köprüsü Yanı, is at the southern end of the overpass which spans the highway on Ziyapaşa Bulvarı, on the right-hand (east) side. Rated at two stars, the Çavuşoğlu has a restaurant, bar, nightclub, car park and 29 decent rooms with bath for US$22/36 a single/double. Discounts are readily granted if the hotel's not full.

If you're willing to spend a bit more you can get luxury at moderate prices – this is not a tourist town. The next best place, with 116 air-con doubles officially priced at US$100, but discounted to as low as US$45, is the four-star *Adana Sürmeli Oteli* (☎ (71) 11 73 21; fax 11 89 73), İnönü Caddesi 142. Its sister establishment behind it, the five-star, 210-room *Büyük Sürmeli Oteli* (bew-YEWK sewr-meh-LEE) (☎ (71) 12 36 00; fax 12 19 45), is an even fancier place, with listed prices of US$120/160 a single/double, but discounts of up to 50% if it's not crowded.

My favourite in this class is the four-star, 77-room *Zaimoğlu Oteli* (zah-EEM-oh-loo) (☎ (71) 11 34 01; fax 11 68 11), Özler Caddesi 72, between the two Sürmeli hotels. Opened in the summer of 1986, the Zaimoğlu charges US$45/57 for singles/ doubles, US$68 for a suite and US$80 for an apartment, all with air-con, TV, minibar and bath. These prices might be discounted somewhat if there are rooms to spare, however.

Places to Eat

If you like spicy food try Adana kebap, the local speciality. Minced lamb is mixed with hot pepper and wrapped around a flat skewer then grilled over charcoal. You'll find other Arab-inspired dishes as the Syrian influence is strong.

The *Yeni Onbaşılar Restorant* (yeh-NEE ohn-bah-shuh-LAHR) (☎ 11 41 78), on Atatürk Caddesi more or less opposite the Tourism Information Office, has changed character recently. By mentioning it here I'm hoping it can regain its old standards of cuisine and service. It's up a flight of stairs in the building called the Özel Sancak İşhanı, with an open-air terrace in good weather (which is most of the time). A full meal of soup, kebap, salad, dessert and beverage (wine and beer are served) should not cost more than US$4 or US$6, probably less.

For even cheaper fare try the *Üç Kardeşler Lokanta ve Kebap Salonu* (☎ 11 73 14), İnönü Caddesi, to the right of the Adana Sürmeli Oteli. The kebaps are good, the hummus spectacular, the service friendly and the prices low. There are lots of similar simple eateries in this area.

Getting There & Away

As an important transfer point for centuries, Adana is well served by all means of transport.

Air Turkish Airlines (☎ (71) 13 72 47; fax 15 70 47), Stadyum Caddesi 32, operates daily nonstop flights between Adana and Ankara (one hour) and İstanbul (1½ hours). There are also two flights weekly in each direction between Adana and Nicosia (Lefkoşe), Cyprus.

Turkish Air Transport (THT) operates two nonstop flights weekly between Adana and İzmir.

An airport bus runs between the airport (☎ 15 91 86) and the Turkish Airlines office (US$2), meeting all Turkish Airlines flights. A taxi into town costs about US$4.

İstanbul Airlines (☎ (71) 13 68 80; fax 13 55 59), Cevat Yurdakul Caddesi, Noyan Apt No 2, has five nonstop flights weekly between Adana and İstanbul, one weekly to İzmir, two to Nicosia, and three to Germany.

Bus Adana's large otogar is active, as you might imagine, with direct buses to everywhere. Some daily services include:

Adıyaman (for Nemrut Dağı) – 370 km, six hours, US$10; seven buses per day, two of these go on to Kahta for an extra US$1

Antalya – 555 km, 12 hours, US$20; a few buses

Alanya – 440 km, 10 hours, US$18; eight buses in summer

Ankara – 490 km, 10 hours, US$16; frequent buses

Diyarbakır – 550 km, 10 hours, US$16; several buses

Gaziantep – 220 km, four hours, US$7.50; several buses

Haleb (Aleppo, Syria) – 300 km, 12 hours, US$30; at least one bus

Kayseri – 335 km, 6½ hours, US$12; several buses

Konya – 350 km, 6½ hours, US$12; frequent buses

Malatya – 425 km, eight hours, US$14; a few buses

Nevşehir (Cappadocia) – 285 km, 5½ hours, US$10; several buses

Şanlıurfa – 365 km, six hours, US$11; several buses

Van – 950 km, 18 hours, US$24; at least one bus

Train The façade of the Adana Gar (☎ (71) 13 31 72), at the northern end of Ziyapaşa Bulvarı, is decorated with pretty faïence panels. Trains depart six times daily for Mersin via Tarsus, a 75-minute trip.

Adana is served by three express trains which make their way up onto the Anatolian Plateau.

The *Erciyes Ekspresi* departs for Kayseri each evening at 5.30 pm, arriving at midnight. Departure from Kayseri is at 4.40 am, arriving in Adana at 10.46 am. One-way tickets cost US$4/5 for 2nd/1st class.

The *Çukurova Ekspresi* departs from Adana each evening at 7.15 pm for Ankara, arriving at 8.05 am. Departure from Ankara is at 8.10 pm, arriving at 8.18 am. One-way tickets cost US$10 for a seat, US$12 for a couchette, US$25/42/60 for a single/double/ triple sleeping compartment.

The *Toros Ekspresi* departs from Adana each evening at 11.30 pm, going via Ankara to İstanbul (Haydarpaşa), arriving at 9.25 pm. Departure from İstanbul is at 9 am, arriving at 6 am. One-way tickets cost US$12/9 in 1st/2nd class; or US$26/46/64 for a single/double/triple sleeping compartment.

ADANA TO ANTAKYA

The very eastern end of the Turkish Mediterranean coast surrounds the Bay of İskenderun and includes the cities of İskenderun and Antakya, in the province of Hatay. Inland from the bay are ruins of a very old Hittite city at Karatepe, and a later Roman one (Anazarbus). On the road are several medieval fortresses. Dolmuşes from Adana run to the town of Kadirli, beyond Anazarbus and before Karatepe. You should be able to reach Anazarbus (by dolmuş and then hitchhike a short way) without too much trouble; you may want to stay the night in Kadirli. Hitching from there to Karatepe is not easy. If you have your own transport this detour is a breeze.

Yılankale

About 45 minutes (35 km) east of Adana is the **Snake Castle** (Yılankale), a fortress perched on a hilltop 2.5 km south of the highway. Built by Armenians and crusaders in the 12th or 13th century, it is said to have taken its name from a serpent which was once entwined in the coat-of-arms above the main entrance (today you'll see a king and a lion, but no snake); other versions have it that this area was once full of snakes. If you have the time, feel free to drive or walk up and have a look around. It's about a 20-minute climb over the rocks and up to the highest point in the fort. There are no services here, no guardian and no admission charge.

To see Anazarbus and Karatepe, make a detour north and east just after the Snake Castle. About 37 km east of Adana is an intersection marked on the left (north) for Kozan and Kadirli, on the right (south) for Ceyhan. Take the Kozan/Kadirli road.

Anazarbus

When the Romans moved into this area around 19 BC they built this fortress city on top of a hill dominating the fertile plain. They called it Caesarea ad Anazarbus. Later, when the Roman province of Cilicia was divided in two, Tarsus remained the capital of the west, and Anazarbus became capital of the east. In the 3rd century AD Persian invaders destroyed the city along with a lot of others in Anatolia. The Byzantine emperors rebuilt it and in later centuries, when earthquakes destroyed it several times, they rebuilt it again.

The Arab raids of the 8th century gave Anazarbus new rulers and a new Arabicised name, Ain Zarba. The Byzantines reconquered and held it for a brief period, but Anazarbus was an important city at a strategic nexus, and other armies came through and took it, including those of the Hamdanid princes of Aleppo, the crusaders, a local Armenian king, the Byzantines again, the Turks and the Mamluks. The last owners didn't care about it much and it fell into decline in the 15th century. Today it's called Anavarza.

The Road to Anazarbus From the main highway follow the Kozan/Kadirli road north to the village of Ayşehoca, where a road on the right is marked for Anavarza/Anazarbus, 4.5 km to the east. If you're in a dolmuş or bus you can get out here and usually hitch a ride pretty easily with a tractor or truck.

At a T-junction you come upon a large **triumphal arch** in the city walls. Through the gate was the ancient city, now given over to crops and pasture, with not much to see. If you turn left, after walking 650 metres you'll reach the remains of an **aqueduct**, several arches of which are still standing. Sometimes there's a gypsy camp set up around them.

Turn right at the T-junction and a 200-metre walk brings you to a little private **'open-air museum'** on the right-hand side of the road. Bits of column and sarcophagi are set in the garden, and an ancient pool has a nice **mosaic** of the goddess Thetis (Nereid), a sea nymph.

To reach the impressive **fortress** on the hilltop dominating the old city and the plain, you can traipse across the fields to a rock-cut stairway, or continue past the open-air museum for several km to a defile cut in the hill. An unpaved road leads through the cut to the far side of a hill, where a farmer's track along the base provides access to the **necropolis**. Ascent of the hill is much easier on this side. Inside are the ruins of a church.

The village of Anavarza has no services though you can get a glass of hospitality tea or a cool drink of water. As the flow of visitors increases, there will probably be some simple eateries and perhaps a pension. If you have camping equipment you can probably find a place to set up camp here.

Heading onward to Karatepe, return the 4.5 km to Ayşehoca and the road north to Çukurköprü and Kozan.

Karatepe

From Ayşehoca head north to Çukurköprü, where the road divides. The left is marked for Kozan and Feke, the right for Kadirli. Take the right fork.

Kadirli (population 50,000), 20 km east of Çukurköprü, is a farming town with a useful little bazaar, a few small restaurants and hotels. The *Aktürk Lokantası* (☎ 4691), facing the shady park with the teahouses in the centre, is simple, cleanish, cheap and good.

From Kadirli to Karatepe the gravel road is easily passable in dry weather, but perhaps a bit uncertain after heavy rains. Hitchhiking is very chancy, though. You might have an easier time hitching if you approach from the south, taking a bus from Adana to Osmaniye, then a dolmuş towards Tecirli and Kadirli and hitchhiking the last 8.6 km to Karatepe; or you can hire a taxi or minibus in Osmaniye to take you round.

It's 21 km from Kadirli to Karatepe through pretty hill country given over to farms and evergreen forests. The **Ceyhan Gölü** (Lake Ceyhan, JEY-hahn) is an artificial lake used for hydroelectric power and recreation. Karatepe (follow the signs) is in the **Karatepe-Aslantaş Milli Parkı** (national park) and **Orman Dinleme Yeri** (forest retreat).

From the Kadirli-to-Osmaniye road it's two km to the forest retreat, which has picnic tables and charcoal grills. A bit farther along is the car park (50c fee), from which it is a five-minute, 400-metre walk uphill through the forest to the hilltop archaeological zone of Karatepe. A building above the car park has toilets, and there are soft drinks for sale.

The occupants of camper vans seem to get away with camping in the car park, though this is probably not officially permitted and there is no dependable source of water (bring your own).

Hittite City This hilltop site, now officially called the **Aslantaş Müzesi** (Lion-Stone Museum), has been inhabited for almost 4000 years, but the ruins you see date from the 13th century BC when this was a summer retreat for the neo-Hittite kings of Kizzuwatna (Cilicia), the greatest of whom was a fellow named Azitawadda.

Halfway up the hill a guard will collect the US$2 admission fee, take your camera (no photography is allowed as excavations are still under way) and offer to lead you around (tip expected). Opening hours for the site are from 8 am to 6 or 7 pm daily in summer.

The remains here are significant. The city was defended by walls one km long, traces of which are still evident. Before arriving at the south gate there is a **lookout point** giving a fine view of the lake, which was not here in Hittite times, of course. The southern entrance to the city is protected by four lions and two sphinxes and lined with fine reliefs showing a coronation or feast complete with sacrificial bull, musicians and chariots. Across the hill at the north gate the lions are even scarier (from an evil spirit's point of view, that is) and the reliefs are even sharper as the stones were buried for centuries and thus protected from weathering. The eyes in the volcanic lion statue are of white stone held in by lead. There are inscriptions in Hittite script; a very long one, with a Phoenician translation, was discovered here and deciphered, which is how we know the history of the city.

Continue past the north gate and bear left to make a circle of the hilltop, ending back at the guard's shed. The road south from Karatepe to the main east-west highway is easier and passes by the ruins of a Roman town.

Hierapolis Castalba
From Karatepe a gravel road goes south down through the hills 8.6 km (the sign reads nine) before joining a paved road. The gravel is fine in dry weather but be careful in rain when there may be mudslides. Once on the paved road head for Osmaniye.

Nineteen km south of Karatepe and six km north of the east-west highway are the ruins of Hierapolis Castalba, with a little castle on a rocky outcrop above the plain about 500 metres east of the road, and columns from a colonnaded street standing in a field. If you clamber up to the fortress, do so for the wonderful view, and not for the building itself, which is badly ruined inside. From the fort you can see the city's **theatre** to the east. Hierapolis Castalba was the capital of a little semi-independent principality paying tribute to Rome. Unfortunately its king, Tarcondimotus I, sided with Pompey in his struggle with Julius Caesar and died at the great battle of Actium. Tarcondimotus II never quite got it together and the little principality faded away not long afterwards.

The road south goes across a bridge and through the village of Cevdetiye before reaching the highway. Head west to reach Toprakkale, about 12 km along.

Toprakkale
At a point 72 km east of Adana the highway divides, skirting the **Earth Castle** (Toprakkale), built of dark volcanic stone about the same time as the Snake Castle. The access road up to the fortress turns off from the westward branch of the highway (Adana to İskenderun); it's 600 metres to the fortress walls, then a few minutes' easy walk into the ruins.

Issos
When you're finished seeing the fortress, head south for İskenderun and Antakya along a fairly perilous road heavy with truck traffic. At Erzin, just over eight km south of Toprakkale, there's a long **aqueduct** in the fields to the right, a remnant of the ancient city of Issos.

Payas
At Payas, also called Yakacık, 35 km south

of Toprakkale, look for the inconspicuous signs in the centre of town (north of Payas's big steel factory) pointing the way (right, west) to the Kervansaray and Cin Kule, one km towards the sea.

The huge Ottoman **Sokullu Mehmet Paşa Kervansaray** was built for the grand vizier of Süleyman the Magnificent and Selim II in the 1570s. Opening hours are from 8 am to 4 or 5 pm daily. It's an elaborate complex of courtyards, Turkish baths, mosque, medrese and covered bazaar – a fortified city in what was then a recently conquered (1516) and still hostile territory. Parts of it look positively Burgundian, which makes me think that Sokullu Mehmet Paşa's architects, who worked under the guidance of Sinan's school, may have restored and expanded the ruins of a crusader church.

Next to the caravanserai is the **Cin Kalesi**, or Fortress of the Genies, a restored little bastion protected by a moat now filled with fig trees. The main gate is a double-bend defensive one which leads to a grassy interior now used as pasture for cattle. The ruins of a small mosque are the only other item of interest. If you walk around the outside of the castle walls you can descend to the moat by means of a stone subterranean stairway at the moat's westernmost point and pick figs.

Farther along down the tarmac road from these two buildings is another little **fortress** with a bent-gate entrance, a keep and gun ports, and there's the ruins of yet another fortress down by the water's edge. You can wander into all three forts at any time of day.

After Payas the road is lined with factories for making steel, cement, fertiliser and the like, all taking advantage of the historic port of İskenderun, 22 km to the south.

İskenderun

İskenderun (population 150,000), 130 km east of Adana, was founded by Alexander the Great in 333 BC and once bore the name Alexandretta, of which İskenderun is a translation. It was the most important port city on this part of the coast until Mersin was developed in the 1960s, but it has retained its importance as a port. Its importance increased during the 1980s with the opening of the oil pipeline from Iraq, and the shutting down of that pipeline during the Persian Gulf War of 1991.

İskenderun was occupied by the English in 1918, turned over to the French in 1919, and included under the French Protectorate of Syria as the Sanjak of Alexandretta. Atatürk reclaimed it for the Turkish Republic (with French acquiescence) in 1938, as he knew it would be of great strategic importance in the coming war (WW II).

There is nothing to hold you in İskenderun as it is just a sailors', brokers' and shippers' town. If you must stop, however, there are several good places to stay in this clean and pleasant city.

Orientation The seashore is on the north side of the city centre. Turn left (south) near the railway station to reach the minibus terminal and the otogar, two buildings a block apart. Turn right (north) from the highway and follow Osman Gazi Caddesi, a wide avenue, to Atatürk Bulvarı, the waterfront boulevard, with its hotels, banks and restaurants. The main square, on Atatürk Bulvarı between Şehit Pamir and Ulu Cami caddesis, is marked by a pretentious patriotic statue (*Abide*, monument) on the waterfront; there are several old buildings dating from the French Protectorate as well. Most of the town's lodgings are within a few blocks' walk of the Abide.

Information The Tourist Information Office (☎ (881) 11620), is at Atatürk Bulvarı 49/B, across the street from the odd Belediye Büfesi and next to the Başpa Pasta Salonu 100 metres west of the Abide. Staff are quite helpful.

İskenderun's postal code is 31200.

Places to Stay Two blocks inland from Atatürk Bulvarı and the Abide is the modest *Kavaklı Pansiyon* (☎ (881) 14608), Şehit Pamir Caddesi, 52 Sokak No 14, a basic but adequate place with friendly staff, a lift, and rooms with running water for US$8/12 a single/double.

The *Kıyı Otel* (☎ (881) 13680), on Atatürk Bulvarı three blocks west of the tourism office, charges US$11/17 for its 30 rooms with balcony (many with sea views), private bath and fan. Tidy marble-topped café tables are set out front on the pavement for breakfast, lunch or a snack, or you can dine in the cheerful, sunny restaurant. They have some large multi-bedded rooms for families.

The best place to stay in town is the three-star *Hataylı Oteli* (☎ (881) 11551), Osman Gazi Caddesi 2, which you may pass as you come in from the highway on your way to the waterfront. The Hataylı has a terrace restaurant on the 5th floor, a breakfast room on the mezzanine and 60 rooms with private baths for US$23/32 a single/double, and US$40 for a double suite.

If the Hataylı is full, try the three-star, 35-room *Cabir Hotel* (☎ (881) 23391; fax 11925), Ulucami Caddesi 16, three short blocks to the west.

South of İskenderun

Past İskenderun the road winds uphill towards Antakya, 60 km away, through the town of Sarımazı (10 km from İskenderun) to Belen, the town at the head of a gorge 15 km south of İskenderun. Belen looks to be an old settlement, and indeed it is, as archaeological excavations nearby have unearthed evidence of settlements dating back to the time of Hammurabi, king of Babylon.

At 147 km from Adana the road passes over the Belen Pass (Belen Geçidi, altitude 740 metres) and then descends to the fertile Amik Plain, the source of Antakya's prosperity.

ANTAKYA

Antakya (population 150,000), also called Hatay (HAH-'tie'), was, until 1938, Arabic in its culture and language. Many people still speak Arabic as a first language, Turkish as the second. You will soon see that there are two Antakyas: the tidy, modern republican one on the western bank of the Asi River (the ancient Orontes) which divides the town; and the older, ramshackle imperial one, with many buildings left from the times of the

Ottoman Empire and the French Protectorate, on the eastern bank.

In the city there's a Roman bridge built under the reign of Diocletian (3rd century AD), an aqueduct, the old city walls, several Arab-style mosques (very different from the Turkish ones) and, most importantly, the Antakya Museum, on the western bank on the southern side of Cumhuriyet Alanı by the bridge. The museum is justly famed for its marvellous Roman mosaics.

History

This is the ancient Antioch, founded by Seleucus I Nicator in 300 BC. Before long it had a population of half a million. Under the Romans it developed an important Christian community (out of its already large Jewish one), which was at one time headed by St Paul.

Persians, Byzantines, Arabs, Armenians and Seljuks all fought for Antioch, and the crusaders and Saracens battled for it as well. In 1268 the Mameluks of Egypt took the city and wiped it out. It was never to regain its former glory.

The Ottomans held the city until Muhammed Ali of Egypt captured it in his drive for control of the empire (1831), but with European help the Ottomans drove their rebellious vassal back. The French held it as part of their Syrian protectorate until 1939. Atatürk saw WW II approaching and wanted the city rejoined to the republic as a defensive measure. He began a campaign to reclaim it, which came to fruition by means of a plebiscite shortly after his death.

Orientation

The modern town is on the western bank of the river, with its Tourism Information Office, PTT, government buildings and museum all ranged around the traffic roundabout named Cumhuriyet Alanı; the Büyük Antakya Oteli, the best hotel in town, is just up the street. The older Ottoman town on the eastern bank is the place to find the bus station (Santral Garajı), a few blocks north of the centre. The city's cheaper hotels are in the eastern part along the river bank promenade.

Information

The provincial Tourism Information Office (☎ (891) 12636) is less than two km north of the PTT, on the western bank at a traffic roundabout. It's open from 8 am to noon and 1.30 to 6.30 pm daily.

Antakya Archaeological Museum

The Antakya Archaeological Museum (Arkeoloji Müzesi) is the prime reason for journeying all the way to Antakya. Admission costs US$2; opening hours are Tuesday to Sunday from 8 am to noon and 1.30 to 5 pm, Monday from 1 to 5 pm. Most labels are in English as well as Turkish. You can photograph the mosaics if you pay a fee.

The first four 'salons' in the museum (Salons I to IV) are filled with Roman mosaics – and what mosaics! Photographs show how they looked in situ, and the tall, naturally lit exhibit rooms show them off well. Seasonal themes, fishing, hunting, war and mythological subjects are all astonishingly well portrayed using the little coloured stone chips. Many of these mosaics came from Roman villas at the seaside and in the suburban resort of Daphne (Harbiye).

Salon V holds exhibits of artefacts recovered from the *tells* (mounds) at Açana and Cüdeyde. The pair of lions serving as column pediments, dating from the 8th century BC, are especially good.

Salon VI has Roman and Byzantine coins, statues, pots, glassware and tools, some dating from the Eski Tunç Devri II (Second Old Bronze Age, 2600-2500 BC). The cuneiform inscriptions are from the Açana excavations.

Cave-Church of St Peter

On the outskirts of town (three km from the centre) is the Senpiyer Kilisesi or Church of St Peter. In this grotto, enclosed by a wall in crusader times, it is said that St Peter preached.

Hours are from 8 am to noon and 1.30 to 6 pm (closed on Monday); admission costs US$1. There is no bus service to Senpiyer. You can walk there easily if it's not too hot; walk north-east out of town along Kurtuluş Caddesi, follow the signs and ask the way. A taxi charges US$2 for the ride, one way.

Daphne (Harbiye)

Dolmuşes run frequently from Antakya's bus station to the hill suburb of Harbiye, the ancient Daphne, nine km to the south; there are less frequent city buses as well. Through a modern residential area and up the hill you come to the **waterfall** on the right (west), just past the Hotel du Liban. Walk down into the wooded valley, which is usually full of Antakyalı vacationers enjoying the cool shade, the little tea gardens (each with a scratchy-sounding cassette player), and the rivulets, pools and falls of cooling water.

Past Harbiye, 42 km farther on, is the **Yayladağı Yazılıtaş Orman Piknik Yeri**, a forest picnic spot near some **ancient inscriptions**. Along the way the road passes near the village of **Sofular**, next to which is a **crusader castle**.

Samandağ

Dolmuşes and Samandağ city buses (Samandağ Belediyesi) run frequently to this seaside suburb 28 km away, following the road south-east past the Antakya Archaeological Museum and over the mountains to the sea.

Samandağ itself is very uninspiring, but go six km north along the beach to Çevlik to see the ruins of **Seleucia ad Piera**, in ancient times Antioch's port town. Dolmuş service is not regular to Çevlik so talk your dolmuş driver into continuing to Çevlik for a small additional fare. Several restaurants here by the sea offer meals in pleasant surroundings; there are a few simple pensions as well.

Seleucia's ruins are not much to look at but a nearby feat of Roman engineering is quite interesting. During its heyday Seleucia lived daily with the threat of inundation from the stream which descended the mountains and came through the town. To remove the threat, Roman emperors Titus and Vespasian ordered their engineers to dig a diversion

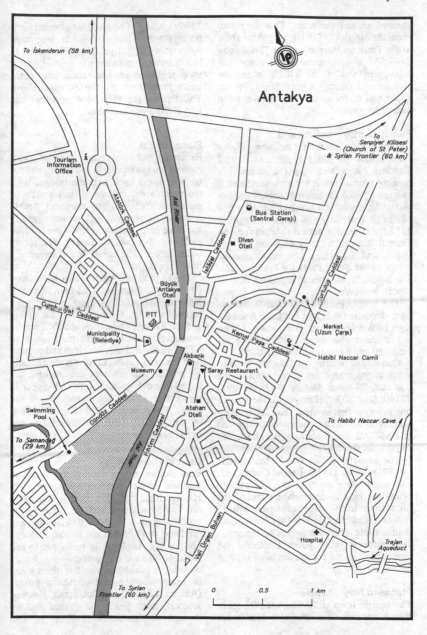

channel around the town. This they did. From the car park in Çevlik, ascend the steps to the **Titus ve Vespasiyanus Tüneli**, pay the US$1 admission fee and a guide will accompany you up the hillside, along the channel and through a great gorge. At the upper end of the channel is an inscription dating the work.

Places to Stay – bottom end

Closest to the bus station is the dumpy *Şeker Palas Oteli* (☎ (891) 11603), at İstiklal Caddesi 79, west across the street. It's nothing special but it's the closest, and it charges US$4/6 for singles/doubles without water. Walk south on İstiklal Caddesi a few blocks to find the *Hotel İstanbul* (☎ (891) 11122), İstiklal Caddesi 14, above the Garanti Bankası halfway between the bus station and the bridge, charging the same prices as the Şeker Palas for better rooms. The hotel's façade is more appealing than its rooms, however.

The *Hotel Kent* (☎ (891) 11670), Köprübaşı, opposite the bridge but back from the river bank a few metres, is no beauty either, but it has double rooms without bath for US$7.50 and a few with bath for US$8.

Continuing southward into the bazaar, south of the bridge and inland a bit, is the one-star, 28-room *Atahan Oteli* (☎ (891) 42140; fax 18006), Hürriyet Caddesi 28, at one time the best in town. The lobby is up one flight. Rooms are somewhat overpriced at US$17/21 for singles/doubles, but comfortable all the same.

The one-star *Divan Oteli* (dee-VAHN) (☎ (891) 11518, 11735), İstiklal Caddesi 62, just a few steps south of the bus station, offers the best accommodation within the immediate vicinity of the bus station, with 23 rooms going for US$10/14/17 a single/double/triple. There are no fans but the cross-ventilation is fairly good. Look for the Pamukbank on the corner; the hotel is close by.

Places to Stay – middle

The best in town is the four-star, 72-room *Büyük Antakya Oteli* (☎ (891) 35860; fax 35869), Atatürk Caddesi 8, an asymmetrical seven-storey white building a few steps away from Cumhuriyet Alanı. The hotel has lots of services including a restaurant, pastry shop, nightclub and bar, and air-con rooms looking onto the river or the town; some have TV. Prices for this cool comfort are US$42/60 a single/double.

Places to Eat

Except for the hotel restaurants, Antakya's eateries tend to be simple and cheap, and are on the eastern bank near the bridge. With most meals you will be offered a plate of pimientos (peppers) and mint, an Arabic touch. Also, you will find hummus readily available here, something one does not find easily in other parts of Turkey. The spring water served with meals is the sweetest I have ever tasted.

I had a good lunch at the *Saray Restaurant* (☎ 17714), Hürriyet Caddesi, Akbank Karşısı, just off the little plaza by the eastern end of the bridge. Go inland from the square and the Akbank a few steps and look for the restaurant. A plain, bright place done in white plastic laminate, it is clean and popular with the locals. Mahmut Akar is the chef and his brother Sami tends the cash register. Tas kebap (the ever-present lamb and vegetable stew), pilav, bread and beverage cost me US$2. The eastern section of town has lots of similar places; the bus station area has even cheaper ones.

Getting There & Away

Bus Dolmuşes run frequently from the southern end of Antakya's bus station to Harbiye (nine km, 15 minutes), Samandağ (28 km, 35 minutes) and the Turco-Syrian border stations at Reyhanlı (for Aleppo) and Yayladağ (for Lattakia and Beirut) throughout the day. Antakya city buses run to and from Harbiye and Samandağ.

Antakya bus station also has direct buses to most western and northern points (Ankara, Antalya, İstanbul, İzmir, Kayseri, Konya), most going via Adana and up through the Cilician Gates. There are also direct buses to major cities in neighbouring countries; travel times to these cities do not include border-crossing formalities, which may add several hours to the trip. Have your visas in advance to hasten formalities.

Daily buses from Antakya serve the following destinations:

Adana – 190 km, 2½ hours, US$5; very frequent buses
Amman (Jordan) – 675 km, 10 hours, US$28
Damascus (Syria) – 465 km, eight hours, US$20
Gaziantep – 200 km, four hours, US$8; frequent buses
Haleb (Aleppo, Syria) – 105 km, four hours, US$12; several buses

Şanlıurfa (Urfa) – 345 km, seven hours, US$14; several direct buses, or change at Gaziantep, from where buses go east to Urfa every half-hour

To/From Syria Syrian visas are not normally issued at the border, but this depends partly upon your nationality and partly upon current regulations. If you plan to travel to Syria and other Middle Eastern countries, plan ahead and obtain the necessary visas in your home country, in İstanbul or in Ankara. At the border you are no longer required to change the equivalent of US$100 into Syrian currency at the official exchange rate, currently only 25% of the black-market rate.

اسكَ اسْتَانْبُول

Central Anatolia

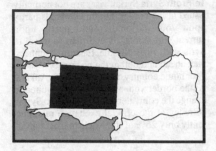

including the very earliest established human communities, which date from 7500 BC. Crumbling caravanserais scattered along the modern highways testify to rich trade routes which flourished for several millennia.

Today, Central Anatolia is still flourishing. Wheat and other grains, fruits and vegetables (including delicious melons) are grown in the dry soil, and livestock rearing is still a big concern. Ankara, Turkey's capital city, is a sprawling urban mass in the midst of the semidesert; Konya and Kayseri, fuelled by the wealth of agriculture and light industry, are growing at a remarkable pace. These cities are quite modern with wide boulevards, apartment blocks and busy traffic. At the heart of each is an old town, a fortress dating from Roman times and a few foundations going back to the dawn of civilisation.

When nomadic Turkish shepherds moved into Anatolia around the year 1100, they found a land which reminded them of Central Asia: semiarid, rolling steppe covered with grass, perfect for their flocks. Mountains and great lakes (some of them salt) broke up the vast expanse of steppe. By the numerous streams, marked with rows of tall and spindly poplars, the nomads finally established villages.

In spring, Central Anatolia is a sea of wild flowers. Great swaths of vivid colour are splashed across the spare landscape in an annual extravagance born of the spring rains. Days are pleasantly warm and nights chilly. In summer the rain disappears and the Anatolian Plateau is hotter and drier, but never humid like on the coasts. As you ride across Anatolia in summer, you will see the dark red of newly ploughed furrows, the straw yellow of grass, the grey and green bands of sandstone in a rock-face. Winter is cold and rainy, with numerous snow falls. You shouldn't be surprised at the snow, for the plateau has an average altitude of 1000 metres.

Though Central Anatolia yields a first impression of emptiness, this is deceptive. The armies of a dozen empires have moved back and forth across this 'land bridge' between Europe and Asia; a dozen civilisations have risen and fallen here,

Ankara

The capital of the Turkish Republic, Ankara (AHN-kah-rah, population three million, altitude 848 metres), was once called Angora. The fine, soft hair *(tiftik)* on Angora goats became an industry which still thrives. Today, Ankara's prime concern is government. It is a city of ministries, embassies, universities, medical centres, gardens, vineyards and some light industry. Vast suburbs are scattered on the hillsides which surround the centre; and most are filled by country people who have moved here in search of work and a better life, which many have found.

Until recently, the principal heating fuel was a soft brown coal called lignite which produces thick, gritty smoke. During the season when heating is used (between 15 October and 15 April), Ankara's air was always badly polluted, but now a pipeline brings clean-burning natural gas to Ankara from Russia. Air quality is expected to improve dramatically as the city converts to this superior fuel. But natural gas will not prevent car exhaust pollution, which is as bad in Ankara as in any other large, car-dependent city. Construction on the city's underground metro system will affect vehicular traffic almost until the year 2000.

You don't need to stay as long in Ankara as you do in İstanbul. Ankara has several significant attractions, but you should be able to tour them all in 1½ to two days, or even a day if you're in a hurry.

History

It was the Hittites who named this place Ankuwash before 1200 BC. The town prospered because it was at the intersection of the north-south and east-west trade routes. After the Hittites, it was a Phrygian town, then taken by Alexander, claimed by the Seleucids and finally occupied by the Galatian tribes of Gaul who invaded Anatolia around 250 BC. Augustus Caesar annexed it to Rome in 25 BC as Ankyra.

The Byzantines held the town for centuries, with intermittent raids by the Persians and Arabs. When the Seljuk Turks came to Anatolia after 1071, they made the town they called Engüriye into a Seljuk city but held it with difficulty.

Ottoman possession of Angora did not begin well, for it was near the town that Sultan Yıldırım Beyazıt was captured by Tamerlane, and the sultan later died in captivity. After the Timurid state collapsed and the Ottoman civil war ended, Angora became merely a quiet town where long-haired goats were raised.

Modern Ankara is a planned city. When Atatürk set up his provisional government here in 1920, it was a small, rather dusty Anatolian town of some 30,000 people, with a strategic position at the heart of the country. After his victory in the War of Independence, Atatürk declared this the new capital of the country (October 1923), and set about developing it. European urban planners were consulted, which resulted in a city of long, wide boulevards, a large forested park with

Hittite Deer Statue

an artificial lake, a cluster of transportation termini and numerous residential and diplomatic neighbourhoods. From 1919 to 1927, Atatürk did not set foot in the old imperial capital of İstanbul, preferring to work at making Ankara the country's capital city in fact as well as in name.

For republican Turks, İstanbul is their glorious historical city, still the centre of business and finance, but Ankara is their true capital, built on the ashes of the empire with their own blood and sweat. It is modern and forward-looking and they're proud of it.

Orientation

The main boulevard through the city is, of course, Atatürk Bulvarı, which runs from Ulus in the north all the way to the Presidential Mansion in Çankaya, six km to the south.

The old city of Ankara, dating from Roman times and including the Hisar (fortress), is near Ulus Meydanı, called simply Ulus (oo-LOOS), the centre of 'old Ankara'. This is an area with many of Ankara's cheapest hotels, restaurants and markets. The most important museums and sights are near Ulus.

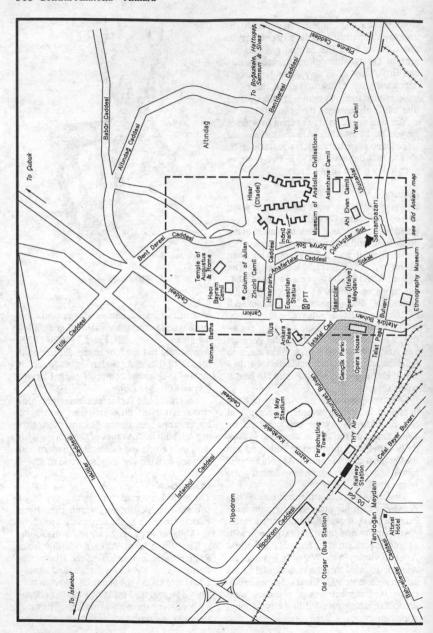

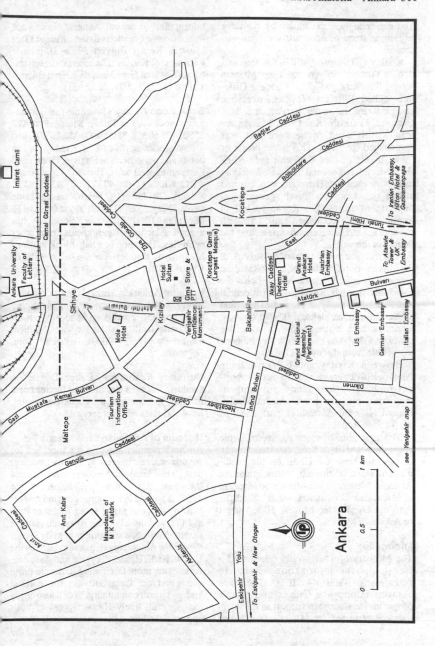

You can recognise the square by the large equestrian statue of Atatürk in the south-east corner.

Kızılay (KUH-zuh-'lie') is the intersection of Atatürk Bulvarı and Gazi Mustafa Kemal Bulvarı/Ziya Gökalp Caddesi. Officially called Hürriyet Meydanı, everyone knows it by the name Kızılay, the 'Red Crescent' (Turkish 'Red Cross') headquarters which used to be here but was demolished long ago. This is the centre of 'new Ankara', called Yenişehir (yeh-NEE-sheh-heer). It has several moderate hotel and restaurant choices. There are also bus and airline ticket offices, travel agencies and department stores. On Kocatepe hill in Yenişehir is the Kocatepe Camii, a modern mosque in Ottoman style which is among the largest in the world.

At the southern end of Atatürk Bulvarı, in the hills overlooking the city, is Çankaya, the residential neighbourhood which holds the Cumhurbaşkanlığı Köşkü, the Presidential Mansion, plus many of the most important ambassadorial residences. The prominent landmark here is the Atakule, a tall office tower and shopping complex with a bulbous top visible from throughout the city.

Between Kızılay and Çankaya along Atatürk Bulvarı are most of the city's important embassies and many government ministries, plus the Büyük Millet Meclisi (Grand National Assembly), parliament of the Turkish Republic.

The first goal of most sightseers is the Hisar (hee-SAHR) or Kale, the citadel on top of the hill. Near the Hisar, on the south-western slope of the hill, is the important Anadolu Medeniyetleri Müzesi or Museum of Anatolian Civilisations, also called the Anadolu Uygarlıkları Müzesi, Hitit Müzesi or Arkeoloji Müzesi.

Information

The Ministry of Tourism has established a free telephone information service in Ankara: call (900) 44 70 90. There are Tourism Information Offices at Ankara's otogar and at Esenboğa Airport in the international terminal (☎ (4) 312 6919). For information in central Ankara, direct your feet and your questions to the office at Gazi Mustafa Kemal Bulvarı 33, a 10-minute walk west of Kızılay. The central administrative office is at Gazi Mustafa Kemal Bulvarı 121 (☎ (4) 229 2631, 229 3661).

Bookshops Ankara's longtime foreign-language bookshop is Tarhan Kitabevi (☎ 417 2550, 425 6030), Selanik Caddesi 19/A, just a few blocks north-east of Kızılay. It has books and periodicals in English, French and German as well as in Turkish. Try also the ABC Kitabevi (☎ 433 2962, 434 3842), Selanik Caddesi 1/A, nearby on the same street. Dünya Aktüel Basın Yayın (☎ (4) 418 6864; fax 418 9155), Konur Sokak 10/A, has a good selection of periodicals from other countries. The shop is a half-block north of Meşrutiyet Caddesi on the west side of Konur Sokak.

Hospital Ankara is Turkey's major medical centre, with hospitals specialising in treating many medical conditions. The city's most up-to-date facility is the Bayındır Medical Centre (☎ (4) 287 9000), Eskişehir Yolu, Söğütözü.

Currency Exchange Merkez Döviz, on Çankırı Caddesi a few hundred metres north of Ulus, just south of the Çiçek Restaurant, has good rates and fast service.

Museum of Anatolian Civilisations

Ankara's premier museum is a must-see for anyone with an interest in Turkey's ancient past. The Anadolu Medeniyetleri Müzesi (Museum of Anatolian Civilisations, ☎ 324 3160) is housed in a restored covered market built by order of grand vizier Mahmut Paşa in 1471, and the adjoining Kurşunlu Han, an Ottoman warehouse. Exhibits heavily favour the earlier Anatolian civilisations such as the Urartu, Hatti, Hittite, Phrygian and Assyrian. Among the more fascinating items are those brought from Çatal Höyük, the earliest known human community. You'll also enjoy the graceful, lively Hittite figures of bulls and stags and the early water vessels.

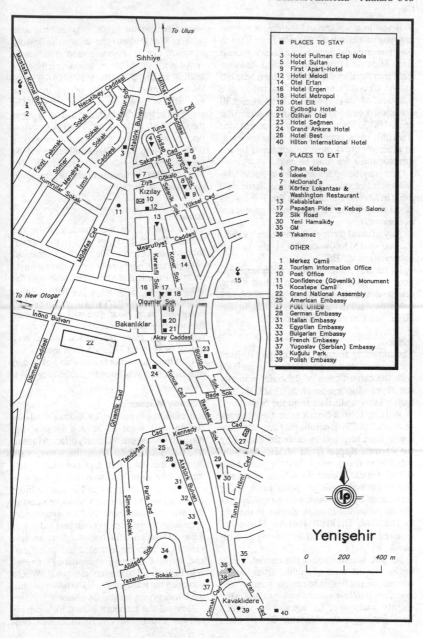

To Ulus

Sıhhıye

Yenişehir

0   200   400 m

PLACES TO STAY

3   Hotel Pullman Etap Mola
5   Hotel Sultan
9   First Apart-Hotel
12 Hotel Melodi
14 Otel Ertan
16 Hotel Ergen
18 Hotel Metropol
19 Otel Elit
20 Eyboğlu Hotel
21 Özilhan Otel
23 Hotel Seğmen
24 Grand Ankara Hotel
26 Hotel Best
40 Hilton International Hotel

PLACES TO EAT

4   Cihan Kebap
6   İskele
7   McDonald's
8   Körfez Lokantası &
    Washington Restaurant
13 Kebabistan
17 Papağan Pide ve Kebap Salonu
29 Silk Road
30 Yeni Hamsiköy
35 GM
36 Yakamoz

OTHER

1   Merkez Camii
2   Tourism Information Office
10 Post Office
11 Confidence (Güvenlik) Monument
15 Kocatepe Camii
22 Grand National Assembly
25 American Embassy
27 Post Office
28 German Embassy
31 Italian Embassy
32 Egyptian Embassy
33 Bulgarian Embassy
34 French Embassy
37 Yugoslav (Serbian) Embassy
38 Kuğulu Park
39 Polish Embassy

If you're a walker and the day is not too hot, you can climb the hillside from Ulus to the museum; otherwise take a taxi. Walk east from Ulus on Hisarparkı Caddesi and turn right into Anafartalar Caddesi, then bear left along Çıkrıkçılar Sokak to reach the museum, which is open from 8.30 am to 5.30 pm, closed on Monday in winter; admission costs US$2. Photography is permitted (for free) only in the central room of the museum; in other rooms it must be approved by the director and a fee must be paid.

You may be approached by a guide who will offer to explain the exhibits. Settle on a price in advance, and be sure that it is understood the price is for your entire group, not per person.

As you stroll through the museum's exhibits, you should know that MÖ is the Turkish abbreviation for BC.

By the way, there are several decent, inexpensive restaurants down the hill on Konya Caddesi, and several charming but slightly more expensive restaurants uphill in the Hisar. See Places to Eat for details.

Hisar

The imposing fortress just up the hill from the museum took its present form in the 800s with the construction of the outer walls by the Byzantine emperor Michael II. The earlier inner walls date from the 600s.

Walk up Gözcü Sokak from the Museum of Anatolian Civilisations past the octagonal tower, then turn left to enter the citadel by the **Parmak Kapısı** (pahr-MAHK kah-puh-suh, Finger Gate), also called the Saatli Kapı (Clock Gate). Within the citadel is a traditional Turkish village, parts of it under restoration by the Ankara municipality. Not too far inside the Parmak Kapısı, to the left, is the **Old Turkish House Museum**, restored and established by the city government.

As you wander about the citadel, you'll notice that all sorts of rubble, from broken column drums to bits of marble statuary and inscribed lintels, has been incorporated in the mighty walls over the ages. The citadel's small mosque, the **Alaettin Camii**, dates

originally from the 1100s, but much has been rebuilt. Wander into the village, following any path that leads higher and soon you'll arrive at a flight of concrete stairs on the right leading to the **Şark Kulesi** (SHARK koo-leh-see, Eastern Tower), where there's a magnificent view over the entire city, all the way to Yenişehir and Çankaya. The tower at the north, **Ak Kale** (White Fort), also offers fine views. The area inside the citadel is being restored. The village ambience will be preserved along with the fortress itself. See Places to Eat for details of the several good restaurants in the Hisar.

Bazaar

Come down from the Hisar, exit by the Parmak Kapısı, and you'll be in the bazaar. Warehouses here are filled with Angora goat hair, and merchants busy themselves with its trade. Turn left and walk down through the bazaar area, lined with vegetable stalls, copper and ironmongers and every variety of household item. Soon you will come to the **Aslanhane Camii** (Lionhouse Mosque), which dates from the 1200s and is very Seljuk in aspect. Go inside for a look.

Continue down the hill on Can Sokak and turn right into Anafartalar Caddesi for Ulus.

Railway Museums

Rail enthusiasts passing by Ankara's railway station will want to have a look at the Railway Museum (Demiryolları Müzesi, ☎ 310 3500). Enter from the street, walk through the main hall and out to the platforms, turn right, and walk along until you come to the museum, a small station building which served as Atatürk's residence during the War of Independence. It's supposedly open daily from 9am to noon and from 1 to 5 pm (closed on holidays). As there are few visitors, it may be locked. Find an official and request, *Müzeyi açarmısınız?* (mew-zeh-YEE ah-CHAR-muh-suh-nuhz, 'Would you open the museum?'). If the time is within the hours given, he should oblige.

Beyond the museum is Atatürk's private railway coach, on the right. It was constructed in Breslau in 1935 and looks very comfy; it's not open to visitors.

Ankara's other railway museum is the Open-Air Steam Locomotive Museum (Açık Hava Buharlı Lokomotif Müzesi), a vast railway yard on the south-western side of Ankara's railway station devoted to Turkey's varied collection of well-used steam locomotives. Access is from Celal Bayar Bulvarı, and is best done by taxi.

Roman Ankara

Roman Angora was a city of some importance, and several significant Roman structures remain. At the north-east corner of the square in Ulus are some buildings and behind them is the first stop on your tour of Roman Ankara. Set in a small park called Hükümet Meydanı (Government Square), surrounded by the Ankara provincial government house and the Ministry of Finance & Customs, is the **Column of Julian** (Jülyanüs Sütunu). The Roman Emperor Julian (the Apostate, 361 63), last of the scions of Constantine the Great, visited Ankara in the middle of his short reign and the column was erected in his honour. Turkish inhabitants later dubbed it Belkız Minaresi, the Queen of Sheba's Minaret, a fanciful appellation if ever there was one.

Walk east from the park, up the hill; turn right, then left to reach Bayram Caddesi and the **Hacı Bayram Camii** (hah-JUH bahy-RAHM), Ankara's most revered mosque, built next to the ruins of the **Temple of Augustus & Rome**. Hacı Bayram Veli was a Muslim saint who founded the Bayramiye order of dervishes in around 1400. Ankara was the centre of the order and Hacı Bayram Veli is still revered by the city's pious Muslims. In recent years the precincts of the mosque have been reordered and landscaped to make a pleasant park.

The temple walls that you see are of the cella, or inner sanctum, which was originally surrounded by a colonnade. First built by the kings of Pergamum for the worship of Cybele, the Anatolian fertility goddess, and Men, the Phrygian phallic god, the temple was later rededicated to Emperor Augustus.

The Byzantines converted it to a church and the Muslims built a mosque and saint's tomb in its precincts. The gods change, the holy place remains sacred.

From Hacı Bayram Camii, walk north on Çiçek Sokak until it meets Çankırı Caddesi. Across this main road, up the hill on the opposite side, is the fenced enclosure of the **Roman Baths** (Roma Hamamları), about 400 metres north of the square Ulus Meydanı. Opening hours are from 9 am to 5 pm, closed on Monday; admission costs US$1. If you're short on money or pressed for time, you can ignore the baths.

The layout of the 3rd-century baths is clearly visible, as is much of the water system. The baths were constructed on a far more ancient city mound, its lowest layers dating from Phrygian times (8th to 6th centuries BC). The baths included the standard Roman facilities: the apoditerium or dressing room, frigidarium or cold room, tepidarium or warm room, and caldarium or hot room. There is some evidence of Seljuk construction above the Roman, and indeed the Ottomans adopted the Roman baths system, which is known today as the Turkish bath.

A column-lined street once extended from the Temple of Augustus & Rome past the baths. Most of the street is now buried beneath buildings and Çankırı Caddesi.

Republican Ankara

In the 1920s, at the time of the War of Independence, Ankara consisted of the citadel and a few buildings in Ulus. Atatürk's new city grew with Ulus as its centre, and many of the buildings here saw the birth and growing pains of the Turkish Republic. A short tour through a few of the buildings tells a great deal about how a democratic nation-state grew from the ruins of a vast monarchy.

War of Salvation Museum The War of Salvation Museum (Kurtuluş Savaşı Müzesi, ☎ 324 3049) is on Cumhuriyet Bulvarı on the north-west corner of Ulus. Photographs and displays recount great moments and people in the War of Independence; captions

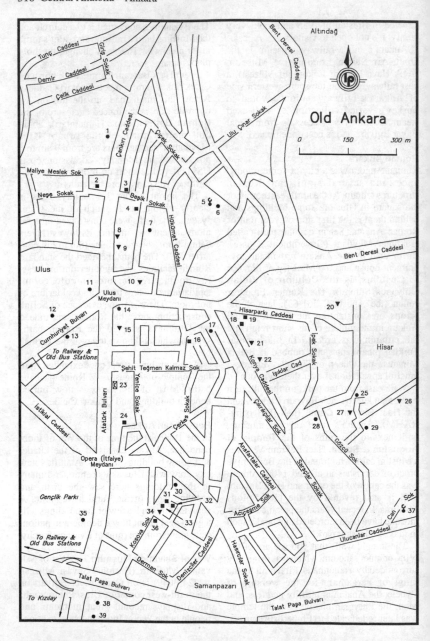

Old Ankara

National Assembly). Before it was Turkey's first parliament, this building was the Ankara headquarters of the Committee of Union & Progress, the political party which overthrew Sultan Abdülhamid in 1909 and attempted to bring democracy to the Ottoman Empire. Opening hours are from 9 am to 5 pm, closed on Monday; admission costs 25c.

Republic Museum The Republic Museum (Cumhuriyet Müzesi, ☎ 310 7140), on Cumhuriyet Bulvarı, just down the hill from Ulus, was the second headquarters of the Grand National Assembly. The Turkish parliament was founded by Atatürk in his drive for a national consensus to resist foreign invasion and occupation of the Anatolian homeland. The early history of the assembly appears in photographs and documents; all captions are in Turkish only but you can visit the assembly's meeting room and get a sense of its modest beginnings. The Grand National Assembly is now housed in a vast and imposing building in Yenişehir. Opening hours are from 9 am to 5 pm, closed on Monday; admission costs 25c.

Across Cumhuriyet Caddesi from the museum is the former **Ankara Palas** hotel, built as the city's first luxury lodging, used by dignitaries and potentates in the early days of the republic. It has been restored and now serves as guest quarters for important official visitors.

Gençlik Parkı & Opera House
Walk south from Ulus along Atatürk Bulvarı and you'll soon reach the entrance to Gençlik Parkı, the Youth Park. A swamp on this site was converted to an artificial lake on Atatürk's orders and the park was included in the city's master plan. It has a permanent fun fair with amusements for children and, in the evening, outdoor cafés with musical performances. Single women should find a café with the word 'aile' (family) in its name.

Notice the small opera house just past the entrance to the park. Atatürk became enamoured of opera during a tour of duty as military attaché in Sofia (1905), and saw to

are in Turkish only. The republican Grand National Assembly held its early sessions here (earlier called the TBMM Müzesi for Türkiye Büyük Millet Meclisi, Grand it that his new capital had a suitable hall for performances as well. The opera has a full season, beginning in autumn. The new Atatürk Cultural Centre will no doubt supplant the quaint old opera house as the preferred venue for operatic productions.

Ethnography & Fine Arts Museums

The Ethnography Museum (Etnografya Müzesi) (☎ 311 9556) is perched above Atatürk Bulvarı, to the east of the boulevard and south of Ulus past Gençlik Parkı. It's an eye-catching white marble oriental structure (1925) with an equestrian statue of Atatürk in front, reached by walking up Talat Paşa Bulvarı from Atatürk Bulvarı. It has fine collections of Seljuk and Ottoman art, craftwork, musical instruments, weapons, folk costumes, jewellery and household items. Also on view is a large and elaborately decorated room used by Kemal Atatürk as his office. Opening hours are from 9 am to 5 pm, closed on Monday; admission costs US$1.

Next door to the Ethnography Museum is the fine arts museum **Resim ve Heykel Müzesi** or Painting & Sculpture Museum in the former headquarters of the Turkish Hearths (Türk Ocağı) movement, open at the same times for the same price.

Ulus Markets

Walk up the hill on Hisarparkı Caddesi out of Ulus and turn right at the first traffic signal onto Susam Sokak; a Ziraat Bankası will be on your right. Bear left, then turn left and on your right will be Ankara's **Yeni Haller** or Vegetable Market, a good place for buying supplies or photographing colourful local life.

Behind the Vegetable Market, on Konya Caddesi, is the **Vakıf Suluhan Çarşısı**, a restored han with lots of clothing shops, a café, toilets and a free-standing small mosque at the centre of its courtyard.

Anıt Kabir

Atatürk's mausoleum (☎ 231 7975), called the Anıt Kabir (ah-NUHT-kah-beer, Monumental Tomb), stands on top of a small hill in a green park about two km west of Kızılay along Gazi Mustafa Kemal Bulvarı. If you saw Ankara from the Hisar or the terrace of the Ethnography Museum, you've already admired from a distance the rectangular mausoleum with squared columns around its sides on the hill.

A visit to the tomb is essential when you visit Ankara. Opening hours are from 9 am to 5 pm (4 pm in winter) every day; the museum closes from 12.30 to 1.30 pm.

Walking along Gazi Mustafa Kemal Bulvarı from Kızılay, you can take a short cut by turning left onto Maltepe Sokak. This becomes Erdönmez Sokak and then meets Gençlik Caddesi. Turn right onto Gençlik Caddesi, then left onto Akdeniz Caddesi and you'll see the back entrance to the park. You may not be allowed to enter by the pedestrian gate, but past it is the car exit road and you can enter there.

Should you take a taxi to the Anıt Kabir's main entrance, from Tandoğan Meydanı up Anıt Caddesi, you'll see the mausoleum as it is meant to be approached. Up the steps from the car park you pass between allegorical statues and two square kiosks; the right-hand kiosk holds a model of the tomb and photos of its construction. Then you pass down a long monumental avenue flanked by Hittite stone lions to the courtyard.

To the right as you enter the courtyard, beneath the western colonnade, is the sarcophagus of İsmet İnönü (1884-1973), Atatürk's close friend and chief of staff, a republican general (hero of the Battle of İnönü, from which he took his surname), diplomat, prime minister and second president of the republic.

Across the courtyard, on the east side, is a museum which holds memorabilia and personal effects of Atatürk. You can also see his official automobiles, several of which are US-made Lincolns.

As you approach the tomb proper, the high-stepping guards will jump to action. Past the colonnade, look left and right at the gilded inscriptions, which are quotations from Atatürk's speech celebrating the 10th anniversary of the republic (in 1932). As you enter the tomb through its huge bronze doors, you must remove your hat (if you don't, a guard will remind you that this is correct protocol). The lofty hall is lined in red marble and sparingly decorated with mosaics in timeless Turkish folk designs. At the northern end stands an immense marble cenotaph, cut from a single piece of stone. The actual tomb is beneath the cenotaph.

The Anıt Kabir was begun in 1944 and finished in 1953. Its design seeks to capture the spirit of Anatolia: monumental, spare but beautiful. Echoes of several great Anatolian empires, from the Hittites to the Romans and Seljuks, are included in its design. The final effect is modern but somehow timeless.

Presidential Mansion

At the far southern end of Atatürk Bulvarı in Çankaya is the Presidential Mansion (Cumhurbaşkanlığı Köşkü). Within the mansion's beautiful gardens is the Çankaya Köşkü, or Çankaya Atatürk Müzesi. This quaint chalet was Atatürk's country residence, set amid vineyards and evergreens. In the early days of the republic it was a retreat from the town, but now the town spreads beyond it. Visits to the mansion's gardens and grounds and to the museum are permitted on Sunday afternoons from 1.30 to 5.30 pm, and on holidays from 12.30 to 5.30 pm, free of charge. Bring your passport.

Take a bus (No 8 or 13) or taxi to the far southern end of Atatürk Bulvarı, where you will find an entrance to the grounds of the Presidential Mansion. Tell the bus or taxi driver that you want to go to the Çankaya Köşkü, (CHAHN-kah-yah kursh-kur). At the guardhouse, exchange your passport for an identity badge, leave your camera, and a guide will accompany you to and through the museum.

The house is preserved as Atatürk used it, with décor and furnishings very much of the 1930s. You enter a vestibule, then turn right into a games room, complete with tables for billiards and cards (the British ambassador was a favourite card partner). The next room is a green (Atatürk's favourite colour) parlour. The large dining room at the back of the house has its own little nook for after-dinner coffee, cigars and brandy.

Upstairs is a formal office, the bedroom and bath, another work room and the library (note the many books in foreign languages).

Downstairs again, to the left of the vestibule is a reception room for dignitaries.

Places to Stay – bottom end

Near Ulus Ulus has numerous inexpensive hotels in its back streets. Most are quiet. The first area to explore is İtfaiye Meydanı, also called Opera Meydanı, across Atatürk Bulvarı from the opera house. At the far eastern end of the square are several small streets, including Sanayi Caddesi and Kosova Caddesi, with almost a dozen cheap little places. At this writing, however, redevelopment is changing the face of this neighbourhood. Whole blocks of buildings are being razed to make way for new construction. Some of the establishments described below may be gone by the time you arrive.

The *Otel Devran* (☎ (4) 311 0485) has, as its official address, Opera Meydanı Tavus Sokak 8, but you'll find it most easily by looking for Gazi Lisesi (a high school) on Sanayi Caddesi, across Atatürk Bulvarı from the opera house and Gençlik Parkı. It's an older building, well used, but with nice touches such as marble staircases, brass trim and little chandeliers. Doubles cost US$14 with shower, US$16 with bath. This is a family hotel.

The two-star, 49-room *Otel Akman* (☎ (4) 324 4140), İtfaiye Meydanı, Tavus Sokak 6, 06050 Ulus, is next to the Otel Devran. It's much more modern, has a lift, car park and bar with colour TV and charges US$14/20 a single/double with bath. The hotel's restaurant is right next door.

The *Otel Erden* (☎ (4) 324 3191), İtfaiye Meydanı, Gazi Lisesi Yanı 23, is beside the Gazi Lisesi, a semi-modern building where double rooms rent for US$14 with washbasin, US$16 with private shower. There's a lift, a car park and a TV room with videos. Here too they cater for couples and single women and discourage single men.

The *Otel Sipahi* (☎ (4) 324 0235), İtfaiye Meydanı, Kosova Sokak 1, on the corner of Azat Sokak across the little side street from the Uğur Lokantası and the Otel Mithat, is another small hotel, costing US$13 for a double with sink, US$15 for a double with shower.

Cheapest rooms are in the *Sahil Palas Oteli* (sah-HEEL pah-lahss; ☎ (4) 310 6935), Anafartalar Caddesi, Hal Sokak 5, next to the Yeni Haller. Where it got its name, the 'Shoreline Palace', I can't say, but on its business card the hotel touts its wares with a little verse which might be translated, 'Clean, quiet, nice; for any purse, good price!'. Waterless rooms go for only US$8 a double.

On the opposite side of the building is the similar *Otel Erzurum* (☎ (4) 324 1527), and the less suitable *Otel Avrupa* (☎ (4) 311 4300), Susam Sokak 9. (Susam Sokak, by the way, translates as 'Sesame St'.) Being near the market, there are numerous cheap eateries here as well.

On the northern side of Ulus, going east off Çankırı Caddesi, is a little street named Beşik Sokak. The *Otel Turan Palas* (too-RAHN; ☎ (4) 312 5225), Çankırı Caddesi, Beşik Sokak 3, Ulus, is quiet though dark and in an area that's developing in commercial importance; it may not survive the wrecker's ball for long. At present, however, rooms with sink go for US$7/12 a single/double. There's hot water for five hours each morning.

A few steps up Beşik Sokak, at its eastern end, is the *Lâle Palas* (☎ (4) 312 5220), Hükümet Meydanı, Telgraf Sokak 5 (look for the jauntily named Frizbi Birahanesi directly across the street). The Lâle is a bit of old Ankara with its marble and brass trim, faded grace and welcome quiet. Doubles with sink cost US$12, with private shower US$15.

Walk down past the Otel Turan Palas and cross to the west side of Çankırı Caddesi and

down the slope to Soğukkuyu Sokak to find more quiet hotels. The *Hotel Suna* (☎ (4) 324 3250, Çankırı Caddesi, Soğukkuyu Sokak 6, charges US$16 for a quiet double room with shower. The neighbouring *Canbek* and *Olimpiyat* hotels are similar, if a bit more expensive.

On Hisarparkı Caddesi due east of Ulus on the way to the citadel, look for the *Hisar Oteli* (☎ (4) 311 9889), at No 6. Also known as the Otel Hamam, it rents rooms for US$7/12 a single/double with sink, and offers the services of its Turkish bath instead of private showers. It's quite noisy, though. The *Hotel Yavuz* around the corner will do if the Hisar is full.

Near Kızılay Near Kızılay, the *Otel Ertan* (☎ (4) 418 4083), Selanik Caddesi 70, a half-block south off Meşrutiyet Caddesi, is the best bet. On a quiet street, with a grape arbour and flowers in the front, it has rooms with shower for only US$14/21 a single/ double; a few bathless singles on the top floor are tiny and unappealing but priced at only US$10.

Places to Stay – middle
Near Kızılay Several good hotel choices are south-east of Kızılay. Go uphill to the south along Atatürk Bulvarı to the next major roundabout, called Bakanlıklar. Akay Caddesi goes east from the roundabout. Karanfil Sokak, one block east of Atatürk Bulvarı, runs between Akay Caddesi and Ziya Gökalp Caddesi, and has several hotels to consider. All except the Ergen have rooms with private bath, TV, air-con and minibar.

The three-star, 52-room *Eyüboğlu Hotel* (☎ (4) 417 6400; fax 417 8125), Karanfil Sokak 73, 06640 Bakanlıklar, is shiny and proper, offering comfortable, quiet rooms for US$45/60 a single/double.

The two-star, 40-room *Otel Elit* (☎ (4) 417 4695; fax 417 4697), Olgunlar Sokak 10, 06640 Bakanlıklar, is on the corner of Olgunlar and Karanfil caddesis. Rates, breakfast included, are officially US$50/74 a single/double, but I was quoted reduced prices of US$32/50 when I last asked.

Across the street from the Elit is the even more comfortable and quiet, three-star *Hotel Metropol* (☎ (4) 417 3060; fax 417 6990), Olgunlar Sokak 5, Bakanlıklar. The 32 rooms rent for US$57/74 a single/double; breakfast costs US$4.50 extra.

Finally, the simple one-star, 56-room *Hotel Ergen* (☎ (4) 417 5906), Karanfil Sokak 48, near Olgunlar Sokak, has a terrace café and charges only US$30/42 a single/double for rooms with bath.

Back on Akay Caddesi, the 27-room *Özilhan Otel* (☎ (4) 417 5066; fax 417 0243), Akay Caddesi 9, Bakanlıklar, is good, clean and cheap. Rooms with private bath cost US$24/34, and you must get one at the back or the traffic noise will keep you awake.

Walk uphill on Akay Caddesi to the big Hotel Ankara Dedeman and turn right onto Büklüm Sokak to find the three-star *Hotel Seğmen* (☎ (4) 417 5374; fax 417 2859), Büklüm Sokak 13, on the corner of Bilerik Sokak. Relatively new and quiet, in a good neighbourhood, the Seğmen's 98 rooms all have air-conditioning, satellite TV, minibar and private bath. You pay US$50/80 a single/double, breakfast included.

The two-star *Hotel Sultan* (sool-TAHN) (☎ (4) 431 5980; fax 431 1083), Bayındır Sokak 35 off Ziya Gökalp Caddesi, is an older, simple but suitable establishment of some 40 rooms, with a lift and its own covered car park, only two blocks from Kızılay. Doubles with bath cost US$40. The restaurant next door can be noisy, however.

More expensive, but also newer and nicer, is the *Hotel Melodi* (☎ (4) 417 6414; fax 418 7898), Karanfil Sokak 10, Kızılay, with two stars and 35 rooms, all with private baths (shower). Rooms are comfortable and the hotel has services such as a bar in the lobby and a little patio out the front set up with umbrella-shaded café tables in fine weather. Rates are US$45/60 a single/double; breakfast costs a very expensive US$5 extra. You may be able to haggle for a lower room price if business is slack. To find the hotel, walk up the hill along Atatürk Bulvarı from Kızılay and take the first street on the left (a tree-shaded, pedestrian-only walk) named Yüksel Caddesi. The Hotel Melodi is a block along this street, on the left-hand side.

Near Ulus Best in this area is the exceptional value offered by the three-star *Otel Karyağdı* (☎ (4) 310 2440; fax 312 6712), Sanayi Caddesi, Kuruçeşme Sokak 4, Ulus, Ankara, with wall-to-wall carpeting, bathrooms with little tubs (showers also), marble trim and even bedside lights bright enough for reading by! Some rooms have TVs. Prices are usually US$26/32 a single/double, though official rates are higher. (Kuruçeşme Sokak, by the way, is just east of İtfaiye Meydanı, and the Otel Karyağdı is just a few steps off the square.)

There is a hotel next to Ankara's old otogar, the one-star, 110-room *Terminal Oteli* (☎ (4) 310 4949; fax 310 4952), Hipodrom Caddesi 3; it's fairly dingy but serviceable and convenient if you're exhausted. Rooms are priced from US$10 to US$12 a single, or US$16 to US$28 a double, the higher prices being for rooms with bath, but you can sometimes haggle for a lower rate. A much fancier hotel is planned for Ankara's new bus terminal, the Yeni Garaj, but it will be some years before it's completed.

Places to Stay – top end

For dignified, well-located four-star accommodation at decent prices, reserve a room at the *Hotel Best* (☎ (4) 467 0880, 468 1122; fax 467 0885), Atatürk Bulvarı 195, 06680 Kavaklıdere, across the street from the American Embassy. The Ankara Chamber of Industry is just to the north; the United Nations representative to the south; and, with such a convenient location, the Hotel Best is often booked solid which is why I urge you to reserve in advance. Rates are US$75/102 a single/double, breakfast included.

The *Hilton International Hotel* (☎ (4) 468 2888; fax 168 0909), Tahran Caddesi 12, Kavaklıdere, 06700 Ankara, is the city's prime place to stay, with 327 plush, modern rooms and suites on 16 floors, near Çankaya and the embassy district, four km south of Kızılay. The hotel's architecture is bold and modern, using traditional Anatolian materials such as coloured stone, brass, glass and lots of greenery too. Many rooms have good views of the city from this hillside perch. Rates are from US$160 to US$210 a single, US$180 to US$230 a double, tax included.

The Hilton's prime competition is the 311-room *Sheraton Ankara Hotel & Towers* (☎ (4) 468 5454; fax 467 1136), Noktalı Sokak, 06700 Gaziosmanpaşa, a cylindrical high-rise which towers above this pleasant residential quarter. Accommodation, service and cuisine are international standard, and prices are similar to those at the Hilton.

Before the opening of the Hilton, the five-star, 194-room *Büyük Ankara Oteli* (Grand Ankara Hotel) (☎ (4) 425 6655; fax 425 5070) was the city's best place to stay. Near the parliament at Atatürk Bulvarı 183, this air-conditioned high-rise has all amenities including a swimming pool (summer only), health club, sauna, tennis court and several shops, bars and restaurants. Service is smooth, polished, experienced. Many rooms have fine views. The price for staying here, on Atatürk Bulvarı near parliament, is US$85 a single, from US$95 to US$140 a double.

Only a few steps north of Kızılay, on Atatürk Bulvarı, is the three-star *Hotel Pullman Etap Mola* (☎ (4) 417 8585; fax 417 8592), İzmir Caddesi, 06440 Kızılay. Comfortable and convenient though not overly fancy, the Mola has 60 air-con rooms with bath, minibar, colour TV with satellite channels and direct-dial phones. There's a restaurant too and many more in the neighbourhood. You pay US$66/85 a single/double.

Finally, a very different sort of accommodation is the *First Apart-Hotel* (☎ & fax (4) 425 7575), İnkilap Sokak 29, 06650 Kızılay, a small modern building on a quiet back street three blocks east of Kızılay. There are 15 comfortable apartments, each with two bedrooms, living/dining room, bathroom and fully equipped kitchen. All apartments have direct-dial phones, colour TVs and furnishings equal to those in a three or four-star hotel. The official rate per apartment for one to four persons is US$110, but I was quoted a reduced rate of US$75.

To find the hotel, walk east on Ziya Gökalp Caddesi from Kızılay to the third street (İnkilap Sokak) and turn right; or walk or drive east on Yüksel Caddesi from Atatürk Bulvarı to the third left, which is İnkilap Sokak.

Places to Eat – bottom end

İtfaiye (Opera) Meydanı Just up the street from the Devran and Erdem hotels are two little kebapçıs, the *Gaziantep Özlem Kebapçısı* and the *Karadeniz Piknik*, very plain, simple and cheap.

For more and better food at only slightly higher prices, try the *Uğur Lokantası* (☎ 310 8396), Tavus Sokak 2. The Uğur specialises in Turkey's regional lamb kebaps. Expect to spend between US$3.50 and US$5 for a full meal here.

Near Ulus The Ulus area has lots of good, cheap restaurants. North of the square on Çankırı Caddesi are several choices with good food, a pleasant atmosphere and low prices. The *Çiçek Lokantası* (chee-CHEK) (☎ 311 5997), Çankırı Caddesi 12/A, a half-block north of the square on the right-hand side, has a pleasant little *havuz* (pool, fountain) in the dining room amidst the white-clothed tables. Dine on soup, kebap, salad and spring water for US$6 or so.

Just north of it is the cheaper *Arjantin Restaurant*, and a *gözlemeci*, a shop selling gözleme, or Turkish 'crêpes'. Thin sheets of bread are fried on a griddle, and a savoury filling such as cheese or potato is added as the bread is folded and folded again, making a delicious snack for less than 50c.

Several restaurants are midway between Ulus Meydanı and the Museum of Anatolian Civilisations. Walking from Ulus along Konya Caddesi you come first to the *Yavuz Lokantası* (☎ 311 8508), Konya Caddesi 13/F, a clean, airy, bright place with some English-speaking staff. It's open long hours every day of the week. Good food at low prices (kebaps for only US$2 or so) is the rule. The restaurant is 1½ blocks east off Hisarparkı Caddesi, about a 10-minute walk downhill (20 minutes uphill!) from the museum. A half-block up the hill from the Yavuz is the *Konya Mevlana Lokantası* (☎ 324 5092), on the corner of Konya and Şan sokaks – a bright, clean, appealing place in an otherwise drab row of shops.

Just a few steps up the hill from Ulus, on the left-hand (north) side of Hisarparkı Caddesi, is a building named the Şehir Çarşısı and, at the back of its courtyard, three small kebap places, the *Mutfak*, the *Misket*, and the *Yeni Amber Lokantası*. They have upstairs family dining rooms and serve that delicious İskender kebap from Bursa for around US$2. There are many equally cheap little eateries on the south side of Hisarparkı Caddesi near the Sahil Palas Oteli and the Yeni Haller market.

Just south of the centre of Ulus is the *Akman Boza ve Pasta Salonu*, Atatürk Bulvarı 3, in the courtyard of the large building at the south-east corner of the square (there are several courtyards – keep looking until you find the right one). Breakfasts, light lunches (sandwiches, omelettes etc) and pastries are the specialities, consumed at tables in the little artificial garden on the open-air terrace. Boza, the fermented millet drink, is a winter favourite. Food is not cheap here, as this is a gathering place for the young and leisured, but the surroundings are very agreeable. Expect to spend from US$4 or US$5 for a light lunch, less for tea and pastry.

Right above the Akman Boza is *Kebabistan* (Kebab-Land, ☎ 310 8080), a budget traveller's dream come true. This busy family-oriented kebap and pide parlour serves good, fresh, cheap pide and kebap all day, every day, to large and appreciative crowds. You can have a filling meal of pide for as little as US$2, kebap for US$3; no alcohol is served. There's a newer, more modern branch of Kebabistan near Kızılay, but the food's better here.

Another good kebap place in the same complex of buildings, is open for lunch only (from noon to 3 pm; closed on Sunday). The *Kocagil Döner Kebap*, at the south-east corner of the courtyard in the building by the equestrian statue of Atatürk, is fancier and caters to a business clientele, but has low prices nonetheless. An excellent meal of soup, döner kebap, rice pilav and a beverage costs less than US$4.

Near Kızılay The streets north of Ziya Gökalp Caddesi and east of Atatürk Bulvarı have been turned into a pedestrian zone packed with places to eat and drink. Cheap, filling snacks such as balık-ekmek ('fish-bread', a simple fried-fish sandwich) and dönerli sandviç (döner kebap in bread) sell for about US$1.25. Selanik Sokak, the first street east of Atatürk Bulvarı, is the nicest. The two streets farther east, İnkilap and Bayındır sokaks, have mostly beerhalls with male customers.

Sakarya Caddesi is parallel to and one block north of Ziya Gökalp Caddesi. Walk along Sakarya Caddesi to the big Sakarya Süper Marketi, the ground floor of which is devoted to snack stands. Just to the right of the market are more snack stands (try the *Otlangaç*) selling İstanbul Çiçek Pasaj-style fried mussels on a stick, Bodrum lokması (sweet fritters), kuzu kokoreç (grilled sheep's intestines) and saç kavurma (bits of lamb fried on a steel parabola).

For good kebap in a sit-down place, find *Cihan Kebap* (☎ 133 1665), Selanik Caddesi 3/B, between Sakarya and Tuna caddesis. It has dinky chandeliers in the dining room, shaded tables out the front by the pedestrian street and good kebaps. A full meal with soup, bread and kebap costs from US$3 to US$4. The *Denizatı Pastanesi* (Sea-Horse Pastry Shop) to the right of the Cihan competes with the *Köksal Pastanesi* across the street for the gilded-youth trade.

South of Ziya Gökalp Caddesi is the Kızılay branch of *Kebabistan* (☎ 417 2222), Karanfil Sokak 15/A, across the street from the Hotel Melodi. The outdoor tables are pleasant, though the food is better in Ulus. Döner kebap with yoghurt, salad and a soft drink costs less than US$3.

Even nicer is the nearby *Papağan Pide ve*

Kebap Salonu (☎ 425 7815), Karanfil Sokak 63, around the corner from the Hotel Elit and Hotel Metropol. The shady vine-covered terrace, complete with tinkling fountain, is the perfect place for a meal of soup, kebap and salad for less than US$3.

For those who need a Big Mac fix, there's a *McDonald's* (☎ 431 5956), at Atatürk Bulvarı 89, just north of Kızılay on the east side of the boulevard.

Places to Eat – middle

Near Ulus Many of the eateries described above as 'bottom end' are of interest to all travellers.

The *Akman Lezzet Lokantası* (☎ 311 1086), Tavus Sokak 4, is right next to the Otel Akman near İtfaiye (Opera) Meydanı. Prices are moderate for Turkey, low for anywhere else, and you can get a good full meal for US$5 to US$8 per person. Opening hours are from 11.30 am to 11 pm daily.

In the Citadel (Hisar) The hottest restaurant development in Ankara recently is in the hilltop citadel. Chefs and restaurateurs are buying up historic houses within the citadel walls and restoring them as restaurants. All are open every day from 11 am to midnight, and all serve alcoholic beverages.

The historic restaurant trend was begun at the *Zenger Paşa Konağı* (☎ 311 7070), Doyran Sokak 13, now a virtual museum with a dining room on top. The cuisine is appropriately Ottoman, featuring gözleme (folded wafer-thin bread with vegetable filling), mantı (Turkish ravioli), and köfte or şiş kebap served on a hot tile. Full meals cost less than US$10; alcoholic beverages are served. The views from the dining room are spectacular, the several museum rooms fascinating. Zenger Paşa, by the way, is Mr Erkal Zenger, an electronics magnate who established the restaurant. Signs point the way through the Parmak Kapısı, then to the left.

If you go through the Parmak Kapısı and walk straight on for several hundred metres you will come to the *Kınacılar Evi* (☎ 311 1010), Kalekapısı Sokak 28, on the right.

This lofty Ottoman *konak* (mansion) is open from 11 am to midnight every day, serving Ottoman and modern Turkish cuisine in gracious old salons decorated in 19th-century style. Full meals cost from US$5 to US$15 per person, drinks included.

Ankara Evi (☎ 311 6566), Hisarparkı Caddesi, İnönü Parkı İçi, is an old Ankara house set in İnönü Parkı, a 15-minute walk uphill from Ulus. Menu and surroundings are similar to those of the other Ottoman restaurants in the citadel. Another historic restaurant to try is the *Boyacızade Konağı Kale Restaurant* (☎ 311 1945, 310 2525), Berrak Sokak 9, a 19th-century mansion with wonderful city views and strolling musicians providing entertainment as you dine.

Near Kızılay The place to look for good, moderately priced food near Kızılay is along Bayındır Sokak, to the east of Atatürk Bulvarı and south of Ziya Gökalp Caddesi. You can't go wrong at the *Körfez Lokantası* (keur-FEHZ) (☎ 131 1459), Bayındır Sokak 24, a half-block north of Ziya Gökalp Caddesi. Though there are indoor dining rooms, the terrace is better in fine weather. It's simple, pleasant and unpretentious, with many kebaps priced under US$3 and fish dishes for around US$4 to US$7. The bread served here is freshly made, flat, unleavened village bread, which is wonderful. The restaurant's name means 'gulf' and the speciality is fish, so feel free to order that; it will be good, even in this land-locked city.

Next door to the Körfez is the *Washington Restaurant* (☎ 131 2219), Bayındır Sokak 22/A, a longstanding favourite with much fancier surroundings, diligent service, Turkish and continental cuisine. Try the filet mignon, and you'll be surprised at the high quality and moderate prices.

Another good seafood place with a club-style atmosphere is *İskele* (☎ 433 3813), Sakarya Caddesi, Bayındır Sokak 14/C (Bayındır Sokak is the third street east of Atatürk Bulvarı). Start with fried mussels or a shrimp casserole (karides güveçi), and go on to grilled or poached fish, and you'll pay from US$10 to US$12, with wine or beer included. İskele is closed on Sunday.

Kavaklıdere Kavaklıdere, the up-market residential district south of Bakanlıklar, up the hill towards Çankaya, has a good assortment of restaurants. Take a bus south (uphill) along Atatürk Bulvarı and get out at Kuğulu Park next to the Polish Embassy (Polonya Büyükelçilik), then walk east one short block between them to Tunalı Hilmi Caddesi.

Black Sea cookery is the speciality at *Yeni Hamsiköy* (☎ 427 7576), Bestekar Sokak 78, off Tunalı Hilmi in Kavaklıdere. The beautiful terrace is open in fine weather, with local and foreign patrons feasting on hamsi (fresh anchovies) served in omelettes, dolmas or corn bread; there's also kara lahana (black cabbage) and other Black Sea specialties. The food and service are excellent, and prices are moderate, at US$10 or so per person. Alcohol is served, and the restaurant is open for lunch and dinner every day.

Yalumsu. (☎ 420 3752), Tunalı Hilmi Caddesi 114/J 2-3, right at the edge of Kuğulu Park, specialises in seafood. There's a table d'hôte menu with drinks for US$14 for two people, and this is the best deal. Ordering à la carte, seafood plates cost around US$4 or US$5.

For excellent Chinese cuisine, try *Silk Road* (☎ 427 6150, 426 4621), Bestekar Sokak 88/B, off Tunalı Hilmi Caddesi. The ancient Silk Road started in Turkey and went to China, a connection this restaurant exploits. Expect to spend about US$15 per person.

GM (☎ 426 3763), Tunalı Hilmi Caddesi 113/1, by the Pamukbank, has a fine international menu, careful service, excellent food, and full meals priced around US$15 per person.

Getting There & Away

In Turkey, all roads lead to Ankara. Its role as governmental capital and second-largest city guarantees that transportation will be convenient.

The old Ankara otogar is one block north-west of the Ankara railway station. In a wing of the railway station is the Turkish Airlines terminal. The railway station and the otogar are separated, appropriately, by the Ministry of Transportation (Ulaştırma Bakanlığı). This whole transportation complex is about 1.25 km from Ulus and three km from Kızılay. Many buses heading down the hill along Cumhuriyet Bulvarı from Ulus will take you there; from Kızılay and Bakanlıklar, take bus No 44 ('Terminal').

Air Ankara has good international and domestic connections by air to Esenboğa Airport (☎ (4) 398 0000), 33 km north of the city centre. Turkish Airlines (THY, ☎ (4) 312 4900 for information, 309 0400 for reservations; fax 312 5531) has offices next to the railway station, and at Atatürk Bulvarı 167/A, Bakanlıklar. Turkish Air Transport (THT, ☎ (4) 419 1492; fax 417 3526) is at Atatürk Bulvarı 125, Bakanlıklar, but you can make reservations at any Turkish Airlines office or travel agency.

THY operates the big jets on long-distance routes; THT has mostly smaller propeller-driven 'commuter' aircraft running shorter routes. İstanbul Airlines (☎ (4) 432 2234, 431 0920; fax 431 1632), Atatürk Bulvarı 83, Kızılay, also has many nonstop flights.

Most flights by THY require a stop or a change of aircraft in İstanbul. Most one-way fares from Ankara on THY and THT cost between US$70 and US$100; İstanbul Airlines' fares are somewhat lower. Here is a list of nonstop flights; many more flights are available via connection in İstanbul. All schedules are subject to change:

Adana – daily (THY)
Antalya – Friday and Sunday (THT)
Baku (Azerbaijan) – Wednesday (İstanbul Airlines)
Bursa – Tuesday and Thursday (THT)
Dalaman – Sunday (THT)
Diyarbakır – daily (THY); one or two daily (THT)
Elazığ – Wednesday and Saturday (THT)
Erzincan – Tuesday and Thursday (THT)
Erzurum – daily (THY)
Gaziantep – daily (THY)
İstanbul – six or more flights daily (THY); at least one daily (THT); Tuesday, Wednesday, Thursday, Saturday (İstanbul Airlines)

İzmir – two or more flights daily (THY); Monday and Friday (THT); Tuesday (İstanbul Airlines)

Kars – one-stop Wednesday and Saturday, via Elazığ (THT)

Malatya – daily (THY; Tuesday, Thursday and Saturday (THT)

Nicosia (Lefkoşa) – daily except Monday (THY)

Şanlıurfa – Tuesday and Thursday (THT)

Trabzon – daily (THY)

Van – daily (THY); Tuesday and Thursday (İstanbul Airlines)

The Turkish Airlines air terminal (☎ (4) 312 4900; for reservations 309 0400) at the railway station has a bank branch for currency exchange, a restaurant and bar and is open daily from 7 am to 8 pm. Ticket sales and reservations counters are open between 8.30 am and 7.45 pm, on Sunday from 8.30 am to 5.15 pm.

Other international airlines sometimes have flights to Ankara, or connections with Turkish Airlines' flights at İstanbul. The addresses of offices in Ankara follow:

Aeroflot
    Cinnah Caddesi 114/2, Çankaya
    (☎ (4) 440 9874)
Air France
    Atatürk Bulvarı 231/7, Kavaklıdere
    (☎ (4) 467 4400)
Alitalia
    Emek İşhanı, 11th floor, Kızılay
    (☎ (4) 425 3813)
British Airways
    Atatürk Bulvarı 237/29, Kavaklıdere
    (☎ (4) 467 5557)
KLM
    Atatürk Bulvarı 127,
    3rd floor, Bakanlıklar (☎ (4) 417 5616)
Lufthansa
    İran Caddesi 2, Kavaklıdere
    (☎ (4) 436 6156, 467 5510)
Sabena World Airlines
    Tunalı Hilmi Caddesi 112/1, Kavaklıdere
    (☎ (4) 467 2535)
Singapore Airlines
    Tunalı Hilmi Caddesi, Bülten Sokak 17/3, Kavaklıdere, (☎ (4) 468 4670)
Swissair
    Cinnah Caddesi 1/2A, Kavaklıdere
    (☎ (4) 468 4846)

Bus Every city or town of any size has direct buses to Ankara. From İstanbul there is a bus to Ankara at least every 15 minutes throughout the day and late into the night.

Ankara's gigantic ultra-modern bus terminal, the Yeni Garaj (New Garage) is five km due west of Bakanlıklar and the Grand National Assembly building, on Bahçelerarası Caddesi (Konya Devlet Yolu) just north of İsmet İnönü Bulvarı (Eskişehir Yolu). Scheduled to open in 1992, construction delays have postponed its opening, though it may well be in service by the time you arrive. If not, you will have to suffer the old otogar, one long block north-west of the railway station and Turkish Airlines' city terminal.

To the Turks, the old Ankara otogar is a busy terminus. To foreigners not knowing the place or the language, it is a frightful chaos of crowds, touts, noise, roaring behemoths and indecipherable signs. Take courage. After a little bit of reconnoitring and searching and with the help of the touts and the ticket agents, you can be on your way before too long. It may be confusing but it is not sinister.

As Ankara has many buses to all parts of the country, it is often sufficient to arrive at the otogar, baggage in hand, and let a hawker lead you to a ticket window for your chosen destination (no charge for the lead). It might be a good idea, however, to wander through the rows of ticket kiosks to see if there is a more convenient departure time. If you

arrive in Ankara by bus, take a few moments to check on schedules to your next destination. Buy your ticket and at the same time reserve your seat, if you can.

Numerous bus companies have offices near Kızılay on Ziya Gökalp Caddesi, Gazi Mustafa Kemal Bulvarı, İzmir Caddesi and Menekşe Sokak. Buying your ticket here will save you a trip to the otogar. Several premium bus companies, including Varan and Ulusoy, have their own terminal facilities near the Yeni Garaj. The Varan ticket office (☎ (4) 417 2525) is south of Kızılay on the east side of Atatürk Bulvarı. Details of some services from Ankara follow:

Adana – 490 km, 10 hours, US$ 13 to US$16; frequent buses daily
Amasya – 335 km, five hours, US$9; frequent buses daily
Antalya – 550 km, 10 hours, US$17; frequent buses daily
Bodrum – 785 km, 13 hours, US$20; a dozen buses daily
Bursa – 400 km, 6½ hours, US$11; hourly buses
Denizli (Pamukkale) – 480 km, seven hours, US$12; frequent buses
Diyarbakır – 945 km, 13 hours, US$20; several buses daily
Erzurum – 925 km, 15 hours, US$23; several buses daily
Gaziantep – 705 km, 12 hours, US$20; frequent buses daily
İstanbul – 450 km, six hours, US$9 to US$20; virtual shuttle service
İzmir – 600 km, 8½ hours, US$14.50 to US$20; buses at least every hour
Kayseri – 330 km, five hours, US$8; very frequent buses daily
Konya – 260 km, 3½ hours, US$8; very frequent buses daily
Marmaris – 780km, 13 hours, US$22; a dozen buses daily in summer
Nevşehir – 285 km, 4½ hours, US$8; very frequent buses daily
Samsun – 420 km, eight hours, US$14; frequent buses daily
Sivas – 450 km, eight hours, US$13; frequent buses daily
Sungurlu (for Boğazkale) – 175 km, three hours, US$4; hourly buses
Trabzon – 780 km, 12 hours, US$24; several buses daily

You can also buy through tickets to Damas-cus (Şam) for US$50, Tehran for US$65, and to other eastern destinations.

Train Train service is good between the Ankara Garı (railway station, ☎ (4) 310 6515, 311 4994) and several major cities. See the Getting Around chapter for a description of train travel and the top trains, and the Getting There & Away sections of the İstanbul and İzmir chapters for descriptions of train service between Ankara and İstanbul or İzmir. The top trains – *Fatih Ekspresi, Mavi Tren, Ankara Ekspresi, İzmir Mavi Tren* – are quite good. Here are some notes on other trains serving Ankara – prices and schedules are subject to change.

Çukurova Ekspresi The *Çukurova Ekspresi* departs from Ankara daily at 8.10 pm hauling one-class coaches, couchette cars and sleeping cars to Adana (arrives 8.18 am) and Mersin (arrives 8.53 am). The return trip departs from Mersin at 6.41 pm and Adana at 7.15 pm, arriving in Ankara at 8.05 am. One-way tickets between Ankara and Adana or Mersin cost US$10/12 in a coach/couchette. Fares in a sleeping compartment cost US$24/42/58 for one/two/three persons.

Doğu Ekspresi The *Doğu* (doh-OO, east) is scheduled to arrive in Ankara from İstanbul at 5.27 pm, and depart from Ankara at 6.15 pm for Kayseri, Sivas, Erzincan (arrives 1.51 pm), Erzurum (arrives 6.11 pm) and Kars (arrives 10.58 pm) daily, but it usually falls behind schedule.

Running from east to west, the *Doğu* is scheduled to arrive in Ankara at 6 am and depart for İstanbul (Haydarpaşa) at 7 am. A one-way 1st/2nd-class ticket from Ankara costs US$11/7.75 to Erzincan, US$14/9.50 to Erzurum, and US$16/11 to Kars. To travel from Ankara to Kars in a sleeping compartment costs US$30/52/66 for one/two/three persons.

Karaelmas The one-class 'Black Diamond' runs daily at 7.55 am to the Black Sea coalmining centre of Zonguldak, arriving at 7.10 pm, for US$5. The return trip departs from

Zonguldak at 9.20 am, arriving in Ankara at 8.08 pm.

Vangölü/Güney Ekspresi The *Vangölü Ekspresi* and *Güney Ekspresi* share a common route from İstanbul (daily at 9 pm) via Ankara (arrive 7.05 am, depart 10.40 am) to Sivas, Malatya and Elazığ Junction. East of the junction, the train continues on Tuesday, Thursday and Sunday as the *Vangölü* (Lake Van) *Ekspresi* to Tatvan and Monday, Wednesday, Friday and Saturday as the *Güney* (Southern) *Ekspresi* to Diyarbakır and Kurtalan (east of Diyarbakır).

These trains haul sleepers and 2nd-class coaches. A one-way 1st/2nd-class ticket from Ankara costs US$15/10.50 to Tatvan, US$13/10 to Diyarbakır. The fare in a sleeping car is from US$30/52/72 for one/two/ three people.

Getting Around

To/From the Airport The airport is 33 km north of the city. Havaş airport buses, US$2.50, are supposed to depart from the air terminal in Ankara 1½ hours before domestic flight times, and 2¼ hours before international flight times. They may leave sooner if they fill up, however, so claim your seat on the bus at least two hours before flight time. Minimum check-in time at the airport for any flight is 45 minutes before departure time.

When your flight arrives in Ankara, don't dawdle in the terminal because the Havaş bus will depart for the city within a half-hour after the flight has landed and there may not be another bus for several hours depending upon flights. Taxis between the airport and the city cost from US$15 to US$20.

Bus Ankara is served well and frequently by an extensive bus and minibus network. Signboards on the front and side of the bus are better guides than route numbers. Many buses marked 'Ulus' and 'Çankaya' ply the entire length of Atatürk Bulvarı. Those marked 'Terminal' go to the railway station and old otogar. Routes are subject to change

as construction for Ankara's metro system blocks streets and diverts traffic.

City bus tickets cost 40c and can be bought from little ticket kiosks at major bus stops or from shops and vendors displaying a sign reading 'EGO Bilet Bayii' or 'EGO Bileti Satılır', or some other phrase with 'EGO Bilet' in it.

Metro Construction is well under way on Ankara's metro system. The first line will run from Kızılay north-west via Sıhhiye, Maltepe and Ulus to Batıkent, a distance of 14.6 km. The station at Kızılay will also serve the Ankaray, the city's new east-west suburban rail system. Construction is scheduled for completion by 1996, but the inevitable delays will no doubt carry it towards or beyond the year 2000.

Taxi The drop rate is US$1 and an average trip costs from US$2.50 to US$3.50 during daylight hours, 50% more at night. The lower fare would be for a trip from the otogar or railway station to Ulus; the higher fare, to Kızılay or Kavaklıdere.

Car See the Getting Around chapter for details on hiring cars. Do not rent a car to drive around Ankara, and if you have a car, park it and take public transportation. Traffic patterns seem whimsically illogical, local drivers delight in speed, danger and chaos, and signs are woefully inadequate.

If you plan to hire a car and drive beyond Ankara, there are many small local companies, and the major international firms have offices at Esenboğa Airport and in the city centre. Details of some of these follow:

Avis
  Tunus Caddesi 68/2, Kavaklıdere
  (☎ (4) 467 2313)
Budget
  Tunus Caddesi 39/A, Kavaklıdere
  (☎ (4) 417 5952, 427 8071; fax 425 9608)
Europcar
  (National, Interrent, Kemwel),
  Küçükesat Caddesi 25/C, Bakanlıklar
  (☎ (4) 418 3430, 418 3877; fax 417 8445)

Hertz
    Akay Caddesi, Kızılırmak Sokak 1/A,
    Bakanlıklar (☎ (4) 418 8440)
Thrifty
    Köroğlu Caddesi 65/B, Gaziosmanpaşa
    (☎ (4) 436 0505, 436 0606)

South Central Anatolia

KONYA

Standing alone in the midst of the vast
Anatolian steppe, Konya (population
600,000, altitude 1016 metres) is like some
traditional caravan stopping-place. The
windswept landscape gives way to little
patches of greenery in the city, and when
you're in the town you don't feel the loneli-
ness of the plateau. In recent years Konya has
been booming. The bare-looking steppe is in
fact good for growing grain and Konya is the
heart of Turkey's very rich 'breadbasket'.
Light industry provides jobs for those who
are not farmers. Much of the city was built
within the last 10 years but the centre is very
old. No-one knows when the hill in the centre
of town, the Alaettin Tepesi, was first settled
but it contains the bones of Bronze Age men
and women.

Plan to spend at least one full day in
Konya, preferably two, but not a Monday as
the museums will be closed. If your interest
in Seljuk history and art takes flame you
could easily spend another half or full day.
As it takes a good half-day to reach Konya
from anywhere, and another half-day to get
from Konya to your next destination, you
should figure on spending at least two nights
in a hotel here.

It's important to remember that Konya is
a favourite with devout Muslims and a fairly
conservative place. Take special care not to
upset the pious, and look tidy when you enter
mosques and the Mevlana Museum. If you
visit during the holy month of Ramazan, do
not eat or drink in public during the day. This
is a courtesy to those who are fasting. (For
Ramazan and other religious dates see The
Calendar section of the Facts for the Visitor
chapter.) Also, the dervishes do not whirl all

the time. They usually only dance during the
Mevlana Festival in December (see Festivals, following).

History

The city has been here a very long time.
Neighbouring Çatal Höyük, 50 km to the
south, is thought to be the oldest known
human community, dating from 7500 BC.

The Hittites called Konya 'Kuwanna'
almost 4000 years ago but the name has
changed over the years. It was Kowania to
the Phrygians, Iconium to the Romans and
now Konya to the Turks.

Under Rome, Iconium was an important
provincial town visited several times by the
saints Paul and Barnabas, but its early Christian community does not seem to have been
very influential.

Konya's heyday was during the 1200s,
when it was capital of the Seljuk Sultanate
of Rum, the last remnant of an earlier Seljuk
empire.

The Seljuk Turks ruled a powerful state in
Iran and Iraq, the Empire of the Great
Seljuks, during the 1000s. Omar Khayyam
was their most noted poet and mathemati-
cian. But Great Seljuk power was frag-
mented in the early 1100s, and various parts
of the empire became independent states.
One of these states was the Sultanate of Rum,
which encompassed most of Anatolia.
Konya was its capital from about 1150 to
1300. In that period, the Seljuk sultans built
dozens of fine buildings in an architectural
style decidedly Turkish, but with its roots in
Persia and Byzantium.

'Mevlana' Celaleddin Rumi

The Sultanate
of Rum also produced one of the world's
great mystic philosophers – Celaleddin
Rumi, called Mevlana by his followers. His
poetic and religious work, mostly in Persian
(the literary language of the day), is some of
the most beloved and respected in the Islamic
world.

Mevlana was born in 1207 in Balkh, near
Mazar-i Sharif in modern Afghanistan. His
family fled the impending Mongol invasion
by moving to Mecca and then to the Sultan-

ate of Rum by 1221, reaching Konya by 1228. His father Baha'uddin was a noted preacher and Rumi grew to be a brilliant student of Islamic theology. After his father's death in 1231, Rumi studied in Aleppo and Damascus but returned to live in Konya by 1240.

In 1244 he met Mehmet Şemseddin Tebrizi, called Şemsi Tebrizi, one of his father's Sufi (Muslim mystic) disciples. Tebrizi had a profound effect on Rumi, who became devoted to him. An angry crowd of Rumi's own disciples put Tebrizi to death in 1247 because of his overwhelming influence on the brilliant Rumi. Stunned by the loss of his spiritual master, Rumi withdrew from the world to meditate and, in this period, wrote his great poetic work, the *Mathnawi* (called *Mesnevi* in Turkish). He also wrote many *ruba'i* and *ghazal* poems, collected into his 'Great Opus', the *Divan-i Kebir*.

Rumi died late in the day on 17 December 1273, the date now known as his 'wedding night', as he was finally united with Allah. His son, Sultan Veled, organised Mevlana's followers into the dervish brotherhood of the Mevlevi (Followers of The Guide), and established the ceremony of its sema.

Though the Mongol invasion soon put an end to Seljuk sovereignty in Anatolia, the Mevlevi order prospered. In the centuries following Mevlana's death, over 100 dervish lodges were founded throughout the Ottoman domains in Turkey, Syria and Egypt, many endowed by members of the ruling class. Numerous Ottoman sultans were Sufis of the Mevlevi order.

Republican Reforms Under the Ottoman Empire, dervish orders exerted a great deal of influence on the country's political, social and economic life. Their world-view was monarchist, arch-conservative and xenophobic in most cases. Committed to progress, democracy and separation of religion and state, Atatürk viewed the dervishes as an obstacle to advancement for the Turkish people, so he saw to it that the dervish orders were proscribed in 1925. Many of the mon-

asteries were converted to museums. The Mevlana opened as a museum in 1927.

Though outlawed, several of the dervish orders survived as fraternal religious brotherhoods, stripped of their influence. The Whirling Dervish tradition was revived in Konya in 1957 as a 'cultural association' which preserves a historical tradition. The annual Festival of Mevlana held in mid-December (see Festivals, following) is officially encouraged as a popular – not a religious – event. Groups of dervishes are also sent on cultural exchange tours to other countries, performing the ceremony from Helsinki to Hawaii.

The dervishes are no longer interested in politics but neither are they truly a 'cultural association'. Young novices are recruited at puberty and devotion to the principles of the order can still be lifelong. Konya's dervishes whirl today to celebrate a great tradition and, as they have been doing for over 700 years, to worship and to seek mystical union with God as Mevlana taught.

Orientation

The city centre is the hill Alaettin Tepesi, crowned with a great Seljuk mosque and surrounded with the city's best Seljuk buildings. From the hill, Alaettin Caddesi goes south-east 500 metres to Hükümet Alanı (Government Plaza, also called Konak), with the provincial and city government buildings and main post office. East of Hükümet Alanı the boulevard changes name to become Mevlana Caddesi and goes another 500 metres to the tourism office and the Mevlana Museum, the Whirling Dervish museum which is Konya's prime attraction. Hotels are located along Alaettin/Mevlana Caddesi and near the Mevlana Museum.

The bus station (otogar) is 3.5 km due north of the centre. The railway station (istasyon) is about three km due west.

Information

Konya's official Tourism Information Office (☎ (33) 51 10 74; fax 11 45 20) is at Mevlana Caddesi 21, across the square from the Mevlana Museum. Opening hours are from

8.30 am to 5 pm, Monday to Saturday. The staff speak English, French and German here and will offer to sell you a swell carpet along with the free information.

Across the street is the Konya Kültür ve Turizm Derneği (Konya Culture & Tourism Association; ☎ (33) 51 62 55, 51 82 88), where you can buy books on Konya and cassette tapes of Mevlevi music.

Konya's postal code is 42000.

Seljuk Turkish Architecture

The centre of Konya is Turkey's best 'outdoor museum' of Seljuk architecture. The Seljuks built wondrous doorways to which small buildings were attached. While the buildings themselves are often starkly simple on the outside, the main portal is always grand and imposing, sometimes huge and wildly Baroque. The interiors are always harmoniously proportioned and laid out, and often decorated with blue and white tiles. Tiles of other colours are sometimes found but they rarely have red in them as the fusing of vivid reds on faïence was a later Ottoman accomplishment.

You can walk to all of the buildings described here but it would be tiring to do so in one day.

Mevlana Museum

The first place to visit in Konya is the Mevlana Museum (Mevlana Müzesi), the former monastery of the Whirling Dervishes, open every day from 9 am to noon and from 1 to 5 pm (3 to 5 pm on Monday); admission costs US$2. On religious holidays the museum (really a shrine) may be open for longer hours. Women may want to cover their heads and shoulders when they enter. You will see many people praying and pleading for Mevlana's intercession. For Turkish Muslims, it is a very holy place.

Enter through a pretty courtyard with an ablutions fountain and several tombs, then remove your shoes and pass into the **Mevlana Türbesi**, or Tomb of Rumi. The sarcophagi of Rumi and his illustrious followers are covered in great velvet shrouds heavy with gold embroidery. It gives the powerful impression that this is a sacred place. The tombs of Mevlana and his son have great symbolic turbans on them.

The Mevlana Türbesi dates from Seljuk times. The mosque and room for ceremonies were added later by Ottoman sultans (Mehmet the Conqueror was a Mevlevi adherent and Süleyman the Magnificent made large charitable donations to the order). Selim I, conqueror of Egypt, donated the Mameluke crystal lamps.

In the rooms adjoining the sepulchral chamber are exhibits of dervish paraphernalia: musical instruments, vestments, illuminated manuscripts and ethnographic artefacts. The rooms off the courtyard by the entrance, once offices and quarters for the dervishes, are now furnished as they would have been at the time of Mevlana (during the 1200s), with mannequins dressed in dervish costumes.

The Mevlevi Sema Rumi's teachings were ecumenical. He stressed the universality of God and welcomed any worshipper, of any sect or following, to join in worship. Non-Muslims were regularly invited to witness the ceremony.

The Mevlevi worship ceremony, which traditionally takes place on a Monday evening ('Tuesday morning' in Islamic thinking) is a ritual dance representing union with God.

The dervishes enter, dressed in long white robes with full skirts which represent their shrouds, on top of which they wear voluminous black cloaks symbolising their worldly tombs; their tall conical red felt hats represent their tombstones.

The ceremony begins with a chant by the *hafiz*, a celebrant who has committed the entire Koran to memory; he intones a prayer for Mevlana and a verse from the Koran. A kettledrum booms out, followed by the breathy, plaintive song of the *ney*, or reed flute.

The sheikh *(şeyh)*, or master, bows, then leads the dervishes in a circle around the hall. As the dervishes pass the sheikh's ceremonial position at the head of the hall, they bow

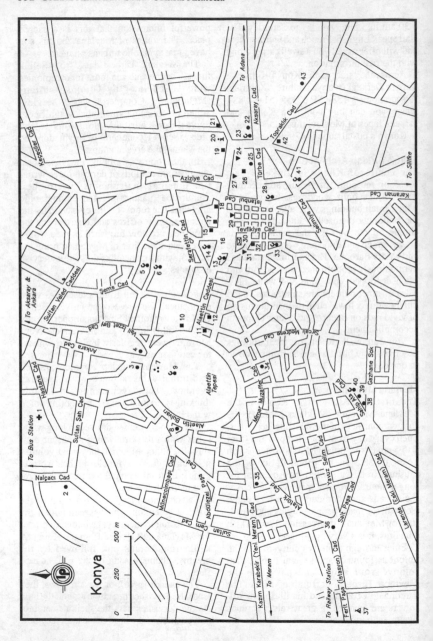

Konya

to one another. After three circuits, the dervishes drop their black cloaks, which symbolises their deliverance from the cares and attachments of this world. One by one the dervishes, arms folded on their breasts, approach the sheikh, bow, kiss his hand, receive instructions whispered in their ears, then spin out onto the floor as they relinquish the earthly life to be reborn in mystical union with God.

The male choir and the orchestra of small drums (*bendir*), gourd viol (*rebap*) and bow (*kemançe*), and open-tube reed flute (ney) begins the music, and the dervishes unfurl their arms and begin to whirl.

By holding their right arms up, palms upwards, they receive the blessings of heaven and communicate them to earth by holding their left arms down, palms downwards. Pivoting on their left heels, the dervishes whirl ever faster, reaching ecstasy with a blissful expression. As they whirl, they form a 'constellation' of revolving bodies which itself slowly rotates. The dance master walks among them to make sure each dervish is performing the ritual properly. After about 10 minutes, all at once, they stop and kneel down. Rising, they begin again; the dance is repeated four times, with the sheikh joining the last iteration. After the whirling, the hafız again chants poetical passages from the holy book.

The breathy, haunting music of the ney is perhaps the most striking sound during the ceremony. Each musician 'opens' (makes) his own instrument from a carefully chosen length of bamboo-like reed, burning the finger-holes to a mathematical formula. The ney is thought to have its own soul, like a human, and 'opening' it liberates the soul, which comes out in its music.

Selimiye Mosque Outside the entrance to the Mevlana Museum is the Selimiye Camii, endowed by Sultan Selim II (1566-74). Construction on the Ottoman-style mosque started during Selim's term as governor of Konya, before his accession to the throne.

Leave the museum, turn left, walk between the Selimiye Camii and the museum and cross the wide street. You'll see a verdant cemetery, the **Üçler Mezarlığı** (urch-LEHR meh-zahr-luh) where you can take a stroll. If you cut through the cemetery at the proper angle, you will emerge near the Koyunoğlu Museum.

Koyunoğlu Museum

The fine Koyunoğlu Museum (Koyunoğlu Müzesi), 750 metres from the Mevlana Museum, was donated to the city by a private collector who seemed to collect everything. Opening hours are from 9.30 am to noon and from 2 to 5 pm; admission costs US$1. The few labels are in Turkish only.

The modern museum building has three levels. Downstairs are collections of minerals, weapons, fossils, stuffed birds and an atrium filled with plants and live birds. The main floor has exhibits of ancient coins: Roman, Seljuk and Ottoman; sculptures, glass, jewellery, Bronze Age implements and a photo display of old Konya. Upstairs is the ethnographic section including kilims and carpets (one bears a map of Turkey); illuminated manuscripts and Korans; miniature paintings and clocks; and 19th-century clothing, bath clogs, weapons, household items, coffee sets, musical instruments, embroidery and needlework.

Next door to the museum is the **Koyunoğlu Konya Evi**, a quaint and delightful little old-fashioned house which shows vividly how a Konyalı family lived a century ago. Leave your shoes at the carved wooden door, put on sandals as all Turks used to do and inspect the small ground-floor room with its silk carpet. There is another, smaller salon on the ground floor as well. Upstairs the rooms are traditionally furnished with lots of carpets, kilims, low benches, pillows, a fine tray-table and lots of turned wood. The picture is of the museum's founder.

Alaettin Mosque

Except for the Mevlana Museum, many of Konya's principal sights are near the Alaettin Tepesi or Aladdin's Hill, at the western end of Alaettin Caddesi. The eastern slopes of the hill are set with tea gardens. The ancient Alaettin Camii (mosque) is right on top of the hill.

The mosque of Alaeddin (or Alaettin) Keykubat I, Seljuk Sultan of Rum from 1219 to 1231, is a great rambling building designed by a Damascene architect in the Arab style and finished in 1221. Over the centuries it was embellished, refurbished, ruined and restored. Renovation began in 1973, when the structure was near collapse, and is still under way. When it is completed the mosque will be opened as a museum, but for now you must be content to view the exterior.

Though hardly as harmonious as an Ottoman work by Sinan, it is impressive. The interior is a forest of old columns surmounted with recycled Roman and Byzantine capitals, with a fine, carved wooden pulpit (1156) and a marble prayer niche. In the courtyard, restorers discovered the graves of eight Seljuk sultans.

On the north side of the Alaettin Tepesi, the scant **ruins of a Seljuk palace** are protected by a concrete shelter.

Great Karatay Seminary

The Great Karatay Seminary (Büyük Karatay Medresesi), now called the Karatay Museum (Karatay Müzesi), is a Seljuk theological seminary just north of the Alaettin Tepesi. It houses Konya's outstanding collection of ceramics and tiles. It is open from 8.30 am to noon and from 1.30 to 5.30 pm. Admission costs US$2.

The school was constructed in 1251-52 by the emir Celaleddin Karatay, a Seljuk diplomat and statesman. It has a magnificent sculpted marble doorway.

Inside, the central dome is a masterpiece of Seljuk blue tilework with gold accents. The effect suggests the heavens with stars of gold. The Arabic inscription in Kufic style around the bottom of the dome is the first chapter of the Koran. The triangles below the dome are decorated with the names of the first four caliphs who succeeded Muhammed; the Arabic letters are highly stylised.

Note especially the curlicue drain for the

Büyük Karatay Medresesi

knocked off by lightning less than 100 years ago.

At the time of this writing the museum is closed for renovation, but it should have reopened by the time you arrive. Besides, the exterior is the most impressive part of the building. When it was last open, the exhibits showed Seljuk motifs used in wood and stone carving, many of them similar to those used in the tile and ceramic work. In Islam, images of creatures with souls (humans and animals) are forbidden as idolatry, but most great Islamic civilisations had artists who ignored the law from time to time. Most Islamic art is geometrical or nonrepresentative, but you will still see birds (the Seljuk double-headed eagle, for example), men and women, lions and leopards.

central pool: its curved shape made the sound of running water a pleasant background noise in the quiet room where students studied.

The museum's collection of tiles includes interesting coloured ones from Seljuk palaces in Konya and Beyşehir. Compare these to the later Ottoman tiles from İznik.

Seminary of the Slender Minaret

Around the Alaettin Tepesi on its western side is the Seminary of the Slender Minaret, (İnce Minare Medresesi), now the Museum of Wood & Stone Carving. Don't enter the building immediately, for half of what you came to see is the elaborate doorway with bands of Arabic inscription running up the sides and looping overhead. This religious school was built in 1258 on the order of Sahip Ata, a powerful Seljuk vizier, who may have been trying to outdo the patron of the Karatay Medresesi, built only seven years earlier.

The doorway is far more impressive than the small building behind it. The minaret beside the door is what gave the seminary its popular name of 'slender minaret'. Over 600 years old, most of the very tall minaret was

South of the Alaettin Tepesi

Several other significant Seljuk monuments lie south of the city, in a warren of little streets. If you can find Ressam Sami Sokak, it will lead you to the following sights.

Not far from the Alaettin Tepesi on Ressam Sami Sokak is another Seljuk seminary, the Crystalline Seminary (Sırçalı Medrese), now a museum of funerary monuments. As always, the portal is grand and highly decorated. The tiles on the exterior give the seminary its name. Sponsored by a Seljuk vizier, construction was completed in 1242. The inscriptions on the gravestones inside are often very fine, done in a variety of Arabic scripts. Symbols of rank – headgear, usually – served to tell the passer-by of the deceased's important role in life. The museum is closed for renovation as of this writing, but you can still enjoy a view of the marvellous façade.

Konya's small **Archaeological Museum** is a few blocks south along Ressam Sami Sokak, in the grounds of the Sahip Ata Mosque Complex (Sahip Ata Külliyesi), which, besides the mosque, includes a dervish monastery and Turkish bath. Museum hours are from 8.30 am to noon and from 1.30 to 5.30 pm. Admission costs US$1. The entire complex was finished in 1283. Note especially the portal to the mosque with its tiled minaret and prayer niche.

Not far from the Sahip Ata Külliyesi is the city's small **Ethnography Museum**, open during the same hours as the Archaeological Museum. Admission costs US$1.

Other Mosques & Tombs

As you wander around town, you will pass other buildings of interest. The **Şemsi Tebrizi Camii**, containing the tomb (1300s) of Rumi's spiritual mentor, is just north of Hükümet Alanı, off Alaettin Caddesi. The **Aziziye Camii** (1874) is a work of Ottoman late Baroque in the bazaar; it's the one with twin minarets bearing little sheltered balconies.

The **İplikçi Camii** (1202) on the main street, Alaettin Caddesi, is perhaps Konya's oldest mosque, built on orders of the Seljuk vizier Şemseddin Altun-Aba. The **Şerefettin Camii**, off Mevlana Caddesi near Hükümet Alanı, was constructed in 1636. Near the PTT on Hükümet Caddesi is the **Hacı Hasan Camii**.

The Bazaar

Konya's market area is behind the modern PTT building. Walk through the city bus-parking area, along the east side of the Koli PTT (the parcel branch) and to the left of the shoeshine stand, then straight along Çıkrıkçılar Caddesi. Besides shops selling all manner of things, there are lots of inexpensive eateries here.

Meram

If you have a spare morning or afternoon, take an excursion (less than 10 km) to Meram, a pleasant, shady suburb west of the city. It's been a getaway destination for Konya city dwellers for at least 1000 years. Minibuses (15 minutes, 40c) depart from the market area not far from the Mevlana Museum.

Çatal Höyük

You can drive or arrange a taxi excursion to Çatal Höyük, the Neolithic site touted as the world's oldest human community (50 km south-east of Konya) but there is little to see except the setting. The prehistoric artefacts have been removed to museums, particularly the Museum of Anatolian Civilisations in Ankara.

The 13 layers of the tumulus date from 6800 to 5500 BC. When excavated by British archaeologist James Mellaart in and after 1958, the mound yielded houses with wall paintings, human bones, and crude baked earthenware mother-goddess figurines.

Festivals

The Mevlana Festival, held in mid-December, culminating on the 17th, the anniversary of Mevlana's 'wedding night' with God. The festival features numerous performances of the sema, or Mevlevi rite. Tickets are sold in advance, and should be bought in advance. Contact the Tourism Information Office or the Konya Culture & Tourism Association for information. Reserve your hotel room in advance, as well. If you can't make it to the festival, plan to see the İstanbul dervishes perform in the Galata Mevlevi Tekkesi near Tünel Meydanı.

Enjoying a Water Pipe

Places to Stay – bottom end

Near the Alaettin Tepesi Several streets just east of the Alaettin Tepesi on the south side of Alaettin Caddesi have good, clean, cheap, fairly quiet hotels. This is prime city-centre real estate, however, and as Konya develops some of these little places are sure to fall to the wrecker's ball.

The first street to the right (south) as you walk along Alaettin Caddesi from the Alaettin Tepesi is Karahüyüklü Sokak, and on it is the *Bulvar Oteli* (☎ (33) 51 37 66), at No 3, renting clean little waterless rooms for US$7/10 a single/double. *Otel Nur*, a few steps farther along, is similar.

The next street east from Karahüyüklü is Emirpervane Sokak, where you'll find the *Otel Kanarya* (Canary Hotel) (☎ (33) 51 15 75), at No 4. This is a homy place where rooms with three beds and no water go for US$7/10/13 a single/double/triple. Showers cost an additional US$1 cold, or US$1.50 hot. Be sure to note the safe in the lobby which bears the legend 'Milner's Patent Fire-Resisting Strong Holdfast Safe'.

Near Mevlana Museum On a quiet street south of Mevlana Caddesi (opposite the Töbank) and west of the Mevlana Museum is the *Otel Köşk* (☎ (33) 52 06 71), Mevlana Caddesi, Bostan Çelebi Sokak 13. It's a convenient place which charges US$9/11 for a single/double with sink, US$16 for a double with shower. Many rooms have three and four beds, good for families or small groups. Also here is the simple but clean *Derviş Oteli* (☎ (33) 51 16 88), Bostan Çelebi Sokak 11/D, charging US$8/16/20 for a single/double/triple with private shower.

The tidy *Petek Oteli* (☎ (33) 52 09 01), Çıkrıkçılar Caddesi 42, Vali Konağı Arkası, is behind the PTT in the midst of the bazaar. It charges the same prices as the Köşk for even nicer rooms. Not far away is the *Yeni Köşk Oteli* (☎ (33) 52 06 71), Yeni Aziziye Caddesi, Kadılar Sokak 28, run by Mr Mustafa Sarıoğlan. Clean and tidy, it features rooms with private showers for US$14/20 a single/double, a breakfast room and car park.

Otel Tur (☎ (33) 51 98 25), Eşarizade Sokak 13, behind the Güzel Sanatlar Galerisi, just down from the tourism office, is only a half-block from the traffic roundabout by the Mevlana Museum. It has very basic bare-bulb double and triple rooms which go for a high US$19 a double with private shower, but it's modern and clean and you can often haggle the price down.

Camping You can camp at the *Şehir Stadı*, the sports complex just east of the railway station on İstasyon Caddesi.

Places to Stay – middle

City Centre The three-star, 82-room *Selçuk Otel* (☎ (33) 51 12 59; fax 51 33 78), is near the Alaettin Tepesi, just north off Alaettin Caddesi. Modern and conveniently located, it rents comfortable, quiet rooms with bath and TV for US$36/52 a single/double.

Just east of Hükümet Alanı, the tidy two-star, 31-room *Şifa Otel* (☎ 51 92 51; fax 52 16 14), Mevlana Caddesi 11, provides decent rooms with private shower at US$24/36 a single/double, breakfast included. Whatever you do, don't make a phone call from this place. My short call to the USA cost US$6 per minute.

Hotel Balıkçılar (☎ (33) 51 29 69; fax 51 32 59), Mevlana Karşısı 1, is right across the street to the south-west of the Mevlana Museum. Its 48 three-star rooms all have minibars and TV sets, and cost US$36/52 a single/double. The location is very convenient.

Hotel Şahin (☎ (33) 51 33 50; fax 55 44 66), Hükümet Alanı 6, 42030 Konya, right in the centre on the main street, is an older hotel. The rooms have been updated and equipped with TVs and minibars, but the ones facing the busy street are quite noisy. The staff are polite and helpful and prices are US$30/50 a single/double with shower.

The three-star, 100-room *Hotel Dergah* (☎ (33) 51 11 97; fax 51 01 16), Mevlana Meydanı 19, 42040 Konya, very near the tourism office, is a convenient hostelry overpriced at US$36/58 a single/double for rooms with private bath (some with tubs as well as showers). The rooms at the front have views of the Mevlana Museum across the square, but are also subject to street noise.

The one-star *Başak Palas* (bah-SHAHK pah-LAHS) (☎ (33) 51 13 38), Hükümet Alanı 3, 42050 Konya, facing the provincial government building midway along Alaettin Caddesi, is an older place with 40 renovated rooms. Rooms with sinks only (hot and cold water) cost from US$20 to US$25 a double; with private bath (tub and shower), US$28/34 a single/double. You can often haggle these prices down, though.

Near the Otogar The three-star *Özkaymak Park Oteli* (☎ (33) 53 37 70; fax 55 59 74), right across the park from the otogar, has 90 simple rooms with shower going for US$36/49 a single/double.

Hotel Sema 2 (☎ (33) 53 25 57), Yeni Terminal, is also next to the otogar, with 33 rooms priced at US$12/15 for a single/double with sink, or US$30 for a double with bath.

Places to Eat
Konya's speciality is fırın kebap, a rich, fairly greasy joint of mutton roasted in an oven. They also make excellent fresh pide topped with minced lamb, cheese or eggs, but in Konya pide is called etli ekmek (bread with meat). Dürüm (roll) is thin flat bread topped with a filling, then rolled up.

The best cheap fare is available on Çıkrıkçılar Caddesi in the bazaar, behind the PTT. Go past the PTT Telefon Müdürlüğü, turn left, and look for the six small eateries clustered together here, charging from US$1 to US$3 for a full meal. *Kabakçı Usta'nın Yeri* at Çıkrıkçılar Caddesi 10/D, serves lots of good cheap ready food for breakfast, lunch and dinner. There are even two streets-ide tables.

At No 19 is the *Şambaba Börekçi*, serving pide called etli ekmek (bread with meat) for only US$1. See it made fresh right before your eyes. To the right of the Şambaba at No 21, the *Hisar Lokanta* has excellent döner kebap. *Lokanta Celil* right across the street does a decent İskender (Bursa) kebap.

Nearby is the *Çağlar Lokantası* (☎ 52 40 42), with lots of ready-food dishes as well as etli ekmek; the upstairs aile salonu may be more pleasant than the downstairs room. To the left of the Çağlar at No 15 is the *Özen Etli Ekmek Salonu* (☎ 52 32 70), serving more of the same.

Just off Çıkrıkçılar Caddesi on Başaraldı Sokak is the *Örnek Lokantası* with ready food, etli ekmek, and tereyağlı börek (flaky pastry made with butter), all at low prices. The upstairs aile salonu is for couples and women alone.

On Bostan Çelebi Sokak near the Köşk and Derviş hotels, look for the *Öztemel Konya Fırın Kebap Salonu*, specialising in the local oven kebap, and, right next door, the *Huzur 2 Lokantası* with lots of ready food. A meal costing more than US$4 is unusual.

Famous for its meat dishes is the *Hanedan Et Lokantası* (☎ 51 45 46), Mevlana Caddesi 2/B, at the south-eastern end of Hükümet Alanı. Clean and bright, with white plastic tables, it is open every day and serves excellent fresh pide, döner kebap, köfte and vegetable dishes. Full meals cost from US$3 to US$5.

Mesut Bolu Lokantası, Mevlana Caddesi 3, across from the Hotel Dergah, has white tables and chairs, lots of air and light, and serves an assortment of Turkish dishes including Konya's fırın kebap. No alcoholic beverages are available. Fırın kebap with salad, bread and soft drink might cost US$3 or so. The 'Bolu' in the restaurant's name refers to the town of Bolu, in the mountains on the Ankara to İstanbul highway, home of Turkey's best chefs.

Nearby is the popular *Şifa Lokantası* (shee-FAH, health) (☎ 52 05 19), Mevlana Caddesi 30, only a short stroll from the Mevlana Museum. It's a modern if simple dining room with tablecloths and full meals for US$3 or US$4. No booze is served here either.

The *Çatal Lokantası* (chah-TAHL) (☎ 51 44 39) is just behind the Tourism Information Office, near the Mevlana Museum. This eatery is a simple, tidy kebap place which serves no alcohol but has good food at low prices. Expect to pay US$4 or less for a full lunch or dinner.

Getting There & Away

Turkish Airlines has an office at Alaettin Caddesi 22, Kat 1/106, (☎ (33) 51 20 00, 51 20 32), on the north side of the street not far from the Alaettin Tepesi.

Konya has some rail service from İstanbul, but most transport is by road (bus). There is an airport, but no scheduled service at present, though there may be soon.

Bus Konya's otogar is 3.5 km from the city centre at Hükümet Alanı (Konak). To travel from the otogar to the centre there are municipal buses and more convenient minibuses (Konak-Otogar, 40c) waiting at a rank near the Özkaymak Park Oteli, just outside the otogar. Some of the minibuses continue to Mevlana Meydanı, next to the Tourism Information Office and the Mevlana Museum.

When the road south via Beyşehir and Akseki is fully improved and opened to bus traffic, travel times (and distances) to Alanya, Antalya and Side will be reduced dramatically, perhaps to only four or five hours. Details of some bus services follow:

Adana – 350 km, 6½ hours, US$12; frequent buses
Adıyaman (Nemrut Dağı) – 720 km, 16 hours, US$30; change at Adana
Aksaray – 140 km, 2½ hours, US$4.50; frequent buses
Alanya – 480 km, 10 hours, US$18; change buses at Silifke or Antalya
Ankara – 260 km, 3½ hours, US$8; frequent buses
Antalya – 365 km, seven hours, US$12; several buses daily
Bursa – 500 km, 8½ hours, US$14; several buses daily
Denizli (Pamukkale) – 440 km, seven hours, US$11; several buses daily
İstanbul – 660 km, 12 hours, US$20; frequent buses
İzmir – 575 km, eight hours, US$14; buses at least every two hours
Nevşehir (Cappadocia) – 226 km, 3½ hours, US$6; several buses daily
Silifke – 218 km, four hours, US$6; frequent buses
Side – 440 km, nine hours, US$20; a few buses daily, or change at Antalya

Train City buses, running at least every half-hour, connect the railway station with the centre of town. If you take a taxi from the railway station to Hükümet Alanı, it will cost about US$2.

There is no direct rail link across the plateau between Konya and Ankara. The best way to make this journey is by bus. Between İstanbul (Haydarpaşa) and Konya you can ride either of the two following daily trains.

İç Anadolu Mavi Tren The 'Inner Anatolia Blue Train' departs from İstanbul (Haydarpaşa) daily at 11.15 pm and arrives in Konya the next day at 12.35 pm.

On the return trip, the train departs from Konya at 8.10 pm, arriving at Haydarpaşa at 9.05 am. A one-way ticket costs US$12, or US$14.50 in a couchette. This train continues beyond Konya to Karaman, arriving at 2.25 pm; departure from Karaman for Konya and İstanbul is at 6.20 pm.

Meram Ekspresi The *Meram Ekspresi* departs from İstanbul (Haydarpaşa) at 6.40 pm, arriving in Konya the next morning at 8.10 am. Departure from Konya is at 4.35 pm, arriving at Haydarpaşa at 6.30 am. A one-way ticket costs US$12/8 in 1st/2nd class. The fare for a sleeping compartment is US$32/56/75 for one/two/three persons.

Getting Around

As most of the sights in the centre are easily reached on foot, you only need public transport to get to the bus and railway stations. Konya's efficient system of minibuses does this well. A light-rail system (trams) should be in operation by the time you arrive.

SULTAN HANI

The highway between Konya and Aksaray crosses quintessential Anatolian steppe: undulating grassland, sometimes with mountains in the distance. Along the way, 110 km from Konya and 45 km from Aksaray, is the village of Sultan Hanı, which has one of several Seljuk hans bearing that name. The Sultan Hanı is 500 metres from the highway. You can visit it on any day in summer from 7 am to 7 pm for US$1.50, and you should, if possible, as it is a fine and impressive example. It was constructed between 1232 and 1236, during the reign of the Seljuk sultan Aladdin Keykubat I. Nearby is the *Kervan Pansyion & Camping* (☎ (4817) 1411, 1325), and other cheap pensions; follow the signs to find them.

AKSARAY

Aksaray (population 90,000, altitude 980 metres) is another of those farming towns (lots of potatoes) where a bed and a meal are its most important features, though you can amuse yourself well enough if you have a spare hour. More to the point, Aksaray is a good base for visits to Ihlara.

It's one km from Aksaray's otogar to the main square. For tourism information, apply to the local tourism office in the jandarma headquarters on the main square with the other government buildings. Signs point the way.

Aksaray's postal code is 51400.

Things to See

The **Zinciriye Medresesi** dates from Seljuk Turkish times, when it was built by the local dynasty of Karamanoğulları emirs. It has been restored several times over the past seven centuries. It is now the local museum, with displays of pots and inscriptions arranged around the courtyard and in the rooms. But it's the building itself which is interesting. It served as a theological college and a han as well. To find it, walk downhill past the Toprak and Çardak hotels, turn right, and walk one short block to the museum.

If you have an evening free, wander into the older part of town to Çerdiğin Caddesi (also called Nevşehir Caddesi), where there are some **old stone houses** and a curious **brick minaret** leaning at a pronounced angle. Built in 1236 by the Seljuks, it is touted by a nearby sign as the 'Turkish Tower of Pisa'.

The **government buildings** on the town's main square have been nicely restored. A short way up the hill is the **Ulu Cami**, with a good façade and an interesting pulpit.

Places to Stay – bottom end

Aksaray has several bottom-end hotels behind the Vilayet (government building) on the main square. The *Toprak Oteli* (☎ (481) 11308), *Çardak Oteli* (☎ (481) 11246) and *Mutlu Oteli* (☎ (481) 11073) all charge US$4 a single, US$7 for a waterless double.

Across the street and up a few steps from the Otel Ihlara (described below) is the *Hitit Pansiyon* (☎ (481) 11996), Kılıçaslan Mahallesi, Otel Ihlara Karşısı, a little apartment house turned into a pension *alla turka*. You remove your shoes and put on clean slippers when entering. The lobby is decorated with carpets, kilims, low couches (called *sedir*) and pillows. The guest rooms upstairs are bare and waterless but the front ones are large and have balconies. Bathrooms down the hall are small but tiled and clean. The price for a double room is US$18.

The *Aksaray Aile Pansiyon* nearby is similar; as is the *Ihlara Pansiyon* (☎ (481) 16083), Eski Sanayi Caddesi, 1 Nolu Sokak, charging US$9 for a clean waterless doubles.

If you're camping, head for the *Ağaçlı Turistik Tesisleri*, a luxury camping ground at the main highway intersection, where you can pitch your tent or park your camper van for US$3, plus the same amount again for each person in your party.

Places to Stay – middle

The two-star *Otel Vadi* (☎ (481) 14326, -7), one block from the main square, is the best value. With 35 rooms with shower and a restaurant, it's comfortable for one night, and charges US$18/24 a single/double. Breakfast is an additional US$2 per person.

Hotel Yoğuran (☎ (481) 15490), 3 Nolu Hükümet Caddesi, in the midst of the bazaar a half-block from the Vilayet building, is among the city's newer and more interesting places to stay because of its location. Rooms with private shower cost US$20 a double, a few dollars more if you want a TV set also.

The alternative is the three-star, 64-room *Otel Ihlara* (☎ (481) 11842, 13252), Kılıçaslan Mahallesi, Eski Sanayi Caddesi, two blocks from the main square on a quiet back street (follow the signs, or ask). A bit plusher with a lift, restaurant and fairly quiet rooms with private baths, its official rates are US$35/55 a single/double, breakfast included, but on my last visit I was quoted rates only a third as high as these.

The top place in town is the *Ağaçlı Turistik Tesisleri* (Ağaçlı Touristic Establishments) (☎ (481) 14910; fax 14914), Ankara-Adana Asfaltı, Nevşehir Kavşağı, out on the highway at the main intersection with the roads to Nevşehir and Niğde. If you have a car, this place will be convenient. Two motels are within its green and shady gardens.

The *Melendiz Motel* charges US$35/45 a single/double, breakfast included. The *Ihlara Motel* charges a bit less, US$30/40 a single/double. Other services abound, including an inexpensive cafeteria, a more formal restaurant, gift shops, swimming and wading pools and a fuel station.

Places to Eat

Except in the better hotels, there are only simple restaurants. The place to look is behind the Vilayet building, near the cheap hotels. Here you'll find the *Zümrüt Restaurant* (zurm-RURT) (☎ 12233), *Çardak* (chahr-DAHK) (☎ 11926) and *Aksaraylı Restaurant* (AHK-sah-rahy-luh) (☎ 13386), all serving tasty if simple meals for under US$3.

Getting There & Away

There are direct buses from Aksaray to Ankara (230 km, 4½ hours), Nevşehir (65 km, 1½ hours), Niğde (115 km, two hours) and Konya (140 km, 2½ hours). There are also regular dolmuşes in summer to Ihlara Köyü (45 km, one hour), the starting place for visits to the Ihlara valley.

IHLARA (PERISTREMA)

Forty-five km south-east of Aksaray, partly along a rough unpaved road, is Ihlara, at the head of the Peristrema gorge. This remote and somewhat forbidding valley was once a favourite retreat of Byzantine monks. Dozens of painted churches, carved from the rock or built from the local stone, have sur-

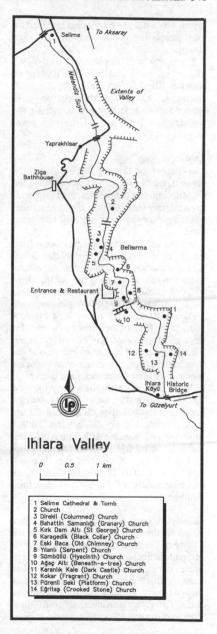

Ihlara Valley

0   0.5   1 km

1 Selime Cathedral & Tomb
2 Church
3 Direkli (Columned) Church
4 Bahattin Samanlığı (Granary) Church
5 Kırk Dam Altı (St George) Church
6 Karagedik (Black Collar) Church
7 Eski Baca (Old Chimney) Church
8 Yılanlı (Serpent) Church
9 Sümbüllü (Hyacinth) Church
10 Ağaç Altı (Beneath-a-tree) Church
11 Karanlık Kale (Dark Castle) Church
12 Kokar (Fragrant) Church
13 Pürenli Seki (Platform) Church
14 Eğritaş (Crooked Stone) Church

vived. The wildly beautiful area is visited by tour buses but is far less touristy than Göreme.

Start early in the day and you'll enjoy the trip more, particularly in the middle of summer. The hike up the gorge, along the course of the stream Melendiz Suyu, is wilder and more exciting than touring the well-trodden paths amidst the rock-hewn churches at Göreme.

Things to See

The scenery on this trip, especially on the descent into the gorge, is as wonderful as the ancient churches themselves. Plan on spending a full day seeing Ihlara. If you're coming out from Aksaray, the drive will take some time.

At the south-eastern (upper) end of the gorge, on the rim near the village Ihlara Köyü, is a modern installation with a restaurant, souvenir shop and ticket booth, where you buy a ticket for US$2 and enter any time from 8.30 am to 5.30 pm.

You must descend a very long flight of stairs to the floor of the gorge and wander for several hours to see the various churches. Though there are simple eateries along the way in the gorge, you might want to pack a picnic or at least take snacks and drinks.

Signs mark the **churches** along the way. The most interesting, with the best paintings, are the Yılanlı Kilise, Sümbüllü Kilise, Kokar Kilise and Eğritaş Kilisesi. Farther down the valley are the Kırk Dam Altı Kilise, Bahattin Samanlığı Kilisesi, Direkli Kilise and Ala Kilise. Several of the churches, notably the Çarıklı, Elmalı and Karanlık, are closed because of the risk of structural damage.

Güzelyurt Less than 10 km from Ihlara Köyü on the road east to Derinkuyu is the village of Güzelyurt. It gets top marks for its efforts to attract tourists, including welcome arches over the entry roads, signs in English marking the few old churches and 'monastery valley'. Though hardly Göreme or Ihlara, Güzelyurt is an interesting old Cappadocian farming village of stone houses, orthodox churches converted to mosques, lush fields, valleys, streams and gardens all barely touched by tourism.

Places to Stay

There are a few small pensions between the village and the entry to the gorge. The *Vadibaşı Pansiyon* is a neat village house charging US$8 per person for bed and breakfast. It's 750 metres from the entry at the rim of the gorge, and the same distance into the village. The *Pension Anatolia* is fancier, charging US$16 a double for a waterless room, breakfast included. French is spoken at the *Family Pension*.

You can camp at the entry to the gorge: US$3 for a tent, plus US$1.50 per person.

In Belisırma Köyü in the valley you'll find the *Aslan Camping & Pansiyon* (☎ (481) 13780), with 30 beds in tents which rent for US$6 a double.

Places to Eat

The restaurant at the rim entry to the gorge has the best view, but a limited menu. A full meal still costs around US$6 or US$7. Simple eateries operate in the village (*Mehmet Işık's Restaurant*) and the valley (two along the trail, one in Belisırma Köyü) during the touristy summer months.

Getting There & Away

Bus The rim entry to the gorge is 1.5 km from the village of Ihlara Köyü, 45 km from Aksaray and 95 km from Nevşehir. Ihlara Belediyesi buses run several times daily from Aksaray's otogar, charging US$1.50 one-way.

Car If you have a car, your visit is made much easier. From the main Aksaray to Nevşehir highway, turn south (right, if you're coming from Aksaray) at a point 11 km east of the intersection of the Ankara to Adana and Aksaray to Nevşehir highways. After making this turn, go about 23 km to another right turn marked for Ihlara Vadisi. The road passes through Selime village, with numerous rock-hewn buildings, and then three km farther on it runs through Yaprak-hisar; both villages are dramatically surrounded by rock and marked by Göreme-style fairy chimneys. After 13 km you come to Ihlara Köyü, where you turn left to reach, after another km or so, the entry point at the rim of the gorge.

It is also possible to come to Ihlara from the underground cities of Kaymaklı and Derinkuyu (52 km), or vice versa. From Derinkuyu, proceed south towards Niğde, but turn west (right) at the village of Gölcük (signs mark the turn-off). Drive through fertile potato and grain-farming land and up into the mountains (wonderful scenery) through Sivrihisar and Güzelyurt.

Güzelyurt has its own very unimpressive underground dwelling and a mosque built in Byzantine times as a church dedicated to the theologian Gregory of Nazianza (born in 330 AD). The scenery on this drive is dramatic and beautiful. Sixty km after Gölcük, turn left for Selime and the road to Ihlara.

UZUN YOL
The drive from Aksaray or Ihlara to Nevşehir takes you along one of the oldest trade routes in the world, the Uzun Yol or Long Road. It linked Konya, the capital of the Seljuk Sultanate of Rum, with other great cities of the sultanate (Kayseri, Sivas and Erzurum) and ultimately with the birthplace of Seljuk power in Persia.

Following the Long Road today takes you past the remains of several hans, including the impressive and well-preserved **Ağız-karahan** (1243) on the south side of the road about 13 km east of Aksaray, open daily from 7 am to 6 pm for a small fee; the **Tepe-sidelik Hanı** (also called the Öresin Hanı, 13th century) on the south side about 20 km east of Aksaray; and the **Alay Hanı** (12th century), badly ruined, on the north side of the highway about 33 km east of Aksaray. All are marked by signs.

KIRŞEHİR
Midway along the road from Ankara (190 km) to Cappadocia (100 km) lies Kırşehir (population 85,000, altitude 978 metres). It's an ancient city, famous in Ottoman times as the centre of the mystical Ahi (Akhi) brotherhoods, the Muslim equivalent of the Masonic lodges. The Ahi brotherhoods were founded in the 14th century as secret religious societies among members of the crafts guilds, particularly the tanners' guild. Their political power grew to the point where the sultans had to reckon with them.

The founding father and inspiration of the Akhi brotherhoods was Ahi Evran (1236-1329), a tanner whose family came from Khorasan. He lived and died in Kırşehir. His mosque and tomb are Muslim places of pilgrimage.

Kırşehir is a provincial capital with a few old buildings and a few cheap, basic hotels. You should have no trouble finding your way around.

Orientation
The city centre is at Cumhuriyet Meydanı, the main traffic roundabout with the ugly modern clock tower. Almost everything you'll want and need is within a five-minute walk of here. The main commercial street running out of the square is Ankara Caddesi, and a few steps along it is the PTT. Hotels, restaurants, and the Ahi Evran Türbesi are a short walk farther along Ankara Caddesi. The Cacabey Camii is on the opposite side of Cumhuriyet Meydanı from Ankara Caddesi.

Information
The Tourism Information Office (☎ (487) 11416), Cumhuriyet Meydanı, Aşık Paşa Caddesi, is right at the city centre; follow the signs. If it's open (hours are supposedly from 8 am to noon and from 1 to 5 pm daily), the chances of finding a knowledgeable person who speaks English are virtually nil. All the sights are well marked by signs, though, usually with wonderful, hilarious translations.

Kırşehir's postal code is 40000.

Things to See
The **Ahi Evran Camii ve Türbesi** or Ahi Evran Mosque and Tomb, also called the Ahi

Evran Zaviyesi (Dervish Lodge), are simple stone structures, obviously very old.

The amusing translated sign notes that Ahi Evran 'was founder of saints philosophy and he had striven hard with skin art', meaning he was a tanner. Pilgrims in their 'Friday best' are usually crowded into the small rooms in prayer.

Just off the traffic roundabout is the **Cacabey Camii** (mosque; that's JAH-jah-bey), built by the Seljuk Turks in 1272 as a meteorological observatory and theological college. It's now used as a mosque.

The black and white stonework draws the eye here. The **Alaettin Camii** dates from Seljuk times as well. You may also see a number of tombs dating from the 1300s.

Places to Stay & Eat

The cheap hotels in town charge about the same prices for the same well-used, spartan and somewhat dismal rooms: about US$5/9 a single/double for a room with sink, or US$7/11 for a room with shower.

The *Ahi Oteli* (☎ (487) 11700), on Ankara Caddesi, M Ali Yapıcı Bulvarı, is just off Ankara Caddesi facing the Ahi Evran Camii, and is a marginally better and quieter place to stay than the nearby *Anadolu* and the *Banana*.

The *Otel Anadolu* (☎ (487) 11826), Ankara Caddesi 20, across the main street from Ahi Evran, is well worn but cheap, and has a lift. The *Otel Banana* (☎ (487) 11879), next door at Ankara Caddesi 26, is virtually identical.

The new three-star *Terme Hotel* (☎ (487) 22404; fax 18148), Terme Parkı, on the outskirts of town near the Terme Kaplıcaları hot springs, provides Kırşehir with 132 bath-equipped rooms at US$35/46 for a single/double, a Turkish bath, and a swimming pool. Follow the signs to find it.

As for meals, places on Ankara Caddesi can fill this need as well. *Kebap 49* is right on the corner near the Ahi Oteli; the *Sofra Restaurant* is a few steps away in the opposite direction, more or less across the street from the Ahi Evran Türbesi.

Cappadocia

Cappadocia, the region between Ankara and Malatya, between the Black Sea and the Taurus Mountains, with its centre at Kayseri, was once the heart of the Hittite Empire, later an independent kingdom, then a vast Roman province. Cappadocia is mentioned several times in the Bible.

Today the word survives as a name for one of Turkey's most visited tourist areas, the moonscape around the town of Ürgüp and the Göreme Valley. You won't find the name on an official road map, so you'll need to know that the area extends from Kayseri in the east (north-east of Ürgüp), Aksaray to the west, Hacıbektaş to the north and Niğde to the south.

For all its apparent barrenness, the mineral-laden volcanic soil is very fertile and Cappadocia today is a prime agricultural region with many fruit orchards and vineyards. Little wineries experiment with the excellent grapes, sometimes with pleasant results. Irrigation schemes should greatly increase the productivity of the region.

Another source of wealth is carpet-making and while the women in Cappadocian villages toil at their looms, Kayseri is a hotbed of persistent rug dealers. But Cappadocia's new economic dimension is tourism. People come from all over the world to visit the open-air museum of the Göreme Valley, to explore the rock-hewn churches and dwellings in surrounding valleys, to gaze on the fairy chimneys and to plumb the depths of the underground cities at Derinkuyu and Kaymaklı, south of Nevşehir.

History

The history of Cappadocia began with the eruption of two volcanoes, Erciyes Dağı near Kayseri and Melendiz Dağı near Niğde. The eruptions spread a thick layer of hot volcanic ash over the region which hardened to a soft, porous stone called tufa, or tuff.

Over aeons of geological time, wind, water and sand erosion wore away portions

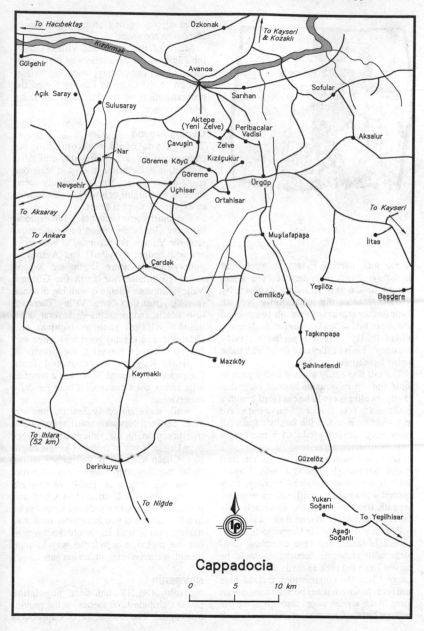

Cappadocia

0   5   10 km

A crusader

of the tuff, carving it into elaborate and unearthly shapes. Boulders of hard stone, caught in the tuff and then exposed by erosion, protect the tuff directly beneath from further erosion. The result is a column or cone of tuff with a boulder perched on top, whimsically called a *peribaca*, 'fairy chimney'. Entire valleys are filled with these weird formations.

The tuff was easily worked with primitive tools and the inhabitants learned early that sturdy dwellings could be cut from it with a minimum of fuss. One could carve out a cave in a short time and, if the family expanded, more easy carving produced a nursery or storeroom in almost no time.

When invaders flooded across the land bridge between Europe and Asia, Cappadocians went underground – literally. They carved elaborate multi-level cave cities beneath the surface of the earth and only came to the surface to tend their fields.

Christianity arrived in Cappadocia and its adherents found that cave churches, complete with elaborate decoration, could be carved from the rock as easily as dwellings. Large Christian communities thrived here and rock-hewn churches became a unique art form. Arab armies swept through in the 7th century but the Christians retreated into their caves again, rolling stone wheel-doors across the entrances.

Many of the caves and villages were inhabited by the descendants of these early settlers until our century, when the disintegration of the Ottoman Empire forced the reorganisation of the Middle East along ethno-political lines.

Getting Around

Though you could see something of Cappadocia on a lightning day trip from Ankara, it is far better to stay at least one night in the region. You could easily spend three or four nights or a week if you wanted to explore all there is to see.

The most convenient bases for explorations are Ürgüp, the region's tourist centre; Göreme Village, the favourite of backpackers and budget travellers; and Avanos, a pottery-making centre. Ürgüp and Avanos are a 10-minute ride from the Göreme Valley; Göreme Village is walking distance (one km) from the Göreme Valley. There are also hotels and pensions in several other nearby villages such as Uçhisar and Ortahisar, and several good mid-range and luxury hotels in Nevşehir, the provincial capital. Kayseri is separated from Cappadocia by around 70 km and a range of hills and is not a convenient base for daily excursions.

While there are convenient dolmuş services between Nevşehir and Ürgüp, public transportation to the valleys and villages near Ürgüp is not as frequent as one might like. Cheap tours allow you to see all the sights, but they often dump you into a carpet or souvenir shop in the middle of nowhere for two hours (ask about this when you book). You can rent mopeds and motorcycles in a few places. If you have more time than money, plan to walk and hitchhike throughout the region, a wonderful way to tour, though it can be tiring in the hot sun.

NEVŞEHIR

Nevşehir (NEHV-sheh-heer, population 60,000, altitude 1260 metres) is the provincial capital. The moonscape of Cappadocia is not much in evidence here but it's very close by. Nevşehir is a transfer point and a base for visiting the underground cities at Kaymaklı and Derinkuyu.

Orientation

Nevşehir's main street is called Atatürk Bulvarı; along its eastern reaches on the way to Göreme it changes names to become Yeni Kayseri Caddesi. The main north-south road, Lale Caddesi, intersects with Atatürk Bulvarı at the centre of the town. The new otogar is less than one km north of the centre towards Gülşehir.

Information

The Tourism Information Office (☎ (485) 12717), Atatürk Bulvarı (Yeni Kayseri Caddesi), is a few hundred metres east of the main intersection. Look for a small white building on the right-hand side. It's open every day in summer from 8.30 am to noon and from 1 to 5.30 pm. Staff are well informed and quite helpful. Nevşehir's postal code is 50000.

Things to See

There is little to see or do in Nevşehir proper except perhaps for Monday's **market** or a climb up to the **citadel** to enjoy the view and be importuned into buying some of the locally handmade lace. Have a look at the **Nevşehirli İbrahim Paşa Külliyesi**, the mosque complex at the southern end of the Hotel Şehir Palas.

Sultan Ahmet III's grand vizier İbrahim Paşa (1662-1730), sometimes called Damat İbrahim, was a great builder, having supplied his sovereign with many romantic palaces and lodges in İstanbul. He was one of the first great men of the empire to have been influenced by European fashions. He was born in humble conditions in the village of Muşkara, and when he became rich and famous he returned to his village to found a new city (*nev*, new; *şehir*, city). Along with his New City, İbrahim founded this mosque complex (1726), consisting of the mosque, a seminary, a school, a library, a water fountain and a hamam. The mosque and hamam are still

in business. Bath hours at the hamam are from 7.30 am to 9 pm.

The **Nevşehir Museum** (Nevşehir Müzesi) is one km out along Yeni Kayseri Caddesi on the road to Göreme and Ürgüp. Opening hours are from 8 am to noon and from 1.30 to 5.30 pm; admission is US$1. The arrangement is the familiar one: an archaeological section with Phrygian, Hittite and Bronze Age pots and implements, up through Roman, Byzantine and Ottoman articles; and an ethnographic section with costumes, tools, manuscripts and jewellery.

For excursions from Nevşehir, readers of this guide have found the Tulip Travel Agency (☎ (485) 15022), Aksaray Caddesi 1, owned by a Dutch-Turkish couple, to be especially helpful.

Underground Cities

For sheer fascination and mystery, the places to see are the underground cities south of Nevşehir along the road to Niğde: Kaymaklı, 20 km south of Nevşehir; Mazıköy, 10 km east of Kaymaklı; and Derinkuyu, 10 km south of Kaymaklı. Board a bus or minibus at the proper minibus stop in Nevşehir (see map); they depart every 30 minutes or so and charge US$1.50 for the ride. Kaymaklı Belediyesi operates regular buses from Nevşehir's otogar, and there are others to Niğde.

Kaymaklı The countryside around Kaymaklı has no enchanting fairy chimneys or sensuously carved valleys, yet the stone is the same soft volcanic tuff which allowed early residents to develop the real estate cheaply.

At Kaymaklı, an unprepossessing farming village of white houses and unpaved streets, an unimpressive little cave in a low mound leads down into a vast maze of tunnels and rooms. From the highway, follow the signs which indicate a left (east) turn, or ask for the Yeraltı Şehri (YEHR-ahl-tuh shehh-ree, Underground City). The entrance is one block east of the highway and it's open from 8 am to 5 pm (the 6.30 pm in summer) every day; admission costs US$2.50. Collapse of some of the underground tunnel network has

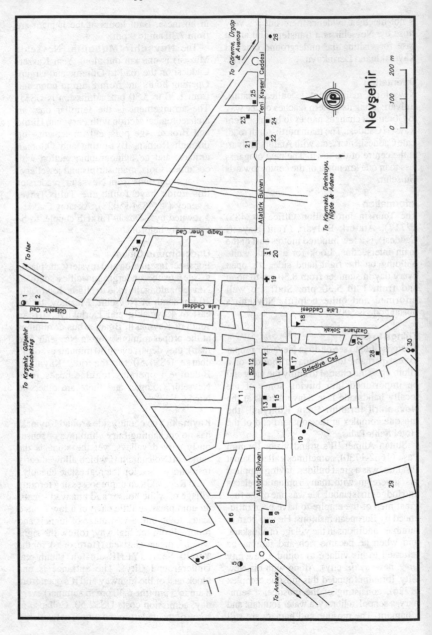

Nevşehir

To Göreme, Ürgüp & Avanos

Yeni Kayseri Caddesi

To Kaymaklı, Derinkuyu, Niğde & Adana

Atatürk Bulvarı

To Nar

To Kırşehir, Gülşehir & Hacıbektaş

Gülşehir Cad

Raşıp Üner Cad

Lale Caddesi

Lale Caddesi

Gazhane Sokak

Belediye Cad

Atatürk Bulvarı

To Ankara

0   100   200 m

■ PLACES TO STAY

2 Hotel Şekeryapan
3 Otel Altınöz
4 Hotel Hisar
6 Hotel Kaymak
7 Bulvar Palas
8 İpek Palas Oteli
9 Kemer Pansion
13 Hotel Epok
14 Hotel Şems & Aspava Restaurant
15 Koç Palas Otel
17 Hotel Nur
21 Hotel Nisa
23 Hotel Seven Brothers
24 Hotel Dilara
25 Hotel Orsan
27 Hotel Lale
28 Şehir Palas Hotel

▼ PLACES TO EAT

11 Park Restaurant
14 Aspava Restaurant & Hotel Şems
16 Divan Restaurant
18 Hanedan Restaurant

OTHER

1 Otogar (Bus Station)
5 Aksaray Dolmuş Station
10 Market
12 PTT
19 Hospital
20 Tourism Information Office
22 Valilik (Provincial Government Building)
26 Nevşehir Museum
29 Kale
30 İbrahim Paşa Mosque

limited what's to be seen here, but progress is being made clearing the rubble.

Little arrows guide you into the cool depths. (Space yourself to travel in a gap between larger groups.) As you go down, it's like entering a huge and very complex Swiss cheese. Holes here, holes there, 'windows' from room to room, paths going this way and that, more levels of rooms above and below. Without the arrows and the electric wires, it would be fearfully difficult to find the way out again. If you wander off along another passage, separated from the group by only a few metres, you can hear what they say, you can converse with them, but you can't find your way back to them! Suddenly a foot comes into view and you realise that they're on the next level, almost above your head!

If you look carefully, signs of the troglodyte lifestyle are everywhere: storage jars for oil, wine and water, communal kitchens blackened by smoke, stables with mangers, incredibly deep wells. Soon you no longer find it impossible to believe that tens of thousands of people could have lived here happily year-round, deep within the earth. It's even suspected that there were underground passages which connected Kaymaklı with its sister city of Derinkuyu, seven km away, though the tunnels have yet to be fully excavated.

Mazıköy Just north of the turn-off for Kaymaklı's Yeraltı Şehri is another turn-off east marked for Mazıköy Yeraltı Şehri, 10 km along. Nestled in a valley enclosed by the now-familiar sheer rock cliffs is the village of Mazıköy, with its central town square. Buy your ticket here (US$2) whenever there's anyone around, then follow the inevitable lad to the entrance just off the town square.

The underground levels are much more distinctly defined here. Speaking tubes (the guide calls them *telefon)* kept people on different levels in touch; there were shafts for air and light as well.

On top of the valley wall is a necropolis with slot-like graves. Your boy guides will show you the stone shelter supposedly used for the *güvercin postası* (carrier-pigeon mail service).

At this writing the village has few services, but you can get simple meals and beds now, and fancier ones will follow.

Derinkuyu Its name means 'deep well', and this underground city, 10 km south of Kaymaklı, has larger rooms arrayed on eight levels. Prices and opening times are the same as at Kaymaklı. Derinkuyu is perhaps a bit less touristy but both places have been discovered.

Derinkuyu has several restaurants near the main square. There's also the Hotel Ali Baba, and others, though once you've seen the underground city there's little reason to stay. You might have a look at the mosque, obviously built as a church, and the large monastery church (in good condition, complete with bell tower) on the main road just 100 metres south of the turn-off for the underground city.

Places to Stay – bottom end

Nevşehir has hotels in all price ranges, though low-budget possibilities are not as good here as in Göreme Village.

From the main intersection at the city centre, walk uphill on Atatürk Bulvarı past the Aspava Restaurant and Hotel Şems, and turn left at the next street, Belediye Caddesi, to find the tidy little *Hotel Nur* (☎ (485) 11444), behind a little marble fountain at Ada Sokak 2, which is quieter than those places right on the boulevard, and just as cheap. Rooms cost US$5/9 a single/double.

Continue along Belediye Caddesi two short blocks to a more comfortable but expensive longtime favourite, the *Hotel Lale* (☎ (485) 11797), just west of the intersection with Lale Caddesi. The rooms with bath are quite comfortable for what you pay: US$8/16 a single/double.

Continue uphill on Atatürk Bulvarı past the Hotel Epok (see Places to Stay – middle, following) and turn left to find the *Koç Palas Otel* (☎ (485) 11216), Hükümet Caddesi 1, facing a little square on the left-hand (south) side of Atatürk Bulvarı. The charge for a waterless double is US$11.

Farther up the hill along Atatürk Bulvarı several small cheap hotels on the left-hand side are affected badly by street noise. There's the *İpek Palas Oteli* (☎ (485) 11478), Atatürk Bulvarı 99, charging US$4.75/7.50 a single/double with washbasin. You have a good chance of actually getting hot water here.

Right around the corner from the İpek Palas is the *Kemer Pansion* (☎ (485) 11751), Aksaray Caddesi, Yiğit Galeri Bitişiği 3/1, an old renovated stone building with a darkish lobby but lighter rooms. Prices are about the same as at the İpek for the waterless rooms, but you get the benefit of a roof terrace here.

A short distance uphill from the İpek Palas is the slightly seedier *Bulvar Palas* (☎ (485) 11695), Atatürk Bulvarı 101, which rents clean waterless rooms at the same rates. The triples have washbasins in them.

Just a bit farther along is the Aksaray dolmuş station, once the main otogar, with several hotels nearby, including the *Hotel Kaymak* (☎ (485) 15427), Eski Sanayi Meydanı 11; you'll see its sign. Older but presentable and convenient, it has elephant-foot toilets (but regular baths in the common bathrooms) and charges US$7/10/12.50 a single/double/ triple for a waterless room. The lobby bears a primitive mural showing a steel factory.

Camping There are several camping places along the road to Ürgüp, none of which is outstanding. Rates are generally US$2 per person, and another US$2 or so for a tent or caravan.

Follow the signs to Ürgüp and shortly after leaving Nevşehir you will come to the *Dinler Turizm Mocamp*, behind a Türk Petrol station. Rates are about US$3 per adult, almost as much for tent or vehicle. The nearby *Koru Mocamp* has elicited a few complaints from readers.

Places to Stay – middle

Only 100 metres south of the otogar is the relatively new three-star *Hotel Şekeryapan* (☎ 485) 14253; fax 14051), Gülşehir Caddesi 8, with a lift and 37 comfy rooms, all with private showers, priced at US$20/30 a single/double, breakfast included. There's a restaurant, Turkish bath and sauna, terrace bar and lounge as well.

Hotel Seven Brothers (☎ & fax (485) 14979), Yeni Kayseri Caddesi, Tusan Sokak 25, is a new two-star, 24-room hotel on a quiet street on the way to Göreme. There's a lift and restaurant, and posted room prices of

US$14/22 a single/double, but I was quoted US$11/16 when I asked.

Among the old stand-bys is the *Hotel Orsan* (☎ (485) 12115; fax 14223), Yeni Kayseri Caddesi 15, right across the street from the aforementioned Hotel Seven Brothers. The lobby and public rooms are covered in the wonderful Turkish carpets of the area, many of which feature crimson; they make a strong impression. The 95 three-star rooms (all with shower) rent for US$25/32 a single/double, breakfast included. The Orsan is slightly dearer than other hotels because it has a small swimming pool.

The new two-star, 29-room *Hotel Dilara* (☎ (485) 15567; fax 12739), Yeni Kayseri Caddesi 2, on the south side of the main street across from the Orsan, is a fine place with similar prices, but watch out for road noise.

The two-star, 60-room *Hotel Epok* (☎ (485) 11168), Atatürk Bulvarı 39, is on the main street in the middle of town. Though it's nice enough, it suffers from street noise and I'd suggest that you look first at its even more attractive and comfortable sister hotel, the *Şehir Palas Hotel* (☎ (485) 15329), Camii Kebir Caddesi 41, not far away. Walk downhill past the Epok, turn right at the next street, and walk two blocks to the large tawny stone building which is the hotel. Designed with echoes of the local architecture and traditional building materials, the Şehir Palas offers comfy, quiet rooms with bath and balcony; the only noise here is from the minaret. Rooms cost US$25/38 a single/double, breakfast included – somewhat higher than at the simpler Hotel Epok.

The one-star, 25-room *Hotel Şems* (☎ (485) 13597; fax 10834), Atatürk Bulvarı 29, above the Aspava Restaurant a few blocks west of the centre along the main street, is newish, nice and reasonably priced at US$15/24 a single/double. Rooms at the front of the hotel may be noisy.

Places to Stay – top end

About three km east of the centre of Nevşehir on the Ürgüp road stands the big five-star, 350-room *Nevşehir Dedeman Hotel*

(☎ (485) 19900; fax 12158), the town's first five-star accommodation. Guest rooms have all the luxury accoutrements, including air-con, TVs, minibars and the like. Two restaurants, four bars, a swimming pool, Turkish bath, sauna, courts for volleyball, basketball and tennis – it's all yours for US$85/125 a single/double. The hotel is often busy with tour groups.

Though not as lavish in its services, the new four-star *Otel Altınöz* (☎ (485) 15305; fax 12817), Ragıp Üner Caddesi 23, has 120 equally comfortable air-conditioned guest rooms renting for much less: US$50/60 a single/double, breakfast included. Turkish bath, sauna, disco, restaurants and bars are all yours to enjoy, and the location is quiet.

Places to Eat

For general purposes, the central *Aspava Restaurant* (☎ 11051), Atatürk Bulvarı 29, is a good bet for ready food, kebaps and pide at low prices. You can figure on spending from US$3 to US$4 for a full meal.

Just down the street from the Hotel Nur on Ada Sokak is the *Divan Restaurant* (☎ 12735), similar to the Aspava in offerings and price, but without the noisy street. It's open for breakfast.

The *Hanedan Restaurant* (☎ 11179), Gazhane Caddesi 18/A, specialises in kebaps and does a thriving take-away business. A plate of lamb kebap, a salad and a glass of ayran (the yoghurt drink) costs less than US$3.

The *Park Restaurant* (☎ 14487), across Atatürk Bulvarı from the Hotel Epok and up the hill through the park, is where Nevşehir's movers and shakers come in the evening to have a drink and talk politics, sport, and business. Waiters quietly bring plate after plate of meze, grilled meat or chicken, various soups and stews and a few desserts. It's not fancy, but there's a view. A full lunch or dinner costs from US$6 to US$7.

Getting There & Away

Bus Apart from using the new otogar on the north side of the town, some Nevşehir buses and minibuses use the old otogar, now called the Aksaray bus station, uphill to the west along Atatürk Bulvarı. Here are details for other destinations:

Adana – 285 km, 5½ hours, US$10; several buses daily

Aksaray – 65 km, 1½ hours, US$2.50; frequent minibuses and buses

Ankara – 285 km, 4½ hours, US$8; very frequent buses daily

Denizli (Pamukkale) – 665 km, 10 hours, US$18; one bus daily

İstanbul – 725 km, 10 to 12 hours, US$15 to US$20; a few buses nightly

Kayseri – 105 km, 2½ hours by bus, 1½ hours by minibus, US$4; very frequent buses and minibuses

Konya – 226 km, 3½ hours, US$6; several buses daily

Yozgat (via Kayseri) – 300 km, five hours, US$8

From Nevşehir you might be going south to the underground cities of Kaymaklı and Derinkuyu, already described. If so, you may want to visit Niğde as well. If not, skip the following section and head for Ürgüp and Göreme.

NİĞDE

Niğde (NEE-deh, population 75,000, altitude 1216 metres) was built by the Seljuks 85 km south of Nevşehir. If you are passing through, you might want to have a look at the buildings the Seljuks and the Mongols left behind. Not far out of town is an ancient monastery hewn from the volcanic stone.

Orientation

The marketplace is conveniently marked by a clock tower (saat kulesi). The centre of town life is between the clock tower and the Vilayet (government building), which is a few short blocks to the north-west on Atatürk Meydanı (sometimes called Hükümet Meydanı), the main square. It's one km from the otogar to the Vilayet; on the way you pass near the hill with the Alaeddin Camii.

Information

The Tourist Information Office (☎ (483) 11261), İstiklal Caddesi, Vakıf İş Hanı 1/D, just off the main square, is open daily (except Sunday) from 8.30 am to noon and from 1.30 to 5.30 pm.

Süngür Bey Camii

The **Alaeddin Camii** (1223), on the hill with the fortress which dominates the town, is the grandest mosque. But the Süngür Bey Camii at the foot of the hill by the marketplace (Thursday is market day) is, for me, the city's most interesting building. Restored by the Mongols in 1335, it is a curious and affecting blend of architectures. Windows around the ground floor differ in style and are highly carved; on the upper storey are blind lancet arches instead of windows. The rose window above the north window bears a six-pointed 'Star of David', a motif you'll see used elsewhere. The big, stolid, square doors with fine carving are unusual. Recent restorations have done wonders for the exterior stonework but have filled the interior with reinforced concrete which is quite ugly and jarring. The north galleries are a conglomeration of architectural styles. The mihrab is wonderfully carved and almost Chinese in appearance.

The **Ak Medrese** (1409) is now the town's museum. Also take a look at the **Hüdavend Hatun Türbesi** (1312), a fine example of a Seljuk tomb; and the **Dış Cami**, an Ottoman mosque with a carved mimber inlaid with mother-of-pearl.

Eski Gümüşler Monastery

It's 10 km from the clock tower in Niğde to the rock-hewn monastery of Eski Gümüşler, east of town. Coming from Nevşehir, an intersection near a Mobil fuel station on the main highway is marked for Niğde (right, west) and Eski Gümüşler (left, east), four km. It's actually 4.75 km. Minibuses operated by the Gümüşler Belediyesi run out here from Niğde. Ask for Eski Gümüşler (ess-KEE gur-mursh-LEHR) and take the bus to the end of the line. You can also hitch to the site.

In the village of Gümüşler you will find refreshing tea, soft drinks and snacks to consume. In autumn, at harvest time, the villagers pick such a wealth of apples from

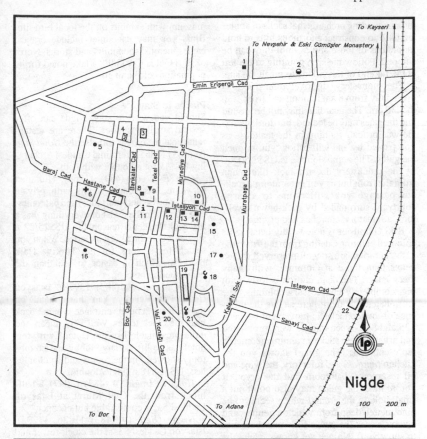

Niğde

0   100   200 m

To Kayseri
To Nevşehir & Eski Gümüşler Monastery

Emin Erişergil Cad
Baraj Cad
Hastane Cad
Bankalar Cad
Tekel Cad
Muradiye Cad
Muratpaşa Cad
İstasyon Cad
Bor Cad
Vali Konağı Cad
Kaleiçi Sok
İstasyon Cad
Sanayi Cad
To Bor
To Adana

	PLACES TO STAY		3	Polis (Police Station)
			4	PTT (Post Office)
1	Hotel Stad		5	Hüdavend Hatun Türbesi
8	Otel Evim		6	Hastane (Hospital)
10	Niğde Oteli		7	Vilayet (Government Building)
12	Otel Murat		11	Tourism Information Office
13	Hotel Taciroğlu		15	Saat Kulesi (Clock Tower)
14	İpek Palas Oteli		16	Müze (Museum)
			17	Kale (Fortress)
	PLACES TO EAT		18	Alaeddin Camii
			19	Bedesten (Covered Market)
9	Niğde Şehir Lokantası		20	Ak Medrese
			21	Süngür Bey Camii
	OTHER		22	Railway Station
2	Oto Terminalı (Bus Terminal)			

the surrounding orchards that sacks of apples are used to construct enormous bins to hold mountains of loose apples until they can be shipped. Follow the sign pointing to the left at the far end of the village to reach the site.

The monastery, discovered in 1963, is open daily from 8 am to noon and from 1.30 to 5.30 pm. The guardian may not be around and the gates may be locked, but don't worry. He was probably sitting in the teahouse as you passed by and will follow you to open the gates. The admission fee is US$1.50.

The monastery doesn't look like much from the front but as you enter along a rock-cut passage you will come to a large courtyard surrounded by rock-hewn dwellings, a refectory, churches and crypts.

Eski Gümüşler is noteworthy because its coloured paintings, dating from the 7th to the 11th centuries, are so well preserved (much better than those at Göreme), with many faces intact. The main church is lofty, with big, completely unnecessary columns. The cross-hatch line motif here shows the influence of the iconoclastic movement between 725 and 842, when images were prohibited and artists had to stick to painting geometric representations. The guard shows you the kitchen *(mutfak)* and refectory, the wine and oil reservoirs, bathroom and the crypt. If you're nice, the guide may also point out a small hole in the ground which seems to be nine metres deep from which a gentle wind always issues (he puts a little pinwheel in it to show you). No-one yet knows where the hole leads or what other rooms and tunnels there may be in this labyrinth, though explorations are continuing.

Sultan Marshes Bird Sanctuary

Well over 250 species of birds visit the Sultansazlığı Kuş Cenneti (Sultan Marshes Bird Paradise), 60 km north-east of Niğde (80 km south-west of Kayseri), east of the Kayseri-Niğde highway south of Yeşilhisar. Though little developed for tourism, bird-fanciers may want to explore the marshes and seek out the observation tower at Ovaçiftlik, on the road to Yahyalı. It offers good views across the marshy lake Eğri Göl, and a little

museum with exhibits on the local bird life. Birds you may encounter include cranes, eagles, herons, spoonbills and storks. North of Eğri Göl is Yay Gölü, a lake noted for its populations of flamingos.

Places to Stay

Should you want to stay, Niğde can offer several small hostelries. There are restaurants near the otogar and also the *Hotel Stad* (☎ (483) 17865), Terminal Caddesi 6, charging US$15 for a double with bath.

Otel Evim (☎ (483) 11860), Hükümet Meydanı, has simple rooms with private baths (showers and short tubs) and balconies. The hotel is in the midst of everything, has a lift, and charges a reasonable US$15/22 a single/double, breakfast included. When you search for it, look for the Türkiye Halk Bankası, which is easier to see than the neighbouring hotel.

Otel Murat (☎ (483) 13978), İstasyon Caddesi 46, Belediye Yanı, has a façade on the main street but its entrance is at the back near the clock tower. Well kept, clean and quite presentable like the Hotel Evim, this hotel has no lift, no large lobby and no tubs (only showers) in the rooms and so charges less: US$14/18 a single/double.

Hotel Taciroğlu (☎ (483) 13047), a half-block from the Otel Murat at İstasyon Caddesi 55, is comparable but cheaper.

Niğde Oteli (☎ (483) 11826, 11208), İstasyon Caddesi 83, at the clock-tower end of İstasyon Caddesi, is clean (with over-enthusiastic help) but passable, and certainly cheap: rooms with washbasin cost US$4/6 a single/double.

İpek Palas Oteli (☎ (483) 18255), to the right of the old Belediye building near the clock tower, has presentable, simple rooms with clean sheets (but no running water) for US$3/5 a single/double.

Places to Eat

Besides the restaurants near the otogar, you might try the *Niğde Şehir Lokantası*, to the right of the Pamukbank on İstasyon Caddesi; it's closed on Sunday, though. The *Aile*

Pastanesi, near the statue of Atatürk on the main square, has an outdoor shaded terrace.

Getting There & Away

Niğde's otogar has buses to most nearby destinations, but perhaps only one or two per day. There is frequent service to Adana (205 km, 3½ hours, US$6), Aksaray (115 km, two hours, US$3.50), Kayseri (130 km, 1½ hours, US$3.50) and Konya (250 km, 3½ hours, US$8).

Service to Nevşehir (85 km, 1½ hours) is fast and frequent, with minibuses departing from the otogar every hour on the hour from 5 am to 6 pm.

CAPPADOCIAN VALLEYS

East out of Nevşehir, the rolling terrain is sandy. After a few km the panorama of Cappadocia begins to unfold: distant rock formations become visible as fairy chimneys, and valleys with undulating walls of soft volcanic ash fall away from the road. In the distance, the gigantic snow-capped peak of the volcano, Erciyes Dağı (Mt Aergius), floats above a layer of cloud.

No matter where you make your base, several moonscape valleys with painted churches and troglodyte dwellings will draw your attention. The Göreme Valley is the most famous of these, but nearby Zelve is less touristy, and the valleys at Soğanlı even less so. Here are descriptions of these Cappadocian wonders, followed by details of places which make convenient base camps: Göreme Village, Ürgüp, Avanos, Gülşehir and Hacıbektaş.

Dolmuşes run from some of the villages to the Göreme Valley in summer. From Ürgüp, look for the Göreme Müze dolmuş at the otogar. It leaves when it fills up and costs US$1. Avanos Belediyesi buses travel the route from Avanos via Çavuşin, Göreme and Uçhisar to Nevşehir every 30 minutes in summer from 6.45 am to 6.15 pm, for US$1.

Tours of the sights in the region are offered by several agencies for around US$10 to US$15 per person, and considering the heat of the sun and the difficulties of transport, it's not a bad idea. The catch, of course, is that you spend some of your valuable time sitting in shops to which the minibus has brought you. The tour company gets as much as 30% commission on everything you buy in the shops. But the tea is free and the 'shopping' can be just a rest from walking in the sun. If you don't want to waste time in a shop, find a company which does not have the enforced shopping.

To hire an entire taxi or minibus, with driver, for a full-day tour of all Cappadocia, starting at Ürgüp or Nevşehir, costs from US$50 to US$80.

Whichever way you go, wear flat shoes for going up the metal-rung ladders and stairways, and take a torch (flashlight) if you have one. Refreshments, snacks and light meals are available at all of the valleys.

Göreme Valley

Of all the Cappadocian valleys, Göreme is without doubt the most famous, and rightly so. Approaching it from the Ortahisar inter section by the Hotel Lapis Inn, the road descends steeply into a maze of little valleys, ridges and cones. The rich flood plain of each valley blazes with bright patches of green crops or is dotted with tidy rows of grapevines. Halfway down the hill, 1.7 km from the Hotel Lapis Inn, is the entrance to the **Göreme Açık Hava Müzesi** or Göreme Open-Air Museum, open from 8.30 am to 5.30 pm. Admission costs US$3. Parking for cars costs US$1, for motorcycles and mopeds it's about 40c.

It's easy to spend most of a day walking the paths here, climbing stairways or passing through tunnels to reach the various churches. The primitive 11th-century paintings and frescoes in several are outstanding. In between churches, the utter improbability of the landscape floods over you: the lovely, soft textures in the rock, the fairytale cave dwellings, the spare vegetation growing vigorously from the stark but mineral-rich soil. If you're smart, you'll get to the valley early in the morning in summer and space yourself between tour groups. When lots of people crowd into one of these little churches they block the doorway, which is often the only source of light. They then 'look at the paintings' in the dark!

Walking into the valley from the entrance, you come first to the **Rahibeler Manastırı**, or Nun's Convent, a large plain room with some steps up to a smaller domed chapel with frescoes. Across the way is the similar Monk's Monastery. From this point you can follow a loop path around the valley in either direction. Here are the sights you come to if you walk clockwise.

The path winds past various vistas and unmarked churches; the large grooves in the church floor are burial crypts. The **Çarıklı Kilise** or Sandal Church is named for the 'sandals' in the floor opposite the doorway. This one has lots of good frescoes, especially one showing Judas's betrayal (in the arch over the door to the left). Near the Sandal Church is a small unmarked chapel with a fresco of a man on horseback – St George, no doubt.

The **Karanlık Kilise** or Dark Church, among the most famous and fresco-filled, is currently undergoing two years of restoration work by Turkish and Italian artisans. It will probably be open by the time you visit. The church took its name from its former condition when it had very few windows. The lack of light preserved the vivid colour of the frescoes which, among others, include scenes of Christ as Pantocrator, Christ on the cross and his betrayal by Judas. Past the Dark Church is a **refectory** with tables and benches cut right from the rock.

The **Yılanlı Kilise**, Snake Church or Church of the Dragon, has frescoes on part of the vault and iconoclast designs on the other. On the left wall, St George and St Theodore attack the dragon yet again.

The **Barbara Kilise**, or Church of St Barbara, is a good example of the severely plain decoration used during the iconoclastic period (725-842) when images were outlawed. There are a few fairly worn post-iconoclast frescoes of the Virgin Mary and St Barbara. On the right are three more chapels, with carved crosses in the apse and primitive line drawings.

The **Elmalı Kilise** or Apple Church has a

Karanlık Kilise (Dark Church)

stunning display of frescoes. There are eight small domes and one large one, and lots of well-preserved paintings. Where's the apple? Some say the Angel Gabriel, above the central nave, is holding it.

The last church on the loop is that of **St Basil**, with somewhat disappointing frescoes.

Outside the enclosure and down the hill a few steps along the road is the **Tokalı Kilise** or Buckle Church, among the biggest and finest of the Göreme churches, with frescoes telling the stories of Christ's miracles. There's a little chapel downstairs. If a guardian is not on duty and the gate to the church is locked, get someone to come. Then get them to turn on the lights (*ışıklar*, uh-shuk-LAHR).

Farther down the hill and along the road to Göreme Village are many more churches, most minor and unimpressive. The region once had hundreds of little chapels. Signs point the way to the **Nazar Kilise** and the **Saklı Kilise**, which are worth a visit.

Göreme Village (formerly called Avcılar), 1.5 km east of the Open-Air Museum, is small but busy with backpackers, farm wagons and tractors. If you take the time to explore the village's winding streets, you will see many buildings carved in the rock. There's even a flour mill.

Çavuşin & Zelve

From Göreme Village, the Avanos road leads north four km to Çavuşin, with its **Church of John the Baptist** near the top of the cliff which rises behind the village. A half-km north of the village, along the road, is the **Çavuşin Church** (look for the iron stairway).

A side road from Çavuşin heads up another valley five km to Zelve, which is almost as rich in churches and strange panoramas as Göreme, but much less well organised. Halfway along the road are groupings of curious 'three-headed' fairy chimneys near a row of souvenir stalls. If you're walking from Göreme Village, a footpath starts from Çavuşin and saves you a few km to the road junction, but it is more difficult walking on the path than on the road; take your pick. Zelve is seven km from Avanos, by the way.

Zelve was a monastic retreat. Opening hours are from 8.30 am to 5.30 pm and admission costs US$2. The several valleys here do not have nearly as many impressive painted churches, though there are a few you should see. They are marked by signs.

The **Balıklı Kilise** or Fish Church has fish figuring in one of the primitive paintings, and the more impressive **Üzümlü Kilise** or Grape Church has obvious bunches of grapes, but mostly iconoclastic decoration. Look also for the **Değirmen** (Mill). Unfortunately, erosion continues to destroy the structures in the valley, and some parts may be closed because of the danger of collapse.

There are restaurants and tea gardens just outside the archaeological site for refreshments.

Valley of the Fairy Chimneys

From Zelve, go 400 metres back down the access road and turn right on a paved road marked for Ürgüp. Two km brings you to the village of **Aktepe** (Yeni Zelve), where you'll find the *Yörem Restaurant* with simple Turkish food at simple prices. Bear right, follow the Ürgüp road further uphill and, after less than two km, you'll find yourself in the Valley of the Fairy Chimneys (Peribacalar Vadisi).

Though many Cappadocian valleys hold collections of strange volcanic cones, these are the best formed and most thickly clustered. Most of the rosy rock cones are topped by flattish, darker stones which have caused the cones to form. Being harder rock, the dark cap-stones sheltered the cones from the rains which eroded all the surrounding rock, a process known to geologists as differential erosion.

As of this writing the valley is open and free, but the local authorities scenting a tourist dollar gone unseized, will no doubt soon erect a ticket kiosk and charge an admission fee.

If you continue to the top of the ridge, you will find yourself on the Avanos-Ürgüp road, with Avanos to the left, Ürgüp to the right. By the way, a sign here indicates that it's three km to Zelve, when in fact it is more than five.

Uçhisar

Uçhisar, 15 km east of Nevşehir and five km south-west of Göreme Village, is dominated by the Kale ('castle'), a tall rock outcrop riddled with tunnels and windows, and visible for miles around. Now a tourist attraction (open from 8 am to 8.30 pm in summer for US$1), it provides panoramic views of the Cappadocian valleys and countryside. There is less to see and do in Uçhisar than in villages such as Göreme and Ürgüp, but that also means there are fewer tourists.

Places to Stay Uçhisar also has its own collection of little pensions, hotels and restaurants, many especially popular with French tourists. The *Hakan Pension & Res-*

taurant is in the centre not far from the Kale. Down by the PTT on the edge of Güvercinlik Valley is the *Pension Méditerranée*, fairly fancy (more like a hotel) but with fabulous views and a nice roof restaurant. The *Villa Motel Pansion* (☎ (4856) 1089), on the other side of the PTT, is a nice stone building. The *Erciyes Pension* (☎ (4856) 1090) next door is similar. Beyond these is the *Kaya Otel* (☎ (4856) 1007), carved into the volcanic tufa, and formerly operated by Club Med. Its *Bindallı Restaurant* is Uçhisar's best. Beyond the Kaya is the *Başaran Pension* (☎ (4856) 1222) which advertises its *vue superbe sur la vallée*.

Mustafapaşa

Called Sinasos when it was an Ottoman Greek town before WW I, Mustafapaşa is today the relatively undiscovered gem of Cappadocia. Stop and have a look around, ask at the tourism office for the keys to the old churches, and relax. A good hotel is the *Hotel Cavit* (☎ (4868) 5186), run by a retired army officer, where for US$7 per person per day you get a family-style welcome and breakfast of fresh milk from the cow and home-made fruit preserves from the orchard.

Soğanlı

This valley, about 35 km south of Ürgüp via Mustafapaşa and Güzelöz, is much less touristy than Göreme or Zelve. But the pressure of tour buses is getting so bad at these places that the tour operators are searching for new parking places and Soğanlı may be one of them. Even so, it's an interesting and beautiful place to explore. It is not easy to get to by public transportation, however. Try to find a dolmuş from the otogar in Nevşehir or Ürgüp, but this is chancy. Otherwise you'll have to take a taxi or hitch.

The valleys of Aşağı Soğanlı (Lower Onion Valley) and Yukarı Soğanlı (Upper Onion Valley) were, like Göreme and Zelve, largely monastic. Turn off the main road and proceed five km to the village, where signs point out the **Tokalı Kilise** or Buckle Church on the right, reached by a steep flight of worn steps, and the **Gök Kilise** or Sky Church to the left across the stream bed. Follow the signs, walk up the stream bed 50 metres, then go up on the left to the church. The Gök is a twin-nave church, with the two naves separated by columns, ending in apses. The double frieze of saints is badly worn.

At the point where the valleys divide, the villagers have posted a billboard map indicating the churches by number. The village square is to the left. In the village square are the Soğanlı and Cappadocia restaurants, toilets, shops and a telephone.

The churches are open from 8.30 am to 5 or 6 pm with a break for lunch; an admission fee of 50c to US$1 is payable at each church. The churches, listed according to the villagers' numbering scheme, follow:

1 Ballık (Honey-Hive)
> This church is of little interest.
2 Tokalı
> described in Soğanlı section
3 Gök
> described in Soğanlı section
4 Karabaş (Black Head)
> In the right-hand valley, this church is covered in paintings showing the life of Christ and also Gabriel and various saints. Look for the pigeon in the fresco, showing the local influence. Pigeons were very important to the monks, who wooed them with dovecotes cut in the rock.
>
> The dovecote across from the Karabaş Kilise has white paint around its small window entrances to attract the birds; the sides of the entrance are smoothed so the birds cannot alight, but must enter. Inside, a grid of poles provides roosting space for hundreds of birds which dump manure by the kg onto the floor below. The monks gathered the manure, put it on the grapevines and got the sweetest grapes and the best wine for miles around.
>
> In the yard between the church and the dovecote is a refectory, with tandoor ovens in the ground (note the air-holes for the fires). The monks lived apart but dined communally.
5 Kübbeli & Saklı (Cupola & Hidden Churches)
> These two churches are also in the right-hand valley, across the stream bed and high on the far hillside. The Kübbeli is interesting because of its unusual Eastern-style cupola. The Hidden Church is just that – hidden from view until you get close.
6 Yılanlı (Snake Church)
> Farthest up the right-hand valley, this church has

frescoes darkened by smoke and age, but you can still make out the serpent to the left as you enter.

7 Geyikli (Deer Church)
This is up the left-hand valley, above the village square, but it's not very impressive.

8 Tahtalı (Wooden Church)
The farthest of the churches up the left-hand valley, it is also dull.

Yellow Caravanserai

The Seljuk-era Yellow Caravanserai (Sarı Han) is six km east of Avanos along a road marked for it. It was restored in the late 1980s, and is now open as a museum from 9 am to 1 pm and 2 to 6 pm every day, for US$1. The elaborate Seljuk portal is, as usual, quite impressive. Inside, it is the standard plan with a large court where animals were loaded and unloaded, and a great hall where people and animals could escape the weather. Above the portal is a small mosque. If you climb to the top of the walls, try to ignore the liberal use of concrete in the restoration.

GÖREME VILLAGE

Göreme Village (Göreme Köyü), set among towering tufa cones and honeycomb cliffs and surrounded by vineyards and fields, is a magical place. At dawn and dusk the swifts dart, swoop and dive amidst the cones before settling into their niches cut from the rock. There is much birdlife in Göreme because there are lots of places for birds to nest.

This village, 1.5 km west of the Göreme Open-Air Museum, grew explosively during the 1980s as Turkey's tourism boom swept over it. What was once a sleepy farming village named Avcılar is now chock-a-block with little pensions, camping grounds and restaurants. It is the prime place to stay for those travelling on a budget because the beds and meals are cheap and good and the sights are within walking distance.

Information

There is a little local tourist office across from the bus station and the Belediye – go there with any complaints about local businesses. Göreme Village's postal code is 50180.

Places to Stay

Pensions are found everywhere in the village and along the road to the Göreme Open-Air Museum. Prices for beds range from US$3 to US$5 or even US$8 or US$9 per person, but most are of the cheaper variety. Many pensions have areas where you can camp for even less money. Rooms cut into the volcanic tufa are a bit claustrophobic but far cooler than rooms in modern buildings.

Travellers arriving in Göreme head for the favoured few pensions recommended in guidebooks. Off-season, these places get most of the business and can afford to be well-kept and well-run. In summer, they fill up early and often, and the overflow spills into the lesser places. Pension owners have formed a cooperative which has an office near the bus station in Göreme. Find the office and you'll get guidance to the various pensions in town.

Perhaps the most popular lodging with backpackers is Mustafa and Ruth Yelkalan's *Rock Valley Pension* (☎ (4857) 1153), well up the valley from the village centre. Part of the allure is the price (US$9 for a waterless double), also the good meals (many vegetarian) available from the kitchen.

Köse Pansiyon (☎ (4857) 1294), also well up the valley, is run by Mehmet and Dawn Köse and has hosted backpackers for years. It's very plain, with beds on the floor village-style; there's a dining room and camping ground as well. Rates are low – US$9 a double for waterless rooms.

Other good pensions up at this end of the valley include the *Keleş Cave Pension* (☎ (4857) 1152) and the *Tabiat (Natural) Pansion*.

The *SOS Motel-Pansiyon-Restaurant* (☎ (4857) 1134) has two types of lodgings: the pension with beds in dorms at US$5 each, or 'motel' rooms with private showers for US$14 a double. Modest but attractive in the Greek Islands way, it has some rooms carved from the rock. Look for it near the popular but posh Ataman Restaurant.

Just down the road from the SOS is the *Halil Carved Pansiyon*, which is similar, with some rooms carved right from the rock.

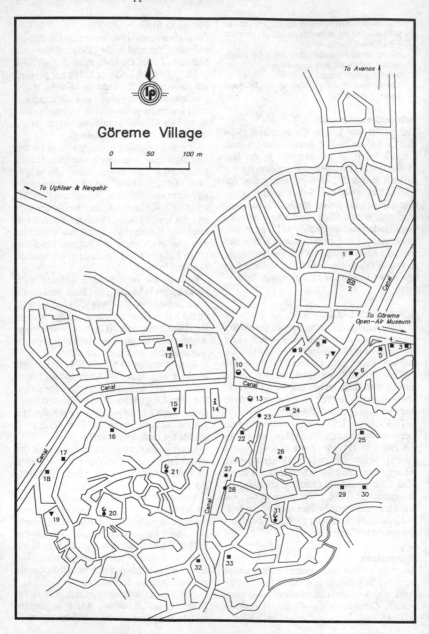

Göreme Village

0   50   100 m

To Avanos ↑

To Uçhisar & Nevşehir

To Göreme
Open-Air Museum

■ PLACES TO STAY

1   Tan Pansiyon
3   Peri's Pansiyon
4   Ufuk (Horizon) Pension
5   Paradise Pension
8   Esen Pension
9   Turkish House Pension
11 Köşk Pension
12 Asma Pension
16 Kemer Pansiyon
17 SOS Motel-Pansiyon-Restaurant
18 Halil Carved Pansiyon
22 Göreme Pension
24 Star Pension
25 Cave Hotel Melek
29 Sarıhan Motel Pansion
30 Arif Pension
32 Köse Pansiyon
33 Rock Valley Pension

▼ PLACES TO EAT

6   Pizza Tardelli
7   Yöre Spaghetti Evi
15 Mehmet Paşa Restaurant
17 SOS Motel-Restaurant-Pansiyon
19 Ataman Restaurant

    OTHER

2   PTT
13 Dolmuş Station
14 Tourism Information
10 Otogar
20 Aydınlık Camii
21 Orta Cami
23 Belediye (Municipality)
26 Castle (Kale)
27 Garden
28 Fountain
31 Gaferli Camii

Tan Pansiyon (☎ (4857) 1445), operated by the assistant mayor of the town, is very friendly, and charges US$7 for a clean double room with shower. Meals are good here as well.

For more comforts, try the *Cave Hotel Melek* (☎ & fax (4857) 1463), 150 metres uphill from the main street. You enter a small multi-level courtyard, then a village-style lounge with low seats and a fireplace adjoin-

ing the dining room. Guest rooms, in the buildings or carved into the tufa, cost US$13 a waterless double and US$13/18 a single/ double with private shower, breakfast included. The Melek takes Dutch groups, and may be full.

Just a few dozen metres uphill from the Melek is the similarly quiet and comfortable *Sarıhan Motel Pansion* (☎ (4857) 1216), with good views of the town and rock-cut rooms for US$13/18 a single/double, breakfast included.

Tuna Pension (☎ (4857) 1376) has Turkish-English management, hot water, clean beds and cave-style rooms, a laundry, and a single price of US$4 per person.

Ufuk (Horizon) Pension (☎ (4857) 1157), run by Mr İsmail Arığ, has received several good reports from readers. Rooms cost US$7 a double with shower. Also good is the *Esen Pension* (☎ (4857) 1278), for the same prices.

Other pensions which readers have liked in the past include the *Divan*, *Kemer* and *Peri's Pansiyon*.

For charming but slightly pricier accommodation, see the following descriptions of the Ataman and Mehmet Paşa restaurants.

Camping Several readers have recommended the *Dilek Camping*, 50 metres along the road to Göreme Open-Air Museum. The facilities are clean, the staff are friendly, and there's a swimming pool, which is comforting after a hot hike-filled day. The price for a tent and two persons is US$4.

Places to Eat

Most pensions in Göreme provide meals and most are similar – good and cheap. Most eateries in the town serve wine and beer.

Yöre Spaghetti Evi, on the main street, is popular with budget travellers who enjoy its good sunset views, though the food is not particularly cheap. A plate of dolma (stuffed vine leaves) costs over US$1, as does a beer. The *Sedef Restaurant* next door has a nice roof terrace.

Pizza Tardelli (☎ 1330), across the main street, is plain but not unpleasant, with big windows, some streetside tables, and a menu listing roast chicken, pizzas, spaket bolonez (spaghetti Bolognese), Turkish favourites, and wine and beer.

Mehmet Paşa Restaurant (☎ (4857) 1207; fax 1463) is in the Konak Türk Evi (Turkish Mansion-House), a nicely restored Cappadocian grandee's house (1825) with an open-air terrace and several charming dining rooms (some in the harem), and a bar. The menu lists a mixture of Turkish, Ottoman and continental specialities. You can expect to spend from US$8 to US$15 for a full meal. There are several rooms for rent as well.

The *Ataman Restaurant* (☎ 1310; fax 1313), up the valley behind the village in rock-hewn chambers is the most touristy. Clearly aimed at the bus-tour clientele who arrive frequently and abundantly, it provides good food and service in pleasant and certainly unusual surroundings.

The rock-hewn dining rooms are decorated with Turkish crafts. The menu is limited but passable; wine and beer are served. Expect to spend from US$6 to US$10 per person for a full meal with drinks here. There are 38 rooms for rent here as well.

Getting Around

Öz Cappadocia Tour (☎ (4857) 1159), by the bus station in the centre of the village, is one of several agencies in Göreme which rents mountain bikes, mopeds and motorcycles. Its prices for eight-hour rentals are fairly typical: US$8/10 for an old/new bicycle, US$14 for a moped (fuel included), US$30 for a motorcycle (fuel included). You must leave your passport as a security deposit.

Rainbow Ranch, uphill on the way to the Cave Hotel Melek, rents horses and organises excursions into the countryside. Contact the staff for prices and schedules.

ORTAHİSAR

The village of Ortahisar, about three km south-east of the Göreme Valley, is near the intersection of the Nevşehir to Ürgüp and Göreme roads. A Cappadocian farming village at heart, Ortahisar's new-found

importance comes from its strategic location so close to the access roads and the famous painted churches. From Ortahisar you can hike to various lesser churches in the surrounding countryside.

Ortahisar's postal code is 50650.

Places to Stay

The village centre, 1.5 km from the intersection, has several small pensions. Try the *Dönmez* and the *Gümüş* on the street by the PTT, the *Yalçın* (on the way to Ürgüp) and the more comfortable *Hotel Göreme* (☎ (4869) 1005) on the main square, a simple but clean, airy and cheerful place renting rooms with new tiled baths for US$10/12/15 a single/double/triple. If it's full, try the *Hotel Selçuk* across the street.

Hotel Yükseller (☎ (4869) 1450; fax 1451), Kayseri Caddesi, Ürgüp Yolu, is fairly fancy at US$30 a double, but for this you get a swimming pool, comfy bath-equipped room, and a quite good restaurant.

Ortahisar's prime place to stay is the very comfortable four-star, 252-room *Hotel Lapis Inn* (☎ (4869) 1470; fax 1480), Göreme Kavşağı, Ortahisar, 50560 Ürgüp, Nevşehir. It's right at the Göreme turn-off on the Ürgüp-Nevşehir road.

A large, box-like, modern place, it features a rich use of black-and-white marble and polished limestone in the spacious lobby. Rooms have dark wooden furniture, twin beds and bathrooms with marble vanities, and tub and shower baths.

Hotel services include a TV lounge, games room, piano bar, restaurant and a large shopping area. Rates, including breakfast, are US$40/54/65 a single/double/triple, US$80 for a 'suite' (a larger double room with TV and minibar).

You can walk the two km to the Göreme Valley easily from here.

ÜRGÜP

Twenty-three km east of Nevşehir and seven km east of Göreme Valley is the town of Ürgüp (population 10,000, altitude 1060 metres), at the very heart of the Cappadocian wonderland. Life in Ürgüp is divided between farming and tourism, and a hotel might share a stretch of land with a vineyard or alfalfa field. Because of the volcanic soil, sufficient water and abundant sunshine, the town is surrounded by a rich landscape of grain fields, vineyards and clusters of beehives.

Many of the buildings in the town are made of the local tawny limestone with a pronounced grain. Some of the older houses have fine bits of carved stone decoration. Quite a number of Ürgüp's citizens still live or work, at least part of the time, in spaces carved out of the rock. Ürgüp's main street has a sprinkling of antique and carpet shops, a Tourism Information Office and several restaurants.

Information & Orientation

Ürgüp is a small town and, with the help of the map in this book, you'll find your way around in no time. The Tourism Information Office (☎ (4868) 1059) is at Kayseri Caddesi 37, down the hill from the main square behind a garden. The town's museum is right next door and is open every day from 8.30 am to 5.30 pm.

Turkish Bath

Near the otogar is the Tarihi Şehir Hamamı (☎ (4868) 2241), Cami Karşısı, a historic building (1902) of uncertain provenance. It looks as though it may once have been a small church. Today it is a thoroughly touristy hamam with touristy prices: US$8 for a bath. Men and women are admitted together, which never happens in traditional hamams.

Wine Festival

The abundant sunshine and volcanic soil of Cappadocia are excellent for viticulture, resulting in delicious sweet grapes. Several small local wineries have carried on the Ottoman Greek tradition of making wine from Cappadocia's grapes. Ürgüp puts on a wine festival and tasting during the first week in June, when you can sample the products of small wineries such as Turasan, Duyurgan Bağcılık and Yemenici, and the

large quasi-governmental Tekel, during the festival at special events. Contact the Tourism Information Office for details.

Several wines are available anytime in bottles, such as Turasan's Peribaca light red, Duyurgan's dry white Algan, the hearty red Cappadocia from Mustafapaşa, and Tekel's Ürgüp white and Çubuk red, both quite cheap. Tekel has a *satış yeri* (sales point) on Suat Hayri Ürgüplü Caddesi across from the Ürgüp Oteli.

Places to Stay – bottom end

Ürgüp has numerous pensions in which you can get a bed in a clean but spartan room for about US$3 to US$5 per person. The prime area for cheap pensions and hotels is the quarter called Sivritaş Mahallesi, especially Güllüce and Elgin sokaks.

Güllüce Sokak is the street south of Kayseri Caddesi, the main street. Four pensions here charge US$3.50/5.50 for a waterless single/double room. Coming from the centre, you first reach the *Hotel Kuzey* (☎ (4868) 1874), which also has a double bedded room with private shower for US$7.50. Breakfast costs another US$1.40 per person. Next along is the *Sarıhan Pension* (☎ (4868) 2264), then the *Merkez Hotel Pension* (☎ (4868) 2746), at No 14. Look for the similar *Sepetçi Pansiyon* next.

The *Hotel Anatolia* (☎ (4868) 1487), on Kayseri Caddesi one block north of the Sepetçi Pansiyon, is a similarly priced place that's a favourite with backpackers despite the road noise.

The cheapest place on Elgin Sokak is the *Family Pansion Villa* (☎ (4868) 1906), which is OK inside, though not much to look at from the outside. Doubles cost US$10/14 without/ with bath. You can camp in the garden for much less.

Hotel Divan (dee-VAHN) (☎ (4868) 1705), Elgin Sokak 4, has its own tiny camping area in the garden, as well as rooms for US$5 to US$8 a single, US$10 to US$15 a double, US$12 to US$17 a triple. The higher prices are for rooms with shower.

Hotel Eyfel (☎ (4868) 1325), Elgin Sokak

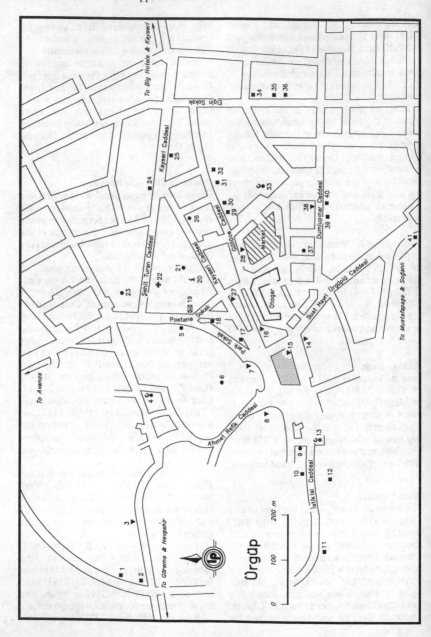

Ürgüp

8, is the class act on the street, with a tiny swimming pool.

The watering hole raises the prices somewhat but all of the rooms have private

showers and cost US$12/17/20 a single/double/triple. Campers can pitch their tents at the back of the house.

On Dumlupınar Caddesi south of the market are several hotels, most of them not cheap, with the exception of the *Kale Otel* (KAH-leh) (☎ (4868) 1069), Dumlupınar Caddesi 29, on the upper floor. It has double rooms with sink for US$8, or US$11 with private shower.

The *Yeni Hitit Hotel* (hee-TEET) (☎ (4868) 3131; fax 8565), Dumlupınar Caddesi 47, offers outstanding value for money. Well-kept and moderately priced, it has clean rooms – some with one double and one single bed – with showers and marvellously kitschy fairy-chimney nightlights, for US$14/19 a single/double, breakfast included.

Up the street from the otogar past the Turkish bath are more pensions. The *Hotel Asia Minor* (☎ (4868) 1645; fax 1520), İstiklal Caddesi 38, also called the Küçük Asya, is a nice stone village house converted to lodgings. Rooms are tiny but the showers are OK and the front terrace is a good place to take it easy. Prices are moderate at US$11/16 a single/double, with shower.

Also up the hill on a side street past the Turkish bath is the *Hotel Elvan* (☎ (4868) 1191, 1291), Dutlu Cami Mahallesi, Barbaros Hayrettin Sokak 11, a pension run by Ahmet and Fatma Bilir. Rooms are in odd places around a small courtyard; some are carved from the stone, with vaulted ceilings and wall niches. All are well kept, with tidy tiled showers and plenty of hot water. Prices are US$12/18 a single/double; breakfast costs an extra $2 per person.

The *Göreme Pansiyon* and *Hotel Şato* (☎ (4868) 1146) are two halves of the same building just off Kayseri Caddesi. A homy, quiet place decorated with lots of carpets, kilims and cicims, its rooms are fairly cool in summer. They cost US$12/18 a single/double, but the owner is often ready to haggle over a lower rate.

Hotel Park (☎ (4868) 1883), Avanos Caddesi 20, across the street from the PTT, is simple but comfortable, with some good views of the countryside. East-facing rooms have balconies, but the street out the front can be noisy. Prices for rooms with shower are US$12/18 a single/double, breakfast included.

Camping Many of the small pensions mentioned will allow you to pitch your tent and use all of their facilities for a very low fee.

Places to Stay – middle

Want to live in a cave? Of the many troglodytic hotels, the best is the *Esbelli Pension* (☎ (4868) 3395; fax 8848), Turban Girişi, Çeşme Karşısı, up the long hill from the main square, across the road from the big Turban Motel. The Esbelli, an old village house parts of which reputedly date from Roman times, has been lovingly restored and now boasts rooms with modern baths, a sun deck-terrace, and a modern kitchen at your disposal. Rates are US$35/50 a single/double, excellent breakfast included.

The *Hotel Alfina* (☎ (4868) 1822; fax 2424), on İstiklal Caddesi on the road into town from Nevşehir, a 10-minute walk back up the hill from the otogar, also has cave rooms. The Alfina can truly be called troglodytic, with 32 comfortable rooms hewn from the volcanic rock (the cutter's tool marks are still visible). Each room has one small window, clean modern baths and there's a pleasant terrace restaurant so you can escape from your cave-person existence now and then. The price, at US$28/38 a single/double, is hardly prehistoric, but how many times do you get the chance to live in a cave? This place is not for claustrophobes, though.

Hotel Surban (☎ (4868) 1603; fax 2025), Yunak Mahallesi, PO Box 55, is uphill on the road towards Nevşehir – a walk from the centre – near the Hanedan Restaurant. New and comfortable, it offers value for money: good rooms with bath for US$24, breakfast included.

The *Taşsaray Hotel* (☎ (4868) 2344, 2444), Mustafapaşa Caddesi 10, made of tawny sandstone, is 400 metres from the otogar along the Mustafapaşa road. It's a comfortable, modern hotel with restaurant,

lobby and lift; each room has a bath and a balcony. Some have nice views. Prices are moderate at $42 a double with shower, breakfast included.

Places to stay – top end

Most of Ürgüp's fancier hotels are one to two km out of town along Kayseri Caddesi. Best of the lot is the four-star, 230-room *Perissia Hotel* (☎ (4868) 2930; fax 1524), PO Box 68. The hotel's several square, box-like buildings set amidst lawns and gardens echo the local architecture, but provide all the luxury services, including swimming pools, restaurants, bars, and a disco. Rooms cost US$55/70/90 a single/double/triple, breakfast included.

Places to Eat – bottom end

An Ürgüp speciality is kiremit kebap, a large patty of minced lamb baked on a clay tile. The tile draws off some of the grease, and keeps the meat hot after it's served. Other strange ways of cooking lamb, such as saç kavurma (sizzling bits of lamb on a steel parabola like an inverted wok) are also popular here.

On the main square is the *Cappadocia Restaurant* (☎ 1029), with a few outdoor tables and many more indoor, fairly attentive service and decent three-course meals for around US$4 or US$5. The nearby *Sofa Restaurant* (☎ 2300), across the square in the courtyard of an old han provides competition, and many readers prefer it to the Cappadocia. Meals cost about the same.

Cheaper restaurants are found on Dumlupınar Caddesi, south of the market. The *Kent Restaurant*, more or less across the street from the Yeni Hitit Oteli on Dumlupınar Caddesi, has saç kavurma and kebaps sautéed on clay tiles for less than US$2. Next door is the *Kardeşler Pizza Restaurant*, specialising in good cheap pide (for as low as 90c) and kebaps. Both of these restaurants serve breakfast.

Also near the otogar is the *Set Kebap Salonu*, between the otogar and Dumlupınar Caddesi. Besides good cheap kebaps, it has streetside tables, and little nearby traffic.

On Suat Hayri Ürgüplü Caddesi, near the entrance to the otogar, is the *Uğrak Restaurant*, with a few outdoor tables on the busy street corner and full meals for US$3.

For pastries and sweets, there are the *Zümrüt Pasta Salonu* (☎ 1685), Dumlupınar Caddesi 26 and the *Merkez Pastanesi* (☎ 1281), the best in town, on the main square. A large glass of tea (duble çay) and a portion of cake costs around US$1.

Places to Eat – middle

The town's most prominent and fancy place is the *Şömine Cafe & Restaurant* (☎ 8442), which takes its name from the French word *cheminée* (fireplace). Just off the main square, its high terrace provides indoor and outdoor tables. Ürgüp-style kebaps baked on tiles are a speciality. Grilled meats cost from US$2 to US$4, full meals with drinks from US$8 to US$12. The Şömine is open every day from 8 am to midnight.

The *Han Çirağan Restaurant* (☎ 1169, 1621) is at the far end of the main square in an old village stone house behind a vine-covered garden. The plain, vaulted interior dining room is simple but not unpleasant. The menu offers a welcome change from the standard kebaps and ready foods, listing some regional dishes. I had a good dinner of soup, salad, a meat course, melon for dessert and a half-bottle of local wine for less than US$10. If you skip the wine you'll spend much less.

Hungry for fish? That's the speciality at the *Hanedan Restaurant* (☎ 1266), uphill from the centre on the road to Nevşehir. The fish are alive in an aquarium near the entrance. Choose the one you want, and make sure to ask the price first. Full meals cost upwards of US$12 or so.

Getting There & Away

Bus Bus and minibus service is frequent and convenient in high summer with less frequent service in winter. Details of some daily services follow:

Adana – 308 km, six hours, US$10; one bus
Ankara – 308 km, five hours, US$8; at least seven buses in summer
Antalya – 485 km, 11 hours, US$20; at least one bus in summer
İstanbul – 748 km, 11 hours, US$17; at least two buses
Fethiye – 780 km, 14 hours, US$18; at least one bus in summer
Kayseri – 80 km, 1½ hours, US$2.75; hourly minibuses from 7 am to 7 pm
Konya – 250 km, four hours, US$7; at least three buses in summer
Nevşehir – 23 km, 30 minutes, 60c; minibuses every half hour
Pamukkale – 690 km, 11 hours, US$13; at least one bus in summer

Getting Around

Minibuses run the tourist circuit hourly each day from June to September, departing from Ürgüp for the Göreme Valley, Göreme Village, Zelve, Avanos etc. You can hop on and off anywhere around the loop, but each ride costs 50c.

In summer it's usually fairly easy to hitch-hike as well. Agencies in town rent bicycles, mopeds and motorcycles at prices similar to those given in the Göreme Village section.

Car The major international car companies – Avis, Europcar (National), Hertz and Inter-rent all have franchisees with offices near Ürgüp's main square, within one block of the otogar. For more details on renting cars, see the introductory Getting Around chapter.

AVANOS

North of Göreme, on the banks of the river Kızılırmak, lies Avanos (AH-vah-nohs, population 12,000, altitude 910 metres), famous for pottery making. The town's workshops turn out pots, ashtrays, lamps, chess sets and other utensils and souvenirs moulded from the red clay of the Kızılırmak or Red River. On the outskirts along the Gülşehir road are several tile factories making clay blocks (*tuğla*) and roof-tiles (*kiremit*) for building construction.

For some reason, Avanos is particularly popular with French travellers. Every pension in town is connected in some way with at least one carpet shop, pottery factory or travel agency, or perhaps all three. If you're not staying here overnight, Avanos is a good place to have lunch or at least a çay break. Wander around the town a bit, looking in the workshops.

Avanos has banks, a PTT, pensions, hotels, restaurants, pharmacies and other such necessities.

Information & Orientation

Most of the town is on the north bank of the river, but several pensions are on the south. Besides, the town is small enough for you to get around on foot easily enough. There is a small Tourism Information Office (☎ (4861) 1360). The postal code for Avanos is 50500.

Things to See

Avanos is a handicrafts town and its citizens sponsor the annual Avanos Elsanatları Festivalı (Avanos Handicrafts Festival) for three days in late August.

On the main square, by the shady little park-cum-tea garden, is a marvellous **monument** in a pool. Made entirely of red clay pottery, it shows an amazingly lifelike potter at work. Below it is a scene depicting a woman and a girl weaving a Turkish carpet – another Avanos craft. On the left side is a bearded, short-clad, camera-carrying tourist holding a bunch of grapes and laughing while standing on a huge pair of hands: is this God's gift to Avanos? At the back of the monument is a woman on a donkey with a child peering out of a saddlebag. On the right side is a self-portrait of the monument's creator, H Ömer Taşkın, who finished the work in 1974.

Have a look in one of the **pottery workshops**. Several in the town welcome visitors and even sponsor pottery classes. To find the workshops, go behind (north of) the pottery monument and turn right just after the Şanso-Panso restaurant. Along this street are several potteries, on the way to the Panorama Pension. There are other potteries scattered throughout the town.

The town's **hamam** is in Orta Mahalle, west of the Hotel Venessa, was built at the end of the 1980s with tourists in mind. Named the Alaadin Turkish Bath, it is a Disneyfied version of the traditional style, using local sandstone and red tiles for the roof. As of this writing it's still plagued with heating problems, which may or may not be fixed by the time you arrive.

Excursions

Several travel agencies with offices on the main plaza, including Kirkit Voyages and Point de Rencontre run excursions and tours to other parts of Cappadocia. Kirkit, run by the owners of the Kirkit Pension, is particularly interesting, with one-week treks on foot, by mountain bike or on horseback priced between US$500 and US$600 per person, everything included. Contact the agencies for details.

Özkonak Underground City

North of Avanos is the village of Özkonak, beneath which is a small version of the underground cities to be seen at Kaymaklı and Derinkuyu. It's not nearly so dramatic or impressive as the larger ones, but it is less crowded. The town's muezzin found it in the garden of his house.

Dolmuşes run infrequently from Avanos to Özkonak. Leave Avanos on the Gülşehir road; after 4.5 km, look for a road on the right (badly marked) for Özkonak, 9.5 km farther along. Once you arrive in the village, turn right at a crude sign pointing the way to the Özkonak Yeraltı Şehri (underground city). There is another right turn and, at a fuel station, yet another right. Less than two km brings you to the car park. (You can also reach Özkonak via the main road to Kayseri; a sign points the way.)

The site is open from 8.30 am to 5 pm, more or less; admission costs US$1. The muezzin, Mr Latif Acer, or the site guardian will greet you with bits of German, English or French, and show you to the entrance, right beneath the car park. Take a jumper or jacket and a torch (flashlight) if you have them. The muezzin fixed the place up himself, adding the electric lights. He says that he's shown so many visitors through the chilly rooms that he's contracted rheumatism. The admission fee is a tip given after the tour. He or a boy will take you through, pointing out a room with a wine reservoir

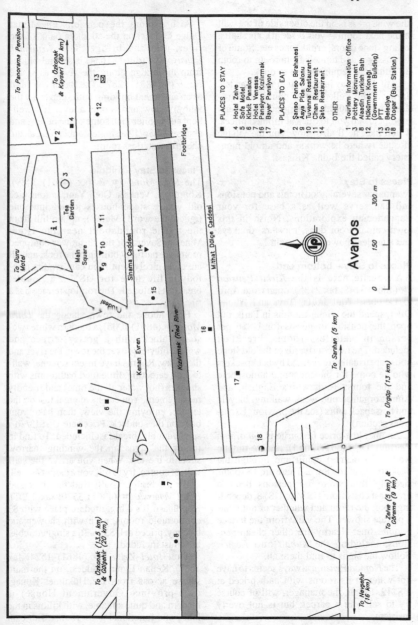

Avanos

0   150   300 m

To Panorama Pension

To Ozkonak & Kayseri (80 km)

Footbridge

To Duru Motel

Main Square

Tea Garden

Sinama Caddesi

Kenan Evren

Kızılırmak (Red River)

Mithat Dölce Caddesi

Ünlesi

To Ozkonak (13.5 km) & Gülşehir (20 km)

To Nevşehir (16 km)

To Zelve (5 km) & Göreme (9 km)

To Orgüp (13 km)

To Sarıhan (5 km)

PLACES TO STAY

4   Hotel Zelve
5   Sofa Motel
6   Kirkit Pension
7   Hotel Venessa
16   Pansiyon Kızılırmak
17   Bayer Pansiyon

PLACES TO EAT

2   Şanso Panso Birahanesi
9   Asya Pide Salonu
10   Tuvanna Restaurant
11   Cihan Restaurant
14   Şato Restaurant

OTHER

1   Tourism Information Office
3   Pottery Monument
8   Alaadin Turkish Bath
12   Hükümet Konağı
     (Government Building)
13   PTT
15   Belediye
18   Otogar (Bus Station)

(the wine press is on the other side of the wall in the next room – you'll see it), air shafts, rolling stone doors, grindstones etc. Some of the passages and tunnels from room to room are quite low, requiring you to duck.

Latif Acer may invite you in for some tea, show you his collection of photos and articles dealing with his underground city and attempt to sell you textiles at inflated prices. If you like, he'll also show you the village mosque (where he works) and an old monastery called the Belha Kilisesi.

Places to Stay

Avanos has several good hotels and pensions and can serve well as a base for your Cappadocian explorations. Noise in this town comes from dogs, roosters, donkeys and a nuclear-powered muezzin.

Places to Stay – bottom end

A favourite here is the *Kirkit Pension* (☎ (4861) 3148; fax 2135), open from April to October. Your hosts, Tovi and Ahmet Diler, spend the winter months in Paris, but open the pension to guests for US$6 per person in waterless rooms, breakfast included. The two courtyards of the old stone house are usually frequented by backpackers who've come for the congenial atmosphere and the tours: Tovi, who's English, and Ahmet organise one-week walking, bicycle and horseback tours (see the previous Excursions section).

Another low-price favourite is *Panorama Pension* (☎ (4861) 1654), a five-minute walk (250 metres) uphill and through the back streets of the town. There are 18 rooms sleeping from two to four persons; bed and breakfast costs from US$4 to US$8, depending upon the room and whether or not it has a private shower. The view from the terrace is quite fine. Nearby are other cheap pensions, including the *Kubalı* and *Kemer*. Follow the signs to find them all.

The *Nomad Pension* always seems to have hot water in its rooms with bath priced at US$12. Erhan, the manager, will of course try to sell you a carpet, but is not overly insistent.

Also explore the pensions on Mithat Dülge Caddesi on the southern bank of the river, near the bridge. The *Kızılırmak Pansiyon* (☎ (4861) 1634) is several blocks from the bridge along the river, as is the *Bayer* (☎ (4861) 1287). The Bayer was built as an apartment building with shop (now the lobby) below and rooms above. It's well-kept and homier than some of the others, and charges US$6/12 a single/double for a clean, cheerful waterless room.

Places to Stay – middle

The *Sofa Motel* (☎ & fax (4861) 1489), Köprübaşı, Venessa Oteli Yanı, is four nice old village stone houses joined into one (ignore the word 'Motel'), up the hill from the traffic roundabout near the Hotel Venessa. Several of the 23 shower-equipped rooms are partially built into the rock, and all are quite nicely kept. You can live the troglodytic life here for US$22 a double, breakfast included. The rooftop terrace has a fine view.

High above the town stands the *Duru Motel* (☎ (4861) 1005), a modern white two-storey block with a grassy terrace and wonderful views over the town, the river and the valley. Rooms have insect screens, wall-to-wall carpeting, little tiled bathrooms with showers (hot water all the time) and friendly management. You can have breakfast on the terrace, enjoying the view, then bake your body on the sundeck. Prices are US$13/20 a single/double, breakfast included. To find it, follow the signs up the winding, narrow street to the top. When you arrive the staff will, of course, try to sell you a carpet as well.

By the bridge you'll find the three-star *Hotel Venessa* (☎ (4861) 3570; fax 1201), Köprübaşı. It's a big, modern place with 83 comfortable rooms, each with shower and balcony, priced at US$26/36 a single/double, breakfast included.

The *Hotel Zelve* (☎ (4861) 1524; fax 1687), Kenan Evren Caddesi, on the main square across from the Hükümet Konağı (Sub-province Government House) is modern and quite suitable, with kilims in the lobby and functional guest rooms with bath going for US$20/30 a single/double, buffet breakfast included.

Across the bridge on the road to Göreme are a number of three and four-star hotels, intended for the group trade but available to individual travellers as well. These include the four-star, 84-room *Hotel Altınyazı* (☎ (4861) 2010; fax 1960), the four-star, 178-room *Hotel Yıltok* (☎ (4861) 2313; fax 1890), and three-star, 46-room *Hotel Palansaray* (☎ (4861) 1844; fax 2079).

Places to Eat

For simple meals, the *Cihan Restaurant* (jee-HAHN) (☎ 1045) on the main square is a popular ready-food and broiled-chicken place open for all three meals, and usually full. Lunch or dinner might cost US$3 or US$4; get there before the food runs out.

The *Sofra Restaurant* (☎ 1324), Hükümet Konağı Karşısı, next to the Hotel Zelve and facing the government building, is similar – nothing fancy, but serviceable.

The *Tuvanna* (☎ 1497) is slightly fancier and more expensive, but not by much, with şiş kebap and small beefsteaks priced from US$3 to US$4, full meals from US$8 to US$12.

Şanso-Panso Birahanesi, up the slope of the main square behind the pottery monument, on the right, serves Efes Pilsen beer and food and is the closest you'll come in Avanos to a taverna. Also here is the *Meydan Pide Salonu*, to the left of the Point de Rencontre travel agency, serves cheap pide at outdoor tables. There's another good, cheap pide place, the *Tafana Pide Salonu* (☎ 1862), Kenan Evren Caddesi 47, a block to the south, nearer to the river.

The *Şato Restaurant* (☎ 1485), on the river just south of the Tuvanna, has a nice situation and decent food for around US$8 to US$10 per person, drinks included. For dinner and entertainment, try the *Dragon Restaurant* (☎ 2170), 1.5 km west of the Hotel Venessa along the Gülşehir road. Popular with tour groups, this cave-club provides food, drink, as well as Turkish folk and belly-dancing most summer evenings.

Expect to spend a total of about US$20 for the entire evening.

For pastries, I like the *Aytemur Pastanesi*, near the Tuvanna, where one of the special banana rolls and a large glass of tea goes for under US$1.

In the evening, the *Bambu Bar*, Atatürk Caddesi 78, just east of the Hotel Venessa and Sofa Motel, is woody and atmospheric.

Getting There & Away

Avanos Belediyesi buses run to Ürgüp and Nevşehir periodically throughout the day.

GÜLŞEHİR

Some 23 km west of Avanos is Gülşehir (population 10,000). It has several unimpressive rock formations on the outskirts: **Karşı Kilise**, or St John Church; an unexcavated underground city; and **Açık Saray**, rock formations with a few insignificant churches. In the centre of the village stands the **Karavezir Mehmet Paşa Camii & Medrese** (1778), an Ottoman mosque and its college (now a library).

Gülşehir has several good hotels, including the fancy Swiss-run *Kepez Hotel* (☎ (4866) 1163; fax 1639), on the flat-top hill in the midst of the town. The Kepez is attractively built of local sandstone, with the finish done by Swiss craftsmen brought in expressly for the job. Rooms have marble floors and showers, with the heating in the floor; reading lights of a special design invented by the hotel's owner and builder, Mr H W Peter; and three cosy restaurants. 'All is to a Swiss standard', says owner Peter. The cost to stay here is US$26 per person, breakfast and dinner included.

Hotel Gülşehir (☎ (4866) 1028), on the northern outskirts by the river, is a three-storey hotel surrounded by greenery, with older rooms in a motel-style block, newer ones in the hotel. Airy, decently furnished rooms with bath go for US$35 a double, breakfast included. It has a camping area and a swimming pool, as well as a restaurant. The hotel is open only during summer.

HACIBEKTAŞ

A clean and pleasant town, Hacıbektaş, (population 10,000) is on the north-western outskirts of the Cappadocian region, 27.5 km west of Gülşehir. It is famous not for its churches or troglodyte dwellings, but as the home of Hacı Bektaş Veli, founder and spiritual leader of the Bektaşi order of dervishes. Born in Nishapur (Iran), Hacı Bektaş (1248?-1337?), inspired a religious and political following that blended aspects of Islam (both Sunni and Shiite) and Orthodox Christianity. Bektaşi Dervishes, who were often scorned by mainstream Islamic clerics, developed a wide following in Ottoman times, attaining considerable political and religious influence. They were outlawed along with all other dervish sects when the Turkish Republic was founded.

The Bektaşi spiritual philosophy developed in the borderlands between the Turkish and Byzantine empires, where guerrilla fighters from both sides had more in common with one another than they did with their sovereigns in Konya or Constantinople. Their liberal beliefs caught on with the common people, and the ideas of the Bektaşis are still an important force in Turkish religious life today. The believers gather in Hacıbektaş each August on pilgrimage to the saint's tomb.

Things to See

There's only one thing to see really, the **Hacı Bektaş Monastery**, officially called the Hacıbektaş Müzesi, open from 8.30 am to 12.30 pm and 1.30 to 5.30 pm, closed on Monday. Admission costs US$1. Plaques are in Turkish, with some in English. Though it's called a museum, you should remember that it is a sacred place.

Several rooms in the museum are arranged as they might have been when the dervishes lived here, including the **Aş Evi**, or kitchen, with its implements; and the **Meydan Evi**, where novice dervishes were inducted into the order. Other rooms have musical instruments, costumes, embroidery, turbans and other artefacts of the order, as well as relevant old photographs.

You can enter the **saint's tomb** in the garden at the far end of the building. Remove your shoes before stepping inside, as this is a place of prayer.

Places to Stay

Across the street from the monastery is a market and shopping complex, and the simple but overpriced *Hotel Hünkar* (☎ (4867) 1344), with clean rooms and telephone-style showers going for US$14 a double. The management is friendly.

Out on the Ankara road, one km from the monastery, is the *Hotel Village House* (☎ 1628, 1046), with 26 modern rooms priced at US$17/22 a single/double, breakfast included. It's a nice little three-storey hotel with restaurant and bar. Guest rooms have balconies and tiny private 'telephone' showers.

KAYSERİ

Once the capital of Cappadocia, Kayseri (KAHY-seh-ree, population 500,000, altitude 1054 metres) is now a booming farm and textile centre. In the shadow of Erciyes Dağı (Mt Aergius, 3916 metres), the sleepy old conservative town surrounding the ancient black citadel became a bustling city of modern, apartment-lined boulevards during the 1980s. These two aspects of Kayseri aren't completely comfortable together, and something remains of old Kayseri's conservative soul.

In Turkish folklore, the people of Kayseri are the crafty dealers. Though every merchant you meet in the bazaar will not fit this image, you are sure to be persecuted by at least one carpet dealer. They hang out where tourists go – in front of hotels, outside the tourist office, near the popular restaurants. On my last visit it took a mere 90 seconds between the time I set foot in the city and when I first heard those dreaded words, 'Hey, wanna buy a carpet?'. Kayseri is at the centre of a region which produces many of Turkey's loveliest carpets, and you may do well shopping here. But if you don't buy, the rug merchant who has been following you for days will be there at the bus station, waving and weeping, as you pull out of town.

If you're passing through on your way to Cappadocia, take a few hours to tour Kayseri, meet some of the very hospitable Kayserilis who are not carpet touts, and visit the many wonderful Seljuk buildings and the nice bazaar. Those heading east might want to see the sights, spend the night, and get an early start the next morning. Besides the sights in town, there are two superb Seljuk caravanserais north-east of the city, off the Sivas road.

History

This was Hittite country, so its history goes way back. The first Hittite capital, Kanesh, was earlier the chief city of the Hatti people. It's at Kültepe, 20 km north-east of Kayseri off the Sivas road. There was probably an early settlement on the site of Kayseri as well, though the earliest traces which have come to light are from Hellenistic times.

Under the Roman emperor Tiberius (14-37 AD), the town received its name, Caesarea, and later became famous as the birthplace of St Basil the Great, one of the early Church Fathers. Its early Christian history was interrupted by the Arab invasions of the 600s and later.

The Seljuks took over in 1084 and held the city until the Mongols' arrival in 1243, except for a brief period when the crusaders captured it on their way to the Holy Land.

After Kayseri had been part of the Mongol Empire for almost 100 years, its Mongol governor set up his own emirate (1335) which lasted a mere 45 years. It was succeeded by another emirate (that of Kadı Burhaneddin), then captured by the Ottomans (seized during the Ottoman interregnum by the Karamanid emirs), later taken by the Mamelukes of Egypt, and finally conquered by the Ottomans again in 1515, all in just over 100 years. Those were exciting times in Kayseri.

Orientation

For orientation, use the black-walled citadel (hisar or İç Kale) at the centre of the old town just south of Cumhuriyet Meydanı, the huge main square. Another convenient point of reference is Düvenönü Meydanı, 350 metres west of the citadel along Park Caddesi. The railway station is at the northern end of Atatürk Bulvarı, over a half km north of Düvenönü Meydanı. Kayseri's otogar is over one km north-west of the citadel (750 metres north-west of Düvenönü Meydanı) along Osman Kavuncu Caddesi. Mimar Sinan Parkı, a vast expanse north of Park Caddesi, has some of the city's most outstanding Seljuk buildings.

Information

The Tourism Information Office (☎ (35) 31 11 90, 31 92 95) is beside the citadel at Kağnı Pazarı Hunat Camii Yanı No 61, open from 8.30 am to 5 pm daily. Follow the signs. Kayseri's postal code is 38000.

Citadel

Many of Kayseri's interesting buildings are either found near the citadel, on Cumhuriyet Meydanı or on Düvenönü Meydanı.

The citadel which has been restored and turned into a tourist shopping bazaar, was built by Emperor Justinian in the 500s, and extensively repaired by the Seljuk sultan Keykavus I around 1224. In 1486, the Ottoman sultan, Mehmet the Conqueror, made major repairs. With Erciyes Dağı looming over the town, it's not surprising that the hisar should be made of black volcanic stone. At several points within the citadel you can climb flights of stairs up to the top of the walls – there are no guardrails, though.

Hunat Mosque & Seminary

Kayseri has several important building complexes which were founded by Seljuk queens and princesses. East of the hisar is a complex which includes the mosque Hunat Hatun Camii (1228), built by the wife of the Seljuk sultan Alaettin Keykubat, plus the tomb of the lady herself, and bits of a Turkish bath.

Next to the mosque is the seminary Hunat Hatun Medresesi (1237), now Kayseri's **Ethnographic Museum** open from 8 am to 5 pm; admission costs US$1. Displays in the

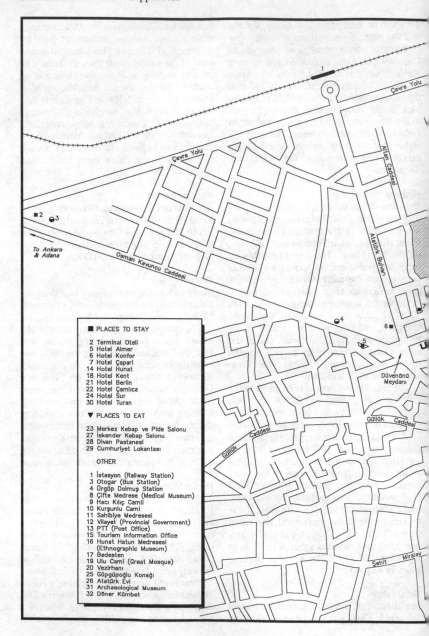

PLACES TO STAY

2 Terminal Oteli
5 Hotel Almer
6 Hotel Konfor
7 Hotel Çapari
14 Hotel Hunat
18 Hotel Kent
21 Hotel Berlin
22 Hotel Çamlıca
24 Hotel Sur
30 Hotel Turan

PLACES TO EAT

23 Merkez Kebap ve Pide Salonu
27 İskender Kebap Salonu
28 Divan Pastanesi
29 Cumhuriyet Lokantası

OTHER

1 İstasyon (Railway Station)
3 Otogar (Bus Station)
4 Ürgüp Dolmuş Station
8 Çifte Medrese (Medical Museum)
9 Hacı Kılıç Camii
10 Kurşunlu Cami
11 Sahibiye Medresesi
12 Vilayet (Provincial Government)
13 PTT (Post Office)
15 Tourism Information Office
16 Hunat Hatun Medresesi
  (Ethnographic Museum)
17 Bedesten
19 Ulu Cami (Great Mosque)
20 Vezirhanı
25 Güpgüpoğlu Konağı
26 Atatürk Evi
31 Archaeological Museum
32 Döner Kümbet

To Ankara & Adana

Çevre Yolu

Altan Caddesi

Atatürk Bulvarı

Osman Kavuncu Caddesi

Düvenönü Meydanı

Güllük Caddesi

Güllük Caddesi

Şehit Miralay

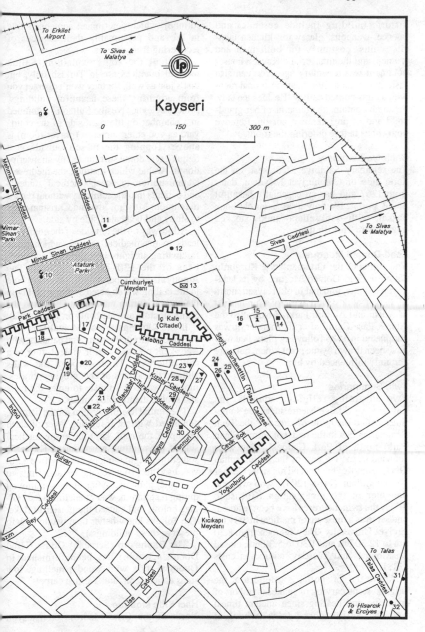

Kayseri

0   150   300 m

To Erkilet Airport

To Sivas & Malatya

To Sivas & Malatya

Mehmet Akif Caddesi

İstasyon Caddesi

Mimar Sinan Parkı

Mimar Sinan Caddesi

Atatürk Parkı

Sivas Caddesi

Cumhuriyet Meydanı

İç Kale (Citadel)

Kaleönü Caddesi

Park Caddesi

Seyit Burhanettin (Talas) Caddesi

Nazmi Toker (Bankalar) Caddesi

Turan Caddesi

Kızılay Caddesi

İnönü

27 Mayıs Caddesi

Tennuri Sok

Cevik Sok

Yoğunburç Caddesi

Bulvarı

Bey Caddesi

Kıcıkapı Meydanı

Lise Caddesi

To Talas

Talas Caddesi

To Hisarcık & Erciyes

9

11

12

13

10

15

16

14

17

18

20

19

23

28

27

24

26

25

29

21

22

30

31

32

historic building include ceramics and faïence, weapons, glassware, kitchen utensils, coins, costumes for both men and women, and the interior of a Kayseri household as it was a century ago. You can also visit Lady Hunat's tomb, an octagonal room with a high-domed ceiling. Besides the lady, the tomb contains the remains of her grandchild and of an unknown person. Remove your shoes before entering the room.

Sahibiye Seminary

The seminary Sahibiye Medresesi, on the north side of Cumhuriyet Meydanı, dates from 1267 and has an especially beautiful Seljuk portal. It's now used as an old book bazaar, with booksellers' shops stocked mostly with Turkish titles.

Lead-Domed Mosque

You can spot the Ottoman-style **Kurşunlu Cami** or Lead-Domed Mosque by its lead-covered dome, unusual in old Kayseri, north of Park Caddesi and west of Cumhuriyet Meydanı and Atatürk Parkı. Also called the Ahmet Paşa Camii after its founder, it was completed in 1585 following plans that may have been drawn by the great Sinan, but were certainly influenced by him.

Twin Seminaries

Two adjoining religious schools, the Gıyasiye ve Şifaiye Medreseleri, are sometimes called the Çifte Medrese or the Twin Seminaries. Set in the midst of Mimar Sinan Parkı north of Park Caddesi, they were founded as the bequest of the Seljuk sultan Giyasettin I Keyhüsrev and his sister Gevher Nesibe Sultan (1165-1204), who was the daughter of the great sultan Kılıçaslan. Today the twin medreses have been restored, and serve as a museum of medical history for Erciyes University. They're open from 8.30 am to 12.30 pm and 1.30 to 5.30 pm, closed on Monday and Tuesday; admission costs US$1.

Above the left portal is a replica of the original stone carving of snakes (symbols of medicine and healing since ancient times) and the Seljuk *çark-i felek* (wheel of fortune), which determined someone's fate in life and presumably their chances of recovering from disease.

Most of the signs explaining Seljuk medical practices are in Turkish only, but that's just as well, for they won't distract you from admiring these beautiful buildings. Princess Gevher Nesibe Sultan is entombed in a chamber on the right side of the courtyard as you enter; a mescit (prayer-room) is above. Topping the mescit outside is a Seljuk-style dome surrounded by an inscription in Arabic which instructs the medrese's administration to accept medical students and patients into the seminary without regard to religion: Muslim, Jew and Christian were to study and be healed side by side.

A doorway on the left side of the courtyard leads to the medical section, which gives fascinating insights into the medical practices of the 13th-century Seljuks. The **Ameliyathane** (Operating Room) has a hole in the ceiling which acted as a 'spotlight' on the patient during operations (I assume the Seljuk doctors operated only on sunny days).

In the **Akıl Hastanesi** (Mental Hospital) is a suite of tiny cells for mental patients, who were kept one to a cell if violent, four to a cell otherwise. Holes through the walls allowed the sounds of encouraging phrases, running water and music to enter the cells and soothe the troubled minds.

The central heating system for the hamam, combined with an insulating layer of earth on top of the roof, kept the entire medical side of the building warm during Kayseri's sometimes frigid winters. (The rooftop earth was used to grow vegetables and fruits to feed the patients. After it was removed during restoration, water penetrated the ceilings below, and caused the plaster to flake. The Seljuks knew better than we do how to preserve these buildings.)

The **Başhekim** (Sertabib) **Odası** (Head Doctor's Room) has been furnished in Ottoman style with wood panelling, low sofas called sedir, and Turkish carpets.

Hacı Kılıç Mosque

North of the Çifte Medrese on İstasyon

Caddesi is the mosque (1249) of the Seljuk vizier Abdülgazi, called the Hacı Kılıç Camii, with some very fine Seljuk architectural detail, especially in the doorways.

Great Mosque

Kayseri's Great Mosque (Ulu Cami) is near Düvenönü Meydanı. It was begun in 1135 by the Danışmend Turkish emirs and finished by the Seljuks in 1205. There's been a lot of repair and 'restoration' over the centuries, but it's still a good example of early Seljuk style.

Bazaar

West of the hisar, east of Düvenönü Meydanı and south of Park Caddesi is Kayseri's tidy, shady bazaar, which you should definitely explore, fending off carpet dealers as you go.

Set at the intersection of age-old trade routes, Kayseri has been an important commercial centre for millennia. Its several Ottoman covered markets have recently been beautifully restored.

The Bedesten, built in 1497 on orders from Mustafa Bey, was first dedicated to the sale of textiles, but now is given over to carpet sellers. The Vezirhanı was constructed in 1727 on the orders of Damat İbrahim Paşa, and now houses shops selling carpets, wool and cotton. The Kapalı Çarşı (Covered Bazaar) was built in 1859, restored in 1988, and now has 500 shops selling necessities to local people, not tourist goods.

Seljuk Tombs

Among Kayseri's other Seljuk archaeological treasures are several of their distinctive tombs. The **Döner Kümbet** (deur-NEHR kewm-beht) or Revolving Tomb is about one km south-east of the hisar along Talas Caddesi. Though it doesn't (and never did) revolve, its cylindrical shape suggests turning, and as you view its marvellous and elaborate Seljuk decoration (1276), you will at least revolve around it. This was a lady's tomb. Nearby is another, the **Sırçalı Kümbet** (1300s), which used to be covered in coloured tiles and topped by a pyramidal roof.

You may spot other *kümbets* in and around Kayseri.

Historic Houses

Just south-east of the citadel is the **Güpgüpoğlu Konağı**, a fine stone mansion dating from the 1700s, now opened as a museum. The main hall (Sofa), larder, Selamlık (men's quarters) and Haremlik (women's and family quarters) have been decorated in period style, and the fine woodwork on the ceilings beautifully restored.

Near the Güpgüpoğlu Konağı is the **Atatürk Evi**, the house where Atatürk stayed when he visited Kayseri. It's also now a museum.

Archaeological Museum

The city's Archaeological Museum is out near the Döner Kümbet, to the east by the railway. The museum houses the finds from Kültepe, site of ancient Kanesh, including the cuneiform tablets which told historians much about the Hittite Empire. Hittite, Hellenistic and Roman statuary, plus exhibits of local ethnography, help to make it worth a visit. Opening hours are from 8 am to noon and from 1 to 5.30 pm daily except Monday; admission costs US$1.50.

Kültepe (Kanesh-Karum)

Appropriately named 'Hill of Ashes' in Turkish, this archaeological site 20 km east of Kayseri was originally settled around 4000 BC. The town of Kanesh came to prominence during Old Bronze times (around 2500 to 2000 BC) when Zipani, king of Kanesh, joined an alliance of Anatolian kings against the powerful king of Akkadia (Mesopotamia), Naram Sin.

By around 1850 BC, Kanesh was the most powerful kingdom in Anatolia. The neighbouring Assyrian commercial centre of Karum, specialising in metals, was among the oldest and richest bazaars in the world. Then a great fire destroyed Kanesh-Karum. It was rebuilt and by around 1720 BC was the Hittite city of Nisa, capital of King Anitta who conquered the pre-Hittite rulers of

Hattuşaş (Boğazkale) and made that a Hittite city.

Today you reach Kültepe by heading east out of Kayseri along Sivas Caddesi. Eighteen km along, just before a BP fuel station, is a road to the left marked for 'Kültepe Kaniş Karum'. Just over two km from the main road is the site marked 'Kültepe Kaniş' and, 200 metres farther along, 'Karum'.

The size and height of the mound is the most impressive thing about the site, showing that ancient Kanesh-Karum was indeed an important city. But signs warn you not to go near the excavation trenches, so there is little to see except the few exhibits in the small museum. The best finds are in the Archaeological Museum in Kayseri.

About 600 metres beyond Karum is the farming village of **Karahöyük**, a collection of old stone houses near a graveyard of rough-cut tombstones, providing a glimpse of real country life.

Caravanserais

North and east of Kayseri are several beautiful restored Seljuk caravanserais. Anyone with a serious interest in Seljuk architecture will want to see them. It's also a good excuse for getting out of the city and seeing a bit of the countryside and of village life.

Haggle with a taxi driver for an excursion to the Sultan Han and Karatay Han, and you will probably end up with a figure of US$20 to US$30 for the entire car. If time and money are short, bargain for just the Sultan Han; you can stop at Kültepe if you like, as well. If only money is short, try to find a bus which will drop you at the Sultan Han (start early in the day), and then trust to luck in catching something back to Kayseri.

Sultan Han The Sultan Han is on the highway, 45 km north-east of Kayseri. Besides being a fine example of the Seljuk royal caravan lodging, it has been beautifully restored so it is easy to appreciate the architectural fine points. The han was finished in 1236; restoration was carried out only a few decades ago. Don't let the locked gate worry you. Shortly after your car draws up, a boy

will come running with the key and a booklet of tickets; admission costs US$1.50. Opening hours are supposedly from 9 am to 1 pm and from 2 to 5 pm (till 7 pm in summer), but in fact the han is open whenever the guardian can be found.

Tour the inside, noticing particularly the elegant snake motif on the little mosque's arches. Climb up to the roof if you like, but don't neglect a walk around the exterior as well. Note the lion-faced water spouts on the walls, and the plain towers of varying design.

Karatay Han If you have time, take your taxi to the Karatay Han, in a Turkish village now well off the beaten track. From the Sultan Han, head back towards Kayseri and take the turn-off south or east to Bünyan. Pass through Bünyan heading towards Malatya, and about 30 km along there is a road on the right for Elbaşı. Follow it for five km to Elbaşı, and four km beyond to Karatay, also called Karadayı. (Coming from Malatya, look for a turn-off marked 'Karatay Han, 10 km' about 35 km west of Pınarbaşı.)

The Karatay Han, built in 1240 for the Seljuk vizier Emir Celaleddin Karatay, was once on the main east-west trade route. It was restored in the 1960s, and is yet another fine example of high Seljuk art. A visit to the Karatay Han gives you a glimpse into the life of a Turkish village as well.

Erciyes Dağı

Erciyes Dağı or Mt Aergius (3916 metres), as it was known in Roman times, is an extinct volcano 26 km south of Kayseri. It is one of Turkey's few ski centres, with a chairlift, beginners' lift, and a ski lodge, the *Kayak Evi* (Ski House, ☎ (35) 32 89 71) with 100 beds.

Leave the city by the road to the airport *(havaalanı)* and the village of Hisarcık (14 km). Minibuses go as far as Hisarcık frequently during the day; you must hitch or take a taxi (US$10) the last dozen or so km to Tekir Yaylası (2150 metres) and the ski lodge. Equipment can be rented at the ski lodge.

Though fairly good for skiing (for Turkey), Erciyes is rather inhospitable to hikers. Short walks can be made from the ski lodge, but longer treks require planning, good equipment and a guide. For full information, see Lonely Planet's *Trekking in Turkey*.

Places to Stay – bottom end

Hotel Sur (SOOR) (☎ (35) 31 95 45, 31 39 92), Cumhuriyet Mahallesi, Talas Caddesi 12, offers good value in a convenient location. Doubles cost US$14 for one large bed or twin beds, or US$16 for two beds (one double, one single), both with private shower. Walk south-east along Talas Caddesi from the citadel, with a remnant of the city walls and the Sivas Kapısı (Sivas Gate) on your right. Turn right after passing the wall, then right again, and you'll see the hotel. Don't mind the crowd of men gathered in the street; they're waiting to do business at the local employment office.

In the bazaar is the tidy and fairly quiet *Hotel Çamlıca* (CHAHM-luh-jah, ☎ (35) 31 94 26), Bankalar Caddesi, Gürcü Sokak 14, with serviceable rooms priced at US$15 a double with washbasin, US$18 with shower. It's a bit difficult to find. From the Divan Pastanesi (see Places to Eat), turn right off 27 Mayıs Caddesi and take the third street on the left, Nazmi Toker Caddesi, known to the locals as Bankalar Caddesi (Banks Street), for obvious reasons. After you come to an intersection, walk one block more along the curving street to the hotel.

Near the Çamlıca is the *Hotel Berlin* (☎ (35) 31 52 46), Maarif Caddesi, Yeni Han Çıkmazı 12, only a block from the Vezirhanı. On a quiet dead-end street, it offers good clean double rooms with sink for US$12, or with shower for US$14, breakfast included. *Hotel Titiz* (☎ (35) 31 71 39; fax 31 22 46), Maarif Caddesi 7, just down the street from the Çamlıca, is modern, clean and presentable at US$16/24 a single/double with private shower. Some rooms have TVs.

Lower prices? Behind the Hunat Mosque & Ethnographic Museum near the Tourism Information Office is the *Hotel Hunat* (☎ (35) 32 43 19), Hunat (or Zengin) Sokak 5, a simple, cheap, convenient, quiet place

with waterless rooms priced at US$4/6 a single/double.

The *Hotel Kent* (☎ (35) 31 24 54), Camikebir Mahallesi, Camikebir Caddesi 2, near Düvenönü Meydanı, is more modest and much-used. Rooms with shower here go for US$12/16 a single/double.

Places to Stay – middle

Kayseri has seen several good new hotels open in the last few years near Düvenönü Meydanı. The two-star, 44-room *Hotel Çapari* (☎ (35) 31 49 91; fax 31 89 53), Donanma Caddesi 12, is hidden away on a back street just one block north-east of Düvenönü Meydanı. The location, though a bit difficult to find at first, proves to be a quiet one. All rooms have private baths and TVs, and cost US$22/38 a single/double, breakfast included. There's a restaurant and bar.

Hotel Konfor (☎ (35) 20 01 84; fax 31 79 11), Atatürk Bulvarı 5, is a few dozen metres north of Düvenönü Meydanı on the left. Attractively modern, its rooms are quite comfy and well located, and cost the same as those at the Çapari.

Facing Düvenönü Meydanı on its southwest corner is the three-star *Hotel Almer* (☎ (35) 20 01 88, 20 79 70; fax 20 79 74), Osman Kavuncu Caddesi, with very comfortable rooms equipped with TV, minibar and air-conditioning costing US$28/42 a single/double, breakfast included.

The older two-star *Hotel Turan* (too-RAHN) (☎ (35) 31 19 68, 31 25 06), 27 Mayıs Caddesi, Turan Caddesi 8, is Kayseri's old faithful, having served travellers for many decades. Rooms, though old, are still serviceable, and priced at US$20/30 a single/double. The staff are ready to haggle here, and if business is slack you may pay less. The hotel has a roof terrace and a Turkish bath.

Next to the otogar is an emergency-only lodging, the nominally one-star *Terminal Oteli* (TEHR-mee-NAHL) (☎ (35) 36 46 74), Osman Kavuncu Caddesi 176, with 21 rooms for US$20 a double with private shower, US$16 a double with just a washbasin.

Places to Eat

Kayseri is noted for a few special dishes, among them pastırma (from the same root-word as pastrami?) – salted, sun-dried veal coated with çemen, a spicy concoction of garlic, red peppers, parsley and water. It takes about a month to prepare, has a very strong flavour, tends to stick in your teeth and despotically rule your breath for hours, but once you acquire the taste you look forward to returning to Kayseri. The darker the pastırma, the longer it has been allowed to age. Shops in the centre will sell it to you for picnics (try 100 grams); before you buy, ask for a sample (*Bir tat, lütfen*, beer TAHT lewt-fehn, 'A taste, please').

Other Kayseri specialties include sucuk (soo-JOOK), a spicy sausage; salam (sah-LAHM), Turkish salami; tulum peynir (too-LOOM pehy-neer), hard cheese cured in a goatskin; and bal (BAHL), honey. Few of these things, with the exception of pastırma, will appear on restaurant menus, so you must buy them in food shops for picnics.

The *İskender Kebap Salonu* (☎ 31 27 69), 27 Mayıs Caddesi 5, by the citadel, one floor above street level, has been serving good Bursa-style döner kebap for several decades. It has a good view of the busy street, and low prices of about US$3 to US$4 for a meal of kebap, ayran and salad. The general dining room is one flight up; the much nicer aile salonu with flowers on every table is another flight up via a stairway from the general dining room.

Across the street is the *Merkez Kebap ve Pide Salonu* (☎ 31 29 62), with similar fare, including fresh pide. The nearby *Cumhuriyet Lokantası* (☎ 31 49 11), two doors down 27 Mayıs Caddesi from the Divan Pastanesi, is a good choice for ready food or roast chicken.

The *Divan Pastanesi* (☎ 35 11 27) is a good, fancy pastry shop on 27 Mayıs Caddesi a block south of the citadel, on the corner of Mevlevi Caddesi. Have their Şam fıstıklı baklava (many-layered flaky pastry sweet with pistachio nuts) and a büyük çay (large glass of tea) for about US$1.50.

The bazaar has numerous good cheap eateries. Follow Mevlevi Caddesi from the Divan Pastanesi and take the first street on the left to find the *Şamdan Lokantası* (☎ 31 58 20), one flight up. It's quiet and cheap, with a small balcony and decent food.

Near the Hotel Berlin is *Kebabcı Hilmi* (☎ 31 40 75), a tidy, busy kebap grill in a passageway on Yeni Han Çıkmazı, the same street as the Berlin. Kebaps cost between US$1 and US$2.

Getting There & Away

Air Kayseri's Erkilet Airport is connected with İstanbul by four nonstop flights per week by Turkish Air Transport (THT) (☎ (35) 31 10 01). Buy your tickets at the Turkish Airlines office (same phone) at Sahibiye Mahallesi, Yıldırım Caddesi 1. As of this writing, there is no air service to Ankara. An airport bus (US$1.50) connects the city with Erkilet airport. Catch the bus 1¼ hours before flight departure time, or be at the airport at least 30 minutes before the scheduled departure time.

Bus Being at an important north-south and east-west crossroads, Kayseri has lots of bus service. To get to the citadel from the otogar, walk out the otogar's front door, cross the avenue and board any bus marked 'Merkez' (Centre), or take a dolmuş marked 'Terminal-Şehir'. A taxi to the citadel costs US$2.

Details of bus services to and from Kayseri follow:

Adana – 335 km, 6½ hours, US$12; several buses daily

Ankara – 330 km, five hours, US$8; hourly buses

Gaziantep – 371 km, 6½ hours, US$12; several buses daily

Kahramanmaraş – 291 km, five hours, US$10; several buses daily

Malatya – 354 km, six hours, US$10; several buses daily

Nevşehir – 105 km, 2½ hours by bus, 1½ hours by minibus, US$4; very frequent buses and minibuses

Sivas – 200 km, 3½ hours, US$6; frequent buses daily

Ürgup – 80 km, 1½ hours, US$2.75; hourly minibuses from 7 am to 7 pm

Train Several daily trains connect Kayseri with Ankara and points east; see the Ankara section for details. The only convenient train is the *Vangölü/Güney Ekspresi* combination which arrives in Kayseri during the day; the *Doğu Ekspresi* stops at Kayseri in the middle of the night, and the *Çukurova Ekspresi* bypasses the city.

The train between Kayseri and Malatya takes 10 hours, if it's on time; the bus is much quicker. There are no good train connections north to the Black Sea; better to take a bus, or the train to Sivas, then a bus to Samsun.

To get into town from the railway station, walk out of the station, cross the big avenue and board any bus heading down Atatürk Bulvarı to Düvenönü Meydanı.

North Central Anatolia

The region north-east of Ankara and north-west of Sivass has a little of everything: ancient Hittite ruins, gritty industrial cities, graceful old Ottoman towns, mountain scenery and plains.

Most travellers make stops in this region on their way to somewhere else. Going to the Black Sea coast, it's worth seeing Amasya and Tokat, and Çorum can provide lodgings if your itinerary demands it. But a few destinations are worth excursions in themselves: the well-preserved Ottoman town of Safranbolu; the Hittite ruins at Boğazkale, near Sungurlu; and the historic city of Amasya, situated in a dramatic river gorge.

SAFRANBOLU

For many years Safranbolu (population 35,000, altitude 350 metres) was a closely guarded secret: a small town of wonderful well-preserved Ottoman houses hidden in the hill country 250 km north of Ankara. Turkish architects, painters and photographers knew about it and exploited its artistic potential. Only the most adventurous travellers wandered through it, often by accident, on their way to the Black Sea coastal town of Amasra.

Safranbolu's charms have now been discovered, but not over-exploited. The town, 10 km north of the gritty steel-manufacturing city of Karabük, is not on the most heavily travelled tour bus routes. You must still make a special effort to make your way to Safranbolu. Once you do, you'll enjoy walking along the narrow, twisting cobbled lanes and seeing traditional trades and crafts practised just as they were in Ottoman times.

History

A settlement was founded here between 200 and 1500 BC, and was subject to the usual conquest, rule, exploitation and enjoyment by Hittites, Paphlagonians, Persians, Lydians, Romans and Byzantines. Under the Turks, the rulers were the Danışmends, Seljuks, Çobanoğlus, Çandaroğlus and Ottomans. During the 1600s, the main Ottoman trade route between Gerede and the Black Sea coast went through Safranbolu, bringing commerce, prominence and wealth to the town. Wealthy patrons established caravanserais, mosques and Turkish baths. Safranbolu produced many men and women who were successful in commerce and government, and who shared their success with their birthplace by endowing charitable foundations.

During the 1700s and 1800s the wealthy families of Safranbolu built spacious mansions of sun-dried mud bricks, wood and stucco. The families of the surprisingly large population of prosperous artisans built less impressive but similarly sturdy, harmonious homes, and a surprising number of these buildings survive today. About 20 to 25% of Safranbolu's population during the 19th century was Ottoman Greek, most of whom moved to Greece during the great exchange of populations following WW I. Their principal church, dedicated to St Stephen, has been restored as Kırankoy's Ulu Cami (Great Mosque).

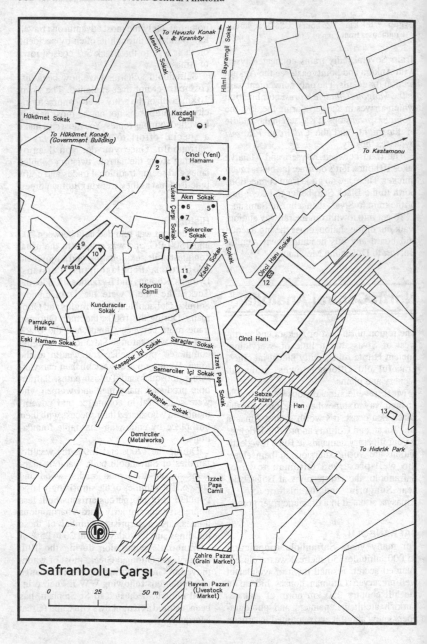

Safranbolu–Çarşı

0   25   50 m

1   Main Square & Bus Stop
2   Safranbolu Kültür ve Turizm Derneği
    (Culture & Tourism Association)
3   Hamam – Men's Entrance
4   Hamam – Women's Entrance
5   Asmaaltı Lokantası
6   Merkez Lokantası
7   Özkan Lokum Shop
8   Municipal Information Office
9   Tourism Information Office
10 Boncuk Café
11 Belediye (Municipality)
12 PTT
13 Kaymakamlar Evi (Museum)

Orientation

Coming via Karabük, you arrive in the modern part of Safranbolu called Kıranköy, arrayed along the ridge of a hill and formerly called Misaki Milli by its Ottoman Greek inhabitants. If you continue uphill from the traffic roundabout you will reach the section called Bağlar (baa-LAHR), with its centre at Köyiçi, which has many interesting old houses.

Turn right (south-east) at the roundabout and go 1.7 km, down the hill, up the other side and down again to reach the centre of Old Safranbolu (Eski Safranbolu), the Turkish section called Çarşı (Market), also called Şehir (City). On Saturday a busy market does in fact take place in the main square, marked by the Kazdağlı Camii (1779) The few modern hotels are in Kıranköy, but most of what there is to see is in Eski Safranbolu and Bağlar.

Information

Çarşı has two tourism offices. Follow the signs to the government Tourism Information Office (☎ (464) 23863), 100 metres from Çarşı's main square along Arasta Sokak in the arasta (collection of Ottoman-style shops) formerly occupied by Safranbolu's cobblers. There is also an information office sponsored by the local Safranbolu Culture & Tourism Association (Kültür ve Turizm Derneği; ☎ (464) 21047) just off Çarşı's

main square on Arasta Sokak, marked by signs. Safranbolu's postal code is 67700.

Historic Architecture

In Ottoman times, prosperous residents of Safranbolu maintained dual households. In winter they occupied their town residences in Çarşı, situated at the meeting-point of three valleys and protected from the winter winds. During the warm months they moved to summer houses amidst the vineyards of Bağlar ('Vines'). After establishment of the iron and steel works at Karabük in 1938, modern houses built by factory staff encroached on the old neighbourhoods of Bağlar.

Some of the largest houses had interior pools which, though big enough to be swimming pools, were not used as such. The running water cooled the room and gave a pleasant background sound. The best and most accessible example of this is the **Havuzlu Konağı** ('Mansion with Pool'), now operated as a hotel by the Turkish Touring & Automobile Association. See Places to Stay for details.

Several historic houses have been restored and opened as museums. As time goes on and funds allow, more places are being saved from deterioration. Houses generally have two storeys and from 10 to 12 rooms. The largest houses were divided into *selamlık* (men's quarters) and *haremlik* (women's and family quarters).

Best of the restored houses is the **Kaymakamlar Evi**, open from 8.30 am to 12.30 pm and 1.30 to 5.30 pm (closed on Monday). Admission costs US$1. As you enter, old farm implements, an old telephone switchboard and a *çıkrık* (spinning wheel) are displayed in the area once reserved for storage and stabling animals. Climb the stairs and remove your shoes (as is traditional in Turkish houses) to see the gracious old rooms. Note especially the trundle beds and the closet for bedding which converts into a bathroom. The rooms on the middle floor, with fireplaces, were used in winter. The top-floor rooms, cooler and airier, were used in warmer weather.

Other Historic Buildings

Çarşı's most famous and imposing structure is the large stone **Cinci Hanı** (1645), a cara-vanserai presently under restoration. Right by Çarşı's main square is the **Cinci Hamamı**, built along with the Cinci Hanı and still in service. With separate baths for men *(Erkekler Kısmı)* and women *(Kadınlar Kısmı)*, lots of creamy marble, and glass dome lights which let in dramatic rays of sunshine. It is a worthy place to come clean for less than US$1.

The large **Köprülü Mehmet Paşa Camii** (1662), by the arasta with the Tourism Information Office, is presently under restoration. The **İzzet Paşa Camii** (1796) was restored extensively in 1902-03.

Walk uphill past the Kaymakamlar Evi to reach **Hıdırlık**, the so-called kale (citadel), which was never a fortress despite its modern bits of crenellated wall. On top of the hill is a park offering excellent views of the town, and two türbes (tombs) dating from the 19th century. Safranbolu did have a citadel, by the way. Its last remnants were removed in the early 1900s to make way for the ornamented **Hükümet Konağı** (government building) on the hilltop across the valley.

Safranbolu's traditional character is now protected by regulation. Efforts are also being made to preserve the artisans' shops and trades. Most of the active shops and artisans are in the streets south of the Cinci Hamamı and the Köprülü Camii.

Bağlar has many wonderful old houses, but at this writing they are not organised for viewing. The tourism authorities are taking steps to do this, however, and you may be able to take a house tour when you arrive.

Excursion to Yörükköy

Another, smaller, less renowned village of old houses is Yörükköy (which translates oxymoronically as 'Nomad Village'), 11 km east of Safranbolu along the Kastamonu road. So far tourism has hardly touched it, even as far as transport is concerned. Though increasing demand may result in a dolmuş being laid on, for now you must haggle with a Safranbolu taxi driver to take you there, wait for two hours as you explore the village, then return. This should cost less than US$10.

Places to Stay & Eat

Not having a lot of tourism, Safranbolu does not have many hotels, and those it has are often full. No doubt the number of good little pensions and 'boutique' hotels in restored mansions will increase dramatically in future.

Kıranköy In the new part of town is the *Zalifre Pansiyon* (☎ (464) 20530, 21760), a simple modern place charging US$4 per person in waterless rooms.

Much fancier is the two-star, 20-room *Uz Otel* (☎ (464) 21086; fax 22215), a modern place built to resemble an old Safranbolu house. Restaurant, bar, and shower-equipped guest rooms are yours for US$22/32 a single/double, breakfast included.

The Safranbolu Municipality maintains a guesthouse called the *Belediye Misafir-hanesi* (☎ (464) 23643), or Belediye Sosyal Tesisleri, 500 metres down the road from the Uz Otel. If it's not being used for official functions it often accepts travellers in its bath-equipped guest rooms for US$12/18 a single/double.

The *Gülen Hotel*, downhill from the roundabout, has simple waterless rooms for US$4 per person.

Besides the Uz Otel's good restaurant, you can try the *Çelik Palas Restaurant* next door, which has a pleasant terrace, and the cheaper *Yeni Hayat Lokantası* on the road to Çarşı. *İmren Lokumcu* is famous locally for its lokum (Turkish delight), and has a branch shop in Çarşı's arasta, near the tourism office, as well.

Çarşı The most charming lodgings in Safranbolu are undoubtedly at the *Havuzlu Konak* (☎ (464) 12883; fax 23824), Mescit Sokak, 400 metres uphill from Çarşı's main square on the way to Kıranköy. This metic-ulously restored mansion, sometimes called the Asmazlar Konağı after its former owners, is enclosed behind high walls 1.4 km from the roundabout in Kıranköy, opposite the turn-off for the Bartın-Zonguldak road. Enter and look to the left to see the house's fine pool, right in the centre of the main room, surrounded by low sofas and small brass-tray tables at which guests have breakfast.

The 11 guest rooms upstairs have showers, and fairly authentic period furnishings which are spare but charming. Sound-proofing is at a minimum – this is authentic, too, so almost everything you say can be heard in adjoining rooms – but this is a minor inconvenience.

The basement restaurant has marble floors and an arched fireplace, used frequently to lend cheer to the room. The menu lists such Ottoman delights as mıklama (fried eggs, tomatoes, spinach, ground lamb, onions and pastırma), and gözleme, the Turkish version of Breton crêpes. The more exotic dishes tend to be available only when the hotel is relatively full; otherwise it's şiş kebap. Portions are large and prices are moderate: less than US$8 for soup, salad, main course and beer.

Also in Çarşı is the *Merkez Restaurant*, plain, clean and typical, with three-course meals for US$2.50. Next door is the *Özkan*, a beautiful old sweets shop. Near the arasta, the *Boncuk Café* is one of the town's most congenial places, a modern Safranbolulu's conception of what an 'antique' café should be. Food, drink and company are good.

Getting There & Away
Though there are a few direct buses to Safranbolu, most drop you at Karabük's grimy otogar, from where you take a minibus (50c) for the last 10 km to Kıranköy. If you're driving, exit from the Ankara-İstanbul highway at Gerede and head north, following signs for Karabük.

Getting Around
Minibuses (40c) roll along the route from Çarşı's main square over the hills to Kıranköy and up to the Köyiçi stop in Bağlar every 30 minutes or so throughout the day, solving the transport problem quite nicely.

SUNGURLU
Going to the Hittite cities of Boğazkale and Alacahöyük from Ankara takes you through Sungurlu, where you must change buses. You may want to stay the night here as well. A commerce and farming town 175 km (three hours) east of Ankara, Sungurlu has nothing to detain you except its transport and lodging services. There is no otogar. Buses and minibuses drop you on the highway or in the centre of town.

Orientation
The town centre (Şehir Merkezi), 500 metres off the main highway, is marked by an old clock tower next to a fountain with a Hittite bull statue in front of the Belediye Başkanlığı (Municipality); the commercial centre (Çarşı) is 200 metres farther up the hill, marked by a statue of Atatürk. Minibuses to Boğazkale depart from this commercial square. Don't let the taxi drivers tell you that the minibuses don't run on Sunday; they do.

Places to Stay & Eat
Otel Ferhat (☎ (4557) 1333), in the Çarşı just off the square with the Atatürk statue, and around the corner from the Türkiye Vakıflar Bankası, is tattered but cleanish and charges only US$3.50 per person in waterless rooms. The *Günay Pide ve Kebap Salonu* next door is tidy with pretensions to décor, and serves good fresh Turkish pizza cheaply.

The nominally two star *Hotel Gündoğan* (☎ (4557) 3636), Çankırı Caddesi, Belediye Sarayı Yanı, near the clock tower, more or less behind the Emlak Bankası, next to the Belediye building, has cheap serviceable double rooms for US$6 waterless, or US$7 with shower.

In the middle range, the situation is much better. One km east of the commercial square, on the highway, stands the *Hitit Motel* (☎ (4557) 1042, 1409), on the Ankara-Samsun Yolu. The sign can be hard to spot: it's between the Petrol Ofisi fuel station and the Renault garage. The motel has 23 rooms on two floors set amidst pretty gardens surrounding a swimming pool (usually empty). Prince Charles stayed here in May 1992 while on a private birding-watching trip to Turkey. The restaurant has good food and service, the guest rooms have private showers and balconies looking onto the grounds, and prices are quite reasonable: rooms cost US$20/30/40 a single/double/triple. In the restaurant, expect to spend from US$5 to US$7 per person for lunch or dinner, drinks included. Avoid breakfast, which is overpriced and terrible.

Getting There & Away

Getting to Sungurlu is easy: take one of the hourly buses from Ankara's otogar.

Getting away from Sungurlu demands that you make a choice. From beside the Sungurlu Kaymakamlığı government building near the Atatürk statue in Sungurlu you can catch a Boğazkale Belediyesi minibus operated by the village (US$1) for the 30-km, 40-minute ride to Boğazkale; this is the cheapest way to go. Minibuses run throughout the day, with the last run departing from Boğazkale at 5 pm, the return trip from Sungurlu departing at 6 pm.

Or you can hire a taxi or minibus to give you a tour of Boğazkale and Alacahöyük, including a ride to the top of that exhausting hill, for US$30 for the entire car, about twice as much for a 15 to 20-person minibus.

BOĞAZKALE & THE HITTITE CITIES

Before our own century very little was known about the Hittites, a people who commanded a vast empire in the Middle East, conquered Babylon, and challenged the Egypt of the pharaohs over 3000 years ago. Though their accomplishments were monumental, time has buried Hittite history as effectively as it has buried the Hittites themselves. Only a few references to them, in the Bible and in Egyptian chronicles, remain.

In 1905 excavations began at the site of Hattuşaş, the Hittite capital near the Turkish village of Boğazkale (also called Boğazköy), 200 km east of Ankara off the highway to Samsun. The digging produced notable works of art, most of which are now preserved in Ankara's Museum of Anatolian Civilisations. Also brought to light were the Hittite state archives, written in cuneiform on thousands of clay tablets. From these tablets, historians and archaeologists were able to construct a history of the Hittite Empire.

The Hittites spoke an Indo-European language. They swept into Anatolia around 2000 BC and conquered the Hatti, from whom they borrowed both their culture and their name. They established themselves here at Hattuşaş, the Hatti capital, and in the course of a millennium enlarged and beautified the city. From about 1375 to 1200 BC, this was the great and glorious capital of the Hittite Empire.

Most of the Hittite artefacts are now in Ankara's museum, though there is also a small museum in Boğazkale.

Orientation

Boğazkale (population 2500) has several hotels, camping grounds and restaurants, a teahouse and a few shops. It's a small farming village with a sideline in tourism. Coming from Sungurlu, you enter the village beneath a welcome arch over the road. From the arch and the neighbouring Aşikoğlu Motel it's 100 metres up the street to the museum. Across the street from the museum is the İlçe Sağlık Ocağı (medical clinic), the primary school and the grammar school.

If you are coming from Yozgat, you follow a road which comes over the mountains from the south-east and skirts the eastern part of the archaeological zone. The view of the ruined city from this road is very fine.

South of the village, up on the hillside, sprawl the extensive ruins of Hattuşaş. It's exactly one km from the welcome arch to the ticket kiosk, and another 2.5 km up the hillside to the farthest point, the Yerkapı (Earth or Sphinx Gate) or along the road which loops through the ruins. The separate site of Yazılıkaya is about three km uphill from the ticket kiosk along another road.

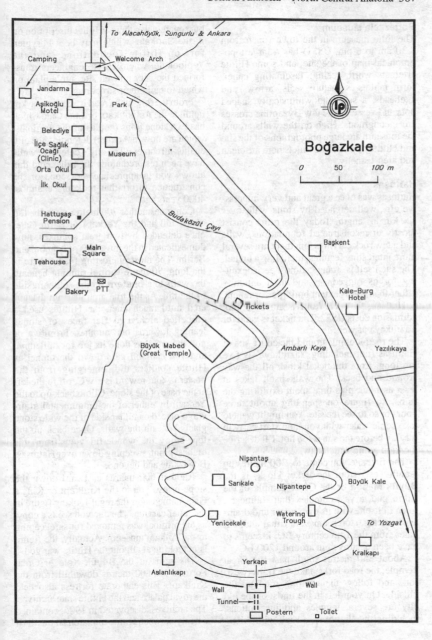

To Alacahöyük, Sungurlu & Ankara

Camping

Welcome Arch

Jandarma

Aşıkoğlu Motel

Park

Belediye

İlçe Sağlık Ocağı (Clinic)

Museum

Orta Okul

İlk Okul

Hattuşaş Pension

Budaközüt Çayı

Boğazkale

0   50   100 m

Başkent

Main Square

Teahouse

Bakery   PTT

Kale–Burg Hotel

Tickets

Büyük Mabed (Great Temple)

Ambarlı Kaya

Yazılıkaya

Nişantaş

Sarıkale

Nişantepe

Büyük Kale

Yenicekale

Watering Trough

To Yozgat

Aslanlıkapı

Yerkapı

Kralkapı

Wall

Wall

Tunnel

Postern   Toilet

Boğazkale Museum

The little museum in the town (open from 8.30 am to 6 pm, US$1) has a large topographical map of the site, and some Hittite artefacts worth seeing: fascinating cuneiform tablets, signature seals, arrows and axeheads, a saw, and whimsically shaped pots and vessels. The few Byzantine crosses are incongruous. High on the walls around the museum are large photographs of the site and Hittite objects. The toilets here are clean and aren't smelly.

Hattuşaş

Hattuşaş was once a great and very impressive city, well defended by stone walls over six km in length. Today the ruins consist mostly of reconstructed foundations, walls and a few rock carvings, but there are several more interesting features, including a tunnel. The site itself is strange, almost eerie, exciting for its ruggedness and high antiquity rather than for its extant buildings or reliefs.

Hattuşaş is open from 8 am to 5 pm; admission costs US$2. The ticket is valid for Yazılıkaya as well.

The road looping around the entire site of Hattuşaş (not including Yazılıkaya) is five km long, from the ticket kiosk all the way around and back. The walk itself takes at least an hour, plus time spent exploring the ruins, so figure on spending about three hours or so to see the site. You might want to take some water with you, and start early in the day before the sun is too hot. I'll describe the loop going anticlockwise.

The first site you come to, 300 metres up (south-west) from the ticket kiosk, is the **Büyük Mabed** or the Great Temple of the storm god, a vast complex that's almost a town in itself, with its own water and drainage systems, storerooms and ritual altars. It dates from the 14th century BC; it seems to have been destroyed in around 1200 BC.

About 350 metres south past the Great Temple, the road forks; take the right (west) fork and follow the winding road up the hillside. On your left in the midst of the old city are several temples and inscriptions, including the **Nişantaş**, a rock with a long

but severely weathered Hittite inscription on it; the **Sarıkale**, which may be a Phrygian fort on Hittite foundations; and the **Yenicekale**, where Hittite engineers transformed the very uneven site into a plain on which to build their structures.

From the fork in the road it's about one km uphill to the **Aslanlıkapı** or Lion Gate which has two stone lions (copies of the originals, which are now in Ankara) defending the city against all comers. The city's defensive walls have been restored along the ridge, and this allows you to appreciate the scope of the construction effort that took place almost 4000 years ago.

Continue another 700 metres up to the top of the hill and the **Yerkapı** or Earth Gate, once defended by two great sphinxes, now domesticated in the museums of İstanbul and Berlin. The most interesting feature here is the long, 70-metre **tunnel** running beneath the walls to a **postern** on the southern side of the hill. As the true arch was not discovered until much later, the Hittites used a corbelled arch, two flat faces of stones leaning towards one another. Primitive or not, the arch has done its job for millennia, and you can still pass down the tunnel as Hittite soldiers did, emerging from the postern. Your reward is a WC, off to the left at the base of the slope. Climb back up to the Yerkapı by either of the monumental **stairways** placed on either side of the wide stone glacis beneath the walls. Once back up the top, enjoy the wonderful view from this highest point, sweeping down over Hattuşaş, Boğazkale and beyond.

Another 600 metres eastward down the slope brings you to the **Kralkapı** or King's Gate, named after the regal-looking figure in the relief carving. The one you see is a copy, as the original was removed for safekeeping to the Ankara museum. Actually, the figure is not a king at all, but the Hittite war god.

The ruins of the **Büyük Kale** or Great Fortress are 800 metres downhill from the Kralkapı. This elaborate fortress also held the royal palace and the Hittite state archives. The archives, discovered in 1906, contained a treaty between Hittite monarch Hattusili III and pharaoh of Egypt Ramses II written in cuneiform on a clay tablet. From the fortress it's just over one km back to the ticket kiosk.

Yazılıkaya

The Turkish name (yah-zuh-LUH kah-yah) means 'inscribed rock', and that's what you find at this site just under three km from Boğazkale. Follow the signs from the ticket kiosk. The road circles a hillock called Ambarlı Kaya, on top of which there were more Hittite buildings, before crossing a stream and climbing the hill past the Başkent restaurant, pension and camping ground (you might want to stop here for refreshments or lunch).

Yazılıkaya was always a naturalistic religious sanctuary open to the sky, but in the later Hittite times (13th century BC) monumental gateways and temple structures were built in front of the natural rock galleries. It is the foundations of these late structures that you see as you approach Yazılıkaya from the car park.

There are two natural rock galleries, the larger one to the left, which was the empire's sacred place, and a narrower one to the right, which was the burial place of the royal family. In the large gallery, the low reliefs of numerous conehead gods and goddesses marching in procession indicate that this was the Hittite's holiest religious sanctuary. The Hittites had 1000 gods, but fewer than 100 are represented here. The most important Hittite deities in 1200 BC were Teshub, the storm god, and Hepatu, the sun goddess.

Alacahöyük

There is less to see at Alacahöyük, but Hittiteophiles will want to make the trip to the site, 25 km north of Boğazkale. As at the other Hittite sites, movable monuments have been taken to the museum in Ankara, though there is a small museum on the site, and a few worn sphinxes and good bas-reliefs have been left in place. This is a very old site, settled from about 4000 BC.

To get there, leave Boğazkale heading north-west on the Sungurlu road, and after 13.5 km turn right at the road marked for

Alaca and Alacahöyük. (Coming from Sungurlu, turn left about 11 km after turning onto the Boğazkale road.) Go another 11.5 km and turn left for Alacahöyük, nine more km along.

As of this writing there is no dolmuş service. The villagers told me they preferred to get rides with trucks, as the truck drivers charge less than the minibus drivers. Thus you will have to do the same, or hire a taxi or minibus to take you to the ruins and back (about US$10 from Boğazkale). You should be able to get dolmuşes as far as the town of Alaca, 18 km from Alacahöyük; from there you must hitch rides. To head onward, you can walk seven km west to the Sungurlu-Çorum highway where there is frequent bus traffic.

Alacahöyük is now a farming hamlet with a humble main square on which stands a fountain, a PTT, a souvenir shop, a bakery and a modest grocery.

The little museum is right by the ruins, and both are open from 8.30 am to noon, and from 1.30 to 5.30 pm, closed on Monday. As this is a small village operation, you may even be able to beg your way in on Monday. The admission fee for everything is US$1.

In the tidy little museum you can inspect tools used in the excavations, and finds from the Chalcolithic and Old Bronze ages. A handy ant farm-style glass case shows the stratigraphy of Alacahöyük's 15 layers of history. The layers are arranged as follows:

1 Phrygian Age (1200-600 BC)
2-4 Old Hittite and Great Hittite Empire Age 2000-1200 BC)
5-9 Old Bronze Age (3000-2000 BC)
10-15 Chalcolithic Age (5500-3000 BC)

The exhibits are not labelled except according to period. Note also the Hitit Çağı Banyo Teknesi, a Hittite-Age bathtub. Downstairs in the museum is its ethnographic section, which many people find more absorbing than the ancient potshards.

At the **ruins**, signs are in Turkish and English. The site is self-explanatory. The **monumental gate**, with its lions guarding the door and its very fine reliefs down in front, is what you've come to see. The reliefs show storm-god worshipping ceremonies and festivals with musicians, acrobats, priests and the Hittite king and queen. Off to the left across the fields is a **secret escape tunnel** leading to a postern as at Hattuşaş.

Leaving Alacahöyük, signs for Sungurlu lead you seven km out to the Sungurlu-Çorum highway by a road not shown on many maps. Turn left (south-west) for Sungurlu (27 km), right for Çorum (42 km) and Samsun (210 km).

Still interested in Hittites? You can visit the very earliest Hittite capital at Kültepe, near Kayseri in Cappadocia, but there is little to see there. Karatepe, east of Adana, is worth a visit, though.

Places to Stay & Eat

There are several small hotels in Boğazkale; most are open only from May to mid-October.

A good first choice is the *Hattuşaş Restaurant & Pension* (☎ (4554) 1013), on the main square in the village, renting rooms for US$6 per person. This standard breeze-block building is well located so you can walk easily to the museum and to Boğazkale.

Next choice is the *Başkent Restoran, Pansiyon & Campink* (☎ & fax (4554) 1037), Yazılıkaya Yolu Üzeri, Boğazkale, Çorum, one km from the museum on the road to Yazılıkaya and Yozgat, with 18 tidy little rooms with twin beds. Hot-water (flash heater) showers at the end of the block are also clean. Rooms cost US$12 a double, but you can haggle if the pension's not full and it's late in the day. The camping ground is the best at Boğazkale. The restaurant, with its white laminate tables, dark wood trim and red tile roof is pleasant, and has a nice view of the ruins, but is often filled by tour groups at lunch time.

Just 400 metres farther up the hill from the Başkent along the Yazılıkaya road is the *Kale-Burg Motel* (☎ (4554) 1189), which looks fancier than it is. Very simple double rooms with showers added as an afterthought

cost the standard US$12. The camping ground is primitive.

The last choice for lodging and dining is the first one you'll see as you enter from Sungurlu, the 25-room *Aşikoğlu Turistik Moteli* (ah-SHEE-oh-loo) (☎ (4554) 1004), Boğazkale, Çorum, right by the welcome arch, open from mid-March to November.

A very simple double room with sink and shower (no toilet) costs US$12 – but the price goes up and down depending on who's asking, and when. The hotel also has a restaurant with edible food at premium prices, around US$5 or US$6 per person for a meal. Both places are heavily used by tour groups. Behind the jandarma post by the welcome arch is the Aşikoğlu's camping ground, which is pretty basic, and will do for a night, but there are better ones.

Atila Camping (☎ (4554) 1101) is just over one km west of the welcome arch and the Aşikoğlu Motel on the Sungurlu road. There's a restaurant, but the primitive camping ground is inconvenient and there's no shade.

Getting There & Away

You can make a day's excursion from Ankara to Boğazkale. With your own car you can stop at Boğazkale on the way to the Black Sea coast at Samsun. Otherwise, come by bus as described in the Sungurlu and Yozgat sections.

If you don't want to make the hike around the ruins when you arrive in Boğazkale, you may be able to find a taxi to give you a tour for around US$10.

If you'd like someone else to take charge of all the arrangements, several tour operators in Ankara run tours to Boğazkale for US$75 per person. Look for their advertisements in the *Turkish Daily News* or try Konvoy Tur (☎ 426 7624, 426 3110; fax 467 4608), Atatürk Bulvarı 233/8, Kavaklıdere, Ankara; or Angel Tours (☎ 436 1216; fax 437 6344), Kahramankadın Sokak 17, Gaziosmanpaşa, Ankara.

YOZGAT

About 35 km south-east of Boğazkale and on

the Ankara-Sivas highway is Yozgat (population 50,000, altitude 1301 metres). It's an unprepossessing provincial capital founded by the Ottomans in the 1700s. Now the main highway through town is lined with modern Turkish waffle-front apartment buildings. In contrast is the Nizamoğlu Konağı, a 19th century Ottoman house now used to hold ethnographic exhibits. Yozgat has those three things travellers need: hotels, restaurants and an otogar.

Orientation

The old main road, a block north of the highway, is more pleasant than the highway, Ankara Caddesi. Walk two blocks north to reach the main square, Cumhuriyet Meydanı with its old clock tower, Vilayet building, PTT, and an old Ottoman building now serving as local army offices; the sultan's monogram is still emblazoned in the tympanum. The Büyük Cami (or Çapanoğlu Camii, 1778), one long block west of the clock tower, is a late Ottoman work. Yozgat's otogar is less than one km east of the main square, an easy walk. To find your way to the main square from the otogar, go out the front door and turn right.

Five km south of Yozgat is Çamlık Milli Parkı (Pine-Grove National Park).

Places to Stay – bottom end

Right next door to the otogar is the *Pınar Otel & Lokanta* (☎ (473) 11997), Ankara Caddesi. The inauspicious entry is past smelly toilets. The rooms are OK, nothing special, but noise is a big factor here: the highway is out the front, the otogar is at the side, and a mosque is at the back. There is a wonderfully luxuriant vine in the 2nd-storey hall. Double rooms with sink cost US$7.

On the main square are two more places. The *Otel Hitit* (☎ (473) 11269), Cumhuriyet Meydanı, Sakarya Caddesi, has almost been worn out by long and frequent usage. Doubles with washbasin go for US$7, with shower for US$9. Next door is the *Hotel Saray* (☎ (473) 12032, 14333), Cumhuriyet Meydanı 1, an old place with high ceilings and far outdated décor. Here you have a

choice of rooms with shower (US$10 a double) or with washbasin (US$8); the rooms with showers sell out fastest.

Places to Stay – middle

The nicest place in town is the fairly dowdy one-star, 44-room *Turistik Yılmaz Oteli* (☎ (473) 11361, 11107), Ankara Caddesi 3, 66200 Yozgat, on the highway in the middle of town. The serviceable rooms here, all with private shower, are supplemented by a lift, restaurant, bar and a Turkish bath. Rates are from US$17 to US$19 a single, US$26 to US$32 a double, but you should haggle for a reduction. Rooms with a bathtub as well as shower cost more.

Places to Eat

The dining room in the *Yılmaz Oteli* is where visiting business types dine, but the locals like the *Ömür Lokantası* down the hill a few steps from the clock tower. It's basic, but I had a good biftek, salad, ayran, fıstıklı baklava and a large glass of tea for US$3. The *Merkez Restaurant*, facing the main square near the clock tower, is more light and airy, with similar prices.

Getting There & Away

Like with travelling to Sungurlu, getting to Yozgat is easy: catch a bus from the otogar in Ankara (220 km), Kayseri (250 km), or Sivas (230 km). For most other destinations, you must change buses at one of those cities. All three are a three-hour, US$6 ride from Yozgat.

Occasional minibuses run from Yozgat to Alaca, from which you can hitch to Alacahöyük, or catch an onward minibus to Sungurlu. There is some minibus service to Boğazkale, but you may have to hire a taxi (US$30, up to four persons) or minibus (US$55, up to a dozen persons) to give you a full tour around: the ride to the site, two hours to look around, and return to Yozgat.

ÇORUM

Set on an alluvial plain on a branch of the Çorum River, Çorum (population 130,000, altitude 801 metres) is an agricultural town and provincial capital. As with so many settlements in Turkey, its origins extend back into the mists of history. People have been living here for at least 4000 years.

If you're travelling north or east by bus you may have to stop in Çorum. As a modern farming centre, it has little to hold your interest unless you're a chickpea addict. Çorum is Turkey's chickpea capital, and you'll see the chalky little pulses served up mostly as *leblebi* (dry roasted), which Turks love to munch while sipping rakı. The town's main street is lined with *leblebiciler* (chickpea roasters).

Orientation

The clock tower marks the centre of tidy and business-like Çorum. The PTT, Belediye, and tourist office are all within 100 metres of it. The otogar is one km from the clock tower along İnönü Caddesi.

Information

The Tourism Information Office (☎ (469) 17717, 18502) is in the Yeni Hükümet Konağı, A Blok, Kat 4, No 8 (New Government Building, Block A, 4th floor, office 8). More convenient is the little streetside office in the Kültür Bakanlığı Güzel Sanatlar Galerisi (Ministry of Culture & Fine Arts Gallery) building uphill from the clock tower on the right-hand side.

Walking Tour

Çorum has a small Byzantine kale (fortress) on a hilltop, and a Seljuk mosque, the 13th-century Ulu Cami (Great Mosque). Most of the other old buildings are Ottoman.

About 400 metres from the otogar is the museum Çorum Müzesi (open from 8.30 am to 5 pm every day for US$1), with a small but interesting and eclectic collection of Hittite, Byzantine-Roman and Ottoman exhibits. Ethnographic exhibits cover Turkish life during the last century. If you're stuck for an hour or two in between buses, go out the main entrance of the otogar, turn left, then left again at the traffic roundabout. The museum is in the copse of pines on the

right-hand side at the next roundabout, across the street from the Turban Oteli.

Places to Stay & Eat

Çorum's hotels are geared not to tourists but to the commodity brokers who buy and sell chickpeas in bulk. You will be welcomed as an interesting and exotic guest.

Most hotels are along the main street (İnönü Caddesi) between the museum and the clock tower. *Aygün Oteli* (☎ (469) 13364), not far from the museum and the Turban Oteli, is old but carefully maintained. Double rooms with shower are officially priced at US$13, but I was quoted US$10 when I hesitated.

The two-star *Hotel Kolağası* (☎ (469) 11971; fax 15451), İnönü Caddesi 97, one km from the otogar, charges US$16/22 a single/double for its rooms with shower.

Hotel Merih (☎ (469) 18379), facing the clock tower on İnönü Caddesi, is oldish and a bit expensive, but there's little to choose from in Çorum. Doubles with sink go for US$15, with shower for US$18; breakfast costs extra.

The fanciest place in town is the *Turban Oteli*, near the museum, charging slightly more than the Kolağası.

As far as food goes, there are several little restaurants just outside the otogar, and many more in the back streets of the centre, a block or two from the clock tower.

Getting There & Away

Çorum, on the main Ankara-Samsun highway, has good bus connections. Details of some services follow:

Alaca – 60 km, one hour, US$2.50; several minibuses daily

Amasya – 95 km, 1½ hours, US$4; several buses daily

Ankara – 242 km, 3½ hours, US$4 to US$6; frequent buses

Kayseri – 274 km, four hours, US$8; several buses daily

Samsun – 176 km, three hours, US$6; frequent buses

Sungurlu – 70 km, one hour, US$1.75; very frequent buses

Yozgat – 104 km, 1½ hours, US$4; several buses daily

AMASYA

Amasya (ah-MAHSS-yah, population 65,000, altitude 392 metres), capital of the province of the same name, was once the capital of a great Pontic kingdom. On the banks of the Yeşilırmak (Green River), surrounded by high cliffs, Amasya's dramatic setting adds interest to its numerous historic buildings: the rock-hewn tombs of the kings of Pontus, some fine old mosques, picturesque Ottoman half-timbered houses and a good little museum. Set away from the rest of Anatolia in its tight mountain valley, Amasya has a feeling of independence, self-sufficiency and civic pride.

History

Despite appearing to be a small, sleepy provincial capital, Amasya has seen exciting times. It was a Hittite town, and was conquered by Alexander the Great. When his empire broke up, Amasya became the capital of a successor-kingdom ruled by a family of Persian satraps. By the time of King Mithridates II (281 BC), the Kingdom of Pontus was entering its golden age and ruled over a large part of Anatolia. During the latter part of Pontus's flowering, Amasya was the birthplace of Strabo (circa 63 BC to 25 AD), the world's first historian.

Perhaps he felt constrained by Amasya's surrounding mountains, because he left home and travelled through Europe, West Asia and North Africa, and wrote 47 history and 17 geography books. Though Strabo's history books have mostly been lost, we know something of their content because he was quoted by many other classical writers.

Amasya's golden age ended when the Romans decided it was time to take all of Anatolia (47 BC) and call it Asia Minor. After them came the Byzantines, who left little mark on the town, and the Seljuks (1075) and Mongols (early 1300s), who built numerous fine buildings which still stand. In Ottoman times, Amaysa was an important power-base when the sultans led military campaigns into Persia. A tradition developed that the Ottoman crown prince should be taught statecraft in Amasya, and test his

knowledge and skill as governor of the province. The town was also noted as a centre of Islamic theological study, with as many as 18 medreses and 2000 theological students in the 19th century.

At the end of the Ottoman Empire, after WW I, Mustafa Kemal (Atatürk) escaped from the confines of occupied İstanbul and came to Amasya via Samsun. At Amasya he met secretly on 12 June 1919 with several friends and hammered out basic principles for the Turkish struggle for independence. The monument in the main square commemorates the meeting; other scenes depict the unhappy state of Turks in Anatolia before the War of Independence. Each year, Amasyalıs commemorate the meeting with a week-long art and culture festival beginning on 12 June.

Orientation

The otogar is at the north-eastern edge of town and the railway station, at the western edge. It's several km from either terminal to the main square, marked by a statue of Atatürk and a bridge across the river. Most of the town (including the main square, the bazaar and the museum) is on the southern bank of the river. On the northern bank are various government and military offices, the tombs of the Pontic kings, and the kale (citadel). You may want to take a bus, minibus, or taxi to and from the otogar and the railway station, but everything else is within walking distance.

Information

The Tourism Information Office (☎ (378) 83385) is in Mehmetpaşa Mahallesi at Mustafa Kemal Bulvarı 27 in a kiosk on the riverbank just north of the main square. Some leaflets are available; the staff speak English, French or German. Amasya's postal code is 05000.

Historic Houses

Start your sightseeing with a walk around the town, admiring the old Ottoman houses along the river. One of them on the north bank, the **Hazeranlar Konağı**, dates from the 1800s. It was finely restored in the early

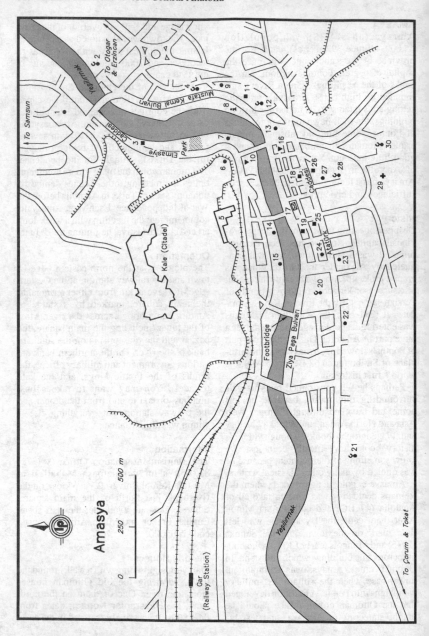

Also on the north bank of the river are the Vilayet (government building) and Belediye Sarayı (Municipality); beside the latter is the shady **Belediye Parkı** with tea and soft drink service, and entertainment some evenings. There are numerous nice old houses here as well, still in use and occupied . Walk beneath the railway line directly behind the huge military building on the river (near the Turban Hotel), and you will enter a neighbourhood of such houses.

Pontic Tombs

Looming above the northern bank of the river is a sheer rock face with the easily observed rock-cut Kral Kaya Mezarları, or Tombs of the Pontic Kings, carved into it. Cross the river, climb the well-marked path towards them and you'll come to the **Kızlar Sarayı**, or Palace of the Maidens. Though there were indeed harems full of maidens here, the palace which stood on this rock terrace was not theirs, but that of the kings of Pontus and later of the Ottoman governors.

Follow the path upward; you may find yourself accompanied by a youthful unappointed guide repeating a few words of German and hoping for a tip. If you don't want a guide, say *İstemez* (eess-teh-MEHZ). In a few minutes you will reach the royal tombs of Pontus, cut deep in the rock as early as the 300s BC, and used for cult worship of the deified rulers. There are 18 tombs in all, but only a few are worth a look. Opening hours are from 8.30 am to 5 pm. Admission costs US$1

Citadel

Above the tombs, perched precariously on the cliffs, is the kale or citadel. The remnants of the walls date from Pontic times, perhaps from those of King Mithridates. The fortress was repaired by the Ottomans, and in the late 1980s in the interests of tourism. Somewhat below the citadel on a ledge is an old Russian cannon which is fired during the holy month of Ramazan to mark the ending of the fast. The view is magnificent.

To reach the kale, cross the northern

1980s, and has been set up as an ethnology museum and gallery for travelling exhibits, usually open from 9 am to noon and 1.30 to 5 pm for US$1 (closed on Monday).

Restoration of the old houses is highly valued by the Amasyalıs. However, many local residents would like to replace old buildings they own (which are expensive to renovate) with more efficient modern structures, so the battle between conservation and progress goes on.

You can stay the night in several historic houses which have been opened as pensions. See the Places to Stay section for details.

bridge near the Büyük Ağa Medresesi and follow the Samsun road for 850 metres to a street on the left marked 'Kale'. It's 1.7 km up the mountainside to a small car park, then another 15 minutes' steep climb to the summit, marked by a flagpole.

Amasya Museum

There's a tidy little museum on Atatürk Caddesi, open from 8.30 am to noon and from 1.30 to 5.30 pm (closed on Monday). Admission costs US$1. The collection includes artefacts from Pontic, Roman, Byzantine, Seljuk and Ottoman times, and there is an ethnographic exhibit.

Perhaps the most interesting exhibits are the wooden doors of the ancient Gök Medrese Camii, the carpets, and the strange baked-clay coffins. The upper floor has more to offer than the lower: note the bronze figure of Teshup, the Hittite storm god, with pointed cap and huge almond-shaped eyes. In the museum garden is a Seljuk tomb, the **Sultan Mesut Türbesı**, now containing some fairly gruesome mummies which date from the Seljuk period and were discovered beneath the Burmalı Cami.

Sights West of the Main Square

Across Atatürk Caddesi from the museum is the **Sultan Beyazıt II Camii** (1486), Amasya's principal mosque, with its medrese, kütüphane (library) and a nice garden.

West of the museum about a half km is the **Gök Medrese Camii** (GEURK meh-drehseh) or Mosque of the Blue Seminary, built in 1276 by the Seljuks. It has a wonderfully ornate Seljuk doorway once covered in blue tiles. Near it are several Seljuk türbes, including the **Torumtay Türbesi**, that of the man who founded the Gök Medrese Camii, (1266). The neighbouring Ottoman **Yörgüç Paşa Camii** dates from 1428.

East of the museum, across Atatürk Caddesi from the Kapalı Çarşı (Covered Market), is the **Taş Han** (1758), an Ottoman caravanserai still used by local traders and artisans. It was originally much larger, but much of it has fallen into ruin. Behind it to

the south is Amasya's famous **Burmalı Minare Camii** or Spiral Minaret Mosque. It's a Seljuk construction (1242) with elegant spiral carving on the minaret, true to its name.

Just to the east of the main square and Atatürk's statue, perched on a rise, is the **Gümüşlü Cami** (Silvery Mosque) which was built in 1326. It was rebuilt in 1491 after an earthquake, in 1612 after a fire, and again in 1688. It was added to in 1903, and the latest restoration was carried out in 1988.

Sights North of the Main Square

North of the main square along the river are Amasya's other historic buildings. The **Bimarhane Medresesi** (Insane Asylum Seminary) was built by the Ilkhanid Mongol governors of Amasya in 1308. The Ilkhans were the successors to the great Mongol Empire of Ghengis Khan. Their architecture reflects styles and motifs borrowed from many conquered peoples. Today only the outer walls of the building stand, stabilised to prevent further deterioration. With the pretty garden in front, this place has a sort of brooding presence. It's open for viewing all the time.

By the way, that large obtrusive building on the opposite bank of the river is an army recreation facility, contributing little to the beauty of the town.

Next along the river is the pretty mosque **Mehmet Paşa Camii**, a fairly early Ottoman mosque (1486), which now serves as the girls' Koran study centre of Amasya. The **Beyazıt Paşa Camii**, a few hundred metres north and just past the bridge, was finished in 1419, and bears many similarities to the famous early Ottoman Yeşil Cami in Bursa. Note especially the porch with marble arches in two colours of stone, the entranceway with gold and blue and the carved doors.

Across the river from the Beyazıt Paşa Camii is the **Büyük Ağa Medresesi** (Seminary of the Chief White Eunuch), built to an octagonal plan in 1488 by Sultan Beyazıt II's chief White eunuch, Hüseyin Ağa. Nicely restored, it still serves as a seminary for boys who are training to be hafız, theologians who have memorised the entire Koran. The medrese is not open to the public, but if the door is open you may peep in to see local boys at their Koranic studies, or playing a quick and refreshing game of football in the spacious yard.

On the southern bank of the river, Ziya Paşa Bulvarı is shady and cool with huge old plane trees. The market section south of here includes an early Ottoman covered bazaar (1483) or bedesten in its narrow streets.

Kaleköy

An interesting excursion can be made to Kaleköy, a village high in the mountains south-east of Amasya, noted for its ruined castle and nice old Ottoman houses. For details, contact Mr Ali Kamil Yalçın, proprietor of the İlk Pansiyon (see Places to Stay).

Yedi Kuğular Gölü

About 15 km west of town is the recently made artificial Yedi Kuğular Gölü (Seven Swans Lake), a favourite stopping-place for birds on their spring and autumn migrations. Trees have been planted and when they mature this kuş cenneti (bird paradise) may be as welcoming to humans as to birds.

Places to Stay – bottom end

There are few hotels in Amasya, and even fewer good ones, but at least they're mostly cheap.

For my money, the best place to stay is Ali Kamil Yalçın's İlk Pansiyon (☎ (378) 81689; fax 86277), Gümüşlü Mahallesi, Hitit Sokak 1, just east of the tourism kiosk by the river (follow the signs). Ali is an architect who discovered the once grand but then dilapidated mansion of Amasya's onetime Armenian bishop, rented it and restored it beautifully to its former grace and charm. The light, airy, spacious salons are now fitted with beds and bathrooms, and offered to travellers for US$10 to US$15 a single, US$15 to US$28 a double, depending upon the room. Some rooms have three beds. There are a few smaller, cheaper rooms with bath off the courtyard. Breakfast costs US$2.50, and is worth every lira; dinners

represent equally good value, and are served in the stone-paved courtyard to a congenial group of guests.

If the İlk Pansiyon is full (as it often is), try the Yuvam Pension (☎ (378) 81324, 12259), Atatürk Caddesi 24/5, on the main thoroughfare 2½ blocks south-west of the Atatürk statue on the north side of the street. Ms Esin and Mr İlker Yener have two pensions, this one in a modern apartment building, and another in a restored Amasya house similar to the İlk Pansiyon about 300 metres farther to the south-west. The restored house, with its quiet garden, is preferable, but both are good choices at US$12 to US$16 a double. Ask about rooms at the eczane (pharmacy/chemist's) at street level, which is where the Yeners are during the day.

Amasya's other cheap lodgings are far less atmospheric. The drab, dingy 31-room Apaydın Oteli (☎ (378) 81184), Atatürk Caddesi 58, is perhaps the most presentable, charging US$5/8 a single/double for a room with sink (cold water only); hot showers cost an additional US$1.50 per person. The common bathrooms have showers with electric-heater shower-heads; there is a Turkish-style splash bath as well. Don't confuse the Apaydın with the truly dismal Hotel Aydın, next to the equally depressing Hotel Ceylan, several blocks farther to the north-east, closer to the main square.

The inaptly named Konfor Palas (kohn-FOHR, Comfort Palace) (☎ (378) 81260), Ziya Paşa Bulvarı 4, by the river, has 36 drab rooms with sinks and charges even less: US$4/6 a single/double; your room may have a balcony looking onto the river. The toilets may give you bad dreams. The similarly priced Örnek Oteli (☎ (378) 8108), Ziya Paşa Bulvarı 2, is across the courtyard, with 13 basic rooms without baths.

Places to Stay – middle

The two-star Turban Amasya Hotel (☎ (378) 84054; fax 84056), Herkiz Mahallesi, Elmasiye Caddesi 20, north of the centre near the Büyük Ağa Medresesi, is a small, fairly quiet 34-room hotel on the riverbank. It has a restaurant and bar with fine views of the river, and rooms with shower for US$22/30 a single/double, breakfast included. It's often filled to capacity by tour groups.

On the main street across from the Yuvam Pension is the new *Hotel Maden* (☎ (378) 84256), above the Ford-Tofaş automobile showroom. Opened in 1992, it's newer than the Turban, but also noisier, at similar prices.

About 28 km north of Amasya on the Samsun road, at Suluova, is the *Saraçoğlu Muzaffer Turistik Tesisleri* (Muzaffer Saraçoğlu's Touristic Installations;☎ (378) 71010, 71783), a small highway motel and restaurant next to a fuel station. Rooms are simple but acceptable, though there is some highway noise. The price for a room with bath is from US$12 to US$18 a single, US$20 to US$26 a double.

Places to Eat

Look for small restaurants in the narrow market streets off the main square (the one with the statue of Atatürk), such as the *Çiçek Lokantası*, which is very basic but cheap and serviceable, with decent roast chicken and ready food. The *Zafer Lokantası*, three short blocks farther along, is also good. The *Elmas Kebap ve Pide Salonu* (☎ 11606), on the same street more or less behind the Hotel Apaydın, is similar, and stays open late in the evening.

There are many small kebapçıs north of the Yuvam Pension in the bazaar streets around the covered market. The *Beslen Kebap ve Pide Salonu* (☎ 83208), Kocacık Çarşısı 18, also has good food and friendly staff.

Ocakbaşı Aile Kebap ve Pide, in front of the Konfor Palas Oteli, is pleasant and not expensive. It has outdoor tables where you can enjoy your freshly baked pide.

For tea in a pleasant garden setting, go to the Belediye Parkı, across the river from the main square, by the town hall.

For nicer dining at a higher price (from US$5 to US$8 for a full meal with drinks), go to the dining rooms in the Turban Amasya Hotel.

Foreign tourists are also welcome at the *Amasya Şehir Derneği* (☎ 11013), in the Öğretmen Evi building overlooking the river at the north end of the bridge opposite the main square. This is a quasi-private club with stark décor but good moderately priced food and drink. Amasya's prominent citizens come here to eat, drink, talk business and while away the evening.

Getting There & Away

Amasya is not far off the busy route between Ankara and Samsun, so buses are frequent. It is also on the railway line between Samsun and Sivas, but the daily trains are quite slow. Some bus companies (Amasyatur, Azimkar) maintain ticket offices on Atatürk Caddesi across from the Belediye building, just east of the Sultan Beyazıt II Camii. Details of some daily bus services follow:

Adıyaman (for Nemrut Dağı) – 650 km, 10 hours, US$20; one bus
Ankara – 335 km, five hours, US$9; several dozen buses
Çorum – 95 km, 1½ hours, US$4; at least eight buses
İstanbul – 685 km, 11 hours, US$18; a dozen buses
Kayseri – 405 km, eight hours, US$15; three buses
Malatya – 460 km, nine hours, US$17; five buses
Samsun – 130 km, 2½ hours, US$4; 10 buses
Sivas – 225 km, four hours, US$8; five buses
Tokat – 115 km, two hours, US$4; nine buses

In addition, there are direct buses to many other destinations, including Adana, Alanya, Antakya, Antalya, Bursa, Diyarbakır, Erzurum, Gaziantep, İzmir, Marmaris and Şanlıurfa.

TOKAT

Tokat (TOH-kaht, population 90,000, altitude 623 metres) is on the southern edges of the Black Sea region and shares in its fertility. It's one of those towns that is half Ottoman and half modern.

History

Its history is very involved and long, starting in 3000 BC and proceeding through the sovereignty of 14 various states, including the Hittites and Phrygians, the Medes and the Persians, the empire of Alexander the Great, the kingdom of Pontus, the Romans, the Byzantines, the Turkish principality of Danismend, the Seljuks and the Mongol Ilkhanids.

Tokatlıs are proud that it was near their town that Julius Caesar said 'Veni, vidi, vici' (I came, I saw, I conquered) in 47 BC after having defeated Pharnaces II, King of Pontus, in a quick and easy four-hour battle.

By the time of the Seljuk Sultanate of Rum, Tokat was the sixth largest city in Anatolia and on important trade routes. The roads approaching the city are littered with great Seljuk bridges and caravanserais testifying to its earlier importance.

After the Mongols rushed in and blew away everyone's composure in the mid-1200s, their Ilkhanid successors took over, followed by a succession of petty warlords who did little for Tokat.

Under the Ottomans, who took the town in 1402, it resumed its role as an important trading entrepôt, agricultural town (the grapes are especially good) and coppermining centre (the copper artisans have been famous for centuries). Significant non Muslim populations (Greek, Armenian, Jewish) were in charge of the town's commerce until the cataclysm of WW I. There is still a small but active Jewish congregation here.

Tokat doesn't get too many tourists, and those who come usually have a quick look at the famous Gök Medrese, the town's museum, then leave.

Orientation

The town centre is the big open square named Cumhuriyet Alanı, where you will find the Vilayet, the Belediye, the PTT and the coyly named Turist Otel. A subterranean shopping centre has added lots of retail space without ruining the spaciousness of the square. Across the main street from the shopping centre is the Tarihi Ali Paşa Hamamı, an old Turkish bath that's a fantasy of domes studded with bulbous glass to let in sunlight.

Looming above the town is a rocky promontory crowned by the obligatory ancient fortress. At its foot is clustered the bazaar and the town's old Ottoman-style houses.

The main street, Gazi Osman Paşa Bulvarı, runs downhill from the main square past the Gök Medrese to a traffic roundabout near which is the otogar, two km from the main square.

Information

The Tourism Information Office (☎ (475) 13753) is in the Vilayet building. Follow the signs in the main square. The far more helpful local tourist office (☎ (475) 18252), presided over by the ever-helpful Mr Erdoğan Horasan, is in the historic Taş Han. Tokat's postal code is 60000.

Blue Seminary Museum

The Blue Seminary (Gök Medrese) is the first thing to see. It was constructed in 1275 by Pervane Muhineddin Süleyman, a local potentate, after the fall of the Seljuks and the coming of the Mongols. Although once used as a hospital, it's now the town museum, next to the Taş Han and the Belediye hotels several hundred metres down the hill from Cumhuriyet Alanı.

The museum is open from 9 am to noon and 1.30 to 6 pm (closed on Monday); admission is US$1. Some exhibit labels are in both English and Turkish, though young students learning English may be on hand to guide you around.

Gök (sky) is also a name for blue, and it is the building's blue tiles which occasioned the name. Very few of these are left on the façade, which is now well below street level, but there are enough tiles on the interior walls to give an idea of what it must have looked like in its glory.

Museum exhibits include Stone Age and Bronze Age artefacts from excavations at Maşat Höyük, relics from Tokat's churches (before WW I there were good-sized Armenian and Greek communities here), tools and weapons, Korans and Islamic calligraphy and an excellent costume display. Also, an ethnographic section has examples of local kilims and Tokat's famous *yazma* art of wood-block printing on gauze scarves.

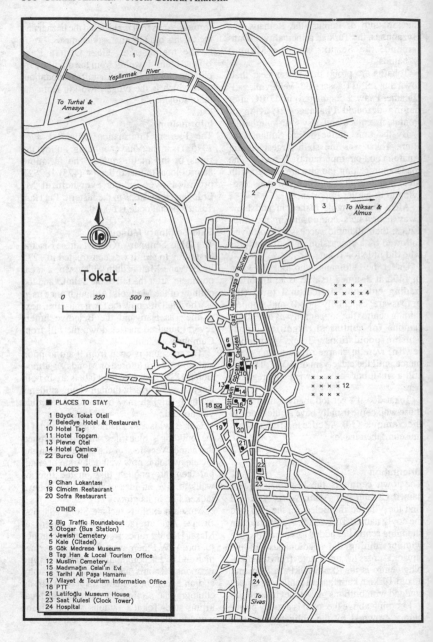

Yeşilırmak River

To Turhal &
Amasya

To Niksar &
Almus

Tokat

0   250   500 m

To Sivas

■ PLACES TO STAY

1 Büyük Tokat Oteli
7 Belediye Hotel & Restaurant
10 Hotel Taç
11 Hotel Topçam
13 Plevne Otel
14 Hotel Çamlıca
22 Burcu Otel

▼ PLACES TO EAT

9 Cihan Lokantası
19 Cımcım Restaurant
20 Sofra Restaurant

OTHER

2 Big Traffic Roundabout
3 Otogar (Bus Station)
4 Jewish Cemetery
5 Kale (Citadel)
6 Gök Medrese Museum
8 Taş Han & Local Tourism Office
12 Muslim Cemetery
15 Madımağın Celal'in Evi
16 Tarihi Ali Paşa Hamamı
17 Vilayet & Tourism Information Office
18 PTT
21 Latifoğlu Museum House
23 Saat Kulesi (Clock Tower)
24 Hospital

One corner of the museum is dedicated to Gazi Osman Paşa, a boy from Tokat who made good as an Ottoman general. After commanding with distinction in the Crimean War, Gazi Osman Paşa led the heroic but doomed 1877 defence of Plevne (in Bulgaria) against a Russian force twice the size of the Ottomans'.

Taş Han & Around

A few steps from the Gök Medrese, on the other side of the Belediye Hotel, is the Taş Han, an Ottoman caravanserai and workshop building which is still in use. Artisans' and craft shops have been set up in the old work spaces, and Tokat's modest *Rus pazarı* (Russian bazaar) flea market is held in the courtyard. Behind the Taş Han are bazaar streets lined with old half-timbered Ottoman houses.

Across Gazi Osman Paşa Bulvarı from the Taş Han, in the fruit and vegetable market, stands the **Hatuniye Camii** and its medrese, dating from 1485 during the reign of Sultan Beyazıt II. You may run across several other old hans and a covered market.

The bazaar's shops have lots of copperware, yazma-printed scarves and local kilims and carpets, some of which have Afghani designs because of the many Afghani refugees who settled here during the Soviet invasion of that country during the 1980s.

Several hundred metres north down the hill from the Gök Medrese, on the same side of the street, is the **Sümbül Baba Türbesi**, a Seljuk-style tomb dating from 1292. Beside it is a road up to the kale, of which little remains but the fine view.

Historic Houses

South of Cumhuriyet Alanı 250 metres on the main street stands the **Latifoğlu Museum House** (Müze Evi), one of the richest 19th-century houses on view in Turkey. It's open from 9 am to noon and 1.30 to 5 pm (closed on Monday) for 50c. Enter through the garden on the north side.

The house's large, gracious rooms are surrounded with low sedir sofas. In the bedrooms, bedding was taken up and stored in cabinets during the day, Asian-style. The sumptuous upstairs rooms, particularly the Paşa Odası (Pasha's Room), is adorned with prominent Star of David motifs, and though this motif was often used in Islamic art, it may be that the house's original owners were Jewish. The wide upstairs hall, light and airy, would have been used in summer only as it was not heated.

Madımağın Celal'ın Evi, Tokat's other well-preserved old house, is on the street to the east of the Tarihi Ali Paşa Hamamı, one block down. The street actually has several old houses, but all, including Madımağın, are still private, and not open to visitors – at least not yet.

Excursions

Zile, 70 km west of Tokat, is near where Caesar battled Pharnaces and afterwards sent his famous one-liner back to Rome. The actual battle site was along the Amasya-Zile road. The town of Zile has a very old citadel, and mosques and hamams dating from the Danışmend, Seljuk and Ottoman periods.

Niksar, formerly Neocaesarea, 54 km north-east of Tokat, was a city of the Pontic kings, then of the Romans. For 40 years after its conquest in 1077 by the Seljuk general Melik Ahmet Danışmend Gazi it was the capital of the Danışmend Turkish Emirate, and today preserves several rare examples of Danışmendid architecture, as well as many Ottoman works.

Turhal, 48 km to the west of Tokat, has an impressive citadel with a network of subterranean tunnels. It, too, was a Danışmendid town, and has several mosques, baths and other buildings to show for it.

Places to Stay – bottom end

Nearest to the otogar (one km) is the *Hotel Gündüz* (☎ (475) 11278), Gazi Osman Paşa Bulvarı 200, suitable if a bit noisy at US$10/16 a single/double with bath. The hotel is just over one km north of the main square – a 10-minute walk.

Among the cheapest places is the old *Belediye Hotel* (☎ (475) 16327), on Gazi Osman Paşa Bulvarı, which charges US$6/8 for a single/double with at least a sink, perhaps a shower.

Across the main street in the bazaar, near the Hatuniye mosque, the *Hotel Topçam* (☎ (475) 11429) is basic (with waterless rooms) but quite cheap at US$7.50 a double.

Up the hill 100 metres is the 26-room *Hotel Çamlıca* (☎ (475) 11269), Gazi Osman Paşa Bulvarı 85, which badly needs renovating. Prices are US$7/10 a single/double with cold-water sink or US$9/13 with hot water and private shower. Get a back room if you need peace and quiet. The nearby *Hotel Taç* (☎ (475) 11331, 20314), in the Birinci Vakıf İşhanı building, charges the same for much better rooms.

Right across the street from the Çamlıca and Taç is the *Plevne Otel* (☎ (475) 12207), Gazi Osman Paşa Bulvarı 83, named for the great pasha's (general's) most famous battle. Posted prices for its rooms are slightly higher than for those at the Çamlıca and Taç across the street, but price reductions are usually offered.

Facing the Vilayet building, just off Cumhuriyet Alanı, is the one-star *Turist Otel* (☎ (475) 11610, 12049), Cumhuriyet Alanı. The rooms with private showers are old but clean and serviceable, and the cosy lobby is decorated with bits of old sculpted stone and local woven and embroidered crafts. Rooms cost US$12/16 a single/double with shower.

Camping Tokat has no organised camping grounds, but you can camp at several recreation areas nearby, including Gümenek (the ancient town of Comana, nine km east); Almus, on the shores of the lake, 35 km east; Niksar Ayvaz hot springs; and Çamiçi forest, 53 km north-east.

Places to Stay – middle

Tokat finally has some middle-range hotels. The new *Burcu Otel* (☎ (475) 27570), Topçam Caddesi 86, just south of the clock tower and 200 metres south of the main square, has quite comfortable rooms with private baths for US$22 to US$25 a double, breakfast included.

The best middle-range bargain in town is the four-star *Büyük Tokat Oteli* (☎ (475) 19863, 16125; fax 13175), Demirköprü Mevkii, on the north-western outskirts just over three km from the main square. Its 60 air-con rooms all have TVs and private baths with tubs, and cost only US$22/30/40 for a single/double/suite, breakfast included. These prices must certainly rise as the hotel's business increases. For now, enjoy the hotel's good restaurant, swimming pool, Turkish bath, barber's shop and boutiques at low rates.

Places to Eat

The local speciality is Tokat kebap: skewers of lamb, sliced potato and aubergine (eggplant) hung on rods and baked (not grilled) in a wood-fired oven. Tomatoes and pimentos (peppers), which take less time to cook, are baked on separate skewers. As the lamb cooks, it releases juices which baste the potato and aubergine. You must try it.

The *Beyaz Saray İskender ve Kebap Salonu*, across the street from the Taş Han and the Belediye Hotel, is a simple split-level place with good Bursa-style döner kebap and a selection of grilled meats and salads. Meals for US$2 are easy to get, though you can spend a bit more.

Behind the Beyaz Saray, in the fruit and vegetable market near the Hatuniye Camii, are little köfte and kebap shops with even lower prices. Try the *Cihan Lokantası* on the corner: you can find it easily if you walk straight out of the Taş Han, across Gazi Osman Paşa Bulvarı, down the alley and into the *sebze halı* (vegetable market). Look for it on the right.

Between the Taş Han and the Gök Medrese, the *Belediye Lokantası*, on the ground floor of the Belediye Hotel, is fancier than the hotel and was for many years the chosen place for local potentates coming to chat, sip and munch in the evening. Expect to spend around US$3 or US$4.

The Turist Otel has a dining room with decent food and service and is a good place to meet other travellers.

The most pleasant place in town is the *Park Restaurant*, to the left of the Belediye on the main square. True to its name, dining tables here are set on terraces amidst evergreens and cooled (in spirit at least) by a tinkling fountain and pool. Come here for a meal or just a relaxing glass of çay. A good feed costs from US$4 to US$6.

Just south of Cumhuriyet Alanı on the main street, on the way to the Latifoğlu Museum House, is the *Sofra Restaurant*, light, airy and more modern, with good meals for US$4 to US$7. The *Cimcim Restaurant* on the west side of the main street serves good fresh pide and – surprise – beer as well. This is also the best place for Tokat kebap.

Getting There & Away

Bus Tokat's modern little otogar is not as busy as some, but buses still manage to get you where you want to go pretty easily. Buses run between the otogar and Cumhuriyet Alanı, but these are infrequent and if your luggage is heavy you may find yourself hiring a taxi for less than US$2 for the two-km ride to the main square. To walk, go 400 metres west to the traffic roundabout, turn

left (south) and it's just over one km to the cluster of hotels, 1.8 km to the main square.

Several bus companies have ticket offices on the south side of the main square, saving you a trip to the otogar to buy onward tickets. Daily services from Tokat include:

Amasya – 115 km, two hours, US$4; about nine buses
Ankara – 440 km, eight hours, US$12; frequent buses
İstanbul – 800 km, 14 hours, US$18; several buses
Samsun – 245 km, 4½ hours, US$7; frequent buses
Sivas – 105 km, two hours, US$4; frequent buses
Yozgat – 240 km, 4½ hours, US$6; hourly buses
   south to Yıldızeli, then hourly buses west to
   Yozgat

To/From Sivas From Tokat you can go east up to Kızıliniş Geçidi (Kızıliniş Pass, 1150 metres) then south into the Çamlıbel Dağları mountain range, up over Çamlıbel Geçidi (Çamlıbel Pass, 2038 metres), down again to Yıldızeli, then into Sivas. Along the way, you leave the lushness of the Black Sea littoral and enter the Anatolian Plateau with its dry red soil. For information on Sivas, see the Eastern Anatolia chapter.

Black Sea Coast

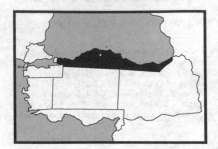

Turkey's Black Sea coast is a unique part of the country; it's lush and green throughout the year with plentiful rainfall. Dairy farming, fishing and tea production are big industries, and there are bumper crops of tobacco *(tütün)*, cherries *(kiraz)* and hazelnuts or filberts *(fındık)*. The hazelnut crop picked for export every year weighs close to 140,000 tonnes.

History

The coast was colonised in the 700s BC by Milesians and Arcadians, who founded towns at Sinop, Samsun and Trabzon. Later it became the Kingdom of Pontus. Most of Pontus's kings were named Mithridates, but it was Mithridates IV Eupator who gave the Romans a run for their money in 88-84 BC. He conquered Cappadocia and other Anatolian kingdoms, finally reaching Nicomedia (İzmit), which was allied with Rome. When the latter came to its defence, Mithridates pushed onward to the Aegean. The Roman response was hampered by civil war at home, but Rome's legions finally drove into Cappadocia and Pontus (83-81 BC), and Mithridates was forced to agree to a peace based on pre-war borders.

In 74-64 BC Mithridates was at it again, encouraging his son-in-law Tigranes I of Armenia to seize Cappadocia from the Romans. He tried, but the Romans conquered Pontus in response, forcing Mithridates to flee and later to commit suicide. The Romans left a small client-kingdom of Pontus at the far eastern end of the coast, based on Trebizond (Trabzon).

The coast was ruled by Byzantium, and Alexius Comnenus, son of Emperor Manuel I, proclaimed himself emperor of Pontus when the crusaders sacked Constantinople and drove him out in 1204. His descendants ruled this small empire until 1461, when it was taken by Mehmet the Conqueror.

While Alexius was in Trabzon, Samsun was under Seljuk rule and the Genoese had trading privileges. But when the Ottomans came, the Genoese burned Samsun to the ground before sailing away.

After WW I, the Ottoman Greek citizens of this region attempted to form a new Pontic state with Allied support. Turkish inhabitants, disarmed by the Allied occupation authorities, were persecuted by ethnic Greek guerrilla bands which had been allowed to keep their arms. It was fertile ground for a revolt. Mustafa Kemal (Atatürk) used a bureaucratic ruse to escape from the sultan's control in İstanbul, and landed at Samsun on 19 May 1919. He soon moved inland to Amasya, and began to organise what would become the battle for independence.

Getting There & Away

Details and schedules are given in the Getting There & Away sections for individual towns. Here is an overview to help you in planning your travels along the Black Sea coast.

Air Turkish Airlines (THY) has daily nonstop flights between Trabzon and Ankara and İstanbul. Turkish Air Transport (THT) has three nonstop flights weekly between İstanbul and Samsun. İstanbul Airlines flies between İstanbul and Trabzon daily except Sunday.

Bus Buses to and along the coast are (as usual) fast, frequent and cheap. The most prominent company is Ulusoy, which has many normal, no-smoking, double-decker and luxury services between Trabzon and many other cities. It's quite easy to take the bus to Samsun from Amasya (130 km), Ankara (420 km), Kayseri (450 km) or Sivas (340 km).

Train The *Karaelmas* express train departs from Ankara daily at 7.55 am, arriving in Zonguldak at 7.10 pm. Departure from Zonguldak is at 9.20 am, with arrival in Ankara at 8.08 pm. Single-class fare is US$5. There is virtually no other passenger rail service to the Black Sea coast.

Boat Turkish Maritime Lines operates car ferries on what amounts to a weekly mini-cruise service between İstanbul and Trabzon. This service departs from İstanbul each Monday evening: calls on Tuesday at Zonguldak, Sinop and Samsun; and on Wednesday at Giresun before arriving in Trabzon on Wednesday around noon. The boat proceeds to Rize by mid-afternoon, and returns to Trabzon to take on westbound passengers and cars at dinner time. On Thursday the boat calls at Giresun, Ordu, Samsun and Sinop, arriving back in İstanbul by mid-afternoon on Friday. The only problem with this service is that tickets sell out fast – well in advance in summer.

Some sample prices (per person, no meals included) to/from İstanbul follow. There are five classes of cabins from cheap 'E' class to deluxe 'A' class, plus aircraft-type Pullman reclining seats, the cheapest way to go.

Port	Seat	Cheap Cabin	Deluxe Cabin	Car
Zonguldak	US$15	$20	$35	–
Sinop	US$22	$28	$55	–
Samsun	US$24	$30	$65	$38
Gireson	US$28	$34	$85	$44
Trabzon	US$35	$42	$100	$52
Rize	US$43	$44	$110	$55

The cruise is fun, but much of the time you will be steaming at night, with no chance of seeing the passing scenery. Also, food and drink on board tend to be expensive (breakfast costs US$3, lunch or dinner US$10), so pack your own supplies. You can stock up in Samsun, as well. If you find the Pullman seat uncomfortable for sleeping or that the room is noisy or smoky, stake out some deck space, roll out your sleeping bag, and spend the night in the fresh air.

Getting Around

With the exception of Amasra, the Black Sea coast west of Sinop has little to offer at present. Its chief city, Zonguldak, is a gritty industrial centre and port town. Access to the western coast is slow and sometimes difficult.

Not so the coast east of Sinop, and especially east of Samsun all the way to Trabzon. The road is scenic and well-travelled by buses, and each town has something to offer. The 360-km ride from Samsun to Trabzon can even be done in a day if you wish. You must take at least a few hours to see the sights in Trabzon, before heading up onto the plateau to Erzurum, or eastward along the coast through the tea plantations to Rize and Hopa.

From Hopa you can climb into the mountains to Artvin in Anatolia's north-eastern corner, a region of exceptionally beautiful scenery described in detail in the Eastern Anatolia chapter.

AMASRA

Amasra (population 7500) is a pleasant coastal town nestled in the shadow of a fortified promontory which juts out assertively towards the coastal sea lanes. This small fishing port is little-visited by tourists, which adds to its charm. If you make it as far as Safranbolu (see the Central Anatolia chapter), you might consider visiting Amasra. It is on the western Black Sea coast 90 km north of Safranbolu and 100 km northeast of Zonguldak, and should not be confused with the similarly named inland city of Amasya 130 km south of Samsun.

Orientation

As you come into Amasra, you pass the museum on the left. If you go straight on you'll reach the eastern beach, which is mostly residential. Turn left at the park and follow Küçük Liman Caddesi around to Atatürk Meydanı (the main square), which serves as an otogar as well. Continue past the Çınar Pansiyon & Restaurant to find half a dozen small pensions and restaurants, plus the entrance to the citadel. The market, held on Tuesday and Friday, is next to the Belediye (Municipality) across the street from the Çınar. There's a small office here for the local Kültür ve Turizm Derneği (Culture & Tourism Association). The government tourist office, rarely open, is off to the east.

Amasra's postal code is 67570.

Citadel

Follow Küçük Liman Caddesi through several massive stone portals to reach the kale (citadel), the promontory fortified by the Byzantines when this small commercial port was known as Sesamos Amastris. The greater fortress seems to have replaced a smaller one erected against Russian adventurers around 861. Rented by the Genoese as a trading station in 1270, Amasra was taken by Mehmet the Conqueror in 1460 without a fight. During Napoleon's invasion of Ottoman Egypt in 1798, French traders doing business in Anatolia were gathered together and interned here as potential enemy agents until 1803. Under the rule of the Ottomans, Amasra lost its commercial importance to other Black Sea ports.

Much of the area within the citadel's walls is now residential. Make your way to the north-western outcrop to enjoy the views from a rocky meadow fragrant with wild figs, iris, bay and thistle, wild mint and sage.

Handicrafts

Throughout the town are scattered woodworkers' shops stuffed with turned-wood trinkets known as *ağaç biblo* (wooden bibelots). The woodworkers of Amasra traditionally carved such utilitarian objects as spoons, forks, distaffs and spatulas, and these things with their no-nonsense design are easy to spot. But as cheap stainless steel and aluminium utensils have invaded their markets, carvers have switched to producing decorative items such as statuettes, lampshades and key rings, none of which have the traditional items' appeal.

Places to Stay

Many cheap hotels are on Küçük Liman Caddesi between the Belediye and the citadel gate. *Otel Pansiyon Belvü Palas* (☎ (3895) 1237), Küçük Liman Caddesi 20, one flight up, has two floors of clean, bare waterless rooms well kept by the resident family of Mehmet Ot. Sunset views are best from rooms Nos 6, 7 and 8. The cost is US$4 per person.

Çınar Pansiyon (☎ (3895) 1018), Küçük Liman Caddesi 1, is slightly more expensive with similar rooms. Just past it is the simpler *Deniz Pansiyon* (☎ (3895) 1309), with a waterfront restaurant and good views.

Try also the *Fatih Pansiyon* (☎ 3895) 1948), Çekiciler Caddesi 36 – the shopping street which crosses the isthmus from north to south. The Fatih is closed in the off season.

Places to Eat

The *Çınar Restaurant*, in the pension of the same name across Küçük Liman Caddesi from the Belediye, is the most prominent, and perhaps the best eating place in town. The *Deniz* next door advertises canlı balık (live fish).

On the same street is *Pump Hamburger*, selling burgers for 60c, köfte (a better choice) for US$1. The nearby *Kupa* is a favourite local drinking place (it features draught beer), but food is served as well.

In the centre of the town near the park, *Köşem Pide ve Kebap Salonu* serves decent-sized portions of good food. It costs from US$2 to US$4 for a full meal. Alcohol is served as well. Right next door is the less fancy *Beyaz Fırın Pide-Kebap Salonu*; the *Saray Aile Pide-kebap Salonu* is a few doors along on the right. You could also try the *Karadeniz Kebap Salonu* in the market.

The shady park is the place to enjoy a cool drink or bracing glass of çay in either the *Café Kumsal* or the *Halikarnas Aile Çay Bahçesi*.

Getting There & Away

The town of Bartın, 10 km south of Amasra, is better served by transport than Amasra proper. You may have to take a bus from Ankara, Karabük, Safranbolu or Zonguldak to Bartın, then change to a minibus to reach Amasra.

AMASRA TO SİNOP

Travelling along the scenic coastal road from Amasra eastward to Sinop is slow going, with mostly local point-to-point minibus services. If you have your own transport it's enjoyable to explore this relatively un-touristed part of the coast, stopping for a swim at Bozköy beach west of Çakraz, to see the boatwrights at work in the town of Kurucaşile, or for a rest in the pretty village of Kapısuyu.

İnebolu (population 8000) reminds one of Amasra in its splendid isolation, but has several hotels, pensions and restaurants to serve travellers.

West of İnebolu, Abana is a modest resort which, in a decade, will no doubt be utterly changed, but is now sleepy and pleasant, with a decent beach. At Ayancık the road divides, with the left (northern) fork being the more scenic route to Sinop.

SİNOP

Sinop (SEE-nohp, population 30,000) is a natural site for a port, and has been one for millennia.

The town takes its name from the legend of Sinope, daughter of the river god Asopus. Zeus fell in love with her, and, in order to win her heart, promised to grant her any wish. Sinope, who didn't fancy marrying him, asked for eternal virginity. Zeus was outwitted, and he allowed Sinope to live out her days in happy solitude at the tip of this peninsula jutting into the Black Sea.

History

Sinop enjoyed a long history as a port beginning with Chalcolithic settlements around 4500 BC, and progressing from there through the Bronze Age and early Hittite period. Colonised from Miletus in the 8th century BC, its trade increased. Successive rulers – Cimmerians, Phrygians, Persians, the Pontic kings (who made it their capital), Romans and Byzantines – turned it into a busy trading centre. The Seljuks used Sinop as a port after taking it in 1214; but the Ottomans preferred to develop Samsun, which had better land communications, sub-ordinating Sinop to this eastern neighbour.

On 30 November 1853, Sinop was attacked without warning by a Russian armada. The local garrison was over-whelmed with the great loss of life. The battle of Sinop hastened the beginning of the Crimean War in which the Ottomans were allied with the British and French to fight Russian ambitions in the Near East.

Orientation

Sinop is at the narrow point of the peninsula, with the road continuing eastward beyond the town to beaches and land's end. The bus station is at the western entrance to the town by the fortified walls. From here the main street, Sakarya Caddesi, goes eastward through the centre 800 metres directly to the Sinop Valiliği (the provincial government headquarters), just north of which are the Tourism Information Office, museum and Temple of Serapis.

From the Valiliği, one can turn right (south) and descend the hill 250 metres past the clock tower and Belediye to the PTT, the prominent Hotel Melia-Kasım and the harbour. East of here the road leads along the shore three km to Karakum Plajı, a municipal beach.

Information

The Tourism Information Office (☎ (376) 15207 or 15298) is next to the museum and the Valiliği. There's a small kiosk also down at the harbour which is open only during high summer. The Turkish Maritime Lines

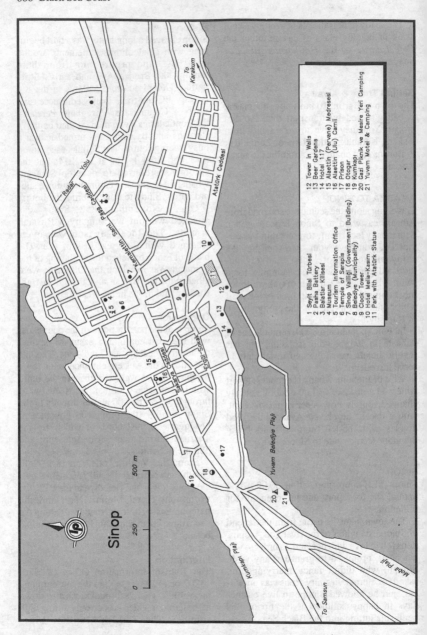

Sinop

500 m

250

0

1 Seyit Bilal Türbesi
2 Pasha Battery
3 Balatlar Kilisesi
4 Museum
5 Tourism Information Office
6 Temple of Serapis
7 Sinop Valiligi (Government Building)
8 Belediye (Municipality)
9 Clock Tower
10 Hotel Melia-Kasim
11 Park with Atatürk Statue
12 Tower in Walls
13 Beer Gardens
14 Hotel 117
15 Alaettin (Pervane) Medresesi
16 Alaettin (Ulu) Camii
17 Prison
18 Otogar
19 Kumkapi
20 Gazi Piknik ve Mesire Yeri Camping
21 Yuvam Motel & Camping

Top: Ottoman houses along the Kızılırmak River, Amasya (TB)
Bottom: Troglodyte dwellings, Göreme (TB)

Top: Black Sea coast near Giresun (TB)
Bottom: Street scene, Safranbolu (TB)

agency (☎ (376) 14122; fax 12781) is by the Hotel 117 on Rıhtım Caddesi, down by the harbour. Sinop's postal code is 57000.

Fortifications

Open to easy attack from the sea, Sinop needed trusty fortifications which it got, beginning with the walls erected in 72 BC by Mithridates IV, king of Pontus. At one time the walls, some three metres thick, were over two km in length.

Across Sakarya Caddesi, south from the otogar, is a prison built into the castle keep – a Seljuk construction converted to a prison by the Ottomans in 1877, and still in use. On the northern side of the otogar down near the shore is an ancient bastion called the Kumkapı (Sand Gate). Another square tower looms above the harbour on the south side of the town.

East of the centre almost to Karakum beach is the Pasha Battery, a gun emplacement built to defend the town during the Crimean War.

Religious Buildings

In the town centre on Sakarya Caddesi stands the **Alaettin Camii** (1267), also called the Ulu Cami. It was constructed on the orders of Muinettin Süleyman Pervane, a powerful Seljuk grand vizier. The mosque has been repaired many times; its marble mihrab and mimber were added in 1429 by the local Candaroğlu emir.

Next to the Alaeddin Camii is the **Alaettin Medresesi**, also called the Süleyman Pervane or Alaiye Medresesi, built in the late 1200s by the selfsame Süleyman Pervane to commemorate the Seljuk conquest of Sinop.

Go eastward uphill from the Sinop Valiliği along Kemalettin Sami Paşa Caddesi to reach the **Balatlar Kilisesi**, a Roman temple converted to a Byzantine church in the 600s. A few traces of frescoes are visible.

Farther uphill, one km from the Valiliği, is the **Cezayirli Ali Paşa Camii** (Mosque of Ali Pasha the Algerian). Within the mosque is the **Seyit Bilal Türbesi**, or tomb of St Bilal, built for Emir Tayboğa in 1297. Seyit Bilal, grandson of Hüseyin (who was a grandson

of the Prophet Muhammed), was blown ashore here in the 600s and put to death by the Byzantines.

Down near the harbour in the market area is the **Tersane Hacı Ömer Camii** (1903) formerly a Gothic church. Next to it is a touching monument, a fountain built in memory of the many Turkish soldiers who died in the surprise Russian attack of 1853. The fountain was built using the money that was recovered from the soldiers' pockets.

Museum & Temple

Just north of the Valiliği is the museum Sinop Müzesi, open from 8.30 am to 5.30 pm (closed on Monday) for US$1. The collection spans Sinop's long history from the Bronze Age to the Turkish War of Independence. A collection of Greek Orthodox icons reminds that the Black Sea coast was heavily populated by Ottoman Greeks until the War of Independence and the subsequent exchange of populations with Greece.

In the museum's garden are a few remains of an ancient **Temple of Serapis** (the Egyptian embodiment of Apollo) excavated in 1951.

Beaches

The waters of the Black Sea are chillier than those of the Aegean or Mediterranean seas, but can be refreshing nonetheless.

As you approach the town, turn right (south) a few hundred metres west of the otogar and prison and descend to the shore to find the Yuvam Belediye Plajı (municipal beach), a forest camping area, and the Yuvam Motel. On the north side of the peninsula near the Kumkapı is another small beach where the water is cooler.

Three km east of the harbour on the southern shore is the Karakum beach, officially styled the Özel İdare Karakum Yüzgeç Tatil Köyü, with a pay beach of black sand, restaurant, nightclub and a nice camping ground with shady tent sites and electrical hook-ups.

Across the peninsula on the northern shore is Akliman, a long beach backed by forest and adjoined by the Hamsaroz fjord.

Places to Stay
Look first for cheap lodgings down by the harbour. *Hotel 117* (☎ (376) 15117, 11579), Rıhtım Caddesi 1, was once Sinop's prime place to stay, and though it has been superseded it is still alright. Rooms with bath and water view are available for US$14 a double.

Within one block of the Hotel 117 and the neighbouring Ziraat Bankası are many cheaper places. Directly inland one block from the Hotel 117 is the tidy *Karahan Oteli* (☎ (376) 10688), in a little courtyard. Rooms with sinks and insect-screens cost US$5/8 a single/double.

Otel Denizci and *Otel Meral* are right across the street from the prominent Ziraat Bankası. Of these two, the Meral is the better choice, but there are pensions which are quieter.

Yılmaz Aile Pansiyonu (☎ (376) 15752), at No 11 on the little street east of the PTT Evi and Hotel 117, charges less (US$3.50 per person and US$1.25 for hot showers), but offers less as well. Slightly farther inland half a block is the similar *Pansiyon Alkan* (☎ (376) 15761).

The best place to stay in town is the two-star *Hotel Melia-Kasım* (☎ (376) 14210, -1; fax 11625), Gazi Caddesi 49. It's 250 metres south of the Valiliği, just east of the harbour on the waterfront. The location is good, with sea views from many rooms, but the nuclear-powered nightclub may keep you up till all hours of the night. Rooms cost US$25/32 a double for land/sea views, breakfast included.

Camping South-west of the otogar near the Yuvam Belediye Plajı are two camping grounds. *Gazi Piknik ve Mesire Yeri*, 300 metres south-west of the main road, is better. You camp in full shade with fine views of the sea. There are tables and benches, and even a playground for the children. Transport to the town centre is handy along the main road. The charge of US$3 per site is rarely levied at slow times of the year.

Farther along the same road, 700 metres off the main road (two km west of the Valiliği), the *Yuvam Belediye Dinlenme Tes-*

isleri camping ground is fairly dismal, with shadeless sites with hook-ups, but it has a fairly nice restaurant with a shady terrace.

The camp sites at Karakum (☎ (376) 15117), 3.5 km east of the Valiliği along the southern shore are nice and shady, with hook-ups, and cost about US$3 per site.

Places to Eat
Özgür Aile Lokantası (☎ 15425), half a block inland from the Hotel 117 at Ortayol Sokak 8, has cheap ready-food soups, stews and other dishes. It's easy to get a full meal for US$3. *Karadeniz Lokantası* (☎ 11956), a tidy eatery directly inland across the street from the Hotel 117, serves breakfast, lunch and dinner at good prices, but no alcohol.

East of the Hotel 117 along the waterfront are various beer gardens, including the *Barınak Café*, which also serves light meals. But the best restaurant here is the *Restaurant Uzun Mehmet*, facing the end of the dock. A signboard lists prices: breakfast goes for less than US$2; full lunches and dinners from US$4 to US$8, slightly more for fish.

Getting There & Away
Details of bus services from Sinop's small otogar follow:

Ankara – 436 km, nine hours, US$13
İstanbul – 702 km, 12 hours via Kastamonu and Karabük, US$17
Karabük (for Safranbolu) – 300 km, six hours, US$9
Samsun – 168 km, three hours, US$5
Trabzon – 513 km, six hours, US$9; change at Samsun

There is no direct bus service between Sinop and Amasra.

Getting Around
Dolmuşes run through the town from the otogar in the west to Karakum on the south-eastern shore. The fare is 30c.

SİNOP TO SAMSUN
On the Samsun road 86 km south-west of Sinop is Bafra, a town known as a centre of the Black Sea tobacco-growing region. There is no reason to stop, though if you need

a meal there are numerous small restaurants on the main square near the Hükümet Konağı (government headquarters). A few rather forlorn hotels can provide lodging in an emergency.

SAMSUN

Burned to the ground by the Genoese in the 1400s, Samsun (sahm-SOON, population 325,000) has little to show for its long history. It is a major port and commercial centre and the largest city on the coast. Your reason to stop here would be to change buses, have a meal or find a bed.

Orientation

The city centre is Cumhuriyet Meydanı (Republic Square), just north-west of a large park with an equestrian statue of Atatürk, and, just south-east of the statue, there's the Vilayet (provincial government headquarters). A handy landmark is the Hotel Yafeya on the north-west side of Cumhuriyet Meydanı.

The railway station is one km south-east and the otogar just over two km south-east of the centre along the shore road Atatürk Bulvarı. Any city bus or dolmuş heading north-west through Samsun will drop you at Cumhuriyet Meydanı.

The main business street with banks, PTT and restaurants is Kazım Paşa Caddesi (sometimes called Bankalar Caddesi), one block inland (south-west) from the shore road, running north from Cumhuriyet Meydanı.

Information

Samsun's Tourism Information Office is north-east of the Atatürk statue across Atatürk Bulvarı. The Directorate of Tourism (☎ (36) 15 28 87) is at 19 Mayıs Mahallesi, Talimhane Caddesi 6. Samsun's postal code is 55000.

Places to Stay – bottom end

Samsun has lots of good cheap hotels close to the town centre. Make your way to the Atatürk statue and Vilayet building just one block south-east of Cumhuriyet Meydanı.

Stand midway between these two landmarks and walk inland one block to the futuristic mosque Merkez Camii. You've just walked through Kale Mahallesi, an area crowded with cheap hotels such as the *Otel Altay* (☎ (36) 31 68 77), Meşrutiyet Sokak 5 a clean, friendly place charging only US$7/11 a single/double with shower. *Otel Özlü* (☎ (36) 35 60 39), Himai Etfal Sokak 5, charges similar rates, but its rooms are not as good.

In the surrounding streets are several other choices, including the passable *Otel Sönmez* (☎ (36) 31 26 69), the borderline *Otel Menekşe* (☎ (36) 31 98 35), and the very basic but cheap *Otel Bahar*.

The *Hotel Gold* (☎ (36) 11 19 59), Orhaniye Geçidi 4, represents the best value for money. It's a good, quiet, clean place renting rooms with bath for US$12/18 a single/double.

Another area to explore for cheap hotels is around Gaziler Meydanı in the bazaar. Walk north-west along Kazım Paşa Caddesi to the Gökçe Otel (on the right), but turn left and walk several short blocks to Gaziler Meydanı with its small, modern mosque. Two hotels on Hacı Hasur Sokak have raised their prices unconscionably since I mentioned them in this guide, however.

Right at the otogar is the 44-room *Otel Terminal* (☎ (36) 11 55 19), fairly run-down but serviceable if you've been on a bus all day. Singles/doubles with bath cost US$12/16.

Places to Stay – middle

The three-star, 96-room *Hotel Yafeya* (☎ (36) 11 65 65; fax 15 11 35), Cumhuriyet Meydanı, has modern furnishings with lots of natural wood. The roof restaurant and bar offer decent food and good views of the city. Prices for the comfortable – if somewhat noisy – rooms with bath are from US$20 to US$25 a single, US$25 to US$30 a double; larger suites with TV and minibar cost slightly more.

Just around the corner, on Kazım Paşa Caddesi, is the two-star *Vidinli Oteli* (☎ (36) 11 60 50; fax 11 21 36), at Kazım Paşa

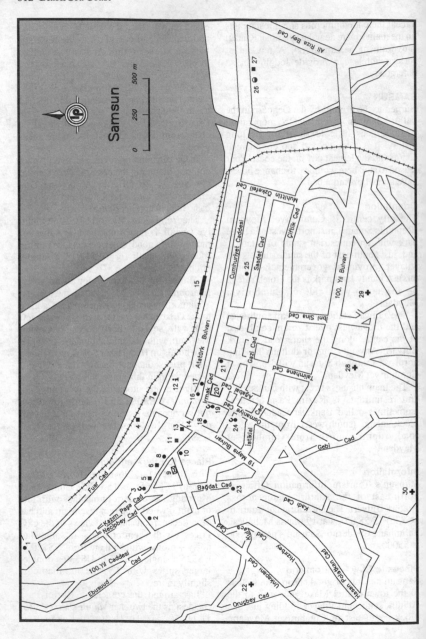

Samsun

0   250   500 m

■ PLACES TO STAY

4 Turban Büyük Samsun Oteli
5 Gökçe Otel
6 Hotel Burç
11 Vidinli Oteli
13 Hotel Yafeya
27 Otel Terminal

OTHER

1 Turkish Maritime Lines Passenger Terminal
2 Belediye (Municipality)
3 Ulu Cami
7 Archaeological Museum
8 Turkish Central Bank
9 PTT
10 Turkish Airlines Office
12 Tourism Information Office
14 Cumhuriyet Meydanı
15 Railway Station
16 Atatürk Statue & Park
17 Vilayet
· 18 Bus Ticket Offices
19 Merkez Camii
20 Kale Mahallesi
21 Directorate of Tourism
22 Hospital
23 Hamam
24 Mosque
25 Police
26 Otogar
28 Hospital
29 Hospital
30 Hospital

Caddesi 4. It's a passable and convenient place with 65 rooms with shower, priced at US$13/24 a single/double, breakfast included.

Walk north-west along Kazım Paşa Caddesi to find more hotels. A few blocks along is the small one-star *Hotel Burç*, (BOORCH) (☎ (36) 11 54 80), Kazım Paşa Caddesi 36. The 38 rooms with bath go for US$12/17 a single/double. Get a quiet room off the main street.

Around the corner from the Burç is the one-star, 35-room *Gökçe Otel* (☎ (36) 11 79 52), Ferah Sokak 1. All rooms here seem to have small balconies opening onto a quiet side street; some rooms have partial views of

the sea. Services include a lift, rooftop bar, TV lounge and restaurant. Rates are slightly more than at the Burç. Both the Burç and the Gökçe are often filled with bus-tour groups from Balkan countries.

Places to Stay – top end

The city's best place to stay is the four-star *Turban Büyük Samsun Oteli* (☎ (36) 11 07 50; fax 11 07 40), Sahil Caddesi, on the shore just north of Cumhuriyet Meydanı, set in its own spacious gardens. Services abound: swimming pool; tennis court; nightclub; pastry-shop café; games room; and, of course, a comfortable bar and dining room. The 117 air-con rooms cost from US$50 to US$66 a single, US$75 to US$100 a double, depending upon whether you have a sea view (more expensive) or a land view; breakfast is included.

Places to Eat

The hotel areas also have lots of small, good restaurants. Look for the *San Restaurant* on the corner of Irmak Caddesi and Hürriyet Sokak, directly opposite the Vilayet, two blocks south-east of Cumhuriyet Meydanı. This is the most pleasant place; it's near the park and offers meals for US$4 or less. A few steps to the north-west (towards the Hotel Yafeya), facing the park, are the *Ravza Restaurant*, which serves good meals and cheap lahmacun (Arab-style pizza), and the adjoining *Zirve Pide ve Kebap Salonu*, another kebap, pide and lahmacun place. *Birtat Pastanesi*, next in this row, satisfies desires for sweets and puddings.

On the corner of Irmak and Osmaniye caddesis is the *Oba Restaurant*, and a few steps down Osmaniye Caddesi is the *Ovalı Restaurant*, where you can have wine or beer with your meal.

Ezgi Akçaabat Köfte Salonu, Kazım Paşa Caddesi 31 across from the Hotel Burç, serves good cheap köfte and other dishes. It tends to be open when other places are closed, such as on holidays and at breakfast time.

At the northern end of Kazım Paşa Caddesi is a small square called Saathane

Meydanı with a modern clock tower and numerous small, cheap eateries.

The dining room at the *Büyük Samsun* is perhaps the best in town, and not overly expensive. In the evening it has live entertainment and full meals for US$10 if you order Turkish dishes, about twice as much if you go for the kordon blö (cordon bleu steak), fileminyon mantarlı (filet mignon with mushrooms), fish or fondue.

Getting There & Away

Air Turkish Air Transport (THT) has nonstop flights between İstanbul and Samsun on Monday, Wednesday and Friday. Make your reservations at the Turkish Airlines office (☎ (36) 11 34 55, 11 50 85), Kazım Paşa Caddesi 11/A.

Bus Samsun seems to offer at least one bus service per day to every important destination in Turkey, and very frequent buses to logical next destinations. Though there are daily trains between Samsun and Sivas, the train trip takes over 12 daylight hours, and is hardly worth it when the bus makes the same trip in about half the time. Details of some daily bus services follow:

Amasya – 130 km, 2½ hours, US$4; 10 buses
Ankara – 420 km, eight hours, US$14; frequent buses
Artvin – 615 km, 10 hours, US$18; several buses
Giresun – 220 km, four hours, US$4; frequent buses
İstanbul – 750 km, 12 hours, US$20; several buses
Kayseri – 530 km, nine hours, US$16; a few buses
Sinop – 168 km, three hours, US$5; several buses
Sivas – 345 km, 6½ hours, US$12; a few buses
Trabzon – 365 km, six hours, US$12; frequent buses
Yozgat – 275 km, 7½ hours, US$13; a few buses

Boat For details of the Turkish Maritime Lines car ferries between İstanbul and Trabzon, stopping at Samsun, see the beginning of this chapter. The Turkish Maritime Lines agent (☎ (36) 11 46 45; fax 11 46 44) is Türer Alemderzade, by the harbour.

EAST TO TRABZON

Two of Anatolia's great rivers, the Kızılırmak and the Yeşilırmak, empty into the sea here on either side of Samsun. The rivers have built up fertile deltas which are now planted with corn and tobacco crops amidst scenes of bucolic contentment. Each house has a lush lawn from its door to the roadway, and each lawn has its own fat cow.

Ünye

Ünye (EURN-yeh, population 40,000), a small port town amidst hazelnut groves, is 95 km east of Samsun. It shares a similar history to Sinop, Samsun and other Black Sea coastal towns, with the exception that the great Turkish poet Yunus Emre, who wrote during the early 1300s, is thought to have been born here.

Seven km inland from the town along the Niksar road stands Ünye Kalesi, a fortress built by the Byzantines to protect this pass to the interior.

In the centre of Ünye, you might note that the Eski Hamam Turkish bath was once a church.

Ünye's bus station is 500 metres southeast of the Atatürk statue in the centre.

Places to Stay As you approach Ünye coming from Samsun, the road skirts the beaches and passes a number of camping grounds, pensions and seaside motels, including the *Gölevi*, *Europa* and *Camping Derya* (☎ (373) 13473); more development is on the way.

The *Belediye Çamlık Motel* (☎ (373) 11333), in a pine forest on the shore just under two km west of Ünye, is well-used but pleasantly situated and not overly expensive for what you get. A double room with bath and sea view costs US$16, or US$20 for a two-room suite with small kitchen.

The nearby *Pansiyon İpek Yolu* (☎ (373) 12643), a tidy, modern place on the shore nearby, is slightly cheaper. *Motel Kumsal* (☎ (373) 14490), farther west of the town, is also worth considering.

There are other small hotels in the town such as the *Otel Kılıç* (☎ (373) 11224), Cumhuriyet Meydanı, Hükümet Yanı 4. It's on the main square next to the government headquarters (Ünye İlçe Hükümet Konağı), and provides good clean rooms with showers for US$9/13/15 a single/double/triple. Some front rooms have balconies. Beware the minaret noise from the neighbouring Saray Camii, however.

About 60 metres south-east of the main square just inland from a park are the *Rainbow Pansiyon*, the *Gökkuşağı Pansiyon* and the *Hotel Çınar* (☎ (373) 11148), adjoining one another on a narrow street called Belediye Sokak. All are about the same, and charge about the same as the Otel Kılıç, but the Kılıç is preferable.

Places to Eat The main square has a few good cheap eateries. Between the Ziraat Bankası and the Belediye just inland from the waterfront are the *Nur Pide Salonu* for cheap Turkish pizza, and the *Oney Karadeniz Pide Salonu* which serves other foods as well.

Ordu

Riding eastward from Ünye, the road passes through the attractive town of Perşembe, then through Bolaman, with many fine (though dilapidated) old Ottoman frame houses.

Seventy km east of Ünye is Ordu (population 110,000), another fishing port with some nice old houses. When approaching the town from the west, you pass a small *orman piknik yeri* (forest picnic spot).

Orientation The centre of town is at the Atatürk bust by the Aziziye (Yalı) Camii, where there's a town plan on a signboard. The bazaar is just inland. The modern otogar is 1.5 km east of the main square, but the dolmuş station for local routes is just east of the main square. You can buy bus tickets at offices just inland from the mosque by the main square.

Information The Tourism Information Office (☎ (371) 10662) is in the Vilayet building, A Blok, one flight up, in offices Nos 21 and 22. There's also a municipal office on the ground floor of the Belediye (☎ (371) 14178), just east of the mosque on the main road. The Turkish Maritime Lines agent (☎ (371) 11013) is Eroğlu Nakliyat, Sahil Caddesi, Eroğlu Apartımanı. Ordu's postal code is 52100.

Museum The Pasha's Palace & Ethnographic Museum (Paşa Konağı ve Etnoğrafya Müzesi) is an interesting little museum 500 metres uphill from Ordu's main square past the Aziziye Camii. It's open from 8 am to 5 pm (on Monday from 10 am to 1 pm) for US$1. Follow signs reading 'Müze – Museum'.

The 19th-century house, a pale yellow box decorated with wedding-cake trim, has a fairly tame ethnographic exhibit downstairs. The upper floors, however, bring to life the Ottoman lifestyle of the 19th century. The bedrooms, guest rooms and salon are all fully furnished with period pieces, costumes and embroidery.

Places to Stay & Eat *Otel Kervansaray* (☎ (371) 11330), Kazım Karabekir Caddesi 1, just east of the Aziziye Camii and inland from the dolmuş station, is old fashioned but serviceable, charging US$12 for a double room with shower. There's a clean restaurant on the ground floor.

Across the street from the Kervansaray is the cheaper *Otel Başak Palas* (☎ (371) 14165). There are many other such small places in the bazaar nearby.

The two-star, 39-room *Turist Oteli* (☎ (371) 14273, 19115), Atatürk Bulvarı 134, is a bit noisy perhaps but moderately priced at US$15/20 a single/double. This is where the hazelnut traders stay.

Even fancier and newer is the three-star *Belde Hotel* (☎ (371) 13987; fax 19398), several km west of Ordu at Kirazlılimanı, charging US$25/35 a single/double for rooms with private bath, TV and minibar. There's a swimming pool here as well.

Besides the hotel restaurants, Ordu has many small eateries in the bazaar. The *Merkez Lokantası*, on the east side of the Aziziye Camii, right by the dolmuş station, fills the bill fairly cheaply.

Giresun

The town of Giresun (GEE-reh-SOON, population 78,000), 46 km east of Ordu, was founded some 3000 years ago. Legend has it that Jason and the Argonauts stopped here on their voyage to the fabled kingdom of Colchis (Georgia), on the eastern shores of the Black Sea, in search of the Golden Fleece. The Argonauts supposedly stopped at a nearby island (Büyük Ada) where Amazon queens had erected a shrine to Ares, god of war.

After the Romans conquered the Kingdom of Pontus, they discovered that the locals had orchards full of trees bearing delicious little red fruit. One theory holds that the ancient name for the town, Cerasus, is the root for many of the names for the fruit – *cherry* in English, *cerise* in French, *kiraz* in Turkish – as well as for the town's modern name. Cherries are still important here 20 centuries later.

You can see the ruins of a medieval castle (Giresun Kalesi) above the town. In the eastern part of the city, a disused Greek Orthodox church has been turned into the Şehir Müzesi (City Museum).

Orientation The centre of Giresun is the Atapark, the park holding the statue of Atatürk, on the main road. The Belediye (Municipality) is just inland from the park. The main commercial street is Gazi Caddesi, going uphill inland from the Belediye. The bus station is four km west of the centre; if you're coming from the east and heading west, have the bus drop you at the Atapark. Bus companies have ticket offices near the Belediye.

Dolmuşes to Görele, Espiye and Tirebolu use a more convenient lot, one long block east of the Atapark on the main road. The PTT is uphill from the Belediye.

Information The main Tourism Information Office (☎ (051) 23190, 13560) is two flights up in the Özel İdare İşhanı on Fatih Caddesi, a block inland from the Atapark, but there's an even more convenient office (☎ (051) 16790) facing the Atapark.

The Turkish Maritime Lines office (☎ (051) 12382; fax 21734) is at Giresun Liman İşletmesi, Atatürk Bulvarı, Akgül Apartımanı 542/3.

Giresun's postal code is 28000.

Kalepark If you have some time to kill in Giresun, the things to do are to eat hazelnuts and chocolate bars containing hazelnuts, and walk 1.5 km uphill to the Kalepark, the 'Castle Park' which is perched on the steep hillside above the town. The beautiful shady park offers panoramic views of the town and the sea, tables for picnickers and tea-sippers, bosky groves for lovers, and barbecues for grillers. It's busy on weekends.

No public transportation serves the park, so you must hike there. Walk inland uphill from the Atapark on Gazi Caddesi and turn left one block past the Otel Kit-Tur; this is a short cut, not passable for cars. When in doubt, ask directions for the Vilayet or the Kale. The prominent mansion on the hillside above the minibus lot is the Vilayet, near a mosque which was obviously once a church.

City Museum The Şehir Müzesi, with its run-of-the-mill collection, is housed in a disused church 1.5 km around the promontory east of the Atapark on the main road.

Festivals The grandly named International Black Sea Giresun Aksu Festival, held annually on 20 May, is a delightful pagan holdover. Traditionally celebrated by Ottoman Greeks on 7 May according to the Julian calendar (Gregorian, 20 May), the festival hails rebirth, fecundity and the coming of the new growing season. Locals say the festival dates back to the days of the Hittite fertility gods: Priapus, the phallic god; Cybele, the Anatolian earth-mother goddess; and other such worthies.

Festivities begin at the mouth of the creek Aksu, where participants pass through a trivet, then through seven double pieces and one single piece of stone to boats waiting at the shore. The boats sail around Büyük Ada while the voyagers cast pebbles representing the last years' troubles into the water. Returning to the town, everyone eats and drinks, and drinks some more.

Places to Stay – bottom end The *Hotel Bozbağ* (☎ (051) 11249, 12468), Arifbey Caddesi 8, is in a quiet location one block up the street from the Belediye. The spacious lobby/lounge has a TV and a canary (the canary's programme is better than the TV's), and shower-equipped rooms that are decently maintained and clean. Rates are US$7/10 a single/double; hot water is on in the evenings only.

You pay the same but get less at the *Otel Cem* (☎ (051) 23425), Gazi Caddesi 6, next to the Garanti Bankası, uphill behind the Belediye on the main street.

Places to Stay – middle The best bet is the two-star, 20-room *Hotel Çarıkçı* (☎ (051) 11026; fax 14578), Osmanağa Caddesi 6, a half-block east of the Belediye. A building almost a century old has been beautifully restored and nicely furnished, and now provides comfortable rooms with private bath for US$17/26 a single/double, breakfast included.

Giresun's status address is the three-star *Otel Kit-Tur* (☎ (051) 20245, 23032; fax 23034), Arifbey Caddesi 2, two short blocks uphill from the Belediye along Gazi Caddesi. Modern rooms with TV and private bath – and some with water views – cost about the same as at the Çarıkçı.

The *Giresun Oteli* (☎ (051) 12469, 13017; fax 16038), on the Black Sea side of the highway one block north of the Belediye, was once the town's best hotel, but now suffers from road noise. Still, it offers excellent water views, which are yours for US$15/20 a single/double.

Places to Eat The *Deniz Lokantası*, next to the Belediye and the Ulusoy bus ticket office, is simple, cheap and open from early in the morning to late at night.

Directly behind the Hotel Bozbağ (on the other side of the block) on a street reserved for pedestrians is the more modern but still cheap *Halil Usta Lokantası*. There are several other eateries on this street as well, and you can dine outdoors in fine weather.

On Osmanağa Caddesi near the Hotel Çarıkçı are several beerhalls which serve light meals and snacks.

Giresun to Trabzon

From Giresun, it's another 150 km to Trabzon. Along the way, the road passes through several small towns, including **Espiye** with the castle Andoz Kalesi and the attractive town of **Tirebolu**, with a tree-lined shore drive (the highway) and two castles (the St Jean Kalesi and Bedrama Kalesi). Tirebolu also has a Çaykur tea-processing plant, which signals your arrival in Turkey's tea country.

Just east of Tirebolu is a good long stretch of pebble beach. Take a Görele dolmuş to reach it.

Görele is the next town eastward, and after it is **Akçakale**, where you'll see the ruins of a 13th-century Byzantine castle on a little peninsula, marked by a prominent sign.

TRABZON

Once called Trapezus, and later Trebizond, the modern town of Trabzon (population 200,000) is Turkey's eastern Black Sea port. Goods come to Trabzon by sea and continue overland by road to Georgia, Armenia, Azerbaijan and Iran.

Though it is 20th-century commerce which has given Trabzon new life, the town actually performed a similar role in the 1800s, when the trade was mostly British. Trabzon gained a romantic reputation in the English-speaking world as a remote trading outpost, though its truly cosmopolitan days of traders, consulates and international agents were long past.

Trabzon is taking on a cosmopolitan air again, however. With the collapse of the Soviet Union and the opening of formerly closed borders, citizens of the Soviet Union's successor republics have flooded across the border into Turkey in search of the benefits of free enterprise.

Being the largest city closest to the Georgian and Armenian borders, Trabzon has seen a great influx of these people. They come to sell whatever they can bring from home, and to buy Turkish consumer goods unavailable in their own countries. Some of these seat-of-the-pants traders will no doubt become rich in legitimate commerce, others in trading contraband. The influx has brought a certain proportion of petty criminals, and also what the Turks call the women of the Natasha Syndrome: those willing to sell themselves to provide for their families or to make enough money to begin a legitimate business at home.

History

Trabzon's recorded history begins around 746 BC, when colonists originally from Miletus (south of Kuşadası) came from Sinop and founded a settlement with its acropolis on the *trápeza*, or 'table' of land above the harbour.

The town did reasonably well for 2000 years, occupying itself with port activities, until in 1204 the soldiers of the Fourth Crusade seized and sacked Constantinople, driving its noble families to seek refuge in Anatolia. The imperial family of the Comneni established an empire along the Black Sea coast in 1204, with Alexius Comnenus I reigning as the emperor of Trebizond.

The Trapezuntine rulers became skilful at balancing their alliances with the Seljuks, the Mongols, the Genoese and others – it didn't hurt to be cut off from the rest by a wall of mountains, either. Prospering through trade with Eastern Anatolia and Persia, the empire reached the height of its wealth and culture during the reign of Alexius II (1297-1330), after which the place fell to pieces in 'byzantine' factional disputes marked, as one historian put it, 'by unbelievable degeneracy and cruelty'. Even so, the Empire of Trebizond survived until the coming of the Ottomans in 1461.

When the Ottoman Empire was defeated after WW I, the many Greek residents of Trabzon sought to establish a Republic of Trebizond echoing the old Comneni empire,

but Atatürk's armies were ultimately victorious.

Nowadays the main reasons for visiting Trabzon are to see the church of Aya Sofya (1200s); to poke around in the old town; to visit Atatürk's lovely villa on the outskirts; and to make an excursion through the alpine scenery to Sumela, a dramatic Byzantine monastery carved out of a sheer rock cliff.

Orientation

Trabzon is built on a mountainside. The port is at the centre of town, with the ancient acropolis on the 'table', now occupied by the main square called Atatürk Alanı (or Meydan Park), rising to the west of it. Most government offices, airline offices, hotels and restaurants are in and around Atatürk Alanı. The Belde İskenderpaşa Oto Parkı is an underground car park, just east of the İskender Paşa Camii beneath a tea garden, charging US$2 per day.

Many of Trabzon's most interesting sights are west of the square along Uzun Yol (oo-ZOON yohl, Long Road), also sometimes called Uzun Sokak.

The post office is on Kahramanmaraş (or simply Maraş) Caddesi, which extends west from Atatürk Alanı. At this writing the PTT is being rebuilt, and you must go down a passage at Kahramanmaraş Caddesi 74, or otherwise around the block, to reach the temporary post office. Banks are on Atatürk Alanı and Kahramanmaraş Caddesi.

Buses bearing the legend 'Park' or 'Meydan' go to Atatürk Alanı. Trabzon's otogar is three km east of the port on the landward side of the shore road. The airport is eight km east of the town.

Information

The Tourism Information Office (☎ (031) 11 46 59, 13 58 18), on Atatürk Alanı near (Akbulut) Boztepe Caddesi, is on the main square, very convenient to most of the town's hotels. Staff speak English, French or German and are very helpful and well informed.

The Turkish Maritime Lines agency (☎ (03) 11 20 18, 11 70 96; fax 12 10 04) is

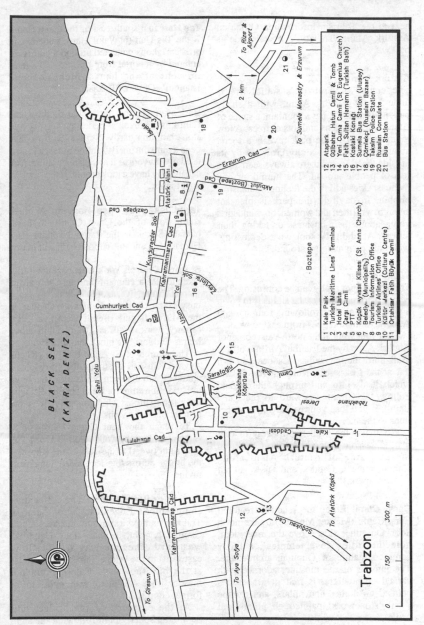

Trabzon

BLACK SEA
(KARA DENIZ)

1	Kale Park
2	Turkish Maritime Lines' Terminal
3	Hotel Usta
4	Çarşı Camii
5	PTT
6	Küçük Ayvasıl Kilisesi (St Anne Church)
7	Belediye (Municipality)
8	Tourism Information Office
9	Turkish Airlines' Office
10	Kültür Merkezi (Cultural Centre)
11	Ortahisar Fatih Büyük Camii
12	Atapark
13	Gülbahar Hatun Camii & Tomb
14	Yeni Cuma Camii (St Eugenius Church)
15	Fatih Sultan Hamamı (Turkish Bath)
16	Kostaki Konağı
17	Sumela Bus Station (Ulusoy)
18	Çömlekçi (Russian Bazaar)
19	Taksim Police Station
20	Russian Consulate
21	Bus Station

0   150   300 m

To Rize & Airport
To Sumela Monastery & Erzurum
To Erzurum
Boztepe
To Atatürk Köşkü
To Aya Sofia
To Giresun

Sahil Yolu
Cumhuriyet Cad
Kahramanmaraş Cad
Gazipaşa Cad
Erzurum Cad
Akbulut (Boztepe) Cad
Atatürk Alanı
Kunduracılar Sok
Uzun Yol
Tekfurlık Sok
İskele Cad
Sarafoğlu
Tabakhane Köprüsü
Tabakhane Deresi
Kale Caddesi
Telahane Cad
Söğüksu Cad
Cami Sok

2 km

next to the Tourism Information Office on Atatürk Alanı. Trabzon's postal code is 61000.

Atatürk Alanı

The centre of Trabzon's social life is undoubtedly Atatürk Alanı, with a shady park in its midst. It has a fountain, a statue of Atatürk, tea gardens and lots of trees. A few moments' rest in the park reveals a secret about Trabzon: it is a city crowded by its hillside location and there always seem to be lots of people around. The humid air and overcast skies add to the feeling of claustrophobia. In daylight the park is pleasant enough, with men and women, boys and girls going about their business or taking their leisure. At night it's somewhat depressing, with only men hanging around.

Walking Tour

Trabzon's topography can be confusing. The best way to see many of the sights is to go on a walking tour. The following tour starts at Atatürk Alanı and goes from east to west.

Start your walk at the north-west corner of Atatürk Alanı by the İstanbul Airlines office. Walk north along Gazipaşa Caddesi and turn left at the first street, Kunduracılar Sokak, which leads into and through the bazaar. Follow this street westward to the Çarşı Camii; if you lose your bearings, ask directions to the mosque.

(To make the walk from west to east instead, take an Erdoğdu dolmuş (30c) from the east side of Atatürk Alanı along Kahramanmaraş Caddesi and ask to get out at the Atapark.)

Çarşı Camii

Enter the recently restored Çarşı Camii (Market Mosque) by the north door. On either side above the inner door, note the little 'dove temples', a fairly common feature of Ottoman architecture. The interior of the mosque, adorned with crystal chandeliers, is rich in arabesques painted on domes and pillars, and trompe l'oeil 'stonework' painted on pillars and walls.

Taş Han

Just south-east of the Çarşı Camii is the Taş Han (or Vakıf Han), traders' and artisans' shops collected around a courtyard entered by a portal from the street. It's reminiscent of the hans which surround İstanbul's Covered Bazaar.

Bedesten

On the north side of the Çarşı Camii is Trabzon's Bedesten, a very old stone building partly in ruins. Said to have been a mint during Byzantine times, it is now used by sawyers as it awaits restoration. You can usually have a look around if the sawyers are at work.

Tarihi İskender Paşa Hamamı

A block south-west of the Çarşı Camii on Paşahamam Sokak is the Tarihi İskender Paşa Hamamı, an ancient Turkish bath still in use.

St Anne Church

Walk west past the Tarihi İskender Paşa Hamamı and turn left at the second street, Kazazoğlu Sokak, to reach busy Maraş (or Kahramanmaraş) Caddesi at the Müftü İsmail Efendi Camii, a 19th-century work. Walk eastward uphill along Maraş Caddesi one block and turn right.

The church of St Anne Basilica (Küçük Ayvasıl Kilisesi) is among the city's oldest churches, having been built during the reign of Byzantine emperor Basil I in 884-85, with later renovations. Unfortunately, it is not usually open for visits.

To reach the Yeni Cuma Camii or St Eugenius Church, walk south to Uzun Yol, then right (west) to the Tabakhane Köprüsü, the bridge across the steep-sided Tabakhane ravine.

St Eugenius Church

The 13-century church of St Eugenius, patron saint of Trabzon, is now a mosque: the Yeni Cuma Camii. To reach it, walk along Uzun Yol westward (the one-way traffic flows eastward) to the bridge Tabakhane Köprüsü at the big Tabakhane Camii. From this mosque it's a 400-metre walk uphill to the former church.

At the east end of the bridge, take Sarafoğlu Sokak uphill following the signs

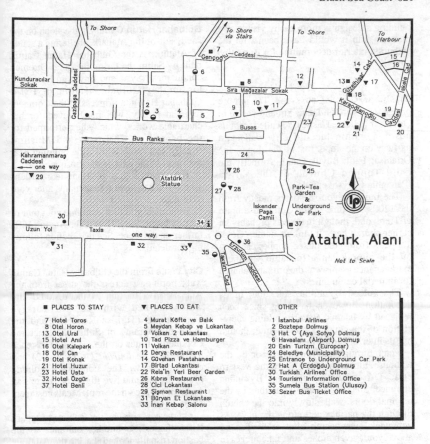

Ataturk Alanı

Not to Scale

■ PLACES TO STAY

7 Hotel Toros
8 Otel Horon
13 Otel Ural
15 Hotel Anıl
16 Otel Kalepark
18 Otel Can
19 Otel Konak
21 Hotel Huzur
23 Hotel Usta
32 Hotel Özgür
37 Hotel Benli

▼ PLACES TO EAT

4 Murat Köfte ve Balık
5 Meydan Kebap ve Lokantası
9 Volkan 2 Lokantası
10 Tad Pizza ve Hamburger
11 Volkan
12 Derya Restaurant
14 Güvehan Pastahanesi
17 Birtad Lokantası
22 Reis'in Yeri Beer Garden
26 Kıbrıs Restaurant
28 Cici Lokantası
29 Şişman Restaurant
31 Büryan Et Lokantası
33 İnan Kebap Salonu

OTHER

1 İstanbul Airlines
2 Boztepe Dolmuş
3 Hat C (Aya Sofya) Dolmuş
6 Havaalanı (Airport) Dolmuş
20 Esin Turizm (Europcar)
24 Belediye (Municipality)
25 Entrance to Underground Car Park
27 Hat A (Erdoğdu) Dolmuş
30 Turkish Airlines' Office
34 Tourism Information Office
35 Sumela Bus Station (Ulusoy)
36 Sezer Bus Ticket Office

to the Fatih Sultan Hamamı. At the top of the slope bear right onto Bilaloğlu Sokak at the Lalezar Pastanesi. This street changes names to become Cami Sokak and continues uphill. Near the top of a particularly steep portion, look to the right along Yeni Cuma Çıkmazı Sokak and you'll see the old stones of the church-mosque.

Tradition holds that Eugenius, an early Christian living here, raged against the priests of Mithra and was martyred. His skull was miraculously discovered on this spot shortly after the arrival of the Comneni imperial family, driven from Constantinople by the Fourth Crusade. The church was built in the 1200s, but badly damaged in a fire in 1340, and modified during repairs.

After Mehmet the Conqueror took the city in 1461, he performed his Friday ablutions in the nearby baths, proclaimed the church a mosque, prayed there, and ordered the construction of the minaret.

The mosque's north door is often locked, but the east door, reached by the courtyard to the left, may be open if the *bekçi* (guardian) is about. The building is elegantly simple, lofty and light, with three parallel naves and a transversal topped by a cupola. The building's design is more easily visible as a mosque than it would have been with the elaborate interior decoration of a Byzantine church.

Ortahisar Camii

Cross the Tabakhane bridge westward on Uzun Yol and you're in Ortahisar (Middle Castle), so called from its position within the old city walls and halfway up the slope. Just up the slope is the Ortahisar Fatih Büyük Camii, formerly the Gold-Topped Church of the Virgin (Panaghia Chrysokephalos).

The building you see dates mostly from the 1200s, the time of the Comneni Empire of Trebizond, though there was probably an earlier church here. It took its name, 'Gold-Topped', from gold-plated copper cladding on the cupola, an affordable Comneni extravagance as this was the principal church for imperial ceremonies.

The golden Byzantine splendour of its decoration, however, has long since been replaced by Islamic austerity, aiding appreciation of the church's architecture, though not its interior furnishings.

Enter through the northern door by the teahouse, turn right and walk to the western end. This was the original Byzantine entrance. Standing in the exonarthex by the original doors, walk slowly into the church through the narthex and along the nave. As you walk, watch arch after arch open up above you (seven arches and fake arches in all), pointing upwards, lifting you eye and presumably your spirits heavenward by an almost cinematic effect. As you move forward the building seems almost to rise and expand before you, culminating in the lofty lightness of the dome, formerly ablaze with gold mosaics.

The apse of the church at the eastern end retains some traces of beautiful Byzantine stonework. The carved work in the mihrab looks to be Seljuk, no doubt brought here from some other building.

Continue westward along Uzun Yol for several hundred metres to the Gülbahar Hatun Camii.

Gülbahar Hatun Camii

Up the slope on the south side of the Atapark, sheltering a statue of Atatürk, is the Gülbahar Hatun Camii, built by Selim the Grim, the great Ottoman conqueror of Syria and Egypt, in honour of his mother Gülbahar Hatun in 1514. Gülbahar Hatun, a princess of the Comneni imperial family, was much loved for her charitable works, which she performed for the benefit of Christians and Muslims equally. Her tomb is the little building near the street to the east of the mosque.

The Atapark has pleasant tea gardens where you can have refreshments after your long walk.

You can, if you like, continue your tour of the city by catching a bus to the Atatürk Villa farther up the slope. See that section following for details.

City Walls

From the Gülbahar Hatun Camii, walk north-east across the street from the Atapark to a bastion in the restored city walls, marked with 'TC' for Türkiye Cumhuriyeti (Turkish Republic) and the *tuğra* monogram) of Sultan Mehmet the Conqueror. Enter on the west side to reach the *Zindan Restaurant* (☎ 12 32 32) and enjoy the view. The stone-walled dining rooms are one and two flights up; there's an open-air terrace on the roof. Meals cost from US$6 to US$9.

On the east side, by the teahouse Atapark Kiraaathanesi, is another entrance to the bastion (usually locked) beside the elaborate marble Ottoman **Abdullah Paşa Çeşmesi fountain** (1844).

Back to Atatürk Alanı

Dolmuşes (30c) run from the north-west corner of the park by the Gülbahar Hatun Camii eastward along Uzun Yol to Atatürk Alanı.

If you walk, stop for a look at the **Kostaki Konağı**, a typical 19th-century Trabzon town mansion a half-block south of Uzun Yol at Zeytinlik Caddesi 10. It is presently being restored to become a museum.

Boztepe

Up the hillside south-east of the main part of

town is a lookout and the Boztepe Piknik Alanı with a fine view of the city and the sea. In ancient times Boztepe harboured temples to the Persian sun god Mithra and to Apollo. Later the Byzantines built several churches and monasteries here, ruins of which still remain.

To get to Boztepe from Atatürk Alanı, take a bus labelled 'Park-Boztepe Bld Dinlenme Tesisleri' (Park-to-Boztepe Municipal Recreation Facilities) or a Boztepe dolmuş (from a side street on the north side of Atatürk Alanı). The route goes uphill 1.5 km to the local orthopaedic hospital, then another 700 metres to a beautiful forest with the picnic facilities.

Up the hill, past the picnic area about three or four km, are the ruins of the former **Kaymaklı Monastery**, boasting some fine frescoes. The monastery is now part of a farm and at this writing it is unmarked, so finding it in the maze of hillside paths can be difficult. Perhaps in future there will be signs.

Aya Sofya

The Aya Sofya Müzesi (Haghia Sophia or Church of the Divine Wisdom) is three km west of the centre on a terrace which once held a pagan temple. The site is above the coastal highway, reachable by city bus or dolmuş from Atatürk Alanı (look for a 'Hat C' (Route C) dolmuş on the north (lower) side of the square).

The church is now a museum, open from 8.30 am to 5 pm (closed on Monday in winter); admission costs US$1. Built between 1238 and 1263, its design was influenced by Eastern Anatolian and Seljuk motifs, though the excellent wall paintings and mosaic floors follow the style of Constantinople. Tombs were built into the north and south walls. Next to the church is its bell tower, finished much later, in 1427. This was a monastery church, but nothing remains of the monastery.

Atatürk Villa

The Atatürk Köşkü or Atatürk Villa ('Atatürk Povillion' on some signs), accessi-

ble by city bus or dolmuş, is five km southwest of Atatürk Alanı, above the town with a fine view and lovely gardens. The white villa was designed in a Black Sea style seen much in the Crimea, and built between 1890 and 1903 for the wealthy Trabzon banking family named Karayannidis.

The family gave it up when Atatürk visited the city in 1924. (Atatürk visited Trabzon and stayed there only three times briefly, the last time in 1937.) Upon his death in 1938 the villa, and all the rest of his estate, became national property. The villa is now a museum with various bits of Atatürk memorabilia.

Being a patriotic site, the villa and its well-kept gardens are open every day, from 9 am to 5 pm; admission is 50c. Local students who are studying foreign languages act as volunteer guides, though you can stroll through on your own if you like.

To get to the villa, take a city bus from the bus stop on the lower (north) side of Atatürk Alanı, more or less behind the Tourism Information Office. Buses depart at 20 minutes past the hour, passing the Gülbahar Hatun Camii along the way, and arriving at the villa 25 minutes later. Get off at the Atatürk Köşk stop. The return trip takes only 15 minutes. The round trip costs 30c.

Russian Bazaar

The influx of petty traders from the former Soviet lands has been so great that Trabzon's city government has accommodated them in the Russian bazaar. At Çömlekçi, on the main highway due east of Atatürk Alanı at the bottom of the hill, a line of bus shelters some 300 metres long has been turned into a flea market.

For a small admission fee you are admitted to the shelter, to be greeted by displays of hardware, toys, Armenian brandy, Russian vodka, caviar, clothing, electric appliances, watches, crockery, household wares, car parts, cameras etc. There's a lot of surplus military matériel – rubber life rafts, lanterns etc – which the Soviet state produced in abundance. Prices and quality are both generally low, and haggling is essential.

Sumela Monastery

The Greek Orthodox Monastery of the Virgin Mary at Sumela, 46 km south of Trabzon, was founded in Byzantine times (500s), and was abandoned in 1923 upon the founding of the Turkish Republic, after hopes of creating a new Greek state in this region were dashed. The monastery clings to a sheer rock wall high above evergreen forests and a rushing mountain stream. It is a mysterious, eerie place, especially when mists swirl among the tops of the trees in the valley below. Don't miss Sumela, as it is among the most impressive and fascinating sights in Turkey. Note that on Wednesdays, when the ferry from İstanbul arrives in Trabzon, Sumela is crowded with cruise passengers.

The way to Sumela is along the Erzurum road. One km and a half north of the town of Maçka is a dramatic rock formation of basaltic columns resembling in minature California's Devil's Postpile or Ireland's Giant's Causeway. Unfortunately the road passes through a tunnel behind the formation, so you may not see it. At Maçka, 30 km south of Trabzon, you turn left for Sumela, also signposted as Meryem Ana, because the monastery was dedicated to the Virgin Mary.

About 3.5 km from Maçka (12.5 km from Sumela) is *Sumela Camping*, a stream-side camping ground. Another 2.5 km takes you through Coşandere village, where there's an old Ottoman humpback bridge.

The road winds into dense evergreen forests, following the sinuous course of a rushing mountain stream. Mists may drape the tops of the trees and the air becomes much cooler. Peasant houses look like those in alpine central Europe. The road is subject to landslides, and may be impassable after heavy rains.

As you approach Sumela, you must stop at the entrance to the national park and pay an admission fee of 70c for entry to the park, it costs US$1.50 more if you plan to visit Sumela, plus US$1.75 for a car. Students pay reduced fees. Opening hours vary with the amount of daylight, but are generally between 9 am and 6 pm.

At the end of the road is a lovely shady park with picnic tables and fireplaces by a roaring brook, and several A-frame shelters for rent. (No camping is allowed in the park.)

The head of the trail up to the monastery begins in the picnic area. This trail is steep but easy to follow, and is the one most people use. There is another trail which begins farther up the valley. To find it, follow the unpaved road past the picnic area, cross the stream and head up into the forest.

You climb through forests and alpine meadows, ascending 250 metres in about 30 to 45 minutes. There are glimpses of the monastery as you climb. In the autumn just before the snows arrive, a beautiful sort of crocus, called *kar çiçeği* (snowflower) blooms in the meadows.

Much of the monastery is closed as restoration progresses. The various chapels and rooms here are mere shells or façades but have a good deal of fine fresco painting, some of it with gilt. Many of the paintings are the worse for wear, as bored shepherd boys used them as targets for pebble attacks. In recent years, antiquity thieves and black marketeers have been a problem as well.

Getting There & Away Ulusoy runs buses to Sumela in the warm, tourist-filled months, departing not from the otogar in Trabzon but from a special terminal just uphill from the tourism office off Atatürk Alanı. The trip takes about 40 minutes and costs US$2.

There are also sometimes dolmuşes running to Sumela and back. Drivers will sometimes agree to take your luggage, hold it while you visit Sumela, and drop you at the otogar around 3.30 pm so you can head out of town.

You can take a taxi-dolmuş round-trip for US$7 per person; stop by and reserve your seat the day before at the taxi stand facing the Hotel Özgür. For a taxi proper, look in the main square; wait under banners proclaiming prices of US$45 or so for a car holding five persons. The price includes the ride there, a two-hour wait and the ride back to Trabzon.

Places to Stay – bottom end

There is very little good value for money in Trabzon hotels. Many of the cheap hotels are filled with traders and prostitutes from the former Soviet republics (all indiscriminately called 'Russians' by the Trabzonlus.) With lots of willing customers, there is little incentive to maintain cleanliness. Even if good standards are maintained, a change of management may bring in a completely different clientele and standards may drop in a matter of weeks.

The heart of the cheap hotel area is in the district called İskender Paşa Mahallesi, off the north-east corner of Atatürk Alanı on Güzelhisar Caddesi, near where İskele Caddesi (officially named Şehit İbrahim Karaoğlanoğlu Caddesi) begins its descent to the harbour.

Hotel Anıl (☎ (03) 11 95 66, 22617), Güzelhisar Caddesi 10, is a modern place with friendly staff, clean rooms (some with showers), and some street and nightclub noise in the north-facing sea-view rooms. As usual, the baths could be better kept. A room with sink costs US$8/16 a single/double, or US$11/19 with shower.

Otel Can (that's 'John') (☎ (03) 11 47 62), Güzelhisar Caddesi 2, is modern and tidy, with tiny but good rooms, a TV lounge on the upper floor, and friendly management. Rooms with sink for US$13 a double are the best deal: the rooms with add-on showers (for a few dollars more) are so small that the person relaxing in bed gets wet feet when the other person showers. The *kat banyo* (shared showers) are fine.

Otel Kalepark (☎ (03) 11 34 45), Güzelhisar Caddesi 33, is similar to the Anıl and Can, and charges similar prices, but has a few rooms without running water for US$7 a single.

Otel Ural (☎ (03) 11 14 14), Güzelhisar Caddesi 1, across from the Otel Can, is old-fashioned, quietish, drab but serviceable for US$10 a double with sink.

Erzurum Oteli (☎ (03) 12 54 27), Güzelhisar Caddesi 15, has disappointed as many readers of this guide as it has satisfied, but it will do at a pinch. Rooms with minuscule add-on showers cost US$14 a double; there's hot water in the evenings only. It's quiet, though, an advantage it shares with the nearby and equally undistinguished *Otel Güzelyurt* (☎ (03) 11 57 16), Güzelhisar Caddesi 12/A.

Off of İskele Caddesi is a quiet place. *Hotel Huzur* (☎ (03) 12 11 71) is hidden away down a dead-end alley to the right (east) off İskele Caddesi just before it turns. It's surprisingly good, quiet and cheap – US$7/12 a single/double for a room with a tiny shower. A few rooms even have sea views.

Otel Konak (☎ (03) 11 23 65), İskele Caddesi 27, offers rooms with sea views and showers (but not toilets) for US$14 a double, but there's lots of street noise.

New in 1992, the *Hotel Toros* (☎ (03) 21 12 12), Gençoğlu Sokak 3/A, has clean, quiet rooms without running water for US$5 per bed, or US$6.75 per bed with private shower. To find it, start on the north side of Atatürk Alanı and walk up the side street to the left of the Meydan Kebap restaurant.

Hotel Benli (☎ (03) 21 10 22), Cami Çıkmazı Sokak 5, is just off the eastern end of Atatürk Alanı, up the hill behind the Belediye and the İskender Paşa Camii. It's an odd place with strange staff and 42 well-used rooms which rent for US$10/14 a single/double with sink, slightly more with shower.

Places to Stay – middle

Trabzon has only one suitable hotel in the middle price range. Trabzon needs at least one top-end hotel, and it should be built soon.

The three-star *Hotel Usta* (☎ (03) 11 28 43, 11 21 95; fax 12 37 93), Telgrafhane Sokak 1, across from the İskender Paşa Camii on the north-eastern corner of Atatürk Alanı in a fairly quiet yet convenient location, is currently the best in town, with 76 renovated rooms, all with bath. It's often full because the other ostensibly middle-range hotels are so horrible. Services include a lift and car park; it's a fairly quiet location. Rates are a somewhat high at US$35/50 a single/ double, breakfast included.

The nominally two-star *Hotel Özgür* (☎ (03) 11 13 19, 11 27 78; fax 11 39 52), Atatürk Alanı 29, has 45 rooms (all with bath or shower), most of which suffer from the traffic noise from the square, or late-night music noise from the hotel's own nightclub. Rates are US$24/33/40 a single/double/ triple. Though most rooms have twin beds, others have double beds, five have three beds, and five are junior suites.

The 42-room *Otel Horon* (☎ (03) 11 11 99, 11 22 89), Sıra Mağazalar Caddesi 125 (also called Şehit Teğmen Kalmaz Caddesi), rates one-star and has a variety of rooms with a variety of beds and plumbing options over-priced at US$16 to US$28 a single, US$30 to US$38 a double. Lower prices are for rooms with sinks only; higher priced rooms have private shower.

Places to Eat – bottom end

Look around Atatürk Alanı and you will see many small restaurants.

Derya Restaurant, across from the Belediye on the north-east corner of Atatürk Alanı, has a full selection of ready food. Full meals can be had for around US$3. It's especially busy at lunch. Look also for the *Volkan* and *Volkan 2* a few steps to the west.

Also here is the *Tad Pizza ve Hamburger*, across from the İskender Paşa Camii, a reasonably accurate approximation of a US-style pizza parlour. Pizzas cost from US$2.25 to US$3, burgers are only half that.

Büryan Et Lokantası, just off the south-west corner of Atatürk Alanı across from the Turkish Airlines office, specialises in grilled meats but also has a full selection of soups and stews. The foods displayed at the back are the best, including chicken-and-cheese şiş kebap.

Another clean, convenient place with good stews on the south side is the *İnan Kebap Salonu*, across from the tourism office.

On the north side of Atatürk Alanı is *Murat Köfte ve Balık*, a simple grill place serving fish and lamb meatballs. The fish is best at lunch time when the place is most active. Prices depend upon what's in season, but uskumru (mackerel) which grills well goes for US$1.50 to US$3 per fish; alabalık (trout) costs more.

Meydan Kebap ve Yemek Lokantası, on the north-east corner of Atatürk Alanı, is bright, hectic, crowded and noisy – a real human fuel-stop. But it does a very tasty çevirme piliç (rotisserie chicken).

Cici Lokantası ('Cute Restaurant'), on the square's east side, offers decent, cheap food and has fluorescent lights, a ceiling fan and a tactile stalactite ceiling that is a finish-plasterer's nightmare. It opens early, making it good for breakfast.

If you want to drink beer or wine with your meal, your choices are less congenial. The *Kıbrıs Restaurant* (☎ 11 76 79), Atatürk Alanı 17, on the east side near the Cici, has a small and rather plain dining room at street level and a bigger one upstairs. Dishes include the Turkish classics, and a meal might cost from US$6 or US$8, more if you have fish.

Şişman Restaurant (☎ 12 34 45), on Kahramanmaraş Caddesi just west of the square on the left-hand (south) side, has a *yazlık* (an open-air terrace) on the upper floor. It's drab, with stained tablecloths and mediocre food, but alcohol is served. Meals cost from US$5 to US$10.

For a beer and snacks, try *Reis'in Yeri* (the sign says 'Reis Fıçı Bira'), a little Tuborg beer garden at the beginning of İskele Caddesi.

At the *Güven Pastahanesi* (☎ 12372), Güzelhisar Caddesi 5/A, you can get a good breakfast and, later in the day, excellent pastries and puddings. Have the hususi Laz böreği (special Laz pastry), flaky pastry top and bottom with a cream filling (US$1).

The proprietor, Mr Gündüz Akay, can lead you on a trek to Çamlıhemşin in the Kaçkar mountain range where there are hot springs, as well as lots of wildlife and beautiful mountain scenery.

Your guide, Gündüz Bey, speaks German as well as Turkish.

Getting There & Away

As the commercial hub of the eastern Black Sea coast, transport to and from Trabzon is easy by bus, air and sea. Note that the Turkish-Georgian border crossing at Sarp is presently open only to nationals of Turkey and the former Soviet republics. Citizens of other countries must cross by boat to Batumi (see following).

Air For information on transport to and from the airport, see Getting Around, below.

Turkish Airlines has daily nonstop flights between Trabzon and Ankara and İstanbul. The Turkish Airlines office (☎ (03) 11 34 46, 11 16 80) is on the south-west corner of Atatürk Alanı.

İstanbul Airlines also flies nonstop between İstanbul and Trabzon daily except Sunday, at fares lower than the competition. Its office (☎ (03) 12 38 06, 12 33 46; at the airport, 12 33 27) is on the north-west corner of Atatürk Alanı at Kazazoğlu Sokak 9, Sanat İş Hanı.

Bus Trabzon's modern otogar, three km east of the port, is served by buses and dolmuşes running along the coastal road and up to Atatürk Alanı (see the following Getting Around section).

The otogar has a left-luggage area (emanet) with prices posted, a maternity room (kreş) for nursing and changing babies, a restaurant, cafeteria, barber shop (kuaför) and shops in which to buy food and sundries for the journey.

The price of your journey depends to some extent on the comfort of your bus. In addition to its regular buses, Ulusoy operates especially comfortable double-decker 'Neoplan' buses to the most popular destinations, including Ankara and İstanbul, and you pay from 5 to 10% more for the comfort. Details of some daily services follow:

Ankara – 780 km, 12 hours, US$22 to US$26; frequent buses
Artvin – 255 km, five hours, US$12; frequent buses
Erzurum – 325 km, eight hours, US$15; several buses
Hopa – 165 km, three hours, US$7; buses at least every half-hour
İstanbul – 1110 km, 19 hours, US$20 to US$32; several buses
Kars – 525 km, 12 hours, US$18; change at Erzurum or Artvin
Kayseri – 686 km, 12 hours, US$24; several buses
Rize – 65 km, one hour, US$2; Rize Belediyesi shuttle buses
Samsun – 365 km, six hours, US$6; frequent buses
Van – 745 km, 17 hours, US$15; a few, direct or via Erzurum

Boat For information on the İstanbul, Samsun and Trabzon ferries, see the beginning of this chapter.

At this writing the land border at Sarp between Turkey and the Republic of Georgia is open only to Turks and former Soviet citizens. Others must cross by boat. Travel between Trabzon and Batumi (Georgia) by hydrofoil (deniz otobüsü, 'sea bus') is possible but frustrating. First you must get a visa from the former USSR consulate 200 metres south-east from the south-east corner of Atatürk Alanı (look for the police guard booth). The consulate is only open on Monday from 9 am to 1 pm, and on Tuesday and Thursday from 9 am to noon and 3 to 5 pm. After obtaining your visa, you must get boat tickets down by the harbour. The boat may or may not leave on time, and may or may not have a place for you. Many swindlers work the rackets concerning these boats and tickets to ride on them. One hopes the situation will soon improve.

Getting Around

To/From the Airport The airport bus (US$1) leaves the Turkish Airlines office at the south-west corner of Atatürk Alanı for the airport 90 minutes before each scheduled Turkish Airlines flight.

You can also take a Havaalanı ('Airport') dolmuş from a side street on the north side of Atatürk Alanı.

To/From the Bus Station To reach Atatürk Alanı from the otogar, cross the shore road in front of the terminal, turn left, walk to the bus stop and catch any bus with 'Park' in its name; the dolmuş to catch for Atatürk Alanı is 'Garajlar-Meydan'. A taxi between the otogar and Atatürk Alanı costs less than US$4.

Dolmuş Routes Dolmuşes departing from Atatürk Alanı will take you to most sights. Route descriptions are included with the previously mentioned sightseeing information.

TRABZON TO ERZURUM

Heading south into the mountains by road, you're in for a long but scenic ride.

Carrying Liquids

Before you get on the bus, take charge of any liquid-filled containers in your luggage. The atmospheric pressure here at sea level is much greater than it will be in the mountains. If you have a full water bottle in your pack at Trabzon, it will have burst or at least leaked by the time you reach Gümüşhane. If you're descending to Trabzon from Erzurum, your water bottle will collapse and leak due to the increase in pressure as you descend. It's best to carry liquid-filled containers with you as hand luggage and adjust the pressure as you travel.

Sights En Route

Along the highway south, you zoom straight to Maçka, 35 km inland from Trabzon, and then begin the long, slow climb along a serpentine mountain road through active landslide zones to the breathtaking **Zigana Geçidi** (Zigana Pass) at an altitude of 2030 metres. The landscape is one of sinuous valleys and cool pine forests with dramatic light. At the pass there is a small restaurant, grocery and teahouse.

The dense, humid air of the coast disappears as you rise and becomes light and dry as you reach the south side of the **Doğu Karadeniz Dağları** (Eastern Black Sea Mountains). Along with the landscape, the towns and villages change. Black Sea towns have a vaguely Balkan appearance, while places higher up look distinctly central Asian. Snow can be seen in all months except perhaps July, August and September.

An extensive programme of road improvement is under way: the widening of this ancient caravan route will cause traffic delays for years to come.

Gümüşhane, about 125 km south of Trabzon, is a small town in a mountain valley with a few simple travellers' services, but not much to stop for except the scenery. By the time you reach **Bayburt**, 195 km from Trabzon, you are well into the rolling steppe and low mountains of the high Anatolian Plateau. Bayburt has a big **medieval fortress** and simple travellers' services. The road from Bayburt passes through green, rolling farm country; in early summer wild flowers are everywhere.

Exactly 80 km west of Erzurum is the **Kop Geçidi** (Kop Pass) at an altitude of 2400 metres. A **monument** here commemorates Turks who fought for this pass for six months under the most dire conditions during the War of Independence. Countless soldiers lost their lives. A memorial ceremony is held annually on 15 May.

From Kop Pass, the open road to Erzurum offers fast, easy travelling.

EAST FROM TRABZON
Uzungöl

East of Trabzon 56 km is the town called Of. Go south 25 km up the Solaklı creek valley through the town of Çaykara, then another 16 km along a rough road to Uzungöl (Long Lake, altitude 1100 metres) to enjoy the mountain air and perhaps hike in the countryside.

Uzungöl is a popular destination for local people on weekend outings, so it's best to come during the week, though dolmuşes are much easier to find on weekends. To stay the night, call ahead to the *İnan Kardeşler Tesisleri* (☎ (0446) 6021) which has 50 beds for US$12 each, and serves simple but delicious meals of local trout for around US$8.

Rize

Seventy-five km east of Trabzon, Rize (REE-zeh, population 60,000) is at the heart of Turkey's tea plantation area. The steep hillsides which sweep upward from the shore are thickly planted with tea bushes. Local men and women bear large baskets on their backs, taking the leaves to the processing plants. The tea is cured, dried and blended here, then shipped throughout the country. A few years ago there was a shortage of processed tea due, some say, to bad industry planning, and at that time all Turkish eyes were on Rize. In this country, a shortage of tea spells imminent social collapse.

Pazar

Pazar, the town at the mouth of the stream Fırtına Çayı, has at least 12 hotels for the tea traders, but nothing else to hold your interest. Rates are uniformly US$8 to US$12 a single, US$10 to US$16 a double with private baths. These are more comfortable lodgings than you'll find in the small villages in the high mountain valleys.

Çamlıhemşin & Ayder

East of Rize about 40 km, just before Ardeşen, a road on the right (south) points the way to Çamlıhemşin (19 km), a village deep in the Kaçkar mountain range which serves as the jumping-off place for treks into the mountains. Peaks in the range rise to almost 4000 metres. You can explore the area on your own or organise a tour by talking to Mr Gündüz Akay at the Güven Pastahanesi in Trabzon.

Don't confuse Çamlıhemşin with the separate village of Hemşin, in another valley to the west.

As you ascend into the mountains, there's a frail but ancient humpback bridge 10 km from the coastal highway, and another just past Çamlıhemşin just under 20 km from the highway.

If you need to stay in Çamlıhemşin, there's the simple Otel Hoşdere (☎ (0568) 1104, 1145), with a restaurant, in the town centre.

Just beyond Çamlıhemşin, the road continues on the western bank of the Fırtına Çayı up to Çat (1250 metres), a mountain hamlet used as a trekking base.

If you turn left and cross a modern but derelict bridge just above Çamlıhemşin, follow the signs for Ayder Kaplıcaları. Ten km farther along at Şenyuva is another graceful humpback bridge, and also the Sisi Pansiyon, operated by Savaş and Doris Güney, who organise treks into the nearby mountains. A-frame bungalows at the Sisi Pansiyon cost US$20, or you can camp with your own tent for a fraction of that.

Ayder (1300 metres), eight km past Şenyuva, is a yayla (high-pasture) village proud of its two kaplıcalar (hot springs) with water reaching temperatures of 56°C (133°F). Small, simple hotels here cost US$5 per person, and basic but congenial restaurants provide sustenance. Local guides can lead you on excellent mountain hikes taking one day or more. For full information on hiking in the Kaçkar range, see Lonely Planet's Trekking in Turkey.

Getting There & Away Domuşes make several runs daily between Pazar on the coast and Çamlıhemşin, in some cases continuing to Ayder. Passengers are mostly shoppers from the villages, which means that the dolmuşes descend from the mountain villages in the morning and return from Pazar in early afternoon.

Hopa

The easternmost Turkish port on the Black Sea coast, 165 km east of Trabzon, is Hopa (population 18,000). Once a sleepy little port, Hopa has grown rapidly to serve the flood of traders and truckers who attempt to satisfy the appetites of the commerce-starved former Soviet republics. The town's growth has been chaotic, and Hopa has lost even the vestigial charm it once had. Only stop here if you must.

At the Georgian frontier, 30 km to the east is a border-crossing point at Sarp. At this writing, only people living in the region are allowed to cross here. Foreign visitors must cross by boat from Trabzon; see that section for details. If you cross, you can visit Batumi, the pretty Georgian seaside resort which was once an Ottoman town.

Places to Stay & Eat Most of Hopa's hotels are on the eastern side of the stream Sundura

Çayı along the waterfront street called Orta Hopa Caddesi, are usually filled with Russian and Turkish truckers and traders, and suffer from constant truck noise. Most have restaurants.

Best of the lot is the one-star *Hotel Papila* (☎ (0571) 3641, 2641; fax 2975), charging US$17/25 a single/double for clean rooms with shower.

There's also the *Cihan Hotel* (jee-HAHN) (☎ (0571) 1897, 3201; fax 1898), 200 metres west of the Papila at Orta Hopa Caddesi 7, almost as comfortable but a bit more expensive. Try haggling.

The cheaper places are clustered around the PTT (where the buses and minibuses stop), 200 metres west of the Hotel Cihan. The *Hotel Devran* (☎ (0571) 1091) and the neighbouring *Otel Vayıçlar* (☎ (0571) 1059) are both quite cheap – as well they might be – and filled with Russians.

Much better are the *Otel Ak* (☎ (0571) 2511) and the bigger *Hotel Huzur* (☎ (0571) 1095), on the west side of the Sundura Çayı just east of the Artvin road. Rooms cost from US$8.50 to US$11 a single, US$11 to US$16 a double. The *Antep Pide ve Lokanta*, to the right of the Hotel Ak, serves meals.

Getting There & Away Direct buses from Hopa to Erzurum depart early in the morning. If you miss the direct bus, you can catch a later bus to Artvin (1½ hours, US$1.50), then an onward bus from Artvin. For information on Artvin, see the Eastern Turkey chapter, after Erzurum and Kars.

Eastern Anatolia

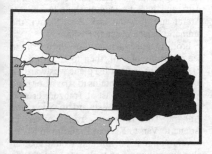

Eastern Turkey is a land of adventure where each event of the day seems to take on the character of some fabled happening. You might go to bed at night disappointed because Mt Ararat was covered in cloud Early next morning the mountain will take you by surprise, intruding into your consciousness, shining in the sun outside your hotel window. Or you might be riding along a rough road and suddenly come upon the ruins of a medieval castle, not marked on any map, not described in any guidebook. Every day reveals some new notion of epic events.

The east is not as well developed as western Turkey. You will see fewer tractors in the fields and more draught animals. Instead of grain-harvesting machinery, you might come across farmers threshing and winnowing in the ancient manner.

The people are no less friendly than in other parts of Turkey but they are more reticent and not, generally speaking, used to seeing and dealing with foreigners (except in the hotels and tourist offices). It may take a little more time for the friendliness of the adults to emerge, but not so with the children. Every single one will simply *have* to find out where you come from and what language you speak. When travelling, be prepared for the distances. You may ride for hours to get from one town to the next. When you get to that town, there may not be many hotels to choose from. And the one you want – particularly if it's the best in town – may be fully booked. Travelling in eastern Turkey is certainly not as comfortable as it is in the west. But if you are adaptable and out for adventure, this is the place to find it.

Warning

As this guidebook goes to press, I cannot recommend travel to south-eastern Turkey (to Diyarbakır, Mardin, Bitlis, or points south or east of them) due to the continuing Kurdish insurgency. If you do plan to travel to this area, be sure to contact your embassy or consulate in advance, ask about current conditions, tell them your plans, and ask their advice. Travel only during daylight hours, only on major highways (or preferably by air) and restrict your stops to major towns and cities.

Getting There & Away

If you're touring by public transport, you may want to consider flying to or from the eastern region. Buses, as always, go everywhere; there are even direct buses to İstanbul from most large eastern cities such as Erzurum, Van and Diyarbakır. Though there are some trains, they're usually not as comfortable nor as fast as the bus.

Air Turkish Airlines (THY) flies daily between İstanbul/Ankara and Diyarbakır, Erzurum, Gaziantep, Malatya, Trabzon and Van. Turkish Air Transport (THT) flies daily from Ankara to Diyarbakır, twice weekly to Elazığ, Erzincan, Kars and Şanlıurfa, and three times weekly to Malatya. İstanbul Airlines has flights between İstanbul and Trabzon daily except Sunday, and twice weekly between İstanbul and Ankara and Van. Check with the airline for schedules.

Bus Services to and from Ankara are frequent. Routes running east-west are generally not a problem, but north-south services can be infrequent, so allow plenty of time and check departure schedules as soon as you can.

Train From Ankara via Kayseri, there are three major eastern rail destinations: Erzurum, Kurtalan/Diyarbakır and Tatvan/Van. The Erzurum line goes on to Kars and in good times goes as far as the Armenian frontier, with a connecting train to Moscow. The Van line used to go on to Iran, with a connection to Tabriz and Tehran. This connection has been severed for years, but because of recent developments in Iran it may be revived. South of Elazığ, this line branches for Diyarbakır and Kurtalan.

For information on trains serving these routes, see Getting There & Away in the Ankara section of the Central Anatolia chapter.

Getting Around

The eastern mountains and high plateaux are subject to long and severe winters. I don't recommend travelling out east except from May to September and preferably in July and August. If you go in May or September, be prepared for some quite chilly nights. A trip to the summit of Nemrut Dağı (2150 metres) should not be planned for early morning except in July and August. In other months the mountaintop will be very cold at any time and bitterly cold in early morning. There may also be snow.

Most visitors touring this part of the country make a loop through it, starting from Amasya, Tokat, Kayseri, Trabzon, Adana or Antakya. Such a trip might follow one of the itineraries below.

From Amasya, Tokat or Kayseri, head via Sivas and Malatya to Adıyaman then Kahta to see Nemrut Dağı, then either north-east to Erzurum, Doğubeyazıt, Kars and Artvin, or south to Şanlıurfa and via Mardin to Diyarbakır for its ancient walls and mosques.

Starting from Adana or Antakya, go to Adıyaman and Kahta via Gaziantep. After seeing Nemrut Dağı, head south to Şanlıurfa, east to Mardin and north to Diyarbakır.

From Diyarbakır, head east through Bitlis

and around the southern shore of Van Gölü (Lake Van), stopping to see the Church of the Holy Cross on the island of Akdamar, before reaching the city of Van. Then head north to Ağrı and east to Doğubeyazıt to see Mt Ararat and also the İşak Paşa Sarayı, the dramatic Palace of İshak Pasha.

From Doğubeyazıt head north to Kars to see the ruins of Ani, then to Erzurum. At Erzurum you can catch a plane westward, or toil through the mountains to Artvin, or head for the Black Sea coast at Trabzon, or start the return journey westward to Sivas and Ankara. This itinerary, from Kayseri or Adana to Van to Kars to Erzurum to Sivas, covers about 2500 km and would take an absolute minimum of 10 days to complete by bus and/or train. It's better to take two weeks or more.

Car Special warnings are in order for those driving in the east. Fuel stations are fewer, roads can be significantly worse, and Kurdish separatist activity must be taken into account.

Fill your fuel tank before setting out, carry bottled water and snacks, plan on spending more time than you think the drive will actually take, and try to do most of your travelling in the earlier part of the day. Avoid driving in the evening or at night.

Roads in the extreme east of the country, and particularly in the north-east, are often riddled with potholes which break tyres and dent rims if hit at speed. When filled with rainwater it is impossible to tell the depth of, or judge the damage capacity of the potholes. They occur seemingly at random in otherwise smooth roads, and necessitate slow driving even on good stretches. If you break a tyre, even to the extent of gashing the sidewall open, a good Turkish *lastikçi* (tyre-repairer) can probably fix it – unbelievable but true.

As long as the Kurdish separatist unrest continues in the south-east there will be numerous military and police roadblocks. When you approach a roadblock, slow down and be sure you interpret the soldiers' signals correctly. When there is the slightest doubt about the signal, stop. If you misinterpret a signal and unintentionally run a roadblock, there may be serious consequences.

North-Eastern Anatolia

Mountainous and remote from the cosmopolitan atmosphere of Ankara and İstanbul, north-eastern Anatolia is a large slice of the 'real' Turkey, relatively unchanged by the tourist flood which swept over the western and central sections of Anatolia during the past decade.

As with much of Anatolia, cities and towns here date their foundation in millennia, not centuries. The Hittites, Romans, Persians, Armenians, Georgians, Arabs and Russians have all battled for control of these lands.

This is Seljuk country. Sultans of the first Turkic empire in Anatolia (during the mid 1200s) built impressive mosques, medreses, caravanserais and baths in Sivas and Erzurum which are not to be missed by anyone with a lively interest in architecture. The beautiful mountain scenery and historic Armenian and Georgian churches of extreme north-eastern Anatolia (around Artvin and Kars) are among the most powerful attractions in this region. The mountain trekking in the Kaçkar range between Erzurum and Artvin is excellent.

The following description of north-eastern Anatolia moves from west to east, from Sivas via Divriği, Erzincan and Erzurum to Artvin and Kars.

SİVAS
The highway comes through Sivas, the railway comes through Sivas, and over the centuries dozens of invading armies have come through Sivas (population 250,000, altitude 1285 metres), often leaving the town in ruins when they left.

Today it is a fairly modern and unexciting place which is full of farmers, yet at its centre are a few of the finest Seljuk Turkish buildings ever erected.

History
The tumulus at Maltepe, near Sivas, shows evidence of settlement as early as 2600 BC. Sivas itself was founded, as far as we know, by the Hittite king Hattushilish I around 1500 BC. Ruled later by the kings of Assyria, the Medes and the Persians, it came within the realms of the kings of Cappadocia and Pontus before being claimed by Rome. The Romans called it MegalopolisMegalopolis, which was later changed to Sebastea, which the Turks shortened to Sivas.

Byzantine rule lasted from 395 to 1075, when the city was taken by the Danişmend emirs. Danişmend rule was disputed by the Seljuks, and Sivas changed allegiance from one side to the other several times between 1152 and 1175, when the Seljuks took it – until the Mongol invasion of 1243.

Even after the Mongols were succeeded by the Ilkhanids, Sivas's travails weren't over. Taken by the Bey of Eretna in 1340, it succumbed to Tamerlane in 1400, and soon after (in 1408) to the Ottomans.

In more recent times Sivas gained fame as the location for the Sivas Congress, which opened on 4 September 1919. Atatürk came here from Samsun and Amasya, seeking to consolidate the Turkish resistance to Allied occupation and partition of his country.

He gathered as many delegates from as many parts of the country as possible, and confirmed decisions which had been made at a congress held earlier in Erzurum. These two congresses were the first breath of the revolution and heralded the War of Independence.

Orientation
The centre of town is Konak Meydanı, in front of the Vilayet Konağı building (provincial government headquarters). Near it are most of Sivas' important sights, hotels and restaurants.

The railway station (Sivas Gar) is 1.5 km south-west of Konak Meydanı along İnönü Bulvarı. After you arrive in Sivas by rail, walk out the station's front door to the bus stop on the station (south) side of İnönü Bulvarı. Any bus running along this major

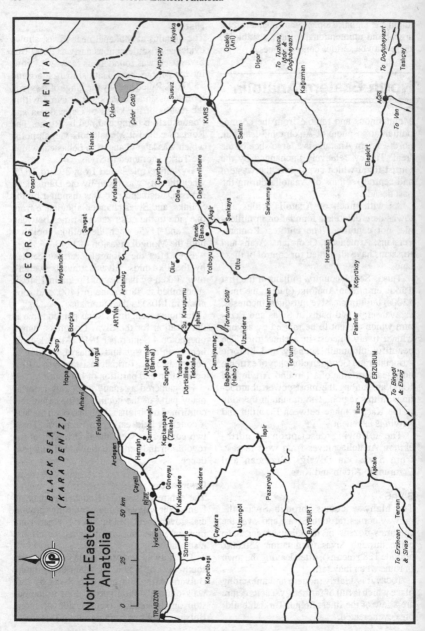

road will trundle you to or from the station. If in doubt, just ask the driver, 'Konak?'.

The bus terminal (Sivas Otogar) is over two km south-east of the centre, and difficult to find on foot. Transport to and from the terminal is by taxi, with a ride to Konak Meydanı costing US$2, less to the cheap hotels.

All of the sights except one are conveniently grouped in a pleasant park at Konak Meydanı; the other building to see is a short walk away.

Information

The Tourism Information Office (☎ (47) 21 35 35, 21 35 06; fax 23 00 20) is in the Vilayet Konağı building facing the main square, open Monday to Friday from 9 am to 5 pm. The postal code for Sivas is 58120

Çifte Minare Medrese

The Çifte Minare Medrese (Seminary of the Twin Minarets) has, as its name explains, a pair (çift) of minarets. Along with its grand Seljuk-style portal, that's about all it has, as the medrese building behind the portal has long been ruined. Finished in 1271, it was commissioned by the Mongol-Ilkhanid vizier Şemsettin Güveyni who ruled here.

Şifaiye Medresesi

Directly opposite the Çifte Minare is the Şifaiye Medresesi (İzzettin Keykavus Şifahanesi, Darüşşifa), a hospital medical school which ranks as one of the city's oldest buildings. It dates from 1217, when it was built on orders of the Seljuk sultan İzzettin Keykavus I, whose architect used stylised sun/lion and moon/bull motifs in several places in the decoration.

Look to the right (south) as you enter the courtyard to see the porch which was closed up and made into a tomb for Sultan İzzettin upon his death in 1219. Note the beautiful blue tilework and Arabic inscriptions. The main courtyard has four eyvans, or niche-like rooms, with the sun and moon symbols on either side of the main (east) eyvan.

The building's main court is now planted in grass and surrounded by tea gardens,

leather, carpet and souvenir shops. Unfortunately, each establishment has its own music system, so there's little chance of enjoying a quiet moment here.

Kale Camii

Near the Çifte Minare, back towards Konak Meydanı a bit, is the Kale Camii (1580), an Ottoman work constructed by Sultan Murad III's grand vizier Mahmut Paşa.

Bürüciye Medresesi & Museum

A few steps east of the Kale Camii, near the gazebo with an ablutions fountain up on top and a WC beneath, is the Bürüciye Medresesi, built in 1271 by Muzaffer Bürücirdi, who is entombed in it (inside, to the left, with the fine tilework). It now serves as Sivas' museum. With a grassy courtyard, pleasant and blissfully quiet tea gardens with tables and chairs, and sedirs (low sofas) in the eyvans, it's a wonderful place for a rest and refreshment. Historic carpets and kilims decorate the walls.

Sivas Congress & Ethnography Museum

North-west of the Kale Camii across İnönü Bulvarı is the Ottoman secondary school building which was the site of the Sivas Congress on 4 September 1919. Today it is the Sivas Congress & Ethnography Museum (Sivas Kongresi ve Etnoğrafya Müzesi), open from 9 am to 5 pm (closed on Monday). Admission costs 75c. Enter on the north-west side – coming from the Kale Camii and the park, you must walk around to the far side of the building. Displays are captioned in Turkish only, being of interest mostly to local patriots and students.

Great Mosque

The town's other sights are south-east of Konak Meydanı along Cemal Gürsel and Cumhuriyet caddesis. Walk to the southern end of the park and turn left (east) onto Cemal Gürsel Caddesi.

The Ulu Cami, or Great Mosque (1197) is Sivas' oldest building of significance. Built during the reign of Kutbettin Meliksah, it's a

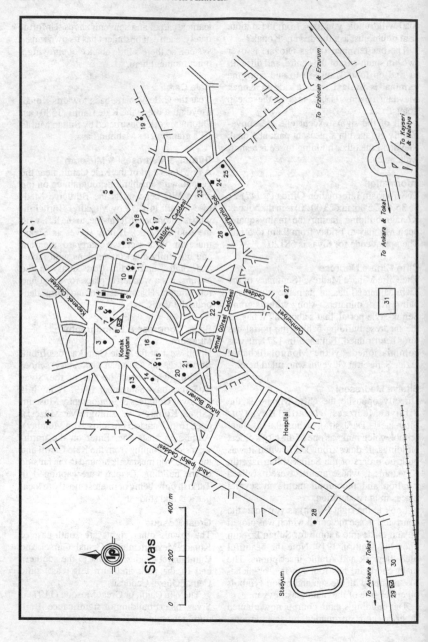

Sivas

To Erzincan & Erzurum

To Kayseri & Malatya

To Ankara & Tokat

To Ankara & Tokat

Atatürk Caddesi

Kepenek Caddesi

Kurşunlu Sok

Cemal Gürsel Caddesi

Cumhuriyet Caddesi

İnönü Bulvarı

Abdi İpekçi Caddesi

Konak Meydanı

Hospital

Stadyum

0   200   400 m

large, low room with a forest of 50 columns. The brick minaret was added in 1213. Though it's not as grand as the more imposing Seljuk buildings, it has a certain old-Anatolian charm.

Gök Medrese

Just east of the Ulu Cami, turn right (south) on Cumhuriyet Caddesi to reach the Gök Medrese, or Blue Seminary, built in that bumper year of 1271 at the behest of Sahip Ata, the grand vizier of Sultan Gıyasettin II

Keyhüsrev, who funded the grand Sahip Ata mosque complex in Konya and many other buildings throughout the Seljuk realm.

The façade of the building is wild and exuberant in its decoration. Although built to the traditional Seljuk medrese plan, in this one the fancy embellishments of tiles, brickwork designs and carving are not just on the doorway, but on windows and walls as well. The blue tilework gave the school its name, 'gök' (sky) being an old Turkish word for 'blue'.

If you want to take a photograph, come in the afternoon when the shadows have gone.

Places to Stay – bottom end

Sivas suffers from a lack of tourists, so its hotels are not kept up to visitor standards. There are no hotels near the bus or railway stations.

The inexpensive hotels in the first 500 metres south-east of Konak along Atatürk Caddesi are uniformly drab and dingy, and expensive for what you get. *Otel Özden* (☎ (47) 21 12 54), Atatürk Caddesi 21, is typical, with cleanish but depressing rooms for US$10 a double with sink, US$13 a double with private shower. There's a lift, management is friendly, and the location is farily convenient, though noisy.

The cheaper, better hotels are 700 metres south-east of Konak Meydanı, at the junction of Atatürk Caddesi and Kurşunlu Sokak.

Among the newer places in this area is the *Otel Fatih* (☎ (47) 23 43 13), Kurşunlu Caddesi 15, charging US$10 for a double with private shower (subject to increasing with demand). The hotel has a lift and central heating. The neighbouring *Otel Çakır* (☎ (47) 22 45 26) is similar, at the same price.

Even cheaper is the tidy and friendly *Otel Evin* (☎ (47) 21 23 01), Atatürk Caddesi 176, offering rooms with and without sink for US$5/7 a single/double. The owner says he'll light the fire for a shower on demand. Around the corner on Kurşunlu Sokak is the very similar *Otel Yuvam* (☎ (47) 21 33 40), which may be slightly quieter.

Places to Stay – middle

All of the middle-range hotels are 250 metres south-east of Konak Meydanı.

The *Otel Sultan* (☎ (47) 21 29 86; fax 21 93 46), Eski Belediye Sokak 18, across the street from the German Consulate, has 30 double rooms which were restored a few years ago. It offers decent, quiet value for US$23/35 a single/double with private shower and TV.

Competing with the Sultan for the carriage trade (such as it is) is the nearby 33-room *Otel Madımak* (☎ (47) 21 24 89), around the corner at Eski Belediye Sokak 4. The lobby and restaurant are bright and fancy and may actually rate the two stars the hotel has been awarded, but the rooms tend to be much plainer and only functional. Though posted prices are like those at the Sultan, you can haggle for rates approaching US$16/27 a single/double with private bath and TV if the hotel's not full.

Sivas's old standby, the two-star *Otel Köşk* (KURSHK) (☎ (47) 21 11 50), Atatürk Caddesi 11, has a restaurant, a lift and 44 fairly noisy, heavily used double rooms with bath priced at US$23/35 a single/double with private bath and TV. A buffet breakfast is included.

Places to Eat

Sivas has no lack of good inexpensive places to eat. For a range of foods at the lowest prices, find 1. Sokak (that's 'Birinci Sokak') in Sularbaşı Mahallesi, behind the PTT just off the eastern side of Konak Meydanı. The Aliağa Camii is halfway up the slope, and below it are several small, cheap restaurants good for a quick feed for US$1.50 to US$3. The appropriately named *Doy-Doy Lokantası* ('Stuff-Stuff') is cheapest, the *Nimet* and *Anadolu* the nicest. *Güleryüz Kebap* is the best for a variety of kebaps, including grills, İskender (Bursa) kebap, and spicy-hot Adana kebap. Several of the restaurants here serve sulu yemek (soups and stews) as well as cheap, good pide.

For slightly nicer surroundings, try the *Cumhuriyet Et Lokantası* on Atatürk Caddesi near the Hotel Köşk between the Pamukbank

and Garanti Bankası. Besides the expected döner kebap and köfte, it serves Konya fırın kebap (roast lamb). A full meal costs from US$3 to US$6; no alcohol is served.

Turn down the street between the Hotel Köşk and the Pamukbank to find the *Yeni Merkez Lokantası* and the *Erdemli Et Balık Lokantası*, both tidy and quiet, each with an aile salonu (room for women and couples), the latter serving fish as well as meat.

Across Atatürk Caddesi from the Hotel Köşk is *Hakan Baklavacı*, where Sivas's gilded youth gather (the girls in one upstairs room, the boys in the other) to eye one another warily and to consume delicious baklava and other sweets for US$1 or so per portion.

For fancier meals with alcoholic beverages, you must resort to the dining rooms of the middle-range hotels.

Getting There & Away

As it is on Turkey's main east-west highway and is also a transit point from north to south, Sivas is well served by rail and bus.

Bus Sivas otogar, 2.2 km south of Konak Meydanı, is difficult to find if you're on foot. Likewise, it's difficult to walk from the otogar to Konak, so you'll probably end up taking a taxi (US$2). The otogar has its own PTT branch, a restaurant and pastry shop, a shoeshine stand and an *emanetçi* (left luggage/checkroom).

Bus traffic is intense in all directions, though many of the buses are passing through, so it's impossible to know whether seats are available until a bus arrives. Details of some daily services follow:

Amasya – 225 km, four hours, US$8; five buses
Ankara – 450 km, eight hours, US$13; frequent buses
Divriği – 175 km, 3½-hours, US$7; several buses
Diyarbakır – 500 km, nine or 10 hours, US$16; several buses
Erzurum – 485 km, nine hours, US$18; several buses
İstanbul – 900 km, 12 hours, US$20 to US$24
Kayseri – 200 km, 3½ hours, US$6; hourly buses
Malatya – 235 km, five hours, US$11; several buses
Samsun – 341 km, six hours, US$13; several buses
Tokat – 105 km, two hours, US$4; frequent buses

Train Sivas is a main rail junction for both east-west and north-south lines. The two main east-west expresses, the *Doğu Ekspresi* and the *Güney/Vangölü Ekspresi*, go through Sivas daily. See the Ankara Getting There & Away section in the Central Anatolia chapter for details of these trains.

KANGAL & DİVRİĞİ

South-east of Sivas, 175 km over recently improved roads and on the rail line, lies Divriği, where a ruined castle stands guard over two magnificent Seljuk buildings. Along the way at Balıklı Kaplıca (Çermik) is a medical curiosity.

Balıklı Kaplıca

On your way to Divriği, the uninteresting farm town of Kangal, east of the Sivas-Malatya road, offers no reason for you to stop. But 15 km east of Kangal at Balıklı Kaplıca (or Çermik) off the Divriği road is a curious – even bizarre – health spa for those with psoriasis. Sufferers of this disease, which causes dry, scaly, itchy, unsightly patches on the skin, come to Balıklı Kaplıca ('Hot Spring with Fish'). They relax in the pools of hot mineral water, and let the resident fish nibble away at the scaly skin. The combination of the water and the fish is said to offer some relief, at least a portion of which must be comic relief.

Divriği

Divriği (DEEV-ree, population 25,000), a town hidden beyond a mountain pass (1970 metres high) in a fertile valley, is visited by relatively few tourists, foreign or Turkish. It's a nice old-fashioned Turkish mountain town with an economy based on agriculture. The narrow streets are laced with grapevines and paved in stone blocks and its houses are still uncrowded by modern construction.

Uphill from the town centre stand the Ulu Cami (Great Mosque) and Darüşşifa (hospital). Both were founded in 1228 by the local emir Ahmet Şah and his wife, the lady Fatma Turan Melik. Beautifully restored and preserved, these buildings sit, far from anywhere, and are a wonderful work of art hidden in the boondocks.

Divriği has a few basic lodging places, some simple restaurants and banks for changing money.

Ulu Cami Both of Divriği's architectural treasures are actually part of the same grand structure. Say 'Ulu Cami' (OO-loo jah-mee) to anyone in town, and they'll point the way 250 metres up the hill to the complex. The guardian will open the buildings, show you around, and expect a tip of US$1 at the end of the short tour.

The northern portal of the Ulu Cami is simply incredible, with geometric patterns, medallions, luxuriant stone foliage and intricate Arabic-letter inscriptions bursting free of the façade's flatness in a richness that is simply astonishing. It is the sort of doorway which only a provincial emir, with more money than restraint, would ever conceive of building. In a large Seljuk city, this sort of extravagance would have been ridiculed as lacking in taste. In Divriği, it's the wonderful, fanciful whim of a petty potentate shaped in stone.

The northern portal is most of what there is to see, although the north-western one has some fine work as well. The mosque's interior is very simple, with 16 columns and a plain mihrab.

Darüşşifa Adjoining the Ulu Cami is the hospital, plainer and simpler outside except for its requisite elaborate portal. Inside, eclecticism and odd ingenuity reigns: the floor plan is asymmetrical, the four columns all dissimilar. The octagonal pool in the court has a spiral run-off, similar to the one in Konya's Karatay Medresesi, which allowed the soothing tinkle of running water to break the silence of the room and to soothe the patients' nerves. A platform raised above the main floor may have been for musicians who likewise soothed the patients with pleasant sounds.

Seljuk Tombs As this was once an important provincial capital, you will notice several hexagonal or octagonal drum-like structures throughout the town. These are the traditional kümbets or Seljuk tombs. Ahmet Şah's tomb is near the Ulu Cami, as are several earlier ones dating from 1196 and another from 1240.

Places to Stay Even those travellers on the lowest budget will have to make hard decisions once they look at the hotels in Divriği. But at least there are hotels and, as more tourists come, these will no doubt improve.

The *Otel Ninni* (☎ 1239) charges US$5 for a double room without water; the common shower and toilet are down one floor from some of the rooms. The *Hotel Değer* next door is even more basic. Both hotels are on the main commercial street in the centre of town.

Getting There & Away With your own car, you can drive in and out; there is no road onward towards Erzincan.

Three or four buses run between Divriği and Sivas daily, continuing with Ankara and İstanbul. The trip between Sivas and Divriği takes about 3½ hours and costs US$7. Divriği's bus station is on the highway southwest of the village.

Coming from Malatya, you can take a bus as far as Kangal, near the turn-off for Divriği, and wait for the Divriği bus to stop on its way through.

The rail line from Sivas to Erzurum passes through Divriği. Check the schedules, allow for late arrival of trains in Sivas, and you may be able to catch a train to get you to Divriği conveniently. However, buses are faster and more frequent.

You can continue eastward by train from Divriği to Erzurum, about 6½ hours away, though you may have to stay overnight in Divriği and catch a train the next day.

The Divriği railway station is about two km south of the Ulu Cami.

ELAZIĞ

Elazığ (EHL-lah-zuh, population 200,000, altitude 1200 metres) was founded only in the 19th century at a place known as Mezraa.

In 1834 Sultan Mahmut II gave his vizier Reşit Mehmet Paşa the duty of reasserting Ottoman imperial control over the semi-independent provincial lords of the region. The pasha proclaimed Mezraa a provincial capital and installed an army garrison. Later, under the reign of Sultan Abdülaziz, its governor gave it the name of Mamuretülaziz, later shortened to Elaziz and, in republican times, to Elazığ.

Today Elazığ is a farming centre and university town, though its importance as an entrepôt was ended when the lake cut it off from main roads to the north and east. Viticulture is important; Tekel, the government spirits company, raises its big dark-red *öküzgözü* ('ox-eye') grapes in the region.

If you're passing through and need a place to stay for the night, plan to spend an hour or two seeing the Urartian treasures in the archaeological museum, and the ruins of ancient, earthquake-ruined Harput, five km north of Elazığ.

Orientation & Information

The city centre is the intersection of İstasyon, Gazi and Hükümet caddesis, near the İzzet Paşa Camii. The Belediye (Municipality) is

Top: Nomad's tent, Doğubeyazıt
Bottom: İshak Paşa Sarayı, Doğubeyazıt

Top: At the Balıklı Göl (Carp Pool), Şanlıurfa (TB)
Bottom: The summit, Nemrut Dağı (Mt Nimrod) (TB)

here as is the Tourism Information Office (☎ (81) 11 10 04, 11 23 79), at İstasyon Caddesi 35 in the İl Halk Kütüphanesi (provincial library) building. The main administrative office (☎ (81) 12 21 59) is in the Hükümet Konağı (provincial government headquarters) eight long blocks west on Gazi Caddesi.

Elazığ's postal code is 23000.

Archaeology Museum

On the campus of Euphrates University (Fırat Üniversitesi) on the outskirts of the city, the Elazığ Archaeology & Ethnography Museum (Elazığ Arkeoloji ve Etnografya Müzesi) holds artefacts discovered during the excavations which preceded the inauguration of the Keban Dam (Keban Barajı) in the 1960s.

The dam, north-west of Elazığ, caused the flooding of the valleys surrounding Elazığ to the north. Before the new lake was created, an archaeological rescue project excavated many likely sites. Among the most valuable finds were Early Bronze Age royal seals, gold jewellery, and a cuneiform inscription from the time of Menua, king of Urartu.

Harput

It was Harput, not Elazığ, which had the long and eventful history, effectively ending in the 19th century when it was ruined by earthquakes. Guarded by its photogenic castle, Harput was an important way-station on the Silk Road to and from China and India, but with the earthquake and the building of Elazığ, its importance was greatly diminished.

Today besides the castle you can visit the Great Mosque (Ulu Cami), dating from the 1200s; the Church of the Virgin Mary (Meryem Ana Kilisesi), and the Arap Baba Mescit and tomb, a Seljuk work.

Places to Stay

There are not a lot of places to stay in Elazığ, but they'll do. For low prices, try the Erdem Oteli (☎ (81) 11 22 12), in the centre at İstasyon Caddesi 19, with rooms for US$7/10 a single/double.

If you can afford it, the two-star Beritan Hotel (☎ (81) 11 44 84; fax 12 79 70), Hürriyet Caddesi 24, has 68 comfortable rooms with private baths going for US$18/26 a single/double. The town's best is the two-star, 100-room Büyük Elazığ Hotel (☎ (81) 12 20 01; fax 11 18 99), Harput Caddesi 9, charging about the same. Both two-star places have restaurants and bars.

ERZİNCAN

Like other north-eastern Anatolian cities, Erzincan (EHR-zeen-jahn, population 100,000, altitude 1185 metres) is very old. Unlike other cities, Erzincan has little to show for its great age, as it lies at the heart of Turkey's earthquake zone. Major quakes in 1939, 1983 and, most recently, on 13 March 1992, have left hardly anything of historical or architectural interest. What you see today is a modern farming town whose people wait bravely with apparent nonchalance to face the next devastation.

Besides old buildings, earthquakes have effectively erased Erzincan's old street plan. The modern main street is broad and arrow-straight, lined with shops, hotels and restaurants.

Should you need to stop, hotels along the main street can provide basic no-frills lodging. Erzincan's best is the three-star, 30-room Roma Hotel (☎ (023) 11016; fax 33530), Ordu Caddesi, 102 Sokak No 1, where a comfortable room with bath costs US$18/28 a single/double. The two-star Urartu Hotel (☎ (023) 11561), at Cumhuriyet Meydanı, is larger with 58 rooms and slightly lower prices.

As for restaurants, the Anıl and Kaya on the main street are good, the latter especially so for döner kebap served with the local flat paper-thin bread, salad and soft drink for US$3.

TERCAN

Midway on the age-old highway between Erzincan and Erzurum stands Tercan (TEHR-jahn, population 12,000, altitude 1475 metres), yet another ancient settlement with a momentous history. A town of farmers and herders, Tercan is set in a fertile river valley accented by huge rock outcrops to the south. Just west of the town, where the highway and railway cross the river, is an ancient stone bridge badly ruined, with most of its arches fallen.

The reason to stop in Tercan is to see the Tomb of Mama Hatun (Mama Hatun Türbesi), built between 1192 and 1202, unique in Anatolian architecture. It's uphill through the town 250 metres off the highway next to the Mama Hatun Kervansaray.

The tomb proper is surrounded by a high, thick circular wall which you enter through a portal decorated in bands of unusual Kufic script. Inside, the circular wall is pierced by 12 eyvans in which lesser notables could be entombed; several cenotaphs indicate burials below. The south-west mihrab niche faces Mecca from this easterly location.

Climb the stairs to the right of the entrance portal to get a view of the tomb and the surrounding cemetery. The eight-lobed tomb proper stands in the centre of the circle, oriented to the points of the compass with the door to the south. Its roof resembles an umbrella. The space above the actual burial chamber is still used for prayers, and thus may be open.

The neighbouring caravanserai is topped by a forest of chimneys (in this cold climate). The western door, facing the town on the opposite side of the caravanserai from the tomb, is the one likely to be open.

Though much repaired and rebuilt over the centuries, this caravanserai still exhibits some unusual features. Its long entry hall is lined with eyvans, leading to a singularly large eyvan across the courtyard from the entrance. Conical caps on the bastion tops are an odd feature.

Should you need to stay the night, Tercan has one tiny spartan hotel, the *Kaloğlu*, on the main street. There are simple restaurants as well.

ERZURUM

Erzurum (EHR-zoo-room, population 300,000, altitude 1853) is the largest city on the high plateau of Eastern Anatolia. It has always been a transportation centre and military headquarters – the command post for the defence of Anatolia from Russian and Persian invasion. Under the republic, it is assuming a new role as an eastern cultural and commercial city. There is a university here.

Erzurum, with its severe climate and the sparse landscape, lacks the colour and complexity of İstanbul or İzmir, but makes up for it with a rough frontier refinement. Although unused to seeing a lot of foreigners, the local people still give travellers a warm welcome. Many more women wear the veil here and a few are in purdah. The old men go to prayer early and often. In contrast, the town is busy with armed forces officers striding purposefully through its streets and squadrons of troops being trucked here and there.

When there's no fighting to do, Turkish commanders tend to order the troops to plant trees which are everywhere in Erzurum. The orderly, modern tree-lined boulevards provide a welcome contrast to the arid, almost lifeless appearance of the surrounding oceans of steppe.

For tourists, Erzurum is a transfer point with air, rail and bus connections. But if you stay the night (or even two nights) here, you'll be able to occupy your free time visiting some very fine Turkish buildings and a lively market area. You can also take a scenic excursion to the Tortum Valley and the village of Yusufeli in the mountains on the way to Artvin.

History

In Byzantine times Erzurum was called Theodosiopolis after the emperor who founded it on the ruins of an earlier settlement in the late 5th century. The powers in Constantinople had their hands full defending this town from Arab attack on several occasions. The Seljuks took it after the Battle of Manzikert effectively opened Anatolia to Turkish settlement in 1071. Being in a strategic position at the confluence of roads to Constantinople, Russia and Persia, Erzurum was conquered and lost by armies (in alphabetical order) of Arabs, Armenians, Byzantines, Mongols,

Persians, Romans, Russians, Saltuk Turks and Seljuk Turks. As for the Ottomans, it was Selim the Grim who conquered the city in 1515. It was captured by Russian troops in 1882 and again in 1916.

In July 1919, Atatürk came to Erzurum to hold the famous congress which, along with the one at Sivas, provided the rallying cry of the struggle for independence. The Erzurum Congress is most famous for its determination of the boundaries of what became known as the territories of the National Pact – those lands which would be part of the foreseen Turkish Republic. Atatürk and the congress claimed the lands which, in essence, form the present Turkish state and rejected any claim or desire to any other formerly held Ottoman lands. The phrase at the time was, 'We want no more, we shall accept no less'.

Orientation

Although the old city of Erzurum was huddled beneath the walls of the kale, the new Erzurum, which has grown up around the old, has broad boulevards, traffic roundabouts and an open, airy feeling, part of which comes from the dry wind which blows constantly.

You can walk to everything in the centre (Old Erzurum), including the railway station, but you will need a taxi or bus to get to and from the otogar, the airport and one of the top hotels.

Besides the main otogar north-west of the centre, there is the Gölbaşı Semt Garajı on the north-eastern outskirts, with minibus services to points north and east.

In Old Erzurum, a convenient point of reference is Gürcü Kapı, once the 'Georgian gate' in the city walls. It is marked by a chunky stone fountain at a traffic intersection 600 metres up the hill (south-east) from the railway station.

Modern Erzurum's main street is Cumhuriyet Caddesi, renamed Cemal Gürsel Caddesi along its western reaches. The two parts of the street are divided at the centre by a traffic roundabout bearing a large statue of Atatürk, a pool and fountain and the name Havuzbaşı.

It is almost three km from the otogar to the centre of town (where you'll find the Belediye and Vilayet), and two km from the otogar to the Havuzbaşı roundabout. From the otogar to the railway station is 2.5 km.

Erzurum's sights are conveniently grouped in the old part of town, within easy walking distance of one another.

Information

The Tourism Information Office (☎ (011) 15697, 19127) is on the south side of Cemal Gürsel Caddesi at No 9/A, one block west of the Havuzbaşı traffic roundabout. The postal code is 25000.

Money Erzurum Döviz, on Cumhuriyet Caddesi just west of the Yakutiye Medresesi next to the big Inter-Erzurum Toyota showroom, changes cash only, daily from 10.30 am to 1.30 pm and 2.30 to 7.30 pm. The only bank in Erzurum which seems to exchange travellers cheques is the Türk Ticaret Bankası (the sign says 'Türkbank') in Gürcü Kapı.

Bookshop When in need of a week-old foreign periodical, try the Kültür Sarayı book and tape shop at Cumhuriyet Caddesi 38, opposite the Yakutiye Medresesi.

Twin Minaret Seminary

At the eastern end of Cumhuriyet Caddesi is the Çifte Minareli Medrese (1253) or Twin Minaret Seminary, open every day from 8.30 am to 5.30 pm. Admission costs 75c.

The Çifte Minareli was built by Alaettin Keykubat II, son of the Seljuk sultan known for his many great building projects. Enter through the towering limestone portal topped by its twin minarets made of brick and decorated with small strips of blue tile. The main courtyard has four large niches and a double colonnade on the eastern and western sides. Stairways in each of the corners lead to the students' cells on the upper level.

At the far (southern) end of the courtyard

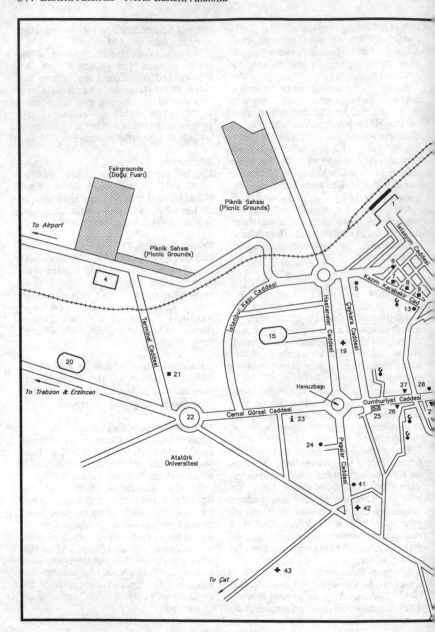

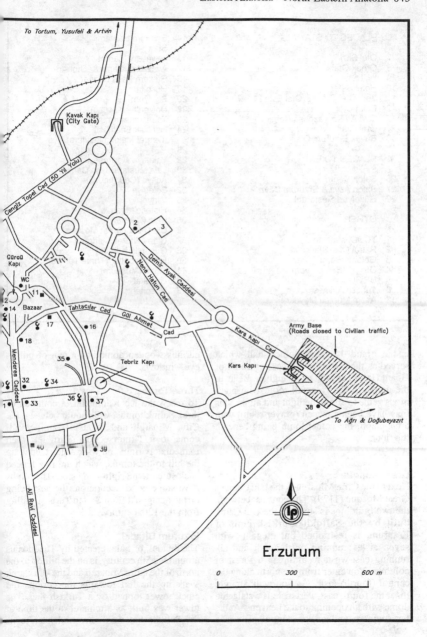

To Tortum, Yusufeli & Artvin

Kavak Kapı
(City Gate)

Cengiz Topel Cad (50 Yıl Yolu)

Gürcü
Kapı

WC

Bazaar

Tahtacılar Cad

Gül Ahmet Cad

Nene Hatun Cad

Demir Ayak Caddesi

Menderes Caddesi

Tebriz Kapı

Kars Kapı Cad

Army Base
(Roads closed to Civilian traffic)

Kars Kapı

To Ağrı & Doğubeyazıt

Ali Ravi Caddesi

Erzurum

0   300   600 m

is the grand 12-sided domed hall which served as the Hatuniye Türbesi or Tomb of Huant Hatun, the sultan's daughter. Beneath the domed hall is a small room with ingenious vents to allow the light and air in. This may have been a mescit (prayer room) with a cenotaph, the actual tomb being beneath the floor.

Great Mosque

Next to the Çifte Minareli is the Ulu Cami or Great Mosque (1179). The contrast between the two buildings is striking: the Ulu Cami, built by the Saltuklu Turkish emir of Erzurum, is restrained but elegant, with seven aisles running north-south and six running east-west, resulting in a forest of columns. You enter from the north along the central (fourth) aisle. As you walk straight in, at the fourth east-west aisle is a stalactite dome with an opening to the heavens. At the far southern end of the central aisle is a curious wooden dome and a pair of bull's-eye windows.

Three Tombs

To reach the Üç Kümbetler, a complex of three Seljuk tombs, walk south between the Çifte Minareli and the Ulu Cami; you'll come to a T-intersection. Turn left then immediately right and walk a short block up the hill to the tombs, which are in a fenced enclosure on the right-hand side. The tombs have some good decoration, the best being on the octagonal Emir Sultan Türbesi, dating from the 12th century.

Erzurum Citadel

The citadel, or kale, erected by Theodosius around the 5th century, is on the hilltop to the north of the Çifte Minareli and the Ulu Cami. Walk up the hill towards the curious old clock tower topped by a Turkish flag. The tower was built as a minaret in the time of the Saltuks but was converted later to its time-keeping function. It stands by the entrance to the kale.

The kale is open from 8 am to noon and from 1.30 to 7.30 pm in summer; admission costs 75c.

Within the kale walls you will probably encounter a group of boys playing football. Once they notice you, the game will end and they will run up to ask where you come from and to try their one phrase in English, which is usually 'Do you speak English?' or 'What is the time?'.

Besides the boys, the kale harbours a few old cannons with Russian or Ottoman inscriptions and a disused prayer room. It's difficult to get to the top of the walls for a view. The boys will recommend that you climb an electricity tower, but this is probably not a good idea. If the guardian takes a liking to you, he may allow you to climb the clock tower for the view.

Ottoman Mosques

Return to Cumhuriyet Caddesi then head west and you will pass on the north (right) side the small Ottoman **Caferiye Camii**, constructed in 1645 upon the order of Ebubekiroğlu Hacı Cafer.

Cross over the busy intersection, on the south-eastern corner of which stands the Vilayet, and you come to the **Lala Mustafa Paşa Camii** (1563), on the north-western corner. Lala Mustafa Paşa was a grand vizier during the golden age of the Ottoman Empire, and his mosque is a classical Ottoman work of the high period. It may have been designed by Sinan or one of his followers.

Yakutiye Seminary

Just to the west of the Lala Mustafa Paşa Camii is the Yakutiye Seminary (Yakutiye Medresesi), a Mongol theological seminary dating from 1310 and built by the local Mongol emir. Its portal copies the Seljuk style and is well worth a look, especially the lions. The minaret borrows from Seljuk architecture as well. There is a türbe adjoining the school at the back, which was meant to be used as the emir's tomb but never was.

The school is not open to visitors, though many Erzurumlus enjoy the surrounding park.

Erzurum Museum

The museum Erzurum Müzesi (☎ 11406) is several long blocks south-west of the Yakutiye Medresesi. Walk west along Cumhuriyet Caddesi to the Havuzbaşı roundabout, then turn left (south) and walk up the hill. The museum is just before the next intersection, on the left (east) side of the street. It's a 15-minute walk, or you can take any bus climbing the hill from Havuzbaşı.

The museum is open from 8 am to noon and from 12.30 to 5 pm, closed on Monday; admission costs US$1. Some exhibits are labelled in English.

The museum's collection is interesting primarily for its ethnological displays. There are beautiful carpets and kilims, Ottoman costumes and home furnishings, and a purloined Russian church bell. One case documents the massacre and mass burial of the Muslim inhabitants of the village called Alaca Köyü by Armenian insurgents at the beginning of the century.

Besides the ethnological collection, the museum has some fragments of Seljuk tiles and Urartian pottery, and some pottery and jewellery found in Hellenistic and Roman tombs.

Bazaar

Erzurum's market areas are scattered through the old part of the city. As the streets are narrow and winding (as usual), it is not easy to direct you on your walk. Start your wanderings at the Lala Mustafa Paşa Camii, then walk north along the street next to the mosque. You will pass the Rüstem Paşa Çarşısı or Market of Rüstem Pasha, which is the centre for the manufacture and sale of black amber prayer beads. For a look at the shops, go to the upper floor.

Just down the street from the Rüstem Paşa Çarşısı is the small **Pervizoğlu Camii** (1715). Along Kavaflar Çarşısı Sokak you'll find many tinsmiths who sell handmade cookers, heaters and samovars – all prized in this cold climate.

Continuing downhill in the market district will bring you, finally, to İstasyon Caddesi, the street leading to the railway station and the numerous hotels in this district.

The **Erzurum Hamamı** at the bazaar end of İstasyon Caddesi has received praise from many readers of this guide as one of the better hamams in Turkey. Unfortunately, it is usually open to men only.

Excursion to the Georgian Valleys

Many visitors to Erzurum make an excursion northward into the Tortum Valley (Tortum Vadisi) to enjoy the dramatic mountain scenery and to visit some of the old Georgian churches in little farming villages. For details, see the Georgian Valleys section, following, for information on travelling between Erzurum and Artvin.

Visiting Pasinler

Pasinler Belediyesi buses shuttle frequently between Erzurum and Pasinler 38 km to the east. You can hop on one to make a day excursion to see the Hasankale fortress and to enjoy the Pasinler hot springs. For details, see Pasinler in the following Erzurum to Kars section.

Places to Stay – bottom end

Erzurum is a low-budget traveller's dream, with many very cheap places to stay not far from the town centre. As for the upper end, there are no hotels in the luxury class, but several sufficient, comfortable three-star places.

Erzurum's inexpensive lodging places are scattered throughout the old part of town and are especially thick along Kazım Karabekir Caddesi (KYAA-zumm kah-rah-beh-KEER), north-east of Gürcü Kapı, not far from the railway station and the bazaar.

Otel Arı (☎ (011) 13141), Ayazpaşa Caddesi 8, is good and cheap, with double rooms from US$6 to US$8. Your room may have a sink, or shower, or toilet, or a combination

of these, but hot water is available only in the communal showers. The hotel is right next to the Ayazpaşa Camii (ask for that). From Gürcü Kapı, walk uphill on the street to the left of the Türk Ticaret Bankası ('Türkbank' on the sign) and when it widens into a square go left towards all those 'Avukat' signs.

Nearby is the *Otel Evin* (☎ (011) 12349), Ayazpaşa Caddesi, Bedendibi Sokak 12, down the street from the better known Hotel Çınar. The Evin has clean beds for US$4.50 and double rooms for US$8.50. Some rooms have views of the town. Hot water for Turkish splash-baths comes from the simple water heaters in which the hotel owner builds a fire half an hour before your appointed shower time.

The *Yeni Otel Çınar* (☎ (011) 13580), Ayazpaşa Caddesi 18, is a little more comfortable, but also costs more: US$9 with sink, US$12 with shower for a double room. To find these two hotels, look for the Gürpınar Sineması (a cinema) in the bazaar. Opposite it is a little street leading to the Çınar.

Beginning in Aşağı Mumcu Meydanı, the little square at the south-eastern (bazaar) end of Kazım Karabekir Caddesi, walk north-west along the Kazım Karabekir Caddesi to find the following hotels.

The 32-room *Hitit Otel* (☎ (011) 11204), at No 26, is just off the little square. A room with sink costs US$8/11 a single/double, US$10/13 with private shower. It'll do, particularly if the other hotels on the street are full. Next door is the similarly priced *Örnek Otel* (☎ 11203), Kazım Karabekir Caddesi 8, a similar place with 35 rooms, all with private showers. It's a bit like a barracks though, and has a weird colour scheme, but Turkish families love it.

Next along the street is the much better 55-room *Otel San* (☎ (011) 15789, -90), Kazım Karabekir Caddesi 10, which has a friendly management, a lift, cracked linoleum, a well-worn lobby, and guest rooms with neat beds and towels. Rooms cost US$10/14 for a single/double with shower, US$8 for a double with sink, and US$16 for a triple with bath.

The one-star *Otel Polat* (☎ (011) 11623; fax 44598), Kazım Karabekir Caddesi 4, next along the street, is a step up in comfort and price, with a lift, a family atmosphere, pretensions to modernity and style and 60 rooms, each with a bath, for US$13/21/26 a single/double/triple. The lift does not inspire confidence. It is the one on the left; the 'lift' on the right is actually a telephone booth.

Places to Stay – middle

Otel Oral (☎ (011) 19740; fax 19749), Terminal Caddesi 3, is perhaps the best hotel in the city. Its 90 two-star rooms all have showers or baths and cost US$28/40 a single/double, US$50 for a suite. It suffers from street noise, however, and its inconvenient location demands that you go everywhere by taxi or minibus. In the warm months, when you must have the windows open for ventilation, request a room at the back *(arka tarafta)* without fail.

The 50-room, nominally three-star *Büyük Erzurum Oteli* (☎ 16528; fax 22898), Ali Ravi Caddesi 5, is older than the Oral but has a more convenient location just up the hill from the Belediye and Vilayet. The staff speak some English. The hotel is old-fashioned and drab, with small rooms and slightly faded furnishings, but it's comfortable enough. Rates are high at US$30/42 a single/double. Dinner in the hotel's dining room costs from US$7 to US$10 per person. As always, front rooms may be noisy.

Other hotels are distinctly more modest than the Oral and Büyük Erzurum and are basically at the bottom end. They are mentioned here because their more desirable locations may cause their prices and quality to rise in future.

One middle-range hotel is very near the railway station and the bazaar. It's the 36-room, two-star *Hotel Sefer* (☎ (011) 13615, 16714), İstasyon Caddesi, near Aşağı Mumcu Meydanı. Convenient, but certainly not fancy, it officially charges US$32/42 for a single/double room with bath, but almost always offers substantial reductions to the likes of US$11/16. The entrance is decrepit; the guest rooms are better.

Places to Eat – bottom end

As with hotel prices, meal prices in Erzurum are low. Kebap places are, as usual, among the cheapest and best. Just opposite the Akçay Otel on Kamil Ağa Sokak is the *Mulenruj Kebap Salonu* (that's 'Moulin Rouge') (☎ 19783) which has a large main dining room and a smaller mezzanine at the rear. The döner kebap tends to be a bit salty for my taste, but a meal of it, along with some kuru fasulye (beans in tomato sauce), pilav and a soft drink came to US$3.50. Several other kebapçıs are within a few steps of the Mulenruj.

A stroll along Cumhuriyet Caddesi reveals several slightly fancier places. The *Salon Çağın* (☎ 19320) is near the traffic roundabout nearest the Yakutiye Medresesi, on the south side of the street. Clean, bright and cheery, it has very tasty food and on Sunday makes the house speciality, mantı (Turkish ravioli). A light lunch of sebzeli kebap (lamb stew with vegetables), bread and soft drink costs US$2.25.

Across the street is the fancier *Salon Asya* (☎ 21243). The menu includes a large variety of kebaps, including tereyağlı (with butter) and Bursa kebap. Meals cost from US$3 to US$4.

For cheap pide, try the *Park Pide Salonu* (☎ 22554), facing the front door of the Yakutiye Medresesi from across the park and across the side street. A tiny place, it's clean, the pide is good and the price is only from 50 to 75c.

Several cafés and pastry shops on Cumhuriyet Caddesi are useful for a quick bite or breakfast. Best is the *Kılıçoğlu Antep Baklavaları*, two doors west of the Salon Çağın. Bright and modern, it sells excellent buttery baklava with tea for US$1. *Patisserie Zirve*, farther west down the hill from the Salon Çağın, is good for pastry and tea, or breakfast. *Café Kuğu* is mostly for drinks. *Café Kandil*, east of the Salon Çağın, is just a hang-out for cool locals.

On Kazım Karabekir Caddesi, try the *Vatan Lokantası* opposite the Hotel Polat, a block behind the Hotel Sefer. The Vatan has an excellent selection of sulu yemek (ready food, mostly stews) at lunch. Its white table-cloths are thriftily covered in transparent plastic. Full meals can be had for around US$3.

Places to Eat – middle

Erzurum's best, since 1928, is the *Güzelyurt Restorant* (☎ 11514, 19222), directly facing the Yakutiye Medresesi across Cumhuriyet Caddesi. With white tablecloths, soft light-ing, quiet music, experienced black-clad waiters – the Güzelyurt is a culinary oasis in rough-and-ready Erzurum. Have the house speciality, mantarlı güveç – a delicious cas-serole of lamb, pimientos (sweet peppers), onions, tomatoes, mushrooms and cheese. It's big enough for two people if you've already had several appetisers. Your bill should not exceed US$5 to US$8 per person. Alcohol is served.

Getting There & Away

Being the main city in eastern Turkey, Erzurum is well served by all modes of trans-port.

Air Turkish Airlines (☎ (011) 11904), at 100 Yıl Caddesi, SSK Rant Tesisleri 24, at the north-western end of Kazım Karabekir Caddesi, has a daily flight from İstanbul via Ankara to Erzurum, and return. The airport bus (US$1.75) meets every flight and stops at the otogar on the way into town. For the trip back to the airport, it leaves the Turkish Airlines office 1¾ hours before flight time and stops at the otogar along the way. A taxi to or from the airport, 10 km from town, costs around US$5.

Bus The otogar, three km from the centre along the airport road, handles most of Erzurum's intercity traffic. City bus No 2 passes by the otogar and will take you into town for 20c. The otogar has snack shops and a restaurant.

Just up the hill from the railway station along İstasyon Caddesi, at Gürcü Kapı where the bazaar begins, are the offices of numer-ous bus companies. You can buy your

onward tickets here and save yourself a trip out to the otogar.

Details of some daily services from Erzurum's otogar follow:

Ankara – 925 km, 15 hours, US$23; several buses
Artvin – 215 km, four hours, US$9; several buses
Diyarbakır – 485 km, 10 hours, US$16; several buses
Doğubeyazıt – 285 km, 4½ hours, US$10; five buses
Erzincan – 192 km, four hours, US$8; frequent buses
İstanbul – 1275 km, 21 hours, US$17 to US$23; several buses
Kars – 205 km, 3½ hours, US$6; several buses
Sivas – 485 km, nine hours, US$18; several buses
Tortum – 53 km, one hour, US$2; several dolmuşes
Trabzon – 325 km, eight hours, US$15; several buses
Van – 420 km, 7½ hours, US$18; several buses
Yusufeli – 129 km, three hours, US$6; several dolmuşes

For Iran (if you already have your visa), take a bus to Doğubeyazıt, from where you can catch a minibus to the Iranian frontier.

The Gölbaşı Semt Garajı, about one km north-east of Gürcü Kapı through the back streets, handles minibuses serving towns to the north and east of Erzurum, including Ardanuç, Ardeşen, Arhavi, Çayeli, Fındıklı, Hopa, Pazar, Rize, Tortum, Şavşat, Şelale and Yusufeli. The Gölbaşı Semt Garajı can be difficult to find unless you take a taxi. Look for the Hotel Ersin and a Petrol Ofisi fuel station; it's behind the Petrol Ofisi station.

Train The Erzurum Garı is at the northern end of İstasyon Caddesi, 600 metres north of Gürcü Kapı, over a km from Cumhuriyet Caddesi. You can walk to or from the station to most hotels except the Oral. City buses depart from the station forecourt every half-hour and circulate through the city. A taxi should cost less than US$3, no matter where you go in town.

Erzurum has good rail connections with Ankara via Kayseri, Sivas, Divriği and Erzincan. Express trains cover the distance between Erzurum and Ankara in about 28 hours – if they're on time. For details of trains serving Erzurum, refer to Getting There & Away in the Ankara section of the Central Anatolia chapter.

Getting Around

Hat 2 (Route 2), covered by city buses and dolmuş minibuses, goes between the district of Yoncalık by the citadel westward along Cumhuriyet Caddesi as far as the otogar.

GEORGIAN VALLEYS

The mountainous country north of Erzurum towards Artvin was once part of the medieval kingdom of Georgia, and has numerous churches and castles to show for it. The trouble you take to see this region will be amply rewarded. The mountain scenery is at times spectacular, the churches, which share many characteristics of Armenian, Seljuk and Persian styles, are interesting and seldom visited. If you happen to be visiting in mid-June, the orchards of cherries and apricots should be in bloom – a special treat.

History

Georgian culture, now centred in the Republic of Georgia (formerly the Georgian Soviet Socialist Republic), is old and highly developed. The Georgian kingdom was founded in the Mingrelian lowlands and Caucasus Mountains at the eastern end of the Black Sea around the 4th century BC. Known in Europe as Colchis, it was the legendary home of Aeëtes and Medea, possessors of the Golden Fleece sought by Jason and his Argonauts.

Georgia was independent until around 100 BC when King Mithridates VI of Pontus conquered it for a short while. Dominated by Rome and the Persian Sassanids, the country was converted to Christianity by St Nino of Cappadocia in the mid-300s.

The partly Armenian dynasty of the Bagratids had gained control of Georgia by the 500s. Though they maintained good relations with the emperors and patriarchs of Byzantium, Georgia was briefly conquered and ruled by the Arabs in the early 700s.

After the Arab invasion the Byzantine emperor was nominal ruler of the districts north of Erzurum (named Tao and Klarjeti in Georgian), but real power was in the hands of local Georgian princelings. One among them, King Ashot I Kuropalates, began

building a true Georgian kingdom, seizing territory from the Byzantines and the Arabs, and building churches. Building continued under his successors David the Great and Bagrat III.

In the early 100s, the Byzantines retook effective control of Tao and Klarjeti in an effort to stave off invasion by the Seljuk Turks. The Seljuks were not to be put off, however, and Alp Arslan, sultan of the Great Seljuks of Persia, took Georgia and Armenia in 1064 on his way to the fateful defeat of the Byzantines at Manzikert (1071) which would open all of Anatolia to Turkish settlement.

The Great Seljuk state soon disintegrated into a welter of principalities, allowing King David II ('the Restorer') of Georgia to reunite the Georgian lands under his rule in 1125.

David's great-granddaughter, Queen Tamara (1184-1213), or Thamar, was a master of statecraft and strategy both military and political. Having extended her kingdom's borders greatly, she reigned over the flowering of medieval Georgian culture. Unfortunately for her country, she died just as the Mongol storm was gathering in the east.

The Mongols swept through Georgia in the 1200s, to be followed by Tamerlane in the late 1300s. King Alexander I divided his kingdom into three for his sons, which led to a more rapid decline in Georgia's fortunes. By 1555 much of the country had been partitioned between the Ottomans and the Persians.

During the 1700s, the Georgian kings, threatened by the Turks to the west and the Iranians to the east, pledged their allegiance to the Russian tsar, but the tsar was no less hungry for territory than his imperial neighbours. In 1801 King George XIII ended the history of the Georgian kingdom by abdicating in favour of the tsar, who took control.

Getting Around

The small mountain villages in these valleys are a delight to explore, but transport is not easy. You can see the most if you have your own car. Failing that, consider finding other travellers to share the cost and hiring a taxi for a day's excursion from Erzurum, perhaps ending at Yusufeli, which you can use as a base for further exploration. Public transport to and from most of the villages consists of a single minibus which heads down to Erzurum early in the morning for the market, returning in the afternoon.

Bağbaşı (Haho)

About 25 km north of Tortum is a turn-off on the left (west), near a hump-back bridge, to this village, called Haho by the Georgians. Go 7.5 km up the unpaved road through orchards and fields to the village. Stop at the Belediye and teahouse and ask for the *kilise anahtarı* or church key; no doubt a guide will accompany you for the last 600 metres up the road to the church, which is now the village mosque. The church, which dates from the 10th century, is still in fairly good repair, thanks to its continued use for worship. The guide will show you several reliefs reminiscent of those at Akdamar.

Öşk Vank

Another 15.5 km north of the Bağbaşı turn-off, in a wide valley with the river to the left (west) of the highway, is the road to Öşk Vank, seven km off the highway and up into the mountains. You must ford the river and wind up the road to the village, where you can't miss the big, impressive church. Most of the roof is gone, but there are still traces of reliefs and paintings. This was a monastery church, built in the 10th century. The *Coşkun Çay Evi*, to the right of the church, is used by foreigners dropping in for a glass of tea.

Tortum Gölü

North of Öşk Vank, the highway skirts the western shore of Tortum Lake (Tortum Gölü), which was formed by a landslide about three centuries ago. The 48-metre Tortum Şelalesi (waterfall), in the grounds of the TEK (Türkiye Elektrik Kurumu), is only worth seeing in the winter when there's plenty of water. In summer, the meagre flow

of water is diverted to the hydroelectricity plant. The lake is a beautiful spot for a picnic, but the guard at the gate to the TEK grounds asks US$6 for admission to see the falls – an outrageous price.

A few km north of the lake at Çamlıyamaç is a lookout across the valley and the mountains to the Tortum Çayı river gorge cut through the banded rock. If you stop at the lookout, children from the green oasis below will no doubt be on hand to sell you whatever fruit is in season in this land famous for its orchards.

İşhan

Heading north from the lake, take the road on the right marked for Olur and go six km (exactly 50 km from the Vank road) to a turn-off on the left for İşhan, marked by a sign reading 'İşhan Kilisesi'. This village is another six km up a rough, steep, muddy road carved out of the mountainside and probably impassable during wet or icy weather. If there have been heavy rains, the road may be washed out.

The scenic mountain village is worth seeing, as is its church, 100 metres past the village and down the hill. On one side of the church is a fountain and a toilet. The front of the church faces an open space, while the back nestles into the hillside. This was the Church of the Mother of God, built in the 8th century and enlarged in the 11th. There are some traces of fresco inside and a horseshoe arcade in the apse, and several reliefs on the exterior, including one of a lion.

There are several other churches and castles to visit to the east of İşhan along the Olur road. For details, see the Yusufeli to Kars section, following.

Return to the Olur road, go back the six km to the highway and go north towards Artvin. In the 8.5 km between the Olur road and the Yusufeli road, the highway goes through a dramatic gorge, wild and scenic, with striking bands of colour in the tortured rock of the sheer canyon walls. The Yusufeli turn-off is at a place called Su Kavuşumu (Water Confluence), where the waters of the Tortum Çayı and the Oltu Çayı join the

Çoruh Nehri (Çoruh River). A sign reads, 'Meyve Cenneti Yusufeline Hoş Geldiniz' (Welcome to Yusufeli, Paradise of Fruit). From the turn-off, it's 10 km up the Çoruh Valley to the town.

Yusufeli

The swift Barhal Çayı rushes noisily through Yusufeli (population 4500, altitude 1050 metres) on its way to the Çoruh River nearby. Yusufeli is kept neat and tidy in the best tradition of alpine towns. The local people are friendly, though they think it a bit much that foreigners spend vast sums of money and come long distances to to risk their lives rushing down the foaming Çoruh River, white-water rafting and kayaking.

A one-minute stroll shows you all of metropolitan Yusufeli: Halim Paşa Caddesi, the main street; the Belediye facing the main market street next to the river; the three banks (İş, Ziraat and Halk) and the few little hotels and restaurants. You passed the town's hospital (Devlet Hastanesi) on the road in. Yusufeli's postal code is 08800.

Georgian Churches Yusufeli is a convenient base for visits to the churches at Barhal and Dörtkilise. As of this writing there is limited dolmuş service to these villages, but soon no doubt the dolmuş drivers will wise up and offer day-long tours to these and other Georgian churches in the region.

Barhal (officially called Altıparmak, altitude 1300 metres), 32 km north-west of Yusufeli high in the mountains over a very slow unpaved road, preserves a fine 10th-century Georgian church long used as the village mosque. The church and the village's mountain setting are well worth the bumpy two-hour dolmuş ride or drive.

Dörtkilise ('Four churches'), 13 km south-west of Yusufeli via Tekkale, is the location of a ruined 10th-century Georgian church and monastery. The church is similar to, but older and larger than, the one at Barhal, and it takes less time and effort to see it. If you don't have a car, take a dolmuş towards Kılıçkaya or Köprügören and get out at Tekkale, then hike six km to Dörtkilise.

Places to Stay The hotels are of the most basic type, with beds (that's all) in waterless rooms. Virtually all charge US$3/5.50 a single/double. With the visitor flow to Yusufeli increasing rapidly, there may be more comfortable lodgings in the near future.

The cleanest place at my last inspection was the *Hotel Hacıoğlu* (☎ (0589) 1087), on Mustafa Kemal Caddesi. The adjoining *Hotel Damla* is much less appealing.

Facing one another on the east bank of the river by the rickety suspension footbridge are the *Hotel Aydın* (☎ (0589) 1365) and the *Hotel Çoruh*. To see a room, apply in the respective teahouses, of which this little street has more than its share. The *Hotel Sema* is also on the riverside.

The *Hotel Çelik Palas* (☎ (0589) 1507), right next to the mosque, is also a good choice, though the minaret noise will wake you at dawn.

The other hotels including the *Çiçek Palas Oteli* (☎ (0589) 1333) and *Dumlu* are less appealing.

Camping Cross the footbridge from the town centre and follow the signs to find *Akın Camping* and *Greenpeace Camping*, both very simple and cheap.

Places to Eat *Mahzen Fıçı Bira* (or Öğretmenler Lokalı) and *Kaçkar Fıçı Bira*, next to each other on the far side of the river near the footbridge, have the most pleasant situation. Draught beer (fıçı bira) is a strong point, as are the balconies right over the river.

Mavi Köşk Et Restaurant, entered by an inconspicuous stairway next to the Hotel Sema, is as posh as Yusufeli gets. Satin tablecloths, an elaborate (for Yusufeli) sound system, and a TV add to its charm. Prices are not much higher (about US$4 or US$6 for a meal), and alcoholic beverages are served.

The *Saray Lokantası* on the main street is the local cheap favourite for ready food at lunch time, but can be hot and crowded then.

Getting There & Away It's 130 km between Erzurum and Yusufeli. Dolmuşes depart from Erzurum's Gölbaşı Semt Garajı several times daily for Yusufeli and other towns and villages in the Georgian valleys.

Yusufeli to Kars

The fscenic drive up the valley of the Oltu Çayı from Yusufeli to Olur is along a good paved road. The aptly named Taşlıköy (Stony Village), 22 km east of the İşhan turn-off, illustrates the rough living in this harsh if beautiful region: the low stone houses with sod roofs are built half into the earth to escape the rigours of the winter cold.

Just north-east of the Olur road, look north-east from the bridge over the Gölbaşı to see a **ruined Georgian castle** perched on a rock spur, one of many in the region.

Continue south to Yolboyu, the junction with roads east to Bana (Penek) and Göle, and south to Oltu. At Yolboyu, **twin castles** on opposite sides of the stream guard this fertile valley, the eastern gateway to the mountainous region.

There's an even grander **citadel** at Oltu, south-west of Bana and 36 km south of the Olur castle.

Penek (Bana), 11 km east of Yolboyu, has a fine **7th-century Georgian church** set in a riverside meadow one km south-east of the road across the Penek Çayı. Though the church is worth a visit, access is difficult and only for the truly devoted Georgian church goer.

From Bana church it's seven km north-east to the Şenkaya turn-off and another three km to the village of Akşir. About 17 km past Akşir in a particularly lush and narrow valley is the western end of Değirmenlidere village, a collection of **low stone houses** with wood portals – an eerie sight when unoccupied – which serve as summer quarters for transhumant herders.

At the upper end of Değirmenlidere, the road emerges from the mountain valleys and the countryside opens by surprise into vast rolling steppe. The quality of the road surface deteriorates markedly here, the potholes slowing your vehicle's speed to a crawl. The surface doesn't improve until some 30 km before Kars.

For information on Kars and Ani, see those sections following.

ARTVİN

Artvin (ahrt-VEEN, population 28,000, altitude 600 metres) is the capital of the province bearing the same name. You can approach Artvin from Yusufeli (75 km, 1¾ hours) or from Hopa on the Black Sea coast (70 km, 1½ hours). Sit on the right-hand side of the bus coming up from Hopa to get the best views.

If you come from Hopa, or go there from Artvin, remember that any liquid-filled containers in your luggage will expand as you ascend into the mountains or contract as you descend to the Black Sea coast. They will leak in either case. Keep liquid-filled containers with you and open them periodically to adjust the atmospheric pressure.

The ride to Artvin via either route is wonderfully scenic. As you approach the town you will notice medieval castles guarding the steep mountain passes. During the third week in June, a pasture seven km from Artvin called the Kafkasör Yaylası becomes the scene of an annual festival, the Kafkasör Kültür ve Sanat Festivalı (Caucasus Culture & Arts Festival). The main events are the bull wrestling matches *(boğa güreşleri)*. Enquire in town.

Orientation

Artvin is still a small town easily negotiated on foot, except for the trip to and from its otogar.

Artvin is perched on a high hill which rises steeply above a bend in the Çoruh River. Its main street, İnönü Caddesi, is lined with the government offices and bureaus required of a provincial capital – Valilik (the provincial headquarters, also called Hükümet Konağı), the Belediye (Municipality), Forestry Service, Electricity Board, lots of banks etc. (The Belediye is served by no fewer than three teahouses within 15 metres of its front door, and no doubt it's here that the town's *real* business is done.)

The street parallel to İnönü Caddesi and one block up the slope is called Cumhuriyet

Caddesi. Most hotels are within a block or two of the Valilik.

Artvin's otogar is in Köprübaşı (sometimes called Çarşı), the riverside district at the foot of the hill. Minibuses (Artvin Belediyesi Halk Münübüsü, 30c) shuttle passengers between the town centre and the otogar at Köprübaşı. Bus companies maintain ticket offices in the town centre as well as at the otogar.

Artvin's postal code is 08000.

Places to Stay

Being a rough, small, poor provincial town, Artvin has no good hotels, no matter what your budget. The cheap hotels here are also subject to use as brothels by women who've come from the former Soviet Union. A hotel used primarily as a brothel will still rent you a room; that is, it will not have a neon sign advertising that it is a brothel. You must figure that out for yourself. At this writing the hotels recommended following are legitimate lodging places, but this is subject to change.

The *Yeni Şafak, Konak* and *Trabzon* are all dispiriting, even at US$2 a bed. The hopefully named *Otel Kültür Palas* (☎ (0581) 1118), across İnönü Caddesi from the Valilik and down a few steps on Hamam Sokak, is not quite as dire as the others. Unfortunately, it is also usually full of 'Russians' (citizens of the former Soviet republics). The Şehir Hamamı (Turkish bath) is only a few metres away, guaranteeing a good bath at least.

One step up in price and 'comfort' is the *Hotel Genya* (☎ (0581) 1192, 1136), İnönü Caddesi 23, just up from the İş Bankası. You pay US$9 for a double room, which may or may not have a sink in it.

More or less across İnönü Caddesi from the Genye is Artvin's best, the *Karahan Otel* (☎ (0581) 1800), İnönü Caddesi 16, though the hotel entrance is up the hill on the opposite side of the building. The 48 shower-equipped rooms here are dingy but serviceable, and much better than the appallingly drab and sordid lobby. Staff are friendly and helpful, however. Prices are quite high for what you get at US$20 to US$24 a single, US$25 to US$30 a double.

The *Kafkasör Tatil Köyü Dağ Evleri* (Caucasus Holiday Village Mountain Chalets, ☎ (0581) 1814, 2936) are simple lodgings near the Kafkasör meadow. Ask at the Karahan Otel or the Belediye about access.

Places to Eat

Artvin's best restaurants are the dining room of the Karahan Otel and the *Efkar Restaurant* at the foot of İnönü Caddesi where it turns to descend the slope. Both have smoke-soiled windows and scratchy music, but some of the food can be surprisingly good. A three-course meal with a huge beer costs about US$4.

For even cheaper fare, explore the upper reaches of İnönü Caddesi by the Yapı Kredi Bankası. *Kadir'in Yeri* at No 56 is good for döner kebap, the nearby *Çınar Lokantası* for soups and stews. *Kuğu Kebap*, across from the Şafak Oteli in the centre, has good döner also.

For tea, pastries and light meals, try the *Akın* and the *Köşk*, across the street from one another near the Yapı Kredi Bankası on İnönü. The *Durak Çay ve Kahvaltı Salonu* directly across from the Valilik advertises 'Breakfast' (in English) but is much more of a local teahouse.

Getting There & Away

The roads from Artvin to Hopa and Erzurum are fairly good, smooth and fast.

Minibuses depart from Artvin frequently in the morning and early afternoon for Yusufeli, Hopa and Rize, circulating through the upper town looking for passengers before descending to Köprübaşı and the otogar. As Turizm, one of the major companies serving this region, has a ticket office on İnönü Caddesi across from the Valilik. Details of some daily services from Artvin follow:

Erzurum – 215 km, four hours, US$9; several buses and dolmuşes

Hopa – 70 km, 1½ hours, US$4; frequent dolmuşes

Kars – 270 km, five hours, US$12; two buses (6 and 10 am)

Samsun – 577 km, eight or nine hours, US$18; one or two buses

Trabzon – 255 km, five hours, US$12; frequent buses

Yusufeli – 75 km, 1¾ hours, US$3.50; several dolmuşes

There are also several minibuses daily to these towns and villages of the region:

Ardahan – US$9
Ardanuç – US$1.50
Göle – US$9
Meydancık – US$5
Narman – US$9
Oltu – US$5
Şavşat – US$3
Tortum – US$7.50

ARTVİN TO KARS

The most direct route between Artvin and Kars is via the old Georgian town of Şavşat. The road deteriorates east of Şavşat, so plan on taking more time for the journey than the distance alone might indicate. The southern road via Ardanuç is little more than a track; go via Şavşat. Both roads meet at Ardahan, then go on via Gölebert and Susuz to Kars.

If you have your own vehicle, start early from Artvin (or Kars) and plan to take at least one excursion to one of the several Georgian churches within a short distance of the main road. Take some water and snacks along, whether you go by bus or car. If you have your own car, it's a good idea to fill your fuel tank before setting out on this journey.

Ardanuç, on the southern route, boasts a large **Bagratid fortress**. Beyond it 14 km is the village of Bulanık, and a few km off the main road, the 10th-century **church of Yeni Rabat**.

On the road to Şavşat just after passing the Ardanuç turn-off, look for a stone bridge and a sign to Hamamlı. This village, just over six km off the main road, boasts the fine 10th-century **Georgian church of Dolishane** (now a mosque). Back on the main road, another 12 km brings you to Pırnallı village and the trailhead for the 30 to 45-minute hike up to the 9th-century **Georgian monastery** and **church of Porta**.

Another **fortress** guards the western approach to Şavşat. From here you can make an excursion north via the Veliköy road 10 km to Cevizli to see the 10th-century **monastery church of Tbeti**, ruinous but still beautiful in its setting.

After traversing the rough road east of Şavşat, the simple town of Ardahan appears as an oasis of civilisation. There are a few very basic services, but you will want to press on to Kars for the night.

ERZURUM TO KARS

The highway east leaves Erzurum and climbs into a landscape of wide vistas, rich irrigated fields and the inevitable flocks of cattle and sheep.

Pasinler

Hasankale fortress, 38 km east of Erzurum, dominates Pasinler (population 22,000, altitude 1656 metres) from its rock promontory. Much of the triple-walled fortress, reached by a block-paved street on the west side of the highway, is in good repair (some restored). It dates from the 1330s when the Ilkhanid emir Hasan had it built. Extensive repairs were made later by the Akkoyunlu leader Uzun Hasan.

The town is conservative in the eastern way, with pious, fiery-eyed, white-bearded men; and many women completely enveloped by burlap-coloured chadors.

Pasinler is famous in the region for its hot springs (kaplıcalar). From the main intersection next to the Belediye, cross the railway line, turn left and continue 800 metres to the baths and the adjoining *Hotel Kale* (☎ (0187) 1538) which charges US$12/17 a single/double for a tidy, quiet room with shower.

For more modest budgets, the *Hotel Park*, a block west of the Belediye in the market, is about the best cheap bet.

The highway and the rail line follow the broad flood plain of the Aras Nehri (Aras River) from Pasinler eastward 43 km to Horasan.

In Horasan you may see the **Çoban**

Köprü, a 16th-century stone bridge designed, it is said, by the great Sinan.

At Karakurt, the road leaves the river valley to climb into the mountains through pine forests, passing one fertile mountain pasture after another on its way to Sarıkamış.

Sarıkamış

Sarıkamış (sah-RUH-kah-mush, population 25,000, altitude 2125 metres), a lumbering town 152 km east of Erzurum, has a small ski resort, a huge army base, a forestry headquarters and, on its eastern outskirts, a big shoe factory.

The army base and a stone monument on the eastern outskirts are poignant reminders of a military disaster. In December 1914, during the early days of WW I, the Ottoman Third Army was encamped for the winter at Sarıkamış, defending this approach to Anatolia against an equal force of Russian troops. The egomaniacal Enver Paşa, effective head of the Ottoman war effort, ordered his troops to attack and push eastward – a disastrous tactic in midwinter. (Mustafa Kemal (Atatürk) was astounded and appalled when he heard of the order.) The Ottomans lost 75,000 troops to cold, hunger and casualties. The Russians counterattacked and took Erzurum.

Places to Stay Sarıkamış has two hotels, better than any found in Kars. If you normally stay in middle-range hotels, consider staying in Sarıkamış and taking day trips to Kars.

The *Turistik Hotel Sarıkamış* (☎ (0229) 1176, 2152), Halk Caddesi 64, is in the centre of town, marked prominently by signs. Although the hotel is not fancy, the lobby is colourfully decorated with local carpets and kilims, and the rooms are well kept and fairly cheerful. The dining room is quite serviceable. Rooms cost US$16/32 a single/double with bath and breakfast.

The *Hotel Akın* (☎ (0229) 2233), one block down the street, is simpler and cheaper.

The *Sarıkamış Kayak Tesisleri* (Ski Facilities) are four km west of the town centre

marked by the Belediye building. From the Belediye, follow the signs 1.5 km to the railway line, cross it and continue past the ghostly shells of crenellated stone warehouse and factory buildings. Three km from the Belediye turn right by a crude brickyard, and up the hill to the ski lift. The simple ski lodge (kayak evi) has some older rooms and a new accommodation building. You may be able to find lodging here in summer, and certainly can in winter.

KARS

East of Sarıkamış, the highway climbs out of the lush mountain valleys and away from the evergreen forests to vast rolling steppe with mountains in the distance. It is in this sea-of-grass setting that you find Kars (population 80,000, altitude 1768 metres), an agricultural and garrison town dominated by a permanently lowering sky and fierce, wet weather.

You will see lots of police and soldiers in Kars, and every one of them can tell you without hesitation the precise number of days he has yet to serve in Kars before he can go west to 'civilisation'. As for the locals, a harsh climate and a rough history has made them, for the most part, dour and sombre, though not impolite.

Dominated by a stark, no-nonsense medieval fortress (rebuilt in 1855) which is still used as part of the city's defences, Kars was a pawn in the imperial land-grabbing game played by Turkey and Russia during the 19th century. The Russians captured Kars in 1878, installed a garrison, and held it until 1920 and the Turkish War of Independence, when the republican forces retook it. One of the large mosques was obviously built as a Russian Orthodox church.

You have no doubt come to Kars with the intention of visiting Ani, if not it doesn't make much sense to come here. While you're in Kars, however, there are a few things well worth seeing.

Orientation

The Russians must have had great plans for Kars. They laid it out on a somewhat grandi-

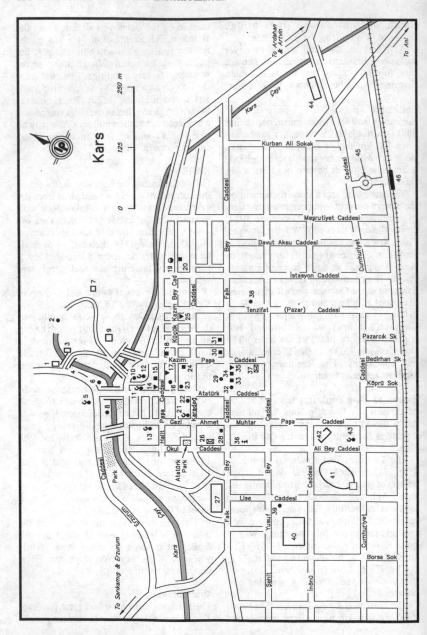

■ PLACES TO STAY

15 Hotel Güngören
18 Hotel Temel
20 Yılmaz Oteli
24 Asya Oteli
30 Otel Hayat
31 Topçu Palas Oteli
33 Otel Kervansaray
34 Hotel Nur Saray & Doğu Kars Bus
     Ticket Office

▼ PLACES TO EAT

14 Yeşilyurt Restaurant
17 Lale Pastanesi
25 Nil Restaurant
35 Güzelyurt Lokantası

OTHER

1 Mazlum Ağa Hamamı
2 Kars Kalesi (Castle)
3 İlbeyioğlu Hamamı
4 Taş Köprü
5 Laçin Bey Camii
6 Namık Kemal House
7 Beylerbeyi Sarayı
8 Cuma Hamamı
9 Church of the Apostles
   (Kümbet Camii)

10 Bastion in City Walls
11 Aliağa Camii
12 Evliya Camii
13 Yusuf Paşa Camii
16 Russian Bazaar
19 Otogar
21 Merkez Camii
22 Belediye (Municipality)
23 Turkish Air Transport (THT)
     Ticket Office
26 PTT
27 Emniyet (Security Police HQ)
28 Gazi Ahmet Muhtar Paıa HQ
29 Belediye Hamamı
32 Cihan Kars Bus Ticket Office
36 Tourism Information Office
37 PTT (Çarşı Branch)
38 Temizlik İşleri
     (Ani Bus Departure point)
39 Jandarma
40 Vilayet
41 Stadyum
42 Hospital
43 Fethiye Camii
     (ex Russian Orthodox Cathedral)
44 Museum
45 Atatürk Statue
46 Gar (Railway Station)

ose grid plan which, only now, over a century later, is being fulfilled. Nonetheless, almost everything in Kars is within walking distance, except perhaps the railway station and the museum. The new bus station is about 10 km west of Kars, but shuttle buses run to the old bus station in the town.

Information

The Tourism Information Office (☎ (021) 12724, 12300), Ordu (also called Ali Bey) Caddesi 140, is open from 8.30 am to 5.30 pm daily in summer, closed weekends in winter.

Kars Museum

The museum Kars Müzesi is worth seeing. Opening hours are from 8 am to 5.30 pm, nominally closed on Monday, but with so little to do in Kars, the staff is usually on duty anyway. Admission costs US$1.

The museum's oldest exhibits date from the Old Bronze Age. Roman and Greek periods are represented, as are Seljuk and Ottoman times. Several photo exhibits show excavations at Ani and there are shots of Armenian churches in Kars province. The chief exhibit is a pair of carved doors from the town's main Orthodox church (now a mosque) and a Russian church bell from the time of Tsar Nicholas II (1894-1917).

You should not miss the ethnographic exhibits upstairs, as this area produces some very fine kilims, carpets and cicims (embroidered kilims). Costumes, saddlebags, jewellery, samovars and a home carpet loom complete the exhibit.

A curiosity designed for local consumption is the Katliam Bölümü (Genocide

Section), one showcase displaying a few photos and documentation (all in Turkish) regarding the massacre of Muslims by Armenian forces in the early part of the century.

Behind the museum is the railway coach in which representatives of Russia's Bolshevik government and the fledgling Turkish Republic signed (in 1920) the protocol ending the Russian occupation and annexation of Kars.

Church of the Apostles

Although called the Drum-Dome Mosque (Kümbet Camii), the Church of the Apostles was built between 932 and 937 by the Bagratid king Abas. It was repaired extensively in 1579 when the Ottomans rebuilt much of the city. The porches were added to the ancient structure in the 19th century. The relief carvings on the drum are of the apostles.

Locked and seemingly abandoned, the church awaits restoration as a museum, which may happen if Kars ever develops enough of a tourist trade. For now, the only way to see the interior is to peek through the doors on the south-west (river) side.

Stone Bridge

Not far from the church is the Taş Köprü (Stone Bridge), which dates from the 15th century. It was repaired in 1579 along with everything else in town, but was later ruined by an earthquake after which it was rebuilt to its present form by the local Karaoğulları emirs in 1719. Ruins of the Ulu Cami and a palace called the Beylerbeyi Sarayı are nestled beneath the castle (kale) near the bridge.

Kars Castle

No doubt there has been a fortress at this strategic spot since the earliest times, but records show that one was built by the Saltuklu Turks in 1152 and torn down by Tamerlane in 1386. It was rebuilt upon the order of the Ottoman sultan Murat III by his grand vizier Lala Mustafa Paşa in 1579. Further repairs were made in 1616 and 1636. Although the Kars Kalesi is still an active

military base, it is open free to visitors most afternoons. Ask at the tourism office before walking up the road which passes the Church of the Apostles and the ruined palace known as the Beylerbeyi Sarayı.

The kale was the scene of bitter fighting during and after WW I. When the Russian armies withdrew in 1920, the control of Kars was left in the hands of the Armenian forces which had allied themselves with Russia during the war. Civilians, whether Christian or Muslim, suffered oppression and worse when under the control of irregular troops of the opposing religion. As the slaughter of Christian Armenians occurred in some parts of eastern Turkey, there was also slaughter of Muslim Turks and Kurds around Kars until the republican armies took the kale.

Historic Houses

The best example of a traditional Kars house is the **Gazi Muhtar Paşa Headquarters** on the corner of Faik Bey and Gazi Ahmet Muhtar Paşa caddesis. The stone house with elaborate wood trim and a sod roof was used as headquarters by Gazi Ahmet Muhtar Paşa, commander of the Ottoman forces during the Russian war in 1877. Later a school, then for a while the tourist office, it is not now open for visits.

The other house with a history is not much to look at, but its former occupant, Namık Kemal (1840-88), played a significant role in the development of modern Turkey. Born in Tekirdağ, the son of the Sultan's court astronomer, he became a government translator. An interest in European society and philosophy led him to translate the works of Rousseau and Montesquieu, and then to expound a similar political philosophy in plays, essays, articles and poems.

Kemal advocated Turkey's adoption of European political, technical, economic and social advances, but did so in the context of devout Islam. He reinterpreted European progress for an Islamic context, adapted it to Islamic traditions, and made it more acceptable to traditional Muslims. Kemal's calls for 'freedom and fatherland' got him into trouble with the sultan. He died in internal exile on Chios, but his ideas were eagerly absorbed by the Young Turks and by Mustafa Kemal (Atatürk).

Turkish Baths

The Belediye Hamamı is right across Faik Bey Caddesi from the Hotel Kervansaray. The Muradiye Hamamı at the citadel end of the Stone Bridge is for women only. Kars, perhaps because of its cold climate, has many other warm steamy baths as well.

Places to Stay

The hotel lineup in Kars is as depressing as the town's weather, but at least most hotels are cheap. Electricity and water stop unexpectedly and frequently.

The best value for money is at the *Hotel Temel* (or Temel Palas, ☎ (021) 11376), Kazım Paşa Caddesi 4/A. Clean and relatively pleasant rooms with private shower cost US$9/14 a single/double. There's a decent restaurant, and a lift which few people use because of the constant danger of being stranded inside when the electricity goes off without warning.

The flashiest hotel is the *Hotel Güngören* (☎ (021) 18113; fax 11296), Halit Paşa Caddesi, Millet Sokak 4. Opened in 1990, it already reflects hard use, but each room has a private bath with tub and shower. A hamam and grill restaurant are at your service. Rates are US$11/14/20 a single/double/triple. The location is quiet. The same warning about the lift applies.

The 38-room *Otel Kervansaray* (☎ (021) 11990), Faik Bey Caddesi 124, is old but decently kept by its old-fashioned management. Double rooms come waterless or with sink for US$7, or with shower (but no toilet) for US$11; you can haggle for discounts if it's not busy. Rooms at the back are quieter. The hotel has its own locked car park, and the Belediye Hamamı is right across the street.

A few doors down from the Kervansaray, the *Hotel Nur Saray* (☎ (021) 11364), Faik Bey Caddesi 208, has rooms with sink only (none with shower), but boasts clean sheets and cheap prices of US$6.50 a double.

One block east, the *Topçu Palas Oteli* (☎ (021) 11946), Faik Bey Caddesi 169, and the *Otel Hayat* (☎ (021) 13586) are similar.

The 30-room *Yılmaz Oteli* (☎ (021) 11074, 12387), Küçük Kazımbey Caddesi 14, near the bus terminal, was once the best in town. Its 30 rooms cost US$10/16 a single/double with shower. There's a tidy restaurant. To find it from the otogar, walk through a passage in the big long building on the east side of the bus lot (the ticket offices are on the west side).

The 33-room *Asya Oteli* (☎ (021) 12299), Küçük Kazım Bey Caddesi 50, is very grubby and run-down, but quiet. Rooms with shower go for US$6/10 a single/double; there are a few cheaper bathless singles. Kars's Russian Bazaar is right across the street.

Places to Eat

Kars is noted for its excellent honey. If you ask, you should get it for breakfast on a plate next to a smear of butter. Mix the honey and butter and spread it on bread. Several shops along Halit Paşa Caddesi near the Temel and Güngören hotels sell Kars honey and also the local kaşar peynir ('kosher' mild yellow cheese). One such is the P Ş Mandıra at No 158, more or less across from the Vakıfbank.

The decent little *Güzelyurt Lokantası* is a few doors down from the Hotel Kervansaray on Faik Bey Caddesi. It serves all three meals, including breakfast with Nescafé.

The *Nil Restaurant* not far from the Hotel Yılmaz is good for a bowl of hot soup at breakfast time, but my favourite place for breakfast is the *Lale Pastanesi*, Halit Paşa Caddesi 166. Most of the day it sells just dry cakes and biscuits, but its kahvaltı (breakfast) is Kars honey, butter, a half-loaf of fresh bread, and tea or hot, sweet milk. The shop has a fine view of the citadel through the front windows.

The *Otogar Restaurant* upstairs from the otogar, is alright if you need a meal before getting on your bus. Walk beneath it to the *Yılmaz Oteli*, which has a decent dining room.

The local notables meet to eat and drink at

the *Yeşilyurt Restaurant*, Halit Paşa Caddesi
113, an old Russian place with oiled board
floors, and high-ceilings. Food and service
are acceptable if not exceptional; alcohol is
served. A full meal with drinks costs from
US$4 to US$6 per person.

For ocakbaşı (open-grill) dining, try the
restaurant at the Hotel Güngören.

Things to Buy

Kars carpets *(Kars halıları)* are coarse of
weave and simple of pattern and colour, but
appealing for their boldness. Many of the
yarns used are undyed, retaining the natural
colour of the fleece. Any dealer in town will
quote you a price of so many liras or dollars
per sq metre. There are several grades of
carpets, and thus several price ranges. Once
you've found a carpet you like and have
agreed on a price per sq metre (haggle!), the
carpet is measured, yielding the final, exact
price.

These are not fine Turkish carpets, but
they are earthy, attractive, sturdy and inexpensive, although heavy and bulky to carry
home.

Getting There & Away

Bus Kars has two bus stations, the new one
near the museum about one km from the
centre, and the old one near the bazaar.
Dolmuşes shuttle between the new otogar
and the town centre.

The major companies here are Cihan Kars
and Doğu Kars, with ticket offices at both
otogars and on Faik Bey Caddesi between
Atatürk and Kazım Paşa caddesis, near the
Hotel Kervansaray.

Details of some daily services follow:

Ankara – 1100 km, 18 hours, US$20; a few buses
Artvin – 275 km, 5½ hours, US$9; a few buses
Doğubeyazıt – 240 km, four hours, US$8; see note
  following
Erzurum – 205 km, 3½ hours, US$6; several buses
Sivas – 653 km, 12 hours, US$20; a few buses
Trabzon – 525 km, 12 hours, US$18; a few buses
  (change at Erzurum or Artvin)

For Ani (45 km, 50 minutes), see the transport notes in the Ani section following.

For Doğubeyazıt a special warning is in
order. At this writing there are very few
direct buses from Kars to Doğubeyazıt. The
usual way to get there is to take a bus to Iğdır
then another bus to Doğubeyazıt. You may
have to wait in Iğdır less than an hour or for
many hours, you can't know which.
However, this does not stop the transport
sharks in Kars from selling you 'direct'
tickets from Kars to Doğubeyazıt at
premium prices. When you reach Iğdır your
bus may stop like all the rest, and you must
wait in a bus company office for the next bus
to Doğubeyazıt. The ticket you bought may
indeed take you all the way from Kars to
Doğubeyazıt, but not on the same bus.

Train One might hope that the Kars garı
(railway station) would be a 19th-century
Russian architectural extravagance, but
unfortunately it's a drab, crumbling,
characterless modern structure. A statue of
Atatürk greets you as you approach, and a
valiant old steam locomotive, mounted in
front of the station, evokes a more romantic
age of rail travel.

Two trains daily run out to the Armenian
border at Doğu Kapı. The slow *Akyaka
Postası* departs each Friday afternoon for
Ahuryan, just across the border in Armenia,
returning to Kars in the early evening each
Tuesday.

Two trains shuttle daily between Kars and
Erzurum. The *Karma* local train departs
from Kars daily at 2.40 pm, arriving in
Erzurum about six hours later (the bus takes
3½ hours). The *Doğu Ekspresi* departs from
Kars daily just before midnight bound for
Erzurum (about 5½ hours) and ultimately
for İstanbul's Haydarpaşa station. A one-way
ticket between Kars and Erzurum costs
US$3.75/2.50 in 1st/2nd class.

ANİ

The ruined city at Ani, 45 km east of Kars,
is striking. Its great walls, over a km in
length, rise to challenge you as you drive
across the wheat-covered plains and into the
Turkish village Ocaklı Köyü. Within the
walls is a medieval ghost town set in grassy

fields overlooking the deep gorge cut by the stream Arpaçay, which forms the boundary between the Turkish Republic and the Armenian Republic.

During the Soviet period, Ani was within the 700-metre no-man's-land imposed by Moscow on the Turkish border. Visits to the ruins were governed by the strict terms of a protocol agreed upon by Moscow and Ankara. Today the mood is much more relaxed, and few of the old rules apply.

History

Anahid, the Persian goddess equivalent to the Greek Aphrodite, was worshipped by the pagan Urartians, and has left her name on this great city as Ani.

On an important east-west trade route and well served by its natural defences, Ani was selected by King Ashot III (952-77) as the site of his new capital in 961, when he moved here from Kars. His successors Smbat II (976-89) and Gagik I (990-1020) reigned over Ani's continued prosperity. But after Gagik, internecine feuds and Byzantine encroachment weakened the Armenian state.

The Byzantines took over the city in 1045, then in 1064 came the Great Seljuks of Iran, then the Kingdom of Georgia, and for a time local Kurdish emirs. The struggle for the city went on until the Mongols arrived in 1239 and cleared everybody else out. The Mongols, who were nomads, had no use for city life, so they cared little when the great earthquake of 1319 destroyed much of Ani's beauty – not to mention infrastructure. The depredations of Tamerlane soon after were the last blow: trade routes shifted, Ani lost what revenues it had managed to retain, and the city died.

Information

To visit Ani, which stands so near the border of the Armenian Republic, you must have permission from the Turkish authorities. Start by filling in a form at the Tourism Information Office, then take it to be stamped at the Emniyet Müdürlüğü (ehm-nee-YEHT mew-dewr-lew, Security Directorate), two blocks west on Faik Bey

Caddesi, where police officials in green uniforms will routinely approve your application. Then proceed to the Kars Museum to buy your ticket (US$2); tickets are not sold at Ani proper. Ani is open from 8.30 am to 5 pm.

Getting There & Away

Transport can be a problem. Kars is in that stage of development when local sharks try to monopolise transport to a tourist site and raise the prices unconscionably. You may find it difficult to find reasonably priced transport, or you may have to haggle like mad.

You should have little trouble getting the necessary permit by yourself, even if you speak no Turkish.

The cheapest transport (US$1.25) is the municipal bus to Ocaklı which makes one run daily from Kars to Ani, departing from the Temizlik İşleri building on Pazar Caddesi between Faik Bey and Şehit Yusuf Bey caddesis at 6.30 am. It returns from Ani (Ocaklı Köyü) around 4 pm, but the transport sharks (including, allegedly, at least one person in the Tourism Information Office) will do their best to keep you off it.

A typical ruse is to tell you that the municipal bus 'broke down', or doesn't run anymore, but that you can catch a cheap dolmuş from in front of the tourism office at 8.30 am for US$6 per person round-trip. When you arrive at the tourism office, you are told that the dolmuş broke down but that a taxi (which happens conveniently to be waiting right there) will take you to Ani for several dollars more (per person) than the dolmuş fare.

On your return trip from Ani, the villagers of Ocaklı may tell you that the bus has already left and that you must take a taxi. They do it for the same reason as do the people in Kars – they get a kickback from the taxi driver.

It is often possible in the summer months to hitchhike to Ani. Get your permit the day before, if possible. Start early in the morning and take some snacks and lots of drinking water. Hitching from Ani to Kars, start by mid-afternoon (2.30 pm) at the latest or you may be left on the road.

Touts in the town will be sure to let you know that Doğu Kars runs a daily minibus or two out to Ani from Peron 9 in the old otogar for US$7 per person round-trip, including waiting time at the site. If they say there are not enough people, hang around at the tourism office or talk it up in your hotel, gather a group and hire a four-seat taxi (US$20) or a nine-passenger minibus (US$45) for the excursion. Agree on a definite amount of waiting time at the site. Two hours is the minimum; many visitors find this too short a time.

Touring the Ruins

Ocaklı Köyü, clustered at the foot of the great walls, is a typical Kurdish-Turkish village: stone houses with sod roofs topped by TV aerials. You'll smell the distinctive pungency of burning *tezek*, cakes of dried dung used for fuel. There are a few snack and drinks stands but no other services. Village children will volunteer to guide you in exchange for tourist treats: coins, *bonbons*, empty plastic water bottles, pens, cigarettes.

Enter the ruined city through the Alp Arslan Kapısı, a bent double gate named for the Seljuk sultan who conquered Ani in 1064.

Your first view of Ani is stunning: wrecks of great stone buildings adrift on a sea of grass, landmarks in a ghost city where once more than a hundred thousand people lived. Use your imagination to see the one and two-storey buildings which would have crowded the city's streets, with the great churches looming above them. Today birdsong is almost the only sound carried on the constant breeze, and the tangy scent of mint rises from underfoot as you walk.

The shepherds of Ocaklı Köyü pasture their flocks on the lush grass which grows on top of the undulating field of rubble from Ani's collapsed buildings. During your explorations, you're sure to be approached by a shepherd wanting to sell you *eski para* (old coins) or perhaps a bit of coloured tile unearthed in the ruins.

Follow the path to the left and tour the churches in clockwise order.

Church of the Redeemer The Church of the Redeemer dates from 1034-36, but only half of the ruined structure is still standing, the other half having been destroyed by lightning in 1957.

St Gregory (Tigran Honentz) Beyond the Redeemer church, down by the walls separating Ani from the gorge of the Arpaçay, is the Church of St Gregory (Tigran Honentz, 'the Illuminator'), called the Resimli Kilise (church with pictures) in Turkish. Named for the apostle to the Armenians, it was built by a pious nobleman in 1215, and is in better condition than most other buildings at Ani. Be sure to see the frieze carved on the east and south exterior walls, as well as the frescoes inside depicting scenes from the Bible and from Armenian church history.

Convent of the Virgins Follow the paths south-west and down into the Arpaçay gorge to visit the Convent of the Virgins (Kusanatz), enclosed by a defensive wall. The scant ruins of a bridge across the river are to the west.

Cathedral Up on the plateau again, the cathedral ('Fethiye Camii') is the largest and most impressive of the churches. Ani cathedral was begun by King Smbat II in 987, and finished under Gagik I in 1010. Trdat Mendet, the cathedral's architect, also oversaw repairs to the dome of Sancta Sophia in Constantinople, brought down in the earthquake of 989.

Ani became the seat of the Armenian Catholicos (pontiff). As the grandest religious edifice in the city, it was transformed into a mosque whenever Muslims held Ani, but reverted to a church when the Christians took over.

The cathedral demonstrates how Armenian ecclesiastical architecture emphasises height above all else: the churches are not long nor wide so much as high – a reaching towards heaven.

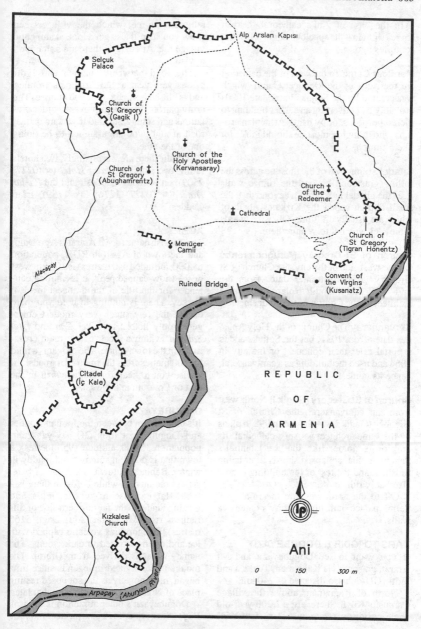

Ani

In the case of Ani's cathedral, heaven comes right in – the spacious dome fell down centuries ago.

Menüçer Camii To the west of the cathedral are the ruins of the Menüçer Camii, which was created by the Seljuks in the late 1000s probably by converting an earlier building to sacred purposes, or by using Armenian artisans who thought a mosque should look a lot like a church.

Citadel South-west of the mosque across the rolling grass and beyond the ruined walls rises the citadel İç Kale and, beyond that, the small church called the Kızkalesi, both of which are usually off limits. Obey the guards if they tell you not to venture here.

Church of St Gregory (Abughamrentz) On the west side of the city, the Church of St Gregory (Abughamrentz) dates from the mid-1000s and was built to plans by the same architect as the Church of the Redeemer.

Kervansaray The Church of the Holy Apostles dates from 1031, but the Seljuks added a portal after their conquest of the city in 1064 and used the building as a caravanserai, hence its name.

Church of St Gregory (Gagik I) North-west from the caravanserai, the Church of St Gregory (Gagik I) was begun in 998 to plans by the same architect as Ani's cathedral. Its ambitious dome, like that of İstanbul's Sancta Sophia, collapsed shortly after being finished, and the rest of the building is now also badly ruined.

Off to the north-west are the ruins of a Seljuk palace built into the city's defensive walls.

KARS TO IĞDIR & DOĞUBEYAZIT

If you want to see Doğubeyazıt and Mt Ararat, go south via Kağızman, Tuzluca and Iğdır (UH-duhr), a distance of 240 km.

North of Kağızman, above the village Çamuşlu Köyü, there are 12,000-year-old **rock carvings** (*kaya resimleri*, kah-YAH reh-seem-leh-ree) which the villagers can show you. You'll also get a look at authentic village life. At Tuzluca, there are **salt caves** to visit.

The road between Tuzluca and Iğdır passes very near to the Armenian frontier, and is closed between dusk and sunrise. The army patrols the area to prevent border violations and smuggling, and if you are on that road at night you are assumed to be doing one or the other.

In Iğdır there are, surprisingly, two hotels rating two stars: the *Latif Hotel* (☎ (0227) 2509), on Karadağ Caddesi; and the *Parlar Hotel* (☎ (0227) 1276; fax 1759), İrfan Caddesi 39.

AĞRI

The Turkish name for Mt Ararat is Ağrı Dağı, and the town of Ağrı (ah-RUH, population 65,000, altitude 1640 metres) is 100 km west of the snow-capped peak. It is a strong contender for the title of the drabbest town in Turkey. There is nothing to hold you there except the few small, very modest emergency-only hotels: the *Otel Can* and *Otel Salman*, within a block of the main crossroads in the town centre. The otogar is a mud lot 500 metres from the main crossroads. I'd advise you to head for Doğubeyazıt in the east or Erzurum in the west.

DOĞUBEYAZIT

It's only 35 km between the Iranian frontier and Doğubeyazıt (doh-OO-bey-yah-zuht, population 36,000, altitude 1950 metres), a town that is dusty in summer and muddy in winter. Behind the town is a range of bare, jagged mountains, while before it there is a table-flat expanse of wheat fields and grazing land. On the far northern side of this flatness rises Mt Ararat (Ağrı Dağı, 5165 metres), an enormous volcano capped with ice and often shrouded in dark clouds. The name Ararat is derived from Urartu. The mountain has figured in legends since time began, most notably as the supposed resting place of Noah's Ark. But more on that later.

Doğubeyazıt's other attraction is the İşak Paşa Sarayı, a fortress-palace-mosque

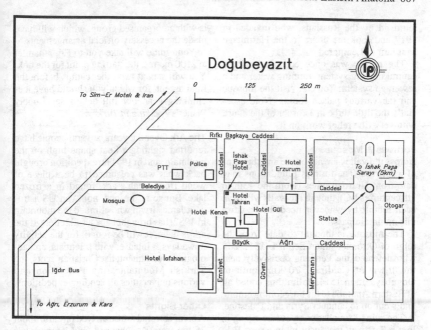

complex perched on a terrace five km east of town.

Information

Doğubeyazıt, called 'Dog Biscuit' by its admirers, has no Tourism Information Office, but hotel desk clerks can usually provide the information you need. The town is small and easily negotiated on foot. Its postal code is 04400.

Note that it may be very difficult, if not impossible, to make a long-distance or international telephone call. The PTT can seldom get a line for you.

You may want a guide to show you the sights around Doğubeyazıt or to arrange a climb up Mt Ararat. One guide recommended by readers of this book is Mr Mehmet Arık of Til-Tur Travel (☎ (0278) 2414, 2374), Çarşı Caddesi 53.

İşak Paşa Sarayı

Head east, five km from town, to get to İşak Paşa Sarayı. It's a pleasant walk and you'll have lots of company. Dolmuşes often pass nearby, especially on weekends, otherwise a taxi driver will demand about US$6 for a return-trip tour, waiting time included. Admission to the site costs US$2 and it's supposedly open from 8 am to 5 pm, but it may close earlier in winter. Drinks are available at the site.

Although ruined, the 366-room fortress-like palace has many elements which are in good condition. The mosque was used for prayers until about a decade ago and the central heating system, which needs some work, is a surprise in that it's there at all.

The building was begun in 1685 by Çolak Abdi Paşa and completed in 1784 by his son, a Kurdish chieftain named İshak (Isaac). The architecture is an amalgam of Seljuk, Ottoman, Georgian, Persian and Armenian styles. A grand main portal leads to a large courtyard. The magnificent gold-plated doors which once hung on the portal were removed by the Russians, who invaded in 1917 and took the doors to the Hermitage Museum in Leningrad.

The palace was once equipped with a central heating system, running water and a sewerage system. You can visit the mosque and the various palace rooms. Note especially the little türbe in a corner of the court, with very fine relief work on it.

Fortress & Mosque

Across the valley are a mosque and the ruins of a fortress. The fortress foundations may date from Urartian times (from the 13th to 7th centuries BC), though the walls will have been rebuilt by whoever needed to control this mountain pass.

The mosque is thought to date from the reign of Ottoman sultan Selim I (1512-20), who defeated the Persians decisively near the town of Çaldıran, 70 km south of Doğubeyazıt, in 1514. Selim thus added all of Eastern Anatolia to his burgeoning empire and went on to conquer Syria and Palestine.

The ruined foundations you see rising in low relief from the dusty plain are of Eski Beyazıt, the old city, which was probably founded in Urartian times circa 800 BC.

Mt Ararat

Mt Ararat (Ağrı Dağı) has two peaks when seen from Doğubeyazıt. The left-hand peak, called Büyük Ağrı (Great Ararat) is 5165 metres high, while Küçük Ağrı (Little Ararat) rises to about 3925 metres.

The best time to view the mountain is at sunrise or within an hour or two thereafter, before the clouds obscure it. Any viewing requires good, clear weather.

You can climb Mt Ararat but you need written permission from the authorities in Ankara, and then you must have an approved guide. The mountain is dangerous: severe weather, ferocious sheep dogs, rock and ice slides, smugglers and outlaws can turn an adventure into a disaster. Getting the necessary permission can take several months unless you do it through a Turkish agency, then it may get done in six weeks.

The only legal way to go up the mountain is with an organised group, which will have made the necessary official arrangements.

Your guide will take you to Eli, a hamlet at 2100 metres, the starting point for the trek. You will stay at two other camps before the final ascent, for which you should have ice-climbing gear. For full details see Lonely Planet's *Trekking in Turkey*.

The Ark   Over the years, several people have reported sighting a boat shape high on the mountain, and in 1951 an expedition brought back what was presumed to be a piece of wood from Noah's ark, found in a frozen lake. But so far no-one, not even US astronaut James Irwin who climbed the mountain in 1982, has brought back a full report. If the ark is there, it will be found, for the activity nowadays is intense, with scientists, archaeologists, fundamentalist Christian sects, the Turkish Mountaineering Federation and various universities all sending expeditions.

Other Sights

A bit of celestial refuse arrived on earth about 35 km from Doğubeyazıt, and its mark has now been added to the regular circuit of things to see near Doğubeyazıt. Ask at your hotel for more information.

Another good day trip is to the sulphur hot springs at Diyadin, where you can bathe in the pools and explore a river which flows into a cave.

Places to Stay – bottom end

My favourite among the cheap places to stay is the tidy *Hotel Tahran* (☎ (0278) 2223), Büyük Ağrı Caddesi 86, up the street from the big Hotel İsfahan. Modern and clean, it charges US$12 for a double with a private shower.

Another good choice is on the main street several blocks from the Hotel İshak Paşa. It's the *Hotel Erzurum* (☎ (0278) 1708, 1080), on Belediye Caddesi, a bit more expensive for what you get, with waterless rooms going for US$10, but it's fairly new as Doğubeyazıt hotels go.

The *Saruhan Hotel* next door is very cheap (US$4 per person), but in exchange for very basic accommodation offers good views of Mt Ararat and İşak Paşa Sarayı.

There are three small hotels on Emniyet Caddesi, the street between the prominent İshak Paşa and İsfahan hotels. The *Hotel Kenan* (☎ (0278) 1303, 2009), on Emniyet Caddesi, has a restaurant, a nice lobby and good rooms, though the hallways are shabby. The price is a bit high at US$9/14 a single/double with bath. The *Hotel İlhan* (☎ (0278) 2055), on Emniyet Caddesi, has very plain, basic accommodation in waterless rooms, but free hot showers and charges US$9 a double. The *Hotel Nur*, nearby, is similar.

The *Hotel Gül* (☎ (0278) 1176, 1479), Güven Caddesi 34, behind the Hotel Kenan in the next block, is very cheap, but is often fully booked with religious Iranian tourists. Double waterless rooms cost US$8 a double, plus another US$1 for a bath. The *Hotel Kıbrıs* (☎ (0278) 1407), on Güven Caddesi, is a better choice at US$5 per person. Some rooms have views of Mt Ararat.

Camping *İshak Paşa Cafeteria*, very near the İşak Paşa Sarayı, allows travellers to roll out their sleeping bags in a room off the dining room for US$1.75 per person. Good hearty meals are served as well.

Places to Stay – middle
Rising above the mud-brick roofs and TV aerials of Doğubeyazıt is the two-star *Hotel İsfahan* (☎ (0278) 1139, 2045; fax 2044), Emniyet Caddesi 26. Its 73 double rooms with showers on five floors cost US$25/38/46 a single/double/triple. It's modern and comfortable, with lots of kilims and carpets in the lobby and lounge, as well as its own lift and car park. The restaurant is the best in town. The hotel often caters to high-energy trekking groups.

Perhaps the most comfortable accommodation in Doğubeyazıt is at the three-star, 125-room *Sim-Er Moteli* (SEEM-ehr, ☎ (0278) 1601, 2254; fax 3403), PK 13, İran Transit Yolu, a modern 130-room establishment five km east of town on the highway to Iran. It's a comfortable, quiet, light and pleasant place surrounded by its own

grounds. The rooms are decorated in restful colours and have shiny-clean tiled bathrooms, locally made woollen blankets and craftwork decorations. With a shower, rooms cost US$28/40 a single/double, and the set-price meal costs US$10. There's a 30% reduction on room rates for children.

The two-star *İshak Paşa Hotel* (☎ (0278) 1245, 2406), Emniyet Caddesi 10, at the intersection of Emniyet and Belediye caddesis a block from the Hotel İsfahan, is simpler than the aforementioned hotels, but lower in price. It has 21 rooms on four floors, each with a tiled shower and balcony. There is a restaurant and bar and rooms cost US$16/28 a single/double.

Places to Eat
The main street has three or four kebapçıs, one of which advertises (in English), 'All Kinds of Meals Found Here'. The *Gaziantepli Kebap Salonu* is not bad. The restaurants in the two top hotels are good.

The *Kristal Pastahanesi*, on Emniyet Caddesi to the left of the Hotel Kenan, offers a Turkish breakfast for US$1 and afternoon tea and pastry for about the same price. It's a fancy place for this town, with plastic laminate tables, ice-cream parlour chairs and a separate aile salonu at the back.

Getting There & Away
From Doğubeyazıt, bus services are limited and mostly go via Erzurum. Details of (mostly daily) services follow:

Ankara – 1210 km, 22 hours, US$30; one direct bus
Erzurum – 285 km, 4½ hours, US$10; five buses
Iğdır – 51 km, 45 minutes, US$2; several dolmuşes
İstanbul – 1550 km, 28 hours, US$30; two direct buses
Kars – 240 km, four hours, US$8; a few buses
Van via Ağrı, Patnos and Erçiş – 315 km, 5½ hours, US$12; several buses to Ağrı, change for Van
Van via Çaldıran – 185 km, five hours, US$12; direct dolmuş every few days; more frequent service planned

INTO IRAN
Once you accept the cultural peculiarities of the Islamic Revolution, travel in Iran can be

enjoyable. The people are mostly very friendly and helpful. To visit or travel through Iran you must have a visa, theoretically obtainable from an Iranian embassy or consulate, but this may depend on the fluctuating currents of international relations.

It may take anywhere from a week to a month or more to obtain a visa. You may have to first obtain a visa for the country you will enter when you leave Iran; you may be asked to show a bus or airline ticket out of Iran. Be prepared for some Middle Eastern bureaucratic hassles. See the Visas & Embassies section in the Facts for the Visitor chapter, and contact your embassy in Ankara for details on current availability and requirements for visas.

The border crossing near Doğubeyazıt may take as little as one hour. You may be asked to pay an unofficial fee (ie, a bribe) by the Iranian officials. The Bank Melli branch at the border changes cash dollars or pounds or travellers cheques into Iranian rials (tomans). It may not change Turkish liras, but you may be able to exchange liras at banks farther into Iran.

From the border you can take a taxi to Maku, then an Iran Peyma bus from Maku to Tabriz.

South-Eastern Anatolia

Turkey's south-eastern region shares some characteristics with the north-east: its history is involved and eventful, its landscapes dramatic, and its tourist traffic much lighter than that on the congested Aegean and Mediterranean coasts. But apart from these things, the regions are dramatically different.

South-eastern Anatolia is mostly hot, dry country with elevations ranging from Şanlıurfa's 540 metres to Van's 1725 metres. The people are mostly Kurdish, and farming is their principal occupation. With the inauguration in 1992 of the gigantic Atatürk Dam, keystone of the vast South-east Anatolia Project (Güneydoğu Anadolu Projesi, GAP), this poor but fertile land began to get the water it needs to become the country's most abundant producer of crops.

Kurdish Separatism

Turkey's Kurdish minority, numbering an estimated 10 million people, is dispersed throughout the country, with significant communities in the major cities. By some estimates there are nearly a million Kurds living in İstanbul alone. But only in the south-east do Kurds come close to constituting a majority of the regional population.

The Kurds of south-eastern Anatolia have complained for years that the taxes collected in this underdeveloped region went to Ankara but none of the money came back to them in the form of government investment or services. The GAP project is answering that complaint, and the south-east promises to become a very wealthy area indeed. Besides the exponential increases in crop yields and the amount of arable land, the vast new lakes formed by GAP will provide abundant new sources of hydroelectric power, as well as revenue from tourism and fish aquaculture.

The new wealth may temper – or aggravate – Turkey's decade-old Kurdish separatist movement. Periodically through Ottoman and republican times, some Kurds in south-eastern and east-central Anatolia have dreamed of building a separate and independent Kurdish state uniting the Kurdish minorities in north-western Iraq, eastern Turkey, northern Syria and north-western Iran.

In recent years the separatist movement has been led by the Kurdistan Workers Party, known as the PKK. The group's terrorist activity takes place mostly in south-eastern Turkey, but there have been attacks against Turkish troops and civilians in north-eastern Anatolia and even in such cities as Ankara, Antalya and İstanbul.

The level of battle (for so it is) between the Turkish authorities and the Kurdish separatists ebbs and flows. It is to be hoped that peace will soon reign again in south-eastern Anatolia. Please read the warning at the beginning of this chapter about travel to this region.

GAZİANTEP

Known throughout most of its long history as Aintab, the city of Gaziantep (population 550,000, altitude 855 metres) was called Antep by the Ottomans. In April 1920, when the Great Powers were carving up the Ottoman lands, Antep was attacked and besieged by French forces. The city's nationalist defenders held out for 10 months before finally surrendering, a feat later recognised by the Grand National Assembly when it granted the city the title of Gazi, meaning Defender of the Faith (or War Hero). Since that time, the city has been called Gaziantep.

Despite its remarkably long history, Gaziantep today is a large, modern city with only two sights to interest visitors: the kale (citadel) and the museum.

Otherwise, Gaziantep offers a number of comfortable hotels at mid-range prices. As a bonus, you can enjoy a good number of culinary treats: the city and the region are known for excellent grapes and olives, for the soft Arabic 'pizza' called lahmacun (LAHH-mah-joon) and for pistachio nuts. This is the pistachio (şam fıstığı, SHAHM fuhss-tuh) capital of Turkey.

You can bypass this city without great feelings of guilt. If you do stay the night, have some lahmacun, buy a supply of delicious pistachios (about US$8 per kg in the shells; more without shells), spend an hour looking at the kale and museum the next morning, then get back on the road.

History

Archaeologists have sifted through some of the dirt which forms the artificial hill beneath the kale, and have found prehistoric artefacts dating from Neolithic times (7000-5000 BC). But the history begins when small Proto-Hittite, or Hatti, city-states grew up between 2500 and 1900 BC.

Hittites and Assyrians battled for this region until it was taken by Sargon II, king of Assyria, in 717 BC. The Assyrians ruled

for almost a century before being overcome by the Cimmerians, a Crimean people driven from their traditional lands by the Scythians. The Cimmerians swept through Anatolia destroying almost everything that lay in their path, setting an example that would be followed by numerous uncreative hordes which showed up in later history.

The Cimmerians cleared out and the Persians took over from 612 to 333 BC. They were followed by Alexander the Great, the Romans and the Byzantines. The Arabs conquered the town in 638 AD and held it until the Seljuk Turks swept in from the east in the 1070s.

With the crusades, Antep's history perks up a bit, but most of the action and romance took place in Urfa. The crusaders didn't stay long before the Seljuks took over again, and Antep remained a city of Seljuk culture, ruled by petty Turkish lords until the coming of the Ottomans under Selim the Grim in 1516.

Orientation

Gaziantep is fairly large, and you will have to take public transport to get from the bus or railway station to the centre. For reference purposes, the centre of the city is the intersection of the main roads named Atatürk Bulvarı and Hürriyet Caddesi next to the Hükümet Konağı (Provincial Government House).

The Devlet Hastanesi or State Hospital, another useful landmark, is a few blocks past the Hükümet Konağı on Hürriyet Caddesi. Most of the services you might need, including banks, post office, pharmacy, cheap and moderate restaurants, pastry shops, florists, pistachio-nut shops, a newsagent and even a hamburger joint are within one block of the intersection of Atatürk Bulvarı and İstasyon Caddesi.

The most recommendable hotels are also within a block or two of the Hükümet Konağı. The museum is about half a km from here and the kale is about half a km from the museum – an easy and pleasant walk.

The otogar is two km from the Hükümet

Konağı: walk out the front door of the otogar to the main road, turn right, walk half a block to the 'D' sign, and take a 'Devlet Hastanesi' minibus, or one of the less frequent city buses from the nearby bus stop. Don't listen to the taxi drivers when they say, 'There are no minibuses that take you into town'.

The railway station is almost as far out of town. The 'Devlet Hastanesi' minibus passes near it; walk from the station to the first large intersection to find the minibus. A taxi to the centre costs about US$2.50.

You can see the hill with the kale from many places in the city, and thus it serves as a handy landmark. Look for the highest hill, which bears a two-minaret mosque as well as the kale.

Information

Gaziantep's Tourism Information Office (☎ (85) 14 06 03, 10 59 69) is near the Hotel Kaleli at Hürriyet Caddesi, Güzelce Sokak 28/A. There is a Provincial Tourism Directorate (İl Turizm Müdürlüğü) on Atatürk Bulvarı. Very few of the staff speak anything but Turkish and only a few hand-out materials are available.

Gaziantep's postal code is 27000.

Kale

Head for the citadel first. The road to it begins just opposite the museum, which is next to the stadium.

The citadel was first constructed, as far as is known, by the emperor Justinian in the 6th century AD, but was rebuilt extensively by the Seljuks in the 12th and 13th centuries. The massive doors to the fortified enclosure may well be locked, but at least have a look at them. As you approach the kale bear right around the massive walls. Don't go through what appears to be an enormous stone gateway; this is actually the fosse (dry moat), straddled in ancient times by a drawbridge high above. Around to the right of the fosse you will come to a small mosque, opposite which is a ramp leading up to the citadel doors. If they're open, proceed across the wooden bridge which spans the fosse and into the kale.

The surrounding quarter is one of artisans' workshops, old stone houses and little neighbourhood mosques. Trucks for hire are gathered at one side of the kale, heirs to the ancient carters and teamsters.

Gaziantep Museum

The museum Gaziantep Müzesi (☎ 11 11 71), next to the stadium on İstasyon Caddesi, is open from 9 am to 5.30 pm, closed on Monday. Admission costs US$1. Surrounded by the requisite sculpture garden, the museum holds something from every period of the province's history, from mastodon bones to Hittite figurines and pottery to Roman mosaics (three fairly good ones) and funeral stones complete with portraits of husband and wife, to an Ottoman ethnography room of kilims, carpets and furniture heavily worked in mother-of-pearl.

Places to Stay

Gaziantep's accommodation is resolutely middle-range, with nothing much at the bottom and top ends of the price scale. There are no hotels near the otogar or the railway station. Most of the hotels are within a block or two of the Hükümet Konağı, either on Atatürk Bulvarı or on Hürriyet Caddesi

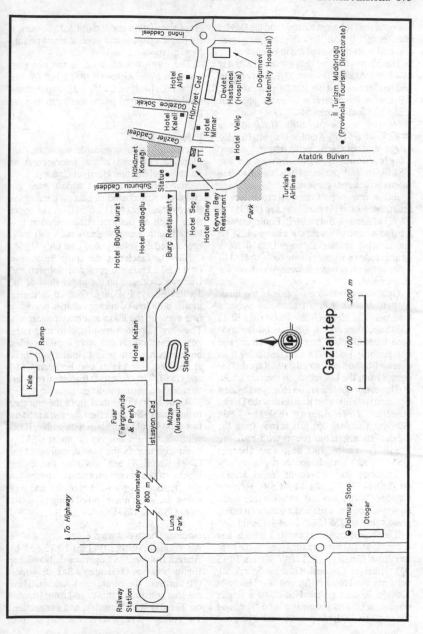

between the Hükümet Konağı and the Devlet Hastanesi. I'll start with the cheaper places and end with the best place in town.

The 35-room *Hotel Veliç* (☎ (85) 12 23 41, 11 17 26), Atatürk Bulvarı 23, is fairly bright and modern, with a lift and its own car park. All rooms have private showers and cost US$12/18 a single/double.

Nearby is the 50-room *Hotel Güney* (☎ (85) 11 68 86), Atatürk Bulvarı 10, also bright and modern, with lift and sauna. Singles/doubles with shower go for US$18/26, but the hotel has two bathless rooms which rent for less.

Just a few steps from the crossroads at Hükümet Konağı is the *Hotel Seç* (☎ (85) 11 52 72) at Atatürk Bulvarı 4/B. Equipped with a lift and central heating, it charges US$7 a single with private shower, US$10 for a double room without private bath, or US$14 a double with private shower. Watch out for street noise.

On the opposite (north) side of the intersection Atatürk Bulvarı becomes Suburcu Caddesi. The *Hotel Güllüoğlu* (☎ (85) 12 43 63), Suburcu Caddesi 1/B, has all the standard medium-class comforts, is clean, and charges only US$14/18 a single/double for a room with shower. Enter the hotel around the corner from the baklavacı on the side street.

Three more hotels are on Hürriyet Caddesi between the Hükümet Konağı and the Devlet Hastanesi. *Hotel Alfin* (☎ (85) 11 94 80), Hürriyet Caddesi 25, just across from the Devlet Hastanesi, has rooms with bath, lift, breakfast room and bar, and charges US$17/22/30 a single/double/triple.

The one-star, 45-room *Hotel Mimar* (☎ (85) 11 79 92; fax 14 44 59), Hürriyet Caddesi 24/C, has 40 comfortable bath-equipped rooms, a lift and a garage. It offers good value at US$18/25 a single/double.

The traditional favourite, which has accommodated tourists for years, is the two-star *Hotel Kaleli* (☎ (85) 10 96 90; fax 10 15 97), Hürriyet Caddesi, Güzelce Sokak 50, between the Hotel Alfin and the Hükümet Konağı. Rooms go for US$28/40 a single/double, or US$58 a triple in a suite. The hotel has two lifts, 70 large guest rooms with good

cross-ventilation and small tiled showers, a rooftop restaurant and several small private parking spots.

The city's newest hotel is the two-star, 42-room *Hotel Katan* (☎ (85) 10 69 69; fax 10 66 66), İstasyon Caddesi 58, opposite the stadium. It charges prices similar to those at the Kaleli.

Places to Eat

Gaziantep's recommendable restaurants are likewise clustered at the intersection of Atatürk Bulvarı and Hürriyet Caddesi.

Just across Hürriyet Caddesi from the Hükümet Konağı and its plaza is the *Keyvan Bey Restaurant* (☎ 11 26 51), on the upper floor, with an outdoor terrace section festooned with green vegetation. A full meal here based on kebaps need cost only US$4.

Slightly fancier is the *Burç Restaurant* (☎ 11 30 12) on the corner of Suburcu and İstasyon caddesis, on the upper floor of the Ticaret Sarayı building. Glassed-in dining rooms with lots of crimson drapes provide a fine view of the plaza and busy crossroads. They are favoured by pistachio magnates, government chiefs and other local notables, but meals here are priced similarly to those at neighbouring places cost between US$4 and US$7. The restaurant features live entertainment on some evenings.

Right across the street from the entrance to the Ticaret Sarayı is *Best Burger,* a modern fast-food hamburger shop with edible, if not wildly authentic, burgers for under US$2.

Finally, there's the roof restaurant at the Hotel Kaleli. Green and blue fluorescent lights make everyone look somewhat ghostly, but it's pleasant and airy and well above the street noise. A full dinner can cost from US$5 to US$8.

Getting There & Away

Air Turkish Airlines (☎ (85) 10 15 65, -6), Atatürk Bulvarı 38/C, operates daily nonstop flights between Gaziantep's Sazgın Airport (20 km from the centre) and Ankara. There are also nonstop flights to and from İstanbul on Tuesday and Saturday, and connections via Ankara every day. The flight from

Ankara takes just over an hour; from İstanbul, it's one hour and 40 minutes. An airport bus departs from the downtown office on Atatürk Bulvarı 90 minutes before flight time and costs less than US$2.

Bus The modern otogar is two km from the town centre and the bus service is frequent and far-reaching. Details of some daily services follow:

Adana – 220 km, four hours, US$7.50; several buses
Adıyaman & Kahta (Nemrut Dağı) – 210 km, four hours, US$8; several buses
Ankara – 705 km, 12 hours, US$20; frequent buses
Antakya – 200 km, four hours, US$8; frequent buses
Diyarbakır – 330 km, five hours, US$11; frequent buses
Mardin – 330 km, 5½ hours, US$12; several buses
Şanlıurfa – 145 km, 2½ hours, US$5.50; frequent buses

Train The *Toros Ekspresi* departs daily from İstanbul (9 am) and Gaziantep (4.05 pm), arriving in the opposite city about 30 hours later, having made stops in Ankara, Kayseri, Niğde and Adana. A one-way 1st/2nd-class ticket all the way costs US$15/10.50. The fare in a sleeping car is US$30/52/72 for one/two/three people.

An alternative is to take the overnight *Çukurova Ekspresi* from Ankara to Adana, then proceed by bus.

GAZİANTEP TO ŞANLIURFA

The road from Gaziantep to Şanlıurfa is very hot in summer, yet the land is fertile, with fig orchards, olive trees, cotton and wheat.

At Nizip, there is a turn-off south for **Karkamış** (Carchemish), a neo-Hittite city which flourished around 850 BC, about the time Akhenaton occupied the throne of Egypt. Though Karkamış assumed the role of Hittite capital after the fall of Hattuşaş, there is little left to see, and you must see it with a military escort so you don't get shot at as a smuggler – it's hardly worth the trip.

At Birecik you cross the Euphrates River (Fırat Nehri). The town has a **ruined fortress**, rebuilt and used by the crusaders. In spring (March or April), the town holds a traditional festival in honour of the **bald ibis**, which used to winter here, but is now on the verge of extinction. Authorities had established an **ibis feeding and protection station** to give the birds meat and eggs, and even built wooden houses for them following plans provided by the Turkish Wildlife Protection Society and World Wildlife Fund.

As you head east, the land becomes rockier and less fertile. The highway is crowded with oil tankers shuttling between the Turkish oilfields and the refineries in Batman and Siirt. By the time you approach Şanlıurfa, the land is parched, rolling steppe roasting in the merciless sun. The landscape is changing, however, as the gigantic Southeast Anatolia Project comes online, bringing irrigation waters to vast tracts of otherwise unarable land.

KAHRAMANMARAŞ

Formerly known as Maraş, the sonorous new name of this city (population 250,000, altitude 568 metres) was given to it in 1973 in honour of its role during the War of Independence. Maraş was occupied by French troops after WW I, and the populace showed such a fierce resistance to French rule that parliament added *Kahraman* (Heroic) to its traditional name – belatedly – half a century later.

The site of the city has moved repeatedly over the centuries, the present site having been chosen by the Dülkadır emirs during the 1300s. Wars and earthquakes have destroyed much of old Maraş, but if you need to stop for a meal or for the night you can spend a few hours pleasantly enough – and you will see very little indeed of other tourists.

Today Maraş is a modern city set where the agricultural plain meets the slopes of Ahır Dağı (Horse Mountain, 2301 metres). It's a farming centre with vast, rich crops of cotton and potatoes in the surrounding countryside. Copper working is also important. The Maraşlıs enjoy riding around on motorcycles with sidecars – convenient in this sunny, dry climate.

History

Marqasi was the capital of a principality which sprang up after the collapse of the Hittite Empire based at Boğazkale/Hattuşaş in 1200 BC. Destroyed by King Sargon of Assyria in the 700s BC, it rose again under the Romans, who called it Germaniceia.

The Byzantines employed its citadel as an eastern defence-point against Arab invasion, but the Arabs took it (in 637) anyway. The Byzantines reclaimed it in later centuries, but while the Byzantines were dealing with the Seljuk invasion up north, control of Germaniceia passed in 1070 to an Armenian strongman named Philaterus. He ruled over a large kingdom briefly, until 1097, when it was conquered by the crusaders and then returned to Byzantine control.

A succession of Kurdish, Seljuk and Turcoman emirs and sultans ruled the city until it was conquered by the Ottoman sultan Selim in 1515. Maraş had a significant Armenian population until the War of Independence, after which many from this community fled to neighbouring Syria or abroad.

Orientation

The city's otogar is 100 metres to the west of the main highway on Azerbeycan Bulvarı. This major thoroughfare continues west 400 metres to the archaeology museum, and beyond it 900 metres to Kıbrıs Meydanı (Cyprus Square), in the heart of the business district. Many hotels are near Kıbrıs Meydanı, or along the 400-metre stretch of Atatürk Bulvarı which goes west from Kıbrıs Meydanı to the Ulu Cami (Great Mosque), an ancient building which marks the traditional centre of the city. There are no hotels near the otogar.

The railway station (TCDD – or DDY – Gar) is at the foot of Cumhuriyet Caddesi, just east of the main highway, two km northeast of Kıbrıs Meydanı. There are no hotels, restaurants or other services nearby.

Information

The Tourism Information Office (☎ (771) 26590), is off Azerbeycan Bulvarı at Yeşiltepe Sokak 2, Gölkari Apartımentı, 1st floor. The postal code for Kahramanmaraş is 46000.

Historic Buildings

Start your walk around at the **Ulu (Acemli) Camii**, built in a Syrian Arabic style in1502, during the time of the Dülkadır emirate. Note especially its tall and unusual minaret, which has survived the depredations of earthquakes and invaders relatively intact. Across the park to the south-west is the recently restored tomb of the founders. The **Çukur Hamamı** Turkish bath is nearby as well.

The **citadel** (kale) to the south has been rebuilt and repaired over the centuries, and looks as if it has. There is nothing to see now but the gates and walls.

To the north a few steps is the **Taş Medrese**, a seminary dating from the 1300s. The **Taş Han** was the city's caravanserai.

South-west of the Ulu Camii up the wooded slopes is a neighbourhood of **old Ottoman houses**, some in good repair.

Kahramanmaraş Museum

The museum Kahramanmaraş Müzesi, 900 metres east of Kıbrıs Meydanı along Azerbeycan Bulvarı (400 metres uphill from the otogar), is open from 8 am to 5 pm (weekends from 9 am to 5 pm, Monday from 10 am to 1 pm). Admission costs US$1. Exhibit labels (when they exist) are usually in Turkish, with a few in English.

Exhibits include dinosaur bones found in the region, and a dozen very fine Hittite stelae covered in fascinating, lively reliefs. An Assyrian border marker is covered in cuneiform inscriptions. Other exhibits cover every period from the Old Bronze and Hittite to Ottoman. The ethnographic section is rich in textiles, costumes done in cloth of gold, inlaid woodwork, and beautiful local kilims.

Places to Stay & Eat

Because it is an agricultural trading centre, Kahramanmaraş has several comfortable two-star hotels right in the centre off Kıbrıs Meydanı.

Otel Kazancı (☎ (771) 34462; fax 26942),

just uphill a few steps from Kıbrıs Meydanı, is perhaps the best: central, yet quiet and charging US$18/28 for a single/double with bath.

One block to the north-east is the cheaper but still quite good *Otel Büyük Maraş* (☎ (771) 33500; fax 28894), Milli Egemenlik Caddesi 7, charging only US$12/21 for a single/double with bath.

The two-star, 80-room *Hotel Belli* (☎ (771) 34900; fax 18282), across Kıbrıs Meydanı from the two previously mentioned hotels, is somewhat older but still good, charging US$14/20 for a single/double with bath.

Maraş is noted for several culinary specialties, among them saç kavurma, bits of lamb fried on a convex steel griddle; and külbastı, grilled lamb chops with çemen (cumin, the spice made from ground fenugreek seeds) red pepper and garlic. Most famous of all is hakiki Kahramanmaraş dövme dondurma (authentic Maraş beaten ice cream), made with so much glue-like binder that it withstands the city's intense summer heat, can be displayed hanging on a hook like meat, and eaten with knife and fork. For a sample, try the elaborate *Yaşar Pastanesi & Ice Cream Palace* next to the Hotel Belli.

Getting There & Away

Maraş shares in the traffic which crisscrosses the region from Kayseri to Gaziantep and from Adana to Malatya. Most of the bus services originate somewhere else, and may or may not have onward seats. Details of some daily services follow:

Adana – 190 km, 3½ hours, US$8; frequent buses
Adıyaman – 164 km, three hours, US$7; several buses
Antakya – 185 km, four hours, US$8; several buses
Gaziantep – 80 km, one hour, US$2; very frequent dolmuşes depart from beside the Hotel Kazancı on Kıbrıs Meydanı
Kayseri – 291 km, 5½ hours, US$10; several buses
Malatya – 226 km, 4½ hours, US$9; several buses

NEMRUT DAĞI

The Commagene Nemrut Dağı (NEHM-root

dah-uh), not to be confused with a mountain of the same name on the shores of Lake Van, rises to a height of 2150 metres between the provincial capital of Malatya to the north and the village of Kâhta in Adıyaman province to the south. It's part of the Anti-Taurus range.

The summit was formed when a petty, megalomaniac pre-Roman king cut two ledges in the rock, filled them with colossal statues of himself and the gods (his 'relatives'), then ordered an artificial mountain peak of crushed rock 50 metres high to be piled between them. The king's tomb may well lie beneath those tonnes of rock. Nobody knows for sure.

Earthquakes have toppled the heads from most of the statues, but many of the colossal bodies sit silently in rows, and the two-metre-high heads watch from the ground.

When to Visit

Plan your visit to Nemrut between late May and mid-October, and preferably in July or August. The road to the summit becomes impassable in the snow. Remember that at any time of year, even in the heat of summer when the sun bakes the valleys below, it will be chilly and windy on top of the mountain. This is especially true at sunrise, the coldest time of the day. Take warm clothing and a windbreaker on your trek to the top, no matter when you go.

Tours from Cappadocia & Şanlıurfa

It is possible to take minibus tours from Cappadocia to Nemrut. The tour from Cappadocia takes two days, costs about US$75, and involves many hours of breakneck driving, but you may want to consider it if your time is limited. There used to be tours from Şanlıurfa as well, but the flooding of the old highway by the new lake has forced tour operators to change plans. Perhaps by the time you arrive, the tours from Şanlıurfa will include a fast speedboat ride on the lake to Kahta.

History

Nobody knew anything about Nemrut Dağı until 1881, when an Ottoman geologist making a survey was astounded to come across this remote mountaintop full of statues. Archaeological work didn't begin until 1953, when the American School of Oriental Research undertook the project.

From 250 BC onwards, this region was the borderland between the Seleucid empire (which followed the empire of Alexander the Great in Anatolia) and the Parthian empire to the east, also occupying a part of Alexander's lands. A small but strategic land which was rich, fertile and covered in forests, it had a history of independent thinking ever since the time of King Samos circa 150 BC.

Under the Seleucid Empire, the governor of Commagene declared his kingdom's independence. In 80 BC, with the Seleucids in disarray and Roman power spreading into Anatolia, a Roman ally named Mithridates I Callinicus proclaimed himself king and set up his capital at Arsameia, near the modern village of Eski Kahta. Mithridates prided himself on his royal ancestry, tracing his forebears back to Seleucus I Nicator, founder of the Seleucid Empire to the west, and to Darius the Great, king of ancient Persia to the east. Thus he saw himself as heir to both glorious traditions. He married a Parthian princess.

Mithridates died in 64 BC and was succeeded by his son Antiochus I Epiphanes (64-38 BC) who, born of a Parthian mother, consolidated the security of his kingdom by immediately signing a non-aggression treaty with Rome, turning his kingdom into a Roman buffer against attack from the Parthians. His good relations with both sides allowed him to grow rich and to revel in delusions of grandeur. As heir to both traditions, he saw himself as equal to the great god-kings of the past. It was Antiochus who ordered that the fabulous temples and funerary mound be built on top of Nemrut.

Antiochus must have come to believe in his own divinity, for in the third decade of his reign he sided with the Parthians in a squabble with Rome, and in 38 BC the Romans deposed him. Commagene was alternately ruled directly from Rome or by puppet kings until 72 AD, when Emperor Vespasian incorporated it for good into Roman Asia. The great days of Commagene were thus limited to the 26-year reign of Antiochus.

Orientation

Visitors to Nemrut Dağı have traditionally used the provincial capital of Adıyaman (ah-DUH-yah-mahn, population 150,000, altitude 669 metres) or the nearby village of Kahta (ky-YAHH-tah, population 60,000) as a base for their ascent, though the route via Malatya is popular too. In recent years the Malatya route has gained in popularity.

In the late 1980s the economy and topography of this area were greatly affected by two developments: the filling of the vast lake behind the GAP project's Atatürk Dam, and the discovery of oil near Kahta. Though Kahta is where the oil is, it is Adıyaman, the provincial capital, which has benefited from an influx of money for building and development.

Adıyaman's citizens are not particularly welcoming to foreign tourists. The minibus drivers and tour touts in Kahta are often crooked, and pestilential in the way they follow and badger you to take their over-

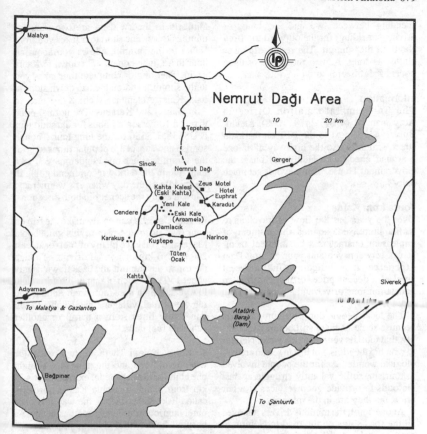

Nemrut Dağı Area

0   10   20 km

priced tours. But there's more to see along the Kahta route, so you may decide to bear with the unpleasantness.

The road to the top from Malatya via Tepehan can also be covered in a day, or with an overnight stay in the village of Büyüköz near the summit, where there are simple pensions and a basic but adequate hotel. By taking the Malatya route, visitors miss seeing the several sights along the Kahta-Nemrut road, such as Arsameia. The cost is about the same by either route (if you don't get ripped off). If you decide to go via Malatya, refer to the section on that city.

Distances among these points are as follows:

Adıyaman to Kahta – 35 km
Adıyaman to Malatya – 190 km
Kahta to Nemrut – 70 km
Gölbaşı to Malatya – 121 km
Malatya to Nemrut – 110 km.

Whichever way you go to the summit, pack a bottle of water and some snacks such as dried fruit, biscuits and nuts, as the journey can take between six and eight hours and services along the way are limited. Plan on spending between two and 2½ hours of driving (or riding) for the outward trip from Kahta to the summit. The return trip takes almost as long. Add to these two or three hours of sightseeing at the various sites.

Information

The Tourism Information Office in Adıyaman (☎ (8781) 2478, 1008), Atatürk Bulvarı 41, is next to the PTT on the main street, which is also the highway. If no one is around, check at the Hükümet Konağı, the Government House. You may not get much help.

Tours from Kahta

Over the years, as the flow of travellers to Kahta increased, so has the number of unpleasant characters who interject themselves between you and your Nemrut Dağı experience. It is difficult to find a decent hotel at a decent price, difficult to find an honest minibus driver and a tour worth the money.

The local people don't welcome tourists because some of them still believe, incredibly, that tourists venture to the top of Nemrut to worship the idols, not just to see an archaeological wonder. As for the people involved in tourism, some valiantly struggle against the odds to provide good services at a fair price, but they are in the minority.

At one point, the minibus drivers removed all the road signs on the road to Nemrut in order to make it difficult for tourists to get up the mountain in their own cars. Other tricks involve bait-and-switch: you agree with a minibus driver on a tour price and a departure time to get to the summit by sunrise, but the driver never shows up. However, another driver *just happens* to be waiting across the street from your hotel and will take you up for twice the price. And with construction on the road to Nemrut, local drivers will tell you that you won't be able to make it in your own car (untrue) and that you should take a minibus tour instead.

If you run into difficulties in Kahta, write to the Ministry of Tourism, Eskişehir Yolu, Ankara, to let them know about it.

Minibus In theory, there are two standard minibus tours. The short tour takes you from Kahta to the summit, allows you about an hour there, then comes right down to Kahta again. The long or complete tour takes you to the summit, and on the trip down stops at Eski Kale (Arsameia), Yeni Kale (next to Eski Kahta) and Karakuş. The normal price to rent a 10-person minibus for the short tour is US$35, US$50 for the long tour. Though sunrise and sunset are popular times to be at the summit, either one condemns you to a long ride in the dark. I recommend going in the middle of the day when it's warmer and you can enjoy the scenery in both directions.

Private Car You can easily make the trip on your own using the map in this guidebook. Make sure you have plenty of fuel for at least 200 or 250 km of normal driving. Though the trip to the summit and back down is only about 150 km, much of that will be driven in low gear, which uses more fuel. Should you run out of fuel, villagers may be able to sell you a few litres from a barrel or another vehicle's fuel tank.

To Kahta Kalesi There are two roads, the winding old one and the new, fast, straight one built for the petroleum extractors. It's 24 km from Kahta to Kahta Kalesi, formerly called Eski Kahta. Along the way this once purely agricultural landscape has become a busy oil field with nodding pumps, storage tanks and earthmoving equipment.

The Mt Nimrod National Park (Nemrut Dağı Milli Park) is entered at Karakuş, 10 km from Kahta. This hilltop, like that on Nemrut, is artificial, created to hold the graves of royal ladies of Commagene. A black eagle *(karakuş)*, its head missing, tops one of the several columns marking the site. The summit of Nemrut is clearly if distantly visible from Karakuş, it's the highest point on the horizon to the north-east, off the black eagle's right shoulder.

Nineteen km from Kahta and five km before Kahta Kalesi, the road crosses a **Roman bridge** built in honour of Emperor Septimius Severus (194-211 AD), his wife and sons, long after Commagene had become part of Roman Asia. Of the four original columns (two at either end), three are still standing. Some historians think that the missing column was removed by one of the sons, Caracalla, when he murdered the other son, Geta, in 212.

As you leave the bridge, there should be a sign pointing to the right for Nemrut Dağı and Gerger; the road to the left near Heracles Camping is for Kahta Kalesi.

You approach Kahta Kalesi along the valley of a stream called the Kahta Çayı. Opposite the village are the ruins of a Mameluke castle (1300s), now called **Yeni Kale** (yeh-NEE kah-leh, New Fortress), which you can explore. It bears some Arabic inscriptions; the Mamelukes were originally a Turkic people, but they were assimilated into Egyptian society.

You can engage a guide in Kahta Kalesi to lead you up a trail to the summit. There are lodging possibilities as well. The Demiral family, which has traditionally provided lodgings, now does so only for organised groups which reserve in advance. *Heracles Camping*, at the road junction, will do at a pinch, but there are much nicer places farther along at Damlacık.

Eski Kale (Arsameia) About a km up the road from Kahta Kalesi, a road to the left takes you the two km to Eski Kale, the ancient Commagene capital of Arsameia. Admission costs US$1.50. Walk up the path from the car park and you'll come to a large stele with a figure (maybe female) on it. Further along are two more stelae, a monumental staircase and, behind them, an opening in the rock leading down to a cistern.

Another path leads from the first path to the striking stone relief which portrays the founder of Commagene, Mithridates I Callinicus, shaking hands with the god Heracles. Next to it is a long inscription in Greek and to the right is a tunnel descending through the rock. The locals will tell you the tunnel goes all the way to the valley floor below, though it has not yet been cleared of

the centuries of rubble. Archaeologists believe it is a dead-end.

Above the relief on the level top of the hill are the foundations of Mithridates' capital city. The view is magnificent from here. If you stop at Arsameia on your way down from Nemrut, this is the perfect site for a picnic.

To the Summit Three km upward from Eski Kale is Damlacık, where there are simple restaurants and camping places, a jandarma post and a Red Crescent first-aid station. Try the *Garden Camping*, which has a delightful shady location and a small swimming pool, or the *Damlacık Pension & Camping*. After Damlacık the paved road gives way to one of stabilised gravel.

The next settlements are Kuştepe (seven km), then Tüten Ocak (three km). After Narince the road becomes rougher and steeper. Another seven km east of Narince is a turn-off to the left marked for Nemrut, which you want to take; to continue straight on would take you to the village of Gerger. At this road intersection is the *Boğaz Café*, on the right.

Continue up the mountain five km to the hamlet of Karadut, which has a few small pensions and restaurants. The backpackers' choice here is the *Apollo Pansiyon, Restaurant & Camping* (☎ 1246). The price of a bed is US$4.50, shower fee included. If you stay you'll have to take a minibus from Karadut to reach the summit. A passing minibus may charge US$2 or more; to rent an entire minibus for a trip to the summit and back to Karadut costs about US$20. At the upper end of Karadut village is the *Karadut Kamping & Restaurant.*

North of Karadut, the last half-hour's travel to the top is on a steep road paved in black basalt blocks and still fairly rough. There are two lodging places along the road. The 30-room *Hotel Euphrat*, 9.5 km from the summit, charges US$20 per person for bed, breakfast and dinner.

The *Zeus Motel*, a mountain inn seven km below the summit, was closed on my last visit due to rockslide damage. Should it reopen, it's worth considering for lodgings or a meal.

At the Summit You're well above treeline when you climb the final ridge and pull into the car park at the summit. Just up from the car park is a building with toilets, a café for snacks and hot tea, soft drinks and souvenirs. The staff may allow you to sleep on the floor of the café, but it's *very* cold. The attendants don't seem to mind if you park a camper van in the car park overnight, or if you camp discreetly. This permissive attitude may change if lots of people camp at the same time.

Beyond the building is the pyramid of stones; it's a hike of less than one km (15 or 20 minutes) over the broken rock to the western temple. Sometimes donkeys are on hand to carry you, but this is not much help since staying on the donkey is almost as difficult as negotiating the rocks on your own. Admission to the archaeological site costs US$3.50.

Antiochus I Epiphanes ordered the construction here of a hierothesium, or combination tomb and temple:

I, great King Antiochus, have ordered the construction of these temples, the ceremonial road, and the thrones of the gods, on a foundation which will never be demolished.... I have done this to prove my faith in the gods. At the end of my life I will enter my eternal rest here, and my spirit will join that of Zeus-Ahura Mazda in heaven.

Approaching from the car park, you see first the western temple and behind it the conical tumulus, or funerary mound, of fist-sized stones.

At the western temple, Antiochus and his fellow gods sit in state, though the bodies have mostly been tumbled down along with the heads. But at the eastern temple the bodies are largely intact, except for the fallen heads, which seem more badly weathered than the heads at the west. On the backs of the eastern statues are inscriptions in Greek.

Both terraces have similar plans, with the syncretistic gods, the 'ancestors' of Antiochus, seated in this order, from left to right:

first is Apollo, the sun god – Mithra to the Persians, Helios or Hermes to the Greeks; next is Fortuna, or Tyche; in the centre is Zeus-Ahura Mazda; to the right is King Antiochus; and at the right end is Heracles, also known as Ares or Artagnes. The seated figures are several metres high; their heads alone, about two metres tall.

Low walls at the sides of each temple once held carved reliefs showing royal processions of ancient Persia and Greece, Antiochus' 'predecessors'. Statues of eagles represent Zeus.

The flat space next to the eastern temple, with an 'H' at its centre, is a helipad which accepts the arrival of the wealthy, the important and the fortunate. It stands on the site of an ancient altar. In the valley below, about three km from the summit, is the *Güneş Hotel*, of use mostly to those coming up Nemrut from Malatya. The Güneş charges US$18 per person for bed and breakfast with supper and a hot shower included.

Places to Stay

You can stay in Adıyaman, Kahta, Malatya or on the mountain slope. Adıyaman is for those looking for lodgings in the middle range, Kahta for those travelling on a budget. For lodgings on the mountain, refer to the description of the trip up Nemrut Dağı.

Adıyaman Now a boom oil town, Adıyaman (postal code 02100) is a gritty concrete wasteland stretched along several km of the highway (Atatürk Bulvarı). Most of Adıyaman's lodgings have been commandeered by Türk Petrol (TPAO) for their engineering staff. As the boom continues, new hotels will be built and the pressure should ease.

The three-star, 54-room *Bozdoğan Hotel* (☎ (878) 13999; fax 13630), on Atatürk Bulvarı near the western end of town, is the town's best, with a good bar, restaurant, and swimming pool. Rooms with bath cost US$32/50 a single/double. Air conditioning and TV are to be added in future – so they say.

A short distance farther east along Atatürk

Bulvarı at the junction with Turgut Reis Caddesi near the Vilayet is the two-star *Hotel Serdaroğlu* (☎ (878) 13331, 14841; fax 11554), quite comfortable but presently leased to the oil company. If rooms become available, prices will be close to those charged at the Bozdoğan.

The *Motel Beyaz Saray* (☎ (878) 14907), Atatürk Bulvarı 136, on the highway in the eastern part of town, has a small swimming pool and acceptable but unexciting rooms with shower, but is now full of oil company personnel.

Not far away is the *Motel Sultan* (☎ (878) 13493, 13377), Atatürk Bulvarı YSE Yanı, and like the Beyaz Saray, leased to TPAO.

Next door to the Sultan stands the *Motel Arsameia* (☎ (878) 12112, 13131), Atatürk Bulvarı 148, a standard Turkish hotel with double rooms and shower, leased to the oilies.

Kahta The oil boom is changing the face of Kahta (postal code 02400) rapidly, and most of the information given here will probably be out of date by the time you arrive. New hotels are being built, so you will have a better selection than can be mentioned here.

While hotels in Adıyaman are filled with oilies, Kahta's slightly cheaper 'motels' are often filled with bus-tour groups. Virtually any Kahta hotelier will expect you to participate in one of his minibus tours up Nemrut, and whatever bargain you get on the hotel room may be neutralised by the markup on the tour.

The cheapest and best of the pensions is the *Anatolia Pension* (☎ (8795) 2479), run by Mr Orhan Kılıç and his family. Large, light, airy rooms cost US$6 a double. Breakfast (which costs extra) is served in the garden.

Hotel Mezopotamya (☎ (8795) 3533, 3577), on the western outskirts of Kahta, charges according to demand. Rooms with bath might cost anywhere from US$12 to US$35 a double, breakfast included. The same can be said for the *Hotel Nemruttours* (☎ (8795) 1967, 3781) directly opposite.

At the junction with the Nemrut road is the *Hotel Kommagene* (☎ (8795) 1092), PK 4, a converted house with fly-screens on the windows, and lots of Turkish carpets and kilims to lend atmosphere. It charges US$14/20 a single/double with bath for its much used and very basic rooms. The hotel has a bar and a camping area.

Across the Nemrut road from the Kommagene is the *Nemrut Family Pension*, a newer alternative to the motels at slightly lower prices.

Places to Eat

The *Kent Restaurant*, on the north side of the main highway (Mustafa Kemal Caddesi) in the centre of town, has been here for years and still turns out decent, cheap fare at low prices. To the east is the similar *Özen*, to the west the more modern *Yudum* (☎ 5245), Mustafa Kemal Caddesi 23. At any of these, two plates of food and a drink cost about US$3.50.

Getting There & Away

Adıyaman and Kahta are served by frequent buses, but nothing else. There are air and rail services to Malatya.

Bus Dolmuşes run between Kahta and Adıyaman (35 km, 30 minutes, US$1.75) throughout the day. From Kahta you can travel by bus easily to Malatya (225 km, three hours, US$7). There are two direct buses daily; or change at Adıyaman.

Reaching Diyarbakır is a problem. The new lake behind Atatürk Dam flooded the highway five km east of Kahta, and one must now endure a series of slow, infrequent ferry crossings in order to follow the old highway via Siverek to Diyarbakır or via Hilvan to Şanlıurfa. New roads will be constructed to speed land transport, but this may take years. You may find yourself travelling the long way via Gaziantep.

Should you decide to take the slow ferries eastward, you will enter that fabled cradle of civilisation, the watershed of the Tigris (Dicle, DEEJ-leh) and Euphrates (Fırat, fuh-RAHT) rivers. The partly submerged highway east from Kahta goes via Akıncılar and Çaylarbaşı to the east-west highway (53 km). Turn right (west) at the highway for Şanlıurfa, 70 km from the junction; or left (east) 23 km to Siverek, and another 116 km to Diyarbakır, a total distance of 192 km.

MALATYA

Going from Adıyaman via Gölbaşı to Malatya, the highway crosses the Reşadiye Pass (Reşadiye Geçidi) (1510 metres) and through a dramatic rock-bound gorge before descending to Malatya (mah-LAHT-yah, population 350,000, altitude 964 metres), a modern town grown large and rich on agriculture. This is the apricot capital of Turkey, and after the late-June harvest thousands of tonnes of the luscious fruit are shipped throughout the world. Malatya's cherries, almost as good as the apricots, are harvested from early to mid-June. The citizens of Malatya celebrate the end of the harvest with an apricot festival in July.

Other than excellent fruit, this city, the birthplace of İsmet İnönü (Atatürk's right-hand man) and Mehmet Ali Ağca (who shot Pope John Paul II), has little to offer the tourist except the alternate route up Nemrut Dağı.

History

Malatya is at the crossroads of major trade routes today as it has been since Neolithic times. There was an early Assyrian settlement here, and a Hittite one. After the fall of the Hittite Empire, various city-states emerged, among them Milidia (or Maldia), a name preserved for over 3000 years and now pronounced Malatya.

The Assyrians and Persians conquered the city alternately, and later the kings of Cappadocia and Pontus did the same. In 66 BC Pompey defeated Mithridates and took the town then known as Melita, and later Melitene. The Byzantines, Sassanids, Arabs and Danışmend emirs held it for a time until the coming of the Seljuks in 1105. Then came the Ottomans (1399), the armies of Tamerlane (1401), the Mamelukes, the Dülkadır emirs, and the Ottomans again (1515).

When the forces of Egypt's Mohammed Ali invaded Anatolia in 1839, the Ottoman forces garrisoned Malatya, leaving it in ruins upon their departure. The residents who had fled the war returned and established a new city at Malatya's present site.

Orientation

Malatya stretches for many km along İnönü/Atatürk Caddesi, its main street, also called Kışla or İstasyon Caddesi. Hotels, restaurants, banks and other services are near the main square with its statue of İnönü, the Vilayet building and the neighbouring Belediye (Municipality). The Belediye Parkı, on the north side of İnönü Caddesi facing the İnönü statue, is a convenient landmark.

The new otogar is about six km west of the centre just off the highway. The old otogar, which is still used for some dolmuş services, The railway station (istasyon) is also on the outskirts several km west of the centre. City buses and dolmuşes marked 'Vilayet' operate between the station and the centre.

Information

The Tourism Information Office (☎ (821) 17733) is in the centre on İnönü Caddesi above the Tütünbank, open Monday to Friday from 9 am to 5 pm. There is also a small tourist information office in the otogar, where a tourism official will be on hand to greet you and urge you to sign up for one of the tours to the top of Nemrut Dağı (for details see following).

Old Malatya

Eleven km north of the centre at Battalgazi are the remains of Old Malayta (Eski Malatya), the walled city inhabited from early times until the 19th century.

The modern Turkish village of Battalgazi has grown up in and around the ruined but still impressive **city walls** strengthened by 95 towers. The walls have lost all of their facing stone to other building projects, and apricot orchards now fill what were once city blocks, but it is easy to see that this was once a great city.

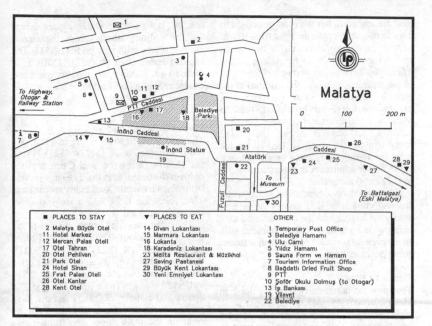

Malatya

0   100   200 m

■ PLACES TO STAY

2 Malatya Büyük Otel
11 Hotel Merkez
12 Mercan Palas Oteli
17 Otel Tahran
20 Otel Pehlivan
21 Park Otel
24 Hotel Sinan
25 Fırat Palas Oteli
26 Otel Kantar
28 Kent Otel

▼ PLACES TO EAT

14 Divan Lokantası
15 Marmara Lokantası
16 Lokanta
18 Karadeniz Lokantası
23 Melita Restaurant & Müzikhol
27 Sevinç Pastanesi
29 Büyük Kent Lokantası
30 Yeni Emniyet Lokantası

OTHER

1 Temporary Post Office
3 Belediye Hamamı
4 Ulu Cami
5 Yıldız Hamamı
6 Sauna Form ve Hamam
7 Tourism Information Office
8 Bağdatlı Dried Fruit Shop
9 PTT
10 Şoför Okulu Dolmuş (to Otogar)
13 İş Bankası
19 Vilayet
22 Belediye

The **Ulu Cami** (1224), on the main square, is a Seljuk work dating from the reign of Alaettin Keykubat I. The **Silahtar Mustafa Paşa Hanı** (caravanserai) on the main square is an Ottoman work dating from the 1600s, but restored recently.

Buses (No 3 or 4, Battalgazi) will take you there if you find yourself with time on your hands in Malatya.

Malatya Museum

The museum Malatya Müzesi, open from 8.30 am to noon and 1.30 to 5.30 pm (closed on Monday), is almost a km from the centre (follow the signs). Admission costs US$1; labels are in Turkish only.

The collection is the standard stuff, everything from Palaeolithic, Chalcolithic and Old Bronze Age through to Roman and Byzantine times. There are some finds from the excavations at Aslantepe and also from the Lower Euphrates Project, an archaeological rescue mission conducted by Middle East Technical University (Ankara) and İstanbul University in the Euphrates valley before the Keban Dam flooded it several decades ago.

Hamams

Malatya has lots of Turkish baths. The Historical Municipal Bath with Sauna (Tarihi Saunalı Belediye Hamamı) faces the Malatya Büyük Oteli. The modern Sauna Form ve Hamam is on a side street nearby, as is the Yıldız Hamamı. A simple bath costs US$2, more if you have massages etc.

Tours to Nemrut Dağı

The tourism office organises minibus tours (daily from April to mid-October) which seem to be hassle-free. Have your overnight gear with you and meet at the front door of the tourism office at 11.30 am any day (even on weekends when the office is closed).

The minibus comes and picks you up at noon for the four-hour ride up Nemrut through dramatic scenery. The last 30 km of road are unpaved, but the road goes right to the summit, closer than the road from Kahta.

After enjoying the sunset for two hours, you descend two km to the *Güneş Hotel*, where you have dinner and spend the night. In the morning, you take the minibus to the summit for an hour at sunrise before returning to the hotel for breakfast, then to Malatya, arriving around 10 am.

Costs (per person) include the US$12 round-trip for the minibus, US$10 for the hotel (including dinner and breakfast), and US$3.50 for admission to the national park, or US$25.50 altogether.

It is possible to ascend from Malatya and descend via Kahta. Hike across the summit with your baggage to the car park and café building and ask around for a minibus with an empty seat; or hitch a ride with a tourist going down to Kahta.

Places to Stay

You must be particularly wary of noise in Malatya. The last night I stayed here (a week night), heavy traffic along the main street did not abate until 2 am, and started up again in earnest at 5 am. I got less than four hours' sleep.

Places to Stay – bottom end

Best of the cheap lodgings in the centre is the *Park Otel* (☎ (821) 11691), on Atatürk Caddesi across from the Belediye. For US$9/11/13 you get a double room with sink/shower/two rooms. Though clean, it is noisy, so get a room at the back.

Otel Kantar (☎ (821) 11510), Atatürk Caddesi 81, has only bathless rooms, but the staff are friendly and a double room with sink costs US$10. As always, make sure you get a quiet room. The nearby *Otel Pehlivan* (☎ (821) 12609), Cumhuriyet Caddesi 26, is run by the same people and costs the same.

Up the street from the Hotel Sinan on the same side, midway to the Otel Kantar, is the old-fashioned *Fırat Palas Oteli* (☎ (821) 11241), Atatürk Caddesi 30, not as nice as the others but certainly cheap at US$5/8.50 a single/double for a waterless room.

Otel Tahran (☎ (821) 23387), PTT Caddesi 20, is a good place and is quiet except for the dolmuş stand across the street. Double rooms with sink go for US$11. The *Mercan Palas Oteli* (☎ (821) 11570), PTT Caddesi 14, is dingy and old, but quiet and cheap, charging US$7 a double for waterless rooms.

Places to Stay – middle

The best hotel in town is the two-star, 52-room *Malatya Büyük Otel* (☎ (821) 11400; fax 15367), facing the Yeni Cami, a block north of the Belediye Parkı. The large private bathrooms have tubs, and many rooms have TVs. Rates are US$25/32 a single/double, breakfast included.

The other star-rated hotels are just to the east of the Vilayet. The one-star, 35-room *Hotel Sinan* (☎ (821) 12907, 13007), Atatürk Caddesi 16, has eight floors, a lift, a restaurant and bar, and charges from US$14 to US$20 a single, from US$17 to US$25 a double. The more expensive rooms have private baths and more amenities. Being right on the main street, the front rooms suffer from noise.

A bit farther east, up the hill on the opposite side of the main street, is the one-star, 50-room *Kent Otel* (☎ (821) 12175, 12813), Atatürk Caddesi 151. Prices and services are similar to those at the Hotel Sinan.

Places to Eat

Very near the Tahran, Mercan and Merkez hotels, on İnönü Caddesi across from the İş Bankası, is a line of restaurants – *Marmara, Divan, Saray, Güngör* – specialising in fluorescent lighting, quick service and good, cheap food. The *Marmara* and *Divan* are most pleasant, but at any of these places you can fill up for US$3 or less.

Just down the street from them, drop in at *Bağdatlılar*, a dried fruit shop, for a look at its splendid array of dried apricots and many other dried fruits, nuts and snacks both sweet and salt.

A fancy place for pastries is the *Sevinç Pastanesi*, facing the Otel Kantar on Atatürk Caddesi. Gleaming showcases are stuffed with all sorts of sweet treats. There are tables at the back.

A few doors uphill from the Kent Otel at Atatürk Caddesi 137 is the *Büyük Kent Lokantası* – clean, bright and friendly. It's excellent for soups and stews as well as for döner kebap. There's an aile salonu; meals cost between US$3 and US$6.

At PTT Caddesi 29 next to the Otel Tahran is *Lokanta* (☎ (821) 59988), clean, white and shiny bright, a modern, up-market, proper place for Malatya's gilded youth. The food is good and moderately priced; no alcohol is served.

Another quiet place is the *Karadeniz Lokantası*, facing the Belediye Parkı.

Yeni Emniyet Lokantası (☎ 11562), south behind the Belediye, is Malatya's old standby for drinking, eating and talking. The ground-floor dining room reminds one of a railway station waiting room, but there's a nicer room upstairs and a roof terrace as well. Hundreds of bottles of rakı stand ready behind the bar. Food is good and service eager; meals cost from US$6 to US$10, more if you drink a lot.

Melita Restaurant & Müzikhol (☎ 24300), next door to the Hotel Sinan in the Turfandalar İşhanı building on the upper floor, is where local potentates meet to eat, drink, and listen to the tremulous organ music. Though fancy for Malatya, it is still surprisingly moderate in price, charging around US$4 to US$6 for a full dinner with drink. The organ can be a bit much, though.

Getting There & Away

There are many people interested in buying, selling, trading, growing and eating apricots, so Malatya is served by air, rail and bus.

Air Turkish Airlines (THY, ☎ (821) 11922, 14053), Kanalboyu Caddesi 10, Ordu Evi Karşısı, has one nonstop flight daily between Malatya's Erhaç Airport and Ankara, with connections to İstanbul and İzmir. The airport bus costs US$1.50 and leaves the Turkish Airlines office 90 minutes before flight departure time.

Turkish Air Transport (THT) also has nonstop flights to and from Ankara on Tuesday, Thursday and Saturday, with connections for İstanbul. Contact the Turkish Airlines office for reservations and information.

Bus Malatya's new otogar is on the western outskirts of the city; the old otogar, used for some short-run service, is north of the centre. Dolmuş minibuses (25c) run between each otogar and the Şoför Okulu Durağı (Driving School Stop), a dolmuş stand on PTT Caddesi facing the Otel Tahran.

Malatya bus service includes daily trips to the following destinations:

Adana – 425 km, eight hours, US$14; a few buses
Adıyaman – 190 km, three hours, US$7; frequent buses
Ankara – 685 km, 11 hours, US$18; frequent buses
Diyarbakır – 260 km, 4 hours, US$8; frequent buses
Gaziantep – 250 km, four hours, US$8; a few buses
İstanbul – 1130 km, 18 hours, US$28; a few buses
Kahta – 223 km, three hours, US$7; two morning buses
Kayseri – 354 km, six hours, US$10; several buses
Sivas – 235 km, five hours, US$11; several buses

Train Malatya's istasyon can be reached by a dolmuş (25c) from the Belediye Parkı, or by 'İstasyon' city bus.

The city is served daily by express train from İstanbul (Haydarpaşa) and Ankara via Kayseri and Sivas. On some days it's the *Vangölü Ekspresi*; on other days it's the *Güney Ekspresi*, heading eastward for Diyarbakır and Kurtalan. See Getting There & Away in the Ankara section of the Central Anatolia chapter for details.

ŞANLIURFA

Dry, dusty and hot – this is the way Şanlıurfa (population 270,000, altitude 540 metres) appears at first glance. You may think, 'What importance could such a town in the middle of nowhere possibly have?'. When you get to know Urfa (as it's commonly called), you'll find that it's known for a shady park with several pools and great religious significance, a richness of agricultural produce, a

cool and inviting labyrinthine bazaar, and its great historical importance.

Urfa gives a mixture of impressions. In the shadow of a mighty medieval fortress, saintly old men toss chickpeas into a pool full of sacred carp or gather at a cave said to be the birthplace of the patriarch Abraham. In the cool darkness of the covered bazaar, shopkeepers sit on low platforms in front of their stores, as was the custom in Ottoman times. The chatter of Turkish is joined by a babble of Kurdish and Arabic, with the occasional bit of English, French or German.

You must spend at least one night in Urfa and a full day, or at least a morning, to see the sights and get lost in the bazaar. You may also want to make an excursion south to Harran, the biblical town of beehive houses near the Syrian frontier.

History

The mysterious laws of geography ruled that this dusty spot would be where great empires clashed again and again over the centuries. Far from Cairo, Tehran and Constantinople, Urfa was nevertheless where the armies, directed from those distant capitals, would often meet. Urfa's history, then, is one of wreckage.

Urfa has been sizzling in the sun for a long time. It is thought that more than 3500 years ago there was a fortress on the hill where the kale now stands. Called Hurri (Cave) by the Babylonians, the people built a powerful state by military conquest simply because they knew what a chariot was and how to use it in battle (few of their neighbours had heard of the chariot). But the Hittites finally got the better of the Hurrites, despite the latter's alliance with the Pharaohs of Egypt. Around 1370 BC, the Hittites took over. After the fall of Hattuşaş, Urfa came under the domination of Carchemish.

The alliance with Egypt produced an interesting cultural exchange. After Amenhotep IV (Akhenaton) popularised worship of the sun as the unique and only god, a similar worship of Shemesh (the sun) was taken up here. Sun-worship (one would think it might be shade worship instead!) was not just a religious belief, but a political posture. It defied the cultural, political and religious influence of the nearby Hittites, by adopting the customs of the Egyptians, who were a safe distance away.

After a period of Assyrian rule, Alexander the Great came through. He and his Macedonian mates named the town Edessa, after a former capital of Macedonia, and it remained the capital of a Seleucid province until 132 BC when the local Aramaean population set up an independent kingdom and renamed the town Orhai. Though Orhai maintained a precarious independence for four centuries, bowing only slightly to the Armenians and Parthians, it finally succumbed to the Romans, as did everyone hereabouts. The Romans did not get it easily, however. Emperor Valerian was badly defeated here in 260 AD and subsequent Roman rulers had a hard time over the centuries keeping the Persians out.

Edessa pursued its contrary history (witness the sun worship) by adopting Christianity at a very early time (circa 200 AD), before it became the official religion of the conquerors. The religion was so new that for Edessan Christians the liturgical language was Aramaic, the language of Jesus and not the Greek on which the church's greatness was built. Edessa, having pursued Christianity on its own from earliest times, had its own patriarch. It revelled in the Nestorian

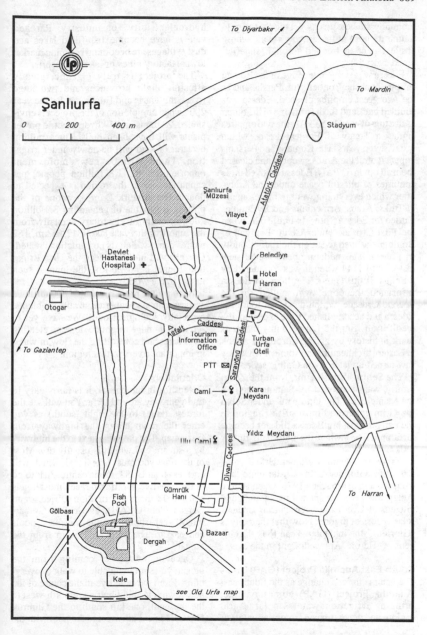

monophysite heresies as yet another way to thumb its nose at its faraway rulers, whose armies so often trooped through and flattened everything.

Edessa was at the outer edge of the Roman Empire near the frontier with Persia, and as the two great empires clashed, Edessa was shuttled back and forth from one to the other, as in a tug-of-war. In 533 AD the two empires signed a Treaty of Endless Peace which lasted seven years. The Romans and Persians kept at it until the Arabs swept in and cleared them all out in 637 AD. Edessa enjoyed three centuries of blissful peace under the Arabs, after which everything went to blazes again.

Turks, Arabs, Armenians and Byzantines battled for Edessa from 944 until 1098, when the First Crusade under Count Baldwin of Boulogne arrived to set up the Latin County of Edessa. This odd European feudal state lasted until 1144 when it was conquered by a Seljuk Turkish emir. The 'loss' of Edessa infuriated the pope, who called for the Second Crusade, which never set foot near Edessa and accomplished little except to discredit itself. But the Latin county made its mark in history by giving Europeans a look at Eastern architecture and some of what they saw turned up later in the Gothic style.

The Seljuk Turkish emir, from the Zengi family, was succeeded by Saladin, then by the Mamelukes. The Ottomans under Selim the Grim conquered most of this region in the early 1500s, but Edessa did not become Urfa until 1637 when the Ottomans finally took over.

As for its modern sobriquet, Urfa became Şanlıurfa (Glorious Urfa) a little more than a decade ago. Even since 1973, when Heroic Antep was given its special name, the good citizens of Urfa have been chafing under a relative loss of dignity. Now that their city is 'Glorious', the inhabitants can look the citizens of 'Heroic' Antep straight in the eye.

South-East Anatolia Project (GAP) Urfa's character is in for a change as the South-east Anatolia Project (GAP) comes on line, bringing irrigation waters to large arid regions and generating enormous amounts of hydroelectricity for industry. Parched valleys have become fish-filled lakes and dusty villages are becoming booming market towns, factory cities or lakeside resorts.

The project is truly gigantic, greatly affecting eight provinces and two huge rivers, the Tigris and Euphrates. By the year 2005 when completion of the project is envisioned, 22 dams and 19 hydroelectric power plants will have been built. Three million hectares of land will be newly under irrigation. There will be new employment opportunities for 1.8 million people; per capita income in the region is expected to double. The Atatürk Dam, keystone of the project, is capable of generating 8.9 billion kilowatt-hours of electricity annually from the runoff of the vast lake (817 sq km, 162 metres deep) which its construction created. One element in the project, the Urfa Irrigation Tunnel is, at 26 km, the longest such tunnel in the world.

Such a huge project, capable of enormous success, can also generate sizable problems, especially ecological ones. We have yet to see what damage might be done by creating huge lakes and controlling the flow of water in important rivers in this region.

Orientation

Except for in the bazaar, it is fairly easy to find your way around Urfa. You will see the fortress (kale) to the right (south) as you enter the town along the highway from Gaziantep. The otogar is next to the highway by a stream bed which is usually dry. Most of the time you must take a taxi, which will cost less than US$2, to the centre. Ask to go to the Belediye in order to reach most hotels and the Tourism Information Office, or to Dergah (dehr-GYAH), also called Gölbaşı (GURL-bah-shuh), for the mosques, pools and bazaar. The latter is 1.5 km from the otogar.

Once in town after coming from the otogar, you should be able to walk to everything. From the Belediye in the centre of the new town it is about half a km north-west to the museum, one km south to the Gümrük Hanı, 1.5 km south-west to the pool with the fish (Dergah or Gölbaşı) and two km south-west to the kale (fortress).

Information

The Tourism Information Office (☎ (871) 12467) is at Asfalt Caddesi 3/B off Sarayönü Caddesi, not far from the Belediye and the top hotels. In summer, it tends to be open most of the day, including Sunday, though there may be a lunch break.

Except for the museum, Urfa's sights are in the oldest part of town, at the foot of the fortress.

Gölbaşı

This is the area which includes the **pools of the sacred carp**, the Rızvaniye and Abdurrahman mosques and the surrounding park. The name means 'at the lakeside', and while the pools hardly constitute a lake, it is easy for Urfa's citizens to amplify the size of these cool, refreshing places in their minds.

On the northern side of the pool, called the Balıklı Göl, is the **Rızvaniye Camii** and Medresesi. At the western end of the pool is the **Abdurrahman Camii** and Medresesi, also called the Halil ur-Rahman Camii, a 17th-century building with a much older (early 1200s) Arab-style square minaret which looks suspiciously like a church's bell tower. You may walk in and look around the Abdurrahman Camii as you like.

Legend had it that Abraham, who is a great prophet in Islamic belief, was in old Urfa destroying pagan gods one day when Nimrod, the local Assyrian king, took offence at this rash behaviour. Nimrod had Abraham immolated on a funeral pyre, but God turned the fire into water (the pool) and the burning coals into fish (the carp). You can sip the sacred water from a subterranean spring within the mosque.

The two pools, this one and the nearby Ayn-i Zeliha, are fed by a spring at the base of Damlacık hill, on which the kale is built.

Local legend-makers have had a field day with the fish in the pool, deciding that they are sacred to Abraham and must not be caught lest the catcher go blind. You can buy food for the fish from vendors at the pools-ide, even though signs say, 'In the interests of the fishes' health, it is requested that they not be fed'.

Instead of feeding the fish, take a seat and a shady table in one of the tea gardens and have a cool drink or bracing glass of çay to ward off the heat of the day. (Hot tea will make you perspire, thus cooling you down.) There are restaurants in the park (see Places to Eat).

Dergah

This area, to the south-east of the pools and the park, has several mosques. The **Mevlid-i Halil Camii** holds the tomb of a saint named Dede Osman, a cave which harbours a hair from the Beard of the Prophet and another cave called Hazreti İbrahim'in Doğum Mağarası or **Prophet Abraham's Birth Cave**, in which, legend has it, the Prophet Abraham was born. You can visit any and all of these wonders for free, but do so quietly and decorously. Abraham's birth cave has separate entrances for men and women, as it is a place of pilgrimage and prayer.

A new, large, Ottoman-style mosque stands to the west of the birth cave to supplement the smaller prayer places.

Next door to the birth cave is a complex of mosques and medreses called **Hazreti İbrahim Halilullah** (Prophet Abraham, Friend of God), built and rebuilt over the centuries as an active place of pilgrimage. To the east, on Göl Caddesi, is the **Hasan Paşa Camii**, an Ottoman work.

Fortress

Depending upon your reference source, the fortress (kale) on Damlacık hill was built either during Hellenistic times or by the Byzantines or during the crusades or by the Turks. No doubt all are true, as one could hardly have a settlement here without having a fortress, and it was normal for fortresses to be built and rebuilt over the centuries. In any case, it is vast and can be reached by a cascade of stairs.

You enter between a pair of columns which local legend has dubbed the Throne of Nemrut after the supposed founder of Urfa,

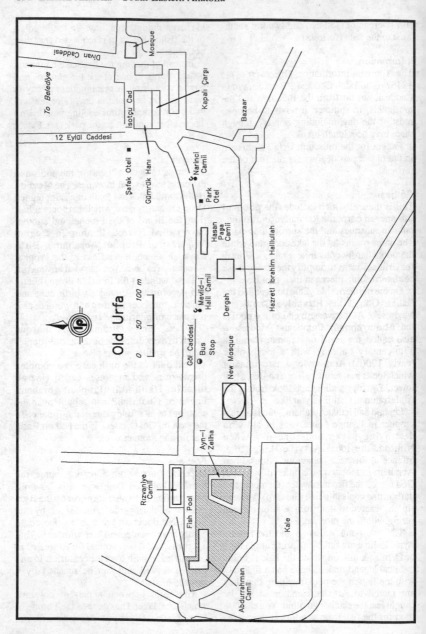

Old Urfa

0   50   100 m

the biblical King Nimrod (Genesis 10: 8-10). Once inside the kale precincts, you will confront the possibility of broiling in the sun while your fellow travellers are resting in the cool shade of the park by the pools.

Bazaar

Urfa's bazaar is less than 500 metres east of the pools. The first place to visit is the old **Gümrük Hanı** or customs depot, an ancient caravanserai. To the left (south) of the caravanserai courtyard is the **Kapalı Çarşı** or covered bazaar, which has not changed much in several centuries, except for some of the products.

After you've visited the Gümrük Hanı, just wander. Urfa's bazaar reveals dozens of fascinating scenes from traditional life.

Şanlıurfa Museum

Up the hill to the west of the Vilayet building, off Atatürk Caddesi, is the museum Şanlıurfa Müzesi, open from 8.30 am to noon and from 1.30 to 5 pm daily (on Monday, from 1.30 to 5 pm only). Admission costs US$1.50. Exhibits are labelled in Turkish and English.

Renovations in 1988 brought marble floors, good lighting and attractive exhibits. Surrounding the museum, in its gardens, are various sculptures, and on the porch as you enter are several mosaics, but only one is worth a look. Inside, noteworthy artefacts include neolithic implements, Assyrian, Babylonian and Hittite relief stones, and other objects from up through Byzantine, Seljuk and Ottoman times. Large photos and diagrams explain the use of many otherwise inscrutable objects.

Upstairs is the ethnology section, which is interesting, but exhibit labels are in Turkish only.

Prophet Job's Site

Otherwise known as Eyüp Peygamber Makamı, Prophet Job's Site is off the Harran road and is marked by signs. Visit free at any time. Eyüp (Job), standard-bearer of the Prophet Muhammed, passed through Urfa with the Arab armies riding into Anatolia to attack Constantinople. Local legend holds

that he became ill here, but was cured (or at least made to feel a bit better) by drinking water from a spring on the outskirts of town. The **spring** is now in a grotto next to a mosque within a walled grove of evergreens.

Places to Stay – bottom end

Urfa has numerous inexpensive hotels and two relatively fancy places, grouped conveniently in two areas: the centre of the town and near Abraham's cave. There are no lodgings around the bus station.

Two cheap hotels are adjacent to the bazaar and Gölbaşı. The *Şafak Oteli* (☎ (871) 31157), Göl Caddesi 4, is the better, with waterless rooms renting for US$5/8 a single/double. Haggle! The hotel faces the Gümrük Hanı across Göl Caddesi. Unfortunately, it also catches the full sun and can be oppressively hot.

Rooms at the *Park Otel* (☎ (871) 31095), Göl Caddesi 101 (100 metres to the west), are even plainer and without sinks, but doubles are even cheaper.

Between Dergah and the centre of town is the modern shopping district. Just off the main street in a quiet location is *Otel İstiklal*, Sarayönü Caddesi, Zincirli Kapı 4/E. It has a vine-shaded courtyard and a small terrace restaurant. Its cool, fairly quiet rooms and usually hot showers cost US$9 a double.

In the centre near the Belediye, several cheap hotels face the expensive Turban Urfa Oteli. The *Otel 11 Nisan* (☎ (871) 11089), Sarayönü Caddesi 141, is a small, simple family place with bathless rooms renting for US$9 a double. Nearby on Sarayönü Caddesi, the *Hotel Güven* (☎ (871) 31700) charges just a bit more for its bathless rooms.

Behind the Turban Urfa Oteli you'll find more choices. The *Hotel İpek Palas* (☎ (871) 31546), Köprübaşı 4, has singles/doubles for US$5.50/10.50 with private showers.

Just around the corner is the *Cumhuriyet Palas* (☎ (871) 34828), Köprübaşı 6, which is also quiet, but cheaper.

Hotel Kapaklı (☎ (871) 35230, 32016), on Sarayönü Caddesi near the corner of Asfalt Caddesi, is very near the Tourism Information Office and offers a choice of rooms with or without bath and air-con for US$11 to US$18. Some rooms are quiet, some aren't.

Places to Stay – middle

Middle-range hotels may have evaporative air-cons – noisy machines which blow out the cooled air at gale force.

The newest three-star hotel in town is the *Koran Hotel* (☎ (871) 31809, 32332; fax 21737), on the main highway. All 54 rooms have air-conditioning, minibars and TVs. Rates are US$35/50 a single/double.

Urfa's traditional favourite is the three-star *Hotel Harran* (☎ (871) 34743, 32860; fax 34918), on Atatürk Bulvarı, directly opposite the Belediye. All 54 rooms have evaporative air-cons and private bathrooms, and some have TVs and refrigerators. The hotel also has a good terrace restaurant and a Turkish bath. Rooms cost US$35/50 a single/double.

A few steps to the south (right) is the one-star *Turban Urfa Oteli* (☎ (871) 33520, 33521), with 53 basic but serviceable rooms, all with telephone, twin beds and tiny showers. Some of the guest rooms, as well as the lobby, restaurant and bar, are air-conditioned. Rooms cost US$30/44 a single/double. Prices include breakfast and dinner. The rooftop restaurant is pleasant, but some of the prices aren't. The staff have a reputation for brusqueness.

Places to Eat

Urfa's culinary specialties include çiğ köfte (minced uncooked mutton), içli köfte (a deep-fried croquette with a mutton filling) and Urfa kebap (skewered chunks of lamb or minced lamb rissoles – broiled on charcoal and served with tomatoes, sliced onions and hot peppers). For a snack, try künefe, a sweet pastry with a cheese filling.

Places to Eat – bottom end

Inexpensive eateries are plentiful, and the richest concentration of them is near the Hotel İpek Palas and Cumhuriyet Palas on Köprübaşı Çarşısı. The *Güney Lokantası* (☎ 32237) at No 3/D is an example. Ceiling fans keep the hot air moving, refrigerated cases keep the drinks cold, the location keeps the noise at bay and the chef fills his steam table with various stews, vegetable dishes, pilavs and soups each day. A simple meal costs from US$2 to US$3. Similar restaurants are only a few steps away.

Perhaps the most pleasant place for an inexpensive meal is in the park at Gölbaşı. The *Turistik Göl Gazinosu, Lokanta & Aile Çay Bahçesi* (Touristic Lake Club, Restaurant & Family Tea Garden), next to the Balıklı Göl, has a family dining area, a video cassette player and a prohibition against alcoholic beverages. I had domatesli kebap (köfte grilled with chunks of tomato and served with chopped scallions, grilled hot peppers and huge flaps of flat village bread). With a tankard of cool ayran, the cost was US$4. Tea is cheap, Turkish coffee costs twice as much and soft drinks three times as much as tea.

Places to Eat – middle

Urfa is one of those towns in which the best hotels also hold the best restaurants. There is general agreement that the terrace restaurant of the Hotel Harran is the best place to dine. Service is attentive and polite, the food is good, alcoholic beverages are served and the open-air terrace at the back of the hotel several floors up is very pleasant. All this comes at a price, however. A dinner of tavuk şiş (chicken brochettes), mixed salad, bread and beer costs around US$8 to US$10.

Getting There & Away

Although Urfa is supposedly served by rail, the station is at Akçakale on the Syrian frontier, 50 km south of the town. The nearest airport is at Diyarbakır. Therefore, Urfa is best reached by bus.

Bus The otogar has a restaurant and pastry shop and a left-luggage depot. As it is on the main highway serving the south-east, Urfa has plenty of bus traffic, but most buses are passing through, so you must take whatever seats there are. Details of some daily services follow:

Adana – 365 km, six hours, US$11; several buses
Ankara – 850 km, 13 hours, US$18; several buses
Diyarbakır – 190 km, three hours, US$7; frequent
  buses
Erzurum – 665 km, 12 hours, US$18; a few buses
Gaziantep – 145 km, 2½ hours, US$5.50; frequent
  buses
İstanbul – 1290 km, 24 hours, US$38; a few buses
Kahta (for Nemrut Dağı) – 375 km, four hours, US$9;
  a few buses to Adıyaman, change for Kahta
Malatya – 395 km, seven hours, US$14; a few buses
Mardin – 175 km, three hours, US$7.50; several buses
Van – 585 km, 10 hours, US$20; a few buses

HARRAN

And Terah took Abram his son, and Lot the son of
Haran his son's son, and Sarai his daughter in law, his
son Abram's wife; and they went forth with them from
Ur of the Chaldees, to go into the land of Canaan; and
they came unto Harran, and dwelt there.

Genesis 11: 31

So says the Bible about Harran's most
famous resident, who stayed here for a few
years back in 1900 BC. It seems certain that
Harran, now officially called Altınbaşak, is
one of the oldest continuously inhabited
spots on earth. Now its ruined walls and Ulu
Cami, its crumbling fortress and beehive
houses give it a feeling of deep antiquity.

Harran's ancient monuments are interesting, though not really impressive. It is more
the lifestyle of the residents that you may
find fascinating. They live by farming and
smuggling and now await the wealth
expected to come with the development of
the South-east Anatolia Project.

History

Besides being the place of Abraham's
sojourn, Harran is famous as a centre of
worship of Sin, god of the moon. Worship of
the sun, moon and planets was popular hereabouts, in Harran and at neighbouring
Sumatar, from about 800 BC until 830 AD,
although Harran's temple to the moon god
was destroyed by the Byzantine emperor
Theodosius in 382 AD. Battles between
Arabs and Byzantines amused the townsfolk
until the coming of the crusaders. The fortress, which some say was built on the ruins
of the moon god's temple, was restored when
the Frankish crusaders approached. The cru-

saders won, and maintained the fortress for
a while before they too moved on.

Things to See

Before even reaching the town you'll see the
hill surrounded by crumbling walls and
topped with ruined buildings. Besides the
gates and city walls, the most impressive of
the ruins, in which some good mosaics were
found, is the **Ulu Cami**, built in the 8th
century by Marwan II, last of the Umayyad
caliphs. You'll recognise the square minaret
(very un-Turkish) of the mosque.

On the far (east) side of the hill is the
fortress, in the midst of the beehive houses.
As soon as you arrive, children will run to
you and crowd around, demanding coins,
sweets, cigarettes, empty water bottles and
ballpoint pens. Whether you hand out some
of these treats or not, they'll continue their
demands. Expect to have an escort as you
tour the ruins.

Getting There & Away

If you have your own car, you must go to
Harran. Without a car, you must decide
whether the three to four-hour 100-km
round-trip from Urfa should be done by taxi
(US$35 to US$40 for the car and driver) or
by minibus tour (US$5 to US$9 per person).
If you're interested in the minibus tour, be
advised that there are several tours in town
and that not all give good service. Ask other
travellers who have just taken the tour, and
see what they say. The minibus normally
departs from Urfa at 9.30 am, returning at
1.30 pm from Harran.

While Harran is now officially called
Altınbaşak, you will see signs in both names.
Leave Urfa by the Akçakale road at the
south-east end of town and go 37 km to a
turn-off to the left (east). From there, it's
another 10 km to Harran. As you approach
the site you come to a jandarma post, across
from which is a small restaurant, a camping
ground and a souvenir shop. There is no
accommodation in Harran, though this will
no doubt soon change.

DİYARBAKIR

The Tigris (Dicle, DEEJ-leh) River flows by the mighty black walls of Diyarbakır (dee-YAHR-bah-kuhr, population 375,000, altitude 660 metres). As with many Turkish cities, this one has grown beyond its ancient walls only in the last few decades. Farming, stock raising, some oil prospecting and light industry fuel the Diyarbakır economy.

The city prides itself especially on its watermelons. A brochure published for the annual watermelon festival in late September states:

In olden times, our watermelons had to be transported by camel as they weighed 90 or 100 kg. They were carved with a sword and sold in the market.

The brochure also says that nowadays the prize-winning melons at the festival weigh a mere 40 to 60 kg.

Today Diyarbakır, lying in the midst of a vast, lonely plain at the centre of the Kurdish separatist insurgency, is like an armed camp. The military presence is predictably large, and the tension is palpable.

Traditional life continues nonetheless. Many of the men wear the traditional baggy trousers, and older women have black head coverings which often serve unofficially as veils. Visiting men from Syria and Iraq have the long jellabah robes and keffiyeh (head scarves) of Arab lands, and the women may even be in purdah, wearing the black chador.

The tawdry chaos of signs in the city's centre, the narrow alleys, the mosques in the Arab style with black-and-white banding in the stone – all these give Diyarbakır a foreign, frontier feeling. The people, predominantly Kurds, tend to be taciturn and not particularly outgoing in their dealings with foreigners, and the street urchins are annoying. In summer it's very hot here, so avoid hotel rooms just beneath the building's roof or rooms that get full late-afternoon sun.

History

Considering that Mesopotamia, the land between the Tigris and Euphrates valleys, saw the dawn of the world's first great empires, it's no surprise that Diyarbakır's history begins with the Hurrian Kingdom of Mitanni circa 1500 BC, and proceeds through domination by the civilisations of Urartu (900 BC), Assyria (1356-612 BC), Persia (600-330 BC), Alexander the Great and his successors the Seleucids.

The Romans took over in 115 AD, but because of its strategic position the city continued to change hands numerous times until

it was conquered by the Arabs in 639 AD. Until then it had been known as Amida, but the Arabs settled it with the tribe of Beni Bakr, who named their new home Diyar Bakr, The Realm of Bakr.

I'd like to make this city's history simple for you, and say that when it was conquered by the Seljuks in 1085 or the Ottomans in 1515 it became a peaceful place, but this isn't so. Because it stands right in the way of invading armies from Anatolia, Persia and Syria, it was clobbered a lot more.

Orientation

Although the city has grown, your concern will be with the old part within the walls, except for the bus and rail stations west of the old city.

Old Diyarbakır has a standard Roman town plan, with the rough circle of walls pierced by four gates at the north, south, east and west. From the gates, avenues travel to the centre where they meet. Since Roman times, several sections of wall have been razed and a few new gates opened.

The railway station is at the western end of İstasyon Caddesi. From the station, this street goes east to the Urfa Kapısı (OOR-fah kah-puh-suh, Edessa Gate), the city's eastern gate. Inside the walls, the continuation of İstasyon Caddesi is named Melek Ahmet Caddesi or sometimes Urfa Caddesi. To go downtown from the station, walk out the front door, go to the first big street and wait on the left (north-east) corner of the far side for a dolmuş going to Dağ Kapısı.

The otogar is north-east of the city where Elazığ Caddesi (also called Ziya Gökalp Bulvarı) intersects the highway. Travel along Elazığ Caddesi to the centre and you will pass the Turistik Oteli just before penetrating the walls at the Dağ Kapısı (DAAH kah-puh-suh, Mountain Gate), the northern gate, sometimes also called the Harput Kapısı. From this gate, Gazi Caddesi leads to the centre. To get downtown from the otogar, take a dolmuş to Dağ Kapısı, 3.5 km away. Don't let people tell you that there are no dolmuşes and that you must take a taxi.

Information

The Tourism Information Office (☎ (831) 12173) is in the new city north of the walls at Lise Caddesi 24, Onur Apartmanı. Ask for LEE-seh jah-deh-see, which runs west from Elazığ Caddesi about three blocks north of the Dağ Kapısı. The office is about 3½ blocks along. The central tourism office is in the Kültür Sarayı on the 6th and 7th floors (☎ 10099, 17840).

Diyarbakır's postal code is 21000.

The Walls

The city's old walls are extensive – almost six km long – and are the first item on most people's list of things to see. In recent years it has become unsafe to walk along the top of the walls because of robbers. If you go, do so with a group.

Although there were Roman and probably earlier walls here, the present walls date from early Byzantine times (330-500 AD).

The historic names for the **gates** in the walls are the Harput Kapısı (north), Mardin Kapısı (south), Yenikapı (east) and Urfa Kapısı (west). The massive black basalt walls are defended by 72 bastions and towers, many of them gathered around the İç Kale (EECH-kaleh, citadel or keep) on the north-eastern corner, overlooking the Tigris. Of the gates, the Harput Kapısı or Dağ Kapısı is in the best condition.

Perhaps the most rewarding area of the walls to explore for inscriptions and decoration is the portion between the İç Kale and the Mardin Kapısı, going westward (away from the river). Start at the Mardin Kapısı near the Deliller Han, a stone caravanserai now restored as a hotel. Climb up to the path on top of the walls, walk along and you'll pass by the **Yedi Kardeş Burcu** (Tower of Seven Brothers) and **Malikşah Burcu** (Tower of Malikşah, also called Ulu Badan). The view of the city from on top of the walls is good and enables you to get your bearings and to see how the Diyarbakırlıs live. You must descend at Urfa Kapısı, but you can climb up again on the opposite side of İstasyon Caddesi.

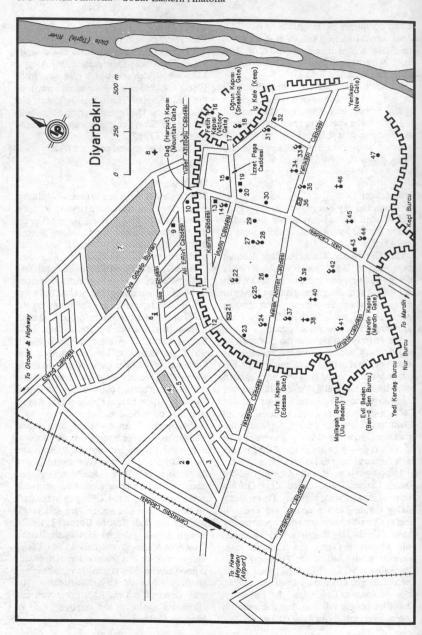

Diyarbakır

Mosques

Diyarbakır has many mosques, but the most interesting is the **Ulu Cami**, built in 1091 and extensively restored in 1155 after being damaged by fire. The mosque is rectangular in plan – Arab-style, not Ottoman. Its founder was Malik Şah, an early sultan of the Seljuks. Across the courtyard from the Ulu Cami is the Mesudiye Medresesi, now used as offices. Across the street from these buildings is the **Hasan Paşa Hanı**, a caravanserai dating from the 16th century, now used by carpet sellers and souvenir vendors.

Black-and-white stone banding is a characteristic of Diyarbakır's mosques, many of which date from the reign of the Akkoyunlu (White Sheep Turkomans) Dynasty. One of these is the **Nebi Camii** (1530) at the main intersection of Gazi and İzzet Paşa/İnönü caddesis.

The **Behram Paşa Camii** (1572), in a residential area deep in the maze of narrow streets, is Diyarbakır's largest mosque and is in a similar style. The **Safa Camii** (1532) is more Persian in style, with a grand and highly decorated minaret.

The **Kasım Padişah Camii** (1512) is also famous for its minaret, but it's the engineering that draws the interest – the huge tower stands on four slender pillars about two metres high, lending it the name Dört Ayaklı Minare or Four-Legged Minaret.

Atatürk Villa

The Atatürk Köşkü or Villa is interesting not because the Turkish leader spent much time here (he didn't), but as an example of upper-class Diyarbakır architecture. It has horizontal zebra stripes and an airy eyvan court facing pretty gardens.

Museum

Diyarbakır's museum is in the Fuar Sahası (fairgrounds) off Ziya Gökalp Caddesi, next to the Devlet Hastanesi. To get there, leave the old city through the Dağ Kapısı. Besides the usual archaeological and classical finds and the obligatory ethnological rooms, it has collections showing the accomplishments of the Karakoyunlu (Black Sheep Turkomans) and Akkoyunlu, powerful tribal dynasties which ruled much of Eastern Anatolia and Iran between 1378 and 1502.

The Akkoyunlu formed a pact with the Venetian Empire against the Ottomans, but were defeated by Mehmet the Conqueror in 1473. After 1497, the Safavid Dynasty founded by Shah Ismail took over Iran, putting an end to more than a century of Turkoman rule in this area.

Places to Stay – bottom end

The area around Dağ Kapısı has numerous little inexpensive hotels. Some are on İnönü Caddesi, as are the more expensive places. A favourite is the *Van Palas Oteli,* in a narrow side street off the south side of İnönü Caddesi, next to the Hotel Derya. The manager is into his work and sits around the courtyard fountain trading stories with visitors, playing backgammon or helping them to apply henna. Simple rooms are inexpensive, from US$2.75 to US$5 per person, but it's the spirit of the place that makes it popular.

The *Hotel Köprücü* (KEURP-reu-jeu, ☎ (831) 12963), İnönü Caddesi, Birinci Çıkmaz, is on a tiny dead-end street off İnönü Caddesi near the Büyük Otel. It's quiet, except for the call of the muezzin from the Nebi Camii next door, and offers a choice of rooms without running water or with a private shower, costing from US$4.50 to US$6.50 a single and from US$8 to US$11 a double.

Near the Derya and Büyük hotels are two more cheap places. The *Hotel Malkoç* (☎ (831) 12975), İnönü Caddesi, Sütçü Sokak 6, is an aile hotel charging US$8/11 a single/double with shower. Next door is the *Hotel Kaplan* (☎ (831) 13358), İnönü Caddesi, Sütçü Sokak 14 – a very quiet location. It has clean rooms, lots of hot water, big towels and similar prices.

If you can't find a room at the places listed, take a look at the *Otel Kenan* (☎ (831) 16614), İzzet Paşa Caddesi 20/B, next to the Otel Saraç. It's well worn, but the rooms are kept up fairly well. Some rooms have private baths and all smell a bit musty, but cost only

US$7 a double with a private shower. The hotel has a lift.

Moving up in quality a little, the first choice is the one-star *Hotel Derya* (☎ (831) 14966), İnönü Caddesi 13, less pretentious than some other places and offering very good value at US$14/20 a single/double for its 28 rooms with shower. It's often full.

Next in line is the one-star, old and fairly beaten-up *Otel Saraç* (sah-RAHCH, ☎ (831) 12365), İzzet Paşa Caddesi 16, almost next door to the more expensive Demir Otel. The 35 rooms are drab and simple, but cost only US$13/19 a single/double, with shower or bath.

The older one-star, 29-room *Hotel Aslan* (ahss-LAHN, ☎ (831) 13971), Kıbrıs Caddesi 53, is a few steps from the Dağ Kapısı. It costs US$13/18 a single/double for older rooms overlooking the gate in the city walls, but has a lift. Don't confuse it with the Aslan Palas next door.

Places to Stay – middle

Of the moderately priced places along İzzet Paşa Caddesi, several, such as the *Akdağ* and *Sürmeli,* are under long-term lease to oil prospecting companies and do not rent rooms to others.

The nicest place to stay, despite the relative simplicity of its accommodation, is the *Otel Büyük Kervansaray* (☎ (831) 43003), in the Deliller Han, a converted caravanserai on Gazi Caddesi near the Mardin Kapısı in the city walls. Very comfortable rooms with bath in a historic building cost US$36/55 a single/double, breakfast included.

Most of the middle-range hotels are on İnönü Caddesi or its continuation, İzzet Paşa Caddesi. The four-star, 58-room *Demir Otel* (☎ (831) 12315; fax 24300), İzzet Paşa Caddesi 8, at the intersection with Gazi Caddesi, a short distance south of Dağ Kapısı, is the old standard. With fairly good housekeeping, phones in the bathrooms and what passes for luxury in Diyarbakır, it charges US$35/60 a single/double, subject to haggling. The air-con is often too ineffective, though.

The nearby two-star, 75-room *Büyük Otel*

(beur-YEURK, ☎ 15832; fax 12444), İnönü Caddesi 4, is cheaper, with the trappings, but not the comforts, of a luxury hotel. Rooms cost US$26/38 a single/double with bath.

The newer two-star *Hotel Kristal* (☎ (831) 40297; fax 40187), İnönü Caddesi, Sütçü Sokak, has 30 comfortable rooms priced like those at the less comfortable Büyük.

Just outside the Dağ Kapısı is the veteran 57-room, two-star *Turistik Oteli* (☎ (831) 25003; fax 44274), Ziya Gökalp Bulvarı 7, built in 1953 but well kept, with spacious public rooms and guest rooms. It's a comfortable period piece and prices reflect this extra comfort. Rooms cost US$30/42/50 a single/double/triple with a private bath. Because of street noise, it's best to get a room at the back.

Places to Eat

Kebap places are everywhere and solve the dining problem easily and cheaply (for US$3 to US$4) most of the time. Many are near the junction of İnönü/İzzet Paşa and Gazi caddesis, near the hotels.

A stroll along Kıbrıs Caddesi from Dağ Kapısı westward will reveal several small, cheap places to eat, including the *Büryan Salonu* (☎ 24372), Kıbrıs Caddesi 17, for kebaps (a sign notes that you can pay in US$ or DM); the *7 Kardeşler*; and the *Kent Restaurant* (☎ 10899), Kıbrıs Caddesi 31/A, which has outdoor tables in the alleyway.

The *Babaman Lokantasi* (☎ 15887), on Kıbrıs Caddesi, serves a sebzeli kebap (vegetable and lamb stew), pilav and soft drink for less than US$3.50. It even has a summer dining area on the upper level, overlooking the walls and tea gardens.

For slightly fancier meals, head for the hotel restaurants in the *Demir* (a rooftop terrace) and the *Turistik*, or go to the air-conditioned *Güneydoğu 21 Sofra Salonu* (☎ 42597), İnönü Caddesi 32/A, near the Derya and Büyük hotels. The Turkish classics are served behind huge front windows in a Diyarbakır-style white décor. This is where the city's gilded youth (and gilded elders, for that matter) meet to eat, paying from US$6 to US$9 for a full meal.

There are also some pastanes in the centre, good for breakfast or a snack. I always seem to end up having a breakfast of su böreği (steamed noodle-like pastry with white cheese) at the *Şeyhmus Pastanesi* on the north-eastern corner of the intersection of İnönü/İzzet Paşa and Gazi caddesis. Despite it's being one of the town's fanciest pastry shops, the breakfast costs less than US$2, even with a large glass of tea.

Late in the afternoon, get baklava at the *Ünal Pastanesi,* a few steps south of the intersection on Gazi Caddesi in a building called the Merkez İş Hanı. Plush easy chairs and fake marble tables provide the décor while the cook provides a fine selection of various styles of baklava selling for between US$1 and US$1.50 per portion.

Getting There & Away

Air Turkish Airlines (☎ (831) 40428, 43366), Kültür Sarayı Sokak 15, Yenişehir, serves the city's Kaplaner airport with daily nonstop flights to and from Ankara, with connecting service to İstanbul. Additional flights to and from İstanbul on Monday and Friday are nonstop. Note that these flights fill up in advance, so reserve ahead. If you can't, you might try going standby as often there are no-shows.

Turkish Air Transport (THT) also has daily nonstop flights between Ankara and Diyarbakır, with extra ones on Monday, Wednesday, Friday and Sunday. Reserve through Turkish Airlines.

Bus Many bus companies have ticket offices in town on Kıbrıs Caddesi or in other spots near the Dağ Kapısı. Minibuses to Mardin depart not from the otogar but from the centre of town, leaving by the Urfa Kapısı hourly. Details of daily services on the main routes follow:

Adana – 550 km, 10 hours, US$16; several buses
Ankara – 945 km, 13 hours, US$20; several buses
Erzurum – 485 km, 10 hours, US$16; several buses
Kahta (Nemrut Dağı) – 192 km, three hours, US$8; several buses
Malatya – 260 km, four hours, US$8; frequent buses
Şanlıurfa – 190 km, three hours, US$7; frequent buses

Sivas – 500 km, nine or 10 hours, US$16; several buses

Van – 410 km, seven hours, US$14; several buses

Train Train service to the south-east is neither speedy nor dependably on time, so you may prefer to take the bus.

Diyarbakır is connected with Ankara by the *Güney Ekspresi* which runs eastward on Monday, Wednesday, Friday and Saturday, departing from Ankara at 10.40 am, stopping at Kayseri and Sivas before arriving in Diyarbakır at 12.42 pm the next day. The train continues eastward to Batman and Kurtalan.

The return service from Diyarbakır departs at 1.35 pm on Monday, Wednesday, Friday and Sunday, arriving in Ankara at 4.10 pm the next day.

For ticket prices, see the Ankara section of the Central Anatolia chapter under Getting There & Away.

The *Güney Ekspresi*'s schedule connects with that of the *Anadolu Ekspresi*, allowing direct train travel between İstanbul and Diyarbakır via Ankara.

MARDİN

About 175 km east of Urfa and 100 km south of Diyarbakır is Mardin (mahr-DEEN, population 60,000, altitude 1325), an odd and very old town crowned with a castle and a set of immense radar domes, all overlooking the vast, roasted Syrian plains. There is a certain amount of smuggling trade with Syria (in sheep for example, which are much more expensive in Syria than in Turkey) and lots of Kurdish separatist activity, but other than that, Mardin sizzles and sleeps.

This town had a large Christian community and there are still a few Syriac Christian families and churches. On the outskirts is the monastery of Deyrul Zafaran in which Aramaic, the language of Jesus, is still used as the liturgical tongue.

Mardin is not particularly well equipped with hotels and restaurants and is perhaps best visited on a day trip from Diyarbakır if you prize your comforts. Travelling on the cheap, it makes sense to take a bus from Urfa to Mardin, stay the night if you're in no hurry, then take a minibus north to Diyarbakır.

History

The history of Mardin, like that of Diyarbakır, involves disputes by rival armies over dozens and dozens of centuries, though now nobody cares. A castle has stood on this hill from time immemorial.

Assyrian Christians settled in this area during the 5th century. In the 6th century, Jacobus Baradeus, bishop of Edessa (Urfa), had a difference of opinion with the patriarch in Constantinople over the divine nature of Christ. The patriarch and official doctrine held that Christ had both a divine and a human nature. The bishop held that He had only one (mono) nature (physis), that being divine. The bishop was branded a Monophysite heretic and excommunicated. He promptly founded a church of his own, which came to be called the Jacobite (or Syrian Orthodox) after its founder.

At the same time and for the same reason, the Armenian Orthodox Church and the Coptic Church in Egypt were established as independent churches. In the case of the Jacobites, control from Constantinople was no longer a problem, as the Arabs swept in and took control soon afterwards. The Monophysites were also able to practice their religion as they chose under the tolerant and unconcerned rule of the Arabs.

The Arabs occupied Mardin between 640 and 1104. After that, it had a succession of Seljuk Turkish, Kurdish, Mongol and Persian overlords until the Ottomans under Sultan Selim the Grim took it in 1517.

Orientation

Perched on a hillside, Mardin has one long main street, Birinci Caddesi, running for about two km from the Belediye Garajı at the western end of town through the main square Cumhuriyet Meydanı to Konak, a small square with the Hükümet Konağı and military buildings at the eastern end.

Everything you'll need is along this street or just off it. City buses and intra-city dolmuşes run back and forth along the street. If you are driving your own car, leave it in the car park at Cumhuriyet Meydanı and walk to the hotels and things to see.

Information

The Tourism Information Office (☎ (841) 11665) is on Meydanbaşı Caddesi in the İl Halk Kütüphanesi (provincial library) building. Mardin's postal code is 47000.

Sultan İsa Medresesi

Dating from 1385, this seminary is the town's prime attraction. Walk east from the main square to the Hotel Başak Palas, then left (north) up the stairs to a large and imposing doorway. The doorway is what you have come to see, as there is little to see inside. The ancient building is used in part as a private residence.

Mardin Müzesi

The museum Mardin Müzesi (☎ 1664) is set up in one courtyard of the Sultan İsa Medresesi. You can enter through the door with the flagpole and sign. You may have to shout for the watchman.

The museum's opening hours are from 8.30 am to 5.30 pm every day; admission is free. It holds bits of statuary, but you've really come to admire the building and the view across the vast plains towards Syria.

Kasım Paşa Medresesi

Built in the 1400s near the western end of town, below the main street, you'll have to ask for guidance to find the seminary Kasım Paşa Medresesi.

Ulu Cami

This ancient mosque, built in the 11th century, is an Iraqi Seljuk structure. It's below (south of) the main street at Cumhuriyet Meydanı. As Mardin's history has been mostly one of warfare, the mosque has suffered considerably over the centuries, particularly in the Kurdish rebellion of 1832.

Deyrul Zafaran

In the rocky hills east of the town, six km along a good but narrow road, is the monastery of Mar Hanania, called Deyrul Zafaran. This means the Saffron Monastery in Arabic, a name which, legend says, was given because saffron crocuses were used in the mortar of the building. It was once the seat of the Syrian Orthodox patriarch. Though the patriarchate is now in Damascus, the monastery still has the modest trappings due to the patriarch and continues its charitable work of caring for orphans.

As you drive to the monastery, you will doubtless notice a hillside on which a motto has been written with white stones, 'Ne Mutlu Türküm Diyene' (What Joy to the Person Who Says, 'I am a Turk'). Atatürk originally uttered the phrase as part of his campaign to overcome the Turkish inferiority complex imposed by Europe and the USA. Here, though, it has a different significance, reiterating the government's commitment to the unity of the country against the efforts of Kurdish separatist groups.

The first sanctuary on this site, now included within the monastery, was dedicated to worship of the sun. In 495 AD the first monastery was built. Destroyed by the Persians in 607, it was rebuilt, to be looted by Tamerlane six centuries later.

You can visit the monastery any day without prior arrangement. As there is no public transport, you must take a taxi from the town centre, which will cost about US$8. Haggle for a set price to include the return journey and an hour's waiting time.

Enter the walled enclosure through a portal bearing a Syriac inscription. An Orthodox priest will greet you and hand you over to one of the orphans for a guided tour.

First comes the **original sanctuary**, an eerie underground chamber with a flat ceiling of huge, closely fitted stones held up as if by magic, without the aid of mortar. The guide says that this room was used ages ago by sun worshippers, who viewed their god rising through a window at the eastern end. A niche on the southern wall is said to have been for sacrifices.

The guide then leads you through a pair of

300-year-old **doors** to the **tombs** of the patriarchs and metropolitans who have served at Deyrul Zafaran.

In the chapel, to the left of the altar as you face it, is the **patriarch's throne**. It bears the names of all the patriarchs who have served since the monastery was refounded in 792. To the right of the altar is the **throne of the metropolitan**. The present stone altar was carved to replace a wooden one which burnt about half a century ago. The chapel is fairly plain and simple, but the primitive art is wonderful, especially the carved furniture and paintings. Services are said in Aramaic.

The next rooms on the tour hold several **litters** used to transport the church dignitaries, and also one of several **wells** in the monastery. In a small side room is a 300-year-old **wooden throne**. The **mosaic work** in the floor is about 1500 years old.

A flight of stairs takes you up to the suite of guest rooms, very simple accommodation for travellers and those coming for meditation. The **patriarch's suite**, a small, simple bedroom and parlour, are here. On the walls of the parlour are pictures of the patriarch (who lives in Damascus) with Pope John Paul II. Another picture shows an earlier patriarch with Atatürk.

As you leave the parlour, take a moment to enjoy the fine view of the mountains. Other monasteries, now in ruins, once stood farther up the slope. Some of the water for Deyrul Zafaran comes from near these ruins, through underground channels excavated many centuries ago.

At the end of the tour you may want to tip the guide. He'll refuse at first, but will probably accept when you offer a second or third time.

Places to Stay

All of Mardin's hotels are basic and cheap. Few are pleasant.

East of Cumhuriyet Meydanı are several small, modest hotels, such as the *Yıldız Oteli* (☎ (841) 11096), Birinci Caddesi 391, where plain rooms without plumbing will cost you US$4/6.50 for a single/double. The public showers have cold water only.

The *Hotel Bayraktar* (☎ (841) 11338, 11645) is on the main street facing Cumhuriyet Meydanı, with its other side overlooking the plains. It is Mardin's best hotel, with 50 rooms on eight floors reached by a lift, and a terrace restaurant where the notables gather. All rooms have showers and cost US$20 a double.

In the unlikely event that both these places are full, continue east to the *Hotel Başak Palas* and the even simpler *Hotel Şirin Palas*, on the main street beneath the Sultan İsa Medresesi.

Places to Eat

The only real restaurant, although nothing special, is at the Hotel Bayraktar (☎ 11647), which overlooks the square. Ask about prices before you order, as my simple meal turned out to be surprisingly expensive at US$6.50.

There are several small, very inexpensive eateries east of the Bayraktar along the main street. Ask prices when you order.

Getting There & Away

Several buses run daily from Urfa to Mardin. Minibuses run about every hour between Mardin's Belediye Garajı and Diyarbakır's Mardin Kapısı (Mardin Gate in the city walls), for US$3. The 100-km journey takes about 1¾ hours.

BİTLİS

Travel eastward from Diyarbakır 88 km and you'll reach the town of Silvan from where it's another 22 km to Malabadi. Just east of here is the Batman Suyu, a stream spanned by a beautiful hump-backed **stone bridge** built by the Artukid Turks in 1146. It is thought to have the longest span (37 metres) of any such bridge in existence. With its engaging bend in the middle, it's truly a work of art. Restoration in 1988 has returned it to much of its former stateliness.

Another 235 km brings you to Bitlis (BEET-leess, population 45,000, altitude 1545 metres), an interesting but dusty and somewhat chaotic old town squeezed into the narrow valley of a stream. A **castle** dominates the town and a **hump-backed bridge** and another old bridge span the stream.

The **Ulu Cami** was built in 1126, while the **Şerefiye Camii** and **Saraf Han** (a caravanserai) date from the 16th century. The town was the capital of a semi-autonomous Kurdish principality in late Ottoman times.

Walnut trees surround the town and, in autumn, children stand by the highway with bags of nuts for sale.

Up the hill at the eastern side of the town, on the left (north) side of the road, is an old caravanserai, the **Pabsin Hanı,** built by the Seljuks in the 1200s. Often there are nomads camped near it, their sprawling black tents pitched beneath its crumbling walls.

It's only 26 km to Tatvan, a railhead and western port for lake steamers.

TATVAN

Tatvan is a crossroads town, built for and surviving on the commerce which moves through by road and rail. This includes the Turkish army which is here to protect the country's eastern borders at the traditional invasion points from north, east and south.

The town, several km long and only a few blocks wide, is not much to look at and has only a few poor tourist services. However, its setting on the shores of an inland sea, backed by bare mountains streaked with snow, is magnificent.

You must pass through Tatvan, and you may even make it your base for explorations along the north-western shore of the lake, so here's what you need to know.

Information

The Tourism Information Office (☎ (8497) 2106), at İşletme Caddesi 6, is by the lakeshore

Nemrut Dağı

The mountain rising to the north of Tatvan is Nemrut Dağı, not to be confused with the one near Adıyaman and Malatya with the statues on top. This Nemrut Dağı (3050 metres) is an inactive volcano with a crater lake on top which is beautiful, clear and cold and which should be visited for the view or for a swim

if you normally swim among icebergs. If not, there are hot springs as well. Nemrut is the volcano which dammed up the outflow of Lake Van, causing it to cover its present vast area of 3750 sq km, and to become highly alkaline.

In summer, dolmuşes make the run up the mountain (for around US$6 per person) if there are enough people interested. If you have your own transport, leave Tatvan by the road around the lake to the north marked for Ahlat and Adilcevaz. On the outskirts of Tatvan, look for a left turn near a Türk Petrol station, as this road will take you up the mountain.

Ahlat

Continue northward by car or dolmuş along the lakeshore for 42 km and you'll come to the town of Ahlat, famous for its Seljuk Turkish tombs and graveyard.

History Founded during the reign of Caliph Ömar (581-644), Ahlat became a Seljuk stronghold in the 1060s. When the Seljuk sultan Alp Arslan rode out to meet the Byzantine emperor Romanus Diogenes in battle on the field of Manzikert (Malazgirt; see that section following), he rode out from his base at Ahlat.

In following centuries, Ahlat had an extraordinarily eventful history – even by Anatolian standards – with emir defeating prince and king driving out emir. It's no wonder Ahlat is famous for its cemeteries.

Ahlat, and indeed this whole region, was conquered by the Ottomans during the reign of Süleyman the Magnificent in the 16th century. The fortress on the shore in Ahlat dates from that period.

Tombstones The tombstones are most commonly of grey or red volcanic tuff. The artistry of the Ahlat stonemasons is extraordinary, with intricate web patterns and bands of Kufic lettering. It is thought that Ahlat stonemasons were employed on other great stoneworking projects, such as the decoration of the great mosque at Divriği, near Sivas.

To the right (south) of the highway as you approach the town is **Ulu Kümbet**, the Great Tomb, now in the midst of a field near some houses. Across the highway from it is a little museum, and beyond the museum is a unique Muslim cemetery with stele-like headstones. Over the centuries, earthquake, wind and water have set the stones at all angles, giving the graveyard an unsettling and eerie look.

On the north-western side of the graveyard is the **Çifte Kümbet** (Twin Tomb) and **Bayındır Türbesi** (Bayındır Tomb), with a colonnaded porch and its own small prayer room.

Malazgirt

About 60 km north of Ahlat is Malazgirt (Manzikert), which is greatly important in Turkish history. On 26 August 1071, the Seljuk Turkish sultan Alp Arslan and his armies decisively defeated the Byzantine emperor Romanus Diogenes and took him prisoner. The Byzantine defeat effectively opened Anatolia to Turkish migration and conquest.

The Seljuks established the Sultanate of Rum with its capital at Konya, and other nomadic Turkish tribes came from Central Asia and Iran to settle here. A band of border warriors, following a leader named Osman, later spread its influence and founded a state which would become the vast Ottoman Turkish Empire. It all started here, in 1071, when the heir of the Caesars lost to a Turkish emir.

Adilcevaz

Twenty-five km east of Ahlat is the town of Adilcevaz, once an Urartian town but now dominated by a great Seljuk Turkish fortress, the **Kef Kalesi**, and the even greater bulk of **Süphan Dağı** (4434 metres).

Meltwater from the year-round snow-fields on Süphan Dağı flows down to Adilcevaz, making its surroundings lush and fertile. As you enter town along the shore, the highway passes the nice little **Tuğrul Bey Camii**, built in the 13th century and still used daily for prayer. You can climb Süphan Dağı in summer. For details, see Lonely Planet's *Trekking in Turkey*.

Dolmuşes run between Adilcevaz and Van (Beş Yol) several times daily. If you continue around the lake, you will pass through **Erciş**, a modern town which covers settlements that date from Urartian times.

Places to Stay

Ahlat and Adilcevaz have a few small, cheap pensions. In Tatvan, the few cheap hotels (such as the *Otel Trabzon*, where rooms cost US$4/7 a single/double with washbasin) are very basic and well used, but so is the best hotel in town, the *Vangölü Denizcilik Kurumu Oteli* (☎ (8497) 1777).

Hidden on the shore a short walk from the centre, the old stone building looks as though it is left from Ottoman times, though it may have been built to accommodate railway passengers. It has a serviceable restaurant and the 23 drab, basic and old-fashioned rooms cost from US$15 to US$25 a double, some with private showers. Despite its lack of comforts, this, the best hotel in Tatvan, is often fully booked with tour groups.

Getting There & Away

Tatvan's railway station is about two km north-east of the centre along the road to Ahlat and Adilcevaz; there are infrequent city buses.

The *Vangölü Ekspresi* departs from Tatvan at 9.50 am on Tuesday, Thursday and Saturday bound for Ankara, arriving at 4.10 pm the following day. A one-way 1st/2nd-class ticket from Tatvan to Ankara costs US$15/10.50. The fare in a sleeping car is US$30/-52/72 for one/two/three people. Reserve your sleeping-car space well in advance.

Ferries operated by Turkish Maritime Lines cross the lake from Tatvan to Van on an irregular schedule – while there are supposed to be four boats per day, there often is only one. Don't believe the departure times you're told. You can make the 156-km journey to Van more quickly (two hours) by bus around the southern shore.

AKDAMAR

Between Tatvan and Van, the scenery is beautiful, but there is no reason to stop except at a point eight km west of Gevaş, where you *must* see the 10th-century Akdamar Kilisesi or Church of the Holy Cross. One of the marvels of Armenian architecture, it is perched on an island in the lake. Motorboats ferry sightseers back and forth. You can also make this trip as an excursion from Van.

In 921, Gagik Artzruni, King of Vaspurakan, built a palace, a church and a monastery on the island, three km out in the lake. Little remains of the palace and monastery, but the church walls are in superb condition and the wonderful relief carvings on the walls are among the masterworks of Armenian art.

If you are familiar with biblical stories, you'll immediately recognise Adam and Eve, Jonah and the Whale, David and Goliath, Abraham about to sacrifice Isaac (but he sees the heaven-sent ram, with its horns caught in a bush, just in time), Daniel in the Lions' Den, Sampson etc.

The paintings inside the church are not in the best condition, but their vagueness and frailty seem in keeping with the shaded, partly ruined interior.

Getting There & Away

Dolmuşes run from Beş Yol in Van to Gevaş for US$2. Some of the dolmuş drivers have a racket whereby they take you to Gevaş, then set a high price for the remaining eight km to the boat dock for Akdamar. To beat this, agree on a price all the way to the dock (Akdamar İskelesi) before you board the dolmuş in Van.

Boats to the island (US$3 for the round trip) run about every 30 minutes if traffic warrants this, which it usually does in the warm months, especially on Sundays. If it doesn't, you may have to charter a boat for a special trip, for around US$25 to US$35.) The voyage takes about 20 minutes and an admission ticket to the church costs US$1.

A fairly expensive teahouse and camping area are near the dock.

VAN

Almost 100 km across vast Lake Van (Van Gölü) from Tatvan lies Van (population 150,000, altitude 1727 metres), the eastern railhead on the line to Iran and the largest Turkish city east of Diyarbakır and south of Erzurum.

Van has several claims to fame. It was the Urartian capital city and at the Rock of Van near the lakeshore are long cuneiform inscriptions. Van is also the market centre for the Kurdish tribes who live in the mountain fastnesses of extreme south-eastern Turkey. An excursion to the south-east takes you past the ancient Urartian city at Çavuştepe and the picture-perfect mountain fortress of Hoşap to Hakkari and Yüksekova, deep in the breathtaking scenery of the Cilo Dağı mountains.

History

The kingdom of Urartu, called Ararat in the Bible, flourished in these parts from the 13th to the 7th centuries BC. The Urartian capital, Tushpa, was near present-day Van. The Urartians were traders and farmers, highly advanced in the art of metalwork and stone masonry. They borrowed much of their culture from the neighbouring Assyrians, including their cuneiform writing. Although they emulated the Assyrians, they were at war with them more or less permanently. Even though Urartu was less powerful than Assyria, the Assyrians never completely subdued the Urartians. But when the battle was joined by several waves of Cimmerians, Scythians and Medes who swept into Urartu, the kingdom met its downfall.

With the downfall of Urartu, the region was resettled by a people whom the Persians called Armenians. By the 6th century BC the region was governed by Persian and Mede satraps.

The history of the Armenians is one of repeated subjugation to the rule of other peoples as they occupied a strategic crossroads at the nexus of three great empires in Syria, Persia, and Anatolia. Tigranes the Great succeeded in gaining control of the kingdom from its Parthian overlords in 95

BC, but his short-lived kingdom was soon crushed in the clash of armies from Rome in the west and Parthia in the east.

In the 8th century AD, the Arab armies flooded through from the south, forcing the Armenian prince to take refuge on Akdamar Island. Unable to fend off the vast number of Arabs, he later agreed to pay tribute to the Caliph. When the Arabs retreated, the Byzantines and Persians took their place, and overlordship of Armenia see-sawed between them as one or the other gained military advantage.

The next wave of people to flood through were the Turks. Upon defeating the Byzantines at Manzikert, north of Lake Van, in 1071, the Seljuk Turks marched in to found the Sultanate of Rum and were followed by a flood of Turkoman nomads. Domination of Eastern Anatolia by the powerful Karakoyunlu and Akkoyunlu Turkish emirs followed, and continued until the coming of the Ottoman armies in 1468.

During WW I, Armenian guerrilla bands intent on founding an independent Armenian state collaborated with the Russians to defeat the Ottoman armies in the east. The Armenians, former loyal subjects of the sultan, were looked upon as traitors by the Turks. Bitter fighting between Turkish and Kurdish forces on the one side and Armenian and Russian on the other brought wholesale devastation to the entire region and to Van.

The Ottomans destroyed the old city of Van (near the Rock of Van) before the Russians occupied it in 1915. Ottoman forces counterattacked but were unable to drive the invaders out, so Van remained under Russian occupation until the armistice of 1917. Under the Turkish Republic, a new planned city of Van was built several km from the old site.

Orientation

The highway passing between the town and the lake is the ancient Silk Road (İpek Yolu). In the city, the main commercial street is Cumhuriyet Caddesi, with banks, hotels, restaurants, the Turkish Airlines office and the Tourism Information Office. At the northern end of Cumhuriyet Caddesi, where it meets five other streets, is the square called Beş Yol (Five Roads), with a huge concentration of dolmuş and bus stops.

The city's bus terminal is on the northwestern outskirts, just off the Silk Road.

The two railway stations are the İskele İstasyon or lakeside Dock Station and the Şehir İstasyon or City Station. The City Station is north-west of the centre near the bus terminal, while the Dock Station is several km north-east on the shore.

Van Kalesi (the Rock of Van), the only significant sight, is about five km west of the centre.

Information

The Tourism Information Office (☎ (061) 13675, 12018) is at the southern end of Cumhuriyet Caddesi, at No 127. Van's postal code is 65000.

Van Museum

Off Cumhuriyet Caddesi, not far from the Bayram Oteli, is the museum Van Müzesi which holds exhibits dating back to before Urartian times. Other exhibits include beautiful Urartian gold jewellery, some with amber and coloured glass, Urartian cylindrical seals, and pots from the Old Bronze Age (circa 5000 BC). The Urartu Süsleme Plakaları (jewellery breastplates) from the 9th to 7th centuries BC are particularly fine, as are the bronze belts. Another exhibit has *gemleri* (horse bits) from the 9th and 8th centuries BC.

The ethnographic exhibits upstairs include countless kilims, the flat-woven rugs superbly made by the Kurdish and Turkoman tribes who live in the mountains. At the far end of the room is a sedir or low couch, such as is found in village houses, covered with traditional crafts.

The museum is open from 9 am to 5.30 pm; admission costs US$1. Cameras are not permitted inside, so you must check yours in at the door.

Rock of Van

Dolmuşes to the Rock of Van (Van Kalesi)

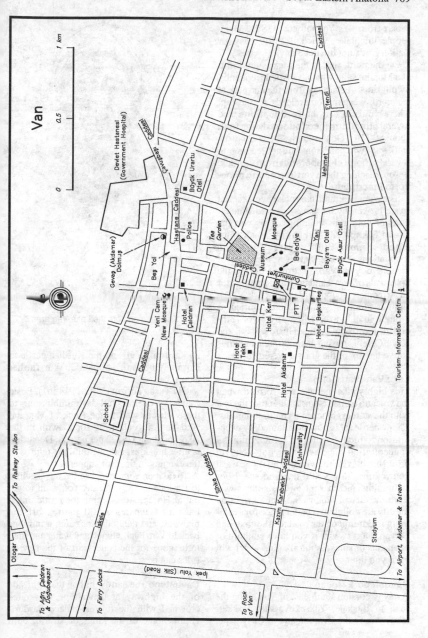

Van

depart from Beş Yol and cost US$1. Many people hitchhike, which is fairly easy, or walk it if it's not too hot a day.

On the north side of the rock is the **tomb** of a Muslim saint which is visited frequently by pilgrims. A stairway from the car park at the north-western corner leads to the top, where you can see the **fortifications** and several **cuneiform inscriptions** dating from about 800 BC. On the south side is a narrow walkway with an iron railing leading to several **funeral chambers** cut from the rock. Before reaching these you pass a **long cuneiform inscription**.

The view south of the rock reveals a flat space broken by the grass-covered foundations of numerous buildings. This was the **site of Tushpa**, an Urartian city which flourished almost 3000 years ago. The foundations you see, however, are those of the **old city of Van**, destroyed during the upheavals of WW I and the futile struggle for an Armenian republic in eastern Turkey. The sight is stunning – a dead city, buried as though in a grave, with only two **16th-century mosques**, the Hüsrev Paşa and Kaya Çelebi, raising their broken minarets above the top of the grass-covered rubble.

Lake Van (Van Gölü)

This highly alkaline lake was formed when the volcano named Nemrut Dağı (not the one with the statues) blocked its natural outflow. The water level is now maintained by evaporation which results in a high mineral concentration. The water is not good to drink, but it's fine to swim in, and if you wash your clothes in it you'll need no soap! For swimming, pick a spot on the shore away from the city of Van, as the waters right by the city are polluted. A better place for swimming is Edremit on the road to Akdamar and Tatvan. Don't swim if you have sunburn or open cuts or sores, as the alkaline water will burn you intensely.

Çavuştepe & Hoşap

A day excursion south-east of Van along the road to Başkale, Yüksekova and Hakkari takes you to the Urartian site at Çavuştepe,

Kurdish man from the Lake Van area

25 km from Van, and the Kurdish castle at Hoşap (Güzelsu), another 33 km further along.

Old Tuşba Turizm (☎ (061) 14561), Posta Caddesi 9, operates full-day minibus tours to these sites as well as the Rock of Van and Akdamar, also allowing for a swim in the lake, for about US$22 per person. Departure is after breakfast and the minibus returns in the evening in time for supper.

To do it on your own, catch a bus heading to Başkale (US$3) and say you want to get out at Hoşap. After seeing the castle, hitch back to Çavuştepe, 500 metres off the highway, and then hitch or catch a minibus back to Van. Pack a lunch and water and plan to be gone for the better part of the day, as rides can be scarce.

Çavuştepe The narrow hill on the right side of the highway at Çavuştepe was once crowned with the fortress-palace Sarduri-Hinili, home of the kings of Urartu, built between 764 and 735 BC by King Sardur II, son of Argisti. Climb the hill to the car park, where there is a guardian to keep you from taking photos (excavations are still underway) and perhaps to show you what there is to see. No admission fee is being charged yet and no drinks or refreshments are available at the site.

Climb the rocky hill to the temple ruins, marked by a gate of black basalt blocks polished to a high gloss. A few of the blocks on the left side of the doorway are inscribed in cuneiform. As you walk around, notice the cisterns for water and, at the far end where the palace once stood, the royal Urartian loo.

Hoşap Castle Back on the road, another half-hour's ride (33 km) brings you up over a hill and down the other side, where the castle Hoşap Kalesi stands perched and photogenic on top of a rocky outcrop. Beneath it is the village of Güzelsu, along a stream. On the left side of the road before the village is a badly ruined caravanserai or medrese. Cross the bridge into the village and follow the signs around the far side of the hill to reach the castle entrance.

The castle, built in 1643 by a local Kurdish chieftain, has a very impressive entrance portal in a round tower. A guardian is supposed to be on duty from 8.30 am to noon and from 1.30 to 5 pm. The guardian will sell you a ticket for less than US$1 and let you walk up into the fortress via a passage cut through the rock. Many of the castle's hundreds of rooms are still clearly visible and the view is good. Across the valley are the remains of mud-brick defensive walls, now badly eroded and looking like a dinosaur's spine. Soft drinks are on sale at the castle entrance.

Places to Stay – bottom end
Van has one decent, modern, comfortable hotel and a good selection of cheaper places. The *Bayram Oteli* (BAH-yee-RAHM, ☎ (061) 11136), Cumhuriyet Caddesi 1/A, is very near the intersection of Cumhuriyet and Yani Mehmet Efendi caddesis. It could use a sandblasting from top to bottom and new

paint, but for now its 72 rooms with beaten-up showers and balconies cost US$10/16 a single/double. Other services available are a lift, car park, hamam and TV lounge.

A similar but slightly cheaper place to stay is the one-star *Hotel Beşkardeş* (BEHSH-kahr-desh, ☎ (061) 11116/7), Cumhuriyet Caddesi 34. It has 40 rooms with balconies going from US$10 to US$14 a single, from US$14 to US$18 a double and from US$16 to US$23 a triple. Prices are lower for rooms with sinks and higher for rooms with shower. The hotel has five floors but no lift.

The cheapest of the more modern hotels is the 63-room *Hotel Kent* (☎ (061) 12519, 12404), behind the Türkiye İş Bankası. Its 63 rooms cost from US$7 to US$10 a single and from US$11 to US$16 a double, with sink or private shower. The paint is fairly new, though the place still looks well used.

The *Hotel Çaldıran* (CHAHL-duh-RAHN, ☎ (061) 12718), on Sıhke Caddesi, two short blocks down towards the lake from Beş Yol and near the Yeni Cami, has 48 clean, cheap rooms priced at US$10/15 a single/double with private shower.

Very popular among backpackers is the old *Hotel Van*, behind the Tekel building not far from the Çaldıran and near the fruit and vegetable market. It's a big old place with minimal maintenance carried out but lots of beds priced at only US$3 a night.

In the bazaar area not far from the Yeni Cami and Beş Yol is the *Lüks Aslan Oteli* (☎ (061) 12469), Eski Hal Civarı. It's a small and simple family concern with pale yellow doors; yellow-striped wallpaper; hot water morning and evening; and many light and airy rooms, some with views of the town (the three-bed corner rooms numbered 103, 203, 303 etc are the best). Prices are good at US$6/10/13 a single/double/triple.

The two-star *Hotel Tekin* (☎ (061) 13010; fax 11366), Küçük Cami Civarı, Nur Sokak 24, near the Little Mosque west of Cumhuriyet Caddesi, has an easily visible sign on its roof. There are 52 rooms in this quiet place and each has its small problems, such as leaky washers, but it's cleaner than most places and offers a bit more comfort for a bit more money. A room costs US$14/19/24 a single/double/triple with private shower.

Camping There is camping at Edremit, 18 km from Van on the way to Gevaş and Akdamar. You can also camp at the moderately priced restaurant near the dock for Akdamar boats.

Places to Stay – middle
The best hotel in town is the 75-room, three-star *Büyük Urartu Oteli* (☎ (061) 20660; fax 21610), Cumhuriyet Caddesi 60. (The hotel is on Hastane Caddesi, near the hospital, despite its Cumhuriyet Caddesi address.) It's a fairly new, modern and attractive place with a spacious lobby, restaurant and bar, mezzanine breakfast room and comfortable guest rooms with private baths. Rooms cost US$36 a single and from US$45 to US$55 a double. The décor draws on Urartian themes as the hotel's designer is a professor of archaeology.

Also quite comfortable is the three-star, 69-room *Hotel Akdamar* (AHK-dah-mahr, ☎ (061) 18100; fax 20868), Kazım Karabekir Caddesi 56 (on the street running west from Cumhuriyet Caddesi near the Tourism Information Office). Rooms cost US$25/36 a single/double with bath. The hotel has lifts, a car park, a terrace restaurant which is among the best in town, and a bar.

The older, more modest two-star *Büyük Asur Oteli* (beur-YEURK ah-SOOR, ☎ (061) 18792), Cumhuriyet Caddesi 126, has 48 rooms in muted colours lit by fluorescence. It also has all the basic services such as lifts, a restaurant and parking. Like the other middle-range hotels, it is heavily used by European tour groups. Rooms cost US$18/34 a single/double with bath.

Places to Eat – bottom end
Van's simple lokantas are bright, big and unfancy. Try the *Şölen Lokantası* (☎ 12855), Kazım Karabekir Caddesi, across from the Hotel Akdamar, or the *Şafak Lokantası* (☎ 11922) next door to the Hotel Akdamar. A plate of İzmirli kebap (meatballs and veg-

etables in broth), rice pilav and a soft drink costs less than US$3.

Cumhuriyet Caddesi has more small restaurants. The *Altın Şiş Fırınlı Kebap Salonu* or Golden Skewer Oven-Equipped Kebap Salon (☎ 12265), is a modern, smoky place (down past the PTT) with a good selection of cheap kebaps.

The *Saray Lokantası* (☎ 11756) is down a side street off Cumhuriyet Caddesi by the Türkiye İş Bankası, towards the Hotel Kent. It's just as cheap as the place on the main street, but quieter.

Up the hill a few steps from the intersection of Cumhuriyet and Kazım Karabekir caddesis is the *Turistik Köşk Restoran* (☎ 12160), with similar food and prices, but a garden dining area behind the main dining room.

For pastries or breakfast, try the *Tuşba Pasta Salonu* (☎ 11069), the fanciest place in town, to the right of the Belediye on Cumhuriyet Caddesi between the Sümerbank and Garanti Bankası. The *Güven Pastanesi* (☎ 16578), across the street from the Hotel Nuh and south of the tea garden next to the Töbank, is a bit less fancy.

Places to Eat – middle
The fanciest and probably the best food is at the Büyük Urartu Oteli and Hotel Akdamar, where a great dinner can cost US$10 but represents good value for money.

Things to Buy
In the shops of Van you will see handwoven craft items, such as kilims and saddlebags, finer than you've ever seen before. The dealers, however, realise that these finely made things will fetch high prices in Paris, London and New York, so you won't find many bargains. You will enjoy seeing the fine selection of good woven items, though. Prices for the normal, common kilims etc will be reasonable. You are under no obligation to buy, so don't feel pressured. Looking at these crafts is a wonderful experience. Some of the dealers speak English.

Getting There & Away

As the 'capital' of the extreme south-east, Van has ready transport. For dolmuşes to the Rock of Van ('Kale'), the ferry dock ('İskele'), the Akdamar boat dock ('Gevaş') and Adilcevaz on the lake's northern shore, go to Beş Yol at the northern end of Cumhuriyet Caddesi.

Air Turkish Airlines (☎ (061) 11768, 11241), Cumhuriyet Caddesi 196, in the Enver Perihanoğlu İş Merkezi building, has daily nonstop flights between Ankara and Van, and connecting flights for İstanbul and İzmir. At this writing there is no airport bus; you must take a short taxi ride.

İstanbul Airlines has nonstop flights between Ankara and Van on Tuesday and Thursday, with continuing service for İstanbul.

Bus Many bus companies maintain ticket offices along Cumhuriyet Caddesi, including the Van Gölü and Van Turizm companies. The larger companies have servis arabası minibuses to shuttle passengers between the downtown office and the bus terminal. As usual, bus traffic to and from Van is fast and frequent. Details of some, mostly daily, services follow:

Ağrı – 230 km, four hours, US$8; frequent buses
Diyarbakır – 410 km, seven hours, US$14; several buses
Doğubeyazıt via Çaldıran – 185 km, five hours, US$12; direct dolmuş every few days; more frequent service planned
Doğubeyazıt via Erçiş, Patnos and Ağrı – 315 km, 5½ hours, US$12; several to Ağrı, then change for Doğubeyazıt
Erzurum – 420 km, 7½ hours, US$18; several buses
Hakkari – 210 km, four hours, US$9 several buses
Malatya – 585 km, 10 hours, US$22; several buses
Şanlıurfa – 585 km, 10 hours, US$20; a few buses
Tatvan – 156 km, three hours, US$6; frequent buses
Trabzon – 745 km, 17 hours, US$30; a few direct buses, most via Erzurum

Train Van used to be served by the *Vangölü Ekspresi* which went right on to the lake steamer at Tatvan and cruised across the lake, resuming its eastward journey to Tehran at

Van's dock (Iskele). Service to Iran has been suspended for several years, but perhaps it will be resumed as Turkish-Iranian relations improve. The ferries still run at irregular intervals, taking four hours to cross the lake to Tatvan. Bring your own food, as only drinks are served on the boats.

HAKKARİ

The absolute, positive dead end of Turkey is Hakkari (hah-KYAH-ree, population 35,000, altitude 1700 metres), 210 km south of Van over a zig-zagging mountain road. The scenery is spectacular. However, the police and army presence in this tinderbox of Kurdish separatism is intense. Expect to be stopped for identity checks frequently, and don't plan to stay long before returning westward.

Buses depart daily from Van for Hakkari. At 112 km is Başkale, notable for its altitude (2450 metres). Yeni Köprü, at 160 km, is the point at which a road left goes to Yüksekova, on the road to Iran, an alternative base for climbs into the mountains – in better times, when political and military conditions allow.

Finally, 210 km from Van you arrive in Hakkari, which has one lodging place, the *Hotel Turistik*, which charges US$10 for a double room.

NORTH FROM VAN

Having come this far, your next goal must be Doğubeyazıt, the town in the shadow of Mt Ararat, at the Iranian frontier on the E23 highway. There is an alternative to the normal Erçiş-to-Patnos-to-Ağrı route. Where the lake ring road turns westward at the town of Bendimahi, continue north towards Muradiye, Çaldıran and Ortadirek. (Dolmuşes leave Van every few days in summer along this route.) The road is unpaved after Çaldıran and is extremely rough in spots between Çaldıran and Ortadirek, but it's usually passable. The road is being improved and is wonderfully scenic. Dolmuşes often stop at a scenic waterfall, volcanic rock formations and a nomad camp.

This route to Doğubeyazıt is only 185 km long, so it saves a few km, but you shouldn't drive along it after 5 pm. The road's officially closed after that hour and Turkish army patrols are on duty to stop smugglers. The patrollers are very friendly if you obey the

regulations, but will be strict after 5 pm. Even during daylight hours, remember to keep your passport handy for identity checks.

Turkish Language Guide

From the time when Turks first encountered Islam around the year 670, Turkish had been written in the Arabic alphabet, the letters of the Koran. However, the Arabic letters did not suit the sounds of Turkish and made the task of literacy very difficult.

Even under the empire, alphabet reform had been proposed in order to promote literacy and progress. But it was Atatürk, of course, who did it in 1928. The story is typical of him: when told that it would take several years of expert consultation to devise a suitable Latin alphabet for Turkish, and then about five years at the least to implement it, he replied, 'The change will be carried out in three months, or not at all'. Needless to say, the new alphabet was ready in six weeks, and three months later the old alphabet was forbidden in public use. And it worked! The president of the republic himself got a slate and chalk, went into the public parks, and held informal classes to teach the people the new letters.

Lonely Planet's *Turkish Phrasebook* has words and phrases that are geared to travellers' needs. Ask for it at your bookshop.

For the meanings of common terms used in this guide, and Turkish words and phrases you might encounter on signs, please refer to the Glossary which follows this section.

Turkish Audio Cassettes

An audio cassette is a big help in learning correct pronunciation. I've made up a 90-minute audio cassette (No. TSK 04) keyed to the Turkish Language Guide, and another cassette (No. TKPB 01) keyed to the *Turkish Phrasebook*. For either cassette, please send your name and address, the stock number of the cassette you would like, and a cheque or money order payable to Tom Brosnahan for US$12 or UK£8 per cassette to Turkish Cassette, c/o Tom Brosnahan, PO Box 563, Concord, MA 01742-0563 USA. Fast letter-mail ('1st-class') postage is included in the price.

If you can't find the Lonely Planet *Turkish Phrasebook* at your bookshop, send US$5 or UK£3.50 to me at the address above, and I'll send you one by letter mail.

Note that this address is for audio cassette and *Turkish Phrasebook* orders **only**. Please send all other correspondence to me via a Lonely Planet office (for addresses, see the back of the title page at the front of this book).

PRONUNCIATION

Despite daunting oddities such as the soft 'g' (ğ) and undotted 'ı' (ı), Turkish is phonetic and simple to pronounce. In a few minutes you can learn to pronounce the sounds reasonably well.

Here are some tips on correct pronunciation in Turkish. Most letters in Turkish are pronounced as they appear. Here are the tricky ones, the vowels and the exceptions.

A, a	short 'a' as in 'art' or 'bar'
â	very faint 'y' sound in preceding consonant, for example Lâleli is lyaah-leh-LEE
E, e	'eh' as the first vowel in 'ever' or 'fell'
İ, i	as 'ee' in 'see'
I, ı	'uh' or the vowel sound in 'were' or 'sir'
O, o	same as in English
Ö, ö	same sound as in German, or like English 'ur', as in 'fur'
U, u	'oo', like the vowel in 'moo' or 'blue'
Ü, ü	same as in German, or 'ew' in 'few'

C, c	pronounced like English 'j' as in 'jet'
Ç, ç	'ch' as in 'church'
G, g	always hard like 'get', not soft like 'gentle'
ğ	not pronounced; lengthens preceding vowel; ignore it!
H, h	never silent, always unvoiced, as in 'half'
J, j	like French 'j', English 'zh', or the 'z' in 'azure'
S, s	always 'sss' as in 'stress', not 'zzz' as in 'ease'
Ş, ş	'sh' as in 'show'
V, v	soft, almost like a 'w'
W, w	exists only in foreign words; not really Turkish
X, x	only in foreign words; Turks use 'ks' instead

An important point for English speakers to remember is that each Turkish letter is pronounced; there are no diphthongs as in English. Thus the name *Mithat* is pronounced 'meet-HOT', not like the English word 'methought', and Turkish *meshut* is 'mess-HOOT', not 'meh-SHOOT'. Watch out for this! Your eye, used to English double-letter sounds, will keep trying to find them in Turkish, where they don't exist.

These examples also demonstrate that the 'h' is pronounced as an unvoiced aspiration (like the first sound in 'have' or 'heart', the sound a Cockney drops), and it is pronounced every time it occurs; it is never combined to make a diphthong. So your Turkish friend is named not 'aa-meht' but 'ahh-MEHT'; the word *rehber*, 'guide', is not 're-ber' but 'rehh-BEHR'. In the old days, English writers used to spell the name *Achmet* just to get people to breathe that 'h', but it didn't work: people said 'otch-met'. Say, 'a HALF'. Now say 'Ah-MEHT' the same way.

GRAMMAR
Grammar is another matter entirely. Though supremely logical and unencumbered by genders and mountains of exceptions, Turkish structure is so different from that of the Indo-European languages that it is completely unfamiliar at first. A few hints will help you comprehend road and shop signs, schedules and menus.

Suffixes
A Turkish word consists of a root and one or more suffixes added to it. Though in English we have only a few suffixes (-'s for possessive, -s or -es for plural), Turkish has lots and lots of suffixes. Not only that, these suffixes are subject to an unusual system of 'vowel harmony' whereby most of the vowel sounds in a word are made in a similar manner. What this means is that the suffix might be -*lar* when attached to one word, but -*ler* when attached to another; it's the same suffix, though. Sometimes these suffixes are preceded by a 'buffer letter', a 'y' or an 'n'.

Here are some of the noun suffixes you'll encounter most frequently:

-*a*, -*e*	to
-*dan*, -*den*	from
-*dır*, -*dir*, -*dur*, -*dür*	emphatic (ignore it!)
-*(s)ı*, -*(s)i*, -*(s)u*, -*(s)ü*	for object-nouns (ignore it!)
-*(n)ın*, -*(n)in*	possessive
-*lar*, -*ler*	plural
-*lı*, -*li*, -*lu*, -*lü*	with
-*sız*, -*siz*, -*suz*, -*süz*	without

Here are some of the common verb suffixes:

-ar, -er, -ır, -ir, -ur, -ür	simple present tense
-acak, -ecek, -acağ-, -eceğ-	future tense
-dı, -di, -du, -dü	simple past tense
-ıyor-, -iyor-	continuous (like our '-ing')
-mak, -mek	infinitive ending

Nouns
Suffixes can be added to nouns to modify them. The two you will come across most frequently are *-ler* and *-lar*, which form the plural: *otel*, hotel; *oteller*, hotels; *araba*, car; *arabalar*, cars.

Other suffixes modify in other ways: *ev*, house; *Ahmet*, Ahmet; but *Ahmet'in evi*, Ahmet's house. Similarly with *İstanbul* and *banka*: it's *İstanbul Bankası* when the two are used together. You may see *-i, -ı, -u* or *-ü, -si, -sı, -su* or *-sü* added to any noun. A *cami* is a mosque; but the *cami* built by Mehmet Pasha is the *Mehmet Paşa Camii*, with a double 'i'. Ask for a *bira* and the waiter will bring you a bottle of whatever type is available; ask for an *Efes Birası* and that's the brand you'll get.

Yet other suffixes on nouns tell you about direction: *-a* or *-e* means 'to'; *otobüs* is bus, *otobüse* (oh-toh-bews-EH), to the bus; *Bodrum'a* (boh-droom-AH), to Bodrum. The suffix *-dan* or *-den* means 'from': *Ankara'dan*, from Ankara; *köprüden*, from the bridge. Stress is on these final syllables *(-a* or *-dan)* whenever they are used.

Verbs
The infinitive form is with *-mak* or *-mek*, as in *gitmek*, to go; *almak*, to take. The stress in the infinitive is always on the last syllable, 'geet-MEHK', 'ahl-MAHK'.

The simple present form is with *-r*, as in *gider*, he/she/it goes; *giderim*, I go. The suffix *-iyor* means about the same, *gidiyorum*, I'm going. For the future, there's *-ecek* or *-acak*, as in *alacak* (ah-lah-JAHK), he will take (it).

Word Order
The nouns and adjectives usually come first, then the verb; the final suffix on the verb is the subject of the sentence:

I'll go to İstanbul.	*İstanbul'a gideceğim.*
I want to buy (take) a carpet.	*Halı almak istiyorum.* (literally 'Carpet to buy want I')

Some Useful Words & Phrases

Greetings & Civilities

Hello	*Merhaba*	MEHR-hah-bah
Good morning	*Günaydın*	gew-nahy-DUHN
Good day	*Günaydın*	gew-nahy-DUHN
Good evening	*İyi akşamlar*	EE ahk-shahm-LAHR
Good night	*İyi geceler*	EE geh-jeh-LEHR

Goodbye	*Allaha ısmarladık*	ah-LAHS-mahr-lah-duhk (said only by the person departing to go somewhere)
Bon voyage	*Güle güle*	gew-LEH gew-LEH (said only by the person staying behind; literally, 'Go smiling')
Stay happy	*Hoşça kalın*	HOSH-cha KAH-luhn (alternative to goodbye)
What is your name?	*Adınız ne?*	AH-duh-NUHZ neh
How are you?	*Nasılsınız?*	NAHS-suhl-suh-nuhz
I'm fine, thank you.	*İyiyim, teşekkür ederim.*	ee-YEE-yihm, tesh-ek-KEWR eh-dehr-eem
Very well	*Çok iyiyim*	CHOHK ee-YEE-yeem
Pardon me	*Affedersiniz*	af-feh-DEHR-see-neez
May it contribute to your health!	*Afiyet olsun!*	ah-fee-EHT ohl-soon (said to someone sitting down to a meal)
May your life be spared!	*Başınız sağ olsun!*	bah-shuh-nuhz SAAH ohl-soon (said to someone who has just experienced a death in the family)
May your soul be safe from harm!	*Canınız sağ olsun!*	jah-nuh-nuhz SAAH ohl-soon (said to someone who has just accidentally broken something)
May it be in your past!	*Geçmiş olsun!*	gech-MEESH ohl-soon (said to someone who is ill, injured, or otherwise distressed)
May it last for hours!	*Saatler olsun!*	saaht-LEHR ohl-soon (said to someone who just emerged from a bath or shower, a shave or a hair cut. It's a corruption of *sıhhatler olsun*)
In your honour! To your health!	*Şerefinize!*	sheh-rehf-ee-neez-EH

Small Talk

yes	*evet*	eh-VEHT
no	*hayır*	HAH-yuhr
I hear you/I get it.	*Ha!*	HAH
Please.	*Lütfen.*	LEWT-fehn
Thanks.	*Teşekkürler.*	teh-sheh-kewr-LEHR
Thanks.	*Sağ Ol.*	SOWL
Thanks.	*Mersi.*	mehr-SEE
Thank you very much.	*Çok Teşekkür Ederim.*	CHOHK teh-sheh-KEWR eh-deh-reem
You're welcome.	*Bir şey değil.*	beer SHEHY deh-YEEL
Pardon me.	*Affedersiniz.*	AHF-feh-DEHR-see-neez
Pardon.	*Pardon.*	pahr-DOHN
Help yourself.	*Buyurun(uz).*	BOOY-roon-(ooz)
friend	*arkadaş*	AHR-kah-DAHSH
What?	*Ne?*	NEH
How?	*Nasıl?*	NAH-suhl

Who?	*Kim?*	KEEM
Why?	*Niçin, neden?*	NEE-cheen, NEH-dehn
When?	*Ne zaman?*	NEH zah-mahn
Which one?	*Hangisi?*	HAHN-gee-see
What's this?	*Bu ne?*	BOO neh
Where is ... ?	*... nerede?*	NEH-reh-deh
At what time?	*Saat kaçta?*	saht-KAHCH-tah
How much/many?	*Kaç/kaç tane?*	KAHCH/tah-neh
How many liras?	*Kaç lira?*	KAHCH lee-rah
How many hours?	*Kaç saat?*	KAHCH sah-aht
How many minutes?	*Kaç dakika?*	KAHCH dahk-kah
What does it mean?	*Ne demek?*	NEH deh-mehk
Give me ...	*... bana verin*	bah-NAH veh-reen
I want ...	*... istiyorum*	ees-tee-YOH-room
this	*bu(nu)*	boo(NOO)
that	*şu(nu)*	shoo(NOO)
the other	*o(nu)*	oh(NOO)
hot/cold	*sıcak/soğuk*	suh-JAHK/soh-OOK
big/small	*büyük/küçük*	bew-YEWK/kew-CHEWK
new/old	*yeni/eski*	yeh-NEE/ehss-KEE
open/closed	*açık/kapalı*	ah-CHUHK/kah-pah-LUH
not ,,,	*... değil*	deh-YEEL
'It exists'	*var*	VAHR
'It doesn't exist', none	*yok*	YOHK
and	*ve*	VEH
or	*veya*	veh-YAH
good	*iyi*	EE
bad	*fenah*	feh-NAH
beautiful	*güzel*	gew-ZEHL

Countries (Informal Names)

Australia	Avustralya	AH-voo-STRAHL-yah
Austria	Avusturya	AH-voo-STOOR-yah
Belgium	Belçika	BEL-chee-kah
Canada	Kanada	KAH-nah-dalı
Denmark	Danimarka	DAH-nee-MAR-kah
France	Fransa	FRAHN-sah
Germany	Almanya	ahl-MAHN-yah
Greece	Yunanistan	yoo-NAH-nee-stahn
India	Hindistan	HEEN-dee-stahn
Israel	İsrail	EESS-rah-yeel
Italy	Italya	ee-TAHL-yah
Japan	Japonya	zhah-POHN-yah
Netherlands	Holanda	ho-LAHN-dah
New Zealand	Yeni Zelanda	YEH-nee zeh-LAHN-dah
Norway	Norveç	nohr-VECH
South Africa	Güney Afrika	gur-NEY AH-free-kah
Sweden	İsveç	eess-VECH
Switzerland	İsviçre	eess-VEECH-reh

| UK | İngiltere | EEN-geel-TEH-reh |
| USA | Amerika | ah-MEH-ree-kah |

Accommodation

Where is ... ?	... *nerede?*	NEH-reh-deh
Where is a hotel?	*Bir otel nerede?*	BEER oh-TEHL NEH-reh-deh?
Where is the toilet?	*Tuvalet nerede?*	too-vah-LEHT NEH-reh-deh?
Where is the manager?	*Patron nerede?*	pah-TROHN NEH-reh-deh?
Where is someone who knows English?	*İngilizce bilen bir kimse nerede?*	EEN-geh-LEEZ-jeh bee-lehn beer KEEM-seh NEH-reh-deh?

To request a room, say:

I want ...	... *istiyorum.*	ees-tee-YOH-room
a double room	*İki kişilik oda*	ee-KEE kee-shee-leek OH-dah
a twin-bedded room	*Çift yataklı oda*	CHEEFT yah-tahk-LUH OH-dah

If you want to be fully correct, say *istiyoruz* for the plural ('We want ...'). For the courageous, string them together:

We want a quiet bathless double room with a wide (double) bed.
Sakin iki kişilik geniş yataklı banyosuz oda istiyoruz.

room	*oda*	OH-dah
single room	*bir kişilik oda*	BEER kee-shee-leek OH-dah
double room	*iki kişilik oda*	ee-KEE kee-shee-leek OH-dah
triple room	*üç kişilik oda*	EWCH kee-shee-leek OH-dah
room with one bed	*tek yataklı oda*	TEHK yah-tahk-LUH OH-dah
room with two beds	*iki yataklı oda*	ee-KEEyah-tahk-LUH OH-dah
room with twin beds	*çift yataklı oda*	CHEEFT yah-tahk-LUH OH-dah
double bed	*geniş yatak*	geh-NEESH yah-tahk
room with bath	*banyolu oda*	BAHN-yoh-LOO OH-dah
room without bath	*banyosuz oda*	BAHN-yoh-SOOZ OH-dah
room with shower	*duşlu oda*	doosh-LOO OH-dah
room with washbasin	*lavabolu oda*	LAH-vah-boh-LOO oh-dah
a quiet room	*sakin bir oda*	sah-KEEN beer oh-dah
It's very noisy.	*Çok gürültülü.*	CHOHK gew-rewl-tew-lew
What does it cost?	*Kaç lira?*	KAHCH lee-rah
cheaper	*daha ucuz*	dah-HAH oo-jooz
better	*daha iyi*	dah-HAH ee
very expensive	*çok pahalı*	CHOHK pah-hah-luh
bath	*banyo*	BAHN-yoh
Turkish bath	*hamam*	hah-MAHM
shower	*duş*	DOOSH
soap	*sabun*	sah-BOON

shampoo	*şampuan*	SHAHM-poo-AHN
towel	*havlu*	hahv-LOO
toilet paper	*tuvalet kağıdı*	too-vah-LEHT kyah-uh-duh
hot water	*sıcak su*	suh-JAHK soo
cold water	*soğuk su*	soh-OOH soo
clean	*temiz*	teh-MEEZ
not clean	*temiz değil*	teh-MEEZ deh-YEEL
laundry	*çamaşır*	chah-mah-SHUHR
dry cleaning	*kuru temizleme*	koo-ROO teh-meez-leh-meh
central heating	*kalorifer*	kah-LOH-ree-FEHR
air-conditioning	*klima*	KLEE-mah
light(s)	*ışık(lar)*	uh-SHUHK(-LAHR)
light bulb	*ampül*	ahm-PEWL

Getting Around

Where is a/the ... ?	*... nerede?*	NEH-reh-deh
railway station	*Gar/istasyon*	GAHR, ees-tah-SYOHN
bus station	*Otogar*	OH-toh-gahr
cheap hotel	*Ucuz bir otel*	oo-JOOZ beer oh-TEHL
toilet	*Tuvalet*	too-vah-LEHT
restaurant	*Lokanta*	loh-KAHN-tah
post office	*Postane*	POHSS-tah-neh
policeman	*Polis memuru*	poh-LEES meh moo-roo
left luggage/checkroom	*Emanetçi*	EH-mah-NEHT-chee
luggage	*bagaj*	bah-GAHZH
suitcase	*bavul*	bah-VOOL
left	*sol*	SOHL
right	*sağ*	SAH
straight on	*doğru*	doh-ROO
here	*burada*	BOO-rah-dah
there	*şurada*	SHOO-rah-dah
over there	*orada*	OH-rah-dah
near	*yakın*	yah-KUHN
far	*uzak*	oo-ZAHK
a ticket to ...	*... bir bilet*	BEER bee-LEHT
a ticket to İstanbul	*İstanbul'a bir bilet*	ih-STAHN-bool-AH
map	*harita*	HAH-ree-TAH
timetable	*tarife*	tah-ree-FEH
ticket	*bilet*	bee-LEHT
reserved seat	*numaralı yer*	noo-MAH-rah-LUH yehr
1st class	*birinci mevki*	beer-EEN-jee mehv-kee
2nd class	*ikinci mevki*	ee-KEEN-jee mehv-kee
for today	*bugün için*	BOO-gewn ee-cheen
for tomorrow	*yarın için*	yah-ruhn ee-cheen
for Friday	*Cuma günü için*	joo-MAH gew-new ee-cheen
one-way trip	*gidiş*	gee-DEESH
round-trip	*gidiş-dönüş*	gee-DEESH-dew-NURSH
student (ticket)	*talebe (bileti)*	tah-leh-BEH
full-fare (ticket)	*tam (bileti)*	TAHM
daily	*hergün*	HEHR-gurn

| today | *bugün* | BOO-gurn |
| tomorrow | *yarın* | YAHR-uhn |

Getting Around – arrivals & departures

When does it ...?	*Ne zaman ...?*	NEH zah-mahn
depart	*kalkar*	*kahl-KAHR*
arrive	*gelir*	*geh-LEER*
eight o'clock	*saat sekiz*	sah-AHT seh-KEEZ
at 9.30	*saat dokuz buçukta*	sah-AHT doh-KOOZ boo-chook-TAH
in 20 minutes	*yirmi dakikada*	yeer-MEE dahk-kah-dah
How many hours does it take?	*Kaç saat sürer?*	KAHCH sah-aht sew-REHR
... hours	*... saat*	... sah-AHT
... minutes	*... dakika*	... dahk-KAH
early/late	*erken/geç*	ehr-KEHN/GECH
fast/slow	*çabuk/yavaş*	chah-BOOK/yah-VAHSH
upper/lower	*yukarı/aşağı*	yoo-kah-RUH/ah-shah-UH
next/last	*gelecek/son*	geh-leh-JEHK/SOHN

Getting Around – air

airplane	*uçak*	oo-CHAHK
airport	*havaalanı*	hah-VAH-ah-lah-nuh
flight	*uçuş*	oo-CHOOSH
gate	*kapı*	kah-PUH

Getting Around – train

railway	*demiryolu*	deh-MEER-yoh-loo
train	*tren*	tee-REHN
railway station	*gar, istasyon*	GAHR, ees-tahs-YOHN
sleeping car	*yataklı vagon*	yah-tahk-LUH vah-gohn
dining car	*yemekli vagon*	yeh-mehk-LEE vah-gohn
couchette	*kuşet*	koo-SHEHT
no-smoking car	*sigara içilmeyen vagon*	see-GAH-rah eech-EEL-mee-yehn

Getting Around – bus

bus	*otobüs, araba*	oh-toh-BEWSS
bus terminal	*otogar*	OH-toh-gahr
direct (bus)	*direk(t)*	dee-REK
indirect (change buses)	*aktarmalı*	ahk-tahr-mah-LUH

Getting Around – boat

ship	*gemi*	geh-MEE
ferry	*feribot*	FEH-ree-boht
dock	*iskele*	ees-KEH-leh
cabin	*kamara*	KAH-mah-rah
berth	*yatak*	yah-TAHK
class	*mevki, sınıf*	MEHV-kee, suh-nuhf

Getting Around – highway terms

hitchhike	*otostop*	OH-toh-stohp
diesel fuel	*mazot, motorin*	mah-SOHT, MOH-toh-reen
petrol, gasoline	*benzin*	behn-ZEEN
regular	*normal*	nohr-MAHL
super	*süper*	seur-PEHR
motor oil	*motor yağı*	moh-TOHR yah-uh
air (tyres)	*hava (lâstik)*	hah-VAH (lyaass-TEEK)
exhaust (system)	*egzos(t)*	ehk-ZOHSS
headlamp	*far*	FAHR
brake(s)	*fren*	FREHN
steering (-wheel)	*direksiyon*	dee-REHK-see-YOHN
electric repairman	*oto elektrikçi*	oh-TOH ee-lehk-TREEK-chee
tyre repairman	*oto lâstikçi*	oh-TOH lyass-TEEK-chee
car washing	*yıkama*	yuh-kah-MAH
lubrication	*yağlama*	YAH-lah-MAH

Note Towns are marked by blue signs with white lettering; villages are marked by white signs with black lettering. Yellow signs with black lettering mark sights of touristic interest. Yellow signs with blue lettering have to do with village development projects.

Post Office

post office	*postane, postahane*	POHS-tah-NEH
post office	*PTT*	peh-teh-TEH
open	*açık*	ah-CHUHK
closed	*kapalı*	kah-pah-LUH
postcard	*kartpostal*	kahrt-pohs-TAHL
letter	*mektup*	mehk-TOOP
parcel	*koli*	KOH-lee
parcel	*paket*	pah-KEHT
small packet (mail category)	*küçük paket*	kew-CHEWK pah-keht
printed matter (mail category)	*matbua*	MAHT-boo-ah
postage stamp	*pul*	POOL
registered mail	*kayıtlı*	KAH-yuht-LUH
express mail, special delivery	*ekspres*	ehks-PRESS
by air mail	*uçakla, uçak ile*	oo-CHAHK-lah, oo-CHAHK-ee-leh
money order	*havale*	hah-vah-LEH
poste restante	*postrestant*	pohst-rehs-TAHNT
customs	*gümrük*	gewm-REWK
inspection (prior to mailing)	*kontrol*	kohn-TROHL
telephone token (large, medium, small)	*jeton (büyük, orta, küçük)*	zheh-TOHN (bew-YEWK, ohr-TAH, kew-CHEWK)

Bank

money	*para*	PAH-rah
small change	*bozuk para*	boh-ZOOK pah-rah
Turkish liras	*lira*	LEE-rah
dollars	*dolar*	doh-LAHR

foreign currency	*döviz*	durr-VEEZ
cash	*efektif*	eh-fehk-TEEF
cheque	*çek*	CHEK
equivalent	*karşılık*	kahr-shuh-LUHK
exchange	*kambiyo*	KAHM-bee-yoh
exchange rate	*kur*	KOOR
commission	*komisyon*	koh-mees-YOHN
charge, fee	*ücret*	eurj-REHT
purchase	*alış*	ah-LUSH
sale	*veriş*	veh-REESH
stamp	*pul*	POOL
tax	*vergi*	VEHR-gee
identification	*kimlik*	KEEM-leek
cashier	*kasa, vezne*	KAH-sah, VEHZ-neh
working hours	*çalışma saatleri*	chal-ush-MAH sah-aht-leh-ree

Days of the Week

day	*gün*	GEWN
week	*hafta*	hahf-TAH
Sunday	*Pazar*	pah-ZAHR
Monday	*Pazartesi*	pah-ZAHR-teh-see
Tuesday	*Salı*	sah-LUH
Wednesday	*Çarşamba*	char-shahm-BAH
Thursday	*Perşembe*	pehr-shehm-BEH
Friday	*Cuma*	joo-MAH
Saturday	*Cumartesi*	joo-MAHR-teh-see

Months of the Year

month	*ay*	AHY
year	*sene, yıl*	SEH-neh, YUHL
January	*Ocak*	oh-JAHK
February	*Şubat*	shoo-BAHT
March	*Mart*	MAHRT
April	*Nisan*	nee-SAHN
May	*Mayıs*	mah-YUSS
June	*Haziran*	HAH-zee-RAHN
July	*Temmuz*	teh-MOOZ
August	*Ağustos*	AH-oo-STOHSS
September	*Eylül*	ehy-LEWL
October	*Ekim*	eh-KEEM
November	*Kasım*	kah-SUHM
December	*Aralık*	AH-rah-LUHK

Health

hospital	*hastane*	hahss-tah-NEH
dispensary	*sağlık ocağı*	saah-LUHK oh-jah-uh
I'm ill.	*Hastayım.*	hahss-TAH-yuhm
My stomach hurts.	*Karnım ağrıyor.*	kahr-NUHM aah-ruh-yohr
Help me.	*Yardım edin.*	yahr-DUHM eh-den

Shopping

shop	*dükkan*	dyook-KAHN
market	*çarşı*	chahr-SHUH
price	*fiyat*	fee-YAHT
service charge	*servis ücreti*	sehr-VEES ewj-reh-tee
tax	*vergi*	VEHR-gee
cheap/expensive	*ucuz/pahalı*	oo-JOOZ/pah-hah-LUH
very expensive	*çok pahalı*	CHOHK pah-hah-luh
which?	*hangi?*	HAHN-gee
this one	*bunu*	boo-NOO
Do you have ... ?	*... var mı?*	VAHR muh
We don't have ...	*... yok*	YOHK
I'll give you ...	*... vereceğim*	VEH-reh-JEH-yeem
this much	*bu kadar*	BOO kah-dahr

Children

child(ren)	*çocuk(lar)*	CHO-jook-(LAHR)
baby	*bebek*	beh-BEHK
diaper	*bebek bezi*	beh-BEHK beh-zee
nursery	*kreş*	KRESH

Cardinal Numbers

0	*sıfır*	SUH-fuhr
¼	*çeyrek*	chehy-REHK
½	*yarım*	YAH-ruhm (used alone, as 'I want half')
½	*buçuk*	boo-CHOOK (always used with a whole number, as '1½', bir buçuk)
1	*bir*	BEER
2	*iki*	ee-KEE
3	*üç*	EWCH
4	*dört*	DURRT
5	*beş*	BEHSH
6	*altı*	ahl-TUH
7	*yedi*	yeh-DEE
8	*sekiz*	seh-KEEZ
9	*dokuz*	doh-KOOZ
10	*on*	OHN
11	*on bir*	ohn BEER
12	*on iki*	ohn ee-KEE
13	*on üç*	ohn EWCH
20	*yirmi*	yeer-MEE
30	*otuz*	oh-TOOZ
40	*kırk*	KUHRK
50	*elli*	ehl-LEE
60	*altmış*	ahlt-MUSH
70	*yetmiş*	yeht-MEESH

80	*seksen*	sehk-SEHN
90	*doksan*	dohk-SAHN
100	*yüz*	YEWZ
200	*iki yüz*	ee-KEE yewz
1000	*bin*	BEEN
2000	*iki bin*	ee-KEE been
10,000	*on bin*	OHN been
1,000,000	*milyon*	meel-YOHN

Ordinal Numbers

Ordinal numbers consist of the number plus the suffix *-inci, -ıncı, -uncu* or *-üncü*, depending upon 'vowel harmony'.

first	*birinci*	beer-EEN-jee
second	*ikinci*	ee-KEEN-jee
sixth	*altıncı*	ahl-TUHN-juh
13th	*onüçüncü*	ohn-ew-CHEWN-jew
100th	*yüzüncü*	yewz-EWN-jew

Turkish Food

Except in the fanciest restaurants, Turks don't have much use for menus. This is a society in which the waiter *(garson,* gahr-SOHN) is supposed to know his business and to help you order. Nonetheless, the waiter will bring a menu *(menü,* meh-NEW or *yemek listesi,* yeh-MEHK lees-teh-see) if you ask for one. The menu will at least give you some prices so you'll know what you will be asked to pay.

Otherwise, you may choose from the menu several times only to get the response *Yok!* (YOHK, None!). The menu, as I said, is not much use. Instead, the waiter will probably say *Gel! Gel!* (Come! Come!) and lead you into the kitchen for a look. In the glass-fronted refrigerator cabinets you'll see the şiş kebap, köfte, bonfile steaks, lamb chops, liver, kidneys and fish which are in supply. Also in the cabinet may be the cheeses, salads and vegetable dishes, if meant to be served cold. Then he'll lead you right to the fire for a look at the stews, soups, pastas and pilavs. With sign language, you'll have everything you want in no time. It's a good idea to ask prices.

If you don't eat meat, ask *Etsiz yemek var mı?* (eht-SEEZ yeh-mehk VAHR muh, Have you any meatless dishes?), or say *Hiç et yiyemem* (HEECH eht yee-YEH-mehm, I can't eat any meat).

Some general words to know are:

restaurant	*lokanta*	loh-KAHN-tah
pastry-shop	*pastane*	PAHSS-tah-neh
'oven' (bakery)	*fırın*	FUH-ruhn
'pizza' place	*pideci*	PEE-deh-jee
köfte restaurant	*köfteci*	KURF-teh-jee
kebap restaurant	*kebapçı*	keh-BAHP-chuh

snack shop	*büfe*	bew-FEH
alcoholic drinks served	*içkili*	eech-kee-LEE
no alcohol served	*içkisiz*	eech-kee-SEEZ
family (ladies') dining room	*aile salonu*	ah-yee-LEH sah-loh-noo
no single men allowed	*aileye mahsustur*	ah-yee-LEH mah-SOOS-tuhr
breakfast	*kahvahltt*	KAHH-vahl-TUH
lunch	*öğle yemeği*	ury-LEH yeh-meh-yee
supper	*akşam yemeği*	ahk-SHAHM yeh-meh-yee
to eat; meal, dish	*yemek*	yeh-MEHK
portion, serving	*porsyon*	pohr-SYOHN
fork	*çatal*	chah-TAHL
knife	*bıçak*	buh-CHAHK
spoon	*kaşık*	kah-SHUHK
plate	*tabak*	tah-BAHK
glass	*bardak*	bahr-DAHK
bill, cheque	*hesap*	heh-SAHP
service charge	*servis ücreti*	sehr-VEES ewj-rch-tee
tax	*vergi*	VEHR-gee
tip	*bahşiş*	bah-SHEESH
error	*yanlış*	yahn-LUSH
small change	*bozuk para*	boh-ZOOK pah-rah

Here is a guide to restaurant words, arranged (more or less) in the order of a Turkish menu and a Turkish meal. I've given the names of the courses (*çorba, et* etc) in the singular form; you may see them in the plural (*çorbalar, etler* etc).

Soup

soup	*çorba*	CHOHR-bah
broth with mutton	*haşlama*	hahsh-lah-MAH
chicken soup	*tavuk çorbası*	tah-VOOK chor-bah-suh
egg & lemon soup	*düğün çorbası*	dew-EWN chor-bah-suh
fish soup	*balık çorbası*	bah-LUHK chor-bah-suh
lentil soup	*mercimek çorbası*	mehr-jee-MEHK chor-bah-suh
lentil & rice soup	*ezo gelin çorbası*	EH-zoh GEH-leen chor-bah-suh
mutton broth with egg	*et suyu (yumurtalı)*	EHT soo-yoo, yoo-moor-tah-LUH
tripe soup	*işkembe çorbası*	eesh-KEHM-beh chor-bah-suh
trotter soup	*paça*	PAH-chah
tomato soup	*domates çorbası*	doh-MAH-tess chor-bah-suh
vegetable soup	*sebze çorbası*	SEHB-zeh chor-bah-suh
vermicelli soup	*şehriye çorbası*	shehh-ree-YEH chor-bah-suh
yoghurt & barley soup	*yayla çorbası*	YAHY-lah chor-bah-suh

Hors d'Oeuvres

Meze (MEH-zeh), or hors d'oeuvres, can include almost anything, and you can easily – and delightfully – make an entire meal of meze. Often you will be brought a tray from which you can choose those you want.

aubergine/eggplant puree	*patlıcan salatası*	paht-luh-JAHN sah-lah-tah-suh
cold white beans vinaigrette	*pilaki, piyaz*	pee-LAH-kee

flaky pastry	*börek*	bur-REHK
red caviar in mayonnaise	*tarama salatası*	tah-rah-MAH sah-lah-tah-suh
stuffed squash/marrow	*kabak dolması*	kah-BAHK dohl-mah-suh
stuffed vine leaves	*yaprak dolması*	yah-PRAHK dohl-mah-suh
	yalancı dolması	yah-LAHN-juh dohl-mah-suh
stuffed with lamb (hot)	*etli*	eht-LEE
stuffed with rice (cold)	*zeytinyağlı*	zehy-teen-yah-LUH
white cheese	*beyaz peynir*	bey-AHZ pehy-neer

Fish

A menu is of no use when ordering fish (*balık*, bah-LUHK). You must ask the waiter what's fresh, and then ask the approximate price. The fish will be weighed, and the price computed at the day's per-kg rate. Sometimes you can haggle. Buy fish in season (*mevsimli*, mehv-seem-LEE), as fish out of season are very expensive.

Aegean tuna	*trança*	TRAHN-chah
anchovy (fresh)	*hamsi*	HAHM-see
black bream	*karagöz*	kah-rah-GURZ
bluefish	*lüfer*	lew-FEHR
caviar	*havyar*	hahv-YAHR
crab	*yengeç*	yehn-GECH
grey mullet	*kefal*	keh-FAHL
lobster	*istakoz*	uhss-tah-KOHZ
mackerel	*uskumru*	oos-KOOM-roo
mussels	*midye*	MEED-yeh
plaice	*pisi*	PEE-see
red coralfish	*mercan*	mehr-JAHN
red mullet	*barbunya*	bahr-BOON-yah
roe, red caviar	*tarama*	tah-rah-MAH
sardine (fresh)	*sardalya*	sahr-DAHL-yah
sea bass	*levrek*	lehv-REHK
shrimp	*karides*	kah-REE-dess
sole	*dil balığı*	DEEL bah-luh
swordfish	*kılıç*	kuh-LUHCH
trout	*alabalık*	ah-LAH-bah-luhk
turbot	*kalkan*	kahl-KAHN
tunny, bonito	*palamut*	PAH-lah-moot

Meat & Kebap

In *kebap* (keh-BAHP), the meat (*et*, EHT) is always lamb, ground or in chunks; preparation, spices and extras (onions, peppers, bread) make the difference among the kebaps. Some may be ordered *yoğurtlu* (yoh-oort-LOO), with a side-serving of yoghurt.

aubergine/eggplant & meat	*patlıcan kebap*	paht-luh-JAHN keh-bahp
beef	*sığır*	suh-UHR
boiling chicken	*tavuk*	tah-VOOK
chateaubriand	*şatobriyan*	sha-TOH-bree-YAHN
chicken in walnut sauce	*çerkez tavuğu*	cher-KEHZ tah-voo
cutlet (usually lamb)	*pirzola*	peer-ZOH-lah
döner with tomato sauce	*bursa kebap*	BOOR-sah keh-bahp

flat bread with minced lamb	*etli pide/ekmek*	eht-LEE PEE-deh, ehk-MEHK
grilled minced lamb patties	*köfte*	KURF-teh
kidney	*böbrek*	bur-BREHK
lamb stew	*tas kebap*	TAHSS keh-bahp
lamb & vegetables in paper	*kağıt kebap*	kyah-UHT keh-bahp
liver	*ciğer*	jee-EHR
meat & vegetable stew	*güveç*	gew-VECH
milk-fed lamb	*(süt) kuzu*	koo-ZOO (SEWT)
mixed grill (lamb)	*karışık ızgara*	kah-ruh-shuk uhz-gah-rah
pit-roasted lamb	*tandır kebap*	tahn-DUHR keh-bahp
pork (forbidden to Muslims)	*domuz*	doh-MOOZ
ram's 'eggs' (testicles)	*koç yumurtası*	KOHCH yoo-moor-tah-suh
roast lamb with onions	*orman kebap*	ohr-MAHN keh-bahp
roast skewered chicken	*tavuk/piliç şiş*	tah-VOOK/ pee-LEECH SHEESH
roast skewered lamb	*şiş kebap*	SHEESH keh-bahp
roasting chicken	*piliç*	pee-LEECH
small fillet beefsteak	*bonfile*	bohn-fee-LEH
spicy-hot roast köfte	*Adana kebap*	ah-DAH-nah keh-bahp
spit-roasted chicken slices	*tavuk/piliç döner*	tah-VOOK/pee-LEECH dur-NEHR
spit-roasted lamb slices	*döner kebap*	dur-NEHR keh-bahp
sun-dried, spiced beef	*pastırma*	pahss-TUHR-mah
tiny bits of skewered lamb	*çöp kebap*	CHURP keh-bahp
veal	*dana*	DAH-nah
wok-fried lamb	*saç kavurma*	SAHTCH kah-voor-mah
wienerschnitzel	*şinitzel*	shee-NEET-zehl

Salads

Each of the Turkish names would be followed by the word *salata* (sah-LAH-tah) or *salatası*. You may be asked if you prefer it *sirkeli* (SEER-keh-LEE), with vinegar or *limonlu* (LEE-mohn-LOO), with lemon juice; most salads (except *söğüş*) come with olive oil. If you don't like hot peppers, say *bibersiz* (BEE-behr-SEEZ), though this often doesn't work.

chopped mixed salad	*karışık*	kah-ruh-SHUHK
	çoban	choh-BAHN
green salad	*yeşil*	yeh-SHEEL
mayonnaise, peas, carrots	*Amerikan*	ah-meh-ree-KAHN
	Rus	ROOSS
pickled vegetables	*turşu*	toor-SHOO
roast aubergine/eggplant puree	*patlıcan*	paht-luh-JAHN
romaine lettuce	*marul*	mah-ROOL
sheep's brain	*beyin*	behy-EEN
sliced vegetables, no sauce	*söğüş*	sur-EWSH
tomato & cucumber salad	*domates salatalık*	doh-MAH-tess sah-LAH-tah-luhk

Vegetables

vegetable	*sebze*	sehb-ZEH
cabbage	*lahana*	lah-HAH-nah

carrot	*havuç*	hah-VOOCH
cauliflower	*karnabahar*	kahr-NAH-bah-hahr
cucumber	*salatalık*	sah-LAH-tah-luhk
green beans	*taze fasulye*	tah-ZEH fah-sool-yah
marrow/squash	*kabak*	kah-BAHK
okra	*bamya*	BAHM-yah
onion	*soğan*	soh-AHN
peas	*bezelye*	beh-ZEHL-yeh
peppers	*biber*	bee-BEHR
potato	*patates*	pah-TAH-tess
radish	*turp*	TOORP
red beans	*barbunye*	bahr-BOON-yeh
spinach	*ıspınak*	uhs-spuh-NAHK
tomato	*domates*	doh-MAH-tess
white beans	*kuru fasulye*	koo-ROO fah-sool-yah

Fruit

fruit	*meyva, meyve*	mehy-VAH
apple	*elma*	ehl-MAH
apricot	*kayısı*	kahy-SUH
banana	*muz*	MOOZ
cherry	*kiraz*	kee-RAHZ
fig	*incir*	een-JEER
grapefruit	*greyfurut*	GREY-foo-root
grapes	*üzüm*	ew-ZEWM
morello (sour cherry)	*vişne*	VEESH-neh
orange	*portakal*	pohr-tah-KAHL
peach	*şeftali*	shef-tah-LEE
pear	*armut*	ahr-MOOT
pomegranate	*nar*	NAHR
quince	*ayva*	ahy-VAH
strawberries	*çilek*	chee-LEHK
tangerine, mandarin	*mandalin*	mahn-dah-LEEN
watermelon	*karpuz*	kahr-POOZ
yellow melon	*kavun*	kah-VOON

Sweets

sweet, dessert	*tatlı*	taht-LUH
baked caramel custard	*krem karamel*	KREHM kah-rah-MEHL
baked rice pudding (cold)	*fırın sütlaç*	foo-roon SEWT-lach
'bottom of the pot' (cold baked pudding)	*kazandibi*	kah-ZAHN-dee-bee
cake	*kek*	KEHK
candied marrow/squash	*kabak tatlısı*	kah-BAHK TAHT-luh-suh
cheese cake	*peynir tatlısı*	pehy-NEER TAHT-luh-suh
chocolate pudding	*krem şokolada*	KREHM shoh-koh-LAH-dah
crumpet in syrup	*ekmek kadayıf*	ehk-MEHK kah-dah-yuhf
flaky pastry, nuts & milk	*güllaç*	gewl-LACH
fruit	*meyve*	mehy-VEH

ice cream	*dondurma*	dohn-DOOR-mah
'Lady's navel', doughnut in syrup	*kadın göbeği*	kah-DUHN gur-beh-yee
many-layer pie, honey, nuts	*baklava*	bahk-lah-VAH
milk & nut pudding	*keşkül*	kehsh-KEWL
pastry	*pasta*	PAHSS-tah
rice flour & rosewater pudding	*muhallebi*	moo-HAH-leh-bee
rice pudding	*sütlaç*	sewt-LAHCH
saffron & rice sweet	*zerde*	zehr-DEH
semolina sweet	*helva*	hehl-VAH
semolina cake in syrup	*hurma tatlısı*	hoor-MAH
shredded wheat in syrup	*tel kadayıf*	TEHL kah-dah-yuhf
shredded wheat with pistachios & honey	*burma kadayıf*	boor-MAH kah-dah-yuhf
stewed fruit	*komposto*	kohm-POHSS-toh
sweet of milk, rice & chicken	*tavuk göğsü*	tah-VOOK gur-sew
Turkish delight	*lokum*	loh-KOOM
walnut, raisin, pea pudding	*aşure*	ah-shoo-REH
yoghurt & egg pudding	*yoğurt tatlısı*	yoh-OORT taht-luh-suh

Other Dishes & Condiments

aubergine baked with onions & tomatoes	*imam bayıldı*	ee-MAHM bah-yuhl-duh
aubergine & lamb (hot)	*karnıyarık*	KAHR-nuh-yah-RUHK
aubergine & lamb pie	*musakka*	moo-sah-KAH
biscuits	*bisküvi*	BEES-koo-VEE
black pepper	*siyah biber*	see-YAH bee-behr
	kara biber	kah-RAH bee-behr
bread	*ekmek*	ehk-MEHK
butter	*tereyağı*	TEH-reh-yah
cheese	*peynir*	pehy-NEER
'cigarette' fritters	*sigara*	see-GAH-rah
flaky or fried pastry	*börek (-ği)*	bur-REHK
fruit jam	*reçel*	reh-CHEHL
garlic	*sarmısak*	SAHR-muh-SAHK
honey	*bal*	BAHL
ice	*buz*	BOOZ
lemon	*limon*	lee-MOHN
macaroni, noodles	*makarna*	mah-KAHR-nah
mild yellow cheese	*kaşar peynir*	kah-SHAHR pey-neer
mustard	*hardal*	hahr-DAHL
oil, fat	*yağ*	YAH
olive oil	*zeytinyağı*	zehy-TEEN-yah-uh
olives	*zeytin*	zehy-TEEN
pastry (not noodles)	*pasta*	PAHSS-tah
pizza, flat bread	*pide*	PEE-deh
salt	*tuz*	TOOZ
spaghetti	*spaket*	spah-KEHT

stuffed (vegetable)	... *dolma(sı)*	DOHL-mah(-suh)
cabbage leaves	*lahana*	lah-HAH-nah
green pepper	*biber*	bee-BEHR
marrow/squash	*kabak*	kah-BAHK
vine leaves	*yalancı*	yah-LAHN-juh
vine leaves	*yaprak*	yah-PRAHK
sugar, candy, sweets	*şeker*	sheh-KEHR
vinegar	*sirke*	SEER-keh
white (sheep's) cheese	*beyaz peynir*	bey-AHZ pey-neer
with ground lamb	*kıymalı*	kuhy-mah-LUH
with white cheese	*peynirli*	pehy-neer-LEE
water	*su*	SOO
yoghurt	*yoğurt*	yoh-OORT
yoghurt & grated cucumber	*cacık*	jah-JUHK

Drinks

İçki (eech-KEE) usually refers to alcoholic beverages, *meşrubat* (mehsh-roo-BAHT) to soft drinks. When waiters ask *İçecek?* or *Ne içeceksiniz?*, they're asking what you'd like to drink.

As for Turkish coffee *(kahve,* kahh-VEH) you must order it according to sweetness: the sugar is mixed in during the brewing, not afterwards. You can drink it *sade* (sah-DEH), without sugar; *az* (AHZ), if you want just a bit of sugar; *orta* (ohr-TAH), with a middling amount; *çok* or *şekerli* or even *çok şekerli* (CHOHK sheh-kehr-LEE), with lots of sugar. When the coffee arrives, the waiter may well have confused the cups, and you may find yourself exchanging with your dinnermates.

Nescafé is readily found throughout Turkey but tends to be expensive, often around 70c per cup.

American coffee	*Amerikan*	ah-meh-ree-KAHN
aniseed-flavoured brandy	*rakı*	rah-KUH
beer	*bira*	BEE-rah
dark	*siyah*	see-YAH
light	*beyaz*	bey-AHZ
draught ('keg')	*fıçı bira*	fuh-CHUH bee-rah
coffee	*kahve(si)*	kah-VEH(-see)
coffee & milk	*Fransz*	frahn-SUHZ
fizzy mineral water	*maden sodası*	mah-DEHN soh-dah-suh
fruit juice	*meyva suyu*	mey-VAH soo-yoo
gin	*cin*	JEEN
hot milk & tapioca root	*sahlep*	sah-LEHP
instant coffee	*neskafe*	NEHSS-kah-feh
lemonade	*limonata*	lee-moh-NAH-tah
milk	*süt*	SEWT
mineral water	*maden suyu*	mah-DEHN soo-yoo
spring water	*menba suyu*	mehn-BAH soo-yoo
tea	*çay*	CHAH-yee
thick millet drink	*boza*	BOH-zah
Turkish coffee	*Türk kahvesi*	TEWRK kahh-veh-see
vermouth	*vermut*	vehr-MOOT
vodka	*votka*	VOHT-kah
water	*su*	SOO

whisky	*viski*	VEE-skee
wine	*şarap*	shah-RAHP
red	*kırmızı*	kuhr-muh-ZUH
rose	*roze*	roh-ZEH
sparkling	*köpüklü*	kur-pewk-LEW
white	*beyaz*	bey-AHZ
yoghurt drink	*ayran*	AH-yee-RAHN

Cooking Terms

baked, oven-roasted	*fırın*	fuh-RUHN
boiled, stewed	*haşlama*	hahsh-lah-MAH
broiled	*kızartma*	kuh-ZAHRT-mah
charcoal grilled	*ızgara*	uhz-GAH-rah
cold	*soğuk*	soh-OOK
hot, warm	*sıcak*	suh-JAHK
puree	*ezme(si)*	ehz-MEH(-see)
roasted	*rosto*	ROHSS-toh
steamed, poached	*buğlama*	BOO-lah-MAH
well-done, -cooked	*iyi pişmiş,*	ee-YEE peesh-meesh,
	pişkin	peesh-KEEN
with egg	*yumurtalı*	*yoo-moor-tah-LUH*
with ground lamb	*kıymalı*	*kuhy-mah-LUH*
with cheese	*peynirli*	pehy-neer-LEE
with meat	*etli*	eht-LEE
with sauce	*soslu,*	sohss-LOO,
	terbiyeli	TEHR-bee-yeh-LEE
with savoury tomato sauce	*salçalı*	*sahl-chah-LUH*
with yoghurt	*yoğurtlu*	YOH-oort-LOO

Glossary

Here, with definitions, are some unfamiliar words and abbreviations you might meet in the text or on the road in Turkey:

acropolis – 'high city', hilltop citadel and temples of a classic Hellenic city

agora – open space for commerce and politics in a classic Hellenic city

aile salonu – 'family room', for couples, families and single women in a Turkish restaurant

akaryakıt – 'liquid fuel', petrol (gasoline), diesel etc.

Allah korusun – God protect me!

apse – semicircular recess for the altar in a church

araç çıkabilir – vehicles entering

arasta – row of shops near a mosque, the rent from which supports the mosque

askeri araç – military vehicle

banliyö – suburb(an)

bedesten – vaulted, fireproof market enclosure where valuable goods are kept

bouleuterion – place of assemby, council meeting-place in a classic Hellenic city

cami(i) – mosque

caravanserai – 'caravan palace', large fortified way-station for caravans

çarşı – market, bazaar

çeşme – spring, fountain

çevreyolu – ring road, bypass

dağ(ı) – mountain

Damsız Girilmez – 'No single males admitted' (Turkish nightclubs)

DDY – Devlet Demiryolları, (Turkish) State Railways; same as TCDD

deniz – sea

deniz otobüsü – hydrofoil

Denizyolları – Turkish Maritime Lines

Dikkat! Yavaş! – Careful! Slow!

dinlenme parkı – (highway) rest area

eczane – chemist's/pharmacy

eski – old (thing, not person)

eyvan – large recess, vaulted or domed, open to a courtyard

figure malzeme – gravel mound at roadside

gazino – Turkish nightclub (not for gambling)

geçit, -di – mountain pass

geniş araç – wide vehicle

hamam(ı) – Turkish steam bath

han(ı) – inn or caravanserai in a town or city

harabe(ler) – ruin(s)

harem – family/women's quarters of a residence (cf *selamlık*)

hazır yemek – food prepared and kept hot on a steam table

heyelan (bölgesi) – landslide (zone)

hisar – fortress, citadel; same as *kale*

Hünkar Mahfili – sultan's special prayer-place in a mosque

imam – prayer leader, Muslim cleric

imaret(i) – soup kitchen for the poor

iskele(si) – landing-place, wharf, quay

İşhanı – office building

kale(si) – fortress, citadel; same as *hisar*

kapı(sı) – door, gate

kaplıca – thermal spring or baths

karayolları – highways

kat – storey (of a building)

kat oto parkı – multi-level parking garage

Katma Değer Vergisi – Value Added Tax

kervansaray(ı) – Turkish for caravanserai

kilim – napless woven wool mat

kilise(si) – church

konak, konağı – mansion, government headquarters

köprü – bridge

köşk(ü) – pavilion, villa

köy(ü) – village

kule(si) – tower

külliye(si) – mosque complex including seminary, hospital, soup kitchen etc

kümbet – vault, cupola, dome; tomb topped by this

küşet(li) – (railway carriage having) couchette(s), shelf-like beds

liman(ı) – harbour

Maaşallah – Wonder of God! (said in admiration or to avert the evil eye)

mağara(sı) – cave

mahalle(si) – neighbourhood, district of a city

medrese(si) – Muslim theological seminary

mescit, -di – prayer room, small mosque

meydan(ı) – public square, open place

meyhane – wine shop, tavern

mihrab – niche in a mosque indicating the direction of Mecca

mimber – pulpit in a mosque

minare(si) – minaret, tower from which Muslims are called to prayer

müezzin – cantor who sings the ezan, or call to prayer

narthex – enclosed porch or vestibule at the entrance to a church

nave – middle aisle of a church

necropolis – 'city of the dead', cemetery

nufüs – population

oda(sı) – room

odeon – odeum, small classical theatre for musical performances

okul taşıtı – school bus

otogar – bus terminal

otoyol – motorway, limited-access divided highway

pansiyon – pension, B&B, guesthouse

park yeri – car park

patika – trail, footpath

pazar(ı) – weekly market, bazaar

PTT – 'posta, telefon, telğraf': post, telephone and telegraph office

rakım – altitude above sea level

Ramazan – Muslim lunar holy month

şadırvan – fountain where Muslims perform ritual ablutions

saray(ı) – palace

sebil – public fountain or water kiosk

şehir – city; municipal

selamlık – public/male quarters of a residence (cf harem)

Selçuk – Seljuk, of or pertaining to the Seljuk Turks

sufi – Muslim mystic, member of a mystic ('dervish') brotherhood

sürücü adayı – student (learner) driver

tatil köyü – holiday village

TC – Türkiye Cumhuriyeti (Turkish Republic), designates an official office or organisation

TCDD – Türkiye Cumhuriyeti Devlet Demiryolları, Turkish State Railways; same as DDY

tehlikeli madde – dangerous cargo

Tekel – government alcoholic beverage & tobacco company

tekke(si) – dervish lodge

THY – Türk Hava Yolları, Turkish Airlines

tırmanma şeridi – overtaking lane

TML – Turkish Maritime Lines, Denizyolları

TRT – Türkiye Radyo ve Televizyon, Turkish broadcasting corporation

tuff, tufa – soft stone laid down as volcanic ash

tuğra – sultan's monogram, imperial signature

türbe(si) – tomb, grave, mausoleum

uzun araç – long vehicle

valilik, valiliği – provincial government headquarters; same as vilayet

vilayet – provincial government headquarters; same as valilik

yalı – waterside residence

yayla – mountain pasture, usually used in summer only

yasak bölge – forbidden zone

yol onarımı – road repairs

yol yapımı – road construction

yol(u) – road, way

zaviye – dervish hostel

Historic Place Names

HISTORIC NAME	MODERN NAME	HISTORIC NAME	MODERN NAME
Adrianople	Edirne	Laodicea	Laodikya
Aintab	Antep, Gaziantep		(Goncalı, Denizli)
Alexandretta	İskenderun	Lycia	Fethiye region
Amida	Diyarbakır	Lydia	Manisa region
Angora	Ankara	Magnesia-ad-Sipylum	Manisa
Antioch	Antakya	Meander (River)	Büyük Menderes
Antioch-in-Pisidia	Yalvaç	Mediterranean Sea	Akdeniz
Antiphellus	Kaş	Miletus	Milet
Ararat, Mt	Ağrı Dağı	Mylasa	Milas
Assos	Behramkale	Myra	Demre, Kale
Attaleia	Antalya	Nicaea	İznik
Black Sea	Karadeniz	Nicomedia	İzmit
Bosphorus	İstanbul Boğazı	Nimrod, Mt	Nemrut Dağı
Byzantium	İstanbul	Olympus, Mt	Uludağ
Caesarea	Mazaca Kayseri	Pamphylia	Antalya region
Cappadocia	Kapadokya	Paphlagonia	Sinop region
	(Nevşehir region)	Pergamon, Pergamum	Bergama
Caria	Milas region	Philadelphia	Alaşehir
Chalcedon	Kadıköy	Phocea	Foça
Cilicia	Silifke region	Phoenicus	Finike
Constantinople	İstanbul	Phrygia	Burdur region
Dardanelles	Çanakkale Boğazı	Proussa, Prusa	Bursa
Dorylaeum	Eskişehir	Sardis	Sart
Edessa	Urfa, Şanlıurfa	Sebasteia	Sivas
Ephesus	Efes, Selçuk	Seleucia of Isauria	Silifke
Euphrates	(River) Fırat	Sesamos Amastris	Amasra
Galatia	Ankara region	Sinope	Sinop
Gallipoli	Gelibolu	Smyrna	İzmir
Halicarnassus	Bodrum	Tarsus	Tarsus
Harran	Altınbaşak	Telmessos	Fethiye
Hattuşaş	Boğazkale	Theodosiopolis	Erzurum
Hellespont	Çanakkale Boğazı	Thrace	Trakya
Hierapolis	Pamukkale	Thyatira	Akhisar
Iconium	Konya	Tigris (River)	Dicle
Ida, Mt	Kaz Dağı	Tralles	Aydın
Ionia	İzmir region	Trebizond	Trabzon
Ilium	Truva	Troy	Truva
Kanesh	Kültepe	Xanthos	Kınık

Index

738 Index

THANKS

Thanks must go to all the following travellers and others (apologies if we've misspelt your name) who used the last edition of this book and wrote to us with information, comments and suggestions. To those whose names have been omitted through oversight, apologies – your time and efforts are appreciated.

Jeroen Aarssen (NL), Gert Aberson (NL), Russell B Adams (UK), Simon Allen (UK), Graham Aller (Aus), Sami Akar (Tur), Erol Akarsh, Mustafa Akyil (Tur), Babak Alizadeh, Lone Andersen (Dk), Ralf Andersen (Dk), Phil, Hilary & Pip Andre (UK), Duncan Angus (UK), Jackie Aplin (UK), Graeme Archer (Aus), MJ Armitage (UK), Georgina Arnold (UK), Mark Ashby (NZ), Sait Aslan (Tur), Beatriz Atesdagli (Tur), Athena Pension (Tur), Steven Augart (USA), P & J Aughey (UK), Lisa Austin (D), Gokhan Aydin (Tur), Karen Ayliffe (UK), Yeni Aziziye (Tur), Phil Baarda (UK), Mette Marie Bach (Dk), Sharon Bacich (Aus), Larry Bailey (USA), Mary Ballantyne (C), Wolfgang Banisch (D), Heidi Banker (Tur), Emrah Banligil (Tur), Martha Barchyn (C), Teye Barhema (NL), Giles Barnard (UK), Judith Barnes (UK), Judy Barton (UK), Hikmet & Fusun Barut (Tur), A Barzilai (Isr), Bonnie Baskin (USA), Teddy Bayersborgen (NL), AL Bayliss (UK), Sahin Baynut (Tur), Nicola Beamish (Aus), Glen Beattie (Aus), William Bechhoefer (USA), Kylie Beckhouse (Aus), Mark S Beiley (UK), Don & Andy Bell (UK), Kirsten Bender (Tur), Garrett Bennett (Aus), EM Bentley (UK), Michael Berendt (Dk), Pollak Bernhard (A), Siebetje Bendien (NL), Diana Benedetto (I), Karen & Terry Bennet-Wright (C), Lorne Berman (C), Gerald Berstell (USA), Hope Beverstein, William Biermaier (USA), Lynn Biggar (UK), Rosemery Biggs (UK), Dr Richard Birchenough, Nigel Bird (UK), Tim Bird (UK), Peter Blackford (Aus), Simon & Peta Blake, Ann & Emily Blake-Dyle (UK), Eugene Blanchard (USA), Marianne Boesen (Dk), Cathy Bolger (USA), Claude Bollag (CH), Osman Boluk (Tur), Patrick Boman (F), Tad Boniecki (Aus), Lianne Bosch (NL), Tamara Boslia (I), Douwe Bouma (NL), Simon Bourke (UK), Ghee Bowman (UK), Ray Bradley (C), Margaret Bramley (NZ), Dr John R Braun (USA), Patti Brawn (C), Doreen Brierbrier (USA), Jari Brinkell (S), D Brown (USA), Joanna Brown (UK), Peter Brown (UK), Steve Brown (UK), Cheree Brown (Aus), Janet Cameron (Aus), Brendan Carmel (Aus), Peter Carstens (NL), Anthony Carter (Aus), MVE Chan (Sin), Mr & Mrs F C Charles (UK), David & Marie Charter, Peter Chesik (UK), Terri Cieka (UK), A Citak (Tur), Richard S Clark (USA), J Clarksen (UK), Tim Colby (C), John Connelly (USA), Jim Connor (UK), Jane Corlett (UK),

Annie Cornet (B), Chris Cowan (USA), A Cox (UK), Simon Crivick (UK), Gail Cryer (C), Elaine Cullen (USA), Mario D'Souza (UK), David Dano (Dk), Janet Davies (UK), Michael Davies (Aus), Graeme Davis (UK), Greet de Bolle (B), Lynne de Lacy (UK), Gerrit Jan de Roo (NL), Alexandra de Stefano (UK), Olivia & Jacque de Vox (SA), Carol Deberding (Aus), Graham Dekker (NZ), Petri Dermout (NL), R Dermus (Tur), Gerard Detusik (B), Osman Ramazon Dikici (Tur), Michelle Dillon (UK), Susannah Dillon (UK), Lani & Aharon Dinun (C), Tony Dolinson (UK), Peter Donaldson (UK), Kemal Donmez (Tur), Ray Donnelly (UK), Mary Doyle (USA), John Duggan (UK), Sheila Durkin (UK), JC Dursley (UK), Don & Pat Eastly (USA), Paula & Edward Echeverria (USA), Dr HM Edge (UK), Ralph Elliot (USA), Wendy Elrick (NL), Amir Elron (Isr), J Engelander (NL), Tony English (UK), Peter & Monica Evans (UK), Gungor Evrensel (Tur), Robert Falk (Aus), Gilliam Farjounel (F), Molly Farr (UK), Edwin Feiat (NL), MH Ferguson (NZ), Jaop Flohil (NL), Jez Ford (UK), John Forde (Tur), Lynda Forster (CH), Knut Fougner (N), Joan Francis (Aus), Rob Frank (NL), Mark Frauden (NL), Tania Friedman (Aus), Mustafa Gakiroglu (Tur), V Galet (B), Jim Gannon (UK), Mike Gardom (UK), Wanda & Curt Garrison (C), Dominick Garton (UK), John Gerch (USA), Renaud Georges (F), Christos Geropoulos (Gr), Victor Gilevitis (Aus), Elisabeth Glasgow (UK), Harrey Goldley (UK), Joe Gordon (USA), Frank Gould (UK), b Graham (UK), Stephen Graham, Jesus Grande (Sp), W Granger (Aus), Ian Gray (Aus), Juliette Gregory (UK), Betsy Griffith (USA), Tina Groen (NL), Kari Grundt (N), James Guest (Aus), Shona Hagger (I), Juliet Haji (UK), M Haley (Aus), Deborah Hallberg (USA), Susan Hamovitch (USA), William Harby (USA), Neville Hardwick (NZ), Mat Hardy (UK), Joanne Harrison (D), D Hartley (UK), Leo Hawkins (Aus), Elaine Hawley (C), N Heaton (UK), Freddie Heitman (USA), Ross Henderson (Aus), Simon Hewett (UK), Jonathan Hibbs (UK), Richard Hillam (UK), Nick Hillman, Lisette von Hilten (B), David & Jennifer Ho (USA), Sharyn Hocking (Aus), Lilian Hoeberechts (NL), Bevin Hoffman (Ita), Mette Holland (Dk), Gary Horntvedt, Maralyn Horsdal (C), Chi-Chin Huang (USA), Dr AG Huber (C), Theo Huckle (UK), Shirley Hudson (USA), Hulya Pansiyon (Tur), D Hunter (UK), A & P Hurrell (UK), Sigve Jacobsen (Dk), Samantha Jagger (UK), SN James (UK), Jan & Klaske (NL), Tim Jarvis (UK), Simon Jeffreys (UK), Tim Jeffreys (UK), Wai Lin Tam Jo, Sarah Jones (USA), Jim Jones (I), Yolanda Kadagan (Tur), Saul Kaiserman (USA), Robin Karidge (UK), Larry & Danna Katzman (USA), Michelle Keeler (Aus), David Keene (UK), Ronald Keijzer (NL), Kathleen Kelly (Aus), Lisa Kelly (Aus), Ruthli Kemmerer (USA), Angela Kent, Barry Kerper (USA), Felicity Kerridge (UK), Jean A Kidd (USA), Jonathan King (USA), Lisa King (UK)

748

Rainer Kirchhefer (D), Miranda Klaaw (NL), Stian Kongsrud (N), D Kornfeld (USA), Dawn Kose (Tur), Wendy Kosonen (USA), Karen Kranmiller (UK), Michael Krause (Aus), Lewis Krimen (USA), Ingolf Kristensen (Dk), Irene Kummins-Hiller (D), Salman Kurt (Tur), Samran Kurt (Tur), Lorr & Sher Lachs (USA), Sonia Lacombe (C), Anne Lancashire (C), Joshua Landy (USA), Neils Langevad, Gregg & Robin Lansing (USA), Carmel Leahy (Aus), Graham Lee (UK), Jean Levasseur (C), Deirdre Linton (UK), Stefan Lipka (UK), Alan Lloyd, Nicola Lloyd (UK), Patricia D Lock (UK), Peggy Lockard (USA), Jean Luc Lodard (F), Tamara London (UK), Julian Longley (UK), Debirah Love (USA), Janine Lovell (Aus), Earl Luetzelschwab (USA), Susanne Lumsden (Aus), Anna & Lars Lundberg (Sw), Grant Lythe (NZ) Liesbeth & Andr Maas (NL), Steve Mabey (UK), Don & Chris MacKennon (Aus), Neil, Sally & Alec Mac-Lennan (UK), Sandy Mactaggart (C), George Main (UK), La Maison du Turc (Tur), A Majdandzic (Aus), Johan Malmborg (Sw), Dr E Martin (UK), Kristof Masschelein (B), Jason Matherly (USA), Theo Mathot (NL), Pat May (Aus), George McClelland (Aus), Barrie McCormick (UK), John McCutcheon (Aus), Gaby & James McIntosh (UK), Maria McKenzie, Peter McLaren (Tur), Frederico Medici (I), Bert Meijer (NL), Steve Menary (UK), Dr Jorgen C Meyer (N), Maria Meylan, Leslie & Carsten Miller (USA), A Moe & D Brown (USA), Wayne Montgomery (Aus), Adrian Morgan (Aus), Kirsten Mowrey (USA), Marieke Mulder (NL), Simon Mumford (Tur), JH Mundler (NL), Claire & Mike Muraoka (USA), Jacqueline Murphy (Aus), Vicki & Paul Murra (Aus), Steve Nash (UK), A Neal (NZ), M Neighbours (UK), Lisa Nicholson (Aus), Bernice Nikiddjuluw (NL), Kari Nordsle, P Norkunas (Aus), Michael O'Dea (Aus), M O'Shea (UK), Mehmet Oz (Tur), Kemal Ozkurt (Tur), Kadir Ozturk (Tur), Paolo Pan (I), John Parsons (Aus), Harry Pearman (UK), BR Pearson (UK), Della Pearson (C), Scott Pearson (USA), R Pelly (UK), Pension Priene (Tur), David Perry (Aus), Edward Peters (UK), Syd Peters (SA), Tine Petersen (Dk), Anna Petherick (NZ), D Phipps (UK), Loretta Picone (Aus), David Pittaway (Aus), Hilde & Dirk Poelman (B), Jonathan Poon (HK), Adrian & Linder Porter (UK), Patsy Pouvelle (F), Lisa Powell (C), Susan Praeger (USA), Peter Pulvermachts (CH), Grace Raube (USA), Jim Reardon (USA), William Redgrave (UK), Robert Reedy (USA), Jerrold Rehmar (USA), Holly & Mike Reiter (USA), Kay Renius (USA), T Richard (USA), Martin Richardson (Aus), Christopher Riley (UK), Louise Roberts (Aus), RW Robinson (Aus), B & J Robson, Neil Rogall (UK), Isobel Rolfe (UK), Susan Roundtree (Ire), Heather Rowland (UK), Philip Royal (UK), Susan Rubin (USA), Zaat Rubrecht (NL), Hernan Ruiz (S), Bartha Rusticiss (NL), Dolores ylee, Ali Sabah (Tur), Maureen & Paul Sadler, Rose Safran (USA), Craig Sands (USA), Stefano Santandrea (I), Cathy Santore (USA), Paul Sargent, Mustafa Sarioglan (Tur), Eero Sarrala (Fin), Mark Sassen (NL), G Saunders (Aus), Michel D Sauve (C), Frans Scheefhals (USA), Joan Scheyie (USA), Karin Schict (Aus), Anne Schneider (USA), Palle Schreuelnas (S), Lou Senini (Aus), William Shackleford (USA), Al Shapiro (UK), Judith & Ittach Shemesh (Isr), Janice Shenfelt (C), Side Pension (Tur), T Sidey (UK), G Silcock, Ellen Simon (USA), Delwyn Simpson (NZ), Iris Sliedrecht (NL), EA Smeeton (UK), Andrew Smith (Aus), Benedict Smith (UK), Hayden Smith (Tur), Frank Snelling (UK), Alexandre Soeur (B), Josef Sofer (Isr), Catherine Somers (Aus), Tom Spreutels (B), Richard Staniforth (C), Mark Stapleton (Aus), Joan Starkey (UK), Mary & Bob Steeves (C), Rich & Carolyn Stevens (C), Jane Stewart (UK), Kathleen Stewart (USA), Joan & Dennis Stokes (Aus), Sheree Storm (USA), Emily Stott (UK), Anna Strowger (UK), Leon Struehx (B), Virginia Stuiber (USA), Margaret Swain (UK), Loren Swearingen (USA), Nick & Hilary Sweeney (USA), Przemyslaw Switakowki (PL), U Switucha (C), S Tadmor (Isr), Andrea Talmud-Maurel (Isr), Tamer Pansion (Tur), Kristian Tangen (N), Michael Tar (USA), Michael Taslitz, Brian Teasdill (UK), Emily Teeter (USA), MP Templeton (UK), Rosalind Thoday (UK), PA Thomas (UK), Steve Toparlak (Tur), Tergut Topcu (Tur), John Tucker (UK), Julle Tuuliainen (Fin), Claudia Uygur (CH), Jan van Assche (B), Adriaan van der Weel (NL), Paul J van Eggelen (NL), Niana van Hees (NL), Linda van Leeuwen (Aus), Peter van Pelt (B), G van Shothorst (UK), Thijs de Ruyter van Steveninck (NL), Irmgard Verburgt (NL), Peter Vergenwen (NL), Mieke Verger (NL), D Vidgen (Aus), P Vollenburg (NL), Florence Vuillet (F), Michael Walensky (USA), Jeanette Ward (Aus), Lynne Watson (C), Mathilda Webb (UK), Vanessa Weigall (UK), M Westrup (NL), Chris Wheatley (UK), Peter Whitehead (UK), Joe Whiteman (UK), Robert Widinski (USA), Pierre Willems (B), Elaine Williams (Aus), Helene Winch (UK), Tony Winters, Joe Wolfgang (USA), Karl Wright (NZ), Dr Avi Yaarvi (Isr), Ali Yagmur (Tur), Ali Kamil Yalcin (Tur), Pat Yale (UK), Rita Yanny (USA), Mary J Yates, Ruth & Mustafa Yelkalan (Tur), Osman Yetimoglu (Tur), Refat Yildeg (Tur), M Yonkers (NL), Denis Young (UK), Marian Zaagman (NL), Joanne Zitko (USA), Bob Zoete (NL)

A – Australia, A – Austria, B – Belgium, C – Canada, D – Germany, Dk – Denmark, F – France, Fin – Finland, I – Italy, Ire – Republic of Ireland, Isr – Israel, N – Norway, NL – Netherlands, NZ – New Zealand, Sin – Singapore, Sp – Spain, Sw – Sweden, CH – Switzerland, Tur – Turkey, UK – United Kingdom, USA – United States of America

Guides to the Middle East

Arab Gulf States
The Arab Gulf States are surprisingly accessible and affordable with an astounding range of things to see and do – camel markets, desert safaris, ancient forts and modern cities to list just a few. Includes concise history and language section for each country.

Egypt & the Sudan - a travel survival kit
This guide takes you into and beyond the spectacular pyramids, temples, tombs, monasteries and mosques, and the bustling main streets of these fascinating countries to discover their incredible beauty, unusual sights and friendly people.

Iran - a travel survival kit
The first English-language guide to this enigmatic and surprisingly hospitable country written since the Islamic Revolution. As well as practical travel details the author provides background information that will fascinate adventurers and armchair travellers alike.

Israel - a travel survival kit
Detailed practical travel information is combined with authoritative historical references in this comprehensive guide. Complete coverage of both the modern state of Israel and the ancient biblical country.

Jordan & Syria - a travel survival kit
Two countries away from the usual travel routes, but with a wealth of natural and historical attractions for the adventurous traveller...12th century Crusader castles, ruined cities, the ancient Nabatean capital of Petra and haunting desert landscapes.

Trekking in Turkey
Explore beyond Turkey's coastline and you will be surprised to discover that Turkey has mountains with walks to rival those found in Nepal.

Yemen - a travel survival kit
The Yemen is one of the oldest inhabited regions in the world. This practical guide gives full details on a genuinely different travel experience.

West Asia on a shoestring
Want to cruise to Asia for 15 cents? Drink a great cup of tea while you view Mt Everest? Find the Garden of Eden? This guide has the complete story on the Asian overland trail from Bangladesh to Turkey, including Bhutan, India, Iran, the Maldives, Nepal, Pakistan, Sri Lanka and the Middle East.

Also available:
Arabic (Egyptian) phrasebook and **Turkish** phrasebook.

Lonely Planet Guidebooks

Lonely Planet guidebooks cover every accessible part of Asia as well as Australia, the Pacific, South America, Africa, the Middle East, Europe and parts of North America. There are five series: *travel survival kits*, covering a country for a range of budgets; *shoestring guides* with compact information for low-budget travel in a major region; *walking guides*; *city guides* and *phrasebooks*.

Australia & the Pacific
Australia
Bushwalking in Australia
Islands of Australia's Great Barrier Reef
Fiji
Melbourne city guide
Micronesia
New Caledonia
New Zealand
Tramping in New Zealand
Papua New Guinea
Bushwalking in Papua New Guinea
Papua New Guinea phrasebook
Rarotonga & the Cook Islands
Samoa
Solomon Islands
Sydney city guide
Tahiti & French Polynesia
Tonga
Vanuatu
Victoria

South-East Asia
Bali & Lombok
Bangkok city guide
Myanmar (Burma)
Burmese phrasebook
Cambodia
Indonesia
Indonesia phrasebook
Malaysia, Singapore & Brunei
Philippines
Pilipino phrasebook
Singapore city guide
South-East Asia on a shoestring
Thailand
Thai phrasebook
Vietnam
Vietnamese phrasebook

North-East Asia
China
Mandarin Chinese phrasebook
Hong Kong, Macau & Canton
Japan
Japanese phrasebook
Korea
Korean phrasebook
Mongolia
North-East Asia on a shoestring
Seoul city guide
Taiwan
Tibet
Tibet phrasebook
Tokyo city guide

West Asia
Trekking in Turkey
Turkey
Turkish phrasebook
West Asia on a shoestring

Middle East
Arab Gulf States
Egypt & the Sudan
Egyptian Arabic phrasebook
Iran
Israel
Jordan & Syria
Yemen

Indian Ocean
Madagascar & Comoros
Maldives & Islands of the East Indian Ocean
Mauritius, Réunion & Seychelles

Mail Order

Lonely Planet guidebooks are distributed worldwide. They are also available by mail order from Lonely Planet, so if you have difficulty finding a title please write to us. US and Canadian residents should write to Embarcadero West, 155 Filbert St, Suite 251, Oakland CA 94607, USA; European residents should write to Devonshire House, 12 Barley Mow Passage, Chiswick, London W4 4PH; and residents of other countries to PO Box 617, Hawthorn, Victoria 3122, Australia.

The Lonely Planet Story

Lonely Planet published its first book in 1973 in response to the numerous 'How did you do it?' questions Maureen and Tony Wheeler were asked after driving, bussing, hitching, sailing and railing their way from England to Australia.

Written at a kitchen table and hand collated, trimmed and stapled, *Across Asia on the Cheap* became an instant local bestseller, inspiring thoughts of another book.

Eighteen months in South-East Asia resulted in their second guide, *South-East Asia on a shoestring*, which they put together in a backstreet Chinese hotel in Singapore in 1975. The 'yellow bible' as it quickly became known to backpackers around the world, soon became *the* guide to the region. It has sold well over half a million copies and is now in its 7th edition, still retaining its familiar yellow cover.

Today there are over 120 Lonely Planet titles in print – books that have that same adventurous approach to travel as those early guides; books that 'assume you know how to get your luggage off the carousel' as one reviewer put it.

Although Lonely Planet initially specialised in guides to Asia, they now cover most regions of the world, including the Pacific, South America, Africa, the Middle East and Europe. The list of *walking guides* and *phrasebooks* (for 'unusual' languages such as Quechua, Swahili, Nepalese and Egyptian Arabic) is also growing rapidly.

The emphasis continues to be on travel for independent travellers. Tony and Maureen still travel for several months of each year and play an active part in the writing, updating and quality control of Lonely Planet's guides.

They have been joined by over 50 authors, 54 staff – mainly editors, cartographers, & designers – at our office in Melbourne, Australia, 10 at our US office in Oakland, California and another three at our office in London to handle sales for Britain, Europe and Africa. In 1992 Lonely Planet opened an editorial office in Paris. Travellers themselves also make a valuable contribution to the guides through the feedback we receive in thousands of letters each year.

The people at Lonely Planet strongly believe that travellers can make a positive contribution to the countries they visit, both through their appreciation of the countries' culture, wildlife and natural features, and through the money they spend. In addition, the company makes a direct contribution to the countries and regions it covers. Since 1986 a percentage of the income from each book has been donated to ventures such as famine relief in Africa; aid projects in India; agricultural projects in Central America; Greenpeace's efforts to halt French nuclear testing in the Pacific and Amnesty International. In 1993 $100,000 was donated to such causes.

Lonely Planet's basic travel philosophy is summed up in Tony Wheeler's comment, 'Don't worry about whether your trip will work out. Just go!'